Dictionary of
Ethics, Theology and Society

Dictionary of
Ethics, Theology and Society

Edited by

Paul Barry Clarke
and
Andrew Linzey

London and New York

First published 1996
by Routledge
11 New Fetter Lane, London EC4P 4EE

Simultaneously published in the USA and Canada
by Routledge
29 West 35th Street, New York, NY 10001

Typeset in Sabon by Datix International Limited, Bungay, Suffolk

Printed and bound in Great Britain by TJ Press (Padstow) Ltd, Cornwall

British Library Cataloguing in Publication Data
A catalogue record for this book is available from the British Library

Library of Congress Cataloguing in Publication Data
A catalogue record for this book is available on request

ISBN 0–415–06212–8

CONTENTS

ADVISORY BOARD

INTRODUCTION

The purpose of this *Dictionary of Ethics, Theology and Society* is an ambitious one: the mapping out of the major ethical, theological and political influences which have come to form Western society, and to demonstrate their continued relevance in a number of areas. These influences and their histories are not of course unrelated, although there are necessarily tensions between them. At times the entangling and conjunction of terms is more than apparent; at times their disjunction is obvious. This is not therefore another Dictionary of Ethics, *or* a Dictionary of Theology, *or* a Dictionary of Society. This Dictionary attempts a bolder, interdisciplinary survey: the detailing and illustration of aspects of what might be called the 'Western mind'.

Whether there can be said to be any such thing as the 'Western mind' is of course contestable; indeed now more than perhaps ever it *is* being contested. It is frequently argued that society has no coherent ideology left, and that complete pluralism in faith and in practice is now inevitable. On some accounts secularization has progressed so far that it is now impossible to relate society and theology, and that we are in a postmodern, post-theological, post-ethical position from which there is no return and nowhere left to go. There is an epidemic of endism, predictably as the millennium approaches; we face the suggestion that we are at the end of history, the end of modernity, the end of politics. On such arguments the linking of the social, the theological and the ethical might seem a quixotic endeavour. Yet the arrogance of such a view – not dissimilar to the now exploded idea that biological evolution has been a narrative destined to culminate in *homo sapiens* as it is today – fails to take into account some serious arguments, arguments which are explored and detailed between the covers of this book.

For such a view fails to appreciate that even – perhaps especially – in its pluralistic forms, Western society continues to be deeply indebted to the Judeo-Christian tradition and its synthesis with political and social thought. Furthermore, whatever the extent of secularization, and however dramatic the challenge of what has been called postmodernism (that useful catch-all term for the current intellectual predicament), the origins of a society determine the range of possibilities that follows; determine them not in an eschatological sense, nor in a mechanistically determinist sense, but in a foundational sense. Whatever the future holds, it will always contain the debts, traces and scars of all that precedes it.

There will, in such a process, be moments of crisis, of apparent breaches with tradition. It is not implausible to suggest that we live in an age experiencing just such fracturings and rifts. Yet a society does not, cannot by definition, abandon its foundations. It can however transform them; and at certain points these transformations will present themselves as revolutionary breaks. But breaks are always breaks *from* something; they are not, as Germany's *Stunde Null* or Cambodia's Year Zero perhaps show, a new beginning with the slate wiped clean; a social ethical and political *tabula rasa*. This Dictionary, then, does not merely attempt to historicize our current position, to read the obituary of a tradition; it demonstrates how deeply that tradition has been written into our society, how each apparent crisis or revolution is in some ways only a palimpsest on what precedes it, and how that tradition has written and re-written itself over such palimpsests as it has developed.

What the current crisis does perhaps suggest

is that the dialogue between the disciplines involved in this *Dictionary* has, without breaking down, become at times a series of monologues among the deaf. The complex interweaving of the terms of the book's title is not reflected when social theorists become committed to rejecting any theological or metaphysical standpoints; nor when there are theologians determined to oppose any social theory without explicitly confessional assumptions. Western thought, in short, is characterized by continuity *and* discontinuity; conformity *and* rebellion; consensus *and* innovation; and yet all of these attributes are part of, and build upon, the very same tradition of thought and practice.

What this suggests is that the ethico-theologico-political moment may be and must be revised, reinterpreted and continuously recreated; but for all the metaphors of revolution and conclusion now in currency – it is continual. In this process, this activity, our actions in the world – actions which are never divorced from the ethical, political or theological – and also our interpretations of or reflections on those actions, are tantamount. Many of the headwords in this book treat issues of abiding concern, forms of thought or behaviour which are invested with sufficient importance to have been ceaselessly considered and acted on; and many treat issues which have recently been invested with an urgency which looks set to grow rather than diminish over the coming years. One thinks particularly of certain issues of sexuality, and even more so, of environmental and animal rights issues. In an age of seemingly limited political options, these are topics which have seen considerable political mobilization and ethical debate in many different areas of society; they are unignorable, but their contexts and histories will not always have been apparent even to those to whom they are most pressing.

A Dictionary of Ethics, Theology and Society is right to cover these issues; it is also right not to ignore the difficulties of the synthesis attempted here. Contributors were not selected with any theological or political perspective in mind, but rather for their expertise and their willingness to engage in an enterprise which has exposed the profitable difficulty of these various strands; to start to unravel a Gordian knot. It

has not always been easy to find academics and experts prepared to consider writing within their own field while maintaining the deliberate aim of embracing other disciplines and perspectives. Interdisciplinary work is arduous and still insufficiently recognized. We have searched out academics, from a wide number of fields, and indeed countries, who have been prepared to push the boundaries of their subject and transgress familiar and well-protected institutional boundaries. For their pluck, resolve and in some cases audacity, we extend our thanks.

The *Dictionary* represents both the strengths and the weaknesses of the current state of interdisciplinary dialogue. In many areas the interchange of ideas is lively and fruitful; in others it seems barely to have begun, as categories of thought on one side or another develop in sterile isolation. Inevitably therefore this *Dictionary* serves as the initiation of a debate and a discussion which is potentially endless. On every page there are links and correspondences, thought-provoking potentialities, which remain to be further explored. The *Dictionary*, as any Dictionary must be, is not the closing off of avenues of thought, but their widening. It traces a heritage and tradition which is still evolving and whose future shape and form is not only unclear but in fact waiting formation. It is not for nothing that tradition has been called the 'seed-bed of creativity'.

As editors, we have not sought to harmonize all the disparate and sometimes apparently disconnected strands of thought – theological, political, sociological, philosophical, anthropological, and ethical – represented here. Each entry must be judged by itself as to how, and to what extent, it continues and develops a deeper understanding of Western tradition and its contemporary manifestations in thought and practice. In our advice to contributors, we have asked them to untangle the intellectual history of a given topic or practice, to illustrate its contemporary relevance, and finally, where appropriate, to make some personal comment or summation to push the discussion onwards. The result in many cases has been an original contribution which both reflects the current state of debate and also engages with it, sometimes excitingly and rarely uncontentiously. It is one of the pleasures of this *Dictionary* that it demonstrates what a rich and as yet not fully tapped resource for human living the tradition described can prove to be.

Our hope is that the *Dictionary* will appeal to new generations of scholars and students frustrated with the artificial barriers which the various disciplines within academic study have erected, and which in some cases have led to a closing of minds rather than an enthusiasm for exploration. There are increasing signs – especially in the field of ethics – that interdisciplinary approaches are being encouraged and supported. Perhaps it is not too much to expect that this *Dictionary* will spur on new interdisciplinary studies, even courses, in ethical theory; for there are no greater theological or political questions today than the ethical. The question as to how and why things are as they are feeds into the question of how we behave, of how we act on society and how it acts upon us; the question of good and of evil.

This *Dictionary* was conceived when we were both Fellows of the Centre for the Study of Theology at the University of Essex: a new Centre concerned specifically with the relationship between theology and society. We would like to extend our particular thanks to the Council of the Centre and its interdisciplinary fellowship for their encouragement and support, and especially to the Administrative Director Lynn Bowman-Burns for her tireless help with the rounds of organization and correspondence. We are also grateful to the Department of Government at the University of Essex, for providing superb facilities ideally suited to the research we have undertaken, and to our wives, Ildi Clarke and Jo Linzey. Many members of Routledge, our publishers, deserve our appreciation. Our thanks to Wendy Morris, who backed our vision; to Mark Barragry, who kept faith with the project during gestation and delivery; and especially to Michelle Darraugh, Robert Potts and Samantha Parkinson, whose expert editorial advice and assistance, not to mention hard work, guided the book through to production.

Paul Barry Clarke and Andrew Linzey
September 1995

NOTES ON CONTRIBUTORS

Vicki Abt received her PhD in social psychology from Temple University in 1972. She is primary author of *The Business of Risk: Commercial Gambling in Mainstream America* (University Press of Kansas, 1985) and numerous scholarly articles and book chapters on risk, leisure behaviour, gambling and addiction. She is currently book review editor for *The Journal of Gambling Studies*. She is on the advisory board of the New York based National Council on Problem Gambling. Dr Abt has often been called to advise local and state officials and has given testimony at several legislative hearings on gambling in Pennsylvania. Dr Abt is currently Professor of Sociology and American Studies at Penn State's Ogontz Campus in the Philadelphia area. She often appears on radio and television programmes dealing with State lotteries, government policies and problem gambling.

Brenda Almond is Professor of Moral and Social Philosophy at the University of Hull. She is Chair of the Society for Applied Philosophy and joint editor of the *Journal of Applied Philosophy*. Her books include *Moral Concerns* (Humanities Press, 1987), *AIDS − A Moral Issue: The Ethical, Social and Legal Aspects* (ed.) (Macmillan, 1990) and *The Philosophical Quest* (Penguin, 1990).

Rex Ambler has been teaching theology at the University of Birmingham since 1968. He studied at the universities of Manchester, Oxford and Amsterdam, before taking up a tutorship in philosophy at Manchester College, Oxford, and then a lectureship in the philosophy of religion at the University of Nottingham. At Birmingham he teaches both philosophical and practical theology. His research interests and writing, however, have focused more on the practical

side. He co-edited a book in 1980, *Agenda for Prophets: Towards a Political Theology for Britain* (Bowerdean Press), wrote booklets, *A Guide to the Study of Gandhi* and *The Relevance of Gandhi in the West* (Housmans, 1986 and 1989 respectively) and a book, *Global Theology: The Meaning of Faith in the Present World Crisis* (SCM Press, 1990). He is presently doing work for two books: one on the crisis of modernity and its implications for faith (a postmodern faith?), and the other on ecological theology. As to other affiliations, he is a member of the Gandhi Foundation, the Green Party, and the Society of Friends.

James Atkinson was the founder and is now Director of the Centre for Reformation Studies, University of Sheffield. Previously he has been Research Fellow at Sheffield, Reader in Theology at the University of Hull, Canon Theologian at Leicester and Sheffield cathedrals, Professor of Theology at Chicago, and Professor of Biblical Studies at Sheffield. He is the author of several works, including *Rome and Reformation* (1965), *Luther and the Birth of Protestantism* (1968), *Martin Luther: Prophet to the Church Catholic* (1983) and *The Darkness of Faith* (1987).

Paul Avis is Vicar of Stoke Canon and four other parishes and a Prebendary of Exeter Cathedral; Honorary Research Fellow in the Department of Theology, University of Exeter and Treasurer of the Society for the Study of Theology; a member of the Church of England's General Synod, Doctrine Commission, and Faith and Order Advisory Group. He is the author or editor of more than a dozen books, including *Anglicanism and the Christian Church* (1989), *Christians in Communion* (1990), *Authority,*

Leadership and Conflict in the Church (1992), and *The Resurrection of Jesus Christ* (1993). He is currently working in the area of fundamental theology – the validity and methodology of Christian theology.

Paul Badham is Professor, Dean of the Faculty of Theology, and Head of the Department of Theology and Religious Studies, at University of Wales, Lampeter. He is co-Director of a unique MA programme in Death and Immortality. His publications include *Christian Beliefs about Life after Death*, *Immortality or Extinction?*, *Death and Immortality in the Religions of the World* and *Ethics on the Frontiers of Human Existence*.

Eileen Barker is Professor of Sociology with special reference to the study of religion at the London School of Economics. Her publications include *The Making of a Moonie: Brainwashing or Choice?* (Gregg Revivals, 1993, first published by Blackwell 1984), *New Religious Movements: A Practical Introduction* (HMSO, 1989, 3rd impression with amendments, 1992), four edited volumes and over a hundred articles. She is currently researching changes in new religions and their members, the New Age, Religion in Eastern Europe and Armenian Diaspora. She is the founder of INFORM (Information Network Focus On Religious Movements), and acted as its Honorary Director from 1988–93. She is the first non-American to be elected as President of the Society for the Scientific Study of Religion.

Stephen C. Barton, BA Hons, Dip Ed (Macquarie University), MA (University of Lancaster), PhD (King's College, London). His present position is Lecturer in New Testament, Department of Theology, University of Durham (since 1988); he is also a non-stipendiary minister at St John's Church, Neville's Cross, Durham. His research interests include New Testament hermeneutics, the social scientific interpretation of the Bible, the theology and spirituality of the Gospels and the theology of the family. Publications include *The Spirituality of the Gospels* (SPCK, 1992), *People of the Passion* (SPCK/Triangle, 1994) and *'Not Peace but a Sword': Discipleship and Family Ties According to Mark and Matthew* (Cambridge University Press, forthcoming).

Richard Bauckham is Professor of New Testament Studies at the University of St Andrews, Scotland. Previously he was Reader in the History of Christian Thought at the University of Manchester. His publications and research interests range widely over the fields of biblical studies, historical theology and contemporary theology. His books include *Tudor Apocalypse* (1978), *Jude, 2 Peter* (1983), *Möltmann: Messianic Theology in the Making* (1987), *The Bible in Politics* (1989), *June and the Relatives of Jesus in the Early Church* (1990), *The Theology of the Book of Revelation* (1993), *The Climax of Prophecy* (1993), and *The Theology of Jurgen Möltmann* (1993).

Zigmunt Bauman is Emeritus Professor of Sociology at the University of Leeds, England.

David Beetham is Professor of Politics at the University of Leeds. He is an expert in European social and political theory. His current research interests are in democratic theory and practice, including a democratic audit of the UK. Publications include *Bureaucracy* (Open University Press, 1987) and *The Legitimization of Power* (Macmillan Press, 1991).

Jeremy Begbie is Vice Principal of Ridley Hall, Cambridge and a member of the Faculty of Divinity, University of Cambridge. He teaches modern systematic theology and has a special interest in the relationship between theology and the arts, especially music. He has lectured extensively in the United States and Canada and is author of *Voicing Creation's Praise* (1991) and *Music in God's Purposes* (1989).

Ted Benton is Professor of Sociology at the University of Essex. He has a long-standing interest in Marxist theory and politics, as well as in other socialist and emancipatory thought and practice. His recent publications include *Natural Relations: Ecology, Animal Rights and Social Justice* (London: Verso, 1993); *Social Theory and the Global Environment* (Routledge, 1994) and with Red-Green Study Group

What on Earth is to be Done? (2 Hamilton Road, Manchester, 1995).

John Berkman is Assistant Professor of Social Ethics at Sacred Heart University in Fairfield, Connecticut. His research interests include the history of ethics and moral theology, and environmental ethics.

Robert Bernasconi has held the Lillian and Morrie Moss Chair of Excellence in Philosophy at the University of Memphis since 1988. He formerly taught at the University of Essex. He works in the phenomenological and hermeneutical tradition and has published articles on many of the leading figures of that tradition. He is the author of *The Question of Language in Heidegger's History of Being* (1985) and *Heidegger in Question* (1993). He is completing a book to be called *Between Levinas and Derrida*. His current research is increasingly concerned with issues in social and political philosophy.

Nigel Biggar is Chaplain of Oriel College, Oxford, where he teaches Christian ethics in the University's Faculty of Theology and at Wycliffe Hall. Among his publications are: *The Hastening that Waits: Karl Barth's Ethics* (Oxford: Oxford University Press, 1993); *Theological Politics: A Critique of 'Faith in the City'* (Oxford: Latimer House, 1988); (ed.) *Reckoning with Barth: Essays in Commemoration of the Centenary of Karl Barth's Birth* (Oxford: Mowbray, 1988); (co-editor) *Cities of Gods: Faith, Politics and Pluralism in Judaism, Christianity and Islam* (Westport, CT: Greenwood Press, 1986).

Anthony Black is a Professor in the Department of Political Science and Social Policy, University of Dundee, Scotland. He has worked on medieval political thought, especially relating to constitutionalism within the church and guilds and corporations. He is currently engaged on a comparative study of Islamic and European political thought from the seventh to the seventeenth centuries. His previous publications include *Council and Commune* (1979), *Guilds and Civil Society* (1984), *State, Community and Human Desire* (1988), and *Community in Historical Perspective* (1989, an edition of a translation from Otto Gierke).

Jose Miguez Bonino, BD (Facultad Evangelica de Teologia, Buenos Aires, 1947), MA (Emory University, 1954), PhD (Union Theological Seminary, NY, 1960), was born in 1924. He is Emeritus Professor of Systematic Theology and Ethics at ISEDET (Protestant Institute for Higher Theological Studies, Buenos Aires). Ordained Presbyter in the Inglesia Evangelica Metodista Argentina, 1947, he has served in several parishes in Bolivia and Argentina. He was a member of the Presidium of the World Council of Churches, 1975–82, and President of the Argentine Permanent Assembly for Human Rights. He is an elected member of the Constitutional Committee for the Reform of the Argentine Constitution. His books include *Room to be People* (Fortress Press, 1979), *Toward a Christian Political Ethics* (Philadelphia: Fortress, 1983), *That They May Have Life: Encounters with Jesus in the Gospel of John* (New York: General Board of Global Ministries, Methodist Church, 1989), *Conflicto y Unidad en la Iglesia* (San Jose, Costa Rica: Ediciones Cebila, 1992) and *Rostros del Protestantismo Latinoamericano* (Buenos Aires: Nueva Creación, 1995).

M.F.C. Bourdillon studied Social Anthropology at the University of Oxford; he has also studied philosophy and theology. He has taught in the Department of Sociology, University of Zimbabwe, for many years, and also in Calabar, Nigeria. With Meyer Fortes, he edited *Sacrifice*. He has written *Shona Peoples, Religion and Society: A Text for Africa* and many other works, his primary research interest being Shona religion and Zimbabwean society generally.

Joseph A. Bracken SJ is Professor of Theology and Rector of the Jesuit community at Xavier University, Cincinnati, Ohio. Author of *What Are We Saying about the Trinity?* (1979), *The Triune Symbol* (1985), *Society and Spirit* (1991), and *The Divine Matrix* (under evaluation); likewise author of many articles on trinitarian theology and process theology in various academic journals; currently interested in the relation between Christianity and Asian religions

(Hinduism, Buddhism, Taoism) in terms of their relative conceptions of ultimate reality.

Paul Brett is Director of Social Responsibility in the Diocese of Chelmsford and a Residentiary Canon of Chelmsford Cathedral. His publications include *Love Your Neighbour: The Bible and Christian Ethics Today* (Darton, Longman & Todd, 1992), *Rethinking Christian Attitudes to Sex* (Centre for the Study of Theology, University of Essex, 1991), and articles on 'Automation', 'Computers' and 'Robots', in *A New Dictionary of Christian Ethics* (SCM Press, 1986).

Charles Brock is Chaplain and Director of Ministerial Education at Mansfield College, Oxford. He is also Minister of Wheatley United Reformed Church and joint Chaplain to Reformed students at the University of Oxford. He teaches the psychology of religion in the Faculty of Theology and Liturgy at Ripon College, Cuddesdon. His publications include *The Lord's Supper* (1986), the sacramental liturgies for the URC Service Book (1989), *Mosaics of the American Dream: America as the New Israel* (1994) and *Sightings of Hope: Stories of Urban/Rural Mission in the URC* (1994).

Paul Custodio Bube is Associate Professor of Religion and Philosophy and Chairperson of the Department of Religion and Philosophy at Kansas Wesleyan University in Salina. His publications include *Ethics in John Cobb's Process Theology* (Atlanta: Scholars Press, 1988), 'From monoculture to polyculture: the possibilities for community', in *Home Territory: Essays on Community and Land*, ed. Wes Jackson and William Vitek (Yale University Press, forthcoming), 'Abortion: law, religion and society', in *Bioethics Forum* (Winter, 1993), among others.

Ian Budge has been Professor of Government at the University of Essex, a leading international department, for fifteen years. Former Chairman of Department and former Director of the European Consortium for Political Research. Visiting Professor, University of Wisconsin (1969–70) and UCI (1989), European University Institute, Florence (1982–5), Science Centre, Berlin (1990)

and Universitat Autonoma, Barcelona (1991). He is the author or co-author of some ten books, and forty articles, mainly on elections, government and parties, and democratic theory. Currently Director of the Manifesto Research Group engaged in comparative research on election and government programmes and their implementation. Recent publications include *Parties and Democracy* (1990), *Party Policies and Government Coalitions* (1993) and (with others) *The New Challenge of Direct Democracy* (1995).

Russell A. Butkus, PhD, is currently Associate Professor of Theology and Religious Education at the University of Portland in Portland, Oregon. He received his BA in Religion from St Lawrence University and his MEd and PhD from Boston College. His longstanding interest is in religious and theological education for social justice. His current research and teaching interest is in the field of environmental theology and ethics. He has lectured widely and is author of a number of publications including 'Some reflections on the economic pastoral: US Catholics in a capitalist context', in *PACE: Professional Approaches for Christian Educators* (April 1988), 'Linking social analysis and curriculum development: insights from Paolo Freire', in *Religious Education* (Fall 1989), 'Dangerous memories; toward a pedagogy for social transformation', in *Religious Education for Social Transformation* (ed. Allen J. Moore, 1989) and 'Character development', in *Harper's Encyclopedia of Religious Education* (ed. Iris and Kendig Cully, 1990).

Lisa Sowle Cahill is Professor of Christian Ethics at Boston College. She is an associate editor of journals including the *Journal of Medicine and Philosophy*, the *Journal of Religious Ethics* and *Concilium*. She has served as president of the Catholic Theological Society of America. She is the author of books and articles on bioethics and on the ethics of sex and gender, including *Between the Sexes: Toward a Christian Ethics of Sexuality*, *Women and Sexuality*, and *Religion and Artificial Reproduction* (with Thomas A. Shannon); and is writing a book on sex, gender, family, and Christian ethics. She has contributed entries to the *Encyclopedia of*

Bioethics (2nd edition) and the *Westminster Dictionary of Christian Ethics* (revised edition).

Gary Calore was born in Frankfurt of American parents. He received his AB from the College of William and Mary in Virginia and his MA and PhD from Bryn Mawr College. He is currently Associate Professor of Philosophy at the Ogontz Campus, Pennsylvania State University. His research interests include classical American philosophy and American popular religion. Among his published works are: 'Foundationalism and temporal paradox: the case of Augustine's confessions', in *Antifoundationalism Old and New*, ed. Tom Rockmore and Beth J. Singer (Philadelphia: Temple University Press, 1992), pp. 57–84; 'Deflating the real: project for a metaphysical reconstruction of time', in *Philosophical Quarterly*, vol. XXXV, no. 2 (June 1995), pp. 175–92.

Hiram Caton has been Professor of Politics and History in the Faculty of Humanities at Griffith University, Brisbane, since 1976, and also heads the School of Applied Ethics. He has bachelor's and master's degrees in Arabic language and civilization from the University of Chicago. He studied philosophy at the University of Freiburg and then Yale University, where his PhD was awarded in 1966. He taught philosophy at the Pennsylvania State University, then moved to the Research School of Social Sciences, Australian National University. He has been Visiting Professor at Harvard University and at the Institute for Contemporary History, Munich, and is associated with the Max Planck Institute for Human Ethology in Andechs, Germany. He has been awarded: National Humanities Fellow (USA), 1982–3; Doctor of Letters degree for distinguished contributions to history, 1989; and was elected Fellow of the Australian Institute of Biology, 1991. He is presently writing *People Power: A Study of Collective Action*.

Ian Clark is Assistant Director of Studies in International Relations at the University of Cambridge and a Fellow of Selwyn College. His research interests lie mainly in the fields of theories of international relations, ethics of war, and the history of nuclear strategic ideas. His

publications include *Limited Nuclear War: Political theory and War Conventions* (Princeton University Press, 1982), *Waging War: A Philosophical Introduction* (Oxford University Press, 1988), and *The Hierarchy of States* (Cambridge University Press, 1989). His most recent book is *Nuclear Diplomacy and the Special Relationship: Britain's Deterrent and America 1957–62* (Oxford University Press, 1994).

Stephen R.L. Clark is Professor of Philosophy at the University of Liverpool, and founder of Philos-L, an e-mail list for philosophers. He teaches ancient philosophy, ethics and philosophy of religion. His research interests include Platonism, the understanding and treatment of animals and the philosophical implications of modern knowledge. Publications include *The Moral Status of Animals* (Clarendon), *The Mysteries of Religion* (Blackwell), *From Athens to Jerusalem* (Clarendon), a three-volume work based on the Stanton and Wilde lectures, *Limits and Renewals* (Clarendon), Read Tuckwell lectures published as *How to Think about the Earth* (Mowbrays) and the Scott Holland lecture published as *How to Live Forever* (Routledge).

Paul Barry Clarke is Director of the major international programme in political theory and political philosophy in the Department of Government at the University of Essex. He has written many articles and books, been widely consulted by governments, ethical advisory groups and policy makers in Australasia and the United Kingdom in areas of concern such as embryo research, euthanasia and AIDS and by institutions in the Baltic states and in China. His recent theoretical writings have centred around the foundations of political philosophy, political science and the philosophy of social science with a special interest in the relation between the traditional conception of theory and theology, the breakdown of the relationship and the rupture with the past. Recent books include *The Autonomy of Politics*, *AIDS: Medicine, Politics, Society, Citizenship*; and (with A. Linzey) *Research on Embryos: Politics, Theology and Law, Theology, the University and the Modern World* and *Political Theory and Animal Rights*. He is currently completing *Autonomy Unbound*, an extensive study of the relation between the theological complex of meanings associated with the origins and construction of the concept of autonomy and its contemporary development in late post modern conditions. This major study is a precursor to a further study of the complex of symbols in the social originary. His book *Deep Citizenship* is to be published by Pluto Press in March 1996.

Priscilla Cohn, PhD, is a Professor of Philosophy at Ogontz Campus, Pennsylvania State University. She has written on the history of philosophy, contemporary philosophers and ethical questions, and is particularly interested in animal rights. She has directed courses on this subject at the University of Madrid's summer school, and has been Visiting Professor at the University of Santiago de Compostela. She has lectured all over the world, and is an associate editor of the animal rights series for Edwin Mellen Press. Since 1991 she has been President of the Advising Committee of the Ferrater Mora Chair of Contemporary Thought, University of Gerona.

Dan Cohn-Sherbok was born in Denver, Colorado and educated at Williams College and the Hebrew Union College where he was ordained as a rabbi. He received a doctorate from the University of Cambridge and has taught Jewish Theology at the University of Kent at Canterbury since 1975. He has been a Visiting Professor at the University of Essex, a Visiting Fellow at Wolfson College, Cambridge, and a Visiting Scholar at Mansfield College, Oxford and the Oxford Centre for Postgraduate Hebrew Studies. He is the author and editor of more than thirty books.

Lavinia Cohn-Sherbok received an MA in Theology from the University of Cambridge and an MA in Elizabethan and Jacobean Studies from the University of Kent. She was formerly Principal of West Heath School, and currently lectures in Religious Studies at Chaucer College, Canterbury. She is the author of *A Short History of Judaism*.

Peter Coleman is Professor of Social Gerontology at the University of Southampton, a joint appointment between Geriatric Medicine and Social Work Studies. A psychologist by background, he teaches social work, medical, psychology and nursing students. His research interests are in the study of identity processes, biography and meaning in ageing, and of the quality of long term care provision with particular regard to psychological survival in advanced old age. His publications include *Ageing and Reminiscence Processes: Social and Clinical Implications* (1986), *Life Span and Change in a Gerontological Perspective* (co-editor, 1985), and *Ageing in Society: An Introduction to Social Gerontology* (co-editor, 1990; 2nd edition, 1993).

Martin Conway is President of the Selly Oak Colleges, a federation of eight colleges in Birmingham involved in adult and higher education, most of which are rooted in Christian inspiration and allegiance, but which are open to people of every creed, culture and tradition. After significant experience on the staff of the Student Christian Movement, the World Council of Churches and the British Council of Churches, he taught 'Church and Society' at Ripon College, Cuddesdon, Oxford, prior to taking up his Selly Oak Colleges' post in 1986. Recent publications include: *That's When the Body Works – the Canberra Assembly of the World Council of Churches as a Foretaste of a Council of the Universal Church* (Birmingham: Selly Oak Colleges, 1991); 'Helping the Ecumenical Movement to move on – Walter Hollenwager and the rediscovery of the value of diversity', in *Pentecost, Mission and Ecumenism: Essays on Intercultural Theology – Festschrift in Honour of W. J. Hollenweger*, ed. J.A.B. Jongeneel (Frankfurt, Bern, Paris, New York: Peter Lang, 1992). Research interests are chiefly in the contemporary worldwide ecumenical movement, including the roots, means and fruits of dialogue between Christians and people of the other major religious traditions within the total human community.

Marie Cornwall is Professor of Sociology at Brigham Young University, Utah. She has a PhD from the University of Minnesota. Her research has focused on the religiosity of latter-day saints, the family and religion, and women's place in religious cultures. She is the senior editor of *Contemporary Mormonism: Social Science Perspectives* (University of Illinois Press, 1994).

Anthony P.M. Coxon is Research Professor in the Department of Sociology and Fellow of the Centre for Theology, University of Essex. He is also Emeritus Professor of Sociological Research Methods, University of Wales. His current research interests include the sociology of sexual behaviour ('The structure of sexual behaviour', *Journal of Sexual Research*, vol. 29, 1992) and the socio-epidemiology of HIV infection and homosexual lifestyles, as Principal Investigator of Project SIGMA (Socio-sexual Investigations of Gay Men and Aids). His earlier research has been chiefly in social stratification (*Images of Occupational Prestige*, 1978; *Class and Hierarchy*, Macmillan, 1979; *Images of Social Stratification*, Sage, 1986) and on the clergy (*The Fate of the Anglican Clergy*, with Bob Towler, Macmillan, 1977), together with methodological work on multidimensional scaling.

Colin Crowder lectures in the philosophy of religion, modern theology and modern atheism at the University of Durham. His work is concerned with the relation between modernity and religious belief – a concern which unites research interests in post-foundationalist philosophy of religion, theology and culture, and a variety of social and educational issues. He is the co-editor of *European Literature and Theology in the Twentieth Century* with David Jasper (1990) and *Theological Perspectives on Christian Education* (1995), with Jeff Astley and Leslie Francis, and the author of several articles in the philosophy of religion. At present, he is editing a volume of essays on Christian non-realism, and developing a Wittgensteinian critique of foundationalism. He is the reviews editor of *Literature and Theology*.

Don Cupitt is a Lecturer in Theology at the University of Cambridge, and a Fellow of Emmanuel College, Cambridge. He is an Anglican priest, and the author of over twenty books,

including, most recently, *Creation out of Nothing* (1990), *What is a Story?* (1991), *The Time Being* (1992), and *After All* (1994).

Charles E. Curran is Elizabeth Scurlock University Professor of Human Values at Southern Methodist University, Dallas, Texas. He has served as president of the Society of Christian Ethics, the Catholic Theological Society of America, and the American Theological Society. He has lectured extensively in the United States and abroad, has published in major periodicals in English and the primary European languages, and has authored and edited over thirty volumes. His latest works include *Catholic Higher Education, Theology and Academic Freedom* (University of Notre Dame Press, 1990), *The Living Tradition of Catholic Moral Theology* (University of Notre Dame Press, 1992) and *The Church and Morality: An Ecumenical and Catholic Approach* (Fortress Press, 1993).

Douglas J. Davies is Professor of Religious Studies within the Theology Department of the University of Nottingham where he has taught since 1974. He has bachelor's degrees both in social anthropology and theology from the University of Durham and did his first research on Mormonism at the Oxford Institute of Social Anthropology. Subsequent research and teaching at the University of Nottingham have included books on the sociology of knowledge in *Meaning and Salvation in Religious Studies* (1984), on *Studies in Pastoral Theology and Social Anthropology* (1986) and on *Mormon Spirituality* (1987). Major studies of religion in Britain have been conducted through the Cremation Research Project, *Cremation Today and Tomorrow* (1990) and through the Rural Church Project funded by Leverhulme Trust, *Church and Religion in Rural England* (1991). He has also written on the history of religion and sociology in the nineteenth century in a biography of *Frank Byron Jevons: An Evolutionary Realist* (1991). His current research focuses on ritual, symbolism and belief in Mormonism, and in cremation and death.

Anthony Dyson is Samuel Ferguson Professor of Social and Pastoral Theology, and Academic

Director of the Centre for Social Ethics and Policy at the Victoria University of Manchester. Recent publications include *The Ethics of In-Vitro Fertilisation* and *Ethics of Biodiversity* (ed. with J. Harris). He specializes in Christian social ethics, in particular, in bioethics.

J. Ronald Engel, PhD, is Professor of Social Ethics at Meadville/Lombard Theological School and Lecturer in Ethics and Society at the Divinity School, University of Chicago. He serves as chair of the Ethics Working Group of the World Conservation Union; is associate director of the Program on Ecology, Justice and Faith in North American Theological Education; is associate director of the Hastings Centre project on nature, polis and ethics; is a member of the executive committee of the International Development Ethics Association; and is on the editorial board of the *American Journal of Theology and Philosophy*. He is author of *Sacred Sands: The Struggle for Community in the Indiana Dunes* (Wesleyan University Press, 1983), is co-editor with Joan G. Engel of *Ethics of Environment and Development* (University of Arizona Press, 1991), co-editor with Joan G. Engel and Peter Bakken of *Ecology, Justice and Christian Faith: A Guide to the Literature 1964–1994* (Greenwood Press, 1995), and is author of numerous articles on religion, ethics and the environment.

G.R. Evans is a University Lecturer in History at the University of Cambridge and works on medieval history and ecumenical theology. She is author of *The Church and the Churches: Towards an Ecumenical Ecclesiology* (Cambridge University Press, 1994), *Method in Ecumenical Theology* (Cambridge University Press, forthcoming); and has edited *Christian Authority: Essays in Honour of Henry Chadwick* (Oxford, 1988), *The Anglican Tradition: A Handbook of Anglican Sources* (SPCK, 1991) *Episcopal Ministry: The Report of the Archbishops' Group on the Episcopate* (Church House Publishing, 1990).

Kathleen Coulborn Faller, PhD, ACSW, is Professor of Social Work at the University of Michigan. She is also Director of the Family Assessment Clinic, a multidisciplinary team that evaluates cases of child maltreatment, and co-director of the Interdisciplinary Project on Child Abuse and Neglect, both at the University of Michigan. She is involved in research, clinical work, teaching, training, and writing in the area of child sexual abuse. She is the author of *Social Work with Abused and Neglected Children* (The Free Press, 1981), *Child Sexual Abuse: An Interdisciplinary Manual for Diagnosis, Case Management, and Treatment* (Columbia University Press, 1988), *Understanding Child Sexual Maltreatment* (Sage Publications, 1990), and *Child Sexual Abuse: Assessment and Intervention* (US Department of Health and Human Services, 1993), as well as a number of research studies and clinical articles in the area of child sexual abuse. She is presently member of the Board of Directors and on the Executive Committee of the American Professional Society on the Abuse of Children.

David A.S. Fergusson is Professor of Systematic Theology and head of the Department of Divinity with Religious Studies in the University of Aberdeen. He is the author of *Bultmann* (London: Chapman, 1992) and the editor of *Christ, Church and Society: Essays on John Baillie and Donald Baillie* (Edinburgh: T & T Clark, 1993).

Kieran Flanagan is Senior Lecturer in Sociology at the University of Bristol. His main work lies in the sociology of religion, specializing in liturgy, religious pluralism, hermeneutics and ritual. Currently he is researching for a book on theology, sociology and culture with the reference to debates on postmodernity. His major work is *Sociology and Liturgy: Representations of the Holy* (London: Macmillan and New York: St Martin's Press, 1991).

Duncan B. Forrester is Professor of Christian Ethics and Practical Theology at the University of Edinburgh; he is also Director of the Centre for Theology and Public Issues. His research interests are largely in the area of theology and its relation to public policy. Among his publications are *Theology and Politics* (1988), *Christianity and the Future of Welfare* (1984) and

Beliefs, Values and Policies: Conviction Politics in a Secular Age (1989).

Michael Freeman is a Reader in the Department of Government and Deputy Director of the Human Rights Centre at the University of Essex. He is author of *Edmund Burke and the Critique of Political Radicalism* and co-editor of *Frontiers of Political Theory*. He has published articles in the philosophy of social science, political theory and historical sociology, and his research interests include the formation of the modern nation-state, revolutions, genocide and human rights. He currently writing a book on the comparative study of genocide and also writes on problems of nationalism and minority rights.

Geoff Gilbert is a Senior Lecturer in the Department of Law and the Human Rights Centre at the University of Essex. His teaching includes international criminal law, the law of evidence, minority rights and the international protection of refugees. His research interests relate generally to the individual and groups in international law. His publications include *Aspects of Extradition Law* (1991) and several articles on international criminal jurisdiction, the root causes of refugee flows and the rights needed by minority groups. He is on the editorial board of the *World Report on Freedom of Thought, Religion, Conscience and Belief* (Routledge, 1996).

Robin Gill is the Michael Ramsey Professor of Modern Theology at the University of Kent at Canterbury. Previously he held the William Leech Research Chair of applied theology at the University of Newcastle. Among his books are *The Social Context of Theology* (1975), *Theology and Social Structure* (1977), *Prophecy and Praxis* (1981), *A Textbook of Christian Ethics* (1985; revised edition, 1995), *Theology and Sociology* (1987), *Competing Convictions* (1989), *Christian Ethics in Secular Worlds* (1991), *Moral Communities* (1992), *The Myth of the Empty Church* (1993), and *Readings in Modern Theology* (1995). He is currently working on a book on moral communities and Christian ethics for the series he edits for Cambridge University Press, *New Studies in Christian Ethics*.

Harvey Gillman was born in 1947 to a Jewish family. He studied modern languages at the Queen's College, Oxford. After several years as a teacher of French, Italian and German, he became a Quaker in 1977 and joined Quaker Peace and Service as Publications Secretary. Since 1981 he has been Outreach Secretary of Quaker Home Service. Publications include *A Minority of One, A Light that is Shining, An Introduction to the Quakers* and *A Portrait of Friends*. He is at present working on a pamphlet on spiritual hospitality and a study pack for attenders of Quaker meetings called *You and the Quaker Tradition*.

Tim Gorringe is the Chaplain of St John's College, Oxford, and Fellow and Tutor in Theology. He is the author of a number of books including one on providence, *God's Theatre* (SCM Press, 1991).

David L. Gosling read physics and undertook postgraduate research in nuclear physics at the University of Manchester prior to reading theology at Cambridge as part of his training for the ministry of the Church of England. He did his doctorate at the University of Lancaster on the impact of science on Indian society. From 1974–84 he taught theology at the University of Hull, then moved to Geneva to become Director of Church and Society of the World Council of Churches. He represented the Council of Churches for Britain and Ireland at the Rio Earth Summit in 1992. He is currently Spalding Fellow in Comparative Religion at the University of Cambridge and a member of staff at Great St Mary's University Church. His research interests include south Asian religion and environmental issues. Publications include *Nuclear Crisis: A Question of Breeding*, ed. with Hugh Montefiore (Prism Press, 1975), *Science Education and Ethical Values*, ed. with Bert Musschenga (World Council of Churches and Georgetown University Press, 1985), *Will the Future Work?*, ed. with Howard Davis (World Council of Churches, 1986), *A New Earth: Covenanting for Justice, Peace and the Integrity of Creation* (Council of Churches for Britain and Ireland/Delta Press, 1992).

Elaine Graham is Lecturer in Social and Pastoral Theology, and Director of the Centre for Feminist Studies in Theology, at the University of Manchester. She previously worked in adult theological education and higher education chaplaincy. Her research interests include the significance of theories of gender in the human sciences for Christian pastoral practice and theology; the relationship between contemporary social theory and Christian theology; and the interface between adult theological education and academic theology. She has published in and review regularly for, *Theology, MC* and *Contact*. She is co-editor, with Margaret Halsey, of *Life-cycles: Women and Pastoral Care* (SPCK, 1993), and is currently preparing a book on practical theology after postmodernism.

Robert Grant has taught for twenty-one years at the University of Glasgow, where he is Reader in English Literature. Previously, he was a Fellow of Trinity Hall, Cambridge, and a lecturer at the University of Sussex. He is author of *Oakeshott* (1990), and also of some seventy essays and reviews (including several other dictionary entries) on literary, aesthetic, political and philosophical topics, in the *Times Literary Supplement, Inquiry, Philosophical Quarterly, History of European Ideas, Shakespeare Studies*, among others. He has lectured widely in the United States and in Eastern Europe.

John W. De Gruchy was born in Pretoria in South Africa in 1939. He studied in South Africa and North America. He obtained a DTh from the University of South Africa in 1971 with a thesis on Dietrich Bonhoeffer and Karl Barth. An ordained minister of the United Congregational Church of Southern Africa. He has served several congregations. From 1968–73 he was Director of Studies and Communications at the South African Council of Churches. Taught in the Department of Religious Studies at the University of Cape Town since 1973. Since 1986 he has been a Professor of Christian Studies. Author of several books and is the editor of the *Journal of Theology for Southern Africa*.

Colin Gunton has been Professor of Christian Doctrine at King's College, London since 1984, and is also Associate Minister of Brentwood United Reformed Church. His recent publications are *The Promise of Trinitarian Theology* (T & T Clark, 1991), *Christ and Creation* (Paternoster, 1992) and *The One, the Three and the Many* (Cambridge University Press, 1993).

Douglas John Hall is Professor of Christian Theology in the Faculty of Religious Studies of McGill University, Montreal. He is the author of some fifteen books and numerous articles, and he lectures widely in the United States, Canada and elsewhere. He was Visiting Professor at the University of Siegen, Germany, in 1980, and Visiting Scholar at Doshisha University in Kyoto, Japan. He holds graduate degrees from Union Theological Seminary, and honorary degrees from Queen's University and the University of Waterloo. His main project is a trilogy of systematic theology in the North American Context.

Daphne Hampson holds advanced degrees in history, in theology and in continental philosophy. She has since 1977 been a Lecturer in Divinity at the University of St Andrews. She is the author of *Theology and Feminism* (Blackwell, 1990) and of numerous articles in feminist theology. Daphne Hampson is a frequent broadcaster, writer and public lecturer.

Francoise J. Hampson is Senior Lecturer in the Department of Law and the Human Rights Centre at the University of Essex. Her interests include the law of armed conflicts, international humanitarian law and international human rights law. She has appeared before the European Commission and Court of Human Rights on behalf of individual applicants and been on fact-finding missions relating to the conflicts in Afghanistan and the former Yugoslavia. She is a Governor of the British Institute of Human Rights and on the Red Cross panel of instruction, nationally and internationally. Publications include 'War and law in conflicts in the Third World', *Third World Quarterly*, vol II, no. 2 (1989), pp. 31–62; 'The United Kingdom before the European Court of Human Rights', *Oxford Yearbook of European Law* 9 (1989), pp. 121–73; 'Fact-finding and the International Fact-Finding

Commission', in Fox and Meyer (eds), *Effecting Compliance*, vol II of *Armed Conflict and the New Law* (British Institute of International and Comparative Law, 1993), pp. 53–82, and 'Means and methods of warfare in the conflict in the Gulf' and 'Liability for war crimes', in P.J. Rowe (ed.), *The Gulf War 1990–91 in International and English Law* (Routledge, 1993).

Daniel W. Hardy was President and Director, Center of Theological Inquiry, Princeton, from 1990 to 1995. Previous appointments include Lecturer and Senior Lecturer in Modern Theological Thought, University of Birmingham, 1965–86, Van Mildert Professor of Divinity, University of Durham and Residentiary Canon of Durham Cathedral, 1986–90. His major publications are *Jubilate Theology in Praise* (with David F. Ford; US title *Praising and Knowing God*), 1984, and *God's Ways with the World* (forthcoming).

Daniel J. Harrington is Professor of New Testament at Weston School of Theology in Cambridge, Massachusetts. He received his doctorate in biblical studies from Harvard University in 1970 and was ordained a priest in 1971. He has been general editor of *New Testament Abstracts* since 1972 and is a past president of the Catholic Biblical Association. The most recent of his fifteen books are *Matthew* in the Sacra Pagina series (which he edits) and *Paul on the Mystery of Israel* (Liturgical Press). He has a long standing interest in the actualization of Scripture both in antiquity and today.

Trevor A. Hart, BA (Durham), PhD (Aberdeen), is Professor of Divinity at the University of St Andrews, Scotland. From 1986 to 1995 he was a Lecturer in Systematic Theology at the University of Aberdeen. His recent publications include *Justice the True and Only Mercy: Essays on the Life and Theology of Peter Taylor Forsyth*, which he edited (T & T Clark, 1995) and *Faith Thinking: The Dynamics of Christian Theology* (SPCK, 1995).

Stanley Hauerwas is Professor of Theological Ethics at the Divinity School of Duke University.

His work ranges widely over issues of theology and ethics. His most recent book was *After Christendom?* (Abingdon Press).

Paul Helm is Professor of the History and Philosophy of Religion, King's College, London. Research interests include the metaphysics of theism, religious epistemology, and John Calvin and Calvinism. He is the author of *The Varieties of Belief* (1973), *Calvin and the Calvinists* (1982), *Divine Revelation* (1982), *Eternal God* (1988), *The Providence of God* (1993) and *Belief Policies* (1994).

Michael Herman did his national service in 1947–9 in the Intelligence Corps, and returned to intelligence work in 1952 after reading Modern History at Queen's College, Oxford. He joined Government Communications Headquarters at Cheltenham and remained there until retirement in 1987, apart from spells in the Cabinet Office (as Secretary of the Joint Intelligence Committee) and in the Defence Intelligence Staff. In 1987–8 he was a Gwillym Gibbon Fellow at Nuffield College, Oxford and since then has been an Associate Member. He teaches on intelligence and military power at King's College, London; is an Honorary Research Fellow at the University of Keele; writes articles and reviews; and is completing a book on intelligence power for the Royal Institute of International Affairs.

Peter Bingham Hinchcliff was born in South Africa in 1929, and is an Anglican clergyman. He is also a Regius Professor of Ecclesiastical History in the University of Oxford and has been a Canon of Christ Church since 1982. His research interests include the history of English theology in the nineteenth century and the history of Christianity in Africa. He is the author of several books including *John William Colenso: Bishop of Natal* (1964); *Benjamin Jowett and the Christian Religion* (1987); *God and History: Aspects of British Theology 1875–1914* (1992). His is a contributor to, *inter alia*, R. Morgan (ed.), *The Religion of the Incarnation: Anglican Essays in Commemoration of Lux Mundi* and J. McManners (ed.), *Oxford Illustrated History of Christianity*.

Simon Holdaway is Reader in Sociology at the University of Sheffield. He is a former police officer who has researched and written extensively about many aspects of policing. In the field of policing his major interests are in the occupational culture of the police and police race relations in particular. He has also researched policy making in, and the governance of, the probation service. His major publications include *Inside the British Police* and *Recruiting a Multi-Racial Police*.

Bernard Hoose is a Lecturer in Moral Theology at Heythrop College, University of London. He is the author of *Proportionalism: The American Debate and its European Roots* and of articles on various topics, including genetic engineering, divorce, justice and various aspects of fundamental moral theology. He has recently been doing research on the ethics of punishment.

Brian Horne is Lecturer in Systematic Theology at King's College, London. His research interests are in the field of aesthetics: especially the relationship between religion and literature; and in particular the work of Dante Alighieri and Charles Williams. In addition to numerous contributions to volumes of essays on theological and literary subjects his publications include *A World to Gain: Incarnation and the Hope of Renewal* (1983) and *Charles Williams: A Celebration* (1995), a collection of essays which he introduced and edited to commemorate the fiftieth anniversary of the death of Charles Williams.

Thomas E. Hosinski is Associate Professor and Chair of Theology at the University of Portland, Oregon. He received his PhD in Christian Theology from the University of Chicago Divinity School. He is a member of the American Academy of Religion and the Catholic Theological Society of America. His research is in philosophical and systematic theology, with a special interest in the doctrines of God and creation, and the relation between science and religion, and process theology. He is the author of *Stubborn Fact and Creative Advance: An Introduction to the Metaphysics of Alfred North Whitehead* (Rowman & Littlefield, 1993) and several articles in scholarly books and journals (including *Process Studies, Religious Studies Review*, and *The Modern Schoolman*). He is a Roman Catholic priest and a member of the Congregation of the Holy Cross.

Fisher Humphreys is Professor of Divinity at the Beeson Divinity School of Samford University in Birmingham, Alabama. He is an ordained Southern Baptist Minister. He has taught Christian theology for more than two decades, and has a special interest in theological method and in the contribution which theologians can make to public policy. He is the author of eight books, the most recent of which is *The Way We Were: The Theology of the Southern Baptists*.

Bob Jessop is Professor of Sociology at the University of Lancaster. He has a strong commitment to post-disciplinary theoretical and empirical work and has lectured and published in sociology, political economy, social policy, and state theory. His current research concerns changing forms of the welfare state, problems of governance, and the future of the nation-state. Among his best-known publications are *The Capitalist State* (1982), *Nicos Poulantzas* (1985), *Thatcherism: A Tale of Two Nations* (1988), *State Theory* (1990), and recent essays on the Schumpeterian workfare state, the nature of the post-Fordist state, and the character of governance. He has recently completed research on the transition to capitalism in Eastern and Central Europe.

Gareth Jones is a Lecturer in Systematic Theology at the University of Birmingham, having been Bampton Fellow at the University of Oxford, and editor of the journal *Reviews in Religion and Theology*. Researching in modern and systematic theologies, his published works include *Bultmann: Towards a Critical Theology* (1991) and *Critical Theology: Questions of Truth and Method* (forthcoming). Jones is currently working on a project on theology and social theory for Polity Press, and co-editing with Lewis Ayres a new series for Basil Blackwell entitled *Challenges in Contemporary Theology*.

Ivor H. Jones, MA Oxon, MA Cantab, MLitt, PhD (Bristol), FRCO, is Principal of Wesley House in Cambridge, and teaches the New Testament. He has had a long career in theological education, having taught at Birmingham, Lincoln, Manchester and Bristol. He is a Fellow of the Royal College of Organists, and the convener for the new Methodist hymnbook, *Hymns and Psalms*. His major interest is in biomedical ethics. He is currently editing a series of biblical commentaries.

Jack Kamerman is Associate Professor of Sociology at Kean College in Union, New Jersey. He received his PhD from New York University. He has written extensively on the sociology of death and suicide, and the sociology of music. He is currently completing research on the survivors of ninety-three New York City police officers who committed suicide between 1934 and 1940. His recent work has focused on generation as a variable in the study of suicide. He is the author of *Death in the Midst of Life: Social and Cultural Influences on Death, Grief and Mourning*.

Alistair Kee is Professor of Religious Studies at the University of Edinburgh. A graduate of the University of Glasgow, he did his graduate studies in New York and taught at the University College of Rhodesia (now Zimbabwe) and at the University of Hull before returning to teach in Glasgow. His main research field is ideology and religion and he is the co-editor of a series published by Cambridge University Press on this subject. His own books include: *The Way of Transcendence*; *Seeds of Liberation*; *A Reader in Political Theology*; *The Scope of Political Theology*; *Constantine versus Christ*; *Domination of Liberation*; *Being and Truth*; *The Roots of Christian Freedom*; *Marx and the Failure of Liberation Theology*; *From Bad Faith to Good News*.

Molly Baer Kramer was born in Illinois in 1968. She is currently researching the English animal protection movement in the nineteenth and twentieth centuries for her doctoral thesis in Modern History at the University of Oxford, where she is a Rhodes Scholar. She has a bachelor's degree in psychology and philosophy from Southern Illinois University (1990), and has completed two years towards a master's degree in environmental studies at the University of Montana.

Bernhard Lang was born in Stuttgart, Germany in 1946. He holds degrees from the universities of Tübingen (Dr theolo.) and Freiburg (Dr habil.). After having taught at the universities in Tübingen, Mainz, Philadelphia (Temple University), he now teaches religion at the University of Paderborn, Germany. He is also an Associated Professor of Religion at the Sorbonne, Paris. His publications include (with Colleen McDannell) *Heaven: A History* (Yale University Press).

Kenneth Leech is M.B. Reckitt Urban Fellow at St Botolph's Church, Aldgate, in East London. He has worked in East London for over thirty years and is author of *Pastoral Care and the Drug Scene* (SPCK, 1970), *Soul Friend* (Sheldon Press, 1977; revised edition, Darton, Longman & Todd, 1994), *Struggle in Babylon: Racism in the Cities and Churches of Britain* (Sheldon Press, 1988), *Care and Conflict: Leaves from a Pastoral Notebook* (Darton, Longman & Todd, 1990), *The Eye of the Storm: Spiritual Resources for the Pursuit of Justice* (Darton, Longman & Todd, 1992), and other works.

Andrew Linzey was born in Oxford in 1952, and is a member of the Faculty of Theology in the University of Oxford. He holds the world's first academic post in theology and animal welfare – the IFAW Senior Research Fellowship at Mansfield College, University of Oxford. He is also Special Professor in Theology at the University of Nottingham. He was formerly Director of Studies of the Centre for the Study of Theology in the University of Essex. He has been Visiting Lecturer in Religious Studies at the University of Prince Edward Island and Visiting Professor of Theology at Saint Xavier University, Chicago. He has lectured and broadcast extensively in Europe, Canada and the United States. His first book, *Animal Rights: A Christian Assessment* (1976) effectively heralded the modern animal rights movement. Since then he has written or edited thirteen books on theology and ethics including other pioneering works on animals: *Christianity and the Rights of Animals* (1987); *Animals and Christianity* (1989); (with Paul Barry Clarke) *Political Theory and Animal Rights* (1990); *Animal Theology* (1994).

Michael Lloyd read English at Downing College, Cambridge. He worked for an Air Ambulance service in Newfoundland and Labrador before training for the Anglican ministry at Cranmer Hall in Durham. He was Curate at St John's, Locks Heath, and then studied for a doctorate on 'The Cosmic Fall and the Free Will Defence' at Worcester College, Oxford. From 1990 to 1994 he was Chaplain and Director of Studies in Theology at Christ's College, Cambridge. He is currently working to complete his thesis and turn it into the first of three volumes on the problem of evil.

Ann Loades is Reader in Theology at the University of Durham. Her current research interests are in feminist theology and ethics, and in sacramental theology. Publications include *Kant and Job's Comforters* (1985), *Searching for Lost Coins* (1988, Scott Holland Lectures), ed. W.A. Whitehouse, *The Authority of Grace* (1981), with J. C. Eaton, *For God and Clarity: New Essays in Honour of Austin Farrer* (1983), *Feminist Theology* (1990), with L. Rue, *Contemporary Classics in Philosophy of Religion* (1991), with M. McLain, *Hermeneutics, the Bible and Literary Criticism* (1992), *Dorothy L. Sayers: Spiritual Writings* (1993).

John Macquarrie was Lady Margaret Professor of Divinity, University of Oxford, and Canon of Christ Church, 1970–86. He is a Fellow of the British Academy (1984) and holds three honorary doctorates. He was educated at Paisley Grammar School and at the University of Glasgow. Appointments include: Royal Chaplains Department, 1945–8; St Ninian's Church, Brechin, 1948–53; Lecturer, University of Glasgow, 1953–62; Professor of Systematic Theology, Union Theological Seminary, New York, 1962–70. His publications include: *An Existentialist Theology* (1955); *The Scope of Demythologising* (1960); *Twentieth Century Religious Thought* (1963); *Studies in Christian Theology* (1966);

God Talk (1967) *God and Secularity* (1967); *Martin Heidegger* (1968); *Three Issues in Ethics* (1970); *Existentialism* (1972); *Paths in Spirituality* (1972); *The Faith of the People of God* (1972); *The Concept of Peace* (1973); *Thinking about God* (1975); *Christian Unity and Christian Diversity* (1975); *The Humility of God* (1978); *Christian Hope* (1978); *In Search of Humanity* (1982); *In Search of Deity* (1984); *Jesus Christ in Modern Thought* (1990).

Brian Mahan recently taught Religious Studies at the University of Colorado at Boulder.

Martin E. Marty is the Fairfax M. Cone Distinguished Service Professor at the University of Chicago; he headed a six-year, six-volume fundamentalism project for the American Academy of Arts and Science and is author of the multivolume *Modern American Religion* (University of Chicago Press).

Stuart D. McLean is Associate Professor of Christian Education and Theological Ethics, Phillips Graduate Seminary, Enid, Oklahoma. Among his interests are root metaphors in understanding both theology and social science. He is author of *Humanity in the Thought of Karl Barth* (Edinburgh: T & T Clark, 1981), 'Basic sources and new possibilities: H. Richard Niebuhr's influence on faith development theory', in *Faith Development and Fowler*, ed. Craig Dykstra and Sharon Parks (1986).

Rosemary Mellor has been Senior Lecturer in the Department of Sociology, University of Manchester, since 1975. Her research interests are in urban sociology and aspects of urban change. Publications include *Urban Sociology in an Urbanized Society* (1977), 'Urban sociology: a trend report', *Sociology* (1988), and 'Transitions in British urbanization', *International Journal of Urban and Regional Research* (1989).

Marcel Merle was Professor at the University of Bordeaux (1950–67) and then Paris (1967–89). He is now Emeritus Professor at the University of Paris I. Main publications: *Sociologie des Relations internationales* (Dalloz, 4th edition, 1988; trans. into Spanish, Portuguese, English and Arabic); *Les églises chrétiennes et la décolonisation* (ed. A. Colin, 1967); *L'église catholique et les relations internationales* (Le Centurion, 1988); *Les acteurs dans les relations internationales* (Economica, 1986); *Forces et enjeux dans les relations internationales* (Economica, 1985); *La crise du Golfe et le nouvel ordre international* (Economica, 1991).

Timothy S. Miller is Associate Professor of History at Salisbury State University, Salisbury, Maryland. He received his PhD in Byzantine history at the Catholic University of America, Washington, DC in 1975. He worked for the Byzantine Research Center at Dumbarton Oaks, Harvard's Institute for the Study of Byzantine Civilization. From 1979 to 1982, Dr Miller taught at the University of Washington, Seattle, where he began work on his study of Byzantine hospitals. In 1982, he received a fellowship from the National Humanities Center in North Carolina to finish his book. In 1983, he began teaching at Salisbury State University in Maryland where he continues to work today. He is presently writing a book on the care of orphans in the Byzantine Empire and has also written several other articles on Byzantine philanthropic institutions and on orthodox monasticism.

Joan Montagnes is a Canadian studying for the Unitarian Universalist ministry at Meadville/Lombard Theological School in Chicago. She has a Masters degree in plant ecology. Her plans are to join these two streams of education into a public ministry in environmental ethics. Besides scientific publications, she has contributed to an upcoming annotated bibliography of Christian environmental justice works.

David H.J. Morgan has been employed in the Sociology Department at the University of Manchester for thirty years. His main interests are family sociology (especially changing perspectives on marriage) and the sociology of gender with particular reference to men and masculinities. He is the author of *The Family, Politics and Social Theory* (Routledge, 1985) and *Discovering Men* (Routledge, 1992). He has also edited several volumes including (with Sue Scott) *Body Matters* (Falmer, 1993).

John Muddiman is G.B. Caird Fellow in New Testament Studies at Mansfield College, Oxford and a lecturer in the Faculty of Theology. He is the author of *The Bible, Fountain and Well of Truth* (Blackwells, 1983) and several articles, including 'The first century crisis', in P. Clarke, F. Hardy, J.L. Houlden, S. Sutherland (eds) *The World's Religions* (Routledge, 1988). His interests extend beyond biblical exegesis and interpretation: he is a member of the second Anglican Roman Catholic International Commission (ARCIC II), and of the Church of England Doctrine Commission. He is also co-Director of the Oxford Centre for the Environment, Ethics and Society.

Michael Nazir-Ali is Bishop of Rochester. He was the General Secretary of the Church Missionary Society from 1989 to 1994. He holds both British and Pakistani citizenship. It was the first time in the Society's history that a Christian from outside Britain has been appointed to this position. He read Economics and Sociology at the University of Karachi, and Theology at Fitzwilliam College and Ridley Hall, Cambridge. His interests have led him to research and study in several fields, including comparative literature, comparative philosophy of religion and theology at the universities of Cambridge and Oxford, the Australian College of Theology, and the Centre for World Religions at Harvard. He has taught at universities in the United Kingdom and Pakistan.

In Pakistan, Michael also taught at Karachi Theological College, worked as a parish priest in a poor urban area, became Provost of Lahore Cathedral and was consecrated the first Bishop of Raiwind. In 1986 he was appointed to assist with the planning and preparation for the 1988 Lambeth Conference, and so joined the staff of the Archbishop of Canterbury. He was the editor of the Report and the Pastoral Letters of the 1988 Lambeth Conference.

Michael serves as a Director of the Oxford Centre for Mission Studies, Christian Aid and until recently was a trustee of Traidcraft. Michael has been a Visiting Lecturer in a number of universities and colleges in the UK, Canada, the USA and Australia. He has travelled widely in Africa, Asia, Australia,

Europe and North America. Michael is also Assistant Bishop in the Diocese of Southwark. He is the author of many articles, and three books, *Islam, a Christian Perspective*, *Frontiers in Christian-Muslim Encounter* and *From Everywhere to Everywhere – A World View of Christian Mission*.

David Nicholls is Vicar of Littlemore, Oxford. He studied politics at the London School of Economics, history at King's College, Cambridge and theology at Yale; he taught politics at the University of the West Indies, and the University of Oxford. He was a trustee of Oxfam for nine years and on the executive committee for three years. He is a Senior Member of St Anthony's College, Oxford, and was, for two years, Chairman of the Society for Caribbean Studies. He has written numerous articles on the Caribbean and is author of *The Pluralist State* (Macmillan, 1975 and 1994), *From Dessalines to Duvalier: Race, Colour and National Independence in Haiti* (Cambridge University Press, 1979; Macmillan, 1989 and 1995) and *Haiti in Caribbean Context* (Macmillan, 1985). He has contributed chapters on Haiti to the *Cambridge History of Latin America*. In 1985–6 he was Hulsean Lecturer at the University of Cambridge and has published the first series under the title *Deity and Domination* (Routledge, 1989 and 1994); a further volume is entitled *God and Government in an Age of Reason* (Routledge, 1995).

E.R. Norman is currently engaged in research in the Department of Government at the University of Essex. Her research interests include the relation between conceptions of the self and politics, the historical transformations of the concept of the self, autonomy and agonistic politics.

Michael Northcott is Lecturer in Christian Ethics and Practical Theology in New College, University of Edinburgh. He was born in London and educated in Kent and at the University of Durham. His publications include *The Church and Secularisation. Urban Industrial Mission in North East England* (Frankfurt, 1989), *The New Age and Pastoral Theology: Towards the Resurgence of the Sacred* (Edinburgh,

1992) and *The Environment and Christian Ethics* (Cambridge, 1995).

Michael Novak is a theologian, author and former US ambassador and holds the George Frederick Jewett Chair in Religion and Public Policy at the American Enterprise Institute in Washington, DC. He received the Templeton Prize for Progress in Religion in May 1994. He has written over twenty influential books in the areas of politics, economics and culture, including *The Spirit of Democratic Capitalism* (1982, 1991), *Catholic Social Thought and Liberal Institutions* (1984), *Will it Liberate? Questions about Liberation Theology* (1986) and *Free Persons and the Common Good* (1989). He also wrote the text of the influential *New Consensus on Family and Welfare* (1987). His latest book is *The Catholic Ethic and the Spirit of Capitalism*.

Helen Oppenheimer was born in 1926, and is a graduate of Lady Margaret Hall, Oxford (philosophy): BPhil, MA (Oxon); DD (Lambeth). She is a writer on philosophical theology and Christian ethics, and taught ethics at Cuddesdon Theological College, 1964–9. She has served on various Church of England commissions, especially on divorce and marriage, including the *Putting Asunder* group and the Root Commission; and on the inter-Anglican Theological and Doctrinal Commission. Books include: *The Hope of Happiness* (SCM Press, 1983); *Marriage* (Mowbrays, 1990), in the series: 'Ethics: Our Choices'. Articles in books and periodicals include: several in *A New Dictionary of Christian Ethics* (SCM Press, 1986); 'Handling life', in *Doctor's Decisions*, ed. G.R. Dunstan and E.A. Shinebourne (Oxford University Press, 1989); 'Reflections on the experience of ageing', in *Concilium* (1991); 'Ourselves, our souls and bodies', in *Studies in Christian Ethics* 4:1; 'Abortion' (ibid. 5:2); 'Ethics and personal life', in the *Encyclopedia of Theology* (Routledge, 1995).

Marco Orrù, PhD (University of California at Davis, 1984), is Associate Professor of Sociology at the University of South Florida. His book *Anomie, History and Meanings* was published by Allen & Unwin in 1987 (a French translation by l'Harmattan Edition-Diffusion is forthcoming).

His research has been published in the *British Journal of Sociology, Archives Europeenes de Sociologie, Journal of the History of Ideas, Sociological Forum, American Sociologist, Journal for the Scientific Study of Religion,* and other professional journals in the US and abroad. He is also a contributor to the *Routledge Encyclopedia of Philosophy.*

David A. Pailin is Professor of the Philosophy of Religion and Head of the Department of Philosophy at the University of Manchester, where he has taught the philosophy of religion and philosophical theology since 1966. He studied at Trinity College, Cambridge, Perkins School of Theology (Southern Methodist University, Dallas) and at the University of Manchester. His publications include *The Way to Faith, Attitudes to Other Religions, Groundwork of the Philosophy of Religion, God and the Process of Reality, The Anthropological Character of Theology* and *A Gentle Touch: From a Theology of Handicap to a Theology of Human Being,* as well as numerous contributions to books and journals. He is currently working on two studies of understanding and truth in theology, and intends to explore further the debates about faith and reason in the seventeenth and eighteenth centuries.

Barrie Paskins has worked in the Department of War Studies at King's College, London since 1971. A philosopher by training, he specializes in the ethics and the literature of war. His publications include *The Ethics of War* (with Michael Dockrill, 1979) and numerous articles on the ethics of military affairs. A member of the Council for Christian Approaches to Defence and Disarmament and of the Conflict Research Society, he was one of the authors of *The Church and the Bomb* (1982).

Michael Pearson is a Lecturer in Philosophy and Ethics, and Head of the Department of Theological Studies at Newbold College, Bracknell in Berkshire. His book *Millennial Dreams and Moral Dilemmas* (Cambridge, 1990) examines the way in which the Seventh-Day Adventist Church has responded to contemporary issues in the realm of sexual ethics. Other published

works, such as the essays in *Abortion: Ethical Issues and Options* (1990) and *Remnant and Republic* (1990) reflect his research interest in the relationship between faith and practice.

John M. Phelan, PhD (NYU), is Professor of Communications and Director of the Donald McGannon Communications Research Center, Fordham University, New York City. He began his career as a teacher of Attic and Homeric Greek, with graduate degrees in classics and philosophy. The founder and designer of the current undergraduate and graduate curricula at Fordham, Phelan also established and heads the McGannon Center for Communication Research focusing on ethical policy issues with international impact. The author of *Media-world: Programming the Public* (1977); *Disenchantment: Meaning and Morality in the Media* (1980); *Apartheid Media: Disinformation and Dissent in South Africa* (1987); and other published works presented in New York, San Francisco, Dubrovnik, and Madrid, among other international venues. Active member of the ACLU National Media Committee, American Pen Freedom-to-Write Committee, and New York's Century Association. Formerly affiliated with Yale University's International Area Studies Center and Columbia University's Media Studies Center.

Caroline Phillips read English at Oxford, and was awarded a PhD from the University of Essex for a thesis on the nature of mystical insight in the work of certain North American poets. She has lectured at the University of Cape Town and the University of British Columbia and is presently Head of English and Religious Studies at the Colchester Institute, Essex.

Roy Porter is a Professor of Social History of Medicine at the Wellcome Institute for the History of Medicine. He is currently working on the history of hysteria. Recent books include *Mind Forg'd Manacles: Madness in England from the Restoration to the Regency* (Athlone, 1987); *A Social History of Madness* (Weidenfeld & Nicolson, 1987); *In Sickness and in Health. The British Experience, 1650–1850* (Fourth

Estate, 1988); *Patient's Progress* (Polity, 1989) – these last two co-authored with Dorothy Porter; and *Health for Sale: Quackery in England 1660–1850* (Manchester University Press).

Clare Rhatigan has a background in applied social studies (including sociology, psychology and social policy), child development and pre-school and primary education. She is also a qualified social worker with a diverse range of professional experience and in a variety of settings. Her principal interests are in children with learning difficulties and their families (including counselling, assessment and advocacy), feminism and issues surrounding women and mental health.

Richard Roberts is Professor of Divinity at the University of St Andrews. He will shortly become Professor of Religious Studies at the University of Lancaster, where he will teach the sociology of religion, religion and social theory and the history of religious and atheistic thought. His current research interests include religion and socio-cultural identity, ethnography, religion and the modernity/postmodernity problem, rhetoric, and gender theory. His publications include *Hope and its Hieroglyph: A Critical Decipherment of Ernst Bloch's Principle of Hope* (1990), *A Theology in its Way: Essays on Karl Barth* (1990), *The Recovery of Rhetoric: Persuasive Discourse and Disciplinarity in the Human Sciences* (co-editor, 1993) and *Religion and the Transformations of Capitalism: Comparative Responses* (editor, 1995).

Neal Robinson was born in the UK in 1948 and is an Anglican priest and a specialist in Islam and Christian-Muslim relations. He studied in the universities of Oxford, London, Birmingham and Paris and is currently Lecturer in Theology and Religious Studies at the University of Leeds. In addition to contributing to several collections of essays and writing numerous articles for academic journals, he is the author of *Christ in Islam and Christianity* (1991) and the editor and translator of *The Sayings of Muhammad* (1991). He is currently completing a book on the Qur'an, which is scheduled to be published by SCM Press in 1996.

Christopher Rowland is Dean Ireland Professor of the Exegesis of Holy Scripture at the University of Oxford and a Fellow of Queen's College. His recent books include *Christian Origins* (1985) and (with Mark Corner) *Liberating Exegesis: The Challenge of Liberation Theology to Biblical Studies* (1990).

Rosemary Radford Ruether is the Georgia Harkness Professor of Applied Theology at the Garrett Theological Seminary and member of the Graduate Faculty of Northwestern University in Evanston, Illinois. She is a frequent contributor to books and magazines on issues of religion and women, peace and justice and ecology. Her most recent book is *Gaia and God: An Ecofeminist Theology of Earthhealing* (San Francisco: Harper, 1992).

Elinor Scarborough is Lecturer in European Politics and Government and Politics Fellow in the Centre for the Study of Theology at the University of Essex. Her publications include *Political Ideology and Voting Behaviour* (1984), *The Scope of Government* (co-editor, 1995), and *The Impact of Values* (co-editor, 1995). She was research co-ordinator for the European Science Foundation Programme Beliefs in Government (1989–95) and is joint series editor of five volumes examining changing attitudes towards government among the publics of Western Europe.

H. Schuurmann, PhD (University of Notre Dame, 1979), is Professor at King's University College in Edmonton, Canada. Previously he has taught at Denison University, Calvin College and Calvin Theological Seminary. He is the co-author (with A. Freddoso) of *Ockham's Theory of Propositions: Part II of the Summa Logicae*, and articles on the concept of theodicy. He is presently working on a book on the problem of evil.

Peter Scott is Professor of Education at the University of Leeds. He was editor of *The Times Higher Education Supplement* from 1976 until 1992. He has written extensively on universities. His books include *Knowledge and Nation* (1990) and *The Crisis of the University* (1984). He is a member of the Academia Europaea and has honorary degrees from the University of Bath and the Council for National Academic Awards.

Peter Sedgwick is Vice Principal of Westcott House, Cambrdige. He was formerly a Lecturer in the Theology Department at the University of Hull, and is an ordained Anglican minister. He has written *The Enterprise Culture* (SPCK, 1991), and co-edited *The Weight of Glory: The Future of Liberal Theology* (T & T Clark, 1991), which was a festschrift for Peter Baelz. He is also Advisor in Industrial Issues to the Archbishop of York, and a member of the Church of England's Industrial and Economic Affairs Committee.

A.D. Smith is Professor of Sociology at the London School of Economics. He took his first degree in Classics at Wadham College, Oxford, studied Politics at the College d'Europe in Brussels and obtained his Masters and Doctorate in Sociology at the London School of Economics. He also holds a Doctorate in the history of art. His teaching and research interests are in comparative and historical sociology, specializing in the study of ethnic identity and nationalism. His publications include *Theories of Nationalism* (1971; 2nd edition, 1983), *The Ethnic Revival* (1981), *The Ethnic Origins of Nations* (1986), *National Identity* (1991), and *Nations and Nationalism in a Global Era* (1995).

Norman Solomon who currently teaches at Oxford, founded the Centre for the Study of Judaism and Jewish/Christian Relations at the Selly Oak Colleges, Birmingham, and was its Director from 1983–94. Prior to that, he was rabbi to several orthodox congregations in the UK. He was a member of the international committee which organized the Oxford (1988) and Berlin (1994) *Remembering for the Future* conferences on holocaust and genocide. From 1985–91 he was editor of the quarterly *Christian Jewish Relations* for the Institute of Jewish Affairs, London. His publications include *Judaism and World Religion* (1991), *The Analytic Movement* (1993). His main research interest now is the impact of modernity on religious thought.

Robert Song is Lecturer in Christian Ethics at St John's College, Durham. He holds a DPhil from the University of Oxford for work in political theology. He has published several articles in the field of Christian ethics, and is author of a forthcoming book on Christian theology and political liberalism (to be published by Clarendon Press). Since 1991 he has chaired the Movement for Christian Democracy.

Bryan Spinks is Chaplain at Churchill College, Cambridge, and an affiliated lecturer in the Divinity Faculty of the University. His research and publications have been in the areas of liturgy and doctrine, specializing in East Syrian liturgy, and the Reformed tradition. He has contributed to a large number of theological journals. His main publications are *Freedom or Order?* (1984); *From the Lord, and the Best Reformed Churches* (1985), *The Sanctus in the Eucharistic Prayer* (1991), *Western Use and Abuse of the Eastern Liturgical Traditions* (1992), *Worship: Prayers from the East* (1993) and with J. R. K. Fenwick, *Worship in Transition* (1995). He has also edited and co-edited three other major books. Bryan Spinks is a member of the Church of England Liturgical Commission.

Timothy L.S. Sprigge, born 1932, was previously Professor of Logic and Metaphysics at the University of Edinburgh and he now teaches there part-time. His books include *Santayana: An Examination of his Philosophy* (1974), *The Vindication of Absolute Idealism* (1983), *The Rational Foundations of Ethics* (1987), and *James and Bradley: American Truth and British Reality* (1993). His interests divide equally between ethics and metaphysics.

Kenneth Surin wrote two books in his career as a philosopher of religion. More recently, he has produced articles on C.L.R. James, ethnographic writing, post-colonial theory, global capitalism and state theory. He is currently Professor and Director of Graduate Studies in the Literature Program at Duke University.

Stephen Sykes has been Bishop of Ely since 1990. Previously he has been Fellow and Dean of St John's College, Cambridge, 1964–74, and Fellow again, 1985–90, Van Mildert Professor of Divinity, University of Durham, 1974–85, and Regius Professor of Divinity, University of Cambridge, 1985–90. He is the author of *The Integrity of Anglicanism* (1978), *The Identity of Christianity* (1984) and *Unashamed Anglicanism* (1995), and has edited a number of other works, including *Sacrifice and Redemption* (1991).

Mary Elizabeth Tanner is currently General Secretary of the Church of England's Council for Christian Unity. Previously she taught Hebrew at Hull and Bristol universities and at the Federation of Theological Colleges in Cambridge. A member of the World Council's Faith and Order Commission since 1976, she is now its Moderator. She was a member of ARCIC II and the Archbishop of Canterbury's Commission on Women and the Episcopate, the Eames Commission. She has published articles in the field of Old Testament, ecumenical theology, Anglicanism and Christian feminism. In 1988 she was awarded a Lambeth DD by the Archbishop of Canterbury and in 1990 received an honorary DD from the General Seminary, New York.

Barry P. Thompson is Canon Theologian of Chelmsford Cathedral in the UK and a Fellow of the Centre for the Study of Theology, University of Essex. He initially trained as a scientist at the universities of St Andrews and Oxford. More recently he has been the Archbishop of York's adviser on industrial issues and Director of the Applied Theology Unit of the University of Hull. While there, he edited the festschrift for A.T. Hanson (*Scripture, Method and Meaning*, Hull University Press, 1987). He has been a consultant to the Church and Society sub-unit of the World Council of Churches and of its Christian Medical Commission. He edited the proceedings of the second WCC International Consultation on AIDS and Pastoral Care, Tanzania 1988. He is convener of the Bioethics Group of the Society of Ordained Scientists and joint editor of the Essex University Papers on Theology and Society.

David M. Thompson, MA, PhD, FRHistS, is University Lecturer in Modern Church History

and has been a Fellow of Fitzwilliam College, Cambridge since 1965. He has been President of the Ecclesiastical History Society since 1993, and convener of the Doctrine and Worship Committee of the United Reformed Church since 1991, and has been active in ecumenical affairs nationally and internationally for nearly thirty years, serving as a member of the Executive Committee of the British Council of Churches in the 1980s.

James Thrower is Professor of the History of Religions and Director of the Centre for the Study of Religions at the University of Aberdeen. He was educated at the universities of Durham (where he read theology) and Oxford (where he read philosophy). Before being appointed in 1970 to a lectureship in the comparative study of religions at Aberdeen, he had taught at the universities of Leicester, Ghana and at Bede College, Durham. He is the author of *A Short History of Western Atheism* (1971), *The Alternative Tradition* (1981), *Marxist-Leninist 'Scientific Atheism' and the Study of Religion and Atheism in the USSR* (1983) and *Marxism-Leninism as the Civil Religion of Soviet Society* (1992). He is currently working on *Theories of Religion*.

Sylvana Tomaselli was a Research Student at King's College, Cambridge, then a Research Fellow of Newnham College, Cambridge (1985–8). She is an intellectual historian working predominantly on the seventeenth and eighteenth centuries. She has written on such topics as mind–body dualism, the history of women, and population theories. Her publications also include a translation of Jacques Lacan's *Seminar II: The Ego in Freud's Theory and in Psychoanalytic Technique*, edited by Jacques-Alain Miller, prepared and annotated by John Forrester (Cambridge University Press and Norton, 1988). She edited *Rape: An Historical and Social Enquiry* (Blackwell, 1986; pb, 1989) and *The Dialectics of Friendship* (Routledge, 1989) with Roy Porter. She has contributed to a number of reference works on the Enlightenment and other subjects. Her book, *Seduction and Civilization: An Enlightenment Perspective on the History of Woman*, will be published by Weidenfeld and

Nicolson. She is also editing Mary Woll-stonecraft's *Vindication of the Rights of Woman* for Cambridge University Press.

Iain R. Torrance is Lecturer in Systematic and Practical Theology, University of Aberdeen, Scotland. He has been joint editor of the *Scottish Journal of Theology* since 1982. Author of *Christology after Chalcedon* (1988). Contributor to *Who Needs Feminism?* (ed. Holloway, 1991), *Justice the True and Only Mercy* (ed. Hart, 1995); *But Where Shall Wisdom be Found?* (ed. Main, 1995); *The Forty Martyrs of Sebasteia* (ed. Mullet, 1995). His research interests include sixth-century theology, bioethics, ethics and the community, Scottish theology.

Thomas S. Torrance is Senior Lecturer in the Department of Economics at Heriot-Watt University in Edinburgh. He holds an MA from St Andrews and a PhD from the University of Edinburgh. Previously, he was a Lecturer in the Department of Logic at the University of Aberdeen. His research interests include: philosophy and the methodology of economics; history of economic thought; open-economy macro-economics. Publications include 'Causation, social science and Sir John Hicks' (with J. T. Addison and J. Burton) in *Oxford Bulletin of Economics and Statistics* 50 (1988), 'The philosophy and methodology of economics', in D. Mair and A.G. Millers (ed.) *A Modern Guide to Economic Thought* (Edward Elgar, 1991), 'Causality and determinism in economics' (with S. A. Draka-polous), in *Scottish Journal of Political Economy* 41 (1994).

Denys Turner is currently H.G. Wood Professor of Theology at the University of Birmingham and formerly Senior Lecturer in Theology in the Department and Religious Studies at the University of Bristol. He is the author of *Marxism and Christianity* (Oxford: Blackwell, 1983); *The Darkness of God* (1995) *Eros and Allegory* (1995) and a number of articles on the relations between Christian theology and politics. From 1989–95, he was Chair of the Catholic Institute for International Relations in London.

John Urry, BA, MA, PhD (Cambridge), has taught at the University of Lancaster since 1970. He is currently Professor of Sociology and Dean of the Faculty of Social Sciences. He has published many books including *The End of Organized Capitalism* (1987); *The Tourist Gaze* (1990); *Economies of Signs and Space* (1993). Research interests include social class, tourism and leisure, the environment, the service industry and social theory. He is editor of the *International Library of Sociology* (Routledge).

Charles Villa-Vicencio is Professor of Religion and Society at the University of Cape Town. The author of over fifty academic articles, his latest books include *A Theology of Reconstruction: Nation-Building and Human Rights* (Cambridge University Press, 1992) and *The Spirit of Hope: Conversations on Politics, Religion and Values* (University of California Press, 1994). His research interests include theology and culture, religion and human rights and religious pluralism.

Alex de Waal completed his DPhil in social anthropology at the University of Oxford, a study of rural famine survival strategies that was published as *Famine Kills: Darfu, Sudan, 1984–1985* (Clarendon Press, 1989). Subsequently he has written widely on issues of famine and human rights in Africa, and was Associate Director of Africa Watch until resigning in 1992 on account of his opposition to the US military intervention in Somalia. Since then, he has been co-Director of the London-based organization African Rights. His most recent publication (jointly with Rakiya Omaar) is *Rwanda: Death, Despair and Defiance* (African Rights, 1994).

Paul Waldau was born in 1950 and is a Religious Studies graduate of the University of California. He pursued graduate work in theology with Langdon Gilkey, David Tracy and Schubert Ogden at the University of Chicago Divinity School, and work in the philosophy of religion with John Hick at Claremont Graduate School. He completed a master's degree in religious studies at Stanford University and a Juris Doctor degree at UCLA Law School. He is currently a research student in the Faculty of Theology in the University of Oxford and a member of Christ Church, Oxford. He is working on a doctoral dissertation, under Keith Ward, on speciesism in the world's religions.

Rachel Walker is a Lecturer in Russian and Soviet Politics and the Director of the Centre for Russian Studies at the University of Essex. She has also taught at the University of Southampton. Her research interests concern ideological process in the Soviet Union and contemporary Russia. Recent publications include, *Six Years that Shook the World: Perestroika the Impossible Project* (Manchester University Press, 1993); 'Glasnost and perestroika', in M. Foley, *The Shape of Political Ideas* (Manchester University Press, 1994); 'The Soviet State and its Demise', in *Eastern Europe and the Commonwealth of Independent States* (Europa Publications, 1994); 'Language and the politics of identity in the USSR', in M.E. Urban, *Ideology and System Change in the USSR and Eastern Europe* (Macmillan, 1992); 'The relevance of ideology', in R.J. Hill, *Restructuring Eastern Europe: Views from Western Europe* (Edward Elgar, 1990).

Pat Walsh is a Lecturer in Medical Ethics at the Centre of Medical Law and Ethics, King's College, London. She is a moral philosopher who has worked at University College, London and at the London School of Economics. Her research interests are in the field of moral and political philosophy and currently she is working on a European-wide study of the moral issues presented by persistent vegetative states.

Charles Wanamaker is an Associate Professor and Head of the Department of Religious Studies at the University of Cape Town, South Africa. He has received academic degrees in the United States, Canada and Great Britain. He has a PhD from the University of Durham, England. He is is a specialist in New Testament and Early Christian studies and socio-historical studies of the emergence of Early Christianity. He is the author of *Commentary on First and Second Thessalonians* in the International Greek Testament Commentary Series.

Colin Ward is a self-employed anarchist author, whose *Anarchy in Action*, first published in 1973 has appeared in eight languages. Most of his many books explore popular and unofficial uses of the environment. His *The Child in the City* and *The Child in the Country* (Bedford Square Press) examine the environmental experiences of childhood. *Talking Houses* and *Freedom to Go* (Freedom Press) apply an anarchist approach to housing and transport. In *Influences: Voices of Creative Dissent* (Green Books) he discusses the thinkers whose ideas have shaped his own.

Albert Weale has been Professor of Government at the University of Essex and co-editor of the *British Journal of Political Science* since 1992. Prior to that he was Professor of Politics at the University of East Anglia, and before that Lecturer in Politics and Assistant Director of the Institute for Research in the Social Sciences at the University of York. His current research interests include modern political theory, especially the theory of justice and the theory of democracy, health politics and comparative environmental policy. His principal publications include *Political Theory and Social Policy* (Macmillan, 1983), *The New Politics of Pollution* (Manchester University Press, 1992) and (with others) *The Theory of Choice* (Blackwell, 1992), as well as a number of edited works and papers.

Jonathan Webber recently graduated from Oriel College, University of Oxford, where he gained a first class degree in philosophy and theology. He is currently researching issues in Christian ethics and the philosophy of religion.

Todd Whitmore is Assistant Professor of Social Ethics in the Department of Theology at the University of Notre Dame, Indiana. He has been a recipient of the Henry Luce III Fellowship in Theology and is a member of the Center of Theological Inquiry in Princeton, New Jersey. His articles have appeared in several journals, including *Theological Studies* and *The Journal of Religious Ethics*. He is the editor of *Ethics in the Nuclear Age: Strategy, Religious Studies, and the Churches* and *The Growing End: Retrieving and Renewing the Thought of John*

Courney Murray (with J. Leon Cooper). His present work is entitled *The Common Good and the Care of Children: Catholicism, American Public Life, and the Challenge of Abortion.*

Yorick Wilks is Professor of Computer Science at the the University of Sheffield. Previously he was a researcher at Stanford AI Laboratory, Professor of Computer Science and Linguistics at the University of Essex and then Director of the Computing Research Laboratory at New Mexico State University. He received his doctorate from the University of Cambridge in 1968 for work in computer programmes that understand written English in terns of a theory later called 'preference semantics'. This has continued to be the focus of his work. He has published numerous articles and five books on artificial intelligence, the most recent of which is *Artificial Believers* (with Afzal Ballim, Lawrence Erlbaum Associates, 1991). He is a Fellow of the American Association for Artificial Intelligence, and serves on advisory committees for the National Science Foundation and the boards of some fifteen AI-related journals.

Michael A. Williams, PhD (Harvard 1977, New Testament and Christian Origins), is Associate Professor of Comparative Religion at the University of Washington, Seattle, WA, and served as chairman of the Comparative Religion Program from 1985–91. He is the author of *The Immovable Race: A Gnostic Designation and the Theme of Stability in Late Antiquity* (1985); editor of *Charisma and Sacred Biography* (1982) and *Innovation in Religious Traditions: Essays in the Interpretation of Religious Change* (1992); author of numerous articles on gnosticism and related topics and translations of ancient gnostic documents. In 1991 he was Visiting Professor with the Faculté de théologie de l'Université Lavel in Quebec, in connection with Laval's Project Nag Hammadi. He has served as chairman of the Nag Hammadi and Gnosticism section of the Society of Biblical literature, and on the steering committee of this and other SBL units treating gnosticism and early Christianity. He is currently on the board of the *Journal of Biblical Literature.*

Rowan Williams was born in South Wales and studied Theology at Cambridge and Oxford. He has taught in various Theological Colleges and universities in Britain, the United States and Africa. Until 1992, he was Professor of Divinity in the University of Oxford, and is now Bishop of Monmouth in the Anglican Church in Wales. He has written several books on Christian doctrine and spirituality, and has a particular interest in the social context of Christian spirituality. His most recent book (1991) is a study of St Teresa of Avila.

John Wilson has held the posts of Professor of Religion, Trinity College, Toronto and Lecturer in Philosophy, University of Sussex. He is currently Lecturer in Educational Studies and Tutor at the University of Oxford Department of Educational Studies. He is the author of numerous books in philosophy, religion and education, including *Equality* (Hutchinson, 1966), *Education in Religion and the Emotions* (Heinemann, 1972) and *A Preface to Morality* (Macmillan, 1987).

Bryan Wilson was Reader in Sociology in the University of Oxford from 1962 to 1993, and Fellow of All Souls. He served as President of the Conference Internationale de Sociologie des Religions (1971–5), and became its first Honorary President in 1991. He has contributed to various encyclopedias, written ten books (and edited a further six) mainly on sociological aspects of religion. Among his more recent publications have been *Religion in Sociological Perspective*; *The Social Dimensions of Sectarianism* and *A Time to Chant: The Soka Gakkai Buddhists in Britain* (with Karl Dobbelaere).

Charles E. Winquist is Thomas J. Watson Professor of Religion at Syracuse University. He is a philosophical theologian working in a secular context. He has authored and co-authored numerous articles and nine books including *Epiphanies of Darkness* (1986), *Theology at the End of the Century* (1990) and *Desiring Theology* (1994).

John Witte, Jr is Professor of Law and Director of the Law and Religion Program at Emory

University in Atlanta, Georgia. He teaches and writes in the fields of legal history, church-state relations, and law and religion, and is the author of some fifty professional articles, and editor of *Christianity and Democracy in Global Context* (1993), *The Weightier Matters of the Law* (1988) and *A Christian Theory of Social Institutions* (1986).

J. Philip Wogaman has been Senior Minister of the historic Foundry United Methodist Church in Washington DC since 1992. After receiving a PhD in social ethics from Boston University (1960), he taught Christian ethics at University of the Pacific (1961–6) and Wesley Theological Seminary in Washington DC (1966–92), serving as Dean of that institution from 1972–83, and currently as affiliated professor. He is a past President of the Society of Christian Ethics of the United States and Canada, and a member of the American Theological Society and the Society for the Study of Christian Ethics (UK). Dr Wogaman's publications include *Christian Moral Judgment* (1989), *Christian Perspectives on Politics* (1988), *Economics and Ethics* (1986) and *Christians and the Great Economic Debate* (1977), among others.

Linda Woodhead is Lecturer in Christian Studies at the University of Lancaster. Her doctoral research was on 'The religion of Rabindranath Tagore'. Her current research is in Christian studies, and she has a particular interest in Christianity in the modern world and in Christian ethics. Her recent publications include 'Feminism and Christian ethics', in Teresa Elwes (ed.), *Women's Voices in Religion* and 'Post-Christian spiritualities', in *Religion*. She is currently engaged in writing a one-volume introduction to Christianity.

John H. Yoder is Professor of Theology in the University of Notre Dame, and a Fellow of Notre Dame's Joan B. Kroc Institute for International Peace Studies. In 1987 he served as Chairman of the Notre Dame Faculty Senate. He served the Mennonite denomination in overseas relief and mission administration, in ecumenical representation, and in seminary education. He served Goshen Biblical Seminary in Elkhart as professor 1965–84 and as President 1970–3. He has served as guest faculty in graduate theological schools in Buenos Aires, Strasbourg, Berkeley, Vancouver, Miami and Melbourne. His research and writing have been in the fields of reformation history, ecumenism, and church renewal, and Christian social ethics. In 1987 he served as President of the Society of Christian Ethics. His best known books are *The Politics of Jesus* and *The Original Revolution* (1972), *When War is Unjust and The Priestly Kingdom* (1985) and *Body Politics* (1992).

Dudley Young teaches in the Department of Literature at the University of Essex. His most recent book, *Origins of the Sacred: The Ecstasies of Love and War* (Little, Brown, 1992), is an inter-disciplinary attempt to align the discourses of anthropology, philosophy and mythology.

ABORTION

Abortion demonstrates perhaps better than any other moral issue the impossibility of segregating 'personal' from 'social' ethics, morality from law, or religious from secular moral argument.

In ethical discourse, abortion is understood as the deliberate choice to terminate a pregnancy through an action which either directly destroys the foetus or causes its expulsion from the uterus before viability. Such a choice is obviously a highly personal moral action. In abortion a person or persons cause the death of another individual member of the species (although whether the foetus is likewise a 'person' is a hotly contested and crucial point in the abortion debate). At the same time, moral views of abortion are closely entwined with social concerns about SEXUALITY, GENDER and FAMILY, and about the social institutionalization of various forms of homicide. The relative influence of these social factors in shaping evaluations of abortion has varied historically as well as culturally.

Historical variation no less characterizes Christian approaches to abortion. While until recent decades the Christian churches had always condemned abortion, they did so for different reasons and in different degrees, and theological opinion has been offered in support of different exceptions to the general prohibition. In contemporary Christianity, the social and political EMANCIPATION of women and their struggle for sexual equality have created strong challenges to the traditional presumption against using abortion as a means of avoiding motherhood. The conflict over gender, sexuality and abortion in the public sphere has also led to debates about the proper relation between law and morality, and about the legitimacy of the involvement of religious bodies in policy formation.

Abortion receives scant attention in Scripture. One frequently cited text in the Hebrew Bible provides that, if a woman is struck and miscarries, the perpetrator shall pay a fine to her husband. If the woman herself is killed, the penalty shall be 'life for life' (Exodus 21: 22–3). The lesser valuation of foetal life is nuanced in the Greek Septuagint translation (early third century BCE), which imports the Greek philosophical distinction between the formed and unformed foetus, regarding only the formed as a 'man' and the killing of it as homicide. Several Biblical texts manifest interest in life in the womb without making explicit reference to abortion (Genesis 4: 1; Job 31: 15; Isaiah 44: 24; 49: 1, 5; Jeremiah 1: 5; Matthew 1: 18; Luke 1: 40, 42). The New Testament rejects magical drugs and potions (*pharmakeia*), which probably included abortifacients (Galatians 5: 20; Revelation 9: 21). Early Christian writings, the *Didache* and *The Epistle of Barnabas*, explicitly condemn both abortion and infanticide, linking the former not only with occult medicine but also with sexual immorality.

The assumption that resort to abortion disguises sexual lust, especially the infidelities of women, continues to characterize condemnations of abortion in the early church, for instance by Clement of Alexandria (the *Pedagogue*) and Tertullian (the *Veiling of Virgins*). Tertullian also exhibits concern for the status of unborn life itself when he defends Christians against accusations of infanticide by going so far as to reject any destruction of what has been conceived (the *Apology*). Elsewhere he characterizes abortion to save the mother as a 'necessary cruelty', but even so does not clearly justify it, arguing, apparently to the contrary, that the foetus lives before birth (*On the Soul*).

Though condemning abortion as at least a sexual sin, Tertullian, Jerome and Augustine propose that only abortion of the formed foetus is homicide. Their premise is that God infuses the human soul, not at conception, but at a subsequent point when the development of the body is adequate. The time of ensoulment was set at forty days for males and ninety for females, according to Aristotle's claims based on his observation of differences in aborted foetuses. The differentiation of the ensouled or animated foetus from earlier forms was endorsed in the medieval period, pre-eminently by Thomas Aquinas, following the Septuagint (*Commentary on Book III of the Sentences of Peter Lombard; Summa Theologiae* II-II. Q 64). At the same time, a contradictory and competing view influenced both patristic and medieval writers sometimes to adopt a more stringent position, treating even sterilization as a form of killing. This was the notion, ignorant of the female genetic contribution, that the male seed contains the whole human being in miniature, so that to waste it is to kill.

The Protestant Reformers share with the prior tradition the assumption that the only proper expression of sexuality is in patriarchal, monogamous, procreative marriage. They take up the question of ensoulment primarily in relation to God's creative and predestining will. Luther and Calvin held that the soul comes into existence with the body at conception, while Melanchthon believed that the infusion of the soul awaited a gradual formation of the body. Calvin characterizes abortion as 'an inexpiable crime' (*Commentaries*, at Genesis 38: 10) and asserts that 'the fetus enclosed in its mother's womb already is a man' (*Commentaries*, at Exodus 21: 22). Anglican and Puritan thinkers of the seventeenth century also condemned abortion, primarily as a sin of sexual immorality, though some alluded to the distinction between formed and unformed foetuses.

In the developing casuistic tradition of Catholicism, authors both before and after the Reformation maintained the distinction of foetal stages. Some debated justifiable abortion, usually to save the mother's life, but also in view of her health and reputation. By the late nineteenth century the Catholic Church had narrowed its teaching on both fronts, treating life as having full value from conception, and ultimately excluding any direct destruction of the unborn even to save the mother's life (in an 1869 Vatican decision against emergency craniotomy during birth). Official Catholic teaching continues, however, to permit so-called indirect abortions, operations directed primarily at relieving a condition of the mother but having as a tolerated secondary effect the death of the foetus she carries. In such cases, the destruction of the foetus itself must neither be carried out directly nor be the means to alleviate the mother's condition. An example of an allowable procedure is a hysterectomy performed on a women who is pregnant but who has uterine cancer.

Although the Reformers invariably conceived of the individual's good in relation to the societies of family, church and CITIZENSHIP, and, like their medieval predecessors, set religious authority on a higher plane than civil government, they also set a new course for ethics through the importance attached to the faith commitment of the individual. By emphasizing faith in God through Jesus Christ even over membership in religious community, the Reformation made it possible for modern Christianity, especially mainstream Protestantism, to envision the moral agent's conscience as the true and ultimate gauge of moral responsibility. This tendency emerged interdependently with the Enlightenment confidence in rationality and autonomous decision, and with the Western liberal democratic political systems which enhanced the legal protection of AUTONOMY, privacy and conscience. The modern recognition of the importance of individual integrity and freedom has only gradually been extended to women. In the industrialized Western nations of the twentieth century, it has come increasingly to entail the view that reproductive freedom is a necessary precondition of women's access to a range of social opportunities traditionally reserved for men. A consequence has been the liberalization of abortion laws.

Religious responses to these social changes can be categorized largely along Roman Catholic and Protestant lines. CATHOLICISM with its unified and hierarchical teaching office, male clergy and medieval theological foundations, has tended to accept women's access to public roles cautiously, and to view motherhood as the ultimate feminine vocation. Catholic moral theology, deriving from penitential practice, also aims at precise conclusions and norms, making these as specific as possible. The result has been exceptionless rules against both contraception and abortion, the latter linked by the Second Vatican Council with infanticide as 'unspeakable crimes' (*Gaudium et spes*, no. 51). The Enlightenment influence is evident in so far as the Catholic position presents abortion in terms of a conflict of individuals – foetus against mother. The Catholic moral tradition, deriving from the essentially philosophical 'natural law' system of Aquinas, also values rationality, justice and public consensus. Catholics are likely to seek and expect a relatively large degree of coherence between religious beliefs, more general humanistic moral values and the civil law.

Protestants rest more confidence in individual accountability to God than in authoritative teaching. The Reformation emphasis on SIN, ambiguity and even paradox in the human condition yields as well a scepticism about absolute moral rules, owing partly to a distrust of reason and of works-righteousness. The Reformers' acceptance of a married clergy, and the development of covenantal traditions about both marriage and religious community, may have accelerated Protestant support for women's social participation, including ordination in many mainstream denominations. Hence, regarding abortion, Protestants are much more likely than Catholics to see it as an individual decision in which unique circumstances must be considered and which cannot be constrained too closely by law. Although abortion may be tragic, and may always be shadowed by moral ambivalence, it cannot be condemned absolutely. An exception to these trends is found in fundamentalist and Biblicist Protestant denominations, which often combine conservative social attitudes with a view of Scripture as warranting unequivocal condemnation of sinners. In such groups, a post-industrial, Western, nuclear family structure is often elevated as a standard against which both abortion and women's roles are evaluated.

The comparative legal scholar Mary Ann Glendon (1987) notes that twentieth-century abortion laws have developed in most European countries as a result of public debate contributing to a revised consensus. Religious groups were not necessarily excluded from the process, even given highly pluralistic cultures (e.g. consultations of British government commissions with the churches in order to offer recommendations prior to policy changes). Of twenty countries studied, only two (Ireland and Belgium) retained blanket prohibitions against abortion. Eleven countries, including Great Britain (England, Scotland and Wales), allowed abortion 'with cause' and after review, although the actual accessibility of abortion varied. Six countries, among them the USA, allowed elective abortion, at least in the first trimester of pregnancy. Glendon argues that the process toward moderate change which occurred in the UK and elsewhere from the late 1960s onward was short-circuited in the USA by the 1973 Supreme Court decision, Roe v. Wade. Roe allowed the woman virtually absolute freedom in terminating a first or second trimester pregnancy, but also isolated her as an individual from the social and economic supports which encourage childbirth (e.g. through health care and family policies). Although the compromise statute likely to have emerged through American legislatures might have been permissive in the first trimester, it might also have used moderate restraints on later abortions to affirm a moral ethos which values childbearing and seeks alternatives to problem pregnancies.

In the USA in particular, the churches are engaged in a struggle either to sustain 'abortion rights' or to redefine abortion policy more narrowly (with the Roman Catholic Church as perhaps the most visible institutional advocate of the latter course). Two issues can be addressed briefly here. Should the morality of abortion be reflected in the law? And should religious groups be influential in shaping law for pluralistic societies? Although not every moral value can be legally prescribed, the law does legitimately address moral decisions which bear on the good of others or on the common good. Key to abortion law is the moral status of the foetus, a conundrum perhaps in principle not definitively resolvable. Although an individual life may begin with conception, even official Catholic teaching acknowledges that the status of such a life as a 'person' is finally unclear and not empirically demonstrable (Vatican 1987). In the absence of conclusive scientific or philosophical evidence which could settle the issue, the task is to shape a reasonable social consensus about the status of foetal life and about its protectability in the face of the mother's conflicting interests. If the foetus has significant value independently of the mother, then its protection may well fall within the proper scope of the law. Criteria of a just and viable law would include that it be non-discriminatory, not create greater evils than it avoids and command enough respect to be enforceable. In a heterogeneous SOCIETY, no individual or group should be excluded from the development of a consensus about law, provided that arguments are articulated in publicly accessible language, which, while non-sectarian, need not be

3

'neutral'. Even ostensibly secular philosophical or humanist positions necessarily owe their identity to particular moral and political traditions, as is certainly true of the liberal democratic positions which have created the very framework for the modern Western abortion debate.

In conclusion, it needs to be noted that the reality of abortion as a social and moral issue extends beyond the Western framework. The majority of the world's women live in highly patriarchal cultures with little access to education and health care, much less to a variety of social roles or reproductive freedom. From a Christian social perspective, considerations of international economic and political JUSTICE must form the most basic foundations of the moral consideration of abortion. Abortion as an individual moral decision is secondary to structures of family and society which drastically limit the moral freedom which a woman, couple or family may have in carrying out the responsibilities of sexuality, MARRIAGE, family, pregnancy and parenthood.

Callahan, D. (1970) *Abortion: Law, Choice and Morality*, New York and London: Macmillan and Collier Macmillan.

Callahan, D. and Callahan, S. (eds) (1984) *Abortion: Understanding Differences*, New York and London: Plenum.

Connery, J. (1977) *Abortion: The Development of the Roman Catholic Perspective*, Chicago, IL: Loyola University Press.

Glendon, M.A. (1987) *Abortion and Divorce in Western Law: American Failures, European Challenges*, Cambridge, MA: Harvard University Press.

Grisez, G.G. (1970) *Abortion: The Myths, the Realities, and the Arguments*, New York: Corpus Books.

Harrison, B. (1983) *Our Right to Choose: Toward a New Ethic of Abortion*, Boston, MA: Beacon Press.

Jung, P.B. and Shannon, T.A. (eds) (1988) *Abortion and Catholicism: The American Debate*, New York: Crossroad.

McBrien, R.P. (1987) *Caesar's Coin: Religion and Politics in America*, New York and London: Macmillan and Collier Macmillan.

Mitchell, B. (1987) 'Should law be Christian?', *The Month* 248 (Second New Series 20): 95–9.

Murray, J.C. (1964) *We Hold These Truths: Catholic Reflections on the American Proposition*, New York: Sheed & Ward.

Noonan, J.T., Jr (ed.) (1970) *The Morality of Abortion: Legal and Historical Perspectives*, Cambridge, MA: Harvard University Press.

Vatican Congregation for the Doctrine of the Faith (1974) *Declaration on Abortion*, Origins 4: 386–92.

——(1987) *Donum vitae (Instruction on Respect for Human Life in Its Origin and on the Dignity of Procreation: Replies to Certain Questions of the Day)*, Origins 16: 697–711.

Lisa Sowle Cahill

ADVENTISM

Christians have differed widely over the centuries in their understanding of what constitutes the KINGDOM OF GOD. Adventist Christians are distinguished by their belief (based on such texts as Acts 1: 11; Revelation 22: 7; 1 Thessalonians 4: 16) that Jesus Christ will make a literal and glorious return to this earth to establish the kingdom.

There was a tremendous upsurge in such belief in the 1830s and 1840s in the USA, particularly in the northeast. In ante-bellum America many believed that, if the current momentum towards social reform was maintained, the millennium of peace and plenty, described in the book of Revelation, could begin very soon. These *post-millennialists* believed that a stable, devout and moral republic would be the vehicle of the kingdom of God. Christ would return to claim the earth after a thousand years of peace (*see* MILLENARIANISM).

Others, however, believed the human race to be too flawed to inaugurate the kingdom. They were convinced that a millennium of peace could begin only after God had intervened directly to halt the downward spiral in human affairs. The focus of attention for these *pre-millennialists* was the imminent, physical return of Jesus to the earth in glory. A lively belief in the imminent dissolution of temporal arrangements had important consequences for the social lives of these Adventists. It lent urgency to missionary activity, and led to the subordination of everyday concerns. Any activity which seemed to express confidence in the long-term future of the established order became suspect. For example, some Adventists, believing procreation now to be pointless, felt that they should abstain from sexual activity. Some withdrew from the abolitionist cause to devote their energies to preaching about JUDGEMENT and the advent, when SLAVERY, along with all other evils, would be eliminated. Others, however, maintained their existing social commitments believing that Christ had told them to be occupied until he returned.

Some were led by their study of Bible prophecy to set dates for the anticipated return of Christ. Attention came to be focused on 22 October 1844. Disillusioned by the uneventful passing of that date, some left the movement to reconsider their lives. Others sought to rationalize the 'great disappointment' by saying that Christ had begun the work of judgement on that date and that his return to the earth would follow the conclusion of that process.

These Adventists came to believe that they were appointed by God to be a reform movement within Christianity. Their role was to call people to renewed faithfulness to the commandments of God, central to which was the observance of the seventh-day sabbath.

Although it was the original intention of these believers to avoid the secularizing effects produced by formal organization, they were obliged to create a legal entity in order to protect their properties, and so in 1863 the General Conference of Seventh-day Adventists came into existence. In the 1870s their missionary work spread beyond America to Europe. By the early years of the new century, the church had embarked on evangelization on a worldwide scale, and by 1994 membership had risen to 8 million.

Since the early days of the movement, urgent proclamation of the advent has been accompanied by a commitment to various humanitarian concerns. Adventist social involvement has tended to reflect the philosophy of the church's charismatic leader, Ellen White (1827–1915), who quickly became established among the believers as one through whom God gave guidance. Her influence on adventism has been considerable. She advocated VEGETARIANISM, a healthy lifestyle and simple preventive medicine as means to personal wholeness long before they became fashionable. Adventists soon established medical and educational facilities and at

the time of writing run a large network of institutions including modern hospitals and health food factories, universities and publishing houses. The Adventist Development and Relief Agency (ADRA) regularly provides emergency aid in many of the world's trouble spots as well as being involved in long-term community projects.

The basic tension within adventism derives from the perceived 'delay' in the advent. That pietism which emphasizes personal preparation for a future kingdom tends to conflict with engagement in matters of contemporary social concern. Religious revivalism and advanced institutionalization lie uncomfortably together. Conservative members wish to preserve the distinctiveness of an adventist worldview with its emphasis on an impending apocalypse. Others, however, are more concerned to see adventism take its place in a free market of religious ideas and commitments. Differences in outlook of this kind tend to derive from ethnic as well as generational sources. As American influence wanes, greater control over the identity and destiny of the church passes into the hands of members from Africa, South America and the world's island communities, places where the greatest growth in membership currently occurs. In such an international community, where it becomes increasingly difficult to obtain consensus on controversial issues such as the ordination of women and the control of finance, there is a general tendency to devolution of power.

Adventism seeks to retain three fundamental items on the spiritual agenda. First, it holds that it is impossible to have confidence in the future of a world faced with environmental and nuclear catastrophe, overpopulation, and the breakdown of social infrastructures. Second, it insists on the importance of the quest for personal wholeness, the harmonious development of the physical, mental and spiritual elements of our being. Third, it seeks to explore the relationship between the wider world and the world within, the tension between a social and a personal ethic.

Christians in the Seventh-day Adventist tradition now face several major challenges. Early Adventists claimed that their message constituted 'present truth', that it resonated with the particular needs of the time. Some traditional adventist concerns in the area of health, spirituality and ecology are now so commonplace that the church may find itself deprived of a unique *raison d'être*. Adventists thus have to sustain hope in the imminent return of Christ as they seek to respond to contemporary social needs. Failure to balance these concerns might well cause a conservative backlash resulting in a strengthened tendency to social isolation, or schism. In short, the Adventist church reflects the much wider social conflict between the forces of SECULARIZATION and FUNDAMENTALISM.

Bull, M. and Lockhart, K. (1989) *Seeking a Sanctuary*, San Francisco, CA: Harper & Row.

Damsteegt, P.G. (1977) *Foundations of the Seventh-day Adventist Message and Mission*, Grand Rapids, MI: Eerdmans.

Froom, L.E. (1971) *Movement of Destiny*, Washington, DC: Review & Herald.

Gaustad, E.S. (ed.) (1974) *The Rise of Adventism*, New York: Harper & Row.

Knight, G. (1985) *Myths in Adventism*, Washington, DC: Review & Herald.

Land, G. (ed.) (1986) *Adventism in America*, Grand Rapids, MI: Eerdmans.

——(1987) *The World of Ellen G. White*, Washington, DC: Review & Herald.

Numbers, R.L. (1976) *Prophetess of Health*, New York: Harper & Row.

Pearson, M. (1990) *Millennial Dreams and Moral Dilemmas*, Cambridge: Cambridge University Press.

Smith, T. (1965) *Revivalism and Social Reform*, New York: Harper & Row.

Michael Pearson

ADVERTISING

Advertis*ing* is a social institution that produces advertisements within a political economy of technical specialization and bureaucratic organization.

An advertise*ment* is any public form of announcement about any entity, usually but not exclusively a commodity, aimed to promote the acceptance or purchase or at least a toleration of, if not a preference for, the entity.

The advertising *agency* is the advanced technological means of soliciting, creating and placing advertisements as well as, frequently, of measuring their effects. The advertis*er* is the client of the agency and pays the bills. Usually a corporate seller of commodities, the advertiser can also be a political party, a government, a public utility, a religion, a social movement, a charity – any entity, in other words, which chooses some medium of the public forum to reach large numbers of the public with a message and is willing and able to pay to do so.

The advertising agency began in the nineteenth century with the advertising agent, usually just a middleman between an advertiser and a medium, most usually the newly mass-produced large circulation newspaper. The agent bought up a large quantity of newspaper space in blocks and then sold those blocks in pieces to various advertisers at a mark-up. In time, the agent expanded his services to include composition of the advertising copy and eye-catching artwork. The modern agency retains this distinction in the account executive as opposed to the creative director. With the addition of more and more services, including research of public wants, needs, fears and hopes as well as follow-up studies of advertising effects on sales, votes or simple acceptance, the more general term *marketing* has grown in use to signify all the varied parts of an orchestrated campaign to 'move' any entity, from soap to Senators, into a market. Advertising in this context is narrowly construed as that part of marketing which creates and places announcements of whatever complexity in whatever mass medium. Marketing goes further not only in services to clients but also in the use of more varied media as well, such as direct mail and telephone calls. A further distinction is often accorded marketing as a quasi-science of analysing what a given market (i.e. a regional or income group or other demographic slice of the general public) can be persuaded to buy, accept or prefer, whereas advertising merely follows an advertiser's need to push an already accomplished product, idea or programme on a given public.

In practice, however, the distinction between marketing and advertising is not clear-cut since most advertising, except for the basic price–availability announcement, is done within the context of marketing and most often through the same agencies, which are still called advertising agencies. The *lis de verbis* can verge on the self-serving and spurious when it is claimed that advertising serves producers while marketing serves consumers, on the disingenuous grounds that marketing gives people what they already want. Marketing is only used to move objects which people need to be persuasively told they need or want, usually at a price. There is no marketing of fresh air unless it comes with a mountain resort or sea cruise.

The confusion is averted if one defines advertising as the multimedia language that marketing speaks, thus making it an integral yet rationally separable part of the industrialization of persuasion.

The vast bulk of advertisements are simply price and availability announcements about basic commodities. A much smaller but culturally significant portion of advertisements promote political parties, candidates for office, public policy positions, or favourable acceptance of various industries, unions or other entities, particularly if they are unpopular for some reason. A fraction, but a most visible fraction, of all types of advertisements compete for attention by adding emotional appeal and differentiating information in an attractive form – anything from the colour red to a full-scale musical comedy television minute. The announcements become elaborate and go far beyond information about the entity. In a context of low demand, high competition or actual public antagonism, advertising agents may seek to exploit psychological needs that may be only factitiously joined to the entity by the advertisement itself. Excesses in this direction have led advertising to be called the art form of bad faith.

As in much else, the social issues raised by advertising are not based on the number of advertisements placed, but on the cultural and social impact of the influential visible advertisements in advanced media that go far beyond the mere announcement of price and availability of commodities. *Ponderantur, non numerantur.*

The social and moral issues raised by the great majority of advertisements are for the most part no different from the standard issues raised by buying and selling (honesty and reliability) or any other form of human intercourse (obligations of truth and faithfulness, compassion, respect for the integrity of individual rights and so forth). Bargaining and barter were and are known in all the cultures that have developed moral and religious traditions, most of which have well-known maxims and principles that deal with the vast spectrum of social and moral issues, from fair weight to marriage contracts, bred in the market-place.

An example of one of these common moral problems found in advertising but not by any means restricted to it or newly created by the modern industrialization of persuasion is the obligation of the speaker to be sincere. Sophists in ancient Greece were condemned by some because they sold their eloquence to the highest bidder. Do the copywriters or art directors for a conservative politician have themselves to be politically conservative? Whatever the answer to this moral question, if it deserves one, it need not spring from special inside knowledge about advertising. Advertisers may lie about the reliability, or true price, or utility of their commodities. These are serious moral and social issues, but not particularly confined to, nor made special by, the context of advertising. People may commit adultery in the back seats of automobiles. This does not raise a special question of automotive ethics.

The issues raised by the *abuse* of advertisements are real, even urgent, but they are issues long with us and long understood. In other words, clear moral wrong is done in situations where the common moral expectations of obligations met and crimes avoided are not fulfilled. But the language spoken by modern marketing, the institution of advertising, may cause social ills unforeseen or unplanned, perhaps even unapprehended, when it works as common expectations suppose.

The institution of advertising, in other words, is something different from the mere sum of all advertisements. It has evolved into a complex structure of its own, intimately interlaced with other institutions of great antiquity, from churches to governments, and in some measure has actually altered these greater, but dependent, institutions. Advertising has grown into the predominant industrial process of communicating with a public in order to obtain its

7

co-operation with or, at very least, its passive acceptance of whatever the advertiser wants. Advertising is the technological management of modern media in the service of the advertiser. It has evolved methods for effective persuasion that put it at the heart of modern propaganda.

Modern advertising is not unlike total high-tech nuclear warfare. Both carry on hoary practices from the dim past but each has so industrialized the process with advanced technologies that the fundamental activity is transmuted into something new that raises questions beyond standard discussions of right and wrong on battlefields or in the market-place. One might say that just as nuclear war has made of the whole planet a potential battlefield, thus raising new questions about war itself, so, too, has modern advertising made of the whole planet an actual constant market-place, thus provoking radical changes in the practice and theory of human intercourse.

In the largest single market, the USA, explicit advertising constitutes 60 per cent of newspaper copy, 52 per cent of magazine pages, 18 per cent of radio time and an average of 27 per cent of television time. More importantly, most influential media are dependent on advertising income. They therefore reinforce, in non-advertising copy or time, the subtexts of conformity, narrow immediate gratifications and non-critical acceptance of established institutions. This is called offering a supportive environment for advertising, which the advertisers have come to expect. Advertisers do not like to waste money on people who cannot afford their products or who do not vote and thus do not support media that might aim at the politically or economically disenfranchised. This force has narrowed the spectrum of aesthetic and political diversity as effectively as outright authoritarian censorship.

Advertising is the principal employer of writers, musicians, composers, artists and actors. The effect of this is to subordinate the independent vision of the artist to the social interests of his current or likely future employers. Looking back through history it is obvious that great art has outlasted its patrons' immediate self-interests, but the themes of the art clearly reflect the worldviews of the patrons, be they Italian Popes, Dutch businessmen, English dukes or the French bourgeoisie.

There is no denying that some of the cleverest, most brilliant, witty, even awesome, art is directly connected with advertising. There is also no denying that much art would not exist if there were no advertising. But the avowedly persuasive marketing context distorts the styles and narrows the range of the admitted cornucopia.

Whilst it is true that advertiser-supported news and opinion media, such as the *The New Yorker* magazine in America and Great Britain's *Guardian* or *The Independent*, may be of higher quality than reader-supported tabloids like the American *National Enquirer* or the British *Daily Mirror*, the former generally share the same viewpoint and values while the latter have a much greater range and scope from admitted trash to scholarly quarterlies and alternative journals of opinion like *Granta* or *Grand Street*. Despite the range, readers (or viewers) who support their own media are few in number and this limits the resources of any communications outside of advertising or state sponsorship.

Advertising, as noted, has made an art of hyperbole and its overwhelming presence has desensitized people to measured statements. It thus inflates public discourse and creates expectation of, and resignation to, exaggeration, misdirection, prevarication, even outright contradiction. Loud and insistent advertising for state lotteries trumpet 'You've got to be in it to win it!' with bells and whistles, while a lightning whisper 'Bet with your head, not over it' follows as a disclaimer and sop to moral objections. Virtually invisible fine print, in other words, has come to television and radio. The circus barker sets the tone for public debate.

Advertising is the capital pump that fuels global media. No broadcasting system in the world is without advertising. It is obvious in the total or mixed market systems that now characterize most of the world; it is less obvious but just as pervasive in mixed market systems such as China or Bulgaria or Zaïre, where the state is the principal advertiser. Advertising agencies are increasingly international organizations with specialists who study local cultures for the appropriate 'hook' or 'angle' that will be effective and inoffensive. The collapse of central planning in the East had its own internal dynamics, but the long reach of advertised and advertising Western music, film, television, fashion – the sacraments of consumerism – played an acknowledged role in making centrally planned economies appear unbearably shoddy and barren. The force of Western advertising in Russia, where basic necessities are scarce and expensive, is breathtaking in its ability to get people to spend a month's salary in an hour on designer jeans or cosmetics.

The Third World, incorrigibly plural as it is, is as one in being affected by advertising's seductive pictures of the good life through consumption. Thus, élites squander scarce resources on Western luxury items and others scramble to migrate to a better life. This is not to deny the original SIN of the powerful pampering themselves or the substantive rationality of seeking escape from poverty, disease and political instability; it is to underscore the enormous power of Western mass culture, the seamless garment of advertising, to legitimate material success as identical with human worth.

This power can override previous powerful allegiances. During the Falklands War, the fiercely anti-British Argentinian populace was flocking to the current James Bond film in Buenos Aires. Bond films, a media pioneer in successful international marketing, are of course a much parodied vehicle for outrageous excess in brand-name luxury. Whether one is amused or awed by the spectacularly supplied superspy, one humbly emulates his love for and dependence on gadgets. The Anglo-American political freight of effortless superiority in both morals and money that this glitzy comic strip carries is of course the subtext of all mainstream advertising.

The traditional defence of advertising agencies for their work is that it is a needed service for what has become a confusing and impersonal market. The village greengrocer or pharmacist has disappeared and one has only ads and packaging and trademarked franchised services to guide one. A growth in candor or a decay of shame may account for the latest industrial apologetic: advertising serves the public and its clients because it adds value to a product by altering purchasers' perception of its value! A car, drug, home, appliance is only as good or bad as you can be made to think it is.

This may account for the ho-hum reaction of electorates to the revelation of corruption and deceit in candidates successfully marketed for high office.

There is no doubt that advertising, as a special industrialized language of persuasion aimed at researched psychological vulnerabilities of a mass audience, cut off from traditional trusted sources of advice, is successful. No greater mark of its achievement is the rush of good causes, like Amnesty International and many others, to utilize its methods and outlets.

Can such means by itself corrupt such ends?

Elliott, B.B. (1962) *A History of English Advertising*, London: Business Publications.

International Advertising Association (1977) *Controversy Advertising: How Advertisers Present Points of View in Public Affairs*, New York: Hastings House.

Leigh, J.H. and Martin, C.R., Jr (eds) (annual) *Current Issues and Research in Advertising*, Ann Arbor, MI: Division of Research, Graduate School of Business Administration, University of Michigan.

Leiss, W., Kline, S. and Jhally, S. (1990) *Social Communication in Advertising: Persons, Products and Images of Well-Being*, Scarborough, Ontario: Nelson Canada.

Marchand, R. (1985) *Advertising the American Dream: Making Way for Modernity, 1920–1940*, Berkeley, CA: University of California Press.

Phelan, J.M. (1980) *Disenchantment: Meaning and Morality in the Media*, New York: Hastings House.

——(1981) 'Affinity and conflict between theology and communication', *Media Development* 4: 28.

——(1991) 'Selling consent', in P. Dahlgren and C. Sparks (eds) *Communication and Citizenship*, London: Routledge.

Real, M.R. (1989) *Super Media: A Cultural Studies Approach*, London: Sage.

Schudson, M. (1984) *Advertising, The Uneasy Persuasion: Its Dubious Impact on American Society*, New York: Basic Books.

John M. Phelan

AGGRESSION

Aggression is a form of behaviour which, whatever its cause or origin, is seen by others as hostile and threatening. In the case of individuals, it may be analysed in terms of criminal behaviour (*see* CRIME) or in non-criminal terms (*see* DOMESTIC VIOLENCE). This entry concerns aggression on the part of organized communities, commonly states (*see* WAR). In this context, aggression can be a neutral term or indicative of the initiation of armed conflict or include a threatening posture without the need for the use of armed force (Holmes, in Elshtain 1992).

The purposes of the United Nations include the suppression of acts of aggression (Article 1). The Security Council determines the existence of an act of aggression (Article 39). It may then order measures necessary for the restoration of international peace and security, including if necessary the use of force. To guide the Security Council, the General Assembly has approved a definition of aggression (Report of the Special Committee on the Question of Defining Aggression, GAOR, 29th Session, Suppl. No. 19 (A/9619), 6 December 1974).

The definition refers back to the UN Charter. Aggression includes the use of armed force against the sovereignty, territorial integrity or political independence of another state or in any other manner inconsistent with the Charter. The first use of armed force by a state in contravention of the Charter constitutes *prima facie* evidence of an act of aggression but the presumption can be rebutted on the facts. The definition does not prejudice the right to self-determination, freedom and independence, as derived from the Charter, of peoples forcibly deprived of that right. In practice, this refers to the independence of colonies and non self-governing territories. There is no right to secession from a sovereign state in international law.

A war of aggression is a crime against the international peace and gives rise to international responsibility. This includes not only an obligation to compensate but also the personal criminal responsibility of the political leaders (*see* WAR CRIMES).

In international law, the only legitimate unilateral uses of armed force are in self-defence or, in the case of colonies and non self-governing territories, force used to achieve self-determination. The international community, in the shape of the United Nations, can authorize the use of force where there is a threat to international peace and security. In theory, an internal situation such as the gross violation of HUMAN RIGHTS could be held to constitute such a threat.

The gross violation of human rights was not, of itself, a ground for unilateral or multilateral armed intervention in the past (*see* LIBERATION THEOLOGY). More recently, the UN has intervened militarily in situations which may be characterized in that way (e.g. Somalia, Rwanda and Haiti). UN concern, whether in the General Assembly, the Security Council or human rights bodies, does not constitute unlawful intervention. The state cannot claim that the matter falls exclusively within its domestic jurisdiction.

The only recognition of the need to correct any injustice in the *status quo* (Niebuhr 1932) is in the field of the right of self-determination of colonies (Mill 1984). In international law, self-determination does not apply to communities within an independent STATE. The failure to recognize internal colonialism (Hechter 1975) contains a risk currently being made manifest. If there is no framework for the expectations of the parties, they may think that the only way to protect themselves or to achieve an acceptable solution is by fighting for it.

The limits of international law reflect a tension between those who see the UN Charter as providing a basis for PEACE, with JUSTICE being sought by other means (Henkin 1979), and those who believe that there can be no peace without justice (McDougal and Feliciano 1961). Such a principle would appear to be as applicable within the state as between states.

Effective deterrent measures against aggression require not merely the absence of conflict but peace-making (Matthew 5: 9). This raises the issue of whether aggression is inherent in the relations between collectivities and whether it can be opposed collectively or only by individual ethics (Niebuhr 1932). If conflict is endemic in a pluralistic and sin-ridden society (Woollard 1972), is there any point in seeking to prevent it?

The social nature of aggression raises the problem of accountability or criminal responsibility. International law does not recognize the criminal liability of states, as opposed to that of political leaders, on the grounds that, *inter alia*, states cannot have criminal intent (see CRIME - *mens rea*). States can, however, be held liable to compensate the victims of aggression. In other words, all the citizenry, whether or not they approved of the aggression, will be affected by its consequences. This raises the issue of collective GUILT.

After the horrors of the First World War, statesmen sought to renounce the use of war as an instrument of national policy. The Kellogg–Briand Pact, or the Pact of Paris, was signed on 27 August 1928 by, amongst others, Belgium, France, Germany, Great Britain, Italy, Japan, Poland and the USA. The failure of the League of Nations to find an effective collective response to the Italian invasion of Abyssinia, the *anschluss* and the German invasion of Czechoslovakia contributed to the discrediting of the Pact and the outbreak of the Second World War. The Pact was legally binding on most major actors in that conflict. In the negotiations leading to the UN Charter, it was sought to do something more modest but more effective. The collective response to acts of aggression after 1945, however, was severely hampered by the Cold War and the power of veto of the permanent members of the Security Council. The only occasions on which the Security Council has functioned even approximately as envisaged by the drafters of the Charter were in relation to Korea and the Iraqi invasion of Kuwait. Cases such as Tibet, East Timor, Hungary, Czechoslovakia, Grenada and Panama were not similarly treated. It would be over-optimistic to believe that the response to the Iraqi invasion of Kuwait is the precursor of a consistent response to such acts. Whilst there is evidence of an appreciation of what needs to be done, such as activities outside the range of previous peacekeeping operations, there is not as yet evidence of the necessary political or financial will. Greater use may be made of regional mechanisms such as the Conference on Security and Co-operation in Europe, the Organization of African Unity and the Organization of American States.

The case of Iraq highlights both the contemporary relevance of the problem of aggression and the difficulties to which its suppression gives rise. Without total surrender, Saddam Hussein could not be put on trial. The Iraqi people are still subject to a sanctions regime and the cease-fire resolution of the Security Council in effect penalizes the people of Iraq for the act of aggression. They are required to compensate those who suffered loss as a result of the occupation of Kuwait, including those whose loss was occasioned by an act lawful under the laws of war (*ius in bello*). The people of Iraq are being treated as though they are in some sense responsible for the invasion. This raises issues of collective GUILT and of the relative or absolute nature of innocence.

The failure of the United Nations and the community of states to address substate issues which could lead to conflict has resulted in situations such as those in Somalia and the former Yugoslavia. The theoretical basis of international law is inadequate. There would appear to be no reason in morality, theology or reality why such a rigid distinction should be drawn between states and substate collectivities.

The situation in Eastern Europe and the former Soviet Empire highlights the need for conflict prevention, peace-making and effective minority rights protection.

Elshtain, J.B. (ed.) (1992) *Just War Theory*, Oxford: Blackwell.

Ferencz, B.B. (1975) *Defining International Aggression: the Search for World Peace*, 2 vols, New York: Oceana.

Hechter, M. (1975) *Internal Colonialism; the Celtic Fringe in British National Development*, London: Routledge & Kegan Paul.

Henkin, L. (1979) *How Nations Behave*, 2nd edn, New York: Columbia University Press.

McDougal, M.S. and Feliciano, F.P. (1961) *Law and Minimum World Public Order: the Legal Regulation of International Coercion*, New Haven, CT: Yale University Press.

Mill, J.S. (1984) 'A few words on non-intervention', in *Collected Works*, vol. XXI, London: Routledge & Kegan Paul.

Nicholson, M. (1992) *Rationality and the Analysis of International Conflict*, Cambridge: Cambridge University Press.

Niebuhr, R. (1932) *Moral Man and Immoral Society*, New York: Charles Scribner's Sons.

Ramsey, P. (1968) *The Just War: Force and Political Responsibility*, New York: Charles Scribner's Sons.

Woollard, A.G. (1972) *Progress: a Christian Doctrine?*, London: SPCK.

Françoise J. Hampson

AGNOSTICISM

The term 'agnosticism', which literally means being in a state of 'not knowing' (*a-gnosis*) with regard to the truth (or otherwise) of religious claims about the nature of reality, is a comparatively recent addition to the vocabulary of religious controversy, particularly compared with 'ATHEISM' which has a linguistic history of well over two thousand years. It was coined, in fact, as recently as 1869 by Professor Thomas Huxley to define his position in controversies over the existence of God at meetings of the London Metaphysical Society, and was quickly adopted by many of the leading anti-religious thinkers of the day and, in particular, by Sir Leslie Stephen whose *An Agnostic's Apology*, published in 1876, did much to popularize the term among the broad mass of thinking people. The position which this term was adopted to express is not new, however. It was given classic expression by the ancient Greek philosopher Protagoras (481–411 BCE) who, in a surviving fragment of his now lost work *Concerning the Gods*, says that with regard to the existence of the gods he cannot 'feel certain that they are or that they are not ... for there are many things that hinder knowledge, the obscurity of the subject and the shortness of life' (fragment 15 in Kirk and Raven (1957)).

A much older term that might be thought to express the position that Huxley was trying to articulate is 'scepticism'. However, the two terms are not equivalent, for the sceptic has traditionally held that there are many other questions, besides the question of the existence of God or the gods, to which the human mind is incapable of finding answers, although the theistic question has certainly, from the time of Pyrrho of Elis (*c.*300 BCE), the founder of the sceptical tradition, been regarded as falling within this category. The two terms do, therefore, overlap and many of the arguments that scepticism developed against dogmatism in matters of religion have been picked up and used by agnostics. Pyrrho's concern seems to have been the search for peace of mind (*ataraxia*); and in a world where there was a proliferation of warring philosophical doctrines, the non-involvement in religious controversy (achieved by abandoning the search for knowledge of those things that it was impossible for the human mind to know about) aided this search. As Sextus Empiricus (*c.*200 CE), our main source for classical scepticism, put it:

> The origin of Scepticism is the hope of attaining *ataraxia*. Men who were disquieted by the contradictions in things and in doubt as to which alternative they ought to accept, were led on to enquire what is true in things and what is false, hoping by the settlement of this question to attain *ataraxia*. The principle of Scepticism is to oppose to every proposition an equal proposition; for we believe that as a consequence of this we end by ceasing to dogmatize.
>
> (*Outlines of Pyrrhonism*, 1.3)

However, Sextus did not, as some have thought, include among 'dogmatic' statements ordinary everyday statements about the world, for: 'the Sceptic acquiesces in the sentiments which are necessary products of immediate experience' (ibid., 1.12). It was with regard to things which were regarded as 'occult' that 'dogmatism' was out of place. As Sextus wrote:

> We say he [the Sceptic] does not dogmatize, using 'dogma' in the sense of 'assent to one of the occult matters of investigation'; for the Pyrrhonean philosopher assents to nothing that is occult.
>
> (ibid., 1.13)

As was argued by Cicero (106–43 BCE) in *On the Nature of the Gods* and again, in the wake of the revival of classical scepticism at the time of the Renaissance and Reformation in Europe, by Michel de Montaigne and St François de Sales, the lesson to be drawn from scepticism is that, as there is no rational way of settling religious disputes, the prudent man or woman would be well advised to stay with well-tried traditions rather than take up with new religions and philosophies. There is some evidence that conservative scepticism is once again re-emerging in the Western world in the 1990s. However, in the brief century or so of its existence, agnosticism has not only not drawn this conclusion but, unlike atheism, has not become associated with any particular political or social philosophy.

Many Christian thinkers have welcomed the reluctance of sceptical and agnostic thinkers to pronounce one way or the other on the question of the existence of God, arguing that knowledge of God rests not on reason but on faith. This was the position taken by Calvin in the sixteenth century, by Kierkegaard in the nineteenth and, more recently, by Karl Barth. The philosopher Immanuel Kant, whose criticism of the traditional proofs for the existence of God is regarded by many philosophers as definitive, wrote in the preface to the second edition of his *Critique of Pure Reason* that he had destroyed such proofs 'in order to make room for faith'. The Roman Catholic Church, however, has continued to maintain that reason can establish limited but genuine knowledge of God. Agnostics, of course, are convinced neither by attempts to prove the existence of God nor by the claim that knowledge of God rests on faith, a claim which many agnostics feel is undermined by the number and variety of both Christian and other faiths on offer in the world. Such agnostics hold that, in the absence of universally agreed criteria for deciding which, if any, of the religious claims and counter-claims found in the world today should be accepted, agnosticism is the only reasonable response that they can make.

One of the reasons that led both Huxley and Stephen to adopt the term 'agnosticism' that continues to weigh with agnostics was that the terms 'atheism' and 'atheist' provoked such a degree of horror among religious believers that their use in religious controversy was not conducive to reasonable discussion. At the outset of his essay *An Agnostic's Apology* Stephen wrote that 'Atheism still retains a certain flavour as of the stake in this world and hell-fire in the next'. He went on to express the hope that the use of the term 'agnosticism' would 'mark an advance in the courtesies of controversy'. It is because of the antipathetic reaction that the term 'atheism' still arouses that many people in Britain and North America, who to all intents and purposes are atheists, prefer to refer to themselves as 'agnostics'. Engels, writing in the latter part of the nineteenth century, referred to such agnostics as 'shamefaced atheists'.

A new element was introduced into the theist/atheist/agnostic controversy in 1936 by the English philosopher A.J. Ayer who, in his book *Language, Truth and Logic*, rejected all of these designations on the grounds that one could not take up a position (either for, against, or not knowing) with regard to what, for him, was a meaningless assertion. Ayer's position was not, however, as novel as he and others seemed to suggest. The famous nineteenth-century atheist Charles Bradlaugh, who consistently refused to call himself an 'agnostic', wrote in his essay 'A Plea for Atheism' (1883): 'The atheist does not say "there is no God", but "I do not know what you mean by God"; I am without idea of God ... I do not deny God because I cannot deny that of which I have no conception' (p. 4). However, others, such as Leslie Stephen, who expressed similar views, felt that such a position is best described by the term 'Agnosticism'. This position with regard to statements about God – a position that to differentiate it from other forms of agnosticism might be called 'conceptual agnosticism' – is perhaps the most widespread attitude in the Western world, not only to the question of the existence of God but to religious claims generally, for it is not just that many thinking men and women in the Western world find it difficult to come to a decision with regard to religious questions, it is that they find the language of religion (and particularly language about 'God') unintelligible. It is for this reason that many Christian theologians regard the articulation of what has become known as 'God-Talk' as being among their most urgent tasks.

Ayer, A.J. (1936) *Language, Truth and Logic*, London: Gollancz.

Bradlaugh, Charles (1883) *Humanity's Gain from Unbelief*, London: Watts and Co.

Cicero (1972) *On the Nature of the Gods*, trans. H.P. McGregor, London: Penguin.

Huxley, T.H. (1894) 'Agnosticism' and 'Agnosticism and Christianity', in *Collected Works*, vol. V, London: Macmillan.

Kierkegaard, Soren (1958) *Johannes Climacus or De omnibus Dubitandum Est*, trans. T.H. Croxall, London: Adam and Charles Black.

Kirk, G.S. and Raven, J.E. (1957) *The Pre-Socratic Philosophers*, Cambridge: CUP.

Macquarrie, John (1967) *God-Talk*, London: SCM Press.

Michel de Montaigne (1987) *An Apology for Raymond Sebond*, trans. M.A. Screech, London: Penguin.

Popkin, Richard H. (1964) *The History of Scepticism: From Erasmus to Descartes*, Assem: Van Goram.

Sextus Empiricus (1933) *Outlines of Pyrrhonism*, in *Works*, vol. 1, trans. R.G. Bury, London: Loeb Classical Library.

Stephen, Leslie (1931) *An Agnostic's Apology and Other Essays*, London: Watts and Co.

James Thrower

AIDS

AIDS (Acquired Immune Deficiency Syndrome) first attracted public attention in Western countries in the early 1980s, as a disease affecting gay men in the Bay Area of San Francisco and, not long afterwards, in New York. It was already at that time affecting the general population in parts of sub-Saharan Africa, although the virus associated with the syndrome, HIV (Human Immunodeficiency Virus), had not been identified.

While the accepted scientific account has been challenged by certain scientists and journalists, the prevailing medical view is that HIV is a health-destroying virus transmitted principally through sexual contact or direct blood-to-blood transmission. This has led to the identification of two other categories to what have come to be known as 'high risk' groups: sex workers (prostitutes) and intravenous drug-users (through the practice of sharing needles). So, notwithstanding the very different African experience, discounted by many as a result of special factors not present in Western Europe or America, AIDS was initially seen in the West as a disease associated with marginal groups, engaged in deviant behaviour for which the individual was personally responsible – guilty – and therefore to be blamed. In this way, it became stigmatized, and associated by some who saw the issue in religious terms with the notions of sin and divine retribution. For these, such Biblical and historical precedents as Sodom and Gomorrah or the ancient Roman Empire could be viewed as warnings of the breakdown of social and political order associated with moral decline and licentiousness.

AIDS is therefore a multidimensional issue, touching not only on medicine and science, but also on politics, sociology, law and economics. Indeed, some of those first involved medically with the disease saw these social dimensions as taking precedence over the purely medical ones. Nevertheless, the main medical features of the disease are striking. First, there is no cure: this is a virus infection and the great modern advances in medicine have not produced cures for virus infection. Medical treatment consists of alleviating the symptoms until the immune system itself overcomes the infection, but AIDS *destroys* the immune system, so creating a medical problem of different dimensions. The best hope, then, is for a vaccine, or for the means to slow down the progress of the disease, but these are long-term measures still at the research stage. Second, there is a long latency period, perhaps as much as ten years, during which a person is infectious to others, though without visible symptoms. At this stage diagnosis is possible through blood-tests, but the issue of testing has itself given rise to controversy for social and legal reasons. Third, and for the individual most importantly, the outcome is in the end fatal, although there may well be a number of years of satisfying and healthy life to look forward to.

The central biological features here, sex and death, are striking in their juxtaposition, perennially having prompted reflection in art, literature, philosophy and theology. From a religious perspective, the pastoral and personal aspects of ministry traditionally involve counselling and discussion of issues surrounding sexuality, as well as advice and support in the context of death and bereavement.

As far as intimate sexual relationships are concerned, the ideal way of life of most major religions, particularly the Judaeo-Christian tradition, emphasizes the centrality of the institution of monogamous MARRIAGE. In another traditional area of religious activity, that of education, it is this ideal which is promoted by mainstream religious leaders, although liberalizing tendencies exist in various churches which adopt a more sympathetic attitude to alternative life-styles and to less restrictive sexual relationships. The advent of AIDS has brought such differences more sharply into focus, for they involve a very different approach to AIDS avoidance and prevention, with consequent irreconcilable differences in approaches to sex education. The logic of the argument is that faithful monogamy provides protection in a practical sense against infection, and that where this cannot be assumed, 'safe sex' – a euphemism for condom-use – is the preferred option.

This issue is becoming increasingly important in those African and Asian countries where the role of the churches in education and guidance is accepted. Here the policy of the World Council of Churches, through such organizations as Churches' Action for Health, is to provide aid and assistance to sensitize local church leaders to the need for HIV/AIDS prevention and care. The health education agenda is broadened, however, by this body, to include empowering women and seeking to combat poverty. The WCC has also convened a consultative group to examine the theological and ethical aspects, as well as the justice and human rights aspects, of the HIV/AIDS epidemic.

AIDS presents a classic confrontation between utility on the one hand and liberty or principle on the other, with the rights of some in conflict with the health or welfare of others. On the personal level, it throws into focus questions concerning relationships, particularly sexual relationships, as well as the wider context in which those relations take place. It supplies another kind of relevance to values such as LOVE, loyalty, trust and the personal sacrifice needed to secure the stability of the FAMILY in the modern world: secret liaisons of one partner carry risk for the other; pregnancy and parenthood are threatened, not only because childbearing itself is another known method of transmitting the virus, from mother to child, but also, as the example of parts of Africa shows, because the middle generation may be missing on a scale unprecedented except in time of war, leaving the very young and the old without means of support. Apart from its impact on the family, the loss of this middle generation may also be a loss to the worlds of politics, government, the arts and literature in these countries.

If the solution is seen, as it often is, in terms of money, AIDS becomes a political as well as a personal issue. Despite their imperfections, solutions such as condoms and needle-exchanges (encouraging intravenous drug-users to safeguard themselves from the risk attached to needle-sharing) must clearly be promoted by governments, so that expenditure on these remedies as well as on scientific research is politically well-justified. But politicians, however well-intentioned, do not have it in their power to end this scourge; it is for individuals, therefore, to recognize that whatever other grounds may exist for a variety of sexual life-styles and experimentation with drugs, AIDS has altered the scale of risk in a way which calls for a fundamental reappraisal of some assumptions of Western liberal societies over recent decades.

Since appraisal of risk, and the ability to act upon that appraisal, is also altered under the influence of alcohol and non-injected drugs, AIDS may provide a prudential motive for what some religious groups have traditionally advocated for other reasons – a more abstemious life-style in these respects, too. In some directions, however, the implications may be less conservative. If homosexual marriage were permitted, then stable relationships and consequent risk reduction for the non-heterosexual might be facilitated (see SAME-SEX RELATIONS). Some would argue for earlier and more extensive sex education to allow the young to assess all such risks competently.

Apart from these personal issues, many issues arise within the specific context of medical ethics. There are issues of medical confidentiality: should a doctor break confidence in order to save the life of a sexual partner who is being unknowingly put at risk? Should patients be tested for HIV before surgery to alert health-workers to risk and the need for special precautions? Should surgeons and dentists be obliged to inform their patients of *their* HIV status? Under what conditions should clinical trials of new drugs or vaccines against HIV be conducted? Should pregnant women be offered early in pregnancy the chance to establish their HIV status with the opportunity of abortion if testing positive?

These questions can only be listed. Answers in all cases are likely to be contested, even from within a shared ethical or religious perspective.

There may be more agreement, however, about the social context in which questions are raised and answered. AIDS disproportionately affects people in poor countries and people in poor neighbourhoods. In Western countries, there is a link with subcultures of the homeless, of drug-users, of prostitutes, as well as with ethnic groups who are counted as deprived by various other measures, such as health and education. With all or most of these, Christianity has traditionally had a special connection, based on the example of its founder, who associated with the socially unacceptable and deprived, and initiated a pattern of compassionate service which is the distinctive mark of practical Christianity. The Christian churches, including the Catholic church responding to the call of Pope John Paul II through its organization Caritas, are now involved in many countries of the world in this caring function in relation to AIDS. Such help may involve everything from fund-raising to personal help: the provision of meals, of shelter or refuge, of nursing and medical care.

Religion in general, and not merely the Christian religion, is particularly concerned with death, and it is not surprising that the long-drawn-out and premature deaths caused by AIDS bring special reflection on life and death, beginning and termination. There is a practical question, too, of whether those who wish to avoid the final stages of the illness should take action to bring that about, and whether a compassionate society should change its laws to make this more a matter of individual choice, at least by permitting access to means and advice on SUICIDE to people outside the medical profession (see EUTHANASIA). And while some will find reflection on death a route to God, others will find themselves confronted in a new and acute way by the ancient religious dilemma of combining faith in God's benevolence and omnipotence with the reality of human suffering.

Almond, B. (ed.) (1995) *AIDS, a Moral Issue: The Ethical, Legal and Social Aspects* (2nd edn), London: Macmillan.

Bayer, R. (1989) *Private Acts, Social Consequences*, New York: Free Press.

Cohen, Elliott D. and Davis, M. (eds) (1994) *Aids: Crisis In Professional Ethics*, Philadelphia: Temple University Press.

Dalton, Harlon *et al.* (eds) (1987) *AIDS and the Law: Guide for the Public*, Yale CT: Yale University Press.

Dominian, J. (1987) *Sexual Integrity: The Answer to AIDS*, London: Darton, Longman & Todd.

Fleming, A.F., Carballo, M. *et al.* (1988) *The Global Impact of AIDS*, New York, WHO, Alan R. Liss, Inc.

McNeill, W.H. (1976) *Plagues and Peoples*, Harmondsworth: Penguin.

Marcetti, A. and Lunn, S. (1993) *A Place of Growth: Counselling and Pastoral Care of People with AIDS*, London: Darton, Longman & Todd.

Miller. H.G., Turner, C.F. and L.E. Moses (eds) (1990) *AIDS, the Second Decade*, Washington, DC: National Academy of Sciences, National Academy Press.

Shilts, R. (1988) *And the Band Played On*, Harmondsworth: Penguin.

Brenda Almond

ALIENATION

The concept of alienation has a long history during which it has exhibited variations of usage and application in a number of different disciplines. The concept can be found in the fields of law, politics, sociology, psychology and theology. The stem is the Latin *alienare* from which by a variety of routes the words alien, alienage, alias, alienate, alienable and similar are derived. While the contemporary usages of the term alienation in sociology and social psychology are both recent, and often excessive, the ideas behind 'alienation' are as old and as basic as reflection upon the human condition.

'Alienation', as used in English, incorporates several different ideas which, in some other languages, are distinguished by different words. A failure to clarify the way in which the word is used often leads to confusion. Such confusion has its source in different applications of the root and in different ideas expressed by the same word and is not confined to the present. Cicero, for example, referred both to *abalienatio*, a term relating to the legal transfer of property, and to *alienatio*, which, in context, appears to have meant something akin to estrangement: to make alien, to separate. Both these usages of the word are still extant. Livius used the word *abalienatio* in the sense of deprivation, to deprive someone of their civic status; while such a usage would now be unusual it would not be impossible or incorrect. Someone deprived of their liberty, for example, can properly be said to be alienated from their liberty. Rousseau speaks of the obverse case of someone depriving themselves of their own liberty, of placing themselves in a condition of SLAVERY and thereby removing all morality and humanity from their acts. St Paul refers to alienation as a separation from the life of God. In Ephesians 4: 18, the Latin Vulgate has him speaking of the Gentiles that they are '*alienatae a vita Die*': alienated from the life of God. Such a usage would indicate also that a life alienated from God would be a life of *hamartia*, missing the mark, often, and crudely, rendered as 'SIN'. To be in a condition of alienation and to be in a condition of 'sin' are different expressions of a common human experience. Luther picks up St Paul's point in his translation of the New Testament using the German terms *Entfremdung* and *Entfremden* to translate '*alienatae*' in a way that is indicative of a loss of a personal relation or a process by which such relations become estranged. This theological use of the notion of alienation requires as its pre-condition certain concepts of self and of personality which are not found in all societies. Indeed they seem to require a particular view of the place of humans in the universe. The theological dimension to the experience of alienation couples a strong sense of self with a relatively weak social structure. Both are perceived as detached from the larger (created) order or in a condition of crisis with respect to that order.

While the use of the term 'alienation' and its correlates can be specifically dated and traced, the ideas behind the word have roots in early accounts of the place of humans in the cosmos. Early Mesopotamian and Egyptian cosmogenic accounts emphasize creation and the situation of humans in the world. Such accounts do exhibit the roots of self-reflection but show, on the whole, little evidence of an internal and questioning reflection. This is probably due to the particular relations holding between perceptions of the structure of the cosmos and the actual structures of those societies. A picture of the cosmos if mirrored precisely in a stable social structure with clear and limited horizons would produce a sense of suffering but not a crucial sense of the human and social roots of the unfairness of that SUFFERING. Hence reflection on the self, or on the social structure, would be displaced into reflection on the cosmic structure. In ancient societies this had the effect of tending to shift the locus of perception for the human predicament away from any sense of personal responsibility for that predicament and of preventing the emergence of a full sense of self-hood. The numerous accounts of quarrels between, or actions of, the gods as explanations for human, social and natural events attest to this form of being as one in which life events are externally controlled. A sense of the external control of life is necessary to, but not sufficient for, the experience of alienation. What is also required is a sense of the self as agent, as one who might be in control but who is not fully in control, or who has lost full control. In this sense of personal agency the gap between the purely theological understanding of alienation as a felt separation from God and the social and political understanding of alienation as a sense of the externalization of control is bridged. That sense of self, which is not automatically present merely because the life is a human life, depended for its emergence on, among other things, a new understanding of (created) order.

Mesopotamian and Egyptian cosmologies do not show any systematic pattern of reflection on the human condition as being in (divine) creation while nevertheless being distinct from (divine) order. This clear disjunction between the perception of that which is and the perceiving self required some breakdown of long-standing social and political order. In Mesopotamia that is shown in the development of the idea of a personal God in the second millennium BC. It is expressed later as an early form of counterfactual reflection on the possibility of averting death in the Babylonian Adapa myth and developed even more fully in the Adamic myth. Eating from the fruit of the tree of knowledge breaks an injunction from God, but also brings about self-reflection. Genesis 3: 7 makes the shift from innocence to reflection clear, 'Their eyes were opened and knowing that they were naked they made aprons for themselves with fig leaves.' Later (3: 22) God says, 'man has become like one of us, knowing good from evil'. It might also have been added that in coming to this knowledge humans also came to a sense of estrangement.

The Biblical creation story illuminates, among other things, the process by which humans come to an awareness of their separation from the world and from God. In the process of becoming aware of their own distinctness they become self-conscious and reflective in their Being. The world, themselves and God become estranged as consciousness and self-knowledge is born. There is, then, considerable evidence to suggest that the ideas necessary to the term alienation first came into use in a theological context before being put to legal use in Imperial Rome and later to social and political use by Rousseau, Hegel and then Marx.

The different ideas included in 'alienation' include separation, estrangement and deprivation or even expropriation. While each of these words can be given a legal meaning, e.g. an estranged relation leading to a divorce, the deprivation of freedom, or the expropriation of property, it is their relation to the self which has been of greatest interest. In part this development is the product of a changing social structure. It is also, in part, the result of an increasing preoccupation with the process by which the self in becoming aware of itself has come into being. While it would be folly to suggest that self-awareness is a purely modern phenomenon, it is clear that the problem of self-awareness and the process of self-formation have come under intense intellectual scrutiny only in late modernity. As concern with and interest in the self and self-reflection have increased, so the concept of alienation has come to be of greater significance than hitherto. It is not true that Christianity gave to the world the concepts of the individual and the self; such concepts are pre-Christian and emerge also in non-Occidental contexts about 500 BC. What Christianity did do, however, was develop and universalize those concepts. The theory of alienation, therefore, has been most developed in Occidental theology and philosophy of religion. It is most fully developed in Hegel's work, largely neglected until after the Second World War. For Hegel, the word which we translate as alienation is given two different expressions in the German original,

Entfremdung, primarily estrangement, and *Entausserung*, to externalize. Hence alienation can be both a state of Being and a process. As a state of Being, alienation must be expressed as alienation from something or from someone, or even from one's self. As a process alienation can be a state of becoming, or of losing a state of Being (*see also* PROCESS THEOLOGY). This simple distinction, often lost in the English translation, expresses both positive and negative features of alienation. *The Phenomenology of Spirit* gives two descriptions of alienation. One is in the form of 'the unhappy consciousness', as exemplified in the internally divided early Christianity which projects some 'essential' nature on to a transcendent being. The second is traced through the decline from the unalienated life of Greece through the fall of Rome to the French Revolution. This decline from the ethical life of Greece is matched by the growth of individualism and atomism. That individualistic world produces a life which is led both in the gap between this world and the 'other' world and in the gap between self-conscious individuality and social substance. It is in CULTURE where mediation between these aspects of consciousness is worked out. The distinction between different forms of being which is expressed in alienation, and mediated through culture, gives rise to the possibility of higher forms of being. That development cannot occur successfully, however, in certain forms of society and alienation results in loss of contact with self, of self-knowing, where the human becomes a stranger not merely to the other but also to the self – the self becomes as other. The development of *geist* is the development in history of self-knowing within which the alienation of spirit is itself overcome and which will be reflected in the relation between social substance and human beings.

Two notable strands of thought about alienation have developed from Hegel's analysis of the concept. One, first attended to in the philosophical and humanistic writings of the early Marx and published only in this century, emphasizes the social dimension of alienation and places its source in specific social conditions. The second, emanating largely from the *existenz* philosophy of Heidegger, and later more explicitly existentialist writings, have tended to concentrate more on the phenomenological condition of man's *Being in the World*. The difference is graphically illustrated, on the one hand, by Marx's belief that a whole human life is to be achieved only through overcoming alienation – a transcendence that can be achieved only through political action – and, on the other hand, by Sartre's earlier claims that the condition of man was such that he was condemned to be the victim of his own freedom. His mode of Being (*pour-soi*) made him a victim for failing to realize his condition of freedom.

It is Marx, perhaps, more than any other writer who has developed the social and political aspects of the concept of alienation. Marx's early writings are resplendent with references to alienation. Following the inspiration of Feuerbach, who had argued that God was a product of the alienated imagination of man, Marx rejected Hegel's idealism. For Marx the source of alienation was to be found in the material conditions of human life. Three terms are used by Marx, sometimes interchangeably and sometimes not. From the concept of *Verausserung*, the contracting of one's labour to another, the idea that through such contraction one's Being becomes the property of another is derived. The result is *Entausserung*, the condition of loss of Being. In the 1844 manuscripts, Marx ties these two concepts to another, *Entfremdung*: alienation of labour, and opens the way for an analysis of alienation based on the institution of private property and the division of labour.

In the 1844 Paris manuscripts Marx distinguishes several different types of alienation: alienation from nature; his own life functions expressed in labour as alienation from the product of that labour and resulting in alienation from himself; alienation from one's species-being so that the species becomes a means to an end; and the estrangement of man from man, so that the other appears as a stranger. (See also EMANCIPATION.) The frequent claim that Marx took private property as the cause of alienation is a gross oversimplification; it is rather that in the first instance property is the outcome, the consequence, of alienation. Later the relation between private property and alienation becomes reciprocal so that eventually private property is

'both the cause and the consequence of alienation'. In *The Communist Manifesto* (Marx 1848), this formulation is distilled into the claim that private property is the practical root of alienation and that the supersession and transcendence of private property (its abolition is the usual and somewhat misleading translation) is at the centre of the communist ideal. The transcendence of private property relations thus becomes a central ·tenet of Marx's practical revolutionary critique at that point in his intellectual development.

'Alienation' is frequently seen as an aberration of the young Marx still preoccupied with the writings of Hegel. The early writings, most of which have come to light only in this century, present a humanist view of Marx which was not clearly evident in the more economically directed work of his later life. Some debate, inspired principally by Althusser, has tended to suggest that the concept of alienation is not central to Marx's work (*see also* MARXISM). Althusser's structuralist reading of Marx, which has had much influence, tends to diminish the role of the human actor in the process of history; history is regarded as 'a process without a subject'. The effect of such a reading is to dehumanize Marx's thought and to diminish his early ethical ideal of what it is to lead a full human life. If the sense of self is diminished, then so is the sense of alienation. It is no accident, therefore, that Althusser's reading of Marx eliminates the importance of concepts cognate with or dependent upon alienation. Such concepts, if taken as other than entirely epiphenomenal, undercut purely structural explanations of social life.

Marx takes religion as a means of controlling the effects of leading a life founded in alienation. 'Religion is the sigh of the oppressed creature, the sentiment of a heartless world, and the soul of soulless conditions. It is the opium of the people', Marx says in a critique of Hegel's *Philosophy of Right*. It is quite possible to take this notion in a quite different way however. It does seem that some form of estrangement is both ineliminable and necessary, a part of the human condition. If so, then it may be that religion is not always and necessarily a means of controlling the grosser effects of alienation, but rather, that some aspect of alienation is a necessary requirement for the religious impulse. Marx suggests as much himself in a short rhetorical dialogue: 'If my own activity does not belong to me,' he asks, 'to whom then does it belong? To a being other than me. Who is this being? The gods?' The gods, he suggests, who in the earliest times produced labour in the service of temple building in Egypt, India and Mexico. As the dialogue develops it becomes clear that the real 'other' is other men and not the gods.

Marx may well be right that a certain kind of alienation does produce such religious or quasi-religious feelings and the conceptions that develop with and justify the feelings and the source of the alienation. It may be the case, however, that the sense of the gap between the inner and the outer part of being is greater in more recent times, and that the possibilities for a sense of alienation have actually increased. The outcome of that may well be expressed as a largely inchoate and frenzied activity. As Marx claimed in his essay *On the Jewish Question*, following the breakdown of feudal forms of order individual egoistic man appeared and with that a 'frenzied movement of the cultural and material elements which form the content of . . . life'.

It is into the gap between the condition of being and the consciousness of that condition that the basis for the theological understanding of the importance of alienation can be found. Erich Fromm expresses this view well: 'the concept of alienation is, in non-theistic language, the equivalent of what in theistic language would be called "sin"'. As noted earlier the concept of sin (*see* SIN) has become largely overlaid with cultural meanings. Its root word *hamartia*, however, literally means nothing more or less than missing the mark, an important connotation of which is, of not being at one with God: of estrangement from God. Some form of alienation or estrangement seems to be an indispensable part of the human condition. This view is developed by Tillich who argues that existence for man contains indispensable, indeed necessary, elements of estrangement. In his *Systematic Theology* he argues that 'Man as he exists is not what he essentially is and ought to be. He is estranged from his true being.' To 'be' is to 'be' in a condition of separation from

oneself. Another way of expressing this might be to say that existence is not the same as Being. Theology is a means of attempting to deal with this problem. For Tillich it is Jesus who provides the exemplar to whom we may appeal in understanding the problem. Jesus had the ability both to face this estrangement and to show how man's existential estrangement or alienation is to be overcome. A completely satisfying solution to the problem of alienation would mean a union not only of men with other human beings but also with the God from whom he is estranged as well. Such a complete elimination of alienation can be longed for but not achieved.

This conception of alienation and its possible reduction, if not elimination, evokes both a political and a theological dimension. For Tillich, the two dimensions of estrangement, from others and from God, appear to be part of the human condition, yet they are only satisfied in Jesus. For Marx, estrangement from others and from self is principally a product of social arrangements. Yet it seems that both projects are bound to some degree of failure. Perhaps some rearrangement of social and political structure may well reduce alienation from others. It seems unlikely, however, that any conceivable such rearrangements would eliminate all forms of alienation. Similarly, if, as for Tillich, it is Jesus that is the exemplar for overcoming the dual elements of estrangement, then it would appear that while non-divine mortals might strive to achieve such a state they are, ultimately, doomed to their mortal condition.

'Alienation' then contains two principal elements, the one social and political, and the other existential: relating to the perception of the human condition. The experience of and expression of these two aspects of alienation is mediated by the self which also provides the bridge between them. The human condition is one in which some degree of sense of estrangement between world and other is probably both necessary and irreducible. Some forms of life may, however, limit the sense of alienation by displacing the perception of the control of life so far away from human affairs that any possible self-hood does not emerge or it is displaced elsewhere as allegedly happens in totemistic cultures. Paradoxically an excess sense or feeling of loss of control of life leads not to alienation but to its elimination through eradication of, or dispersal of, a sense of self. The end point of self-alienation is the end of alienation and the end of self. Conversely some sense of alienation is required for self-hood. By complete contrast, a deliberate and controlled attempt to abandon both sense of self and sense of world is found in the Buddhist idea of *nirvana*.

The assumption commonly underlying many claims about alienation, that alienation is necessarily bad, need not go unchallenged. Whether alienation is bad or good is a judgement to be made in the light of the circumstances of the particular form of alienation and one's judgement about the nature of the human condition itself.

A sense of estrangement from the world and from others not only feeds our creative ability and produces a sense of self and of personal distinctness, it also provides the tension between consciousness of self and the yearning of the self to transcend its very condition of self-hood. It is from within that gap, between the sense of self and the sense of something outside the self, between inner and outer, that the sense of estrangement finds its place. The resulting impulse, when existential, produces what has been described as the mystical, religious, 'haunting realisation of ultimate powerlessness in an inscrutable world, and the unquestioning and thoroughly irrational conviction of the possibility of gaining mystic security by somehow identifying oneself with that which can never be known' (Edward Sapir). The impulse when practical turns to politics – the activity of sharing in the control of one's life – and when scientific-technical to the activity of attempting to control, or even recreate, nature.

The two sides of alienation show clearly the close, if sometimes uncomfortable, necessity of the relation between religion and politics. It is a reasonable goal to attempt, by practical means, to reduce unnecessary manifestations and forms of alienation; such a task is a proper and legitimate role for political and social action. It may also be the case, however, that when unnecessary or harmful forms of social and political alienation have been reduced, the sense of estrangement from God will find a full and proper religious expression: an expression that intellectually can only be partially mediated in the interplay between theology and society.

Althusser, L. and Balibar, E. (1971) *Reading Capital*, trs. B. Brewster, New York: Pantheon.
Feuerbach, Ludwig (1957) *The Essence of Christianity*, trs. George Eliot, New York: Harper and Row.
Hegel, G.W.F. (1977) *The Phenomenology of Spirit*, trans. A.V. Miller, Oxford: Clarendon.
Heidegger, M. (1962) *Being and Time*, trs. John Macquarrie and Edward Robinson, New York: Harper.
Marx, Karl (1843) *On the Jewish Question*
——(1844) *Economic and Philosophical Manuscripts*
——(1848) *The Communist Manifesto* in *Karl Marx, Friedrich Engels: Collected Works*, London: Lawrence and Wishart.
Ollman, Bertell (1971) *Alienation, Marx's Conception of Man in Capitalist Society*, Cambridge: Cambridge University Press.
Sartre, Jean Paul (1956) *Being and Nothingness*, New York: Philosophical Library.
Sapir, Edward (1960) *Culture, Language and Personality*, Berkeley, CA.
Tillich, Paul (1963) *Systematic Theology*, Chicago: Chicago University Press.

Paul Barry Clarke

ANARCHISM

The word derives from the Greek *anarkhia*, meaning without a ruler, and was used in a derogatory sense until, in the mid-nineteenth century in France, it was adopted in a positive way to describe a political and social ideology arguing for organization without government. In the evolution of political ideas, anarchism can be seen as an ultimate projection of both liberalism and socialism, and the differing strands of anarchist thought can be related to their emphasis on one or the other of these aims. Historically, anarchism was a radical answer to the question 'What went wrong?' that followed the outcome of the French Revolution. Conservatives like Edmund Burke and liberals like Alexis de Tocqueville had their own responses. Anarchist thinkers were unique on the political Left in affirming that workers and peasants, grasping the chance to overturn the result of centuries of exploitation and tyranny, were betrayed by the seizure of centralized state power by a new class of politicians who had no hesitation in applying violence and terror, a secret police and a professional army to maintain themselves in power. The institution of the STATE was itself the enemy. They applied the same criticism to every REVOLUTION of the nineteenth and twentieth centuries.

The main stream of anarchist propaganda for more than a century has been *anarchist-communism*, which argues that property in land, natural resources and the means of production should be held in mutual ownership by local communities, federating for innumerable joint purposes with other communes. It differs from state socialism and from Marxist communism in opposing any central authority which, it has always argued, inevitably leads to governmental and bureaucratic tyranny, enforced by terror. *Anarcho-syndicalism* puts its emphasis on the organized workers who, through a social general strike, could expropriate the expropriators and establish workers' control of industry. *Individualist anarchism* has several traditions, one deriving from the 'conscious egoism' of the German writer Max Stirner (1806–56) and another from a series of American nineteenth-century thinkers who argued that in protecting our own AUTONOMY and associating with others only for common advantages we are promoting the good of all. They differed from free-market liberals in their emphasis on *mutualism*, usually derived from the French anarchist Proudhon. *Pacifist anarchism* follows both from the anti-militarism that accompanies rejection of the state with its ultimate dependence on armed force and from the conviction that any morally viable human society depends upon the uncoerced goodwill of its members.

These and other threads of anarchist thought have different emphases. What links them is their rejection of external authority, whether that of the state, the employer or the hierarchies of administration and of established institutions like the school and the church. The same is true of more recent varieties of anarchist propaganda, *green anarchism* and *anarcha-feminism*. Like those who believe that animal liberation is an aspect of human liberation, they claim that the only ideology consistent with their aims is anarchism.

It is customary to relate the anarchist tradition to four major thinkers and writers. The first was William Godwin (1756–1836) who in his *Enquiry concerning Political Justice* set out from first principles an anarchist case against government, the law, property and the institutions of the state. He was an heir both to the English tradition of radical nonconformity and to the French *philosophes*, and although social historians have traced his influence in nineteenth-century organs of working-class self-organization, he was not rediscovered by the anarchist movement until the 1890s.

The second was Pierre-Joseph Proudhon (1809–65), the French propagandist who was the first person to call himself an anarchist. In 1840 he declared that *Property is Theft*, but he went on to claim that *Property is Freedom*. He saw no contradiction between these two slogans, since the first related to the landowner and capitalist whose ownership derived from conquest or exploitation and was only maintained through the state, its property laws, police and army, while the second was concerned with the peasant or artisan family with a natural right to a home, to the land it could cultivate and to the tools of a trade, but not to ownership or control of the homes, land or livelihoods of others.

The third of these anarchist pioneers was the Russian revolutionary Michael Bakunin (1814–76), famous for his disputes with Marx in the 1870s when, for his successors, he accurately predicted the outcome of Marxist dictatorships in the twentieth century. 'Freedom without socialism', he said, 'is privilege and injustice, but socialism without freedom is slavery and brutality' (Bakunin 1973: 110) The last was another Russian of aristocratic origins, Peter Kropotkin (1842–1921). His original reputation was as a physical geographer and in a long series of books and pamphlets he attempted to give anarchism a scientific basis. *The Conquest of Bread* was his manual on the self-organization of a post-revolutionary society. *Mutual Aid* was written to confront misinterpretations of Darwinism that justified competitive capitalism, by demonstrating through the natural history of animal and human societies that competition within species is less significant than co-operation as a pre-condition for survival. *Fields, Factories and Workshops* was his treatise on the humanization of work, through the integration of agriculture and industry, of hand and brain and of intellectual and manual education. The most widely read of all anarchist authors, he linked anarchism both with social ecology and with everyday experience.

Some anarchists object to the identification of anarchism with its best-known writers. They point to the fact that its aspirations can be traced through the slave revolts of the ancient world, the peasant uprisings of medieval Europe, in the ideology of the Diggers in the English revolution of the 1640s and in the revolutions in France in 1789 and 1848 and the Paris Commune of 1871. In the twentieth century, anarchism had a role in the Mexican revolution of 1911, the Russian revolution of 1917 and most notably in the Spanish revolution that followed the military rising that precipitated the civil war of 1936. In all these revolutions the fate of the anarchists was that of heroic losers.

But anarchists do not necessarily fit the stereotype of believers in some final revolution, succeeding where the others failed, and inaugurating a new society or utopia. The German anarchist Gustav Landauer (1870–1919) declared that 'The state is not something which can be destroyed by a revolution, but is a condition, a certain relationship between human beings, a mode of human behaviour; we destroy it by contracting other relationships, by behaving differently' (Buber 1949: 46).

Anarchism has, in fact, an endless resilience. Every European, North American, Latin American and oriental society has had its anarchist publicists, newspapers, circles of adherents, imprisoned activists and martyrs. Whenever an authoritarian or repressive political regime collapses, the anarchists are there, a minority among the emerging ideologists, urging their fellow citizens to learn the lessons of the sheer horror and irresponsibility of government. The anarchist press re-emerged in Germany after Hitler, in Italy after Mussolini, in Spain after Franco, in Portugal after Salazar, in Argentina after the generals and in the Soviet Union after seventy years of suppression. For anarchists this is an indication that the ideal of a self-organizing society based on voluntary co-operation rather than coercion is irrepressible. It represents, they claim, a universal human aspiration.

The main varieties of anarchism are resolutely hostile to organized religion. Blanqui's slogan *Ni Dieu ni maître* reflects their attitude, particularly in countries like France, Italy and Spain, with long anarchist and anti-clerical traditions. But beneath the anarchist umbrella there are specifically religious trends. The novelist Leo Tolstoy (1828–1910) preached a gospel of Christian anarchism, especially in essays like *The Kingdom of God is Within You* which profoundly influenced several generations of pacifist anarchists, as did the social attitudes of the Society of Friends, particularly the Quaker approach to decision-making. Similarly several of the radical tendencies in the Catholic church, particularly the Distributist movement associated with G.K. Chesterton with its links with the ideology of Proudhon, or the Catholic Worker movement in the USA and its later equivalents in Latin America, have been strongly attracted by some aspects of anarchist propaganda. In India, Mohandas Karamchand Gandhi (1869–1948) acknowledged that his campaigns for civil disobedience in the form of non-violent non-co-operation with government and his hopes for self-governing village democracy built around local food production and craft industry derived from Tolstoy, from the archetypal American advocate of individualist anarchism Henry David Thoreau, and from Kropotkin's *Fields, Factories and Workshops*. His work, and that of successors like Vinoba Bhave and Jayaprakash Narayan, has been evaluated from an anarchist standpoint by Geoffrey Ostergaard. And there are, needless to say, Western writers who have discovered strongly anarchist elements in Taoism and Buddhism. One of the best revaluations of the thought of Proudhon, Kropotkin and Landauer was made by the theologian Martin Buber in his book *Paths in Utopia*.

It has even been suggested that anarchist movements themselves resemble 'chiliastic' or 'millenarian' religious sects (see MILLENARIANISM). This view has been propagated by Marxist historians, designating, for example, rural Spanish anarchists as 'primitive rebels'. More recent work by historians and anthropologists has destroyed this interpretation. Those villagers were found to be rational people with a realistic assessment of their situation.

But the mere mention of the millennium leads us to consider the future of anarchism in the twenty-first century. Anarchists argue that if they are simply a marginal curiosity in the evolution of political ideas in the twentieth century, how do we evaluate the major political theories? Some form of theoretical Marxism may survive in universities, but as a ruling ideology it now exists rarely and can survive only in countries where the army and secret police remain loyal and unintimidated by popular discontent. The Fabian variety of socialism through nationalization has been abandoned even by its inheritors. The economic liberalism of the free market, even in the world's richest countries, creates an 'underclass' of citizens with no access to it, while capital investment shifts around the world in search of ever cheaper sources of labour.

From an anarchist standpoint the history of the twentieth century has been an absolute justification of the anarchist critique of the state. It has been the century of the totalitarian state (see TOTALITARIANISM), subverting every other form of human organization into organs of state power. It has consequently been the century of total war, reaching out to enrol every last citizen into the war machine, promoted by rivalry for markets among the great powers and by the free market in weapons, where every local dictator is fed by the state-sponsored arms trade of the rich nations. Similarly anarchists see the anti-clericalism of the nineteenth-century precursors vindicated by the late twentieth-century re-emergence of militant religion, whether in the form of Protestant, Catholic, Jewish, Muslim, Hindu or Sikh FUNDAMENTALISM, as a justification for persecuting, attacking and slaughtering adherents of other faiths.

Finally they see themselves as precursors of universal yearnings for the humanization of work. Kropotkin urged the decentralization of industry on a small scale and its combination with food production for local needs, arguing for 'a new economy in the energies used in

supplying the needs of human life, since these needs are increasing and the energies are not inexhaustible'. He was almost unique in foreseeing current issues in these terms, just as he foresaw the history of economic imperialism in the twentieth century leading to wars which 'are inevitable so long as certain countries consider themselves destined to enrich themselves by the production of finished goods and divide the backward nations up among themselves . . . while they accumulate wealth themselves on the basis of the labour of others' (Kropotkin 1985: 40).

A century and a half of anarchist propaganda has had no visible effect on the world outside. But the concerns it has raised are bound to become the overwhelming social issues of the coming century. Can humanity outgrow nationalism and the religious loyalties that have become inextricably entangled with it? Can we overcome differences without resort to weapons? Can we feed, clothe and house ourselves and stay healthy without the obligation to win purchasing power by selling our time and talent to organizations we hate? Can we organize ourselves to gain a livelihood that does not add to the destruction of our own environment and that of other people and other species, far away?

This series of questions is very far from the preoccupations of any political party with the faintest hope of electoral success. Anarchists are, as they have always been, among the people who, by raising them, condemn themselves to exile to the fringe of political and social agitation. Rejecting both the polarities of the voting system and the simplicities of a *coup d'état* to replace the existing order by the imposition of a new order, the anarchists, whether they want to or not, pursue a path of permanent opposition. They stress that the history of the twentieth century is crowded with new orders, installed and subsequently dethroned at a vast human cost. In predicting this, the anarchists have been steadfastly correct. One of the most interesting and suggestive modern anarchist propagandists was the American writer Paul Goodman (1911–72) who wrote, late in life, that

For me, the chief principle of anarchism is not freedom but autonomy, the ability to initiate a task and do it one's own way. . . .

The weakness of 'my' anarchism is that the lust for freedom is a powerful motive for political change, whereas autonomy is not. Autonomous people protect themselves stubbornly but by less strenuous means, including plenty of passive resistance. They do their own thing anyway. The pathos of oppressed people, however, is that, if they break free, they don't know what to do. Not having been autonomous, they don't know what it's like, and before they learn, they have new managers who are not in a hurry to abdicate. . . .

(Goodman 1972: 47)

Any enquirer, chancing upon his words, will recognize that he is describing not only the problem of anarchism but that of any liberatory ideology. The anarchists emerge from the dilemma with rather more credit than most.

Bakunin, M. (1973) *Selected Writings*, London: Jonathan Cape.
Buber, M. (1949) *Paths in Utopia*, London: Routledge & Kegan Paul.
DeLeon, D. (1978) *The American as Anarchist: Reflections on Indigenous Radicalism*, Baltimore, MD: Johns Hopkins University Press.
Goodman, P. (1972) *Little Prayers and Finite Experiences*, New York: Harper and Row.
——(1990) *Communitas: Means of Livelihood and Ways of Life*, New York: Columbia University Press (first published 1947).
Goodway, D. (ed.) (1989) *For Anarchism: History, Theory and Practice*, London: Routledge.
Kropotkin, P. (1985) *Fields, Factories and Workshops*, London: Freedom Press (first published 1899).
——(1987) *Mutual Aid: A Factor In Evolution*, London: Freedom Press.
Marshall, P. (1992) *Demanding the Impossible: A History of Anarchism*, London: HarperCollins.
Ostergaard, G. and Currell, M. (1971) *The Gentle Anarchists*, Oxford: Clarendon.
Proudhon, P.-J. (1970) *Selected Writings*, London: Macmillan.
Taylor, M. (1982) *Community, Anarchy and Liberty*, Cambridge: Cambridge University Press.
Tolstoy, L. (1990) *Government is Violence: Essays on Anarchism and Pacifism*, London: Phoenix Press.
Ward, C. (1985) *Anarchy in Action*, London: Freedom Press (1st edn, London: Allen & Unwin 1973).
Woodcock, G. (1963) *Anarchism: A History of Libertarian Ideas and Movements*, Harmondsworth: Penguin.

Colin Ward

ANGLICANISM

'Anglicanism' was a term introduced in the nineteenth century (first recorded, according to the 1989 *Oxford English Dictionary*, in 1838 in an essay by the Oxford theologian John Henry Newman). It signified that religious stance constituted by the doctrine and disciplines of the Church of England, and it has become common to use it more broadly in relation to the Anglican Communion as a whole. Another term, 'Episcopalianism', is also common, especially in the USA where the Anglican Church is called 'the Episcopal Church'. This designation emphasizes that church government characteristically includes the episcopacy and avoids the national reference explicit in the term 'Anglican'.

The Anglican Communion, a term coined in 1885, includes an estimated 70 million people in more than 450 dioceses on all the continents of the world. They embrace more than 64,000 individual congregations in 164 countries, organized as twenty-eight independent, self-governing national or regional churches (Provinces). The separate Provinces of the Anglican Communion trace their origins to the expression of Christian faith developed in the Church of England and, through its missionary expansion, throughout the British Isles and directly or indirectly in other lands after the Reformation. All the churches of the Anglican Communion are in communion with the see of Canterbury, freely recognizing the Archbishop of Canterbury as the principal Archbishop and the focus of unity within the Communion.

The doctrine and discipline of Anglicans are strongly shaped by the specific emphases of the English Reformation, in respect of both what was preserved from earlier centuries and what was reformed. This is particularly the case in relation to social teaching. On the matter of church and secular power, early Anglican thinkers embrace viewpoints expressed by a variety of reforming thinkers from the fourteenth century onwards. In moral theology, the English reformers taught explicitly on the basis of medieval concepts, modified in parts by the results of more accurate exegesis of the Hebrew and Greek scriptures. As a result there is considerable breadth of view within Anglicanism, and several strands of thought can be detected.

The major influences upon the English Reformation are (i) the underground movement of protest against and criticism of the church in England, known collectively as Lollardy, dating from the late fourteenth century. Among its targets was the wealth, secular power and venality of the church. At a more public, intellectual level there was (ii) the humanist movement, which was serious, devout and scholarly, and likewise critical of the worldliness of the church and its popular superstitions. This movement proved attractive to the universities, and formed a context receptive to Luther's writings which reached England in considerable quantities between 1517 and 1529. William Tyndale (*c*.1494–1536) conceived the project of an English translation of the New Testament. The third movement of reform concerned (iii) the national political ambitions of the monarch. Throughout the medieval period Church and Crown were engaged in a continuous struggle for power. Clerical privileges were a popular target of attack, and publications expounded the benefits of separating spiritual and temporal realms. When Henry VIII's marriage to Katherine of Spain came under stress through dynastic and diplomatic pressures, a proposed decree of nullity was resisted by Pope Clement VII, under political constraint from the Emperor Charles V who had sacked Rome in 1527.

In these ambiguous circumstances the desire of Henry VIII for a DIVORCE and remarriage acquired major significance. An obscure Cambridge Biblical scholar, who had justified the divorce on canonical and scriptural grounds, was made Archbishop of Canterbury in 1532. Archbishop Thomas Cranmer then assisted Henry in transferring headship of the Church in England from the Pope to himself. (*See* CHURCH AND STATE.) Henry VIII was excommunicated in 1533.

Political conditions now strongly favoured the further course of reform. But despite consultations between Lutheran theologians and English churchmen, and the efforts made by Henry VIII to bring Melanchthon to England, no public document resembling the Lutheran Augsburg Confession (1530) was issued in England

until 1553 (the Forty-Two Articles of Religion, later revised as the Thirty-Nine Articles in 1563).

The advance of reform occurred instead through the King's ruthless suppression and plundering of the monasteries from 1536, the increasing accessibility of the English Bible licensed in 1538 and cautious developments in the direction of an English-language liturgy. The profession of Protestant doctrine was still severely punished, though Henry tolerated his (now married) Archbishop's Protestant sympathies and defended him personally.

Cranmer held the doctrine of the 'godly prince', according to which the monarch was viewed as divinely appointed and anointed (on the precedent of Old Testament kings) to do God's bidding and to defend the Church. With their background in Renaissance HUMANISM, the reformers strongly believed in advancing lay education and supported the reform or founding of colleges and schools. In the socio-economic crisis which developed in the first half of the sixteenth century, Anglican reformers mounted powerful attacks against the avarice of the wealthy which had brought about unemployment and starvation. Bishop Hugh Latimer of Worcester (*c*.1485–1555), the leading preacher of his day, denounced social and ecclesiastical abuses in forthright terms, especially those 'carnal gospellers' who had supported the reformation of the Church for their own enrichment.

After the English Bible the most important influence upon the developing Church was to be its Prayer Books. *The Book of Common Prayer and Administration of the Sacraments, and Other Rites and Ceremonies of the Church After the Use of the Church of England* (1549) was a revision of medieval rites but contained much new material, largely composed by Archbishop Cranmer, who drew on a wide variety of patristic, Eastern, Western and Reformed sources. Three years later it was replaced by a still more Protestant liturgy, revised partly in response to suggestions and demands from English and continental reformers. After a brief and bloody Catholic revival under Queen Mary (1553–8), the book was restored by Queen Elizabeth I in 1559.

In addition to the *Book of Common Prayer*

the Church of England authorized two *Books of Homilies* (1547 and 1563), which contain sermons on a variety of doctrinal and social matters. They teach a moderate Lutheran doctrine of justification by faith, of conversion to God and personal devotion, together with strong insistence on respect for the sovereign and of moral standards for personal and family life.

The defence of moderate reform which retained the traditional pattern of threefold ordained ministry, with an enhanced pastoral character, occupied the best Anglican minds during the reign of Queen Elizabeth. It was taught by theologians that the bishops were for the spiritual government of the nation, united under a divinely appointed sovereign. This theory was given sophisticated theological expression in Richard Hooker's *Laws of Ecclesiastical Polity* (1593–7), against the arguments of Puritans. Both Hooker and later Anglican moral theologians owe much to Aristotle and Thomas Aquinas. The cosmic order is rooted in God's creation of the world and its natural laws. To find one's way as a Christian in the practical detail and ambiguity of human life required a strong doctrine of conscience, on which Bishop Robert Sanderson and Bishop Jeremy Taylor both produced major works in 1660. The seventeenth century saw the development of a theological method which attempted an integrated moral–ascetic theology in a description of a responsible Christian life, lived in full co-operation with grace.

In the eighteenth century church–state relationships changed markedly with the dominance of Parliament over the Crown, and the consequent drawing of bishops into the conflicts of party government. This led to such bitter disputes inside the Church that regular meetings of clergy (Convocations) were abandoned. While faithful pastoral work continued to be carried out in the parishes, there was evidence of considerable subservience to the rationalist and utilitarian spirit of the age.

In this context the Evangelical revival of the mid-eighteenth century made a profound and lasting impression upon the Church of England. The Puritan movement had made much of 'inward religion', and small groups of serious-minded Anglicans were a feature of late seventeenth-century religion. Continental pietism,

especially the Moravian Brethren, played a significant role in the development of the revival, which produced major evangelists, George Whitefield (1714–70) and John Wesley (1703–91), among its leaders. The response of bishops to their large and successful public meetings grew increasingly hostile, but by the end of the century the numbers of evangelicals had grown sufficiently to assure them a place within the church's tradition.

Early Anglican evangelicals of the period 1790–1820 showed a serious concern to maintain a close relationship between faith and personal and social morality. Within a fundamentally conservative conception of political and social order, they undertook major campaigns to improve conditions in prisons, factories and the urban slums and to organize opposition to the slave trade.

Where evangelicals stressed JUSTIFICATION and regeneration, 'High Churchmen' emphasized the apostolic order and authority of the visible church. Oxford became the home of a theological and spiritual movement whose leaders included men like John Henry Newman (1801–90), who subsequently joined the Roman Catholic Church. The character of this movement began to change when its priests took parishes in the poverty-stricken cities of England. Incarnational theology was allied to the pursuit of justice and to social protest in a remarkable combination of conservative theology and radical politics. CHRISTIAN SOCIALISM, a broad and diverse movement from the 1850s, became a significant element in Anglican social thought and practical action.

Both Evangelicalism and the Oxford Movement transformed the Church of England. The former gave it a strong vein of piety and missionary zeal; the latter reinforced its sacramental orientation and saved it from subservience to the state. As a direct consequence of its emphasis upon the apostolical descent of bishops Anglicanism found increasing confidence in its identity outside the legal framework of the English church. The initial expansion of Anglicanism was in the form of port chaplaincies, the outcome of commercial expansion. The eighteenth century saw the opening of the missionary era, and after the American War of Independence the first American bishop was consecrated in 1784 in Scotland (where the Episcopal Church had been disestablished in 1689). The fiction that chaplaincies were under the jurisdiction of the Bishop of London was abandoned. Bishops were appointed in colonial territories and organized their churches on the basis of voluntary compact. The first bishop of New Zealand, G.A. Selwyn (1809–78), was granted a measure of self-government in 1852. Synodical government, in which bishops, clergy and lay people each play a distinctive role, came increasingly to be a characteristic of Anglicanism.

In its church–state relations Anglicanism has inherited a feeling for the importance of politics and government, as a divinely bestowed responsibility, and a conviction that religion belongs to the public domain. Even out of the context of establishment, Anglicans have continued to play a significant part in public life. Archbishop Desmond Tutu, Primate of the Church of the Province of Southern Africa, exemplifies the positive potential of this tradition. In other contexts Anglicans have found themselves impeded by their past association with colonial administrations.

With the geographical spread of Anglicanism came the demand to preserve and foster an international Anglican identity. In the context of considerable anxiety about the spread of Biblical criticism and liberal theology, a proposal was made in 1865 to the Archbishop of Canterbury to convene a synod of bishops from home and abroad. Of the 150 bishops invited, sixty-seven attended the first Lambeth Conference. Ten years later a second conference was held, and the conference has met ever since at roughly ten-year intervals. The body is deliberative and has no legislative power. It meets at the invitation of the Archbishop of Canterbury and constitutes a practical recognition of his authority as the focus of unity. The respective Provinces of the Communion remain legally autonomous bodies.

The social teaching of the Lambeth Conference Reports has tended to favour reform. In 1888 a report considered in a positive way the relations between Christianity and SOCIALISM. In 1908 it welcomed the strengthened movement of representative democracy, encouraging

Christian people to work for justice and social welfare. In a radical reversal of earlier policy, the 1958 Conference affirmed the responsibility of parents for deciding upon the number and frequency of children, including the use of artificial means of the control of conception.

In the inter-war years Anglican social thought was greatly enriched by the work of William Temple, Bishop of Manchester from 1921, Archbishop of York from 1929 and Archbishop of Canterbury from 1942 to 1944. Through his lively concern with social, economic and international questions, Anglicans acquired a voice of considerable authority. The Malvern Conference (1941) was an important landmark in the discussion leading towards the development of the welfare state in Britain. In the same tradition should be counted two major interventions in national politics, reports on *The Church and the Bomb* (1982) and *Faith in the City* (1985), the latter a devastating indictment of decline, decay and social disintegration in British cities. Similar emphases may be discerned in the teaching on 'Christianity and the Social Order' in a 1988 Lambeth Conference Report.

Because the Anglican Communion lacks a universal decision-making body, Anglican theology and social thought embraces a considerable variety of opinion. With the growth of international theologies of liberation since the 1960s denominational theology of all kinds has tended to decline in importance. Increasingly strong emphasis has been placed upon the indigenization of Christian thought and practice. The resources of the Anglican tradition are none the less both considerable and subtle, and have elicited contemporary defence and exposition.

Avis, P. (1989) *Anglicanism and the Christian Church*, London.
Clark, H. (1993) *The Church under Thatcher*, London.
Dickens, A.G. (1992) *The English Reformation*, 2nd edn, London.
Duffy, E. (1993) *The Stripping of the Altars*, London.
Elmen, P. (ed.) (1983) *The Anglican Moral Choice*, Wilton, CT.
McAdoo, F.R. (1949) *The Structure of Caroline Moral Theology*, London.
Norman, E.R. (1976) *Church and Society in England 1770–1970*, Oxford.

Stephenson, A.M.G. (1978) *Anglicanism and the Lambeth Conferences*, London.

Suggate, A.M. (1987) *William Temple and Christian Social Ethics Today*, Edinburgh.

Sykes, S. and Booty, J. (eds) (1988) *The Study of Anglicanism*, London.

Stephen Sykes

ANIMAL RIGHTS

In order to understand contemporary animal rights theory, we need to set it within the context of the historically dominant philosophical modes of discourse about animals to which it is, at least in part, a response or even a development. There are six main ethical theories of the status of animals.

1 *Humanocentric theory*   According to this view, animals have no moral status. Humans have no direct duties to animals except in so far as some human interest is involved. Wanton cruelty may be wrong not because it infringes the rights of animals but because cruelty brutalizes human beings, or leads to similar activity in relation to human subjects. Morality, strictly speaking, only concerns what humans do to humans, or to other subjects in so far as they affect human subjects.

This theory may also be called the classical, or Aristotelian–Thomist view. In terms of systematic theology, it was the virtually unchallenged Christian view until the eighteenth century. As late as the middle of the nineteenth century, Pope Pius IX forbade the opening of an animal protection office in Rome on the grounds that humans had duties to other humans but none to animals. It finds its clearest continuing expression in Roman Catholic moral theology, for example: 'Zoophilists often lose sight of the end for which animals, irrational creatures were created by God, viz., the service and use of man. . . . In fact, catholic moral doctrine teaches that animals have no rights on the part of man' (Palazzini 1962: 73).

There are two main philosophical/theological justifications for this view both derived at least in part from Aristotle and systematized in the Christian tradition mainly through the work of St Thomas Aquinas. First, animals are by divine providence and nature our slaves – given for our use. 'Hereby is refuted the error of those who said it is sinful for man to kill brute animals; for by divine providence they are intended for man's use according to the order of nature. Hence it is not wrong for man to make use of them either by killing or in any other way whatever' (Aquinas 1945: 220–4). Second, animals are by definition non-rational creatures; they cannot therefore possess a mind, or an immortal soul, and are not persons possessing rights. Their *raison d'être* is to serve the higher intellectual species, namely human beings.

Recent Roman Catholic teaching may have modified this stark Thomistic perspective. The encyclical *Sollicitudo Rei Socialis* specifically speaks of the need to respect 'the nature of each being' within creation (1987: 64–5). Moreover, the *Catechism of the Catholic Church* does acknowledge that we owe animals 'kindness' after the example shown by the saints. But the same *Catechism* reaffirms the major elements of Thomist thought. God still destines 'all material creatures for the good of the human race'. It is '*contrary to human dignity* to cause animals to suffer or die needlessly', and 'it is likewise unworthy to spend money on them [animals] which should as a priority go to the relief of human misery' (English translation 1994: 81, 516–17; my emphasis).

2 *Contractualist theory*   According to this view, rights and duties flow from persons who are capable of making contracts or entering into mutual obligations. In short: no duties, no rights. This is a variant of the standard Aristotelian–Thomist position. Aristotle held that justice required rational friendship, a quality which was impossible between those who were not equals, and hence slaves and animals – to take only two examples – were excluded from the moral community (Aristotle 1915: 1161a–b). Aquinas held likewise that friendship was only possible between rational creatures (Aquinas 1918).

We find this view reflected in modern theology, e.g. by Bernard Häring: 'Nothing irrational can be the object of the Christian virtue of neighbourly love. Nothing irrational is capable of the beautifying friendship with God' (Häring 1963: 361–2). The view is both confirmed and modified by the *Catechism* as follows: 'One can love animals; one should not direct to them the affection *due only to persons*' (1994: 517; my emphasis).

Perhaps the best contemporary defence of contractualism is found in the work of John Rawls. While he accepts that it is wrong to be cruel to animals, even that 'we have duties of compassion and humanity to them', he nevertheless concludes that animals are 'outside the scope of the theory of justice' and that it is not possible for a contractualist theory to 'include them in a natural way'. The 'considered beliefs' that we owe duties to animals apparently depend upon a metaphysical view of the world separate from contractualist doctrine (Rawls 1972: 504–12).

3 Humanitarian theory   There are two key elements. First, that humans should prevent unnecessary cruelty and promote kindness to sentient beings, and second, that humans should exercise benevolence or philanthropy towards inferior creatures – not least of all for their own (humans') sake.

This theory, or rather sensitivity, was characteristic of what is now called the humanitarian movement especially dominant in the nineteenth and twentieth centuries and which gave rise to such organizations as the Humanitarian League, the English and American Societies for the Prevention of Cruelty to Animals and the Friends of Animals League (*see* Thomas 1983). This movement was in conscious or unconscious reaction to Thomist scholasticism which failed to include animals, at least directly, within the sphere of human moral responsibility.

The Royal Society for the Prevention of Cruelty to Animals (RSPCA), for example, was founded by an Anglican priest, Arthur Broome, in 1824. He penned the first prospectus of the Society in which he argued:

Our country is distinguished by the number and variety of its benevolent institutions . . . all breathing the pure spirit of Christian charity. . . . But shall we stop here? Is the moral circle perfect so long as any power of doing good remains? Or can the infliction of cruelty on any being which the Almighty has endued

with feelings of pain and pleasure consist with genuine and true benevolence?

(Broome 1823–6: 203–4)

The underlying argument is that cruelty to humans or animals is incompatible with the Christian faith. Indeed the Society recorded in its First Minute Book a resolution that it was a Christian Society based specifically on the Christian faith and on Christian principles (see Turner 1980).

Perhaps the most progressive exponent of this general theory is Humphry Primatt. His *Dissertation on the Duty of Mercy and the Sin of Cruelty to Brute Animals*, published in 1776, maintained that: 'We may pretend to what religion we please, but cruelty is atheism. We may make our boast of Christianity, but cruelty is infidelity. We may trust to our orthodoxy, but cruelty is the worst of heresies' (Primatt 1776: 288).

4 Welfare theory   Weak welfare theory is almost indistinguishable from humanitarian theory but I shall concentrate here on the strongest utilitarian welfare theory propounded by Peter Singer in the 1970s. There are three key elements. First, sentiency (generally defined as the ability to feel pain and suffering) is the only defensible boundary of moral concern between species. Second, once it can be reasonably supposed that a being is sentient, its suffering should be taken into account morally. Third, all sentient beings, human or animal, have an *equal* claim to have their interests considered as individuals (see Singer 1976). Perhaps it is worth pointing out that Singer appears to draw the line at molluscs; everything above is sentient life.

As propounded by Singer this view has no theological basis as such but it is not difficult to provide one. From a theological perspective, the Cross of Christ is God's vindication of innocent suffering. To inflict suffering on innocent, undefended, unprotected beings – provided that the suffering is unmerited and undeserved as of course it always is in the case of animals – is nothing less than intrinsically evil (*see* CRUELTY). It finds its strongest expression theologically in the Oxford sermon of Cardinal Newman in which he argued that suffering inflicted on innocent animals is morally equivalent to that inflicted upon Christ. 'There is something so very dreadful, so satanic in tormenting those who have never harmed us, and who cannot defend themselves, who are utterly in our power, who have weapons neither of offence nor defence, that none but very hardened persons can endure the thought of it.' And he concludes: 'Think then, my brethren, of your feelings at cruelty practised upon brute animals, and you will gain one sort of feeling which the history of Christ's Cross and Passion ought to excite within you' (Newman 1868: 136–8).

The practical upshot of the welfare theory is that animal suffering must be taken with the greatest seriousness and that all sentient beings have an equal claim to moral consideration. But this does not commit utilitarian welfarists to an absolutist position. A utilitarian position is always open to the weighing up of consequences. As Singer himself writes in his *Practical Ethics:* 'if one, or even a dozen animals had to suffer experiments in order to save thousands [presumably Singer here means thousands of the same species], I would think it right and in accordance with equal consideration of interests that they should do so' (Singer 1980: 58). In other words, if it could be shown that the suffering of some animals can save the suffering of many other creatures, it would be justifiable to make them suffer – according to the utilitarian version of the welfare theory.

5 Rights theory   Again, there are three key elements. First, animals are ends in themselves and must not be regarded as means to human ends: as resources, commodities, laboratory tools or units of production. Second, all animals which are – in the words of Tom Regan – 'subjects of a life' have inherent value and therefore possess rights (Regan 1983: 232–65). Third, those beings which possess inherent value possess it *equally*, so it is normally wrong to infringe the rights of *individual* animals no matter the consequences.

There are secular and theological doctrines of animal rights. The secular philosophical view enumerated by Regan argues that animals are complex beings with emotions, desires and interests to such an extent that they bring subjectivity to our world. It is this subjectivity which makes them beings with inherent value. Regan argues

that all mentally normal mammals of a year or more have rights equal to that of humans (Regan 1983: 78).

The theological basis of rights (Linzey 1976, 1987, 1994) holds that, while all creation has value, some beings have rights by virtue of their Creator's right. Animals who are 'Spirit-filled, breathing creatures, composed of flesh and blood, are subjects of inherent value to God' (Linzey 1987: 69). According to this view, animals have 'theos-rights' (literally 'God-rights') because it is the right of God which establishes the specific value of some living beings. In this sense, rights are not awarded, accorded or bestowed but recognized. 'When we speak of animal rights we conceptualise what is objectively owed to animals as a matter of justice by virtue of their Creator's right' (Linzey 1987: 97).

The attainment of animal rights' goals would require a transformation of human society as we know it. Such a society would be characterized by minimum disturbance to animal life and an end to all institutional abuse of animals in agriculture, science and sport.

6 Generosity theory   Drawing on the humanitarian theory (*see* above), one theological view argues that what humans owe animals requires even more than an acceptance of their rights. According to this view, humans have a duty not only to respect the rights of animals but also to be morally generous. 'Drawing upon the notion of divine generosity exemplified in the person of Jesus, I suggest that the weak and defenceless should be given not equal, but greater, consideration. The weak should have moral priority' (Linzey 1994: 28).

The key elements of the argument are as follows. First, humans are the deputized moral agents of God in creation, with a God-given responsibility to care for the earth generally and animals in particular. Second, this human power or 'dominion' over animals should take as its model the Christ-given paradigm of lordship manifest in service. Third, the logic of this Christological paradigm is that the 'higher' should sacrifice itself for the 'lower' and not the reverse. Fourth, animals have an analogous status to that of children; adult humans have a special responsibility to both, and, finally, animals, like children, should be seen as having not equal claim but greater claim upon us precisely because of their vulnerability and relative powerlessness.

The practical upshot of the generosity theory is that humans should generously, self-sacrificially, work to promote the well-being of other creatures. The theological *raison d'être* of human beings is as 'the servant species' (Linzey 1994: 45–61). The idea that humans should seek their advantage, welfare and survival at the cost of other species is replaced by a paradigm in which humans should bear for themselves whatever ills may flow from not using animals rather than inflict suffering and death on creatures which are the subjects of a special trust.

It is difficult to avoid the conclusion that theories 4–6 represent a real intellectual advance in terms of understanding the moral status of animals. Theories 1 and 2 – and even 3 – continue to keep animals out of the sphere of moral justice. Once humanocentric theory is rejected and it is accepted that causing suffering and death to animals is a morally significant issue, then radical conclusions in terms of individual behaviour and social practice must follow. The social world in which we live has been – and still is – largely fashioned by the intellectual heritage of the Aristotelian–Thomist tradition. Hence, we continue to use animals as means to human ends: we hunt, ride, shoot, fish, wear, eat, cage, exhibit, factory farm and experiment upon billions of animals every year.

There are signs, however, that this once monolithic intellectual tradition and practice is breaking down – not least in matters relating to the status of women, environmental ethics, and the debate about the nature of sexuality. The animal rights and generosity theories anticipate an even greater weakening of this tradition and return us to some fundamental insights which have always been present within Western culture (to some degree) but which have been insufficiently recognized and articulated.

For example, the Judaeo-Christian tradition which has in many ways justified and sanctioned the ruthless use of animals has always contained within itself a vision of universal peace inclusive of animal life (Isaiah 11: 1–9; cf. Romans 8: 18–24). Specifically also animals are included within the Noahic covenant (Genesis 9: 3). Karl Barth,

to take only one modern example, maintains that the view of Psalm 36: 6 that God especially preserves humans and animals is 'a thread running through the whole of the Bible; and it first emerges in a way which is quite unmistakable when the creation of man is classified in Gen. 1. 24f with that of the land animals' (Barth 1958: 181).

Progressive theories can claim to have a basis in some layers of Biblical theology and in the notion that God alone is the source of the value of all life forms. From this perspective, 'modern' theories holding strong duties to animals are the result of a revival of an ancient spiritual insight concerning the intrinsic – God-given – worth of animated creatures. In the same way that Judaeo-Christian tradition both justified the subordination of women to men *and also* provided a theological basis for women's equality, so too has the tradition both justified animal abuse and also provided a moral critique of that abuse at the same time. Which perception of animals – the view that they are here for our use, or the view that we should behave generously to them and respect their rights – will prevail only time will tell.

My own view is that there is no real alternative to the inclusion of sentients within the human moral circle. Accepting that, there can of course be room for legitimate discernment and debate. While rights theory holds many advantages in terms of demarcating appropriate moral limits to human behaviour, it does not follow that rights language can – or should – convey everything that needs to be said from a theological or philosophical standpoint about the moral status of animals. Rights language cannot by itself claim to be a comprehensive theory; talk of respect, care, generosity, love and gentleness to animals is not only appropriate but also essential.

The same kind of qualification seems appropriate in relation to questions of goals and strategy. To accept animal rights goals does not mean that all systems of gradual reform should be eschewed; on the contrary 'progressive disengagement from injury' (Linzey 1987: 104f.) seems the most enlightened and effective strategy for moral reformers working for progress with either human or animal causes. One final caveat seems essential: animal rights thinking which eschews the use of sentient animals as means to human ends should also, logically, eschew the use of fellow humans as means to (even moral) ends as well – which means in practice that violence in pursuit of animal rights causes is morally self-contradictory and self-defeating.

Aquinas, St Thomas (1918) *Summa Theologica*, ed. and trans. the English Dominican Fathers, New York: Benzinger Brothers, Part 1, Questions 64.1 and 65.3.
——(1945) *Summa Contra Gentiles*, in *Basic Writings of Saint Thomas Aquinas*, ed. and trans. Anton C. Pegis, New York: Random House, vol. II.
Aristotle (1915) 'Nicomachean Ethics', in *The Works of Aristotle*, ed. and trans. W.D. Ross, London: Oxford University Press.
Barth, Karl (1958) 'The work of creation', *Church Dogmatics*, vol. 3, Part 1, ed. and trans. T.R. Torrance and G.W. Bromiley, Edinburgh: T. & T. Clark.
Broome, Arthur (1823–6) 'Prospectus of the SPCA, 25 June, 1824', *RSPCA Records*, vol. II.
Catechism of the Catholic Church (1994) London: Geoffrey Chapman.
Clarke, P.A.B. and Linzey, Andrew (eds) (1990) *Political Theory and Animal Rights*, London and Boulder, Colorado, MA: Pluto Press.
Clark, Stephen R.L. (1977) *The Moral Status of Animals*, Oxford: Clarendon Press.
Frey, R.G. (1980) *Interests and Rights: The Case Against Animals*, Oxford: Clarendon Press.
Garner, Robert (1993) *Animals, Politics and Morality*, Issues in Environmental Politics, Manchester: Manchester University Press.
Godlovitch, Stanley, Godlovitch, Roslind and Harris, John (eds) (1971) *Animals, Men and Morals: An Inquiry into the Maltreatment of Non-Humans*, London: Gollancz.
Häring, Bernard (1963) *The Law of Christ*, vol. II, London: Mercier Press.
John Paul II, Pope (1987) *Sollicitudo Rei Socialis*, Encyclical Letter, London: Catholic Truth Society.
Linzey, Andrew (1976) *Animal Rights: A Christian Assessment*, London: SCM Press.
——(1987) *Christianity and the Rights of Animals*, London: SPCK, and New York: Crossroad.
——(1994) *Animal Theology*, London: SCM, and Chicago, IL: University of Illinois Press.
Magel, Charles (1989) *Keyguide to Information Sources in Animal Rights*, London and New York: Mansell.
Midgley, Mary (1983) *Animals and Why They Matter: A Journey Around the Species Barrier*, Harmondsworth: Penguin.
Murray, Robert (1992) *The Cosmic Covenant: Biblical Themes of Justice, Peace and the Integrity of Creation*, London: Sheed & Ward.
Newman, John Henry (1868) 'The Crucifixion' (Sermon X), in *Parochial and Plain Sermons*, London, Oxford and Cambridge: Rivingtons, vol. VII.
Palazzini, P. (ed.) (1962) *Dictionary of Moral Theology*, London: Burns & Oates.
Primatt, Humphry (1776) *Dissertation on the Duty of Mercy and the Sin of Cruelty to Brute Animals*, Edinburgh: T. Constable.
Rachels, James (1991) *Created from Animals: The Moral Implications of Darwinism*, Oxford: Oxford University Press.
Rawls, John (1972) *A Theory of Justice*, Oxford: Oxford University Press.
Regan, Tom (1983) *The Case for Animal Rights*, Berkeley, CA: University of California Press.
Rollin, Bernard E. (1989) *The Unheeded Cry: Animal Consciousness, Animal Pain and Science*, Oxford: Oxford University Press.
Ryder, Richard (1989) *Animal Revolution: Changing Attitudes Towards Speciesism*, Oxford: Blackwell.
Singer, Peter (1976) *Animal Liberation: A New Ethics for Our Treatment of Animals*, London: Jonathan Cape.
——(1980) *Practical Ethics*, Cambridge: Cambridge University Press.
Tester, Keith (1991) *Animals and Society: The Humanity of Animal Rights*, London: Routledge.
Thomas, Keith (1983) *Man and the Natural World: A History of the Modern Sensibility*, New York: Pantheon.
Turner, James (1980) *Reckoning with the Beast: Animals, Pain and Humanity in the Victorian Mind*, Baltimore, MD: Johns Hopkins University Press.

Andrew Linzey

ANOMIE

Anomie is a term used by social scientists to conceptualize a condition where social rules are absent (normlessness) or are in a state of normative confusion (captured by the French word *dérèglement*), or where norms are disregarded, in varying degrees, by the members of a society. The word anomie and its orthographic variants anomy and anomia derive from the Greek noun *anomia*, which in turn goes back to the Greek adjective *anomos*, literally meaning without law or without rule. According to Ostwald (1969: 85) the earlier Greek term described 'the asocial behaviour of an individual who defies law-and-order and who acts in contravention of any or all the canons regarded as valid and binding by the society in which he lives'.

In contemporary social sciences, two variants

of the concept have emerged. Anomie (or anomy) refers to a condition of societies or of particular groups within a SOCIETY (Durkheim [1897] 1951; Merton 1938), whereas anomia describes the psychological normlessness of individuals (Srole 1956). But regardless of the distinct emphases on the individual or collective levels, anomie is a central concept in the social sciences because it highlights the fact that social integration and normative stability are not given features of social or individual life. On the contrary, some degree of normlessness and deregulation are the observed norm rather than the exception. More to the point, anomie can be shown to be a desirable trait, not a pathological feature, of modern societies and individuals (Guyau 1887).

The classical Greek literature provided early historical evidence concerning the phenomenon of anomie, and early philosophical disquisitions about anomie's effect on the larger society. In Euripides' *Iphigenia in Aulis* (1090–7) the chorus lamented: 'Godlessness is on the rise, mortals push Virtue aside, *Anomia* governs the Law, and no one is afraid any longer of the divine retribution'. The anonymus Iamblichi, a fifth-century sophist, argued: 'If *anomia* is the cause of such great evils, and law-and-order causes such great goods, it is not possible otherwise to acquire happiness unless one considers law as the guide of his whole life' (fragment 7.17). But the Greek literature also provided early awareness that existing laws and norms are socially constructed phenomena – that they are not inherently compelling. The sophist Antiphon, for instance, reasoned: 'The most profitable means of utilizing justice is to respect the laws when witnesses are present but otherwise to follow the precepts of nature' (fragment 44A).

The Biblical literature offers a rich discussion of anomie (de la Potterie [1956] 1971) and it dovetails with classical Greek thought in presenting two sides of anomie. On the one hand, in the Greek version of the Old Testament *anomia* corresponded to such English terms as wickedness, ungodliness, impiety, injustice, wrong, depravity, evil and, above all, sin and iniquity. The Book of Psalms, where the Greek *anomia* is most frequently found, offers several examples where *anomia* (iniquity) equals *hamartia* (sin).

Here, the transgression of the written law is unqualifiedly condemned. On the other hand, in the New Testament we find an alternative view summarized by the apostle Paul's critique of Judaic legalism, where the spiritual freedom obtained through Christ makes the constraints of the written law obsolete. Paul writes: 'The law is not made for the righteous, but for the lawless [*anomois*] and unruly' (1 Timothy 1: 9). The significant point, in the theological argument of Paul as in the philosophical argument of the sophist Antiphon, is that written laws and norms are instruments for obtaining compliance by the unruly, but these same laws and norms are irrelevant and can be dispensed with if we follow the 'precepts of nature' (Antiphon) or 'the law of the spirit' (Paul). In both cases, the existing socio-historical normative structure is relativized through an appeal to higher principles of conduct (*see* CIVIL DISOBEDIENCE).

Within the social sciences, a dual approach to anomie has also emerged within the writings of Emile Durkheim (1897) and Robert K. Merton (1938). In Durkheim's conceptualization anomie results when the unsocialized, impulsive desires of our human nature are insufficiently disciplined by social values and inadequately restrained by social norms and rules. 'Unlimited desires are insatiable by definition and insatiability is rightly considered a sign of morbidity. . . . [Society] alone has the power necessary to stipulate law and to set the point beyond which the passions must not go' (1951: 247, 249). Thus, 'under weaker restraints, desires and ambitions overflow impetuously' (1951: 364). But Durkheim also acknowledges the beneficial role of *dérèglement*, as he argues: 'The entire morality of progress and perfection is [thus] inseparable from a certain amount of anomy' (1951: 364). Here Durkheim recognizes, perhaps reluctantly, that anomie is necessary for societies to move away from traditional social arrangements toward MODERNITY.

Robert K. Merton's writings also illuminate the dual character of anomie. In Merton's writings, anomie obtains when a disproportionate emphasis on culturally approved goals is coupled with a weakening in the importance of norms for legimately achieving the cultural goals. 'Aberrant conduct, therefore, may be viewed as a symptom of dissociation between culturally defined aspirations and socially structured means' (1938: 674). For Merton, anomie results from the imbalance between cultural goals and institutionalized means, where the former is overemphasized at the expense of the latter. But Merton also shows a different side to anomie by demonstrating that anomie and modernity are inextricably related and go hand in hand. Merton identifies the strong egalitarianism of American society, coupled with an emphasis on a universalistic success goal, as the cause of anomie. In a rigidly stratified society, where people's expectations are differently assigned, anomie would be greatly reduced; but anomie is more likely 'in a society which places a high premium on economic affluence and social ascent for *all* its members' (1938: 680). Merton's reasoning demonstrates that a characteristic of American culture and of modernity in general – equal opportunity for all members of society – is a key factor in the emergence of anomie. Anomie and modernity are thus shown to be inextricably linked.

The theological, philosophical and sociological discussions described above seem to converge in identifying two sides of anomie. On the one hand, normlessness and *dérèglement* are perceived to be problems which threaten social order and the optimal integration of individuals within society. In this respect, to paraphrase Durkheim, anomie is an evil. On the other hand, it is also recognized that some degree of anomie is needed for social change to occur. The great experiment of Athenian democracy in the fifth century BC was accompanied by some cultural and normative anomie. The transition from Judaism to Christianity implied abandoning a normatively structured Judaic tradition in favour of the anomic creativity of the 'law of the spirit'. The emergence of modern industrial democracies is also characterized by the obsolescence of traditional social hierarchies and by an increase in normative flexibility, an increase in anomie. Historically, an overwhelming emphasis has been placed on the dangers of anomic disorder, normlessness and cultural anarchy. But it has also become clear, although less forcefully stated, that social progress and change cannot obtain unless normative restraints are relaxed,

and anomie is acknowledged to be a crucial ingredient of modernity.

The two analyses of anomie at the social level lead to two parallel implications of anomie for societies and individuals alike. On one side is the attempt to seek a remedy to rampant anomie by bringing back community-based values in modern societies, restoring the morality of the traditional *Gemeinschaft*. Modern individualism is perceived to be defective and inadequate in providing the moral glue of advanced societies, and a return to collectivism is perceived to be the answer. On the other side is the realization that highly differentiated societies increasingly need individuals who are capable of autonomous judgement in navigating a complex social world. Anomie, understood as the ability to go beyond the written normative statements of a society and capture the spirit of modernity, is then not something to be fought and suppressed, but rather something to be actively nurtured in the modern individual. Pulled between the competing needs for social order and social change, and between the disruptive and the constructive sides of anomie, social scientists have mirrored the ambivalence of the real world in their own theoretical constructs.

I identified anomie as the normlessness and *dérèglement* which characterize not only problems of social disorganization and deviant behaviour but also desirable innovation, social change and progress. Understanding the ambivalent qualities of anomie should enable us to do justice to the complex social phenomena it seeks to describe. But, more importantly, understanding the ambivalence of anomie should allow us unconditionally to come to terms with the broader ambivalences of social life in general and of modernity in particular.

Besnard, P. (1987) *L'Anomie, ses usages et ses fonctions dans la discipline sociologique depuis Durkheim*, Paris: Presses Universitaires de France.

Clinard, M.B. (ed.) (1964) *Anomie and Deviant Behavior*, New York: Free Press.

Durkheim, E. ([1897] 1951) *Suicide: A Study in Sociology*, New York: Free Press.

Guyau, J.M. (1887) *L'Irreligion de l'avenir, étude de sociologie*, Paris: Felix Alcan.

Merton, R.K. (1938) 'Social structure and anomie', *American Sociological Review* 3(5): 672–82.

Orrù, M. (1987) *Anomie: History and Meanings*, Boston, MA: Allen & Unwin.

Ostwald, M. (1969) *Nomos and the Beginnings of the Athenian Democracy*, Oxford: Clarendon Press.

de la Potterie, I. ([1956] 1971) 'Sin is iniquity', in I. de la Potterie and S. Lyonnet (eds), *The Christian Lives by the Spirit*, Staten Island, NY: Alba House.

Srole, L. (1956) 'Social integration and certain corollaries', *American Sociological Review* 21(6): 709–16.

Marco Orrù

ANTI-SEMITISM

The term anti-Semitism was coined in 1879 by Wilhelm Marr, an anti-Jewish polemicist in Germany, to describe antipathy to the Jewish people. Although this term is technically incorrect since it should include all Semites, it has none the less gained universal currency. Through the centuries hostility to Jews and the Jewish religion has been expressed as a result of numerous causes: political, social, cultural, economic and religious. Depending on the social and cultural conditions, anti-Semitism has taken on a wide variety of forms. In the Greco-Roman world Jews and Judaism were subject to discrimination and persecution. Where Greek power was dominant the typical view was that anything non-Greek was barbaric. The Jewish tradition was thus regarded with contempt. None the less it was only when Christianity emerged in the first century AD that Jews came to be viewed as contemptible and demonic. In its advocacy of anti-Jewish attitudes, the Church drew upon Hellenistic ideas that had penetrated into the Jewish faith. For a number of Jews the Torah was interpreted in allegorical terms, and such a conception was transformed by Christianity into a justification for separating religious meaning from ritual observance. Revival movements in the ancient Jewish world – the disciples of which believed themselves to be the true Israel – also provided a source for the Christian conviction that the Jewish faith constituted the fulfilment of Biblical teaching. Further Gnosticism which grew out of the attempt to harmonize Hellenistic thought with the Jewish tradition added to the Christian denigration of the God of the Hebrew Scriptures. Finally, the Pharisaic spiritualization and universalization of Judaism intensified the Christian determination that the good news of the New Testament should be spread to all people. Christianity thus utilized features inherent in the Judaism of the Hellenistic and Roman period to shape its own identity and distance itself from the faith from which it had originated.

With the emergence of the Christian community, anti-Jewish sentiment in the Greco-Roman world intensified. The early Church believed itself to be the authentic heir to the promises given by God in Scripture: Jesus' messiahship ushered in a new era in which the true Israel would become a light to the nations. Such a vision of the Christian community evoked hostility against the Jewish people, who were regarded as apostate and unrepentant. This animosity was fuelled by the Gospel writers who described Jesus attacking the leaders of the nation. The Church taught that what is now required is circumcision of the heart rather than obedience to the Law: Christians are to remain faithful not to the Torah but to Christ. In proclaiming this Christian message Paul emphasized that the Hebrew people had been rejected by God, and the new covenant had taken the place of the old. In the Epistle to the Hebrews this antithesis between the Jewish people and Christian community is heightened: Christ is conceived as the true eternal Temple in opposition to the earthly and temporal cult of Jerusalem. Such a contrast is also to be found in the Fourth Gospel, which differentiates between the fulfilled spiritual universe of Christianity and a fallen world of darkness represented by the Jews. The New Testament thus laid the foundation for the theological negation of Judaism and the Jewish people.

Following New Testament teaching, the Church Fathers developed an *Adversos Judaeos* tradition which vilified the Jews. According to these writers, just as Jews were guilty in the past of indecency, so they have continued to be a lawless and dissolute people. For this reason all future promises apply solely to the Church. Appealing to Scripture, the Fathers attempted to demonstrate that the conflict between the Church and the Synagogue was prefigured in Scripture. Separated from the Christian message of salvation the Jews have been rejected and are subject to God's wrath. It is the Christian community rather than the Jews who constitute the elect. This is the culmination of the messianic vision of the ingathering of all people to Zion. The Christian faith, the religion of the Roman Empire, serves as the vehicle for bringing God's redemption to humanity, but the Jews are to suffer rejection and misery because of their unwillingness to accept Jesus as the Messiah. Destined to wander in exile, they find no peace. Jewish law has thus been superseded through Christ's death, and it is now the Christian faith alone which offers salvation to the world.

The tradition of anti-Semitism created by the Fathers of the Church continued into the Middle Ages. During the centuries of the Crusades Jews were massacred throughout Western Europe. Although some Christian leaders condemned such barbarism, the masses continued to attack those who stubbornly clung to the Jewish faith. Christian hostility was further intensified by a number of charges levelled against the Jewish population. Repeatedly Jews were accused of murdering Christian children to incorporate their blood into unleavened bread for Passover; such allegations of ritual murder spread from country to country and many Jews were victimized for supposedly committing such atrocious acts. Jews were also accused of blaspheming the Christian faith in their sacred literature, and as a consequence copies of the Talmud were burned. In addition, the Jewish population was blamed for causing the Black Plague by poisoning wells. Those who perished in the Christian onslaught as a result of these allegations prayed for vengeance. In faithfulness to God, these martyrs went to their deaths confident that Christians would suffer eternal torment for their sins.

During the Middle Ages the Jewish community was detested, and the stereotype of the demonic Jew became part of Western culture. Repeatedly during this period Jews were accused of possessing attributes of both the DEVIL and witches. As the personification of EVIL, they were relegated to a subspecies of the human race. Jews were also perceived as magicians *par excellence*, about to work magic against the Christian community; this belief served as the basis for the charge that the Jewish population

desecrated the Host and committed acts of ritual murder. Yet while it is true that Jews did engage in magical practices, they were excluded from non-Jewish circles of sorcerers and witches, and Jewish magic was dependent on the power of good rather than the demonic realm. Thus Christian allegations of this period were based on ignorance and fear. None the less the masses attacked the Jews in their pursuit of the demons, and in this onslaught thousands of innocent victims lost their lives.

Although the Jewish community was expelled from France in the fourteenth century, negative images of Jews continued to play a role in French culture. Catechisms, lives of Jesus and canticles portrayed the Jewish people as tools of Satan. In addition, tracts abounded which denounced the Jews in terms reminiscent of the Middle Ages. In England, Jews were similarly vilified even though the Jewish nation was expelled in 1290. German Jews were also detested – such hostility was most powerfully expressed in Martin Luther's *Against the Jews and the Lies* (1542). Such publications were followed by a wide range of tracts which denigrated Judaism and the Jewish people. Thus despite the existence of powerful court Jews throughout Germany, the Jewish masses lived simple lives and endured considerable hardship during this period.

Similarly in Spain by the fourteenth century Jews came to be regarded with suspicion and hostility. Measures were taken against the Jewish community, and in consequence many Jews embraced the Christian faith to escape attack. Such apostasy as well as the Christian onslaught on Jewry led to the decline of the *aljamas* (Jewish communities), a trend which was resisted by Jewish leaders. During the fifteenth century the Church initiated a new form of persecution. Under Ferdinand and Isabella the Inquisition was established to purge conversos or New Christians – Jewish converts to Christianity as opposed to Old Christians of pure blood – who were suspected of practising Jewish customs. Tribunals were established throughout Spain which applied torture to extract confessions from the guilty – those who refused to confess were cast to the flames. Finally, at the end of the century, an Edict of Expulsion was enacted to rid the country of the Jewish race who had polluted the Christian population.

When the Inquisition intensified its efforts to root out Christian heresy in Spain, Marranos fled to other countries for safety from their Christian persecutors. Many sought refuge in Portugal, where they led a Christian way of life while selectively observing Jewish practices. Following Spanish precedent, the Portuguese Inquisition was established in 1536 and attempted to track down Marranos wherever they lived. Other Marranos were driven to find homes in other lands. Both Turkey and Salonica constituted Marrano refuges from Christian oppression in the sixteenth century. Others went to Antwerp, Venice, Ancona and Bordeaux; in the next century Marranos settled in Amsterdam, Hamburg and London.

In the seventeenth century Polish Jewry was massacred by Cossacks under Bogdan Chmielnicki. In the wake of this Christian onslaught the Hasidic movement encouraged religious pietism, but was severely criticized by the traditional rabbinic establishment. As the community was torn by this conflict, attacks were directed against the Jewish population by Gentiles. Such hostility was paralleled in Russia. Initially Jews were prevented from settling in the country, and with the annexation of Polish territories to Russia in the nineteenth century Jews were regarded by Christians with suspicion and contempt and eventually expelled from the villages where they resided.

During the early modern period the commercial interests of the bourgeoisie, coupled with centuries-old Christian prejudice against Jews and Judaism, evoked considerable hostility toward the Jewish population in Western countries. In Germany, merchants protested against the infidels living in their midst. Jewish trade, they believed, would destroy the economic life of the country and pollute the Christian population. Similar attitudes were expressed in France, where the bourgeoisie resisted Jewish settlement despite the fact that the nobility regarded Jews as financially useful. In Great Britain, Jews were also subject to virulent criticism, and attempts to simplify procedures for Jewish naturalization and to authorize Jews to possess land were met with considerable resistance. In the USA,

however, Jews gained a broad measure of freedom as the country struggled to achieve its independence from England. None the less, despite many of the advances made in the seventeenth and eighteenth centuries, Jewish life did not alter radically from medieval patterns of existence. Stereotyped as foreign and strange, Jews were subject to discrimination and persecution during the early modern period.

Under the banner of the Enlightenment, English free-thinkers sought to ameliorate the condition of the Jews. Such attempts, however, were countered by other writers who attacked Jewry on grounds consonant with the spirit of a rationalist and scientific age. In France, Protestants influenced by the Enlightenment attempted to refute charges against the Jewish population. Yet despite such progressive attitudes, they were unable to free themselves from traditional assumptions about Jewish guilt and divine retribution. In addition, many of the major thinkers of the age encouraged Judeophobia. In Germany an attempt was made to present Jews in a more positive light, but here as well the rise of national self-confidence provoked antipathy toward the Jewish population. Such philosophers as Kant, Fichte and Hegel wrote disparagingly of both Jews and Judaism.

At the end of the eighteenth century the spirit of the Enlightenment stimulated Christian Europe to seek the amelioration of Jewish life. With the establishment of the Napoleonic era, Jewish existence was revolutionized. The summoning of a Great Sanhedrin in France paved the way for Jewish emancipation, and the position of Jewry improved throughout the Continent. In the midst of such social upheaval German Jewish reformers attempted to adapt Jewish worship to modern conditions. To the consternation of the Orthodox, Reform temples appeared throughout Germany. Yet ironically, many enlightened Jews influenced by the Romantic movement were uninterested in what Reform Judaism had to offer. Instead of providing a basis for the resurgence of Judaism, the movement undermined confidence in traditional belief and practice and intensified Christian antipathy to the Jewish way of life. In Russia, the aim of emancipation was to bring about the assimilation of the Jewish community – the

programme of the Tsars was driven by centuries-old Christian hostility to the Jews. From
the Jewish side, responses to these moves throughout Europe to improve the plight of the Jews
were mixed – traditionalists tended to fear that
such steps would undermine Torah Judaism
whereas progressives enthusiastically welcomed
new freedoms and opportunities. The gentile
reaction was equally ambivalent. Although liberals ardently campaigned for equal rights,
many Christians feared the consequences of such
agitation and at the end of the second decade of
the nineteenth century outbursts against the
Jewish population spread from country to
country.

In the enlightened environment of the nineteenth century, Jewish apologists sought to improve the condition of the Jewish population.
In England Benjamin Disraeli, the Tory Prime
Minister, formulated a theory of the Jewish
race which served as the basis for his quest to
grant civil rights to the British Jewry. His advocacy of Jewish emancipation, however, provoked a hostile response from various critics
who denigrated Jewry in terms reminiscent of
previous centuries. Such disparagement was similarly a central feature of French life, as evidenced by the Damascus affair in which the
President of the French Council sided with the
French consuls in Damascus who accused Jews
there of ritual murder. Despite the peaceful
conclusion of this matter, this medieval charge
gave rise to widespread anti-Jewish sentiment
in France. In addition, the Christian myth of
the Wandering Jew who was driven from his
homeland for having rejected Christ became a
predominant image in French literature of the
period and stimulated French Judeophobia as
did the anti-Jewish allegations of French socialists. In Germany the advocates of German
RACISM as well as metaphysical writers critical
of Jews and Judaism generated considerable
ill-will.

During the latter half of the nineteenth century, the Jewish community suffered further
outbreaks of anti-Semitism. In Germany numerous racist publications denigrated the Jewish
people, leading to the creation of political parties which propagated anti-Jewish attitudes.
At the same time the researches of Christian

Biblical scholars tended to undermine the traditional Jewish belief in the authority of Scripture.
Similar attitudes were expressed by a variety of
French authors who denounced both Judaism
and the Jewish nation. Such hostility provided
the background to the Dreyfus affair which
erupted at the end of the century. Falsely accused of treason, Alfred Dreyfus was sentenced
to life imprisonment but subsequently exonerated. The hatred engendered by his trial led a
number of Jews to question whether Jewry
could ever be secured without its own land.
During this period Russian Jewry also experienced widespread persecution culminating in
the pogroms of 1881. Profoundly affected by
such massacres, many Jews emigrated to distant
lands; others sought to improve their condition
through revolutionary struggle. Aware of such
agitation, the Russian authorities became increasingly alarmed. Such concern was intensified
by the publication of the *Protocols of the Elders
of Zion* which alleged that the Jewish people
conspired against society to achieve world
domination.

In the years leading up to the First World
War, Jews became scapegoats for the problems
afflicting German society. Objections were
raised against the assimilation of German Jewry,
and numerous Christian writers protested
against the pernicious influence of Jewish attitudes. Between 1930 and 1933 over 6 million
were unemployed; such a situation led to the
rise of Nazism with its policies of anti-Semitism.
In Russia during the war years Christian anti-
Semites accused Jews of espionage and collaboration with the authorities. With the onslaught
of the revolution, Russian authorities condemned what they believed to be an international Jewish conspiracy, and pogroms occurred throughout the country. In the years
following the war a series of forgeries were
produced to implicate Jews with the revolutionary movement and illustrate the existence of a
worldwide Jewish conspiracy. During this
period British writers also condemned Jewry for
their dishonesty as well as participation in the
revolutionary struggle. In the USA, too, Jews
were subject to discrimination, and a number
of writers blamed the Russian revolution on
the involvement of Jewish activists. French

Judeophobia was similarly animated by perception of the Jewish influence in world affairs.

Anti-Semitic attitudes of the war years crystallized in Hitler's conception of the Jewish people as an evil race seeking world domination. Once the Nazis gained power, they instituted a series of anti-Jewish policies culminating in Kristallnacht during which Jewish property and buildings were destroyed. This event was followed by the invasion of Poland in September 1939 where Jews were massacred. The next stage of Hitler's plan of extermination took place with the invasion of Russia in 1941. Initially mobile killing battalions began the devastation of Russian Jewry; this method of killing was supplemented by the death camps where Jews were gassed. During these years of horror, some German Christians expressed their opposition to these policies, yet many other Church members within and without Germany refused to help the Jews. After the Second World War Germany expressed little remorse or guilt for the destruction of 6 million Jews. Instead most Germans continued to harbour anti-Semitic sentiments. Such attitudes were also manifest in postwar Austria. Similar Judeophobia has been expressed in Britain where neo-Nazis and ultra-rightwing groups advanced the theory of worldwide Jewish conspiracy. French hostility toward the Jews after the war has also led to the condemnation of Zionism, the occurrence of a series of attacks on Jewish property and the resurgence of the nationalist party. Poland and Russia too have witnessed the rise of anti-Semitism despite the absence of a sizeable Jewish community. Most significantly, anti-Jewish attitudes have been spread throughout the Arab world as a result of the creation of a Jewish homeland in Israel.

For twenty centuries then anti-Semitism has been a constant feature of Jewish history. What can be done to overcome this longest hatred? Fortunately in the post-HOLOCAUST world there has been a major effort on the part of the Christian Church to overcome Christian antipathy toward Judaism and the Jewish people. In the last few decades the Roman Catholic Church and the WORLD COUNCIL OF CHURCHES have issued numerous decrees denouncing anti-Semitism and encouraging positive Jewish–Christian encounter. In addition, pioneering Christian scholars have attempted to understand the Jewishness of Jesus – modern CHRISTOLOGY, they believe, must be purged of any anti-Jewish bias. God's enduring covenant with the Jewish nation has also repeatedly been emphasized, and various theories have been propounded to illustrate that Jesus' death and resurrection do not replace God's revelation on Mount Sinai.

In this context the traditional idea of Christian mission has been replaced by the notion of Christian witness. There are thus positive signs of hope as both Jews and Christians stand on the threshold of the twenty-first century. These of course are only preliminary steps toward understanding and reconciliation. Yet, if the negative stereotypes of Jews which have become infused in the Western cultural tradition can be overcome by such positive exploration, then the way may be open to overcoming the hatred of the past.

Cargas, Harry James (1990) *Shadows of Auschwitz*, New York: Crossroad.

Cohn-Sherbok, Dan (1993) *The Crucified Jew: Twenty Centuries of Christian Anti-Semitism*, London: Harper Collins.

Flannery, Edward H. (1985) *The Anguish of the Jews*, New York: Macmillan.

Gilbert, Martin (1986) *The Holocaust*, London: Collins.

Littel, Franklin (1975) *The Crucifixion of the Jews*, New York: Harper and Row.

Parkes, James (1963) *Antisemitism*, London.

Poliakov, Leon (1971–4) *A History of Antisemitism*, London: Routledge and Keagan Paul.

Rubenstein, Richard L. and Roth, John K. (1987) *Approaches to Auschwitz*, London: SCM Press.

Ruether, Rosemary (1974) *Faith and Fratricide: The Theological Roots of Antisemitism*, New York: Seaburgh.

Wistrich, Robert (1991) *Antisemitism: The Longest Hatred*, London: Methuen.

Dan Cohn-Sherbok

APARTHEID

'The degree to which apartheid has divided and compartmentalised South African society is nothing short of astounding.' These words from the report of the Commonwealth Eminent Persons Group, which visited South Africa in 1986, gave expression to the essence of apartheid – literally an ideology of separateness. The report continued: 'The living standards of South Africa's white cities and towns must rank with the highest anywhere; those of the black townships which surround them defy description in terms of "living standards". Apartheid creates and separates them; black and white live as strangers in the same land.' Officially the apartheid era ended with democratic elections in April 1994, although the effects of the system continue to plague every sphere of South African society.

Apartheid was always more than simple RACISM. It was racism deeply rooted in the economic, socio-political, cultural and intellectual identity of South Africa. In what follows, the religious roots of apartheid are traced in relation to its historical evolution, giving special attention to theological debate. Condemned as a sin and a heresy by major churches around the world, as well as by member churches of the South African Council of Churches (SACC) and the Roman Catholic Church in South Africa, apartheid was until recently defended and promoted by the white Nederduitse Gereformeerde Kerk (NGK) as being in accordance with scripture. The constitution of the Nederduitsch Hervormde Kerk (NHK), in turn, still includes a clause limiting church membership to whites.

Racial segregation in South Africa reaches back to the beginning of colonization in South Africa. By the beginning of the nineteenth century racial tension had ripened to the point where armed insurrection broke out on the eastern frontier of the Cape Colony. Yet, when rural and frontier congregations demanded separate facilities and services for black converts, the 1829 synod of the NGK insisted that holy communion be administered to all baptized members 'without distinction of colour'. Growing racism soon, however, gained the upper hand. In 1857 the Synod revoked its earlier decision, arguing that due to the 'weakness of some', blacks and whites should worship separately. In 1881 a separate Sendingkerk (Mission Church) was established for 'coloured' people. The first synod of a separate church for blacks (the NGK in Africa) followed in 1881, while a separate Indian Reformed Church was established as late as 1968. This principle of a separate church for each separate racial group was similarly adopted by the NHK and the Gereformeerde Kerk. The outcome is an ecclesial and theological burden with which the Dutch Reformed Churches (DRC) still live today.

The subjugation and social separation of blacks and whites, of which DRC theology is a reflection, intensified with an efficiency that the Dutch had never been able to attain after the British occupied the Cape in 1806. This is despite the fact that the English-speaking churches which came to South Africa as part of British colonial activity seldom sought to justify racial divisions theologically in the same way as the DRC. Some of the settler churches, however, followed the practice of separate churches for black and white members for missiological reasons. These included the Presbyterian churches and the Baptists. The Lutheran churches adopted a similar stance. The English-speaking churches that theologically affirmed racially integrated churches were in social practice, in turn, almost as segregated as the Dutch Reformed Churches.

By the time of the 1806 occupation, Britain was emerging as the world's foremost capitalist and imperialist power. Its concern was to open the world market to its industrial goods. This policy contributed to the abolition of slavery and the relaxation of some other controls over the labour market causing some Dutch settlers to trek into the hinterland beyond the sphere of British rule. Yet, in seeking a market for their goods, the British also wanted to develop commercial farming as a means of paying the costs of maintaining the colony. This required a steady, tightly controlled labour market, resulting in a series of laws which limited black ownership of land and introduced taxes requiring blacks to sell their labour to white land owners. After the discovery of gold in 1886 and the resultant Anglo-Boer War which gave the British control over the mines, these laws were implemented with a new sense of vigour, to provide cheap labour for the mining industry. New laws were passed restricting the movement of blacks, requiring them to carry passes, introducing job reservation and controlling social practices in a manner that anticipated the panoply of laws that would later constitute statutory apartheid. The willingness of Boer and British settlers to work in alliance with one another after the war, in turn, resulted in a further intensification of segregationist and discriminatory laws.

This alliance was short lived. Old hostilities between the Afrikaner and the English were fuelled by a new kind of Afrikaner nationalism. The 1930s saw the confluence of German philosophic ideas, an Afrikaner contextual form of neo-Calvinism and the zealous promotion of the Afrikaner language movement and culture. The outcome was a chauvanistic philosophy of 'die eie' – the urge to affirm one's own and to be oneself, to the exclusion of others. This gave rise to theological and biblical motifs that would result in an integrated Christian doctrine of apartheid. A philosophical basis for apartheid had emerged, setting the stage for the most comprehensive set of racially based laws the world has ever known when the National Party came to power in 1948.

The apartheid era   The legislation that followed included the *Population Registration Act*, the *Mixed Marriages Act*, the *Group Areas Act*, the *Bantu Education Act* and a range of laws imposing job protection for whites and establishing white political, social and economic privilege. Later would come the establishment of 'independent' and 'self-governing' states for each separate African tribe, and large-scale forced removals of blacks from 'white' areas.

The Defiance Campaign of the 1950s saw the mobilization of blacks against white domination and apartheid in an unprecedented manner. H.F. Verwoerd, prime minister at the time and the architect of grand apartheid, simply insisted that once fully developed, apartheid (separate development) would result in 'happiness, security and stability . . . for the Bantu as well as whites'. 'Create your own future!' he told whites and each separate black group in South Africa.

His utopian ideals were never realized. The Sharpeville massacre followed in 1960 and the banning of the African National Congress and the Pan Africanist Congress came almost immediately, setting the stage for the elimination of all forms of organized black political opposition to apartheid. This lasted until 2 February 1990 when the ANC, PAC and other restricted

organizations were unbanned. Nelson Mandela was released from prison on 11 February 1990. Most apartheid laws were subsequently repealed, with the last legal barrier to racial integration being removed when the first democratically elected government was installed after the elections held on 27 and 28 April 1994.

The theological struggle   Among the first significant theological rejections was the classification of apartheid as 'intrinsically evil' by the South African Catholic Bishops Conference in 1957. The Cottesloe Consultation came three years later in December 1960. It brought together representatives of the WORLD COUNCIL OF CHURCHES (WCC) and South African member churches to work out an appropriate response to the events that resulted in Sharpeville. The consultation effectively rejected apartheid as being contrary to the Bible, and the NGK synods that were members of the WCC, together with the NHK, resigned their membership. The smaller Gereformeerde Kerk had never been a member of the WCC. These developments marked the beginning of a new ecclesial phase in the struggle against apartheid. The Christian Institute was formed in 1963 by Beyers Naudè to counter racism in the churches. It was banned by the government in 1977. The *Message to the People of South Africa* published in 1968 by the South African Council of Churches (SACC), condemned apartheid as a 'pseudo gospel'. The WCC established the Programme to Combat Racism a year later, resolving in 1970 to provide funding for humanitarian purposes to the liberation movements that had resorted to armed struggle against the South African regime. Refused entry to South Africa by the government in 1971, the WCC resolved not to visit South Africa again until apartheid had been eliminated. The first official visit by the WCC to South Africa since that decision took place in October 1991 with the visit of the General Secretary, Dr Emilio Castro, resulting in the historic Cape Town Conference of the WCC.

The theological defence of apartheid by the NGK reached its height with the publication in 1974 of the report of the NGK, *Human Relations and the South African Scene in the Light of Scripture*, providing an explicit biblical and theological defence of apartheid. This led to the declaration of heresy against this church by the World Alliance of Reformed Churches (WARC) in 1982. All the major churches in South Africa (apart from the DRC) adopted similar resolutions of their own. Important in the South African context was the *Belhar Confession* of the NG Sendingkerk, in which theological support of apartheid was declared a matter of *status confessionis*. A variety of other important theological statements on apartheid were published at the time, including the *Kairos Document* in 1985.

The NGK responded with the publication of *Church and Society* in 1986. The document moved away from the explicit theological and biblical support for apartheid, without rejecting apartheid completely. Next came the revision of *Church and Society* in 1990 which came closer to a full rejection of apartheid. It rejected apartheid as implemented on ethical grounds, while refusing to condemn its underlying theology as heretical. This failed to satisfy all the NGK's critics. In November 1990 the most representative conference ever of South African churches met in Rustenburg, declaring itself to be against apartheid. The representatives of the NGK who were present subsequently distanced themselves from certain aspects of this statement.

The Southern African Alliance of Reformed Churches meeting in April 1991 denounced *Church and Society* for not dealing with apartheid as a matter of *status confessionis*. The SACC, at its 1991 National Conference, in turn, suspended a decision on an application for observer status by the NGK until a satisfactory response was received to a number of clarifying questions. The WARC subsequently rejected an application for renewed membership of this body, pending the outcome of unity talks between the black, coloured and white NG churches. Since then the black and coloured NG churches have united to form the Uniting Reformed Church in Southern Africa. The General Synod of the NGK, meeting in Pretoria in 1994, has rejected apartheid as 'sinful'and its theological justification as 'false doctrine' (*dwalleer*). It has committed itself to union with the United Reformed Church. The NGK has renewed its request for observer status in the SACC and in conversation with the WARC agreed that the

acid test of its rejection of apartheid will be the outcome of church union conversations.

Apartheid was formally brought to a close under the government of F.W. De Klerk. The residual structures of apartheid are now being dismantled.

Alberts, L. and Chikane, F. (eds) (1991) *The Road to Rustenburg: The Church Looking Forward to a New South Africa*, Cape Town: Struik Christian Books.

Cochrane, J. (1987) *Servants of Power: The Role of the English-Speaking Churches 1903–1930*, Johannesburg: Ravan Press.

De Gruchy, J. (1979) *The Church Struggle in South Africa*, Cape Town: David Philip; Grand Rapids, MI: Eerdmans.

De Gruchy, J. and Villa-Vicencio, C. (eds) (1983) *Apartheid is a Heresy*, Cape Town: David Philip; Grand Rapids, MI: Eerdmans.

Villa-Vicencio, C. (1988) *Trapped in Apartheid: A Socio-Theological History of the English-Speaking Churches*, Maryknoll: Orbis Books.

Charles Villa-Vicencio

APOCALYPTIC

Apocalyptic is the religious outlook which roots perception of the divine purposes in knowledge obtained through revelation by vision, audition or dream. Such knowledge includes a variety of matters which are of concern to humanity, e.g. the destiny of the world and in particular the nature of God's purpose (whether for the past, present or the future), heaven and hell, knowledge of the divinity and the origin of the world. So in the religion of Second Temple Judaism apocalyptic is a form of religion where superior knowledge of God and the world is based on divine insight which is given outside the conventional processes of reasoned interpretation and beyond the wisdom which the human mind alone could offer.

Apocalyptic is widely linked with a particular form of eschatology in which an imminent expectation of the end of the world is accompanied by the irruption of a new order. The similarities between the earnest expectation for the return of Christ in early Christian texts and some apocalyptic passages in the apocalypses (especially the book of Revelation) led to the view that there was a distinctive apocalyptic ESCHATOLOGY shared by the first Christians. This formed the basis of several pioneering attempts to reconstruct early Christianity as a movement thoroughly dominated by an eschatology in which eager expectation was replaced by disappointment and a waning hope. Much of modern New Testament scholarship has struggled to accommodate itself to this interpretation. This contrasts with a this-worldly political eschatology, consistently maintained in Jewish messianism, in which the future order of things grows within the womb of history. The catastrophic and disruptive are often supposed to be sanctioned by Revelation, though the book hardly offers a consistently otherworldly eschatology, a fact which is hardly surprising given the pervasiveness of chiliastic ideas in the earliest church. More problematic for the view of apocalyptic which sees it as marking an end of history is the fact that all the extant Jewish apocalypses written contemporaneously with Revelation offer an account of this-worldly hope which differs little from other non-apocalyptic sources.

Apocalyptic has at times been seen as a contrast to the religion based on Law such as that found in rabbinic Judaism. The antinomian hue of some early Christian literature has been seen as a continuation of an alternative strand within Judaism in which apocalyptic dreaming was seen as a contrast to the preoccupations of the interpreters of the Law of Moses. It is true that there is a contrast between the minutiae of the discussions which make up the earliest rabbinic texts and the eschatological elaborations of the apocalypses. But the differences conceal as much as they reveal. The particular genre of the rabbinic tractates and the apocalypses provides a reason for the absence of various eschatological elements from the former. Care needs to be taken before drawing conclusions from the content of different types of text about the existence of ideological conflicts between rabbis and apocalyptists.

The assumption that apocalyptic is the religion of the marginal has been a feature of its role in the study of MILLENARIANISM. It is certainly the case that in both Judaism and Christianity apocalyptic has been linked with fringe movements, often of a subversive character, which have threatened the fabric of conventional religion (Sabbatianism in Judaism and the Joachite strand in forms of Franciscan theology are two obvious examples). The urgent expectation of the overthrow of the status quo has been regarded as the outlook of the dispossessed and has constituted a significant part of the investigation of the sociology of apocalyptic. There is evidence from Judaism and Christianity that apocalyptic was not, however, only the property of the marginalized and those who looked forward to an imminent change in the political order. The use made of apocalyptic by very different groups suggests that its dualistic view of the world tells us very little about the sort of people responsible for its writing and dissemination. Many of the pseudepigrapha bear all the hallmarks of works written for particular purposes by an élite at the very heart of society. In saying this we are at once compelled to recognize that the task of writing such works (or even committing traditions to writing) was not a task for the uneducated. Sometimes it may have been carried out by the marginalized as the Dead Sea Scrolls indicate. Nevertheless the sophisticated and articulate are just as likely to have been marginalized as the poor, particularly if they were once in a position to influence affairs.

Apocalyptic visions can function in several ways. First, they could offer a short-cut in the interpretation of scripture to those whose task it was to wrestle with the sacred texts and find meaning in them in the circumstances of their day. Second, we find in apocalyptic that Jewish version of the 'irrational' element in religion which had a particularly vital period in late antiquity. We can discern in apocalyptic a symptom of the influence on Judaism of wider religious and spiritual currents from the Hellenistic world. Third, it is possible to see how the visions of the apocalypses could provide an escape from the unacceptable realities which confronted Jews at the time. The visions which communicated divine insight about the future hope confirmed people in their belief and practice, despite the horrors of the world around them and the lack of evidence of their fulfilment, though knowledge of this world and the secrets of it could so easily become an end in itself and detract from the issues confronting the people of God in this world. Fourth, we may surmise that occasionally apocalyptic functioned as a spur to action and change in this world. In this 'Utopian' type of ideology we may discern the way in which apocalyptic ideas may have impelled the Jewish fighters for freedom to take up arms against the Romans and in desperate straits to believe that God would come to their aid with legions of angels. We cannot be sure how much influence the Jewish apocalypses which are now extant had on those who fought for freedom from Rome (indeed it should be noted that the extant apocalypses are singularly devoid of injunctions to engage in an armed struggle), but something like the beliefs contained in them impelled the rash actions about which Josephus has so much to tell us in his account of the Jewish War. Fifth, the apocalypse proved to be an inadequate and outmoded vehicle of the doctrinal concerns and material needs of the emerging church and rabbinic Judaism and became largely obsolete in both religious communities.

Because apocalyptic has been so consistently linked with eschatology its visionary elements have tended to be ignored. As a result its role in the history of mysticism has not been explored sufficiently. There has remained an eschatological element in mystical religion particularly in Judaism which has led to outbursts of acute messianic fervour. In the Christian mystical tradition the intensity of intimacy with God is evident also in the ancient apocalyptists' quest for the vision of the divine. While the paraphernalia of visions and auditions was frowned upon by some mystical writers such as John of the Cross and the author of *The Cloud of Unknowing*, there is abundant evidence that this is a feature of the mystic's experience. There is some evidence to suggest that radical revolutionary movements were empowered by a mystical element so that inner identification with the divine and the transformative power that was unleashed could at times achieve some external effect in acts of social catharsis and upheaval (e.g. Thomas Muentzer).

A claim to be the recipient of an apocalypse (as was often the case in the apocalyptic literature of Judaism where angelic interpretations of visions are frequent) could lead to some uncertainty over the precise meaning of the contents of the revelation; what was not so easily questioned, except by outright denial, was the certitude of the recipient of that revelation that a direct communication had come from God. Significant movements in the history of religion marked by apocalyptic revelation (including Islam) engendered an unstable situation when the claim to apocalyptic revelation had as its content an innovation in belief or practice rather than merely an affirmation of the status quo. Instances may be noted in the history of the church where resort to that absolute certainty which apocalyptic and mysticism (viewed as the understanding of matters beyond normal human perception) offers can be used to justify unscrupulous and dehumanizing behaviour in the pursuit of some higher goal.

In contemporary Christianity the privileged status presupposed by apocalyptic revelation can be found in contrasting wings of Christian faith and practice. The apocalyptic literature of the Bible has proved to be a fertile ground for understandings of the Christian self-identity. In contemporary Christianity committed to pre-millennialism (a particular sketch of Biblical eschatology based on Daniel, Ezekiel, Revelation and 1 Thessalonians) offers a scenario in which the world is destined to inevitable destruction while the Elect are safeguarded by their divine removal through the Rapture. In view of that prospect the only safe place to be is to be born again and thereby guarantee an escape from the terrors of the end-time. In the light of this the most appropriate course of action is to engage in a mission which will draw as many as possible into that privileged circle and leave a corrupt world to spin inexorably to its foreordained destruction.

LIBERATION THEOLOGY, on the other hand, does not explicitly use the language of apocalyptic and revelation directly to support its claim to privileged knowledge, yet running through its distinctive perspective is the view that the perspective of the poor must be determinative of the mission of the church. It is with them that God is particularly present and action done to and with them is activity directed towards God. God's presence in the world is specifically located in the poor and outcast: to see and help them is to glimpse God and respond to the divine. In other respects also liberation theology draws on the theological perspective of the apocalyptic tradition: reading the signs of the times, the critique of ideology and prophetic theology. Some of that outlook is evident in liberation theology's conviction that the prophetic critique of social arrangements can be done via a mixture of Christian insight and socio-economic analysis. That assessment, however sophisticated, is supported by the view that insight into the true nature of history and institutions is a present possibility (particularly for those who are on the margins of society and benefit little from its goods). Accordingly, ambiguity as a characteristic feature of human experience is resisted and the possibility of real knowledge is opened up which in turn can lead to particular and often controversial forms of action. Thus, for example, in recent years in South Africa the Kairos Document has attempted to read the signs of the times by offering a searching critique of state manipulation of religion, politically anodyne trends in theology and the need for an outspoken prophetic theology which criticizes the status quo from the perspective of the oppressed, thus prompting action to bring about moves to justice.

Such contrasting use of the apocalyptic traditions is by no means a recent phenomenon. Although Augustine's theology discourages both the claim to understand the purposes of God in history and the expectation that the Kingdom of God can come in this world, there was a far-reaching challenge to that view by the Calabrian abbot and commentator on Revelation, Joachim of Fiore. His writings are significant for two reasons. First, his theology is rooted in a complex interpretation of the book of Revelation which resulted in a complex theology of history. More importantly, however, he maintained a close link between the future age of perfection and human history and agency. Specifically, he saw the emergence of two monastic orders as fulfilling the apocalyptic prophecies. The Franciscans in particular (the Dominicans were the other order) attached great significance to Joachim's interpretation of apocalyptic tradition and identified their movement with that kind of decisive eschatological moment. The apocalyptic legacy had a long history in the Franciscan movement (where it undergirded the convictions of some of the more extreme elements) and

contributed to an ongoing story of radical dissent in the Hussite and later movements of the radical reformation. What we find in this tradition is an attitude to eschatology in which human agency had a full part. That contrasts with the opposite effect of a determinist apocalyptic theology rendering humanity powerless in the face of the cosmic forces unleashed.

Challenge to the Churches. The Kairos Document.
McGinn, B. (1992) *History of Western Mysticism*.
Rowland, C. (1982) *The Open Heaven*.
——(1988) *Radical Christianity*, London: Polity Press.
Scholem, G. (1955) *Major Trends in Jewish Mysticism*.

Chris Rowland

ARMAMENT

Armament is the manufacture, transfer and deployment of military weapons (as distinct from civilian weapons for hunting, sport, crime and policing). Which aspects of armament seem most important depends on one's overall attitude to WAR, PEACE, deterrence and VIOLENCE. Some believers in PACIFISM tend to be equally averse to all aspects of armament. A more complicated picture emerges if, as in this article, one is guided by the just-war tradition that some uses of military force may conceivably be legitimate.

Broadly speaking, it is convenient to distinguish three main contexts in which armament and disarmament occur: (a) deterrence among states; (b) conventional warfare between states; (c) irregular warfare as in civil war or armed rebellion.

Armament in the context of military deterrence is probably as old as warfare but has become vastly more important since 1945. Nuclear weapons and modern delivery systems made it possible for states to threaten one another with rapid annihilation. From this terror emerged a new idea of international security. States which can threaten one another with mutual destruction have every incentive to treat one another with extreme caution, so that a nuclear deterrent promises security not only against an opponent's nuclear weapons but also against AGGRESSION and conventional war. Throughout the period of the Cold War, it is argued, deterrence snapped the age-old link between ideological rivalry and conventional war.

With the demise of the USSR, nuclear deterrence ceased to be a relatively simple principle of international security. There were still only five declared nuclear weapons states and these happened to be the five Permanent Members of the UN Security Council (USA, Russia, China, France and UK). A number of other states (including India and Israel) were known to possess nuclear weapons but had no immediate incentive to increase their capabilities. The strongest contenders to become Permanent Members of the Security Council were Japan and Germany, for their economic strength, despite the low profile of their participation in military politics since 1945. There were two principal changes. First, deterrence among the great powers had ceased for the time being to be a major issue, bringing a great variety of intractable regional problems to the top of the political agenda. Second, chaos in the former USSR poured a vast inventory of weapons and a large number of defence scientists into the global arms trade, greatly increasing the 'quality' and quantity of arms available for war and rebellion.

Long-term planning for nuclear deterrence continued, especially in the USA, on the basis that one cannot tell who may need to be deterred in a changing and insecure world. The end of the qualitative arms race between the USA and the USSR made it likely that the pace of military innovation would slow but planners had to take into account the possibility of advanced former-USSR weaponry falling into the hands of aggressive or unstable regimes such as Iraq.

Armament is of course relevant in the context of conventional warfare. There have been numerous wars since 1945 (such as those involving India and Israel) which can be called 'conventional' in the sense that they have been fought between states without nuclear, chemical or biological weapons and with as much scope as there has ever been for the belligerents to observe the laws and customs of war (such as the conventions on the humane treatment of prisoners-of-war). It is very unlikely that these wars were caused by arms or arms races: underlying political tensions were acute and the timing of war cannot be traced to 'technological windows of opportunity'. Without *any* weapons these states could not of course have fought wars against one another but the cutting-off of external sources of supply would almost certainly have encouraged a greater build-up of indigenous weapons manufacture. Denial of weapons from outside the region may have prevented access to *sophisticated* weapons but most of the killing has employed less sophisticated weapons which could have been made locally or obtained in global markets whose regulation would be extremely difficult.

The most important ethical and political issues in conventional warfare thus concern the underlying political tensions, the JUSTICE of the causes for which war is fought or avoided, and the just conduct of war. Armament is a subordinate issue because it simply reflects pre-existing realities.

Armament in irregular warfare raises different questions. Unlike states, rebels are rarely able to make their own weapons except at the extremes of a rebellious peasant's lethal pitchfork or a rebel movement which is in control of territory that it can protect sufficiently to operate arms factories. Between these extremes lies a great variety of 'terrorist'/'liberation' movements whose access to arms is heavily dependent on supplies or money from friendly governments. Throughout the Cold War the great powers armed numerous non-state organizations (such as the rival militias in Afghanistan after the USSR's 1979 intervention). Regional powers were equally generous (such as South Africa towards Renamo in Mozambique).

In the period since 1945 the warfare made possible by this arming of rebels has been 'irregular' in that some, if not all, of the belligerents are non-states. Observance of the laws and customs of war is especially difficult when some of the belligerents lack the discipline of a professional military force and others (states employing 'terror' against their own people) habitually refer to their opponents as 'criminals'.

To consider the question of armament in this kind of warfare is peculiarly difficult because of the vulnerability of unarmed rebels. If they are subjected to GENOCIDE or fierce persecution, how *can* we deny them arms or the money to arm themselves? But if we do help them to arm, are we merely promoting yet one more uncontrollable outbreak of murderous civil strife? This is discussed further in DISARMAMENT.

Thus, in conventional war, armament reflects underlying political tensions. Armament developed a life of its own in the baroque proliferation of military innovations during the Cold War arms races but for the time being issues of deterrence have become less pressing. Perhaps the cruellest dilemmas of armament concern irregular war.

Armament does not happen spontaneously. It is human beings who arm and this raises a number of ethical issues including (a) the moral status of munitions workers and defence scientists, (b) the 'mere possession' of weapons and (c) responsibility in the arms trade.

According to the just-war tradition, direct attacks upon non-combatants are illegitimate. *Clear* examples of non-combatants include babies and the mentally ill who are evidently unable to play an active part in combat, but the full extent of non-combatant immunity is very controversial. Are sane adults to be regarded as combatants on the assumption that they support the war effort? What of agricultural workers 'digging for victory'? A widely shared view is that adults as such are not combatants because they do not, *qua* subjects or citizens, play an active part in controlling the war. Agricultural workers are non-combatant because they are engaged in the non-belligerent activity of food production even if they give it a warlike name such as 'digging for victory'. The makers of weapons (including 'defence' scientists), on the other hand, are engaged in an essentially belligerent activity since the whole point of weapons is that they be usable in war. According to this view, combatants include munitions workers (and defence scientists) as well as the military and that part of the government which controls the military politically because these are the people *actually prosecuting the war effort*.

Suppose, then, that direct attacks upon munitions workers are not ruled out in principle. What are the practical implications? They are no more fair game for any kind of attack than other combatants, for the just-war principles impose severe restrictions upon all killing: combatants may be attacked only with a just cause as a last resort, under the authorization of legitimate authority, with a reasonable prospect of success, and with reason to believe that the good to be obtained will outweigh the certain evil involved in the war effort. If all these conditions are met, it is plausible to argue that targeting munitions workers in their factories and laboratories is as legitimate as targeting enemy soldiers or members of the enemy war cabinet. A difficult question, as regards both soldiers and weapon-makers, concerns their time away from work. It is very widely agreed that soldiers should be able to surrender in appropriate circumstances and in doing so become non-combatant. They are to be kept in benevolent quarantine until the war ends. They must not be killed, ill-treated or pressured to fight against their own side. By the same reasoning captured or conquered munitions workers (or defence scientists) are presumably entitled to be in effect prisoners-of-war, though this is not explicit in the positive law of war.

What of munitions workers in their own homes? It seems that soldiers in their leisure hours can be regarded by some as legitimate targets. For example, the IRA killing of British soldiers drinking off duty in Northern Ireland is usually condemned on the basis that the IRA is waging an *illegitimate* war rather than that off-duty soldiers are non-combatants. Even off duty, it seems to be thought, soldiers are not entitled to feel safe. By the same reasoning, the makers of weapons are presumably legitimate targets of a just war even when they are not at work. If so, they are presumably entitled to expect special protection by their own government.

It is sometimes thought that the possession of nuclear weapons may be legitimate even if their use is not. To fire such weapons is almost certain to violate just-war principles but, it is argued, the weapons are not immoral *in themselves* so having them for deterrence purposes may be legitimate. This argument is most implausible. Theorists and historians of deterrence are virtually unanimous in declaring that deterring an opponent requires both *capability* and *will*. The 'mere possession' of nuclear weapons may constitute a frightening capability but it would be perverse to expect this to deter an opponent from aggression if the opponent did not believe that we might have the will to use the weapons. In a crisis (such as the Cuban missiles crisis of 1962) we must be able to prevent the opponent from counting on us not to use our nuclear weapons. Mere possession will not be enough without the reasonable expectation that we might well fire our nuclear weapons *in extremis*. Bluff will not suffice; something close to the intention to use the weapons is an indispensable part of nuclear deterrence.

Thus, merely possessing nuclear weapons gives no moral let-out from the responsibilities which armaments bring with them. The responsibilities which armaments impose finds another and a tragic illustration at the opposite extreme from nuclear weapons. Consider a ten-year-old child or a berserk adult in possession of a replica gun. Suppose the child is a member of a crowd some of whose older members are stoning troops, or is on a street notorious for snipers when troops are passing. Or suppose the beserk adult is at the centre of a crisis to which armed police have had to be called. The just-war tradition recognizes self-defence as a legitimate cause of the kind of killing that we call war and the positive law of all countries allows police and soldiers to defend themselves. In our example, the child or beserk adult confronts the soldiers or police with a time-urgent threat to which shooting to kill may be an inescapably legitimate response. The mere possession even of replica fire-arms can make the most innocent of human beings into legitimate targets of direct attack.

Between the extremes of nuclear weaponry and replica guns lies a great variety of armaments which become all too readily part of 'the arms trade'. 'Arms trade' is something of a misnomer because it covers not only the sale of weapons for profit but also the transfer of armaments for influence. It is the policy of many governments that, as Denis Healey once put it when he was the British Minister of Defence, this is a legitimate trade of which they seek their fair share. Should 'the arms trade' be thought of in these terms, as a kind of commerce which in essence is little different from any other?

Mainstream modern analyses of the arms trade may be summarized as follows. It is a relationship between *suppliers* and *recipients*. It is driven largely by *demand* on the part of the recipients. They feel that they need arms for whatever defensive or aggressive purposes they happen to have. This creates a welcome opportunity for suppliers. Between 1945 and the collapse of the USSR the suppliers were primarily *states*. Each supplier state had armament needs of its own and the demand from recipients was a welcome opportunity to reduce the burdens of military expenditure through foreign sales or to enhance the benefits of military expenditure by the influence which sometimes derives from the transfer of arms. Private companies were not at liberty to sell arms irresponsibly but were subject to licensing by governments which in turn were restricted by such limitations as the mandatory arms embargo against South Africa. Because arms could be re-exported to prohibited destinations, states had to be careful to ensure that they obtained and enforced end-use agreements, preventing a recipient from passing technology to an unacceptable third party. In time of war, the supply of spares or replacements might be interrupted, preventing the arms trade from directly fuelling conflict and on occasion making it possible to pressure belligerents into a cease-fire. Thus the economic and political benefits of the arms trade were subject to the higher demand for political control.

To this relatively optimistic analysis we must add four kinds of complication. First, the recipients in the arms trade are not always states with a clear and monolithic chain-of-command. It can easily happen that a country's army, navy and air-force develop lively priorities of their own, e.g. for the acquisition of weapons which offer status or prestige, and that weak political control thus results in what can only be called *frivolous* expenditure of desperately scarce resources. Second, the recipients are sometimes not states but 'liberation movements' which are unable to control adequately the weapons which they acquire. Third, effective regulation of arms sales and transfers is likely to be confined to a relatively few high profile cases. The foreign ministry of a potential supplier is quite likely to look very carefully at the transfer of the latest military technologies and at any transfer or sale directly into an area which is at war, but the vast numbers of movements of low-tech weaponry make it almost inconceivable that there can be effective monitoring of the kinds of armament with which most killing is actually done. Fourth, the precipitate collapse of the Soviet Union has resulted in the release on to world markets of breath-taking quantities of weaponry of every kind, from the most to the least sophisticated and possibly including nuclear weapons: there has certainly been evidence of traffic in plutonium.

The arms trade raises many ethical issues. One point which is seldom addressed is that in supplying arms we are doing something analogous to giving a gun to a person with a known history of murder. (Is there *any* state which has never fought an unjust war? Is there *any* rebel group which can be relied on never to do so?) We run the grave risk of *making ourselves accessories to murder*. In this respect the arms trade is no more like other relationships of sale or transfer than selling a gun resembles a trade in sweets or cigarettes. It requires the utmost moral circumspection. What might this mean in public policy? One possibility is for a country to supply arms only on one or both of the following conditions: (a) the supply is part of an explicit treaty obligation or (b) the supply is for published economic gain. Either way, the supply would be subjected to public scrutiny and thus brought within the scope of the principle which requires legitimate authority for a war to be just. Another possibility is to stipulate that arms can be transferred only if the opposition as well as the government in the recipient country is known to support the measure. Taken together, these requirements would severely curtail a supplier country's participation in the arms trade.

But, many will protest, why should we be limited when others are gaining? If we do not supply arms, someone else will, and what about the jobs tied up in such an industry? One can reply partly that suppliers do not always benefit from the arms trade. A deeper thought is that participation in the arms trade raises the basic just-war question which, in its Christian formulation, is: 'Can a Christian, without sin, wage war?' It would be very surprising if the traditional restrictions on war did not also apply to the arms trade.

Freedman, L.D. (1989) *The Evolution of Nuclear Strategy*, London: Macmillan.
O'Brien, W.V. (1981) *The Conduct of Just and Limited War*, New York: Praeger.
Pierre, A.J. (1982) *The Global Politics of Arms Sales*, Princeton, NJ: Princeton University Press.

Barrie Paskins

ART

The universality of art in human social history is well attested: contrary to popular belief, it appears that art is not merely a luxury but a necessity. We know of no people which has done without art in some form. A relationship between art and religious belief has also been widespread, ranging from close interdependence, e.g. in the Byzantine and medieval eras, to uncertainty and suspicion (in much contemporary Protestantism). Much twentieth-century art has chosen to abandon religious iconography altogether even though broadly religious themes have by no means been uncommon.

No simple yet comprehensive definition of art has yet commanded wide acceptance. In the Western tradition, the original meaning of art is skill in making. The word was used by the ancient Greeks to refer, first of all, to crafts that satisfy basic human needs. The Greek and Latin equivalents (*techne, ars*) included broadly everything we might call 'fine art', along with servile and liberal arts. Much current usage limits the meaning of art to painting and sculpture. Furthermore, the word 'art' may signify the work of art, or the creative process itself, or the experience of appreciating art, or some combination of these. With such fluidity of use, it is perhaps best to regard the notion of art as essentially indeterminate, or an 'open-textured' concept which can never be delimited in all possible directions.

From the standpoint of purpose, a distinction has been made (especially since the seventeenth century) between 'useful' arts – specifically directed towards some purpose – and 'fine arts', to be enjoyed for their own sake (though they may also be aimed towards some extrinsic end). A further distinction is sometimes made between 'popular' art – practised and enjoyed by the majority in a social group – and 'high' art – practised and enjoyed by a minority who will typically see their art as superior in quality.

This article will adopt a wide use of the word 'art', to embrace the activities and products associated with the 'fine arts' of music, poetry, drama, literary fiction, visual depiction, architecture, ballet and modern dance, film and sculpture.

Art has been examined from an immensely wide variety of perspectives – historical, philosophical, psychological, sociological, anthropological, semiotic and others. Chief among the disciplines is aesthetics. Aesthetics has sometimes been taken in a fairly broad sense to refer to the investigation of a particular attitude to objects (not necessarily works of art) which attends to their form and structure. More commonly it denotes the study of human behaviour and experience in creating, perceiving and understanding art.

Closely associated with art are a cluster of related concepts. Perhaps the most persistent has been the ancient concept of *beauty*, classically explicated in terms of harmony, proportion, soundness, unity-in-multiplicity and similar qualities. Although beauty may be an aesthetically desirable quality in art, many aestheticians would question the belief that art is qualified by its aspiration towards beauty (Seerveld 1980, Wolterstorff 1980). The notion of *creativity* also often appears in discussions of the arts. It emerged during the Renaissance and was first given formal expression in the Enlightenment. Its original use was as a term in what Nahm has called the 'great analogy' between divine and human making – in some sense we mirror the creativity of God. In common usage it is understood to consist in attributes of an individual such as spontaneity, originality, high intelligence or such-like. It is possible, however, to speak of a social group possessing creative qualities. And a work of art itself can be regarded as creative in the sense that it can initiate significant changes in attitudes and perceptions. Consideration of creativity often leads to discussion of *style*. A style is a language with a vocabulary of artistic forms or motifs and a syntax governing their relationship. For some, integral to true creativity is *inspiration*. Though not prominent

in recent aesthetics it is a concept with a rich and long history, usually denoting the direction of the artist by some external spiritual force.

Discussion of art in a social context also inevitably raises questions about the relation between art and the values, concerns and perceptions prevalent in social systems. A number of distinct issues are involved here. First, there is the question of whether, and in what ways, works of art embody the manner in which an artist perceives the world. Wolterstorff, for example, has argued that there is a 'world behind the work of art', a complex of beliefs and goals on the part of the artist which may range from the trivial to an entire worldview. Second, artistic productions appear to be able to express major themes that occupy members of a SOCIETY, giving voice to ways of understanding that characterize its typical member. However, though art works may reflect in varying degrees the assumptions, beliefs, philosophies, moral codes, political and other ideals of the society or CULTURE to which they belong, they are also the creation of individual artists and may thus conflict with prevailing attitudes. Third, not only do artistic styles shift in relation to social determinants, but the creative ideologies which govern the production and reception of art also change, often in very subtle ways. Fourth, it may well be that in some cases art not only reflects but pre-figures changes about to occur in society (Attali 1985).

Any theological study of the relationship between the arts and society today will have to come to terms with a cluster of influential strands of thought and action sometimes grouped together under the heading of 'MODERNITY'. Together they have contributed towards a cast of mind which tends to demote the arts in favour of other spheres of human endeavour (especially the natural sciences) and treat them as essentially discontinuous with the rest of our experience. (Some would argue that this cast of mind is changing rapidly, especially in the light of studies which indicate a high level of spending by the public on the arts in recent years.)

One of these strands concerns a divorce between art and action. In the eighteenth century, the concept of 'disinterestedness' began to be applied to the fine (as opposed to the useful) arts. If we are to treat a work of art as art, it was urged, we should never regard it as a means to an end. We should attend to the work itself, considering it purely for its own sake. This conviction reached philosophical expression in the work of Immanuel Kant but has had numerous supporters since Kant. Even a brief survey of what our society commonly calls 'works of art' would very probably reveal that the majority were intended, by producer or distributor, for some form of disinterested contemplation. 'No matter what the art, in each case the action that you and I tend to regard as intended is a species of . . . *perceptual contemplation*' (Wolterstorff 1980). It is worth recalling that only in the seventeenth and eighteenth centuries do we see the rise of the museum, art gallery and concert hall. None of these exist, or has ever existed, in lands where modern European civilization is, or was, unknown.

Often linked to disinterestedness is the notion of the 'autonomy' of art, or 'art for art's sake' – the view that art is answerable only to itself, has no social responsibility and must not be assessed according to its correspondence to phenomena beyond itself, such as a moral order, the artist's intentions or the circumstances of its production. A theory usually called 'formalism' (Clive Bell) holds that what is crucial in the enjoyment of an art work is its 'significant form', not its reference. In the 1950s and 1960s, the sculptures of David Smith and Anthony Caro, the paintings of Ad Reinhardt and Robyn Denny, the music of Pierre Boulez and Karlheinz Stockhausen were all examples of works produced by those convinced that art should pursue its own self-referring ends. Such an approach has in part been a reaction to the commercial pressures of industrial modernization. The emergence of an urban culture in the nineteenth and twentieth centuries may have freed artists from aristocratic and church patronage, but this brought with it a pressure to satisfy the demands of the market that mass society presented, a pressure which many artists have often found themselves strenuously resisting.

It is significant that in this century much avant-garde art has tried to overcome the isolation of art by offering new visions of society in which no deep gulf separates 'art' and 'life'. The Futurists (e.g. Umberto Boccioni) and the Situationists (an alliance of European artists who emerged in the late 1950s) are cases in point. Yet because the public invariably fail to respond to such visions, these artists quickly became marginalized and élite. Ironically, avant-garde art today is often institutionalized, adopted into the commercialized establishment in such a way that it is very hard for it to challenge attitudes in any significant way.

Closely bound up with a stress on the autonomy of art are epistemological assumptions, in particular a widespread confidence that the empirical sciences grant us public, certain, clear, reliable and verifiable truth – 'dry truth and real knowledge' (Locke) – while the arts are concerned with matters of entertainment and individual inner dispositions, with little or no bearing on the way things actually are. In reaction, there have been those, like some of the Romantics, who exalt art as the supreme key to unlock reality. Others try to give art epistemological respectability through a strictly 'scientific' aesthetics. But the commoner outlook, generated in part by what is perceived to be the ever increasing success of the scientist, assigns science to the realm of certainty and art to the realm of private taste. Clearly, this makes evaluative judgements about art on the basis of objective criteria extremely hard. It also explains in part the colossal effort often needed to justify public financial support for the arts.

Related to this, and especially characteristic of modernity, is a concept of the artist as chiefly an *imposer* rather than a *discoverer* of value and meaning. The centre of gravity in modern aesthetics has been towards the idea that the artist must impress conceptual patterns, emotions, political attitudes and so forth upon the world, with little emphasis on respecting that which is given to hand and mind. This line of thinking finds pointed expression in the view that art is a bulwark against the chaos and confusion of the world. For the Romantics, art became the place in which inert nature and chaotic history are brought to life by the unifying imagination, a restful place in an otherwise hostile world.

In the wake of such assumptions, it is not surprising that the relation between artist and society has so often been problematic, tending towards the individualization of the artist and a view of an art work as the bare product of a 'creative' individual rather than a means of personal exchange. The ideas of the wayward 'genius' and 'inspiration', confined by the ancients to poets and thinkers, were extended during the Renaissance to other artists and were developed in various ways in succeeding centuries. By the seventeenth century it was a commonplace that artists were likely to have difficult characters and that this might even be a prerequisite of their talent. The 'romantic' conception of the artist – misunderstood, eccentric and unconventional, oblivious of his audience – has cast a significant shadow over our century, albeit often in caricature form. The emergence of the concept of 'avant-garde' art towards the end of the nineteenth century – an art that will by its very nature conflict with received opinion – became a doctrine with a profound influence on subsequent thinking about the arts. (This was undoubtedly affected by the close association of art and politics since the French Revolution: even styles, as opposed to their occasional subject matter, become linked to political views.)

In the last two decades there has emerged a cultural phenomenon – postmodernism – which in some ways has reacted against the characteristic trends of modernity. Provoked by the crises of Western modernity, specifically developments in science and technology, political, social and economic organization, the postmodern outlook is highly suspicious of claims to certainty, fixed knowledge, all-embracing rationalities and theories of progress, stressing instead the plurality, variability and fallibility of all human activity and the worthlessness of searching for fixed foundations of truth. In art theory, it can manifest itself in the attempt by some to deconstruct the social and political myths of high art and urge that art's form and content are not intrinsic to art itself but constructed by readers and perceivers. The 'meaning' of art is radically indeterminate. In extreme forms of postmodernism, such as deconstructionism, language itself becomes the sole domicile of order and meaning. Postmodern art, ironically often fuelled by the demands of market economics, reflects the absence of an over-arching value system in post-industrial society. Typically a host of disconnected images and fragments of earlier styles are freely juxtaposed (e.g. many pop videos, the paintings of Gilbert and George, Pat Steir, the architecture of G. Aulenti).

Theological responses to postmodernism include warm-hearted celebration (Cupitt), attempts to highlight the transcendent dimension of artistic creation (Steiner), calls for a re-grounding of art in the natural order (Fuller, an atheist with theological sympathies), and the search for a non-metaphysical justification of the religious significance of art (Pattison). Theological engagement with the arts in society shows signs of increasing vitality in recent years. It is impossible to predict the course which such discussion will take, but some likely areas for future debate may be indicated.

First, much hinges on whether one believes the material order is itself the bearer of meaning. That God has become incarnate as one of us, and part of God's creation, contains positive encouragement for treating the material world as a proper, meaningful environment for us to explore. Creativity will involve discovery and respect as well as the shaping (and even redeeming) of what is given. In this way creation is neither ignored nor overridden but, by being enjoyed, developed, elaborated and even redeemed, it is enabled to take on another, hopefully richer, meaningful form. (Intriguingly, Peter Fuller's riposte to modernism and postmodernism, from an atheist perspective, moves precisely in this direction.) Second, the relation between the visual and aural is likely to be much discussed. It is sometimes said that ours is an age of the triumph of the visual over the verbal and this is why the arts are today treated so warily by the churches whose first allegiance is to the Word of God, spoken and heard. Perhaps it is nearer the truth to speak of the dominance in Western culture of the audio-visual: we are bombarded with combinations of images and words, yet we are increasingly unable to see or hear anything in depth. The result is the paradox of an audio-visual culture in which Christian audio-visual input has become virtually unheard and invisible. If there is to be a rehabilitation of a Christian sensibility in our time, it is likely that Christians will need to learn from many of the artistic 'classics' of the past about ways of hearing and seeing reality in depth. (It might still be argued that theological approaches to the arts have been for too long dominated by visual metaphors and the tendency to see painting as the paradigmatic art form. The fruitfulness of, say, musical categories has been insufficiently explored. Musical conceptuality may well offer new vigour not only to aesthetics but also to THEOLOGY (Gunton).) Third, if the Christian vocation is not to disengage from the contingencies of history, but to participate in God's purposes for creation as embodied agents in a way which draws on all human capacities, the separation of art from action will be questionable. Wolterstorff is one of many Christian writers who insist that works of art are instruments and objects of action, through which individuals and groups carry out their intentions with respect to the world and their society. They should be understood as inextricably part of the social fabric of human purposes, passions and interests. This need not lead to 'functionalism', where we value a work of art solely because of its usefulness; aesthetic merit is also desirable. It is only to say that abstracting art entirely from the matrices of human action will yield to distortion and inscrutability.

Fourth, with a renewed focus in theology on the Cross and RESURRECTION as disclosing who God is, it is to be hoped that theologies of the arts will increasingly be seen in this light. If at Golgotha, the chaotic and destructive are taken into the rupture of Father and Son, the horror of human brutality and the breakdown of all relationships treated with infinite seriousness, then, as Paul Tillich repeatedly argued, art which passes lightly over the tragic in pursuit of a superficial beauty is in danger not only of self-deception but also of hiding God. Moreover, in the raising of Christ we are given a foretaste of the ultimate re-creation of creation and a final reference point for an art which seeks to move beyond mere depiction to transformation. In so far as art does take its final cue from the resurrection it can be considered a provisional manifestation of future glory (Küng). Fifth, it is reasonable to expect that relational concepts of the human person will be explored more fully and the resources of trinitarian theology will be employed to this end. This might lead to, for example, a re-fashioning of the categories of originality, a rediscovery of the positive contribution of tradition, and the finding of new ways in which the Church in its communality can foster the arts. Sixth, fresh attention should be given to the Holy Spirit. For many of the themes we have mentioned are closely associated with the Holy Spirit – beauty, creativity, inspiration, community. Seventh, if, as some contend, our art is becoming increasingly representational, just at a time when our theology shows signs of becoming more abstract, it may well be that art rather than theology will do much to fashion Christian identity in a de-Christianized Western world. As the art historian would point out, it would not be for the first time.

Attali, Jacques (1985) *Noise: The Political Economy of Music*, Manchester: Manchester University Press.

Begbie, J. (1991) *Voicing Creation's Praise*, Edinburgh: T. & T. Clark.

Burch Brown, F. (1990) *Religious Aesthetics*, Basingstoke: Macmillan.

Dillenberger, J. (1987) *A Theology of Artistic Sensibilities: The Visual Arts and the Church*, London: SCM.

Fuller, P. (1988) *Theoria: Art and the Absence of Grace*, London: Chatto & Windus.

Hewison, R. (1990) *Future Tense: New Art for the Nineties*, London: Methuen.

Pattison, G. (1991) *Art, Modernity and Faith*, Basingstoke: Macmillan.

Seerveld, C. (1980) *Rainbows for the Fallen World*, Toronto: Tuppence Press.

Steiner, G. (1989) *Real Presences*, London: Faber & Faber.

Tillich, P. (1956) *The Religious Situation*, London: Thames & Hudson.

Wolterstorff, N. (1980) *Art in Action*, Grand Rapids, MI: Eerdmans.

Jeremy Begbie

ARTIFICIAL INTELLIGENCE

Artificial intelligence (AI) is an area of applied, or practical, computation that has suffered in a number of ways from its name: at other times and places it has been known as machine intelligence, intelligent knowledge-based systems or even, long-ago, cybernetics. To discover what AI does, or claims (see Barr and Feigenbaum 1982), we shall not advance much by any kind of analysis of the word 'artificial', in contrast with 'natural' or 'human', but rather by listing some of the areas of human performance for which programs have been written to simulate them: playing chess, recognizing shapes and manipulating objects, producing and understanding speech, reading and translating texts, composing music, doing mathematics, composing and executing complicated plans, and so on.

AI's most striking achievements have been among its least practical: computer chess and backgammon players are now among the world's very best. Machine translation between languages, although still of only moderate quality (with perhaps 65 per cent of sentences correctly translated, though at very high speed), has found an eager commercial market.

Any simple definition of AI tends to be both too inclusive and exclusive at the same time. A common one would be: AI is the simulation on a *computer* of distinctively human mental functions. This is too inclusive, in that it would include mere arithmetic, which is distinctively human but better done by pocket calculators than by humans, and not normally considered AI. There is an active area of AI concerned with modelling how people actually do arithmetic, including the mistakes children make learning it. This has the apparently bizarre consequence that correct arithmetic is not AI but computational simulation of bad arithmetic is. On the other hand, much of AI has been concerned with robotics and vision, which models mental capacities that are not distinctively human since we share them with higher mammals.

In spite of this diversity of activity in AI, four areas remain central, in that each has some claim to be the historical core of AI. These are natural language processing (which goes back to the earliest days of machine translation in the 1960s); theorem proving by computer; knowledge representation (which usually means logically based structures representing what we know of the world); and statistically based networks. This last, originally called cybernetics but now often known as connectionism, has had a revival in recent years.

Connectionism denotes the current cluster of AI theories around the notion of very simple computing units, connected in very large numbers and 'learning from experience' by means of shifting aggregated weights in a network (see Partridge and Wilks 1990). Researchers in connectionism and neural nets believe that modelling the brain itself is possible, but conventional AI (which one could take to include the other three approaches listed above, and which can be thought of as rule and symbol based) has always rejected this view and held that the software AI creates models human mental processes but not necessarily the brain itself.

The jury is still out on connectionist work within AI: it is attractive to all those who remain suspicious of over-formal logical approaches, but it does not give much solace, yet, to those who still hanker after 'rules of computer behaviour' in some form for those it cannot produce. So far, its successful programs have not covered any phenomena not already covered satisfactorily by rule-driven approaches.

Only humans do mathematics and use language, and much attention has been paid in AI to both of these phenomena. But some AI researchers associate modelling the essentially human with the replication (not yet achieved) of more intangible attributes, such as emotions (Sloman and Croucher 1981), consciousness (Wilks 1985) and thought itself. The last has been less directly described, since we normally take the use of language or the ability to plan or reason as direct evidence of thought. This identification of thought with behaviour was at the heart of Turing's (1950) highly influential paper on computers and thought. He argued that discussion of whether or not computers could ever be said to think was a waste of time, and essentially philosophical, in a bad sense of the term. His position was close to that of the then fashionable doctrines of Wittgenstein. Turing proposed to substitute for the philosophical question a practical one, one that has become known as the Turing test.

He envisaged a program that could engage in a dialogue with a person via what were then called teletypes. The person was never told they were typing to a machine but was asked to decide a quite different question, namely whether the person on the other end was a man or a woman. Turing suggested that, if a machine could perform so well that the person never detected the machine, then we might as well say the machine thought. Contemporary usage is already approaching what Turing envisaged: people now routinely talk of machines like bank automats deciding and thinking things on the basis of very brief interactions with them.

AI has attracted a range of fundamental criticisms of its aims, methods and even morality. Dreyfus (1972), in an article originally entitled 'Alchemy and artificial intelligence', argued that AI was in the same historical tradition as medieval alchemy, one of whose goals was the creation of a homunculus, an artificial human. Dreyfus's point about historical continuity is correct, though it does not tell against AI in the way he intended, since other alchemical enterprises, such as the better known one of the transmutation of base metals into gold, were simply ahead of their time rather than impossible in principle. Wiener, the father of the term *cybernetics*, also wrote of the continuity with medieval work (1964); in his case the analogy was Jewish, with the Golem, or homunculus, said to have been created by the Great Rabbi of Prague.

A crucial difference between the medieval tradition and AI is that AI seeks explanation as well as construction: in the absence, as now, of extensive information from brain physiology, AI's methodology of simulating intelligent behaviour on machines may yield the best explanations of human cognition that we have. As someone once put it: AI seeks the answer to traditional metaphysical questions (such as what there is and how we know about it) by other means. The search for what is sometimes called 'the architecture of cognition' has widened out from AI to a subject now called *cognitive science*, while the more constructive aspects have become a wider movement called *artificial life* that involves physicists and biologists as well as computationalists.

Dreyfus's criticisms of AI were not about principle but method: in particular he argued that the core AI tradition of logical theorem proving, mentioned above, could not be a foundation for any serious modelling of a human, since humans have receptors (e.g. eyes and ears) and manipulate the world around them from birth in a way current computers cannot. The heart of Dreyfus's case was that humans are embodied and *grow up* in a way that computers do not. This aspect of human life and development is essential to us being the kind of creatures we are, argued Dreyfus. He has since accepted that not all AI is, or need be, logic based, and that the anti-logical, non-representational, learning-oriented approach of connectionism mentioned above is closer to his view of how AI should be pursued.

There is a fairly obvious relation here between these two views of how an artificial human-like construct should be sought and traditional theological views of humans as fully incarnated (a view often identified with Judaic history and thought) as opposed to that of humans as possibly disembodied souls, minds or spirits, a notion closer to the 'dualist' Greek tradition. So, for example, connectionist systems are sometimes said to be *essentially implemented* ones, where hardware and software cannot be wholly separated in the way that has been assumed in traditional AI, where, indeed, it is often claimed as a virtue that software (programs) could be implemented on any hardware (computers). So, McCarthy once gave a classic definition of AI as a study of intelligence *independent of any implementation* in humans, animals or machines.

From within AI, Winograd and Flores (1986) criticized the ability of AI's symbolic-cum-logical representational methods to capture the complexity of continuous, organic phenomena such as are found in biology. Again, Searle (1984) has argued that AI lacks, and must lack, any way of capturing with programs the notion of a mental state, which he takes to be essential to being a human. Somewhat earlier, Weizenbaum (1976) argued, on an essentially ethical and psychiatric plane, that dialogues with computers for therapeutic purposes, like those mentioned earlier as being in the tradition of the Turing test, were harmful to those engaging in them and that AI could cause widespread social damage, because of the depersonalization they induced. No such evidence has ever been produced, nor has it in support of the widespread belief on the Left that AI is a final high point in the ALIENATION and dispensability of the worker under CAPITALISM. On the contrary, it is plain that the higher the level of AI research and development in a country, the lower its UNEMPLOYMENT rate.

The researches described here were essentially practical ones, even if not always resulting in actual programs, to produce an automaton with a roughly human capacity. Papert at MIT always cautioned against what he called the 'superhuman fallacy': he argued that the ordinary everyday faculties of humans (i.e. talking, seeing) were so hard to replicate that no AI research should even consider creating capacities greater than those of a human. In fact, of course, mathematical and scientific calculations are routinely done on computers in ways that could not be performed even by all the people on earth working together, but this kind of computing is normally ruled out as not being AI, as we noted at the beginning.

There have been theoretical discussions of whether a truly superhuman/omniscient machine was conceivable, which would be to say, in traditional terms, to model God rather than a human being. Popper (1950) demonstrated long ago that a machine could not be omniscient (in a defined sense) even if it were composed of every atom in the universe: it would still not be able to predict its own behaviour completely.

There have been similar attempts to set limits, in mathematical/computational terms, to the powers of human-scale machines. Lucas (1964, recently revived by Penrose 1989) argued that Gödel's theorem showed an essential distinction between humans and machines in that the latter could prove theorems but, given the classic theorem on undecidable propositions, there would always be at least one more theorem that the machine could not prove but which a human could see was true. The implication was that if the machine could not prove the theorem, it could not see it was true, and hence there was a firm human–machine distinction. It was fairly easy to dismiss this purported distinction: since the human who knows the theorem to be true has evidence and is not just guessing, there is no reason why a machine, if it can fully simulate the human, should not know that theorem on the same grounds that the human does, shaky though they may be.

Many others have discussed senses in which machines could plausibly be said to have beliefs (there is a full survey in Ballim and Wilks 1991), at least in the sense that to have a belief requires that one can model the situation that others have beliefs different from one's own. This is a fairly weak condition, but it excludes the bank automat which has no information whatever that anyone or anything else has a view *different* from its own of what is in accounts, and so does not have beliefs on this criterion.

There have been serious discussions of the ways in which we might come to attribute a limited notion of responsibility to computers, rather as English courts ascribe a limited notion of blame to dogs (which are not treated as simple machines, or *ferae naturae*; for a discussion see Wilks and Ballim 1991). As computer systems become more complex it will become much harder to assign blame for failure to companies or individual persons, and this will become a serious practical issue.

Ballim, A. and Wilks, Y. (1991) *Artificial Believers*, Norwood, NJ: Erlbaum.

Barr, A. and Feigenbaum, E. (1982) *The Handbook of Artificial Intelligence*, vols I, II, New York: Kaufman.

Dreyfus, H. (1972) *What Computers Can't Do*, New York: Harper & Row.

Lucas, J. (1964) 'Minds, machines and Gödel', in A.R. Anderson (ed.) *Minds and Machines*, Englewood Cliffs, NJ: Prentice-Hall.

Partridge, D. and Wilks, Y. (eds) (1990) *The Foundations of Artificial Intelligence*, Cambridge: Cambridge University Press.

Penrose, R. (1989) *The Emperor's New Mind*, Oxford: Oxford University Press.

Popper, K. (1950) 'Indeterminacy in quantum and classical physics', *British Journal for the Philosophy of Science*.

Searle, J. (1984) *Minds, Brains and Science*, Cambridge, MA: Harvard University Press.

Sloman, A. and Croucher, M. (1981) 'Why robots will have emotions', in *Proceedings of the Seventh Joint International Conference on Artificial Intelligence*, Vancouver.

Turing, A. (1950) 'Computing machinery and intelligence', *Mind*.

Weizenbaum, J. (1976) *Computer Power and Human Reason*, San Francisco, CA: W.H. Freeman.

Wiener, N. (1964) *God and Golem Inc.*, Cambridge, MA: MIT Press.

Wilks, Y. (1985) 'Consciousness and machines', in C. Hookway (ed.) *Minds, Machines and Evolution*, Cambridge: Cambridge University Press.

Wilks, Y. and Ballim, A. (1991) 'Liability and consent', in A. Narayanan and M. Bennun (eds) *Law, Computer Science and Artificial Intelligence*, Norwood, NJ: Ablex.

Winograd, T. and Flores, F. (1986) *Understanding Computers and Cognition*, Norwood, NJ: Ablex.

Yorick Wilks

ASCETICISM

The term asceticism is derived from the Greek *askēsis*, meaning training or exercise. Ascetic practices are found to one degree or another in all major religious traditions but have been more pronounced in Christianity, Islam, Hinduism and certain forms of Buddhism than in Judaism, Confucianism or Taoism. The ascetic practices of other religious and quasi-religious groups, including the Essenes, Stoics, Gnostics, Pythagoreans and Manichaeans, have exerted influence on the development of Christian ascetic ideals. The prevalence of asceticism within a given tradition is often said to correlate with its 'world-rejecting' tendencies, though the term 'world rejection' has been applied so capriciously and tendentiously as to be rendered vacuous. It may be that the psychological origin of ascetic practice is 'the practical observation that an alteration of physical conditions produces a changed condition of the psyche' (Miles 1990: 94). The specific practices associated with asceticism are wide and varied and include sexual abstinence, fasting, meditation, contemplation, solitude, voluntary poverty and the practice of obedience. The intended consequences of ascetic practice are equally numerous and include intellectual acuity, moral regeneration, spiritual transformation, empowerment of the self in the service of God and neighbour, ATONEMENT for SIN, the attainment of religious merit and the propitiation of the gods.

Biblical warrants for Christian asceticism are plentiful. Paul's letters in particular are replete with images of the 'spiritual athlete'. 'Train yourself in godliness, for, while physical training is of some value, godliness is valuable in every way, holding promise for both the present life and the life to come' (I Timothy 4: 7–8). 'Athletes exercise self-control in all things; they do it to receive a perishable wreath, but we an imperishable one' (I Corinthians 9: 25). The gospels tend to place less stress than the Pauline letters on spiritual athleticism and more on the inevitability of self-sacrifice and suffering for those who choose to be disciples of Jesus. 'If the world hates you, be aware that it hated me before it hated you' (John 15: 18). 'If any want to become my followers, let them deny themselves and take up their cross and follow me' (Mark 8: 34; compare Luke 9: 23 and Matthew 16: 24). The New Testament, however, can also be construed as cautioning against excessive attachment to ascetic ideals: 'For John came neither eating nor drinking, and they say, "He has a demon"; the Son of Man came eating and drinking, and they say, "Look, a glutton and a drunkard, a friend of tax collectors and sinners!"' (Matthew 11: 18–19).

The origin of the systematic practice of asceticism within Christianity is contemporaneous with the birth of monasticism in the fourth century. It was then that Anthony of Egypt and other anchorites took to the Egyptian desert in reaction to the increasingly triumphal and 'established' character of Christianity in the wake of the conversion of Constantine in AD 312. In monastic asceticism, the ideal of martyrdom, so dominant in the first three centuries of Christian history, was reaffirmed in sublimated form: dying to the 'world' and the ways of the old self (McGinn 1992: 134; Miles 1981: 32–6). A premonastic 'free-form asceticism' practised by small groups of men and women within village society preceded, and for a time coexisted with, the solitary practice of the anchorites of the Egyptian desert. Both styles of ascetic practice eventually gave way to more highly organized ascetic communities, or *coenobia* (McGinn 1992: 131–9). Developments in cenobitic asceticism, most particularly those associated with the Rule of St Benedict in the sixth century and with the later appearance of Cistercian, Carthusian, Franciscan and Dominican spiritualities, were of profound significance in the formation of Christian ascetic practice. The importance of theologians such as Clement of Alexandria (third century), Pseudo-Dionysius the Areopagite (fourth century) and, most notably, St Augustine of Hippo (fourth century) in shaping Christian ascetic practice derives in part from the influence of their theologies upon monastic practice.

Though the spirituality of many lay Christians in late medieval Europe was shaped by monastic asceticism, manuals of devotion such as Thomas à Kempis' *The Imitation of Christ* (fifteenth century), St Francis de Sales' *Introduction to the Devout Life* (seventeenth century) and John Bunyan's *Pilgrim's Progress* (seventeenth century) became increasingly influential. These manuals often communicated harsh spiritual judgements regarding the relative worth of the body, of human relationships and of creation in general.

Another and equally important non-monastic influence upon the development of Christian asceticism is the emergence of 'inner-worldly' ascetic practices. In Roman CATHOLICISM, the *Spiritual Exercises* of St Ignatius Loyola inspired an ascetic ethos of unparalleled worldly efficacy that thrust the members of the Society of Jesus into a leading role in the Counter-Reformation. Perhaps even more significant is the emergence of the 'Protestant work ethic', the Calvinist ascetic ethos that Max Weber argues to have been of unique importance in the shaping of modern-day Western culture. According to Weber, the necessity of reconciling articles of faith promulgated in the Westminster Confession, especially the troublesome doctrine of predestination, with the spiritual needs of the believer resulted in a pastoral strategy counselling the active repression of thoughts concerning one's ultimate fate and enjoining the believer to embrace intense worldly activity in God's service. Though succeeding in affirming vocational responsibility for the created world absent in earlier 'world-rejecting' ascetic practices (Weber 1964: 166–83), the resultant ethos tended to harbour antipathy toward the mystical elements of earlier ascetic ideals and toward emotionality and passion in general.

Nearly a hundred years ago, William James noted that his 'healthy-minded' liberal Protestant and agnostic contemporaries understood asceticism to refer to the activity of embracing 'mortification for mortification's sake' and therefore judged this practice 'repugnant'. Echoing this same sentiment a century later, Margaret Miles says that 'asceticism is one of the currently least understood and most universally rejected features of historical Christianity' (Miles 1990: 94). But it is H.L. Mencken's playful identification of puritanism with 'the haunting fear that someone, somewhere may be happy' that probably best captures the modern disdain for things ascetical.

Though it is never easy to chart the complex interaction between ideas and the cultural matrices that spawn them, it is safe to say that the writings of Nietzsche and Freud both reflect and inform modern and contemporary suspicions regarding ascetic practice. For Nietzsche, asceticism signifies, among other things, the 'hatred of humanity, of animality, of inert matter; this loathing of the senses . . .; this fear of beauty and happiness' (Nietzsche 1956: 299). His observation that human aggression and anger previously directed outward had, under the tutelage of the 'ascetic priest', turned inward, reducing the self to 'a wild beast hurtling against its cage' (Nietzsche 1956: 214–30), anticipated and probably influenced later psychoanalytic insights on the interrelations between guilt, ALIENATION and the internalization of cultural norms. But it was Freud's notions of the individual and cultural superego functions (Freud 1961: 83–96), and his ingenious and pioneering work in devising therapeutic techniques to mute harsher elements of these, that proved an indispensable prod to the emergence of a countervailing ethos which challenged the ascendant ascetic ethos. The new ethos, described by one theorist as 'the triumph of the therapeutic' (Rieff 1966: 1–47) and more judgementally by others as 'the culture of narcissism', is one in which the maintenance of a sense of well-being takes precedence over social and religious commitments that might disrupt the individual's equanimity with guilt-provoking demands. A review of popular literature and attention to the use of therapeutic vocabulary in everyday conversation suggest the widespread influence of the therapeutic ethos in Western culture as well as its antipathy to ascetic ideals of human conduct.

Ironically, the once subversive exercise in the 'hermeneutics of suspicion' associated with the names of Nietzsche and Freud has become sufficiently commonplace that contemporary defenders of ascetic ideals and practices are able to assimilate such criticisms as a matter of course. The *New Catholic Encyclopedia*, for instance, readily admits: 'What used to be accepted values of asceticism do not readily harmonize with mid-twentieth century knowledge of man or God' (1990: 941). William James, asceticism's earliest champion following the Nietzschean onslaught, distinguished three distinct pathological motives for asceticism – 'obsessive guilt', 'pessimistic feelings about the self' and 'genuine perversions of bodily sensibility' (James 1961: 285–98) – before setting about the task of defending ascetic practice. And Margaret Miles, though also recommending a new form of ascetic practice, judges it best, in the light of traditional asceticism's disparagement of the body and its legitimation of the marginal status of women, to jettison the term in favour of 'Christian practice' (Miles 1990: 103–4).

It is worth noting that many of the more cogent arguments for a critical retrieval of ascetic practice are tied to radical social criticism. Turning to James and Miles again, we note in both cases a strong suspicion of American materialism. For James, who proposes a return to the ascetic ideal of voluntary poverty, the fevered chase after wealth and the exaggerated fear of impoverishment are the most pervasive and powerful inhibitions to moral discernment and compassion. Miles shares James's concern, but broadens his social critique to include suspicion of culturally prescribed strategies for constructing self-esteem and recognition of the 'deadness of exploitive sexuality'. It is her contention that a 'new asceticism' may enable individuals to 'dehabituate' themselves from distorted patterns of action and thought characteristic of some aspects of contemporary culture (Miles 1981: 155–63). Religious activists such as Mohandas Gandhi, Martin Luther King and Dorothy Day have realized in practice something of the same synthesis of asceticism and radical social resistance. Such time-honoured ascetic practices as fasting, contemplation and voluntary poverty figure prominently in their activism. As Peter Van Ness points out, these singular lives embodied 'a new synthesis of traditional religious teachings with contemporary political realities, and even more, they dramatized their teachings by enlisting spiritually disciplined practices in their public struggles' (Van Ness 1992: 269). One senses in such lives a uniquely powerful and credible witness for the revitalization of ascetic practice within the context of prophetic religious activism.

The future of Christian ascetic practice is unclear. No doubt, various proposals and reflections on the emergence of a 'new asceticism' by theologians and other scholars help to clarify the situation somewhat. But there can be little question that what is actually done at the pastoral level will prove determinative. Religious functionaries – priests, ministers, spiritual directors, pastoral counsellors, religious activists – mediate between the classic resources of Christian tradition, its sacred texts, rituals, dogmas, as well as its saints and prophets, and the economic, ideological, psychological and idiosyncratic forces that shape the pastoral needs of the faithful. It is also in the practice of pastoral care that potentially creative antinomies closely related to ascetic practice – those between contemplation and action, the AUTHORITY of tradition and individual AUTONOMY, identity formation and self-transcendence and others – can be more fully embraced and at least partially resolved. A credible ascetic practice for our time will encourage the confession of and liberation from self-centred and collectively shared inhibitions to the love of God and neighbour. It will discover and address such inhibitions as they are manifest not only in the slavish surrender to bodily desires but also in traditional asceticism's newly repented tendency toward the denigration and repression of these same desires. More subtly, it will note inhibitions to spiritual discernment and compassionate service in the studied alternation of surrender and repression that caters to the more refined indulgences of the 'well-balanced' ego.

Brandon, S.G.F. (ed.) (1970) *Dictionary of Comparative Religion*, New York: Charles Scribner's Sons.
Brown, Peter (1990) *Body and Society*, London: Faber & Faber.

Freud, S. (1961) *Civilization and Its Discontents*, New York: Norton.

James, W. (1961) *The Varieties of Religious Experience*, New York: Macmillan.

McGinn, B. (1992) *Foundations of Mysticism*, New York: Crossroad.

Miles, M.R. (1981) *Fullness of Life*, Philadelphia PA: Westminster Press.

——(1990) *Practising Christianity*, New York: Crossroad.

New Catholic Encyclopedia, vol. I (1970), New York: McGraw-Hill.

Nietzsche, F. (1956) *The Birth of Tragedy and the Genealogy of Morals*, trans. Francis Golffing, Garden City, NY: Doubleday.

Rieff, P. (1966) *The Triumph of the Therapeutic: Uses of Faith After Freud*, New York: Harper & Row.

Van Ness, P.H. (1992) *Spirituality, Diversion, and Decadence*, Albany, NY: State University of New York Press.

Weber, M. (1964) *The Sociology of Religion*, Boston, MA: Beacon Press.

Brian Mahan

ATHEISM

The perception of atheism (from the Greek *atheos*, without God) and of atheists in Western societies has changed considerably over the last hundred years. A century ago Robert Flint, Professor of Divinity at Edinburgh University, wrote that 'The prevalence of atheism in any land must bring with it national decay and disaster ... if once the workers of the large cities become atheists utter anarchy will be inevitable' (Flint 1877: 36–7) – a view which reflected not only the predominant perception of atheism of Flint's own day but also that of Western society from the time of Greek antiquity. Plato, in his *Laws*, had prescribed the death penalty for certain kinds of atheists on the grounds that their views undermined both morality and law (Bk X, 908–10), and even John Locke, the great advocate of religious toleration, exempted atheists from the application of the principles he was advocating on the grounds that, as he put it, 'Promises, covenants, and oaths, which are the bonds of human society can have no hold upon an atheist' (*Letter Concerning Toleration*). Atheism, he argued, in that it is not only not a religion but also a

philosophy which undermines all religion, could not come under the privilege of toleration that was rightly claimed by all *bona fide* religions. In England until the Evidence Amendment Act of 1869, atheists, whose word it was believed could not be trusted, could not give evidence in English courts of law, for they were unable, as atheists, to take an oath which was couched in theistic language. Further, until well into the twentieth century, law courts in England were reluctant to give the custody of children to professed atheists – the poet Shelley, for instance, who was not in fact an atheist but had been sent down from Oxford in 1810 for writing a pamphlet *On the Necessity of Atheism*, was legally deprived of the custody of his children on the grounds that he might inculcate them with atheistic views, as was Annie Bessant half a century later. This perception of atheists as *necessarily* untrustworthy and immoral has subsequently given way to a more tolerant attitude and, whilst in some quarters the public profession of atheism may still not be socially acceptable, atheists in Western societies have today, by and large, the same rights, privileges and opportunities as do other members of SOCIETY. The term 'atheism', however, still retains connotations that lead many who are, in fact, atheists to describe themselves by the rather less offensive term 'agnostic' (*see* AGNOSTICISM).

If the perception of atheism in Western societies is as described above, it is not surprising that, over the greater part of the history of these societies, the term 'atheist' has been loosely used as a term of abuse in religious controversy and that many of those who were called 'atheists' have often held quite different opinions. Socrates, for instance, would appear to have been regarded as an atheist by many of his contemporaries, as indeed were the early Christians who, in the polemics of their time, were often described as 'atheists and haters of the human race'.

We must distinguish, therefore, between two types of atheism: *relative* and *absolute*. *Relative atheism* is the denial of some particular, contingent, conception of 'God' in the interest of promoting what is regarded as being a more adequate conception. Such, for example, was the atheism of the ancient Greek philosopher

Xenophanes (570–475 BCE), who rejected what he regarded as the anthropomorphic and amoral representations of the gods found in Homer whilst at the same time suggesting, as a counterpart to this rejection, a conception of God as 'one, eternal and unchanging'. Outwith the Western tradition a similar relative atheism can be found in some of the late hymns of the *Rig Veda* in ancient India (*c*.1000 BCE) where there is a questioning of the existence of the gods of the traditional Hindu pantheon. Of these critics of traditional polytheism, Max Müller wrote: 'Their atheism, such as it was, would more correctly be called Adevism, or a denial of the old *devas* [as the gods of the old Hindu pantheon were called]. Such a denial ... of what was once believed, so far from being the destruction is, in reality, the vital principle of all religion' (1878: 303). Many twentieth-century Christian theologians would agree: the German émigré theologian Paul Tillich, for instance, was extremely critical of the 'patriarchal monarchist' conception of God held by many of his co-religionists and sought to rectify this by putting forward a conception of a 'God beyond God', only to be himself regarded as an atheist by some Christians and not a few Humanists. Up to the eighteenth century relative atheism was the most common form of atheism found within the Western tradition. However, in the eighteenth-century absolute atheism began to manifest itself for the first time since Classical Antiquity.

Absolute atheism is the denial not only of all and every conception of 'God', but also of the very existence of God. Outwith the Western tradition such atheism need not, of course, be irreligious: in the Indian religious tradition, for example, the Advaita Vedanta philosophy, together with the religions of Buddhism and Jainism, have all denied, or at least been agnostic towards, the existence of God, but have not been regarded as any the less religious on account of that denial. Religion is wider than theism. However, within the Western tradition, absolute atheism has, overall, been linked to the rejection of religion. Such rejection, more often than not, has been based on a philosophical naturalism which denies the existence of any reality other than that which is accessible through sense experience, although from the time of the Enlightenment the rejection of religion in the West has also evoked in support the detrimental effects that theistic religious belief is held to have on human societies. Further, from the eighteenth century onwards the difficulty of reconciling belief in a God who is both good and omnipotent with the EVIL that is found in the world appears to have led many more people to reject belief in God than would appear to have been the case in earlier ages, although in India in the sixth century BCE the Jains made use of the argument from evil in their critique of theism.

Absolute atheism is found in almost all the cultural traditions of the world. Its earliest recorded appearance was in India about the sixth century BCE where there arose a materialistic and hedonistic school of thought known as Lokayata or Carvaka. The Lokayata outlook on the world was similar to that associated with the names of Democritus and Epicurus in ancient Greece – an outlook that finds poetic expression in the *De Rerum Natura* of Lucretius – and most of the characteristics of later forms of absolute atheism in both the Indian and in the Western traditions can be found in these two ancient approaches to the world, in that both have a materialistic ontology, an empirical epistemology and a hedonistic ethic, all of which are features of absolute atheism. However, whilst Epicurus advocated a withdrawal from the world of affairs and the cultivation of private friendship, Lokayata sought to divert men's and women's attention away from a religious 'otherworld' towards a proper concern with this, the only world that they believed there is. A vigorous naturalistic (and atheistic) tradition can be found not only in India and in ancient Greece but also in China, where the most famous naturalist Wang Ch'ung (27–97 CE) expressed views similar to those found in Lokayata and Epicurianism.

After its appearance in ancient Greece absolute atheism does not occur again in the Western tradition until the eighteenth-century Enlightenment. The seventeenth-century thinker Thomas Hobbes, who is often regarded as an atheist and was regarded as such by many of his contemporaries, was, on his own admission, not an atheist but a Deist, in that he held that God was necessary to account for there being a world at all, even though, having created the world, God took no further part in its affairs. The first avowed atheist of modern times was the French materialist philosopher Baron d'Holbach (1723–89), the second volume of whose book *The System Nature*, published in 1754, contained a vigorous defence of atheism. From the eighteenth century onwards an increasing number of thinkers advocated absolute atheism and the rejection of all religion, the most well known of whom were Karl Marx, Friedrich Nietzsche, Sigmund Freud and Jean-Paul Sartre. As all of these thinkers regarded the issue between theism and atheism as having been settled in favour of atheism in the eighteenth century, none of them felt the need to argue the case for atheism: all, however, felt the need to explain the origin of the idea of God and the role which theistic religion had played in human societies. This they did by drawing on Ludwig Feuerbach's suggestion that God was a 'projection' of certain aspects of human nature. Thus for Marx religion was 'the fantastic realisation of the human essence in a world where the human essence has no true reality', a fantasy of alienated man which was destined to disappear when a society in which men and women were no longer alienated had been brought into being (*see* ALIENATION). Freud saw belief in God as a projection of the need that he believed men and women have for 'a father figure' to shield them from the terrible realities of life in the world. The most profound discussion of theism in the nineteenth century however, is found in the writings of Friedrich Nietzsche who claimed that what he rather dramatically called 'the death of God' in Western culture was fraught with the most serious consequences for the survival of that CULTURE – consequences of which he believed his contemporaries were oblivious. The foundations of Western civilization having crumbled, the 'philosophers of the future', said Nietzsche, must, as a matter of urgency, address the problem of how to re-establish Western culture on a non-theistic basis. For Nietzsche the controversy surrounding theism was essentially a controversy over the creation of values and a meaningful life in a godless world. This question was also one of the main preoccupations of atheistic existentialist philosophy as popularized by Jean-Paul Sartre and Albert Camus. The consequences of trying to live with an atheistic outlook on life were also explored by the Russian novelist Dostoyevsky in his novel *The Brothers Karamazov* – a novel which was intended to be the first part of a (never completed) larger work which was to have been called *The Atheist*.

The most concerted attempt to date to establish a totally atheistic way of living in the world was that made by Soviet 'scientific atheism'. This enterprise, which was proclaimed by decrees of the Supreme Soviet of the USSR in 1953 to be an integral part of the ideology of Marxism–Leninism, sought to replace religion, at all levels of Soviet society, with a positive and constructive atheistic outlook on life. (*see* COMMUNISM.)

The mention of this ill-fated experiment raises yet again in the Western tradition what is, perhaps, the major *lietmotiv* of the theism–atheism controversy at the present time, and that is the question of the social and cultural consequences of atheism, which in turn raises the further question of how, in what is perceived by many to be a post-theistic (if not, as yet, a post-religious) society, it is possible to establish society on other and more secure (because less problematical) foundations than theism. The civil religion debate, initiated by Robert Bellah and other American sociologists worried about the future development of American society, is indicative of the fear that many people in Western society still have that unless society is founded on theistic or, at the very least, religious foundations, social order, and with it a meaningful way of life, will collapse. Contemporary atheism has still much work to do if it is to allay this fear. Just how much work can be seen from reading Allan Bloom's comments on atheism and culture in the third part of his book *The Closing of the American Mind* (1987).

Bloom, Allan (1987) *The Closing of the American Mind*, London: Penguin (especially pp. 194–216).
Camus, Albert (1945) *The Myth of Sisyphus*, London: Hamish Hamilton.
Feuerbach, Ludwig (1957) *The Essence of Christianity*, London and New York: Harper and Row.
Flint, Robert (1877) *Anti-Theistic Theories*, Baird lecture, Edinburgh: Wm. Blackwood.

Freud, Sigmund (1953) *The Future of an Illusion* and *Civilization and its Discontents*, in *Complete Works*, vol. XXI, London: The Hogarth Press.

Kaufmann, Walter (1954) *The Portable Nietzsche*, New York: Viking Press.

Küng, Hans (1978) *Does God Exist?*, London and New York: Collins.

Marx, Karl, and Engels, Friedrich (1957) *On Religion*, Moscow.

Müller, F.M. (1878) *Lecture on the Origin and Growth of Religions,* London: Longmans.

Sartre, Jean-Paul (1948) *Existentialism and Humanism*, London.

Thrower, James (1981) *The Alternative Tradition: A Study of Unbelief in the Ancient World*, The Hague: Mouton.

——(1983) *Marxist–Leninist 'Scientific Atheism' and the Study of Religion in the USSR*, Berlin: De Gruyer.

James Thrower

ATONEMENT

Atonement denotes the fact of reconciliation between estranged parties. In Christian theology it refers, in the first place, to reconciliation between God and sinful humankind, and its realization is associated decisively with the life and death of Jesus Christ. This association has been conceived in a number of ways, and on this matter (in contrast to, for example, the doctrine of Christ) the Church has been prepared to live with a plurality of interpretations: no one doctrine of the atonement has been officially accorded the status of orthodoxy.

The success of a Christian doctrine of the atonement may be gauged by five criteria: first, the adequacy of its concept of SIN as an existential phenomenon, both moral and corporate; second, its effectiveness in explaining how the life and death of Christ effects transformation in the lives of others; third, the justice it does to the actual historical context of Jesus' life and death; and fourth, the plausibility of its account of the decisive role of Christ in bringing atonement about.

One of the most common terms in which the atonement wrought through Christ has been conceived is that of SACRIFICE. Of the several concepts of sacrifice present in the Hebrew Bible, the main one employed by New Testament authors (especially the author of the Epistle to the Hebrews, but see also Romans 2: 15 and 1 John 4: 10) is that of the sin- or guilt-offering. This views sin as a kind of disease or contamination, and of atonement as a kind of wiping out or cleansing – i.e. expiation – that is effected by the fresh life poured out in the blood of the sacrificial victim (Leviticus 17: 11). Such a conception has the merit of understanding sin not simply as an inner condition affecting the discrete spirits of individuals but as an objective force infecting the social body. It also affirms that atonement is made by another (the victim) and at a very high price (the victim's life). However, it obscures the inner, moral dimension of sin, and offers no explanation of how the victim's death is capable of effecting atonement for others, except in magical terms of the 'cleansing' properties of the victim's blood. Furthermore, although the Hebrew Bible recognizes that the efficacy of a sin-offering requires repentance on the part of the sinner, it fails to establish any intrinsic connection between the sacrifice itself and the subjective transformation of the sinner. The New Testament does not improve upon this sacrificial concept of atonement, but simply affirms that the sacrificial blood of Christ – the Lamb – has (somehow) cleansed human life of sin once and for all. Later Christian theologians, however, did seek to understand Christ's sacrifice, not as the pouring out of some magical purifying agent, but rather as an act of self-giving that pays either a debt owed to God by humankind or a ransom owed to the DEVIL.

This last notion conflates the concept of atonement through sacrifice with another Hebrew Bible concept of atonement by means of a scapegoat (Leviticus 16: 6–10). Here sin is pictured as an EVIL force that can (somehow) be transferred on to a goat and expelled with it out into the wilderness 'for Azazel' – which might mean 'for the demons of the desert'. Church Fathers such as Justin Martyr (*c.* 100–*c.* 165) and Origen (*c.* 185–*c.* 254) understood this as a kind of appeasement or propitiation of evil powers and used it to explain Christ's death as the means by which God pays a ransom to the devil in order to terminate his rights over sinners. Such an account certainly makes it clear that God is the primary agent in the making of atonement and it gives an explanation of how Christ's death is decisive and final in that process. But it does so at the expense of depicting sin in thoroughly extrinsic terms as a kind of quasi-legal debt, and it does not succeed in explaining how Christ's payment of this debt results in the transformation of concrete sinful life, whether individual or social.

The ransom-payment model of atonement presupposes that the devil has power over sinners by some right, and depicts atonement in terms of the fulfilling of a certain natural JUSTICE. The *victory* model also understands sin as a kind of power to which sinners are subject, but here the power is simply hostile and oppressive – it has no justice. Moreover, it has commonly been identified with social and political forces. When St Paul wrote of Christ's victory over 'the principalities, . . . the powers, . . . the world rulers of this present darkness' (Ephesians 6: 12), he was thinking of cosmic spiritual powers in rebellion against God as they expressed themselves in the political tyranny of the Roman state. He was thinking in similar terms of the oppressive legalism of some contemporary Jewish religion when he wrote that Jews as well as Gentiles are 'enslaved to the elemental spirits of the world' (Galatians 3: 19). This specification of the oppressive power of sin has the signal advantage of taking into account the two institutional forces that historically conspired to bring about Jesus' death. In contemporary Christian theology the ranks of the 'powers' have been widened to include all sorts of inordinate human powers (Karl Barth) or idolatries (Paul Fiddes) that hold human beings in thrall – for example, materialism, political absolutism, BUREAUCRACY, technology, fashion, transportation.

Not all contemporary theologians have understood the victory of Christ as a victory over oppressive powers at work in history. Gustav Aulen, for example, understands it as the victory of God's love over God's wrath against sin. This, however, is unsatisfactory because it suggests God possesses a divided self. Moreover, Aulen's account, like the other versions of the 'victory' model, also fails to explain how it is that Christ's death results in decisive victory over the destructive forces let loose by sin.

Theories of the atonement that proceed in terms of *justice* do offer a coherent explanation of how Christ's death is decisively victorious, even if their account of sin and its effects is too abstract. Athanasius (*c*.296–373) proposed that Christ, in taking on human nature and suffering death, paid the debt that God had decreed sin should incur. Thereby Christ made possible the reconciliation of God's love with his truthfulness or integrity.

Anselm (*c*.1033–1109) interpreted sin in feudal terms as a failure to give the divine liege-lord his due honour. This disorder can be rectified in one of two ways. Either restitutive satisfaction is paid to God, together with additional compensation for offended dignity; or the offender suffers eternal DEATH. But since human offenders can give God at most only what they owe, they have nothing further with which to pay such compensation. So they can only be saved from eternal death if someone else, not indebted as they are, pays off their full debt for them. This is the reason for the incarnation and death of the Son of God who, dying as a perfect human being, paid a debt not his own and, dying voluntarily, paid compensation by his merit.

A third theory of atonement of this kind was proposed by John Calvin (1509–64) in terms of criminal justice. Here sin is an offence against the law, not against feudal honour; and atonement can be made only by suffering the appropriate penalty. So the only way in which humankind can be spared the PUNISHMENT that the law demands, without arbitrarily suspending the operations of justice, is by an innocent substitute being punished in their place. This God arranges by having Christ die on the Cross. In so doing, God expresses LOVE for human sinners while maintaining divine justice.

The fact that all three of these models set God's love in some tension with God's constancy or justice is not in itself a flaw, except for those who suppose that God (and God's love) should be so free as to be absolutely unconstrained – even by the demands of God's own integrity. There is, however, a major problem with the retributivist and compensatory concept of justice by which God is supposed to be constrained. For there is good reason to doubt that such a concept should be endorsed by Christians. Jesus himself urges that injury not be met with retaliation, even if it is proportionate (Matthew 5: 38–9), and he places his emphasis firmly on the generous forgiveness of debt (see, for example, the parable of the Prodigal Son in Luke 15: 11–32). It might reasonably be argued that Jesus did not suppose that forgiveness could be effective in realizing reconciliation without repentance on the part of the offender, and that genuine repentance is bound to express itself in the offer of compensation, where that is possible (see the story of Zacchaeus in Luke 19: 1–10). However, strictly speaking, compensation is only possible where material damage has been inflicted. In so far as the damage attaches to a relationship – for example, in the form of slander or betrayal or carelessness – the injury committed cannot be undone, even though the offender might resolve never again to repeat his offence. Therefore, if there is to be reconciliation, the aggrieved must be willing to forgive, to let go of the past, to write off part or all of the 'debt'. What this implies for criminal justice and penal theory is that 'justice' does not consist in some retributive balancing of the books, so that punishment realizes justice by making the offender suffer 'proportionately' to his crime. On the contrary, and in accord with the Hebrew concept of 'JUSTIFICATION', it consists in the rectification of a relationship – the reintegration of a criminal into his community. The main point of a penal system, then, should be to offer forgiveness and to encourage the criminal to become penitent.

In addition to this common defect, Anselm's theory also suffers from a peculiar flaw of its own: namely, an important point of disanalogy between the relationship of a feudal lord with his vassal, and that of God with human creatures. For whereas in the first case the 'debt' is sufficiently objective that someone other than the debtor can pay it, in the second case it is thoroughly subjective. Human creatures owe their Creator their own perfect lives, not just any one. So the fact that Jesus was able to live a perfectly obedient life is good for Jesus but cannot be of any help to someone who was unable. Jesus' success cannot cover someone else's failure – unless, following Athanasius and Karl Barth, one thinks of human life and death as Platonic universals which Jesus has (somehow) transformed by participating in them.

The theory of penal substitution also has a weakness of its own. For whereas the Son of God's offering of himself to suffer punishment instead of human sinners demonstrates God's love for us, it also comprises what we would regard, according to normal canons, as a gross miscarriage of justice: a case of an innocent executed instead of the guilty.

Further, both Anselm's and Calvin's attempts to conceive of the atonement in terms of justice think of sin as an abstract 'debt', and of atonement as a kind of balancing of the moral books. The problem with this conception is that it is hard to relate it intrinsically to our experience of sin as an existential condition. Certainly, these theories do propose an extrinsic relation, arguing that the initiative that God has taken to effect atonement, and the cost suffered in so doing, should move us to gratitude, penitence and obedience – in other words, it should subsequently provoke our subjective transformation. But this still leaves opaque the connection between sin as the 'debt' paid by Christ and sin as disorder and oppression, psychic and social.

More successful in explaining the intrinsic causal link between Christ's life and death and the transformation of sinful life are those theories of the atonement that operate in terms of love. According to R.C. Moberly (1845–1903) Christ, in suffering death obediently, at once identified himself with sinful humanity and confessed the rightness of God's judgement on sin. This compassionate penitence, mediated by the Church (and especially by the EUCHARIST), helps us to recognize the destructive reality of our sin, to take responsibility for it and to turn away from it. Atonement is effected, then, by the ecclesially mediated influence of Christ's compassionate and penitential Spirit. Moberly's theory has recently been given a political turn by the British theologian, Timothy Gorringe. According to him, in Christ God entered into solidarity with oppressed humanity. In so doing, he exposed the lie by which the oppressive powers (of race, nation and capital) sustain themselves – namely, that they are inevitable necessities which must simply be endured – and thus enables the freeing of the oppressed for liberating, humanizing agency. It is this liberating 'education' that the Spirit continues through the Church and its sacraments.

These accounts stand in the tradition of Abelard (1079–1142), who understood the atoning function of Christ's passion and crucifixion as that of revealing God's love – a revelation that has the power to engender a corresponding love in those who behold it. Abelard himself did not quite explain how the Cross reveals the love of God. He assumed that through it God made a sacrifice for us, but he did not tell us in what sense. Recently, Paul Fiddes has helpfully explained this in terms of the dynamics of forgiveness. As he sees it, the one who would forgive must work to create a climate that encourages an offender to take responsibility for their offence, to repent of it and so to accept the forgiveness offered. The forgiver does this by undergoing a costly journey of sympathy in which they identify with the offender. The Passion and Cross of Christ should be understood, then, as comprising the path by which God is identified with humans in the utmost depths of their sinful condition. But as for Moberly, so for Fiddes, Christ's suffering reveals, not only the compassion of God, but also thereby the truth about human sin.

These theories of the atonement have often been accused of being excessively subjective and merely 'exemplarist'. The first charge holds that they do insufficient justice to the 'objectivity' of Christ's role in realizing atonement, and by 'objectivity' is meant the unprecedented, unsurpassable, universal decisiveness – the 'once-for-all-ness' – of what Christ achieved. The question that is posed here is this: if Christ's death is to be understood primarily as a revelation of God's love (and the nature of human sin), why should we regard it as decisive? Aulen's answer is that it is the point where God's love 'overcomes' wrath; but Abelard, Moberly and Fiddes do not avail themselves of this problematic solution. Abelard appeals obscurely to some notion of sacrifice. Moberly speaks of the unique perfection of Christ's penitence, arising out of his uniquely complete identification with both the holy God and sinful humankind. Along similar lines, Fiddes argues that, although eternally loving and compassionate, through the desolation of his Son God experienced the condition of sin, and so identified with sinful creatures, to a unique and absolute degree.

When the accusation of exemplarism is levelled, what is meant is that the revelation of God's love in Christ contributes to the making of atonement merely by providing a moral example for human beings to imitate. The complaint here, then, is that such a theory depreciates the need for the GRACE of God and expects too much of the sheer moral effort of humans. But the charge cannot be sustained; for, as Fidde has made quite plain, these theories represent God's love in Christ, not merely as presenting a moral example, but also as being a powerfully creative influence.

René Girard, the French anthropologist, has proposed a theory of the atonement that moves along lines remarkably similar to those of Moberly and Fiddes, while being much more socially grounded. According to Girard, sin is essentially the universal social syndrome of participation in the struggle for power ('mimetic rivalry'), the refusal to take responsibility for it, and the search for a scapegoat to blame and upon whom to turn the otherwise internecine VIOLENCE. This syndrome is sanctioned by 'sacrificial' religion and by retributive law – 'the powers'. The function of Jesus' life and death was to reveal the radical non-violent love of God, to expose the sinful, violent foundations of religious and political 'PEACE', and thereby to rob the 'victimage mechanism' of its authority. This he did by being patently innocent, suffering the violence unjustly heaped upon him, and yet unilaterally renouncing retaliation.

Girard's theory is successful on a number of counts. First, it takes account of the several different concepts of atonement to be found in the Bible, arguing that the truly Christian understanding of atonement should operate in terms of the victory of divine love over pre-Christian religious and legal institutions of atonement through violent sacrifice or scapegoating. Second, it explains how the suffering of an innocent (e.g. the Suffering Servant of Isaiah 53) can effect reconciliation with God and other human beings – by exposing the injustice of violence, revealing the divinity of non-violent love, and moving the sinner to renounce the first and identify with the second. Third, it identifies the 'powers' in terms that fit the historical circumstances of Jesus' passion and death at the hands of religious and political authorities. And fourth, it explains how love wins its victory over them – by exposing their violent foundations (cf. Colossians 2: 15).

In spite of these strengths, there remain questionable features. First, can sin be reduced to 'mimetic rivalry'? And second, can Jesus' revelation be considered decisive? Do we have reason to suppose, as Girard does, that Jesus was the most innocent and arbitrary, and the least violent, of victims; that he alone succeeded in identifying himself completely with God's Word of love; and that his revelation was therefore not only original but perfectly explicit? Girard's theory of the atonement, for all its strengths, does not yet add up to an orthodox understanding of Christ as God Incarnate. As it stands, it amounts to a kind of Spirit-Christology, according to which Christ is God Incarnate because he alone has become one with God by equalling the perfection of God's love.

The relationship between theologies of atonement and SOCIETY has been two-way. On the one hand, society's assumptions about the nature of justice have shaped theology. That was most obviously the case with Anselm's feudal notion of respect for honour and with Calvin's notion of the retributivist nature of punishment. On the other hand, theories of the atonement have also shaped society. As Boyd Hilton has shown, in Britain from the late eighteenth century into the second half of the nineteenth century the Calvinist doctrine of atonement by penal substitution (unfortunately) helped to foster *laissez-faire* individualism in social and economic thought and policy.

Some ways in which a properly Christian theory of the atonement should bear upon social life are these. First, sin should be understood as having a corporate dimension, as most of the Biblical notions of atonement (sacrifice, scapegoat, victory over the powers) presuppose. What this means, as Barth has pointed out, is that law-abiding citizens should maintain solidarity with their criminal fellows. This obligation constitutes a strong objection to any final expulsion of a criminal from the community – by means of CAPITAL PUNISHMENT, for example. It also constitutes a strong objection to any penal practices that are gratuitously degrading or humiliating.

Second, a doctrine of atonement that really takes its cue from the teachings, the life and the death of Jesus is bound to think primarily in terms of the forgiving love that strives to inspire penitence. This implies a preference for reformative over retributivist penal theory. Not that punishment should have no retributive element: it must be directed at one who deserves it – i.e. at the criminal – and it must impose sufficient loss of liberty upon them to protect innocent neighbours from further depredations. Nevertheless, beyond this, the purpose of punishment should be to encourage the criminal to repent and reform, with a view to being fully restored into the community.

Finally, if atonement is understood to come about by means of Christ's perfect compassion that perfectly reveals the rightness of God's judgement upon sin, and so is powerful to inspire penitence in the hearts of sinners, then the EUCHARIST becomes a powerful engine of social transformation. For in representing the compassionate judgement of God in Christ, it mediates a power that can create a virtuous cycle of penitence or critical self-knowledge, compassion for other sinners in their weaknesses, and forgiveness of the injuries that their weaknesses incline them to inflict. The Eucharist thereby becomes the beating heart of the Christian community, communicating the Spirit to the body of Christ and thereby empowering its members to become epiphanies of the divine compassion, prophets against ruthless and divisive institutions and practices, and agents of social atonement.

Dillistone, F.W. (1968) *The Christian Understanding of Atonement*, Welwyn: James Nisbet.

Fiddes, Paul (1989) *Past Event and Present Salvation*, London: Darton, Longman & Todd.

Girard, René (1987) *Things Hidden since the Foundation of the World*, London: Athlone.

Gorringe, Timothy (1986) *Redeeming Time: Atonement through Education*, London: Darton, Longman & Todd.

Hilton, Boyd (1988) *The Age of Atonement. The Influence of Evangelicalism on Social and Economic Thought, 1785–1865*, Oxford: Clarendon.

Moberly, Elizabeth R. (1978) *Suffering, Innocent and Guilty*, London: SPCK.

Moberly, R.C. (1901) *Atonement and Personality*, London: John Murray.

Moses, John (1992) *The Sacrifice of God*, Norwich: Canterbury Press.

Nigel Biggar

AUTHORITY

In present-day usage an author is commonly the composer of a written text or a score. The older meaning of the word, however, was much wider: an author, *auctor* in Latin, was the creator or founder of any thing, institution or domain. An author was a begetter, a father, an originator or maker, and was seen as having unconditional authority to determine TRUTH and to lay down and enforce the law within the domain that belonged to him. What you have made, you have the right to rule: authorship confers authority.

In this connection we should remember that the female ovum was discovered only in the early nineteenth century. The earlier biological theory was very often patriarchal in the strict sense: the father who sires was the sole originator, the female merely nourishing in her womb the seed that the male had planted therein. Thus traditional ideas about authority were linked with a patriarchal metaphoric, which in turn was supported by a mistaken biological theory.

The cluster of ideas involved in these formulations was of immense power and importance, underlying as it does both PATRIARCHY, monarchy and much of theology. If you are the author, then you are fully *entitled* to respect, gratitude and implicit obedience within your domain and from your offspring. You are expected to lay down the law, and you have a *right* to be believed and obeyed.

As applied to a text, these ideas suggest that the author is the best authority to consult about the true meaning of his or her own work. For the author's creative will is the true and original determinant of meaning, and every sort of literary scholar must therefore seek to discover what the author originally meant to say at the time when the work was composed. Within any institutional context, be it a church, a lecture-room, a playhouse or a courtroom, truth is sought by returning to a founding origin. Enquiry is thus oriented towards a 'primitive' Golden Age when TRUTH was uncontaminated, meanings clearly defined and the Law universally obeyed. This is sometimes called 'the myth of the normative origin', and it has had a wide-ranging influence, not only upon scholarly and interpretative practice, but also upon political theory and religious history.

Even to the present day and in the most liberal Western democracies, we still tend to assume that the authority of parents over their children is near-absolute. At any rate, the idea of children's rights remains relatively undeveloped. Parents still often have the rights, for example, to determine the religious education of their children, and to inflict corporal punishment upon them, and parenthood has long supplied metaphors for the exercise of absolute authority. It is somehow inconceivable that there should be any appeal against God's judgement, or that the earthly King could be charged with breaking his own law; and both were therefore spoken of as 'fathers'.

So we have a very long tradition of linking the concept of authority, its invocation, its justification and its exercise, with theology, with patriarchy and with monarchical structures in society. God has been seen in the image of a Roman *paterfamilias* or an absolute Monarch, and much of religious language and symbolism, ever since the Book of Job, has appeared to say that we human beings can have no *locus standi* from which we might be able to challenge or question the wisdom of God's decrees. Even today it is still possible for a few ultraconservative Catholic Christians and Muslims to argue that DEMOCRACY is incompatible with theism, and not viable as a political theory. For democracy in the end traces all questions of truth and values back to a mere contingent and shifting human consensus, whereas theism traces everything back to its true foundation in God's eternal will.

Until the European Enlightenment such ideas were seldom questioned. The kings of Middle Eastern antiquity traced their descent from gods, and the Pope derived his authority from God's commissioning of Christ and Christ's commissioning of Peter and his successors. Constitutional lawyers and scriptural exegetes alike sought for the original and therefore authoritative and founding meaning of the texts with which they were concerned.

It is as if both civil and religious societies were seen as descent-groups, lineages that can be traced back to one or more Founding Fathers who gave us the Law. Robert Filmer's *Patriarcha* (1680) still traced the divine right of kings back to the authority that God gave Adam over his children. Where people think like this, the task of any reformer must be to remove secondary corruption and restore primitive purity. So people have dreamt of getting back to the good old days when God was close, everyone practised the virtues, and the king was a father to his people.

Those good old days, however, were evidently gone. God was no longer present in person to give immediate guidance. It was therefore usually held that God has appointed some subordinate authority or 'vicar' to act on his behalf. This delegate reveals or interprets God's will, or administers God's Law and executes divine JUSTICE. Such authorities include God's eternal Word Incarnate, the Word written in the Scriptures, those who copy, study and preach the text of the Scriptures, and the priestly ruling class in the Church.

The philosophical chain of authority that underlies this sequence has become clearly understood only recently. There are four levels. The prime or founding authority is the creative will of the author, in which he/she acts to express his/her mind. This creative self-expression is then clothed in spoken words, which are faithfully recorded by an amanuensis in a written text. Fourth and finally, the student of the word written seeks that interpretation of it which is closest to the author's original mind. The order, then, is mental intention, spoken utterance, written text and interpretation.

The subordinate authorities so far mentioned (Scriptures, scribes, priests etc.) may be compared with similar authorities in the STATE: the legislature, the LAW, lawyers, judges and so forth. These are all 'external authorities'. In addition there is within each person's heart the 'internal authority' of conscience, a sense of vocation, private judgement, the inward testimony of the Holy Spirit and so on. The importance of internal authority is recognized both by the state and by the Church, including the Roman Catholic Church. In Catholic moral teaching conscience must always be obeyed, even when its deliverances are at variance with the objectively-valid and correct line taught by the Church. If I have carefully ascertained and weighed the Church's teaching, and yet still find myself in conscientious disagreement with it, then I am described as being in a state of 'invincible ignorance': I must follow my conscience, and shall not sin by doing so. Thus it is not quite correct to call the Roman Catholic system 'authoritarian'. Certainly, painful conflicts between individual judgement and church authority can and do arise; but the individual's freedom of conscience is not in the end overridden. (Or, at least, it should not be.) Rather similarly, the state – at least where it is fairly stable and confident – permits the individual some rights of conscientious objection, to active military service, or to participating in a surgical termination of pregnancy, for example.

One further strand of traditional ideas about authority should be mentioned. Until about the time of Hegel, Western thinkers generally believed in an objective Order of Reason, Plato's 'noumenal' world, in which were vested the unchanging moral and intellectual standards by which human life must at all times and in all places be guided. This belief in objective norms is called by philosophers 'realism', and by ordinary people belief in 'absolutes' or 'objective certainties'. It began to break down in the nineteenth century as people came to recognize that historical change, cultural diversity and the conditioning of thought by language are not shallow but very deep. It seems that all our standards are immanent, and subject to change. But most purportedly authoritative teachers of beliefs and values, faith and morals, have claimed to be in touch with and to represent an unchanging and superhuman order. In a word, they have been Platonists, because they have taught belief in timeless truths and values out-there, a belief which is now is widely questioned.

Since the Enlightenment, indeed, *all* the ideas about authority so far discussed have been subjected to sustained attack. The major lines of criticism have been as follows.

First, Descartes and his successors introduced a new method of doubt and a critical style of thinking. Like a customs officer demanding that we open all our baggage for inspection, the Enlightenment refused to allow any beliefs to be exempt on the grounds of their being traditional, or revealed, or mysterious, or precious. All beliefs must be exposed to the searching eye of reason and have their credentials examined. Although Descartes himself prudently refrained from using his method to question authority in the Church and the state, there were many others who had no such scruples. Inevitably, critical thinking and the method of doubt have progressively undermined all traditional ideas of authority, until it seems that modern society has nothing left to appeal to beyond the consensus of expert testimony and the measurement of public opinion.

Even that, however, is something of a broken reed, for a second line of criticism of authority, also strongly emphasized in the European Enlightenment, makes a very sharp distinction between is and ought, fact and value, indicative and imperative. From the fact that a certain authority commands me to believe or to do something, it does not follow that I ought to believe or obey, unless I have independent grounds for thinking that this authority deserves to be trusted or to be obeyed. But continually to be demanding that every authority (or expert opinion, or public sentiment) thus validate itself is systematically to undermine precisely its authority.

The third criticism of established notions of social and religious authority is at least as old as Herodotus. The exercise of authority ordinarily requires there to be an unchanging order of truth and values. But it has long been recognized that what people count as being true and ethically precious varies, sometimes very greatly, from one society to another, and in different historical periods. In recent thought there have been strong currents of anti-platonism, anti-realism and historical relativism. These doctrines are hard to state without appearing to claim for them precisely the kind of truth that they deny; but this difficulty is (supposedly) avoided by Michel Foucault and his followers, who seek to write the history of systems of thought in as cool and positivistic a manner as possible. Systems of thought, beliefs and values are described, and their changes reported, in a manner that can only be called 'Martian', and which inevitably robs them of any authority they might otherwise be felt to have had for us.

The fourth line of criticism stems from the feminist (see FEMINISM) movement. Feminist writers have argued that a great deal which in the past was portrayed as being natural and part of the entrenched order of things should rather be seen as culturally-established and changeable. As Simone de Beauvoir put it, 'One is not born, but is made, a woman'. Females are in bondage to cultural stereotypes that have been imposed upon them. Feminists further point out the strikingly 'masculinist' character of our traditional ideas of reason and authority. The exemplars of reason and authority, to a startling degree, tend to be masculine divinities who have no consort and lines of unmarried male philosophers and popes. It is suggested that such figures symbolize the masculine principle's total victory over nature, the passions and everything else that is symbolically feminine and therefore irrational and supposedly in need of being governed. Only with Hegel does a more dialectical and heterosexual style of thinking begin to replace the older patriarchal monarchy. The 'Other', woman, is no longer merely ruled; she begins to make an active contribution to the formation and the process of the world.

Finally, during the past century or so there has been something of a discovery of interpretation as being in some sense ubiquitous, and as a creative activity. The theatre director and the orchestral conductor have become important cultural figures. The reading or performance of any work is no longer seen as a simple repetition of the founding meaning imposed upon it by its original creator. Rather, any reading or performance is always an interpretation. The task of the director, conductor, preacher or (indeed) believer is always to re-imagine the text by finding a new way of reading it that will bring it to life in a new way for a new generation. And this new understanding of the necessity for creative reinterpretation has destroyed the old belief in an original authorial intention as the true and authoritative meaning of any work.

We cannot get back to such an original meaning, and in any case we should not even be trying to do so.

In the light of all these lines of criticism it is scarcely surprising that so many people now will accept the moral authority of (for example) the Pope only when he tells them what they already think. As for the authority of the civil law, its intellectual basis is distinctly uncertain: in Britain in 1991–3, politicians were urging people to obey the law and pay a tax, the community charge or 'poll tax', despite the fact that the very same politicians had already acknowledged that the introduction of the tax had been an error and were pledged to abolish it.

What ideas of authority then remain to us? It may be defended as a necessary myth, and justified on utilitarian grounds. We seem willing also to ascribe some authority to people of outstanding gifts or creative and interpretative powers. Fortunately, people still seem to be willing to support leaders whose exercise of authority is constitutional, open to inspection and responsive to the movement of public opinion.

It is impossible to provide a summary bibliography of a topic so vast and so wide ranging. According to their interests, students may wish to pursue the themes sketched above by studying the histories of the Papacy, Biblical criticism, political theory, jurisprudence, ethics, free thought, literary theory or philosophy. Amongst thinkers who have made a significant contribution to the debate one might mention J.S. Mill, H.-G. Gadamer, M. Foucault and J. Derrida. On the neo-conservative side, the names of M. Oakeshott and Alasdair Macintyre are often quoted.

The issues are accessibly introduced in:
Küng, Hans (1971) *Infallible?*, London.
Raz, Joseph (1986) *The Morality of Freedom*, Oxford: OUP.

Don Cupitt

AUTONOMY

Autonomy, from Greek *auto-* and *nomos* (self-law), is the condition of being fully self-legislating or self-governing, free and independent of any external constraint. The earliest use of the term, in the seventeenth century, was political: compare the closely related words autarchy and autocracy, used of an absolute monarchy or despotism. In the Eastern Christian world an autocephalous church is a national church or religious community that appoints its own head and is fully self-governing.

Historically there has been a certain tendency for the language of autonomy to be used in connection with the claims of the Pope, the Russian Tsar, certain churches, etc. This, however, is only an autonomy *vis-à-vis* other earthly institutions. The main tradition of theistic thought has of course always wished to ascribe absolute or metaphysical autonomy to God alone, and has viewed any open challenge to God's sole supremacy as the gravest of all offences. On the basis of Isaiah 14: 12–14, the Fall of Lucifer has been explained as a punishment for the SIN of pride and a presumptuous attempt to usurp God's sovereignty. In traditional Christian thought nobody but God can really be a law unto themselves. In Romans 2: 14f. St Paul speaks of the Gentiles as being a law to themselves, but it is clear that he is not attributing to them moral autonomy in the modern sense, for he goes on to speak of them as guided by a law written in their hearts and witnessed to by their troubled consciences. Thus the moral law that they are to themselves is not of their own making: they find it inscribed upon their own natures by their Creator.

The notion of God's autonomy is not without difficulties. In his *Euthyphro*, Plato first opened the question of whether God creates absolutely, or simply recognizes, the norms of morality and reason. If the latter, then the so-called 'eternal truths' and the moral standard are independent of God. In which case God is seemingly not absolutely autonomous, being guided by norms that are logically independent. Alternatively, if God simply creates the moral standard and the eternal truths, unguided by anything logically prior to that choice, then there can be no explanation of why they should have been set up in just this way and not otherwise. This means that reason's quest for explanation comes up in the end against an inscrutable fiat of the divine will, and is blocked. The believer seems to be left worshipping only power and mystery, for if God is above the law in the same way as the Queen is above the law in the British Constitution, then God cannot be described as being in himself good or even rational, just as the Queen cannot be described as being in herself law-abiding.

Such is the 'Euthyphro dilemma'. Some philosophers believe it can be solved, while others see in it an illustration of the general weakness of 'foundationalist' thinking. They hold that any attempt to explain by referring everything back to an autonomous first principle, or foundation that is itself unfounded, will encounter similar difficulties.

In the Enlightenment the philosophy that traced everything back to God tended to be replaced by an 'I-philosophy' that traced everything back into human subjectivity. Descartes and his successors appeared to treat human consciousness as self-founding and perspicuous to itself. The thinkers of the Enlightenment generally regarded reason and sense-experience as being natural and uncontaminated sources of knowledge. The claim was that human beings could construct their own systems of knowledge and of morality independently of God and tradition.

It was in this context that the idea of the autonomy of the human subject was first promulgated. The outstanding figure is Immanuel Kant (1724–1803). Kant held that in so far as we are rational we must take a deterministic view of the physical world. All events condition each other in the way laid down by Newtonian physics. How then can morality fit into such a vision of the world? Answer: moral principles are unconditional and a priori, being recognized autonomously by pure practical reason and freely adopted as the maxims of one's own action.

Kant thus taught both the autonomy of the moral agent, as self-legislating practical reason and a freely-choosing will, and the autonomy of the moral standard. Being truly a priori and unconditional, moral principles do not in his view depend for their authority either upon the command of God or upon their being built into

the fabric of the world. Kant might thus be regarded as a pioneer of moral non-realism were it not for the fact that on his view there can be only one true and universally-binding morality, acknowledged by all people in so far as they are rational. As in his theory of knowledge Kant holds that we are constrained by reason to build the world in one way only, so in his moral philosophy he holds that we are constrained by reason to formulate only the one true morality.

The strength of Kant's position was that he was able to break with the 'feudal' thinking of the past and assert human autonomy in very bold terms, whilst yet remaining a sort of realist or objectivist in epistemology and ethics. But the weakness of his ethical theory was very soon pointed out by contemporaries: strictly moral considerations were by Kant too sharply separated from facts about human nature, the passions, culture and history. His ethical rigorism and apriorism meant that he could give no account of moral change.

In the Christian tradition, Catholics had long held that 'conscience must always be followed' and Protestants had long insisted upon the right and duty of 'private judgement'. Against this background, Kant's insistence upon the moral necessity for the autonomy of the moral agent has had a marked influence upon subsequent Christian thought. In particular it has raised a question about all those traditional (often, Augustinian) doctrines which appear to represent human beings as being morally impotent or passive and able to act rightly only when God tells them what to do and empowers them to do it. The doctrines in question are those involving the ideas of divine predestination, original sin and the bondage of the will, the need for a revealed morality, prevenient (and, maybe, irresistible) GRACE, the indwelling of the Holy Spirit illuminating, empowering and sanctifying the believer, and so on.

What is to be said about these doctrines? For some, Kant's insistence upon the moral necessity for the full autonomy of the moral agent is a mistaken piece of Enlightenment humanist arrogance and must be rejected. Others accept Kant's point and accordingly either reject the traditional doctrines or reinterpret them in a non-realist or symbolic sense as morally useful guiding pictures. Kant himself, in his book on *Religion within the Limits of Reason Alone*, adopts a mixture of the two approaches.

Much of modern Christianity seems now to accept the concept of the autonomy of the moral agent. At any rate, since the Second World War and the issuing of the UN's Universal Declaration of HUMAN RIGHTS, the mainstream churches have adopted the vocabulary of individual human rights and in a number of countries have defended them vigorously. Such rights certainly include much more freedom to choose one's own values, and shape the course of one's own life, than traditional Christian language envisaged. The implications of this development have perhaps not yet been fully worked out. Reflection on the historical development of doctrine goes back to the Reformation, but general awareness of deep moral change is recent. Yet it is clear now that we both generate such change and have also to adapt ourselves to it constantly.

During the nineteenth century an enormous expansion of historical knowledge took place, and especially knowledge of the history of language, of ideas and of religion. The notion that worldview, beliefs and values are radically different in different cultures became well understood. At the same time Darwinism was making prominent ideas of naturalism, struggle, development, life and the passions. In this context Friedrich Nietzsche (1844–1900) taught the most thoroughgoing version so far of the doctrine of autonomy. For him, everything is historical and everything is a human product. There is no one TRUTH of things out there, no telos or goal, no moral world order, and no one true morality. There are many moralities, faiths and truths, and they are all transient human products. They are symbolic and projected expressions of the will to power – which means, roughly, the will to live by creating a symbolic order in which to live.

On Nietzsche's view the standard type of human being is the artist, a person self-disciplined to live by and for creative expression. Such a person makes life worth living by creating new values and new metaphors.

Nietzsche has various criteria of truth. Following Spinoza's contrast between the active and passive emotions, he prizes most those values and metaphors through which life can most actively and joyfully affirm itself. He often invokes aesthetic criteria, judging people, faiths and ways of life very much as people judge works of ART. More questionably, he makes very extensive use of a contrast between what is healthy and what is sick or decadent.

There is some similarity between Nietzsche's thought and that of earlier radical post-Protestants such as William Blake. Amongst twentieth-century theologians affected by Nietzsche, the most notable early examples were perhaps Albert Schweitzer and Dietrich Bonhoeffer. During the 1960s Nietzsche began to replace Marx as probably the single most widely studied modern philosopher, and radical theology has been especially influenced by him. Thus the Death-of-God theology of the 1960s with its 'Gospel of Christian Atheism' appealed expressly to Blake and Nietzsche. The Christian gospel of redemption is equated with the attainment of full human autonomy *vis-à-vis* God. In Christ, God has died to make us free. God has, so to say, disappeared into our human being, a disappearance foreshadowed as far back as the late Middle Ages when God the Father first began to be represented in human form.

Most recently, postmodernism has been anti-humanist, chiefly because the historical awareness which has dissolved away all concepts of the objective and unchanging has also dissolved away the notion that there is such a thing as human nature. The human self, too, is just another transient and changeable cultural construction.

Among contemporary theologians who have made much of the notion of autonomy are the veteran American Death-of-God theologian T.J.J. Altizer, especially in his writings of the 1960s, and the British theologian Don Cupitt. In 1980 Cupitt applied Kant's argument for the autonomy of ethics to religion, arguing that just as in ethics one can and should learn to do without the encouragement of any external support or sanctions, so too the religious life can and should be pursued autonomously and without the support of realistic belief in God, a supernatural world, etc. In his later books Cupitt has developed his argument steadily further in a broadly Nietzschean and (recently) expressionist direction.

Unpopular though all these ideas are in many quarters, it seems likely that they will remain on the agenda. The rise of FEMINISM since the 1950s is a contributing factor, because feminist analysis has shown the extent to which 'nature' and 'woman' are cultural fictions, the extent to which religious doctrine-systems are culturally conditioned and may need to be criticized and remade, and the sheer depth of the moral changes now taking place in society.

Altizer, T.J.J. (1966) *The Gospel of Christian Atheism*, Philadephia, PA: Westminster Press.
Altizer, T.J.J. and Hamilton, William (eds) (1968) *Radical Theology and the Death of God*, Harmondsworth: Pelican (bibliography).
Cupitt, D. (1980) *Taking Leave of God*, London: SCM.
——(1988) *The New Christian Ethics*, London: SCM.
——(1990) *Creation out of Nothing*, London: SCM/ TPI.
Plato, *Euthyphro*, in *Five Dialogues*, Indianapolis: Hackett, 1986.
Kant, I. (1785) *Foundations of the Metaphysic of Morals*, in H.J. Paton, *The Moral Law,* London: Hutchinson, 1948.
MacLagan, W.G. (1961) *The Theological Frontier of Ethics*, London: Allen & Unwin.
Nietzsche, F.W. (1887) *The Gay Science*, 2nd edn, trans. Walter Kaufmann, New York: Vintage Books, 1974 (and other works).
Raz, J. (1986) *The Morality of Freedom*, Oxford: Oxford University Press.

Don Cupitt

BAPTIST

Baptists comprise a worldwide Protestant (*see* PROTESTANTISM) communion which originated in English Puritanism early in the seventeenth century.

Baptists prefer to express their theological beliefs in confessions which are descriptive of their convictions rather than in creeds to be used prescriptively. They hold many theological beliefs in common with all Christians, such as belief in the TRINITY. They accept much of John Calvin's version of Protestant beliefs. Most Baptists accept the revivalism associated with John Wesley and his colleagues in the eighteenth century. Baptists are committed to the modern missionary movement which began late in the eighteenth century: in 1792 English Baptists sent the cobbler and linguist William Carey to India; and in 1991 the Southern Baptist Convention in the United States had become the largest single missionary organization in the world, supporting more than 7,000 missionaries. Baptists respond to the acids of MODERNITY which the Enlightment released in much the way that other Protestants do: some knowledge élites work to correlate their Baptist beliefs with new scientific knowledge and historical consciousness (William Newton Clarke); many Baptists are influenced unconsciously by the new ideas; a few Baptists are alarmed and resist aspects of modernity either by intellectual apologetics or by organizing institutional resistance (Charles Haddon Spurgeon).

Originally Baptists held two clusters of beliefs which set them apart from other seventeenth-century Protestants. First, as their name suggests, they hold distinctive beliefs about the universal Christian practice of baptism. They believe that the only proper candidates for baptism are intentional believers; hence Baptist churches do not baptize infants. They also believe that the only proper mode of baptism is immersion. In both, Baptists are primitivists in the sense that they intend to return to the practice of the earliest Christian churches.

Second, Baptists are deeply committed to FREEDOM. They believe that religion is genuine only if one accepts it for oneself, and therefore they avoid coercion of any kind. In the government of their churches each congregation is autonomous, and each church member participates in a democratic process to arrive at a congregational decision; in these matters Baptists are similar to their older cousins, the Congregationalists. Furthermore, Baptists believe that GOVERNMENT should be neutral towards religion. Because they attempt to exercise a non-coercive influence upon public as well as private life (they also respect the right of persons of other religious faiths or of no faith to do the same), Baptists are not sectarians. However, they oppose the use of coercive power either by any church upon government or by government upon churches or upon citizens in matters of religion. In 1612 a Baptist layman, Thomas Helwys, wrote to King James I: 'The King is a mortal man, not God, and therefore has no power over the immortal souls of his subjects, to make laws or ordinances for them, and to set spiritual lords over them' (McClellan 1978:12). His book is the first sustained cry for religious liberty in England; he was put in Newgate Prison where apparently he died.

The first Baptist church was founded in 1608 or 1609 by John Smyth, a former Anglican clergyman who had become a Puritan Separatist and had fled with some of his followers for safety to Holland. Influenced by Mennonites there, Smyth baptized himself and then his supporters. By the middle of the century several Baptist churches existed in and around London and were following the practice of believers' baptism by immersion.

Baptists reached America in the 1630s. Roger Williams, a founder of Rhode Island, drew up its charter which promised religious freedom for all citizens. He wrote: 'All the Liberty of Conscience that ever I pleaded for, turns upon these two Hinges: [first], that none of the Papists, Protestants, Jews, or Turks be forced to come to . . . Prayers or Worship; nor, secondly, compelled from their particular Prayers or Worship, if they practice any.' Baptists worked vigorously for the adoption of the Bill of Rights of the Constitution, which begins with the words: 'Congress shall make no law respecting an establishment of religion, or prohibiting the free exercise thereof.' The first national organization of Baptists was formed in 1814, and it divided over the issue of SLAVERY in 1845. Following the Civil War two of the organizations of black Baptists grew into very large denominations. In 1905 the Baptist World Alliance, a loose coalition for co-operative work, was organized. At the end of 1991, 156 Baptist denominations with headquarters in ninety-four countries and with work in 200 countries, comprising 142,000 churches with 37,000,000 members, were members of the Baptist World Alliance; 30,000,000 of these persons belonged to churches in North America. Many Baptist denominations and churches do not belong to the Alliance; the number of Baptists worldwide is estimated to be 70,000,000.

Baptists hold in common the beliefs mentioned above, but they have not responded unanimously to new theological issues. For example, many Baptists resisted the Social Gospel movement, but a leader of the movement, Walter Rauschenbusch, was a Baptist pastor and professor. Again, Latin American Baptists usually refuse to participate in public life, but in the United States Baptists such as Martin Luther King, Jr, and Presidents Jimmy Carter and Bill Clinton have been major public figures, and Baptist theologians such as Harvey Cox have given special attention to political theology. Further, Baptists in the soviet republics welcome charismatic practices, but those in the Southern Baptist Convention resist these practices vigorously. Also, some Baptist denominations belong to national ecumenical organizations and to the WORLD COUNCIL OF CHURCHES.

The principal factor in the growth of Baptists has been their widespread, though not universal, acceptance of the practices of revivalism and of modern missions.

Baptists continue to give their witness concerning baptism to other Christian churches. This creates difficulties for ecumenism (see ECUMENICAL MOVEMENT). Baptists simply do not recognize baptism done by means other than immersion, or any baptism of infants, as scriptural baptism.

Perhaps as a consequence of their having grown from a small, persecuted sect into a large, powerful group in many places, Baptists are less uniform in their commitment to free-dom than they originally were. For example, most Baptist churches still govern themselves democratically, difficult for very large congregations and this together with some loss of confidence that democratic government is a Biblical ideal, has led some Baptist churches to revert to a more presbyterian form of government. Again, the growth of denominational bureaucracies (see BUREAUCRACY) tends to give denominational leaders power over putatively autonomous congregations. Further, some Baptists are alarmed about the religious pluralism of modern nations and about the tendency of pluralism to render religion a private rather than a public matter; they have revised their commitment to government neutrality toward religion on the grounds that, unless government is tilted in favour of religion, it in effect supports a secular ideology. On the other hand, some Baptists continue to point out that the separation of church and state strengthens both entities, that bureaucracies exist to serve congregations not to dominate them, and that congregational decision-making may be difficult but is still the Baptist ideal.

For the future, it is unclear whether Baptists will continue to be faithful to their heritage concerning freedom. Their responses to RACISM have ranged from providing leadership for civil rights movements (Martin Luther King, Jr, Jesse Jackson) to entrenched resistance. Many Baptist denominations are polarized into conservative and progressive factions over theological issues such as the nature of Biblical authority. This may result eventually in the formation of new Baptist denominations, and this, in turn, may inhibit the ability of Baptists to sponsor missionary work.

Allen, C.J. and others (eds) (1958–82) *Encyclopedia of Southern Baptists*, 4 vols, Nashville, TN: Broadman.

Ammerman, N.T. (1988) *Bible Believers: Fundamentalists in the Modern World*, New Brunswick, NJ: Rutgers.

——(1990) *Baptist Battles: Social Change and Religious Conflict in the Southern Baptist Convention*, New Brunswick, NJ: Rutgers.

George, T. and Dockery, D.S. (eds) (1990) *Baptist Theologians*, Nashville, TN: Broadman.

Lumpkin, W.L. (1959) *Baptist Confessions of Faith*, Philadelphia, PA: Judson.

McBeth, H.L. (1987) *The Baptist Heritage: Four Centuries of Baptist Witness*, Nashville, TN: Broadman.

Maring, N.H. and Hudson, W.S. (1963) *A Baptist Manual of Polity and Practice*, Valley Forge, PA: Judson.

Payne, E.A. (1952) *The Fellowship of Believers: Baptist Thought and Practice Yesterday and Today*, London: Kingsgate.

Robinson, H.W. (1946) *The Life and Faith of the Baptists*, London: Kingsgate.

Tull, J.E. (1972) *Shapers of Baptist Thought*, Valley Forge, PA: Judson.

Fisher Humphreys

BLACK MUSLIMS

Black Muslims is the name coined by C.E. Lincoln for an American sect which was founded in 1930 among poor blacks in Detroit and which taught black racial supremacy. Although known to its members as the Lost–Found Nation of Islam, its links with Islam were originally only tenuous. After 1975, however, the parent body moved quickly towards Sunni orthodoxy, changing its name first to the World Community of al-Islam in the West and then, in 1980, to the American Muslim Mission. In 1979 a breakaway group led by Louis Farrakhan revived the original name and doctrines.

Like orthodox Muslims, members of the sect testify that there is no god but Allah and that Muhammad is the messenger of Allah. However, their understanding of what this entails is radically different. Whereas orthodox Muslims believe that Allah neither begets nor is begotten, and is the sole Creator of all races, Black Muslims believe that Allah is human and that he is exclusively concerned with blacks because they are his biological descendants. They hold that the white race is an aberrant creation, invented a mere 6,000 years ago by a rebellious black scientist called Mr Yakub, and destined to be annihilated in Armageddon, which will take place in North America before the end of the century. Whereas orthodox Muslims reject all notions of incarnation and redemption, the Black Muslims believe that their founder Wallace Fard was none other than Allah himself who had come in person to redeem them from their diabolic white oppressors.

Whereas for orthodox Muslims Muhammad the messenger of Allah is the seventh-century Arabian prophet, for Black Muslims he is Fard's successor, Elijah Muhammad, whose advent they maintain was foretold in the Biblical prophecy of the return of Elijah (Malachi 4: 5f.) and in the Qur'anic reference to Allah sending the illiterate a messenger of their own (Qur'an 72: 2). Lastly, whereas orthodox Muslims await a physical resurrection, Black Muslims believe that blacks who respond to Elijah Muhammad's message experience the resurrection here and now, through undergoing moral renewal and becoming conscious that it is time for them to receive justice. They do, it is true, believe in the hereafter, but this is conceived of as the rule of justice on this earth after the whites have been exterminated.

To understand the origin and development of the Black Muslims it is necessary to view the movement against the broad back-drop of American social history. The first Muslims in North America were slaves brought from West Africa but the initial policy of suppressing all African religions denied them the institutional structures necessary for preserving and propagating their faith. At the beginning of the eighteenth century, Protestant missionary societies were given permission to evangelize the slaves on the grounds that Christianity would make them more reliable. Their work resulted in the growth of segregated black congregations and then independent black churches. The abolition of SLAVERY in 1861 did little to alleviate the plight of the blacks who remained an underclass subject to poverty, unemployment and racist abuse. In 1913 Timothy Drew (alias Noble Drew Ali) started the Moorish-Science Movement and taught his followers that they were not to think of themselves as despised Negroes but as Moorish-Americans, descendants of the noble Moors from Africa who had once conquered parts of Europe. Drew's movement was a mixture of Christian revivalism and black nationalism which made use of some of the trappings of Islam. It spread from Newark, New Jersey, to a number of cities including Pittsburgh, Chicago and Detroit, but fizzled out after his death in 1929.

The next year, Wallace Fard (alias Wali

Farrad Muhammad) arrived in Detroit claiming that he had come from Mecca to redeem the American blacks and that they were all of Muslim descent. After three years spent instructing Elijah Poole, the son of an itinerant Baptist preacher, Fard vanished as suddenly and mysteriously as he had appeared, ostensibly returning to Mecca. Poole, whose name Fard changed to Elijah Muhammad, led the Nation of Islam for forty-one years and in its heyday it had over half a million members. He preached strict racial segregation, forbidding his followers to vote, salute the flag or join the armed forces. He encouraged them to be economically independent by starting black businesses and he petitioned the federal government to provide them a black homeland in North America. They adhered to a strict ethical code, abstaining from tobacco, alcohol and drugs and avoiding the use of cosmetics, cinema-going and other activities deemed likely to encourage sexual immorality. Although generally shunned by black intellectuals, the sect thrived amongst the urban poor and was far more successful than the churches and secular agencies in restoring the dignity of some of the most disaffected elements of society including drug abusers and prisoners.

Not all the Black Muslims were outcasts, however. In the 1950s, Malcolm X, Elijah Muhammad's second-in-command, succeeded in attracting better-educated and more affluent blacks. Nevertheless, for many of them the Nation of Islam was a staging post on the way towards Muslim orthodoxy. Then, in 1964, when Malcolm went on pilgrimage to Mecca, he learned from experience that all Muslims are brothers regardless of the colour of their skin (Malcolm X and Haley 1966: 338–47). Realizing that the racist doctrines of the Black Muslims were heretical, and distressed by his leader's involvement in a sexual scandal, he too left the Nation. Thus, even during Elijah Muhammad's lifetime there were those who saw the need for radical changes. They included his son Wallace whom he temporarily expelled three times for disobedience. When Wallace eventually succeeded his father in 1975, he changed his name to Warith to show his determination to break with the un-Islamic ideas associated with Wallace

Fard. He wasted no time in implementing the sweeping reforms which he had long had in mind, and the movement soon became orthodox and respectable. Although he has admitted whites and denied that they are intrinsically evil, Warith has tried to make Islam especially attractive to blacks by exploiting the myth of 'Ethiopianism' which has a long tradition in black religion. He has done this by decreeing that blacks should be called Bilalians, after Bilal the first muezzin who was an Ethiopian slave whom Muhammad enfranchised.

According to Ansari (1981: 139), Warith believes that Fard was a Qadiani (i.e. a member of the self-styled Ahmadiyya Muslims). Since they deny the finality of Muhammad's prophethood, this might account for Fard's designation of Elijah Muhammad as a prophet. There are precedents in Islamic history for some of the other peculiarities of Black Muslim doctrine which Warith has repudiated. For instance several of the extremist Shi'ite SECTS divinized their leaders, and in the twelfth century the Nizaris of Alamut claimed that the resurrection had taken place. Nevertheless, Ansari (1981: 169ff.) is surely right in suggesting that the closest parallels to the Black Muslim claims about Fard and Elijah Muhammad are to be found in contemporaneous black cults of predominantly Christian origin, and that the Black Muslim denial of life after death is a reaction against the 'excessive other-worldliness' of the black churches. However, when Ansari describes the teaching about black and white origins as a 'transparent counter-offensive to the well-entrenched white racist doctrines' he does not go far enough. It is important to recognize that this myth appeals to American blacks because it functions as a powerful THEODICY, explaining why whites are evil and why blacks suffer injustice at their hands (Mamiya 1982: 142).

As the year 2000 approaches, there is likely to be a resurgence of APOCALYPTIC sects of various kinds and in this climate Farrakhan's Nation of Islam will probably thrive at the expense of Warith Muhammad's American Muslim Mission. On the other hand, the American Muslim Mission is the largest Muslim organization in North America and may reasonably expect to continue to enjoy the patronage of the oil-rich Gulf States which see it as an important bridgehead for Islamic mission in the West.

Ansari, Z.I. (1981) 'Aspects of Black Muslim theology', *Studia Islamica* 53: 137–76.

Essien-Udom, E.U. (1962) *Black Nationalism: a Search for an Identity in America*, Chicago, IL: University of Chicago Press.

Lincoln, C.E. (1973) *The Black Muslims in America*, Boston, MA: Beacon Press.

——(1983) 'The American Muslim Mission in the context of American social history', in E.H. Waugh, B. Abu-Laban and R.B. Qureishi (eds) *The Muslim Community in North America*, Edmonton: University of Alberta Press, 216–33.

Malcolm X and Haley, A. (1966) *The Autobiography of Malcolm X*, New York: Grove Press.

Mamiya, L.H. (1982) 'From Black Muslim to Bilalian: the evolution of a movement', *Journal for the Scientific Study of Religion* 21: 138–52.

——(1983) 'Minister Louis Farrakhan and the final call: schism in the Muslim movement', in E.H. Waugh, B. Abu-Ladan and R.B. Qureishi (eds) *The Muslim Community in North America*, Edmonton: University of Alberta Press, 234–52.

Muhammad, Elijah (1957) *The Supreme Wisdom: Solution to the So-called Negroes' Problem*, Chicago, IL: University of Islam.

Neal Robinson

BLACK THEOLOGY

Black theology is concerned with the experience of black people everywhere. Being black is not generally considered to be an advantage. Skin colour is not merely a racial variable – it carries overtones of superiority and inferiority. Almost everywhere in the world, black people are perceived as 'hewers of wood' and 'drawers of water', as physically strong, and as superb athletes, but as mentally inferior, as childlike and, unless given firm guidance by the white races, as potentially criminal. This perception has been reinforced in some Protestant denominations by the identification of the black races with the descendants of Noah's son Ham. Ham, it will be remembered, was unfortunate enough to catch sight of his father naked and in a drunken stupor. In consequence next morning he was cursed by Noah and condemned to be a 'slave of slaves to his brothers' (Genesis 9: 24).

Black theology has arisen in response to this predicament. Like LIBERATION THEOLOGY, which originally grew out of the experience of exploitation and poverty in Latin America, black theology makes an attempt to understand and interpret the Christian message in the light of communal powerlessness. However, a distinction is often made between three different types of black theology. First, there is the theology which has developed in the independent countries of West and Central Africa. Here the emphasis is less on oppression and slavery and more on the reaffirmation of indigenous culture and religion. The aim has been, in the words of Bishop Tshibangu, to evolve a 'theology with an African colour'. In other words, African theology aims to express the eternal truths of Christianity in language and cultural forms which are familiar to and part of the African experience. The second variety of black theology evolved in South Africa under the APARTHEID regime. It grows out of a situation of legalized and systematic exploitation and discrimination. Apartheid was propounded and justified by many of the white South African Churches. The Afrikaners believed that God predestined the white races to rule over the black and that it was part of God's plan that the races should be separate and unequal. For black South Africans, the task has been to examine the Christian message and to preach the dignity and rights of people of all races. The third, and perhaps best-known, variety of black theology has grown out of the black experience of SLAVERY in North America. Like South African theology, it has evolved in response to poverty and powerlessness and it has provided an intellectual underpinning for continuing the civil rights struggle. Again there are clear similarities with Third World Latin American theology and also with feminist theology since all three modes of thought derive from an overwhelming sense of injustice and exploitation. RACISM is its central theme and its avowed aim is to rediscover the liberating message of the God of the Hebrew Bible and the Jesus of the Gospels.

African theology has developed in resistance to the Christianity preached as part of the ideology of colonialism. In the late nineteenth and early twentieth centuries, conversion to Christianity was often seen as a rejection of African culture and as a collaboration

with the European oppressor. As African nationalism developed in the mid-twentieth century, there was an attempt to rediscover indigenous modes of thought – so, for example, in
La Philosophie Bantoue (1949), the European
missionary Friar Placide Tempels expounded
the cosmological ideas of the Bantu tribes.
Drawing on the rediscovery of ancient African
thought, African theology became an attempt
to understand Christianity in a specifically African manner. Thus, for example, E. Bolaji
Idowu in *African Traditional Religion* (1975)
affirmed the validity of African traditions as a
basis for Christian theological speculation and
pastoral practice. This line of thought was endorsed by the Second Vatican Council in the
1960s.

It must be remembered that much of African
culture is not recorded in writing. It is retained
through dance, through song, through ceremony
and through story-telling. For many if not most
Europeans, it is impenetrable. The vitality of
worship and the creativeness of ritual of the
many small African Churches are astounding to
European observers. African theology grows
from such enthusiasm and, arguably, the major
task facing academic African theologians is the
translation of such activity into more universally
communicable forms.

Prominent African theologians include Gwinyai Muzorewa who traces the history of African
theology in *The Origin and Development of
African Theology* (1975) as does Kwesi Dickson
in *Theology in Africa* (1984). John S. Pobee,
who has worked for the World Council of
Churches in Geneva, discusses such doctrines
and phenomena as CHRISTOLOGY, SIN, social organization and POWER in the light of his native
tribal (Akan) culture. In his *Towards an African
Theology* (1979), his declared aim is to promote
a 'genuine dialogue between the Christian faith
and African culture' (p. 22), since 'there are
revelations of the deity other than the revelation
in Jesus Christ' (p. 74). He insists that an African Christian dialogue will not only propagate
Christian truths to the African people, but will
enrich mainstream Christianity itself. Less dependent on the revival and preservation of African culture, and with a greater emphasis on
liberation, is Jean-Marc Ela's *The African Cry*

(1981). Besides works of theory, the practical
pastorates of many prominent clergy should not
be forgotten in any survey of African theology.
Archbishop E. Milingo, for example, the author
of *The World Inbetween* (1984), exercises a
highly significant ministry of healing and exorcism; the activities of many like him are documented by Kalilombe (1985).

Over the years certain themes in African
theology have emerged. On the one hand it
rejects any mode of thought which regards the
European model of economic development and
social organization as the only way forward.
At the same time, the themes in Christianity
which reveal God's presence and interaction
with all peoples, which promote communal responsibility and which teach the interdependence of all creation are particularly emphasized.
The Hebrew Bible is a fruitful source. In identifying elements of Christianity which find an
echo in traditional African culture, not only
are African ways affirmed as being of inherent
value, but European racialism is also rebutted
and self-respect restored to the black peoples of
Africa. Inevitably, however, as mass communication brings an end to the isolation of the 'Dark
Continent', indigenous African culture is likely
to have a weaker hold over its inhabitants. It is
probable then that African theology will move
nearer to its Latin American counterpart and
show increased interest in social justice, human
rights, social reconstruction and human
liberation.

According to the Afrikaner view of history,
the Great Trek was an Exodus experience and
the Afrikaners themselves qualify as the
Chosen People of South Africa. In the same way
as the ancient Israelites were licensed by God to
slaughter and enslave the indigenous people of
Canaan, the white South Africans were entitled
to subjugate and rule over the black. According
to the 1942 draft constitution, 'In obedience to
Almighty God and to His Holy Word, the Afri-
kaaner people recognises its national calling,
manifested in the history of the voortrekers, as
being that of developing South Africa in accordance with the Christian faith' (translated and
quoted by Kalilombe 1989: 207). This historical
understanding led to the system of apartheid –
separate development – by which the whites

gained enormous social and economic advantage at the expense of the black and coloured communities.

Apartheid has been resisted on a political level by such organizations as the African National Congress and the Pan Africanist Congress. Because of its religious roots, it has also been tackled on a theological level. Multiracial organizations such as the Christian Institute (closed down by the government in 1977) and the University Christian Movement have encouraged the development of a distinctive South African Black theology. Collections of essays emerged from seminars in the early 1970s, such as that edited by Basil Moore (1973), stressing the profound injustice of the apartheid system. Predictably the regime did not welcome such initiatives, particularly those emanating from the All-Black South African Students' Organization led by Steve Biko. Biko was the author of *Black Consciousness and the Quest for a True Humanity* (1972) and he died in suspicious circumstances while in police custody. None the less South African theologians have continued to pursue their calling. Such works as Gabriel M. Setiloane's *African Theology: an Introduction* (1986) and Louise Kretzschmar's *The Voice of Black Theology in South Africa* (1986) survey the preoccupations of these thinkers. One of the most prominent thinkers is the Reverend Allan Boesak who was elected President of the World Reform Alliance directly after the white wing of the Dutch Reformed Church had been expelled from that organization. In *Black Theology, Black Power* (1978) and *Black and Reformed* (1984), he argues that Jesus must be seen as the Black Messiah, the liberator and the bringer of God's empowering Holy Spirit. By seeing Christ as one of themselves, black people can learn to love and respect themselves and to rediscover the image of God which is common to all humanity.

Unlike their counterparts in the north of the Continent, South African theologians have not been inclined to emphasize the intrinsic worth of Bantu culture. The apartheid system encouraged precisely that type of thinking in its policy of separate development. Consequently the South Africans have been far closer to the Latin Americans in their stress on social justice (although in general they are not Marxist in orientation). Since the mid-1970s, South African scholars have been making significant contributions to the conferences of the Ecumenical Association of Third World Theologians (EATWT). Most influential of all, however, has been the work of such prominent Churchmen as Bishop Manas Buthelezi (author of 'An African or a Black Theology' (1972)) and Nobel prizewinner Archbishop Desmond Tutu. Through their selfless pastoral ministries and their very public profiles, not only have they shared in the sufferings of their people, but they have brought that suffering to the attention of the world.

It is difficult to predict how theology will develop in South Africa now that the white government has crumbled and DEMOCRACY has been established. It may be that the South Africans will become more interested in their unique African spiritual roots. On the other hand, they may continue to pursue their role as conscience of the regime, preaching their eternal message of justice, freedom and peace and goodwill among men.

Black American theology emerged in the 1960s and 1970s but grew out of the experience of slavery. In the eighteenth and nineteenth centuries, many thousands of black people were captured from their native West Africa and were shipped in appalling conditions across the Atlantic Ocean. The white slaveowners ignored all tribal and religious loyalties. The black slaves were property and, as property, they took on the religion of their masters. However, as many have found before them, there is a strong subversive element in Christianity and this was quickly siezed upon by the slaves. Many Negro spirituals of the nineteenth century draw on the Biblical narratives to express their longing for liberation and justice ('Nobody knows the troubles I've seen, Nobody knows but Jesus ...', 'Go down Moses, Way down to Egypt land; Tell old Pharaoh, Let my people go'.) Even after the Civil War when slavery was abolished in the USA, the black community continued to be exploited. Segregation meant poorer schools, inadequate health care and fewer economic opportunities. Even in the industrial cities of the north, the blacks enjoyed few of the advantages of their white neighbours.

It is no coincidence that many of the civil rights and Black Power leaders were church people. The independent Black Churches provided a training ground for preaching, teaching and social action. In the early years of this century, the resilience and influence of the churches was remarkable. They provided a vision of a successful community based on self-help and mutual interdependence. A formal statement of Black theology did not emerge until 1966 when *A Statement by the National Committee of the Negro Churches* (quoted in Wilmore and Cone 1979: 23–30) was issued. By that time many young Blacks had become disillusioned with the civil rights movement as led by Martin Luther King and had turned to such as Malcolm X and the Black Power movement. Previously it was argued by Joseph Washington in *Black Religion: The Negro and Spirituality in the United States* (1964) that the ideas and values of black Christianity needed to be integrated into contemporary Protestantism. This was totally rejected by Albert Cleage, the Pastor of the Shrine of the Black Madonna in Detroit, Michigan. In his *Black Messiah* (1969) he argued that blacks must free themselves from the oppressive religious doctrines of white Christianity. He maintained that the Hebrew Scriptures were in fact composed by black Jews and were subsequently reworked by the Apostle Paul to make them acceptable to Europeans (*see* BLACK MUSLIMS).

Initially Black American theology primarily developed within the churches, but by the 1970s Black Studies had become a new subject within the university curriculum. Central to academic black theology has been the work of James Cone whose prolific output includes *Black Theology and Black Power* (1969), *A Black Theology of Liberation* (1970), *The Spirituals and the Blues* (1972), *God of the Oppressed* (1975) and *For My People* (1984). Cone teaches at the Union Theological Seminary in New York. He is concerned with exploring the interface between God's Word as revealed in Scripture, on the one hand, and the black experience on the other. He stresses that 'one's social and

historical context decides not only the questions we address to God, but also the mode or form of the answers given to the questions' (1975: 15) and he wrestles with such questions as the role of Jesus Christ in the world today, the meaning of liberation and the relationship between liberation and violence. He is nothing if not combative. He argues that 'Black Theology seeks to analyse the Satanic nature of Whiteness and by doing so to prepare all Non-Whites for revolutionary action' (1970: 8). Later in the same work, he remarks that 'Black Theology will accept only a love of God which participates in the destruction of the White Oppressor' (p. 72) and that the oppressed must serve warning 'that they "ain't gonna take no more of this bullshit, but a new day is coming and it ain't gonna be like today".' (p. 128).

Cone is not working in isolation. Other eminent Black American theologians include Deotis Roberts, G.S. Wilmore, Cecil Cone, G. Eric Lincoln, Cornel West, Charles Long, Vincent Harding, Jacquelyn Grant, Dolores Williams and Kelly Brown. In addition, by 1979 black Americans were in dialogue with the other minorities in the Theology in the Americas Project. They are also involved in the conferences of the EATWT where, for the first time, they have come into sustained contact with Black Africans. Initially there was suspicion. The Americans felt that the Africans were too concerned with the past while the Africans believed that the Americans were obsessed with social and political issues (for a survey of this conflict see Young 1986). Interestingly since the founding of the EATWT relationships have been far more harmonious. The Africans accept that their struggle is also partly a rebuttal of racism and that they too are part of the liberation initiative. The Americans in their turn see that their thinking is enriched by the insights of Africa and that they have much in common with all Third World theologies.

Black theology has provided a searing indictment of traditional Christianity and offers an interesting and radical reappraisal. There is no doubt that it strikes a chord. The most superficial reading of the Exodus story, the words of the eighth-century prophets or the Sermon on the Mount indicates that God is on the side of justice. In the kingdom of God we are promised that the values of this world will be reversed – the lion will lie down with the lamb, the mighty will be cast down from their seats and the meek will inherit the earth. This, however, is only one part of the Christian message. Parallel to the social revolution is promised an otherworldly element – 'Great will be your reward in Heaven'. Karl Marx may have been morally correct in his disapproval of Christianity because it made the proletariat content with disgraceful working conditions in anticipation of future blessedness. None the less a spiritual heaven is a part of the tradition and it is a distortion to ignore it (*see* ESCHATOLOGY).

The emphasizing of certain elements to the exclusion of others is characteristic not only of Black theology but also of all feminist and liberation theologies. All too often Black theology goes one step further. So zealous are its disciples for justice for the Black community that inconvenient facts are simply discounted. An extreme example is the previously mentioned work of Albert Cleage who insists that Jesus was a black Jew. James Cone explains this further: 'It seems to me the *literal* colour of Jesus is irrelevant. . . . Therefore Albert Cleage is not too far wrong when he describes Jesus as a Black Jew, and he is certainly on solid theological ground when he describes Christ as the Black Messiah' (1970: 123). From this he goes on to argue that 'to participate in God's salvation is to cooperate with the Black Christ as he liberates his people from bondage. . . . The new day is the presence of the Black Christ as expressed in the liberation of the Black community' (p. 128).

For better or worse Christianity is a religion based on history. Jesus of Nazareth was a historical person. No doubt it would have been better for the condition of black people in the twentieth century if Jesus had been of African descent. Similarly it would have improved the lot of women if he had had a double X rather than an XY chromosome structure. Unfortunately, however, he was, as a matter of fact, neither black nor female. To maintain that he was black but not literally black is to move into a Looking Glass world where, as Humpty Dumpty said to Alice, words mean what we want them to mean.

It weakens the black theology case to pretend that the liberation of the black community is the only proper concern of the followers of Jesus. Jesus is more than a Black Messiah. He is the Alpha, the Omega, the First and the Last, the Beginning and the End. He is the One in whom all humanity – men as well as women, rich as well as poor, white as well as black – find their true fulfilment.

Biko, Steve (1972) *Black Consciousness and the Quest for a True Humanity,* Durban: Lutheran Publishing House.

Boesak, Allan (1978) *Black Theology, Black Power,* New York: Orbis.

——(1984) *Black and Reformed,* New York: Orbis.

Buthelezi, Manas (1972) 'An African or a Black Theology' in H.J. Becken (ed.) *Relevant Theology for Africa,* Durban: Lutheran Publishing House.

Cleage, Albert (1969) *Black Messiah,* New York.

Cone, James H. (1969) *Black Theology and Black Power,* New York: Seabury.

——(1970) *A Black Theology of Liberation,* New York: Orbis.

——(1972) *The Spirituals and the Blues,* New York: Seabury.

——(1975) *God of the Oppressed,* New York: Seabury.

——(1984) *For My People,* New York: Orbis.

Dickson, Kwesi (1984) *Theology in Africa,* London: Darton, Longman and Todd.

Ela, Jean-Marc (1981) *The African Cry,* New York: Orbis.

Ferm, Dean (1986) *Third World Theologies,* Maryknoll, New York: Orbis.

Idowu, E. Bolaji (1975) *African Traditional Religion,* London: SCM.

Kalilombe, Patrick A. (1985) 'Doing theology at the grassroots: a challenge for professional theologians', *African Ecclesial Review* 24: 148–61.

——(1989) 'Black theology', in David Ford (ed.) *The Modern Theologians,* vol. II, Oxford: Blackwell.

Kretzschmar, Louise (1986) *The Voice of Black Theology in South Africa,* Johannesburg: Raven Press.

Lincoln, C. Eric (ed.) (1974) *The Black Experience in Religion,* New York.

Milingo, E. (1984) *The World Inbetween,* London: SCM.

Moore, Basil (1973) *Essays in Black Theology,* London: C. Hurst.

Muzorewa, Gwinyai (1985) *The Origin and Development of African Theology,* New York: Orbis.

Parratt, John (1987) *A Reader in African Christian Theology,* London: SPCK.

Pobee, John S. (1979) *Towards an African Theology,* Nashville, TN: Abingdon.

Setiloane, Gabriel M. (1986) *African Theology: an Introduction,* Johannesburg: Skotaville Publishers.

Tempels, Placide (1949) *La Philosophie Bantoue,* Kinshasa, Zaïre: Limete.

Washington, Joseph (1964) *Black Religion: The Negro and Spirituality in the United States*, Boston: Beacon.

Wilmore, Gayraud S. and Cone, James H. (eds) (1979) *Black Theology: A Documentary History 1966–1979*, New York: Orbis.

Witvliet, Theo (1985) *A Place in the Sun*, London: SCM.

Young, Joseph U. (1986) *Black and African Theologies: Siblings or Distant Cousins*, New York: Orbis.

Lavinia Cohn-Sherbok

BLASPHEMY

No single understanding of blasphemy (Greek: *blasphēmia*, slander, profane speech) is widely accepted, but most definitions make reference to the idea of *contemptuous or offensive speech about God* – in short, the defamation of the divine. If this were sufficient, blasphemy could be identified in the conjunction of three specific factors: a particular *manner* (insulting), *means* (spoken or written words) and *object* (God). It is true that some religious authorities do narrow the application of the term in just this way, so that phenomena failing to meet these precise conditions are treated as offences less serious than blasphemy. On the other hand, in many religious traditions blasphemy has a much wider scope: its means may include signs and gestures, and its objects may include sacred books, persons, practices and beliefs.

The attempt to establish a comprehensive definition is frustrated in a variety of ways. First, it is hard to plot the position of blasphemy in absolute terms since its conceptual neighbourhood – typically involving ideas like idolatry, apostasy, profanity, sacrilege, heresy and OBSCENITY – has not been noted for semantic stability. Moreover, as the boundaries between 'legitimate' and 'illegitimate' dissent from religious orthodoxy have shifted, so understandings of blasphemy have changed too. It follows that essentialist accounts of blasphemy based on its content alone are unsatisfactory; and even an account geared to the intention of the blasphemer (Perret 1987) can fail to do justice to contextual factors and some good *prima facie* cases of blasphemy (Hoffman 1983, 1989). The identification of blasphemy happens within traditions of *interpretation*, and involves irreducibly local conflicts over the legitimacy of words and actions.

More specifically, understandings of blasphemy vary dramatically between (and within) religious traditions. Jewish thought has reserved the idea of blasphemy for the cursing of God, deeming nothing else capable of being blasphemed as such. This minimalism was perfected in legal developments which made it hard to secure a prosecution for blasphemy, and harder still to commit the offence in the first place. Christian theology, however, extended the scope of the term considerably – if not systematically – and its subsequent career as a pretext for the persecution of dissent is infamous (e.g. Levy 1981). In fact, 'blasphemy' and 'heresy' were virtually synonymous until the former re-emerged at the Reformation as a separate (but still amorphous) idea. Sophisticated theological discussions have done little to defuse the explosive rhetorical force which has been the most obvious feature of Christian discourse on blasphemy. In Islamic thought, ideas similar to that of blasphemy have been conceptually related to infidelity and apostasy. Given the theological structure of Islam, it is far from surprising that not only God but also the revealed Qur'an and the Prophet can (in effect) be blasphemed. This is hardly the beginning of religious diversity – but it is enough to suggest that the attempt to manufacture an 'essential' concept of blasphemy is a hopeless one.

The point about essentialism is important. Secular commentators object most to religious traditions which operate with ideas of blasphemy in excess of a roughly comprehensible theocentric 'essence' – even if this is an ahistorical fiction. But the narrowness or breadth of any particular understanding of blasphemy is not an index of religious sensitivity (as if Muslims were somehow more 'touchy' than Jews): it is a function of the 'grammar' of complex religious identities. Therefore it makes no sense to think that *all* believers should restrict the idea of blasphemy to the vilification of God, since this might falsify the character and content of their belief. Religious ideas, including concepts of blasphemy, can be superficially similar and yet incommensurable in depth.

The concept of blasphemy is intelligible enough at a religious level: in taking blasphemy in their midst seriously, religious groups affirm the seriousness of their commitments. This 'internal' censorship is an inevitable factor in the conservation of group identity; it should not be confused with forms of 'external' censorship which it need not necessarily entail (Alan Unterman, in Cohn-Sherbok 1990). There are, of course, theological critiques of the concept of blasphemy (e.g. Sara Maitland, in Cohn-Sherbok 1990), and even theological celebrations of blasphemy itself (e.g. Sangharakshita 1978), but these do not render unintelligible as such the prohibition of blasphemy within religious communities. Instead, the real problem concerns the intelligibility of the concept of blasphemy at a social and legal level. Can the STATE ever be justified in placing limits on what can be said about religion? In addressing this question, it is helpful to consider some legal developments in England.

Although there have been statutes such as the 1697 Blasphemy Act (repealed in 1967), the crime of blasphemy was originally defined in common law – and there it has been redefined ever since. Successive legal judgements have illustrated changing understandings of blasphemy, and in particular a kind of 'SECULARIZATION': in part, the growing perception that if blasphemy is a crime it is because of its social effects, not its innate sinfulness.

In early modern England, blasphemy was viewed as treason against God as well as against lawful goverment; in other words, the law still embodied and acted upon a theological judgement. But as heresy became a matter confined to the ecclesiastical courts, it was perhaps inevitable that the secular courts would justify their prosecution of blasphemy in less obviously theological terms – by appealing to national rather than divine integrity, for example. 'Christianity being parcel of the laws of England', Lord Chief Justice Hale declared in 1676 (R. v. Taylor), 'therefore to reproach the Christian religion is to speak in subversion of the law.' This was a crucial judgement, drawing on the intimate connection between religion and social stability presupposed by traditional religious communities in their dealings with blasphemy. But Hale's understanding of that connection was highly specific, and thus peculiarly vulnerable to changing social realities.

By the late nineteenth century it was harder to believe that blasphemy was seditious or, indeed, that all attacks on Christianity were necessarily blasphemous. Lord Chief Justice Coleridge's judgement of 1883 (R. v. Ramsey and Foote), that 'if the decencies of controversy are observed, even the fundamentals of religion may be attacked without a person being guilty of blasphemous libel', was therefore very significant. It suggested that blasphemy was unacceptable because it involved offending (as opposed to subverting) society, and argued that blasphemy lay not in *what* was said but *how*. This shift from 'matter' to 'manner' severely restricted the scope of the law. Further restriction was to follow as, for example, when possible provocation of a breach of the peace became a component of the offence.

In the late 1970s the successful prosecution of *Gay News* (*Lemon* 1979) revived a law that had been thought a 'dead letter' for decades. In some ways, the judgement reversed the tendency towards restricting the scope of the law: there was no need to prove an *intention* to blaspheme, and the breach of the peace qualification was attenuated too. But perhaps the case was most significant in showing the final outcome of the secularization of blasphemy: what was held to be at risk was not God's honour, nor the state's integrity, but a group's feelings. That the prosecution was a private one only underlines the point.

The 'privatization' of religion, therefore, and the secularization of the state are the processes which have shaped the modern history of the concept of blasphemy. At one time the religious and social aspects of blasphemy were inseparable. Now blasphemy is usually thought a purely religious concept, a bizarre relic of 'sacred law'; yet it has survived legally, unlike heresy because of its progressive redefinition in *secular* terms. Moreover, the unsustainable theses of the old common law judgements have been abandoned. The law does not assume that Christianity is true, or even morally necessary; nor does it presuppose a connection between blasphemy and sedition, or even between blasphemy and public disorder. Rather, it is the *sensibilities* of Christians, as opposed to their actual beliefs, which are deemed entitled to legal recognition and protection. In short, blasphemy can be judged harmful because the offending of religious feelings can be construed as the harming of interests.

The case for the abolition (without replacement) of the common law offence of blasphemy is a very strong one. First, there is a historical argument: blasphemy laws are utterly discredited by the violent persecution they have legitimized through the ages (Levy 1981, 1993; Walter 1990). Second, there is a legal argument. There are, after all, many serious defects in the existing law. For example: blasphemy seems to have become a 'strict liability' offence, despite a growing stress on intention elsewhere in the law; blasphemy law requires highly subjective distinctions between 'matter' and 'manner', between degrees of offensiveness, and so forth, which are far from straightforward; and it assumes, optimistically, that religious feelings can and should be distinguished from other strongly held feelings (Jones 1980). But the most obvious problem with the law is that it protects the feelings of Christians alone, as British Muslims found out early in the controversy over *The Satanic Verses* in the late 1980s. If the blasphemy law is meant to protect religious sensibilities rather than the content of religious beliefs, it is illogical as well as unethical to confine legal protection to the sensibilities of Christians. And yet to extend the scope of the law would be to introduce many new problems: it would be unfair to protect *some* religions only, and unfeasible to protect *all* – even assuming that 'religion' could be defined. Third, there is the 'free speech' argument: freedom of expression is an absolute good, and its curtailing – the effect of blasphemy law – is absolutely wrong. Grounded in the philosophy and rhetoric of liberal DEMOCRACY, this is the core of the abolitionist case. It has attracted wide support since the publication of *The Satanic Verses*.

The liberal consensus is that there is no more to be said on the subject. But outstanding contributions from Richard Webster (1990) and Simon Lee (1990a,b, 1992) have kept the issue open, and I wish now to join their dissenting voices in sketching some reasons for caution.

First, this liberal abolitionist approach involves an arbitrary deployment of the discourse of rights. In practice, the right to free expression is limited by legislation on race relations, obscenity, public order, libel and so on – and would be unthinkable otherwise. Moreover, it is a right among other rights, including the right to practise one's religion without harassment; the two occur together in both UN and European HUMAN RIGHTS conventions. Therefore talk of the absolute right of free expression being threatened by religious persecution is, at best, misleading and unhelpful. Second, the liberal approach involves the arrogant dismissal of the self-understanding of certain communities. It cannot allow that religion is as important as race (or more so) in determining identity: to do so would be to admit that there can be incitement to religious as well as to racial hatred, and hence to concede the need for legislation parallel to the Race Relations Act. In other words, the liberal approach sustains a specifically Western, secular and reductive account of religious belief as a 'private' matter, distinct from (and liable to conflict with) the moral and political beliefs which all rational people can and should share. Unable to recognize its own cultural contingency, it recasts a real conflict between complex and incommensurable worldviews as a mythical conflict between the universal and the particular, between reason and mere 'feelings'. Thus it advocates a method for resolving conflict while covertly advancing the beliefs of one of the conflicting parties. It may be naïve, therefore, to let 'free speech fundamentalists' dictate the rules of a game in which they are committed players.

So what should happen to the blasphemy law? Neither the *retention* nor the *extension* of the present law can carry legal or moral conviction. But straight *abolition* would not in itself put everyone on an equal footing: because the 'privatizing' of censorship (Lee) and the 'internalizing' of the blasphemy taboo (Webster) would continue to protect Christian sensitivities in an informal way, Muslims (among others) would still suffer disproportionate abuse – and the law's denial that religion significantly constitutes identity would make the situation even worse. There is a strong case, then, for replacing the present law with legislation which will balance conflicting rights while recognizing the duties of citizens in a plural society. A possible new offence could be based on the idea of *group libel*, or *the deliberate outraging of religious feelings* (favoured by the minority report of the Law Commission in 1985), or *incitement to religious hatred*. Each has some kinship with existing legislation (on libel, blasphemy and obscenity, and racial discrimination respectively), but builds in safeguards appropriate to its subject matter. With Lee I think the last of these is the most promising: it leaves the maximum room for free speech (being designed for extreme cases only); it does not rely upon misleading talk about 'feelings'; and it seems to stand the best chance of achieving a workable legal form. Above all, it would take seriously the role of religion in forming social identity, and in so doing rescue the present law's only virtue from its unacceptable setting.

There is nothing parochial about this discussion: similar dilemmas have faced (and will face) legislators in many other countries. Indeed, the way forward proposed by Lee is particularly relevant in that it would bring British law into line with international legal obligations – and these can no longer be ignored in the debate on blasphemy and religious offence in the contemporary world. Where the discussion is in danger of narrowness, in fact, is in its focus on *legal* remedies for social problems. Serious commentators (like Lee and Webster) help us to see that what we need is not so much legislation as imagination: the exercise of sympathy, the ability to look through another's eyes. And this will entail a discipline of discernment: 'there has been too much emphasis on the *right* to free speech and not enough on the rights and wrongs of choosing when, where and how to exercise that right' (Lee 1990a: 20). Theologians could, perhaps, try to salvage, from the bleak history of blasphemy, something relevant to conflict management in a plural society. But they would be better employed, and would be drawing on far richer resources, in helping to foster the imagination and discernment which nurture a common social life in the midst of irreducible diversity.

Asad, T. (1993) *Genealogies of Religion: Discipline and Reasons of Power in Christianity and Islam*, Baltimore: John Hopkins University Press.

Cohn-Sherbok, D. (ed.) (1990) *The Salman Rushdie Controversy in Inter-Religious Perspective*, Lewiston, NY: Edwin Mellen Press.

D' Costa, G. (1990) 'Secular discourse and the clash of faiths: *The Satanic Verses* in British society', *New Blackfriars* 71 (842): 418–22.

Hoffman, F.J. (1983) 'Remarks on blasphemy', *Scottish Journal of Religious Studies* 4(2): 138–51.

——(1989) 'More on blasphemy', *Sophia* 28(2): 26–34.

Jones, P. (1980) 'Blasphemy, offensiveness and law', *British Journal of Political Science* 10(2): 129–48.

Law Commission (1981) *Offences Against Religion and Public Worship* (Working Paper 79), London: Law Commission.

——(1985) *Offences Against Religion and Public Worship* (Report 145), London: Law Commission.

Lawton, D. (1993) *Blasphemy*, Hemel Hempstead: Harvester Wheatsheaf.

Lee, S. (1990a) 'First introductory paper', *Law, Blasphemy and the Multi-Faith Society*, London: Commission for Racial Equality.

——(1990b) *Cost of Free Speech*, London: Faber & Faber.

——(1992) 'Religion and the law: ways forward', in D. Bowen (ed.) *'The Satanic Verses': Bradford Responds*, Bradford: Bradford and Ilkley Community College.

Levy, L.W. (1981) *Treason Against God: A History of the Offense of Blasphemy*, New York: Schocken.

——(1993) *Blasphemy: Verbal Offense Against the Sacred, from Moses to Salmon Rushdie*, New York: Knopf.

Perret, R.W. (1987) 'Blasphemy', *Sophia* 26(2): 4–14.

Sangharakshita, M.S. (1978) *Buddhism and Blasphemy*, London: Windhorse Publications.

Simpson, R. (1993) *Blasphemy and the Law in a Plural Society*, Bramcote: Grove Books.

Sprigge, T.L.S. (1990) 'The satanic novel: a philosophical dialogue on blasphemy and censorship', *Inquiry* 33(4): 337–400.

Walter, N. (1990) *Blasphemy Ancient and Modern*, London: Rationalist Press Association.

Webster, R. (1990) *A Brief History of Blasphemy: Liberalism, Censorship and 'The Satanic Verses'*, Southwold: Orwell Press.

Colin Crowder

BONDAGE

Article 4 of the UN Declaration of Human Rights 1948 states that, 'No one shall be held in slavery or servitude; slavery and the slave trade shall be prohibited in all their forms.' Notwithstanding this it is estimated that there are currently 200 million people in the world who are held in some recognized form of slavery. There are an unknown number of people beyond that who live in some form of bondage or service condition and a further and similarly unknown number of people having the status, or less, of a slave or bondsperson by virtue of having no political identity. Stateless people, refugees, dispossessed peoples, illegal immigrants, and so called 'guest' workers have a status that reduces or even eliminates freedom. The imagery of bondage, servitude and slavery is powerful and may refer to any form of heteronomy. The philosopher David Hume spoke of 'reason' as 'the slave of the passions', relatedly we speak also of being 'a slave to desire', to needs, and to addictions or habits. These phrases, if metaphorical, indicate the absence of AUTONOMY, control over one's self. Strictly understood, however, bondage and slavery is the condition of being under the control of another person, at its worst it may also include a lack of political or even legal status. It may involve the absence of legal personality and even the denial of humanity. It may be temporary or permanent. Servitude by contrast is assumed to be temporary but may *de facto* be permanent. Additionally there is even in so-called free countries and among so-called free people a well established attitude of self-effacing behaviour that often amounts to servility.

Bondage and its more extreme form of chattel slavery, far from being unusual in the modern world, has actually been extended beyond its ancient origins. Even on narrow definitions of bondage and slavery – institutionalized bondage principally, chattel slavery, debt bondage, child slavery – there are now more people worldwide in some form of bondage than at any previous time. If bondage, servility and slavery is defined more widely as the absence of 'having a share in the operations of one's own life' (Rousseau, 1994) then the absence of some kind of position is the privilege of few.

The relation of Christianity to bondage and servility is, in common with some other universalizing modes of thought, two-sided. In its universalism it embodies, like stoicism and humanism, principles that if carried through to their conclusion are opposed to such bondage.

That Christianity has sometimes been comfortable with and indeed even embraced bondage, servility and slavery is due first, to the alternate side of Christianity: its particularism, and second, to the extension of a Biblical view that all Christians are in bondage to God. In consequence an exclusive Christianity has sometimes been blind to the condition of non-Christians while also being indifferent to the secular and other inequalities among those who are included in the domain of Christians.

The particular source of the word *slavery* is *slav*; the present meaning was transferred from the conditions of some of the slavonic peoples of Central Europe who as a result of conquest were held in a servile and inferior condition. The term obtained its present meaning by the ninth century although the institutions of bondage, slavery and manners of servility are known to be several thousand years older and can be found in parts of the ancient world. It is probable that the institution of formal bondage as opposed to the casual, occasional or haphazard, holding of someone at the will of another, came into being with the emergence of kingdoms and representative kingship, evidence of which can be found 2500–3500 BCE. There is some slight evidence, principally archaeological, of human conflict before that time but it was probably occasional, haphazard and disorganized. Representative kingship was probably instituted in an attempt to deal with emergencies facing groups initially related by kin. As such groups threatened others, and were threatened by others, they became a distinct peoples and came to recognize themselves as such. As Hegel was later to point out this recognition of self and other is vital to the formation of bondage. The earliest forms of human self-consciousness were primarily group centred. What was valuable in self-identity was obtained from the identification with the values of the group. That which is familiar is given a higher value than that which is strange and that which is strange is rejected or subjugated. The earliest groups, and therefore the members of those groups, became conscious of their particular identity in opposition to other groups. As they became conscious of themselves so those groups who were successful valued themselves as purveyors of some quality, civilization, humanity, not found in other peoples. The growth of bondage developed alongside the growth of the values of civilization and of humanity. Bondage and slavery is humanity's other; in Hegel's model the bondsman is the antithesis of the master who is human: a sense of humanity is gained against the backdrop of the condition of bondage. Bondage flourishes best in conditions where a people regards itself as having an identity through time and who represents themselves as the purveyor of civilized and human values. Bondage is not, and paradoxically, the invention of barbarous peoples, it is the invention of self-styled civilized peoples regarding themselves as incorporating the highest values of humanity, and who see the stranger as outside those values. Modes of thought that have a strong sense of what counts as group belonging or membership also have a strong sense of what counts as not belonging and of not meeting membership critieria. Historically Christianity has been no more exempt from this process than any another group regarding itself as inculcating thoughtful and civilizing values. Sometimes, and in some respects, the bondsman has EQUALITY on a basis independently of the social group, as before God. Sometimes, and in other respects, that value even if accepted does not carry over into social action.

The ambivalent attitude of Christianity towards the bondsman is shown clearly in the expiation of the vocabulary of bondage and slavery from modern English renderings of the New Testament. The Greek *doulos*, slave, is consistently rendered as servant yet the institution of bondage was, and had been for some time, widespread throughout both the Roman world and Ancient Greece. One of the earliest references to chattel bondage occurs in conjunction with the invention of CITIZENSHIP. In the poetry of Solon, Archon of Athens approx. 490 BCE we find that Athenians are falling into bondage slavery in far off lands as a consequence of the ills that have befallen the city. Those ills Solon regarded as self-imposed, brought about as a consequence of turning from JUSTICE, who, ultimately, cannot be avoided. In Athens by the time of Pericles perhaps $\frac{1}{4}$ to $\frac{1}{2}$ of population were in conditions of chattel

bondage. Citizens led a life primarily of *Skole*, of LEISURE, and that life depended on such bondage. In the nature of things little is known about the inner life of such people, they have a place in ancient literature, in the comedies of Aristophanes, and in the philosophy of Plato and Aristotle, but they are not the writers of that literature or philosophy. People in bondage were despised and ill-regarded, they were not regarded as fully human, but nor in general were they ill treated or wantonly killed by their master. Aristotle, who places friendship as vital to human relations, suggests that one cannot be friends with a bondsman. As an extension of this SAME-SEX RELATIONS with male bondsman was not possible. That female slaves were regarded as available to serve the master indicates not the special status of the female in this respect but that relations with women were always unequal. That Aristotle regarded slavery as a natural condition was to have a profound influence on the Christianity that followed the neo-Aristotelian teachings of Thomas Aquinas and much of medieval scholasticism.

Only in Stoic philosophy was the idea of a universal humanity extended to bondsmen. Zeno's *Republic*, not now extant but influential both in idea and in imagery, seems to have held out the promise of a universal CITY guided by the light of the sun, in which particular differences between people, including differences of sex and race, were eliminated (see Schofield, 1991). Menander wrote of the noble slave. Such philosophy, however, had little practical effect on the lives of such oppressed people. Stoicism was widely adopted in Rome, but its affect on the lives of bondspeople was limited. At the time of early Christianity slavery was a long established and virtually unchallenged practice. One of the few challenges to bondage came, approx. 60 CE, in the writings of the Stoic philosopher Seneca. Seneca (*De Beneficiis*, 3, 18–28; Letter 47 to Lucius) considered that slaves could exhibit qualities of virtue. Slaves and free men have, he argues, a common origin. Slaves, like free men, share the passions in common, to which, he says in true Stoic fashion, they are both bound. It is from this Stoic idea that the notion of men as subject to their passions developed

In Hume it finds its expression as the view that reason is the slave of the passions. In Kant it finds its expression in the view that the truly free man, the autonomous man, acts on reason alone and not merely according to passion and in Hegel in the view that freedom requires consciousness of that freedom. Seneca's view that those in bondage are human is notable for its novelty. In principle the development of Christianity should have brought a serious challenge to the institution of bondage but Christianity found the institution in its Judaic background, in its Greek language and in its Roman institutions. The fact and the imagery of slavery are strong in both the Hebrew Bible and in the New Testament. As Seneca thought a bondsman could be virtuous, or not, so a significant imagery of the New Testament is of the good and the bad slave (Matthew 25: 14–30; Luke 19: 11–27). The imagery of Mark 10: 43, 'whoever has a mind to be the greatest among you must be your servant, and whoever has a mind to be first among you, must be the slave of all' prefigures some of the political imagery of Rousseau's general will. Perhaps most importantly in its universality Christianity admitted Jew and Gentile, rich and poor, slave and freeman to the possibility of salvation. Those in bondage have a soul, hence the difference between master and bondsman is merely an earthly one. As an earthly difference it was, nevertheless, in the view of some major church fathers a natural rather than a conventional difference. By extension some primitive peoples were naturally fitted to servility, a doctrine that influenced some Christian attitudes to the slavery of certain peoples. The difference that this particularism raised was not a difference that Christianity was able to fundamentally challenge until well after the universalizing effects of the humanism of the Renaissance.

The principle figure in the challenge to some major particularizing effects of the church was Dante Alighieri (1265–1321) who was the virtual inventor, or following the early Stoics the virtual re-inventor, of the idea of a universal humanity. The terms *humanitas* and *humana civilitas* which meant a humane or civil manner came in Dante's hands to mean the human race, mankind, a term which included Christians,

Moslems, Jews, and Pagans. The distinguishing feature of human life was to be found in will and liberty. In freedom man's being was unconditioned, existing for its own sake and not for some other end. This idea of the proper mode of human being as unconditioned being was later to be reiterated in Kant's idea of the Categorical Imperative, one formulation of which demands that humanity be treated, in oneself and in others never merely as a means but also as an end in itself. For Dante the proper expression of unconditioned being was to be found in *polizare*, political activity for the sake of being human; POLITICS. For Kant the proper expression of unconditioned being was to be found in morality. Such universalizing sentiments did not, however, find an immediate and direct way into undercutting either the principle or the practice of bondage. Later humanists were able to refer back to Aristotle's view that slavery was a natural condition, argue that some races were not fully human, that one could sell oneself into bondage, or be taken by conquest when one's life would otherwise be forfeit. Through such devices bondage was justified even in the face of declarations asserting the rights of man. James Madison had argued in the Federalist Papers, in 1787, that slaves were part persons and part property; as property they were excluded from government. In *Dredd Scott v Sanford*, 1857, Chief Justice Roger B. Taney for the US Supreme Court held that a Negro could not bring a suit in the court of Missouri. Members of 'the Negro race' were regarded by the constitution 'as a separate class of persons' and those persons who were members of 'the Negro race' are not 'included and not intended to be included, under the word "citizens"', as such they could not exercise the rights and privileges of the union. It followed that the words of the Declaration of Independence did not apply to members of 'the Negro race' who were but part persons.

This acceptance of the idea that there could be part persons in spite of the existence of ideals which were otherwise universalistic and humanistic was widespread. It demonstrates clearly the ability that people have to hold contradictory principles without difficulty or qualm. The challenge to this Janus-faced humanism came from several quarters. The principles of its own destruction had been contained within it, even back to its Stoic origins, but it was from Christianity that the impetus to that destruction came. The claim that all men were bound to God, including the kenotic Jesus, 'who, though he was in the form of God, did not count equality with God as a thing to be grasped, but emptied himself, taking the form of a slave, being born to the likeness of men' (Philippians 2: 6–7), provided a model of equality and universality. When given an appropriate universalistic reading and the appropriate historical circumstances this model evidenced itself in the social and political action necessary to end institutionalized chattel slavery. In England that action came in consequence of the actions of Quakers, who held all men to be equal not merely in a sacral sense but in a secular sense also. These arguments had considerable effect on the growing abolitionist movement led by, among others Thomas Clarkson, William Wilberforce and the Prime Minister, William Pitt. In 1792 a majority in favour of the abolition of slavery was obtained in parliament. In the US Quakers had similarly refused to deal in the trade in humans but, as *Dredd Scott* showed, attitudes which regarded some humans as being in a different class to others ran deep. On September 22nd 1862, during the Civil War, Abraham Lincoln issued the Emancipation Proclamation, which stated that as from the first of January 1863 all people in states in rebellion or parts of states in rebellion would become free. In 1865 the abolition of slavery was recognized in the thirteenth amendment to the constitution.

The abolition of distinctions between people based on origin or ethnic difference formally removed one of the great evils from the West. Such removal, however, deals with only part of the more general problem of subjection. Chattel slavery still abounds in many parts of the world, and even in the west other forms of subjection have been devised that are little better. In Europe and in North America, all guest workers and resident aliens are denied political rights and some social rights in the countries in which they live, work and bring up their children. In some cases there is little or no *de facto* protection against employment conditions which breach the protective legislation available to citizens. Economic migrants, legally resident under various constitutional provisions enacted after the Second World War, may be forced into working conditions below that which is legally prescribed. Illegal immigrants, common in Europe and in North America, have no civil rights, no social rights, no political rights and no ready redress against transgressions against them. In the terms of *Dredd Scott* v *Sanford* 'people' means the 'citizens' of the country. Citizens have meaningful rights, guest workers and illegal immigrants often do not. To that extent they are our new people of bondage, they have become the new form of the other through which civilization affirms itself.

There is an argument, and it is a powerful one, that civilization needs bondage but that the bondsman will ultimately transcend civilization. In the dialectic of the struggle between Master and Bondsman, a centre piece of the *Phenomenology of Spirit*, Hegel shows how consciousness develops through the mediation of the consciousness of the other. If the master treats the bondsman as mere object then his own subjectivity is mediated through an object. Ultimately this is self-defeating for the consciousness of the master for he can affirm his consciousness only through the recognition of the bondsman as a subject of consciousness. The master thus comes to depend upon the bondsman for his own consciousness. The bondsman however, is interacting both with the master and with nature which he transforms, negates, through work. Only the bondsman becomes truly self-conscious, the consciousness of the master is unable to rise above the petty and trivial. It seems to be implied in Hegel's argument that servitude and discipline are required for self-development. That theme is seen at various stages in ancient Judaism and in Christianity. Vogt argues that in Judaism the relation between Jahweh and Israel, people or individuals, was often construed as one of slave to master. In Hegelian terms the tribes of Israel come to form themselves, as a people, to have an identity in bondage to God, with God as their protecting master. As already noted the same theme recurs in

Christianity, although in later Christianity its terms are more individualistic in emphasis. It is this other-worldly acceptance of bondage that largely explains the ambivalent attitude of Christianity towards bondage throughout most of its history. Yet the attitudes of humanism, even until very recently, have been no better. The appeal to the civil values of Ancient Greece and Rome is an appeal to values that were built upon *skole*, leisure, and upon, therefore, the institution of bondage and slavery. Bondage, slavery, servility and subjection are at the very heart of our civilization. The complete abolition of these categories through the acceptance and adoption of universalistic values is unlikely; a lesson of the past is that such values whether sacral or secular are sufficiently general that they can be readily instantiated in conflicting and contestable ways. The abolition of bondage, whatever its form, to be effective will depend not so much on universalistic principles as on particularistic actions. The abolition of such bondage is contingent upon accepting people into particular groups as full members, as citizens with all the rights, duties and powers that such status implies. The message of the latter half of the twentieth century shows the difficulty of that particular and concrete act. (*See also* SLAVERY).

Clarkson, Thomas (1808) *The History of the Rise, Progress and Accomplishment of the Abolition of the American Slave-Trade by the British Parliament*, London: Longman & Co.

Davis, D.B. (1966) *The Problem of Slavery in Western Culture*, Ithaca, NY: Cornell University Press.

Finlay, M.I. (1960) *Slavery in Classical Antiquity*, Cambridge.

Franklin, J.H. (1948) *From Slavery to Freedom*, New York: Alfred A. Knopf.

Hegel, G.W.F. (1979) *The Phenomenology of Spirit*, Oxford: Oxford University Press.

Kristeva, Julia (1991) *Strangers to Ourselves*, New York & London: Harvester Wheatsheaf.

Luther, M. (1990) *On Bondage of the Will*, Revel Fleming.

Rousseau, J.-J. (1994) *Discourse on the Origin of Inequality*, Oxford Paperbacks.

Savage, Elizabeth (ed.) (1992) *The Human Commodity: Perspectives on the Trans-Saharan Slave Trade*, London: Frank Cass.

Schofield, Malcolm (1991) *The Stoic Idea of the City*, Cambridge: Cambridge University Press.

Slavery and Abolition: A Journal of Slave and Post-Slave Studies: Frank Cass. Three issues yearly, London.

Snowdon, F.M. (1970) *The Blacks in Antiquity*, Cambridge, Mass.

Vogt, Joseph (1974) *Ancient Slavery and the Ideal of Man*, Oxford: Basil Blackwell.

Paul Barry Clarke

BUREAUCRACY

The study of bureaucracy (from the French *bureau*, the covering of writing desks, and *cracy*, office: hence government by office) within social science has followed the enormous expansion of professionalized administration across all sectors of industrial society during the course of the nineteenth and twentieth centuries. The best starting point for an understanding of it remains the work of the German sociologist Max Weber, who made the study of bureaucracy a focal point of enquiry in the early years of this century. Weber's distinctive definition of bureaucracy and explanation for its development have achieved classic status, however much they have been subject to later modification and critique.

Before Weber, bureaucracy was usually conceived of as a type of political system (literally 'rule by the bureau') characteristic of monarchical states such as Prussia, and contrasted with representative or parliamentary systems of the British type. Weber's originality was to show how the administrative organization of states such as Prussia was increasingly replicated across the whole range of contemporary institutions, including the capitalist enterprise, the mass political party and the Catholic Church. Bureaucracy was therefore to be defined, not as a type of STATE, but as a system of professionalized administration, embodying the following characteristics: the employment of full-time salaried officials, recruited competitively according to merit and following an established career path; the hierarchical organization of offices, each with a clearly define sphere of competence, following rule-governed procedures and maintaining a written record of every transaction; the impersonal treatment of all business, without favouritism or bias; the accumulation of expertise, through the control of specialized knowledge and the knowledge stored in the files. Taken together, Weber argued, these features made bureaucracy increasingly 'escape-proof', because only such a system was capable of dealing with the complex administrative tasks of a mass industrial society. In comparison with other historical forms of administration (by unpaid amateurs, local notables, collegial bodies or kinship networks), bureaucracy was like a machine compared with non-mechanized systems of production (Weber 1968: ch. XI).

Weber's broadly (though not exclusively) positive judgement about the superiority of bureaucratic administration has formed a key point of analysis and debate for most subsequent writers on the subject. These have largely concentrated their attention on bureaucracy's problems or defects, which can be analysed under the twin headings of bureaucratic inefficiency and bureaucratic power respectively.

Conclusions about the inherent *inefficiency* of bureaucracy have been developed within two quite separate disciplinary fields. Organizational sociologists have argued that the features which Weber identified as contributing to organizational efficiency can just as readily hinder it as promote it. Thus a hierarchical structure can discourage individual responsibility and initiative and prevent information flowing upwards to the point where it is needed for effective decision-making; adherence to rules can produce inflexibility, procrastination and 'red tape'; impersonality fosters administrative indifference and insensitivity to the needs of particular cases; and so on (Blau and Meyer 1971). From this standpoint the term 'bureaucratic' can become an entirely negative one, as in much popular discourse: synonymous with inefficiency, obstructionism and rigidity (see Crozier 1964). And we could counterpose to it an alternative model of a flexible, less hierarchical or rule-governed administrative system which would be especially appropriate where the organizational environment was subject to rapid change or non-routine tasks were to be accomplished (Perrow 1970).

A similar conclusion about the inefficiency of bureaucracy is reached from the standpoint of free-market economics. Here bureaucracy is defined more narrowly than by Weber, as a hierarchical organization operating in a non-market environment, in contrast to a firm, which operates in a competitive market. Government administration is the archetypal 'bureaucracy' in this sense. Precisely because it does not depend upon the sale of its product or service in the market-place, a bureaucracy has no systematic pressure to economize and suffers from all the typical defects of any monopoly: indifference to the consumer, 'feather-bedding' of employees, making unnecessary WORK and so on. Moreover, left to itself, a bureaucracy has an inherent tendency towards expansion, since it is only through organizational expansion rather than organizational efficiency that the rewards and status of senior officials are typically enhanced (Niskanen 1971). This type of economic analysis lay behind the New Right, or neo-liberal, drive towards the privatization of public services and the introduction of market disciplines into the public sector that was characteristic of the 1980s in Britain and the USA.

If one much analysed defect of bureaucracy is its inefficiency, another is the sheer scope of its POWER, and the threat this poses to both DEMOCRACY and individual freedom. Here Weber himself offered a prescient analysis of the way in which the very features that made bureaucracy such an effective form of administration – its continuity and range of operation, its expertise, its professional '*esprit de corps*' – at the same time established it as a formidable structure of power. A particular concern of his political analysis was that this power could be used to control those who were supposedly in charge of policy-making, such as elected representatives or political leaders, who would prove to be dilettantes in the face of bureaucratic expertise (Weber 1968: Appendix II). The popularity of the BBC 'Yes Minister' series bears witness to the continuity of this problem of the democratic accountability and control of professional administrators from Weber's time to our own (Lynn and Jay 1983).

Besides the issue of democratic accountability, there is also the threat to individual liberty posed by the sheer concentration of powers in the hands of a government bureaucracy – its organizational capacity in relation to a disorganized and atomized citizenry, the secrecy with which its knowledge is protected, its control over individual files and so on. Such powers make possible a degree of societal supervision and individual control unknown to post history. Critics of the Soviet system argue that this threat was most fully realized there because of the co-ordination of all administrative organizations by a single party apparatus which was able to suppress all independent initiative within SOCIETY. The Soviet system thus constituted a kind of culminating point of bureaucritic pathology, a final inversion of the relation between ends and means: the administrative means became an end in itself, devoted to the protection and promotion of its own privileges; the instrument for achieving control of societal development on behalf of the people turned into an agent of control over them (see Djilas 1957; Rizzi 1985).

How, then, can those concerned with liberal and democratic values seek to mitigate these dangers? As a start, we should avoid exaggerating them. Professionalized administration of the kind Weber called 'bureaucratic' is indeed a necessary feature of contemporary life, and one required in a democratic system as in any other. There is no doubting that the problems associated with it are accentuated within the monopoly context of GOVERNMENT. However, we also need to avoid the mistake of attributing to the administrative system all the faults of government, whatever their source; of criticizing 'the bureaucracy' for the inadequacy of the rules they administer, or for insufficiencies of funding, the responsibility for which lies with the politicians themselves. In other words, we should avoid making bureaucracy the scapegoat for all the problems of democratic government, or treating its negative features as irremediable rather than as tendencies which can be offset.

Among different strategies for controlling administrative power, we could distinguish, first, the requirement of pluralism: that there be alternative and independent sources of expertise relevant to government policy available both within civil society and within the state system itself (especially to Parliament or the legislature), to prevent a monopoly of knowledge resting with a central bureaucracy. Second is the requirement of openness: that the evidence and arguments on which public policy is based should be publicly known, and that all files not strictly relevant to national security should be open to public inspection or to the relevant individuals if they are personal. A third strategy involves constitutionally guaranteed rights for individual citizens, including a right of redress in the event of maladministration and the enforcement of the rule of law in all state activity by means of an independent JUDICIARY.

Taken together, these strategies will contribute to the efficiency of bureaucracy, as well as to making its power more controllable. The mistake made by free-market theorists is to assume that only a competitive market can guarantee efficiency, whereas it can also be the product of professional norms reinforced by rigorous procedures of public accountability. Of course, the pressures of strict financial targets and budgetary discipline are necessary as well. But we should also recognize that 'efficiency' is a much more contestable idea in a public bureaucracy than in a private organization guided by the single criterion of profitability; and that pressures for cost efficiency can hamper the effective delivery of a service as much as promote it (Beetham 1987).

In conclusion, bureaucratic administration deserves a more nuanced assessment than it has often received. Modern societies cannot survive without it, yet it has an intrinsic tendency to exceed its purely administrative function and for its function to take oppressive forms. Both tendencies are most likely to be minimized by the countervailing institutional arrangements of a vigorously democratic polity.

Beetham, D. (1987) *Bureaucracy*, Milton Keynes: Open University Press.

Blau, P.M. and Meyer, M.W. (1971) *Bureaucracy in Modern Society*, New York: Random House.

Crozier, M. (1964) *The Bureaucratic Phenomenon*, London: Tavistock.

Djilas, M. (1957) *The New Class*, London: Thames & Hudson.

Lynn, J. and Jay, A. (1983) *Yes Minister*, 3 vols, London: BBC Publications.

Niskanen, W.A. (1971) *Bureaucracy and Representative Government*, Chicago, IL: Aldine-Atherton.

Perrow, C. (1970) *Organizational Analysis: A Sociological View*, Belmont, CA: Wadsworth.

Peters, B.G. (1978) *The Politics of Bureaucracy*, New York: Longman.

Rizzi, B. (1985) *The Bureaucratization of the World*, ed. Westoby, London: Tavistock.
Weber, M. (1968) *Economy and Society*, ed. Roth and Wittich, New York: Bedminster Press.

David Beetham

BUSINESS

The term *business* refers to any engagement or activity. By the close of the fifteenth century the term had come to include engagement in a trade or profession: the basis of its current economic meaning. Business is a state in the *vita activa*, the life of action, as opposed to the *vita contemplativa*, the life of thought. As such it is in tension with the contemplative side of life, that mode of being that is regarded as central to spirituality. In spite of the tension between the active and the spiritual life there are features of business that have some theological import. Starting a business is a creative act. It involves multiple relations with others that have the potential for the formation of a voluntary, co-operative, task-oriented community. Even when egoistically driven, business may come to serve the common good of SOCIETY. While business lives under the discipline of profit its consequences are often larger than the mere making of a profit.

Business has been largely neglected by theologians, even during the past century when it has become the quintessential activity of the age. Given its eschatological dimension and its (relative) otherworldliness, Christianity has found it necessary in all ages to lay particular stress on those things that are eternal, quite often at the rhetorical expense of those things that form part of the fabric of daily life. Early precursors of what we would now call business included craft activities, trade and commerce. A few early saints and church fathers saw commercial activities as a means of realizing the Stoic ideal of a single human race. It was chiefly through international commerce that the peoples came to know one another in a peaceful way, apart from invasions by warring armies. But most others, such as St Ambrose (who was born of the landed aristocracy), saw in commerce a low form of activity by which middlemen bought cheap and sold dear, thus (in his eyes) cheating everyone they dealt with. Among poets, spiritual writers and theologians, commerce was usually relegated to quite a low place on the scale of human activities, since it involved worldly preoccupation, relatively superficial worries, intercourse with Mammon and vulgar (if not slightly shady) dealings. Thus, the economic historian Jacob Viner reports that a certain disdain for commerce is altogether typical of Christian history:

> The early Christian Fathers on the whole took a suspicious if not definitely hostile attitude toward the trade of the merchant or middleman, as being sinful or conductive to sin, essentially as involving either necessarily or commonly fraud or exploitation or violation of charity.
>
> (Viner 1991: 39–40)

However, on the precedent of the developing law concerning independent corporations such as burial societies and religious communities, new laws in the Middle Ages permitted the formation of business enterprises and other private corporations at least semi-independent of GOVERNMENT. Given the papacy's sense of universal law, and its deployment of military protection for key highways and bridges, international trade slowly drew European nations into regular commerce with one another. The mendicant friars of the thirteenth through fifteenth centuries faced problems of conscience brought to them by lay persons involved in the increasingly complex worlds of commerce, finance, and such burgeoning industries as silk-making and textiles. The Spanish and Portuguese Jesuits, Dominicans and others became engaged in the exploration and development of the Americas, experiences that drove them to take theological reflection on economics to new depths. Joseph Schumpeter points out that such Scholastics were the first to formulate many of the concepts which were to catch the attention of the founders of the new discipline of economics, such as Scotland's Francis Hutcheson (1694–1746) and Adam Smith (1723–90). The risk–effort theory of business profit is undoubtedly due to the Scholastics. In particular, it may be mentioned that de Lugo – following a suggestion of St Thomas – described business profits as 'a kind of wage' for a social service. No less certain is it that they launched the theory of interest. Adam Smith himself, incidentally, began his career by studies in divinity and moral philosophy and through his teachers knew of the researches of the Jesuit School of Salamanca.

In the encyclical tradition, beginning with Leo XIII's *Rerum Novarum* (1891), business as such received little attention, papal thought being rather more preoccupied with the larger question of *system* raised by such socialists as Proudhon, Marx and Lenin. Leo XIII, followed by Pius XV in *Quadragesimo Anno* (1931) and his successors until John XXIII (1881–1963), condemned socialism outright, while asymmetrically but quite sharply criticizing the liberal market economy. In that era of ideological *laissez-faire*, INDUSTRIALIZATION and URBANIZATION posed a threat to traditional Christian family life. After Leo XIII, popes took care to side with working people, to emphasize the right of association as practised by labour unions, and to call for laws embodying a Christian code of standards for business activity.

Almost simultaneously, there grew up in other Christian communities various forms of CHRISTIAN SOCIALISM, as represented in England by Archbishop Temple (1896–1902) and R.H. Tawney (1880–1962), and in the USA by Walter Rauschenbusch (1861–1918), the founder of 'the Social Gospel' movement. Unlike those socialists whose presuppositions were atheistic and materialistic, Christian socialists typically tried to preserve certain rights to private property, the sphere of society as opposed to that of the state, and some considerable freedom in market exchange, but tempered by law and moral standards. Some, however, did go rather far in their support for nationalization and other forms of state control over the economy. All were witheringly critical of acquisitiveness, the profit motive and traditional business practices. In the Third World, traditional land-holding élites also objected to capitalist businesses (and 'liberalism') but for conservative reasons, just as many corporate leaders in such nations preferred cosy and often corrupt arrangements with government to free markets that would expose them to the rigours of competition.

In his commentary on the economic teaching of the Second Vatican Council (1961–5), Oswald von Nell-Breuning noted that while the Council spoke of businessmen under the titles of 'owner', 'manager' and 'employer', it neglected the most important title of all, 'the entrepreneur'. This omission, he said, was significant because the title 'entrepreneur' highlights the dynamic element in economic systems. Owner/manager/employer – all these belong to the ancient and more static tradition. The agent of change – of invention, discovery and innovation – is the man or woman of enterprise. Even where that enterprise is driven by private concerns, it may well produce public good. The classic form of the justification of society permitting the pursuit of private activities, is that such activities through the regulation of the invisible hand generate public good. As Mandeville put it.

Thus every part was full of Vice,
Yet the whole Mass a Paradice;
. . . And Vertue who from Politicks
Had learn'd a Thousand cunning Tricks,
Was, by their happy Influence,
Made Friends with Vice: and ever since
The Worst of all the Multitude
Did something for the common Good.

(Mandeville 1970: 67–8)

But the entrepreneur, on other accounts, contributes directly to the public good and has become the contemporary basis of capital. Pope John Paul II picked up the changing meaning of capital and emphasized the directly public benefit of co-operative business activity in his hundredth anniversary commemoration of *Rerum Novarum, Centesimus Annus* (2 May 1991). He pointed out that the chief meaning of capital once was land, later the ownership of the means of production, but today is human capital: skills, knowledge, know-how. Human capital is decisive for economic development. It springs from the 'creative subjectivity' of the human person, made in the image of the Creator. In business, this creativity is almost always expressed as 'work for others and work with others', and thus the business form should first of all be understood as a form of community, bound by the laws appropriate to that form of community:

people work with each other, sharing in a 'community of work' which embraces ever widening circles. A person who produces something other than for his own use generally does so in order that others may use it after they have paid a just price, mutually agreed upon through free bargaining. It is precisely the ability to foresee both the needs of others and the combinations of productive factors most adapted to satisfying those needs that constitutes another important source of WEALTH in modern society. Besides, many goods cannot be adequately produced through the work of an isolated individual; they require the co-operation of many people in working towards a common goal.

(p. 32)

A business is not, of course, a total community; it is driven by the specific task of profiting from, discerning and meeting, or even creating and meeting the needs and wants of others. It has a creative and productive function. It supplies employment. It calls forth and depends upon the practice of a quite considerable range of human virtues, among which the Pope includes:

diligence, industriousness, prudence in undertaking reasonable risks, reliability and fidelity in interpersonal relationships, as well as courage in carrying out decisions which are difficult and painful but necessary, both for the overall working of a business and in meeting possible set-backs.

(p. 32)

The Pope points out that the business firm deserves careful and favourable study by Christians, since it 'throws practical light on a truth about the person which Christianity has constantly affirmed'. He also adds penetrating comments about profit:

the purpose of a business firm is not simply to make a profit, but is to be found in its very existence as a *community of persons* who in various ways are endeavouring to satisfy their basic needs, and who form a particular group at the service of the whole of society. Profit is a regulator of the life of a business, but it is not the only one; *other human and moral factors* must also be considered which, in the long term, are at least equally important for the life of a business.

(p. 35)

Such ideals are not of course always met. As new and more rigorous ways of making political institutions accountable must be found so new and more rigorous ways of making economic institutions accountable must also be found. Theology has a part to play in encouraging this and developing new conceptions of business and business ideals. Just as there has developed a considerable specialization of theology concerned with church and state, politics more generally, and the arts, so in our time there is a growing literature on the theology of economics, the theology of the corporation, and business ethics. It can safely be said that most Christians of the world spend a considerable portion of their lives active in the economic system, a great many of them in various nonprofit sectors, but considerably more in for-profit activities. Reflection upon the implications of the Gospel for business activities may therefore be expected to grow in range, depth and intensity. (*See also* URSURY).

Drucker, Peter F. (1983) *Concept of the Corporation*, 2nd edn, New York: Harper & Row.

John Paul II, Pope (1991) *Centesimus Annus*, London: Catholic Truth Society.

Kirzner, Israel M. (1985) *Discovery and the Capitalist Process*, Chicago, IL: University of Chicago Press.

Macfarlane, Alan (1987) *The Culture of Capitalism*, Oxford: Basil Blackwell.

Mandeville, Bernard (1970) *The Fable of the Bees*, ed. Philip Harth, London: Penguin.

Novak, Michael (1992) *The Catholic Ethic and the Spirit of Capitalism*, New York: Free Press.

Schumpeter, Joseph A. (1954) *History of Economic Analysis*, ed. Elizabeth Boody Schumpeter, New York: Oxford.

Tawney, R.H. (1926) *Religion and Rise of Capitalism*, New York: Harcourt, Brace & World.

Viner, Jacob (1991) *Essays on the Intellectual History of Economics*, ed. Douglas A. Irwin, Princeton, NJ: Princeton University Press.

Vorgrimler, H. (1968) *Commentary on the Documents*

of *Vatican II*, 5 vols, London: Herder. 'Part II, Chapter III, Socio-Economic Life. History of the Text by Herbert Vorgrimler. Commentary by Oswald von Nell–Breuning', pp. 288–313.
Weber, Max (1958) *The Protestant Ethic and the* *Spirit of Capitalism*, trans. Talcott Parsons, New York: Charles Scribner's Sons.

Michael Novak
Paul Barry Clarke

CAPITAL PUNISHMENT

Typically, capital punishment is defined as the execution of a criminal by the STATE or some other public authority. That executions have public authority is crucial; executions carried out by vigilantes or lynch mobs cannot be considered 'capital punishment'. According to Augustine, killing criminals without public authority is tantamount to murder. Thus, any theological evaluation of capital punishment relies on a theological analysis of the nature and possibility of civil authority (*see* CHURCH AND STATE). For instance, under what circumstances, if any, may Christians execute their fellow human beings? When, if ever, should the Christian Church grant the state authority to carry out executions?

Answers to questions about secular authority have always been influenced by Christian understanding of the role and authority of the church. As Christian convictions about the church and the world have changed, so have their convictions about capital punishment.

The early church condemns Christian participation in capital punishment. In the third century Tertullian says that 'even if he appeals to the power of the State, the servant of God should not pronounce capital sentences' (*De Idololatria*, ch. 17, Compagnoni, p. 46), and the Councils of Hippolytus, addressing soldiers and magistrates undergoing catechetical formation, say 'let him who wields the power of the sword or the magistrate who wears the purple [criminal judge] renounce his office or else be excluded [from catechesis]'. Similarly, in the early fourth century Lactantius says

> the just man, whose task it is to administer justice, is not permitted even to charge anyone with a capital crime, since it makes no difference whether one kills with words or with the sword: killing as such is forbidden.
> (*Divine Institutiones*, VI, 20; Compagnoni, p. 46)

With its history written in the blood of its many martyrs, the early church clearly recognized that allegiance to Christ was incompatible with the Roman Empire's interest in executing its dissenters, be they 'political', 'religious' or 'criminal'.

Beginning with Emperor Constantine's conversion to Christianity in AD 312, the church's self-understanding and internal discipline undergo profound changes. Prior to Constantine's conversion, the church is a small, often persecuted group within the Roman Empire. Within a century, the vast majority of the Empire considers itself at least nominally Christian. Whereas previously the church viewed the Empire as a pagan institution needing conversion, it now increasingly comes to see divine providence working through the Empire.

With the phenomenal growth of Christianity, it is no longer generally believed that all Christians can live up to the demands of the Gospel. One result of this is the development of a two-tiered ethic in Christianity: that of true Christians whose lives conform to the Gospel, and that of nominal Christians and pagans who live by a less rigorous 'natural' ethic. Many of the demands of the Gospel formerly understood to be binding on all Christians come to be understood as 'counsels of perfection', to be reflected in the lives of the devout few, but not demanded of most Christians. By medieval times, the two-tiered ethic will be firmly in place; the 'Gospel' ethic will be associated with clerics and those in religious orders, and the 'natural' ethic with lay Christians.

With the widespread growth of Christianity, church penitential practices are seen to be insufficient discipline for the needs of a Christian Empire, and the church begins to acquiesce in secular, punitive practices which were formerly forbidden. While the practice of capital punishment continues to be condemned, it is increasingly tolerated. For example, the canons of the Roman Synod continue to affirm that state officials sin in handing down capital sentences, but no longer consider expelling such officials from the church. Similarly, St Ambrose allows judges of capital offences to remain in the church, but recommends that they abstain from the EUCHARIST. The same ambivalence towards capital punishment is expressed by St Augustine, who recognizes the inevitability of state-sanctioned vengeance, but never describes capital punishment by the Empire as a work of the vengeance of God.

By the beginning of the fifth century, the church largely has come to accept the traditional penal practices of a now nominally Christian Roman Empire. However, remnants of early church practice and discipline continue. In the ninth century Pope Nicholas I writes about the newly converted Bulgars, saying

> you must give up your former habits and not merely avoid every occasion of taking life. . . . You should save from death not only the innocent but also criminals, because Christ has saved you from the death of the soul.
>
> (Ep. 97, ch. xxv)

Similarly, clerics continue to be prohibited from any involvement in capital sentences, since they

> are chosen for the service of the altar where the passion of the slain Christ is represented – that Christ who, as Peter expressed it, *When he was reviled did not revile in return.* It is, therefore, not fitting that clerics should strike or kill, for servants should imitate the master . . . second . . . clerics are entrusted with the ministry of the New Law which lays down no capital or corporal penalty. To qualify as *ministers of the new covenant,* therefore they should abstain from such actions.
>
> (Aquinas, *Summa Theologica* 11, 11, 64, 4)

This prohibition continues to the present in Roman Catholic Canon Law, which bars from priestly ordination anyone who has been directly involved as judge or executioner in the carrying out of the death penalty.

Aquinas's work continues to presume the acceptability of the two-tiered ethic, justifying capital punishment on the basis of a natural law understanding of the State. The relation between individuals and community is that between part and whole. As the good of any part is subordinate to the good of the whole, so individual fulfilment is found in serving the common good. With respect to capital punishment, one may have to remove a person to save the community, as one removes a gangrenous toe to save the body. The purpose of punishment is medicinal, not retributive: to heal wounds and to prevent further injury (*Summa Theologica* 11, 11, 66, 6). Capital punishment can be justified if and only if the person has posed and *will continue to* pose a serious threat to SOCIETY.

Martin Luther rejects the medieval two-tiered ethic, for this ethic understands the commands of Christ, such as 'resist not evil', to be counsels of perfection rather than precepts binding on all. That, according to Luther, is to call Christ 'a liar' and 'in error'. Along with the two-tiered ethic, Luther also rejects the related medieval distinction between the functions proper to the church and to the State. In their place, Luther distinguishes true Christians from all other people. True Christians are of the KINGDOM OF GOD, and all others are of the kingdom of the world. If all were true Christians, then laws and princes would be unnecessary. However, since we neither have or ever will have such a world, Christians must respect and contribute to the authority of the State and thus operate in both kingdoms. As children of the kingdom of God, all true Christians are to follow the demands of Christ through being non-resistant *inwardly*, in their own person and in relation with other true Christians. Yet, living also amongst the children of the world, Christians have a duty to protect their neighbours *outwardly* by occupying various judicial positions in civil government, which God has ordained to punish evildoers. In doing so, the Christian 'satisf[ies]' at the same time God's kingdom inwardly and the kingdom of the world outwardly' ('Secular authority', p. 375). All true Christians, cleric or lay, must discern when to inwardly serve the kingdom of God and when to outwardly serve the kingdom of the world.

Luther's appeal for the legitimacy of capital punishment thus goes beyond that of medievals, in that all Christians

> should [they] see that there is a lack of hangmen, beadles, judges, lords or princes, and find that [they] are qualified, you should offer [their] services and seek the place, that necessary government may by no means be despised and become inefficient or perish. For the world cannot and dare not dispense with it.
>
> (Luther, 'Secular authority', pp. 374–5)

According to Luther's dualist vision of church and state, God acts in the kingdom of the world through legitimate GOVERNMENT. Thus, Luther believes that God's own self, working through human agents, passes the capital sentence and performs the execution.

Calvin's view of the State differs from the two previous viewpoints in rejecting either form of dualism: the cleric–laity dualism of Aquinas; the inward–outward dualism of Luther. There is only one norm for all Christians; it must be drawn from the whole of Scripture. It must function as a standard for all people, recognizing that the society cannot live up to the evangelical call of Jesus. Thus the Calvinist view has no place for either a group of Christians (Catholic clerics/religious orders) or an 'inward' stance (the Lutheran non-resistant individual) where following Christ's example of LOVE and non-violence is paramount. However Calvin considers the way of Christ compatible with the death penalty. Thus, Christians who claim that loving one's enemies is incompatible with the exercise of capital punishment are perverting Scripture and the gospel of Jesus Christ.

The view of the Radical Reformation, whose descendants include the Mennonites and Anabaptists, are like the Calvinists in rejecting medieval or Lutheran dualisms. However, they are more like medieval clerics than Calvinists, in that they believe Christ's call to non-resistant love must be embodied in both individual and societal life. With regard to all issues, whether 'public' or 'private', the love of Christ must be the guiding principle. Thus, with regard to capital punishment, the view is that

It is the clear witness of the New Testament, especially of the Epistle to the Hebrews, that the ceremonial requirements of the Old Testament find their fulfillment and their end in the high-priestly sacrifice of Christ. 'Once for all' is the triumphant proclamation of the Epistle. Henceforth no more blood is needed to testify to the sacredness of life, and no more sacrifices are called for to expiate for [human] usurping of the power to kill. With the cross of Christ the moral and ceremonial basis of capital punishment is wiped away.

(Yoder, *The Christian and Capital Punishment*, p. 9)

Having outlined how different theological analyses of the relationship between Church and State have led to different views on capital punishment, we now turn to arguments from Scripture.

The critical Scriptural question with respect to the legitimacy of capital punishment is how Christians are to understand the relationship between the Hebrew Bible and the New Testament. Many Christians who advocate capital punishment acknowledge that the person and work of Christ are primary and that the Hebrew Bible must be read in the light of the New Testament, but in practice they utilize the Hebrew Bible as their moral benchmark. Thus, it is argued that capital punishment is commanded in Genesis 9: 6, 'Whoever sheds the blood of human, by a human shall that person's blood be shed; for in his own image God made humankind', and that the Mosaic law extends this, demanding capital punishment for a variety of offences within the covenant community of Israel, including striking or cursing one's parent, kidnapping, allowing one's ox to negligently kill another person, sorcery, bestiality, idolatry, adultery, wizardry, rebellious sons and non-virginal brides-to-be (Exodus 21: 15–29; 22: 18–20; Leviticus 20: 10, 27; Deuteronomy 21: 18–21; 22: 21).

Advocates further argue that the New Testament generally reinforces the Hebrew Bible on the question of capital punishment. St Paul is understood to affirm that governing authorities have the right to punish offenders (Romans 13: 1–4). As for Jesus, his commands to turn the other cheek, walk the second mile and give up one's coat and cloak are meant to guide the Church, but they are not intended to do away with the natural laws of society.

The ultimate difficulty for Christians who advocate capital punishment while acknowledging that they live under the New Covenant is that they deny the efficacy of Christ's death upon the cross. If capital punishment is still needed to expiate the guilt of the individual, then Christ's death upon the cross is defective in its ultimate purpose.

Thus, other Christians believe that if Jesus Christ is Lord, then Christ's commands must be obeyed in the private and public realms. Christians are to love God and their neighbour, including their enemy. These Christians believe that the cross of Christ does away with all expiation and retribution once and for all. For Jesus Christ replaces the law of retribution with the law of reconciliation (Matthew 5: 23–4). Jesus's pardoning of the woman caught in adultery (a civil offence requiring capital punishment) is not merely an isolated example of mercy. Rather, in saying 'Let anyone among you who is without sin be the first to throw a stone at her' (John 8: 7), Jesus is challenging the presumption that humans can ever authorize the death penalty as judge and/or executioner.

St Paul's discussion of the power of the pagan civil authorities (Romans 13: 1–4) must be understood in the context of Romans 12, which repeatedly prohibits Christians from seeking vengeance against their persecutors. Romans 13: 1–4 is a description of existing Roman authority, rather than a set of normative claims about a Christian civil government. St John's discussion of the state in Revelation 13 is further evidence that the New Testament is not prone to uncritical acceptance of civil authority. With regard to 'the authority does not bear the sword in vain' (Romans 13: 4) as a justification for capital punishment, the 'sword' of Romans 13: 4 is the symbol of judicial authority, but it was not the instrument used by the Romans to carry out capital sentences.

We find a very different set of presuppositions in arguments for and against capital punishment in contemporary Western liberal societies. Theological appeals are relatively rare. The two justifications most strongly at work in modern societies which employ the death penalty are deterrence and retribution.

Deterrence is designed to protect society by preventing possible future crimes. Opponents of the death penalty argue that this 'deterrent' does not work. From a sociological perspective, institution of the death penalty has not reduced crime; nations with the death penalty do not have a lower murder rate than those without it.

Second, there is psychological evidence that capital punishment does not deter. Many murders are 'crimes of passion', thus lacking the element of 'premeditation' necessary for deterrence to be effective. Third, opponents of capital punishment argue that a deterrence rationale could be used to justify the death penalty for lesser crimes (e.g. especially 'white collar' crimes like stock fraud or maliciously creating computer 'viruses') if the penalty would deter a sufficient number of potential criminals. Such arguments have even been used to justify executing an innocent person in a situation of grave community emergency (see John 18: 14). Executing innocents and executing persons for lesser crimes, however, goes against the general sensibilities of modern liberal societies, which hold strongly to the view that only those guilty of a crime ought to be punished, and that the punishment must 'fit' the crime.

Retributivism is the other standard contemporary justification for the death penalty. According to the theory of retributivism, the death penalty is understood as just deserts, an eye for an eye, life for life, and so on. This view will be untenable for any theological viewpoint which accepts the central Christological claim that in the cross is the final expiation of sin, the 'once and for all' that eliminates the need or legitimacy of any bloodletting to testify to the sacredness of life. Having noted this, it is helpful to distinguish a variety of retributivist viewpoints.

The retributivist viewpoint is often understood as simply giving someone what they deserve, given the positive laws of a society. Just as the statutes of the Olympic Games require that a gold medal be given to the fastest sprinter, so the statutes of a State require that a person who kills another in a particular manner be executed. All citizens in the society know ahead of time that if they break a particular law a particular punishment follows. If the society is to respect that person's humanity, to treat the person as a responsible actor, then it is necessary to impose the prescribed punishment. The major theological problem with this view is that it presupposes the justness of the positive laws of a society. Aquinas would say that Christians have a theological perspective from which they can critique secular laws and secular punishments as potentially unjust.

The 'payment' theory is an attempt to justify more deeply the appropriateness of capital punishment. As restitution for theft involves giving up stolen property, so restitution for murder involves giving up one's own life. Opponents of this theory argue that this analogy is problematic. Retribution is not the same as restitution. The murderer is unable to return or restore what the murderer has 'taken'; executing the murderer does not bring back the life of the victim.

The 'satisfaction' theory holds that the suffering of the offender should match that of the victim. Traditionally, it was the desire for revenge which required 'satisfaction', and societies punished offenders to keep friends and relatives from taking *revenge* on the offender or the offender's family, friends, tribe, etc. However, to the extent that punishment is exacted on such grounds, the rationale is more akin to deterrence than retribution, in that the primary goal is social stability rather than the proper retributivist punishment.

The 'satisfaction' viewpoint finds its strongest modern spokesperson in Kant, who argues that murderers must be executed so that 'blood-guilt' will not be fixed on the society. Kant appeals to Hebrew Bible notions of sacrifice and placation. Sins require sacrifices. The spilling of one person's blood requires the spilling of the blood of the murderer. This is required if God's anger is to be placated.

Many contemporary proponents of capital punishment accept versions of Kant's argument. In the 1990s capital punishment is growing in frequency in the USA. When friends and relatives of victims are interviewed, they regularly claim that they cannot rest easily until the murderer has been executed and thus consider the endless sets of appeals a horrible ordeal for them to be put through.

Opponents of the death penalty argue that the need to 'satisfy' the death of a loved one by executing the murderer is a learned response and that much of the frustration and restlessness felt by victims' families is created by the extremely long – ten to twelve year – delays in final sentencing. They point out that in

countries which do not have a death penalty statute in place and where life sentences are handed down relatively quickly, relatives are much less likely to express a desire for a capital sentence. Moreover, such desires for revenge and expiation, while understandable, can be challenged on theological and scriptural grounds, as has been discussed above (*see* ATONEMENT).

Whether retributive demands for capital punishment are that it is 'fair' or 'just', or that this 'satisfies' the soul of the victim, friends of the victim or God, all such appeals embody the deep human desire for revenge. Though liberal societies generally do not like to acknowledge the desire for vengeance, the death penalty is undoubtedly a means by which society institutionalizes its revulsion at particular heinous crimes and a means of re-establishing a social (or even cosmic) order that was broken by the criminal.

Once the appeal of capital punishment is understood in the framework of vengeance or some thinly veiled correlate, the necessity of Christian opposition to capital punishment becomes clear. Theological objections to capital punishment will begin with the claim that all life, guilty or not, belongs to God and is to be given and taken only by God. In the cross of Christ, all demands by God for sacrifice for sin has been ended, and this includes the blood of murderers or any other criminals. For Christians, whether they act as individuals or as agents of the State, are not to usurp God's control over life. Any dualism between cleric and laity, between the individual and society, or between what the Christian community may do and what the State may do cannot be rigidly maintained. If Christian witness is to maintain its integrity, then the life of Christians, whether operating in the Church or in the world, must be one. Since the Church cannot execute sinners because of the call to forgive, Christians should seek the same for those who violate the law in the wider society.

Armed with a distinctive theological rationale, Christians will join their secular counterparts in public debate against capital punishment. Both may rejoice that people are no longer put to death for crimes like forgery or theft, and continue to advocate the elimination of capital punishment wherever the practice continues.

Christians cannot expect to come to any widespread agreement about the immorality of capital punishment as long as they fail to agree that the retributive theory of punishment in general cannot be sustained theologically. If Christians are committed to communities that enact forgiveness and reconciliation, then they will believe that retributive forms of punishment so prevalent in modern societies are a profound distortion of the Gospel.

Aquinas, T. (1962–   ) *Summa Theologica*, vols I–LX, New York: Macmillan.
Augustine, *City of God*, I, xxi, xxvi.
Barth, K. (1961) *Church Dogmatics*, III, 4, Edinburgh: T. & T. Clark, pp. 397–450.
Compagnoni (1979) 'Capital punishment and torture in the tradition of the Catholic Church', in Böckle and Pohier (eds) *Concilium: The Death Penalty and Torture*, New York: Seabury Press, pp. 39–53.
Cottingham (1979) 'Varieties of retributivism', *Philosophical Quarterly* 238–46.
Jonsen and Toulmin (1988) *The Abuse of Casuistry*, Berkeley, CA: University of California Press, ch. 11.
Luther, M. (1961) 'Secular authority: to what extent it should be obeyed', in Dillenberger (ed.), *Martin Luther, Selections*, New York: Doubleday.
Moule, C.F.D. (1965) 'Punishment and retribution: an attempt to delimit their scope in New Testament thought', *Svensk Exegetisk Årsbok* 30: 21–36.
Yoder (1961) *The Christian and Capital Punishment*, Newton: Faith & Life Press.
——(1964) *The Christian Witness to the State*, Newton: Faith & Life Press.

John Berkman
Stanley Hauerwas

CAPITALISM

Economic life arises from the fact that, whereas human needs and wants are without limit, the means for satisfying them, human talent and material resources, are relatively scarce and have many alternative uses.

Capitalism, or the free-enterprise economic system, is a set of institutions that can be used to obtain a solution to the perennial questions of what should be produced, in what quantities, for whom and by what means. Basically, capitalism is a system of social arrangement that consists of private ownership of economically productive assets plus reliance on markets for the provision of allocative signals. By way of contrast, (theoretical) SOCIALISM involves a command economy which comprises state ownership of the means of production and the use of political direction in matters of their allocation and on issues concerning the nature of the final output supplied and its distribution.

As well as the polar cases of capitalism and socialism, we must also refer to market socialism: under this type of structure, the means of production is publicly owned, but market forces provide guidance on the deployment of scarce factor inputs and on the traits of final output. The fourth possible kind of arrangement, namely private ownership coupled with non-market allocative and output decisions, is usually thought of as a primitive precursor of free enterprise. Historically, it is customarily associated with the economic patterns of feudalism and mercantilism.

Intelligent discussion of the characteristics of capitalism, or indeed of any of the other three types of economic formation we have identified, has to involve an appreciation of the fact that in reality no system is ever found in a theoretically pure shape. Thus, in all free-enterprise economies there is always a considerable ingredient of state ownership and of directly state-sponsored activity; and, correspondingly, even in the most totalitarian of socialist command economies, there is always some use made of markets and even of privately owned factors of production. Also, it is never sensible to regard any particular economic system as a method of creating a Utopia: we have to ask, on balance, which sort of system operates in the most comparatively acceptable manner and is most likely to achieve for society the overall objectives required of economic activity.

As just an *economic* system, capitalism is not, of course, coterminous with civil society as a whole. The free-enterprise system rests on and presupposes a large number of non-economic institutions. Chief of these are the institutions of private property, individual freedom of contract, an impartial legal system for the peaceful resolution of disputes and for contract enforcement and, importantly, the prevalence of the moral values of honesty, trust and amic-ability. Moreover, to function successfully, capitalism relies on general moral approval for activities such as individual self-improvement, risk-taking and entrepreneurship. Competition, within agreed legal bounds and according to informal ethical rules, should also have moral endorsement as a legitimate way in which agents can fruitfully co-operate with each other to achieve mutually desirable ends. Capitalism is thus inextricably bound up, implicitly as well as explicitly, with the moral foundation for the types of human conduct indispensable for its successful operation.

The twentieth century has seen no more en-thusiastic advocate of free enterprise than the Austrian-born economist Friedrich A. Hayek (1899–1992), the 1974 recipient of the Nobel Prize. In many books and writings, Hayek argues that the core elements of free enterprise (private property and markets) were never ra-tionalistically invented at a particular point in time, but that they evolved more or less sponta-neously as unintended repercussions of freely determined human activity and decisions. The origins of these components, like those of lan-guage and indeed of civil society itself, are, according to Hayek (1973: 37), the 'product of the action of many men but are not the result of human design'. But once created, both private property and markets are social institutions that can then properly be subjected to thoughtful periodic adjustment (taking into account that any adaptation may itself have unintended conse-quences of unwanted kinds).

Over the period from 1600 to the present day, modern capitalism grew out of the mercan-tilist system that was itself the outcome of the evolution of rural feudalism away from strict local-community self-sufficiency. From the van-tage point of today, mercantilism as espoused by the English merchant Thomas Mun, the French statesman J.B. Colbert and the English author and economic theorist Sir William Petty, is most naturally understood as an undeveloped form of the sort of economic arrangements that were to be advocated in the eighteenth century by philosophers such as David Hume and, most famously, Adam Smith. Mercantilism was an economic system that rested on well-entrenched

private property rights but which also involved very extensive state direction of economic activ-ity, especially in matters relating to foreign trade. For the mercantilists, international trade was an activity more or less akin to war: partici-pants could only prosper at the direct expense of their overseas trading partners. As a conse-quence of this view, mercantilists tended to be strong nationalists and supporters of national economic autarchy behind a high wall of tariff barriers.

For Hume and Smith, the arguments in favour of the mutually beneficial nature of free trade, the international form of the division of labour, were the starting point for the construc-tion of a new theoretical outlook on the charac-ter of economic endeavour. In this viewpoint, excessively pervasive government intervention in the economy was portrayed as grossly ineffi-cient and even corrupt, while individual initia-tive was identified as the major source of greater material well-being for society as a whole. Ac-cording to this perspective, the rightful role of government was to be not an active decision-making agent within particular markets, but rather a respected referee enforcing necessary ground-rules and essential constraints on the behaviour of all market participants.

Adam Smith's *An Inquiry into the Nature and Causes of the Wealth of Nations* (1776) is one of the most influential books ever written on economics and the general doctrines it pro-pounds were widely treated as authoritative until comprehensively modified by the critical analysis of John Maynard Keynes in the 1930s. Two features of Smith's advocacy of free enter-prise, as opposed to the mercantilist system with its widespread role for government control, are worthy of special note and are to be seen in the following renowned quotation from the *Wealth of Nations* (Book IV, Chapter ii):

every individual necessarily labours to render the annual revenue of the society as great as he can. He generally, indeed, neither intends to promote the public interest, nor knows how much he is promoting it. . . . he intends only his own gain, and he is in this, as in many other cases, led by an invisible hand to promote an end which was no part of his intention. Nor is it always the worse for the society that it was no part of it. By pursuing his own interest he frequently promotes that of the society more effectually than when he really intends to promote it.

(p. 456)

First, in this passage, great emphasis is laid on the function of individual self-interest as a dynamic motivator of economic effort. This aspect of Smith's doctrine endures as part of the modern understanding of the operation of free-enterprise economies, whether we are talking about the owners of skill and financial capital or consumers. The early classical economists strongly defended not only the economic efficiency of natural liberty (freedom of individual choice) but also its moral desirability. Second, the passage alludes to a view that many would still want to defend, but which would now, in the light of contemporary economic understanding, have to be stated somewhat cautiously. This is the doctrine that the functioning of competitive markets leads to a self-stabilizing harmony of interests (an optimal allocation of relatively scarce resources) within the economy. This means that if producers and consumers act, within the legal and ethical framework of their own roles, to maximize their profit and satisfaction respectively, then the 'annual revenue of society' will always be at or near its potential for the benefit of all.

By 'invisible hand', Smith is referring to what we would now call market feedbacks and interrelationships. And at one level, this does of course capture an important aspect of the free-enterprise economic system, namely its ability to make more effective use of scattered information in society, concerning particularly the preferences and choices of individual people, than any group of central controllers in a command economy could ever hope to achieve. The competitive market mechanism, by indicating high relative prices for those goods and services in comparatively short supply, gives an indication to profit-seeking entrepreneurs of what would be in their interest to produce should they be willing to shoulder the associated risks. It is above all the enormous capacity of free enterprise to make truly constructive use of dispersed knowledge

that makes it decisively superior, in the real world, to other rival types of economic order.

'Superiority', however, is a comparative concept. And nowhere in the writings of Hume, Smith, David Ricardo, Thomas Malthus, Jean Baptiste Say, or any of the other early classical economists, is the notion ever seriously entertained that the free-enterprise system in practice is perfect and flawless. In this spirit, we shall now rehearse some of the most common reproaches levelled against capitalism. A number of these, indeed, were frankly acknowledged by those we have just mentioned.

The chief problems frequently alleged to be associated with capitalism can be summarized as follows.

1 At the macroeconomic level, there is considerable evidence that the economy is not automatically self-stabilizing when subjected to internal or external shocks, and disequilibrium features such as widespread involuntary unemployment can occur and persist.

2 The owners of established businesses, if left wholly to their own devices, tend over time to seek to restrict the entry of new firms into their particular industry, thus establishing an anti-competitive pattern of restrictive behaviour.

3 Many firms in their operation tend to generate negative externalities (e.g. environmental pollution) and thus untowardly throw a portion of their operating costs on to the general public.

4 Individuals demand public goods as well as private, but market-based firms have no incentive to provide them. (A 'public good', it should be noted, is a good or service which a non-payer cannot be excluded from consuming, and is also a product of such a kind that many individuals can all consume the very same units of output. Typical examples are street lighting and national defence.)

5 On moral grounds, there are certain privately consumable goods and services to which everyone, by virtue of society membership, should have access at an appropriate level of provision. However, the financing of welfare services and of minimum incomes will not occur without proactive government assistance.

107

6 The competitive pursuit of self-interest as the main motivation for economic behaviour leads inevitably to inequality of incomes and lifestyles, and hence is an ethically unsatisfactory foundation for an economic system.

This catalogue of the most familiar criticisms of capitalism is heterogeneous as well as wide ranging. It covers issues which are topics of current dispute amongst professional economists as well as those that do not fall exclusively into the economists' realm.

The conception of beneficent natural harmony permeates the *Wealth of Nations*. And perhaps the most persistently contentious of the long-lasting claims about capitalism is that the system self-stabilizes at an optimal level of resource allocation. An important aspect of this harmony was formulated by the French businessman and economist J.B. Say. In his work, *Traité d'Economie Politique* (1803), Say expounded his celebrated law of markets that 'supply creates its own demand'. In modern language, this amounts to the contention that withdrawals from the circular flow of income, such as savings, at all times automatically equal injections into it, such as investment. This law was accepted for over a century by all the main non-socialist economists as a critical component of the argument that a prolonged episode of resource misallocation, as represented by involuntary unemployment caused by sustained demand deficiency, was impossible. The last of the classical theorists to defend the position that 'aggregate money savings and aggregate money investment must be identical' (but without mentioning Say by name) was the Cambridge economist Arthur C. Pigou in his *Employment and Equilibrium* (1941: 21). Say's law, and along with it the wider perception of the macroeconomy as naturally self-stabilizing in all circumstances, were rejected on both theoretical and empirical grounds by J.M. Keynes in his acclaimed book of 1936, *The General Theory of Employment, Interest and Money*.

Politically Keynes was a Liberal (spelt with a capital L), who believed passionately that a *necessary* condition for a society which respected individual liberty and personal responsibility was the existence of a free-enterprise economy. Keynes's work is not some kind of assault on capitalism as such, but merely on the form of it that developed under the idea that the macroeconomy on its own can always recover to the full employment state should this condition be disturbed.

In the 1950s and 1960s many Keynesian propositions (such as the idea that growth of the money stock only affects the economy through the variation in interest rates) were challenged by monetarism, a school of analysis led by the (1976 Nobel) economist Milton Friedman. In more recent times, a much more powerful attack on Keynesian ideas than that mounted by monetarism comes from the New Classical School, a radical grouping associated in its origin with the American economist Robert E. Lucas. On the basis of the twin assumptions that all markets at all times clear efficiently and that economic agents act on 'rational expectations' (i.e. agents never make systematic errors in their forecasts of future economic variables), the New Classical economists have sought completely to discredit all types of macroeconomic stabilization policies (Lucas 1972).

The dispute between the followers of Keynes and the adherents of monetarist and New Classical theories on the appropriate level of government intervention for a modern capitalist economy is an ongoing debate in economics. No resolution of the central points is even remotely in sight. It is unlikely, however, that the main thrust of Keynes's insights will ever be totally reversed.

Turning now to other commonly asserted criticisms of capitalism, we begin with the important concern that free-market competition tends to degenerate into monopolization and restrictive practices. Surprising though it may be, this tendency was recognized by Adam Smith himself. In Book I, Chapter x, of the *Wealth of Nations*, he comments: 'People of the same trade seldom meet together, even for merriment and diversion, but the conversation ends in a conspiracy against the public, or on some contrivance to raise prices' (p. 145). The point hinted at here, and widely recognized since, is that free enterprise (as conceived by its originators) is emphatically not *laissez-faire*: on the contrary, governments have an obligation to referee markets and to overrule the restrictive practices of sectional interests if they should appear.

On the topic of monopolies, a complication arises in the case of so-called 'natural monopolies'. In economists' terminology, a natural monopoly is a firm that experiences continuing economies of scale as output expands, and thus if consumers are to benefit by being supplied at the lowest possible long-run average cost there is room for only that firm in the industry. Typical of natural monopolies are investor-owned utility companies, and the solution to the problem is for these to operate under the guidance of a government-appointed utility commission so that their pricing and output decisions can be subject to independent review to avoid possible abuse of monopoly power. Again, we see that free enterprise requires an institutional setting where the state has an established role as an umpire of market activities.

The same approach should be taken in reply to most of the remaining objections to capitalism we listed. Governments have a part to play in areas such as pollution abatement, the provision of public goods and the financing of welfare services and minimum incomes. In some cases, in a few of these areas, firms and individuals may act unprompted. For example, the (1991 Nobel) economist Ronald H. Coase has demonstrated that, where property rights are well defined and the transaction costs of action small, an optimal solution to an externality problem is likely to be reached by private bargaining without government intervention (Coase 1960). But, obviously, over the whole band of items we mentioned as being within the scope of market failure, there can in general be no question of precluding government action.

Finally, we come to the pair of objections that capitalism leads to an unequal distribution of income and that, in any case, the motive of self-interest inherent in the system is morally ambiguous (Preston 1991) (*see* CHRISTIAN SOCIAL-ISM). On the first point, while it is clearly true that free enterprise could not function in a rigidly egalitarian setting, it is also the case that such a situation itself could only exist in reality as a deeply unattractive equality of abject poverty enforced by politically authoritarian measures. But once the pure egalitarian option is ruled out, the distributional problem becomes one of degree upon which thoughtful opinion may honestly differ. On the second point, concerning the claim that self-interest is ethically dubious, the answer can only be that this motive is found in all areas of life and is probably a universal aspect of the human condition. This being so, the reasonable question is not whether to rely on self-interest, but rather how to ensure that action so motivated is channelled in such ways that it will tend to benefit rather than harm society. And this is precisely what the free-enterprise system is supposed to achieve when it operates within an appropriately managed institutional setting. On the play of self-interest in society, Keynes (1936: 374) showed great insight into human character when he declared: 'It is better that a man should tyrannise over his bank balance than over his fellow-citizens.'

In the broadest terms, what, realistically, should be expected of an economic system? We suggest that the answer to this has two parts. First, economic life should be efficient in the sense that society's relatively scarce resources should not be misallocated to generate unwanted products but rather should be used to supply goods and services in accordance with consumer preferences. It is a fact of life that only an efficient economy can create the wealth to enable more than a tiny minority of a population to rise above grinding poverty and bare subsistence. Without economic efficiency, there can be neither decent private incomes nor respectable welfare services. Second, in striving for efficiency in the deployment of resources, an economic process should not spawn unmitigated side-effects that are deeply objectionable on moral or other reasonable grounds. In particular and importantly, efficiency should not be sought by reliance on systematic political coercion to effect economic transactions.

It can hardly be contentious to say that capitalism meets these two broad criteria better than any other currently available type of economic system. In most Western countries the twentieth century has seen the development of the welfare state and active stabilization policies, and the overall result has been versions of capitalism largely free of the most undesirable features with which in former decades it was inclined to be connected. The challenge of the future is to make sure that this process of steady improvement continues. Following the collapse of the USSR and its empire in the early 1990s (largely on account of the comprehensive failure of its command economy and the associated harsh totalitarian political regime), we shall certainly be seeing many more *varieties* of capitalism in the time that lies ahead.

Brittan, S. (1988) *A Restatement of Economic Liberalism*, 2nd edn, London: Macmillan.

Burton, J. (ed.) (1986) *Keynes's General Theory: Fifty Years On*, London: Institute of Economic Affairs.

Coase, R.H. (1960) 'The problem of social cost', *Journal of Law and Economics* 3: 1–44.

Dimand, R.W. (1988) *The Origins of the Keynesian Revolution*, Aldershot: Edward Elgar.

Friedman, M. and Friedman, R. (1980) *Free to Choose*, New York: Avon Books.

Hayek, F.A. (1973) *Law, Legislation and Liberty*, vol. I, London: Routledge.

Hutt, W.H. (1979) *The Keynesian Episode: A Reassessment*, Indianapolis, IN: Liberty Press.

Keynes, J.M. (1936) *The General Theory of Employment, Interest and Money*, London: Macmillan.

Laidler, D. and Estrin, S. (1989) *Introduction to Microeconomics*, 3rd edn, London: Philip Allan.

Lucas, R.E. (1972) 'Expectations and the neutrality of money', *Journal of Economic Theory* 4: 115–38.

Mair, D. and Miller, A.G. (1991) *A Modern Guide to Economic Thought*, Aldershot: Edward Elgar.

Novak, M. (1982, 1991) *The Spirit of Democratic Capitalism*, New York: Madison Books.

Parkin, M. and Bade, R. (1988) *Modern Macroeconomics*, 2nd edn, Oxford: Philip Allan.

Pigou, A.C. (1941) *Employment and Equilibrium*, London: Macmillan.

Preston, R.H. (1991) *Religion and the Ambiguities of Capitalism*, London: SCM.

Say, J.B. (1803) *Traité d'Economie Politique* (cited by D.P. O'Brien (1975) *The Classical Economists*, Oxford: Clarendon, pp.159–62).

Smith, A. (1776) in R.H. Campbell, A.S. Skinner and W.B. Todd (eds) *Adam Smith: An Inquiry into the Nature and Causes of the Wealth of Nations*, vol. I, Oxford: Clarendon, 1976.

Thomas S. Torrance

CATHOLICISM

Catholicism's relationship to the whole of society has been shaped by the theological conviction that, while the ultimate end of the Catholic Church's activity is an eschatological one, such an end encompasses human life and activity short of ultimacy. How this relationship between heavenly and earthly CITY shapes the interactions of ecclesial and secular authorities, institutions and communities depends on other informing theological ideals and the historical circumstances in which they operate. It is possible to delineate three broad periods of the relationship between Catholicism and SOCIETY. From Constantine to the Reformation, we have the ideal of Christendom shaped around the concept of papal supremacy in the Holy Roman Empire in an era of the building of that ideal. From the Reformation until the twentieth century we have entrenchment around that same ideal during a period when historical circumstance made the Holy Roman Empire less viable. In the twentieth century we witness the opening to the modern world and a gradual turning away from the ideal of Christendom to that of the dignity of all persons, who are born in the image of God.

This shift from the ideal of Christendom to that of human dignity coincides with the change in the kind of POWER that the Catholic Church exercises in world affairs from instrumental to expressive power. Instrumental power is that which operates through instrumental activities like economic growth and political procedures. Expressive power is exercised through activities such as the symbolic representation of religious beliefs and the articulation of ideals and norms (for more on these terms, see Hanson 1987). While these two forms of power are not mutually exclusive, the Catholic Church has seen its type of power shift from a mixed form, where it both articulated norms and participated in the instrumental execution of them, to a primary emphasis on expressive power. In this historical context of the development, decline and disappearance of the Holy Roman Empire, Catholicism has shifted its theological understanding of its relationship with society by turning from the ideal of Christendom to the concept of the transcendent dignity of the human person.

The first period is the development of the Holy Roman Empire. The fusing of instrumental and expressive power in Christendom was made possible by the Edict of Milan in 313, which granted Christians religious freedom, and the law of 380, where Christianity was made the official religion of the empire. Prior to this point, the Roman church exercised only expressive power in society. The key question during this period was how the emperor and the pope related – who exercised what kind of power and how much – and what rationale was given for that relationship (my treatment of the medieval papacy follows that of Walter Ullmann 1972).

The petrine themes in the rationale for the papacy begin to develop in the fourth century, and they do so coupled with a monarchical structuring of the church that paralleled that of the empire. This, combined with the move of Constantine from Rome to Constantinople led to the tensions between pope and emperor. In 382, a synod in Rome under Pope Damasus declared that the basis of the AUTHORITY of the Roman church was not imperial decrees, but the theological and Biblical basis that the pope is a successor to Peter. The reasoning was built on Matthew 16: 18, where Jesus leaves the care of the churches with Peter. The petrine idea received further support in four ways. First, the theological metaphor of the 'body of Christ', identified Peter – and the popes in succession – as the 'head'. Second, the synod statement was soon supplemented by the 'discovery' of a translation of a document that was purported to be St Peter's last will, where he, in juristic fashion, hands the leadership of the church over to Clement I, the first pope. Third, Leo I added the idea of 'inheritance', further underscoring the juristic nature of the office of the papacy. Finally, the petrine idea with its various supports was perpetuated by means of the issuance of papal decretals, while the Biblical and other textual backings, in turn, provided a basis for the claim that the decretals articulated divine law for humanity.

Imperial challenge to the status of the papacy led to further refinements in the rationale of the latter during the pontificates of Felix III and, especially, Gelasius I. For Gelasius, government required both emperor and pope, but only the pope possessed divine *autoritas*, or authority. This gave the pope pre-eminence in matters pertaining to the Christian society (e.g. ecclesiastical organization, doctrine and jurisdiction). The emperor had the power only to execute the guidelines set down by the pope. This understanding of the relationship between the two powers gave specificity to the petrine doctrine.

The emperor Justinian (527) attempted to reverse this order of priority. Rome had been lost to the Goths. Reconquest of Rome would allow Justinian to restore the Roman church to pre-eminence among churches while setting emperor over pope. Justinian made many declarations on theological issues under the rationale that sacral matters are part of public law. Much of the struggle between pope and emperor throughout the Middle Ages can be understood as an extension of the basic arguments set forward by Gelasius and Justinian.

A major turning point came with the pontificate of Gregory I (590). He recognized that there was no possibility for claims of papal jurisdiction in relation to Constantinople. Thus he turned to the Western and Germanic peoples of Spain, Gaul and Britain where the papal claims of priority were much better received. The West, with its acceptance of the petrine rationale, was more attractive because, with no military force, the church could have political or instrumental power only in lands where its expressive power also held. The turn to the West was in large part dictated by its reception of the theological rationale for the supremacy of the papacy.

When the Frankish king refused to help the pope with the invading Lombards, Pope Zacharius appealed to Pippin the Short, a mayor, who then overthrew the king. Pippin went on to defeat the Lombards. This created the papal state and marked another key point in the period when the Catholic Church extricated itself from its ties to Constantinople and joined with the West. In 754, Stephen II crowned Pippin king.

Both the papal lands and the anointing of the king were backed by a forgery from the late fifth century, the 'Donation of Constantine'. The document describes Constantine giving Pope Silvester, as the successor to St Peter, the lands and the right to create consuls and patricians. Pippin felt himself to be defending the rights of St Peter. Pippin's son, Charlemagne, continued the role of papal protector, and added even more territories to the 'patrimony of St Peter'. This allowed the papacy to cut its ties with Constantinople. In 800, Leo III crowned Charlemagne emperor. Throughout the ninth century, the Gelasian ordering of the relationship between pope and emperor held sway, as indicated by the fact that the former crowned the latter.

A series of weak popes in the tenth and first half of the eleventh century led to attempts by secular rulers to reverse the priority of pope over emperor, particularly during the rule of Otto the Great (936–73). However, the institution of the papacy, with its rationale, continued and allowed for the series of events which marked the relationship between Pope Gregory VII and Henry IV. Gregory strongly forbad lay investiture of ecclesiastical offices and excommunicated Henry for violations, forcing the latter to ask for absolution in 1077. Henry later deposed Gregory and replaced him with Clement III, who crowned Henry emperor.

These tensions continued in the twelfth and thirteenth centuries. Emperors drew upon the Justinian code to argue for the ancient understanding of their power as autonomous and universal, as opposed to the ecclesiastical understanding of the emperor as a ruler who protects the prerogatives of the church. Frederick I Barbarosa elected himself emperor in 1152 without requesting permission from the pope. He also elected his own anti-popes and tried several times, without success, to take Rome. In the meantime, the church attempted to strengthen its own position by refining and buttressing the Gelasian theory. Bernard of Clairvaux gave shape to the 'two swords' theory, which concretized Gelasius' emphasis on the two powers. Papal predominance in the theory was enacted in coronation rites where the pope would give the terrestrial sword to the emperor. Also added to the idea of succeeding Peter was that of the pope being the 'vicar of Christ', the ruler of the universal church who acted as vicariously as Christ would have acted.

A vigorous papacy returned with Innocent III. At the turn of the thirteenth century, he recovered lost papal territories and set in place in Europe again the Gelasian understanding of the relationship between pope and emperor. Under him, further metaphors were added to the rationale for supremacy. Pope and emperor were as sun and moon with the latter receiving light – and power – from the former. They were as soul and body, with the former giving life to the latter.

However, even with the strength of Innocent III, the thirteenth century witnessed the beginning of historical developments that would culminate in the Protestant Reformation. The empire was beginning to break up. By 1314, it had become a German principality rather than a pan-European entity. Politically, separate monarchies were gaining strength. The concept of territorial sovereignty emerged in the early fourteenth century. While the church had a rationale for its relationship to emperors, it had none for its dealings with kings. Economically, the development of towns and the rise of the bourgeois class had begun. Both political and economic developments led to a loss in the instrumental power of the pope. In the fifteenth century, the papacy forged its first 'concordats' with nations. The pope, no longer superior to the nations, had to enter into contracts with them. By the end of the fifteenth century, the papacy was reduced to a power in central Italy.

This was coupled with a loss in expressive power with the rise of Renaissance humanism and the ideas of the natural person and the citizen to oppose the ideas of the Christian and the serf. The spread of vernacular literature abetted this new sense of power in the common person. Yet the church stayed with the petrine rationale and Gelasian theory that had supported papal monarchy and the ideal of Christendom up to this point. The loss of instrumental power was joined with a shift in the way expressive power was articulated in a changing Europe. Aeneas Sylvius Piccolomini, later to become Pope Pius II, said these words:

I prefer to be silent and I could wish that my opinion may prove entirely wrong and that I may be called a liar rather than a true prophet . . . . For I have no hope that what I should like to see will be realized; I cannot persuade myself that there is anything good in prospect. . . . Christianity has no head whom all will obey. Neither the pope nor the emperor is accorded his rights. There is no reverence and no obedience; we look on pope and emperor as figureheads and empty titles. Every city-state has its king and there are as many princes as there are households.

The papacy was not its own best ally. Corruption in the form of simony (the sale of ecclesiastical offices) and pluralism (the possession of more than one office by those who could afford it) weakened a church that was already placed in a precarious position by historical developments outside its control. Efforts at reform failed, and the time was ripe for the forms of church called for by Luther, with his emphasis on the priesthood of all believers, and Calvin, with his broad delineation of offices into those of pastor, teacher, elder and deacon. Catholicism from the sixteenth to the dawn of the twentieth century can be understood under the rubric of the attempt to retain the ideal of Christendom as linked to papal monarchy and the empire in Gelasian fashion in a time when such an attempt was futile given historical circumstances. The result was a church that was often reactionary in its efforts to sustain the unsustainable.

Papal fear of conciliarism and curial resistance to reform at first obstructed efforts to hold a council in the first half of the sixteenth century. However, the Council of Trent convened in 1545. In large part, it affirmed the hierarchical structure of the church and the rationale behind it. Reform of the episcopacy itself led to greater efficiency in carrying out the Tridentine mandates. While the Tridentine Mass ensured uniform expression of the faith the catechism ensured uniform practice. The Inquisition was reconstituted and supplemented by the Congregation of the Index, which issued lists of condemned books. Thus, while the Gelasian form of Christendom was no longer realizable, the papacy could, and did, re-establish control over the church itself, in large part as a means to resist external developments.

The political battle transformed from one between pope and emperor to one between kings and princes, trying to extend the faith of their choice. This period of the religious wars ended with the Thirty Years War (1618–48) and the Treaty of Westphalia, which mandated that each region take the religion of its ruler. With the exception of France, the most powerful and populous countries, including Prussia, Sweden and England, all became Protestant.

The loss of expressive power continued with the onset of the Enlightenment, which emphasized forms of knowledge not dependent on Biblical or ecclesiastical authority. In science, Copernicus, Kepler, Galileo and Newton all contributed to a view of the cosmos that undercut the Aristotelian metaphysics which underpinned the scholastic philosophical thought. This was particularly problematic because scholastic philosophy supported the hierarchical understanding of the universe that paralleled monarchy in both church and society. The call for religious freedom that corresponded to the new intellectual freedom hobbled both Protestant and Catholic establishments, even though states at best recognized only limited tolerance and not full-fledged religious freedom.

The case for Justinianism, which placed emperor over pope in the Middle Ages, was replaced by Gallicanism and, in the eighteenth century, its German counterpart, Febronianism. Here, the effort was by territorial rulers to limit the scope of the papacy and to subordinate the church to the state. Gallicanism is exemplified best in the rule of Louis XIV in France in the late seventeenth century. Louis called the Assembly of the Clergy, which issued the *Four Articles*. The *Articles* recognized the petrine succession but gave the papacy no instrumental authority. The pope was answerable to general councils, and his decrees were dependent upon their reception by the church. He was to have no infallibility separate from the church. A compromise was later reached where Gallicanism was to be taught, but not required, in the universities and seminaries. Still, the structure of the struggle for the age was set. Justinianism was replaced by Gallicanism, and the only hope for resisting the historical forces which made a Holy Roman Empire only a dim hope was a strong papacy. Gallicanism would be opposed by ultramontanism.

Ironically, the event that eventually strengthened ultramontanism's hand was that which most shook the church: the French Revolution. Relations between the church and the Revolution, though not conflictual at first, worsened when revolutionaries required an oath of compliance and reached the point of being beyond repair when they attempted to uproot Christianity altogether, replacing churches with 'Temples of Reason'. Though the secular religions failed, and Catholicism revived somewhat, strained relations with Napoleon – he captured Pius VI – kept the papacy from exercising any significant power in the church. However, Napoleon's loss at Waterloo turned this fortune around. The Congress of Vienna (1814–15) restored the Pope in Rome and the royal family, the Bourbons, in France. But it did not restore the *ancien régime*, as is evidenced in the fact that the state, and not the church, now controlled education, MARRIAGE and DIVORCE. However, an important and ironic consequence of this arrangement was that the church, freed from its ties with the state, could be ultramontane rather than Gallican.

Ultramontanism maintained the ideal of Christendom structured along Gelasian lines. Its primary intellectual spokesperson was Friedrich von Schlegel (d. 1829), who sought a return to the Holy Roman Empire in the form of a European confederation under the pope. Between 1815 and 1830, then, the churches, both Protestant and Catholic, realigned themselves with monarchs with this newly articulated ideal in mind. In opposition, Félicité de Lamennais (d. 1854) argued for the separation of church and state and the necessity of democratic rule for religious freedom and truth.

The major victories for ultramontanism came during the pontificate of Pius IX (1846–78). His Syllabus of Errors condemned eighty propositions supporting a wide array of ills including both SOCIALISM and CAPITALISM, rationalism, naturalism, progress, LIBERALISM and modern civilization. The state of siege continued. The climax was the definition of papal infallibility at Vatican I. The church compensated for the loss of instrumental power by granting the pope ultimate expressive power.

However, it was not simply the political world that had changed, but also the world of ideas. Greater openness to the modern world was necessary if the papacy was to have influence even over Catholics. Two related shifts in Catholic thought occur over the next century. The first is the gradual replacement of the ideal

of Christendom and the hope for restoration of a new Holy Roman Empire with the ideal of the dignity of the human person grounded in the *imago Dei* doctrine. This shift is coupled with a change in church–state theory, from the establishment of Catholicism to the recognition of religious freedom. Although the instrumental power of the church would never be what it once was, the changes inaugurated a period of resurgence in the church's expressive power.

The beginnings of a subtle but important change in church–state theory occurred even during the pontificate of Pius IX. His statement of the error on church–state relations, Error No. 77, struck many commentators as overly strong, suggesting that Catholicism should be established in every state. It read, 'It is no longer expedient that the Catholic religion should be treated as the only religion of the state, all other worships whatever being excluded.' The French bishop, Felix Dupanloup, soon published a commentary which qualified Pius's statement by developing the thesis–hypothesis distinction in the relations between church and state. Here, the ideal or 'thesis' remains the Catholic state. However, there is broader recognition that historical circumstances might necessitate, for the time being, a lesser form of relationship as 'hypothesis'. The arrangements in the United States, Latin America and Belgium, for instance, could be tolerated until circumstances allowed for the establishment of Catholicism.

However, it was Leo XIII's recognition of the need to protect persons against the abuses of industrialism that began the gradual shift in Catholic thought from an emphasis on Christendom to a focus on human dignity grounded in the image of God. The tradition of social encyclicals from Leo through John Paul II may be read as an articulation of the key threats to and requirements of human dignity (my analysis here follows that of David Hollenbach 1979). Leo's encyclical *Rerum Novarum*, written in 1891, focused on the abuses of the unfettered capitalism of the late nineteenth century. Therefore, he stressed what we now call economic rights. In particular, he emphasized the right to adequate remuneration for work and the right to retain the fruits of one's labour in the form of private PROPERTY (*see* BUSINESS).

Forty years later, Pius XI wrote *Quadragesimo Anno* in changed circumstances. The Great Depression, the formation of a communist regime out of the Russian Revolution, and the rise of Fascist dictatorships all required response. Like Leo, Pius emphasized the transcendent worth of the human person. However, the new circumstances required delineation of additional requirements for the protection of human dignity. Pius XI was aware, in a way that Leo was not, that some hierarchical structures are oppressive of human dignity. Pius XII (1939–58) carried forward this awareness and elaborated a list of rights that included both economic and civil-political rights. Of the latter, he lists, among other rights, the right to worship, to religious formation and education and to free choice of a state of life.

The full articulation of a Catholic HUMAN RIGHTS theory based on human dignity arrived with the pontificate of John XXIII. His encyclical *Pacem in Terris* integrated civil and economic rights through the recognition that human dignity is realized only in complex patterns of interdependence. The full recognition of each kind of right therefore depends on the protection and promotion of the other within an intricate web of rights and duties.

A consequence of this recognition of the full array of rights was the re-examination of Catholic teaching on religious freedom. By the time of the Second Vatican Council, Dupanloup's distinction between thesis and hypothesis had developed into a full-blown theory of church–state relations. The Catholic state was the ideal, even if other arrangements could temporarily be tolerated. But the new emphasis on the dignity of all persons, and the corresponding de-emphasis on the ideal of Christendom modelled on monarchy, created a situation where the idea of religious freedom and the recognition of no one institutional arrangement as normative became persuasive. The Second Vatican Council document, *Dignitatis Humanae*, made the new view official.

The key shift in the social situation since Vatican II has been the collapse of Soviet COMMUNISM. How to realize human dignity in this new context? What are the key threats? The encyclical of John Paul II, *Centesimus Annus*, which marks the one-hundredth anniversary of *Rerum Novarum*, begins to provide some answers. First of all, the fall of communism does not entail unqualified approval of capitalism. Any economic system, including capitalism, must be 'circumscribed within a strong juridical framework which places it at the service of human freedom in its totality' (no. 42). Indeed, the risk now is that there will be no attention to the social problems that socialism has attempted – and failed – to address. While the problem of the encroachment of the state has by no means disappeared, even with the fall of Soviet communism, the temptation is to overlook the way in which the reasoning of the market infringes upon other spheres of social life. John Paul warns of the 'affluent or consumer society' which tends toward a materialist reductionism that is analogous to that of communism. A just society requires other points of reference in addition to the market if capitalism is to serve the common good. The encyclical recognizes that there is more than one way to structure such a society. The aim of the document is to provide an 'ideal orientation'. As such it continues in the present stage of history the emphasis on human dignity, realized in society, and protected by the multiple spheres of human activity.

Hanson, Eric O. (1987) *The Catholic Church in World Politics*, Princeton, NJ: Princeton University Press.

Hollenbach, David (1979) *Claims in Conflict: Retrieving and Renewing the Catholic Human Rights Tradition*, New York: Paulist Press.

John Paul II, Pope (1991) *Centesimus Annus*, English translation Vatican City: Liberia Editrice Vaticana.

Tierney, Brian (1980) with selected documents, *The Crisis of Church and State, 1050–1300*, Englewood Cliffs, NJ: Prentice-Hall.

Ullmann, Walter (1972) *A Short History of the Papacy in the Middle Ages*, London: Metheun.

Todd David Whitmore

CELIBACY

Celibacy is the condition of sexual abstinence. The term usually implies male celibacy adopted, with solemn vows, as part of a religious vocation: but in modern usage it may be applied more widely to both sexes and for other motives. A celibate is to be distinguished from a bachelor (or spinster) in that the single state does not arise from lack of opportunity, resources or inclination; and from a virgin in that celibacy implies present continence but not necessarily lack of previous sexual experience.

The phenomenon of celibacy appears in many of the world's religions, for limited periods among adherents generally, and permanently for certain classes of spiritual teachers or leaders. It is of special interest to sociologists of religion, for celibate groups have often exerted influence out of all proportion to their size, and the regard in which celibacy is held is a valuable indicator of the degree to which any religion is world-affirming or world-denying. On this showing, Roman Catholicism, for example, comes closer to Buddhism, while Protestantism is closer to Judaism and Islam. (Of course other criteria produce different alignments.)

That there is a certain tension between the married state and religious practice or leadership in the cult is an early and widespread human perception. It seems to be based on a number of factors: that the act of sexual intercourse itself defiles or debilitates or exposes to the risk of invasion by the DEMONIC; that MARRIAGE creates partisan ties that may conflict with the interests of wider society symbolically represented in the cult; that devotion to the deity ought to override all other attachments and be proved by heroic renunciation of earthly goods, and so forth.

The Israelite tradition reflects these taboos to some extent. It treats emission of semen (Leviticus 15), along with menstruation and contact with dead bodies, as a source of uncleanness requiring purification before access to the cult is restored. Sexual abstinence is expected of priests and soldiers during their periods in Yahweh's service (e.g. 1 Samuel 21: 1–6, cf. Mark 2: 26). But there is no trace of institutionalized, permanent celibacy during the period represented by the Hebrew Bible. Ascetic groups like the Nazirites (Numbers 6: 1–5) or Rechabites (1 Chronicles 2: 55) abstained from alcohol and haircuts but not from sex. Israel refused to recognize celibacy as a superior status; it emphasized, rather, the ethnic

imperative to be fruitful and multiply, and raise up children to Abraham.

Nevertheless, in the first century CE, APOCALYPTIC hopes for the coming Age saw the rise of celibacy within Judaism. There were individual hermits like John the Baptist who declared that God could raise up children to Abraham from the stones of the desert (Matthew 3: 9). He rejected the life of the FAMILY and SOCIETY and sought to recapture the purity of Israel's wilderness experience in preparation for the advent of God. (See also the hermit Banos, who used daily cold baths to deflate sexual desire (Josephus, *Life* 2).) Others joined celibate communities such as, most probably, the Essene monastery at Qumran, where the principle of priestly and military chastity was maintained as a constant, ascetic discipline for all its members. In early Christianity also, celibacy was a response to imminent ESCHATOLOGY. Jesus of Nazareth encouraged his followers to leave wives and children (Mark 10: 29) and concentrate all their efforts on preaching the nearness of the Kingdom in the short time that remained before the coming of the Son of Man (Matthew 10: 23). The community he gathered around him understood itself as an alternative family, in which members were related non-sexually to each other as 'brothers and sisters' (Mark 3: 35). At the same time Jesus endorsed the natural family in certain respects: he insisted on the commandment to 'honour' parents (Mark 7: 10), i.e. to provide for them in their old age from the economic resources of the family unit; and he forbade DIVORCE, despite the Law, as contrary to the original purposes of God which were about to be realized in the coming age (Mark 10: 2–9). In the resurrection, marriage will be unnecessary, superseded by existence 'like the angels' (Mark 12: 25). To what extent Jesus went further and advocated present anticipation of this future state of blessedness is debated. The ambiguous wording of Luke's version of the dispute on the resurrection (20: 35) and the saying on 'eunuchs for the Kingdom' at Matthew 19: 12 may well reflect that shift from eschatology towards the ASCETICISM of a privileged élite which is typical of later developments. And Paul could find no instructions from the Lord to give to the Corinthians on the question of the unmarried (1 Corinthians 7: 12).

Paul was himself unmarried, finding a precedent for his vocation in Jeremiah, the only celibate prophet of Israel (Galatians 1: 15). He recommended the single state to any endowed with the particular divine gift (charisma: 1 Corinthians 7: 7). But the rationale he gave was moderate and practical: he wanted to avoid conflicts of interest between marital duty and Christian service (1 Corinthians 7: 32) and was concerned that the married were more likely to suffer in the 'tribulation' of the last days before the end (1 Corinthians 7: 28). The married were not to refrain from sexual intercourse except occasionally, by mutual consent, for purposes of prayer (1 Corinthians 7: 5). Engaged couples might decide not to proceed with marriage, but it was not a sin if they did not (1 Corinthians 7: 36 f. This passage does not advocate non-sexual cohabitation or 'spiritual marriage' though it was misread later that way). In general the earliest Church was too deeply imbued with traditional Jewish values to elevate celibacy in principle over marriage, as a higher state, however much particular circumstances might make the latter unadvisable. Deutero-Pauline letters assume marriage to be the norm for Christians (Colossians 3: 18 f.; Ephesians 5: 33; 1 Peter 3: 1–7; Hebrews 13: 4) and condemn the vaunted excesses of the ascetics (1 Timothy 4: 3). Nuptial imagery is desexed and appropriated for purposes of religious exhortation (e.g. Revelation 21: 9) but the practical consequence of sexual renunciation is rarely drawn (not even at Revelation 14: 4, where the description of the 144,000 is probably a metaphor for the 'chaste' army of Christ).

In the contemporary pagan world, however, the single state was widely revered. Traditional institutions like the Greek cult of Artemis or the Vestal Virgins in Rome were reinforced by the ascetic strain in philosophy: Pythagoreans, Cynics and Stoics despised the sexual act as a violent and irrational passion, disruptive of mental equilibrium, and with damaging medical side-effects. At the same time, various world-renouncing Eastern CULTS were making major inroads into the Hellenistic world. This setting influenced Christianity both positively and negatively. It provided social models into which the original eschatological vision could be translated and preserved despite its temporal disappointment: in the growing number of celibates among the higher clergy and missionaries, in the vocations of religious widows and 'solitaries' (in Greek 'monachoi', monks), in the cult of virginity, of virgin martyrs and the Blessed Virgin Mary, in the rejection of divorce and serious reservations about remarriage after the death of a spouse, and generally in the rigorous ordering of the private lives of lay Christians by means of the penitential system. On the other hand, the Church, especially in the East, also reacted against ascetical extremism, especially as it became linked with syncretistic and heretical tendencies in doctrine, in the case of Gnostics, Montanists, Encratites and Manichees. In order to keep its hold on society and resist the divisive effects of sectarianism, the Church concentrated its ideal of sexual purity into a special category of 'religious', monks, nuns and clergy, and defended the legitimacy, indeed the obligation, of normal married life for the laity.

The history of clerical celibacy in Christianity is complex and controversial. Broadly speaking, up to the fourth century, priests and deacons could be married and normally were; they could contract marriage after ordination. But there was strong popular feeling against clerical marriages, as is clear from the fact that Church Councils, despite a dissenting minority of largely Western representatives arguing the rigorist case, felt obliged to condemn the practices of boycotting eucharists celebrated by married clergy and of priests' abandoning their wives after ordination 'under the pretence of piety'. At first a vow of celibacy was only demanded when a candidate for ordination had previously committed an offence against chastity. But this was gradually ·extended so that all unmarried candidates were expected to take the vow; marriage was then effectively permitted only before ordination. Furthermore, married clergy were forbidden to remarry if their wives died and those who had married more than once were automatically disqualified from ordination.

After the fall of Rome, East and West moved apart. In the East, legislation was enacted by several emperors against married bishops, chiefly to protect Church property against the possibility of inheritance claims by their children. But the marriages of the lower clergy were left unregulated, except that they should abstain from sexual relations before the liturgy, a rule that has had the effect of preventing the development of daily eucharists in Orthodoxy. In the West, however, particularly in Spain, celibacy for all clergy became the norm. Candidates who were already married were required to take a vow of chastity and to live continently with their wives. But the policing of the bedrooms of married clerics became a major headache for church authorities, and proved the policy unworkable. In the wake of the collapse of the Carolingian Empire in the mid-ninth century and invasions by heathen hordes, clerical marriage and concubinage reached scandalous proportions. The popes of the eleventh century took strong measures to reform the situation and in the process exacerbated to breaking point relations with the East. The Second Lateran Council of 1139 finally eliminated the fiction of theoretically continent clerical marriages and made ordination a legal impediment to the contract of any subsequent marriage.

A similar period of open defiance of clerical discipline occurred in the fifteenth century and again attempts to bring about reform precipitated the second great schism in the Christian Church. At the Council of Trent in 1563, the 'objective' superiority of celibacy over marriage and its requirement for ordination as a matter of ecclesiastical, if not divine, law was affirmed – an action which decisively drove the cohabiting German clergy into the arms of Protestantism.

In Roman Catholicism since 1945, the debate has been reopened, against the background of a dramatic fall in the numbers of priestly vocations. Clerical celibacy is viewed more and more as an unnecessary disincentive to potential candidates for the priesthood, and as a personal deprivation without any of the compensating gains, financial security, social standing, reputation for holiness, that once accompanied it. In a period of liberalization in theology and practice since the Second Vatican Council (1962–5), there has been a flood of applications to Rome for dispensation from priestly vows ('laicization'). Although Paul VI reaffirmed traditional

discipline in his encyclical *Sacerdotalis Coelibatus* of 1967, he readily granted dispensations, unlike his successor John Paul II who has assiduously opposed the trend. However, the desire to promote friendlier relations with Eastern Orthodoxy and to recognize the place of the Uniats (Eastern Catholics), as well as the attempt to encourage conversions from Protestant and Anglican ministers, has mitigated the rhetoric of Roman denunciation of the evil of married clergy, which is now reserved for the threat of women priests. Ironically, however, if the Roman Catholic Church were to ordain women, it could solve the problem of the shortage of clergy and at the same time make it easier to maintain the Latin discipline on celibacy.

In Western secular societies, the dynastic and economic factors that even until recently dominated the institution of marriage have almost entirely given way to those of personal fulfilment and marital companionship. This change has profoundly affected the way procreation is viewed. To have children is everyone's right, but to limit their number is everyone's duty. A curious anomaly follows: huge investments of time and money in the treatment of infertility, and yet widespread practice of medical ABORTION. The modern nuclear family is a weak, fragile institution, liable to break down suddenly on purely emotional grounds, increasingly lacking any social, legal or financial rationale. It is not surprising, therefore, that it has come under attack from several quarters.

What could be called 'the new celibacy' has arisen as one such protest. In contrast to the experiments in communal living and multiple sexual partners of the 1960s, radical critics of Western society are now quite as likely to exalt the single state and advocate complete sexual renunciation. Factors involved here are, first, the growing awareness that we are facing an impending demographic crisis: that the human population of the planet on present trends will stabilize at between 10 and 11 billions in the mid-twenty-first century, which will entail severe pressure on the means of food production, exhaustion of fossil fuel resources, the destruction of all the remaining wild life and a permanent change in the earth's atmosphere (*see* POPULATION CONTROL). Second, there is a range of other contributory factors that favour sexual abstinence, such as the threat of a world-wide AIDS epidemic, harsh legal penalties against RAPE, including rape within marriage, the increased political and financial independence and self-sufficiency of women, the rise of radical feminist consciousness, the availability of AID (artificial insemination by donor) and sperm banks screened to exclude congenital defects. All these factors together have contributed to remove the stigma of being unmarried and to promote the single state, for women and for men, as a preferable alternative. Whether this protest movement will last long, or will gain sufficient momentum permanently to affect the most basic of human drives and the normal pattern of human sexual behaviour, is open to serious question.

The celibate, in religion and in society, remains an ambiguous, counter-cultural figure, standing out heroically for other worldly values, for singleness and integrity, but at the same time liable to be drawn into parallel structures of power that mirror and even manipulate surrounding society.

Blenkinsopp, J. (1968) *Celibacy, Ministry, Church*, New York: Burns & Oates.

Brown, Peter (1989) *The Body and Society, Men, Women and Sexual Renunciation in Early Christianity*, London: Faber & Faber.

Burrus, V. (1987) *Chastity as Autonomy, Women in the Stories of the Apocryphal Acts*, Lewiston: Edwin Mellen.

Cholii, R. (1989) *Clerical Celibacy in East and West*, Leominster: Gracewing.

Cochini, C. (1990) *The Apostolic Origins of Priestly Celibacy*, San Francisco, CA: Ignatius Press.

Delhaye, P. (1967) *New Catholic Encyclopedia*, New York: McGraw–Hill, vol. 3, pp. 369–74.

Eliade, M. (ed.) (1987) *The Encyclopedia of Religion*, New York: Macmillan, vol. 3, pp. 144–8.

Foucault, M. (1986) *The History of Sexuality*, 2 vols, London: Penguin.

Frein, G.H. (1968) *Celibacy the Necessary Option*, New York: Herder & Herder.

Goergen, Donald (1979) *The Sexual Celibate*, New York: Image Books.

Greer, G. (1971) *The Female Eunuch*, London: Paladin Books.

Hodgkinson, L. (1986) *Sex is not Compulsory*, London: Columbus Books.

Lea, H.C. (1867) *A History of Sacerdotal Celibacy*; 4th rev. edn, London: Watts, 1932.

Leclerq, H. (1910) *Dictionnaire d'Archeologie Chretienne et de Liturgie*, ed. F. Cabrol, Paris: Letouzey, vol. 2, columns 2802–32.

Legrand, L. (1963) *The Biblical Doctrine of Virginity*, London: Geoffrey Chapman.

Ranke-Heinemann, Uta (1990) *Eunuchs for Heaven: The Catholic Church and Sexuality*, London: Andre Deutsch.

Rice, D. (1990) *Shattered Vows, Exodus from the Priesthood*, Belfast.

Thomas, G. (1986) *Desire and Denial, Sexuality and Vocation*, London: Grafton.

John Muddiman

CENSORSHIP

Censorship is the activity in which an authority (usually public) attempts to control, limit or suppress publications, information, beliefs, arguments. This activity is defended as being for the protection of (usually) a public good against instability or subversion.

Underlying the whole question of censorship are the questions of the nature of secrecy (with its threats and values) and the authority and stability of a group. Historically, different aspects have been debated. An older view was more social and political. It was concerned with the need of a self-determining people to have access to all the relevant information to make their own decisions. Behind this lay notions of AUTONOMY, and the idea of a *right* to information and publication was developed. Along with this there follow questions of the need for education and discernment, and differing ideals of particular kinds of SOCIETY. This cluster of ideas will be developed later. The focus is changed in post-Enlightenment and post-liberal attacks on censorship. Here, following the growth of individualism, the self-evident good is seen to be the dignity of the individual and that individual's free expression. Freedom of expression leads to the liberation of the person from community. It brings in turn issues of radical subjectivity and relativism (mirrored in modern hermeneutical theory). These ideas will be developed later: in contemporary society the crucial question is whether it is possible to speak of there being a common AUTHORITY in a pluralist culture.

Plato's *Republic* (Books 3 and 10) contains a

classic defence of censorship. First, the poets are attacked for having a lack of knowledge (595a–602c). They only copy the way things appear, and so are at a third remove from the TRUTH. Second, the poets are seen as dangerous: they encourage the desires which ought to be suppressed (605c–608b). For theories of censorship, significant points here are (a) Plato's realist theory of knowledge – truth or an all-encompassing knowledge is available and so should be searched for through education – and (b) society is homogeneous and brittle: it can be threatened by subversive ideals, and controlled and educated by law. This Platonic inheritance has haunted Western understandings.

The Judaeo-Christian tradition is ambivalent. The story of Eve, Adam and the fruit of the tree of the knowledge of good and EVIL implies that there are God-given limits to knowledge. The Hebrew wisdom tradition teaches the value of discernment, silence, institutional stability and the evil of gossip. The Johannine tradition ('you will know the truth and the truth will set you free' (John 8: 32)) blesses enquiry and implies that it will bring its own reward. This is significant for later Christian rejection of censorship.

Some of the early Christian Fathers (Ambrose (d. 397); Augustine (d. 430)) voluntarily submitted their works for prior censorship. The Franciscan Order legislated concerning censorship in the *Constitutiones Narbonnenses* (1260). Censorship was instituted for the entire Church after the invention of the printing press (1453) in the 1487 bull *Inter multiplices* of Pope Innocent VIII (1482–92). This bull was reissued in 1501 and included in the Fifth Lateran Council (1512–17). Pope Leo XIII (1878–1903) gathered up and reorganized later legislation on censorship in the constitution *Officiorum ac munerum* (25 January 1897). Much of this constitution was taken into the Code of 1918. Pius X reinforced the regulations in the encyclical *Pascendi dominici gregis* (8 December 1907).

This censorship of books prior to publication was justified both on the ground of the Church's divine mission, which, it claimed, gave it exclusive control over Biblical interpretation and dogma, and on the NATURAL LAW principle that, just as a father has a right to protect his children, so the Church has a right to protect its members in the matter of their faith and morals. Behind this there lay questionable notions of truth as some kind of static deposit of revelation over which the institutional Church held control.

The Protestant Reformation, appealing to scripture, challenged the authority of the Roman Church's interpretation, and attempted to reformulate a dynamic and living understanding of God in encounter with whom theological statements are made, but who always relativizes anything we can say about God. This in turn provoked a need for the publication of adequate Biblical texts, and an awareness of the provisionality of anything we say about God.

On the secular side, in post-Reformation England, there was an increasing impatience with prior to publication censorship ('prior restraints') as an awareness of the need for documents and argument grew. In his pamphlet *Areopagitica* (1644), John Milton insisted on 'the liberty to know, to utter, and to argue freely according to conscience' as the basic inheritance of the Reformation. On this basis he argued classically for the freedom to publish, upholding a vigorous belief that truth 'needs no policies, nor strategems, nor licensings to make her victorious'. This was instrumental in the abandoning of prepublication censorship in England in 1695. The principle was enshrined in William Blackstone's *Commentaries on the Laws of England* (1765–9) and the First Amendment to the Constitution of the USA (1791).

Nineteenth-century liberalism showed a different slant to the question, moving from the question of freedom of speech (or publication) to defending freedom of expression. Here the classic document was John Stuart Mill's essay *On Liberty* (1859). Mill defended freedom of expression on the grounds, first, that if any opinion is silenced that opinion may still be true. 'To deny this is to assume our own infallibility.' Second, even if the silenced opinion were an error, it might contain a portion of truth, and 'it is only by the collision of adverse opinions that the remainder of the truth has any chance of being supplied'. Third, even if the received opinion were the whole truth, unless it is 'frequently, and fearlessly discussed, it will be held as a dead dogma, not a living truth'. Mill is less sanguine than Milton about the ability of the truth to triumph. The truth is often suppressed. Nevertheless, he is a modern in his recognition of the futility of claiming infallibility and in his insistence that our opinions must be open and gradually yield to fact and argument.

Despite certain lapses, freedom of speech is well entrenched in the Western democracies during the the 1990s. A free press, sanctioned by law, is recognized as a vital part of a free society and a safeguard against TOTALITARIANISM and atrocities. The West must never forget the lessons of the HOLOCAUST. The USA deserves credit for the way it is prepared to wash dirty linen in public.

Freedom to publish is equally entrenched in the West. The dissemination of information has never been easier than it is in the modern world, not just through hard copy, but also through floppy disk, fax, modem and satellite TV. In a computer society, prepublication censorship is impossible. Nevertheless, the explosion in modern information technology brings its own dangers. Truly vast amounts of data are now easily stored and searched. This raises anxieties over public access to databanks. Electronic search programs operate with their own (unintentional) censorship and may present misleading returns. Sissela Bok (1983) has been a robust critic of official secrecy in its many forms.

However, the most intractable contemporary ethical concerns over censorship lie elsewhere. The issue is not 'what may be published?' but 'what may not be published?' Even PORNO-GRAPHY claims to be a mode of expression. Nineteenth-century liberalism separated the public and private realms. It was considered inappropriate to legislate for private morality (note the contrast to Plato). Late twentieth-century pluralism has dismantled the agreed principles of the public realm and given public ('ethnic') status to the private world. Narrative ethics (MacIntyre 1981; Hauerwas 1983) dismiss the notion of abstract and independent ethical principles: values are concrete and arise within communities, which must give up specious ethical imperialism. Postmodern ethicists stress cultural relativity. If this argument is pursued, the pressing question is: how can local moralities avoid being sectarian? If all moralities are local and we are bereft of general principles (there is a late twentieth-century hostility to the Enlightenment), we have no means of deciding between self-righteous interest groups. In the absence of agreed principles, threats are applied. The paradigm instance is the censorship of Salman Rushdie's *Satanic Verses* (1988) by the Muslim world (*see* BLASPHEMY). Another instance is the rise of POLITICAL CORRECTNESS (the threatened liberal establishment) and the censorship and newspeak it imposes. We are faced by crusading fundamentalisms. In attempting to find a resolution, Sharon Welch (1990) argues for an ethic of communication, and Jonathan Sacks (1991) makes a plea for bilingualism: we learn the language of the tribe because that is where we discover our identity, but we must also learn the language of CITIZENSHIP. There are parallels in modern hermeneutical theory where, after a phase of believing that every interpretation had validity, there are new moves to recover an ethic of reading (*see* HERMENEUTICS).

Appignanesi, Lisa and Maitland, Sara (1989) *The Rushdie File*, London: Fourth Estate.
Bok, Sissela (1983) *Secrets*, New York: Pantheon Books.
Gardiner, H.C. (1961) *Catholic Viewpoint on Censorship*, New York: Image Books.
Hauerwas, S. (1983) *The Peaceable Kingdom*, Notre Dame, IN: University of Notre Dame Press.
Itzin, Catherine (ed.) (1992) *Pornography: women, violence and civil liberties*, Oxford: Oxford University Press.
MacIntyre, A. (1981) *After Virtue*, London: Duckworth.
Mill, John Stuart (1859) *On Liberty*, London: Fontana Library, William Collins, 1962.
Milton, John (1644) *Areopagitica*, London: Everyman's Library, Dent, 1927.
Sacks, J. (1991) *The Persistence of Faith*, London: Weidenfeld and Nicolson.
St John-Stevas, N. (1956) *Obscenity and the Law*, London: Secker & Warburg.
Welch, S. (1990) *A Feminist Ethic of Risk*, Minneapolis, MN: Fortress.

Iain Torrance

CHARISMATIC MOVEMENTS

In Christian theology, the term 'charismatic'

refers to the highly subjective, intensely affective and non-rational form of worship identified with 'baptism in the spirit' and its supernatural gifts (*charismata*): 'speaking in tongues' (glossolalia), faith healing, prophecy and exorcism. By extension, in sociological theory the term is used, following Max Weber, to designate a kind of emotionally charged AUTHORITY centred in the leader of a social movement whose personal powers and qualities are recognized by his followers to be extraordinary and to have superhuman or divine origins. Both senses are operative in this article as the development and significance of a particular charismatic movement, the non-denominational Neopentecostal renewal of the mid- to late twentieth century, is considered in the light of Weber's 'ideal type' of charismatic social action.

As understood here 'the charismatic movement' refers to recent manifestations of Pentecostal Christianity that in some way differ from classical Pentecostalism in doctrine or affiliation. Unlike classical Pentecostals, whose denominations are rooted directly in the American Pentecostal revival of the early twentieth century, those who call themselves 'charismatics' most often trace their origins to the widespread renewal of communion in the Holy Spirit that began within the traditional non-Pentecostal churches of the USA in the early 1960s. Charismatics are now part of nearly all Protestant denominations, the Roman Catholic church and, to a very limited extent, the Eastern Orthodox church worldwide. Ecumenical in nature, the movement has manifested itself predominantly in the form of small prayer groups intent on integrating the experience of Spirit baptism and the practice of the charismata into the traditional beliefs and practices of their respective churches without significantly transforming them. Among some Protestant charismatics baptism in the Holy Spirit is regarded as a distinct act of grace. Many Protestants and all Roman Catholic charismatics, however, regard it as a renewal or actualization of that spiritual baptism which all Christians receive in water baptism or on their conversion.

Contingent features of theology and expressive style aside, all charismatic worship involves the ritual re-enactment of Acts 2: 1–4 in which believers recapture the awe, wonder, mystery and joy in the immediate experience of the Holy Spirit. WORSHIP releases the individual believer's power of self-expression while creating an emotional bond with the spiritual community. Witnesses to baptism in the spirit repeatedly refer to a personal encounter with Jesus, a more complete acceptance of him, and a deeper yielding to his importance in their lives. Yet, the aspects most readily identifiable as characteristic of the charismatic renewal are spiritual gifts described in 1 Corinthians 12: 8–10. While this text comprises nine charismata, those that are most central to the Neopentecostal revival are glossolalia, PROPHECY and healing. The significance of the movement, in the eyes of many charismatics, is not so much that it has brought the occurrence of these gifts to the mainline churches, but that it has raised the expectation that they are continuously available and fostered the conviction that they are an essential part of the mission of each local church.

It is widely accepted that, as a distinct religious movement, the charismatic renewal began on Easter Sunday, 1960, when Father Dennis Bennett, rector of fashionable St Mark's Episcopal Church in Van Nuys, California, reported to his congregation that he had spoken in tongues at a private prayer meeting. Exiled by the church hierarchy to a marginal inner-city parish in Seattle, he continued to promote the charismata in the belief that there was no contradiction between his Episcopal confession and Pentecostal experiences. His church grew rapidly, gaining support from many mainline ministers and priests and wide publicity in the mass media. Within a short time many Protestant intellectuals and theologians espoused the cause of the new Pentecost, feeling it possible again to have a direct experience of God. By 1967 the movement began to make inroads among Catholics. In that year professors of theology at Duquesne University led students into the Pentecostal experience. It spread from there to students and faculty of Notre Dame and the University of Michigan, and by the decade's end had filtered down to the local parishes, spawning hundreds of charismatic prayer groups which gathered at conventions numbering in the tens of thousands. Growth of the movement in Great Britain, continental Europe and other parts of the world was similarly widespread (Quebedeaux 1983: 64–72).

As the charismatic renewal gained momentum, its ECCLESIOLOGY modified the experience of the Pentecost. Sectarian Pentecostalism was primarily a religious movement of the black American underclass. Meetings were frequently characterized by spontaneous and highly expressive vocalizations and body gestures. By contrast, Neopentecostal experience, accommodated to white middle-class styles of worship, was subdued. Not only was the practice of charismata generally removed from public worship and made a feature of private prayer meetings, in some cases the very nature of the gifts themselves was subtly altered. Differences in social background between Pentecostals and charismatics were reflected in their respective healing ministries. While Pentecostals emphasized physical healing, charismatics, with a middle-class sensitivity to psychology, focused on healing the emotions. Moreover, glossolalia became less central for Neopentecostals, who at the same time sought and, to a certain extent, achieved legitimacy for this practice in mainstream academic and professional circles (ibid.: 170–3).

With its stress on the need for personal conversion to Christ, the authority of the Bible and the mandate for spreading the Gospel, charismatic renewal shared important theological concerns with Neoevangelicalism. Though many Neoevangelicals considered themselves charismatics, the movement did not accept Neoevangelicalism's demand for doctrinal agreement as the precondition of Christian unity. Rather, it was Spirit baptism – shared experience of the Pentecost – that was seen to be the unifying principle transcending separated believers and denominations.

By emphasizing the recovery of the New Testament charismata, Neopentecostalism represented a remarkable return to experiential religion within the middle classes of Western Christianity of the modern era. It allowed the common believer to recapture the sense of awe and mystery in the universe that had been eclipsed in both Protestant Neoevangelicalism, with its reverence for 'propositional revelation' and Baconian inductive logic in its doctrine of Biblical inerrancy, and Protestant and Catholic liberalism, with its rational and 'demythologized' theology (ibid.: 235–6).

The charismatic movement seemed to gain additional legitimacy and stature with the election of Jimmy Carter to the US presidency in 1976, though by that time mainline acceptance of the new Pentecost had been widespread and it was estimated that one-third of all American Christians thought of themselves as 'charismatic' (ibid.: 80). By 1977 the primary goal of revitalizing Christianity had been largely met and the movement began to lose distinctness, merging with the larger EVANGELICAL mainstream into the potent social and political force of the New Christian Right. The rise of large, well-funded, independent and technologically sophisticated popular television ministries, including those of Pat Robertson, Jerry Falwell, Jim Bakker and Jimmy Lee Swaggart, has both enhanced the movement's reach and potentially altered the nature of the experience it has sought to awaken in both the churched and the unchurched (Frankl 1987: 151, 154).

The status of charismatic renewal as a social movement is demonstrable by its large number of adherents, its prevalence across many denominations and the collective pursuit of objectives that affect and shape the social order in some fundamental respect. Its objective of revitalizing Christianity by reaffirming the belief in the supernatural that has been sapped by rationalism and secularism is also a challenge to what is seen as the dominant ethos of modern Western values. While much of the effort of the movement is directed toward personal conversion, such changes also bring certain institutional and cultural transformations. Generalizing the charisma of the movement involves the very problems described by Weber regarding all types of charismatic action. The charismatic movement's ideology requires personal, i.e. emotional/affective, experience of the power of the Holy Spirit, but efforts to recruit and proselytize require a degree of rational organization. A certain tension thus exists in the charismatic movement between its charisma and its rational activities as a social movement. Weber writes that a charismatically led group is elevated out of the routine of its mundane concerns. Charismatic authority is undermined to the extent that collective action is 'routinized'. In the case of the charismatic renewal, adherents believe that they have been elevated out of the routine of everyday life as they experienced the signs and wonders of the charismata being demonstrated at conferences and on television and reported in books. The various attempts to market the movement, however, have brought a degree of institutionalization that threatens to mechanize the experience and render it inauthentic. To bring the gifts of the Holy Spirit to an audience in the millions, televangelist Pat Robertson, for example, must apply the rationally calculated means necessary to sustain an economic organization dedicated to the mass production of messages. Thus in order for the ministry to survive and advance, the substance of the charismata must appear within the forms dictated by the logic of the broadcast industry. A complex technological infrastructure involving telephone banks, satellite hookups and computerized direct mailing that links converts to elaborately scripted acts of worship amid appeals for donations in popular televised formats, such as the 'talk show' or 'docudrama', for many now constitutes the environment, if not the vehicle, of Pentecostal inspiration (ibid.: 79–101).

It is a widely held belief among charismatics that the wholesale adoption of what is essentially an entertainment medium in order to bring Christians into a more intimate relationship with the Holy Spirit has worked to the benefit of the renewal while not diminishing the mystery and awe of the Gospel's re-enactment (Poloma 1982: 187). Nevertheless, there can be no doubt that visual mass media, to some as yet undetermined extent, have significantly reordered the modalities of profane experience. How the intensely personal and yet communally ecstatic experience of the Pentecost can be transmitted by way of electronically mediated, parasocial interaction without being extinguished or transformed remains an open question.

Anderson, R.M. (1979) *Vision of the Disinherited: The Making of American Pentecostalism*, Oxford: Oxford University Press.

Frankl, R. (1987) *Televangelism: The Marketing of Popular Religion*, Carbondale, IL: Southern Illinois University Press.

Harrell, D.E. (1976) *All Things Are Possible: The Healing and Charismatic Revivals in Modern America*, Bloomington, IN: University of Indiana Press.

Jones, J.W. (1974) *Filled With New Wine*, New York: Harper & Row.

McDonnell, K. (1976) *Charismatic Renewal and the Churches*, New York: Seabury Press.

Poloma, M. (1982) *The Charismatic Movement: Is There a New Pentecost?*, Boston, MA: Twayne.

Quebedeaux, R. (1983) *The New Charismatics II*, New York: Harper & Row.

Weber, M. (1978) 'The nature of charismatic domination', in W.G. Runciman (ed.) *Weber: Selections in Translation*, Cambridge: Cambridge University Press.

Wuthnow, R. (1988) *The Restructuring of American Religion*, Princeton, NJ: Princeton University Press.

Gary Calore

CHILD ABUSE

The components of the term 'child abuse' are of considerable lineage. The compound, however, is recent and reflects the creation and construction of a category of treatment towards others that has been long standing if relatively unproblematic until recently. The term 'abuse' has a Latin root *abusare* but it is not until early modern times that it has found its way into European languages in its present sense as misuse, disuse, ill-treat, violate, defile or pervert. The closest Biblical term is *katachraomi* a compound of *kata*, 'down', and *chraomai*, 'use'. It is used in 1 Corinthians 7: 31 to describe those who 'deal with the world as if they had no dealings with it' and in 1 Corinthians 9: 18 as 'not making full use of my right in the gospel'. The word 'child' is from the Old English *cild*, and appears as a translation of the Biblical *teknon*, where it appears figuratively as the children of, for example, God in John 1: 12, light in Ephesians 5: 8 and the Devil in 1 John 3: 10. As the diminutive *teknion*, it appears in plural form variously in, for example, 1 John 2, 3, 4, and Galatians 4: 28. *Huious* is a son but is also given as the 'children of Israel' in Matthew 27: 9. In 1 John it refers to 'the Son of God'. Related terms are *pais, paidion, paidarion, nepios* and *nepiazo*, the last as used in 1 Corinthians 14: 20 refers to being a babe: 'be babes in evil'. In spite of numerous literal and figurative uses of the terms 'child', 'abuse' and cognates the term child and the term abuse are not placed together.

The absence of any direct Biblical view on child abuse is scarcely surprising. Until recently, the status of children in Western cultures was low, and in many cultures even today the child is regarded as akin to a commodity. In states that have limited WELFARE or that are primarily FAMILY or kinship based rather than individualistic, children contain present and future guarantees for the aged and infirm members of the family. In such cases what appears as exploitation from an individualistic viewpoint may appear as necessary from the viewpoint of a kinship-based system in a SOCIETY that has no state-based welfare safety net. What also emerges from a comparative perspective, historical or geographical, is that the idea of the child as a semi-autonomous being is a construct of individualistic modes of life. Outside of individualism the child is always absorbed into some other network, family, tribe, clan, sib, etc. The right of the father to the power of life over death of his son was developed in its fullest known form in the Ancient Roman institution of *patria potestas*. That power began at birth when a father could reject a newborn child and concluded only with the death of the father. While the father lived the child, whatever its rank in the CITY might be, was never autonomous from the father.

There is some evidence that early European forms of individualism began to make a clear distinction between parents and children in a type of contract theory in which in return for the parents looking after the children at one stage of life the children would look after the parents at a later stage of life. The clearest break between the understandings of the past and the present, however, is to be found in John Locke's claim that the basis of paternal power is the exercise of dominion over the child for the benefit of the child, not the benefit of the parent. This argument is striking for it relies on ideas drawn from traditional Biblical readings, St Thomas Aquinas, and Richard Hooker to show that any POWER, whether it be the power held by a STATE or the power held by a father, is not absolute but a trust. Locke's argument places political power with the people and personal power with the child.

Locke's arguments were not fully developed, however, and, until very recently, still not fully acknowledged. Between Locke and the present stands the growth of the nation-state and the Industrial Revolution. The former gave rise to the individualism on which the idea of the child could be developed. The latter produced previously unheard-of and unthought-of levels of exploitation of people of all ages. As much as anything it was literary accounts of the maltreatment of young people that helped construct the idea of 'the child', and the idea of 'childhood'; an era of life singled out for its protection from the world rather than its exposure to the world. Charles Kingsley's *The Water Babies*, the socially acute observations of the maltreatment of children in the novels of Charles Dickens, and, in the USA, the accounts of childhood years provided by Mark Twain, all contributed to the construction of the idea of a 'child' that could be abused and of a special period of life, 'childhood', that should be engendered, nurtured and protected. It is against that backdrop that not only the idea of child abuse developed, but the idea of a childhood that ought to be something that could be reasonably provided to all young people.

'Child abuse' as defined in contemporary Western societies has come to be specified in particular ways. In formal and professional terms 'child abuse' is now regarded as encompassing a specific range of types of child maltreatment. Four general categories are normally distinguished. In order of reported occurrence these are physical neglect, physical abuse, sexual abuse and emotional maltreatment. In the USA the largest proportion of physical neglect cases involve lack of adequate supervision, and the most frequently reported type of physical abuse is minor cuts and bruises (American Association for Protecting Children 1988). Severe cases like that of Maria Colwell in England in 1973 (Elliot 1991) and Lisa Steinberg in the USA in 1989, tragic though they are, are not representative of most child abuse cases (see CRUELTY).

Although children have not been regarded and even now are not always regarded as capable of abuse in terms of the Western definitions of that phenomenon, some kind of treatment of the child as a less than autonomous being is widespread. Some societies, and in some instances some religions, have sanctioned and still do sanction infanticide, especially of children who are illegitimate, of the wrong gender, or handicapped (Kuhse and Singer 1985; Zigler and Hall 1989). Over time, in Western society and in UN declarations views about the status of children have altered. They have become, in principle at least, progressively less likely to be regarded as chattels and therefore subject to disposal by parents or subject to other harmful acts, and more likely to be viewed as individuals having rights. This changing view of children and what constitutes their maltreatment depends less on moral and religious imperatives and more on economic and structural realities, social and economic forces. For example, indenture, a common recourse for parents unable to support their children and an economically useful institution, was outlawed in most Western jurisdictions in the nineteenth century. As other types of SLAVERY were made illegal, so indenture became defined as child maltreatment. This restriction is not applied universally; for instance it is common in Thailand for rural female children to be sold into prostitution to bring some economic benefit to the village or to the family from which they came. Such practices are now condemned under UN declarations, but realistically it has to be understood that without a satisfactory state backdrop that satisfies reasonable welfare needs the elimination of such practices lies somewhere in the range between the impossible and the miraculous. Formal definitions of child abuse can be given, but their precise content is always relative to actual cultures and actual circumstances. In the West, for instance, to deny a child education would be regarded as neglect, itself a category of abuse. But until there was universal compulsory education, parents could hardly be held to be guilty of educational neglect. Similarly, before condemning other cultural practices too quickly it is essential to pay attention to the matrix of available social possibilities. On the basis of the Kantian moral maxim that 'ought implies can' it would be unreasonable to demand that parents and society should do or conform to that which is not possible: to that which cannot be done.

Clearly given the recent construction of the idea of the child and of a childhood it is not surprising that the notion of child abuse has not attracted professional attention until recently. Only in the last 150 years has child abuse become a focus of professional attention. In the latter half of the nineteenth century, child well-being became a source of concern, especially for the profession of social work. However, the focus was as much on children whose parents were poor, as on children whose parents were abusive. The remedy was the same for both groups of children. They were removed from their parents' homes and placed in institutions or foster homes. In both the USA and Europe, the evolution of social welfare programmes provided economic support for poor families with children, and such children were no longer taken from their parents.

The idea of 'child abuse' fell by the wayside for some years and was 'rediscovered' in the 1960s, when in the USA a group of physicians (Kempe et al. 1962) reported on cases of children presenting at hospital with multiple fractures at various stages of healing. They used the term 'battered child syndrome' to describe the medical conditions of these children. Their work had a considerable impact in North America and in Western Europe. Ultimately it led to increased professional and societal awareness of child abuse and neglect, the development of legislation and institutions to address these troubling problems, and a more sophisticated understanding of child maltreatment and its variations.

Issues of debate are the causes of child abuse and its cures. Cases discovered by Kempe and his colleagues were quite severe and led to hypotheses that parents who engaged in such harmful behaviour were quite disturbed. These professionals also observed that abusive parents were often themselves abused as children. This gave rise to theories about the intergenerational transmission of child abuse. On the other hand, researchers who examined the characteristics of cases reported to child welfare agencies (Gil 1971; Gelles 1977; Garbarino 1988) described environmental stresses, such as poverty, unemployment and social isolation, as key factors leading to child maltreatment. At present most professionals accept that multiple factors play a part in child maltreatment, and models which include parental, victim, family, environmental and cultural factors are espoused.

Although society is likely to intervene regardless of who engages in abusive acts against children, behaviours of special concern are those committed by children's caretakers. In Lockean terms an abuse by a child's carer would be of particular concern for it would be a breach of a special trust. But abuse in any case has to be contextually understood; it is not, as some professionals may think, an absolute. Professionals may fail to appreciate that contributing and causal factors and their relative importance vary based upon type of maltreatment and the individual case. Physical neglect is, as a rule, closely tied to and often synonymous with poverty. In contrast, sexual abuse is likely to have its aetiology in the offender's psychopathology, particularly sexual arousal to children. Physical abuse is often precipitated by environmental stress, but parents may also have significant disturbance, particularly in impulse control. There is also variability in dynamics within the general categories of maltreatment. For example, the amount of disturbance in a parent who inflicts multiple fractures is much greater than that in a parent who bruises a child's arm. Similarly, two mothers may fail to nurture their children, but one may do so because she is overwhelmed by homelessness, poverty and unemployment, and the other because she is an alcoholic.

As a society we have so far invested more effort in identifying child maltreatment than in its prevention and cure. In the USA, and to a somewhat lesser extent in England, prevention programmes, supported by voluntary agencies, have been administered to children in schools and other settings. However, the majority of programmes target sexual abuse and rely upon the victim to resist and report their abuse. Few resources have been employed to teach teenagers appropriate child care and parenting or to provide training for expectant parents.

In both the USA and England, there have been drastic cuts in social welfare programmes, which are probably the most effective means of preventing child maltreatment. As noted above, where welfare programmes are absent or inadequate children come to serve functions that deny their childhood and deny their growth towards autonomy. Welfare programmes not only alleviate the environmental stresses that can precipitate abusive or neglectful behaviour, they are actually necessary conditions to the constitution of the 'child'. Although there has been a dramatic increase in reports of child maltreatment in the last forty years, in fact care of children has generally improved. The expanding number of reports is the result of societal and professional attention to the plight of children, a broadened definition of child maltreatment and new child abuse legislation and policy. However, it is not sufficient to identify and label child maltreatment. Sufficient resources, for broader social welfare programmes and specific services for child abuse, must be invested to remedy particular problems. More generally a society that does not invest in adequate and appropriate welfare programmes undercuts the very conditions that allow for the constitution of the child and the development of childhood. A society that condemns child abuse while cutting back on welfare programmes is generating a social and political fault line of major proportions. It is engaged in a deep and irreconcilable contradiction that can only end at best in tears and at worst in something far more terrible.

American Association for Protecting Children (1988) *Highlights of Official Child Abuse and Neglect Reporting, 1986*, Denver, CO: American Humane Association.

Cicchetti, D. and Carlson, V. (eds) (1989) *Child Maltreatment: Theory and Research on the Causes and Consequences of Child Abuse and Neglect*, Cambridge: Cambridge University Press.

Elliot, D. (1991) 'Substitute family care for children in Great Britain', *Social Services Review* 65(4): 565–81.

Faller, K.C. (1991) *Child Sexual Abuse: An Interdisciplinary Manual for Diagnosis, Case Management, and Treatment*, London: Macmillan.

Garbarino, J. (1988) *Psychological Maltreatment of Children*, Lexington, MA: Lexington Books.

Gelles, R. (1977) *Problems in Defining and Labelling Child Abuse*, Paper presented to the Study Group of the Problems in the Prediction of Child Abuse and Neglect, Wilmington, DE, June.

Gil, D. (1970) *Violence Against Children*, Cambridge, MA: Harvard University Press.

Giovannoni, J. and Becerra, R. (1979) *Defining Child Abuse*, New York: The Free Press.

Kempe, C.H., Silverman, F., Steele, B., Droegmueller, W. and Silver, H. (1962) 'The battered child syndrome', *Journal of the American Medical Association* 181: 4–11.

Kuhse, Helga and Singer, Peter (1985) *Should the Baby Live?* Oxford: OUP.

Locke, John (1690) *A Treatise Concerning the True Origin, Extent and End of Civil Government.*

Mrazek, P.B. and Kempe, H. (eds) (1981) *Sexually Abused Children and their Families*, London: Pergamon.

Polansky, N., Chalmers, M.A., Buttenweiser, E. and Williams, D.P. (1981) *Damaged Parents: An Anatomy of Child Neglect*, Chicago, IL: University of Chicago Press.

Zigler, E. and Hall, N. (1989) 'Physical child abuse in America: past, present, and future', in D. Cicchetti and V. Carlson (eds) *Child Maltreatment: Theory and Research on the Causes and Consequences of Child Abuse and Neglect*, Cambridge: Cambridge University Press.

Kathleen Coulborn Faller
Paul Barry Clarke

CHRISTIAN SOCIALISM

Christian socialism emerged as a distinct movement almost as soon as the word 'SOCIALISM' acquired its contemporary sense (*c*.1830). Marx tilted against it in the *Communist Manifesto* (1848). It shared with secular socialism a background in the Utopian thought of Saint-Simon (1760–1825), Fourier (1772–1837) and Robert Owen (1771–1858). At first Christian socialism was largely Protestant, and the fact that socialism was included in the 'Syllabus of Errors' (1864) inhibited its Catholic development. From the start it had four resources which set it apart from secular socialism: (a) an appeal to a critique of wealth and PROPERTY in patristic and scholastic sources; (b) the possibility of a politically radical reading of the Creed; (c) a tradition of radical dissent which ran through medieval peasant movements, the Hussites, Anabaptists, Levellers and Diggers, and John Bunyan, to the Corresponding Societies of the 1790s; (d) a tradition of church relief work which was easily radicalized. Necessarily it took different forms in different countries.

In England Christian socialism first emerged in the group around J.M. Ludlow (1821–1911), Charles Kingsley (1819–75) and F.D. Maurice (1805–72). Ludlow grew up in France, and it was his experience of the Paris uprising in February 1848 which was the catalyst for the group's formation. Their aims were set out in the journal *Christian Socialist* in 1850. They opposed competition and wished to replace selfishness and conflict with the law of LOVE. Robert Owen's experiments in New Lanark and in America were much in the background, and the group founded various co-operative societies and workers' associations. Kingsley popularized the message in his novels *Alton Locke* and *Yeast* (both 1850). The group was Broad Church, and critical of Tractarianism. Maurice's thought centred on the KINGDOM OF GOD, which existed in God's mind and needed to be reproduced here on earth, but he was suspicious of DEMOCRACY and could not commit himself to universal suffrage. Disagreements between the leaders led to the cessation of the journal within a year, and the group broke up by 1855. Throughout this period Carlyle's views on wage labour (in *Past and Present*) and Ruskin's papers on political economy (*Unto This Last*, 1862) exercised a great influence on Christian socialist thought.

Twenty years later the work of Tractarian slum priests had turned many Anglo-Catholics into socialists. Stuart Headlam founded the Guild of St Matthew in Bethnal Green in 1877. Unlike most Christian socialist groups he demanded the abolition of private property and the immediate redistribution of wealth through taxation. Charles Gore (1853–1932) and Scott Holland (1847–1918) founded the Christian Social Union in 1889 on a broader, though still Anglo-Catholic, basis. When these groups lost their impetus the Church Socialist League was founded in 1906; it believed that 'Christianity is the religion of which socialism is the practice'. After some time this group seemed too church centred for some of its members, and Conrad Noel formed the Catholic Crusade in 1918 which sought 'To break up the Present World and Make a New in the Power of the Outlaw of Galilee'. Though criticized for their liberal and reformist views the theology of Maurice, Westcott (1825–1901) and Charles Gore was central to all these groups. Together, R.H. Tawney (1880–1962) and William Temple (1881–1944) put the concerns of this movement at the heart not only of church but of national life. Many of its ideals were put into practice by the Labour government of 1945. Tawney's *Equality* (1931) was its last manifesto. The Conference on Christian Politics, Economics and Citizenship (COPEC), which Temple called in 1924, was important in preparing the way for what was eventually to become the social thought of the WORLD COUNCIL OF CHURCHES which has insisted on JUSTICE, participation and sustainability. In 1960 Tawney was instrumental in the founding of the Christian Socialist Movement, which is still active and is affiliated to the Labour Party. The Anglo-Catholic Jubilee Group stands more in the tradition of Headlam and Noel.

In Germany Christian socialism finds its roots in the social philosophy of B. Baader (1765–1841), which, in its concept of the proletariat, anticipates Marx, and in a variety of social reform movements. Here as elsewhere 1848 was a crucial year. On the Catholic side Bishop Ketteler (1811–77) pleaded for a 'heroic love of the neighbour', an organization of the working classes and a state social policy. The same year J. Wichern (1808–81), on the Protestant side, spoke of 'Christian socialism' at the first Evangelical Congress, at which his Inner City Mission was inaugurated. From the relief work of these city missions flowed the impulse for Christian DEMOCRACY. Adolf Stöcker (1835–1908), who worked in the Berlin Mission, founded the Christian Democratic Party in 1880 in an attempt to head off more radical socialist parties. Under his impetus R. Todt wrote his book *Radical Socialism and Christian Society* in 1877 setting out the social and political demands of the gospel. The Kantian ethics of Ritschl, under whom Stöcker studied, and the near identification of the kingdom with liberal society characterized this strand of social thought. Another product of the Inner City Mission, F. Naumann (1860–1919), started the important periodical *Die Christliche Welt* in an attempt to bring together Marxism and Protestantism but, increasingly disillusioned by the church, he turned to secular politics.

In sharp distinction from this movement was the work of the Blumhardts. J.C. Blumhardt (1805–80) was rooted in pietism, but combined MILLENARIANISM with a passionate championship of the oppressed. His son Christoph (1842–1919) took a more active political line and represented the Social Democratic Party in Württemberg for six years. For him Christians are engaged in a struggle against the powers of chaos under the slogan 'Jesus is Victor!' P. Tillich (1886–1965) was one amongst many who continued a radical involvement in Christian socialism after the First World War in different movements based in Baden, Berlin and Cologne until they were broken up by Nazism. After the Second World War the Christian socialist impulse in Germany found expression from 1950 onwards in the dialogue with Marxism, looking especially to the Czech theologian J. Hromadka. H. Gollwitzer (1908–93) was the most important theologian involved in this process and was heavily involved in the student uprisings of 1968.

In Switzerland both H. Kutter (1863–1931) and Th. Ragaz (1868–1945) were influenced by the Blumhardts. Kutter's *Sie Müssen!* (1903) broke with Christian socialism, urged a fight against mammon and the establishment of 'the impossible'. Kutter gradually distanced himself from social democracy. Ragaz saw God's hand in socialism, and believed that there was an anticipation of the kingdom in the establishment of a democratic and co-operative society. After the First World War he became the leader of an international peace movement. Both shared an 'eschatological realism' (*see* ESCHATOLOGY) stressing God's lordship of all reality and the possibility of a radical Christian worldliness. K. Barth, at first influenced by them, later took a more critical position, but remained a member of the Marxist Social Democratic Party and, after the Second World War, encouraged Hromadka in his dialogue with MARXISM.

In France the nineteenth century was still dominated by the question whether the Church could support the Revolution, and later by the uncompromising opposition of the Vatican to socialism. Nevertheless Christian socialist positions were anticipated by many writers, especially Villeneuve-Bourgemont (1784–1850), whose 1834 essay *Christian Political Economy* pleaded for workers' organizations. F. de Lamennais, for eighteen years a Catholic priest, sketched a picture of an ideal unity of production and consumption in *Paroles d'un croyant* in 1834, a book which had a Europe-wide impact. Its condemnation later in the year caused him to leave the church. A Catholic Workers Party, expounding corporatist ideas, was founded in the 1870s. At the end of the century Ch. Péguy (1873–1914) put his stamp on a specifically French Christian socialism which passionately combined *mystique* and *politique*. Like William Morris he combined a romantic reading of the Middle Ages, nationalism and Utopian social-ism. The incarnation stood at the heart of his politics, but he was always distanced from the church. French Protestants such as E. Gounelle (1865–1950) and P. Passy (1859–1940) edited important Christian socialist journals and founded the Union of Socialist Christians in 1908. Catholic social thought was continued by theologians such as J. Maritain, H. de Lubac and J. Daniélou, but it was the Second World War which revolutionized French Christian socialism through the involvement of some priests in the resistance and in factory work. The Worker Priest movement was suppressed in 1954, but its impetus was continued in the Christian Marxist dialogue of the 1960s and the widely in-fluential movement 'Christians for Socialism'. In the immediate postwar years E. Mounier, in the journal *Esprit*, advocated a 'third way' between CAPITALISM and COMMUNISM.

In the USA the way for the 'Social Gospel' was prepared by Mennonite and Shaker groups, but also by Unitarians in the school of Joseph Priestley (*see* UNITARIAN). More than 150 Uto-pian communities have been recorded between 1750 and 1850, twenty-five of which were Christ-ian inspired. Discussion of the social dimension of the gospel became more prominent after the Civil War and the rapid industrialization of the north. The Congregational minister Washington Gladden (1836–1918), called the father of the social gospel in America, stood for the right of labour to organize, and wished labour and capi-tal to co-operate. W.D. Bliss founded the Society of Christian Socialists in 1889 which urged that all industrial relations should be based on the fatherhood of God and the brotherhood of man, and published *A Handbook of Socialism* in 1895. The best known theologian of the move-

ment was W. Rauschenbusch (1861–1918), who put forward his views in a series of famous books commencing with *Christianity and the Social Crisis* (1907). The son of a Lutheran immigrant, he had studied at Berlin and visited London, where he met the Webbs and other early Fabians. Like the German Christian social-ists his background was in the ethical teaching of Ritschl. Jesus was a Hebrew prophet prepar-ing people for a righteous social order. All human goodness must be social goodness. The worst form of SIN is that which consecrates WEALTH and property to individual advance-ment at the expense of the good of the whole. In *Moral Man and Immoral Society* (1932) R. Niebuhr continued the concerns of the Social Gospel movement. Christian social thinking in America was radicalized by the Vietnam War and there is now an important school of Marxist Biblical interpreters (N. Gottwald, C. Myers) and of social activists (the Sojourners group).

In review we can identify three major types of Christian socialist thinking, though there are important overlaps between them. There is first the tradition which runs from Maurice, through Gore and Conrad Noel to Temple. This repre-sents a radical reading of the orthodox creed. First and foremost is an appeal to the political significance of the doctrine of the TRINITY. The Athanasian Creed affirmed that God is a unity of persons in which 'none is afore or after other; none greater or less than another: but all three Persons are co-eternal together; and co-equal'. Christian socialists added – in whose image we are made. 'Within this Eternal Com-radeship all men "live and move and have their being"; and so Comradeship is man's natural element, and man out of Comradeship is as unnatural as fish out of water.' The basic princi-ple of socialism, co-operation rather than compe-tition, was understood as implicit in the doctrine of God.

Second, the doctrine of the incarnation is taken to provide a metaphysical foundation for fraternity and EQUALITY. When God takes human nature upon Godself all human beings are consti-tuted as brothers and sisters of the Son of Man. This means that appeals to equality rested on an account, believed to be revealed, of the true nature of reality. In two ways this was marked off from the liberal German and American forms of Christian socialism: it began with revelation, and not with ethics, and it rested on ontology.

An account of the political implications of sacramental practice followed automatically. The twin axioms of socialism were taken to be the importance of the body and of fellowship. For Catholic socialists like Péguy or Noel the use of incense, vestments, lights and music were signs that God had redeemed the body and its appetites. Sacraments and incarnation meant an absolute rejection of the secular/sacred division. 'What God hath joined together, let no man put asunder.' Since the body is the temple of the spirit failure to provide proper nourishment, shelter and rest are sacrilegious. Baptism is the mark that Social Darwinism must be rejected and be replaced with a truly co-operative society of mutual forgiveness. Confirmation is about the true priesthood of all. The Eucharist speaks of commitment to God's kingdom, the sanctity of material things and the new community. The one bread which is broken and shared is taken as a sign of the one world, and its goods, to be taken and shared by all.

It will be clear that, though these doctrines were often sketchily outlined, they anticipated to a remarkable extent the emphases of LIBERATION THEOLOGY, which has also produced politically radical readings of the ancient creeds.

A second major tradition is represented by the German liberals and the American Social Gospel Movement. Here the main focus of discourse is 'the kingdom'. Socialism is not rooted in incarnation but understood as the continuation of a movement which Jesus had initiated, which called people into a fellowship of justice and brotherhood. The prophetic critique of injustice is more important than the doctrines of the creed, and forms the basis for the denunciation of existing injustices. The church is understood as a 'kingdom movement', parallel with, if not destined to supersede, secular socialist movements. Appeal to these themes was not absent from 'incarnational' socialism, but there it was subordinate to what were taken to be more fundamental doctrines. Here too liberation theology has continued ethical reflection, though on the deepened ground of an appeal

both to Marxist and to personalist philosophies (M. Buber, E. Levinas, E. Dussell).

The third, and most ancient, strand in Christian socialist thinking finds its roots in Anabaptist thinking, and the radical dissent of the seventeenth century. This strain is frequently, though not always, millenarian (see MILLENARIANISM). Here the imminent advent of God's kingdom calls present norms into question, and seeks an anticipation of the messianic rule. In this way a millenarian tradition could lead to radical practice, as illustrated by C. Blumhardt. Such messianism has been taken up most comprehensively, in modern times, by the Marxist Ernst Bloch, in his *The Principle of Hope* (1947, revised 1959), which evoked a theological response from J. Moltmann, *Theology of Hope* (1965) that has influenced much recent Christian political thought. Liberation theology has been critical of the failure of European political theology to engage in concrete struggles, but this messianic tradition has also been important to it.

The tradition of radical dissent moved in a deist direction in the eighteenth century, and its impact on Tom Paine, and his importance as a precursor of socialism, cannot be underestimated. For labour pioneers such as Keir Hardie religious dissent and political radicalism continued to run together.

Another aspect which characterized Anabaptist thinking was a critique of the role of the STATE, especially in its judicial function. Here the Marxist goal of the final withering away of the state was anticipated. The most important representative of this view in the second half of the twentieth century has been J. Ellul, whose advocacy of Christian anarchy has appealed both to socialists and to neo-liberals.

For Catholics the encyclical *Rerum Novarum* (1891) has been regarded as the Magna Carta of Christian social thought. It affirms the right of workers to organize, is opposed to the worst excesses of capitalism, but believes private property to be a natural right and wishes to encourage co-operation between capital and labour. Socialism as such continued to be regarded as incompatible with Christianity into the 1960s. Catholic social teaching appealed above all to the medieval critique of USURY, and the twin norms of a just wage and a just price, and tried to establish social norms on the grounds of NATURAL LAW.

The papal affirmation of private property is in tension with very strong condemnations of private property in the Church Fathers, especially Ambrose and Chrysostom, and with a tradition of communist experiments which look back to Acts 4. There has been a confusion, however, in the discussion between questions of lifestyle, the indecency of opulence in the midst of want (as raised, for example, by Ragaz), the question of charity versus justice, and the question of the ownership of the means of production, which is what Marx means by 'property'. When Catholic social teaching affirms the right to property it affirms inequality of wealth, and the duty of charity, though this is modified by reference to the right to common use. A distinction is made, very doubtfully defended on Biblical and patristic grounds, between distributive justice (equality) and commutative justice (justice commensurate with status). As a response to Marx this argument is largely irrelevant because he is concerned with class inequalities which flow from private ownership of the means of production. Christian socialists such as Headlam and Tawney understood this and advocated public ownership. No socialist consensus has emerged as to how to respond to the privatization of nationalized industries in most Western countries.

Marxist discussion made a distinction between Utopian and scientific socialism and, until the 1960s, was scornful of most Christian socialist thought and endeavour ('sprinkling holy water on the heart burnings of the aristocrat'). Utopian socialism began with a vision of the human and with moral imperatives, scientific socialism with an analysis of the functioning of capital. The former tended to be impractical, the latter overconfident of the powers of social engineering. The Christian Marxist dialogue of the 1960s, damaged but not destroyed by the invasion of Czechoslovakia in 1968, was an important forerunner of liberation theology which, in most cases, recognizes the need for a Marxist analysis of both the functioning of capital and class relations. At the same time Marxist thinkers such as M. Löwy have recognized the contribution Christian theology can make to

the elaboration of a socialist ethic and to combating Social Darwinist views of society. There is a tension in Marx's thought between historicism, the doctrine that advancing modes of production will necessarily produce the classless society, and the insistence that human beings are the subjects of their own history. Christian millenarianism links hands with the first strand, and Christian ethics with the second strand.

Though there is no universally agreed definition of socialism it is clear that the term arose in response to the Industrial Revolution, with its vision of 'economic man', and stands for an organization of society which is co-operative rather than competitive, where the individual is always understood in his or her social context, where each according to their ability sees that the needs of all are met, and where the strong are not privileged over the weak. Since theory and practice necessarily inform each other it is clear that, in the construction of such a society, both Jewish and Christian traditions have important resources to offer.

Duroselle, J.B. (1951) *Les Débuts du Catholicisme social en France 1822–1870*, Paris: Presses Universitaires de France.

Groves, R. (1967) *Conrad Noel and the Thaxted Movement*, London: Merlin.

Kupisch, K. (1953) *Vom Pietismus zum Kommunismus*, Berlin: Lettner Verlag.

Lütgert, W. (1927) *Der christliche Sozialismus in 19 Jahrhundert*, Halle: Niemeyer Verlag.

Moody, J.N. (1953) *Church and Society. Catholic Social and Political Thought and Movements 1789–1950*, New York: Arts Press.

Moon, P.T. (1921) *The Labour Problem and the Social Catholic Movement in France*, New York: Macmillan.

Norman, E.R. (1987) *The Victorian Christian Socialists*, Cambridge: Cambridge University Press.

Rauschenbusch, W. (1991) *Christianity and the Social Crisis*, Philadelphia, PA: Westminster.

Raven, C.E. (1968) *Christian Socialism 1848–1854*, London: Cass.

Rowland, C. (1988) *Radical Christianity*, Cambridge: Polity.

Sauter, G. (1962) *Die Theologie des Reiches Gottes beim älteren und jüngeren Blumhardt*, Zurich: Zwingli.

Siefer, G. (1964) *The Church and Industrial Society*, London: Darton, Longman & Todd.

T. J. Gorringe

CHRISTOLOGY

Christology (from *Christos logos*) is the dogmatic or theological articulation of the significance of Jesus of Nazareth according to the Christian faith. For the most part it is distinguished from soteriology, the exposition of Christ's saving significance, by being chiefly concerned with his being, or who he is. Attention is concentrated on who he is in relation to God, the human race and the creation rather than on, for example, the meaning of his atoning death. The distinction, however, is not an absolute one, for the two areas are so closely intertwined that neither can adequately be related without constant reference to the other. Christology has nearly always been subordinate to soteriology in the sense of being developed in support of Christian understandings of salvation. Christ's divinity has accordingly been articulated and defended in support of the claim of the *reality* of human salvation, his humanity in support of the reality of *human* salvation.

The discussion of Christology has taken up a large proportion of the church's intellectual life, especially in the first five and the last three centuries. Only in recent times has much attention been given to the relation between Christology and society, although historians have commented on the way in which different Christological teachings have from the beginning been associated with different political attitudes. The complexity of the subject is revealed by the fact that contrary judgements have been made of the significance of the doctrine of the divinity of Christ – both that it has encouraged an exaggerated respect for constituted AUTHORITY and that it has relativized the power of any earthly ruler and thus undermined uncritical respect for constituted authority. The history of christology can be broadly divided into three phases: the New Testament, the history of theology before the dawn of the modern age, especially the first five centuries after Christ, and the modern age, during which new emphases have been made.

The Christ of the earliest New Testament teaching, that of the epistles, especially Paul's, is in many ways conceived as a social reality. To avoid anachronism, however, we must be aware that there is little or no social thought which is comparable with that of Plato and Aristotle or with modern social theory. While the New Testament books – for example, Acts and Revelation – often reflect an awareness of the political conditions of the day, the writers are mostly concerned with the interests and needs of the young Christian church, a minority community in an empire containing many races, nations and religions. Yet, that said, there is to be discerned in the New Testament a concern for living in community that has important implications for a consideration of theology and society.

By such sayings that 'in Christ there is neither Jew nor Greek, ... neither slave nor free, ... neither male nor female' (Galatians 3: 28), Paul implied that those who are brought into relation to Christ are by that very fact brought into a new form of social relatedness to each other. Such a consideration also underlines much of his moral teaching, and in particular his use of the metaphor of the body, which conceives the local church as a community of particular, diverse and yet mutually dependent members. Similar themes can be found in the rather later gospel of John, where the mutual indwelling of Jesus and his Father is made the ground of the redeemed social relations of the members of the Christian community for which the author was writing.

Suggestions of a similar teaching can also be found in the words of Jesus, particularly where he is represented as saying that the treatment of children, or of those in need, is tantamount to behaviour to him (Matthew 25: 31–46). Another relevant dimension of the Gospels, which is of great contemporary interest, is to be found in the relation of Jesus to the Jewish people. The accounts of the ministry of Jesus begin with his response to John the Baptist's recalling of Israel to her responsibilities as a people. It is also clear that the reasons for his death have something to do with his conception and teaching of the religio-political calling of Israel, as well as with her political situation under Roman rule. The matter, however, is complex and disputed, and it is unlikely that there will ever be agreement as to the precise historical situation.

There is also much dispute about the degree to which later dogmatic teaching of the humanity and divinity of Christ is anticipated in or supported by the teaching of the New Testament. Grillmeier's massive study of the development of early Christology argues for an essential continuity of development, with the Fathers articulating and developing what is already to be found in the texts. It is widely agreed that there are in the book's passages teaching or appearing to assume both that Jesus is of divine status and that he is a full human being. Disagreement centres on the unity and significance of New Testament teaching. Some critics argue that there is such a diversity of teaching that it is wrong to integrate it into dogmatic theses, while others hold that the Bible should be understood not as a repository of dogmatic teaching so much as a report of ancient experience which may be radically different from modern experience of the same matters. Underlying the latter position is the influential teaching of D.F. Strauss (*Life of Jesus*, 1835) that the reports of the early Christians are to be understood as the product of the myth-making tendency of the primitive mind which is so different from the modern mind that the original history is impossible to recover. This article is written in the belief that dogmas of the absolute discontinuity of ancient and modern minds no longer stand up to examination and that, despite weaknesses of emphasis and content, the Fathers were in general right in what they made of the documents.

It could still be argued, however, that the early dogmatic tradition failed to build adequately on the social implications of New Testament Christology and allowed Christian teaching to be overlaid by conceptions of social order which blunted their impact. Despite this it is scarcely surprising that the early centuries were chiefly marked by efforts to establish the distinctive claims of Christianity in relation both to perceived distortions of it deriving from within and to attacks from without. The main attention came to be focused, accordingly, on the questions of the divinity and humanity of Christ and the relation between the two. Yet the treatment of these themes was never abstract in the sense that they were of interest purely as intellectual conundrums. At heart was the nature of God and of God's relation to the world as creator and

redeemer. In that respect, a social concern for the integrity of the church as the community of salvation was never far from the surface. For example, conceptions of the person of Christ which were held to endanger the integrity of the church's WORSHIP were opposed on those grounds.

At the centre of all debate is the doctrine of the incarnation, which teaches, building on texts like John 1: 14, that Jesus is the eternal Son of God become man for the salvation of the world. The way in which such a doctrine affirms the value of human life was drawn out by such theologians as Irenaeus of Lyons in his attacks on the Gnostic devaluation of life in the flesh, and in the occasional early attack on the institution of SLAVERY. After the first teaching of the incarnation there were numerous disputes about the reality of the humanity and divinity of Christ, notably that between theologians centred on Antioch and Alexandria. The former 'school' stressed the humanity of Jesus along with his moral achievement, for they were in general concerned with the redemption of the human will. Earlier representatives came under the suspicion that they saw Jesus as a 'mere man', adopted by God to do his work (the heresy of 'adoptionism'). Later Antiochenes affirmed the divinity of Christ, but found it difficult to give adequate account of the relationship of humanity and divinity: the impression was sometimes given of the eternal Word of God and the man Jesus existing side by side ('Nestorianism' or dualism).

By contrast, Alexandrians stressed the ontological union of the eternal Son of God with the man Jesus. Their emphasis tended to be on salvation of the flesh from corruption, and at the same time on the place of the EUCHARIST in mediating such redemption. Their Christology developed in opposition to the thought of Arius, whose contention that the Son is ontologically inferior to the Father was countered by the arguments of Athanasius and the affirmation of the creed of Nicea in 325 AD that the Son is 'of one substance – one in being [*homoousios*] – with the Father'. Before the controversy broke out Athanasius had written one of the classics of Christology, *On the Incarnation of the Word*, which teaches that Jesus is the presence as man of the eternal co-creating Word, made incarnate to recreate the human race which through SIN was going to destruction. Later Alexandrians sometimes stressed the divinity of Christ so powerfully that his human reality appeared to be in danger, as in the heresy of Apollinaris that the divine Word replaced the human mind of Jesus. This overemphasis was in turn corrected by the Cappadocian theologian, Gregory of Nazianzus, who made much of the saying that 'the unassumed is the unhealed', arguing that if the Son did not take to himself the whole of our humanity, body and soul alike, then we were not truly saved by him.

Classical Christology came, if not to a closure – for parts of the church remained unreconciled – at least to a kind of pause, in the Definition of Chalcedon of 451. This credal formula contained concepts which attempted to mediate between the two opposing tendencies, stressing very strongly at once the oneness of Christ and the fullness of both his divine and human reality. The concepts they used – 'of one substance', 'person', 'nature' – became the currency of almost all Christological teaching until modern times. The unity of Christ's being was expressed by the concept of person, his full divinity and humanity by the affirmation that he was of one substance with on the one hand God the Father and on the other the human race. It is on the latter side that classical Christology revealed its weakness, for later theology appeared to lack the conceptual equipment to give full weight to the humanity of the saviour. It is this which has come into the centre of interest in modern times.

A crucial early modern development was the teaching of Socinus early in the seventeenth century that Jesus was not the pre-existent saviour come to earth but a man equipped by God with divine powers. The value of this challenge to orthodoxy was that it compelled theology to address the Achilles' heel of traditional theology, the treatment of the humanity of Christ. Against Socinus, the Puritan John Owen – whose position was developed in the nineteenth century by Edward Irving – argued that alongside the teaching that the eternal Son became man there was needed also a stress on the fact that as man he was only what he was by virtue of the leading of the Holy Spirit. This was an attempt to obviate the impression sometimes given by orthodox Christology that Jesus' humanity was a cipher because he was simply the instrument of the divine Word.

But the mainstream failed to develop this possibility, and during the Enlightenment the Chalcedonian tradition came under savage criticism, being accused of abstraction and contradiction. There were a number of prongs to the assault, but prominent among them were the arguments of Biblical critics that the dogmatic tradition failed to account for the historical evidence. Prominent here were the posthumously published *Fragments* of H.S. Reimarus (d. 1768), who claimed that the inconsistencies of the gospel accounts were proof that the dogmatic Christology was a deliberate fabrication. The more subtle challenge of his editor, G.E. Lessing (1729–81), to the sufficiency of any historical basis for doctrine helped to generate a quest, which dominated the nineteenth century, for the Jesus of history which effectively replaced in many places the concern for doctrinal Christology. The critique of orthodox Christology was in large measure accepted early in the nineteenth century by Schleiermacher, widely thought to be the century's most important theologian, who developed what became the dominant Protestant tendency. The result was that until well into the twentieth century a basis for the significance of Jesus was sought not so much in the traditional teaching as in the religious experience or moral teaching of the man Jesus, albeit usually a man the quality of whose experience was held to elevate him to a kind of divinity. Most exponents of this approach did not so much deny the divinity of Jesus as attempt to reach it by arguing 'from below', after the example of Socinus, although more radical critics who built on one side of the thought of Hegel held that Jesus' divinity was simply an instance of the divinity of the human race. It should not be forgotten, however, that major thinkers of this era, among them S.T. Coleridge and Søren Kierkegaard, continued to maintain versions of orthodox Christology.

It is in modern times, when Christianity's ecclesiastical institutions begin to be called into question, that the matter of the social relevance of Christology starts to come to the fore. The philosopher Kant (1724–1804) is one of those who associated the concept of the KINGDOM OF GOD with human social reality. Believing any dogmatic Christology to be an offence to human reason and moral AUTONOMY, Kant taught that Jesus is to be understood as the teacher of a pure ethic that can be arrived at by reason independently of him. Kant, however, remained an essentially individualist thinker, unlike two of his major successors, Schleiermacher and Hegel. For the former, it was part of the essence of religion that it take social form, so that Christianity was understood as a form of social life released into history by the influence of Jesus.

It was Hegel, however, who most explicitly developed the social dimensions of Christology. His audacious step was to save the orthodox teaching of the divinity of Jesus by demonstrating its universal social and political significance. Aware of the loss, since the collapse of the medieval synthesis, of a unified basis for social order, he saw in the reconciliation of the human and divine realized in Christ the possibility of a new and modern Christendom. While Søren Kierkegaard saw in all this a reversion to paganism, the 'left' Hegelians, including Marx, saw it as the end of orthodox Christology in a different way, and took the route to atheism, which, they believed, it finally implied.

In the twentieth century, explicitly political and social Christology has come into its own. The early part of the century, from the time of the First World War, was dominated by the often strongly political theology of Karl Barth. Rather than attempting to draw direct lines between Christology and POLITICS, however, Barth employs the mediating concept of revelation. In the early writings, he struck a strongly eschatological note in which Christology was deployed as a weapon against contemporary ETHICS and self-understanding, particularly those making appeal to the experience or teaching of the historical Jesus. The later Christology continued to be used to maintain a distance between any human political order and the kingdom of God. Barth's strongly Christological theology continued to serve him as the basis for political judgements, though the logic of these was not always apparent.

Two other influential approaches to Christology in this century have been those of the Roman Catholic Karl Rahner and the Lutheran Wolfhart Pannenberg, both of whom attempt to come into more positive engagement than Barth with modern approaches to Christology 'from below'. Pannenberg argues that the historical-critical method, especially when applied to the texts about the resurrection, produces a result opposite to that obtained by Reimarus. The reliability of the historical accounts provides the basis for an approach to a Christology that does justice to all the concerns of the dogmatic tradition without the need to accept traditional methods that have come into question. Similarly Rahner, working in a rather different context, calls upon the resources of idealist and existentialist philosophy to produce a Christology in which movements 'from below' and 'from above' are integrated, so that a Chalcedonian Christology can be obtained without the *a priori* methods of the dogmatic tradition.

In contrast to the essentially dogmatic approach of Barth, and what its opponents sometimes claim to be the bourgeois and individualist theology of Rahner, recent political Christology, especially that of the largely Catholic LIBERATION THEOLOGY, has returned to categories deriving from the nineteenth century. This is particularly apparent in the Christology of Jon Sobrino, the subtitle of whose book is 'an outline beginning with discipleship of the historical Jesus'. Much of the thrust of this Christology draws political implications, which have been important particularly in Latin America, from Jesus' concern with the poor and oppressed. The Christology of Jürgen Moltmann represents something of a combination of a dogmatic and political theology. Taking his direction from the evils of this century's wars and political oppression, Moltmann sees in the cross of Christ the healing involvement of God in the SUFFERING of the world.

A salient feature of both the nineteenth-century liberal and more recent liberation Christologies is that they derive opposing political messages by means of essentially the same Christological method. The difference is that one tradition is shaped by Kantian thought, the other by Marxist. This suggests that the political expectations brought to Christology shape the content. While this is inevitable to some degree, suspicion must fall on any attempt to move directly from Christology, especially the modern quest for the historical Jesus, to its social and political implications. The reason is that such a move abstracts Christology from two features of its Biblical context, atonement and the church. According to the New Testament, the motor of social transformation is the forgiveness of sins mediated by the cross of Christ and incorporation into the body of the crucified and risen Christ, the church. That does not preclude a drawing out of the social implications of Christology, but places a question mark against any theology that attempts it without taking account of these two central realities.

Grillmeier, Alois (1975) *Christ in Christian Tradition.* vol. I, *From the Apostolic Age to Chalcedon,* London: Mowbray.

Gunton, C.E. (1983) *Yesterday and Today. A Study of Continuities in Christology,* London: Darton, Longman & Todd.

Hick, J.H. (ed.) (1977) *The Myth of God Incarnate,* London: SCM.

Mackintosh, H.R. (1913) *The Doctrine of the Person of Christ,* Edinburgh: T. & T. Clark.

Moltmann, Jürgen (1974) *The Crucified God,* London: SCM.

Pannenberg, Wolfhart (1968) *Jesus – God and Man,* London: SCM.

Rahner, Karl (1961) *Theological Investigations,* vol. 1, London: DLT.

Schweitzer, Albert (1954) *The Quest of the Historical Jesus,* 3rd edn, London: Black.

Sobrino, Jon (1978) *Christology at the Crossroads. A Latin-American Approach,* London: SCM.

Colin Gunton

CHURCH AND STATE

I consider state in the wide sense of 'any form of government' in what follows.

From its first days, the Christian Church represented itself as a community of exiles or 'resident aliens' in the Roman Empire. To be a Christian was to be a 'citizen' of another commonwealth (Philippians 3: 20) or a member of another race, neither Jewish nor non-Jewish (1 Corinthians 10: 32; 1 Peter 2: 9–10). Such language is found not only in the New Testament but in writers of the sub-apostolic age such as Clement of Rome and the author of the second-century *Letter to Diognetus.* Furthermore, because belonging to the Church is not determined by ethnic origin, the Christian community is in principle open to all, it is a new *humanity,* a new model of how human beings live together. Inevitably, therefore, its very existence produces tensions with existing forms of loyalty and belonging – family, race, political order – especially since these were invested with religious AUTHORITY in the ancient world. The early Christians were regularly accused (at best) of having no interest or investment in the ordering of public affairs and (at worst) of being actively hostile to the existing order.

Hence the consistent apologetic theme that Christians are not actively subversive; their loyalty may be limited but it is real (Romans 13) and the very careful handling in the Gospels and Acts of the attitude of Roman officialdom to Jesus and his followers reflects this concern. The second-century *Acts of the Scillitan Martyrs* shows us Christians on trial insisting that they pay taxes and do not break the law, even though they will not recognize the religious authority of the Emperor. Other writers, like Tertullian and Origen, stress that Christians uphold the PEACE and WELFARE of the Empire by their prayers, even if they will not act as magistrates or fight in the army. Occasionally – as in Revelation – the reaction is more explicitly hostile (though not militantly subversive): the imperial authority is diabolical and will be overthrown in the last days by God.

When Christianity is tolerated and given legal status in the fourth century, the picture changes dramatically in some quarters: the Christian Emperor is seen as holding authority from God, and the interests of Church and Empire become indistinguishable. This is given definitive expression by Eusebius of Caesarea in the early fourth century, and remains a powerful ideology in the background of Eastern Christianity for a long time. But the collapse of the Western Roman administration between 350 and 450 produced a different picture. Augustine of Hippo's great treatise *On the City of God,* written partly in response to the sack of Rome in 410, deals with the whole issue at a much deeper level. It is *not* a discussion of the relations between 'Church' and 'state', but an analysis of two opposing forms of community. The city of God is a commonwealth where all things and persons are in right, ordered relation: God is loved above all, and so all things and persons are loved for what they truly are; this is therefore a community of perfect JUSTICE. The 'earthly' city is any form of social life in which egotism (individual or collective) is allowed to prevail, and God is not honoured: without the love of God, nothing is properly valued, there is no sense of a good that is genuinely and equally for all, and so there is no justice. The Church is *not* identical with the city of God, but the reality of that city can be seen in it; nor is any worldly kingdom identical with the 'earthly' city, though in so far as any state ignores God and the proper love of God's creatures, it slides towards the self-destructive blindness of this pseudo-community. The Church may collaborate with earthly rulers in forwarding justice and peace, but it cannot guarantee their persistence, nor should it seek to defend its own vision by force (Augustine's own justification of the legal suppression of schism and heresy sits uncomfortably with this); it is always at a distance from any earthly order, neither simply hostile nor simply supportive, but at best a critical fellow-worker, with a horizon beyond the success or failure of particular hopes and achievements.

The Western Middle Ages inherited Augustine's scepticism about the *de facto* rulers of the nations. But because of the fluid and uncertain pattern of political authority in the kingdoms of the Dark Ages, the Church increasingly saw itself as a kind of STATE alongside or above others. The Pope was its supreme magistrate, surrounded by a 'high court', and its laws bound the clerical citizens who made it up. At times, these laws conflicted with the laws of the kingdoms and had the effect of creating enclaves in the kingdoms where the local ruler's law did not hold. This produced great tensions, and occasional violence (the murder of Thomas à Becket). The papacy, especially under Gregory VII in the eleventh century and Innocent III in the thirteenth, struggled to maintain the position that ecclesiastical power was superior to royal or customary law in the kingdoms – to the extent of permitting the Pope to depose monarchs. But this was not universally held: we also find theories of the complementary authority of the Pope and the German Emperor (the 'Holy Roman Emperor', who was vaguely believed to inherit something of the status of earlier Roman monarchs) – the 'two swords' of Luke 22: 38 (*see* CATHOLICISM). In very different vein, Thomas Aquinas revives elements of classical republican theory: the commonwealth is a community of responsible citizens, whose legal and social dispositions are indeed held answerable to the revelation of divine 'positive law' through the Church, but who do not require ecclesiastical government to devise basic rational conventions for living together in justice. This is a more optimistic assessment of natural social capacities than Augustine's, though it also provides more concrete criteria for the criticism of political *structures* (notably monarchy, which Aquinas regards with less than total enthusiasm). The dramatic decline in the papacy's moral authority in the later Middle Ages led to an increased interest in some quarters (not least among fourteenth-century Franciscans) in the potential role of the Emperor in guaranteeing the peace of both Church and SOCIETY. The canonist Marsilius of Padua provided the most original and sophisticated defence of the *practical* superiority in legal matters of the monarch, and his works are often seen as the origin of a doctrine of the Church as a 'private' society, i.e. one that exists because people *choose* to belong to it, in contrast to the state. For Marsilius, the ruler expresses the common interest of the populace, while the Church deals only with specific areas of concern; the Church thus has no rights of coercion in the state. This is an unusual – and controversial – development of some aspects of Augustine's thought, but without much of the hinterland of Augustine's overall theory of human nature and desire. And it is worth noting that some Augustinian thinkers in the fourteenth and fifteenth centuries took a radically different position, justifying civil disobedience and even revolt against the state in the name of a theologically defined ideal of justice.

The Reformation period brought to a head the conflict between the papacy and the kingdoms: the only way, it seemed, in which the absolutist nature of papal claims could be countered was by exalting the absolute authority of the local prince. Elements from the thought of Marsilius and John Wyclif, and even from the age of the Emperor Constantine, were drawn in to support such a programme, whose most dramatic results could be seen in the England of Henry VIII, where the King was declared Supreme Head of the Church. The English ideal was a unitary Christian state in which there was no appeal, in temporal or spiritual matters, from the King's jurisdiction. It is a cruder and more localized version of the Eastern Christian (Byzantine) model, though the latter embodied a far clearer doctrine of royal accountability in some respects. On the continent, Luther developed a theology of the 'two kingdoms', the two ways in which God's rule was communicated to us: the realm of the gospel, where souls were nurtured and forgiven and prepared for everlasting life, and the realm of law and coercion, where disorder was restrained and sinners visibly punished. The practical standards of the two were radically different, and the Church could not require the state to behave like a church; yet the state held its authority from God no less than the Church. Other Reformers were less sanguine about the state's autonomy, and Calvin and his followers retained a strong doctrine of the rights of Christians to challenge or resist an unjust state. While Luther believed that God's law could be administered by a Turk as well as a Christian, Calvinists required godliness in the ruler, and their civil loyalty depended on this. More radical Reformers still (like Thomas Müntzer) agitated for an immediate and wholesale transfer to theocracy: numerous pacifist and egalitarian groups developed and survived as self-contained dissident communities within a number of states. The Mennonite churches are perhaps the best-known strand in this tradition.

The sixteenth-century German principle, enunciated to control religious warfare, was that each prince should determine the confessional allegiance of his territory (*cujus regio, ejus religio*). Churches throughout Europe became tied in with the legal structures of the state, as 'by law established', and the rights of religious minorities were often non-existent: this prevailed as much in Catholic as in Protestant states, though there were examples on both sides of civic tolerance. English intransigence encouraged dissidents to take refuge in the American colonies, and the long memory of this helped to fix in the American Constitution the rigid principle of separation between Church and state, and the effective privatizing of religious options.

The English symbiosis of Church and state was provided with a brilliant and far-ranging justification by Richard Hooker at the end of the sixteenth century (*see* ANGLICANISM); but it was shattered irrevocably by the Civil War, and became more and more a fiction. The granting of civil rights to Roman Catholics in 1829 marked a decisive point in its collapse. Vestiges long remained, and the legal 'establishment' of the Church of England still survives. Attenuated as it is, this continues to give the Church of England something of a public voice on matters of social and moral interest; since the Second World War, the Church has regularly produced reports on such questions, issuing from a respectful collaboration between churchpeople and the educated liberal conscience. The ideals of British welfarism owe much to a generation of Christian intellectuals sympathetic to a moderate socialism, Archbishop William Temple being one of the foremost (*see* CHRISTIAN SOCIALISM). Not much of this heritage is left: the language of British politics is both polarized and secularized as never before, and the popularity of individualist and *laissez-faire* economics has eroded interest in the whole idea of a social morality.

Many have concluded that the establishment consensus needs an infusion of a more robust theology (and have looked admiringly at the sometimes rather sharper-edged discussions of the established Church of Scotland, which has long enjoyed a greater administrative independence). Twentieth-century European politics, with its record of APOCALYPTIC tragedy and tyranny, has done much to foster such a theology. Lutheran respect for *de facto* political authority resulted in a shameful degree of political compliance in the Nazi period in Germany (with some noble exceptions, above all Dietrich Bonhoeffer), and it was a Reformed (Calvinist) theologian, Karl Barth, who produced the most original and coherent justification for an active critique of tyranny. For Barth, the state exists to preserve common human life, to restrain destructiveness, and as such works for what the Church works for; when it defends its identity by measures that make it impossible to see it as concerned with the welfare of all, it must be called to account by the Church, and where necessary resisted. Barth applied this equally to the anti-Semitism of the Third Reich and the nuclear policies of postwar Europe.

There is a superficial resemblance to some of the ideas behind Catholic 'Christian Democrat' programmes, which identify an area of purely 'natural' goods, in pursuing which Christians and non-Christians could co-operate (and it should be noted that the Roman Catholic Church since the Second Vatican Council has recognized the civic rights of non-believers). But the crucial difference is that Barth, in the best Reformed tradition, considered (a) that there could be no *final* legitimation for the state except in terms of the purposes of God in Christ and (b) that the supposedly 'neutral' goods of the political life were therefore always to be understood in relation to what fosters the authentic proclamation of the gospel.

Barth stands somewhere between the classically liberal position, modern Anglican or Roman Catholic, for which certain goals can be identified and negotiated without explicit theological elements entering in, and the radical Utopianism that envisages a unitary society obedient to the gospel, whether in the form of old-style theocracy or some of the varieties of LIBERATION THEOLOGY. But one of the most penetrating observations in this area was made by Barth's associate, Ernst Wolf, in 1958: Wolf noted that much theology had become bogged down in seeking a metaphysical definition of 'the State', at the expense of reflecting on 'political virtue'. Ultimately, the question of the relations between Church and state should be a question about how theology reflects on the nature and goals of human co-operation, on those goods that can only be secured by *common* action, and on the character and morality of power. The more we are preoccupied with the theoretical definition of two kinds of human institution, *the* Church and *the* State, the more we lose sight of the

primitive Christian conviction that the gospel is capable of forming a new human community of unrestricted scope, characterized by mutual valuation and nurture ('communion'). The Church in its worship and language sacramentally anticipates this promised renewal, and in the light of this vision tests and challenges other patterns of corporate human life, in the effort to discern what furthers the community of the Kingdom; and this means that the Church is *as likely to be as uncomfortable as it is to be a constructive presence* in any human political context. Its first loyalty will not be to *the* State, in abstract or concrete, though it will not be simply anarchist and Utopian either.

Barth, K. (1954) *Against the Stream. Shorter Post-War Writings, 1946-1952,* London: SCM.
——(1960) *Community, State and Church: Three Essays,* New York: Doubleday.
Figgis, J. N. (1913) *Churches in the Modern State,* London: Longman.
——(1916) *From Gersen to Grotius,* Cambridge: Cambridge University Press.
Gilby, T. (1958) *Principality and Polity. Aquinas and the Rise of State Theory in the West,* London: Longman.
Milbank, J. (1990) *Theology and Social Theory. Beyond Secular Reason,* Oxford:Blackwell.
Skinner, Q. (1978,1980) *The Foundation of Modern Political Thought,* 2 vols, Cambridge: Cambridge University Press.
Temple, W. (1942) *Christianity and Social Order,* London: SCM.
Troeltsch, E. (1931) *The Social Teaching of the Christian Churches,* London: Allen & Unwin.

Rowan Williams

CITIZENSHIP

The word 'citizen' is derived from the Latin root *civitas*. In the early modern political revival in Europe it is found as *citisein* in Middle English, *citéain* in Old French and *citoyen* in Early Modern French. Most generally the term refers to an inhabitant of a city, but more particularly, and significantly, a freeman, a member of a body politic or, in middle to late modernity, a member of a STATE. Citizenship can be understood in two principal senses, that of rights or status, so called passive citizenship, and that of active citizenship which carries responsibilities, duties and the idea of sharing in world-making possibilities with others. Citizenship is a mode of being human that is primarily and predominantly political. The ideas of citizenship have frequently been ill at ease with theological concepts in particular and with religious sentiments in general. Citizenship with its emphasis upon worldliness is frequently taken in theology and religious thought to be a weak and merely contingent attribute of human being, occasionally, if regrettably, desirable, sometimes avoidable and never essential. Such views, while common, are both mistaken and unfortunate, for citizenship is not an addition to, but an integral and indispensable feature of, humanity.

There are two distinct ancient historical sources of the idea of the citizen: Athens and Rome. Both sources contain the two principal elements of citizenship, participation and status. The clearest early expression of the ideals of the citizen as engagement in the operation of one's own life is given in the Solonic moment about 594 BCE. As *Archon* of Athens, Solon, justly regarded by many as the first to embody the ideals of true citizenship, gave laws to Athens that embodied ideals of EQUALITY and participation. These Athenian ideals are best stated by Pericles and echo into the language of citizenship even today. In a panegyric to those fallen in the Peloponnesian war Pericles told the people of Athens that their laws afford justice to all and 'advancement in public life falls to reputation for capacity, class considerations not being allowed to interfere with merit . . . if a man is able to serve the state he is not hindered by the obscurity of his condition' (Thucydides). In contrast to Pericles, who had praised merit above birth, Cicero divided the trades and professions into the liberal and the vulgar and condemned, 'the odious occupation of the collector of customs and the usurer and the base and menial work of unskilled labourers, for the very wages the labourer receives are a badge of slavery . . .'. For such people, who were the vast majority, citizenship was a status, it carried some rights and some duties but excluded the right to participate in the political life of the republic. The value of even a passive form of Roman citizenship was not negligible, however, and was often earnestly sought. The force of,

and value of, Roman citizenship is perhaps best known through the appeal of St Paul, a citizen of both Tarsus and Rome, to Caesar. Arrested in Jerusalem, Paul told those who held him that he was born a citizen of Rome. 'Those about to examine him moved immediately away from him as did the Tribune who was afraid knowing fully that he had bound a Roman citizen.'

Citizenship is a mode of being in the world. It is most fully expressed in the idea of participation, theatrically expressed as actor – Greek, *prosopon*, or Latin, *personae dramatis* – from which the idea of the person as one having a certain kind of legal status, a legal identity, developed. The Christian notion of PERSON by contrast with either the Greek or Roman concepts shifted the notion of the person from drama and from law into the domain of religion and metaphysics. By modelling the idea of human personhood on the personhood of God the idea of the human person began to acquire a status that no legal notion of citizenship or personhood could, itself, complete. More widely, and far more significantly, by giving a divine imagery to the notion of personhood a new image of the rupture between being in the world and being of another world was articulated. In Christianity, and equivalently in many other religions, the life of the spirit and the life of the body are held in tension; this places a strain on what appear to be distinctly secular categories such as citizenship. This rupture can lead to divided loyalties, as the cryptic comment by Jesus to 'render unto Caesar that which is Caesar's and unto God that which is God's' shows. Yet the tension between the secular and the sacral can be pulled to breaking point as is also shown in the conflict between the demands of the authorities of Rome and the conscience of the early Christians that led to their persecution. This tension and persecution led both to claims that Christians were no threat to the secular authorities and to new expressions of the mode of citizenship. The anonymous writer of the *Epistle to Diognetus* claimed that Christians are no threat to secular authorities, but he also made it clear that Christians 'pass their time upon the earth, but they have their citizenship in heaven'. This Stoic-inspired imagery recurred with new force and significance after the collapse of the city of Rome. The early Augustine wrote of the duty of a good citizen as making communal decisions on grounds of common interest. His later work, however, turned away from the temporal world towards the eternal city. Augustine argued that Rome's many gods had failed to protect that depraved city. Rome was an earthly city that had glorified itself and whose members had lived by earthly standards. But Christians were also engaged in another city, a heavenly city, that glorified God and lived according to God's will. He then developed the doctrine of predestination by arguing that the course of a person's life was known to God from eternity: 'By two cities I understand two societies of human beings, one is predestined from all eternity to reign with God, the other doomed to eternal punishment with the devil'. The tension between time and eternity expressed in this claim resulted in a doctrine that dramatically ruptured the life of the spirit and the life of the city and contributed to a major decline in civic values that has never been completely corrected.

Institutionally that separation instanced itself as the split between CHURCH AND STATE. In an intellectual act of reconciliation St Thomas Aquinas, beginning a new tradition in NATURAL LAW theory, wrote both that the law was obtained by reason, by inward reflection, and that virtue consisted in following the law of another. For 'a law is nothing else than a dictate of reason in the ruler by which his subjects are governed. Now the virtue of any subordinate thing consists in its being well subordinated to that by which it is regulated.' On these principles the rupture between the life of the spirit and the life of the world is covered over by that great chain of being where everything in the universe, divine, natural and positive, has its place. The proper place of the ruler is to use reason to give law and the proper place of the subject is to use reason to obey the law given by the ruler. This particular cover to the rupture between the two cities is thin. It removed the idea of AUTONOMY from citizenship concepts and could be used to justify replacing those concepts with subject concepts subordinating civic life to a larger purpose; no intrinsic and autonomous value was placed in the civic life. The rediscovery of that

value required the rediscovery of the value of the life of the CITY found variously in Europe from the thirteenth century but best known, perhaps, in the emergence of, and pride in, city life in the Italy of the *quattrocentro*. Bruni, in a panegyric to Nanni Strozzi that echoed the panegyric of Pericles, praised Florence, its history, its traditions of freedom and civic virtue, and its citizens. Even before Bruni both Dante and Marsilius of Padua had distinguished Church and state and made significant contributions to the theory of citizenship. Marsilius, referring to Aristotle's *Politics*, takes as a citizen one who participates in the civil community, and is insistent that law-making properly 'belongs to the whole body of the citizens or the weightier part thereof'.

The absolutist Bodin rejected the idea of the citizen as a participant in public affairs, arguing that 'It is a very grave error to suppose that no one is a citizen unless he is eligible for public office'. A citizen is a free subject but 'It is therefore the submission and obedience of a free subject to his prince, and the tuition, protection, and jurisdiction exercised by the prince over his subject that makes the citizen'. By contrast for Starkey in an imaginary dialogue of considerable influence 'this succession of princes by inheritance and blood was brought in by tyrannous and barbarous princes, which as I said is contrary to nature and all right reason'. Yet even the most radical of claims to citizenship did not always avoid the sacral imagery. The newly established French National Assembly in 1789 declared 'in the presence of the Supreme Being to recognise the . . . sacred rights of men and of citizens'. As the rights of humans and the rights of the citizen have sacred status, the rights of the citizen are not separate from and additional to human rights, and such rights are, in this imagery, God given and not to be removed by humans. Such fine sentiments were transitory and the French Assembly came to distinguish, as indeed had the normally reasonable German philosopher Immanuel Kant, between citizens who could participate fully in civic affairs and citizens who could not. Active and passive citizenship, participation and status, were not ideas confined merely to Ancient Rome. The tension in the idea of affiliation to a body politic continually stretches between participation and subjection: in some jurisdictions that is clearer than in others.

The newly emerging USA made it clear that citizenship was a matter of law and of jurisprudence rather than of sacred status. In 1857 (*Dredd Scott* v *Sandford*), the Supreme Court ruled that the fine words of the Declaration of Independence did not apply to 'the Negro race', who were regarded by the Constitution 'as a separate class of persons'. The court held that the words '"people of the United States" and "citizens" are synonymous terms, and mean the same thing'. Every citizen was held to be a part of the sovereign people and those persons who are 'Negro' are not 'included and not intended to be included, under the word "citizens"'. The court thus constructed two types of person, those able to exercise all the rights and privileges in the union and those unable to exercise such rights and privileges. In such a case it would not be sufficient to be human to exercise full personhood – it was necessary also to be a citizen. The close relation between citizenship concepts, personhood and humanity emerged with some clarity during mid- to late modernity. 'Man as an individual is entitled to liberty, it is his birth right,' the minutes of the London Corresponding Society asserted (2 April 1792). This requires citizenship for, unless one has the 'right of sharing in the government of his country . . . no man can, with truth call himself free'.

This view of the centrality of citizenship to freedom is not without its critics. Marx claimed that political EMANCIPATION, expressed in, among other things, citizenship rights was only a partial solution to the ills of the time. The idea of citizenship includes the idea of equality, but as the reality of social class within which people live out their real lives is inherently unequal the idea of the citizen was, for Marx, an abstract juridical device for avoiding true human emancipation. An alternative to this view, where citizenship is seen as containing the potential to undercut class inequalities or to change them radically, was given by the sociologist T.H. Marshall in 1949. Marshall divided citizenship into three different aspects: civil, including the right to freedom of movement and the liberty to make contracts; political, including the right to be elected to public office or to be an elector; and social, including the right to welfare provision and to share in the heritage of society. The rights incorporated in the notion of citizenship, according to Marshall, developed at historically different times. The change from feudalism to CAPITALISM exhibited first liberty rights, followed by political rights, and finally social rights as part of a progressive development. The social aspect to citizenship can both erode existing class barriers and produce newly legitimized stratifications. Social rights include the right to education which is a public duty of the individual as well as a personal right, 'for the social health of a society depends upon the civilisation of its members'. Yet education makes equality of opportunity 'in the process of selection and mobilisation' available as a right to citizens. This weakens hereditary privilege and undercuts the traditional class structure. However, education is tied to occupation so the demands of 'citizenship operate as an instrument of social stratification'. Citizenship replaces one form of stratification with another, legitimated, however, on a different basis.

The idea of citizenship is powerful, radical, potentially liberating and humanizing. As the English idealist Muirhead, echoing the sentiments of that influential reforming school of thought, put it: 'To deny one's citizenship is to deny one's humanity.' It is not, however, without its challenges and problems. One kind of challenge is to achieve the aims and ideals of citizenship within the conditions of mass society; as Laski (1928) put it, 'The scale of modern civilisation has of itself done much to deprive the citizen of his freedom' and freedom, as well as equality, is the *sine qua non* of citizenship.

Citizenship is a notion that depends upon, indeed requires, community and participation in that community, yet the demands of and scale of mass society tend to undercut the possibility of community. The direction of modern society has tended to emphasize the value of autonomy, yet autonomy and community are not notions that fit together well. Autonomy depends upon self-direction while community tends to press heteronomy upon actions. Citizenship, at least as developed in Ancient Greece, depended for its effectiveness upon a degree of *homonia*, like-mindedness, between its members, who, even if of different tribes, considered themselves to be of the same people. The membership of contemporary societies of late modernity and postmodernity is often cosmopolitan, heterogeneous and frequently exhibits *heteromonia*, other, or different, mindedness. Here an active and full sense of citizenship is vital if the society is not to break down due to the particularizing tendencies of group or ethnic membership. Nowhere is this problem, and the stakes, seen more clearly than in the countries newly emerging in central and eastern Europe following the breakdown of the Soviet and Eastern bloc. Here there was no pre-existing civil society, civic tradition or tradition of citizenship. In some cases the consequences have been, and will be, disastrous. When the totalitarian structures that have substituted for absent civic values have been removed, or have collapsed, the particularities of ethnicity, nationality or group have outweighed the burgeoning civic tradition of a fledgling civil society. The value and importance of citizenship in such cases is inestimable.

Citizenship concepts contain within them the possibility of stretching outlook and behaviour across the gaps of otherwise different outlooks. To be and to act as a citizen is to act in a capacity that is slightly distinct from the merely personal. For Marx the weakness of citizenship concepts was their abstract and juridical quality. Yet that is in fact their strength for it enables people of what might otherwise be different persuasions to relate together. Indeed, active citizenship is the principal conceptual and practical device for challenging social and political breakdown. If life is without a civic context people become objects of utility, as means to an end rather than ends in themselves, as heteronomous beings: slaves. But that civic context need not be single, unified and monolithic. On the contrary there are clear dangers where loyalty is to a single civic context, for that in turn reduces the diversity of outlook and enhances rather than reduces the possibilities of strife.

Citizenship and self-identity are intertwined; hence dual or even multiple citizenship, as with St Paul, does not narrow but rather broadens the perspective and outlook. Thus the Treaty on European Union signed at Maastricht in 1993 in creating dual citizenship for all its nationals, as citizens of their country and as citizens of Europe, has the clear aim of enhancing and promoting solidarity between its peoples: of transposing *homonia* and *heteromonia*, of bringing together people whose outlook contains significantly dissimilar components. Equivalently, to be, figuratively, both a citizen of an eternal world and a citizen of the temporal world is not to be placed in a series of inescapable conflicts – it is to have a perspective on both positions.

To be engaged with the world is a necessary, though not sufficient, part of being human. The outer form of active world engagement, as participant rather than as subject, is the citizen; the inner sense redounds around relatively clear senses of willing, intending and reflecting. It is both together that combine to produce the idea of human Being. That idea has developed in the wake of participatory ideas of citizenship. Neither in history nor in anthropology are there examples of people who conceive of themselves as human and who then come to develop the idea of citizenship. It is rather that the initial consciousness of exclusivity and superiority led to the concept of the citizen; to the idea of equality and participation. In turn it is those ideas, as *humanitas*, applied to the most universal category, the species, that made the concept of the human possible. Citizenship concepts if rich enough, however, have emancipatory potential and can be used to demand, and to justify, a rise in the standards of human life, and in the very sense of what it is to be human.

Aquinas, Thomas (1945) 'Summa Theologica', in *Basic Writings of St Thomas Aquinas,* ed. Anton C. Pegis, New York: Random House.
Augustine, St (1972) *Concerning the City of God Against the Pagans* (Book xv); Harmondsworth: Penguin.
Bodin, Jean (1955) *Six Books of The Commonwealth,* ed. M.J.Tooley, Oxford: Blackwell.
Cicero (1951) *The Basic Works of Cicero*, ed. M. Hadas, New York: Random House.
Clarke, Paul Barry (ed.) (1994) *Citizenship*, London and Boulder, CO: Pluto.
——(1995) 'Towards a Deep Theory of Citizenship' *University of Essex Papers in Government*, University of Essex.

Hobbes, Thomas (1946) *Leviathan*, Oxford: Blackwell.

Laski, Harold J. (1928) *The Recovery of Citizenship*, London: Ernest Benn.

Locke, John (1963) *The Second Treatise of Government*, ed. P. Laslett, New York: New American Library.

Marshall, T.H. (1949) *Citizenship and Social Class*, London: Pluto.

Marsilius of Padua (1980) *Defensor Padua*, trans. A. Gewirth, Toronto: Toronto University Press.

Marx, Karl (1843) *On the Jewish Question* in *Karl Marx, Friedrich Engels: Collected Works*, London: Lawrence & Wishart.

National Assembly of France (1789) *Preamble to the Declaration of the Rights of Man and of Citizens*.

Rousseau, Jean Jacques (1913) *The Social Contract and Discourses*, trans. G.D.H. Cole, London: Dent.

Starkey, Thomas (1994) *A Dialogue Between Cardinal Pole and Thomas Lupset*, in Clarke 1994 (first published 1878).

Thucydides (1910) *History of the Peloponnesian War*, trans. Richard Crawley, London: Dent.

Paul Barry Clarke

CITY

Derived from Latin *civitas, civitatem* the initial sense is CITIZENSHIP, from whence in the Middle Ages the notion of the city as a place incorporating a body of citizens was derived, and it is from this idea that the current terminology originates. Thus the Middle English *cite*, Old French *cité* and Italian *citta* appear to have come into currency at similar times. Black quotes John of Viterbo, 1250, as offering the formula, 'City means "you dwell safe from violence" ("*Civitas*", *id est* "Cit(ra) vi(m) (hab)itas").' In contemporary usage the term city is commonly interchanged with 'urban area', 'conurbation' and cognate terms. In the process the sense of the idea of the city as consisting of, among other things, a body of citizens, a confraternity held together by a sense of belonging or friendship (*synoicism*) is lost. The idea of the city has considerable symbolic significance both in secular and in sacral terms. In secular terms the city may be taken to symbolize politics and earthly life, from which the sacral must turn. The sacral counterpoint to the earthly city, and what it represents, is to be found in the notion of the

heavenly city, the city of God. The tensions in this idea are deep, manifold, and probably not capable of full resolution in Christian theology (*see* KINGDOM OF GOD).

It is useful to maintain a distinction between a city and mere urbanization. A city is, minimally, a settlement with a reasonably well understood economic pattern of activity and also a symbolic significance to its members and others; a significance often expressed in some kind of legal statement, charter or custom and practice of equivalent significance and importance. A settlement is not, of itself, a city, and mere urbanization does not *per se* constitute a city. It is possible to distinguish between a mere settlement, a proto-city, a garrison, a citadel, a city, and mere urbanization. The drawing and maintenance of such a distinction enables an assessment of the so-called crisis of the cities to be made, and to see that the post-modern urbanization is a form of life beyond the traditional city.

From settlement to city On the best available evidence it appears that the first human beings were nomadic hunter–gatherers with no settled mode of life and no settlements of a permanent nature. *Homo erectus*, widespread in Asia, Africa and Europe for 500,000 years, may have established settlements for temporary recurring use; e.g. Terra Amata near Nice shows traces of huts fifty by nineteen feet square to which the builders returned on a regular basis, perhaps combining nomadic life with occasional settlement. Recent discoveries in Spain show some evidence of collective life in Europe 250,000 years ago. Discoveries of flint in Europe show evidence of early trade routes; an economic precondition of the development of the city. Modern humans, *Homo sapiens sapiens*, show firm indication of settlement activity in Egypt by 9000 BCE. There were established proto-cities covering sites up to 30 acres at Jericho in the Jordan Valley, in Canaan by 7500 BCE and at Catul Huyuk in Anatolia before 7000 BCE. Farming villages spread to Mesopotamia after 7000 BCE and were established in the Yellow River Valley in China by 6000 BCE. Between *c.*3500 BCE and 3000 BCE some form of city life was widely established throughout Mesopotamia, Canaan, Anatolia, the Indus Valley, and in Egypt, although in Egypt the

Pharaoh was not permanently resident at a fixed place, and economic life was not primarily city-centred. City life, as a mode of human Being, was firmly established throughout large areas of the Near East by 3000 BCE: a date which can be taken as an important axis time in the development of the city. By 1600 BCE dynastic cities of officials developed at Cheng-chou and Anyang in China, and the city of Kush in North Africa above the second cataract of the Nile was developing. Some of these early cities were of considerable size. It is estimated that the City of Elba destroyed in 2250 BCE had a population of 26,000. Subsequent to that destruction it was rebuilt and destroyed at least twice more. Some cities were walled early in their history indicating both the protective nature of cities and their strategic importance. The early Sumerian cities may well have been walled as early as early as *c*.3500 BCE, to limit the aggrandizement of their neighbours, and to preserve their independence and AUTONOMY. This indicates that even as early as *c*.3500 BCE the idea of the autonomous city-state had developed: an idea that spread rapidly throughout the Mediterranean and the Near East.

The earliest Biblical reference to a city is in Genesis 4: 16, where it is said that, 'Cain went out from the presence of the Lord, and dwelt in the land of Nod, on the East of Eden'. The reference makes it clear that Cain was no longer in the presence of the Lord when (4: 17) he 'knew his wife; and she conceived and bore Enoch: and he built a city, and called the name of the city, after the name of his son, Enoch.' It is Cain, the man with the mark, the stain upon him, who is cast out from the company of good men and builds the city. Even at this stage, symbolically the earliest point of human life away from Eden, the city is equated with the absence of God, with sexual congress and with secular rather than sacral life. That view continues in some form throughout history, and is not confined to the Judaic and Christian traditions. By Genesis 14: 2 there are 'five cities of the plain', and the form of their life has turned away from God to the point where even hospitality rules are not observed: one of the most serious breaches of conduct in many tribal and tribally-based cultures. The symbolic effects of city life are best exemplified in the account of Lot's wife who was turned into a pillar of salt as a punishment for turning to look back at the cities of Sodom and Gomorrah, cities of the plain, as they were destroyed by God (Genesis 19: 26; Luke 17: 28, 32). It is common to find other and early accounts that make it clear the cities of men gave displeasure to the God(s). Even the Gods, in some traditional accounts, attempted to destroy all men in order to silence the NOISE of their cities at night and obtain some peace and rest (*see* EVIL).

The just city   Not all early accounts of cities and city life are, however, so negative. While the city may symbolize the secular it may also symbolize confraternity and seemliness among humans. It may be regarded as administered by Gods through men, as in the temple cities of the ancient Near East, or it may have a city God as protector as in, e.g., Pallas Athene. It may be administered with attention to some standard of justice and fairness, as with the code of Sargon of Akkad, *c*.2870 BCE or as with the code of Hammurabi 2123–2081 BCE whose stated aim was to uphold justice in the land. Cities may be seen as reflecting, or incorporating, divine harmony or justice. Indeed the universe itself may be regarded as a city, as a common home for gods as well as for men (Cicero: *De Natura Deorum*, bk. II/4). A city is often seen as a place where certain standards of conduct are required if the city itself is to be satisfactory. When the stoic Clement writes, 'A city or a people is something morally good, an organization or group of men administered by law which exhibits refinement', he does not so much introduce a normative account of what constitutes a city as reflect a long standing view that cities are not a mere grouping of people living in the same place. A group of people living without laws would not be a city in this strict sense. By contrast a group living under common standards of justice, but not as a spatio-temporal group, could be a city: a cosmic city. Yet there is a significant change from the idea of the city as incorporating the pantheon of the cosmos, as reflected in, for example, the pharaoh and his viziers, where the pharaoh is himself divine, or in the ancient idea of divine kingship, to the idea of the city as created by the actions of men. This latter development is philosophically best represented in Plato's view that the polis is man writ large. The polis is *anthropolis*. It can be seen also as a central practical project of the Hellenes best represented in the Greek city state.

The unitary city   The Greek city state, the polis, was a major turning point in the development of the city. The polis is not only autonomous and unitary but its membership is confraternal, its basis synoicistic. The city as a unitary, autonomous, and fraternal political community, appears to be a primarily occidental development. Its basis is the establishment of a *sunoikismos* which Plutarch gives as living together, as marriage, as cohabitation. It is also given as *sunoike*, to combine in one city under a metropolis. Ideas related to the root, *sunoik*, are those of dwelling together, cohabiting, binding together as friends as kinsman, a house-fellow, a house in which several people live. The synoicism may be quite deliberate, formal and even sworn. When related to the confraternity of the city it implies a loosening of, or breaking of, the ties of clan or sib. Where clan, sib, tribe, caste, class or other social group predominate the conditions for the development of the autonomous city are not met. Indeed only rarely are most of these conditions met. In the ancient world the ideal is exemplified in the actions of Solon, in the ideals of Plato, subsequently in Aristotle and, partly, in Rome by 500 BCE. It is found in the development of medieval northern European cities, expressed there in the idea of the burgher, and in the civic humanism of the Renaissance. Some form of attempted synoicism is found in Nehemiah who brings the post-exilic people together, 'as one' to renew the covenant and refound the cities, a process described by Voegelin as 'grotesque'; 'the idea of a nucleus of true believers rendered under the genealogical influence, the grotesque result of the post-exilic synoicism' (*Order in History*, Vol. 1, p. 166). The point being made is that if the sib or tribal ties predominate then the synoicism will fail and the city will not develop its full autonomy. The city, in this sense, is its members and not the buildings. In principle a polis could be moved by a collective movement of the politai, even if the ground on which the city was built was chosen with divine assistance.

The act of founding a city may be, as in both ancient Greece and Rome, deliberate, formal and quick. A city may be established in a day; it was intended to last for eternity. Perhaps, as the saying has it, Rome was not built in a day, but, according to Plutarch, it was established or founded on one day, on a site revealed by divinity. The cities of Greece were, similarly, placed on sites chosen after consulting the Oracle at Delphi, itself regarded as the centre of the world, the *omphalos*, and founded in a sacred ceremony. Thucydides recalls the day of the founding of Sparta and the ceremony which established it. Such cities were sacred, placed on sites divinely revealed and with their own protective god. Within the city would be further sacred places; some god inhabited every part of the ancient city. A Roman house had a god of the hearth, and even a god of the space between houses, which in consequence could not be built with party walls. The city was a place for gods, who lived there eternally, and for men who lived there but temporally, and could not be surrendered or left, for that would be to abandon the gods.

The turn from the city   Nevertheless the gods of the city of Rome failed and were effectively vanquished when Alaric sacked Rome in CE 410. 'What folly it is to see any wisdom in committing Rome to such guardians' wrote St Augustine (*The City of God I. 3*). In contrast with the pantheon and the cosmic polity of Greece, Rome and the temple cities, St Augustine sets the monotheism of Christianity and the heavenly city, a part of 'which is on a pilgrimage in this condition of mortality' and which 'knows only one God as the object of worship' (XIX. 17). Part of the heavenly city, its human part, lives in the world, but 'it lives there as an alien sojourner' (XVIII. 1). While there it 'calls out citizens from all nations and so collects a society of aliens, speaking all languages' (XIX. 17). The two cities differ in character, for the earthly city loves the self and the heavenly city loves God, *amor dei*, the former looks for glory from men, the latter finds it highest glory in God (XIV. 28). St Augustine's massive *De Civitate Dei* represents more fully and completely than hitherto a view that the life of the city is to be set against the life of the spirit. It is not, however, a new view either in sentiment or in basic philosophy. The implication that not all is well with the city is a view developed from the founding of the city in Genesis to its apocalyptic destruction as represented in the heavenly Zion and the destruction of the earthly Jerusalem as in the fourth vision of II Esdras (9: 26; 10: 59 Apocrypha). The city of Jerusalem is renewed in Revelation 21 and 22 as a holy city; a new Jerusalem, with no need 'of the sun, neither of the moon, to shine in it; for the glory of God did lighten it' (21: 22, 23). Such views indicate that the life of the city is beyond redemption without renewal by God. Symbolically the city stands for all that is earthly, material and sinful. The earthly city is the repository of the flesh, while the spirit lives elsewhere and denies the material needs of the body. This rejection of the city, both actual and symbolic, resulted in and still does result in embracing the ascetic tradition, the life of the monastic and the life of earthly denial. Here the body is the earthly city, to be opposed, denied and turned from. In practice the sacking of Rome and the rise of the monastic tradition resulted in just such a denial of the life of the city and in a withdrawal from the earthly life associated with the city. The city and the secular, which it represented, came to be subsumed under the control of the papacy. The notion of two distinct domains came to be dominated by the idea of the superior sacral domain under which the life of the city was to be submerged.

The recovery of the city   The recovery of the city in the Western tradition occurred from the eleventh and twelfth centuries onward. With that recovery came a rediscovery of the view of a life autonomous from, distinct from, the sacral. The city again came, in some places, to be based on *synoicism*, friendship and confraternity. The rediscovery of the city as both a place and as a mode of living together in confraternity and freedom was particularly notable in Germany where cities of free-men emerged. Such cities often wrote their own constitutions, elected their own leaders, or restricted already existing leaders under constitutional provisions and provided for their own common security and safety. Similar, if better known, developments in Italy led to raising the status of the city in human life. Marsilius of Padua

distinguished between secular and sacral authority, Machiavelli renewed the Hellenistic idea of distinct modes of life and placed politics firmly in the domain of practical reason where it would not intersect with, or be interfered by, ethical or religious concerns and Bruni, in a recovery of the panegyric of Pericles, extolled the virtues of the citizens of Florence. The city was re-established as an autonomous mode of life, as a significant place in which to live and as a political unit in which its members could take pride and recover the virtues.

The city that was rediscovered and which re-emerged as a distinct form of autonomous life after almost a millennium of near political neglect contained within it the seeds of its own destruction. The conditions which allowed the city to be rediscovered in a political sense were also the conditions which permitted, indeed fostered, the development of the nation STATE. With the development of the idea of a nation of people distinct from either the city or the country the autonomy of the city was subsumed. Thus cities came to seek and to hold charters, or to seek and hold legal personalities as subsidiary organizations. In England where there was no older tradition of independent cities this legal recognition was first obtained in the reign of Edward I (1272–1307) with the granting of city charters. This formal, if substantively almost empty, feature of the English definition of the city is maintained to this day when new charters are sought, and occasionally granted, as with the new city of Sunderland in northern England. The English pattern of defining a city in formal, legal terms is relatively unusual but that early English idea of the city as always and only subsidiary in power and organisation to a higher authority, namely the nation state, is now the standard model throughout the world. In a quite significant and meaningful sense the city can be said to have declined after the emergence of the nation state and to have been replaced with first, modern, and then postmodern forms of urbanization.

The modern city   No clear and precise date can be placed on the founding of the modern occidental city. Its rise coincides with the recovery of the city in the West and so its roots can be found in the period from the twelth to the fifteenth century. The emergence of the terms representing the city in European languages reflects the emergence of the modern city. The breakdown of the feudal order, the rise of INDIVIDUALISM and the widespread change in the mode of association from status to contract in entire populations resulted in population pressures on cities which undercut the idea and ideals of confraternity. The city itself was politically subordinate to the emerging nation state and the coming of INDUSTRIALIZATION changed its nature completely. The city of middle modernity lost its autonomy, its political sensibility and its significant public space. What it gained was industrial and commercial development. Occidental cities had always been characterized by some commercial and entrepreneurial activity in addition to their political significance; in the city of middle modernity this commercial and industrial activity became the mainstay of many cities. Thus one finds cities separated into areas or domains, e.g. financial, commercial, artistic, industrial, residential with city government being predominantly oriented towards the management of services rather than existing as a mode of being in its own right. The government of cities is thus a means to an end, the management of utilities and services, rather than an end in itself: a mode of being together. The change in the function of the city produced a correlative change in the relation between the physical and spiritual centres of the city. The modern city is a place without a unified heart, a unified physical space without a single true public space or a true public function; it is rather a series of partially overlapping, partially private and partially public places, held together by a complex, fragmented and underpowered political structure that is entirely unsuitable for the task. The autonomous and unitary city lost, with the rise of the nation state, first its autonomy and then, with the growth of civil society, its unitary nature. The decline of the late modern city has coincided with the emergence of urbanized patterns of living, thus living in, or close to, the centre of the city, once the preserve of the élite, is often now the preserve of the poor. As cities have declined in importance and significance, so the élites have left the cities for the country or the suburbs. This has produced a continuing cycle of decline in physical cities that will be halted, if at all, only with great difficulty. It is more likely that these cities will be allowed to decline as they are replaced with or supplanted by first the plural and fragmented and then the virtual cities of post-modernity.

The plural city   With few exceptions the unitary city has now been replaced with the post-modern city, a principal social feature of which is a fragmentation expressed as a decline in a single and clearly identifiable centre of authority and a concomitant increase in a plurality and dispersal of centres and places of community. This phenomenon is seen most clearly in the megapoleis of the late twentieth century. Cities such as London, New York, Tokyo, Los Angeles, Mexico City *et al.* have no identifiable centre in other than a purely formal sense. Yet they are places of life and meaningful living. That they are such is due to their constitution as a variety of centres none of which has other than a purely formal priority. From the point of view of those who live in these cities, there is no single centre. Thus the city of London should be understood more properly as the cities of London, the city of New York as the cities of New York and so on. It is in these multiple places within the formal city that people meet, take their sense of belonging, create and recreate their sense of identity and understand their communal mode of being. This has clear political, social and theological consequences. From a political aspect it reduces the significance of existing formal structures. From a social point of view it implies that the formal structures carry little weight compared with the informal generation of immediate place and space, and from a theological point of view it means that it makes little sense to talk of *Faith in the City*, the title of the Anglican Report, we should rather talk pluralistically of 'faiths in the cities'. Lives in the plural cities generate new challenges for those living in such plural circumstances. They can ghettoize, remain tied to a single cultural place or they can seek to reach beyond that, to take their identities from several foci. 'Faiths in the cities' generates new theological and religious challenges. Religious identity, religious allegiance and religious conviction can remain unitary, and thus in tension with other unitary religious identities, allegiances and convictions in the same urban conglomerate. It can diversify as a kind of syncretism, or alternatively, and perhaps more promisingly, it can generate new tolerances and new religious and theological conceptions of identity. The route of unity is in conflict with the imperatives of the plural city and may lead to the kind of disaster seen in, e.g. Sarajevo. The route to syncretism becomes all things to all people and in its lack of specificity risks complete loss of meaningful content. The route to tolerance of religious pluralism requires acceptance that other ways of worship have validity, hence one's own way of worship has no privilege: it is merely the way that those who share that mode of worship do things. This is an important, indeed crucial lesson to learn in a plural society; it is also a vital lesson, perhaps *the* vital lesson, for theology and for religious practice in a plural city. In a plural city, a city that is de-centred, faith, theology and religious practices are also de-centred. That does not diminish their importance for their adherents, but it does locate them in the family of humanly acceptable and desirable religious practices.

The virtual city   The city has played an important role in human affairs for, perhaps, five millennia. Its original founding was probably for safety and security. Later it became a way of life in itself: a mode of being together, and as such the function of the city could not be separated from perceptions of human flourishing. This perception, originally pagan, clashed with the values developing in the sensibilities of the Christians of the early church. The turn away from the city, both as place, and as a mode of life of value in itself presaged the sacking of Rome, but that event confirmed and hastened the portrayal of the earthly city as offering a mode of life inappropriate for those seeking spiritual reward.

The recovery of the city, in Germany and in Italy, was the recovery of the unitary and autonomous city. As it developed so it challenged the authority of the church in its affairs, drawing again a distinction between matters spiritual and matters secular. Yet its own autonomy was in turn challenged by the nation state and its confraternity lost to the rise of individualism

and the associations of civil society. The decline of the autonomous and unitary city is both long term and, with one or two exceptions, almost certainly irreversible: it is the outcome of long term historical trends that have brought the city into conflict with significant features of modern life. That process will almost certainly increase. The decline of the unitary city has been accompanied by the rise of urban areas with multiple places and spaces. In developed countries the growth of private transport has fostered the growth of consumer based suburban centres: places of life only while instrumentally functioning. But as the autonomous and unitary city was modified by the nation state and civil society, so the nation state is itself being modified by tendencies towards supranational organizations and agreements. Relatedly civil society is being modified by changes in methods of communication and changes in modes of exchange relation. Both are being affected by the tendency to a globalization of outlook. The outcome of these tendencies are changes in the way in which people interact and changes in the modes of being together. The first cities brought people together in face to face relations: those meetings were the only form of interaction outside of household or tribe. Meetings now take place in a manifold of situations and utilizing a variety of means. Many such meetings are no longer face to face, and the long term trend is likely to be an increase in the number of such meetings and interactions. In these situations, place and space are notions more of metaphorical significance than of real significance. Place is virtual place rather than actual place, space is virtual space rather than actual space and the locus of such meetings, the point of mutuality, is itself virtual rather than actual. In consequence, the city of the future may well be symbolic, metaphorical and virtual rather than symbolic, metaphorical and actual. The cities of the postmodern world will include such arrangements; already there are virtual banks, virtual research groups, virtual work places, virtual colleges and virtual universities; virtual cities are no great leap of principle. Such cities may take the form of conglomerates or they may take the form of large conglomerates separated by distance but not by significant travelling time. Eura-Lille is itself a small place but consists of a virtual city taking in Paris, London and several other large continental cities all within three hours or less travelling time. Such an arrangement creates a virtual city of over thirty million people; such arrangements are likely to become more common and require re-thinking notions of space, place, membership and association. In the meanwhile large numbers of people live in urban sprawls, but vast numbers of people living together in urban conglomerates of huge size and great sprawl is not in itself the manifestation of a single city, for it has no single heart, no single meaning, and it provides no significant mode of being human together in meaningful interaction. Such arrangements provide no single focus; if they are anything they are overlapping cities, not *a* city. Nor are such places even places of safety. The maxim of John of Vitterbo that, 'city means you dwell safe from violence' would now be reversed by many to read 'city means you go in violence', and safety requires a private rather than a public place: a home, a school, a college, a leisure centre, a club or other association. Not all of these will be replaced by the occupation of virtual space and the creation of new forms of virtual reality, but some will, and this trend is unlikely to be reversed in the conditions of the developed world. In the developing world the trend is often different. The city has there shown the emergence of a new form with the development of some giant city states. Striking examples are found in South East Asia where city states have turned into economic, financial and (increasingly) political powerhouses.

For all its difficulties the city has had a special place in the hearts of human beings; it has represented safety, security and ways of being together. The first cities had religious significance, and that significance lives on in collective memory. Symbolically the city can have spiritual meaning, as Jerusalem has significance to members of several different faiths. Cities can be regarded with dismay, but they can also be regarded as holy, e.g. Jerusalem, or Rome. Cities are often targets in war but they may also be granted special status, as Rome was in the Second World War. The relation between the city and religious experience,

including, but not confined to, Christian religious experience, has always been one of tension; the very idea of faith in the city brings the sacral and the secular together in opposition. Like the meeting point of two tectonic plates is the most dangerous, volatile and explosive area of land mass so the intersection between the sacral and secular has been at its most fraught in the city. Cities mean much to many people, they will be fought over, defended, subject to strife, suffering, war and pestilence when they are attacked and when they need defence. Often the significance of the city is as much in its symbolism, in what it stands for, and that it can stand for so many different things to so many people. The reality of the unitary city is of a place in decline of a mode of being together that has been, or is in the process of being, superseded. The *idea* of the city will always have a special place in the human mind. It will always be a place of tension, including spiritual and religious tension, for in the idea of the city the sacral and secular are in conflict. Yet the actuality of the often ungovernable and frequently decaying urban sprawl that so often now passes for the last physical manifestation of the city of safety will, perhaps more than ever, be regarded with some suspicion and not a little dismay. Everything has changed and yet nothing has changed.

Augustine, St (1972) *Concerning The City of God Against the Pagans,* Harmondsworth: Pelican.

Black, Antony (1984) *Guilds and Civil Society in European Political Thought from the Twelfth Century to the Present*, London: Methuen.

Brown, Peter (1988) *The Body and Society: Men, Women and Sexual Renunciation in Early Christianity*, London and Boston: Faber and Faber.

Clarke, Paul Barry (1994) *Citizenship*, London and Boulder; Pluto Press.

al-Farabi, Muhammed (1985) *Ara ahl al-madina al-fadila*, trans. R. Walzer, *Al-Farabi on the Perfect State*, Oxford: Oxford University Press.

Hammond, Mason (1972) *The City in the Ancient World*, Cambridge, MA: Harvard University Press.

Mumford, Lewis (1961) *The City in History*, New York: Harcourt Brace and World.

Numa Denis Fustel De Coulanges (1980) *The Ancient City: A study on the Religion, Laws, and Institutions of Greece and Rome*, Baltimore and London: The Johns Hopkins University Press.

Schofield, Malcolm *The Stoic Idea of the City*, Cambridge: Cambridge University Press.

Strauss, Leo (1983) 'Jerusalem and Athens', in *Studies in Platonic Political Philosophy*, Chicago: University of Chicago Press.

Voegelin, Eric (1956) *Order in History*, Louisiana: Louisiana State University Press.

Weber, Max (1978) *Economy and Society*, Berkeley CA: University of California Press.

Paul Barry Clarke

CIVIL DISOBEDIENCE

Civil disobedience has been defined as 'a public, nonviolent, conscientious yet political act contrary to law usually done with the aim of bringing about a change in the law or policies of a government' (Rawls 1972: 364). Definitions may vary in detail or emphasis, but most would agree that acts of civil disobedience are public not clandestine; that they are non-violent rather than violent; that they are political yet rooted in a sense of moral outrage; and that their goal is to change a particular law or state policy.

Acts of civil disobedience vary greatly in scope and gravity, but they assume two basic forms. First, they may be acts whereby a specific unjust law (e.g. a racially discriminatory law) is itself disobeyed. Second, they may involve breaking laws other than those in question (e.g. the refusal to pay taxes, strike action) in order to impede the functioning of the STATE. The aim of such action is to draw public attention to particular laws or policies which are morally unacceptable, unjust or unconstitutional. The latter form of civil disobedience requires more justification than the former.

Although such acts are non-violent, they sometimes result in violent reaction on the part of the authorities or opposing groups (*see* VIOLENCE). Situations may arise, however, which lead some proponents of civil disobedience to engage in revolutionary and violent action. While some may argue that civil disobedience and such revolutionary action are on the same continuum, the fact that the former is strictly non-violent in character indicates a qualitative difference between them.

Acts of civil disobedience may be undertaken by individuals on their own, but they often take the form of mass action. Noted twentieth-century instances of civil disobedience are the struggle for independence in India led by Mahatma Ghandi; the Defiance Campaign against APARTHEID in South Africa in the 1950s and again in the 1980s led, amongst others, by Albert Lutuli, Nelson Mandela and Desmond Tutu; the Civil Rights Struggle in the United States of America under the leadership of Martin Luther King Jr; and the struggle of Solidarity against Communist dictatorship in Poland under the leadership of Lech Walesa.

Even though persons engaged in acts of civil disobedience may do so on the grounds of conscience, not all such acts are morally justifiable. Conscience is of fundamental importance, but conscience alone is an inadequate guide or criterion (see Bonhoeffer 1965: 246ff.). On the grounds of the injunction to 'obey the authorities' because they are 'instituted by God' (Romans 13: 1–7), most Christians through the centuries have felt bound by conscience to submit rather than engage in acts of civil disobedience or rebellion (*see* CHURCH AND STATE). Yet, during the first few centuries of church history many Christians were martyred because of their refusal to submit to Roman laws which demanded their denial of their faith. And there has always been a minority which has argued that because Romans 13 presupposes a GOVERNMENT which truly serves the interests of people and the rule of law, situations may arise in which for the sake of conscience it is necessary to obey God rather than human AUTHORITY, whether religious or secular (Acts 5: 29). The problem has been discerning when such disobedience is morally and theologically legitimate.

In the course of the post-Constantinian history of the church, the right to disobey and resist human authority has been most clearly argued by radical reformers rather than by those within the mainstream of Christendom. Yet John Calvin, the sixteenth-century Protestant Reformer who placed such a premium on obedience to authority, acknowledged that situations could arise when civil disobedience and rebellion might be required out of obedience to God (Calvin 1960: 4:20). For some of Calvin's successors, notably the French Huguenots, civil disobedience and resistance became a Christian duty when morally justified. Indeed, the traditional criteria for 'just war' became applicable in determining when civil disobedience, as well as rebellion or REVOLUTION, are appropriate (Beza 1956: 43).

Many Christians have upheld the right of civil disobedience only when the rights of the church or their particular group have been infringed. For example, in his encyclical *Sapientia christiana* (1890) Pope Leo XIII declared that obedience to the state ceases when the church is victimized by the state or when citizens are required to act contrary to church law. However, twentieth-century experience of injustice and tyranny, together with further theological and ethical reflection on the issues, particularly by Christians in situations of oppression, has led to a growing ecumenical consensus that civil disobedience is equally and possibly more legitimate when the rights of the most vulnerable in society are disregarded and infringed by the state. JUSTICE thus becomes the basic criterion for determining the need for civil disobedience.

The prophetic tradition in the Bible not only insists that justice is the foundation for true law, but that the touchstone of justice is the way in which 'widows, orphans, aliens' and 'the poor and oppressed' are regarded and treated. When their rights are transgressed, whether in a legislated form or not, it becomes a moral obligation to oppose such laws and actions.

Yet it does not follow that civil disobedience is appropriate action in all such instances. As in the case of 'just war' theory, acts of civil disobedience should only be resorted to when other options have been explored and have failed. Moreover there must be some reasonable expectation of success, and a reasonable expectation that civil disobedience will not result in anarchy and a general disrespect for the rule of law. The means adopted should not be counter to the desired goal of persuading those in authority to change unjust laws. Civil disobedience thus normally presupposes a democratically elected government which acknowledges the rule of law, however inadequately it puts that rule into practice. In fact, civil disobedience is a democratic act of law-making, a conscientious violation of a particular law or set of laws in the interests of upholding justice and thereby affirming the rule of law.

In some instances tyranny and illegitimacy exist alongside some semblance of DEMOCRACY and respect for the rule of LAW. In these situations acts of civil disobedience as well as armed struggle may both be strategically appropriate and morally justified in bringing about change to specific laws as well as a fundamental transformation of the state. Many Christians, as well as people of other religious and ideological persuasions, argued for such a multiple strategy in the struggle against apartheid in South Africa. Others have argued, however, that non-violent action alone is morally justified and can best achieve the ends sought.

Civil disobedience normally involves personal sacrifice and cost. Its moral power derives not only from the rightness of the cause at hand, but from the willingness of its advocates to act openly, usually for the sake of others rather than themselves, and to accept the consequences of their deeds. In disobeying the law they respect the rule of law, and therefore submit to its authority and to any violent reaction they may encounter. Hence acts of civil disobedience demand discipline and commitment. The willing acceptance of such cost for the sake of justice is an important criterion for establishing the authenticity of those who engage in acts of civil disobedience.

Adams, James Luther (1970) 'Civil disobedience: its occasions and limits', in J.R. Pennock and J. Chapman (eds) *Political and Legal Obligation*, New York: Atherton.

Beza, Theodore (1956) *Concerning the Rights of Rulers over their Subjects and the Duty of Subjects Towards their Rulers*, ed. A.H. Murray, Cape Town: HAUM.

Bonhoeffer, Dietrich (1965) *Ethics*, New York: Macmillan.

Calvin, John (1960) *The Institutes of the Christian Religion*, Book 4, ch. 20, ed. J.T. McNeill, Philadelphia: Westminster Press.

Childress, James F. (1971) *Civil Disobedience and Political Obligation: A Study in Christian Social Ethics*, New Haven, CT: Yale University Press.

King, Martin Luther, Jr (1963) 'Letter from a Birmingham Jail', in *Why We Can't Wait*, New York: New American Library.

Merton, Thomas (1980) *The Non-Violent Alternative*, New York: Farrar Strauss Giroux.

Oosthuizen, D.C.S. (1973) *The Ethics of Illegal Action and Other Essays*, Johannesburg: Ravan.

Rawls, John (1972) *A Theory of Justice*, London: Oxford University Press.

Sharp, Gene (1973) *The Politics of Non-Violent Action*, Boston, MA: Horizon Books.

Thielicke, Helmut (1966) *Theological Ethics*, vol. 1, *Foundations*, Philadelphia, PA: Fortress.

Villa-Vicencio, Charles (1990) *Civil Disobedience and Beyond: Law, Resistance and Religion in South Africa*, Grand Rapids, MI: Eerdmans.

Zinn, Howard (1968) *Disobedience and Democracy*, New York: Random House.

John W. De Gruchy

CLASS

In general usage the term 'class' refers to classification – the partitioning or division of people or things into a series of categories, according to some criterion or common attribute. This is its etymological root, deriving from *classis*, which refers to Servius Tullius' division of the Roman people into six orders of taxation: from the established, tax-paying *assidui* to the poor *proletarii*, 'owning' or producing only their offspring (*proles*), but they in turn were superior to those only countable by head. By its very nature, classification emphasizes the equal position of those within the same class category, and the inequality between the classes. It is therefore a natural language for social inequality.

Sociological usage is akin to common usage, but is more specific. 'Class' features as an example of the more general concept of social stratification: the construction of the social world into strata or layers ordered (or 'graded') according to one or more social attributes or scarce resources – typically wealth, prestige, purity, power, occupation or rank. Implicitly, possession of these attributes is highly valued in the culture concerned; social classification *could* be based upon length of the index finger or hair colour, but these are unlikely to feature as valued attributes and hence serve as a basis for social stratification. Historically, such bases or 'dimensions' have included occupational and ritual purity (Hindu castes), homage and service ('subinfeudation' in the medieval western Estate system), and a major basis for social differentiation in many societies has been SLAVERY versus freedom. In modern industrial societies these bases are more usually economic ownership, occupational prestige, power, educational status and community status.

The historical origin of social differentiation is obscure, but was clearly dependent upon the creation and differential control of surplus from agricultural societies and usually built upon a basic divide, whether an ethnic 'caste line' or a form of slavery, varying from total ownership as a chattel to bond or debt slavery.

Different terminology has been preferred in different periods and societies to refer to similar facts of social inequality: rank, order, station, estate all have a dated but historically-specific provenance; today's terms would more naturally include status and class. But a common differentiator is whether the social arrangement is considered harmonious, consensual (and often God-given) or expressing inherent conflict and incompatible interest – even Plato is reported as disapproving of the fact that the 'undesirable' have higher fertility than 'the best' in a society.

The analysis of social class has been a particular concern of sociologists, developing from earlier work by political economists and concentrated classically upon economic organization that emerged in the Industrial Revolution. Adam Smith provides an excellent starting point for this tradition in his *Wealth of Nations* (1793). He addresses the classic economic problem of the distribution of wealth and division of labour by distinguishing those (classes) who live by rent, wages and profit. With the reduced importance of agriculture and land in industrial society, this reduces to a bipolar opposition of interests (and implicit conflict) between those living from profit and interest and those dependent solely on wages. This forms the basis for Marx's crucial, but unfinished, analysis of class, probably most accessibly advanced in *The Communist Manifesto* (*see* MARXISM). Wedded initially to a Hegelian concept of ALIENATION (especially in his early 1844 manuscripts), and to the 'dialectic' as the mechanism for change, Marx puts class conflict at the forefront of his social analysis, as in his famous aphorism: 'The history of all hitherto existing society is the history of the class-struggle' – following, that is, the Eden-like state of primitive COMMUNISM, and to be superseded by the post-capitalist classless Communist society. Class situations are defined by a group's social relationship to the means of production (basically, ownership and exclusion from ownership). Thus in CAPITAL-ISM the interests of the bourgeoisie are to exploit the proletariat, and the interests of the proletariat are to 'expropriate the expropriators'. This provides the conditions for a class 'in itself', but only by recognition of their own interests, and the fact that these interests are inherently in contradiction to those of the other class, and by means of the class struggle does a class become a class 'for itself', with class consciousness and awareness and pursuing its own interests. This basic structure, of a dichotomous antagonistic opposition, Marx believed characterized all class societies, which differed principally in what form the means of production took (the 'mode' of production, e.g. feudalism, capitalism). Although not a crude mechanist or determinist, he believed that progress towards a communist society was inevitable, and that the 'contradictions' of capitalism were inherent in any class society.

Marx's incomplete analysis has left a legacy of suggested completion and revisionism, and however much the historical detail of his prognoses (such as the increasing pauperization of the proletariat) must be faulted, his influence on the political and sociological analysis of class has been colossal (see Dahrendorf 1959); many later theories have necessarily struggled with his ghost. This is especially true of the other major class theorist in sociology, Max Weber (see Gerth and Mills 1948). Characterizing Marxian class as (economic) class, shared by those who share common life-chances and a common relationship to the market, Weber distinguished it analytically from *status*, the estimation of honour bestowed on positions (typically, but by no means exclusively, occupations in industrial society). In a British context it needs no emphasizing that the WEALTH of the *parvenu* needs legitimation before it becomes recognized by higher, more established echelons. Indeed, where class and status are discordant, the preconditions exist for radical rejection of the basis of the system, rather than assimilation. Weber's interests took him in a radically different direction from Marx, and he became especially concerned with the wider issue of the growth of rationality in industrial society (having its roots in the Protestant ethic, according to his celebrated thesis) and with how the control and manifestation of power has become intricately bound up with bureaucratization in the modern world.

In many ways, European sociology has followed the Marxian tradition whereas American sociology has followed Weber. In empirical studies of class and status, there has been a divergence: American studies and research have tended to concentrate on socio-economic status as a *variable* and Europeans have been more concerned with *categorical* class systems. In the former case, community-based studies have provided accounts of how the social standing of families and individuals relates to such characteristics as education, occupation, house-type and source of income. This has later been generalized to studies of occupational prestige to provide a quantitative scale of socio-economic status. British and European studies often have a more markedly Marxian flavour and tend to concentrate on social class as categorical system, (e.g. the Registrar-General's five-class system in the UK), together with interest in subjective class awareness and class relations and with the question of the *embourgeoisement* of the working class in post-Second World War societies.

More recently these traditions have shown a degree of convergence, with social mobility and status achievement forming the common focus of interest. Much political, ideological (and social scientific) attention has been paid to why increasing class polarization has not occurred, and the role that 'equality of opportunity' (perceptively given the addendum 'to be unequal' by Michael Young) and the mechanism of education has played in increasing access to the higher echelons of society. Social mobility (or, more accurately, individual occupational mobility) has thus become the laboratory for many students of social stratification (see Blau and Duncan 1967; Goldthorpe 1980) and the reigning paradigm in studies of class and stratification, though strongly contested by some Marxists (Westergaard and Resler 1975) and cognitivists (Coxon and Davies 1986). The *effect* of class on other aspects of social life has been extensively examined (see

Reid 1981) and features as an independent variable in almost all sociological studies.

The great majority of studies of class structure have been of the Western (and to a lesser extent the Communist) industrial world, and it may well be that the effective forces of class formation and conflict are now global, involving the Third World against the rest and probably the Western versus the Eastern ex-communist countries.

Religion in general (and theology in particular) has relatively little to say about class *per se*, but this is principally because class is a fairly recent social science concept which is used to interpret the world. The vocabulary used by theology is usually more akin to that of political economists and ethicists, concerned more with rank and (in)equality than with POWER, conflict and stratification. Traditionally, Marxist analyses have been seen as (at best) inimical to Christian accounts (not least because of Marx's avowed materialist and atheist suppositions), and the Marxist desire not so much to interpret the world as to change it (*Theses on Feuerbach* in Marx n.d.) puts it in the role of a rival IDEOLOGY. None the less, Marxism in general and its class analysis in particular has had a degree of influence on areas of social theology (the extent to which papal social Encyclicals utilize such notions is an eloquent testimony), and especially on 'LIBERATION THEOLOGY'. A number of attempts (e.g. MacIntyre [1953] 1971) have been made to relate Marxist or neo-Marxist analyses to Christian theology, and class has probably been one of the more successful areas of debate. Some Christian perspectives accept the social/economic conditioning of religion but argue for a dialectical reciprocal influence (such as Weber's thesis on the relationship between the spirit of capitalism and the Protestant ethic) or distinguish institutional religion (thus effected) from the Christian ethic or incarnational theology. Others seek a common starting-point in Feuerbach's and the early Marx's conceptions of alienation and its Christian counterpart. Yet others see Marxist analyses as giving a secular slant on KINGDOM OF GOD or eschatological ethics (*see* ESCHATOLOGY).

The sociological analysis of religion both precedes and follows the Marxian interpretation, which sees it as an integral part of the class structure and also as being determined by it. The main theological defence against this position has been to concede much of the truth of the latter whilst questioning the former, and differentiating the causes of a belief – a legitimate scientific concern – from the reasons for holding it. The most explicit statement of this dual role is Marx's: if

> it is not the consciousness of man that determines their being, but on the contrary, their social being that determines their social consciousness.
>
> (Marx, Preface to the
> *Critique of the Political Economy*)

then at the very least we can expect Christianity, its historical formations, its institutional forms and its theology, to bear the marks of its social and political creation and development. The most extensive development of this theme is due to Weber's student, Ernst Troeltsch (1931), whose magisterial work first developed in detail the relation between social and religious structure. During its two-volume course he developed (*inter alia*) the ideal types of the church and the sect (and a more shadowy type, mysticism), showing how certain types of religious structure showed (or had a 'selective affinity' for) associated distinctive types of social teaching and relationship to the world. Troeltsch, in using the Weberian 'ideal type', is anxious to stress that it is an analytic construct to which no actual organization may exactly conform, but he recognized (as his successors often forgot) that *both* structures were present in the early church, and sometimes still coexist.

In Troeltsch's account, the church is a 'natural' social structure into which members are born; it is inclusive in scope and universalistic in orientation. The sect, by contrast, is essentially a voluntary organization into which members are converted; it is exclusive and particularistic, making explicit demands of its members.

The church–sect differentiation is also associated with typically divergent doctrine and ethics. The church has a high regard for sacraments as assured means of GRACE, has a wide range of class membership (but one biased towards the middle and upper classes) and has a trained clergy; it needs to emphasize its educational function, since this is its main form of recruitment, and it adopts a basic stance of accommodation to, compromise with, or direct support of the established order. The sect on the other hand is more concerned with the 'correct experience' of its members, recruits typically from the dispossessed, often forgoes regular clergy, and being in ascetic tension with 'the world' rejects any compromise with it. Troeltsch (and Weber) recognized a crucial sociological consequence: the sect is inherently unstable sociologically; it is essentially only valid for one generation and once its members' have children the 'second generation' problem arises – conversion is no longer the only form of admission, and inevitably its structure and form of social teaching approximates to the church. The class overtones of this typology are explicit in the recruitment and membership of the two types: above all, the sect appeals to and recruits from lower status groups and classes, whilst the church is more typically recruited from the middle and upper classes.

The original church–sect distinction is too rudimentary to accommodate all the crucial aspects of religious organization, and it has undergone a good deal of development and refinement. Perhaps the most necessary religious structure to accommodate is the 'denomination', an essentially American organizational form occurring in a pluralistic society, which has become increasingly salient in the last few centuries. In American society, denominations have a far more restricted social base than their counterparts elsewhere, and an aggregated prestige ranking of churches exists (based primarily on the stage at which they arrived from Europe) which complements and reinforces the class structure. Thus whilst 'Protestant', 'Catholic' and 'Jew' represented the 'triple (endogenous) melting pots' of equivalent ways to 'be American', there also exists a consistent ranking, with Unitarian, Episcopalian and Congregationalist denominations enjoying considerably higher regard (and class recruitment, educational level, political preference) than Baptists, Catholics and Pentecostals.

In understanding denominations, H. Richard Niebuhr (1927) (brother of Reinhold) confessed himself driven to sociology:

> The effort to distinguish churches primarily by reference to their doctrine and to approach the problem of church unity from a purely theological point of view appeared to (the author) to be a procedure so artificial and fruitless that he found himself compelled to turn from theology to history, sociology and ethics for a more satisfactory account of denominational differences and a more significant approach to the question of union.

In his analysis Niebuhr examines the structure of the denomination and proceeds to differentiate the 'Churches of the Disinherited' from the 'Churches of the Middle Class' as a way of making sense of doctrinal variation and social structure. The actual process of 'denominationalization' (from sect to denomination) was well charted in a most interesting case study by Pope (1942) where increasing affluence (as a result of sect ASCETICISM) led to more formal organization, a more extended appeal and the employment of a full-time preacher. Even in European countries with histories of established churches, similar aspects are discernible. Thus, Methodism had considerable success in evangelizing the urban working classes (and in the process becoming a 'labour aristocracy'), and Bishop Wickham (1951) showed with considerable historical flair that in England (or, more properly, in Sheffield), and despite its universalistic claims, it was not that the Church of England had lost the working classes, it had never had them for many generations.

There can be no doubt that institutional religion is strongly differentiated, even conditioned, by social class – but so are legal, political and other social institutions. What makes the assertion disturbing to Christians is that it expressly contradicts the universalistic claims of Christianity, and (at least in its Marxian version) implicates religion in the creation and sustaining of power in society.

The notion that religion is conditioned by social class (used as a descriptive sociological notion) is not particularly disturbing; it would be hard to imagine what a social institution would be like that successfully avoided class conditioning. Even on the issue of relationship to the powers that be, there has always been a degree of ambiguity from Paul's time and before. But the more extended universalistic claims of Christianity have made it particularly sensitive to the external criticisms of being particularistic, serving sectional interests, allying itself with power, compromising its pristine values – most of these being encapsulated in the notion of 'class'.

The Marxian account goes on to argue that these factors are not contingent but necessary, and that religion is itself a symptom of class society and of alienation which (like the state) will ultimately wither away at the advent of an eschatological communist society. At this point, the parallel often drawn between Christianity and Marxism as a secular religion is at its most obvious.

Class analysis, then, owes its most explicit meaning and much of its force to the very specific philosophical, ideological (and, let it be said, ethical) system of Marxism, which saw itself as a (indeed, the) scientific system and as needing to combat religion as a false, derivative and narcotic force (however much religion was also presented by Marx as 'the heart of a heartless world', an addition often ignored).

But the Marxian account is far from acceptable from a social science viewpoint; it is incomplete, wrong in a number of its predictions and manifestly needing modification and change to cope (if it can) with the changes in capitalism itself, as Weber and all subsequent social scientists testify.

Even in the more general and neutral sociological sense of class, there is a clear whiff of relativism and partiality in the assertion that institutional religion is class-conditioned, and a sociologically informed theology needs to confront not only the issues of power and class, but also that of status. 'Invidious distinction' and 'conspicuous consumption' (Veblen) and forms of stratification internal to religious institutions (not least the non-theological and sociological aspects of the clergy–laity divide) are largely untouched by theological thought, and Niebuhr's appeal that discussion about unity be informed by

the sociological determinants of ecumenism and unity is still unanswered.

Blau, P.M. and Duncan, O.D.D. (1967) *The American Occupational Structure*, New York: Wiley.
Coxon, A.P.M. and Davies, P.M., with Jones, C.L. (1986) *Images of Social Stratification, Occupational Structures and Class*, London: Sage.
Dahrendorf, Ralf (1959) *Class and Class Conflict in an Industrial Society*, London: Routledge.
Gerth, H.H. and Mills, C.W. (eds) (1948) *From Max Weber: Essays in Sociology*, London: Routledge.
Goldthorpe, J.G. (1980) *Social Mobility and Class Structure in Modern Britain*, Oxford: Clarendon.
Laumann, E.O., Siegel, P.M. and Hodge, R.W. (eds) (1970) *The Logic of Social Hierarchies*, Chicago, IL: Markham.
Lipset, R. and Bendix, R. (eds) (1953) *Class, Status and Power: A Reader in Social Stratification*, Glencoe, IL: Free Press.
MacIntyre, A.C. (1953) *Marxism: An Interpretation*, London: SCM; republished as *Marxism and Christianity*, Harmondsworth: Pelican, 1971.
Marx, K. (n.d.) *On Religion*, London: Lawrence & Wishart.
Marx, K. and Engels, F. (1962) *Selected Works*, vols 1 and 2, London: Lawrence & Wishart.
Niebuhr, H. Richard (1927, 1957) *The Social Sources of Denominationalism*, New York: Meridian.
Pope, Liston (1942) *Millhands and Preachers*, New Haven, CT: Yale University Press.
Reid, I. (1981) *Social Class Differences in Britain*, 2nd edn, London: Grant McIntyre.
Smith, Adam (1793) *An Inquiry into the Nature and Causes of the Wealth of Nations*, London: Strahan & Cadell.
Troeltsch, E. (1931) *The Social Teaching of the Christian Churches*, vols 1 and 2, trans. O. Wyon, London: Allen & Unwin.
Weber, Max (1950) *The Theory of Social and Economic Organization*, trans. A.M. Henderson and T. Parsons, Glencoe: Free Press.
Westergaard, J. and Resler, H. (1975) *Class in a Capitalist Society: A Study of Contemporary Britain*, London: Heinemann.
Wetter, Gustav, S.J. (1958) *Dialectical Materialism*, trans. P. Heath, London: Routledge.
Wickham, E.R. (1951) *Church and People in an Industrial City*, London: Lutterworth.

Anthony P.M. Coxon

CLERGY

The generic term 'clergy' (as opposed to 'laity', Greek *laoi*, people) is usually used to refer to the ordained ministry of the Church. The term is an abbreviation of 'clerk in [Major or Holy]

Orders', deriving from the Latin *clericus* (clerk) from the Greek *kléros* (lot, estate). In traditional Christianity, Major Orders consist of Bishop (from *episcopos*, overseer), Presbyter/Priest (from *presbuteros*, elder) and Deacon (from *diakonos*, servant), and in non-episcopal reformed Christianity the term 'minister' (servant) is the normal generic term.

With the exception of the Religious Society of Friends (Quakers) and a few SECTS, all Christian churches have some form of 'set apart' and ordained ministry, claiming derivation in various divergent ways from the New Testament and apostolic Christianity. From the early patristic period to the Reformation, virtually all Christianity developed an episcopal system, which evolved into a territorial unit of the diocese (with a bishop) and subdivided into parishes served by clergy in priest's orders. At the Reformation a renewed emphasis on the Word and the functions of preaching and evangelization often led to a radical break with the highly sacramental, and particularly Eucharistic, pattern of ministry which had developed. Anglicans (and to a lesser degree Lutherans) kept the episcopal structure and 'succession', whilst Reformed and other Protestant churches focused the authority of ordination on the 'inward call' and its legitimation by the congregation or Church court.

Traditionally Christianity restricted ordination to males, although some evidence suggests that instances existed of women being priests and some early schismatic groups had women clergy. In Protestant churches, women have been assigned a 'deaconess' role for some time, and women in religious communities have clearly exercised a ministerial, if not a priestly, role. In this century, the Anglican Church has begun to ordain women to the diaconate, priesthood and latterly to the episcopate (*see* WOMEN'S ORDINATION).

Functions of the clergy have been varied, depending chiefly on whether they have been allocated a 'cure of souls' as a parish clergyman or not. If so, the functions are primarily occupational and usually pastoral and worship linked ('Word and Sacraments'); if not, some other (typically people-oriented) occupation is followed and clergy functions become more narrowly sacramental or worship linked.

Churches differ also on the permanence of the clerical state; Catholic, Orthodox and Anglican (and to a lesser degree Lutherans) treat Holy Orders as lifelong, and usually as having an 'indelible' nature; Reformed (and especially Congregational) churches treat the congregation's call as critical and may even, as in the case of Baptists, treat a person as having reverted entirely to lay status if not exercising a congregational pastorate. In early, and increasingly in modern, Christianity a part-time non-stipendiary ministry occurs.

The principal divergences between Christian communities with respect to the ordained ministry have come to centre on *episcopacy* – its nature, necessity and succession – and upon the exercise of *priesthood*. The traditional view, which crystallized in the patristic period and has become normative to Catholic, Orthodox, other ancient Eastern and (to a varied extent) Anglican communions, is that the bishop is the essential, normative focus of the tradition of teaching, unity, orthodoxy, AUTHORITY and sacramental validity of the church. The Church of Rome views this authority as emanating from the See of Peter, the Orthodox from local patriarchs in communion with the Ecumenical Patriarch, and Anglicans from a common collegiality and link to the See of Canterbury. This authority is often viewed as being guaranteed by episcopal succession by laying on of hands and commissioning in an unbroken chain from apostolic times, though the historical defensibility of this view is debatable. ANGLICANISM exhibits a greater degree of variance in views of the necessity of episcopal ordination, from the *esse* (absolute necessity), through the *plene esse* (necessary for 'fullness') to the *bene esse* (necessary for the goodness of the church), and Lutherans and Methodists differ in whether they have bishops, claim any succession or ascribe any importance to the fact.

Parish priests, who owe their authority and allegiance to their bishop, exercise pastoral/teaching, sacramental and preaching roles from that source, and the diaconate has become little more than a probationary year before ordination as a priest. In the Protestant traditions, the ministers or pastors have owed their authority to different non-episcopal sources and often minister to a non-parochial 'gathered' congregation – or as in British Wesleyanism are itinerant – where worship and their role in the congregation is concentrated more on preaching of the Word than on the sacrament/s. Unlike their episcopally ordained fellows, their presence is not necessary for the valid celebration of the sacraments.

In sociological terms, however, clergy of different denominations in the Western world today share a very similar position and range of functions and are susceptible to very similar stresses and rewards. The ecumenical movement has led to re-examination not only of theological and historical bases of difference but also of the sociological contexts in which ministry is exercised, and divisive issues such as women's ministry, charismatic experience, sexual issues and the liberal/traditional theological divide often cross-cut existing church boundaries. Eastern Orthodoxy remains largely untouched by such convergence (at least at grass-roots level), and new sectarian movements are often outside – and intend to stay outside – any ecumenical contact, and their clergy exhibit similarly divergent status.

The New Testament presents nothing resembling a single, stable pattern of ministry in the post-Resurrection Church, though most current patterns claim representation there, perhaps with good reason. Although some aspects of current understanding of the development of Christian ministry are conjectural (and probably owe more than would have been allowed in past centuries to contemporary forms of Jewish religious leadership), there seems initially to have been both 'charisma-based' ministries, which, as Weber noted, are often inherently unstable and prone to institutionalization, and 'ordained' ministries, which soon emerged as localized communities gathered round the bishop and his deacons who assisted him, with the presbyters having a historically problematic role. Some believe the difference between the presbyters and the bishops to have been virtually non-existent, others that the difference was that presbyters represent an office whilst the episcopate (and indeed the 'serving diaconate') is a function. However, by 170 CE a universal pattern had emerged, testified by Ignatius of Antioch, of local Christian communities gathered round a single *episkopos*, with his deacons and presbyters. Bishop Lightfoot (1868) in a seminal and still widely accepted article argues three points to explain this transition: that the paradigm structure was the Church in Jerusalem (with James as 'bishop'); that by the second half of the second century presbyters were being elevated to the episcopate, and that the bishops were not localized apostles since the latter were by their very nature itinerant.

In view of later developments it is important to stress that in this period the presbyter was in no way given the title, or considered to be, a priest (*iereus*, *sacerdos*). Priesthood was well-nigh universal in all religions (see James 1955), and the Jewish priesthood was viewed as being fulfilled and superseded in Jesus as High Priest. Whilst the priestly title was transferred figuratively to the Church as people of God, and even to the bishops, it was never interpreted as applying to (let alone applying primarily to) the presbyterate (see Murray, in Lash and Rhymer 1970; Congar 1967). The 'sacerdotalizing' of the presbyterate had to await the third and fourth centuries.

In the pre-Constantine patristic period there was no recognizable clergy in the modern sense, and the laity took a very active part in matters as diverse as the liturgy and appointment of bishops, and even attendance at Church Councils. This changed dramatically and irrevocably with Constantine's recognition of Christianity, and the period up to the end of the Middle Ages was marked by a clericalizing of the Church and what Gabriel Le Bras (see Leclercq 1970) has called the 'exaltation of the clergy' accompanied by the dramatic growth of monasticism. Clergy pay came increasingly from lands (benefices), from mass stipends for particular individuals or groups and occasionally from work (but not trade). In the West, but never the East, CELIBACY was fitfully imposed on parish clergy, though it was never universally adopted until the Counter-Reformation. The separation of clergy and laity was paralleled by that between bishops and priests, as bishops transferred more and more of their erstwhile functions to parish priests and became allied to (and sometimes in effect appointed by) feudal nobility. As the Middle Ages developed, the clergy developed sociologically into a hierarchically ordered feudal estate, which was only saved from becoming a caste by its predominant infertility.

The Reformation and Counter-Reformation witnessed a major reorganization of the clerical estate and the emergence of quite different models of ministry. Although the style of clericalism often affected Protestant ministers quite as much as Catholic priests, the structures were different and the removal or weakening of the episcopal oversight concentrated more power in the parish minister's hands. The schisms in Reformed Christianity and the proliferation of sectarian structures saw the re-emergence of older forms of charismatic and itinerant ministry, and even its rejection entirely (*see* CLASS). Yet the relationship with the state remained problematic, and whilst the Peace of Augsburg principle of *cuius regio, eius religio* (the [prince's] religion in that [prince's] territory) secured some stability in the sixteenth century, nonconformist dissent continued to be a feature of Protestantism. In Roman Catholicism, the reforms of the Council of Trent brought a renewed concern with the 'formation' or training of priests by the seminary system, though explicit training for the clerical role (as opposed to academic education) was largely eschewed by Anglican and Protestant churches until this century. The nineteenth and twentieth centuries have also seen the revival of the Religious Life (see Moorhouse 1969) not only in ANGLICANISM but also, to a much lesser extent, in Lutheranism and the Reformed churches; the Taizé community is the best-known example. As in the Roman Catholic tradition, Anglican religious orders have played a significant part in clergy training.

Sociology came late on to the social science scene, and comparatively little research has taken place on the clergy, especially outside the USA (see Moberg 1962). In part this is because sociology has tended to view religion as derivative, and also because the social position of clergy in contemporary society is sociologically anomalous. Clergy fit in uneasily in the occupational structure. Thus, at different times and places clergy have been an estate, a class of religious specialist 'set apart', a sacrificing priesthood, itinerant preachers, cultic mediators, pastoral country gentlemen, charismatic leaders, congregational managers. In the last century, the clergy formed a prototypical profession, and whilst many characteristics in contemporary society make clergy recognizable religious professionals they are also divergent, marginalized and atypical (Fichter 1961; Moberg 1962). In many industrial societies it is not even clear whether they form an occupation, and if they do, they are again unusual. Their social prestige is generally judged high (typically alongside middle and lower professionals), but the titles 'priest' and 'minister' have much higher prestige than would be predicted from the usual predictors of income and educational level, and they show more variation in rating than almost any other occupation. In part this may be due to changes in recruitment of clergy, as denominations have attempted to make it open to a wider range of class background than has been usual in the past. Most denominations have also adopted some version of seminary or professional training in this century.

The second half of this century has witnessed a rapid SECULARIZATION in the industrialized Western world (Wilson 1966; MacIntyre 1967), and this has had a major effect on the clergy in the sense that congregations have dropped, whole sectors of the population have become indifferent to religious issues – and vocations to the clerical and religious life have systematically declined. Rates of decline differ in different traditions and in different parts of the world, but there are few signs of a reversal of this trend. Within the ministry, there has often been a dramatic loss of self-confidence and a questioning of traditional roles and functions as they experience role-strain and conflict (see Blizzard 1956). Responses to these ambiguities have also been varied, from a resurgence of fundamentalist and traditionalist conceptions to a radical questioning of the status and role of clergy (Towler and Coxon 1979). The 'crisis in recruitment', loss of vocations and loss of men and women leaving the ministry and religious life has equally affected the Roman Catholic church and led to questioning of recent models of priesthood and its correlates (such as CELIBACY) insisted on by the Papacy. The necessity for full-time and life-time ministry is also under question in several denominations.

Many of these trends and divergences now cross-cut denominational boundaries and the future of the clergy depends in large part on the effect of changes now affecting the church at large. On a worldwide scale, renewal and expansion of Christianity are evident in the Third World (Africa, Latin America), whilst contraction and concentration of resources typify Europe and North America. Because SECTS have a far more fluid and potentially adaptable structure and preach a simpler, if fundamentalist, message and can take the initiative and adapt much more quickly than traditional churches, theirs is often the success at least in the short run.

Change is occurring in a domino-like way; developments such as married and women clergy, part-time and time-limited ministry and lay involvement have already occurred in some churches, and are likely to come even in the Roman Catholic Church despite current papal and curial opposition. Ecumenical progress at one time seemed predicated on non-episcopal churches 'taking episcopacy into their system', but New Testament and theological scholarship has shown that contemporary forms of episcopacy and priesthood badly distort the original pattern of ministry, to such an extent that all church polities will need rethinking.

Current trends show a threefold pattern: consolidation and change towards more collegial (episcopal) authority and a more egalitarian ministry among the larger Catholic, Anglican and Protestant churches. But these changes in all instances provoke a traditionalist reaction, and whilst a coalition of Orthodox and traditional Catholics and Anglicans is as unlikely as a merger of fundamentalist protestant sects, it is difficult to see sociologically how they can be held within their larger denominations. In current movements, clergy-theologians naturally play a high-profile role. But studies of serving clergy have shown the paradox that after ordination parish clergy become increasingly suspicious and hostile to theological innovation and change. In the middle term, economic constraints are as likely to produce change in patterns of ministry as theological rethinking, and at least in the West this is all taking place against a significant backdrop of increasing secularization and the marginalization of the clergy. In this context Christian churches and their clergy sociologically cannot (and perhaps theologically cannot) revert to the established pattern of previous centuries.

Blizzard, S.W. (1956) 'The minister's dilemma', *Christian Century*, 25 April.
Congar, Y., OP (1967) 'The different priesthoods: Christian, Jewish and pagan', in *Priest and Layman*, London: Burnes Oates.
Fichter, Joseph H., SJ (1961) *Religion as an Occupation*, Notre Dame, IN: Notre Dame University Press.
James, E.O. (1955) *The Nature and Function of the Priesthood; A Comparative and Anthropological Study*, London: Mowbray.
Lash, N. and Rhymer, J. (eds) (1970) *The Christian Priesthood*, 9th Downside Symposium, London: Darton, Longman & Todd.
Leclercq, J. (1970) 'The priesthood in the patristic and medieval church', in N. Lash and J. Rhymer (eds) *The Christian Priesthood*, 9th Downside Symposium, London: Darton, Longman & Todd.
Lightfoot, J.B. (1868) 'The Christian ministry', in *St Paul's Epistle to the Philippians*, London, pp. 179–267.
MacIntyre, A.C. (1967) *Secularization and Moral Change*, London: Oxford University Press.
Moberg, D.O. (1962) *The Church as a Social Institution*, Englewood Cliffs, NJ: Prentice Hall.
Moorhouse, G. (1969) *Against all Reason: The Religious Life in the Modern World*, London: Weidenfeld & Nicolson.
Towler, R.C. and Coxon, A.P.M. (1979) *The Fate of the Anglican Clergy: A Sociological Study*, London: Macmillan.
Wilson, B.R. (1966) *Religion in Secular Society*, London: C.A. Watts.

Anthony P.M. Coxon

COMMUNISM

The relationship between communism and religion, Christianity in particular, is an intimate and fascinating one and not easily summarized.

At root, communism and Christianity share the same philosophical preoccupations that have animated European civilization for most of its history (Kolakowski 1978: 11): namely, the preoccupation with human imperfection and the search for means to overcome it; and the preoccupation with, and desire to overcome, the apparent duality of being represented by the contingency of existence on the one hand and the desire for perfect self-knowledge in perfect union with non-contingent being (i.e. the absolute or the divinity) on the other hand. They share the same underlying structure of reasoning in so far as they both assume that the march of history is progressive, teleologically determined and its outcome ordained. And they share a similar solution to the problems of imperfection and duality which, in the case of Christianity, takes the form of the ultimate perfectibility of the soul and its union with God in Heaven, and, in the case of communism, takes the form of the perfect SOCIETY (HEAVEN) on earth which is non-exploitative, painless, and represents both the ultimate perfectibility of human nature and the ultimate union of humanity with itself. In fact, it would not be too far-fetched to say that communism is, in many ways, a secularized religious idea.

Where communism and Christianity differ, however, is in their philosophical presuppositions about the perfectibility of human nature and in their consequent appreciation of the means appropriate to achieve their ends. Christianity in general assumes that human nature is given and is essentially and originally imperfect, and consequently preaches individual redemption and individual salvation through faith in, and union with, God. The idea of community, or communion, is also central to Christianity, as are the related notions of Christian fellowship and self-sacrifice. But, at base, Christianity is fundamentally about the spiritual self-improvement of the individual for which the individual is ultimately rewarded after death. Communism, by contrast, assumes that human nature is both plastic and perfectible; that human imperfection therefore has its sources in social conditions not in human nature and that it can consequently be overcome through collective action to transform those conditions. Communism therefore demands collective action and transformation, violent if necessary, in order to bring about the ideal state of being in *this* world. Communism certainly requires self-improvement, spiritual commitment and self-abnegation from the individual in order for collective action to come about, but the end to this process is not individual perfection but the transcendence of the

individual for the greater good and the ultimate perfection of the community as a whole.

The means and, in some respects, the ends of the Christian and communist traditions are therefore diametrically opposed. But both, in their different ways, attempt to deal with a fundamental problem of human existence, namely, the relationship between universalism and particularism, between the individual and the community, between purposive individual action and the social structures that constrain or enhance it. Neither manage to solve the problem, however, because both are too absolute in their solutions. The Christian preoccupation with the individual has been so complete that the established churches have been unable, on the whole, to deal with the social consequences (inequality, conflict, exploitation) that have followed from unalloyed INDIVIDUALISM. By the same token, the communist preoccupation with EQUALITY and community has been so complete that the communist movements, and in particular the ruling communist parties, have been quite unable to deal with the exigencies and motivations of individual existence. The original duality that they attempted to resolve has therefore merely been repeated with the consequence that both traditions have been undermined.

This intimacy of desires and concerns has led to some cross-fertilization and exchange over the centuries, despite differences over means and the 'corporality' of the desired end. It has also, however, led to the most bitter and destructive antagonism.

The original source of the word 'communism' is the Latin *communis*, meaning 'common'. *Communis* is also the root of the word 'communion', an idea that has been central to Christian practice from the earliest times, and that continues to be sacred in modern church practices, since it expresses both the communication and union of Christians with God, and the communication and union of Christians with each other in the fellowship of the church. Indeed, *communis* may have itself derived from the Latin *com* (common) plus *unus* (*unio,-onem*) meaning 'oneness' or 'union'. The earliest Christian communities appear to have practised a form of 'communism' based, among other things, on the principle of equality and the transcendence of property relations, as laid down, for example, in Acts 2: 44: 'And all who believed were together and had all things in common'. And Christian communism seems to have been widespread in the early church up to the third or fourth centuries and thereafter in many monastic orders after the fall of Rome (*see* CHRISTIAN SOCIALISM). Even today some monastic forms of life still describe themselves as practising communism.

The ASCETICISM of these early communities and their insular preoccupation with the creation of God's kingdom on earth (derived in part from their belief in Christ's second coming), however, was subjugated to, and marginalized by the development of ecclesiastical hierarchies and the growing power of the 'established' churches which accompanied the latter's identification with the pre-modern (and the modern) state. Their founding ideas were not entirely lost, though, but were subsequently resurrected, e.g. by medieval sectarians and the practices of later non-conformist religious groups. They were also echoed in the commitment of modern communist movements to egalitarianism, fellowship and brotherhood, their hostility to private property, and a certain monastic asceticism in their attitudes to private life (at least in the early days of their creation). It was the gradual development of capitalism from the sixteenth century onwards, however, that created the conditions for the emergence of modern communist and socialist movements and laid the foundations for bitter confrontation between these movements and the church.

In its modern sense, the first use of the word 'communism' is generally attributed to one Goodwyn Barmby who, according to his own account (cited in the *Oxford English Dictionary*), invented it during a conversation with some disciples of Babeuf (then called Equalitarians) in the year 1840. Prior to that 'socialism' and 'socialist' were the more generally used terms whatever the particular arguments of a given individual. Barmby went on to found the London Communist Propaganda Society and the Universal Communitarian Society in 1841, but he has subsequently been lost in the mists of obscurity, largely, one suspects, because he was

overshadowed by more illustrious contemporaries like Karl Marx. Barmby's own use of the term was clearly influenced by religious Utopianism, since he referred to himself in 1842 as 'the Pontifarch of the Communist Church', and wrote approvingly in 1843 of 'that holy millennial communitive life' which is represented by the 'Communion Table'. He was clearly also acquainted with the ideas of Gracchus Babeuf, an early exponent of radical socialist (i.e. communist) ideas (see Kolakowski 1978: 184 ff.). Babeuf was fiercely opposed to all inequality and to private property as its primary source and sought to eradicate them both by conspiratorial means. Barmby was therefore drawing on both the religious and political heritage of the term. It is not clear, however, that Barmby deserves full credit for its invention. As already noted, even by the 1840s it had had a long historical lineage. Moreover, by the 1830s, according to Kolakowski, a distinction had already begun to emerge between the terms 'communist' and 'socialist'. The former was 'in general used by those radical reformers and utopians who demanded the abolition of private property . . . and absolute equality of consumption, and who did not rely on the goodwill of governments or possessors, but on the use of force by the exploited' (ibid., 187); while the latter, *au contraire*, was increasingly applied to those who advocated both less radical ends and less radical means to overcome the depredations of capitalism and who sometimes looked to the 'goodwill of governments' and/or the possessors of wealth to effect the necessary changes in their own enlightened self-interest. Communists and socialists were certainly fundamentally united in their concern at the increasing misery and exploitation that the uncontrolled wealth accumulation and the unbridled competitiveness promoted by the capitalist order were giving rise to, but this common concern by no means presupposed agreement either on means or ends (*see* SOCIALISM). Perhaps, therefore, Barmby was merely first to name in print what had already emerged in practice. Whatever the case, the mid-nineteenth century saw the development of communism as an identifiably distinct tendency within the more general socialist tradition.

It was the work of Karl Marx and Friedrich

Engels, however, that consolidated this trend. And it was from Marx that the modern communist parties, and the Soviet Communist Party (CPSU) above all, claimed to derive their inspiration.

Marx sought to avoid both the dilemmas of Utopianism with its sterile focus on the (unachievable) ideal, the dilemmas of historical fatalism (Kolakowski 1978: 6) and the dilemmas of moralism, by rooting his theories in the concrete analysis of the workings of the capitalist system. In so doing he recuperated many of the preoccupations of previous centuries. He also laid some of the foundations for the modern confrontation between communism and religion.

For Marx, capitalism represented the apotheosis of human ALIENATION from its own nature, its 'species-being' as he called it in his early writings. The capitalist system had alienated individuals from their labour, the products of their labour, and from their fundamental humanity through the concentrated private ownership of capital; the operation of commodity relations; and the coercive power of the state wielded in the interests of the property-owning capitalist class. It had transformed individual labour into a burdensome necessity and an alienated commodity and destroyed its life-enhancing and creative aspects. Moreover, capitalist competition and the drive for profit had sundered class from class and individual from individual. It had destroyed both community and fellowship, promoting greed in their place. It had also immiserated the mass of the working population even as it produced an abundance of goods. Religion figured in this analysis largely as an instrument of power and subjection that perpetuated the capitalist order at the ideological level by positing capitalism as the natural order of things and getting individuals to accept their lot in this world. Marx also argued, however, that religion was a symptom of the deeper economic causes which underlay human misery and exploitation. In this respect, religion was not only an instrument of subjection, it was also an expression of suffering and the desire for relief on the part of the oppressed and exploited majority (see McGovern 1984: 250–1).

Communism, for Marx, represented the overcoming and negation of these social imperfections. The immense productive capacity of capitalism would not be destroyed, but the exploitation that had limited its consumption and the competition and commodification that had alienated individuals both from their labour and from each other would be transformed through the agency of revolutionary working class action. Thus communism posited the final negation of class exploitation and ALIENATION through the communal sharing of all property; direct production according to need and equality of consumption; and the final dissolution, or 'withering away' in the classic phrase, of the state both as an instrument of coercion and as an organizing principle of society. The elimination of CLASS and competition not only would remove the need for coercion and the exercise of power, it would also remove the need for politics, ideological and religious obfuscation and all the other snares and entanglements that had rendered capitalist society opaque and unintelligible to those who lived in it. Communist society was to be a transparent and harmonious totality that functioned for the common good which, almost by definition, was also and simultaneously the individual good. Moreover, the working class, as the agent of this transformation, would not bring all this about because of some ethereal preference for, or religious faith in, the ideal, but because it was in the material interests of all workers and of all oppressed people to collaborate in what, effectively, was the achievement of their liberation. The working class, as the class which concentrated in its own experience the exploitation and suffering of all the oppressed, would therefore become the universal agent of human emancipation and of human self-realization because it could do no other.

This vision has fired millions to rebel during the course of the twentieth century. The revolutions sparked off in its name have largely succeeded only in replacing the old forms of oppression with new ones, but one frequent feature has been an attack on religion.

Marx was certainly opposed to religion, but his analysis did not necessarily presuppose a militant ATHEISM. Given that, for Marx, religion was a symptom of underlying economic causes, it therefore followed that religion would only disappear once the material conditions producing it had been eliminated. A militant 'war' against religion was therefore both beside the point and, certainly as far as Engels was concerned, potentially counterproductive: the attempt to abolish religion prematurely would only help 'it to martyrdom and a prolonged lease of life' as Engels put it (McGovern 1984: 263). At the same time, however, the writings of both Marx and Engels were sufficiently ambiguous on the question of religion to allow for the possibility of a militant atheism should conditions allow for it. Such was the case in Russia at the time of the revolution in October 1917, and the USSR was to become the paradigmatic example of communist antagonism to religion.

The Bolshevik Party (later to become the CPSU) was overtly antagonistic to religion from the outset. This antagonism derived partly from Marx and Engels; partly from the Bolsheviks' exaggerated belief in the infallibility and omnipotence of science; and partly from local conditions at the time of 1917.

Russian Orthodoxy was the dominant religion of the tsarist state and was intimately associated with it. Almost from its inception (in the tenth century) the relationship between CHURCH AND STATE had been one of 'caesaropapism' in which the tsarist state repeatedly asserted its control over the Church, a control the Church accepted in return for wealth and power. Russian Orthodoxy therefore became the state religion and as such was extremely intolerant of other religions which were almost always suppressed or persecuted (see Steeves 1989 for an account). It also effectively became an administrative arm of government with the result that its top functionaries grew extremely wealthy and powerful and were widely perceived to be authoritarian and corrupt. The Bolsheviks' theoretical objections to religion were therefore reinforced by the evident fact that Russian Orthodoxy was, indeed, an instrument of class rule and state power in pre-revolutionary Russia.

In principle, the Party's analysis of religion allowed for two different practical approaches to its treatment. On the one hand, the Marxist explanation that located the causes of religion in material conditions implied that there was nothing to be gained from attacking religion directly. On the other hand, the close theoretical identification of religion with the logic of class exploitation also presupposed an open confrontation with, and struggle against it at the political level that ran counter to this deterministic argument. Lenin sought to get round the problem by making a distinction between the ecclesiastical hierarchy, which could readily be identified with the state and was therefore a legitimate target of class struggle, and the religious beliefs of individuals which had to be treated with respect and allowed to fade naturally. In practice, however, it proved very difficult to attack one without attacking the other and this, coupled with Bolshevik optimism of the will and impatience for change, rapidly gave rise to a militant atheism that challenged religion head-on.

The worst depradations occurred under Stalin. The years 1929–41, which witnessed the rapid and ruthless transformation of Soviet society, also witnessed policies that amounted to an attempt at the wholesale destruction of all religion. By 1939, 'religious institutions in the Soviet Union were devastated. No denomination had a central organization. Only four Russian Orthodox bishops in the whole country [out of 163] remained out of prison' (Steeves 1989: 91). Some 17,000 churches had been closed and hundreds of thousands of believers, whatever their religion, were either executed or languished in the camps. Stalin might have succeeded in his aim of destroying all visible signs of religious belief had it not been for the German invasion of June 1941. In the aftermath of the invasion the Russian Orthodox Church, under the leadership of its acting leader Metropolitan Sergius Stragorodsky, played such a central part in rallying the population to the defence of the country that Stalin ceased his attempts to liquidate it altogether and entered into a 'concordat' with the religious establishment that once more enabled open religious activity under the control of the state. The result was that believers throughout the country reopened their churches.

Thereafter, the persecution of religion became more intermittent. Nikita Khrushchev returned to the attack between 1960 and his ousting in 1964, but Brezhnev and certainly

Gorbachev adopted much more nuanced approaches. Gorbachev, indeed, actively sought to incorporate religious believers back into society as loyal citizens (see Steeves 1989 for an account).

What is most interesting about the Soviet experience is that neither direct physical destruction nor the more subtle approaches introduced after Stalin succeeded in eradicating religion from the USSR. Both the Russian Orthodox Church and Islam (in the Central Asian republics) were able to reconstitute themselves as functioning hierarchies and functioning churches when conditions allowed and a plethora of nonconformist groups continued to maintain an existence in the underground.

There are a number of possible reasons for this resilience.

Most obviously, the persistence of religious belief vindicated Engels' caution and merely served to demonstrate yet again what some 2,000 years of human existence has shown, namely, that persecution may succeed in destroying communities but rarely succeeds in destroying the ideas and beliefs they died for. The response of the Russian Orthodox Church and other religions to communist persecution was to go underground or into exile abroad and to adapt religious observance to the exigencies of the time.

Second, the Russian Orthodox Church, in particular, also proved to be extremely adaptable both institutionally and spiritually. At the political level, some ten centuries of close association with state power made it possible for the Orthodox leadership both to contemplate, and practise, humble submission once it became clear that open opposition would not succeed – although it should be noted in passing that this complicity with the Soviet state has put the Russian Orthodox establishment under something of a cloud since the collapse of the USSR in 1991. More importantly, however, the structure of Orthodox belief and its intimate association with Russian culture and identity made it almost impossible to eradicate. The Orthodox claim that it was doctrinally and theologically complete (as of AD 787) and its consequent emphasis on liturgy, the direct experience of ritual and the concrete representation of

spirituality and Orthodox values through iconography and a highly developed artistic culture (see Steeves 1989: 24 ff.) meant that Russian Orthodoxy appealed to the heart as much as to the head and was therefore not particularly susceptible to reasoning of any kind. Equally, its central role in the founding myths of the Russian state and the Russian people gave it a cultural potency that had little to do with religion *qua* belief in God and that was therefore entirely beyond the reach of atheistic agitprop.

Third, the Party's ideological practices entirely failed to engage with the nature or substance of religious belief. For example, once Stalin had declared socialism achieved in 1936 the Party's explanation of religion as rooted in material economic causes and class struggle simply made no sense; no more than did its subsequent attempts to explain religion by describing it as a 'survival of the past' that continued to linger in the minds of people. Since, according to the Party's simplistic epistemology, material conditions were supposed to determine consciousness there was simply no logic to the argument and religious believers could remain largely untouched by it. More importantly, however, the Party's dogmatic obsession with collectivism in all things failed to address the existential needs of Soviet citizens as individuals. The new ethics and morality that the Party sought to impose consisted largely of Utopian assertions about the 'ideal communist' and, in any case, stood in stark contrast to the types of behaviour that Soviet citizens actually had to engage in in order to make the system work. In fact, the dogmatic collectivism of the Party resulted in its opposite, rampant individualism without ethical or moral boundaries except for those provided by religion.

Above all, perhaps, the belief in the eventual arrival of communism required almost as great a leap of faith as the belief in God. In the absence of rational refutation on the part of the CPSU, it is therefore possible to surmise that the spiritual well-springs of religious belief either remained untouched or fused the two into a syncretic whole that enabled people to combine belief in God with belief in the possibility of communism. After all, from the individual point of view, why not have the benefit of both:

believe in the possibility of heaven on earth as well as the possibility of reward in the hereafter. Put another way, the Communist Party, for all its scientism, did nothing to undermine faith, but rather, if anything, exploited it.

Neither communism nor the second coming of Christ have materialized. Nor have the Christian or communist traditions managed to solve the fundamental problems of human existence. Since the human misery to which both the communist and the heavenly Utopias were said to provide the ultimate solution, however, has not yet disappeared but is, if anything, increasing, it would be as foolish to assume that the demise of the Soviet Union means the demise of all communist critique, as it would be to predict the final disappearance of religion.

Berdyaev, Nicolas (1969) *The Origin of Russian Communism*, Ann Arbor, MI: University of Michigan Press.

Billington, James H. (1966) *The Icon and the Axe. An Interpretive History of Russian Culture*, New York: Random House.

Dunn, Dennis J. (ed.) (1983) *Religion and Communist Society*, Berkeley, CA: Berkeley Slavic Specialities.

Ellis, Jane (1986) *The Russian Orthodox Church: A Contemporary History*, Bloomington, IN: Indiana University Press.

Kolakowski, Lezsek (1978) *Main Currents of Marxism*, vol. 1, Oxford: Oxford University Press.

Kolarz, Walter (1966) *Religion in the Soviet Union*, New York: St Martin's Press.

Lane, Christel (1978) *Christian Religion in the Soviet Union*, London: Allen & Unwin.

McGovern, Arthur F. (1984) *Marxism: An American Christian Perspective*, New York: Orbis Books.

Parsons, Howard L. (1987) *Christianity Today in the U.S.S.R.*, New York: International Publishers.

Pospielovsky, Dimitry (1984) *The Russian Church under the Soviet Regime, 1917–1982*, 2 vols, Crestwood, NY: St Vladimir's Seminary Press.

Steeves, Paul D. (1989) *Keeping the Faiths. Religion and Ideology in the Soviet Union*, New York: Holmes & Meier.

Rachel Walker

CONSERVATISM

Unlike its main rivals SOCIALISM and LIBERALISM, and notwithstanding the efforts of Aristotle and Hegel to provide one, conservatism is notably reluctant to equip itself with any fully worked-out intellectual justification. Indeed, a sceptical aversion to doctrine and IDEOLOGY generally is the most distinctive feature of modern conservatism, which began (with Burke) as a reaction to the French Revolution and later became a significant strand in Romantic anti-rationalist thought. Of all political outlooks conservatism is the least self-consciously 'political', and is rooted (according to Oakeshott) in a widely shared, extra-political disposition to prefer an established, well-tried manner of doing things to ideal or theoretical alternatives. Hence conservatism is to a large extent independent of party. Its opponents, however, usually regard it as a disingenuous, self-interested defence of social imperfections on the part of those who stand to lose most by their abolition.

The conservative will typically reply that imperfections attend every human arrangement and that to attempt to eliminate them at a stroke, rather than cautiously and piecemeal, will not only bring greater imperfections in its train but will also destroy the genuine amenities which have grown up alongside them. For example, the socialist's attempt to 'abolish' inequalities not only destroys hard-won existing liberties but also introduces a worse, because more systematic, inequality, on account of the huge increase in governmental power needed for the purpose. On the other side, the liberal's impatience, in the name of freedom, to discard moral and economic constraints weakens the socio-cultural norms which make freedom a value, and along with them the motive to defend it.

Though not natural democrats, conservatives usually regard the status quo as just (or acceptable) so long as the majority are visibly content with it. (It was on some such premise that, in 1867, the Conservative politician Disraeli 'dished the Whigs' by greatly extending the franchise.) But conservatives will often claim also that, in a mature society, the status quo serves the interests even of the least advantaged better than any alternative. For all have an interest in social order, social order requires political order (Hobbes), political order is the creature of POWER (Machiavelli), and power is made both more acceptable and more secure by its gradual diffusion. By a series of historical compromises, emergent interests are granted official recognition (e.g. as an opposition, an electorate or a professional association) and are thus absorbed into an ever-widening establishment. In this manner power is at once domesticated, made the object of consensus, and to some extent removed from the directly political arena. PROPERTY is both an immediately tangible form of power and a security against other more coercive kinds. Since the owner has an overwhelming interest in his property, and thus in the political order which secures his rights in it, conservatives have always seen wider ownership as a means to future political stability.

Conservatives, nevertheless, do not support any given social order merely because it exists (unless the sole alternative is anarchy). What counts are the terms on which it exists, and the means by which it is maintained. Communists in the collapsing Soviet empire were not genuine conservatives (despite being so labelled) because the order they defended had proved incapable of compromise. Since it could be maintained only by force, it was unable ever to acquire AUTHORITY, i.e. to secure its subjects' consent. (Conservatives would normally define consent as unforced obedience, irrespective of whatever current beliefs – in divine right, say, or in universal suffrage – may chance to underpin it.)

Contrary to general opinion, therefore, change is central to the conservative outlook. Conservatives are for change so far as it leads (or has led) to consensus, against it only as it leads away from it. Stability lies neither in promiscuous innovation nor in immutable rigidity (which may provoke the very unrest it is meant to avert, and is also a feature of most Utopias) but in continuity. In a 'normal' society the status quo is actually a slowly shifting aggregation of diverse but interconnected phenomena which retains its organic unity even throughout long-term changes in its identity. The conservative conception of change is not a concept of progress towards some ultimate goal (since goals, like societies, change over time), but simply of a process, to be managed or accepted as circumstances, established wisdom and the foreseeable future dictate. Hence conservatism is often described as essentially pragmatic.

Conservatism is particularist and context-specific. Its concern is always with *this* society

and *these* values. Hence it is as various in its content and priorities as the societies in which it appears. Nevertheless, conservatives everywhere prize what may be called 'natural' patriotism (including that of rival nations), but generally despise the ideological nationalisms concocted by parvenu dictatorships. They may find themselves seriously at odds with their own state, however, if the state is at odds with SOCIETY and CULTURE. The underlying intuition is that the individual, even to himself, is strictly inconceivable apart from those things, a fact which must give him the strongest possible motive to preserve them (as his property does to defend the state which protects it). Abstracted from society and culture, he becomes the atomic, undifferentiated individual of liberal theory, who lacks the definitive uniqueness of real-life individuals and whose universal 'rights' are matched by no substantive duties, since every historic context in which they might disclose themselves (and in which rights might be meaningful and effective) has been discounted *a priori*.

Conservatives believe in 'my station and its duties' rather than in Kant's 'duty for duty's sake' (F.H. Bradley's distinction). With Hume and Burke, they associate duty less with reason than with sentiment, and wherever possible seek political recognition for the immediate attachments which (in their view) provide the individual with his deepest fulfilment and sense of purpose. Among them are his attachments to country, locality, FAMILY, CLASS, role, profession, religion, friendships and wider voluntary associations. Each, in the normal case, is a source of security and an object of duty and loyalty, and each, accordingly, is more or less imbued with personality, in other words, is conceived in moral terms.

THE STATE (at least in principle) is generally thought of as the guardian of all these subordinate 'natural' allegiances and the embodiment or completion of their ideal unity (Voegelin's 'existential representation'). Hence it too is quasi-personal, deserving of praise or blame, love or hatred, accordingly as it does or does not fulfil its office. The state cannot impose this or any other unity *ab extra*, in the totalitarian manner, without destroying its own authority.

Rather, it must be permeable to cultural influence, which is only another way of saying that its authority, or right to command, ultimately depends upon consent. (As Simone Weil observed of rights generally, an authority which no-one acknowledges is not worth very much.)

Formal DEMOCRACY and universal suffrage are less productive of consent than evidence of its prior existence. Abstractly regarded, as the touchstone of legitimacy, they concede too much to the idea that political society is a contract (Hobbes, Locke, Rousseau) and that the subject's only obligations are those he has deliberately chosen. They tend moreover to call into question the legitimacy of other generally accepted arrangements, past and present. What is not in doubt is that for the state to represent (and protect) the culture from which it stems requires something like parliamentary government, the rule of law (which is to say, a relatively stable body of law and an independent judiciary to which the administration and all other powers are accountable) and a multiplicity of subordinate institutions and associations each possessing some degree of officially recognized AUTONOMY.

The state and its laws are an outgrowth of civil society, which the state cannot otherwise either properly represent or presume authoritatively to regulate. State and society are nevertheless distinct, and should remain so. For wholly to conflate them is to remove their mutual constraints and so deliver the subject, and all subordinate associations, to the absolute tyranny of majorities. Wholly to separate them, on the other hand, is by definition to make the state's power unaccountable, and to deliver culture, society and the individual to an alien autocracy which will not long suffer such alternative objects of duty to exist.

The animating principle of liberalism is freedom; of socialism, EQUALITY. That of conservatism is order, and perhaps also, as Roger Scruton has suggested, happiness (cf. Aristotle). In conservative eyes liberalism signifies too little order and socialism too much. Too little order results in moral pluralism and ANOMIE (i.e. existential rootlessness, the perception that, being underwritten by no objective authority or necessity, what one does and is are superfluous).

Together with so-called 'disenchantment' (the evacuation of human meaning from the cosmos and its replacement by value-free scientific understanding), *anomie* is widely regarded by sociologists such as Durkheim, Weber and Berger as the endemic disease of MODERNITY, and a major source of unhappiness.

Too much order, on the other hand, is destructive of freedom. The conservative's 'order' differs as much from the socialist's as his or her 'freedom' does from the liberal's. As construed by conservatives, freedom and order are not contraries, but complements. For socialism, at least at its totalitarian extreme, order lies in the common pursuit of premeditated collective goals, which necessarily conflict with those of individuals. The 'order' which conservatives prize is neither monolithic nor formulable as any kind of 'goal'. It is merely whatever emerges from the multitude of spontaneous choices made in response to culture's informal promptings and constraints, and under the formal constraints of law: in a word, culture itself, in its ongoing, mobile totality. Hence, though cultural values can and should be upheld, as law can only be made, by GOVERNMENT (which thus secures an initial or provisional order), government can neither predict nor impose the order which results.

Although conservatives have traditionally been suspicious of both capitalism and economics, their conception of society bears a strong structural resemblance to the market economy as described by Hayek. The difference lies in conservatism's insistence (shared, in fact, by the later Hayek) that politics is prior to economics and that, whatever may be the case in the market, choices in the socio-political sphere are prompted by other considerations than individualistic self-interest. Furthermore, neither economic nor (still less) moral *laissez-faire* is any guarantee of a happy or desirable society. The freedom which counts is not that celebrated by Mill, and satirized by Matthew Arnold, of simply doing as one likes, subject only to others' equal right to do the same. Nor is it that merely of doing what is harmless (which for Mill was the same thing). It is rather the freedom to pursue, with the endorsement of state and culture alike, one's deepest and most permanent attachments. This freedom, spontaneously to fulfil the unspoken common destiny by doing as one knows one ought, is denied by the totalitarian state, where the only duty is to, and determined by, itself. And it is also undermined by liberalism, which, declining to uphold any particular values, relegates all such to the sphere of arbitrary private 'conscience' where (the conservative will say) they must eventually wither for lack of support.

Were they not already familiar, conservative views on other issues could easily be deduced. A conservative will rather entrust his country's security to traditional alliances and the balance of power (and when those fail, to war) than submit its sovereignty to any supposed international authority. He will understand crime and punishment in the everyday language of moral agency rather than in neutral, quasi-scientific terms. He will support the welfare state, but not one so extensive as to erode private initiative and responsibility and confer undue political influence on its employees. He may be indifferent to hierarchy, or support it as a natural concomitant of authority, but will neither destroy it where it is appropriate nor pursue it for its own sake. He may countenance and even celebrate ethnic and cultural diversity, so long as it nurtures an underlying moral consensus and a common allegiance. And the same goes for religion, which, believer or not, he will always respect and must always take seriously. For he will recognize it as at once the most integrative and the most disruptive of all social forces, and as resting, like his own otherwise sceptical politics, on a pious acceptance of the given, of a way of life which carries its meaning within it and (for those immersed in it) needs no justification.

It is tempting to associate the conservative's acceptance of imperfection with the theological doctrines of the FALL of Man and original sin. But such a link, if plausible, need signify no more than that the conservative takes humanity as he or she finds it, and accordingly, not anticipating its overnight transformation, is inclined to be tolerant. The radical, on the other hand, may be more disposed to authoritarianism, precisely because he or she believes in the malleability of human nature and the possibility of

secular redemption. It should be noted, however, that, in very modest unassertive versions, these same beliefs are also not wholly foreign to conservatism.

St Augustine's position *vis-à-vis* such matters is interesting. He sees government less as evidence, in its imperfection, of man's innate sinfulness than as, like SLAVERY, a providential, exemplary punishment for it. (Compare de Maistre's yet more gloomy metaphysical rationalizations of coercion, cruelty and violence.) Government serves also, even in pagan states, to establish an 'earthly peace' which permits undistracted devotion among its Christian subjects who, so long as it demands no observances contrary to Christian conscience, owe it conditional obedience.

None of this seems especially conservative when set beside the genial Aristotelianism of St Thomas Aquinas. For Aquinas, if this world were all-in-all, the good state would indeed be the highest good, since, by guaranteeing justice and security, it enables man's natural sociability to achieve its full secular *telos*. Moreover, seen in the perspective of man's transcendent destiny, the good state, even if pagan, does not cease to be a good. For in improving people morally, it also puts them on the road to salvation.

Its contractual basis apart, Hobbes's generic defence of government is usually regarded as conservative. Its central assumption of universal egoism has led some to see it as a secular politics of original sin. What makes this view less than wholly persuasive, however, is the reflection that people, if they hope to survive in the absence of a protecting authority, have no alternative but to look to their immediate interests, and can therefore scarcely be blamed for doing so.

Aristotle (1978) *Politics*, ed. and trans. E. Barker, New York: Oxford University Press.
Ashford, Nigel and Davies, Stephen (eds) (1991) *A Dictionary of Conservative and Libertarian Thought*, London: Routledge.
Burke, Edmund (1982) *Reflections on the Revolution in France*, ed. Conor Cruise O'Brien, Hardmondsworth: Penguin English Library.
von Hayek, F.A. (1982) *Law, Legislation and Liberty*, London: Routledge & Kegan Paul.
Hegel, G.W.F. (1967) *The Philosophy of Right*, ed.

and trans. T.M. Knox, New York: Oxford University Press.

Kirk, Russell (ed.) 1982 *The Portable Conservative Reader*, Harmondsworth and New York: Viking Penguin.

Oakeshott, Michael (1991) *Rationalism in Politics and Other Essays*, ed. T. Fuller, Indianapolis, IN: Liberty Press.

O'Sullivan, Noël (1976) *Conservatism*, London: Dent.

Scruton, Roger (1984) *The Meaning of Conservatism*, 2nd edn, London: Macmillan (1st edn 1980).

——(ed.) (1991) *Conservative Texts: an Anthology*, London: Macmillan.

Robert Grant

CONTEXTUAL THEOLOGY

Contextual theology – or better, contextuality *in* THEOLOGY – refers to a methodological phenomenon affecting a broad spectrum of contemporary Christian theology. It would be misleading to discuss contextual theology as if it were a school of thought such as liberal theology or neo-orthodoxy; for the contextual approach cuts across many movements in systematic theology and ethics, not all of them mutually compatible. What such movements as LIBERATION THEOLOGY, BLACK THEOLOGY, women's or feminist theology and theologies developed in and for specific cultures (e.g. Korean 'Minjung' theology) have in common is chiefly their determination to give 'the context', i.e. the socio-historical *hic et nunc*, an active role in the articulation of the meaning of the faith. They are 'contextual' because and in so far as they consider the situation in which theological work is undertaken to be a positive, contributing factor in the practice of the discipline.

The concern for contextuality in theology contrasts with – and is usually a reaction to – historically dominant and still-powerful ecclesiastical conventions which regard the substance of Christian *doctrina* as fixed and unchanging. According to the latter, the task of the theological community is to preserve what has been 'handed over' (*tradere*) from the past and to discover how best to *communicate* it to contemporaries. The necessity of communication naturally entails some at least minimal consideration of the particularities of the present

situation; but in these conventions the accent falls upon the 'given' character of that which is to be communicated. Responsible theology in this view means sustaining the 'eternal' veracity of revealed TRUTH (*theologia eterna*) whilst inculcating it under the conditions of time and space. Thus it is said of a well-known Princeton theologian of the nineteenth-century that he boasted that in all of his long career he had had to change nothing.

Contextuality in theology on the contrary assumes that (a) *theology* as distinct from *doctrine* or dogma only occurs where there is a meeting between past traditions and the present realities, (b) historical and situational changes are not superficial but of profound theological significance, since history is the scene of God's providential *dominium* and (c) analysis of the specifics of 'the context' therefore constitutes a vital component in the *praxis* of theology. The concern of those in whom this thinking is operative, consequently, is not in the first instance to keep faith with some doctrinal or confessional tradition but, from the perspective of scripture and tradition, to *engage their 'world'*. This does not imply nonchalance with respect to the history of doctrine, though that may be a temptation in some contemporary theologies; it does imply, however, that 'the tradition is made for humanity and not humanity for the tradition'.

The genesis of such a shift in perception as is evidenced by the prominence of contextuality in contemporary Christian thought is not easily traced, but two factors – one theoretical and one practical – can be discerned as driving towards this orientation.

The theoretical factor is the modern 'discovery' of history. While human beings have always been conscious of time, MODERNITY conditioned us to recognize the radical temporality of all that we are and do. Theological 'orthodoxies' have resisted the implications of this recognition, fearing that it would wholly relativize truth. But nineteenth- and earlier twentieth-century religious experience demonstrated that 'truth' frozen in inflexible systems of belief is incapable of engaging reality. Neither 'conservative' nor 'liberal' orthodoxies were able prophetically to address the rise of National Socialism in Germany. Through the intellectual–spiritual struggles of thinkers like Barth, Bonhoeffer, Tillich, Reinhold Niebuhr, Karl Rahner and Simone Weil, many Christians have learned that only a living truth can engage the living. TRUTH is not something possessed by the church and called, for example, 'The Gospel'. On the contrary, 'Gospel' is discovered, always anew, as the church lives *between* the testimony of the tradition and the spirit of the times (*Zeitgeist*).

In one sense, this is not new. 'Great' theology has always involved such dialogue. Augustine, Aquinas and Luther were all of them 'contextual' theologians. The difference between them and contemporary thinkers for whom the context is significant is that the latter are acutely conscious of the contextual factor. Luther did not *think of himself* as doing theology in response to a quite specific *Zeitgeist*; he simply did it. Today it would be impossible for a thoughtful Christian writer not to know that she or he reflects, and is responding to, historical-topographical particularity. This awareness, which is an extension of modern historical consciousness, creates a new sensitivity to *change* and engenders a fundamental suspicion of all static perceptions of reality.

Perhaps, however, this theoretical factor would not have achieved a breakthrough into concrete expressions of contextuality apart from certain practical dimensions of contemporary church and society. As long as theology could be 'done' under the auspices of European Christianity, almost exclusively by (often celibate) males working within *relatively* homogeneous ecclesiastical communities and under *relatively* stable economic and cultural conditions, the Christian profession of faith could seem to be adequately set forth in dogmatic/systematic summas that paid little conscious attention to 'the context', while in fact transmitting to all the world a highly explicit if hidden 'Christendom' context. God and 'the things of God', it could be assumed, being eternal and immutable, must be presented to North American Indians in the same way as to French or German peasants. 'Man' and 'the world', it could be assumed, were essentially the same wherever they were found — apart, of course, from the necessary racial, CLASS, GENDER and civilizational distinctions already accounted for in the Systems!

Given such assumptions, it is not surprising that expressly contextual emphases in theology first became visible in those places, communities and persons beyond the pale of established Christendom. Wherever marginalized Christians achieved sufficient self-knowledge and self-confidence to recognize that their particular experiences of reality were *not* accurately represented in the dominant traditions of Christendom, some began to insist that their specific contexts must be taken seriously not only ethically but theologically. Thus African-Americans, women and the oppressed of Latin American and other Third World settings were the first to develop *working* contextual theologies, even when that particular nomenclature was not employed.

Since the end of the Second World War, significant minorities throughout the world have become keenly aware of the *explicitness* (the pain!) of their own situations and, simultaneously, of the ambiguous nature of much that has been passed on to them as if it were revealed truth. Theologians like Gutierrez, Koyama, Ruether, Cone and many others have developed critical theologies in which they test the authenticity of received traditions by applying criteria drawn from the history of oppression, marginalization and sheer 'difference'. Such theologies have provided graphic models of Biblical and doctrinal interpretation (e.g. 'hermeneutics of suspicion') which are applicable to all theological reflection, and mandatory for all theology which intends to dialogue with 'the world'.

It would indeed be difficult for Christian thinkers to *ignore* the impact of contextuality in theological thought. Not only has this emphasis influenced the liveliest contemporary movements in theology; not only does it seem indispensable for all who want to comprehend and alleviate the great ethical problems of our historical period, all of which raise questions about the Judaeo-Christian tradition as Christendom has represented it; but beyond that it can hardly be overlooked that much of this emphasis stands in direct continuity both with (a) *Biblical* thought and the best of the Christian tradition, including especially (b) the entire *apologetic* tradition and (c) important aspects of the Reformation of the sixteenth century.

(a) With regard to Biblical thought, it is

increasingly recognized that the *prophetic* tradition of Israel and of Jesus was never well represented by dogmatic or systematic theological systems which, basing themselves on substantialistic ontologies gleaned from the tradition of Athens and its successors, were incapable of responding to the ever-changing *relationships* which constitute historical existence. Contextual theologies have been foremost in recovering the 'relational' ontology of the tradition of Jerusalem.

(b) Like the apologetic tradition from Augustine to Tillich, contextual theology is highly motivated by its desire to achieve points of contact with the world. Where it differs from the apologetic tradition is that it is more explicit in its intention to '*change* the world' (Marx), and in what could be called its *place* consciousness. Apologetic theology (for instance as represented by Tillich or Rahner) is especially conscious of 'the times', but its generally European positioning has regularly blinded it to distinctions between 'places', with the result that it frequently, unwittingly, carried Euro-American cultural assumptions into the mission field as though they were simply Christian.

Finally, contextual theology can find a 'usable past' (Marty) in the Reformation heritage, including aspects of the Catholic reform. It is true that the Reformation all too soon gave way to the kind of 'scholasticism' against which most contextual theologies today still have to do battle. But at the heart of Reformation faith was 'the Protestant principle' (Tillich) with its critique of every 'pretention to finality' (Reinhold Niebuhr), as well as the insistence that the church is *always* under necessity to re-form itself and its message according to the testimony of the divine Spirit (*semper reformanda*). Also in the radical wing of the Reformation, as in post-Reformation pietism (e.g. Zinzendorf, Wesley), the charismatic element implies an ongoing attention to the possibilities and problems of the present as distinct from the preservation of past verities.

Thus even in the tradition there may be more to justify a strong contextual component in theology than to corroborate the position of the critics of contextuality.

No theology is without its attendant dangers.

The danger of contextuality is that it can become myopically fixated upon a 'context' too narrowly understood, whether temporally or spatially. The correctives for this are close at hand, however. Against a short-sighted concentration upon the 'now', those pursuing this method are well advised to engage in a continuous and earnest struggle with *all* the received traditions of the faith; and against the parochialism of the 'here' contextual theologies should (and to some extent have) become pioneers in the deliberate cultivation of a *global* Christian awareness and the development of new and vital experiments in ecumenicity (*see* GLOBAL THEOLOGY).

Gutierrez, Gustavo (1973) *A Theology of Liberation*, trans. Sister Caridad Inda and John Eagleson, Maryknoll, NY: Orbis Books.
Hall, Douglas John (1985) 'On contextuality in Christian theology', *Toronto Journal of Theology* 1(1): 3–16.
——(1989) *Thinking the Faith: Christian Theology in a North American Context*, Minneapolis, MN: Augsburg/Fortress Press.
Koyama, Kosuke (1984) *Mount Fuji and Mount Sinai: A Pilgrimage in Theology*, London: SCM.
Lindbeck, George A. (1984) *The Nature of Doctrine: Religion and Theology in a Postliberal Age*, Philadelphia, PA: Westminster Press.
Ruether, Rosemary (1983) *Sexism and God-Talk: Towards a Feminist Theology*, Boston, MA: Beacon Press.
Sölle, Dorothee (1990) *Thinking About God: An Introduction To Theology*, London: SCM, and Philadelphia, PA: Trinity Press International.
Song, C.S. (1982) *The Compassionate God*, Maryknoll, NY: Orbis Books.

Douglas John Hall

CONTRACEPTION

Contraception aims by various means to prevent conception or pregnancy after sexual intercourse. Some have distinguished contraception, as affecting the act of sexual intercourse, from sterilization, which affects the sexual faculty or power to procreate, but the more common understanding today views sterilization as a form of contraception when it is used to prevent pregnancy. ABORTION disrupts an already existing pregnancy or conception and thus differs from contraception, although abortion too is used for fertility control.

The ancient world of both East and West knew the reality of contraception either by avoiding insemination in the female vas or by employing potions or magic. The term *contraception*, however, is of twentieth-century origin. Despite the long recognition of contraception and some use of it, the practice of contraception became widespread throughout the world only in the twentieth century and especially in recent times. The widespread use and acceptance of contraception today truly constitutes a revolution. Many different factors help to explain this. New contraceptive techniques have been developed especially in more recent times – the condom (originally in the seventeenth century but manufactured on a wide scale only in the twentieth century), male and female sterilization (started at the turn of the century but much easier and more readily available today), and the pill and the IUD (very recently). Contemporary science continues to look for new and better methods of contraception.

The increased life expectancy of all human beings, massive improvements in infant and child health care and development, the requirements of an increasingly industralized society, the growing acceptance of sexual relations apart from procreation, and especially the changing role of women in society have all contributed to the growing acceptance of contraception. Contemporary discussion has sensitized the whole world to the need for POPULATION CONTROL – a position first proposed by Thomas Malthus at the very end of the eighteenth century. Malthus's solution at that time advocated moral restraints such as delayed MARRIAGE and not contraception. In our day the most common forms of contraception are sterilization, both male and female (comparatively simple procedures have made sterilization much more popular today), the pill and the IUD (medical considerations have slowed the use of these methods), diaphragm, condom, periodic abstinence or natural family planning, foams, and coitus interruptus.

The Christian opposition to contraception developed in early Christian times. The Jewish emphasis on fertility did not favour contraception. Some Greek and Roman philosophers (Plato, Aristotle, Pliny the Elder) apparently saw no moral problems with contraception but the Stoics (e.g. Musonius Rufus) using their theory of NATURAL LAW insisted that sexual intercourse exists for the purpose of procreation. Contraception in early Christian times was also associated with prostitutes and others who had extramarital relationships. The early Christian condemnation of contraception (Clement of Alexandria) accepted the Stoic rule of marriage and intercourse existing for procreation as a middle position between the Gnostic Right that opposed all use of sex in imitation of Jesus and the Gnostic Left that extolled freedom to use SEXUALITY in any manner. The influential St Augustine strongly supported the understanding of marriage and sexuality as ordered to procreation in opposition to Manicheanism – a position Augustine himself had earlier held. The procreative rule and the condemnation of contraception thus became a part of the Christian tradition. One must also note the rather negative appreciation of sexuality as somehow or other connected with original sin that was very prevalent in the early church. Even after the split between Eastern and Western Christianity (eleventh century) and the Protestant Reformation (sixteenth century) Christian teaching agreed in condemning contraception for spouses.

Christians in the nineteenth and twentieth centuries had to confront the changing social, cultural, economic, medical and demographic circumstances mentioned above as well as the changed understandings of sexuality in marriage. Protestantism in general continued to condemn artificial contraception although Protestant lay women and men were involved in the birth control movements especially in the Anglo-Saxon countries. The Church of England became the first Reformed church to accept officially the morality of artificial contraception. The Lambeth Conferences of 1908 and 1920 condemned birth control. Some Anglican statements favourable to birth control appeared in the 1920s. In 1930 the Anglican bishops of the Lambeth Conference adopted by a vote of 193 to 67 a resolution describing complete abstinence as the primary and obvious method when a moral obligation exists to limit or avoid parenthood, but other methods may be used (Fayley 1960: 194–5).

In the USA the Committee on Marriage and Home of the US Federal Council of Churches in March 1931 issued an influential statement in which the majority of its members supported the morality of the careful and restrained use of contraceptives by married people. This document recognized the need for spacing and limiting children to safeguard the health of both mother and child and to protect the livelihood and stability of the FAMILY. The committee even referred to overpopulation although as a fairly distant prospect. The document also recognized the love union or mutual affection achieved through sexual relationship without an explicit relationship to procreation. The Federal Council of Churches, apparently because of the controversial nature of the report, did not act upon it. In the ensuing years the major Protestant churches and Protestant theologians and ethicists have accepted contraception as a way to practise responsible parenthood. Protestants on the whole have vigorously reacted to the worldwide population problem and have advocated the use of contraceptives in this regard. Contemporary theologians in the Eastern Orthodox Churches have also generally come to accept the morality of contraception as a way of carrying out the responsibilities of responsible parenthood (Fagley 1960: 195–209).

Undoubtedly the social, cultural, economic, medical and demographic factors mentioned above also influenced this change in Eastern orthodoxy and in PROTESTANTISM. However, as the 1930 document from the Committee of the US Federal Council of Churches pointed out, the Christian tradition was open to development by expanding procreation to include the health and well-being of the child and of the whole family including the parents and by recognizing the love union aspect of marital sexuality even apart from procreation.

In the contemporary discussion some Protestant thinkers have also accepted premarital sexuality although most Protestant churches retain the traditional teaching against it. However, in practice those who engage in premarital sexuality are often counselled to use contraception to avoid pregnancy and sexually transmitted diseases.

The Roman Catholic Church's official teaching has steadfastly opposed artificial contraception for spouses. Pope Pius XI in 1930 in obvious reaction to the Church of England strongly condemned artificial contraception in his encyclical *Casti Connubii*. Official Catholic hierarchical teaching has sanctioned the use of rhythm or periodic continence, but in the 1960s explicit debate about the morality of contraception arose for the first time within Roman Catholicism. The popes (John XXIII and Paul VI) set up a commission to study the question, but in 1968 Pope Paul VI issued the encyclical *Humanae Vitae* reiterating the condemnation of contraception. The natural law requires that 'each and every marriage act must remain open to the transmission of life' (*Humanae Vitae*, n. 11). The pope was heavily influenced by the constant past teaching of the church condemning contraception. *Humanae Vitae* itself recognizes that in practice Catholic married couples might not be subjectively guilty of grave sin in using contraception. Note that the official hierarchical teaching does not rest simply on an overriding concern for procreation but rather on an analysis of the marital act. *Humanae Vitae* (n. 12) refers to 'the inseparable connection, willed by God and unable to be broken by man on his own initiative between the two meanings of the conjugal act: the unitive meaning and the procreative meaning'. Such a rationale also condemns artificial insemination even with the husband's semen.

Pope John Paul II and the official hierarchical teaching continue to condemn firmly artificial contraception while accepting rhythm or natural family planning. Many Catholic theologians maintain the legitimacy of dissent both in theory and in practice for Catholics with regard to this teaching. These theologians reject the reasoning of the encyclical and point out some of its defects – a physicalism which identifies the human moral act with the physical structure of the act; an excessively deductive methodology; a simple act analysis that does not give enough importance to persons and the convenant relationship of marriage; a dependence on outdated biological understandings; and a failure to appreciate the contemporary dimensions of the issue ('the signs of the times'). Some theologians defend the papal teaching by maintaining that contraception necessarily involves a contralife will and falsifies the inner truth of conjugal love itself. In practice Catholic married couples seem to use contraception in about the same numbers as non-Catholics.

On the contemporary scene the social aspect of contraception has become the primary area of discussion. Three issues stand out – government population policies, feminist reaction, and the provision of contraception to minors.

Governments have responded in different ways to the population problem. Today most agree on the need for a holistic approach which sees the regulation of birth involving social, cultural and economic dimensions as well as contraceptive dimensions. Governmental policies concerning population control run the gamut from education, motivation, provision of contraceptive devices, incentives, penalties and outright coercion. These programs should be evaluated in terms of both freedom and JUSTICE. Less coercive policies are easier to justify but some maintain that in dire circumstances coercive measures might be necessary.

Concerns of FEMINISM have strongly shaped the contemporary discussion. Feminist ethics stresses the intimate connection between the personal and the political and begins with the experience of women's oppression in order to unmask and do away with patriarchal structures (see PATRIARCHY). The emphasis on the freedom, equality and participation of women in sexuality, marriage and society in general has encouraged the increased use of contraception. However, feminist ethics strongly criticizes the patriarchal practice of male-dominated medicine especially in the area of reproduction which takes place in the woman's body. Too often women have had to bear both the burdens and the dangers of contraception.

Emotional debates have erupted in the USA over schools providing contraception to young teenage students without parental consent. Opponents stress the invasion of the rights of parents and the promotion of promiscuity. Defenders recognize that such teenagers are often sexually active and it is better to prevent disease and pregnancy.

By giving human beings greater control over their fertility, contraception definitely promotes the good of humankind. However, contraception like other techniques remains limited. Some problems of different sorts exist with all forms of contraception. In addition contraception can be abused; e.g. contraception has made it easier to engage in irresponsible sexual encounters. Contraception also constitutes a significant power. Women, for example, have often borne the burden of contraception and the health dangers connected with it (e.g. the pill and the IUD). The strong and powerful at times have coerced the poor and the vulnerable. In summary, contraception can be judged a very significant but limited human good which can be abused.

Boyle, J.P. (1977) *The Sterilization Controversy*, New York: Paulist Press.

Fagley, R.M. (1960) *The Population Explosion and Christian Responsibility*, New York: Oxford University Press.

Fletcher, J. (1954) *Morals and Medicine*, Princeton, NJ: Princeton University Press.

Grisez, G., Boyle, J. *et al.* (1988) *The Teaching of Humanae Vitae: A Defense*, San Francisco, CA: Ignatius Press.

Kaiser, R.B. (1985) *The Politics of Sex and Religion: A Case History in the Development of Doctrine, 1962–1984*, Kansas City, KS: Leaven Press.

Noonan, J.T. (1965) *Contraception: A History of Its Treatment by the Catholic Theologians and Canonists*, Cambridge, MA: Belknap, Harvard University Press.

Paul VI, Pope (1968) 'Humanae Vitae', *Acta Apostolicae Sedis* 60: 481–503; translated as 'Humanae Vitae' (Human Life), *Catholic Mind* (September): 35–48.

Pius XI, Pope (1930) 'Casti Connubii', *Acta Apostolicae Sedis* 22: 539–92; translated as 'On Christian marriage', *Catholic Mind* 29 (1931): 21–46.

Wogaman, J.P. (ed.) (1973) *The Population Crisis and Moral Responsibility*, Washington, DC: Public Affairs Press.

Charles E. Curran

CORPORATISM

Corporatism refers to a relationship of consensus and collaboration between economic interest groups, especially producers' groups, and the political authorities. It draws attention to the legitimacy, real or alleged, of associations amongst all of those engaged in a given line of production and commerce in a given place, and to their right to exclusive control over their trade. Such associations are called 'corporations' (a translation of such Roman law terms as *universitas, corpus, collegium*), but no reference is intended to 'corporations' in the modern English sense of BUSINESS firms.

As a *historical* concept, corporatism refers to the role played by craft guilds in pre-modern economic organization and socio-political life, e.g. in Europe from the twelfth century onwards. The essence of the guild system was the power to control entry to the guild (of shoemakers, fish-traders and so on) and so the right to practise a given craft in a city. Guilds, and through them CITY governments, attempted to regulate prices, wages and the quality of goods. In France and The Netherlands, the guild system lasted into the eighteenth century, and in some German lands into the nineteenth. In France under Colbert and in Russia under Peter the Great it formed part of STATE policy, often in conjunction with mercantilism. Guilds also existed in traditional Indian and Chinese society. They were an especially important factor in many cities in the Islamic world, and they were used in Ottoman state policy.

A variety of relationships between the guilds and the city authorities was developed. In Europe there were prolonged periods of collaboration. In some German, Flemish and Italian towns, guilds were incorporated as 'members' into the ruling civic council; on the other hand, in towns dominated by long-distance commerce, such as Venice and Lübeck, they were subordinated to the 'senate' of merchant capitalists. Such pre-modern civic regimes are called corporatist in so far as the guilds and the political authorities formulated a common policy on such matters as tariffs, prices, wages, the quality of goods and working conditions. On the other hand, although the Calvinist Johannes Althusius of Emden, in his *Politica Methodice Digesta* (*Systematic Digest of Politic*) (1603), recognized the place of craft guilds in urban constitutions, there was little corporatist theory before the nineteenth century.

As a *political* concept, corporatism has had two almost distinct lives. Originally, it referred to a body of proposals for politico-economic reform centred upon a core of social theory. This developed in the middle and later nineteenth century, often but not solely under the influence of Christian social thought, both Protestant and Catholic. Much of the basic strategy of corporatism may be found in Hegel's *Philosophy of Right*, ed. A.W. Wood, Cambridge, 1991, paragraphs 207, 250–6, 308–11. Other notable theorists included, in Germany, Karl Marlo (1810–65) and Albert Schäffle (1831–1903), whose *Bau und Leben des sozialen Körpers* (*Structure and Life of the Social Body*) was published in 1875–8 and ran to many editions; and, in France, the Catholic Albert le Mun (1841–1914), Léon Duguit (Professor of Law at Bordeaux 1886–1928) and Joseph Paul-Boncour who published *Le fédéralisme économique* in 1900.

In the view of such writers, SOCIETY and political economy should be reorganized around vocational work groups, to include all people in a given area of production (such as the coal industry, the steel industry and so on): employers, managers, employees, perhaps investors. These were to form a single corporation for each trade and to be responsible for decision-making and management in all matters affecting their work and business, such as prices, wages, product quality, organization of labour, investment. They were to watch over the admission and training of new members and the social welfare of the workforce.

Corporatists held a variety of views about the proper relationship between corporations and the GOVERNMENT. The general view was that corporations should develop on the initiative of those in industry and should be largely self-governing. Some, including Durkheim and G.D.H. Cole, suggested that they should be represented in a second chamber of the national government. The internal structure of the corporation, and the degree of DEMOCRACY within it, varied with different thinkers.

The core of social theory was a kind of communitarianism. Individuals are at the core of their being interdependent but their natural community is not the nation-state, or it is only partially so. Many aspects of individuals' lives draw them into fellowship; above all, shared membership of a craft or practice of a profession creates a genuine community. Thus corporatists, partly due to the influence of Christian THE-OLOGY, steered a middle course between individualism and collectivism: individuals cannot live except as members of groups, yet they are deeply attached to a wide variety of groups (*see* CHRISTIAN SOCIALISM). Among these, it was argued, the occupational group had gained steadily in importance. 'A professional community creates between its members an interdependence, a real and positive solidarity, analogous to that engendered by a territorial community' (Paul Boncour). 'Solidarity' connoting fraternity but with a scientific basis, was a key word among corporatists.

While never gaining the sort of mass following enjoyed in some countries by SOCIALISM, corporatism won support among certain groups in, for example, Belgium, Germany and Austria-Hungary. It was attractive to Christian intellectuals because it offered an alternative both to the injustices of *laissez-faire* CAPITALISM and to the (at that time) potentially irreligious and statist ideals of socialism. It appealed to the Protestant notion of the spiritual importance of an individual's calling to a specific economic or professional task. The medieval craft-guild system gave it, in the eyes of some, a respectable Catholic pedigree. Corporatism was explicitly endorsed in Pope Pius XI's encyclical *Quadragesimo Anno* (1931).

The most original and interesting exponents of corporatism were Otto von Gierke (1841–1921), a Lutheran from Prussia, and Emile Durkheim (1858–1917), the French sociologist and humanist, who in fact combined it with aspects of socialism. Gierke incorporated his ideas on corporations into an organicist doctrine of human societies, as an expression of *Genossenschaft* (comradeship): individuals find their identity in groups, and social consciousness flows through groups and individuals in such a way that groups must be regarded as possessing not only legal but real collective personality (*Gesamtpersönlichkeit*). This may be seen in the medieval cities and their guilds, and today in the impressive variety of cultural and economic associations. These ought to share in the

sovereignty wrongfully monopolized by the territorial state. Durkheim's corporatism sprang directly from his distinction between the 'mechanical solidarity' of early society and the 'organic solidarity' of modern industrial society. As social roles become specialized, people's real life brings them more and more into occupational categories as plumbers, lawyers and so on. But because all morality (*morale*) is socially based, 'there are as many *morales* as there are different professions' (Durkheim 1969: 43–4). Therefore corporations must become one of the bearers of social morality in an individualist age, reawakening the ethical spirit in industry and commerce by providing a social framework within which all those engaged in a trade can treat one another as members of a single community. This would link the productive process to norms of JUSTICE recognizable by all participants and so provide the basis for a new system of industrial law. Durkheim was typical of corporatists in wanting to avoid industrial conflict and class war by putting relations between employers and employees on a new footing. Only professional groups could provide the structure and language within which claims could be meaningfully asserted and judgements command internal assent. Durkheim did not seem to consider that such corporations might succumb to collective self-interest.

By such moral and legal means, corporatists hoped that the problems of POVERTY, inequality and violent revolution could be overcome. By socializing its members, the corporation would give everyone a sense of their rightful place in society, would in fact give them just rewards for labour without endangering social stability. The dignity of labour would be restored. Corporatism joined with the English tradition of Ruskin and Morris in 'guild socialism', e.g. in the young G.D.H. Cole's *Guild Socialism Restated* (1920).

As originally conceived, corporatism was never put into practice. From the 1920s onwards attempts were made to implement a form of corporatism as a third way avoiding the alleged evils of both free market capitalism and socialism, in Fascist Italy, Franco's Spain, Salazar's Portugal, and in Ireland and some Latin American countries. In most of these cases, however, it was the state which set up and controlled the corporations and their activities, usually as a move in the struggle against the left. In Ireland, it is true, the Fianna Fail party claimed to stand for a distinctively Catholic programme; while in Mexico a special relationship developed between government and organized labour. But the general result was that corporatism as a whole became discredited through its apparent connection with Fascist or authoritarian regimes.

In the 1970s, the term corporatism was revived and since then has enjoyed a new life with a fundamental change of meaning, commonly qualified as 'neocorporatism' or 'liberal corporatism'. It was now being used to *describe* the way in which peak organizations of industrialists (analogous to the Confederation of British Industries) and of labour (analogous to the Trades Union Congress in Britain) were engaging with government ministries in 'tripartite concertation', the purpose being to promote steady economic growth through the co-ordination of wages, prices and industrial and social policy. The perceived pattern of such 'corporatism' was also used as a tool of analysis for the agricultural sector, the relationship between government and professions such as medicine and social work, and so on. The central features were best described, without using the term 'corporatism', in Rokkan's analysis of Norway:

> The crucial decisions on economic policy are rarely taken in the parties or in Parliament: the central area is the bargaining table where the government authorities meet directly with the trade union leaders, the representatives of the farmers, the smallholders, and the fishermen, and the delegates of the Employers' Association. These yearly rounds of negotiations have in fact come to mean more in the lives of rank-and-file citizens than the formal elections. . . . This two-tier system of decision-making places the Cabinet in an intricate position: it stands at the top of the electoral hierarchy but it is only one of four corporate units at the bargaining table.
>
> (1966: 107)

In Norway, Sweden and Switzerland this process had begun during the interwar years. After 1945 it developed in The Netherlands, the Federal Republic of Germany, Austria and elsewhere. In Sweden the Slatsjobaden Agreement (1938) between employers and unions determined how negotiations over wages and redundancies would be handled. Under Austria's *Sozialpartnerschaft*, a commission of representatives from industry, agriculture, the labour unions and the government controls all collective bargaining and some prices, and can initiate economic and social policy. In the Federal Republic of Germany, *Konzertierte Aktion*, sometimes referred to as a new *contrat social*, developed under the grand coalition around 1967. These corporatist methods, giving exclusive bargaining and participatory rights to privileged organizations, proved rather effective in dealing with the economic problems of the post-1973 recession. In Britain, however, while the National Economic Development Council was set up with similar components in 1962, efforts at collaboration by the Wilson, Heath and Callaghan governments never got beyond temporary and fragile agreements on wage restraint. Since the advent of the determinedly anti-corporatist Thatcher government, corporatism has frequently become a term of abuse in British politics.

This (neo)corporatism had roots in attempts at consensual economic management from the later nineteenth century and the interwar period. It was most effective in countries which, unlike Britain, had aggregated, centralized labour unions. The role of large socio-economic organizations developed in step with the political system, of which they became as it were a part. This could occur either as an attempt to stabilize economic policy when there was a change of government or in periods of coalition government, of which it was the obvious counterpart – as in The Netherlands and Austria; or again during periods of prolonged rule by one party (as in Sweden), when it was in the interests of those who might have been represented by the party out of power (in this instance, the employers) to accept what consultation was on offer. Such trends clearly cross the boundary between 'state' and 'civil society'.

Political scientists and economists referred to

all this at first as a kind of pluralism, or alternatively as a kind of consensual planning. The term 'corporatism' was introduced by Schmitter in a celebrated article in 1974 in order to draw attention to an alleged similarity between the nineteenth-century ideals and the evolution of twentieth-century political economies. Schmitter and others emphasize the permanent and quasi-official nature of the collaboration, insisting with reason that this was fundamentally different from the *ad hoc* and voluntary relationships between government and other associations implied by the term 'pluralism'. Yet the term 'corporatism', although now well established, was in some ways an odd choice. What it had in common with the earlier movement of thought has seldom been explicitly stated, and one suspects it does not go beyond a rejection of confrontation and conflict in industrial relations. In other respects, neocorporatism is very different from what earlier corporatists had prescribed: management and labour retain their separate organizations. No corporations in the nineteenth-century sense have developed. It is no doubt for this reason that in recent literature on the subject genuine insights have been infected with semantic pedantry. The phenomena in question could have been described just as adequately as a variant of étatisme or of late capitalism, as some suggest. Again, while those who emphasize the importance of these phenomena claim to be writing as political scientists, they tend to adopt a moral stance for or against such things. But in any case a new phase in industrial capitalism seems to have been identified.

Black, Antony (1984) *Guilds and Civil Society in European Political Thought from the Twelfth Century to the Present*, London: Methuen.
——(1992) *Political Thought in Europe 1250–1450*, Cambridge: Cambridge University Press.
Bowen, R.H. (1947) *German Theories of the Corporative State with Special Reference to the Period 1870–1919*, New York: Russell & Russell.
Cawson, Alan (1986) *Corporatism and Political Theory*, Oxford: Blackwell.
Durkheim, Emile (1969) *La morale professionelle*, in *Leçons de Sociologie*, Paris: Presses Universitaires de France (translated as *Professional Ethics*).
Lehmbruch, G. and Schmitter, P. (eds) (1982) *Patterns of Corporatist Policy-making*, London: Sage.
Lewis, J.D. (1935) *The Genossenschaft-theory of Otto von Gierke*, University of Wisconsin Studies in Social Sciences and History 25, Madison, WI: University of Wisconsin.
Najemy, John (1982) *Corporatism and Consensus in Florentine Electoral Politics 1280–1400*, Chapel Hill, NC: University of North Carolina Press.
Rokkan, S. (1966) 'Norway: numerical democracy and corporate pluralism', in R. Dahl, (ed). *Political Oppositions in Western Democracies*, New Haven, CT: Yale University Press.
Schmitter, P. (1974) 'Still the century of corporatism?', *Review of Politics* 36: 85–131. Reprinted in Schmitter, P. and Lehmbruch, G. (eds) *Trends towards Corporatist Intermediation*, London: Sage, pp. 7–52.
Wiarda, H.J. (1981) *Corporatism and National Development in Latin America*, Boulder, CO: Westview Press.

Antony Black

COUNTRYSIDE

Countryside is that part of the land that is not town. A land without towns also has no countryside, any more than one without hills has valleys. But it is also to be distinguished from mere wilderness: the line between the desert and the sown distinguishes that land that has been worked by human hands from what grows of itself. The very notion of a 'countryside', distinct from the ordinary working environment of city-dwellers, and of a 'CITY', protected from the more obvious forms of wildlife, is of fairly recent origin. Exactly how this division is conceived depends upon particular histories. Urban Americans may conceive 'the untamed wilderness' as something through which they struggled to the Promised Land or as a Paradise to be preserved from human intervention. That slant on issues of use or conservation is not easily maintained in a populous, and clearly human-made, country. Urban Britons conceive 'the countryside' as the Eden from which they have been banished, and wish rather to preserve the blend of human and non-human that they romantically remember. As Williams (1973) has pointed out, the notion that rural serenity has but recently been disrupted can be traced back to the early Middle Ages or beyond. Like fairies, rural peace has always recently departed. Such wilderness, or seeming wilderness, as can be found up on the moors or highlands or down in wetlands and forsaken scrub may sometimes be admired, but most 'countryside' is understood to be managed by the farming community for the support and recreation of the urban population. Townsfolk wish the countryside still to persist (and sometimes dream of living there), but do not always recognize the needs of 'countryfolk' when those conflict with the townies' idealized pasture. Both sides in this conflict of image and desire may believe that the countryside is 'closer to nature' than the town. Townies, although their ancestors usually fled to towns to escape a life of unrewarded and unending labour, may indulge fantasies of pre-industrial happiness without themselves being willing to surrender the least consumer durable; countryfolk may pity the townies' separation from the soil while simultaneously defending their own practices by speaking of the countryside as 'the farmer's factory'. It has been suggested that the Tudor revolution cost Britain the chance of creating a prosperous peasantry, and Distributism (the project of returning property in land to the people) is one hidden element in British political life.

Two questions arise. First, who owns the land? Second, what is to count as the good health of the land? Much of the European countryside (not being wilderness) is the direct product of human labour and control. The patchwork quilt of little fields and hedgerows in southeastern England is the product of those very enclosures that drove so many of the poor away from such land as they had enjoyed, just as the grandeur of the highlands is a consequence of willed deforestation and the import of sheep 'to eat up men'. Miniature prairies devoid of flowers, birds and butterflies will be no less a product of historical change. The changes that were once resisted will soon, some think, be defended in their turn against invasive change. The command given in Leviticus not to plough up all the land, nor take up all the crop, was expressly intended to leave enough for the poor and the wild creatures, who also 'seek their food from God'. But it also admitted their, literally, marginal status (*see* ANIMAL RIGHTS). Once agreed that we can remake the land who shall set limits to this? Is there any content to the notion of a 'healthy land' which those who use or control it should seek to preserve?

The first answer to the question of ownership must be the Lockean: they own it who mix their labour with it over centuries, if they have left as good for others. It does not follow that *farmers* own it, since the labour of their servants and hired hands was and still is crucial to their fortune. Nor does it follow that those who changed it least have less claim on what they used and needed – which was the excuse that Europeans have used to legitimate the eviction of less intensively agricultural peoples. Lawful inheritance may be the best that any peaceful STATE can handle, but the historical reality is that the countryside was taken from its cultivators by armed force, and those who now inherit it (whether by descent or purchase) are receivers of stolen goods. Country and town alike are made by the unsung efforts of the human and non-human poor. So Lockean owners, in any long-settled landscape, must turn out to be the peoples, including all the furred and feathered tribes who lie among the trees and grasses. They are the rightful owners – but may not be the actual controllers. The actual masters of the land may not live there: they are instead the state officials or industrial magnates who command farmers to grow more or less as state policy or politics require. At the same time, the countryside must be seen still to embody such ideals of 'natural living' as most appeal to townies and to countryfolk alike. We get 'close to nature' through country walks or sports even while we, or our masters, command that nature to be transformed, again, to suit our passing purposes (*see* HUNTING). Past masters of the land made great estates (as well as wildernesses), in which the many peoples of the land had some – though little – standing. Factory farmers, and the governments that have created them, have preferred to exterminate the inconvenient birds, beasts and butterflies (*see* FARMING). An age which lends a little POWER to the common folk may seek to allow such creatures back into the land, if only to give people things to wonder at. If the countryside is the people's playground it may at least be allowed or encouraged to be the wild things' livelihood again. Or else it may be poisoned and degraded by those who, just as much as agribusinessmen, see the land only as material for them, a suitable place for festivals.

If only farmers owned the land, if it was indeed their factory, then we might concede that they should use it as the market and the state dictate. If the people in general have a claim on the land made by their ancestors' labours, and now sustained by their purchases and their tax revenue, then the countryside cannot be just a factory, but also a playground. If we acknowledge the claims of bird and beast as well, then, however reluctantly, we might concede that neither farmer, rambler nor raver, as it were, has sole rights in the land. But there is a larger issue. The Lockean claim was always that our ownership was transient: we hold the land in trust, and own (at best) the fruits of our labour in it. The sole abiding owner, so religious tradition has it, is God, and God's are the cattle on a thousand hills. This is not to say, of course, that 'God made the country and Man made the town'. Human beings, like all others, are co-operative or complaining fellow-workers in both town and country: God is no more absent from the town than Nature itself is. What we mix our labour with does not owe its being to us, nor can we guarantee the product. What we hold from God, in trust, we hold on terms, and those who betray those terms, Leviticus assures us, will find the land taken from them. Then will the land enjoy her sabbaths in the long years of our exile.

Instead of treating the land, the countryside, as a commodity, so Aldo Leopold urged, we should think of it as a community on which we depend. The laws of that community are those of liberty: to allow as much liberty to each inhabitant as is compatible with equal liberty for all. Common ownership, although this may sometimes be appropriate, all too often turns into bureaucratic ownership. The large land-owning families and companies have no good historical title. It may well seem best to insist on the neglected ideal of Distributism: to recreate a prosperous peasantry.

Chesterton, G.K. (1926) *The Outline of Sanity*, London: Methuen.
Cobbett, W. (1967) *Rural Rides*, Harmondsworth: Penguin (first published 1853).
Glacken, C. (1967) *Traces on the Rhodian Shore*, Berkeley, CA: University of California Press.
Jefferies, R. (1979) *Hodge and His Masters*, London: Quartet Books (first published 1880).
Keith, W.J. (1975) *The Rural Tradition*, Brighton: Harvester.
Leopold, Aldo (1968) *Sand County Almanac*, New York: Oxford University Press.
Locke, J. (1960) *Two Treatises of Government*, ed. P. Laslett, Cambridge: Cambridge University Press.
Nash, R. (1973) *Wilderness and the American Mind*, New Haven, CT: Yale University Press.
Pye-Smith, C. and Hall, C. (eds) (1987) *The Countryside We Want*, Bideford: Green Books.
Rackham, O. (1986) *The History of the Countryside*, London: Dent.
Shoard, M. (1980) *The Theft of the Countryside*, London: Temple Smith.
Thomas, K. (1983) *Man and the Natural World*, London: Allen Lane.
Williams, Raymond (1973) *The Country and the City*, London: Chatto & Windus.

Stephen Clark

COVENANT

In the sense in which it is found most widely, the term covenant designates a firm agreement between two or more parties, whereby each is bound by promise to perform in certain ways toward the other(s). In a more specifically theological sense, it designates the decisive agreement between the Lord God and the people of Israel, through which each promised to be faithful to the other and God to bless and protect the people. For Christians, this was re-established in Jesus Christ as a new relation between God and his people.

Where people promise certain behaviour toward others (e.g., 'my word is my bond'), such a promissory arrangement is a covenant. Often such direct, firm promises, which are regarded as binding in simple situations, are the precursors of more carefully worked out agreements; they presume the reliability of the parties involved and anticipate that they will be honoured in the performance. In most cases, beyond the public expression and recollection of the promises, no institutional or legal formalization is involved, and the action of a third party is not invoked except as a witness or where adjudication is necessary. Hence, covenants appear most frequently in societies without a fully developed political order.

Insofar as it is a promissory agreement between people and God, a covenant declares the responsibilities of human beings toward each other to be interwoven with their relationship with God, their promises and performance toward each other confirmed and enriched (blessed) by their relation of promise with God. And it is in the blessing of God that the very conditions are provided which make life and relationships possible – a place to dwell, protection, etc.; this is why there is often a close relation between covenants with God and creation by God. Because of the direct association of human (promissory) relationships with those with God, the notion of covenant is one of the most important and enduring of religious ideas, and an important contribution to conceptions of the basis of human society – how human beings are gathered together, and on what basis this occurs. For those who covenant with each other and with God, it is the primary 'self-thematization' (Luhmann) of their society, and the necessary foundation of more developed forms of sociopolitical order.

The notion of covenant is a complex and dynamic one. It is complex because triadic, typically concerned with the action of this person or social group toward that, the establishment of certain expectations for this action, and the blessings from God which occur when these conditions are met. It is dynamic because, in a fundamental sense, it has to do with the right deployment of the energies of human life in society from and toward their ultimate source in God. Understood in that way, the word covenant signifies something as basic as human social life ordered as God's life (see TRINITY).

These characteristics lead to difficulties in classifying covenant as an idea. As triadic, it is not – despite the modern predilection for doing so – associated primarily with individual intentions and choices: the issue is what this person or group does, or should do, toward these others, and what should be done in each case, and what will (or will not) be done by God. As dynamic, covenant has more to do with the actual performance of specific concrete responsibilities – and therefore the fulfillment of certain norms for behaviour – than it is an idea which is to be understood.

While they are promissory in character, covenants are nonetheless definite. They begin in particular historical events with the making of certain promises whereby relationships and responsibilities are established, involve crucial aspects of the behaviour of those involved, set out norms for the future behaviour of the parties in some expressed form of agreement, and often include means for the settlement of matters of difference: all of these with reference to the active involvement of God, celebrated in particular places with ritual acts. While they are definite in these respects, and therefore have the effect of regularizing the behaviour of those involved, they are also comprehensive in their significance for the parties involved, exclusive in the loyalty they demand ('You shall make no covenant with them or with their gods'), and determining for their future actions.

The exact form which covenants take varies with the development of the societies involved, the complexity of their life and organization and context. There is no ideal type to which they always conform, but all share certain features: they identify the giver of the covenant, usually one who graciously bestows the relationship (that is, the covenant), in the process retelling benefits conferred in the past from which the others should derive a sense of obligation; future behaviour under certain circumstances is specified as stipulations in case-law form ('if . . . , then . . . '); and the blessings or curses which will be forthcoming are listed, perhaps with reference to how they will be conferred.

Such covenants have consequences for other central features of human life and action. With a covenant, freedom is no longer abstracted from social relationships, nor is it arbitrary; it is within given relations and follows specified norms. Strikingly, however, these norms are not regarded as compromising freedom, but as the situation in which freedom receives positive shape, and where God is acknowledged as interwoven with the relationship, God is construed as blessing or enlarging freedom through the structure of responsibilities (ordinances) created by the promises given in covenant. Life shaped by the performance of these responsibilities is blessed.

While their history is very complex, covenants were of great significance in ancient near eastern life, and similarly in the biblical tradition. Thereafter, both in Judaism and Christianity, they were the major foundation for religious communities. As societies become more complex, however, they were typically overtaken by more institutionalized forms of agreement. But they remain significant, since they are instrumental in the formation of new communities and frequently serve as the ideal for the very sociopolitical arrangements which displace them.

Covenants were well-developed as early as the third millenium BC, when they were a chief means for the establishment of new relationships, both small- (familial) and larger-scale (societal). Early life in the ancient near east shows extensive use of covenants as instruments of the identification of social groups through the regulation of their internal life and external relationships. Since they are often means of regularizing social relationships following subjugation, the focus is often on the power of the ruler and the necessity of obedience, with the gods invoked as witnesses and guarantors to the oath, hearing and intervening, favouring and disfavouring, sustaining and penalizing. The form of the covenants was: a preamble naming the lord who grants the agreement; a recalling of the benefits already received and which may be expected; stipulations which provide norms for behaviour; provision for the deposit and reading of the documents recording the agreement; suprahuman witnesses validating the agreement; promised rewards or punishments.

In the Hebrew Bible, two types of covenants are found, one probably transitional (the covenant of God with Israel) and the other promissory (the Abraham and David covenants). The first is exemplified in the Sinai covenant, in which the Decalogue was given by the Lord God (Yahweh) to the Israelites with Moses as the intermediary. While in some respects similar to the obligatory or obediential form seen elsewhere in the near east, this covenant was focused more on benevolence in social relationships, with a correspondingly benevolent provision by God (e.g. 'When you buy a Hebrew slave, he shall serve six years, and in the seventh he shall go out free, for nothing'), than on submission to obligations. It seems to have emerged in a time of simple communities, as the means by which a practical unity was achieved amongst diverse peoples. Preserved in two conflated traditions, one locating it at Sinai and the other at Horeb, one as a sacred meal in the presence of God (Exod. 24: 1f., 9f.) and sanctioned by a decree of the Lord (Exod. 34: 10–28) regulating worship, sacrifice and feasts, the other as the Decalogue repeated to the people (who promise to follow it) after a rite of purification.

The general form of this covenant followed that mentioned above, with the covenant-giver identified as Yahweh, the God who had delivered the Israelites from bondage; the covenant is established by a free and unconstrained act on God's part, and the people may accept or reject with either blessing or enmity the result. The covenant with this God constituted the people as a new kind of community, and lent it stability amidst the rapid changes to which it was subject thereafter. It provided norms for social life, referring especially to those situations which were problematic.

This was a simple, economical way of developing peaceful unity in a society which had not differentiated itself to such a degree as to require institutions and political order. Although frequently misunderstood, its force was not primarily legal. Its chief characteristic was the free grace through which it had been constituted by God, and the freedom by which the people were to respond – albeit a freedom shaped by definite obligations. Interestingly, conduct which met these obligations was difficult to perceive. 'The Sinai covenant, therefore, marked the beginning of a systematic recognition that the well-being of a community cannot be based merely upon socially organized force, nor can the political power structure be regarded, as in ancient pagan states, as the manifestation of the divine, transcendent order of the universe' (Mendenhall and Herion 1992).

The second type, the promissory, is found in the Abrahamic–Davidic covenant. Of the two forms which were widespread in the area, treaties and grants, this followed that of a grant. The covenants with Abraham and David were therefore 'gifts bestowed upon individuals who excelled in loyally serving their masters', Abraham by serving God and following his mandate (Gen. 26: 5), David by serving God with truth, righteousness and loyalty (I Kings 3, 6). In each case, there were gifts conferred, the land in the one instance, dynasty in the other (Weinfeld). As the gift was given unconditionally and in perpetuity, so it was expected that the service which had brought it would be continued.

The understanding of this promissory covenant is revised in the light of events which call into question the perpetuity of the gift. The exile of Northern Israel, the destruction of Jerusalem and the disruption of the dynasty appeared to contradict the unconditional grant of land and dynasty. As a result, revisions were made (by the Deuteronomist to the Book of Kings, and by Deuteronomy to the accounts of the Patriarchs) to make the covenant conditional upon the loyalty of the grantee to the grantor. The covenant could include scattering and disruption by God, and yet in the end allow return to God: 'for the Lord your God is a compassionate God; he will not . . . destroy you; he will not forget the covenant that he made . . . with your fathers' (Deut. 4: 31). In effect, the covenant is enlarged to include exile by God, repentance and the renewal of divine grace. This is only a step away from predictions of the establishment of a new covenant 'written upon the heart' (Jeremiah).

Since the covenant is a constant point of reference throughout the Hebrew Bible, there are many variations of interpretation which cannot be mentioned here. Amongst them, however, is a tendency to concentrate on specific obligations. With Ezra and Nehemiah in the fifth century, for example, there is a covenant (recapitulating Deuteronomic history) addressed to God, enacted by representatives of the community and making observance of the 'law of God' the condition for receiving the blessings of God. This identified the Sinai covenant with the reservoir of legal tradition, and the community as those lineally descended from Abraham. The free conferral of social order by God upon those who responded freely in following this

order was radically changed into life in conformity with law.

Not infrequently drawing upon prophetic anticipations of a new covenant (cf. Jer. 31: 31–4), Jesus (Lk. 24: 27) and Paul (II Cor. 3; 4–18) compared the old covenant with the new. And pre-Christian and Christian scriptures were soon differentiated in these terms. While specific reference to covenant is not widespread in the New Testament, the issue of the nature and kind of relationship constituted between people by God's action in Christ was of signal importance. Since – at least in the promissory form seen in the Abrahamic-Davidic covenant – covenants were always connected in the Hebrew Bible with the ways in which human freedom was shaped from and through the promises of God, the theme of covenant (if not the word) is present wherever human relationships are seen to be reconstituted by and in Christ as the one through whom the promises of God are present.

The relation between the two 'dispensations' has been much discussed in Christian theology. In general, the Christian dispensation is seen as the 'fulfillment' of the promises of the old covenant, not in the sense of a relative betterment but as a transformation of the terms in which covenants are to be seen, as a radical self-giving in which human relationships are enlarged and enriched. To be 'in Christ', therefore, constitutes a qualitatively different form of human relationships marked by faith, hope and love (cf. I Cor. 13). Hence it signifies a new form of society, the church, identified not by its political order but by 'how these Christians love each other'.

After displacement in the West by increasing use of Roman forms of social order, both generally and within the church, the issue of covenant reemerged in doctrinal form in the sixteenth century Reformation, when Zwingli and Bullinger used it as a defence against the Anabaptists in and near Zurich. The topic was taken up by Calvin and others, and further developed in seventeenth century 'federal theology' which emphasized God's covenantal dealings with the human race. Subsequently, it spread to Germany, the Netherlands, England, Scotland and early American life in New England.

Covenant theology in this case provided a format for salvation history, in which God entered first into a covenant of nature or works and afterward (after the fall of Adam and thus the entire human race) into a covenant of grace. The 'covenant of grace' was bestowed on human beings despite their sinful condition as a mark of the sheer grace of God: through the merits of Jesus Christ, they were forgiven and accepted as the children of God. This in turn was seen as founded on still another covenant in the Trinitarian life of God, between God the Father and God the Son: as the Father loves the Son and gives him a people and all authority over them, the Son loves the Father, delights in his will and has shared his glory forever; God the Father and God the Son contract with each other for the salvation of the human race, the Father commissioning the Son as mediator, the Son accepting and performing the commission. By the covenant of grace, the life and salvation achieved by Christ is offered by God to all humanity. But, since belief occurs only through the special grace of the Holy Spirit, the covenant of grace is actually for God's elect only.

This analysis of covenant was more effective as a general elucidation of the character of God's fidelity to humanity as based in the relations of the Trinity than it was in showing how the binding promises between human beings were capacitated by promissory divine action. In form, therefore, it was closer to the obligatory covenant in the Hebrew Bible than to the promissory. Secondly, in differentiating between a covenant of grace offered to all and inspiration of belief in the few by the Holy Spirit, it advocated the separation of pure from impure, and thereby restricted the church (as formed by covenants) from participation in the organic church-and-community social life then emerging. Thirdly, by so elevating 'utter individual choosing', it threatened to undermine the possibility of reliable promissory covenants.

The twentieth century has seen important retrievals of the notion of covenant, but primarily in the uses already reviewed. Barth's theology, for example, provided a brilliant restatement of covenantal theology; but the fundamental tendencies and problems of the Reformed covenantal tradition remained. Likewise, there has been wide use of the notion of covenant in ecumenical affairs and sacramental theology. But these have not led to significant redevelopment of the notion or its practice.

While the general character and form of covenants remains nearly the same, the history of covenants reveals certain variations and developments, in both the concept and its practice. Fundamentally, a covenant always remains the expression of a promise to perform in certain specified ways towards the other(s), and is regarded as binding by the parties involved.

There are clearly variations in the extent of the responsibilities thus established. Where the commitments actually made are few, the covenant can be severely limited in its scope as a vehicle for social unity and for relationship with God. Certainly in the history of Israel, however, and differently for the early Christians, the extent of the responsibilities undertaken is much greater; and the importance of covenant as formative for society and its relationship with God is much more profound. Then the covenant – or in Paul's terms, being 'in Christ' – is a primary avenue for the blessing and enrichment of God to constitute the well-being of the society, and with it the freedom and social structures of society.

There is also a variation and development – although not an irreversible one – in the form of covenants. The earliest covenants were largely obligatory, focused on the power of the grantor 'backed' by the gods as guarantors, with the emphasis on regulation and obedience. The 'grace' with which such covenants were established was a form of power, and the obligations were inflexible. In both the Sinaitic covenant, and much more emphatically in the promissory (Abraham–David) one, the 'grace' was a bestowal of benefits in return for loyal service; and continued service was expected, but the benefits did not cease if the service was not as expected. It was not cut off, but included the possibility of scattering and disruption (of dynasty), and restoration upon repentance. These were profound developments in the character of God, human obligations, and the dynamic relation between the two. They clearly anticipated the 'new covenant' established in Jesus, where God was at one with the people in their social obligations, struggling to restore social justice in accordance with divine justice.

A further development was in the character of the responsibilities undertaken. One clear tendency was in the direction of ever more specific obligations expressed not as promises but as laws, laws governing the relations between people which were seen as the 'law of God'. From this position, the history of covenant was restrospectively interpreted as the history of laws, which invited further legal refinement. This was a departure from the promissory conception of covenant, which had minimized institutions and formalized expressions. It reflected the more complex social structures of latter-day Israel. And it brought a severe reaction from the early Christians, who emphasized a new freedom in Christ – beyond (but not against) laws. But the Christians themselves, retreating from promissory covenants, later resorted to legalized social structures in church and social life. Both the Roman hierarchical social structure used in much church order, and also the Reformed/Puritan 'covenant of grace', have left lasting legacies of obsession with governmental structure, law and legal protection.

Both as idea and as practice, covenant remains basic to theology and its contribution to human affairs. At the same time, its significance is by no means as fully recognized as might be expected, and discussions – particularly constructive ones – of the topic are relatively rare, whether in theology or elsewhere.

There are major issues today regarding all human relations, seen most acutely in the widespread preoccupation with the 'other', the person or group most significantly different whose presence leads to self-consciousness and altered conditions of being (different depending on the symmetry of power). These issues are also manifest in the suspicion about all pacts, whether macrosocial or microsocial. At the same time, there is little confidence that existing agencies are capable of reversing these suspicions, because they are themselves the products of the very social bonds which are so suspect.

At the root of these problems is the question of trust, whether to trust or distrust others. This is extremely closely related to the question of community, whether there is community or not. The two – trust and community – become realities simultaneously, as they are believed in and practised. And their reality is closely tied to belief in their antecedent and continuing possibility, as constituted by the divine.

It is in its combination of these realities, in idea and practice, that the importance of covenants resides. For that reason alone, promissory covenants will be central to the renewal of reliable social relationships at all levels, and a necessary basis for every other kind of social relationship, informal or formal. That is, a covenant – the co-presence of trust, community and divine provision – will be a necessary precondition and motivation of more contractual forms of social relationship.

The idea and practice of covenants, as thus understood, require revival through careful consideration and disciplined use. The process will begin in learning, even before words, that the 'other' is not an enemy, but one who is to be treated hospitably and loved. It will continue in trusting faithfully and justly. So the community which was already present from the beginning will be expressed, and it will deepen as trusting moves from 'seeing through a glass darkly' to meeting 'face-to-face'. Even where there is failure, the trust and community will not collapse, because the relationship of trust and community will include alienation, repentance and forgiveness.

Tracing the development of such trust and community does not tell us what inspires people to create and sustain them, however. Why should people not be separated in self-protective isolation, or engage in legal manoeuvres to manipulate others? Claims about the logical priority of social relationships to individual identity, or the utilitarian value of trust and community, do not provide a sufficient basis for them. The answer to these questions – which badly needs to be recovered – is to be found in the antecedent and continuing possibility provided for them by God. What most urgently needs to be uncovered is how God is the promissory basis of all social life. That will require us to appreciate the mystery of the God whose own life is the promise of humanity, who suffers to redeem us from the failure of our trust and community, and who imparts the energy for all human relationships – the mystery of the character and life of the Trinitarian God.

Allott, P. (1990) *Eunomia: New Order for a New World*, New York: Oxford University Press.

Barth, K. *Church Dogmatics*, vol. III, Edinburgh: T. & T. Clark.

Boff, L. (1986) *Ecclesiogenesis: Base Communities Reinvent the Church*, Maryknoll, NY: Orbis Books.

Farley, E. (1975) *Ecclesial Man: A Social Phenomenology of Faith and Reality*, Philadelphia, Fortress Press.

Gratton, C. (1982) *Trusting: Theory and Practice*, New York: Crossroad.

Mendenhall, G.E. and Herion, G.A. (1992) 'Covenant' in *Anchor Dictionary of the Bible*, vol. I, pp. 1179–1202, Garden City, NY: Doubleday.

Nicholson, E.W. (1986) *God and His People: Covenant Theology in the Old Testament*, Oxford, Oxford University Press.

Seligman, A. (1992) *The Idea of Civil Society*. New York: The Free Press.

Weinfeld, M. (1993) *The Promise of the Land*, Berkeley, CA: University of California Press.

Daniel W. Hardy

CREATION

Within the single term creation, two notions jostle each other. One is creation as the field of relevant preconditions for life which, depending upon circumstances, structure the life of a people or grasp the structure or condition of the universe, the world, humanity and human beings and the relations between them all – providing an integrated account conducive to better understanding and well-being. The other is creation as normative states or processes whose existence, structure or dynamic is established as such by some normative authority: why there is something rather than nothing, or this state of affairs rather than that. Hence, creation can refer to any factors taken as important to the determinative shape and purpose of the universe, the world and human beings, and also to their derivation from an ultimate constitutive state or agency.

In the first sense, the term is closely related to cosmology, the study of the overall structure and evolution of the universe, to cosmogony, which considers the means by which this structure came about, and to other wide-ranging studies of the world and humanity; all retain a concern for establishing the truth of their conclusions, although without necessarily addressing issues about how this truth is established as such. In the second sense, creation is more closely related to theological cosmology and cosmogony, which consider the normative authority by which the shape and purpose of the universe, the world and human beings are constituted and originated, and how the practice of human life in the world is rendered symmetrical with this shape and purpose.

It is important to recognize that creation is not only a matter of straightforward inquiry into a field and its constitutive reality, but also an issue co-present with most others as their context, in which their preconditions are specified. If, for example, one traces primal features of life such as freedom or salvation, creation is co-present as the configuration of life in the world which makes freedom possible or provides the circumstance within which redemption can occur. In this sense, creation is indirectly present in most central issues, interwoven with them as their context. If there is a universe – or world or life or humanity – the preconditions for its possibility are present in it as creation; and concern with creation has to do with specifying these. How is this universe actual, and how within it is the world as it is, and human beings as they are? What are the conditions for their actuality, and how are they to be sustained by each of them?

These concerns are seen widely in modern science (e.g. the 'anthropic principle', the selectivity of conditions in the universe favourable to the emergence of human beings who can observe it), in modern ecological concerns (what is the dynamic of relations by which life in the world is rendered possible, and how they are to be sustained), and in recent phenomenological and aesthetic accounts of humanity. In more specifically theological accounts, these are questions about how the proper relation between the universe, the world, and human life is to be sustained through symmetry with the purposes of God, and the asymmetries of ignorance and carelessness – and the antisymmetries of refusal and SIN – are overcome.

Creation is a collective designation for all fundamental understanding of the universe, the world, humanity, and the basis for their constitution. In the wide-ranging inquiries to which such concerns give rise, reference to creation serves as a validation ('this is the case') or as a statement of ultimate context ('this applies universally'). In this connection, the major question is what provides such finality or ultimacy and how it does so. What sort of 'primary principle' might occupy such a place, and how would it be operative in regions such as the universe, the world and humanity? In what way is it primary, as detached and exerting influence from this detachment, or as inherently related to the universe? Is its effect occasional or pervasive?

Closely associated is the question of the 'nature' of the universe, the world and humanity. Are they complete in their essentials, or requiring further completion? Are they in unimpaired condition, or somehow lacking in integrity or soundness? Whichever is the case, how does their situation reflect the operation of the 'primary principle' to which creation alludes?

As regards the universe, the world, humanity and their elements, what is the intrinsic importance of each, and how are they ordered in relation to each other? Do they occupy a fixed hierarchical order of preference in 'orders of creation', from lowest to highest – with each lower one the stage or instrument for the higher? Or are they more close-knit in dynamic interrelations, each requiring due recognition – and honour where appropriate – from the others?

Deeply built into these questions are issues about the very possibility of understanding creation – whether creation, cosmology and cosmogony are possible except as speculative extrapolations from the very limited data available to human beings. Insofar as any of their features are seen to be universal and necessary, by what means are they established as such? The questions are perhaps most acute where issues of the 'primary constitution' or 'ultimate principle' are involved. Can human beings do more than provide themselves with meaningful symbolizations of the situation in which they exist?

Despite such searching and far-reaching questions, the possibility of a coherent notion of creation, traced to its constitutive factors and a creative principle, is crucial to the well-being of human beings and to the existence of the world. Unless there is a well-founded normative structure for the universe, which provides for the full integrity of the world and of humanity in their relations, there is unlikely to be much future for either one. This is the significance of past and present debates about creation.

Most fundamental inquiries about the universe, the world and humanity, even about fundamental aspects of animate and human life, as well as about their nature and purpose, may be considered aspects of the theme of creation. What makes all of them aspects of creation is that they are concerned to depict the factors determinative for the universe, the world and humanity – its origins, unity and order, the character and direction of its movement, how human beings are to be at home in it, and the most fundamental constitution of each: each and all as arising from the divine.

The most enduring of such explorations seems to give voice to 'the instinct that there exists a spontaneous harmony between our spirit and [cosmic] reality, . . . the very quality which allows our spirit to grasp reality, not only from one specific and superficial viewpoint, but by means of a deep sympathy with its inner structure and its fundamental evolution' (Bouyer 1988: 23).

The passion of this spirit, however, is for greater harmony, particularly through knowledge: 'He who does not know what the world is, does not know where he is. And he who does not know for what purpose the world exists, does not know who he is, nor what the world is' (Marcus Aurelius). Such explorations and inferences take many forms: mythic, symbolic, ritual, historical, philosophical, theological and scientific.

During the course of history, the concern for creation brought a kind of harmony to the explorations. The major issues were established by relating them to others – the world and humanity were correlated, and both were related to their primary principle, God. In most cases, conceptions of the universe, the world, humanity and God were inseparable from each other, even if views varied according to which was given primacy and how it was conceived. Sometimes, as in pantheism, universe and world were equated and made coeternal with the divinity dwelling in it, endowed with soul and mind as well as matter and body, and human beings mirroring this as microcosms; in such a case, finite things were modifications of the infinite substance (God) which exceeded them. Or, as for Hegel, God was Absolute Spirit manifesting itself historically in physical and psychical nature, to be known through knowing the world and the self, which were seen as the indwelling of divinity itself. Sometimes, as in classical theism, God was a transcendent One standing above all as prime mover, from whom the multiplicity of intelligible and sensible things derived as degrees of being; their task was to achieve the being proportioned to them at source.

In rare cases, the harmony of definitions of world, humanity and God was eliminated through reducing all to one, as in materialism. In this case, the world was said to be all there is, and it could be reduced to primal elements whose order is accidental, not necessary or designed by God. In such a case, the laws of the universe were immanent in its fabric, those of its own matter in motion; and human beings were to make the best of their uncertain situation by their own mental powers and practical will.

Within the creation-located interrelatedness of universe, world, humanity and God, a variety of other issues were dealt with, for example those of number, structure and limit. First, were there many worlds in an infinity of time or space, or only one which matches God's 'most wise and excellent contrivance of things' (Newton)? Second, how were the universe and world structured? Several notions predominated: the world as animate with a soul, its diverse individuals associated for the common good according to their nature and function; the world (visible and invisible) as a divinely instituted society, under divine law; and the world as machine, interdependent moving parts related through linear causation. Third, were they limited, with origin and end, and how? Some suggested their coeternity with God, others that they began and would end according to the purposes of God.

Each of these, however, raised questions about the relation of world and humanity to God. Was this relation as body to soul, society to monarch, or machine to designer? If the universe and the world were animate, with the perfection of parts relative to whole appropriate to an animal, and the soul diffused through it, it was created godlike by God – as a body to God's soul. This widespread view was rejected by Christians (Augustine, Aquinas) as compromising the position of God, who possessed all the perfection of the world in a more eminent way; God's relation to the world was properly viewed as a king present in the world in power. If, in the second case, the world was conceived socially, with things ordered to each other, there was less difficulty for Jews and Christians, for whom things were ordered by God according to their dignity and worth. Divine reason (*logos*) had endowed the world and humanity with a perfection of order (the common good), and governed it by directing each thing to its own end; but ultimately the goal of such government was not the goodness of the world but divine goodness itself – beyond the world. Even in the third case, when the world was seen as a mechanical system, Christians could claim that such a world must proceed from the 'counsel and dominion of an intelligent and powerful being' and be directed – even if only inscrutably – by final causes. A problem emerged only in the determinism of world and humanity which accompanied this view.

Within a harmony of knowledge induced by common concern for creation, there were the possibilities for an integrated view of the world, its people and the purposes of God. And insofar as these were traced to God, the view was seen as having normative authority, one which sufficed for the ordering of human life, not least in its social structure.

In the form in which it was dominant in the West, the teaching of creation followed biblical teachings and the formulations of Augustine, Aquinas and Calvin. This asserted that the world was made finite and orderly out of nothing (*creatio ex nihilo*) by God's agency, conceived as contingent, sustained by its Creator as the 'external basis' (Barth 1945) of God's covenant with humanity, and through redemption by Jesus Christ moved toward its end by the Holy Spirit.

As befits the action of a free and omnipotent God, nothing else – external influence or preexistent matter – was involved. There was no necessity that there should be a creation, nor was its form limited by pre-existing materials, but what resulted from God's free act was a world fully formed and independent; no further creation was necessary. In its structure, the world was ordered by the Creator both as a whole and in each part, its order following an hierarchical arrangement, human beings under God but exercising God's dominion over sub-human creation. As 'priests of creation', human beings were to understand and serve it.

Despite the completeness of its creation, the world was also limited, contingent upon the sustaining providential activity of God. Its future was not in its self-improvement, but in the continuing activity of God to preserve and govern it to bring it to its true end. Its Creator was not simply a bare transcendent cause but one continuously related to creation in electing, redeeming and glorifying the people of God in Jesus Christ by the Holy Spirit.

In this view is seen the integrated view of the world and its people under the sovereign and free God which had normative authority for Western society for a millennium at least. In many respects, its influence has persisted even with a diminished orbit to the present day.

But the force of 'creation', not only in this view but as generally harmonizing different concerns and grounding views of the world and humanity in God, gradually declined – to one primarily used within communities for which this view of creation retained its integrative and normative force. This was largely, it appears, because the difficulty of harmonizing increasing ranges of knowledge and tracing the result to God simply became too great. 'Just as primitive peoples found that unity and completeness led to a vast and unwieldy patchwork of uneasy alliances in order that everything could find a place, so the medievals' desire to harmonize all knowledge into a Theory of Everything became unmanageably complicated' (Barrow 1991: 7).

Closely associated with this collapse was the growing power of knowledge as the proper goal of expert inquiry. Explorations were limited by reflectively-prescribed standards which precluded knowledge of the main elements upon which discussions of creation had been centered – 'the world', 'the soul', and 'God' (Kant). The goals of the new 'science' left the possibilities of

the old 'creation' in abeyance, together with all the God-laden possibilities for life which they had fostered.

With the dissolution of creation as harmonizing all in relation to God, there emerged a wide and growing range of concerns whose coherence with each other is limited to the light which each may cast on the others, and whose normativity is self-established. They are distributed amongst a burgeoning range of embracing disciplines: logic and mathematics, theoretical physics, cosmology, physics, chemistry, astronomy, earth sciences, biology, zoology, botany, anatomy, neurology, genetics, animal behaviour and ecology, anthropology, sociology, psychology, linguistics, economics, political science, history and ethics, and all the concerns special to each of the foregoing. These have brought decisively new perspectives to the topics which had figured in ancient discussions of creation.

Such explorations have brought a new depth of field to perceptions of the order and dynamics of the world and life itself. If creation had designated the preconditions relevant to life in the world and their ultimate constitution by a normative authority, this new depth of field penetrated to new aspects of these preconditions, to undreamed-of ways in which they were configured, leaving it unclear how these might cohere or be constituted by an ultimate authority. In effect, they outstripped the conceptions familiar to older views of creation, and the capacity of a view of creation to harmonize understanding of the world and humanity by reference to God. At the same time, however, they offered new evidence of the possibility that the way human beings think may be made congruent with the structure of the world, a possibility which many would claim arises from the common origin of mind and physical world in the activity of God.

One major area of advance has been in cosmology, where the discovery in 1965 of cosmic background radiation has confirmed the origin of the world in a fiery explosion (the 'Big Bang') about fifteen billion years ago. Either the view that this origin is instantaneous or the speculation that a momentary origin is offset by quantum effects (Hawking) may be accommodated in the assertion that God is ontologically responsible for the world's existence. Much of the subsequent history of the universe is now traced as a process of differentiation in which chance and necessity combine in a 'free process' (Polkinghorne 1994), with its productiveness resting on delicate balances of physical laws; only in such a world could human beings emerge capable of self-conscious life (the 'anthropic principle'). The view resembles Newton's conviction that the (in his case mechanistic) order of the world matched the wise counsel of its designer. In this case, there is no clear hope for the future of cosmic history: it is uncertain whether the expansion from the original explosion, or the contraction of gravity, will prevail, the one bringing death by decay (into low-grade radiation) and the other death in a cosmic melting pot.

A second major area of advance has been in the explanations offered in the time-neutral world of quantum physics, the invisible world of elementary particles and their relations (molecules, atoms and subatomic particles). Quantum theory suggests that the microscopic world is indeterminate – that is, it is unclear how it may be measured: if we know the position of an electron, we cannot know its movement, and vice versa. This leads to the view that all observation and interpretation imply some degree of observer-participation, which disturbs the common sense notion of objectivity. The theory opens new possibilities for complementary interpretations and interactions beyond those previously available.

A third area of new depth has been in the time-directional world of macroscopic physics. In two questions in particular, there have been striking developments. Einstein's theory of special relativity led to the conclusion that the simultaneity of events is not absolute, as if occurring in absolute time, but depends on the state of motion of the observer. As a result, Newton's absolute time was abolished, and time related to space (space-time). A further stage was reached in Einstein's theory of general relativity, which connected matter and space-time. Both theories opened new insights into the nature of the contingency of the world.

Other significant areas of exploration have been concerned with the order and dynamics of the world. Whereas the success of the sciences had been due to their practice of tracing complexities to simpler processes, new attention has been given to complexity and the spontaneous formation of order in chaos. Even thermodynamics, the loss of order which occurs as energy is used, was found to operate differently in non-equilibrium systems (Prigogine 1984).

The final issue which must be mentioned is the discoveries illuminating the nature and origins of animate and human life, reaching from evolutionary theory to the generation of new forms of biological organization at all levels, from DNA to the human mind. What have emerged are new depictions of the history of the emergence of life, and of the nature and organization of living organisms, which combine physico-chemical understanding with other forms of observation. No longer fixed forms completely created and ordered at the beginning, life appears as a dynamic history diversifying into different forms and kingdoms (bacteria, eukaryotic cells, fungi, plants, animals and humans), with differences not only genetic (arising from the 'inherent instability of genetic material' and 'inherently dynamic and inherently directionless' [Layzer 1990]) but – in higher forms – related to physical, psychic and cultural capacities and circumstances.

With the coherence and grounding in the activity of God offered by the traditional Christian account of creation undermined by such explorations, there are new attempts to restore coherence by theoretical and narrative means. One tells of the growth of order in the universe, providing a 'new scientific worldview [which] embraces and reconciles quantum physics, macroscopic physics, molecular and evolutionary biology, and modern neuroscience' (Layzer 1990). Others seek a 'theory of everything', searching for unchanging constants of nature defined in many dimensions whose 'shadows' are observable in the changing three-dimensional universe. Still others attempt to tell the 'universe story', a complex historical account of the emergence of the universe and world as we know them (Swimme and Berry 1994). In each case, the coherence is inner-worldly and without reference to the ultimate authority constitutive for it, God.

With approaches to creation (in the traditional and Christian meanings) left in abeyance by most people today, but increasing pressure – arising from supracognitive and ethical concerns – to recover an integrated and normative view of the preconditions for the universe and human life, it is likely that creation will regain its significance in future debate. Early signs of this are evident in the wide and lively interest in issues of science and theology, their affinities (historical, methodological and conceptual), their mutual benefits and the possibilities for mediating between them (Barbour 1990).

The terms in which a renewal of understanding of creation is undertaken will be of particular importance. Unless the issue is confined to the position of delineating the preconditions and their grounding in normative authority, as authoritative for a private community, it will be necessary to incorporate the new insights which have arisen during recent centuries.

If so, however, are these insights to be treated in fragmentary fashion as indicative of new possibilities for a natural theology (Polkinghorne 1994; Peacocke 1993)? While that approach may allow the retrieval of elements of traditional views of creation, it will fail to provide an integrated account of the preconditions for the universe, the world and human life as from God, of the sort provided previously. Following long-standing precedent, it is more likely that, in dialogue with new scientific understanding, a more comprehensive reconsideration of the conditions of the world as arising from God's action will be necessary. In the final section, we outline a theological view of creation sensitive to the challenges of traditional Christian understanding of creation and those of new scientific understanding, although space precludes synthesizing them here.

One difficult preliminary confronted by those who wish to redevelop creation is the question of knowledge. It is axiomatic for finite human beings that they can consider creation only from the 'inside' or as 'participants' – as those who stand within the limitations and possibilities which it affords them. They are not denied access to creation and its derivation from God, however. They have the possibility of knowledge of creation so far as their position and capacities (by nature, history and development) allow it, while they are also limited to what is available to them through their particular position in it.

A major problem for understanding of creation is that the ultimate authority to which such understanding is referred is frequently so much less interesting and well-thought than the history and infrastructure of the universe, the world and humanity. Fundamental to creation, therefore, is the existence of a creator from whose abundance the richness of creation as we know it originates and continues, as distinct from (say) a bare causal principle which might trigger or boost it. Such a creator is unbounded, incomparable and radically alive, not an empty infinite but one with a fullness of being, truth, goodness and beauty, and hence the complete source of all such things in creation. As a mystery which lies 'beyond' the very relational field constituted by it, the fullness of the Creator is known only as that which actively constitutes this field. In other words, the character of the creator is known through its activation of the relational field called creation.

A second challenge is to discern the manner of the creative act of this Creator. It is the fullness of the Creator's being, truth, goodness and beauty which constitutes it as personal ('I am') and free, free to be fully and radically self-giving through acting to originate that which is other than God. It is this which gives rise to the notions of 'world' and 'humanity', designating in the one case not a bounded totality characterized by its own self-independence and in the other case not a complete product with its own autonomy, but those which have their wholeness and freedom contingently, from the radical self-gift of God. That is, the nature, structure and history of the world and humanity are found not in their self-standing but in the radical – but contingent – gift of being, truth, goodness and beauty by the Creator.

The question of origination which often dominates discussions of creation has to do with the radicality of these gifts by the Creator, not with forms of efficient causation no matter how powerful. Likewise, the notion of *creatio ex nihilo* (creation from nothing) derives from the denial of any source from which creation might have derived other than the Creator's existence, truth, goodness and beauty. Both are expressions of the contingency of the relational field comprised by creation (that is, the universe, world and humanity) on the radical self-gift of the Creator.

A further challenge is to understand the implications for the structure and dynamics of the world. While it is important to stress the contingency of the world and humanity on the radical self-gift of God, such contingency must not be misunderstood. Being, truth, goodness and beauty are fully realized in God, and are as constant in the self-giving of God as they are in God; they are faithfully given to the world and humanity. It is this which confers upon both together (the relational field of world and humanity), as well as those which comprise each, an inalienable character, what is proper to their existence together, beyond which they cannot go with impunity. Furthermore, the gift establishes the quality of relations for the relational field, for elements of the world and human beings separately and together: they are to be related as those who realize the being, truth, goodness and beauty in others through care and compassion, not through self-serving which makes others instrumental to inflated needs.

What of the purpose of the world? It is important to recognize that in the constitution of creation, the being, truth, goodness and beauty which are fully realized in God cannot be completely given to finite beings, lest the finite be overcome by the infinite. The radical self-giving of God is for the world and humanity to be themselves – and true, good and beautiful as such. The gift therefore forms the continuing course of the world and humanity, the future whose arrival depends on the readiness of the recipient to receive it. In other words, the fullness of God is present both in the gift of the condition of the world and humanity and in a purposive determination to which they may respond. Joining these two facets leads to the paradoxical statement that the world and humanity may in time become what they already are.

This awareness of creation provides it with some of its most remarkable features. The field of relations (of creation) which is the self-gift of God is a *plenum*, but not one fully realized.

The first of these two features accounts for the seemingly infinite depth of the conditions which we know as the world and humanity, that which inflames the interest of those who wish to find and know its fundamental character. The world and humanity are legitimate concerns for time-neutral observation. The second of the two accounts for the indefinite dynamism of the world and humanity, in which they are seen as cosmically and historically open. Because they are always moving toward an as-yet incomplete goal, they can be known only by anticipation. The world and humanity are legitimate concerns for time-filled observation. The intersection between the two concerns and kinds of investigation – time-neutral and time-filled – is always a murky one, each always implying the other.

It was stressed earlier that God's self-gift is of the field of relations between God, the world and humanity. The same coupling of firmly given conditions with cosmic and historical openness and purposiveness, is found in the field of relations within world, humanity and God and between them. The radically loving self-gift of God does 'shift the boundaries of being', not only originating that which is separate but constituting a unity between God and the other which does not compromise the other's being in filling it. That 'shift', in which God embraces humanity in what the Hebrews called 'covenant', has many ramifications for the social relations between human beings and for the relations between humanity and the world. In each case it invests them with fixed obligations which are expressed as laws, and also indefinitely extends these responsibilities to include radical self-giving, compassion and care for each other and the world – expressed as anticipations of need. This is the basis for the ethical implications of creation.

As seen earlier, the personal character and freedom of the Creator arise from fullness of being, truth, goodness and beauty. These characteristics arise within creation through the radical self-gift of the Creator, and are found throughout the field of relations in humanity and with the world. Precisely because this fullness of personhood and the freedom which flows from it are given to human beings, and to the world itself, however, there is the possibility of a

195

radical reversal in which the gift and its qualities (truth, goodness and beauty) are alienated from their source (who is in turn treated as alienating) and taken as properties of the world and humanity. Even the constancy of the gift is taken over as these are considered intrinsic to those to whom God has given them. The result, evil in the case of the world and sin for humanity, radically dislocates all the relations proper to human beings in the world and fixes them within severely restricted conditions and purposes, thereby denying them both the true conditions of their being and the true future which they might otherwise anticipate. Such a dislocation can only be fully remedied by the radical self-gift of the Creator in creation as Redeemer, conferring new life in the presence of evil and sin. Creation, fully seen, is the precondition for redemption and eschatology.

Barbour, I.G. (1990) *Religion in an Age of Science*, San Francisco: Harper & Row.

Barrow, J.D. (1991) *Theories of Everything: The Quest for Ultimate Explanation*, Oxford: Clarendon Press.

Barrow, J.D. and Tipler, F.J. (1986) *The Anthropic Cosmological Principle*, Oxford: Clarendon Press.

Barth, K. (1945) *The Doctrine of Creation*, Vol. III/1 of *Church Dogmatics*, Edinburgh: T. & T. Clark.

Bouyer, L. (1988) *Cosmos: The World and the Glory of God*, Petersham, MA: St Bede's Publications.

Buckley, M.J. (1987) *At the Origins of Modern Atheism*, New Haven, CT: Yale University Press.

Davies, P.C.W. (1983) *God and the New Physics*, London: Dent & Co.

Hawking, S.W. (1988) *A Brief History of Time*, London: Bantam Press.

Layzer, D. *Cosmogenesis: The Growth of Order in the Universe*, New York: Oxford University Press.

Pannenberg, W. (1994) *Systematic Theology*, vol. 2, Grand Rapids, MI: William B. Eerdmans.

Peacocke, A.R. (1993) *Theology for a Scientific Age*, Minneapolis, Fortress Press.

Polkinghorne, J.C. (1994) *The Faith of a Physicist*, Princeton: Princeton University Press.

Prigogine, K., and Stengers, I. (1984) *Order Out of Chaos: Man's New Dialogue with Nature*, London: New Science Library.

Rolston, H. (1987) III, *Science and Religion*, New York: Random House.

Russell, C.A. (1985) *Cross-Currents: Interactions Between Science and Faith*, Leicester, Inter-Varsity Press.

Russell, R.J., Murphey, N., and Isham, C. (eds) (1993) *Quantum Cosmology and the Laws of Nature: Scientific Perspectives on Divine Action*, Vatican City State: Vatican Observatory.

Russell, R.J., Stoeger, W. R., and Coyne, G. V. (eds) *Physics, Philosophy and Theology: A Common Quest for Understanding*, Vatican City State: Vatican Observatory.

Swimme, B. and Berry T. (1994) *The Universe Story*, London: Arkana.

Tanner, K., *God and Creation in Christian Theology* (1988) Oxford: Basil Blackwell.

Torrance, T.F., *Divine and Contingent Order* (1981) Oxford: Oxford University Press.

Daniel W. Hardy

CRIME

The word *crime* signifies an offence in the public domain as opposed to a mere private injury. It appears to have been developed from the Latin *crimen*, a term that indicates the giving of a judgement against an offence, the offence itself or its related accusation. The substantive existence of crime as opposed to its terminology can be definitely and distinctively traced to the earliest written accounts of our CULTURE and its predecessors and there is every reason to think it pre-dates those accounts. Some kind of formal understanding of, recognition of and PUNISHMENT of deviance is also found in cultures widely different from our own. Even very early cultures give formal accounts of crime and related punishments. The Code of Hammurabi, seventeenth century BCE, lays down specific offences and specific punishments. In the early Hebraic experience the Decalogue sets out basic and non-negotiable edicts that lay down patterns of expected behaviour and prohibits deviance from those expectations. The story of Adam, important to much Christian THEOLOGY, lays down the first interdiction, given by God, not to eat from the fruit of the tree of knowledge. On this account the first crime, however, is not the actions of Eve but the actions of the Serpent in tempting Eve (Ricour 1967). The Hebrew Bible contains the Decalogue as a set of prime interdicts as well as subsequent subsidiary laws. One account of the distinction between the early Hebraic accounts of crime and the Christian account of crime is that in the latter the crime is effectively completed when the condition of mind is met. Hence, 'for out of the heart come evil thoughts, murder, adultery, fornication, theft, false witness, slander' (Matthew 15: 19) and in the addition to the Decalogue given in *The Beatitudes* Jesus says: 'You have heard that it was said "You shall not commit adultery". But I say to you that every one who looks at a woman lustfully has already committed adultery with her in his heart' (Matthew 5: 27–8). The shift shown here is crucial for it is the precursor of the *mens rea* component of crime: a crime cannot be a crime unless the mental state is appropriate. The mind must be sound, the intention must be there, the deed must have been done, the agent must have performed the deed and the deed must have been illegal for the crime to have been complete. Exceptions are strict liability offences, a speeding offence for instance, where intention is not significant.

Crime can be approached from several standpoints; two principal ones are first, legal, and second, as a case or form of deviance. Legal approaches seek to understand crime in general, rather than particular crimes.

> Of course, the definition [of crime] tells us nothing about what acts *ought* to be crimes, but that is not its purpose. Writers who set out to define a crime by reference to the nature of the act, on the other hand, inevitably end by telling us, not what a crime is, but what the writer thinks it ought it to be; and that is not a definition of crime.
>
> (Smith and Hogan 1988: 22)

The legalistic analysis can be divided into two camps. The classical view of crime saw it as a moral code, with morality affecting both definition and sanction. (In *Shaw* v. *DPP* Lord Simonds asserted that 'there remains in the courts of law a residual power to enforce the supreme and fundamental purpose of the LAW, to conserve not only the safety and order, *but also the moral welfare* of the state'; and that the King's Bench was the *custos morum* of the people and had the superintendency of offences *contra bonos mores*. 'Shaw's case', concludes Lord Devlin, 'settles for the purpose of the law that morality in England means what twelve men and women think it means – in other words, it

is to be ascertained as a question of fact' (Smith and Hogan 1988: 20).)

As for punishment, the then Lord Justice Denning put it: '[the] punishment inflicted for grave crimes should adequately reflect the revulsion felt by the great majority of citizens for them'. Nevertheless, it has to be granted that the moral theory of criminality is an insufficient definition, for some crimes are amoral and some immoral acts are not crimes; certain strict liability offences lack a moral complexion and in most countries adultery, for example, is not a crime. Moreover, the moral theory tends to assume a unitary view of morality – that everyone accepts the same acts or omissions to be immoral. That is difficult to believe with regard to the pluralistic society in Britain and it is even more difficult to agree with in relation to the broader international community.

The definition of crime in general by legal scholars is no longer dependent on morality and this gives rise to a second approach, the modern procedure-oriented approach typified by the writings of Kenny, Smith and Hogan and Glanville-Williams. This sees domestic crime as being determined, in whatever manner, procedural or substantive, by the state, which is in authority over its subjects for the protection of society at large. Kenny defined crimes as wrongs whose sanction is punitive and is in no way remissible by any private person but is remissible by the Crown alone, if remissible at all. Kenny has been thoroughly criticized, but the essence of his arguments has been developed by Glanville-Williams.

> A crime must be defined by reference to the legal consequences of the act. . . . A crime then becomes an act that is capable of being followed by criminal proceedings, having one of the types of outcome (punishment *etc.*) known to follow these proceedings.
>
> (Glanville-Williams 1955: 123)

Smith and Hogan adopt the 'practical test' of whether the proceedings may result in the punishment of the offender to determine whether the proceedings are criminal. A sovereign body and the correct type of procedure are thus essential. Such definitions rely on a vertical society with the state in authority over its citizens. Other elements in the modern definition of crime include enforcement procedures, special sanctions and the punishment of offenders. As Winfield pointed out, crimes are defined in terms of punitive sanctions. 'The essence of [criminal] punishment is its inevitability . . . no option is left to the offender as to whether he shall endure it or not'; whereas, in a civil case, 'he can always compromise to get rid of his liability with the assent of the injured party'. Indeed, in the Engel case, the European Court of Human Rights held that 'In a society subscribing to the rule of law, there belong to the "criminal" sphere deprivations of liberty liable to be imposed as a punishment, except those which by their nature, duration or manner of execution cannot be appreciably detrimental.' Thus, criminal sanctions are different in nature to civil ones.

Before leaving the legal definition, although it does not formally form part of an analysis of crime, as opposed to particular crimes, some consideration of *mens rea* for offences needs to be undertaken. Not all domestic crimes require *mens rea*, but all serious crimes do: there is an inherent element in most crimes that the accused should not be guilty unless he was conscious of his actions. It is as if the moral constraint of breaking the accepted code has to be rejected before one can commit a crime. Here we see the influence of that theological tradition from the Beatitudes to St Paul, St Augustine and latterly Kant in making it clear that intention, the heart, is crucial to the assessment of personal conduct.

The sociological definitions of crime, three of which will be looked at here, tend to be wider than the merely legal. The first approach is that of the classical school. The classical tradition is represented by Thomas Hobbes, Cesare Beccaria and, in particular, Jeremy Bentham. In 1789 Bentham outlined a general theory of crime. Bentham argued that crime is part of the natural consequence of unrestrained human tendencies to seek pleasure and avoid pain. Thus, for Bentham, crimes will occur whenever the pleasures produced by them exceed any associated pain that could occur. Bentham called the pleasurable and painful consequences sanctions and divided them into four groups: physical, religious, moral and political. Physical sanctions are those consequences of behaviour that follow automatically. Using Gottfredson and Hirschi's (1990) example of intravenous drug use, the effects are apparently pleasurable, but there is the attendant risk of accident, infection and DEATH. For the classicist, therefore, there is a natural constraint on all crime. Turning to religious sanctions, Bentham was writing at a time when the Church had a much greater role in everyday life and where the fear of the hereafter would be a more pressing leverage in general on society. With regard to moral sanctions, Bentham saw the actions of neighbours and the community as one of the most important sources of pleasure and pain to the individual. He refers to the power of popular sanction as a reward or punishment for behaviour. Implicit is the concept of STIGMA. Finally, in discussing political sanctions, Bentham used his pleasure/pain theory to justify state sanctions of individual behaviour. As Gottfredson and Hirschi note, however, Bentham's interpretation of crime is quite narrow as his theory does not distinguish between criminal and non-criminal acts. They go on to point out, though, that crime was eventually distinguished from other forms of behaviour by concentrating on the notion of political sanctions, pleasures and pains manipulated by the STATE. Thus, the classical definition of crime referred only to those acts attracting a political sanction where the state imposed the punishment.

More recently, the determinists, such as Hartung, Radzinowicz, Bonger and Bock, tend to be more interested in why people commit crimes than what is a crime, but their analysis is premised on Walker's so-called declaratory theory that crime is 'taken as a declaration of what the society in question condemns'. The final sociological view is that of Lombroso, a positivist, who argued that responsibility is dependent on the needs of society. If the society defines an act as a crime, then criminal responsibility arises. In all three sociological approaches, however, crime is a social construct: by reference to whether the act attracts state sanction, society's condemnation of the act or society's definition of the act as criminal.

If the definition of crime has not received much attention from sociologists, that is because they have been more interested in, first, why society determines particular forms of action as deviant and, second, why people fall into particular types of deviant behaviour that are criminal, the study of which is criminology. Thomas and Hepburn (1983) provide an admirably clear definition. Criminology is 'the objective, systematic study of how criminal laws are enacted, why some people break these laws, how we and our representatives react to the breaking of law, and our methods of dealing with convicted offenders'. Issues of criminology might influence our interpretation of crime in several ways. The first is that of victimless crimes. What is a crime without a victim? Hart (1963) suggests that it is an attempt 'to legislate morality for its own sake'. Schur (1965) notes that it refers to the willing exchange, among adults, of strongly demanded but legally proscribed goods or services. It is easy to identify the perpetrator and the object of the crime where it is a violent assault or offence against PROPERTY, such as theft, but it becomes more difficult, as Schur suggests, where the crime is directed at the state or is merely a breach of morality. The foremost crimes without victims are seen as homosexuality, drug abuse, sado-masochism and ABORTION. However, apart from the first, many would question the victimless character of the remainder; for instance with drug abuse the FAMILY often suffers (*see* DRUG ADDICTION). Another problem area concerns women and criminality. Klein and Kress point out that the

> changing nature of women's position in the workforce and in the family has given rise to a new set of issues concerning women [and crime, such as] . . . the increasing rates and fluctuating patterns in women's offences [and a] . . . portrayal of a new 'violent' woman by the media.
>
> (Klein and Kress 1981)

In recent years there have been several sensationalized accounts in the press of murders by women within the family which conveniently ignore the fact of an increase in crimes against women. The traditional criminologists have focused their views on female criminality around biological and psychological attributes of women, as though these aspects were a woman's sole and determinative function, ignoring external influences such as gender-based oppression. Thus, Klein and Kress argue, one must turn to radical criminology for a proper view of how the definition of crime is to be interpreted with respect to women. The radicals reject the legal and traditional sociological definitions as being self-fulfilling, starting instead with a basic 'notion of HUMAN RIGHTS to self-determination, dignity, food and shelter and freedom from exploitation'. Crimes are then those activities which violate those rights, such as APARTHEID, colonialism, SEXISM and RACISM. According to radical criminologists, crime will only be eradicated when there has been a fundamental transformation of society to effect greater JUSTICE and EQUALITY. These views have also been the basis of LIBERATION THEOLOGY, outlined by writers such as Boff and Gutierrez, particularly in relation to life in Latin America. Even the traditional church's teaching can be used to justify these arguments on occasion.

> There is neither Jew nor Greek, slave nor free, male nor female. . . . Now listen, you rich people, weep and wail because of the misery that is coming upon you. Your wealth has rotted, and moths have eaten your clothes. Your gold and silver are corroded. Their corrosion will testify against you and eat your flesh like fire. You have hoarded wealth in the last days. Look! The wages you failed to pay the women who mowed your fields are crying out against you. The cries of the harvesters have reached the ears of the Almighty. You have lived on earth in luxury and self-indulgence. You have fattened yourselves in the day of slaughter. You have condemned and murdered innocent men, who were not opposing you.
>
> (Galations 3: 28; James 5: 1–6; New International Version)

The theological view of crime depends initially on the interdictions provided by the Decalogue, the modification by Jesus and the development of that model by, among others, St Augustine,s

Aquinas, Kant and modern theologians. Many people have an understanding of right and wrong, of good and evil, and such understanding affects the ways in which we conduct our daily lives. Aquinas argued that humans have FREE WILL and so are masters of their actions. On this account criminals are condemned for their wrong acts for they are autonomous beings sovereign over their own actions. Relatedly one strand of Pauline theology has it (Romans 13) that GOVERNMENT is merely exercising its God-given authority when prosecuting and punishing crimes. Unfortunately, government is not infallible and, being constituted from that which is human, sometimes displays their fallen nature in punishing the wrong people for doing what is right (1 Peter 4).

Set against the standard theological model of the AUTONOMY and sovereignty of persons is a recent view that understands the very concept of the person, the very concept of a particular person and the very idea of humanity as a construct. On this view individual people are bearers of social structures; in Althusser's words, 'History is a process without a subject.' Where such a view is held, crime is a Spinoza-like attribute of the whole structure, as are particular crimes and particular criminals. Post-structuralist accounts treat crime in a similar way, seeing it as constituted from discursive practices (see DECONSTRUCTION). In recent liberal-communitarian debates a similar point has been made; if the self is not prior to society in some Augustinian–Thomist–Cartesian–Kantian way but is fashioned in social circumstances, then how and in what sense can it be said to be responsible for its actions, blamed? Correlatively how can someone else properly be praised for their actions? (See, for example Sandel 1982.) Such arguments are not entirely new, although they do grow from the sociological perspective, the view that society plays a part, perhaps a major part, in the formation of social selves, social individuals. The US defence lawyer Clarence Darrow repeatedly argued, and with great success, that his clients could not be guilty as charged for their actions were the products of their circumstances. In the UK, Baroness Wootton was one of the first to make a similar point with respect to punishment. There was no single person who was responsible for the crime, she argued; who then should one punish? Her solution to crime was the removal of the causes of the crime and rehabilitation, not punishment.

Even if these views are not fully accepted there can be little doubt that conditions of, for example extreme poverty may generate circumstances that encourage the crime of theft. More radically, causing or permitting the continuation of poverty can be seen as criminal. Certainly, as John Locke pointed out 300 years ago, taking advantage of one in poverty is an abuse unworthy of any Christian. For Christians the traditional starting point is that the person committing the crime is at the centre of their actions, but one must then go on to ask why and in what circumstances that person committed the crime and consider the other wider, surrounding issues. The parable of the Good Samaritan would suggest that the Christian should not stand by while crimes are committed against individual victims, and indeed in some jurisdictions there are Good Samaritan laws, but, again more radically, is it right to stand by while violations of human rights are perpetrated in the name of the state leaving people in poverty and suffering discrimination? The actions of developed states condemn those people living in the Third World to a life of deprivation – is it criminal to stand by and let this happen, through ignorance, weakness or our own deliberate fault?

For individuals convicted of a crime, what is available to change their behaviour? Is it enough to incarcerate them in prison, regardless of the conditions, hoping that the stigma alone will have beneficial effects, or does society have a responsibility to provide basic humane conditions and a rehabilitative structure (see ATONEMENT)? A reasonably judged theological perspective can combine traditional views of the sovereignty of the person with contemporary views of the effects of society on the constitution of the person by encouraging crime to be viewed in a rehabilitative and redemptive perspective (see CAPITAL PUNISHMENT).

Althusser, L. (1971) *Politics and History*, London: New Left Books.

Boff, L. (1974) *Jesus Christ Liberator*, London: SPCK.

Devlin, P. (1962) 'Law, democracy and morality', *University of Pennsylvania Law Review* 110: 635–57.

Glanville-Williams (1955) 'The definition of crime', *Current Legal Problems* 8: 107.

Gottfredson, M.R. and Hirschi, T. (1990) *A General Theory of Crime*, Stanford, CA: Stanford University Press.

Hart, H.L.A. (1963) *Law, Liberty and Morality*, Oxford: Oxford University Press.

Klein and Kress (1981) 'Any woman's blues', in T. Platt and P. Takagi (eds) *Crime and Social Justice*, London: Macmillan, ch. 6.

Locke, John *A First Treatise on Government*.

Packer, J.I. (1973) *Knowing God*, Downers Grove, IL: InterVarsity Press.

Platt, T. and Takagi, P. (eds) (1981) *Crime and Social Justice*, London: Macmillan.

Ricour, Paul (1967) *The Symbolism of Evil*, New York: Harper & Row.

Sandel, Michael, J. (1982) *Liberalism and the Limits of Justice*, Cambridge: Cambridge University Press.

Schur, E.M. (1965) *Crimes without Victims*, Englewood Cliffs, NJ: Prentice-Hall.

Smith, J. and Hogan, B. (1988) *Criminal Law*, London: Butterworths.

Spinoza *Ethics*.

Thomas, C.W. and Hepburn, J.R. (1983) *Crime, Criminal Law and Criminology*, Dubuque, IA: Brown.

Wootton, Barbara (1950) *Social Science and Pathology*.

——(1959) *Testament for Social Science*.

Young, J. and Matthews, R. (1992) *Rethinking Criminology: The Realist Debate*, London: Sage.

Clare Rhatigan
Geoff Gilbert

CRUELTY

'Cruelty' is by definition the unjustifiable infliction of pain and suffering. If a particular instance of inflicting pain is deemed cruel, it cannot be justified; if it can be justified it cannot be deemed cruel. Christian tradition has always held that there are certain acts of such immorality that they can never be justified no matter the circumstances. The Roman Catholic Encyclical *Veritatis Splendor* reaffirms this view: 'there are objects of the human act which are by their nature "incapable of being ordered" to God, because they radically contradict the good of the person'. Thus, 'there exist acts which *per se* and in themselves … are always seriously wrong by virtue of their object'. These acts are 'intrinsically evil', such that 'a good intention or particular circumstances can diminish their evil but they cannot remove it' (John Paul II, 1993: 122–4). The precise nature and range of this concept is often debated, but it traditionally includes acts of 'mental and physical torture' (ibid., p. 123; *see* CHILD ABUSE). Traditionally, then, acts of cruelty have been deemed to be beyond moral redemption; cruelty is unjustifiable because it cannot be ordered to God and is therefore repugnant to the human person. Humphrey Primatt insists that cruelty is 'atheism', 'infidelity' and 'the worst of heresies', and that 'a cruel Christian … beareth the name of Christ in vain' (Primatt 1776: 228–9).

There is continuing debate concerning the justifiability of inflicting pain. Common justifications include appeals to teleological/consequential benefits that may accrue from, for example, painful medical operations or reformatory punishment, as well as claims that the individual may have merited painful punishment in some way. The Eighth Amendment to the US Constitution, for example, rules that 'cruel and unusual punishment' is unacceptable penal practice. This phraseology has led to the debate over CAPITAL PUNISHMENT, in the USA at least, often being couched in terms of 'justification' by the consequences of deterrence or that an undesirable has been removed from society or, most commonly, by the belief that a murderer has merited the death penalty or has forfeited the right to his or her own life. Similarly in modern warfare, the disproportionate amount of pain and injury caused by certain weapons, such as dumdum bullets and napalm, has led to these being branded 'cruel' and unacceptable, and the debate continues over whether this restriction should extend further to include, for example, biological, chemical and nuclear weaponry.

While there has never been a total Christian prohibition on inflicting pain as something always and everywhere evil in itself because the possibility of particular justifications is not denied, there is a strong disposition within the tradition to regard *certain forms* of pain infliction as morally inexcusable. An obvious example of this is the infliction of pain on 'innocents', notably in the just-war tradition. The category of innocents should include children, sentient foetuses (see Robinson 1977, 1985), the mentally ill and animals (see ANIMAL RIGHTS). The view of C.S. Lewis that 'So far as we know beasts are incapable either of sin or virtue: therefore they can neither deserve pain nor be improved by it' (Lewis 1957: 103) cannot be gainsaid, and applies equally to children as well as to certain vulnerable classes of adult humans. By definition, the morally innocent cannot merit pain or benefit from it. Neither can they consent to pain (which rational adults can and sometimes do) or have the effects of pain softened by an intellectual comprehension of the circumstances.

The categorization of these 'always unjustifiable' kinds of pain as forming a particular moral class of their own requires explanation. One theological rationale is supplied by John Henry Newman in his sermon 'The Crucifixion' delivered in 1842. Newman emphasizes the similarity between the cruel barbarity of the crucifixion and cruel behaviour towards animals and children, claiming that through witnessing the latter one can 'learn to feel pain and anguish at the thought of Christ's sufferings' (Newman 1868: 135). Exploiting the Christological metaphor of the 'lamb of God', Newman maintains the moral equivalence of the cruelty inflicted on innocent beings, such as children and animals, and the horror of the crucifixion: 'there is something so very dreadful, so satanic in tormenting those who never have harmed us, and who cannot defend themselves, who are utterly in our power, who have weapons neither of offence nor defence . . .' (ibid., pp. 136–7). Christian sensitivity to innocent, undeserved and unmerited suffering should arise 'directly out of the Christian conviction that Christ was himself the subject of unmerited suffering and that his life and teaching as a whole require the exercise of humility, mercy and self-costly love'. Furthermore, it seems that the Christian cannot but condemn acts of cruelty: 'If this pattern of life is expressive of God's will – indeed, as Christians have traditionally claimed – God's actual self-revelation, we reach here the very limits of compatibility' (Linzey 1992: 17).

Newman's thesis anticipates the modern argument against child or animal abuse that is based upon what may be termed varying 'ontologies of vulnerability' (see Robinson 1992; Clarke and Linzey 1988). According to this view, it is the sheer vulnerability and defencelessness of the victim that should make certain kinds of behaviour abhorrent. Although Christians have sometimes been reluctant to include animals within the circle of moral protection, historically the question of cruelty to children is a product of concern about cruelty to these other, weaker beings. In 1884 in the USA, Henry Bergh, the founder of the American Society for the Prevention of Cruelty to Animals, brought one of the first successful prosecutions against cruelty to children under extant legislation against cruelty to animals. This led in turn to the founding of anti-child-cruelty societies in both the USA and the UK. In the UK, the founding of the National Society for the Prevention of Cruelty to Children, in the same year, was indebted to members of the Royal Society for the Prevention of Cruelty to Animals who provided the initial impetus as well as material assistance (see Moss 1961; Turner 1964; Owen 1965).

It is often argued, both within and without the Christian tradition, that some instances of the infliction of pain and suffering on animals and children are justified teleologically by a greater good, such as medical research (see VIVISECTION) and the exercise of parental discipline respectively (see McCarthy 1960). Such arguments beg a major ethical question: can the infliction of pain, especially on innocents, ever be justified by consequentialist appeals? The strength of the traditional position lies in its emphasis upon the concept of 'intrinsic evil', and its refusal to embrace relativism or consequentialism. However, unless theological or metaphysical appeals are allowed, it is difficult to hold any absolutist ethical position.

The weakness of the traditional view does not lie in its absolutism, but in its failure to reflect fully on the meaning of its own basic terms, such as 'intrinsic evil', and to consider their relevance in changed circumstances. For example, Newman's view of the Christ-like innocence of children and animals represents a moral extension of traditional doctrine which has received very little consideration, and yet the issue of the rights of the morally innocent and vulnerable can conceivably unite, even reconcile, traditional theology with some aspects of modern sensibility. The implicitly theological notion of the moral priority of the weak has far-reaching implications which are addressed as much in non-theological literature as in theological literature (see Linzey 1994).

The place of cruelty in a universe created by an omniscient, omnipotent, perfectly good God forms a major philosophical and theological issue. As a part of the 'problem of evil' debate, various theodicies have been proposed to show that the existence of pain and suffering inflicted by others neither constitutes evidence against the existence of an all-powerful, loving God nor commits one to the belief that God is cruel. These theodicies all justify the existence of pain and suffering teleologically, claiming that, for example, God is with the sufferer (and to be with God is an incommensurate good), or that human cruelty is necessarily a possibility if humans are to be significantly free (and freedom is an outweighing good). The danger with all such explanations is that success in 'justifying' pain may result in Christian indifference to the reality of evil in the world (*see* THEODICY).

Adams, R.M. and Adams, M.M. (eds) (1990) *The Problem of Evil*, Oxford: Oxford University Press.

Anscombe, G.E.M. (1981) 'War and Murder', in *The Collected Papers of G.E.M. Anscombe*, vol. III, Oxford: Blackwell.

Clarke, P.A.B. and Linzey, A. (1988) *Research on Embryos: Politics, Theology and Law*, London: Lester Crook Academic.

Farrer, A. (1966) *Love Almighty and Ills Unlimited*, London: Collins.

Geach, P. (1977) *Providence and Evil*, Cambridge: Cambridge University Press.

Hick, J. (1975) *Evil and the God of Love*, 4th edn, London: Collins.

John Paul II, Pope (1993) *Veritatis Splendor*, Encyclical Letter, London: Catholic Truth Society.

Lewis, C.S. (1957) *The Problem of Pain*, London: Collins, Fontana.

Lewis, C.S. and Joad, C.E.M. (1950) 'On the pains of animals', *The Month* 3(2): 95–102.

Linzey, A. (1992) *Cruelty and the Christian Conscience*, Nottingham: Lynx Educational Trust.

——(1994) *Animal Theology*, London: SCM, and Chicago, IL: University of Illinois Press.

McCarthy, J.C. (1960) *Problems in Theology*, vol. II, *The Commandments*, Dublin: Browne & Nolan.

Moss, A.W. (1961) *Valiant Crusade: The History of the RSPCA*, London: Cassell.

National Society for the Prevention of Cruelty to Children (1991) *The Needs and Rights of Children, Child Protection Agenda 1991*, London: NSPCC.

Newman, J.H. (1868) 'The Crucifixion', in *Parochial and Plain Sermons*, vol. VII, London: Rivingtons.

Owen, D. (1965) *English Philanthropy*, London: Oxford University Press.

Primatt, H. (1776) *Dissertation on the Duty of Mercy and the Sin of Cruelty to Brute Animals*, Edinburgh: T. Constable.

Ramsey, R.P. (1961) *War and the Christian Conscience*, Durham, NC: Duke University Press.

Robinson, D.M. (1977) 'Reflections on the rights of fetuses and other animals', Address to the Annual Convention of the American Political Science Association, 1–4 September.

——(1985) 'On fetal pain', A Statement prepared for the Senate Judiciary Committee, Subcommittee on the Constitution, 21 May.

——(1992) 'The standing of the fetus', *The World and I* (May): 517–29.

Teichman, J. (1986) *Pacifism and The Just War*, Oxford: Blackwell.

Turner, E.S. (1964) *All Heaven in a Rage*, London: Michael Joseph.

Andrew Linzey
Jonathan Webber

CULTS

The concept of 'cults' (in the plural) is generally to be differentiated in everyday usage from the concept of 'cult' (in the singular). Whereas in the singular the term includes, among various meanings, a cluster of distinctive beliefs and practices, which may be sustained by particular groups within or outside a given religious tradition, in the plural the term refers to a category (albeit loosely defined) of separate religious bodies. Thus, in the singular, the term cult applies to patterns of devotion such as the special reverence manifested in the cult of Our Lady of Fatima, or the cult of the Sacred Heart, or the cult of saints. In older works on the sociology of religious organization, e.g. in the classic text of Joachim Wach, the term is employed only in this sense. In plural usage, which has grown in recent decades, the allusion is generally to new movements which canvass patterns of belief and practice that deviate substantially from those of older settled church and denominational bodies. However, the literature has paid relatively little attention to the need for a formal definition of the concept.

Although the term is often loosely used, and in everyday currency frequently carries strong pejorative connotations, some sociologists have sought to give more specificity to the term. Today, they generally distinguish what is designated as a cult from the other established categories of church, sect and denomination. Roy Wallis has brought greater analytical rigour to this distinction, in particular by reference to two specific variables: (a) the character of a movement's epistemology; and (b) whether the operation of the religious body generates tension between it and the wider society. Both the church-type organization and the sect seek to establish an authoritative epistemology, or, to put the matter in other terms, each claims unique legitimacy for its teachings and religious practice. The denomination and the cult, in contrast, are epistemologically individualist, allowing their members a certain liberty of conscience. They do not, in other words, claim exclusive legitimacy, but admit a certain pluralism of belief and concede equal, or near-equal, warrant to some other similarly oriented movements. With regard to the tension variable, the church and the denomination are both well accommodated in SOCIETY and operate with little or no tension arising. In contrast, between on the one hand the sect and the cult and on the other hand the wider society, there is persistent and endemic tension. That tension is often made apparent in complaints from the general public particularly about intrusive religious performances or proselytizing activities. It issues at times in brushes between cult (or sect) adherents and the law, and in periodic claims by these minority groups for exemption from the normal legal obligations of citizens, particularly in the case of cults in matters of health. It is the recognition of the common circumstances of tension *vis-à-vis* the wider society that induces some commentators to confuse cults and SECTS, and to use both these designations interchangeably, and almost always to disparage them. Thus, while cults have in common with sects a tendency to be ill-accommodated within society, cults differ

from sects in that they do not claim unique and exclusive legitimacy.

The exclusivity of the sect is made manifest in its assertion of a monopoly of ultimate truth; in its claim to a unique warrant for its religious practice; and in its demand that its votaries should not be affiliated with, or even remotely associated with, any other religious body: it might also demand that they dissociate themselves from the everyday activities of the rest of society (*see* FUNDAMENTALISM). In contrast, the cult is frequently quite eclectic in its teachings, and displays some willingness to tolerate other systems of thought and practice. It has neither the organizational means nor the explicit intention to control its members in this respect and has not evolved an ideological defence of its own distinctive teachings to a point where it sees all other bodies of doctrine as necessarily EVIL.

Cults are organizationally less stable than sects, and fail to require from their participants binding obligations to the movement. Unlike sects, cults are at best only rudimentarily institutionalized. They may, at times, be little more than the expression of passing enthusiasm for particular ideas or spiritual exercises (conspicuously so in the case of religious phenomena in underdeveloped societies, e.g. in the numerous Melanesian cargo cults). They are often volatile with respect to their teachings, and new ideas or changed organizational arrangements may often be embraced without difficulty, and may equally easily be jettisoned. As movements, they tend to lack firm boundaries and this, with the changeability of teachings and the frequently unsystematized acceptance of various kindred patterns of thought and practice, implies a lack of cohesion among adherents, many of whom may see themselves as relatively uncompromised seekers on a spiritual quest rather than as committed members of an organization. They may simultaneously be questing in diverse directions, participants in what has been termed the 'cultic milieu', the social context in which devotees of various movements meet, exchange views, and sometimes switch from one pattern of practice to another and back again.

Whilst this degree of volatility and instability is not invariably a feature of all cults, it typifies groups covered by the concept and distinguishes them from sects. Cults do, however, sometimes seek to divest themselves of just these characteristics, and a pattern of development may at times be discerned in which some cults have gradually acquired mechanisms for boundary maintenance, devices by which to retain and enhance adherents' sense of identification with the group, and policies of sharpening the distinctiveness of their own position relative to those of other groups which thus become increasingly seen as rivals and competitors. This evolutionary process is a transformation of a cult into a sect, and is analogous to the more celebrated transition by which sects, in some instances, have gravitated towards a denominational stance. The features of the process are evident as eclecticism is disciplined and the exclusivity of the cult's distinctive teachings is increasingly affirmed. This type of development has been impressively documented by Wallis in *Salvation and Protest* for the early history of Christian Science, and in the more recent evolution of the Church of Scientology from the original therapeutic cult of Dianetics. Mary Baker Eddy and L. Ron Hubbard, respectively the leaders of these two movements, initially made only limited claims to the exclusive loyalty of their following, but increasingly by virtue of a variety of administrative measures each came to take a firmer line against those who 'adulterated' the authorized teaching with alien ideas or practices.

Whilst epistemological individualism may be taken as the most decisive criterion of what is to be called a cult, there are other frequent (but not invariable) characteristics which are typical and to which more importance has been attached by some writers. Among these is the tendency for cults to attract an unstable following who are often only rather loosely and perhaps transitorily attached. A distinction must be made, however, between the usually small core group of adepts, some of whom may be involved in the affairs and organization of the movement full-time, and for whom the cult is a virtually totalistic experience, and the mass of followers, for whom association with the cult is far from exacting anything like this level of commitment. The distinction between core and rank-and-file members is marked in many cult movements: thus, it has been indicated in the Divine Light Mission between the so-called 'premies' and the other devotees; in the Church of Scientology between staff members (and especially those who were employed on L. Ron Hubbard's ship headquarters, the so-called 'Sea-Org') and the ordinary 'pre-clears' who constitute the mass attenders at the movement's courses; and between the trainers and the ordinary meditators in Maharishi's Transcendental Meditation. Whilst total dedication might be demanded from the core members, over whom firm control might be exerted, the ordinary adherents in such organizations have only a segmentary attachment, the remaining areas of their lives and their everyday concerns being relatively little affected by their participation in the cult and in its attendant observances.

It follows that the term 'membership' is itself often less applicable to involvement in a cult than it is in other organizations, and it is sometimes the case that the participant is more of a client than a devotee – although cases vary. The client–practitioner relationship tends in particular to prevail where the cult has, as is frequently found, a strong concern with a system of therapy. Such a relationship is typical of movements which make yoga, massage, meditation, mind control and positive thinking a part of their central practice. It is worthy of note that some essentially therapeutic movements that have little or no explicitly religious doctrine are, in popular usage, as readily designated as cults as are spiritual groups of the kinds referred to above.

Associated with the foregoing characteristics is also the essentially ephemeral nature of cults. In general, cults attract and recruit individuals separately (rather than as whole families) and there is little tendency for cult attachment to persist in families or to give rise to the type of generational transmission of religious belief that occurs normally in the case of established sects (such as Jehovah's Witnesses, Christadelphians, Exclusive Brethren, or even Pentecostalists, for example). Contingent on the lack of any exclusivism of belief or association, and on the circumstance of cult adherents generally, there can be no expectation that cult devotees will practise endogamy, and hence little prospect of creating any generational succession in cult adherence. The cult is much less tribe-like than the sect, and lacks the strong sense of, sometimes almost ethnic, identity that characterizes sect allegiance.

The term 'cults' has also been freely, if not always appropriately, applied to religious movements that arise from outside the central indigenous religious traditions of a society, and particularly to movements of exotic provenance, such as the Divine Light Mission, the International Society for Krishna Consciousness, Rajneeshism and Soka Gakkai International; to movements of an occultist orientation, such as Theosophy, Druidism, Wicca, and the congeries of groups that are embraced under the rubric of NEW AGE spirituality; and also to quasi-scientistic mind-control movements, such as the Forums Network (est), Exegesis and Scientology. As is evident from this extensive application of the term, the concept lacks specificity and scholarly consensus, and is used to cover a diverse range of religious, spiritual and therapeutic bodies, some of which meet to only a limited degree the criteria which sociologists have sought to establish for a more rigorous use of the term.

Some commentators have taken as a *sine qua non* of cults the presence of a charismatic leader (*see* CHARISMATIC MOVEMENTS). Whilst such leadership is certainly sometimes evident in movements that are, on other criteria, appropriately designated as cults, not all cults possess such leadership. Some are relatively impersonal systems of spiritual practice (such as Rosicrucianism and Wicca) in which no clear overall leadership pattern prevails. When a charismatic leader does emerge, it is often the case that he (or she) may come to insist on a pattern of exclusive allegiance and epistemological authoritarianism that is more characteristic of the sect.

Obviously, not all among the highly diverse contemporary examples of spiritual bodies readily or neatly fit into the categories employed by sociologists, and inevitably some movements will at times be referred to in different ways. (It is only thirty years since a reputable theologian in a much respected work on Christian Science, MORMONISM, the Seventh-day ADVENTISTS and Jehovah's Witnesses, all of which sociologists would instantly identify as sects, entitled his study, *The Four Major Cults*.) The attempt of sociologists to clarify the term, and to liberate it from the derogatory implications which it often carries both in common usage and sometimes as used by theologians, has, as yet, had only limited success.

Since the early 1960s, hundreds of new religions have emerged in Western countries, to leave unmentioned the prolific spawning grounds in contexts as diverse as those of South Africa and Japan. Sociologists have generally employed the cumbersome term 'NEW RELIGIOUS MOVEMENTS' to categorize them, in an effort to avoid the negative connotations popularly attached to the term 'cults', as well as to avoid the difficulty created by the absence of a stable definition.

Barker, E. (1989) *New Religious Movements: A Practical Introduction*. London: HMSO.

Beckford, J.A. (1985) *Cult Controversies*, London: Tavistock.

Bromley, D.G. and Hadden, J.K. (eds)(1993) *Religion and the Social Order*, vol. 3: *The Handbook on Cults and Sects in America*, Greenwich, CT: JAI Press.

Bromley D.G. and Hammond, P.E. (eds) (1987) *The Future of New Religious Movements*, Macon, GA: Mercer University Press.

Campbell, C. (1972) 'The cult, the cultic milieu, and secularization', *A Sociological Yearbook of Religion in Britain 5*: 119–36.

Wach, J. (1944) *The Sociology of Religion*, Chicago, IL: Chicago University Press.

Wallis, R. (1979) *Salvation and Protest*, London: Frances Pinter.

——(1984) *The Elementary Forms of the New Religious Life*, London: Routledge.

Wilson, B.R. (1973) *Magic and the Millennium*, London: Heinemann.

Wuthnow, R. (1978) *Experimentation in American Religion*, Berkeley, CA: University of California Press.

B.R. Wilson

CULTURE

In the contexts covered by the present work, the word culture has at least half a dozen distinct, though related, meanings, each successively narrower than the last. In its generic, broadest sense (where it is the concern of so-called philosophical anthropology), 'culture' denotes the whole realm of thought and behaviour whose patterns are not genetically but socially transmitted. Even when their behaviour is learnt, the social animals interact in more or less rigid, species-determined ways; what distinguishes human social behaviour is its almost infinite variability. Animal behaviour is usually explicable directly in terms of its biological function; *pace* sociobiology, however, it is by no means clear that the same is true of human behaviour.

The following are among the reasons for doubt. Much if not most human behaviour seems biologically superfluous. Eating and sexual activity, for instance, are hedged about by all kinds of non-nutritional and non-reproductive considerations. Again, human behaviour, unlike animal behaviour, is self-conscious, and usually has an independent, non-biological significance for the agent. Human beings give themselves articulate reasons for their actions, of which only the very simplest ('I am hungry', for example) are easily reducible to biological motives. *Per contra*, a supposedly 'unconscious' biological motive could never, by definition, constitute a reason for the agent. Finally, animal behaviour may plausibly be seen as the outcome of evolutionary adaptation to a relatively constant natural environment. Human beings, however, continuously modify both their social and their natural environments in ways whose consequences are unpredictable, so that, although their *capacity* to respond to changing circumstances is innate, their actual, specific responses cannot be, since no genetic programme containing them could ever have had time to evolve.

'Culture' in this generic sense is conventionally contrasted with *biological* 'nature' (the so-called 'nature/nurture' distinction). But that is not to say that culture is not 'natural'. In Aristotle's view, for example, the essence of culture is reason (in that culture consists of things done for reasons), and reason is as biologically 'natural' to humans as instinct is to animals. Culture is similarly contrasted with *physical* 'nature', even though, like biology itself, it must be presumed ultimately to be rooted in it. This distinction lies behind the idea (articulated most notably by Dilthey) that cultural and natural phenomena require for their explanation two quite different kinds of study.

We speak also of individual culture*s*, meaning thereby to distinguish them not from nature or from animal societies but (with the sociologist and social anthropologist) from each other. A culture is a particular human SOCIETY together with all its characteristic tools, possessions, ways and conceptions of life; the term, indeed, is often used interchangeably with 'society'.

This usage presupposes, first, that a culture is not a heap of unrelated phenomena but an organic whole, so that each feature of it, whatever its biological explanation, also has meaning in relation to the others. Second, each culture's particular *Gestalt*, or constellation of features (even when some of its features are found in other cultures, or common to all), makes it unique. While not positively necessitating it, both these presuppositions favour 'cultural relativism', the idea that cultures are to be assessed, not by any external standard, but only in relation to their own implicit or explicit aims. So too does the fact that a culture is not only a historic formation, but is also aware of being so, so that it conceives itself in terms of a past, a present and a future. In all these respects a culture resembles an individual, and thus possesses (and is thought by its members to possess) a quasi-personal identity.

There are two kinds of social-scientific 'functionalism', one supportive of cultural relativism, the other not. According to the first (typified, say, by E.E. Evans-Pritchard), every feature of a culture contributes to the maintenance of the whole as a self-conscious and self-contained system. The second, exemplified by such thinkers as A.R. Radcliffe-Brown and B. Malinowski, judges cultural features, and cultures as a whole, by their success or failure in meeting certain ulterior, universal or independently conceived goals such as happiness, utility, survival, etc.

If we subtract from a culture in the sense just given all its concrete physical and institutional components, we are left purely with its ideational aspects, and arrive at 'culture' as a property of a 'society' (its 'consciousness'), which is notionally separable from it. Culture in this sense effectively means 'common culture', i.e. whatever ideas, beliefs and values are generally shared by all members of a society, and are thus seen as definitive of it.

On one view, broadly Marxist or Marxist-influenced, the character of a culture in this sense can be seen as 'determined' by its material (non-ideational) 'base', whether that be economic (its structures of ownership and production) or political (its structures of power). On another view, for example Nietzsche's (at least in some of his writings), it is determined by the dominant racial, sexual or biological 'type'. On a third, Freud's, it is determined by unconscious extra-social forces within the individual or collective psyche, accordingly as those forces themselves have been socially repressed, indulged or sublimated.

Yet a culture as a distinct, coherent and self-sustaining system of beliefs is peculiarly difficult to 'explain' in this epiphenomenal fashion, since it seems to those immersed in it to need no explanation, being self-evidently 'natural' and 'true'. It is not clear how legitimately one may substitute the observer's perspective for the believer's, since to ignore the believer's perspective is effectively to remove from the thing to be explained its most essential feature. On the other hand, to say that a belief can be 'understood' only by its believers opens the door to, and justifies, almost any kind of superstition or absurdity. Dilthey and Weber recommended a kind of imaginative empathy, whereby the observer projects himself into beliefs he does not necessarily share, but unfortunately this so-called *Verstehen* is more easily practised than defined.

The word 'culture' (it will be convenient to add) is often used to mean 'subculture', as in 'youth culture', 'regional culture', 'middle class culture'. Sometimes this usage relates to a whole complex of material, practical and ideational phenomena, at other times to IDEOLOGY alone. Such a culture is not fully autonomous since it is defined, and defines itself, by reference to the wider culture surrounding it.

More circumscribed still than culture in the senses so far given are those 'cultures' pertaining solely to leisure, or all that Aristotle understood by *scholē*. One such, 'high' culture, often goes by the name of 'culture' alone. High culture, popular culture and their subdivisions are those elements of a total culture which transcend its explicitly practical, utilitarian or survival-related concerns. (The latter may well include much of its morality and religion.) *Scholē* is the sphere of purely spontaneous or 'useless' activities, and the ideas, material objects and institutions associated with them. 'Useless', of course, does not mean worthless, since an end in itself is both useless by definition and the underlying source of value in all those 'useful' things (e.g. work) necessary or instrumental to its realization.

Culture in this sense comprises SPORT, entertainment and recreation ('popular culture'); the world of liberal intellect (i.e. the cultivation of knowledge for its own sake); and the arts and the 'higher' aesthetic realm generally ('high culture'). (The last two categories show a substantial overlap, in practice if not in theory.) It may be noted, furthermore, that if such pursuits are considered merely as a rehearsal for work, or a necessary relief from it (the light in which Mill in his *Autobiography* regarded Wordsworth's poetry), they remain essentially utilitarian; that despite their 'uselessness', many of them demand a high degree of effort, skill and dedication; and also that, although in recognition of their 'private' and superficially unserious character they are considered to lie for the most part outside the public jurisdiction, they are frequently governed by an internal ethic of great severity.

Many thinkers, Ruskin and William Morris for example, have acknowledged the importance of leisure, in recommending that work, or the labour necessary for physical sustenance, should also as far as possible seem worth performing for its own sake (as in crafts, the applied arts and the liberal professions). To that extent its 'real' value will be wholly independent of its market or exchange value. The intuition is that a person's personality, fulfilment and self-respect are most deeply bound up with his or her voluntary pursuits. This is perhaps why, in gregarious activities of the kind, the chief penalty for 'unethical' behaviour (as in the professions) is disgrace.

Narrowest of all, at least from the point of the number of its representatives, is 'high' culture, which, as already noted, is an important subclass of leisure culture. High culture is peculiar in that, although at least *de facto* a minority preserve, it aspires to more than subcultural status, implicitly pretending to speak for culture as a whole. Is it thus nothing more than the ideology of a *political* élite, designed to consolidate that élite's dominance, either by advertising or by concealing it?

This question will be considered shortly. Meanwhile, the following things seem generally to be true of high culture. To have acquired it is a personal accomplishment, often accompanied by a certain social grace. It is a quality more of taste and sensibility than of intellect, though it presupposes a fairly high degree of intelligence, as it does also of aptitude and motivation. It requires an EDUCATION or apprenticeship, formal or informal, over and above that necessary simply for ordinary unreflective membership of society. *Qua* education, it is never complete, and also (like *scholē* generally) has no goal other than itself. High culture is an object of esteem, and more rarely of resentment, among those who do not possess it, when they are not simply indifferent. Finally, though high culture is unavoidably local in its immediate origins, and has often (particularly in music) shown a self-consciously nationalist, ethnic or 'popular' tendency, it is generally outward-looking and open to cosmopolitan influence. The two things are not incompatible. For example, far from despising his foreign counterparts, a 'nationalist' composer is quite likely to admire them for pursuing, in their different ways and traditions, the same things as himself.

Large claims have been made for high culture, particularly since the Romantic period and the rise, during the eighteenth century, of the discipline of aesthetics. High culture, or more specifically art, has been thought to provide the intimations of unity, value and meaning in experience which were once provided by religion, and are now threatened by the 'disenchanted' perspective of science. (The term 'disenchantment' was first used in this connection by Schiller, and has entered sociological discourse through Weber, who thought disenchantment the essence of MODERNITY.)

Aesthetic experience, indeed, whether of ART or of nature, may actually be 'superior' to religion, in the sense that, not being propositional, it is immune to refutation. It involves no substantive claims to the effect that, contrary to appearances or expectation, such-and-such happened or is the case (i.e. is revealed truth). In short, aesthetic experience does not depend on belief. At the most it depends, at least where art is concerned, on Coleridge's 'willing suspension of disbelief'. It is not a belief as to fact, but a fact itself. It is not enunciated, but simply enacted and confirmed in the subject's consciousness. Its affinity is not with doctrine but, despite its 'high' designation, with everyday, unreflective cultural experience.

Christian thinkers such as Newman and Eliot have fired impressive broadsides at the essentially pagan (and largely Aristotelian) idea that high culture – art and philosophy, in effect – suffices fully to realize its devotees' human *telos*. The reason is obvious, namely that, if true, the notion must make Christian belief superfluous. The problem of 'belief' seems not to arise in less rationalistic or intellectual religions such as Hinduism, Confucianism, Shinto and the largely civic cults of ancient Greece and Rome. There – and, one might almost add, in medieval popular Christianity too – belief is virtually indistinguishable from practice, i.e. from RITUAL, routine observance, *pietas*, and even ordinary virtue and moral conduct (as those are locally understood). No formal subscription to any definite schedule of articles is required. The consequence is to invest everyday culture with a more numinous, less 'disenchanted' quality than it will display under some more modern, self-consciously theological version of Christianity, where positive belief is likely to be comparatively scarce, arduous, intense and (perhaps) otherworldly.

Matthew Arnold claimed that, despite its disengagement from the vulgarities of practice (as typified largely by government and commerce), high culture nevertheless served an important practical end. The 'cultivated' outlook – sensitive, tentative, educated, scrupulous, empirical – not only issues in 'gentlemanly' behaviour (i.e. minimizes social friction) but also moderates the dogmatism and self-confident ignorance which would otherwise wholly monopolize the worlds of religion, morals and politics.

It might seem as though Arnold were opposing high culture to both common and popular culture (he has certainly often been accused of aestheticism). It is true that high culture is and must be opposed to (complacent) ignorance, crudity and bad taste. But, in a healthy society, so also ought common and popular culture to be. There is no intrinsic conflict between high and popular culture since, though both belong to *scholē*, their purposes in general are different.

It should be noted, however, that many of high culture's most prized possessions – Dickens and Verdi, for example – have also, from the beginning, displayed an enduring 'popular' appeal. The reason, no doubt, is that so-called high culture (when it is not mere aestheticism) is actually an imaginative reworking, and a non-utilitarian JUSTIFICATION of the common culture's deepest, most serious and most definitively 'human' purposes. A culture lacking those things would be 'Philistine', i.e. deficient in high culture and hostile to it, for the reason that it would lack high culture's vernacular roots.

The following observations may suffice to confirm the interdependence of high and common culture. In itself, high culture is the property of no particular socio-economic class. Its representatives are quite literally 'in a class of their own', one open to anybody appropriately qualified, and conferring no *ex officio* membership upon the rich, the powerful or the well-born. Finally, the suppression, by former Communist regimes, of genuine (as opposed to 'official') high culture merely increased the esteem in which it was held by educated and uneducated alike. It became the voice of an underground, but still living, common culture. This example ought finally to scotch the once fashionable 'New Left' contention that culture generally, but particularly high culture, is merely and always the servant of 'ruling class' interests.

In modified form, the latter idea has recently resurfaced in debates concerning the literary canon. In keeping with its name (which means JUDGEMENT), criticism has traditionally ascribed greater value to some works than to others. Opponents of the alleged 'canon' thereby created frequently stigmatize it as both elitist and Eurocentric (to say nothing of sexist, racist, etc.). The charge is so patently absurd as to call its very sincerity into doubt. For the greatest high cultural value has almost invariably been accorded to works of 'universal' import, i.e. to those (European or otherwise) with the widest observable cross-cultural and trans-historical appeal. The idea was that such works, however parochial their fictional setting or actual provenance, must somehow speak to, and for, 'human nature' at large.

Two further points deserve note. First, apart from that of ends-in-themselves (about which more shortly), values are comparative. Most things valued, consequently, show at least some disposition to group themselves into an incipient canon. Some opponents of the supposed literary canon, anti-Eurocentrists and the like, must presumably agree, since they have an 'alternative' canon on offer. What they would contest is that any canon, and any values, can be other than fundamentally political. In their view, aesthetic or literary values are an ideological illusion, designed to entrench political hierarchy at the very heart of culture, and to do so the more effectively by concealing their true (conservative) origin and purpose. It follows that 'subversion' must be the order of the day.

What is not, as a rule, disclosed is why subversion is politically preferable to establishment (which after all includes opposition); how, other than in its subversiveness, the 'alternative' canon is superior; and why, once aesthetic 'AUTONOMY' has been exposed as a sham, one should continue to wage proxy political war at the aesthetic level at all (where the alternative canon is bound to be at a disadvantage). Further, if art and culture are no more than POLITICS in disguise, why have they survived where politics are permitted, and disguises are therefore unnecessary?

Others reject canons and canonicity *per se*, and with them any notion of objective or quasi-objective value. The result, as in the radical post-structuralist Derrida, is an extreme subjectivist relativism (*see* DECONSTRUCTION). Yet it is impossible seriously to advance any position, including the last-mentioned, without implicitly claiming for it a certain objective value. Hence it appears that extreme relativism, like extreme scepticism, is self-contradictory and can only be entertained – as Derrida in fact entertains it – as a kind of joke. There is thus no reason why, if it cannot be advanced seriously, anyone should be obliged to take it seriously.

Second, aesthetic judgements do not necessarily entail a formal canon. Although they aspire to objectivity, they are neither made, nor validated, by reference to any ideal and inflexible standard of perfection, since none such exists. (If it did, artistic change and development would be neither visible nor possible, while criticism would consist entirely in the mechanical application of rules.) Like people and cultures, works of art may be prized precisely for their uniqueness and individuality, which is to say, for their incomparability. (And they are often virtually incomparable anyway, because of differences in genre, medium, period, etc.)

In which case, they cannot be ranked in any absolute hierarchy. Shakespeare may reasonably be rated above his contemporary and fellow-dramatist Webster in the areas in which they invite comparison. But this is not to derogate from Webster's own idiosyncratic, if lesser, achievement, nor to allege that Shakespeare somehow makes Webster superfluous. Indeed, although it is clearly absurd, except in some very abstract or formal respects, to put *Batman* and Shakespeare (along with their respective cultural 'kinds') on a level, it is certainly not unreasonable to allow even to *Batman* its characteristic uses and merits.

The implications of the controversy for the scriptural canon are not altogether clear. A scriptural canon can easily be seen as an instrument of political control since, unlike art and literature, it both claims divine AUTHORITY (not to say authorship) and lays down an explicit rule of life. Thus any GOVERNMENT which can command a monopoly of scripture and scriptural interpretation (especially if it can do so unnoticed) has its legitimation problems solved for as long as its subjects continue to believe in scripture. At the same time, however, scriptural religion, like both high and common culture, has often found itself radically opposed to the temporal power. (This reflection will hardly weigh with those who object to all authority, spiritual and temporal alike.)

As suggested above, literary values not only can but do survive in the absence of any formal canon. Where scripture is concerned, however, what counts is not its aesthetic worth (which may be minimal, and is always irrelevant), but its authenticity, i.e. whether it is, or is not, the revealed Word of God. First formalized at the Council of Laodicea (363), the Christian canon emerged more or less by custom and consensus out of three centuries of religious practice, and has continued to be modified.

In this respect it resembles a literary tradition. But to challenge the very idea of a scriptural canon is to challenge the whole concept of 'scripture' as such, and thus any religion based on it. It seems unlikely that a scriptural religion, once the authenticity of its scriptures had been questioned to destruction, could simply be resolved back once more into its original unrationalized cultus. On the other hand, since a text's divine inspiration must ultimately be an article of faith, and as such independent of empirical proof or disproof, the scriptural canon seems no more vulnerable today than religion as a whole, or than any of its other fideistic components.

Unlike ordinary truths, religious 'truths' are not matters of knowledge (*see* TRUTH). They are definable, rather, as those things, such as the written Word of God, in which people really and fundamentally believe. On the other hand, people believe in them precisely because they are 'true'. belief is a self-sustaining system in just the same way as, according to Evans–Pritchard, a culture is, and, more dubiously, as language is alleged to be by structuralists and their successors. It follows that to defend it, as to embrace it, inevitably involves a certain circularity.

Arnold, Matthew (1869) *Culture and Anarchy*, ed. J. Dover Wilson, Cambridge: Cambridge University Press, 1963.

Dilthey, Wilhelm (1976) *Dilthey: Selected Writings*, ed. H.P. Rickman, Cambridge: Cambridge University Press.

Eliot, T.S. (1948) *Notes Towards the Definition of Culture*, London: Faber & Faber.

——(1982) *The Idea of a Christian Society* (1939) *and Other Writings*, London: Faber & Faber.

Hatch, Elvin (1973) *Theories of Man and Culture*, New York: Columbia University Press.

Kroeber, A.L. (1952) *The Nature of Culture*, Chicago,

IL: University of Chicago Press (especially Section I, 'Theory of Culture').

Scruton, Roger (1983) 'Emotion and culture', in *The Aesthetic Understanding*, London: Methuen.

——(1990) 'Aesthetic experience and culture', in *The Philosopher on Dover Beach*, Manchester: Carcanet.

Williams, Raymond (1966) *Culture and Society 1780–1950*, Harmondsworth: Penguin.

Wilson, Bryan R. (ed.) (1970) *Rationality*, Oxford: Basil Blackwell.

Robert Grant

DEATH

Death, the cessation of life, is a topic that it raises almost innumerable philosophical, theological and social questions. Closely associated with the notion of death – usually restricted to human death – is that of immortality, which, in turn, is usually understood as the immortality of the human SOUL. As soon as we discuss immortality, we are confronted with questions concerning the nature of such an immortal SOUL. Is it divisible? How is it related to the (mortal) body. Stating the problem in this fashion seems to demand that we have a dualistic conception of human being as one creature composed of both body and soul. If so then is the body really the prison of the soul as Plato said? Or is the material body influenced by an immaterial mind as Descartes insisted and, if so, how does this influence take place? Thus, the notion of death raises questions concerning the nature of a human being, and what the relation is between the brain and what we might call the mind or perhaps the spirit or soul.

The notion of death raises ethical problems concerning how we ought to live our life. This would hold true whether there is or is not a possibility that at death we will be held responsible for our actions. The denial of an afterlife and thus the denial of rewards and punishments for our behaviour during this life does not solve ethical problems. ABORTION is still a controversial question regardless of one's position concerning immortality, as is EUTHANASIA. The Hemlock Society and the suicide machine of Dr Kevorkian, dubbed by some Dr Death, has aroused a great deal of comment, both pro and con. Similarly, the morality of the death penalty (see CAPITAL PUNISHMENT) is debated, especially in the USA which seems to be opposing a worldwide trend in the reinstatement of this punishment.

SUICIDE is another problem closely associated with the notion of death. The morality of suicide has been discussed since the ancients. Plato, for example, maintained that the gods forbid us to kill ourselves since we are their property and they decide when our life is to end, not us. Christians also tended, at certain periods at least, to frown upon suicide for much the same reasons, while the Stoics saw suicide as a blessed relief from useless suffering. 'Eternal law', says Seneca, 'has never been more generous than in affording us so many exits from life . . .' (Seneca 1958: 204).

Yet another ethical problem associated with death is that of WAR. If death is something that is not desirable, then questions about the possibility of a just war must also be investigated. In discussing war, it is common to ask questions about the behaviour of the combatants. Similarly, questions concerning the legitimacy of killing non-combatants, such as women and children, the use of torture and so forth are also raised.

The contemplation or awareness of our own death has been discussed not only by recent philosophers such as Heidegger and Sartre but throughout the history of thought. According to some thinkers the inevitability of death gives our life meaning, while others have held that death makes life meaningless or absurd. Philosophers have also asked whether we can experience our own death and how we experience the death of the 'other'. For example, Augustine tells us how the death of a friend diminishes his own life and raises the possibility of his own death: 'Wherever I looked, I saw only death' (Augustine 1961: 76 [IV, 4, 9]). On the other hand, Lucretius and Epicurus see death as something completely outside of life. Epicurus says, 'Death . . . is nothing to us, seeing that when we are, death is not come, and, when death is come, we are not' (Epicurus 1925: 651 [X, 125]).

In recent times we have been forced to redefine the moment of death. No longer can we simply say that a person is dead when his or her heart stops for there are now machines which can perform the functions of the heart. At present in the US death is described in terms of the absence of brain waves. In the UK the criterion of brain stem death is used instead. The development of sophisticated technology has also raised a number of ethical problems since not only is it now possible to save the lives of people who in the past would have died, but in some cases technology has allowed people to continue to live in a state of coma for months and even years. Karen Ann Quinlan lived for months on life-support systems and then survived for another nine years in a coma being fed artificially (*see also* EUTHANASIA). A more recent case receiving attention concerned an attempt in Germany to keep a brain-dead pregnant woman alive in the hope that she would be able to give birth to a healthy child.

So far, all the problems we have discussed have involved human death, but if philosophy involves drawing lines and discussing the nature and boundaries of concepts, one must ask why we limit the notion of death to our own death since it is quite clear that animals die as do plants, for both plants and animals are living things. With the development of ethology, many people have asked if animals other than human animals have an awareness of death. For instance, elephants have been observed burying dead elephants: they cover them with soil and branches. They 'fondle and examine' the bones and tusks of dead elephants (Moss 1982: 33). It has also been observed that elephants will walk on either side of a wounded or sick elephant as if to support him; bulls have been seen lifting and carrying off another wounded bull (ibid.). Do they, perhaps, realize that the sheer weight of a fallen elephant can quickly cause his lungs to collapse and thus cause death? Do they have an awareness of death? The same question can be asked not only about dolphins since they also have been known to support the body of a sick dolphin or even a drowning person, but also about those trained chimpanzees that can distinguish between photographs of animate and inanimate objects. Do they have some conception of life and thus of death? There is experimental evidence to suggest that chimpanzees have the ability to recognize themselves in a mirror. Does such an ability mean that they are self-conscious and does this in turn mean that they might have a sense of their own end or death? From an integrationist perspective such an idea makes sense.

Rather than attempt to answer even some of these questions, all of which have a long and complex history, I would prefer to discuss death from another perspective. Ferrater Moras (*Being and Death: An Outline of Integrationist Philosophy*) uses the idea of death, using it as a kind of leitmotif to explain his own philosophy. He says:

> As to the problem of death, 'integrationism' is meant to designate a point of view according to which we should not be allowed to confine 'death' to any privileged area of reality but only to project whatever we can say about this area to the whole of reality. What Aristotle claimed of Being, we can claim of death, namely, that 'it can be said in many ways.' Thus, I wish to maintain that, although every existing entity ceases to be, and hence in a manner of speaking 'dies,' only certain entities actually 'die' without ever 'ceasing to be.' In fine, the continuum of reality includes different types of 'mortality.'
> (Ferrater Mora 1965: 13)

This approach leads Mora to discuss death in inorganic nature, death in organic nature, human death, and survival and immortality.

While it sounds strange to talk about death in inorganic reality, we can easily talk about such realities in terms of elements and structures, and if we can do that, we can talk about change and the disappearance of structure and its ceasing. Mora maintains that reality can be described by means of two limiting concepts, such as being and meaning, and furthermore, what is described will be a continuum. His view of this continuum is one in which

> we can speak of a progression of the capacity to cease until the level of death is attained. Everything that ceases participates in death, while at the same time death is not entirely comprehensible unless we keep in mind the general and universal phenomenon of cessation to which it is indissolubly attached.
> (ibid.: 69)

To speak otherwise would be to consider inorganic nature as something utterly different from, and alien to, humans. It would cut humans off from nature, and present us with a troublesome dualism. Perhaps we can understand this continuum if we consider the physical nature of a human being for, although we tend to forget it, we can describe ourselves in purely physical terms as being two-thirds water, which in turn is made up of hydrogen and oxygen, which is made up of atoms composed of electrons and protons and so on. Thus, human physical death can be described not only in terms of emotions and experiences but also in terms of disease, in terms of cells, the exchange of chemicals through cell membranes, and so on. Ferrater Mora is not a reductionist; he is not asserting that as physical beings we are reduced to nothing more than the action of our physical components. Rather, he is claiming that, as physical beings, we are linked to inorganic nature, although we are not reduced to it.

It is perhaps much easier to compare human death to death in the organic world for in the death of animals, at least the so-called higher animals, we can recognize certain similarities with our own ageing and death. Many of us have watched a favourite companion animal grow old: a dog's muzzle will turn white just as our hair does. The ageing animal is less playful, less active and so on. Even the process of dying is similar: a favourite cat gets breast cancer and dies as the disease progresses.

If through Darwin we have learned of the continuity of living creatures, through Ferrater Mora's thought we can also understand dying as a kind of continuity. The continuum of which the latter speaks is more inclusive than that of Darwin since it encompasses the whole of reality, including simple structures, while the great biologist primarily concerned himself with what Richard Dawkins called 'complicated things', namely, living creatures (Dawkins 1986: 1). If these descriptions of ceasing to be and death lead us to conclude that there is a continuum of reality, then we can ask if this continuum has any moral implications in much the same way as did James Rachels in *Created from Animals: The Moral Implications of Darwinism* (1990).

In that book, Rachels explained that traditional morality depends on the belief that humankind is special, unique, more important or has a higher value than any other animal. According to Rachels,

Darwinism undermines both the idea that man is made in the image of God and the idea that man is a uniquely rational being. Furthermore, if Darwinism is correct, it is unlikely that any other support for the idea of human dignity will be found. The idea of human dignity turns out, therefore, to be the moral effluvium of a discredited metaphysics.

(Rachels 1990: 5)

Although Ferrater Mora provides a broader philosophical or ontological basis for understanding Darwin, the ideas of both thinkers cause us to reject the notion of humanity as special, as cut off from what Ferrater Mora calls the organic world. The analogy can be carried further. We talk of the death of planets, the death of stars and even the death of the universe. From such a perspective human animals are not special, or not different 'in kind', but only different 'in degree'. Is it anything more than our might that permits us to put non-human animals in small cages, often for life, because we prefer their death from disease rather than our own. Is it not merely our power that allows us first to destroy predators and then to destroy prey on the grounds that the 'natural order' is already disturbed? Is it not a kind of concupiscence that allows us to raise animals under completely unnatural conditions and then to slaughter them for food? Rachels claims that we have to rethink our obligations to other living creatures (*see* ANIMAL RIGHTS). In re-thinking those obligations we have to bear in mind that death, like life, is part of a continuum that includes the whole of the universe.

Augustine (1961) *Confessions*, trans. R.S. Pine-Coffin, Baltimore, MD: Penguin Classics.
Dawkins, R. (1986) *The Blind Watchmaker: Why the Evidence of Evolution Reveals a Universe Without Design*, New York and London: W.W. Norton.
Epicurus (1925) in Diogenes Laertius, *Lives of Eminent Philosophers*, trans. R.D. Hicks, Cambridge, MA: Harvard University Press, Loeb Classical Library.
Ferrater Mora, J. (1965) *Being and Death: An Outline of Integrationist Philosophy*, Berkeley and Los Angeles, CA: University of California Press.
Heidegger, M. (1962) *Being and Time [Sein und Zeit]*, trans. J. Macquarrie and E. Robinson, New York and Evanston, IL: Harper & Row.
Lucretius (1951) *The Nature of the Universe*, trans. R.E. Latham, Baltimore, MD: Penguin Classics.

Moss, C. (1982) *Portraits in the Wild: Animal Behavior in East Africa*, 2nd edn, Chicago, IL: University of Chicago Press.

Plato (1961) 'Phaedo', in E. Hamilton and H. Cairns (eds) *The Collected Dialogues of Plato*, Princeton, NJ: Princeton University Press, Bollingen Series LXXI.

Pojman, L. (1992) *Life and Death: Grappling with the Moral Dilemma of Our Time*, Boston, MA, and London: James & Bartlett.

Premack, D. (1986) *Gavagai! or The Future History of the Animal Language Controversy*, Cambridge, MA: MIT Press.

Rachels, J. (1990) *Created from Animals: The Moral Implications of Darwinism*, Oxford: Oxford University Press.

Sartre, J.-P. (1956) *Being and Nothingness: An Essay on Phenomenological Ontology* [*L' être et le néant: essai d'ontologie phénoménologique*], trans. H. Barnes, New York: Philosophical Library.

Seneca (1958) 'Suicide', in *The Stoic Philosophy of Seneca: Essays and Letters*, New York: W.W. Norton.

Priscilla Cohn

DECONSTRUCTION

Deconstruction means to take apart or uncouple terms that have been taken to be coupled or structured together, to de-structure, to de-construct. Deconstruction contains great radical potential for it shows how what appears natural or given has been structured by tradition and shows how what appears natural and necessary is merely contingent. A primary opposition is that between speech and writing. The received view is that writing derives from speech but, it is argued, when this relation is deconstructed it appears as not necessary, and falsely inverted. The revelation of this inversion shows that the western tradition of thought is logocentric and falsely privileges the presence of God and man. Every structure, it is argued, contains within it the possibility of its own deconstruction, and the moment of structure for the western tradition of THEOLOGY, philosophy, ETHICS and SOCIETY is, poetically at least, best revealed as that point when Plato said to Adimantus in Book II of *The Republic* 'and how may we speak correctly of the gods', *theologia*. At that point he introduced theology into the world, the critical reflection and discourse upon something other-worldly. When he says that we may speak correctly of the gods he implies that there is a TRUTH about the gods that can be known to reason independently of language. That truth is the provenance of the philosopher, who in the metaphor of the cave given in Book VII turns around from the flickering shadows on the wall towards the light. The *periagoge*, the turning around, is the turn towards truth, a truth that can be known independently of the life in the shadows. In a third act Plato makes the philosophers the king and expels the poets from the Republic. In these three acts Plato set the scene for the western philosophical tradition, and for the rational part of the western theological tradition. Deconstruction calls that entire tradition into question by denying that there can be truth, even presence, outside of language, or that there is a reality other than the flickering shadows on the wall, and by returning the poets to the Republic and expelling the philosophers. Deconstruction is the most thorough going challenge to philosophy and to metaphysics, both of which are regarded as at an end. As the entire rational foundation of theology rests on the tradition of metaphysics and philosophy together with its sedimented concepts, arguments and methods, the deconstruction of philosophy is, also, the deconstruction and end of theology.

Deconstruction is usually associated with post-structuralist continental philosophy; it draws upon Nietzsche, Saussure, and Roland Barthes among others. Its best known representative is Jacques Derrida, but while formally recent, its roots are deep, as deep as the moment of the expulsion of the poets from the Republic. Deconstruction is a mid- to late twentieth-century phenomenon but it is no more than the return of the poets who have been biding their time for two and a half millennia and having returned, have returned with sufficient vigour to expel the philosophers and the theologians and reclaim the Republic. Such a dramatic reversal of tradition could not be placed with one or even a few people, it is rather a consequence of a reversal of several related features of western intellectual life. Prime among these are the death of the subject, the death of God and the linguistic turn.

To be a subject is to be in the world in a way that couples consciousness with that which is not conscious, for example, nature, objectivity. This mode of being is quite distinct from mythopoetic forms of life that do not take the world as an object distinct from themselves, as with, for example, Australian Aborigines or Ancient Egyptians. The break towards the distinction in consciousness between subject and object is embedded in the construction of nature, an event that can certainly be traced back to Thales and no doubt predates that. Even so, subjectivity and self were conceived as being dispersed as a form of inter-subjectivity in the tribe, household and polis. *Phrenes*, mind, is, in Ancient Greece, frequently referred to as located partly outside of the individual; as dispersed. That dispersion was collected and focused in the Christian idea of the PERSON, as made in the image of God, as standing before God as an individual, as seeking justification before God as an individual, not as a member of a tribe or household or polis or other form of group. The inward reflexivity present in Greek thought became radically reflexive (Taylor 1989), turning in on itself to produce an inward life centred on the 'I'. This 'I', expressed as an individual entity in St Augustine, became the single centre of consciousness in Descartes. Descartes in seeking certainty, in seeking a rational ground for incorrigible knowledge, found it in the contents of his consciousness, a consciousness that he regarded as transparent, clear all the way down. Incorrigibility had been placed firmly in individuality by St Augustine. Looking for certainty about his own existence he proclaimed that this was not something about which he could be mistaken, 'If I am mistaken I exist', he proclaimed in *The City of God*. If I think, argued Descartes, then I must be a thinking substance: '*cogito ergo sum*', 'I think, therefore I am'. The argument of course is deeply flawed; the fact that there is thinking does not warrant the existence of the singular 'I', and that 'I' cannot guarantee its transparency, indeed its transparency seems completely undercut by the possibility of self-deception. That one can deceive oneself is possible only against the idea of the self as having layers of being, hidden behind various guises and disguises.

Even the presence and placing of the veils is concealed from the inquiring self. In Kant the subject became the centre of the knowing universe and the centre of the moral universe. Against Hume, who thought the self a bundle of impressions, he argued that a merely passive self was impossible, knowledge was active, and experience ordered by the categories of the mind. Morality resided in autonomous action, unconditioned by any desire. The subject was complete, individual, and sovereign over their actions. As Kant put it, in *The Groundwork of the Metaphysics of Morals*, this was only an ideal, but it was a persuasive ideal, though also a problematic one. The Augustinian–Cartesian–Kantian subject was detached from the world as subject to object, as self against nature. For Descartes that there was a world outside of subjectivity was a certainty dependent upon the existence of God. If the certainty in God collapsed, the certainty of the world collapsed. For Kant, the world appeared as phenomena ordered by the categories of the mind. The difficulty here is how does one know that there is a world that matches the categories? Perhaps there are merely disordered, chaotic apperceptions, whose order is merely an apparency of the mind. Perhaps the apperceptions are merely properties of the mind and there is no world at all. Kant had no clear answer to this kind of difficulty. The relation between the mind and the world was, he said, 'a happy coincidence', an answer that, while not notable for its fulsomeness, is perhaps the best available given the basic perspective. That perspective is given by the *problematique* of the western philosophical and theological tradition. Once subjectivity was assumed as something individual and as something distinct from the world as object, the sceptical line of reasoning began. And scepticism can never answer its own questions. A premise of solipsism will never yield a successful argument to the conclusion that there are other people in the world. And the Platonic–Augustinian–Cartesian–Kantian tradition shifted from scepticism to solipsism; to the problem of other minds. How, it was asked, could one know the existence of other minds? And neither Descartes nor Kant had entirely satisfactory answers to that. For Descartes the solution rested on an argument to the existence of God, but if that failed, as it must, for there are no rational arguments to that conclusion, so other minds, other people, faded from reality and became mere appearances. For Hobbes, for Leibniz, for Hume and for Kant nothing outside of the individual mind could be certain, there was no certainty of an external world and no assurance of people in it. What began as an exercise in expelling the poets from the Republic ended with no one left in the Republic other than a lone, sceptical, and peculiarly autonomous, philosopher king.

If the rise of the subject culminated in the rise of *the* subject, an autonomous, sovereign and lone individual, the death of the subject was consequent upon the discovery that there were indeed others. The foundational insight is to be found in Rousseau's *Discourse on the Origin of Inequality*. Love of self, a natural and entirely healthy and necessary feeling, turned in social situations, Rousseau argued, into selfish love, *amour propre*, pride. The difference between the savage and the civilized man, he thought, was that 'whereas the savage lived within himself, civilized man lived without himself, in the eyes of others'. The argument for intersubjectivity found in embryonic form in Rousseau was developed more fully by Hegel. In the *Phenomenology of Spirit* Hegel attempted to show the grounds of consciousness and of subjectivity. Subjectivity, he maintained, developed only in interaction with others. To be conscious of oneself as a subject, as an individual being, did not exclude other minds; on the contrary, it required it. The assumption that one had subjectivity could be satisfied only against the presumption of other minds. If others were regarded as objects, as Cartesian beasts, then the respect shown to the self would be the respect shown by another that was mere object, or mere beast, or mere mechanism. To be regarded as a subject by an object was impossible if subjectivity and self-respect were to be maintained. Hence consciousness was always intersubjective. But if consciousness was intersubjective, then one could not consistently talk of the autonomous and sovereign subject; hence the beginning of the death of the subject.

Hegel's insight was followed throughout a

wide range of western thought. In the early part of the twentieth century the sociologist Max Weber argued for an ideal type of individual action that placed the understanding of the action on the meaning given to that action by the agent. In a devastating critique Alfred Schutz showed that the meaning of an action must always make reference ultimately to an intersubjective background, an agent's action was always an action in a matrix or web of understanding. In sociology and in anthropology it was shown that self-understandings were taken from others, the self was a mirror of others' perceptions of others, the 'I' was not the only way of self-regard, the 'me', also, perhaps even more crucial to self-understanding, was social, indicated the way in which one was regarded by others. But if the self and subjectivity was a social product, a construct, then the autonomous subject was problematic, perhaps even dead. That the autonomous subject had been a philosophical and social construct seemed to be born out by the discoveries of anthropology and history. Marcel Mauss showed how the concept of person was developed in the west through a particular and peculiar Christian embellishment of role concepts. Leo Strauss showed how totemic cultures managed without the regular use of proper names, and Clifford Geerz (1973) showed how proper names could be subsumed and hidden to the point of secrecy. Reference to the unique, fixed and constant self was clearly a western construct and a problematic and unsatisfactory one at that. The very terminology of the subject shows in its ambiguity its problematic status. A subject is the subject of consciousness, but the subject of consciousness is also subject to that consciousness, as prisoner, as subject rather than citizen. Perhaps the death of the subject brings the rise of the citizen self. In any case the notion is sufficiently problematic to cause speculation, in Jean Luc Nancy's peculiarly intriguing question, of 'Who comes after the subject?'

The death of the subject is linked to the death of God. The phrase is Nietzsche's. It is, perhaps, prophetic; it is clearly born of acute observation; it is remarkably insightful. Nietzsche observed the tendencies towards SECULARIZATION, the way in which God had disappeared from the practical lives of much of humanity, the way that in many cases, including many religious movements, God had been placed in the service of man. Feuerbach made a similar point, saying that God was a projection of human need, the product of ALIENATION. The insight was seized upon by Marx in his attempt to turn Hegel around. Hegel had started with the assumption of God as a self-positing being seeking absolute knowing. Human CULTURE was following that discovery, and western history was the medium through which Geist would express itself. In a very real sense western history was God-given. Marx took Feuerbach's claim that God was a projection of human need, understood as material and economic emmiseration, as alienation from world, from the objects of one's labour, from self and from others as one's species being. Religion, he argued, was 'the sigh of the oppressed, the heart of the heartless, the opium of the people'. To be emancipated required not freedom to WORSHIP as one pleased, but to be emancipated from religion. The end of alienation would itself end the psychological and material conditions in which the projection that was God had developed; it would lead, in Nietzsche's phrase, to the death of God. As intellectual arguments made against the rationalism and logocentrism of western philosophy these arguments are powerful, if not decisive. But set against the backdrop of a general decline in religious belief, the decline of religious AUTHORITY – indeed the decline of authority in general – and mere secularization, they gave intellectual weight to those willing to be persuaded or those wavering on the edge of religious disconviction.

Coupled with the death of the subject and the death of God is one of the most powerful and decisive shifts in intellectual understanding in the western tradition of thought: the linguistic turn. Its effects can hardly be overstated. The linguistic turn has no single source, it is a part of a general shift in western thought. It rests on a single and devastatingly simple observation: words, statements and terms in language refer to words, statements, terms and concepts in language. This seems so basic, so obvious, indeed almost so trite, that its revolutionary impact takes some grasping. It is this: if linguistic

terms refer to other linguistic terms then they do not refer to things in the world. If that is so, then language is not about the world at all, it is always and only about language. And truth is not based on correspondence to events, or states of affairs in the world. The assumptions underlying this remarkable claim, remarkable only for its late appearance in western intellectual life, comes from distinct sources, one philosophical, the other linguistic.

The philosophical problem arises from the attempt made in the early part of this century to give an account of the relation between language and the world. Language, it was argued, provided a picture of the world: the so-called picture theory of meaning. The theory is a descendent of nominalism, found in scholasticism, in Hobbes and in the Port Royale School, and lampooned to great effect in Jonathan Swift's *Gulliver's Travels*, where some of the characters, rather than speaking, carry large numbers of objects around with them and display the objects to each other to convey meaning. Nominalism runs into considerable difficulties over the problem of linguistic universals; general categories, for example colours. A colour is not a particular, in the way that 'this pencil' is a particular, hence the universal 'white' cannot be learnt by, e.g. pointing to 'this' white object. Indeed, as Wittgenstein pointed out in a devastating critique of his early philosophy, ostensive definition, definition by pointing to objects, is always ambiguous. The action of pointing as an ostensive definition is only understood in an already existing linguistic framework. That framework is obtained in the practice of the language, hence the meaning of a word is not given by the object to which it apparently refers but by its use. But if it is given by its use then does it refer to the world at all, or merely to other terms, in what Wittgenstein called the 'language game'? Games, as is well known, have rules that constitute and regulate them, but the rules are entirely arbitrary; play is just play and a game to someone who does not understand its rules is incomprehensible. The attempt to test the truth of propositions against events in the world always founders on an infinite regress. Consider the following example given by Tarski. How does one test the claim that the 'snow is white'. 'The proposition the "snow is white" is true if and only if the "snow is white".' But notice the double quotation marks around the proposition that incorporates the truth claim. That truth claim is contained in a linguistic formulation. And there is no way out of this, for any attempt to widen the claim merely refers to a larger linguistic formulation. Put another way: 'everything is in quotation marks'.

In linguistics the same kind of observation was made by Saussure. Saussure distinguishes between *parole*, the speech act or utterance, and *la langue* the matrix or language relations from which the speech act is drawn. Language depends upon a 'signifier', the word or other linguistic token, and the 'signified', the concept, but there is no fixed, clear or given link between the signifier and the signified, for the sign is arbitrary. Meaning is obtained from the differential relations in the matrix of language, and not from some clear, fixed and non-arbitrary relation with an objective world, a world distinct from the subject. While the basic observations that Saussure made are now common, if not universal, intellectual currency, there are two features about it that fed directly into deconstruction. First it is synchronic, second it privileges speech. Saussure took it that the science of semiotics could decode linguistic systems understood synchronically, across space. This fixed the structure of language by eliminating its diachronic dimension and he took it that speech preceded writing.

The first of these observations, that language can be understood synchronically, is characteristic of structuralism in that it fixes a system at a point in time, sets up a totality and closes it to future possibilities. Indeed such totalities are impossible, for if meaning is given in the fluid movement of a linguistic matrix then that matrix can never contain the diversity of possible meanings. Structuralism founders on its own restrictive contradictions. The second observation that speech is the precursor to language is at the heart of western philosophy and theology. And it is this presumption as well as the possibility of closure that Derrida deconstructs. Not only had Plato expelled the poets from the Republic he had also shown a marked dislike

for the introduction of writing. Speech, dialogue, was privileged, and writing given second place. The word came first. This logocentrism was also placed at the heart of western Christianity. When John wrote, 'In the beginning was the word (*logos*) and the word (*logos*) was with God and the word (*logos*) was God' (John 1:1), he made it clear that western Christianity was to follow Plato's logocentric approach to reason. But what is a word without the language on which to draw, without the linguistic matrix within which it makes sense? Wittgenstein had argued that a private language was impossible. The development of a private language would depend on consistency of use. This would depend on memory, on an accurate recall of which word had been used in which way or which concept that it stood for. No one could be sure they could do that. Nor could the problem be solved by setting down the language as written signs or tokens for it would require an unerring memory to recall the relation between the written token, the spoken word, and the concept. Hence the impossibility of a private language. A language could, however, be public, intersubjective, for here the collective and shared experience would provide a foundation for mutual self-correction. The same point can be found in Saussure's writing, although he did not grasp the implication of his own work here. If meaning is taken through difference, then the language is always prior to the speech act on which that act draws. In other words, Plato and St John notwithstanding, it is not the word that comes first, but the matrix from which the word is drawn. As Derrida has it, the western tradition that has privileged the spoken word over writing rests on an error at its very roots, for writing is prior to speech. The implications of this are, if correct, clear; Plato's dislike of writing, his preference for speech, resulted in the logocentrism that led to the rise of the subject with all that followed. Yet it was a foundation that was flawed, for in the beginning was *not* the word – it was the text.

But the attack does not stop there. Structuralism with its emphasis on synchronicity, closure and totality presents meaning as fixed. But meaning is not only the consequence of difference in the matrix of language, it is also never final, but always in the future, always deferred. By playing on the notions of difference and deferment Derrida reaches what he calls *différance*: a deferment that leaves meaning open and makes closed meaning systems impossible.

If language is prior to speech, then the tradition that places the presence of the speaker prior to that which is spoken is mistaken. Hence the subject is a fiction of a flawed tradition. But if closed meaning systems are impossible, then not only is the subject challenged, so is the text. The implications of this for that part of theology that rests on a textual study of the Bible as a received and closed body of work are clear. At its starkest there is no such received and closed body of work; *The* Bible does not exist, for its boundaries are blurred to a point that disrupts the text, turning critical exegesis merely into a series of encounters with sedimented aspects of always translated and never recovered prose. The relation between the reader and the text is not that between subject and object for that distinction is untenable, it is instead an internal relation between the reader and the text. But who is the reader and what is the text? If the boundaries of the text are blurred, so are the boundaries of the reader. Logocentrism had privileged the subject, in this case the reader, but the collapse of logocentrism trampled on, indeed danced on the grave of an already dead subject. Who then is the reader? Certainly not a fixed, static subject with clear boundaries, an unproblematic sovereign 'I'. For Jean Luc Nancy the question provided by the death of the subject was 'Who comes after the Subject?'. Here the question is twofold, 'What comes after the text and who comes after the reader?'

The challenge to traditional biblical scholarship is clear, but the issues go deeper than those of the academy. Certainly deconstruction offers challenges to traditional biblical scholarship, and if even a small part of the arguments raised by deconstruction are accepted the challenge to FUNDAMENTALISM is so great as to place that position in serious intellectual difficulty. But these are, ultimately, academic problems; the challenges, however, go deeper than those of mere exegesis, interesting and exhilarating as that might be. Christianity rests on a concept that the PERSON is a single individual whose actions are autonomous and who will be justified as an individual not as a member of a group. Deconstruction challenges this very understanding of subjectivity and the self, for who is it that is to be justified (*see* SOUL)? Who is it that is to stand before God and explain themselves? How can a dispersed, let alone a dead subject seek justification? Yet further difficulties arise. If logocentrism, as Plato and St John had it, is impossible, rests on an error born of a distaste for that which is new, then how can there be a monotheistic God? For if the beginning is not with the word (*logos*) but with *la langue* then there can be no God although there may be many, admittedly deconstructed, gods.

In the radically deconstructed world, there is no reality other than the flickering shadows of the cave. There is no truth to be sought and no autonomous life to be led. For radical deconstruction there are no certainties and no necessities, for everything is contingent. Our mode of being is mere happenstance, and one compounded on the sedimented errors of times long past. If the more extreme claims of deconstruction are correct then life has no meaning, it is nothing; radical deconstruction is NIHILISM taken to its extreme limits. How then should it be regarded? First, it seems clear enough that the metaphysical realism that lay at the heart of the western tradition of thought is insupportable. Generations of argument from Aristotle onward have shown that the idea of an independent and real world is one that is difficult to sustain. REALISM is, at most, what Putnam has called internal realism, it relates observer and observed internally not as separate entities. As Clarke has shown, the world is always known under descriptions, under concepts, *haecittas*, and there is no world independent of the descriptions given of it that can be used to establish some greater truth. It follows that, while the more extreme claims of deconstruction might be set aside, indeed that 'not to philosophize' is, paradoxically and inescapably, 'still to philosophize' (Levinas), it is clear that there is no biblical text independent of the encounter with the text; at the very least the text and the reader stand in an internal relation to each other. It also seems evident that the western tradition of thought is the product of merely contingent circumstances.

When that tradition is examined at its roots, the very errors and arrogances, political and intellectual manoeuvrings and sheer bad faith that sometimes went into the development of one line of thought rather than another are evident. When the tradition is deconstructed by challenging its foundations on its own terms, from within, then its central presuppositions are exploded. Of course that explosion does not of itself warrant the conclusion that it is false, but it does stretch credibility, and it certainly stretches credibility to privilege it over other traditions, equally contingent, if different.

This difference, this otherness of custom, practice, culture, institution, religion, ideology, belief, ethics, politics and theological equivalences, is challenging, for it admits otherness, admits particularism, and admits that Christian universalism is no more than a hegemonic formation. The alternative is eschatological necessity, the view that God really did write western history, and that western history, *qua* Hegel, represents world history. All other cultures, all other particularities, are subsumed to western eschatology and its hegemonic drive. But not only is that ESCHATOLOGY successfully deconstructed, it also makes all human life meaningless. If the life falls outside the eschatological path, then it is worthless, if the life falls within the eschatological path then its present meaning is deferred in favour of some future meaning. It is paradoxical that this very criticism levelled against Marxist eschatology was ignored by those professing an alternative, if other-worldly, eschatology.

These lessons, if built into western thought and practice, have several intriguing and challenging consequences. First, ethical theory and practice must be built not upon the assumption of universalistic premises of dubious value. It must instead deal with otherness, with alterity, with difference and the respect for difference. Second, there does seem good reason to think that the weaker, if not stronger, consequences of deconstruction lead to a support for a liberal politics of some kind. Liberality is supportive of alternatives in a way that other forms of political life have not, hitherto, been. But, as Rorty has pointed out, there is no way in which liberal politics can be justified on grounds external to

itself and its tradition; there is no final truth to liberal politics, it just is *our* tradition, it just is the way *we* do things. We justify our liberal attitudes by affirming what we already have, not by seeking grand metaphysical truths on which to rest, or modify, our current practices. Third, western theology can no longer justify the making of world-historical claims, and can no longer justify deep eschatology. Indeed it becomes impossible to talk of western theology at all, for that assumes a unity of thought and outlook inconsistent with the pluralism generated by the deconstruction of 'tradition'. If theology is to survive at all, it will survive only as *theologies*, as a multitude of competing voices in an increasingly noisy world.

Finally the challenges generated by a weak deconstruction of our thought are twofold. First, we can accept the nihilist consequences and fall into despair, dismay, angst and misery or second, we can embrace the possibilities generated and rise to the challenge. To be freed from the tradition, to have the hold of the past weakened, may be frightening or it may be exhilarating. It is exhilarating in that it gives us the opportunity to make of ourselves what we will, to accept that what we are is the product of what we are and not given by some external force. What is not an option is the wholesale dismissal of the challenges raised by deconstruction; some of it may be set aside, but too much remains, and will remain, for it to be ignored. The recognition that the flickering shadows on the wall is all is liberating. To learn to live with uncertainty combines angst and exhilaration in a peculiar internal equilibration and to admit the poets back into the Republic is scarcely a disaster if it teaches us that our ethics, our politics, our theology and our narrative life structures have as yet unknown and untried poetic possibilities.

Cadavo, Eduardo, Peter Connor and Jean Luc Nancy (eds) (1991) *Who Comes After the Subject?*: New York and London: Routledge.

Clarke, Paul A.B. (1988) *The Autonomy of Politics* Aldershot and Brookfield: Avebury/Gower.

Critchly, Simon (1992) *The Ethics of Deconstruction: Derrida and Levinas*, Oxford: Blackwell.

Derrida, Jacques (1978) *Writing and Difference*, trans. Alan Bass, London: Routledge and Kegan Paul.

Descartes, Rene A *Discourse on Method* (various editions).

Geerz, Clifford (1973) 'Person Time and Conduct in Bali', in Clifford Geerz, *The Interpretation of Cultures*, Basic Books.

Hume, David (1978) A *Treatise of Human Nature*, ed. L.A. Selby-Bigge, Revd Peter H. Nidditch, Oxford: Clarendon Press.

Kant, Immanuel (1976) A *Critique of Pure Reason*, trans. Norman Kemp-Smith, London: Macmillan.

Levinas, Emmanuel 'God and Philosophy', *Le Nouveau Commerce*, 30–1 (1975), 97–128 and in *The Levinas Reader*, ed. Séan Hand (1989) Oxford: Basil Blackwell.

Marx, Karl and Friedrich Engels (1975) *Collected Works*, London: Lawrence and Wishart.

Maus, Marcel (1985) 'A Category of the Human Mind: the Notion of Person; the Notion of Self', trans. W.D. Halls in *The Category of the Person: Anthropology, Philosophy, History*, ed. Michael Carrithers, Steven Collins, Steven Lukes, Cambridge: Cambridge University Press.

Plato *The Republic* (various editions).

Putnam, Hilary (1978) *Meaning and the Moral Sciences*, Boston, MA, London and Henley: Routledge and Kegan Paul.

Rorty, Richard (1989) *Contingency, Irony and Solidarity*, Cambridge: Cambridge University Press.

Saussure, Ferdinand *Course in General Linguistics*, trans. Wade Baskin, London: Peter Owen, 1960; Fontana, 1974.

Schutz, Alfred (1972) *The Phenomonology of the Social World*, London: Heinemann.

Taylor, Charles (1989) *Sources of the Self: The Making of the Modern Identity*, Cambridge: Cambridge University Press.

Weber, Max (1957) *The Theory of Social and Economic Organization*, trans. A.M. Henderson and Talcott Parsons, Glencoe: The Free Press.

Wittgenstein, Ludwig (1968) *Philosophical Investigations*, trans. Elizabeth Anscombe, Oxford: Basil Blackwell.

Paul Barry Clarke

DEISM

The term 'deism', derived from the Latin *deus*, has the same etymological basis as 'theism', derived from the Greek *theos*, and in the seventeenth century the terms were sometimes used interchangeably. For instance, in the Preface to his translation of George Rust's *A Discourse of the Use of Reason in Matters of Religion* (1683), Henry Hallywell describes 'Deists' as pleading only for 'a Natural Religion in opposition to any Particular Mode or Way of Divine Revelation'. Accordingly, while 'they profess to acknowledge a God and Providence', they have 'withal a mean and low esteem of Scriptures and Christianity' as if a 'fair and rational Account' could not be given of Christianity. He then states that this 'Theism' [*sic*] is 'opposite to the Christian Religion as Christian'.

'Theism' has since come to have a neutral connotation as referring generally to those who believe in the reality of God, but 'deism' has kept a perjorative connotation. Its use resembles that of the description 'radical': what a person means by the description 'deist' is primarily determined by contrast with that person's own position. The term 'deist' is thus employed by people to describe critically the contents of a religious belief which is not 'atheist' but whose views on the reality, will and activity of God are, in their judgement, seriously deficient. This pejorative use of the term is illustrated by George Pearson's Hulsean Lectures for 1834, *The Character and Tendency of the Principles and Opinions of Infidel and Deistic Writers*, in which he attacks 'deists' for their 'infidelity' and declares that, 'though varying in character and degree, all agree in this one respect, in the violence with which they assail the great doctrines and evidences of revealed religion'.

As far as the term 'deism' may be held to connote a positive position, it has come to refer to the belief that, while some supreme being exists who is the ultimate source of being and ground of value, this being does not interfere in the processes of nature and of history by way of particular providential actions (including acts of revelation). It is therefore largely (if not wholly) irrelevant to human thought and action. Deism's formative model of God is consequently often held to be illustrated by the activity of a clockmaker who, having constructed ('created') a self-sustaining mechanism, does not tamper with it but leaves it to go through its motions without interference.

The first reference to 'deists' seems to be in the dedicatory letter to the second volume of Peter Viret's *Instruction Chrétienne* (Geneva, 1564). Comparing them with Epicureans, he describes them as people who hold that, in contrast to atheists, 'they are not without God' as the creator. They 'shew no regard', however, to the person and doctrine of Jesus Christ and, while outwardly conforming to religious practices, inwardly they 'laugh at all religion'. Some of them have a belief in immortality; others do not.

What is generally regarded as the classical era and location of 'deist' thought began about a century later and is predominantly English. With the exception of Lord Herbert of Cherbury (who died in 1648), those who are held to constitute the major exponents of English deism flourished in the period from John Locke to David Hume. The canonical list of the major figures seems to have been determined to a large extent, however, by such critical studies as Philip Skelton's *Deism Revealed: Or, The Attack on Christianity Candidly Reviewed*, first published in 1749, and John Leland's much longer *View of the Principal Deistical Writers*, first published in 1754. Starting with Herbert of Cherbury (1583?–1648), the list usually includes Charles Blount (1654–93), John Toland (1670–1722), Anthony Collins (1676–1729), William Wollaston (1660–1724), Matthew Tindal (1657?–1733), Thomas Woolston (1670–1731), Bernard Mandeville (1670–1733), Anthony, Earl of Shaftesbury (1671–1713), Thomas Chubb (1679–1746), Thomas Morgan (?–1743), Henry St John, Viscount Bolingbroke (1678–1751), and Peter Annet (1693–1769). Skelton and Leland also include Thomas Hobbes (1588–1679) and David Hume (1711–76). Leland discusses the latter at some length, but it is doubtful whether this classification is justified. While, for example, Hume's views on miracles, particular providences, immortality and the origin of belief in God resemble those found in deistic works, his main concern in relation to religious thought seems to be that of showing the unsatisfactoriness of all arguments which purport to establish the reasonableness of theistic belief. He is therefore more accurately to be regarded as a sceptic whose criticisms threaten the alleged rational justification of all theistic belief, whether orthodox or 'deist'.

It is a mistake, however, to infer from the production of such lists that the deists formed a clearly identifiable group with an agreed set of ideas. Their works show that this is not the case. In the first place, the widespread charge that Herbert of Cherbury was the father of English deism is questionable. Although he held that the essential content of true religion was provided by certain common notions which, when properly apprehended, were recognized to be true by all right thinking people, he also believed in the efficacy of prayer, immortality, special providences and revelatory guidance.

Second, there seems to be no single doctrine, let alone a set of doctrines, which all those alleged to be deists share and by which they can be separated from others. In his Boyle Lectures for 1705, *A Discourse concerning the Unchangeable Obligations of Natural Religion, and the Truth and Certainty of the Christian Revelation*, Samuel Clarke (1683–1740) distinguishes four types of deist: the first believe that there is a God but that God has no dealings with the world; the second believe that all that happens in the world is directed by God but that God has no interest in morality; the third have basically satisfactory beliefs about the attributes and activity of God but deny post-mortem existence; the fourth, whom he calls 'the only *True Deists*', believe about God and morality only what can be determined by 'the Light of Nature alone' and deny all claims to revealed insights into the divine nature and will. Other critics are not only unimpressed by the deists' intellectual case, they also doubt the sincerity of their alleged concern for what was called natural religion (i.e. the religious beliefs and practices that could be established by rational reflection). Daniel Waterland (1683–1740), for example, condemns the deists as standing for 'a *personal* religion of their *own* carving' which in practice is characterized by '*libertinism* only and irreligion'. Careful examination of the works of those commonly held to be deists, furthermore, tends to emphasize rather than to eradicate the differences between their ideas. Consequently, Harold Hutcheson is justified in stating (in an article on Herbert of Cherbury in the *Journal of Philosophy* for 1946) that if even 'the most prominent [of the deists] ... shared a common creed' or if even a majority of them 'consciously took "a common philosophical position", no one to my knowledge has yet succeeded in stating that creed or position'.

Third, it is unsatisfactory to attempt to

identify deists by their approach rather than by their doctrines, namely as those who take the canon of reason seriously and hence attempt to promote a form of religious belief that is rationally justified. This is because such an approach is found in far more than those traditionally dubbed deist. Although a few writers on religion challenge in principle the applicability of the canon of reason to religious belief, most consider that authentic belief must be reasonable and can be discerned to be so. Where such people disagree is not over the canon of reason but over what satisfies its demands. Reference to this approach is useful, however, since it indicates that it is unjustifiable to divide religious thought at this time into a series of discrete groupings. Rather it is to be perceived to be a continuum (or, perhaps better, a multidimensional series of them) stretching from those whose radical endorsement of the canon of reason leads them to espouse virtual, if not professed, ATHEISM to those who hold that the whole EVANGELICAL faith can properly be regarded as 'reasonable'.

In this complex intellectual situation, those who are traditionally called deists characteristically consider that what reason requires (or allows) them to believe is less extensive than what those who so describe them consider to be authenticated by reason. It is therefore not at all surprising to find that it is hard to draw a clear line between the views of some reputed to be deists and the views of others such as Ralph Cudworth (1617–88) and other Cambridge Platonists, John Locke (1632–1704) and John Tillotson (1630–94). Furthermore, the major apologists for orthodox Christianity against deism, such as Samuel Clarke, Richard Bentley (1662–1742), George Berkeley (1685–1753), Joseph Butler (1692–1752) and, somewhat later, William Paley (1743–1805), fundamentally agree with their opponents on the need to show the reasonableness of the faith which they defend.

While the major contributions to (and the liveliest debates about) deistic ideas appeared in England, on the Continent leading deistic writers include Voltaire (1694–1778), Hermann Samuel Reimarus (1694–1768), Jean–Jacques Rousseau (1712–78), Gotthold Ephraim Lessing (1729–81) and, in some respects, Immanuel Kant (1724–1804). In America Benjamin Franklin (1706–90), George Washington (1732–1809) and Thomas Jefferson (1743–1826) held what may be regarded as deistic ideas. Its most vigorous proponent there, however, was Thomas Paine (1737–1809) in whose works a popular form of deism becomes linked with radical political movements.

The variety of positions, frequently at variance with each other, that are generally denoted by the label 'deist' suggests that the label is of dubious value for studies of religious thought in the seventeenth and eighteenth centuries. It is liable to mislead rather than to be usefully informative. Consequently, while in view of its widespread usage it is unrealistic to expect historians of thought to drop the term, it is important for those who meet it to ask what precisely is intended by it in each context. In addition, however, all uses of the term may also be justifiably held to point to a more critical (and in some cases an extremely critical) aspect of a movement of thought in which attempts are made to understand religious faith (and particularly the Christian faith) in a way that is neither unreflectively bigoted nor completely sceptical. For some this way involves replacing what they judge to be required by Christianity with a more 'reasonable' faith; for others it means discerning a properly 'reasonable' version of Christianity. The controversies about deism in the seventeenth and eighteenth centuries are thus an important, albeit widely neglected, chapter in the story of the modernizing, secularizing and universalizing of theistic belief.

Furthermore, while use of the label 'deist' is questionable in the history of thought, its use to designate a current position comparable with some past position is even less satisfactory. The formative background of ideas has changed so much since the eighteenth century that it seems to verge on misrepresentation to use the same term to describe beliefs about the divine, however unorthodox, held by persons of the early eighteenth century and beliefs held by persons of the late twentieth century. What gives the practice some legitimacy, however, is the sad fact that many, both theistic believers and their critics, who happen to live in the late twentieth century apparently still inhabit intellectually a long-dead era so far as their religious convictions are concerned.

Byrne, Peter (1989) *Natural Religion and the Nature of Deism: The Legacy of Deism*, London: Routledge.

Cragg, Gerald R. (1950) *From Puritanism to the Age of Reason: A Study of Changes in Religious Thought Within the Church of England, 1660–1700*, Cambridge: Cambridge University Press.

——(1964) *Reason and Authority in the Eighteenth Century*, Cambridge: Cambridge University Press.

Harrison, Peter (1990) *'Religion' and the Religions in the English Enlightenment*, Cambridge: Cambridge University Press.

Lechler, G.V. (1841) *Geschichte des englischen Deismus*, Stuttgart/Tübingen.

Leland, John (1754) *A View of the Principal Deistical Writers that have Appeared in England in the Last and Present Century*, London.

Redwood, John (1976) *Reason, Ridicule and Religion: The Age of Enlightenment in England, 1660–1750*, London: Thames & Hudson.

[Skelton, Philip] (1751) *Deism Revealed: Or, The Attack on Christianity Candidly Reviewed*, 2nd edn, London.

Stephen, Leslie (1902) *A History of English Thought in the Eighteenth Century*, 3rd edn, London.

Stromberg, Roland N. (1954) *Religious Liberalism in Eighteenth-century England*, Oxford: Oxford University Press.

Sullivan, Robert E. (1982) *John Toland and the Deist Controversy: A Study in Adaptations*, Cambridge, MA: Harvard University Press.

David A. Pailin

DEMOCRACY

During the twentieth century democracy has come to be much admired. By the middle of the twentieth century, partly under the pressure of the rising expectations of citizens and partly in response to the terror of totalitarian systems in the 1930s and 1940s, it became popular to claim the title democratic for a political system. Even one-party authoritarian states like those of the former Eastern Europe wanted to identify themselves with the aspiration towards democracy, and often incorporated the term into the name of the state itself, as was the case with the German Democratic Republic. Since the collapse of COMMUNISM in Eastern Europe, and the move towards multi-party systems of government in Africa and Latin America, the notion has become widespread that democracy is not

only desirable but also necessary as a form of GOVERNMENT in the modern world. One writer, in the early flushes of post-communist enthusiasm, even went so far as to proclaim the 'end of history' and the view that liberal democracy would soon be triumphant throughout the world. Subsequent events, most notably the growth of nationalist movements in Eastern Europe and the crushing of the democratic movement in Tiananmen Square in Beijing in which student demonstrators protesting for greater democracy were forcibly broken up by government troops, have shown that this is a facile optimism. But they have also shown the need to make clearer what are the intellectual and moral foundations for a belief in democracy.

There is a sense in which the principles of democracy are secular ideals. Much contemporary democratic theorizing has grown out of the Enlightenment, a movement that was characterized by Peter Gay in *The Enlightenment*, his intellectual history of the eighteenth century as the rise of modern paganism. Certainly both the French and American revolutions of the eighteenth century, important landmarks in the development of modern democracy, drew upon classical inspiration and often self-consciously modelled their political programmes on ideals of popular sovereignty in Greece and Rome. Perhaps more importantly, the growth of the idea of democracy required the view that the task of government was not to make its legislation correspond to a divinely given NATURAL LAW, but instead to derive collective choices from the will of the people, where the people are regarded as responsible for the ordering of their own lives.

Writers on democracy typically distinguish two major institutional forms: direct democracy and indirect or representative democracy. In a direct democracy all citizens participate in the making of important collective decisions, whereas in an indirect democracy the role of citizens is to elect representatives who are the ones who will take policy and legislative decisions. Historical examples of direct democracies include classical Athens, the Puritan New England townships, the Swiss cantons and small-scale pre-literate societies. In the twentieth century, however, the dominant form of democratic government has been the representative variety. In such systems political parties compete with one another for a winning share of the popular vote and hence for the right to be represented in the legislature and to form the government. Consistent with this general principle, there are many possible variations in types of goverment, e.g. presidential versus parliamentary systems, federal versus unitary systems or two-party versus many-party systems. Moreover, in order for any form of democratic competition to take place, representative democracies typically also require a battery of associated political and civil rights, e.g. freedom of association, freedom of expression, freedom from arbitrary arrest and so on. For these reasons we may speak about such systems as 'constitutional democracies'.

The view that constitutional democracy in its present form is a justifiable form of government has not always been widespread. The traditional preference of many leading writers, following Aristotle, was for a 'mixed' constitution, comprising monarchical, aristocratic and popular elements that, it was alleged, would secure stability in government. Parliamentary representation was not of individuals, as it is in modern constitutional democracies, but of estates based on property ownership or of geographical entities such as cities. In many of the struggles over democratic reform in the nineteenth century the term 'democracy' was used as a term of abuse, akin to the notion of 'anarchy'.

This distrust of democracy reflected a long tradition of political thought in the West, going back to Plato for whom democracy was seen as government by the mob prone to erratic movements of opinion and liable to manipulation by demagogues. Outside the Western tradition the existence of imperial states in China and India did not lend themselves to democratic theorizing. Although in the Western Christian tradition attention has been paid to questions of political theory by theologians such as Augustine and Aquinas, the dominant question has been that of securing government rule corresponding to the demands of natural law, rather than prescribing a particular form of popular government. Even historical examples of direct democracies did not live up to modern ideals. Thus, women were typically excluded from the exercise of political power, so that we may say that the ideal of all adults controlling their collective lives through discussion, debate and the vote is a relatively recent one. It is difficult not to see it as a product of the rise of individualism more generally.

Within contemporary accounts of democracy there are many theoretical variations and many arguments for and against any particular form of democratic government, but with some oversimplification it is possible to distinguish two broad classes of opinion about democracy. On the one hand there are those, e.g. James Mill or Joseph Schumpeter, who conceive of democracy principally in terms of its being accountable government; on the other there are those, e.g. John Stuart Mill or Paul Tillich, who conceive of it as being a form of participatory or self-government. According to the first conception the chief merit of democratic over non-democratic forms of government is that those who hold the reins of political power are made accountable for their actions, in the sense that they have to explain and justify the policy choices that they make, and ultimately may be removed if their account of what they are doing is found wanting. The essential function of democracy in this conception is to select a government, but it is equally important to prevent the government from using its position of preeminent power to tyrannize over SOCIETY. One of the virtues of democracy, on this conception, is that it allows for the peaceful transfer of political power.

According to the second conception, democracy is a form of life in which the members of society participate, and the merit of a democratic government is that it expresses at a collective level the ideal of a people's self-government, just as liberty at the personal level expresses the ideal of moral autonomy. The function of government in this conception is to represent the popular will and emphasis is placed upon the ability of the government to act in the public interest. The exercise of the virtues of CITIZENSHIP by individuals, e.g. serving on public bodies or being willing to defend the social order by resort to arms, has a high place in this second, participatory conception of democracy.

The distinction between democracy as accountable government and democracy as self-government is related to, though not identical with, the distinction between direct democracy and representative democracy. Participatory accounts of democracy favour direct democracy where this is possible, but as Dahl and Tufte have shown, the size of modern societies renders full and regular participation by all members of society in every important decision impossible. Indeed, even if social life were decentralized to small units the size of ancient Athens, the supposed home of participatory democracy, there would still not be enough time for everyone to have their say. To have a simple direct democracy would require political communities no larger than a few hundred members, for by the stage at which the political unit involved thousands some element of indirect representation would have to have evolved. For these practical reasons, the modern ideal of democracy has to encompass the practice of representative government and cannot be limited to village-size communities. It is possible that developments in modern technology, e.g. two-way interactive video, will be able to overcome some of the problems associated with size, but until then participatory theorists have to stress the opportunities for increased participation in representative democracy, e.g. measures to decentralize decision-making to local units of government.

If the difference between the ideal of democracy as accountable government and the ideal of democracy as self-government does not correspond to the difference between direct and indirect democracy, wherein lies the distinction? One way of expressing the distinction is in terms of whether the function of democratic institutions is seen primarily as restraining the arrogance of POWER of those in government or primarily as enabling the government to act in accordance with the will of the people in the formulation of public decisions. Proponents of democracy as accountable government are impressed by the potential for the misuse of power, and are concerned to prevent lawful government degenerating into tyranny. Their primary reason for favouring democratic over non-democratic institutions is that they wish to ensure that rascals in government can be thrown out when need be. Proponents of democracy as self-government see a more positive role for the exercise of political power, provided it is exercised in accordance with the will of the people. On this view the purpose of democracy is not simply to avoid bad government but also to promote good government. Good government will of course avoid tyranny, but it will also provide economic security to citizens through a welfare state and advance collective or common interests, e.g. protection from pollution and the development of an ethic of civic responsibility.

Behind these contrasting accounts of democracy there typically lie contrasting accounts of human interests and human motivation. The view of accountable government often assumes a pessimistic view of human nature, nicely captured in James Madison's remarks (*The Federalist Papers* 10):

> what is government itself but the greatest of all reflections on human nature? If men were angels, no government would be necessary. If angels were to govern men, neither external nor internal controls on government would be necessary. In framing a government which is to be administered by men over men, the great difficulty lies in this: you must first enable the government to control the governed; and in the next place oblige it to control itself.

In other words, given that human motivation inclines people to seek power over one another for their own ends, the task of someone seeking to frame a democratic, or as Madison would have put it republican, constitution, is to establish those institutional devices that will prevent the lawful exercise of power from degenerating into tyranny.

The quotation also clearly illustrates the idea common to many versions of democracy as accountable government, namely that politics is an essentially *instrumental* activity which is not about the exercise of the virtues of citizenship but rather about making collective arrangements to the mutual benefit of those who live in a society. For this view the STATE, as the instrument of collective action, is rather like an insurance company which guarantees certain forms of security but does not require a moral commitment from those who benefit from its actions.

Moreover, for proponents of the view of accountable government, democracy is related to motivation not simply as an effect but also as a cause. Since the emergence of the modern democratic movement in the nineteenth century critics have not been found wanting who have been prepared to allege that democracy would lead to a form of mass society and collective mediocrity. The allegation is not simply that the majority would enact unjust legislation, for which the prime example for these writers is the compulsory redistribution of private property, but that the political culture of a democracy inevitably leads to a stifling uniformity that inhibits persons of genius and talent.

For those who hold to the ideal of self-government a different account of human motivation and commitment is required. Typically a more optimistic view of human nature is taken, particularly with regard to the ability of citizens to take an intelligent and dispassionate view of public affairs. In the so-called 'funeral oration' in Thucydides' *The Peloponnesian War* there occurs one of the earliest recorded praises of democracy. The orator in question is Pericles who praises the ancient Athenians for their willingness to make personal sacrifices for the common good, particularly the willingness of citizens to fight for the independence of Athens. In *The Social Contract* Rousseau argued that the members of a self-governing community would decide their common affairs in accordance with the idea of a 'general will' that would capture the sense of what was in the public interest. And in *On Representative Government* John Stuart Mill thought that the principal justification for democracy flowed from the tendency of a democratic political system to provide opportunities for public service in which individuals could enlarge their sympathies and acquire a broadened outlook enabling them to act in the public interest. For Mill, as for Rousseau and Pericles, democracy was not simply a means by which individuals made arrangements for matters of common security and interest, but it was also an education in citizenship and collective action.

The choice between these contrasting conceptions of democracy raises many complex issues of social science and political theory that are currently the subject of much debate. Yet, despite the complexity of the issues, the choice can still be guided by argument and evidence. One approach is to explore how far each conception is consistent with what we may take to be the underlying rationale and justification for democratic government in the first place. There are many reasons for favouring democratic over non-democratic forms of government. Indeed, one of the reasons why democratic institutions are justified is that they seem to lie at the confluence of a range of rather disparate considerations. Thus, one set of reasons for finding democratic governments preferable to non-democratic governments is that the consequences of democracy are on the whole better, in terms of things like living standards and the protection of civil rights, than the consequences of non-democratic government – a central motive behind the revolutions of Eastern Europe in 1989. Yet another set of reasons for finding democracy preferable to other forms of government is that the ideal of AUTONOMY and self-government at the collective level finds expression in democratic government in a way that cannot be true in non-democratic government. Government is simply one way in which persons living together determine a common collective course of action, and even among angels, contrary to Madison, we may presume that collective discussion would be necessary in order to agree upon and co-ordinate a common course of action.

Much turns at this point upon the question of how far individuals can be expected to internalize a sense of the common good. Proponents of democracy as accountable government are not entirely consistent on this score. Thus, although the *Federalist Papers* incline to the view that government is best regarded as a protection against human selfishness, John Jay, in one of the early papers (2, p. 39), describes the delegates to the convention in Philadelphia which drew up the US constitution as being without awe for power and uninfluenced by 'any passions except love for their country'. Joseph Schumpeter, who was generally sceptical of the extent to which people could take an intelligent interest in public affairs, nevertheless insisted that a stable democratic order required citizens to internalize a sense of self-restraint so that not too great a burden was placed upon the functions of government. Thus, even on modest conceptions of democracy some room has to be found for the idea that individual citizens can rise above their own narrow concerns in order to take into account the effect of their actions upon the public good, and from this point of view the assumptions about human nature implicit in participatory accounts of democracy seem implicit in any form of democratic theory.

An important theme among critics of participatory conceptions of democracy is the possibility of the tyranny of the majority. Schumpeter, for example, was keen to distinguish popular and rightful government action, arguing that one could imagine a fully functioning democracy which persecuted religious dissent as did Calvin's Geneva and that Jews were only able to escape the effects of popular ANTI-SEMITISM in the Middle Ages by sheltering under the protection of the church and of princes. Despite John Stuart Mill's advocacy of a participatory version of representative government, he too was worried by what he perceived to be the tendency towards mediocrity in mass societies. In both cases the thought seems to be that elements of élitism are necessary to counterbalance some of the destructive tendencies inherent in the growth of democracy.

Although such arguments are widespread, it is difficult to obtain unambiguous evidence to support them, and much evidence seems to point in the opposite direction. Because representative democracies presuppose certain political freedoms (see freedom), e.g. freedom of association and freedom of expression, the protection and development of democracy is often coextensive with the protection and development of a broader range of constitutional freedoms. Moreover, abuses of civil rights within democratic societies, e.g. racial inequalities in the southern states of the USA or discrimination against Catholics in Northern Ireland, are typically sustained by political devices like the gerrymandering of constituency boundaries or the denial of the suffrage to members of oppressed groups which are hardly consistent with the ideals of political equality and participation that underlie democracy. For these reasons, it may well be that the fears of the tyranny of the majority have been significantly overrated.

To say that the principles of constitutional democracy enjoy widespread support is not to assume that governments around the world will increasingly become democratic in form. Poverty, the pressures of nationalism, ethnic tensions and religious fundamentalism may well threaten the willingness of citizens in different countries to adopt a policy of give and take that seems essential to the stability of democratic political systems. On the other hand, developed economies involve a complexity of control that authoritarian systems, with their lack of popular involvement, find difficult to manage. However, as the experience of India since independence attests, perhaps the strongest element keeping democracies in being is the belief sufficiently widespread among the political classes that democracy is something valuable in itself. If democracy is to survive and flourish that sentiment needs to take deep root.

Barber, Benjamin (1984) *Strong Democracy*, Berkeley and Los Angeles, CA: University of California Press.

Dahl, R.A. (1956) *A Preface to Democratic Theory*, Chicago, IL, and London: University of Chicago Press.

Duncan Graeme (ed.) (1983) *Democratic Theory and Practice*, Cambridge: Cambridge University Press.

Held, David (1987) *Models of Democracy*, Cambridge: Polity.

Lijphart, Arend (1984) *Democracies*, New Haven, CT and London: Yale University Press.

Lively, Jack (1975) *Democracy*, Oxford: Basil Blackwell.

Mill, James (1965) *Essay on Government*, Indianapolis, IN: Bobbs–Merrill (originally published 1820).

Mill, John Stuart (1861) *On Representative Government* (originally published 1861, many editions).

Pennock, J. Roland (1979) *Democratic Political Theory*, Princeton, NJ: Princeton University Press.

Schumpeter, Joseph (1954) *Capitalism, Socialism and Democracy*, 4th edn, London: Allen & Unwin.

Albert Weale

DEMONIC

The demonic is a symbol rather than a concept and it takes two forms: a specific belief in the existence of 'demons', spiritual entities which oppress and sometimes possess human beings who are then seen as 'demon-possessed' or 'demonized'; and a more general sense in which the term is used of distorted, corrupt, EVIL structures and beliefs. The two senses are not incompatible, and it is possible to hold both together. Usually, however, those who hold to belief in demons as literal beings tend to have an individualized approach, while those who hold the second view tend to think in social and political terms.

Paradoxically the opposite of the word symbol (from *sun ballo*, to throw together) is diabolos, DEVIL (from *dia ballo*, to divide, fragment, break up). Early Christian writers saw Satan as the author of division and fragmentation. 'Satan has broken us up.' In its original sense the word *daimon* simply refers to power as in the related word *dunamis*. The word does not in itself indicate EVIL: thus *eudaimonia* refers to the good life, a state of human fulfilment. Yet there is throughout most spiritual traditions the recognition of the ambiguity of power and its potential for corruption. Within the Christian tradition the symbolism of the demonic is used of warped institutions within a fallen world order, but these institutions are also related to cosmic spiritual forces which are believed to stand behind the earthly structures. Wink argues that the demonic is a way of speaking about both the external structures and the inner spirituality (the *daimon*) of those structures.

While the demonic symbol is wider and more complex in scope than the language of evil spirits, the two aspects are linked. The power of evil is seen as manifested in the presence of evil spirits, variously named as Satan, Beelzebub and so on. Satan is only referred to three times in the Hebrew Bible, and there is no developed doctrine of demonology there. However, the association of oppressive political powers with cosmic forces of evil and cosmic warfare begins to appear in the Book of Daniel and in the APOCALYPTIC literature of the inter-testamental period (e.g. Jubilees, Enoch and the Qumran War Scroll). In the APOCALYPTIC material there is a strong sense of spiritual warfare taking place within the context of earthly upheavals. The demonic is beginning to emerge as a vital symbol within Jewish theology.

Both aspects of the demonic are present in the New Testament where the casting out of demons is a central part of the ministry of Jesus. In the gospel accounts the demons have no power unless they are embodied in people. The exorcisms appear in every strata of the synoptic tradition and it is impossible to disentangle them from his ministry as a whole: indeed in Galilee they were his main activity. Here the activity of Satan, the ruler of this world, assumes a more prominent place. Satan holds *exousia* (authority) over the world (Matthew 4: 8). The conquest of the world is seen as a victory over Satan who is seen as falling like lightning from heaven (Luke 10: 18). It is sometimes claimed that the exorcisms of Jesus are signs of the presence of the KINGDOM OF GOD but it is more accurate to see them as a preparation for the kingdom. Yet the coming of the kingdom, and the centrality of the Cross in the process of its coming, is certainly seen as a conquest over Satan's power. God delivers people from the dominion of darkness and transfers them into the kingdom (Colossians 1: 13). The prince of this world is cast out in the lifting up of the Son of Man (John 12: 31). The kingdoms of the world are to become the kingdom of God (Revelation 11: 15).

The language of 'the powers' is used in Paul's letters in relation to fallen structures within the world. Here such terms as *angeloi*, *daimoniai*, *archai* and *exousiai* represent forces which control the operation of evil in the world. They are 'the rulers of this age', the 'principalities and powers', 'the elemental spirits of the world' (1 Corinthians 2: 6–8; Ephesians 6: 12; Galatians 4: 3; Colossians 2: 8, etc.). Christ is portrayed as raised above the powers (Ephesians 1: 21) and the church's task as that of announcing the mystery of God to the powers (Ephesians 3: 10). In the Book of Revelation the Roman imperial power is portrayed as a beast, associated with the cosmic evil force of the dragon/serpent (Revelation 12). While the beast, the Babylon of earlier history, is used as a symbol of spiritual evil, this evil is seen as concretely manifested in the workings of the Roman state machine. Evil is concretized in very specific locations and practices, and the demons must be named. So the early Christian writer Origen claimed that demons were associated with specific territories.

The demonic symbolism has been present in some form in every phase of Christian history, though the influence of rationalism and 'liberal' approaches to theology and to pastoral care has discouraged any central concern with it. Approaches to demons and to exorcism became a focus of attention in the 1970s as a result of the resurgence of the occult within the USA and Europe, and of the application of the demonic symbol to personal and societal dimensions of life. The language of the demonic and of 'burning out the mark of the beast' was rediscovered in the context of the Vietnam War and of RACISM. At the same time, the rise of the CHARISMATIC MOVEMENT after 1967 led to a new interest in demon possession as one aspect of the renewal of healing ministry and of the exercise of the gifts of the Spirit. As the apostles were told to cast out demons (Mark 16: 17), so, it was felt, this ministry is necessary for Spirit-filled Christians today. However, in the 1970s there was some irresponsible use of exorcism, including a widely publicized death after an exorcism in 1975, and this led to a fear of this area of ministry among many, and to a marginalizing of the occult and magical as an area for specialists. However, within classical black Pentecostalism and within the charismatic renewal the 'ministry of deliverance' is seen as part of the normal ministry of the Christian community. Crude forms of Pentecostal theology have tended towards two misleading and dangerous views: a tendency to associate the demonic exclusively with internal spiritual possession; and a crude literalism in the understanding of the symbol. In some quarters demons are seen everywhere and provide a simple explanation of a wide range of happenings. Cardinal Suenens has referred to this as 'demonomania'. The novels of Frank Peretti are a good example of simplistic use of demonology, and they fit successfully into the spiritual culture of the USA. So the power of the symbol is decreased as it is trivialized.

In fact the occult, while it is only one facet of spirituality, does represent a form of the demonic in which power replaces LOVE, and individualism is dominant. The acquisition of personal spiritual power takes over, and religion is twisted into a form of magic. Religion thus becomes a way of exercising spiritual power. Interest in the occult seems to be related historically to the misuse of political power as evidenced most noticeably in the rise of Nazism.

The early Christian church believed that everyone was possessed prior to baptism, and the exorcism was an integral part of the baptismal liturgy. Water symbolizes the realm of the demonic powers, the irrational uncontrollable elements in the universe. God's victory over evil is symbolized, as in the psalms and prophetic writings of Israel, in terms of a conquest over the primal chaos represented by the sea (e.g. Psalm 74, Isaiah 51, etc.). So in baptism Christians 'put the sea of eternal death behind them and leave their demonic enemies drowning in the font' (Farrer 1951).

In psychiatric writing the demonic is sometimes seen as a way of describing neurosis (Freud) or psychosis (May 1974) while R.D. Laing (1975) insisted that both usages were no more than forms of language and did not explain anything. The demonic occurs in psychopathology as a way of describing a state of corporate derangement and possession. Jung used the symbol in relation to Nazism which he saw as a state of corporate possession or demonic condition of the nation.

The demonic symbol is a symbol of distortion, of persons and systems which have betrayed their purpose. Over time it has itself been distorted. It is best to see the demonic symbol as a way of expressing the reality of evil, both in its inner spirituality and in its external manifestation.

Berkhof, H. (1962) *Christ and the Powers*, Scottdale, PA: Herald Press.

Farrer, A.M. (1951) *A Study in St Mark*, London: Dacre Press, p. 87.

Kelly, H.A. (1985) *The Devil at Baptism: Ritual, Theology and Drama*, Ithaca, NY: Cornell University Press.

Laing, R.D. (1975) *The Angels of Darkness*, BBC Radio 3, 27 October.

May, R. (1974) *Power and Innocence*, W. W. Norton.

Peretti, Frank (1986) *This Present Darkness*, West-chester, IL: Crossway.
——(1989) *Piercing the Darkness*, Westchester, IL: Crossway.
Reicke, Bo (1946) *The Disobedient Spirits and Christian Baptism*, Copenhagen: Ejnar Munksgaard.
Ricoeur, Paul (1967) *The Symbolism of Evil*, New York: Harper & Row.
Russell, J.B. (1988) *The Prince of Darkness: Radical Evil and the Power of Good in History*, Ithaca, NY: Cornell University Press.
Wink, Walter (1968) *Unmasking the Powers*, Philadelphia, PA: Fortress Press.
——(1974) *Naming the Powers*, Philadelphia, PA: Fortress Press.
——(1992) *Engaging the Powers*, Minneapolis, MN: Fortress Press.
Yap, P.M. (1960) 'The possession syndrome', *Journal of Mental Science* 106: 442.

Kenneth Leech

DEONTOLOGY

'Deontology' was coined by Jeremy Bentham but employed by him in a sense directly opposite to that in which it is currently used. For Bentham, 'deontology' was directly related to the maximization of the happiness of the community. Currently, deontology is that approach to ethics which lays stress on the central importance of obligation and permission. It recognizes that there may be some actions which are morally obligatory no matter what the consequences, and so is sharply contrasted with consequentialism, though some ethical systems (e.g. that of Joseph Butler) combine elements of each. The word derives from the Greek word *deon, deontos*, ought.

Deontology is closely allied to an understanding of ethical obligation in terms of rule-following, even exceptionless rule-following, where the obligatoriness is understood to be grounded in some general fact or facts. In principle such rules may embody one or an indefinite number of duties. It is also allied to the idea that certain actions or practices are worthwhile in themselves and not merely for some state of affairs which they produce.

Three possible ways of grounding obligatoriness have been widely canvassed. One is to ground it in some distinctive fact or facts about human nature or natural laws about human beings. Such facts must be universal, and capable of making plausible the linkage between certain duties and human well-being or flourishing. Such a view faces two formidable difficulties. One is Hume's celebrated objection about values (in this case obligations) not being deducible from facts (facts about human nature). The other is to make plausible the way in which particular duties are thus deducible or, if not deducible, then strongly supported by the facts. Why do certain rules constitute duties and not other rules? This is a particularly challenging difficulty when it is faced with the competing views of human nature and of human flourishing to be found in modern pluralist cultures.

A second way is to ground obligatoriness in the human will. If, as with Immanuel Kant's famous attempt to do this, the will is not an arbitrary volition but the will of a human being in so far as he is rational and free, this view certainly survives the charge that it makes the content of moral duty wholly arbitrary. For Kant holds that, in so far as human beings will the moral law by a true employment of their practical reason, they will in fact all will the same moral law; the law-making members of the Kingdom of Ends will coincidentally frame the one moral law.

But even if such law-making powers are granted to human beings, the difficulties Kant's ethics face are formidable. The highly abstract character of his moral philosophy makes deriving maxims, specific moral injunctions, a hazardous and contentious business. Kant himself believed it was possible to derive rules from the moral law, notably one about promise-keeping, on the grounds that if promises were breakable at will the very idea of a SOCIETY would collapse. This is not a lapse into consequentialism on Kant's part, provided that his argument is taken as a remark about what constitutes a human society. Kant's excessively abstract understanding of duty was modified by Hegel and others in the post-Kantian tradition.

Kant's ethics, or this aspect of it, may be thought of as an inversion, in true Enlightenment fashion, of the classic Christian view that moral duties are grounded in the will (i.e. the command) of God. Kant simply substitutes the will of man for the will of God (*see* AUTONOMY).

The third influential way in which the obligatoriness of certain rules is grounded is by connecting obligatoriness with the will of God. Provided that the will of God is sufficiently specific and can be readily identified, such an approach overcomes the problem of indefiniteness that plagues Kant's ethics. And if God is the Creator with rights of ownership or lordship over his creation, then the problem of is and ought can also be met.

However, such a view carries difficulties of its own, particularly over the exact connection between obligatoriness and the divine will. Is the mere will of God sufficient for obligatoriness? Could God will anything and in so doing make it obligatory? Or is God bound to recognize certain necessary moral values, and divine will simply endorse and announce these? If so, does such an arrangement not compromise God's sovereignty?

The most plausible response to these difficulties is to deny any contingent connection between the will and the moral character of God by appealing to divine unity, even to divine simplicity, and in addition to argue that, while consistently with his moral character God might impose different obligations on other species of rational creatures (e.g. Martians) than on *homo sapiens*, the obligations imposed on humankind are non-contingently connected with human character as a creature made in the image of God.

What any version of deontological ethics requires is a procedure for adjudicating between conflicting duties. If there is a conflict between telling a lie and saving a life, which is to take precedence and on what grounds? If certain duties are more important than others, in virtue of what are they more important? It will hardly do to claim that the providence of God will never lead anyone into a situation in which duties clash. The same problems arise if the duties are treated as only *prima facie*.

It is often claimed that it is not possible to have duties without God ('If God does not exist, everything is permitted'). The appeal of this view will depend on how plausible it is to ground duties in a purely secular understanding of human nature – for even Kant's Enlightenment ethics requires the postulation of God's existence – or, less ambitiously, on how plausible it is to appeal to intuitions, e.g. about killing or CRUELTY, possessed irrespective of theological view. In any case it is not obvious that the only form that theological ETHICS can take is deontological: why could not the commands of God be rules as understood by the rule-utilitarian?

Bentham, Jeremy ([1834] 1983) *Deontology*, ed. A. Goldworth, Oxford: Oxford University Press.
Butler, Joseph ([1726] 1970) *Fifteen Sermons*, ed. T.A. Roberts, London: SPCK.
Flew, Antony (1966) *God and Philosophy*, London: Hutchinson.
Helm, Paul (ed.) (1981) *Divine Commands and Morality*, Oxford: Oxford University Press.
Kant, Immanuel ([1785] 1953) *Groundwork of the Metaphysic of Morals*, trans. H.J. Paton as *The Moral Law*, London: Hutchinson.
Quinn, Philip L. (1978) *Divine Commands and Moral Requirements*, Oxford: Clarendon Press.

Paul Helm

DETERMINISM

The term 'determinism' is derived from the Latin *determinare*, to bound or limit, yet the idea of boundaries, limits, or causes, to human action can be traced to the earliest written records. The idea of some kind of determimism, of some kind of cause or boundary to human action can also be found in every known culture. No culture and no society, construes itself as being completely free or completely unbounded. The ways in which the bounds or limits are construed does, however, vary vastly from society to society and is often revealing of the deeper underlying ethical, theological and social conceptions that societies have of themselves. Thus a society that sees itself as determined by the actions of the gods, or of a God, is substantially different from a society that sees its general structure determined by natural causality. No society and no ethical system is completely free from some conception of causality but such conceptions of causality have often been bound up with theological perspectives. It must be doubted whether any conception of causality is completely free of mythical or theological traces or sediments or even whether such a conception of causality or determinism is possible. The secular society of the modern or post-modern West is no exception to this general observation. On the contrary its conception of causality has been so directly and significantly affected by its religious and theological perspectives that these two perspectives are probably incapable of complete disentanglement. The effect of this is to ameliorate some of the grander claims of determinism in both theological and secular domains.

To say that some action or event is determined means that it is caused or conditioned. It is often opposed to the idea of FREE WILL. A cause can almost always be assigned to actions and events at the phenomenal level but it does not follow from that narrow observation that the wider thesis or doctrine or determinism holds. The doctrine of determinism is usually taken to refer to the claim that all actions and/ or events are determined and stand in a strict causal sequence to each other. Thus no action can be free and no event undetermined. The notion of determinism now runs much wider than conceptions of actions and events; so much so that it would be better to think of many determinisms rather than a single deterministic idea. However, it is in relation to caused events and the relation between them and freedom that determinisms found their best early expression.

The puzzle of determinism and freedom is well stated in its earliest form by Epicurus who while primarily and predominantly a determinist thought that the atoms might on occasion swerve from their course. This led Cicero to remark that Epicurus, 'says that the atom although thrust downwards by its own weight and gravity makes a very slight swerve. To assert this is more disgraceful than to be incapable of defending what he wants' (Cicero 69–70). The claim and counter claim made here is at the very basis of the problems of the many kinds of determinisms that have subsequently arisen. In spite of their many differences all determinisms raise a core issue about the relation of freedom to the world in which we find ourselves.

Determinism is sometimes taken to be equivalent to fate, pre-destination, and pre-ordination: notions that have considerable religious significance in some doctrines. Usually, however, these notions can be distinguished from each other for they rest on different conceptions of causality. In the *Metaphysics* in an analysis that still dominates discussions of causality, Aristotle distinguished four different conceptions of causality; efficient, formal, final and material. The efficient cause of an event is that event prior to it that produced the event in question. Thus the efficient cause of the artefact of a bed made by a carpenter is the actions of the carpenter. The formal cause is the form 'or idea of the bed, the final cause is its purpose, goal or end, *telos*, and the material cause is the matter from which the bed is composed, the wood.

Final causes or teleological causes have been developed most fully in those aspects of Hebraic and Christian thought that have been impressed with APOCALYPTIC thought and with the finality of last days. In Christian thought this idea is often expressed as the coming of the KINGDOM OF GOD on Earth or the *Parousia*. It is found expressed in dramatic form in *Revelation* but also in the gospels and the belief of the earliest Christians that the final days of the return of Christ on Earth would take place in their life time. The idea of a final cause is later found in St Augustine's notion of the elect or *praedestinatio*, those who had been chosen from the beginning of eternity to find their place in the Kingdom of God. The notion recurs frequently in those doctrines still prevalent that there is an elect or in those sects that depend on some kind of MILLENARIANISM. Its secular form can be found in numerous forms. For example, it emerges in embryonic form in Kant's theory of History: the idea that there is a condition of virtue and happiness which is at some point in the future. It turns up again in Hegel's conception that the end of history is the condition of *sittlichkeit*, the ideal ethical order and yet again in Marx's view that the end of history is the communist society. All such models are secularized versions of the *parousia*, drawn themselves from a mix of the APOCALYPTIC tradition, Aristotelian conceptions of final causality and an Augustinian conception of world history underpinned by a linear account of time.

Models of final causality have been undercut by attempts to reduce them to efficient causality. In efficient causality event 'a' at time t_1 precedes event 'b' at time t_2, so the cause of the light coming on is the prior turning of the appropriate switch. By contrast teleological causality has it that the cause of the flicking of the switch that led to the light being turned on is the end, goal, purpose, or *telos* of having the light on. If that is the case then it seems that the explanation of event 'b' at time t_2 is the cause of event 'a' at time t_1 and that seems to make the direction of causality run in reverse.

Conceptions of reverse causality do seem to underlay some theological conceptions of action and some social and political conceptions of action. The apocalyptic and eschatological traditions have it that there is some pre-determined end state of the universe, or last days. If there is some already determined future state then actions prior to that time are determined by that future event. That does seem to make the conception of causality run backward but it also devalues the meaning of present actions. Present actions have no present significance: it is rather that they are meaningful only against their sacrifice to the future. The clearest examples are in those quasi Marxist theories (not subscribed to by Marx incidentally, who claimed in all seriousness that he was not a Marxist) that arose particularly after the *Second International*. The crude determinism that developed out of that programme appeared to sacrifice actions in the present to some final end. The claim that the revolution is 'inevitable', where this means 'must occur' subverts all actions to this future event. Hence the suffering of the present is meaningful not in its own right but because it leads to some higher goal at the end of history. But such theories here only echo their earlier Christian apocalyptic–eschatological model: the suffering of the present is justified by some event in the future. In such models it appears that the meaning of one's life makes sense only against the conception of something that has not yet happened and in which one may well not participate.

Such teleological explanations are frequently considered to be fundamentally flawed. It may be that the goals associated with an act appear to lead to that act, but this, it is argued, is an illusion, for the dispositional state that gives rise to the goal can, it is argued, be reduced to a form that makes it explicable in terms of efficient causes. Hence a disposition can ultimately be reduced to its prior causes e.g., experience, biology, genetics, and those causes then become the efficient cause of the disposition. If what appear as psychologically self-sufficient, mental states and dispositions, are themselves explicable in terms of prior causes then the goal of an action is not its cause. The implication of this is that the action can, in principle, be explained ultimately in terms of efficient causality.

In Hume's widely adopted model the conditions of efficient causality are met when events are temporally successive, contiguous in time and space and occur on a regular basis. This weak model of causality, sometimes referred to as the regularity theory of causation, has the merit of avoiding any metaphysical commitment to underlying mechanisms, causal powers or religiously inspired end states. It relies instead merely on observable relations and psychological dispositions.

In practice the notion of efficient causality is often held with some metaphysical commitment and some view of causal powers. Hume's sceptical viewpoint forbade the connection of regularity with any underlying mechanism but others take efficient causality to include causal powers and modal claims. The model of efficient causality is then taken in a strong sense. On the regularity model all one can say about a particular causal relation between 'a' and 'b' just is that the term cause describes the relation 'a' regularly occurring before 'b' where 'a' and 'b' satisfy the contiguity criteria. On the causal power or modal model, however, it would be claimed that the statement, 'whenever "a" then "b"' expressed a relation of necessity. It is not that 'a' and 'b' are related only in terms of regularity it is rather that 'a' causes 'b' in the sense that 'a' brings 'b' about.

The earliest attempt to give a complete explanation from matter to human action, ethics, jurisprudence and politics in terms of efficient causality understood in a strong sense is found in the work of Thomas Hobbes. Hobbes starts from the premise that all life is but matter in motion and every aspect of life can be explained in terms of the accidents of bodies. Hobbes's theory is strongly deterministic and he rules out completely the notion of FREE WILL. Nonetheless Hobbes has a strong view of human freedom and he is the first, and one of the best known, examples of someone who is prepared to argue that a strong conception of efficient causality is compatible with a strong conception of freedom.

Compatabilist arguments usually take the form that the causality underlying the determinism rests in a different domain to freedom and that the two domains do not intersect. Hobbes's model is paradigmatic of this kind of argument. Determinism is opposed to free will, but freedom is opposed to coercion. Hence if someone is not coerced into an action or physically impeded from performing an action they are free. If someone is coerced or impeded then they are not free. The issue of underlying causality has nothing to do with the question of freedom. Such views were strongly rejected by Rousseau and by Kant on the grounds that morality required that the will be free.

What is at stake in disagreements of this kind are differences about practical reason but also about the metaphysical status of the PERSON. From Kant's perspective practical reason demands that the actor be undetermined. Even in our own times the broad perspective taken on responsibility seems to favour a view that actions are not determined. It is not clear, however, that all forms of practical reason require such a claim. It is perfectly comprehensible to conceive how one would hold someone responsible for an action even if that action was determined at some metaphysical level and what the general requirements of the practical reason involved would be. Our own pre-Augustinian history is resplendent with such models illustrating that they are, in principle and in practice, possible.

The conception of self and person held by Hobbes on the one hand and Rousseau or Kant on the other is quite different. For Hobbes the conception of the self is weak, perhaps even epiphenomenal, whereas for Rousseau and Kant the conception of the self is strong. Weak conceptions of the self are usual in deterministic arguments, for if actions are determined then the mental states, dispositions and even consciousness of the actor are also caused. If the mental states, dispositions and consciousness of the actor are caused then the actor cannot be said to have a distinct self for the self is always explicable in more fundamental terms.

The promise of the kind of determinism found in efficient causality is the explanation of all actions and future predictions. The ideal is the mechanistic Humean–Laplacian conceptually closed, if spatially infinite, universe where everything is stable and if every present condition was known then in principle all future states would be predictable. Such knowledge, if obtainable, would result in a power of the kind expressed in Auguste Comte's positive philosophy, 'To know in order to predict, to predict in order to control'. As a programme the potential control over the universe promised by knowledge of causes and the determining of events and actions was a significant hallmark of modernity. Determinism, in the sense that one can determine the nature of the world and its environment was at the very heart of the Enlightenment project and its successors. By modelling the conception of determinism on efficient causality the shackles of earlier conceptions of fate and providence that had placed human beings at the mercy of divine forces or providence were broken. In its place was substituted efficient causality where the formal function of God was to start the mechanism of the universe according to knowable laws but not to interfere with those laws once started. This is Aristotle's prime mover, that which moves everything else but which is not itself moved, or Hobbes's first cause where God begins the chain of causes and effects. In such models God is at the beginning of the universe and causal in that sense. As God is omniscient so he knows the end state as a matter of knowledge, but it is not some end state of the universe that determines its present condition. The distinction here is between knowing and causing. For example to know what someone will do is not to cause that action and it is not to determine it. There are many cases where we know very well how someone will behave or react in a certain situation. That knowledge is not, however, a cause of their actions. Similarly a God standing outside of time may well perceive or know what the state of things will be at the end of time. But this knowledge does not warrant the fatalistic claim that such an end state was determined or caused by God's knowledge.

Most modern and contemporary notions of causality are based on efficient causality: an idea that promises much and delivers little. Indeed it is not clear it can deliver anything of significance. The Laplacian model of the universe depends on a stable and closed system and is unsustainable. It assumes that there is a closed totality of states of affairs that can be known in principle. By contrast, however, a universe that contains reflexive knowers is always open and not subject to the kind of closure demanded of the Laplacian model. The act of knowing and reflecting on the 'knowledge' of the totality changes the totality and the act of knowing and reflecting on that totality changes that next totality and so on. The implication of this is that a universe perceived by a reflexive knower is always open. That knower may be God or human beings or other reflexive beings, in either case every act of knowing changes the condition and changes the universe. Another way of putting this is that the universe is never completely describable for every description would need to include both itself and the changes wrought by that description. It is always impossible where there are reflexive beings in the description to both include the description and the effects of the description. To attempt to do so is to change the totality so that it requires a redescription, that redescription requires another redescription and so on. It seems that the enterprise of giving a complete description of the universe is impossible either in principle, or in practice. Consequently the Laplacian (or any structurally similar) model of the universe is impossible.

The more general implications of this argument apply to smaller systems than the universe. This restricts in a quite definite and distinct way what can be said about any system that includes knowers. For slightly different but not completely unrelated reasons there are also general restrictions on what can be said about any but the most simple systems even where knowers are not involved. The state of a system can be completely described only if the determining points in it can be accurately known. That

condition cannot be met of any but the simplest systems. This is not a restriction that is likely to yield to more sophisticated analysis for it is a general restriction of principle. At the microlevel it is found in the principle of uncertainty, first enunciated by Heisenberg, whereby a complete description of both the position and momentum of an atomic particle can never be given. At the macro level it is found in any system that is sensitive to its starting conditions. An uncertainty in those conditions will result in predictive errors. Those errors will always occur unless the starting conditions are precisely known. This is impossible, hence some uncertainty is always present.

Even at the more limited level of events a determinism based on efficient causality can offer little. Much of what is significant and important about the natural and the social world is found in systems and in structures. Attempts to explain changes in systems merely in terms of efficient causality seem doomed to failure. Natural systems are complexes of interacting components that are never completely closed. They do have components that have efficient causes but such causes are never completely determinative of the state of the system at some future point in time. It may even be the case that the course of many natural systems can never be known beyond a certain period. Weather systems are probably just unpredictable beyond a few weeks and some are so unstable that even that may not be possible in all cases. Human and social systems are almost certainly not predictable at all, or even significantly understandable, in terms of efficient causality. That notion for all its apparent strengths and attractions seems not to be significant in a larger sense. That seems to imply that a different conception of causality is required for such systems.

Human affairs seem to be bounded more by structures than by efficient causes. One well known kind of causal claim of that kind, takes a role form. In such cases the cause of someone's acting in a particular way was due to their role. That role in turn is describable in institutional terms. Thus the cause of someone dressing in blue, and standing in the middle of the road waving their arms is that they are a traffic policeman on duty. The explanation of the event phenomenon, waving arms and so on does not meaningfully yield to explanation in terms of efficient cause. It may well be the case that waving arms in a particular way has a neurological and biological counterpart, but explaining the actions of a traffic policeman on duty in such terms is to miss the point. Such an explanation would say nothing of what it is to be a policeman, to be on duty and so on. Nor can it. Those terms are always and only role and institutional terms and not reducible to some mechanistic or efficiently causal explanation.

It does not follow from this failure of the appropriateness of efficiently causal explanations in such cases that the action is not determined. On the contrary it may well be the case that the actions of the policeman are determined by his role and his play in the relevant institution(s). Any such determinism would be structural: the social structures in which people are engaged determine their actions. As with many other determinisms this too can be held in a weak or in a strong sense. In a weak sense it is the view that structures constrain what someone does but do not directly cause it. It is the agent that is the cause of their own actions. In a strong sense this kind of determinism takes it that agents are constructed or constituted in and by structures, they do not have an independent existence. The strongest expression of this kind of perspective is well represented in Althusser's claim that 'History is a process without a subject.' What is at stake here as in the earlier difference between Hobbes on the one hand and Rousseau and Kant on the other is the strength or otherwise given to the notion of self. It it is fully constituted by external factors then it has no independence and cannot be a cause of actions and if the self is fully determined then it might be thought that everything meaningful to people was determined. In some post-modernist thought this position is held and held quite strongly.

By contrast weak structural determinism takes it that there are agents who are the cause of actions but those actions take place in social contexts. Giddens, for instance, has it that agents bring about changes in structures but structures bring about changes in agents; the

relation between them is reflexive. Marx put this idea well when he said that 'men make history but they do not make it in conditions of their choosing'. This kind of theory takes it that structures are enabling as well as constraining. Structures may present barriers and restrictions but they are also necessary for action to take place at all. This latter point is both valid and important. An agent in an otherwise empty universe would be no sort of agent at all. It would have nothing to do and nowhere to act. Even if it had complete omnipotence over itself it would still have no universe into which to act, and without a sense of otherness would have no sense of self. Such a radically free being would be completely determined in the sense of being completely bound for it would be a prisoner of its own emptiness. By contrast a structured universe without agents would itself be nothing: a totality without the knower. That there are knowers makes the totality impossible and that the totality is impossible provides an assurance that neither it nor the reflexively constituted beings in it can ever be completely determined. To be reflexive is always to be underdetermined.

Althusser, L. (1972) *Politics and History*, London.
Aristotle (1941) *Metaphysics*, trans. W.D. Ross, in Richard McKeon (ed.) *The Basic Works of Aristotle*, New York: Random House.
Augustine of Hippo (1972) *Concerning the City of God Against the Pagans*, Harmondsworth: Penguin.
——(1964) *On Free Choice of the Will*, trans. Anna S. Benjamin and L.H. Hackstaff, Indianapolis: Bobbs-Merril.
Cicero *On the Nature of the Gods* I.xxv Loeb Classics.
Giddens, Anthony (1984) *The Constitution of Society*, Cambridge: Polity Press.
Heisenberg, Werner (1949) *The Physical Principles of the Quantum Theory*, Dover Publications Inc.
Hobbes, Thomas (1968) *Leviathan*, Harmondsworth: Penguin.
Hume, David (1975) *Enquiries Concerning Human Understanding and Concerning the Principles of Morals*, ed. Peter H. Nidditch, Oxford: Clarendon Press.
Kant, Immanuel (1964) *The Groundwork of the Metaphysics of Morals*, trans. H.J. Paton, New York: Harper and Row.
Marx, Karl (1975) *Karl Marx, Friedrich Engels: Collected Works*, London: Lawrence and Wishart.

Rousseau, J.-J. (1994) *Discourse on the Origin of Inequality*, Oxford Paperbacks.
Stewart, Ian (1990) *Does God Play Dice?*

Paul Barry Clarke

DEVELOPMENT

Development is a term which, in its application to the growth both of individual organisms or persons and of whole societies, came into use only in modern times, starting from the end of the eighteenth century. It stood for an idea of the gradual unfolding of a fuller form that was present as a pre-determined destiny, or as a potential, 'in germ'. It derived its sense from the characteristically modern visions of evolution and progress.

'Development' implies more than a mere change and even more than 'growth'. It implies a change with a clear-cut direction, and a 'growth' which leads a living organism or a person or a society towards the 'proper' mature state. What the proper mature state is like is known in advance and could be spelled out with some precision; that state sets a standard by which the current shape of the developing entity is evaluated and the degree of still persisting 'underdevelopment' is diagnosed. 'Development' implies as well that to move towards the fully developed form is the course which is 'normal' for the entity in question to take; the absence of such a movement is a sign of some abnormality, presents a problem, requires a remedial action.

Development has therefore become first a political and then a theoretical issue in social sciences and economics, under the influence of the vindications raised and voiced with growing force by the populations disprivileged in the global distribution of wealth and resources. The state reached by the affluent countries of the West has now become the worldwide definition of the destiny of societal evolution; the path leading to that state is to be recapitulated by the rest of the world. Thus 'development' has been pressed into the centre of world politics by the nationalist demands of new states eager to bridge the gap dividing them from the rich and powerful nations of the industrialized West. In the view of both the nationalist élites and Western theories elaborated in response, the enviable WEALTH and standard of living were reached in the West as the result of industrial expansion fuelled by capital saving and investment, and this was exactly the historical course which other countries, belated and thwarted in their 'development', should follow.

It was clear from the start, however, that the Western itinerary leading to their present state of affluence and power cannot be reproduced. First, the very awareness of the 'problem of development' made a tremendous change. The original INDUSTRIALIZATION, URBANIZATION, economic growth in the West were not consciously envisaged or anticipated; they happened without advance knowledge of where were they leading. It was only in retrospect that the idea of 'development' was applied in historiography of the West, and social, psychological, political and cultural transformations were re-described as stages in development – a movement 'with a pointer'. In contrast, the presence of Western wealth as a vivid and agitating example has created a sense of urgency in the contemporary world; it has called for deliberate mobilization of resources, grand designs of social engineering, ubiquitous state intervention: a purposeful action with the end defined in advance, rather than allowing for a diffuse and spontaneous process and the plurality of uncoordinated initiatives which secured the growth in the West. Second, the world in which the first industrial nations lifted themselves to their present level of affluence has been changed beyond comparison, and their 'lifting themselves' was precisely the main cause of that change. Unlike the pioneering countries of the West, their would-be imitators find themselves in a very different, and much harsher, world: they must act from a position of inferiority, in competition with adversaries much stronger and more resourceful then they are.

The combination of the political pressures toward recapitulating what is now seen as the 'Western development' on the one hand and of the practical impossibility of doing it on the other confronted the theorists and the practitioners of development with a task not much easier than that of squaring the circle. Both theory and practice are the site for bitter disagreements showing over the years few signs of abating. Most theorists, though, agree that the pattern of the 'developed' West is indeed the universal meaning of progress and well-being; reaching that pattern is what the countries by comparison undeveloped, or not fully developed, should in ideal circumstances do. The majority of theorists differ solely in their diagnoses of the roots of backwardness and the remedies they prescribe. In recent decades, most opinions on these two subjects were shaped in the ongoing dispute between the theoretical perspectives of *modernization* and *dependency*.

By far the most influential proponent of the first perspective was Walt Whitman Rostow, the author of the 'theory of stages': there is a fixed series of stages which every country (every national economy, treated as a relatively self-enclosed and self-sustained whole) must pass on the way to 'full development'. The stages follow each other in a logical order, each preparing the ground, and determining the likelihood, of the next. Before the development begins, there is the 'traditional' society, characterized by pre-Newtonian technology, ascriptive social structure and absence of capital savings and investments; the crucial passage is the 'take-off', caused by the accumulation of surplus, loosening of the social structure and the appearance of a new élite willing to reinvest rather than consume its riches. In view of this theory, the absence or delay of the 'take-off' stage could only be explained by the presence of some 'obstacles to economic growth' *inside* a given society. Attempts at explanations were widely and repeatedly made, with imperfections of the potentially modernizing élite and resistance of the would-be modern producers remaining the two most favoured subjects.

The search for the 'constraints to economic growth' was conducted mostly in terms of the 'crucial watershed' between the *traditional* and the *modern* SOCIETY, ECONOMY, CULTURE or mentality, deemed decisive for the chances to embark resolutely on the development route. As to the élite, most accounts related directly or obliquely to Max Weber's classic analysis of the link between the Protestant ethic, with the 'this-worldly ASCETICISM' and thus delay of gratification it promoted to an extent never encountered in other religions, and the 'spirit of CAPITALISM' which more than anything else expressed itself in refraining from today's enjoyment of wealth in the name of the magnified profits of the future. As to the potential labour force needed by a modern economy, 'traditionality' of workers was singled out as the main obstacle: if a modern worker must think in terms of 'how best may I use my labour to attain the highest possible returns', the 'traditional' worker tended to think in terms of 'how much do I need to labour in order to satisfy the needs I have'. All in all, the 'take-off' was identified with the 'untying of needs', or in other words with taking the lid off consumer wants and the desire for self-enrichment. As long as the needs remained fixed and thus the population by and large remained immune to the attractions of the market, the stimuli meant to prompt and boost economic growth stayed ineffective.

The 'dependency' perspective developed in direct opposition to the theory of modernization by stages: it denied that passing the stages in their 'natural' succession is, given enough time, inevitable; that such a passage, if it occurs, is prompted by socio-cultural transformations internal to the society in question; and that the reason why the 'take-off' does not take place in the majority of the disprivileged countries is the delay in the said transformations. Instead, theories advanced from the 'dependency' perspective insisted that by far the major cause of economic backwardness is precisely the presence in the world of highly 'developed', economically and politically powerful states. According to these theories, non-development is not a stage in the chain leading to the 'take-off', but a *relation* which not only may last indefinitely but tends to deepen and become even more prospectless over time. The original theory elaborated from the perspective of dependency was advanced by Andre Gunder Frank. It considered the contemporary economy as a global system, sharply divided between a 'metropolis' which dominates the system and many peripheral 'satellites' with AUTONOMY severely constrained by that domination. The satellite status distorts the 'natural' course native economies could have taken; the actual course is determined by the needs and pressures of the metropolis, external to the satellite countries and indifferent to their interests. Dire poverty and further deterioration in the living standards observed currently in many countries of the third World are not the outcome of their 'traditionality', but a secondary, artificially induced condition contrived by the global economic system and a direct outcome of the distorting impact of the systemic metropolis. If the 'modernization' theory focuses almost entirely on inner springs of development and plays down the impact of external factors, the 'dependency' theories, in contrast, tend to assign to the global-systemic factors a role which the critics of such theories deem grossly exaggerated. Both perspectives can be charged with one-sidedness; none can account for the astounding diversity of individual cases of economic success or failure.

Most theories of development advanced from both perspectives assume that becoming 'developed' is a good thing, not universally attainable yet universally desired. This, however, is not necessarily the case. Barrington Moore Jr, the perceptive analyst of diverse routes through which various societies travelled to their present modern state, concluded that there is no evidence anywhere that the majority of people actively desired the industrial society and the turbulence it brinks in its wake; but there is ample evidence that they have not had such a desire. Industrialization, always coupled with the uprooting of customary ways of life and a secure network of human affinities, as well as, for many people, considerable loss of autonomy, is responsible for a lot of hardship with which the victims are not prepared to cope. It is not necessary either that the left behind and relatively impoverished populations who resent the economic privileges of the affluent modern countries unreservedly admire the way of life associated with such privileges and wish it for themselves. Wealth and income as the sole measure of human worth is not universally considered as able to give life a meaning; neither is the rampant, often selfish, individualism of the 'pursuit of happiness' type universally desired as a right substitute for ethical principles of life and proper compensation for the values only such

life could sustain. Material comforts which 'development' is so apt in supplying are not universally approved of if they come, as is often the case, together with the loss of spiritual depth and moral concerns. Finally, nowhere thus far has economic development succeeded in eradicating human misery; raising the 'objective' level at which the poverty line is drawn does not eliminate the humiliation and degrading effects of relative deprivation.

It is for this reason that alongside the theory and politics concerned solely with the best ways of promoting development and hardly ever questioning the desirability of the end itself, one can find standpoints (often, though not always, religiously inspired) from which radical or moderate objections to development, at least in the shape defined by the acceptance of superiority of the affluent countries, are voiced. Traditions of such resistance go back to the Russian 'populism' of the nineteenth century, which first promoted the idea of an 'alternative way', meant to preserve and cultivate, rather than uproot, the ethically charged native legacy. Many observers consider the recent rise of religious FUNDAMENTALISM within the domains of all major religions as a further chapter in the history of that populist tendency; as a sign that the forces resisting the advance of the 'developed' form of life, previously marginal, now gather strength in the face of weakening global power and self-confidence in the West and particularly of the ever more evident harmful consequences (social, psychological, ethical, ecological) of untamed commerciality and consumerism – the consequences with which, however undesirable they may be, the 'developed' societies are ill prepared to cope.

Cipolla, Carlo M. (1976) *Before the Industrial Revolution*, London: Methuen.
Foster-Carter, Aidan (1985) *The Sociology of Development*, Ormskirk: Causeway Press.
Goldthorpe, John E. (1984) *The Sociology of the Third World: Disparity and Development*, Cambridge: Cambridge University Press.
Kitching, Gavin (1982) *Development and Underdevelopment in Historical Perspective*, London: Methuen.
Landes, David S. (1969) *The Unbound Prometheus*, Cambridge: Cambridge University Press.
Moore, Barrington, Jr (1966) *Social Origins of*

Dictatorship and Democracy, Harmondsworth: Penguin.

Rostow, Walt Whitman (1971) *The Stages of Economic Growth*, Cambridge: Cambridge University Press.

Roxborough, Ian (1979) *Theories of Underdevelopment*, London: Macmillan.

Zygmunt Bauman

DEVIL

The Devil, also commonly known as Satan, is conceived as the arch opponent of God, the source of all EVIL in the world, and the one tempting humanity to SIN according to traditional Christian thought. The word 'devil' derives from the Greek *diabolos*, a term originally meaning 'slanderer'. The Septuagint used it for the Hebrew satan, a word meaning 'accuser' or 'adversary'. Normally in the Hebrew Bible, including in the book of Job, the term 'satan' is not used as a proper name. Instead it refers to a member of the heavenly court who functions to accuse people before God. He is God's agent, not God's opponent. Only in 1 Chronicles 21: 1 does the word 'satan' become the name of an individual opposing God. The Chronicler employs Satan in a 'simpleminded THEODICY' to free God from blame for David's sin (cf. 2 Samuel 24), but in the process he opened the way for the 'rapid and spectacular rise to power of the independent evil ruler of human affairs' (Forsyth 1987: 122–3). Through a complex process of myth making this figure, associated with other names like Belial and Mastema, was linked to various historical and mythical opponents of God until in the developing APOCALYPTIC tradition of sectarian Judaism God was thought to have one great cosmic opponent, Satan or the Devil, who directed the evil deeds of Israel's oppressors as well as those of fellow Jews against the elect community. Because Satan was thought to have been a member of the heavenly court originally, he provided the model of the intimate enemy for sectarian Jews (Pagels 1991).

Christianity took over the dualistic conception of a cosmic struggle between God and the Devil from apocalyptic Judaism. To this it added the myth of the resurrected and ascended Jesus Christ who would lead the eschatological victory of God over Satan and his human and heavenly followers (Matthew 25: 41; Hebrews 2: 14; Revelation 20: 4–10). As in sectarian Judaism, those opposing the followers of Christ were viewed as servants of Satan (2 Corinthians 11: 14–15) or children of the Devil (John 8: 44). This negative labelling reinforced the identity of the Christians as the people of God, accounted for opposition to them and distanced them from the corrupting influence of outsiders, especially their religious competitors. The New Testament writings also make clear that Satan played a role in the folk religion of Jesus and his followers. The Devil, as the prince of demons, was thought to be responsible for human illness and disability (Mark 3: 22–7; Acts 10: 38; 2 Corinthians 12: 7). Thus, by exorcising demons (*see* DEMONIC, Jesus and his followers engaged in overpowering the Devil.

In combating the cosmic dualism of GNOSTICISM the Patristic Church contended that the Devil was a rebellious angel, not a genuinely independent power (Forsyth 1987). Thus cosmic dualism was rejected in favour of Pauline ethical dualism, making sin the fundamental problem to be overcome. Augustine claimed the Devil's original sin was pride and then found in this the paradigm for all human sin. At the level of popular Christianity the Devil and his demonic agents were thought to be responsible for all evil in human experience. Entry into the Church included ritual exorcism making it the one part of society free from the power of the Devil. In the late Empire, when all but the Jews had become Christians, the idea of the witch, whose pact with the Devil against Christ rendered him or her totally evil, emerged to account for the persistence of evil in an otherwise Christian world (Brown, in Douglas 1970).

In the twelfth century when the Church began to confront potential rivals the idea developed that heretics worshipped the Devil. This vilification of religious competitors by the Church was clearly intended to marginalize them within society and justify their destruction. Around this period the inquisitions began to direct their attention against the ancient practice of magic and witchcraft claiming that witches, who were said to worship Satan and engage in sexual orgies with him, were part of an organized attack on Christian society (Cohen, in Douglas 1970). The development of this myth led to illness, infertility, crop failure and death being attributed to the work of witches in league with Satan. This in turn created a SOCIETY that was quick to condemn and punish innocent people who were perceived as threats to the social order.

In the contemporary world two distinct tendencies have emerged. On the one hand, since the Enlightenment with its anti-supernatural bias the very concept of the Devil as a personal evil force has become problematic for many in Western civilization. For this reason the Devil plays only a minor role in much contemporary Christian THEOLOGY. Where the term 'Devil' does occur it has largely been demythologized, becoming a symbol or metaphor (Russell 1985) for the malevolent forces of destruction and evil emanating from human volition, or resulting from social interaction and the structures created by human beings. For many theological thinkers the idea of a personal devil has become repugnant because it threatens to absolve humanity of its personal and corporate responsibility for the existence of evil (Williams 1990). On the other hand, for many the Devil remains a formidable spiritual foe seeking to lure people to their destruction through sin. Christian Fundamentalists, with their pre-scientific worldview, often go further, claiming that contemporary society is under increasing assault from Satan (e.g. Christenson 1990; *see* FUNDAMENTALISM). They contend that Satanism, the active pursuit of evil by those worshipping the Devil, is on the increase through organized Satanic cults. Hicks (1991) has documented the considerable impact which this view has had since 1980 on law enforcement workers in the USA many of whom attempt to explain a variety of crimes in terms of Satanic activity. The Devil clearly remains part of contemporary folklore (Hicks 1991), providing a popular explanation for evil and deviancy from societal norms among a significant group of contemporary Christians.

While the Devil's role in serious theological reflection has waned in the modern world, Satan remains a powerful force for evil in the mind of popular Christianity. Unfortunately, by attributing ultimate responsibility for evil to a supernatural force, and by understanding evil in moralistic terms and as deviancy from societal norms, many Fundamentalist Christians appear to deny any personal culpability for the fundamental evils of modern society and avoid the need to engage in creating a world where the root causes of evil such as RACISM, unequal distribution of resources and exploitation are overcome.

Christenson, E. (1990) *Battling the Prince of Darkness: Rescuing Captives from Satan's Kingdom*, Wheaton, IL: Victor Books.
Douglas, M. (1970) *Witchcraft Confessions and Accusations*, London: Tavistock.
Forsyth, N. (1987) *The Old Enemy: Satan and the Combat Myth*, Princeton, NJ: Princeton University Press.
Gellner, E. (1974) *The Devil in Modern Philosophy*, Boston, MA: RKP.
Hicks, R.D. (1991) *In Pursuit of Satan: The Police and the Occult*, Buffalo, NY: Prometheus Books.
Karlsen, C.F. (1987) *The Devil in the Shape of a Woman: Witchcraft in Colonial New England*, London: W.W. Norton.
Pagels, E. (1991) 'The social history of Satan, the "intimate enemy": a preliminary sketch', *Harvard Theological Review* 84: 105–28.
Russell, J.B. (1977) *The Devil: Perceptions of Evil from Antiquity to Primitive Christianity*, Ithaca, NY: Cornell University Press.
——(1981) *Satan: The Early Christian Tradition*, Ithaca, NY: Cornell University Press.
——(1985) *Lucifer: The Devil in the Middle Ages*, Ithaca, NY: Cornell University Press.
——(1986) *Mephistopheles: The Devil in the Modern World*, Ithaca, NY: Cornell University Press.
Williams, D.D. (1990) *The Demonic and the Divine*, ed. S.A. Evans, Minneapolis, MN: Fortress Press.

Charles A. Wanamaker

DISARMAMENT

'To disarm' is 'to reduce national armaments' while the adjective 'disarming' means 'conciliating, instantly gaining goodwill or favour (e.g. of a manner, a smile)'. These definitions are not an adequate guide in military contexts, where a 'disarming first-strike capability' may involve genocidal attacks with nuclear weapons and where scholars find it imperative to distinguish between disarmament and arms control. We follow the strategists in applying 'disarmament' to every sort of destruction or reduction of weapons save natural decay and destruction in use (e.g. destroying a bomb by dropping it in anger), and we contrast disarmament with arms control, which may permit or require *increases* in ARMAMENT if these are agreed to be necessary. Of course, the reduction or increase may be in the assets of a 'liberation movement' rather than in 'national armaments'.

The most effective form of disarmament is also the least attainable: general and complete disarmament would presumably put an end to WAR by removing the weapons with which it is fought. The prospect of this is so remote that more limited measures need to be considered. Broadly speaking, it is convenient to distinguish nowadays three main types of context in which disarmament might be proposed: (a) deterrence among states; (b) conventional warfare among states; (c) irregular warfare as in civil war or armed rebellion.

During the Cold War, each of the superpowers came to possess probably far more weapons than were required according to their own concept of security by deterrence. There was ample scope for cuts before either side became anywhere near endangering its deterrent. This allowed critics of deterrence to argue that deep cuts in weapon inventories could be made, if necessary on a unilateral basis, to demonstrate goodwill and thus to create the conditions for improved political relationships and movement away from the moral nightmare of reliance on nuclear weapons. Opponents of what they called 'one-sided disarmament' said that it would be better in both favourable and unfavourable conditions to proceed through multilateral arms control negotiations. Under favourable conditions, arms control would move the great powers towards shared responsibility for security. When conditions were unfavourable, negotiation would remain a channel for communication and a valuable diversion from deadlier expressions of mutual animosity. This complicated debate was ended (for the time being) not by one side's winning the argument but by the demise of the USSR.

In the immediate aftermath of the Cold War, the USA was so overwhelmingly the strongest military power that deterrence among current nuclear weapon states was not a prominent issue. Of far more urgent concern was the possibility that enemies in some of the world's sharpest political conflicts would acquire and use nuclear, chemical or biological weapons. If the spread of these weapons to a pair of enemies was reasonably well balanced then Cold War theories of deterrence offered some comfort in the thought that the balance of terror *forces* states to act responsibly. But well-balanced proliferation cannot be guaranteed and some doubt that all states are as inherently rational as the superpowers were during the Cold War. It can also be pointed out that the superpowers typically had the option of whether to confront or avoid one another at many points of tension whereas many regional conflicts are unavoidably localized, so that crises are bound to offer fewer options of retreat or avoidance.

Might some kind of disarmament be the best response to this potential spread of non-deterrent nuclear (and chemical and biological) weapons? Part of the answer may well lie in the Non-Proliferation Treaty (NPT). This is an agreement between possessors of nuclear weapons and non-possessors. The non-possessors undertake not to acquire nuclear weapons and to submit to international measures of verification. The possessors undertake to share the benefits of civil nuclear power and to negotiate in good faith for the reduction of their nuclear arsenals. There is little in the Treaty to encourage a non-possessor to sign but a great many non-possessors have judged it to be in their security interest to forgo the nuclear weapons option and to have this formalized in the NPT. Alas, some of the likeliest proliferators have refrained from signing, and it is open to any state to withdraw from the Treaty. Though the NPT is thus a useful measure of voluntary multilateral disarmament (mostly non-acquisition rather than destruction), it is by no means the whole solution to the postwar nuclear weapons problem.

Another kind of multilateral measure might be a regional arms control agreement whereby enemies agree to exclude nuclear weapons from their region. But the prospects of success are bound to be poor. If states are so hostile that they think it worth their while to acquire nuclear weapons for use against one another, any negotiations between them are likely to be a channel for animosity rather than the striking of a harmonious bargain.

If regional powers cannot deny themselves nuclear weapons and cannot be trusted to become the possessors of stable deterrents then the possibility of outside intervention has to be considered. Iraqi experience provides a good illustration of some of the difficulties. Israel acted unilaterally to destroy a reactor which it believed to be capable of helping Iraq to acquire nuclear weapons. As a possessor of nuclear weapons in all but name, Israel was in an invidious position. If a case can be made for its action, it is perhaps that Israel's interests are such as to guarantee that its nuclear weapons programme is aimed at a stable deterrent whereas Iraq's stated rejection of Israel's right to exist confirmed in words what deeds also show, that Iraq is an aggressive state which is prepared to use whatever weapons it possesses (including chemical weapons against its own Kurdish subjects). Following the invasion of Kuwait, destruction of Iraq's capacity to wage aggressive war was an aim of the coalition forces. Attempts were made during and after the war against Iraq to destroy Iraq's ability to make and deliver nuclear weapons.

It is unlikely that every state acquiring nuclear weapons will do so as part of a political stance which is as flagrantly aggressive as Iraq's. This raises some very difficult questions. First, when Iraq invaded Kuwait many countries wanted to look the other way and to avoid becoming involved. Without the determination of the USA to act against a power which had affronted its status in the Middle East it is perfectly possible that even AGGRESSION as flagrant as Iraq's against Kuwait might not have elicited a response sufficient to counter the aggression and deprive the aggressor of a nuclear weapons capability. Where great power interests are less directly involved, may the will be lacking to prevent the spread of nuclear (and chemical and biological) weapons to dangerously unstable regions and aggressive powers? Second, if the will exists, can its exercise avoid the shortcomings illustrated by Israeli unilateralism? The multilateral response of the war to restore Kuwait was made possible by Saddam Hussein's astonishingly simplistic affront to both international law and American interests. The cause of non-proliferation is unlikely to be as well served in future.

Arms do not cause wars (*see* ARMAMENT) and it is unlikely that disarmament can prevent them. What of arms control negotiations, whose agreed outcome may be to reduce or destroy certain categories of weapon systems or their removal from certain especially sensitive regions? The prospects are not good. States which are close to war tend to be deeply mistrustful, so that any significant agreement would have to meet a very high standard of verifiability. Also, weapons are so diverse that the scope for technical difficulties is enormous. Communication is better than none, so negotiations may well be worth supporting, but a substantive outcome is not to be expected.

Rebels probably depend on gifts of weapons or money to a much greater extent than states, so that the responsibility of donors is at its greatest in this kind of warfare (*see* ARMAMENT). Conversely, intervention to prevent or curb political chaos may well be imperative and this may require us to rethink many cherished views about self-determination. During the period of the inter-war League of Nations, it was still accepted that there were parts of the world which were not yet ready for self-government and which could therefore legitimately be subjected to external rule. They became Mandated Territories. The states to which mandates were entrusted were required to prepare them for self-government. After the Second World War, there was ever-increasing hostility to such paternalism (a sexist word for what might better be called 'parentalism'). Anti-imperialism was radically opposed to the continuation of government by mandate but social and political disintegration in the period since the Cold War has been so rapid and intense that reconsideration may be necessary.

The former Yugoslavia provides an example. At the time of writing, the Muslim population of Bosnia-Herzegovina is virtually defenceless against its Serbian enemies and unable to trust its recent Croatian allies which it suspects of aiming to share the region with Serbia, driving out Islam. Understandably, there are calls in the

Moslem world to arm the victims of this internal aggression, but it is not clear that such armament can hope to be any more constructive than the arms poured into Afghanistan following Soviet intervention there in 1979. An alternative approach might be to seek international recognition that Bosnia-Herzegovina is ungovernable at present, is a threat to regional security (not least through the pressure of its refugees on fragile European democracies) and needs to be taken under benevolent external control. The mandate for such a move would presumably require the intervening power(s) to disarm the factions within the country and to return it to independence under an effective government as soon as possible.

The obstacles to such an action are formidable. We have already mentioned anti-imperialism. The political realist will remind us that the League of Nations mandates were conferred on imperial powers which had their own imperial reasons for wishing to supervise the territory, whereas the motives for reconsideration are an apolitical concern for HUMAN RIGHTS and a desire to contain local conflicts which do not give any state a positive reason for wishing to garrison the troubled area. (And history may rule out some of the states best equipped to intervene. For example, no-one wants Germany, the most perturbed recipient of refugees from the former Yugoslavia, to exercise a mandate there.) The disincentives to becoming involved in such a mandate are formidable, not least the size and fire-power and casualties to be incurred by a force adequate to the task of disarming a passionately divided society at war with itself.

Such difficulties may have to be faced now that the brutal simplicities of the Cold War have ceased to set limits to a myriad of ethnic conflicts. The word 'disarmament' has come to have a warmly comforting sound, but may soon be connected above all with painful and invidious interventions.

Vincent, R.J. (1974) *Nonintervention and International Order*, Princeton, NJ: Princeton University Press.
Waltz, K.R. (1981) *The Spread of Nuclear Weapons: More May Be Better*, London: IISS.
Williamson, R. (1992) *Profit Without Honour?*, London: CCADD.

Barrie Paskins

DISPOSAL

Disposal refers to the ways human bodies are treated after DEATH. Burial, including burial at sea, has been the traditional Christian form of disposal but cremation is a growing modern practice.

Bodily RESURRECTION, the identity of the dead and the immortal SOUL are three crucial ideas associated with disposal in Christianity. Burial became the central rite of early Christian disposal because it imitated the burial of Christ, and was the prelude to resurrection. The identity of the dead is closely related to the way bodies are treated at death. Traditionally, when the dead are identified as Christians, through baptism and church-membership, their bodies were thought to have a future and should be treated in ways that prepared them for the day of resurrection.

Early Christianity adopted both the Jewish idea of a resurrection of the body and the Greek belief in an immortal soul. (Traditional Indian ideas of transmigration and reincarnation were never accepted by Christianity.) In practice, Christians have tended to view the disposal of the body as one aspect of death, and the departure of the soul as another.

In early Christian centuries cremation was widespread in pagan Europe but it rapidly gave way to burial under the spread of Christianity whose theology favoured the grave.

Many churches were built over the buried remains of early martyrs, who were believed to be meritorious people whose souls were already in HEAVEN. Many sought burial close to them, hoping to gain some spiritual benefit. Once such a martyr-church (*Martyrium*) was full, bodies were placed outside, giving rise to graveyards.

The martyr's death was associated with baptism involving a symbolic death to the old life and a birth to new life in Christ. As ideas of burial, baptism and death became closely linked, so did martyr-churches and places of baptism (Baptistries). The dead continue to play a significant part in church life as, for example, in Roman Catholic churches where many altars contains a martyr's relic, acknowledged by the priest as he kisses the altar at the start of each Mass. Eastern Orthodox Christians also use relics, placing them in the corner of each altar-cloth. In the twelfth century relics were widely collected and pilgrimages were made to places honouring them. In modern times families commonly visit the graves of relatives because disposal of bodies seldom means forgetting the dead.

Contemporary Christians bury their dead in various ways under the influence of local custom. In many European countries and the USA the dead are viewed in their coffins before being buried. Traditionally they were kept at home for a few days before burial, but as more people die in hospital this custom is rapidly declining and the dead are kept at funeral homes prior to their burial. Throughout the nineteenth and twentieth centuries the disposal of the dead has increasingly been taken on by professional Funeral Directors. Bodies are very often embalmed, making them look more life-like, prior to burial or cremation. In modern Western societies, the bodies of the dead are left in their graves after burial, in what can be called single disposal of the body. Exhumation, the removal of bodies from the ground, is regarded as undesirable, occurring only by order and for legal purposes. But, historically, the bones of the dead have sometimes been exhumed and placed in official ossuaries, especially from overcrowded graveyards of city churches. This ceased with the growth of large civic cemeteries in the nineteenth and twentieth centuries.

In traditional Mediterranean Christian cultures, especially Greek Orthodox ones, a form of double funeral rite is well known. Bodies are seldom embalmed, and several years after burial the grave is re-opened and, if the corpse has fully decomposed, the bones are removed to an ossuary with church rites and popular customs.

Strong pressure began in nineteenth-century Europe to establish cremation as a legal funerary option. Many cemeteries were filling, and burial of the poor often lacked dignity. In 1832 the Anatomy Bill passed through the British Parliament ending the practice of giving the bodies of

convicted murderers to doctors for dissection. In 1834 new Poor Law legislation permitted the dissection of corpses of those who died as paupers. This was little encouragement for paupers knowing that they might be dissected instead of murderers (Richardson 1987: 207).

The new Anatomy Act stimulated the growth of Friendly Societies who provided proper funerals for those who would otherwise be left to the state and dissection. This led to the drive to have a 'respectable' as opposed to a pauper's funeral.

In Britain numerous eminent Victorians supported the move towards cremation with Sir Henry Thompson, surgeon to Queen Victoria, spear-heading reform by founding the Cremation Society of Great Britain in 1874.

Although a few were cremated on private land the breakthrough for cremation came when the baby son of eccentric Dr William Price died. Having trained in medicine in London, this Welshman reckoned himself a high priest of the Druid order, then undergoing a romantic revival. Aged 83 he fathered a baby, named it Jesus Christ, and on its death cremated it on a mountain in South Wales. A public outcry lead to his arrest but the decision at his trial, in February 1884, was that cremation was legal as long as it caused no public nuisance.

This encouraged the Cremation Society. A crematorium built at Woking in Surrey performed the first legal cremation in Britain in March 1885 and, after a slow start, cremation became increasingly popular; by 1968, more were cremated than buried. By the 1990s the cremation rate levelled out at approximately 70 per cent, a high rate compared with other Christian cultures.

Countries with Protestant backgrounds have higher rates of cremation than traditionally Catholic countries. The Lutheran Protestantism of Denmark (67 per cent) and Sweden (61 per cent) matches the Anglical Protestantism of Great Britain (70 per cent) and contrasts with Catholic France (6 per cent), Ireland (3 per cent), Italy (1 per cent) and Spain (3 per cent). In July 1963 the Catholic Church declared it acceptable for Catholics to be cremated, and in 1966 also allowed priests to conduct crematorium services. The Catholic Church opposed

Growth of crematoria in Britain		
Period	Number	Cumulative
1885–99	4	4
1900–9	9	13
1910–19	1	14
1920–9	6	20
1930–9	34	54
1940–9	4	58
1950–9	73	131
1960–9	73	204
1970–9	15	219
1980–9	4	223

Cremation as percentage of all deaths for 1990			
Australia	47	Irish Republic	3
Austria	9	Italy	1
Belgium	20	New Zealand	56
Canada	33	Spain	3
Denmark	67	Sweden	61
France	6	Switzerland	59
Hungary	22	USA	17

cremation partly because Freemasons supported it, for Catholicism opposes Masonry.

Cremation rates also depend on geography since crematoria tend to be built in urban areas for economic reasons, though some rural areas also tend to be more attached to the tradition of local graveyards.

Cremation shows the importance of linking theological and sociological analyses in describing and interpreting human activity, and in dispelling popular misconceptions.

In practical terms, the body is kept in the coffin and placed in a crematory or furnace preheated to a high temperature. The coffin, and then the body, burns rapidly so that after approximately one and a half hours only human ashes and pieces of larger bones remain. These are crushed in a machine called a cremulator. The powdery remains weigh approximately 6 pounds or just under 3 kilograms. Only one body at a time can be accommodated in cremators, and the ashes of each individual are kept separate and dealt with after each cremation.

In Britain ashes are normally buried or scattered on reserved gardens. Some British families place them in sites of personal significance, while some countries like Sweden insist that ashes are buried and not removed for personal placement.

Anthropological theory can help explain differences in funeral practices. So, for example, the social anthropologist Robert Hertz devised a theory for tribal peoples in Indonesia which can also be applied to modern Europe. Hertz showed that some peoples engaged in double funerary rites. First the dead were buried until the flesh rotted away, in what he called the 'wet' phase of the rites. Then, in the 'dry' phase, the bones were placed somewhere special, signifying the change of the identity of the dead as they obtained new identity as ancestors. This approach can be applied to modern burial and cremation to link theological and sociological views on the dead. Two sorts of interpretations will provide examples.

In the first interpretation burial is the primary phase conducted by human beings, normally a priest, while the secondary phase is believed to take place in the future when God resurrects the dead person. Humans perform the first, God performs the second, within a total double RITUAL.

In the second interpretation the burial of the body is one dimension of the rite, and the passing of the soul is the second. The first is performed by Man, while the second occurs as the soul follows its own supernatural course.

In both these interpretations the first phase is natural and the second supernatural. In both, the first phase represents earthly time while the second belongs to eternity. Both interpretations also presume that people believe in life after death (Davies 1990: 30). But research shows that, in Britain, more than half the general public do not believe in an afterlife, a factor associated with the process of SECULARIZATION. For these people cremation gives a new opportunity for understanding human identity in relation to disposal, but still in a two-phased rite.

The first phase is the cremation of the body, and the second involves doing something with the ashes. The distinctive feature of this possibility is that ashes can be used to express aspects of the dead person's former life, being placed in a garden, river, mountain, golf course, etc. These all refer to the past personality of the dead, and to memories for the living, but not to some future eternal identity. In a similar way some people also want their dead pets cremated, showing how animals can also be invested with an identity of their own.

Cremation may have become popular because it answers a symbolic need for those who do not believe in an afterlife and who dislike the idea of rotting in the earth. But, equally, it appeals to those with afterlife beliefs who interpret it in terms of the soul leaving the body after death and who think little of the body itself. Its rapid reduction to ashes can emphasize the belief both in the soul passing on its own way and in the final end of the individual concerned. In this sense cremation is doubly successful compared with burial.

In the nineteenth century city cemeteries were said to be a health hazard, and cremation was pursued as a sanitary necessity. The motto of the British Cremation Society is 'Save the Land for the Living', which expresses some modern thoughts about the ENVIRONMENT. But throughout the 1980s it was increasingly obvious that cremation also had some negative environmental consequences in producing quantities of gases, some of which were undesirable as far as the atmosphere was concerned. This led to the installation of emission-monitoring equipment at crematoria, with constant attempts to increase the efficiency of the cremation process.

In conclusion it might be suggested that the change of emphasis from traditional forms of burial to cremation shows the influence of secularized values with decreased belief in life after death. Ashes privately placed suggest an increased emphasis on personal relationships and the individual identity of the dead person.

Aries, P. (1974) *Western Attitudes Towards Death*, Baltimore, MD: Johns Hopkins University Press.

Bloch, M. and Parry, J. (eds) (1982) *Death and the Regeneration of Life*, Cambridge: Cambridge University Press.

Chidester, D. (1990) *Patterns of Transcendence, Religion, Death, and Dying*, Belmont, CA: Wadsworth.

Curl, J.S. (1972) *The Victorian Celebration of Death*, London: David & Charles.

Davies, D.J. (1990) *Cremation Today and Tomorrow*, Nottingham: Grove Books.

Hertz, R. (1907) 'A contribution to the study of the collective representation of death', reprinted in R. Needham (1960) *Death and the Right Hand*, London: Cohen & West.

McManners, J. (1981) *Death and the Enlightenment*, Oxford: Clarendon.

Metcalf, P. and Huntingdon, R. (1991) *Celebrations of Death*, Cambridge: Cambridge University Press.

Richardson, R. (1987) *Death, Dissection and the Destitute*, London: Routledge.

Douglas J. Davies

DIVORCE

In present society there is a tendency to see divorce both as a source of individual unhappiness and as an index or cause of wider social disorder. However divorce might be evaluated, few people in conducting these debates have any doubts as to the meaning of the term. To be divorced represents a clear legal status, the achievement of which is usually accompanied by clearly defined practices such as the establishment of separate households and agreements over the divisions of property and about the maintainance of, custody over or access to any children.

Divorce is frequently equated with marital breakdown although it is clear that the two need not be the same. Taking a wider historical or cross-cultural approach will serve as a reminder that definitions of divorce are by no means straightforward and in all cases depend upon the particular understandings of MARRIAGE in a given society. This interdependence between understandings of divorce and of marriage may be seen in the history of divorce in European societies and in the emerging distinctions between divorce, annulment and separation. In the case of 'annulment', it was the business of the church courts to determine whether a so-called marriage could be treated as if it had never legally taken place. Such an approach provided some, often limited, opportunities for individuals to exploit ambiguities in existing marriage laws and practices to obtain what was in effect a 'divorce', moreover a divorce which permitted the partners to 're-marry'. Separation, 'from bed and board', was also often seen as a form of officially sanctioned divorce although one which denied the partners the opportunity for re-marriage. Such limited opportunities for *de facto* divorce depended almost entirely upon ecclesiastical understandings and ecclesiastical power. Further, the extent of such formal control over informal marital practices could vary considerably. As one historian vividly notes:

> Prayer, murder, suicide, bigamy, separation, jumping backward over a besom, desertion, wife sale, all were alternatives to formal divorce.
>
> (Phillips 1991: 91)

There will be variation, not only in formal codifications and informal practices, but also in the social significance and meaning that divorce assumes. Clearly, the social meaning of divorce will vary according to the extent to which considerations such as PROPERTY, the family name and public position are at stake. But of equal importance has been the extent of and possibilities for the expression of more locally based popular disapproval of 'divorce' or irregular marital practices. Such variations within societies are always important, but especially prior to the development of centralized state institutions.

From a comparative perspective it is also important to see that the social meaning of divorce and marriage can vary considerably between societies. For example, the social meaning of divorce may be quite different in those societies where the marital tie is not seen as the sole or primary bond that an adult person may have and where obligations to kin and families of origin may be seen as being of equal or greater importance. What a comparative approach may tell us is that divorce is not simply a measure of the quality of interpersonal relationships but must also be understood in terms of the wider sets of social-structural pressures, the networks of relationships and expectations within which the partners individually or jointly are involved and the strength and effectiveness of local public sanctions.

In more complex societies it is necessary to consider those agencies that develop particular interests in marriage and sexual behaviour. Religious institutions are of major importance here, especially to the extent to which they are linked to or implicated in wider social or political practices. For example, much although not all, of the variation between European countries can be explained by the different size and political influence of Catholicism. Historians note that for Britain, as for many parts of Europe, divorce was relatively easy up to the tenth century. From that time, we see the rise of the mainstream Christian position of hostility to divorce culminating in the codification of ecclesiastical law dealing with marriage and divorce at the Council of Trent, 1560–3. With the Reformation, there is the beginning of a divergence between Protestant and Catholic positions with England, however, remaining at the more restrictive end of the continuum. The growth of secular ideologies together with the declining institutional influence of the church led to further weakenings of the absolute prohibitions against divorce; again, England remained somewhat apart from these wider trends. Since the Second World War, however, influential Anglican opinion moved sharply in favour of recognizing divorce and also came to recognize the possibility of the re-marriage of divorced persons within church. The latter part of the twentieth century was often characterized in terms such as 'the tide of divorce' although it would be wrong to see the dramatic increases that took place in many parts of the world as being simply a function of more permissive legislation. Legislation itself reflected wider trends and changes in social and economic life.

One way of viewing the changing attitudes to and legislation concerning divorce is as part of a long-term shift in marriage from institution to relationship. While such a formulation is not without its ambiguities it is one which has a wide currency amongst not only social scientists but also other professionals, including CLERGY. The recognition of divorce and the formal elimination of notions such as 'guilty party' or 'matrimonial offence' could be seen as representing the triumph of a relational view of marriage.

This is not to say that the rising rates of divorce in the latter half of the twentieth century have been accepted without concern. It is, rather, that the nature of the concern has shifted. At one level, divorce is understood as a personal problem requiring the mobilization of care, support and advice for those undergoing the experience of divorce. As a social problem, divorce is probably seen less as a social EVIL in its own right and more as an element in a whole range of other social issues. Here, much of the concern focuses upon the children and upon the range of disadvantages associated with single-parent households, many of which now are created as a consequence of divorce.

Further rises in the divorce rate always attract comment and although it can be maintained, inverting the common formulation, that two out of three marriages do *not* end in divorce there is clearly some concern about the changes which may be reflected in such rises. Some sociologists have written of a 'tipping point' in such issues, the point at which what was once regarded as abnormal or deviant now comes to take on an air of normality even where statistically the practices may still be a minority phenomenon. Divorce becomes less of a stigmatized status and more of an established status passage. However, this passing of the 'tipping point' is not the same as universal approval and concerns continue to be expressed that divorce has gone 'far enough'.

The rise in divorce rates has obviously encouraged speculation as to its causes. More permissive legislation is clearly only part of the answer. One important factor which receives a place in most accounts is to do with the changing position of women in the societies under consideration. This is given plausibility by the fact that most petitions for divorce are initiated by women. Here emphasis has been placed on the rising proportion of married women in paid employment, the extension of political, economic and social rights to women and the growth of feminist thought. Cumulatively, these changes have provided greater opportunities for women to have an independent life outside marriage and have probably produced a reduced tolerance of abuse and exploitation within the home (*see* FEMINISM).

Some emphasis may also be given to the changing patterns of social control in relation to marital behaviour. It can be argued that the relatively limited legal opportunities for divorce in previous centuries were often reinforced by strong, more locally based, patterns of informal control from the wider network of family and community. It is here that we may note differences between Catholic and Protestant countries. It is not simply a question of divorce being condemned more rigorously in one faith than another, although theological differences are important. It is also a reflection of the fact that CAPITALISM and INDUSTRIALIZATION developed earlier and more extensively in Protestant countries and that these major historical developments had the effect of weakening the wider nexus of social controls over individual behaviour. That this cannot be the complete answer, however, is indicated by the case of England which was early in terms of industrialization but relatively late in terms of divorce reform.

The absence or decline of constraints is usually seen in conjunction with the growth or presence of more positive encouragement. In the first place there are, parodoxically, rising expectations concerning marriage. This is clearly linked to the idea of marriage being seen in more relational terms than in institutional terms. People, it is argued, expect more from marriage in terms of personal fulfilment and individual happiness and the marital tie becomes the central adult relationship. However, there are also good reasons to suppose that such expectations cannot be completely fulfilled, e.g. the contrasts between the realities of domestic life with small children and the ideals of the fulfilling marital relationship. Thus, such expectations contribute to strains within the marital relationship while holding out the possibility of their realization in a new relationship.

A second aspect of these more positive sanctions is to do with ideologies of individualism and self-realization. The focus on the more relational aspects of marriage may be seen as part of a wider set of values to do with individual freedom and the right of individuals to shape their own lives. Further, modern economic rationality entails the rejection of traditional controls. However, the varied experiences of former communist countries with respect to divorce indicates that capitalism alone cannot be used to account for the rising divorce rates; however, it may be argued that both capitalist and former communist countries were committed, in varying ways, to values of MODERNITY and economic rationality.

It should be stressed that there is still a lot of work to be done here and many issues to be explored. It may be seen, however, that religion should not simply be viewed as a source of constraint although this was very clearly the case in the past. As Christianity came to endorse a more relational understanding of marriage and family relationships (perhaps in opposition to the more impersonal expectations of commerce or politics) so, paradoxically, it gave some encouragement to divorce.

Gibson, Collin S. (1994) *Dissolving Wedlock*, London: Routledge.
Gillis, John (1985) *For Better, For Worse: British Marriages 1600 to the Present Day*, Oxford: Oxford University Press.
Goode, William J. (1993) *World Changes in Divorce Patterns*, New Haven and London: Yale University Press.
Lewis, Jane, Clark, David and Morgan, David (1992) *Whom God Hath Joined Together: The Work of Marriage Guidance*, London: Routledge.
Phillips, Roderick (1991) *Untying The Knot: A Short History of Divorce*, Cambridge: Cambridge University Press.
Stone, Lawrence (1991) *Roads to Divorce: England 1530–1987*, Oxford: Oxford University Press.

David H.J. Morgan

DOMESTIC VIOLENCE

Domestic violence indicates a phenomenon without identifying the agents responsible for it. It has to do with the abuse of power in intimate relationships, normally those of a household where 'good enough' intergenerational caring should exclude physical and/or sexual abuse, emotional abuse, extreme neglect, the witnessing of violence between the household's members, and substance abuse (Gelles and Loseke 1993). Child battering may be perpetrated by adults of either sex, as well as by siblings and older children outside a household, or by visitors to it, e.g. baby-sitters (The Violence Against Children Study Group 1990; Corby 1993). Male violence towards women may take the form of physical battering (Dobash and Dobash 1970, 1992) and/or RAPE (Matoesian 1993). Female

violence towards men is most likely to be an act of self-defence or a reaction to repeated attacks on a woman and/or children. The evidence for claims of equivalence in VIOLENCE between partners needs careful attention (Dobash and Dobash 1992: 258–84). The main focus of the present entry is on violence between men and women.

Concern with violence against children has sometimes given momentum to making their point of view central to thinking about them (Parton 1985; Parton and Ferguson in The Violence Against Children Study Group 1990). Until the 1970s it seems that society's concern was primarily with protection *from* children, and with the attempt to control delinquents. The present period of considering their interests *as persons* in the light of the traumas which may be inflicted upon them may be said to have begun with the formation of societies for the protection of children in the late nineteenth century. Marked development since the Second World War has resulted from the work of paediatricians such as C. Henry Kempe and his publication of work on the 'battered child syndrome', a clinical condition which may result in permanent injury or death. The capacity of those in positions of trust to harm children, or to fail to protect them, and the limits of understanding, prevention and inter-agency intervention continue to render violence to children an intractable area of social concern. Public sensitivity in the UK developed in particular as a result of the inquiry into the death of Maria Colwell in January 1973.

The history of attention to violence against women and its interrelationship with CHILD ABUSE in the nineteenth and twentieth centuries has most notably been documented and analysed by Linda Gordon (Gordon 1988, 1992). Particular emphases in her work are on the necessity of seeing families as *conflictual* as well as harmonious, and on the unpredictability and ambivalent emotions that characterize intimate relationships. She provides evidence of the negotiating strategies employed by both sexes to make better lives for themselves and their children. Crucial factors include economic dependence or independence, the ability to separate or divorce and the extent of support and intervention from outside a household. The twentieth-century women's movement prompted a renewed focus on child-battering and on abuse and violence between men and women. For women, the possibility of finding a household context where isolation is overcome and, beyond that, of finding economic independence, are central to escaping from a violent household. The problems are cross-cultural, though some of the triggers for violence are peculiar to certain cultures, e.g. issues about dowry payments. The founding of 'Women's Aid' organizations and of refuges for battered women and their children (notably the refuge in Chiswick in 1972) marked a new phase in response to domestic violence (Cohen 1992). An indication of its prevalence is represented by the claim that it is *severe* in one in fourteen marriages in America. And whereas between 1967 and 1973 the Vietnam War cost the USA some 39,000 casualties, during the same period 17,500 American women and children were killed by family members (Walrond-Skinner 1993: 65–7).

It appears that domestic violence may take place once there is commitment to a permanent relationship with another adult, and that more precisely it has to do with the social institution of MARRIAGE as traditionally constructed. In part this accounts for the ambivalent behaviour of women who may eventually leave a violent household after coming to terms with difficulty with the fact that the violence will not stop, and the relationship cannot be restored, unless and until that relationship can be renegotiated at a fundamental level. In the last twenty years, much has been learned about the therapies which enable those who have suffered from domestic violence to embark on one of the *many* roads to recovery (Sandford 1990; Kirkwood 1993). It also seems that domestic violence is related to male possessiveness and jealousy, expectations about women's domestic and sexual 'services', a sense of 'right' to punish women for perceived wrongdoing, and to the maintenance of male authority in a household. Intimacy does not in, of and by itself remove conflicts of interest between members of a household, but there is nothing inevitable about the resolution of such conflicts in favour of male dominance. A distinctive feature of multidisciplinary study of domestic violence at present is

attention to issues of GENDER, POWER and control, and to the ways in which women without a proper sense of self and of their own dignity as human persons may be so incapacitated by habits of self-denial that they are unable to take care of themselves (Parton and Hearn, in The Violence Against Children Study Group 1990; Yllö, in Gelles and Loseke 1993). Any perspective which helps to illuminate domestic violence and recovery from it is to be welcomed.

In so far as religious traditions mediate gender constructions to a SOCIETY, or reflect those of a society, they need careful evaluation when an area of human behaviour as serious as domestic violence manifests itself. It is arguable that the Christian tradition, for one, has fostered SEXISM, i.e. the belief that persons are superior or inferior to one another on the basis of their sex, and that female inferiority is expressed in passivity, dependence, bodiliness, being emotional, weak and childlike in the worst senses of that word. It is worth remembering that the phrase 'rule of thumb' originated in the English common law position that a man might beat his wife with a stick no thicker than his thumb. Until very recently, marriage rites provided reinforcement for such habits of male dominance, as do readings from the so-called household codes of the New Testament. The most troublesome of these is 1 Peter 3: 1–9, which urges submission on Christian wives, so that their silence and chastity might aid in the conversion of their unbelieving husbands. Such texts need to be relegated to the Graeco-Roman slave-owning households in which they may have had some point. The teaching of forbearance, meekness, forgiveness, obedience and self-sacrifice coupled with a sense of inferiority may well play its part in rendering women unable to resist male violence (Pellauer *et al.* 1987; Thistlethwaite 1990).

Social scientists and Christian institutions address the complexity of the issues somewhat differently. Social scientists themselves reveal major divisions of opinion between those who study the phenomena and those who want to mobilize for social change. Study of domestic violence is well advanced, critical and constructive, and if we now agree that domestic violence is wholly unacceptable this represents a major change in sensibility. The social changes needed to free households from violence as a mode of conflict resolution are of no mean order, however. Yet violence is not inevitable, nor is its transmission between the generations, and nor is it impossible to recover from it. It must be the responsibility of Christian institutions not only to eradicate damaging gender constructions from their doctrines and liturgies and forms of teaching, but to learn about appropriate modes of assistance and intervention in the interests of renewed hope and possibilities for those of all ages and either sex who suffer from domestic violence.

Cohen, S. (1992) *The Evolution of Women's Asylums Since 1500. From Refuges for Ex-Prostitutes to Shelters for Battered Women*, New York: Oxford University Press.

Corby, B. (1993) *Child Abuse. Towards a Knowledge Base*, Milton Keynes: Open University Press.

Dobash, R.E. and Dobash, R.P. (1970) *Violence Against Wives*, New York: Free Press.

——(1992) *Women, Violence and Social Change*, London: Routledge.

Gelles, R.J. and Loseke, D.R. (eds) (1993) *Current Controversies on Family Violence*, London: Sage.

Gordon, L. (1988) *Heroes of Their Own Lives. The Politics and History of Family Violence, Boston 1880–1960*, New York: Viking.

——(1992) 'A right not to be beaten. The Agency of Battered Women, 1880–1960', in D.O. Helly and S.M. Reverby (eds) *Gendered Domains. Rethinking Public and Private in Women's History*, Ithaca, NY: Cornell University Press.

Kirkwood, C. (1993) *Leaving Abusive Partners. From the Scars of Survival to the Wisdom for Change*, London: Sage.

Matoesian, G.M. (1993) *Reproducing Rape. Domination through Talk in the Courtroom*. Cambridge: Polity.

Parton, N. (1985) *The Politics of Child Abuse*, Basingstoke: Macmillan.

Pellauer, M.D., Chester, B. and Boyajian, J. (1987) *Sexual Assault and Abuse. A Handbook for Clergy and Religious Professionals*, New York: HarperCollins.

Sandford, L. (1990) *Strong at the Broken Places*, New York: Random House.

Thistlethwaite, S. (1990) *Sex, Race and God, Christian Feminism in Black and White*, London: Chapman.

Violence Against Children Study Group, The (1990) *Taking Child Abuse Seriously. Contemporary Issues in Child Protection Theory and Practice*, London: Unwin Hyman.

Walrond-Skinner, S. (1993) *The Fulcrum and the Fire: Wrestling with Family Life*, London: Darton, Longman & Todd.

Ann Loades

DRUG ADDICTION

The word 'drug' is unscientific and imprecise in origin. Derived from the German *droge vate* (dry casks), it came to be applied, wrongly, to the contents of the casks. In international and conventional usage the word has come to refer to substances which affect the central nervous system, though many drugs do not affect it. Thus a commonly accepted international definition treats a drug as 'any substance that, when taken into the living organism, may modify one or more of its functions'. (A satirical version of this definition sees it as 'any substance that, when administered to three rats in a laboratory, produces a scientific paper'.) 'Drugs' is a simple way of referring to psychochemicals which affect the central nervous system by acting on chemical transmitters in the brain. Drugs mimic substances in the brain, activating receptor sites. As a result of the ingestion of a drug, changes in behaviour will occur – sedation or slowing down of motor activity, stimulation, the killing of physical and mental pain, changes in the nature of perception and so on. Drugs may be animal, vegetable or mineral, or synthetic. While many drugs derived from plants are very ancient (cannabis, opium, coca), others have only been identified or synthesized during the last hundred years (heroin, amphetamine and a range of combinations) or since the 1950s (the minor tranquillizers, many antidepressants, and anti-psychotic agents). The production of centrally acting drugs for therapeutic reasons is a major part of the international pharmaceutical industry.

The concept of addiction derives from the Latin *addicere*, to assent, a word used in the Roman law courts where, in debt cases, the debtor himself or herself was often given to the creditor as a slave and became *addictus*, delivered into slavery. The link between addiction and SLAVERY goes back to early literature. The addict is seen as enslaved to a substance, though often a willing and devoted slave. Thus Anthony Chute's *Tobacco* (1595) glorifies tobacco as a nymph to whom one pledges devotion, and there are many such expressions of dedication to a drug. Many drugs are seen as sacred or even sacramental substances – peyote among native Americans, cannabis among Rastafarians, LSD among many of the gurus of the 1960s mystical counter-culture. The quest for chemical ecstasy or enhanced consciousness is both ancient and widespread. Ronald Siegel sees the desire for intoxication as one of four basic biological drives (along with hunger, thirst and sex).

The terminology of drug use and addiction is confusing. Usually misuse refers to intermittent misapplication of the drug, abuse to continuous misapplication, but both terms assume that there is some objective way of knowing what constitutes misuse and abuse. Moreover the terms are used loosely and often interchangeably. It used to be common to distinguish addiction (involving physical dependence) from habituation. The Departmental Committee on Morphine and Heroin Addiction in 1926 defined an addict as 'a person who, not requiring the continued use of a drug for the relief of the symptoms of organic disease, has acquired, as a result of repeated administration, an overpowering desire for its continuance, and in whom withdrawal of the drug leads to definite symptoms of mental and physical distress or disorder'. However, in 1964 the World Health Organization abandoned the language of addiction for that of dependence, producing the following definition.

Drug dependence is a state of psychic or physical dependence, or both, on a drug, arising in a person following administration of that drug on a periodic or continuous basis. The characteristics of such a state will vary with the agent involved and these characteristics must always be made clear by designating the particular type of drug dependence in each specific case.

Since the mid-1960s, a period marked by the growth of amphetamine use by young people, it has been widely recognized that physical withdrawal symptoms and tolerance are not necessary to the idea of drug dependence.

It has been said that 'the literature of addiction is highly repetitive, sometimes unreliable, and often based on misinformation' (Lindesmith 1968). In recent years, particularly in the USA, the terms 'addict' and 'addictive' have come to be used loosely and generally, e.g. in relation to societies, corporations, churches. The distinction between 'soft' and 'hard' drugs, while still common, is misleading and inaccurate. The term 'narcotic' (which means sleep-inducing) is extremely confusing since it is often used of drugs which do not have this effect. There has also been considerable debate on the whole concept of 'addiction' as a form of compulsive behaviour rather than a chosen lifestyle and identity.

Popular writing and discussion has tended to stress drugs such as heroin and cocaine and to ignore alcohol (which is also a drug, though one often finds the phrase 'alcohol and drugs'), tobacco and the widely prescribed hypnosedatives and tranquillizers. In 1987 it is estimated that 79,128 people in the UK died from alcohol- and tobacco-related causes, compared with 230 from other drugs. The prescribing of centrally active drugs of the sedative, tranquillizer and antidepressant type has been increasing since the 1950s. By 1974 9 million prescriptions for psychoactive drugs were issued in England and Wales.

There are many ways of dividing centrally acting drugs into categories. A simple method is to divide them into sedatives (barbiturates, methaqualone, alcohol), stimulants (amphetamine, cocaine), intoxicants (cannabis, alcohol), psychedelics (mescalin, LSD, STP) and opiates (morphine, heroin). But the same drugs can be used in a variety of ways. Thus alcohol is both sedative and intoxicant, LSD can be used as intoxicant or stimulant, etc. Often drugs which have been used for many years acquire new patterns of usage within a given subculture. Thus free base cocaine ('crack') is now common among urban youth. Derivatives of amphetamine such as MDMA ('Ecstasy') have become common in the UK in the 'rave' scene since 1989, although MDMA was synthesized in 1914. The use of drugs for religious or mystical purposes did not begin with the hippies of 1966. Nitrous oxide was used with such intent by

Coleridge and was documented by William James, while LSD was used in therapy at Powick Hospital in the early 1950s.

Attitudes to the treatment of addiction are as varied as the drugs themselves. The emphasis on the family and the therapeutic community is central to many approaches. Alcoholics Anonymous with its 'Twelve Step Programme' has provided a model for groups involved with other forms of dependence. Therapeutic communities may be based on group work models, while some are rooted in a religious tradition. Chemical approaches will include the use of substitute drugs as in methadone maintenance. Contrary to much mythology, many addicts cease their use of a drug as a result of some life crisis without going through any 'programme'.

In Britain the first major legislation was the Dangerous Drugs Act 1920. The recommendations of the Departmental Committee on Morphine and Heroin Addiction in 1926 (the Rolleston Committee) led to what has been misleadingly called 'the British system'. Drugs such as heroin and cocaine, on the Rolleston policy, can be prescribed under certain conditions. There is evidence that such a policy does keep both addiction, crime and (in recent years) HIV infection through injection under control. In the USA, where these drugs are illegal, the link between addiction and criminal syndicates is one of the major social problems. In the USA, heroin addiction rose from 471,000 in 1990 to 701,000 in 1992. In Britain the total figure for all known drug addicts (not including alcohol) was 20,802 in 1991. During 1991 there were 8,000 new notifications. The heroin figures rose from 5,639 in 1989 to 6,923 in 1990. However, today most of the heroin, cocaine and amphetamine is of illicit origin, and most addicts remain unknown to the Home Office. Policies to deal with drugs may do more damage than the drugs themselves. It has been estimated that 90 per cent of the current costs of drug abuse are costs relating to policy implementation. Policy can increase actual abuse.

In various religious traditions, orthodoxy is linked with sobriety. An ancient Christian hymn of St Ambrose speaks of 'joyfully drinking of the sober intoxication of the spirit' (*laeti bibamus sobriam ebrietatem Spiritus*). There are parallels in Jewish and Hindu spirituality. In both Jewish and Christian worship, alcohol is used ceremonially. Religion itself can be a form of addiction. The link between dependence and spiritual immaturity needs further reflection.

Blakeborough, Eric (1986) *No Quick Fix: A Church's Mission to the London Drug Scene*, Basingstoke: Marshall Pickering.

British Journal of Addiction.

Davies, J.B. (1992) *The Myth of Addiction*, Chichester: Harwood.

Edwards, Griffith and Busch, Carol (1981) *Drug Problems in Britain: A Review of Ten Years*, London: Academic.

International Journal on Drug Policy.

Lindesmith, A.R. (1968) *Opiate Addiction*, Chicago, IL: Aldine Press.

May, Gerald G. (1987) *Addiction and Grace*, New York: Harper & Row.

Musto, David F. (1987) *The American Disease: Origins of Narcotic Control*, Oxford: Oxford University Press.

Schaef, Anne Wilson and Fassel, Diane (1988) *The Addictive Organisation*, New York: Harper & Row.

Scott, P.D. and Marshall, J. (1991) *Cocaine Politics*, Berkeley, CA: University of California Press.

Siegel, Ronald K. (1989) *Intoxication*, New York: Simon & Schuster.

Steinberg, Hannah (ed.) (1969) *The Scientific Basis of Drug Dependence*, J. & A. Churchill.

Szasz, T.S. (1975) *Ceremonial Chemistry*, London: Routledge.

Trebach, A.S. (1982) *The Heroin Solution*, New Haven, CT: Yale University Press 1982.

Weil, Andrew (1972) *The Natural Mind*, Boston, MA: Houghton Mifflin.

Whynes, D.K. and Bean, P.T. (eds) (1991) *Policing and Prescribing: the British System of Drug Control*, London: Macmillan.

Kenneth Leech

ECCLESIOLOGY

'Ecclesiology' is a theological rather than a political or sociological term. It refers to the disciplined and critical study of the Christian Church from a theological point of view. Although ecclesiology clearly has a practical dimension in pastoralia, liturgy and Church government, it is essentially a branch of Christian doctrine and accordingly has a prescriptive intention: it aims ultimately to say what the Church should be and how it should carry out its tasks. It is therefore normally informed by belief and commitment.

However, in order to arrive at its prescriptive conclusions – proposed for Christian belief and action – ecclesiology will certainly include descriptive, phenomenological aspects and here it will rely on historical and sociological studies of the Church as an empirical worldly phenomenon. It will also have an analytical, critical dimension: it will not merely celebrate the Church's past glories, such as they are, but will also sit in judgement on the failings and shortcomings of the Church in history and in the present. In this respect it will draw not only on 'internal' sources of critique, such as the Biblical prophetic material and the major reforming insights of Christian history (e.g. the Protestant Reformation and the theological renewal of the Second Vatican Council of 1962–5), but also on secular traditions of critique, especially broadly Marxist ideological criticism. It is at these two points – phenomenological description and ideological criticism – that the theological discipline of ecclesiology is particularly open to insights and information derived from 'secular' disciplines beyond the 'household of faith'. In conclusion, ecclesiology may be defined as the critical study of the governing paradigms of the Church's self-understanding.

Ecclesiology is a broad topic in THEOLOGY, embracing several departments of theological study that impinge on the nature of the Church: WORSHIP and liturgy, sacraments and discipline, ministry and pastoralia, AUTHORITY and leadership, Church government and Christian unity (ecumenism). Clearly these topics all invite analysis and comment from the social sciences: this analysis will be comparative, relativistic and critical and may be viewed from within the Church, by theological students, conservative theologians and Church leaders, as reductionist and subversive. Some classical ecclesiologies – Roman Catholic, Orthodox or Protestant – claim that the nature of the Church, including its outward political aspect or polity (papal, episcopalian or presbyterian), is bestowed transcendentally by God as part of salvation history and is not subject to the judgement of human reason. They assert that the ultimate integrity of the Church is guaranteed by divine providence, so that the apparent vicissitudes of Christian history become retrospectively baptized as the unfolding of divine purpose. Some modern theologians regard the social sciences as occupying a tendentious stance in relation to Christian faith, rather than as offering ideologically neutral tools for analysis and clarification. They see no place for ecclesiological analysis by merely human methods and techniques that are not subordinated to divine revelation. Rare are the theologians (e.g. F. Schleiermacher) who accept that the outward face of the Church in history – its political aspect – is purely contingent and cannot detract from the abiding validity of the inward essence of faith. However, once it is accepted, in continuity with the dynamic of the Reformation, which sees the Church as continually reforming itself in the light of divine perfection and the requirements of its mission (*Ecclesia reformata semper reformanda*), that the critique of Christianity belongs to the very essence of Christianity, a welcome is assured for the commentary offered by the social sciences.

The aspects of ideological critique that are particularly relevant to ecclesiology concern the distribution of POWER in the religious community. This comes to focus in several areas: the bearing of political paradigms on Church government and the relation of CHURCH AND STATE; the models of authority that pertain in the Church (traditional, bureaucratic and charismatic, to follow broadly Weber's typology); the ideological investment in the formulation and enforcement of official doctrine (dogma) which reflects sectional interests and refracts and distorts divine revelation; and the deconstruction of patriarchy in the Church by feminist theology. To avoid overlapping with other entries in this *Dictionary*, we shall confine our present discussion to the first of these areas – the political aspects of ecclesiology. However, it may be useful first of all to note areas where a socially enlightened ecclesiology is particularly topical in late twentieth-century Western Christianity.

Pluralism Traditional Christianity has upheld in its teaching (and frequently imposed by force) the ideal of unanimity of belief and uniformity of practice. This aspiration has belied the reality of diversity and conflict in the Church from New Testament times to the present day. Theological pluralism is a product, not only of the creative fertility of the theological imagination working on the data of divine revelation, but also of the diversity of social and cultural settings in which theology is carried on, and is a response to the emergence of new challenges to Christian belief and practice – notably from the world of the physical and medical sciences. Recent theology has begun to make a virtue of necessity and to seek a theological rationale for theological pluralism (Rahner, Sykes). In this endeavour, full weight should be given to social and ideological factors. Pluralism is also a factor in ecumenism.

Ecumenism The mainly twentieth-century quest for the reunification of the separated Christian churches has been pursued through practical projects for enhancing fellowship at the local level (degrees of co-operation leading to degrees of communion) and through theoretical projects for reconciling or transcending doctrinal differences (bilateral and multilateral conversations). Social and ideological considerations are important in both, to enable ecumenists and theologians to penetrate beneath the cerebral surface of divisions to the aggravating social and psychological factors. Contrived schemes of unity and paper reconciliations of doctrines are inevitably superficial. Ecumenism needs social science expertise if its efforts are to have that depth of understanding that endures. A wider dimension of ecumenism that is now coming to the fore is inter-faith relations.

Inter-faith relations Long established patterns of mutual condemnation, confrontation and proselytization between the major world faiths is giving way – at least in those parts of the great religious communities touched by Western liberalism – to mutual respect and a desire for dialogue leading to deeper mutual understanding. As well as studies of agreement and difference between the major faiths, there is also a need for each faith to develop a theology of inter-faith relations – a rationale for tolerance, respect, dialogue, co-operation and joint participation in various acts of prayer and worship where appropriate. Mutual understanding cannot come about by trading theological tenets alone, but needs to take into account differences in cultural traditions and diverse ways of interpreting reality as a whole, embodied in myth, RITUAL and social norms. Thus social science is vital to inter-faith dialogue.

Evangelism Whether evangelism is understood in terms of preaching at great crusades, quiet witness to one's neighbour, or social involvement motivated by compassion, its effectiveness will be enhanced if Church leaders have an informed perception of the status of religious beliefs in their society, of the nature and extent of SECULARIZATION and of the persistence of sacred values and symbols (common religion). The empirical work of the sociology of religion and its theoretical interpretation are clearly indispensable here (*see* EVANGELICALISM).

Leadership Declining Church attendance, shortage of ordained ministers, financial constraints and uncertainty about the role of the CLERGY have all conspired to direct attention to what can be learned from secular studies of leadership and management. The skills to define aims, to motivate volunteers, to delegate responsibility and to administer resources of plant, money and manpower are at a premium. In leadership itself the work of W.R. Bion on the dynamics of small groups has been rightly influential in alerting us to the danger of encouraging immature dependence and the imperative of the 'task' or 'work' of the group (Avis 1992).

Feminism Traditional Christianity has been characterized by patriarchy and androcentrism. Sacred symbols have reflected patterns of worldly domination as these have become projected on to the transcendent. In the light of feminist aspirations, Christian theology has recently been compelled to face the question whether a Father God, a male Saviour and a ministry confined to men are intrinsic to the Christian revelation or are to be regarded as a one-sided exaggeration of a sacred reality that transcends the distinction of male and female and is simply distorted by gender stereotypes. Conservative Christians, led by the Vatican, and so-called post-Christian feminists (M. Daly, D. Hampson) take the first view and for different reasons maintain that Christianity cannot distance itself from dominantly male images of the sacred. Liberal Christians, including Christian feminists (female and male), take the second view and have begun to use complementary feminine images of God, to construct an androgynous Christology, to create inclusive liturgies and to campaign for the admission of women to the sacred ministry. In all this the insights of the social sciences have been crucial in suggesting that the apparent differences in role and aptitude between men and women are largely (if not entirely) culturally conditioned (Avis 1989b).

Therapy   If one aspect of the *Zeitgeist* broadly labelled 'NEW AGE' is ecological, the other is certainly therapeutic. The 'turn to the subject' in modernity, that can be traced through Protestant individual responsibility, Kantian epistemology and Romantic sensibility, no longer simply celebrates subjectivity but is also troubled by it – with the result that self-expression frequently adopts a therapeutic mode. Happily for Christian theology, this tendency harmonizes with the Biblical theme of the healing of humanity's physical, social, moral and spiritual ills through God's salvation that makes one whole. Since post-modernity purports (at least) to disown the rampant individualism of recent Western culture, therapy demands a corporate dimension. This is reflected in the popularity of group therapy: we feel that we are more likely to be healed in a community than in the one-to-one therapeutic relationship of traditional depth psychology (it is also cheaper). Correspondingly, the Church comes to be seen as a therapeutic community in which individuals can find the unconditional acceptance that echoes the baby's experience of the nursing mother and which remains the essential prerequisite of the therapeutic situation. Here again ecclesiology is taking a leaf out of the social science (psychology and psychotherapy) agenda (Avis 1989b).

Turning now to the political and juridical aspects of ecclesiology, we may focus on the two rival political models for the Church's organization and government that have dominated Western Catholicism (including Anglicanism) and continue to exist in tension today.

The Christian communities reflected in the greater part of the New Testament literature lacked an overt polity and a political dimension. They were charismatic communities (in Weber's sense): dynamic, volatile, comparatively unstructured and sitting light to all wordly ties. Itinerant apostles and evangelists gathered believers together by preaching the gospel, passing on the traditions of the life, death and resurrection of Jesus, and ritual actions of baptism and the breaking of bread. A threefold crisis brought an end to this phase of the Christian movement and called for a more settled, formal and structured existence for the Church: the expected *parousia* or second coming of Christ did not materialize and longer-term planning became necessary; the Gentile mission exploded the original bounds of a purely Jewish movement and demanded means of control, communication and consultation, such as the Council of Jerusalem depicted in Acts 15; the death of the apostles removed the authoritative living source of tradition and called for normative written sources of teaching.

The development of the nascent Christian Church from these beginnings evinces the phenomenon dubbed by Weber 'the routinization of charisma': the emergence of structures and forms of worship and ministry, including the principle of transmitted authority, the concept of office rather than gifts, standards of belief and norms of practice, investment in property and stipendiary provision for officers of the Church who emerged as a distinct order or caste. In the New Testament, the Pastoral Epistles begin to reflect these developments which are confirmed in the sub-apostolic age with the first signs of a monarchical episcopate as the guardian and embodiment of catholicity (Ignatius of Antioch).

We see then already, at the turn of the first century, a tension emerging between two principles that would continue to exist in conflict throughout subsequent Christian history: the monarchical and the conciliar. Both are forms of CATHOLICISM: they presuppose that the Christian Church exists as a universal, visible, divine society with God-given means and structures through which divine grace, leading to salvation, is bestowed. Catholicity is not a monolithic concept but exists in various permutations of these two fundamental and rival models – the monarchical and the conciliar.

Monarchical catholicism in the history of Western Christianity is a centralized, hierarchical ecclesiology in which plenary authority (*plenitudo potestatis*) is concentrated in the papacy regarded as an absolute monarchy by analogy with imperial government. (There are also episcopal forms of monarchicalism – though much attenuated in the modern Church – in which prelates rule their dioceses by decree without consultation or appeal.) In the period before the Great Schism of 1378 when the cardinals elected a replacement pope, giving rise to parallel structures of jurisdiction running throughout Europe even down to parish level, canon lawyers and theologians readily supplied the popes with ever more inflated claims to bolster their authority against 'secular' rulers. The Church was defined as a *regnum ecclesiasticum* (James of Viterbo), a divinely commissioned monarchical government. In late medieval monarchical papal theory the Pope was free to say and do whatever he pleased and was answerable to no-one. The Pope, it was claimed, could do whatever God could do (Panormitanus). The Pope's pleasure had the force of law and he could dispense his subjects not only from positive law but even from natural law and from the teaching of the gospels according to the letter. The canonists asserted that the Pope had no equal on earth and that every creature was subject to his jurisdiction. The Pope was invested with God's power on earth and was truly a demi-god. The canonists' statements are to be taken at face value since hyperbole was alien to them (W. Ullmann).

As the successor of Moses (who exercised temporal as well as spiritual authority) and of Peter (who wielded two swords on behalf of Christ), the Pope had temporal power as well as spiritual jurisdiction. Though this temporal power was normally delegated to 'secular'

rulers, it authorized the Pope to depose emperors and kings, release subjects from their oath of allegiance, take away empires and kingdoms from their rulers and award them to others, confiscate property, expel persons from public office, interfere in the administration of inheritances and inflict temporal punishments such as flogging, imprisonment and exile. There was no higher court of appeal than the Pope, not even the emperor, for spiritual power included and exceeded temporal power (*Ecclesia continet imperium*). There was no rule that fell outside the boundaries of the Pope's jurisdiction (*Extra ecclesiam non est imperium*), not even heathen empires, for since the reign of God was universal, so must be the rule of God's vicar on earth. What was envisaged by the theorists of untrammelled monarchical catholicism was nothing less than ultimate papal world government.

The twofold papal claim of spiritual and temporal sovereignty reflected the high medieval conception of a unified, hierarchical world. The unity of reality is the fundamental presupposition of medieval thought (Gierke). To deny this was tantamount to heresy (*Duo principia ponere, haereticum est*). 'Throughout the whole Middle Age there reigned, almost without contradiction or qualification, the notion that the oneness and universality of the Church must manifest itself in a unity of law, constitution and supreme government' (Gierke).

Monarchical Catholicism finds expression in teaching, jurisdiction and sacramental power. In teaching it holds that the Roman magisterium has a dogmatic authority equal to – and in practice greater than – a General Council of the Church. In jurisdiction it claims an immediate universal jurisdiction of the papacy, superior to both provincial synods and the authority of the local bishop. In sacramental power it sees all authority to administer sacraments as flowing down from its God-given source in the papacy, so that there can be no true priestly orders or efficacious sacraments outside of communion with the Pope.

These features of monarchical Catholicism persist in modern Roman Catholicism. They received definitive form in the First Vatican Council (1869–70) and were not retracted in the Second which continued to maintain the supreme, full and immediate authority of the Pope over all churches and Christians by virtue of his office. Even the authority of bishops, to which Vatican II attempted to do belated justice, is nugatory apart from their relation to the Pope.

Conciliar Catholicism, articulated notably by Ockham, Marsilius, Gerson and Cusanus and defined by the General Councils of Pisa (1409) and Constance (1414), located plenary authority in the whole Church, of which the papacy is the servant and councils (local, provincial and general) the executive expression. Conciliar thought recognized national identities and aspirations, accepted subsidiarity, welcomed academic contributions and gave a (limited) role to the laity. The Reformation, in its ecclesiological aspect, was a violent outburst of conciliar theology. Continental and Anglican Reformers alike appealed to conciliar principles and urged a free General Council which would be called and presided over by the secular magistrate rather than the Pope. Today the great world Protestant communions practise a conciliar ecclesiology and the WORLD COUNCIL OF CHURCHES perpetuates the conciliar ideal.

In ANGLICANISM, the English Reformation perpetuated monarchical Catholicism, merely transferring the prerogatives of the Pope to the crown. In its Erastian phase, under the Tudors and Stuarts, the sovereign ruled the Church as a department of state, though with lipservice paid to the authority of the Convocations of Bishops and lower clergy. In the power struggle that ensued, the crown was the loser and English Anglicanism has operated by a system of checks and balances for the past three centuries in which the monarchical element has gradually diminished and the conciliar element steadily increased, until today the crown has titular and symbolic authority only in the Church as in the state (but no less real and important for that). Anglicanism has its modern origins in the conciliar ideals of the immediate pre-Reformation period and – with its conception of dispersed authority – aspires to practise conciliar Catholicism (Avis 1989a).

A conciliar ecclesiology is hostile to hierarchy and therefore to patriarchy. It is conducive to the egalitarian images of the Church as the Body of Christ or the people of God. It places a high value on mutual attention, understanding and consultation and therefore is receptive to the insights of feminist theology. It requires undergirding by a personalist and relational theology of communion, grounded in baptism and expressed in a common EUCHARIST, and therefore retains much potential for the ecumenically minded Church of the future (Zizioulas 1985; Avis 1990).

Abbott, W.M. (ed.) (1966) *The Documents of Vatican II*, London: Chapman.

Avis, P. (1989a) *Anglicanism and the Christian Church*, Edinburgh: T. & T. Clark; Minneapolis, MN: Augsburg/Fortress.

——(1989b) *Eros and the Sacred*, London: SPCK; Wilton, CT: Morehouse.

——(1990) *Christians in Communion*, London: Chapman Mowbray; Collegeville: Liturgical Press.

——(1992) *Authority, Leadership and Conflict in the Church*, London: Mowbray; New York: Trinity Press International.

Gierke, O. (1900, 1958) *Political Theories of the Middle Age*, Cambridge: Cambridge University Press.

Rahner, K. (1965–) *Theological Investigations*, London: Darton, Longman & Todd.

Tierney, B. (1955) *Foundations of the Conciliar Theory*, Cambridge: Cambridge University Press.

Ullmann, W. (1955) *The Growth of Papal Government in the Middle Ages*, London: Methuen.

Zizioulas, J. (1985) *Being as Communion*, New York: St Vladimir's Seminary.

Paul Avis

ECOLOGICAL THEOLOGY

Theology comes from two Greek words *logos* (word) and *theos* (God) and is commonly defined as discourse about God. Ecology comes from two Greek words *logos* and *oikos* (home) and is commonly defined as the study of the earth as our home or, more strictly, as the study of living beings in their interconnectedness and interdependence. How then is theology as the study of God relevant to the study of the earth as our home, and vice versa?

One response is that the two disciplines are related but only negatively. Theology, it may be pressed, speaks primarily of other realities than the economy of the planet earth. In his well-known article, Lynn White Jr attacked the other-worldliness of Christianity as responsible for our present ecological crisis. 'Despite Darwin, we are *not*, in our hearts part of the natural process. We are superior to nature, contemptuous of it, willing to use it for our slightest whim.' This contempt stems directly from our Judaeo-Christian heritage. 'What we do about ecology depends on our ideas of the man–nature relationship. More science and more technology are not going to get us out of the present ecologic crisis until we find a new religion or rethink our old one' (White 1967: 1206).

Since then it has become commonplace among environmentalists to view the Judaeo-Christian tradition as a contributor to the current ecological crisis, if not the main originator of it, or, at the very least, as part of the problem rather than part of the solution. This view is not confined to environmentalists. The well-known exponent of animal liberation, Peter Singer, has argued that the 'Judaeo-Christian religious tradition is our foe' (Singer 1987: 7).

Historically, there are three major strands that have contributed to the ambivalence of the Judaeo-Christian tradition towards ecology.

Humanocentricity   I mean by this the closed circle of moral obligation. According to this view, everything other than the human is not included within the sphere of direct duty (see 'Humanocentric theory' in ANIMAL RIGHTS). The human good is therefore presupposed as the only moral good. For example in Thomist teaching, not only do we not have any direct duties to the non-human – except in so far as some human interest or property is involved – but also we have no duty of charity as such. 'The love of charity extends to none but God and our neighbour . . . the word neighbour cannot be extended to irrational creatures since they have no fellowship with man in the rational life' (Aquinas, *Summa Theologica*, Q. 65, Art. 1).

But it is not only in the Catholic tradition that such humanocentricity flourishes. Karl Barth reflects the tendency equally strong in the Reformed tradition to see creation as background or theatre to the real revelation in humanity alone. 'He who in the biblical message is called God is obviously not interested in the totality of things and beings created by Him, nor in specific beings within this totality, but in

man . . .' (Barth 1962: 337). Neither is this tendency limited to classical presentations of creation doctrine. It emerges frequently as a motif in contemporary apologetics. Hans Küng, for example, argues in the context of his analysis of the moral teaching of Jesus that 'God wills *nothing but* man's advantage, man's true greatness and his ultimate dignity' (Küng 1978: 251; my emphasis).

Dualism   The Western theological tradition has been characterized by a tendency to make distinctions (and separations) between flesh and spirit, mind and matter, rational and non-rational, and persons and things. The upshot of this tendency has been to make the non-human second class and marginal in both theology and ethics. Alec Whitehouse describes this tendency when it comes to the mind/matter and rational/non-rational dualisms: 'Those who believe that man's chief and highest end is to glorify God and fully to enjoy him for ever are frequently disposed to treat as fully actual, and to envisage as finally actual, *only what is incorporated into the activity of rational agents.*' Thus: 'Aristocrats of the mind are unwilling to be comfortably or uncomfortably at home with the world's minerals, vegetables and animals' (Whitehouse 1981: 205–11; my emphasis).

Thomist tradition has usually distinguished between three kinds of souls: 'vegetative' souls for vegetables, 'animated' souls for animals, and 'rational', incorporeal, souls for humans. The result of this tendency has sometimes been to collapse the world into two kinds of entities – 'persons' and 'things'. We find the clearest expression of this view in the work of one nineteenth-century Jesuit, Joseph Rickaby, who wrote thus in an influential textbook on moral philosophy: 'There are persons in our regard and there are things. Brute beasts, not having understanding and therefore not being persons, cannot have any rights. . . . We have no duties of any kind to the lower animals, as neither to sticks and stones' (Rickaby 1889: 248; cf. Davis 1958: 258 f.).

Instrumentalism   I mean by instrumentalism the notion that all creation exists for human beings or for the use and service of human beings. It seems indisputable that the scholastic element within the Judaeo-Christian tradition has consolidated the Aristotelian notion that the non-rational creation exists for and belongs to the rational creation. 'If then nature makes nothing without some end in view, nothing to no purpose', argues Aristotle, 'it must be that nature has made them all [animals and plants] for the sake of man' (Aristotle, *The Politics*, 1, viii; 1989: 79).

It is this view which is taken over with very little qualification by Aquinas. 'There is no sin in using a thing for the purpose for which it is ... Dumb animals and plants are devoid of the life of reason; they are moved, as it were, by another, by a kind of natural impulse, a sign of which is that they are naturally enslaved and accommodated to the uses of others' (Aquinas, *Summa Theologica*, Q. 64, Art. 1).

Few would deny the continuing force of these ideas, although how well grounded theologically they are or how far they belong intrinsically to the Judaeo-Christian tradition is a matter of continuing dispute. Attfield, for example, is adamant that 'the tradition which holds that in God's eyes the non-human creation has no value except in its instrumental value for mankind has Greek rather than Hebrew sources' (Attfield 1983: 23; cf. Sorabji 1993).

Given the continuing dominance of these negative strands, it is worth noting the religious, even mystical, flavour of the two insights in which modern ecology appears to be rooted: (a) the intrinsic value of all living beings, and (b) the interdependence of all living beings forming an interconnected whole. The 'first basic principle' of deep ecology is defined as the 'well-being and flourishing of human and non-human Life on Earth have value in themselves. These values are independent of the usefulness of the non-human world for human purposes' (Devall and Sessions 1985: 70). Indeed Arne Naess, the founder of deep ecology, who with George Sessions penned this basic principle makes clear the intuitive basis of the movement in an interview. He says:

There is a basic intuition in deep ecology that we have no right to destroy other living beings without sufficient reason. Another norm is that, with maturity, human beings will experience joy when other life forms experience joy, and sorrow when other life forms experience sorrow. Not only will we feel sad when our brother or a dog or a cat feels sad, but we will grieve when living beings, including landscapes, are destroyed. In our civilization, we have vast means of destruction at our disposal but extremely little maturity in our feelings. Only a very narrow range of feelings have interested most human beings until now.

Indeed Naess goes on to argue that 'The main point is that deep ecology has a religious component, fundamental intuitions that everyone must cultivate if he or she is to have a life based on values and not function like a computer' (Naess, in Devall and Sessions 1985: 75).

When these intuitions are laid bare, it is not difficult to see how they can be construed as consonant with, if not integral to, a Christian cosmology or worldview that can be said, *pace* Barth, to be implicit in the *kerygma*. A Trinitarian sketch might go something like this.

1 The insight that the creation and living beings within it have an irreducible, non-utilitarian value is deducible from a theocentric worldview in which the Creator establishes – independent of all humanocentric perspectives – the value of each and every living creature.
2 The insight that the world is interdependent and interconnected is deducible from the doctrine that Christ as the *Logos* is the ground and goal of creation itself, indeed that, as the *Logos*, Christ is the prefiguring unity of all creation to which modern ecological sensitivity points.
3 The insight that human sensitivity and responsibility towards creation is a moral obligation is deducible from the pneumatological doctrine that humans are called to co-operate with the Spirit in the work of anticipating the kingdom and the new creation in Christ.

In sum: God as Father, Son and Holy Spirit cannot be neutral, indifferent or hostile to that creation which is created, sustained and which will also be redeemed. This way of addressing and redressing the imbalance of the tradition was underlined by Robert Runcie: 'At the present time, when we are beginning to appreciate the wholeness and interrelatedness of all that is in the cosmos, preoccupation with humanity will seem distinctly parochial. . . . We need to maintain the value, the preciousness of the human by affirming the value, the preciousness of the non-human also – of all that is' (Runcie 1988: 13–14).

Despite the important connections between Christian Trinitarianism and ecology, there are some significant points of tension. We gather these under five heads.

Humanocentricity versus biocentricity
Ecologists have been understandably critical of humanocentricity. But there is a tendency in some ecological writing to resist the idea that humans are unique or special in any sense. For example, Sallie McFague suggests that the 'fifteen-billion year evolutionary story does not privilege any particular body, let alone a lately arrived one on a minor planet in an ordinary galaxy (the human body!)' (McFague 1993: 38). But such a tendency obscures the need for a moral humanocentricity in the sense of appealing to humans to do the job which only they can do as moral agents, namely clear up the ecological mess for which they are largely responsible. If humans are the commissioned and deputized moral agents of God in creation some moral humanocentricity seems inevitable. Humans – at least to a unique degree – are fundamental to the purposes of God in restoring creation and co-operating with the Spirit. Indeed, some forms of eco-theory require a strong view of human management, especially of their own species.

Equality versus hierarchy   The argument for biocentric equality is understandable as a protest against traditional moral exclusivism. But to affirm that all living things are inherently or intrinsically valuable does not necessarily commit us to the view that all life has the same or equal value in God's eyes. The attempt within the Christian tradition to isolate certain features as inherently valuable in themselves (soul, person, rationality, sentience) may not be mistaken, but the fundamental question is how we view these values or goods in relation to individual species and individual animals.

Individualism   versus   holism   Some

eco-theories may go to the opposite extreme of valuing creatures *only* in their relation to the whole. For example, Aldo Leopold is well known for his dictum that 'a thing is right when it tends to preserve the integrity, stability, and beauty of the biotic community' (Leopold 1949: 217). This view has been dubbed 'environmental fascism' since it implies that 'the individual may be sacrificed for the greater biotic good' (Regan 1983: 361). The underlying question of the relationship between individual and community rights in creation has yet to be fully resolved in eco-theology.

Immanence versus transcendence   Some eco-theologians are so disturbed by the emphasis placed on divine transcendence rather than immanence that they appear to reject a transcendent God altogether. Anne Primavesi expresses this logic when she writes: 'If nature is seen as 'not God', then this licenses human control over it' (Primavesi 1991: 146). But this rejection of transcendence fails to consider the possibility that God's qualified absence may be the very factor which enables both human freedom and also creation itself. What kind of creation would it be if God were literally in everything? There must come a point where the sacralizing tendency becomes inimical to a proper doctrine of creation as creation. For if sacralization is taken to its limit, God becomes simply another creature insufficiently powerful actually to transform and redeem suffering in the creation itself.

Nature versus natural law   So taken by scientific narratives of the interdependence of the world, some eco-theologians appear to accept as 'givens' a number of natural processes as though they constituted either a new natural law or something approaching a new revelation. 'If the earth is our home, then we need to attend to some of its most basic house rules' (McFague 1993: 57). But to discover certain natural processes is one thing, to claim them as normative or prescriptive is another. This comes into focus when parasitical nature is under discussion. McFague writes:

That nature is red in tooth and claw, that survival involves eating and being eaten, is everywhere evident. And we obviously participate in this pattern – hunger, destruction, sacrifice, waste, death, pain and suffering are intrinsic to this picture, and therefore to our lives and actions as well. Whether the relationships on our planet are predatory, symbiotic, or harmonious (and nature displays all these types) each and every creature, including human ones, is, for good or evil, intertwined with the life and death of others. We are locked together on our planet into a common destiny. We cannot go it alone.

(McFague 1993: 63)

But such a view can, if pressed, result in a failure to perceive moral transcendence. Humans are now invited to imitate the predatory dimension of creation as something inexorably given by the Creator and which is read as a fundamental moral law. In the words of Matthew Fox: 'eat and be eaten' is the 'law of the Universe' (Fox, in Fox and Porritt 1991: 14–15). But such a view refuses the category of natural evil and also the whole possibility of a redemptive God who has cosmic salvation in mind (see Linzey 1976, 1987, 1994).

My own view is that the eco-insights concerning the inherent value of living beings and their interconnection should be regarded as integral to Christian doctrine and a theocentric view of creation. They are, in other words, misplaced *theological* insights. That they now form part of a 'secular worldview' is a sign that the Judaeo-Christian tradition has been insufficiently reflective of its own insights and uncourageous in relation to its own theology. Moreover, the growth of eco-thinking, despite its many limitations, is a rebuke to some of the unexamined and unhelpful assumptions that linger on unchecked in the tradition. The challenge is whether theologians can now engage these insights propounded in a secular setting but with ethical sensitivity and sufficient theological discernment.

Aquinas, St Thomas (1918) *Summa Theologica*, ed. and trans. the English Dominican Fathers, New York: Benziger Brothers, Part II, Question 64, Article 1, and Question 65, Article 1.
Aristotle (1985) *The Politics*, ed. and trans. T.A. Sinclair, London: Penguin.
Attfield, Robin (1983) *The Ethics of Environmental Concern*, Oxford: Basil Blackwell.

Barth, Karl (1962) *Church Dogmatics*, vol. 3, Part 4, ed. and trans. T.R. Torrance and G.W. Bromiley, Edinburgh: T. & T. Clark.
Davis, Henry (1958) *Moral and Pastoral Theology*, vol. II, London: Sheed & Ward.
Devall, Bill and Sessions, George (1985) *Deep Ecology: Living as if Nature Mattered*, Salt Lake City, UT: Peregrine.
Fox, Matthew and Porritt, Jonathon (1991) 'Green spirituality', *Creation Spirituality* 7(3) (May–June).
Griffin, Susan (1994) *Woman and Nature: The Roaring Inside Her*, London: Women's Press.
Johnson, Lawrence E. (1991) *A Morally Deep World: An Essay on Moral Significance and Environmental Ethics*, Cambridge: Cambridge University Press.
Küng, Hans (1978) *On Being a Christian*, London: Collins.
Leopold, Aldo (1949) *A Sand County Almanac*, New York: Oxford University Press.
Linzey, Andrew (1976) *Animal Rights: A Christian Assessment*, London: SCM.
——(1987) *Christianity and the Rights of Animals*, London: SPCK and New York: Crossroad.
——(1994) *Animal Theology*, London: SCM and Chicago, IL: University of Illinois Press.
McFague, Sallie (1993) *The Body of God: An Ecological Theology*, London: SCM and Minneapolis, MN: Fortress Press.
Primavesi, Anne (1991) *From Apocalypse to Genesis: Ecology, Feminism and Christianity*, Minneapolis, MN: Fortress Press.
Regan, Tom (1983) *The Case for Animal Rights*, Berkeley, CA: University of California Press.
Rickaby, Joseph (1889) *Moral Philosophy*, vol. II, London: Longmans.
Ruether, Rosemary Radford (1993) *God and Gaia: An Ecofeminist Theology of Earth Healing*, London: SCM and New York: HarperCollins.
Runcie, Robert (1988) 'Address at the Global Forum of Spiritual and Parliamentary Leaders on Human Survival', Unpublished paper, 11 April.
Singer, Peter (1987) (interview) *The Animals' Agenda* (September): 7.
Sorabji, Richard (1993) *Animal Minds and Human Morals: The Origins of the Western Debate*, London: Duckworth.
Spretnak, Charlene (1986) *The Spiritual Dimension of Green Politics*, Santa Fe, NM: Bear.
White Jr, Lynn (1967) 'The historic roots of our ecological crisis', *Science* 155(3767) (March): 1203–7; reprinted in Donald Van de Vere and Christine Pierce (eds) *The Environmental Ethics and Policy Book: Philosophy, Ecology, Economics*, Belmont, CA: Wadsworth, 1994, pp. 45–55.
Whitehouse, Alec (1981) 'New heavens and a new earth', in Ann Loades (ed.) *The Authority of Grace: Essays in Response to Karl Barth*, Edinburgh: T. & T. Clark.

Andrew Linzey

ECONOMY

The word 'economy' is derived from two Greek words, *oikos* and *nomos*, which together refer to the ordering of the household (Meeks 1989). Economic life, in ancient Greek society, fundamentally centred around the management of households as, in a certain sense, it still does. The term came to be used by early Christians as one of the metaphors for God's rule, as in the New Testament reference to the 'household of God' (Ephesians 2: 19) in which all Christians have membership. The term 'ecumenical' (Greek *oikoumene*) thus refers to the inclusive household of God in which Christians are to reflect the unity of a household, despite theological conflicts and denominational differences. The biblical theme of 'stewardship' follows closely from the Greek *oikonomos*, for the latter can be taken to mean the management of the material affairs of the household by a 'steward' appointed to that task.

In contemporary usage, the economy is the sum of the institutions and processes for the production and distribution of scarce values. Economic systems vary greatly, both historically and in the contemporary world. But all economic systems organize the production and distribution of scarce values. The latter include, most obviously, material goods, such as food, clothing, shelter, aesthetic objects, playthings, implements, vehicles etc. Such material necessities as air and water normally have existed plentifully enough that we do not always think of them as 'economic' goods, but even air, at least pure air, is sufficiently scarce that costly measures to preserve its purity are very definitely a part of the economy. The economy also includes non-material values, such as patents, copyrights and legal options. Anything that is valued but is also inherently limited in supply is at least potentially economic by nature.

Economic thought encompasses ideas about work, including specialized roles and socializations. It includes consideration of the basis, rights and limitations of PROPERTY. It includes thought about social rewards or punishments designed to motivate or regulate production and distribution. Disputes over WEALTH and POVERTY are perennially important in economic thought – whether great disparities of wealth and income are morally acceptable and, if not, what could be done about them. Economic thought includes conflicting interpretations of the proper role of GOVERNMENT in economic life: Should the public own all or most of the instruments of production and commerce? Should government seek to control the business cycle? Should it redistribute wealth and income? Should it prohibit certain forms of commerce? How far should government go in advancing a nation's economic interests in international competition?

Most theological ideas have some bearing upon economic issues. This may be especially true of doctrines of CREATION having to do with divine purposes expressed through the created, tangible order (*see* ECOLOGICAL THEOLOGY). A key question here is whether divine intent is self-evident in the structures of nature, in some variation of NATURAL LAW doctrine, or whether our perceptions of the natural order are ultimately governed by divine revelation. Doctrines of SIN and GRACE, with variant conceptions of the limitations and possibilities of human nature, are pertinent to questions of economic incentive and economic power. Doctrines of stewardship and vocation express the accountability of human economic interests and activities to God.

Prior to the eighteenth century, economic thought was not considered to be distinct from THEOLOGY, philosophy and ETHICS. Ancient Greek philosophy dealt with questions of property, WORK, poverty and commerce in relation to political and moral philosophy. Thus, Plato's communal economic theories are an aspect of his views of the well-ordered society, as explored in *The Republic*, and Aristotle's rejection of lending money at interest is an aspect of his overall philosophy of ends. The Hebrew prophets understood poverty and economic exploitation through the damage done to human beings in community, a moral sensitivity also embodied in Hebrew law codes. Christian patristic writings almost uniformly treat economic selfishness as a serious spiritual issue, while raising searching questions about great disparities of wealth and income (Gonzalez 1990). Until the sixteenth century, Christian thought generally followed

Greek and Hebrew precedence in condemning usury, defined as the taking of interest for loans, despite the inconveniences this imposed upon commerce (*see* USURY). Until well beyond that century, it would have been unthinkable to have treated economics as a separate, independent sphere of human knowledge.

Such an independent conception of economics began to emerge in the eighteenth century, with the development of mercantilist theories and, especially, with the publication of Adam Smith's *The Wealth of Nations* in 1776. While he was himself both a clergyman and a moral philosopher, Smith laid the foundations for independent economic thought by asserting the independence of economic life. His view that the public good would best be served through a free market in which all participants sought their own self-interests (the 'invisible hand') was a big step toward severing the relationship between moral virtue and economics.

Much of the nineteenth- and twentieth-century debate over theology and economics has been defined by the relative independence of economic thought. Even Marxist SOCIALISM, perhaps the most radical alternative to Smith's free market vision, assumed the independence of economics. For the past two centuries, Christian thought has wavered between capitalist and socialist poles, but it has found it difficult to subordinate either capitalist or socialist theory within a broader theological perspective. Christian socialist tendencies during those centuries have been represented by the Briton F.D. Maurice, the American Walter Rauschenbusch, the Swiss Leonhard Ragaz and, more recently, the Liberation Theologians of Latin America and other parts of the world (*see* CHRISTIAN SOCIALISM). Christian capitalist thought has been represented during this period by the nineteenth-century Bishop William Lawrence (USA) and twentieth-century Anglo-American neo-conservatives like Robert Benne (USA) and E.R. Norman (UK), although most twentieth-century Christian economic thinking has supported CAPITALISM to some extent (Atherton 1992; Wogaman 1993). Much twentieth-century Christian economic thought has been summarized in documents of the ECUMENICAL MOVEMENT (Protestant and Eastern Orthodox) and in

papal encyclicals (Roman Catholic). While the former have generally been influenced more by socialist tendencies and the latter have reflected a more conservative orientation, both the ecumenical movement and Roman Catholicism have sought to recover a central place for theological reflection in economic thought. Both have insisted that economic life must be judged not by economic performance alone but by the concrete effects of policies and practices upon human beings. Both have been explicitly critical of the easy Smithian assumption that the market mechanism, left alone, will automatically yield social justice and human well-being.

Theology has an important impact upon economics at six points.

1 The most decisive question is whether theology can affirm the material world, as such, at all. Earliest Christianity confronted that issue through the Docetic controversy, in which some Christian thinkers treated the material world as fundamentally alien to the life of the spirit. Had that view prevailed, Christianity would have developed in radically different ways, if it could have developed at all. Christian orthodoxy, however, stayed within the inherited Jewish mainstream by continuing to affirm that 'the earth is the Lord's, and all that is in it' (Psalm 24, NRSV). The New Testament letter to the Colossians expressed this by identifying the God of Jesus Christ with the creation of 'things visible and invisible' and by asserting that in Christ 'all things hold together' (Colossians 1: 16, 17, NRSV). By affirming the world and identifying its creation with the same God whom we meet in Christ, Christians paved the way for a more detailed theological analysis of how different aspects of the material order, including economic institutions and practices, advance or impede God's purposes.

2 Granted the theological importance of the material world, the central economic tasks of production follow. If basic needs are to be met, there must be adequate quantities of food, clothing, shelter, medical supplies and the related instruments of production, transportation and communication (*see* BUSINESS). People must be trained and deployed

adequately to provide production and services. Fulfilling the needs of production can also give rise to dilemmas. For example, in order to stimulate production, incentives may have to be offered that undermine our sense of community. Some harmful products may perform desirable economic functions. Theological analysis, therefore, must attend to the specifics of production.

3 Production of goods and services can thus be seen as an important sphere in which people respond to or resist God. Economics is an important part of the stage on which human interaction with God is played. Since the Reformation it has become more and more acceptable theologically to refer to economic activity as a part of our vocation and even to think of human creativity as participation in the creative work of God. Not every form of work can be characterized as a 'calling', but many can. On the other hand, many forms of work having no significance in the economic exchange system could be a part of one's calling when understood theologically. For example, there might be no financial compensation for visiting somebody in hospital or providing leadership for a neighbourhood youth group. But such activities are, in the fuller theological sense, also expressions of Christian vocation.

4 If economics has important effects upon individuals, it is equally true that it affects interpersonal relationships and the life of whole communities. According to much theological thought, the relationships bonding human beings to one another in community are ultimately an expression of our kinship in God. The material infrastructure of a community – its roads, parks, utilities, educational facilities, public transportation, courts, museums – is a major aspect of a community's economy. But real community is also related to the economic opportunities of its people and the extent of economic inequalities dividing them. The American Catholic bishops' economics pastoral made this point in proposing a community participation criterion of an acceptable economy: to be acceptable, an economic system must enable all within a society to be participants (Roman Catholic Bishops, US

1986). By this standard, poverty is morally significant not only because its victims' material needs are not met but also because the poor cannot be in normal social relationships with the rest of the community.

5 Some theological views are entirely human centred, but there is a greater tendency in the late twentieth century for theologians to think of the cosmos as a value to God quite apart from humanity. The issues to which this change of orientation points are complex; they at least mean that humanity has great stewardship responsibility for its own ENVIRONMENT (Nash 1991). Such stewardship is also a point of economic accountability, and it occasions dilemmas, as, for instance, when environmental stewardship threatens industries basic to needed production and to the provision of jobs.

6 All economic life also entails the distribution and exercise of POWER. Economic power conveys power over the lives of people and, commonly, over political institutions. Theological support for civil rights and equitable distributions of political power also imply broad distributions of economic power. The ideological debates between supporters of socialism and of capitalism may not be as readily resolvable theologically as some Christians have hoped. But the debate itself helps illuminate the centrality of issues of human power as expressed through economics (Wogaman 1977).

The economy, in whatever form it has taken, has always been an important aspect of human existence, and economic life has generally been a central part of social thought. But Christian economic thinking has to be shaped to fit contemporary social/economic realities.

The dramatic and unexpected collapse of Soviet and Eastern European Marxist socialism at the beginning of the 1990s has fundamentally altered late twentieth-century Christian discussion of economic issues. Whereas only a few years earlier, socialism had captured the imagination of large numbers of Christian intellectuals, the changes in Eastern Europe abruptly undermined confidence that socialism really could be the wave of the future. The free market mechanism, already dominant in North America and Western Europe, became overnight the economic panacea of the formerly socialist countries as well. The effects of this historic transformation have not been limited to the ideological debate between capitalism and socialism as such; they have also placed a cloud over governmental involvements in economic life, for whatever purpose.

That cannot long continue. For one thing, the free market mechanism has manifestly failed to undergird basic human values at a number of points, such as the elimination of poverty, the provision of health care (in free market situations like the USA) and the conservation of the environment. For another thing, the market mechanism cannot be sufficiently responsive to the will of the community unless government is permitted to play a significant economic role. The changed world situation does mean, however, that Christian economic ethics has new issues to think through. Socialist Christians may need to take new stock of the inventive and productive successes of the free market and ask, in new ways, how those values can best be preserved in a broader economic design. Capitalist Christians, on the other hand, may need to take the failures of the market more seriously while asking how successful aspects of the socialist agenda can be affirmed (Atherton 1992).

Meanwhile, the global economic development is proceeding rapidly. Christian economic thought, if it is to participate responsibly in the conversation over the terms of that development, needs to recognize the enduring reality of transnational corporations (Stackhouse 1987), the continued injustice and instability of global economic disparities of wealth and income (Preston 1991) and the intimate relationship between global economic insecurities and political tensions. The new global situation requires creative new thinking about how an international economic order can best be structured.

In this writer's view, the distinctively Christian contribution to thought about the economy has become more, not less, important. Christians cannot claim special technical insight into the various mechanisms of contemporary economic life. They do have important intellectual resources to bring to bear in the analysis of the relationship between the economy and core meanings and values. These resources include a recognition of the intersection between personal stewardship and vocation, on the one hand, and broader issues of social justice, on the other. Christians can never accept easy assumptions about the automatic functioning of the market mechanism to enable the sum of individual acts of selfishness to yield overall social good. Christians are realistic about the effects of human sin, but they are also creative in addressing historic opportunities.

Atherton, John (1992) *Christianity and the Market: Christian Social Thought for our Times*, London: SPCK.

Benne, Robert (1981) *The Ethic of Democratic Capitalism: A Moral Reassessment*, Philadelphia, PA: Fortress Press.

Gonzalez, Justo L. (1990) *Faith and Wealth: A History of Early Christian Ideas on the Origin, Significance, and Use of Money*, San Francisco, CA: Harper & Row.

Meeks, M. Douglas (1989) *God the Economist: The Doctrine of God and Political Economy*, Minneapolis, MN: Fortress Press.

Nash, James A. (1991) *Loving Nature: Ecological Integrity and Christian Responsibility*, Nashville, TN: Abingdon Press.

Preston, Ronald H. (1991) *Religion and the Ambiguities of Capitalism*, London: SCM.

Roman Catholic Bishops, US (1986) *Economic Justice for All: Pastoral Letter on Catholic Social Teaching and the U.S. Economy*, Washington, DC: National Conference of Catholic Bishops.

Smith, Adam (1776) *An Inquiry into the Nature and Causes of the Wealth of Nations*.

Stackhouse, Max L. (1987) *Public Theology and Political Economy: Christian Stewardship in Modern Society*, Lanham, MD, and London: University Press of America.

Weber, Max (1958) *The Protestant Ethic and the Spirit of Capitalism*, trans. Talcott Parsons, New York: Scribner's (originally published 1904-5).

Wogaman, J. Philip (1977) *Christians and the Great Economic Debate*, London: SCM; Louisville, KY: Westminster/John Knox Press.

——(1986) *Economics and Ethics: A Christian Enquiry*, London: SCM.

——(1993) *Christian Ethics: A Historical Introduction*, Louisville, KY: Westminster/John Knox Press.

J. Philip Wogaman

ECUMENICAL MOVEMENT

The movement towards the visible unity of the

Church is the response to the High Priestly Prayer of Jesus recorded in John 17. Very early on in the Church's life the unity of the Church, together with its holiness, catholicity and apostolicity, became an article of faith confessed in the Creed. The response to the call for unity has never been entirely absent from the life of the Church. After the division between East and West in the eleventh century and the division of the Western Church in the sixteenth century there were always those who sought to heal the divisions. Nevertheless, the result of the divisions was that Christian communities lived apart, interpreted the Gospel in isolation and defined themselves over against one another.

The stirrings of the modern ecumenical movement lie in the nineteenth century within groups like the YMCA (1844), the Evangelical Alliance (1846) and the Student Christian Federation (1880) which saw the potential for unity. It was the meetings of the missionary societies in 1888, 1900 and Edinburgh 1910, however, that gave birth to the modern ecumenical movement. Many working overseas for the spread of Christianity saw the contradiction between the Gospel message and the rivalry of competing churches (see MISSION).

Bishop Charles Brent, an Anglican from the USA, discovered at Edinburgh that Christian unity must be grounded on the basis of sound agreement in faith. In 1927 the first Faith and Order Conference brought together Anglicans, Lutherans, Protestants and some Orthodox who set out an agenda of faith, sacraments, ministry and ecclesiology which has remained the focus of the ecumenical, theological agenda ever since.

Two years prior to Lausanne another ecumenical group gathered to consider problems of WAR and PEACE, race, EDUCATION, capital and labour in what came to be known as the Life and Work Movement.

It was the different streams represented by Faith and Order, Life and Work and World Aid that eventually came together in 1948 in Amsterdam in the First Assembly of the World Council of Churches. This event marked a watershed in the ecumenical movement when churches, as churches, committed themselves to a common search for the unity of the Church.

Between 1948 and the present day the work of the WORLD COUNCIL OF CHURCHES (WCC) has been focused in seven World Assemblies, the last in Canberra in 1991. During these years the Council has become more representative. Well over 4,000 churches are members. Although the Roman Catholic Church is a full member only of the Faith and Order Commission official observers play an important part in other parts of the Council. The increased participation of Orthodox Churches has significantly affected the Council's work and has deepened a common spirituality and worship life. Further, what began as a white, Western, male gathering of church leaders now embraces women and men, CLERGY and laity from the different continents and cultures. As the community has broadened, members have added new concerns to the agenda which sometimes exist in tension. The challenge to the Council is to maintain its central mandate to call the churches to visible unity while seeing how the various agendas of social, ethical and political concerns, not least the most recent concern for justice, peace and the integrity of creation, are related to its primary vocation.

At the same time as Christians have learnt to work and pray together at the world level, national and regional councils of churches have encouraged churches to work together in the regions in accordance with the Lund Principle, never to do apart what can already be undertaken together. The Roman Catholic Church is a member of a growing number of these regional councils.

A new impetus in the ecumenical movement came in the 1960s as a result of Vatican II. An understanding of the relationship between the Roman Catholic Church and other churches expressed in the Decree on Ecumenism opened the way for new partnerships. The Roman Catholic insistence on the need for agreement in faith, sufficient and required, to undergird the unity of the Church led to the setting up of a complex network of bilateral theological talks. In the last twenty-five years Anglicans, for example, have talked to Lutherans, Methodists, Orthodox, Reformed and Roman Catholics while the Roman Catholics have talked to the Orthodox, Disciples of Christ, Methodists, Lutherans, Anglicans, Reformed,

Pentecostals etc. The texts from these theological conversations have helped to show how much churches hold in common even where differences were once thought to be intractable. They point to what diversity may be held in unity and where outstanding areas of difference remain. The understanding of the nature of the Church as *koinonia* (communion) together with the recognition of the degree of communion which already exists is perhaps the most important contribution to ecumenical ECCLESIOLOGY.

These dialogues have fed one another and there has been a constant interchange with the work of the multilateral conversation in the World Council of Churches' Faith and Order Commission. This is illustrated in the most well-known of all ecumenical texts, *Baptism, Eucharist and Ministry*. The agreements reached between the Oriental Orthodox and the Orthodox churches are some of the most advanced.

Alongside the efforts of theological dialogue the work and witness of the WCC has provided a constant reminder to the churches that unity in faith and sacraments ought never to be divorced from unity in action for a more just, participatory and sustainable society. The unity and renewal of the Church and the unity and renewal of human society belong together. In the 1950s the work for a 'responsible society' predominated. In the 1960s, with the increasing challenge from the Third World, the model of development and rapid social change became the emphasis. The 1966 Church and Society World Conference examined different social-ethical views of change, including revolutionary action for justice. In the late 1970s the Just, Participatory and Sustainable Society became prominent with the theme of sustainability making a new contribution to the emerging global awareness. 'Liberation' became a central theme of the ecumenical movement. The Programme to Combat Racism and the work on a Community of Women and Men in the Church encouraged Christians worldwide to work together to overcome divisions in human community between black and white, men and women. The impetus was not simply for a more just and equitable society outside the Church but challenged the churches themselves to examine relationships within their own life. In the 1980s and

the 1990s a major new emphasis developed in the area of the search for JUSTICE, peace and the integrity of creation (JPIC). The JPIC movement encouraged Christians to covenant together locally, nationally and regionally to work on issues of peace, justice and environmental protection, to affirm life (*see* ECOLOGICAL THEOLOGY). The result of all this is a growing awareness in the ecumenical movement that ecclesiology and ETHICS belong together. The unity of the Church involves becoming what some call 'moral community'.

Within this broad ecumenical movement with its many partners and multiple concerns there have been some notable unions of churches and closer alliances. The birth of the Church of South India (1947), the Church of North India (1970) and the Church of Pakistan (1970) brought into union churches of Anglican, Methodist, Reformed and Congregational traditions. Other united churches include the United Church of Canada (1925), the Church of Christ in China (1927), the United Church of Christ USA (1957), the United Reformed Church in the UK (1981), etc.

Among formal commitments made between churches which commit the partners to closer living are the Bonn Agreement between Anglican and Old Catholics (1931), the Leuenberg Agreement between churches in the Reformed tradition (1973) and the Meissen Agreement between the Church of England and the Evangelical Church in Germany (1991). Currently proposals for further agreements include the proposed Concordat in the USA, one between Lutherans and Reformed in the USA, Methodists and Lutherans in Sweden and the *The Porvoo Common Statement* between the Anglican Churches of the British Isles and the Nordic and Baltic Lutheran Churches.

Formal agreements between churches whether at world level or regional level are of little avail without the growth into unity at the local level. Unity cannot be imposed, it must grow among local churches. The view of unity remains 'the all joined in each place to the all in every place'. In many places Christians are learning to share together in a life of prayer, in joint service and mission. Co-operating parishes, local ecumenical projects and the annual Week of Prayer for Christian Unity (begun in 1908 and given new direction in 1935) is where unity is experienced as a reality.

There are signs that the despondency which was a reaction to failed union schemes, the not always positive response to the publication of ecumenical texts and the dramatic changes in Eastern Europe with the resulting tensions between the Orthodox and Roman Catholic Church is giving way in the mid-1990s to a renewed commitment to the ecumenical endeavour. Work for unity is seen as a gift of God and as the calling of the Church. Unity is for the appropriate adoration of the Triune God and for the sake of the Church's mission. All of this is most clearly set out in the statement from the Canberra Assembly (1991) of the World Council of Churches: *The Unity of the Church as Koinonia: Gift and Calling.*

Baptism, Eucharist and Ministry (1982) Lima Text, Faith and Order Paper 111, Geneva: WCC.

Bell, G. (1924–58) *Documents on Christian Unity 1920–57*, 4 vols, Oxford: Oxford University Press.

Boegner, M. (1970) *The Long Road to Unity*, London: Collins.

Fey, H. (1970) *A History of the Ecumenical Movement*, vol. ii, *The Ecumenical Advance, 1948–1968*, London: SPCK.

Goodall, N. (1964) *The Ecumenical Movement*, 2nd edn, Oxford: Oxford University Press.

Lossky, N. (ed.) (1991) *Dictionary of the Ecumenical Movement*, Geneva: WCC.

Meyer, H. and Vischer, L. (eds) (1984) *Growth in Agreement, Reports and Agreed Statements of Ecumenical Conversations on a World Level*, Geneva: WCC.

Neill, S. (1968) *The Church and Christian Union*, Oxford: Oxford University Press.

Neill, S. and Rouse, R. (eds) (1954) *A History of the Ecumenical Movement*, vol. i, *1517–1954*, London: SPCK.

Till, B. (1972) *The Churches Search for Unity*, Harmondsworth: Penguin.

Mary Tanner

EDUCATION

Education has a dual existence – as a set of values, often intimately related to an overall account of the human condition and the likely, or desired, trajectory of SOCIETY; and as a set of institutions and other operational arrangements through which these values are, or are supposed to be, realized. Education, therefore, is both a normative system concerned with inculcating values, moral and technical, and transmitting (and transforming) appropriate knowledge and skills, and also an administrative system, a collection of schools, colleges and universities which both express these values and reflect wider social and cultural infrastructures created by historical circumstances.

In the earliest times there was rarely open conflict between education's twin forms because those individuals and groups who embodied society's predominant values, whether sacred or secular, were generally those also directly responsible for its educational institutions. Under modern conditions, however, there is much greater scope for serious dissonance between these two aspects of education, the normative and the organizational, because those who shape social values, now more likely to be politicians than priests, are no longer necessarily the same as those directly responsible for the management of educational institutions and because both groups, the value-setters and the educational practitioners, have become diverse and volatile. One of the most powerful themes of educational change, therefore, has been the steady drift over the centuries from organic to pluralistic interpretations – in terms of both values and organization.

In this double context education has fulfilled three broad roles. The first is to socialize mainly but not exclusively young people into the dominant CULTURE in order to enhance social solidarity and, less benignly, reinforce ideological hegemony. In the largely Christian societies which most European nations continued to be until the nineteenth century, and in the Islamic world still today, the latter purpose took on a transcendent character. The good society and the godly society were elided. More recently education's SOCIALIZATION role has come under more critical scrutiny. It is seen as increasingly problematical in terms both of the need for intellectual openness and of the democratic constitution of society.

The second role, closely related to the first, is to help to form the division of labour. While older social stratification, in particular the formation of élites, was determined by other mechanisms such as birth, charisma or military prowess, education is a key component of the professionalization characteristic of modern society. Also the sophistication of technology has led to a more exact, and exacting, division of labour and the triumph of expertise over experience has offered education a more central role in determining this division.

The third role is individual enlightenment, contributing to personal empowerment and creating the conditions for social EMANCIPATION. This role is more recent, dating back no further than the eighteenth century, although it is now assumed by many to be the main aim of education. So long as the ends of human society were seen as subordinate to 'given' TRUTH, whether revealed through religion or embodied in political and ideological hegemonies, the idea of individual enlightenment could not take proper hold. Although individualism has deeper historical roots, its expression through education is a product of the Enlightenment and characteristic of modern secular societies. According to Socrates (as reported by Plato) ultimate wisdom rests in the realization that 'I do not know', but it is only in the last two-and-a-half centuries that the radical scepticism on which the choices inherent in individual enlightenment ultimately depend has become entrenched as the dominant intellectual mode.

The emergence of education as a distinctive entity is conventionally dated to the age of Plato and Aristotle in Greece at the end of the fifth and beginning of the fourth centuries BC; the former established his eponymous academy, giving separate institutional form to the practice of education, while the latter created an intellectual system that was to endure in broad outline for more than a millennium, providing education with a powerful normative structure able to transcend its immediate social environments and cultural contexts. However inexact and insubstantial the historical record of their achievements, they bestowed a rich rhetorical inheritance which, refined through the Hellenistic and Roman periods and sustained by medieval Islam and Christendom, continued up to and beyond the beginnings of the modern age – and which still provides a powerful component of contemporary educational thought.

Arguably too much emphasis has been placed on this Classical–Islamic–Christian tradition at the expense of other educational traditions, e.g. in China and India. The organizational and intellectual achievements of the latter are certainly impressive. Yet the hegemony of the 'Western' tradition, broadly defined, in the twentieth-century world cannot be denied. Whether this is due to the inherent and historical characteristics of this tradition, in particular its creation of special-purpose institutions distinct from other social and religious organizations and the emergence of intellectual systems designed to transcend the immediate and the given, or to recent and contingent phenomena, the perhaps accidental alignment with the triumphant values of modernity and, in particular, the spectacular successes of science and technology, is difficult to resolve.

In any case the extent to which the 'Western' tradition of education can be regarded as a continuous phenomenon is doubtful. In modern times it has undergone a series of fundamental shifts. In the sixteenth and seventeenth centuries the idea of a dynamic science, with its disturbing cultural reverberations, had to be incorporated. In the seventeenth and eighteenth centuries the emergence of philosophy, as a science of ultimate things, rivalling and surpassing religion posed a further challenge. There followed a series of shocks, each more radical and more rapid than the last – the 'invention' of the affective personality (combined with a much stronger belief in individual creativity, even human perfectibility), begun in the age of sensibility in the later eighteenth century and carried through to the age of Freud in the early twentieth; the erosion of long-established habits of social deference in a period of revolution; the emergence of entirely new patterns of social and economic organization associated with the new industrial order; and the creation of a mass society in our present century.

To each education had to respond, either normatively or organizationally and often both. Jean-Jacques Rousseau was a key figure in the 'invention' of personality. In his writing, notably *Emile*, he challenged the long-held view of wisdom and truth as having an independent pre-existence, whether in the Platonic spheres or as revealed religion. Rather they were expressions of the natural goodness of humanity. In the next century the Arnolds, father and son, tried to maintain, and renew, more traditional conceptions of education in an age of rapid industrial change and advancing democracy – Thomas through his practical efforts at Rugby, so widely emulated, and Matthew as a critic-commentator, the author of *Culture and Anarchy* and other influential texts, and as a schools inspector engaged in the early formation of state systems of education.

The American educator and philosopher John Dewey, responding to the new pressures of the twentieth century, constructed a pragmatic model of education which he attempted to put into practice at the famous University of Chicago experimental school. Convinced of the interconnectedness of all human experiences and suspicious of traditional philosophical dualisms, he argued that children learnt by doing; their interests and aptitudes, not abstract ideas or transcendent values, should be placed at the heart of the curriculum. Another key figure in the development of educational thought, Jean Piaget, active in the mid-twentieth century, explored the child's gradual and difficult accumulation of a logical apparatus, beginning with mere reflexes and ending with higher-level understanding.

The ideas of Rousseau, the Arnolds, Dewey and Piaget continue to resonate through education. From the 'invention' of human personality have been derived notions of subjectivism, relativism, child-centred learning. Out of the crucible of the industrial and democratic revolutions has been refined a confused commitment to aristocratic standards and democratic élites, and the idea of a cultural 'canon' to encapsulate, in Matthew Arnold's own words, 'the best that has been thought and done'. From Dewey and other optimist-pragmatists has come the idea of a topic-centred rather than content-derived curriculum, easy to recognize in its contemporary disguise as 'competencies'. And from Piaget has flowed the belief that education must be structured in terms of developmental psychology.

During the same two centuries education has become one of the central services provided by the modern state. Just as nations were once judged by their success in war, today their maturity is likely to be assessed in terms of their commitment to educating and training their citizens. The motives for this long-haul shift from small educational systems largely based on voluntarist principles to mass systems in which the state has become the majority stakeholder (if not the monopoly supplier) are various.

Among these have been the desire to enlarge individual enlightenment, to promote social justice and so cohesion, and to inculcate patriotic values, especially significant in revolutionary societies determined to impose codes of republican virtue, and the need to raise cultural standards, and civic consciousness, among voters and to increase skill levels to keep pace with economic and technological advances. Whatever weight has been attached to these various motives at different times and in different places, educational systems certainly and arguably institutions have become complex organizations subject to all the opportunities and constraints typical of large-scale bureaucracies.

Most current issues in education reflect either the interplay among the various components within the 'Western' tradition or its organizational situation as a key public service – or, generally, a combination of both. For example, the argument between those who support a relevant curriculum, whether expressed in a vocational context (i.e. 'competencies') or a political one (i.e. 'political correctness'), and those who press the claims of a 'canon' to provide cultural continuity and promote traditional standards re-echoes the different views of the Arnolds and of Dewey. Similarly Rousseau and Piaget agree in stressing the primacy of individual consciousness in education (as opposed to those, following Plato, who see education as a social laboratory or, in the case of Marx, factory), but disagree about the nature of that consciousness.

General trends are difficult to identify. It can be speculated that, at present, in educational theory and practice attention is shifting from the psychology of learning, at any rate in terms of the individual pupil, to the inter-personal dynamics of the classroom and the role of 'systems' within large institutions. It can be argued with greater certainty that, in educational policy-making, the tendency is to create greater organizational flexibility while increasing

275

normative control. In Britain the move away from the central control of schools by local education authorities, and the attempt instead to create an internal market among schools, are an example of the former, while the establishment of a National Curriculum in schools and of a national framework for vocational qualifications in further education is an example of the latter. The present tendency is a reversal of the pattern that prevailed in the 1960s when tight organizational control was maintained over schools and colleges which, nevertheless, were permitted considerable normative discretion.

However, whether the present trend to looser organization and tighter normative control can be maintained is open to doubt. The former is perhaps more accurately interpreted as a futile effort to ignore the inescapable organizational consequences of mass education systems, and the latter as a naïve attempt to deny the normative pluralism, even instability, characteristic of modern society. Three more fundamental questions about the future of education concern deeper issues. First, what is the critical-cultural role of education within a mass society in which hierarchies of value and, more radically, notions of discrimination carry little weight?

Second, in much narrower instrumental terms what is the function of education, as a distinctive organization with transcendent values, in a society that is already moving beyond the modern to assume a post-industrial or post-modern configuration? Organizations of all kinds are likely to be prey to a radical volatility, while the claims of transcendence may dissolve into a just-in-time playfulness. Third, to what extent has education, like other manifestations of MODERNITY, been living off the accumulated capital of religious beliefs and ethical systems it has so destructively interrogated and, most recently, categorically denied?

Archer, Margaret (1979) *Social Origins of Educational Systems*, London: Sage.
Arnold, Matthew (1932) *Culture and Anarchy*, ed. J. Dover Wilson, Cambridge: Cambridge University Press.
Bruner, J.S. (1972) *The Relevance of Education*, Oxford: Oxford University Press.
Dewey, John ([1916] 1944) *Democracy and Education*, New York: Free Press.
Gruber, H.E. and Vonèche, J.J. (eds) (1977) *The Essential Piaget: An Interpretative Reference and Guide*, London: Routledge & Kegan Paul.
Gutmann, Amy (1977) *Democratic Education*, Princeton, NJ: Princeton University Press.
Maclure, J. Stuart (1965) *Educational Documents England and Wales 1816 to the Present Day*, London: Methuen.
Peters, R.S. (ed.) (1967) *The Concept of Education*, London: Routledge.
Rousseau, J.–J. (1911) *Emile*, London: Dent.

Peter Scott

ELDERLY

People of 60 years and more comprise a steadily increasing proportion of the world's population. This poses a complex challenge to many of the current structures within SOCIETY. Improved support systems are needed for the growing numbers of frail elderly people. But just as important is the creation of opportunities for service for the vastly larger numbers of healthy older people who have the experience and time to make major contributions. A broad ranging consideration of ageing is required which builds on insights from the biological and social sciences, the humanities and THEOLOGY. We need to find a balance within two dialectical patterns of thought: recognizing the strengths as well as the frailties of old age; and allowing room for the emergence of new customs while respecting the traditional values and roles associated with old age. The variety of conditions that can occur within human ageing demands a flexibility of pastoral response to interpreting spiritual meaning and meeting spiritual needs, as people move, often within short periods of time, from situations of contribution to others to a situation of dependence on them. Inspirational models are provided not only in literature but also in living practice within many societies around the world. But such heritage should not be used to hinder the development of new ways of growing old. Demographic change alone means that the experience of old age cannot be the same in the future as in the past.

Up to the present century, elderly people in most times and places of the world were a small part of the population. Nevertheless attention to their needs and position in society belied their numerical unimportance. The historical roots of attitudes to old age within Western society have been the subject of much study, but the conclusions are complex (Achenbaum 1985). The Hebrew Scriptures provide some of the most influential images of age. The range of themes in these writings is very broad: historical accounts which are realistic in their depiction of POWER and frailty and which above all demonstrate the importance of FAMILY life for all age groups; calls within the prophetic and psalmist writings for greater sensitivity to the needs of elderly people; and explicit focus on the personal dimensions of ageing, especially physical deterioration, within the wisdom writers (Dulin 1988). The New Testament perspectives provide a contrast, because although they repeat Jewish prescriptions not to neglect the old they have a different view of the life course. As a result of the much stronger stress on an ongoing life with God beyond DEATH, old age appears to have of itself no special importance. While it is clear that the early church did try to recognize and benefit from the wisdom of its older members, there is no parallel with the great respect and dignity shown to older people within Eastern traditions and religions. Although these are not part of the roots of Western culture, they are vital to include in any consideration of ageing within today's multi-ethnic societies. Buddhism and Hinduism provide a more focused approach which stems perhaps from the fact that the original Buddhist insights on the meaning of life were based on an explicit confrontation with the painful realities of deterioration with ageing. Hindu thinking about old age was also transformed as a result, recognizing ageing as a final stage of life with a special task appropriate to it (Tilak 1989).

Christianity and Western society have also been built on the foundations of classical civilization which as with the Hebrew Scriptures provides a rich mixture of contrasting pictures of late life. Western culture appears to have developed with ambivalent attitudes towards age, with some eras and societies emphasizing more respectful images, others the woes. A decisive shift in attitudes, however, seems to have occurred in the late eighteenth century, for which the most striking evidence comes from research on social indices on the east coast of the USA. Older people became less likely to be respected on account of their age. According to some of the original proponents of the view that INDUSTRIALIZATION and modernization led to an increase in negative attitudes to old age, this trend started to go into reverse in the USA from the 1960s. We thus appear to be living at a time not only of growth of the world's elderly population but also of change in societal attitudes (Bond, Coleman and Peace 1993). There is an increased sensitivity to the damaging impact of 'ageism' (the unjustified attribution of characteristics to people on the basis of age alone) and a greater willingness on the part of some older people themselves to campaign for recognition of their potential (as in the 'Grey Panthers' movement in the USA) and to reject terms such as 'elderly' with its negative connotations.

Ageing in the sense of decline of physical and mental functioning is a relative matter. The health of the average 75 year old at the present time in Britain and comparable Western countries is equivalent to that of a 60 year old at the turn of the century. Deterioration is increasingly focused in the higher age ranges, those over 80 years. This is the group in many Western populations which is growing markedly in numbers over the coming twenty years. The population age structures of northern and western Europe, with 20 per cent or more over the age of 60 years, have lost their traditional pyramidal form and are becoming increasingly rectangular. This pattern is being followed by the advanced countries of North America and the Pacific region and is predicted to become common over most parts of the world in the course of the next century. Grave concern is already being expressed about the situation in Third World countries where traditional means of support are being depleted by the movement of younger people to the cities to find work (Tout 1989).

It is vital none the less to see the phenomenon of the ageing of the world's population in a positive light, in which the enjoyment of a long life ceases to be only the privilege of a small minority. A further indicator of new ways of thinking is the adoption of the concept of the 'third age' to depict that period of life which begins when considerations of earning a living and raising a family cease to predominate and individuals become free to choose for themselves how to spend their time in developing their talents and contributing to society in new ways. Laslett (1989) argues that the conditions for creating a flourishing third age already exist in many Western societies. The Christian churches and other religious organizations have been slow to participate in these developments and need to take up vigorously the challenge of offering people in their fifties and sixties the opportunities for reflection on the directions their lives could now take.

The distinction between the 'young-old' and the 'old-old' leads to the use of the term the 'fourth age' to indicate the period of growing disability and dependence that many people, but not all, have to face as they survive into their eighties and beyond. Here the social and pastoral considerations are somewhat different, although developments in modern technology should allow many people to carry on with third age activities even if they are, for example, wheelchair bound. Dementia, which is the disability most related to advanced old age, poses particular problems. The provision of adequate support systems is crucial. As families have decreased in size and their mobility has increased, many elderly people find themselves living in isolated circumstances as they become more dependent. It is important to recognize the related issues of GENDER and ethnicity, since it is mainly older women who live alone, often with inadequate pensions, and members from minority ethnic groups who are further disadvantaged. Social and health services tend to focus their resources on individuals without other available support and have come to assume overmuch from those family members who are available and willing to help. Social policy statements now recognize that, as well as raising standards of domiciliary and residential care, more support needs to be given to the so-called informal carers. It is important too not to neglect the psychological needs of elderly people at this stage of life. Studies on survival in advanced old age show that many display remarkable abilities to come to terms with their situation. Others show tenacity in clinging on to a sense of their

selves rooted in their past lives. Creative ideologies and strategies are required to help elderly people maintain self-respect under physically deteriorating conditions, and secular studies acknowledge the important role of religious faith in these processes (Tobin 1991).

Ageing within modern society requires a fresh approach from Christian pastoral work. The traditional model which focuses on sustenance through the losses and suffering which accompany old age remains essential. But its ready acceptance of people's situations and their interpretatons of these situations can result in missed opportunities for more creative intervention in people's lives: e.g. by challenging their implicit values, seeking family dialogue over problems relating to care and channelling the elderly person's talents into continuing uses. Of all modern theorists about the course and meaning of the life span, Erik Erikson has probably had the greatest impact on pastoral theologians. His writings on old age have been particularly influential because of his conception of old age as an essential part of the life-span and because he has continued to write on these themes well into his own eighties (Erikson et al. 1986). His concepts of 'generativity' and 'integrity' have particular resonance. It is important for the churches to set examples in providing opportunities for elderly people to provide care and LOVE and in combating the loss of intergenerational links. More possibilities can also be created in liturgy to celebrate the passing on of faith by listening to the witness of faith of older people (Whitehead and Whitehead 1982). As well as giving witness to the past, ageing invites a vision of the future which transcends the finiteness of the individual's life-span. In this context the diminishments of age can be seen to have value (as in the Hindu tradition). Late life can be envisaged as a time which marks the coming together of an individual's historical identity and his or her appropriation of a Christian eschatological identity (Gerkin 1989).

If there is one point which should be emphasized in conclusion, it is the need for a more discriminating approach to older people. There is great inequality of income and of living circumstances among older people which requires critique. The churches' traditional ministry of support continues to be vital, especially for those suffering from dementia and those who care for them. But at the same time the churches must be careful to rid themselves of damaging ageism. This is not so easy as many older people are often ageist themselves, not surprisingly since throughout their lives they may have thought in prejudiced ways about age. In a society where older people's traditional roles as grandparents and as culture bearers are threatened, the churches should be to the fore in providing opportunities for them to offer service and witness.

Achenbaum, W.A. (1985) 'Societal perception of aging and the aged', in R.H. Binstock and E. Shanas (eds) *Handbook of Aging and the Social Sciences*, 2nd edn, New York: Van Nostrand Reinhold, pp. 129–48.

Bond, J., Coleman, P. and Peace, S. (eds) (1993) *Ageing in Society: An Introduction to Social Gerontology*, 2nd edn, London: Sage.

Dulin, R.Z. (1988) *A Crown of Glory: A Biblical View of Aging*, New York: Paulist Press.

Erikson, E.H., Erikson, J.M. and Kivnick, H.Q. (1986) *Vital Involvement in Old Age: The Experience of Old Age in Our Time*, New York: Norton.

Gerkin, C.V. (1989) 'Pastoral care and models of aging', *Journal of Religion and Aging* 6: 83–100.

Laslett, P. (1989) *A Fresh Map of Life: The Emergence of the Third Age*, London: Weidenfeld & Nicolson.

Tilak, S. (1989) *Religion and Aging in the Indian Tradition*, Albany, NY: State University of New York Press.

Tobin, S.S. (1991) *Personhood in Advanced Old Age: Implications for Practice*, New York: Springer.

Tout, K. (1989) *Ageing in Developing Countries*, Oxford: Oxford University Press.

Whitehead, E.E. and Whitehead, J.D. (1982) *Christian Life Patterns: The Psychological Challenges and Religious Invitations of Adult Life*, New York: Image Books, Doubleday.

Peter G. Coleman

EMANCIPATION

From its source in Roman Law, in which context it signified a setting free (of wife or child) from paternal AUTHORITY (the *patria potestas*), the term emancipation (Latin: *emancipare*) came to be applied from the seventeenth century onwards in an extraordinarily wide range of extended and metaphorical uses. In addition to wives and children, potential subjects of emancipation came to include colonial churches, and colonized peoples, slaves, victims of various civil disabilities (such as, for example, Catholics in England prior to the 1829 Catholic Emancipation Act), apprentices, wage-labourers, non-Christians and other sinners, believers in superstition, and many other categories. Similarly, the 'chains' or constraints from which these subjects were to be freed, or emancipated, were very diverse: the economic power of employers, the force of tradition, or a priestly élite, the temptations of Satan, the disadvantages of legal restraints or prohibitions, the imposition of military force and so on. In general, to be emancipated was to be free of the constraints imposed by these various intellectual, moral, cultural, legal, economic or military impositions.

Though often used to refer to specific categories of subject and specific sources of unfreedom, from the seventeenth century onwards a distinctively Western and modern sense of universal human emancipation emerged. Closely associated with the European Enlightenment, this involves a certain view of the human being as an autonomous, self-conscious, freely choosing individual. On this view, each individual is equally possessed of the faculties of experience, reason and will. Everyone is therefore capable of independently arriving at well-founded beliefs, both about his own nature and about the world he inhabits. Moral principles, and the ability to choose to obey or disobey them, are also matters accessible to the autonomous individual.

Notoriously, however, actual societies did not recognize these attributes: hierarchies of priests mediated between God and the individual believer; freedom of choice in matters of GOVERNMENT, taxation, religious belief and many other matters were systematically overridden. For many believers in this 'enlightened' view of human AUTONOMY and EQUALITY, the French and American revolutions which established the first distinctively modern constitutional states were seen as bringing about an all-round emancipation from the constraints and impositions of traditional rule, of 'patriarchal' authority. In this tradition, then, the concept of emancipation is closely connected with the achievement of those liberties (generally legally defined and protected) which go to make up CITIZENSHIP in the modern liberal state: freedom of conscience, of expression and of association, freedom from arbitrary arrest, and the protection of PROPERTY.

However, it soon came to be clear that this sense of emancipation suffered from a number of limitations if it were to be considered as genuinely universal in scope. For one thing, as early feminists were quick to point out, the freedoms it protected were largely those of men (later feminists have added that the ideal of human individuality against which social arrangements were measured was itself a masculine construct). For other critics, it was plain that the right of property for some entailed a life of dependence and exploitation for others, whilst 'equality under the law' was a mere formality for those unable to afford access to the courts.

By the mid-nineteenth century, socialist and communist thinkers, most notably Karl Marx, had developed these criticisms into a systematic critique of the Enlightenment view of emancipation as realized in the modern 'bourgeois' state. Certainly Marx viewed the establishment of universal civil and political rights as progress, but he insisted upon a distinction between *political* emancipation and full *human* emancipation. The political community established in the modern liberal state intimated, in an ideal form, the future human community, but was subverted by the atomistic and exploitative relations which continued to characterize social and economic life. In a SOCIETY still dominated by private property and competition, the STATE could be no more than an expression of competing private interests and a means of preserving existing inequalities.

For Marx and his associates, the Enlightenment ideal of the self-sufficient, self-interested, rationally calculating individual, far from constituting a vision of universal human nature, was a mere ideological expression of the type of socially regressive and possessive individual produced by bourgeois society. The modern liberal state both failed to give real content to those universal rights it proclaimed for its individual

citizens and consolidated a system of social and economic relations which obstructed the historical development of a new, wider and richer form of human fulfilment than the Enlightenment had been able to imagine.

This vision of emancipation as a historical transformation which would enable the realization of human potentials not so far even recognized was a distinctive outcome of the radicalization of German idealist philosophy. However, it had marked analogies with, and, it could also be argued, had its historical source in, Christian ESCHATOLOGY. Nevertheless, in this secular form, the communist vision of human emancipation implied not only an account of the future earthly 'good life' but also an interpretation of human historical processes as so many steps towards its eventual realization.

For the early Marx, full human emancipation, or 'self-realization', was defined negatively as the overcoming of all the forms of estrangement which afflicted human kind in the epoch of private property: separation from one's own activity in coercive labour, separation from one another in exploitative and instrumental relations, a fragmentation of the self and, above all, estrangement from nature. Positively, the emancipated state was defined in terms of the transcendence of private property in a communal regulation of production for need, a transcendence in which a species-wide co-operation would enable the full development of each individual. The content of this great co-operative project Marx defines as the 'humanization of nature': the overcoming of human estrangement from nature will take the form of creative (practical, aesthetic, spiritual) transformation of nature, such that humans will recognize themselves in the products of their activity.

This view of emancipation differs substantially from those which were characteristic of the seventeenth- and eighteenth-century cultures and which, indeed, persist in modern liberal social and political theory. First, the perceived autonomy which is positively valued in both visions is taken to be a 'given' attribute in the liberal tradition. To protect it, one needs to prevent other individuals or the sovereign power from interfering in the individual's private sphere. On the more radical, Marxian view, personal autonomy is an *acquired* capacity which requires both material resources and an appropriate setting of enabling social relationships. A reordering of society is a necessary condition for the universal realization of individual autonomy. But the differences go deeper than this. On the Marxian view, autonomy involves not just freedom to choose and to act in accordance with one's choices, but also the opportunity to explore and develop new senses of self – to become a kind of being to whom new *possibilities* of choice become available. This developmental view of the individual was, for Marx, inseparable from his developmental view of the social context with which the individual would develop. Above all, human emancipation in this new sense meant an augmentation in human powers of creative co-operation. This contrast between the dominant liberal and the radical conceptions of emancipation is often characterized in terms of a distinction between 'negative' and 'positive' liberty: the distinction between the right not to be interfered with and the right to govern one's own life.

Although some vision of a future communal organization of social life, organized around the co-operative meeting of need as against the competitive acquisition of profit, continued to provide the moral standard underlying Marx's later writings, the full-blooded Utopian vision of the early writings was never recalled. Marx also soon came to reject his earlier philosophical view of history as a single line of march towards the communist future, and there is reason to believe he also dropped his commitment to the early vision of a full reconciliation of humanity with nature.

In the twentieth century, disillusionment with the degeneration of the Russian revolution into an oppressive dictatorship led to a revival of interest in the moral vision of the earlier works of Marx, and to the development of a distinctively Western neo-Marxian tradition of critical theory. Most closely associated with the names of Theodor Adorno, Max Horkheimer and, more recently, Jürgen Habermas, this tradition abandoned the classical Marxian expectation of proletarian revolution, but sought to retain the moral vision of a future good life to sustain their implacable hostility to the economic and especially cultural forms of late CAPITALISM. For the earlier writers, authentic art, philosophical reflection or fantasy provided intimations of the continuing possibility of a qualitatively different and more humanly fulfilling life. In more recent years, Habermas has tried to anchor this vision in an analysis of the conditions of human communication, especially speech. Implicit in the use of speech is an acknowledgement of the equal right of a partner in dialogue to question what is said, to introduce new topics of conversation and so on. Though these conditions are generally denied in our familiar contexts of asymmetrical power relations, of 'distorted communication', the 'ideal speech situation' is still evoked as a regulative ideal.

Yet another distinctively twentieth-century departure stems from the diffusion into the wider culture of certain concepts of psychoanalysis – the concept of the unconscious, in particular. There are certainly much earlier uses of the term 'emancipation' to signify a liberation from sinful thoughts or desires, but the systematic development in Freud's work of a theory of the complex internal structuring of the self takes this notion much further. For Freud, neurotic symptoms – paralyses, compulsive acts, phobias and the like – should be 'read' as so many symbolic expressions of inadequately repressed early emotional traumas. The continued presence in the unconscious of the powerful affective content of these traumas explained their eruption in often bizarre forms in later life. But Freud and his followers extended those ideas well beyond neurotic symptoms to explain forgetfulness, slips of the tongue, dream sequences and so on, which are commonplaces of everyday life.

Just as the Marxian view of emancipation had challenged the liberal idea of personal autonomy by emphasizing its conditionality on external, material and social-relational supports, the Freudian view brought to light the extent to which unrecognized or unacknowledged inner, psychic forces may inhibit personal development, issue in compulsive or irrational behaviour or, more generally, deprive people of their capacity to be in charge of their own lives. For orthodox psychoanalysts, the route to emancipation (at least in so far as it was attainable at all) was not social revolution but the development of self-understanding through a therapeutic relationship with a psychoanalytic specialist.

However, as Wilhelm Reich and many of the advocates of critical theory, most notably Herbert Marcuse, were able to show, links could be made between the inner psychic conflicts diagnosed by the psychoanalysts and the demands made by a particular kind of (late capitalist) civilization upon its subjects. In his later work Freud had himself made these connections, though he had taken the pessimistic stance that the psychic suffering imposed by the requirements of advanced civilization was 'fatefully inevitable'. Marcuse and others disagreed: new, more open and diverse forms of familial relations, a playful and aesthetic relation to one another and to nature, were on the historical horizon, blocked only by the economic, cultural and political interests which prevailed in late capitalist (and state socialist) societies.

Since the 1960s the centrality of Marxian views of emancipation has given way to a plurality of radical visions – some of them quite new, others bearing the imprint of earlier 'Utopian' socialist and anarchist traditions of thought. The so-called 'second wave' of feminist thought and practice has brought with it a deep challenge to the visions of human fulfilment carried forward by each of the earlier traditions: their emphases on autonomy, self-realization, productive mastery of nature, allegedly reveal a masculine ideal of humanity. Feminists differ widely as to the alternative views they advocate. Some are willing to embrace a revaluing of a feminine ideal of caring, nurturing and closeness to nature, whilst others seek to break free of all traditional gender stereotypes as unnecessary constraints on the free development of human diversity. Comparable developments have taken place in those movements dedicated to the emancipation of oppressed racial and cultural minorities. In general, the shift has been away from demands to be included on equal terms within the existing cultural, economic and legal framework towards an emphasis on their own distinctive cultural forms and identities. Emancipation is now understood as the full recognition of these distinctive forms, as against the uniform assimilation which is the alleged implication of universalistic versions of emancipation.

Widespread concern about impending global environmental catastrophe, also dating from the late 1960s, has also provoked a wide range of radical proposals for a qualitatively different relationship between humanity and nature. Many of these 'GREEN' Utopias echo themes from earlier Utopian socialist and anarchist writers, but they are distinctive in centring their accounts of the 'good life' around sustainable and harmonious relationships to the natural ENVIRONMENT. In some of these visions, non-human animals, and even non-living aspects of nature, are to be valued in their own right, and are thus also to be considered subjects in need of emancipation (see ANIMAL RIGHTS).

Adorno, T. and Horkheimer, M. (1979) *Dialectic of Enlightenment*, London: Verso.

Barrett, M. (1980, 1988) *Women's Oppression Today*, London: Verso.

Eckersley, R. (1992) *Environmentalism and Political Theory*, London: University College Press.

Gorz, A. (1994) *Capitalism, Socialism, Ecology*, London: Verso.

Held, D. (1980) *Introduction to Critical Theory*, London: Hutchinson.

Keat, R. (1981) *The Politics of Social Theory*, Oxford: Blackwell.

Marcuse, H. (1969a) *Eros and Civilization*, London: Sphere Books.

——(1969b) *An Essay on Liberation*, Boston, MA: Beacon Press.

Plumwood, V. (1993) *Feminism and the Mastery of Nature*, London and New York: Routledge.

White, S.K. (1988) *The Recent Work of Jürgen Habermas*, Cambridge: Cambridge University Press.

Ted Benton

EMBRYO RESEARCH

Embryo research originated in the middle part of this century ostensibly as a consequence of demands to deal with infertility in humans and to increase production in animals. The term 'embryo' is derived from the medieval Latin *embryon* and is generally regarded as referring to an early *foetus*, *in utero*; before birth. In humans the term embryo is usually restricted to the first four months after conception. Other terms that apply to unborn humans are zygote, up to fourteen days after conception, and foetus, from four months to birth. Such terms are quite arbitrary. They are constructs devised for convenience and have no basis that would warrant any normative significance. Within these terms embryonic research would apply, in humans, to that period between fourteen days and four months. In practice, experiments on the unborn at that point in gestation and outside the womb, *in vitro*, are disallowed in most jurisdictions and, at the moment at least, technically impossible. By convention, however, the term embryonic research includes, indeed is confined to, research on zygotes. Additionally, technical restrictions make research on an embryo of more than a few days currently impossible.

In many western jurisdictions legal restrictions limit the time during which embryo experimentation is permitted: fourteen days after conception is a common cut off point. Embryo experimentation on human zygotes has excited considerable moral and theological concern, for, as with ABORTION, the point at which such experimentation (or termination) is permitted, or not, defines the line that separates a member of the moral community from that which is not a member of the moral community. In theological terms that line is drawn at the point at which the life, or potential life, is regarded as sacred, or not, as the case may be. All societies draw some line at which a new being has membership rights, it may be at birth, or at naming, or at conception. In some societies infanticide prior to a certain point, 30 days or longer is not regarded as problematic (Kuhse and Singer 1985).

In ancient Rome a new born child was not accepted into the moral community and had no rights until the father picked it up after its birth (Brown 1990). Even then it was subject to the father's power of life over death, *patria potestas* (Maine 1917). Such practices define the group by setting points at which inclusion is permitted and exclusion disallowed. In western societies the tendency has been to see the category of the human in naturalistic terms, and/or sacral terms, rather than as a social category; hence infanticide is not permitted, live birth conferring automatic membership and full rights, if not full duties.

Embryo experimentation, like abortion has shifted the issue of membership and, possibly, rights to a point before birth and has brought western societies directly to face the conflict that has arisen between definitions of humanity given in terms of nature or convention. What appeared natural, the notion of the human, appears now, on some accounts, to be a matter of convention. As an issue embryonic research cuts to the very deepest concerns that we have about the status of life. More starkly, perhaps, than any other issue, embryonic research brings what appears as natural in theological guise, the category of the person and the category of the human, face to face with what appears conventional in social guise.

The potential biological transformations that embryonic research can engender bring us more starkly than almost any other issue face to face with what Sellars has called 'the myth of the given'. Embryonic research is a potential scientific response to the cultural transformations, the break with the past and the abandonment of the 'myth of the given' that is the hallmark of the post-modern revolution. Such is the apparent completeness of the break with the past that embryonic research has thrown up, that it has been thought to represent a major challenge for current ethical categories and modes of thought.

There is a widely held, if problematic, view that research on embryos may take two distinct forms; therapeutic and non-therapeutic and that each of these can be justified independently (Clarke and Linzey 1988: 63). Hence a justification for therapeutic research would not automatically justify non-therapeutic research and vice-versa. Therapeutic research in its strictest sense is directed at the well being of individual embryos. Non-therapeutic research, by contrast, is directed not toward the well being of an individual embryo but utilizes an individual embryo to some further end, for example, the understanding of genetic defects or the alteration of the germ line. Both kinds of research raise serious moral problems, but the problems and their basis are somewhat different in emphasis, if not in kind.

Therapeutic research might include methods designed to distinguish between healthy and unhealthy embryos, improving the medium of culture so that embryos survived better outside the womb while awaiting transplantation, improving the method and success of freezing embryos or improving the methods of thawing and implanting embryos. On the face of it such research will benefit individual embryos. Non-therapeutic research might include the extraction of cells from embryos with a view to cloning the embryo, to determining the basis of particular genetic disorders and to manipulating the characteristics of future generations. It is the fear of the latter with its potentially eugenic programme (*see* EUGENICS) that has raised most fears. In practice the distinction between therapeutic and non-therapeutic research is a thin one. Therapeutic research, rarely, if at all, benefits an individual embryo; that requires therapeutic intervention. If it is of benefit at all it is of benefit to some future embryo and is quite frequently destructive of the embryo involved in the 'therapeutic' research.

The moral and theological problems that embryonic research engenders are three-fold. First, if embryonic research is destructive of a particular embryo, to what extent, if at all, does that matter? Second, if embryonic research is directed towards an alteration of the germ line (the genetic make-up of future generations) to what extent does that matter? Additional problems are thrown up by the methods used to re-implant and to see the manipulated embryo through to term, to birth. That process, consequent upon IVF, or *in vitro* fertilization poses its own moral problems for some theologians. Third, that the act of CREATION involved in the creation of new kinds of life is a break with past theological perceptions of God as creator and humankind as created.

The destruction of a particular embryo matters only if that embryo has moral or spiritual value. In western societies, at least, there are few who would doubt that a child at the moment of birth has a moral value. By extension it is widely, although not universally regarded, that a child in the womb after the point of viability, approximately twenty to twenty four weeks gestation, had a legal and possibly moral value. For that reason most jurisdictions that permit abortion restrict that kind of intervention to the period before viability. On some accounts, however, viability is not the relevant criterion; all life from the moment of conception has value; all life that is conceived is sacred. At conception, it is argued, the potential life has come into being and taken a determinate and unique form. Indeed, on some accounts, ensoulment has taken place, on other accounts, particularly St Thomas Aquinas, following Aristotle, ensoulment takes place later; shortly after conception. More generally it might be held that a human life begins at conception and human rights, or at least respect and dignity, stem from that time. This kind of position has been reinforced by Pope John Paul II,

> . . . the use of human embryos or foetuses as an object of experimentation constitutes a crime against their dignity as human beings who have a right to the same respect owed to a child once born, just as to every person.
> *Evangelium Vitae*, 1995

A view that the conceptus is valuable does not necessarily rest on theological arguments. The equivalent secular argument is that any life that is potentially unique is valuable. A unique potential life and being, it is argued, is created at the moment of conception and is, therefore, valuable; to destroy that is to destroy a unique potential human being.

The second major problem that embryonic research engenders concerns its potential effect on future members of the human race. The alteration of the germ line matters to the extent that eugenics, whether positive or negative, is regarded as morally and theologically acceptable or unacceptable. Negative eugenics, in the sense utilized here, is the destruction of those characteristics in a population that are regarded as undesirable. The classic case was the eugenic programme of Nazi Germany when Jews, gypsies, homosexuals, and other minorities were forcibly and brutally removed from the population, isolated and destroyed. By contrast, positive eugenics is the breeding of, or encouragement of the breeding of, certain characteristics in a population. An example might be breeding or altering the germ line of a population to eliminate certain diseases. At present count, there are some four thousand diseases that are known to have determinate and definite genetic causes.

The removal of those diseases from the human population seems to be attractive and has the promise of benefit for a population. Further benefit might be obtained by the removal of certain characteristics that seem decidedly unfortunate, cancers, cystic fibrosis, Down's syndrome, and other conditions. That programme, even if it were thought desirable, quickly shades over into the possibility of the removal of, for example, dental caries, premature ageing, baldness, red hair, or a thousand other characteristics that fail to appeal to some one or some group or other. Taken yet one step further eugenic programmes based on embryonic research could attempt to shape psychological factors, work and skill factors, orientation towards certain occupations or whatever. If it is admitted that such a eugenic programme should be carried out, i.e., 'What sort of people should there be?', to utilize a phrase of Jonathan Glover, then a further question raises itself, who should decide? Parents or state? Employers or insurance companies?

What examples of this kind show is how easy it is, at least in argument, to slide from attempts to provide techniques of benefit to particular couples, or particular embryos, to research that has potentially sinister consequences. The slope might be slippery and some means has to be found to prevent slides. In this respect many western jurisdictions have been active both in inquiries, in legislation and in licensing practices and have shown some concern to limit the practice and effect of embryonic research. In practice this has meant returning to the basic question that embryonic research throws up and attempting to define the point at which life, with all its rights, and with all the respect due to life, begins.

The clearest legal expression of early rights is to be found in *The Inter-American Convention on Human Rights* section 4.1 of which states that: 'Every person has the right to have his life respected. This right shall be protected by law, and in general, from the moment of conception'. That declaration makes it clear that personhood commences from the moment of conception, and indeed this is the point made clear in *Evangelium Vitae*. In classic Church doctrine there is a distinction between persons

and things. An embryo is not a thing, therefore it must be a person. As a person it has a SOUL, or a potential soul, and the embodiment of that soul may not be destroyed by others.

Set against this theological view, however, is a claim that personhood is a social characteristic; a person is that kind of being that exhibits substantial degrees of rationality and shows the possibility of moral interaction with others (*see also* PERSONS). Such a definition may even be equated with what it is to be human. Peter Singer expressed a view of this kind in evidence to an Australian Senate Select Committee that was looking into the provision of legislation restricting embryonic research: 'A human being is a being possessing, at least at a minimal level, the capacities distinctive of our species, which include consciousness, the ability to relate to others, perhaps even rationality and self consciousness'.

In the United Kingdom the issue of embryonic research merited a Royal Commission headed by Mary, now Baroness, Warnock. The Committee was given the task of deciding whether or not to permit embryonic research. It attempted to determine a clear point at which life could be said to have a moral significance of such weight that interfering with it would be morally unacceptable. They concluded that such a point was not derivable from the scientific evidence relating to the development of the foetus. 'The timing of the different stages of development' was critical but once the 'process has begun there is no particular part of the developmental process, that is more important than another; all are part of a continual process.'

Even so the committee was impressed by the event that was the formation of the primitive streak, the beginnings of spinal development that took place after fourteen days. They reasoned that such an event indicated a clear genetic formation. Such an event did not, of itself however, have *moral* significance. Had the committee come to that kind of conclusion it would have been challenged for producing moral conclusions from natural events: a naturalistic fallacy. Instead the committee argued that it was necessary to make a cut off point beyond which embryonic research would not be permitted, 'in order to allay public anxiety' (Warnock 1984: 65). That cut off point was fourteen days and the fourteen day period has been incorporated into UK legislation; a similar period has been adopted, for similar reasons, in a number of western jurisdictions.

While there is no current evidence that embryonic research has led to massive alterations of the germ line in humans such alteration has taken place in animal lines. That alteration has been sufficiently radical in some cases to produce trans-genic animals, for example, crosses between sheep and goats: 'shoats' or 'geeps'. Such life forms are potential subjects of patent claims, as artefacts rather than as natural beings. Genetic research generally, it is claimed, has the possibility of blurring the distinction between nature and convention; a distinction that is prevalent from Aristotle onwards, and embryonic research is no exception to the elision of this crucial distinction. From a theological perspective it is sometimes thought that embryonic research places God's right to creation in the hands of humanity.

Against this view it is often claimed that the idea of nature is itself a culture product, and an early Hellenistic one at that. On some recent, deconstructive (*see* DECONSTRUCTION) re-appraisals of the origin of the idea of 'nature' it appears that there is no given that is nature, it is instead a myth: 'the myth of the given'. Indeed some of the foundations of early Christianity rest on the, undoubtedly Hellenistically inspired, idea that dominion over nature was given to Adam: that is to say humanity. In later tradition that dominion came to be understood as domination (Clarke and Linzey 1988). Indeed the idea that the fixed past was unrecoverable and that we shared in the openness of the future was accepted by an Anglican Report, whose members argued that the world was possibly

> in process towards an as yet unrealised goal . . . are we bound to accept the natural order of things, just as it is, or is nature a morally neutral order upon which we may impose what we perceive to be good purposes.
>
> (Church of England 1989)

In this framework it is quite possible that part of a Christian response was to work towards even quite radical change where that change was perceived as in accord with God's own purpose.

Embryonic research has, undoubtedly, been of benefit to some couples who would otherwise have been childless. It does, however, raise more questions than have yet been answered, perhaps even can be answered. Embryonic research is *par excellence* an issue that challenges almost all hitherto existing ethical categories (*see* ETHICS) and has shown how what appears as an ethical and theological issue transforms itself into a theo-politico-ethical issue. This transformation is common of ethical issues in the conditions of late MODERNITY and is probably indicative of the future development of such issues.

The example of embryonic research is fruitful in this respect. The distinction between therapeutic and non-therapeutic research seems attractive, yet it turns out to be one of dubious value. As yet there is little, if any, therapeutic research that is not potentially harmful to, or destructive of, individual embryos. Such research, the freezing of embryos, the attempt to find new and better cultures and mediums in which to keep embryos has been costly in the loss of embryos. An equivalent form of experimentation on human beings that was so costly in terms of human life would not be permitted and would be regarded with considerable horror. That it is permitted on embryos indicates that society has taken a clear decision that excludes very early human life from its membership, even from its concerns; that it has indeed classified such cellular structures as not human in a moral or religious sense.

Once this is perceived as the central issue, it becomes an ethico-political issue for the central concern is about what counts as human in a theological sense, an ethical sense and a legal and political sense. These definitions rest on different criteria and reflect different, often incommensurable, concerns. Criteria of inclusion and exclusion in a plural society are always open to contestation and always subject to political debate. In a monolithic society what counted as criteria of membership could be given by some AUTHORITY, by church, or by state for instance, and is not debatable; for what is given with authority in such circumstances appears both natural and objective. In a plural society and in one where traditional conceptions of a unified moral and theological authority have collapsed, dividing lines and concepts are contestable (Clarke 1979). In such cases what has been regarded as an unproblematic theological and ethical issue for the last few hundred years may appear as a point at which we commence living and reliving the ethico-political moment (*see also* ETHICS).

Embryonic research, with its concerns about what counts as life, and with its concerns about the margins of life, more than almost any other issue brings social membership issues to the fore. As it does so it shifts the balance of early membership criteria from a once uncontested arena of theological edict to the agonistic pluriverse of contemporary political arenas. That produces uncertainties, in this case the uncertainties are both challenging and threatening. When we define the point in gestation before which we may experiment on an embryo we assert its otherness and define ourselves. In this case the definition has turned out to be less than clear, less than easy, and its implications less than comfortable.

Brown, Peter (1990) *The Body and Society*, London: Faber and Faber.

Church of England, Board for Social Responsibility (1985) *Personal Origins: A Report of a Working Party on Human Fertilisation and Embryology*, London: CIO Publishing.

Clarke, Paul Barry (1979) 'Eccentrically Contested Concepts', *British Journal of Political Science* vol. 9.

Clarke, Paul Barry and Linzey, A. (1988) *Research on Embryos: Politics, Theology and Law*, London: LCAP.

——(1990) *Political Theory and Animal Rights*, London: Pluto Press.

Clarke, Paul Barry and Tonti-Fillipini, N. (1986) *Obligation in a Caring Profession*, Melbourne: St. Vincent's Bioethics Centre.

Jakabovits, Lord Immanuel (1984) *Human Fertilisation and Embryology – A Jewish View; Submissions to the Warnock Committee and the Department of Health and Social Security*, London: Office of the Chief Rabbi.

Kuhse, Helga and Singer, Peter (1985) *Should the Baby Live?* Oxford: Oxford University Press.

Mahanohey, John (1984) *Bioethics and Belief*, London: Sheed and Ward.

Maine, Henry (1917) *Ancient Law*, London and Toronto: J.M. Dent.

Singer, Peter and Wells, Deane (1984) *The Reproductive Revolution*, Oxford: Oxford University Press, p. 84.

Warnock, Mary (1984) *Report of the Committee of Inquiry into Human Fertilisation and Embryology*, London: H.M.S.O. Cmnd 9314.

Paul Barry Clarke

ENTERPRISE

Enterprise is defined as the establishing of a BUSINESS for the principal purpose of profit and growth. An entrepreneur is an individual who establishes and manages a business in this way. The entrepreneur is characterized principally by innovative behaviour, and will employ strategic management practices. An entrepreneurial venture engages one of Schumpeter's categories of behaviour: profitability; growth; innovative strategic practices. Enterprise should be distinguished from small business venture: any business which is independently owned and operated but is neither dominant in its field nor engages in any innovative practices. Small business owners and ventures may therefore change into being entrepreneurs and enterprises. Both small business owners and entrepreneurs will combine the furthering of personal goals and the pursuit of WEALTH. Typically the business will be seen as an extension of the personality (cf. Birley 1989). It may also provide the primary source of income, and take up the majority of the entrepreneur's or business owner's time and resources.

The history of the term is not originally economic. Malory's *Arthur* describes the enterprise of battle; the common sixteenth-century definition is one of taking in hand an expedition or adventure, usually fraught with danger. There was often a military connotation as in Machiavelli's *The Prince* (1527). It is interesting that by the eighteenth century the early use of enterprising, which often carried the pejorative description of foolhardy or scheming (cf. Marvell, *Reh. Transp.* 1672), had become favourable, and applied to merchants (cf. Gibbon, *Decline and Fall*).

The reason for the change lies in French economic theory. Richard Cantillon's *Essai sur la nature du commerce en general* (1755) drew attention to the function of the entrepreneur as someone who bore economic uncertainty. Anyone who bought and sold intentionally at uncertain prices assisted the working of the economy. It was left to later eighteenth- and early nineteenth-century economists (Quesnay, Baudeau, Turgot and especially Jean Baptiste Say) to apply this theory to different sectors of the economy.

Nevertheless the terms 'enterprise' and 'entrepreneurship' were regarded as obsolete in classical British economic theory from A. Smith to Marshall. Alfred Marshall (1842–1924) was Professor of Economics at Cambridge, and his *Principles of Economics* (8th edn, 1920) became the standard economic textbook on value, price and distribution for decades. He influenced the USA through his disciple Frank W. Taussig of Harvard. Prices adjusted to marginal costs, which were affected by the availability of plant, material and workers. This was because English theory was based upon a normal state of equilibrium, where the market cleared itself from the multiple reactions of businessmen, consumers, investors and workers to the price mechanism. Unknown elements were excluded from the argument, especially social and cultural factors such as enterprise. In addition the great growth of small business ventures, which to later economic historians were seen to be ideal examples of enterprise, were in Victorian Europe regarded as ventures which gave return on capital. Although Marx refers occasionally to enterprise in *Capital*, the main emphasis is on CAPITALISM and capitalist owners.

The great breakthrough in economic theory on the role of enterprise occurs in Joseph Schumpeter's writings. As early as 1912 he focused on the entrepreneur as the motor of the business cycle. However, his work was not translated from German into English until 1934, after he had accepted a chair at Harvard University. His *The Theory of Economic Development* (1934) and his more famous *Capitalism, Socialism and Democracy* (1942) drew attention to the relationship of interest and profit to progressive change. The entrepreneur took risks, engaged in innovative practices and utilized his personal characteristics. This theory had enormous influence.

Nevertheless, there was a profound irony in Schumpeter's writing, for he believed that mature capitalism had now rendered the role of the entrepreneur obsolete, for different reasons from that of classical British economics. Instead the multinational corporation could itself engage in innovation and risk-taking behaviour. In turn such corporations could be nationalized by the state, and the entrepreneur would be replaced by SOCIALISM. J.K. Galbraith's *The New Industrial Estate* (1967) draws heavily on Schumpeter's analysis.

However, other economists were not as convinced as Schumpeter that the rediscovered entrepreneur was as obsolete as might be thought. Ralph Harris, and the Institute of Economic Affairs (IEA) in London, united Austrian monetarist economics (Hayek, Friedman) with entrepreneurial theory in a series of works on competition and the freemarket. The election of the 1979 Conservative Government gave the IEA great prominence. The political dimension of their views was developed by a series of Conservative ministers, including Lord Young and Sir Keith Joseph. The term 'enterprise culture' was born; its first use was probably at the 1985 Conservative Party Conference at Blackpool by Lord Young, in a lecture entitled 'Britain resurgent'.

At the same time there was a growth in small businesses, which had been a declining feature of many West European economies for several decades (cf. *The Bolton Report* 1971 for a government study of small firms in the UK). There were several critical responses to the concept of an enterprise culture by British church leaders, including David Jenkins, Bishop of Durham, and Stanley Booth-Clibborn, Bishop of Manchester. It was difficult to disentangle the 1980s debate on enterprise from that of capitalism or the New Right. A defence of capitalism was offered by the American Roman Catholic theologian Michael Novak, but enterprise has attracted less theological attention. Nevertheless, the renewed interest in Schumpeter's theory, and the rise in small businesses across Europe (especially in Eastern Europe), appear to suggest that enterprise and entrepreneurship will outlive its association with New Right philosophy in the 1980s. Since most theologies of work were predicated of large, fairly stable companies with predictable patterns of behaviour and employment, the return to an expanding and vigorous small firms sector with highly innovative patterns of behaviour must require a reconsideration of a theology of work and of wealth creation. Concepts of creativity, dynamic change and individual leadership (with a consequent emphasis on the notion of character) could play a part here. There are also ethical issues of the regulation of enterprise, and the compatibility of the concept with that of environmental responsibility.

The question of environmental taxation becomes important here. Taxation on employment only serves to reduce jobs. Increasingly economists are examining the tax mechanism to control consumption (VAT) and energy use (the tax on fossil fuels). Enterprise needs to be placed in two frameworks. One is that of state regulation, which is done most easily by a combination of taxation and regulatory bodies. The other is the moral framework, which is the contribution that enterprise can make to the long-term creation of jobs. Some political commentators in the 1990s realized that the only source of long-term job creation would come from a combination of high quality training and enterprise creation. The moral framework that can be provided by theology and political philosophy is seen in the quality of social life which enterprise can provide, if it is harnessed to clear, social goals such as full employment and employee participation in work. Environmental protection requires making the external costs of pollution internal to the polluters themselves. Therefore the market is itself used to regulate the environment. Nevertheless, some environmentalists would challenge the whole concept of traditional economic theory, and the place of enterprise within it. The New Economics would argue for a wholesale redefinition of economic theory. Enterprise remains a concept which is accepted by some theologians and philosophers but resisted by others (e.g. Michael Northcott).

Birley, Sue (1989) 'The start-up', in Paul Burns and Jim Dewhurst (eds) *Small Business and Entrepreneurship*, London: Macmillan.
Burns, Paul and Dewhurst, Jim (eds) (1989) *Small Business and Entrepreneurship*, London: Macmillan.
'Enterprise', 'Entrepreneur', *Oxford English Dictionary* (1989), Oxford: Oxford University Press.
'Entrepreneurship', *International Dictionary of the Social Sciences* (1968), London: Macmillan/Free Press.
Galbraith, J.K. (1987) *A History of Economics*, London: Penguin.
Keat, Russell and Abercrombie, Nicholas (1991) *Enterprise Culture*, London: Routledge.
Northcott, Michael (forthcoming) *The Environment and Christian Ethics*, Cambridge: Cambridge University Press.
Novak, Michael (1989) *Catholic Social Thought and Liberal Institutions*, New Brunswick, NJ and Oxford: Transaction Publishers.
Riddell, Peter (1989) *The Thatcher Decade*, Oxford: Blackwell, especially ch. 4, 'Enterprise culture'.
Schumpeter, Joseph A. (1934) *The Theory of Economic Development*, Cambridge, MA: Harvard University Press (originally published 1912).
——(1942) *Capitalism, Socialism and Democracy*, New York: Harper and Brothers.
Sedgwick, Peter (1990a) 'Freedom, well-being and the enterprise culture', *Studies in Christian Ethics* 3 (1).
——(1990b) 'The enterprise culture as a new world for the churches', *Crucible*, July–September.
——(1992) *The Enterprise Culture*, London: SPCK.

Peter Sedgwick

ENVIRONMENT

Environment is a wide-ranging and value-laden topic which traverses many disciplines and aspects of Western thought. The word has evolved from the old French *en viro*: to form a ring, to surround or to encircle. Thus, the word 'environment' has its origin in the perception of a difference between inner and outer, centre and periphery. Most typically this difference is associated with the boundary between human beings and the rest of nature. Discussion of the environment quickly moves into scientific, cultural, ethical, religious and ultimately metaphysical considerations. This is evident in the fact that the term is now at the centre of a transformation in Western ways of thought about the place of human beings in the cosmos and is the subject of political controversy. 'Environmental concern' may or may not be considered a laudatory activity depending upon how one understands and values the world.

Three guide posts are necessary to find one's way through the tangle of ideas involved with the concept of the 'environment' and its many contemporary uses, such as environmental issues, environmental ethics, environmental sciences, environmental psychology, and environmental art.

First, and most fundamental, is the notion that existence is dialectical. Its most general trait is individuality-in-community, or diversity-in-unity. Human beings, no less than other species, carve their lives out *against* their environment and *out of* their environment. Our environment is neither entirely hostile (otherwise, it would slay us), nor entirely supportive (otherwise, we would stagnate). This means that whatever differences distinguish human beings from their environments are relative, not absolute. There can be no ultimate dualism, or ultimate identity, of organism and environment, self and other, human and non-human nature, the one and the many.

Recognition of this is due largely to the influence of the picture of nature drawn by the modern biological and physical sciences. These sciences converge in the evolutionary model of organism and environment as mutually interacting systems. Many contemporary references to the environment carry meanings derived from this model: for example, the notion of the environment as the aggregate of conditions and influences which affect the life and development of an organism or group of organisms; the ecosystem, defined as all the interdependent systems in a given geographical area; and carrying capacity, which is the total number of species or group of species that an ecosystem can support indefinitely.

The second guide post necessary to understand the meaning of the environment in contemporary social thought is the simple, but oft neglected, contention that human ideas and values *regarding* the environment influence how humans treat the environment. It follows that the quality of the actual environment, and, dialectically, the quality of human life, is determined in large part by the adequacy of these ideas and values. The rapid deterioration of the human environment in recent years has resulted in widespread questioning of the attitudes and concepts about the environment that inform Western culture. There is a growing recognition that human beings have for centuries modified their environment through their cultures and that this relationship is now dysfunctional.

The third guide post that is necessary is the realization that virtually *all phases* of Western thought since ancient times have tended to see the environment as empty of value, and as the fitting object of human manipulation and domination. This assumption is being challenged in many contemporary fields of enquiry and in popular thought by the so-called 'environmental movement'. There is a growing awareness that the environment is the bearer of intrinsic values and the mediator of ultimate values, and thereby the background and source for the creation of distinctly human values. Thus (to name a few), the environment carries the value of life-support, including the support of human life; economic value; recreational value; scientific value, or the value of scientific enquiry as an intrinsically worthwhile activity; aesthetic value; historical value; culture-symbolization value; character-building value; and religious value (the environment as a holy place where we come near to ultimacy).

Since prehistoric times, there has been an increasing perception of distance between humanity and its environment which culminated in the West with the scientific revolution in the seventeenth century. There has been a small reconciliation of humanity and nature since then through the work of the nineteenth-century romantics, the natural sciences and the environmental movement. We caution the reader against any monolithic reading of the history of environmental attitudes in Western thought. The topic is immense and there are many minority reports embedded in the major trends.

The first records of human attitudes toward the environment are the cave paintings of the palaeolithic people. These paintings, made in deep caverns, were of animals in the hunt. Anthropologists speculate that the paintings were the end product of a RITUAL which began with a descent into a cave, symbolizing humanity impregnating the earth with bounty. For the palaeolithic people, it was necessary for humans to take a masculine procreating role in the creation of a fruitful environment, i.e. to induce the goddess to provide animals for the hunt.

In the ancient Near East, where agriculture began, the cycles of the Nile dominated people's attitudes toward the environment. Each year their lands would flood and the flooding made the land fertile. These cycles were understood to be created and not natural: the work of a creator deity, or several deities. Ra, the sun god, and Osiris, who represented the rising and dying vegetation on the river banks, were intimately associated with the Nile and its seasons. Agricultural practices set the seed for hierarchical relationships in society. Surplus food required managers and allowed some individuals to leave the fields and become artisans. Agriculture also led to the first major environmental damage with land clearing, overgrazing and trampling, and an increase in population size. Furthermore, agricultural civilization began to define the differences between nature and society.

The mythopoeic conceptions of the male and female principle in the land as goddess and horned consort prevailed from the palaeolithic to the early Greeks. The temples of the latter were placed high in the mountains in view of double peaks and gently mounded hills perceived as the embodiment of the masculine and feminine in nature. The temples symbolized a delicate balance between the human-constructed environment resting within the natural environment. However, the Greeks began to see themselves as set further apart from nature. This is apparent in classical philosophy. Aristotle and his followers, aided by collections made on the excursions of Alexander the Great, began the tradition of natural history. While some strands of this tradition have retained a sympathetic identification with nature, the primary development led toward an increasing objectification of plants and animals. Classical philosophy conceived humans as unique in nature because of their ability to rationalize. The temples in the later Greek period were built to enclose huge human-like images of deities which could maintain a constant vigil over the surrounding horned mountains and peopled valleys.

The Hebrew scriptures relate that God has given humanity the responsibility to be stewards of the land (Genesis 2: 15). This testament further distances humans from their environment by affirming that humanity alone is created in the image of God. None the less, right relationship with God means having the right relationships within SOCIETY and with the environment. It was humanity, not nature, that disobeyed God, as the Noahic covenant indicates (Genesis 8).

The Christian scriptures were written as a continuation of the revelation of God as seen by the Hebrews; however, over time, they became interpreted through classical, Gnostic and neo-Platonic philosophy which transformed the perception of nature from a blessed part of CREATION to a realm in need of salvation. The doctrine was accepted that all of creation fell with Adam. In medieval Europe, two contradictory trends are visible. In one, evident in the great cathedrals and the theological synthesis of Thomas Aquinas, every part of the cosmos is analogous to every other part. Natural theology found evidence of a divine creator in the perfection of nature. In this view, humans lived in an organic, hierarchical universe, bound together in a great chain of being. In the second view, evident in the Frankish calendars of the ninth century which show men coercing the world around them (ploughing, harvesting, chopping trees, butchering pigs), human control of the environment was conceived to be the redemption of nature from a state of chaotic depravity. It was this second trend that conditioned the growth of Western science and technology.

The distinctly 'modern' view of the environment is apparent in the work of Isaac Newton (1642–1727) who conceived of nature as an impersonal, God-created machine which has been set in motion and is now left to run on its own. This mechanistic understanding of the environment continued through to the nineteenth century and is still present in much thought today. Frances Bacon (1561–1626) claimed that through science and technology humanity could more fully understand this machine, and thus build the new Jerusalem on earth. Réné Descartes (1596–1650) removed humanity even further from the natural environment by developing a philosophy of mind/body dualism. The environment became something to be avoided in deference to the development of subjective experience.

The Western idea of environment was

radically altered with the discovery of the New World. Here was an unmeasured land mass in a state of wilderness. Endless coastline and forests gave the double illusion of a new Eden and terrifying wildness. Montaigne (1533–92) and others wrote of the New World as an earthly Paradise, the Isle of Youth and the Land of Perpetual Spring. But after some exploration Europeans began to find this new land unpredictable and alien to their idea of what paradise was supposed to be. They began to bring back tales of sea monsters, giants and walking corpses. This contributed to a deep-seated ambivalence in the West toward nature, vacillating between sentimental idealization and unnatural fear and hostility. Perhaps most important to humanity's attitudes toward the environment, the European explorers found in the Americas, Africa, Asia and Australia a seemingly inexhaustible source of raw materials to fuel the Industrial Revolution. This confirmed the idea that Providence created the natural environment for the exclusive use and enjoyment of humans. The modern notions of progress and exploitation were joined.

The Romantic movement of the eighteenth and nineteenth centuries was, in part, a reaction to the distance put between humanity and its environment by these several developments. It was a reaction against quantification and objectification of the natural world and the growing discomfort of urban life. The roots of the Romantic movement can be traced back to Gilbert White (1720–93), a country pastor in Selborne, England, who presented an Arcadian image of rural life in his famous *Natural History of Selborne*. Poetry and literature became an important vehicle for the Romantic movement in its fight against the mechanical model of nature and rising industrial civilization. The works of authors such as Johann Wolfgang Goethe, William Wordsworth, Ralph Waldo Emerson and Walt Whitman embodied an organic model of nature and a self-conscious shift towards aesthetic models of perception. This cultural effort to restore harmony with the environment led to the formation of the popular environmental movement and the founding of such organizations as the English Society for the Prevention of Cruelty to Animals (1824) and the American Sierra Club (1892) (*see* ANIMAL RIGHTS).

Charles Darwin's *The Origin of Species* (1859) and George Perkins Marsh's *Man and Nature* (1864) combined elements of both romantic and scientific thought. Darwin argued for the co-evolution of the moral sentiments of sympathy and benevolence with the evolution of proto-human societies. Marsh argued that, although we are absolutely dependent on nature, we have the capability to destroy it. Therefore we must learn to obey her laws or perish. The work of Darwin and Marsh returned humanity to a place within the environment.

After the Second World War, technology and populations exploded, vastly increasing the destructive impact of human activities on natural processes. Rachel Carsen's *Silent Spring* (1962), Paul and Anne Ehrlich's *Population, Resources, Environment* (1970) and Barry Commoner's *Closing Circle* (1971) alerted the English-speaking world to this situation and helped spark the new environmental movement.

There are four primary strands in the twentieth-century Western environmental movement. The first, associated with such wilderness preservationists as John Muir in the USA and George Macaulay Trevelyan in England, carried the romantic protest into action for the sake of recreational, aesthetic and religious environmental values.

The second, associated with figures like Richard Martin and the formation of organizations like the Royal Society for the Prevention of Cruelty to Animals in Britain, argued for the rights, preservation and inherent value of non-human life-forms.

The third, associated with such figures as Ernst Haeckel in Germany, Henry Cowles and Aldo Leopold in the USA and Arthur Tansley in England, drew upon the new science of ecology as a basis for regulating disruptive human interventions in natural cycles, such as the food chain, and for maintaining the biological integrity of watersheds and other ecosystems.

The fourth, associated with Jules Clavé in France, Dietrich Brandis in Germany and Britain, Elias Landolt in Switzerland and Gifford Pinchot in the USA, extended modern methods of scientific and economic management to the problem of assuring a maximum sustainable yield of renewable resources for present and future generations.

These four strands – wilderness preservation, the humane movement, ecology, and resource conservation – came together in the 1960s in the emergence of a truly international environmental movement dedicated to reconciling the processes of modern industrial development and environmental protection in a global context. At the 1972 United Nations Stockholm conference Barbara Ward and Réné Dubos recommended that the United Nations adopt an environmental ethic for one earth. This year also marked the founding of the Club of Rome which effectively popularized the environmental limits to growth. The Stockholm conference was followed by a series of international conferences on environment-related topics: population, food, human settlements, water, desertification, and new and renewable energy resources. In 1987, the World Commission on Environment and Development, in *Our Common Future*, proposed the idea of 'sustainable development' as the unifying goal of humanity's relations to the global environment.

The present environmental crisis is a legacy of dualistic environmental thought. Some of the most relevant environmental issues are in the areas of JUSTICE, health, energy, global issues, public interest and biodiversity.

On the issue of justice environmentalists are often accused of favouring the obligation to preserve plants, animals and natural areas over obligations to underprivileged humans in society. Many people perceive a conflict between human needs and requirements for a high quality environment. For example, the Malthusian Garrett Hardin has written that complete justice will lead to complete catastrophe; that is, if society attempts to feed, clothe and house all of the world's poor, resources will be so scarce that all of the world's population will suffer.

Many are attempting to overcome this conflict between human and non-human rights through the concept of eco-justice: a combination of distributive justice and environmental preservation. The main assumption of the idea of eco-justice is that humans and the environment are being exploited by the same structures: economic profit, hunger for power and society's manipulative mentality. Some feminists are in the front lines of this argument. They assert that there can never be justice or liberation for any person or for the environment until patriarchal structures of domination and hierarchy are dismantled.

Although there are disputes over what constitutes a high quality environment, it is generally agreed that such an environment is conducive to the health and well-being of all. Since the birth of technology, people have been exposed to an increasing number of chemicals the effects of which are not adequately understood toxicologically or ecologically. Cancer, respiratory diseases, psychobehavioural disorders, birth defects and mental disorders can all be caused by artificial environmental factors. In general, the costs of environmental damage and health care are carried by the public sector, whereas the benefits of efficiency and profit are held by the private sector.

Limits on non-renewable energy sources such as oil and gas have sparked interest in more sustainable energy technologies such as solar, geothermic or wind power, although sustainable energy technology is currently thought to be cost ineffective.

NUCLEAR ENERGY is in many ways a relatively 'environmentally friendly' energy source because very little of the resource is necessary for the amount of energy produced, relative to hydropower or coal power. Also, it produces no air pollution, needs no massive dams and does not require that natural areas be flooded. But, as of yet, there is no safe method to dispose of nuclear waste. Moreover, power plants can and do have accidents which could lead to massive explosions, endangering human life and ecosystems on a global scale.

Depletion of the ozone layer, global warming and population growth are environmental issues which are not restricted to local areas; their effects are felt by the entire biosphere. The ozone layer, in the upper stratosphere, prevents the sun's carcinogenic ultraviolet rays from reaching the earth's surface. Chlorofluorocarbons and other free radicals released from air-conditioners, refrigerators and aerosol propellants break down the ozone layer.

Scientists predict that global temperatures will increase because of increasing amounts of artificially produced gases in the atmosphere,

293

especially methane and carbon dioxide. These gases prevent heat from the sun from reflecting back into space. The results of global warming are increased sea levels (due to polar ice-cap melting), desertification and the extinction of many species.

The Club of Rome predicted in 1974 that, if present trends continue, the carrying capacity of the earth may be reached in the next hundred years. This means that the earth will not be able to support all the people in the world. As the twenty-first century nears, many of the world's problems are due to competition for limited essential resources. Yet, society continues to sanction economic and population growth without regard for consequences. The certain catastrophe that lies ahead can be avoided by a paradigm shift from quantitative growth to qualitative or sustainable development.

Public concern for the environment is growing. But efforts to act in the public sphere call into question the effectiveness of contemporary social institutions. The common good is inadequately represented in decision-making, and the burden of proof is on the public rather than on the offenders. Moreover, public access to information is often limited. Changes in environmental attitudes and priorities depend on changes in political, educational, religious and economic institutions.

Concern for biodiversity is a concern for the diminishing variety and variability of organisms within a specific geographical area, as well as a concern for diminishing variation of genetic material, species, habitats, ecosystems and human cultures on a global scale. If present rates of species extinctions continue, one-quarter of all plant and animal species existing in the mid-1980s will be extinct in the next twenty-five years. Those concerned with the problem of biodiversity argue that humanity is destroying the precious results of millions of years of evolution and many potential resources for the future. To institute ecojustice, i.e. justice for all humanity in conjunction with the practice of environmentally sound resource use, is the current challenge to DEMOCRACY.

Our attitudes toward the environment have distanced us from the environment of which we are a part. In Western thought, humanity has become the measure of all things, and all things are to be measured by humans. Thus, it is customary in Western thought to distinguish sharply between the non-human physical (or 'natural') environment and the artificial or cultural environment. Most such distinctions only serve to obscure the fact that human beings, and all their cultural products, are infolded, involved and engaged within the living, terrestrial environment. These distinctions may serve a more positive function today, however. They may be used to point to the fundamental choice now before humankind. This choice is whether humanity will continue on its historical trajectory toward encapsulation within a humanly manipulated environment, with the rest of nature exploited and managed for the sake of some alleged 'unique' or 'superior' human essence or cultural good; or whether humanity will awaken to the incalculable richness of wild and spontaneous values spread across the whole natural environment, and realize that each step it takes to eliminate, reduce and violate these values is also a step toward the demise of much we have known and celebrated by the name of 'human spirit'.

Barbour, I.G. (1980) *Technology, Environment and Human Values*, New York: Praeger.

Evenden, N. (1985) *The Natural Alien: Humankind and Environment*, Toronto: University of Toronto Press.

Glacken, C.J. (1967) *Traces on the Rhodian Shore: Nature and Culture in Western Thought from Ancient Times to the End of the Eighteenth Century*, Berkeley, CA: University of California Press.

Hardin, G. and Baden, J. (1977) *Managing the Commons*, San Francisco, CA: W.H. Freeman.

Holmes, R., III (1988) *Environmental Ethics: Duties to and Values in the Natural Environment*, Philadelphia, PA: Temple University Press.

Hughes, D. (1975) *Ecology in Ancient Civilizations*, Albuquerque, NM: University of New Mexico Press.

Meadows, D.H., Meadows, D.L., Randers, J. and Beherns, W.W., III (1974) *The Limits to Growth*, New York: Universe Books.

Petulla, J. (1980) *American Environmentalism: Values, Tactics, Priorities*, College Station, TX: Texas A & M University Press.

Southwick, C.H. (1976) *Ecology and the Quality of Our Environment*, New York: Van Nostrand.

Worster, D. (1979) *Nature's Economy, The Roots of Ecology*, New York: Anchor/Doubleday.

J. Ronald Engel
R.J.S. Montagnes

EQUALITY

The principle of human equality has never received universal assent. Aristotle, the pre-modern, asserted in Book 1 of *The Politics* that slaves were suited by nature, rather than by convention, to their lot, and thought women obviously unfitted to exercise political POWER. Nietzsche, the incipient post-modern, reviled Christian ethics as a slave morality and looked forward to the dawning of the day of the super-man. Between and beyond these two there have been plenty of thinkers and philosophers who have been sceptical of the claims of equality. Moreover, religions as diverse as Hinduism and Christianity have institutionalized various forms of inequality ranging from the caste system in the case of the former to the racial institutions legitimized by fundamentalist South African Calvinism or the BAPTIST sects of the southern states of the USA in the case of the latter.

Yet, though not universal, the belief in equal-ity has been widespread. St Paul was able to claim that in Christ the distinction was abol-ished between Greek and Jew, circumcised and uncircumcised, barbarian, Scythian, slave and free man, and that in Christ there was neither male nor female (Galatians 3: 26–9). Pascal, ever sensitive to the effects of human vanity, said in the *Pensées* (II, 25, 48) that it was only because kings were habitually surrounded by their panoply of power that they inspired fear and even the most excellent judge in the world would have his reasoning disturbed by a nearby fly. In *The Groundwork for the Metaphysic of Morals* Kant secularized the Christian idea of the equal worth of souls in the sight of God in his categorical imperative which required moral agents to act in such a way that they treated humanity never simply as a means but always at the same time as an end in itself.

Outside the Christian tradition a similar set of ideas can be found in many religious and philosophical traditions. The Stoics held to the idea of the universal light of reason in everyone, as represented in Seneca's idea that all human beings had the potential to pursue virtue, a notion that also occurs in the Confucian tradi-tion with Mencius's idea that the capacity for morality, especially sympathy with others, is common to humanity. In *The Qur'an* (49: 13) it is said that the most honourable person in the community is the most pious – a clear inversion of the status hierarchy of the day. Breakaway movements from Hinduism, like the Jains, the Buddhists and the Sikhs as well as sectarian movements within Hinduism itself, have been motivated in part by the idea of equality. Fi-nally, for secular utilitarians like Bentham, a fundamental requirement of social morality was that everyone should count for one and no-one for more than one.

To hold to an idea of fundamental human equality is not, however, to share any particular view about the ordering of SOCIETY and the distribution of privileges, income, rank and status. Having noted that there was no distinc-tion in Christ between slave and free man, St Paul was apparently happy to go on and instruct slaves to obey their masters. He did of course insist that masters should treat their slaves justly, but the structured inequality of the institu-tional practice was left untouched. Although Stoic political thought at various times appears to have entertained radical political ideas, Sto-icism under the Roman Empire came to be asso-ciated with the policy of cultivating personal indifference to the misfortunes inherent in the Empire's vast inequalities. Kant is quite happy to assume, it appears as a matter of course, that only PROPERTY-owning adult males should have the right to vote. And James Mill, Bentham's disciple, whilst prepared to relax the property qualification, would restrict the franchise to males over the age of 40. In short, a belief in the moral equality of all persons can coexist with a belief in the legitimacy of social, political and economic inequalities.

There have been movements that have re-sisted this bifurcation of ideal and practice. According to The Acts of the Apostles the early Christians held all things in common. The Stoics of the Hellenistic period developed a political theory that attacked inequalities of wealth and power, a view that has been claimed to have influenced the egalitarian sentiments of John Chrysostom. The Levellers of the seventeenth century, particularly their radical wing the Diggers, believed in a more equal distribution of power and property than prevailed at the time. In the twentieth century the *kibbutz* movement has sought to implement ideals of equality in possessions and power in accordance with ideals drawn from traditional Judaism and modern socialism. And many in the twentieth-century environmental movement have favoured small-scale communal living as a way of overcoming inequalities of status and power tied to an ecologically destructive way of life, which they associate with industrial capitalism. Yet, the ethos of these movements, and in particular their withdrawal from the dominant social order in the form of alternative communities, can suggest a rather pessimistic conclusion, namely that the ideal of equality is most likely to be achieved amongst those who self-consciously cut themselves off from the majority of their fellow human beings. Perhaps the pessimism of this conclusion is only exceeded by its paradox.

It is helpful when considering the idea of equality to recognize that the concept is used both as an account of what human beings are and as a prescription of how social institutions ought to be arranged. The two senses, the descriptive and the prescriptive, are linked by the claim that because human beings share a common equality they should be treated with equal respect in certain fundamental ways. The connection between these two senses of the term equality is not intended to be analytic, however, but a substantive moral assertion. Perhaps the best way of bringing this out is to note that statements about equality are always incomplete in themselves. To say of persons that they are equal is an elliptical way of saying that there are certain respects (e.g. the capacity to feel pain or the capacity for a sense of self-respect) in which they share common characteristics and that it is in virtue of those characteristics that social institutions should be arranged in certain respects (e.g. in terms of the absence of formal or informal discrimination) to recognize and respond to the putative underlying equality.

Clearly the crucial intellectual question in thinking about the concept of equality concerns the link between the descriptive and the prescriptive senses of the term. Can the recommendations for greater equality in the arrangement of social institutions be grounded in an account of humans as equal in certain morally relevant respects? Moreover, the historical treatment of the notion of equality raises the question of whether the varied practical implications with which the idea of equality has been associated mean that the principle lacks a significant core meaning. If SLAVERY, the exclusion of women from political participation and large inequalities of WEALTH or income are thought by many leading thinkers to be compatible with an acknowledgement of moral equality, can the idea be thought to have any definite content, or does it merely connote a vague sentiment?

One way of expressing the idea of equality is to say that all human beings possess equal moral worth and therefore should be accorded equality of respect in the way they are treated by others, the idea here being to get behind differences of social rank and status to the treatment of persons as ends in themselves possessing a certain common humanity. Moreover, the capacity to have a sense of respect depends as much upon the structure of social arrangements as upon the treatment by other individuals. Historically this means that the protest against disrespect has come to be associated with a protest against various forms of privilege thought to bestow unequal respect, especially inequalities of political power, economic advantage and social status. Inequality in the distribution of the vote, in occupational and social status or in income and wealth are all means by which disrespect may be shown to individuals. By extension, and more positively, the claim to an equal franchise becomes a claim for equal political participation, the claim to equality of occupational status becomes a claim for an equal sharing of the benefits of co-operative economic life, at least in so far as equal effort is involved in contributing to those benefits, and the claim for the abolition of privileges becomes a claim for a society built upon the idea of common membership rather than competitive privilege. Thus, the practical meaning of the principle of equality comes to be that social life should be so organized that it ensures equal concern and respect for all persons.

If the ideal of equality is interpreted in this way, at least two questions must be faced. First, is the notion of equal moral worth intelligible in the absence of an explicitly theological background that would locate the origin of the putative equal worth in the care and concern of a creator who loves and cherishes the creation? After all, theistic expressions of the idea of moral equality are tied to a broader metaphysics, and even non-theistic versions of the ideal, e.g. in Stoicism and Confucianism, seem to be related to a particular understanding of the cosmic order. Second, even if the grounds of human equality are rendered independent of a theological rationale, are there any specific institutional implications that may be thought to follow from the idea of equality alone?

Turning to the first of these questions, it is clear that the issues involved raise larger questions about the autonomy of ethics and the relationship between God's commands and the principles of right. It is a large, and much discussed, question whether what is commanded is right because it is commanded or whether God only commands what is independently right. If the former position is taken, then any principle that requires agents and institutions to treat persons as deserving of equal respect will flow from the commands of God and will be grounded in those commands. On the other hand, if the right can be identified independently of God's commands, even though God would only ever command the right, then there exists the logical space to recognize that a notion of human moral equality is conceivable without an explicitly theological background. Whatever it is that secures the autonomy of ethics will also secure an independent source of human moral worth. Whilst recognizing the complexity of this ancient controversy, it is at least a plausible option to take the latter of these two sides and to suppose that we can identify features of the human person as such that would qualify all those who satisfy the criteria for being such persons for an equal moral status.

What features of the person might be relevant here? The most common candidate among writers on equality is the capacity for rationality and reflection that underlies moral AU-TONOMY and enables persons to be sources of value. Each person has a life to lead that is uniquely his or hers, and in leading that life persons cannot escape the need to decide upon their own purposes, plans and priorities. Moreover, a person's ability to carry out their chosen plans and purposes depends upon a sense of their own self-worth. To be treated as less than an equal of other persons is to undermine that sense of self-respect and self-worth. These features of the human person cannot, of course, provide a logically watertight deductive grounding for the principle of equality, since there is no contradiction, strictly speaking, in someone acknowledging these features of the human person and yet denying that they have any relevance to the question of the right treatment of persons. Yet, though not logically watertight in this sense, the observation that moral autonomy is distinctive of PERSONS is surely suggestive of a particular moral point of view.

Suppose, then, that we can give some definite content to the idea of equality. What might be thought to be its practical implications? I have suggested that egalitarian thought conceives of the principle as having implications for the allocation of political power, the distribution of economic advantages and the privileges of social status. However, the ideal of equality is insufficient on its own to carry these practical implications. For example, any proposal for the sharing of political power or economic resources has to be subject to a test of feasibility. Ought implies can, and if it is impossible to accomplish the proposed redistribution of benefits or advantage then there seems little point in proposing it except as an intellectual exercise.

In fact, it is far from clear that a commitment to the principle of equal moral worth is incompatible with acknowledging that large inequalities of power, wealth and status are sometimes justifiable. There are a number of arguments that can be deployed to show the compatibility of personal moral equality with institutional inequality. Thus, political power, when justifiably exercised, will provide the conditions of security and order which are the necessary conditions for morally autonomous individuals to carry out their plans and projects. However, effectively to organize political power will require the deployment of expertise and AUTHORITY, which will necessarily place greater influence in some hands than others, arguments that are even more telling if the authority of the STATE extends over a large territorial area as is invariably the case with the modern State.

Similarly, inequalities in the allocation of economic advantages may be justified if they serve as incentives the effect of which is to increase productivity in the ECONOMY at large which are to the benefit of everyone. Indeed, probably the leading contemporary theory of social justice, that of John Rawls, adopts the principle that inequalities of economic reward are justified provided that they have the effect of working to the advantage of the least well-off in society by raising their incomes higher than they would otherwise have been.

Finally, it has been urged by W.G. Runciman that we can distinguish between forms of behaviour in which there is inequality of respect and those where there is inequality of praise. If the members of a society give prizes to their best athletes, musicians or public servants, then this need imply no inequality of respect provided there are no invidious social distinctions implied in the practice, as there would be for example if prizes were given only to white or to male athletes, musicians and public servants. So, even in a society that recognized equal moral worth, it might be possible to find a distribution of the marks of praise and esteem that was far from equal.

If these arguments are taken seriously, then there is no reason why in principle a purportedly egalitarian society, in the sense of a social order whose members shared a commitment to the principle of equal respect, should not display quite marked inequalities in various dimensions of social inequality, including political power, income and status. The inference is thereby cut from moral principle to social and political prescription.

In strict logic this conclusion is correct. From the moral premise of equality it is impossible to derive any straightforward recommendation for social equality. However, there is a problem with simply accepting this agnostic conclusion as the basis for public policy and institutional design. The difficulty is that arguments that are valid in abstract reasoning can disguise a lack of concern for equality motivated not by moral sentiment but by negligence or bad faith. Marks of esteem for achievement can early turn into badges of privilege; the claim for incentives can be a front for simple competitive advantage; and the effective organization of political power always has the potential for high-handedness and tyranny. This is not to say that bad faith is always present in the advancement of these arguments, but when considering questions of institutional arrangements we need always to take into account not only the validity of the arguments but also their potential for misuse.

If this viewpoint is adopted, we lose the purity of the inference from moral equality to social institutions, but we observe a strengthening of the arguments for greater equality in institutions and practices. Effective political power should be rendered accountable to protect against its abuse, the free play of economic forces may need to be modified to correct for an undue influence from sectional economic interests and the scale and value of esteemed rewards would need to be limited in order to prevent their degenerating into marks of unequal respect. The growth of democratic institutions and of the welfare state in the twentieth century provide examples of how these principles might be implemented in practice. Moreover, certain precautionary principles can be adopted in scrutinizing institutional inequalities to ensure that they are not erected on bad faith principles. For example, social inequalities compatible with equality of respect would not be cumulative, and there ought to be reason to assume that politicians and other wielders of power would not be drawn predominantly from the rich or the high born. Second, such inequalities that do exist ought not to run along the lines of what the US Supreme Court has termed 'suspect categories', e.g. those that correspond to ethnic or gender divisions within the population, without there being intense scrutiny of why this might be so.

Paul Tillich argued in his *Systematic Theology* (III, 200) that attempts to actualize social and political equality started in Stoicism rather than Christianity and thereby that the modern democratic concern for greater equality had Hellenistic roots. There is much insight in this observation, but it both underestimates the strength of dissident egalitarian movements within the Judaeo-Christian tradition and overestimates the extent to which the conception of the Stoic cosmopolis was held to be valid for all humanity rather than the virtuous. We might also just as well say that attempts to actualize social and economic equality had to wait upon the Enlightenment with its view that social and economic arrangements were modifiable in the light of human understanding about how social institutions worked.

If a connection can be established between the moral principle of equality and the design of social institutions, does this mean that the ideal of equality finds its content solely in those institutional practices? It is at least arguable that this is not so. From the viewpoint of individuals the world may seem an impossible thing to change, and their own social position may be one of inferiority and disadvantage. In these circumstances, the idea of moral equality independently of its instantiation in any institutional order should provide comfort. Those slaves to whom St Paul was writing should never have been happy, but neither should they have lost their self-respect.

Dworkin, Ronald (1986) *A Matter of Principle*, Oxford: Clarendon.
Erskine, Andrew (1990) *The Hellenistic Stoa*, London: Duckworth.
Nagel, Thomas (1979) 'Equality', in his *Mortal Questions*, Cambridge: Cambridge University Press.
Pennock, J.R. and Chapman, J.W. (eds) (1967) *Equality: Nomos IX*, New York: Atherton.
Rawls, John (1972) *A Theory of Justice*, Oxford: Oxford University Press.
Raz, Joseph (1986) *The Morality of Freedom*, Oxford: Clarendon.
Runciman, W.G. (1970) '"Social" equality', in his *Sociology in its Place and Other Essays*, Cambridge: Cambridge University Press.
Tawney, R.H. (1964) *Equality*, London: George Allen & Unwin.
Tillich, Paul (1968) *Systematic Theology*, vol. III, Digswell Place: James Nisbet.
Williams, Bernard (1972) 'The idea of equality', in Peter Laslett and W.G. Runciman (eds) *Philosophy, Politics and Society* (second series), Oxford: Basil Blackwell.

Albert Weale

ESCHATOLOGY

Eschatology, in the Christian tradition, is the doctrine of the last things, i.e. those events which will occur as a consequence of God's judgement of humanity, the end of the temporal order and the inauguration of a different, transcendent reality (which is given different status in different texts; cf. below). As one particular form of APOCALYPTIC or 'seeing of the heavenly secrets', eschatology is intimately related to such concepts or events as the KINGDOM OF GOD, the last JUDGEMENT, the coming of Messiah, the return of the Spirit and the re-establishment of God's sole AUTHORITY in the world.

Eschatology, consequently, most often appears as a form of written testimony; i.e. it comes down to contemporary THEOLOGY recorded as earlier, apocalyptic descriptions of what will happen at the end of time and, arguably most importantly for early Christianity, when that end will occur. An example of such an eschatological text is the 'little apocalypse', Mark 13 (and parallels). The defining characteristics of this eschatological discourse, as with the overwhelming majority of others, is its concern with the objective data of the last things; what is sought is knowledge of God's will in this respect, because such knowledge heralds power and influence within the earliest Christian communities.

As indicated in a text such as Mark 13, its power and influence is manifested in the testimony of how this knowledge affects the social conduct and hope of the community; for eschatological knowledge, at heart, is interested in an authority expressed in terms of information concerning the end of time. This quality of eschatology, found at every level of the New Testament, recurs throughout the Christian tradition, even to the twentieth century, where the question of the status of eschatological discourse has preoccupied theologians such as Barth and Moltmann and philosophers such as Heidegger and Bloch.

All of these qualities – knowledge, POWER, authority – coalesce in earliest Christianity into a general eschatological conviction, sometimes more sharply drawn but always present, in which the approaching immanence of transcendent realities is expressed in objective terms. Knowledge of this immanence, therefore, is expressed prophetically, taking the character of promise. As such, early Christian eschatology is inevitably related to the expected return/arrival of Messiah, in the form of Jesus of Nazareth. As with such a concept as the kingdom of God, consequently, early Christian eschatology is integral to the Christology of the New Testament, to the extent that one is justified, like Barth, in affirming the *necessarily* eschatological character of any Christian theology if that theology has any concern for the canonical records.

Effectively, therefore, early Christian eschatology functioned to determine the specific conduct of believing communities as they awaited the decisive event of which their leaders – be they apostles, prophets, or writers – claimed transcendent knowledge; such was the essential nature of a level of discourse, the common currency of which was hope and expectation. It is unsurprising, consequently, that modern New Testament critics have sought to relate eschatology to ethics in the early Christian communities. This, however, is to miss the point; for the knowledge claimed by exponents of early Christian eschatology is not employed for moral guidance, but rather for criticism and anticipatory judgement in their nascent churches (cf. Acts 4). Such eschatological knowledge, in other words, validates activity of social construction and destruction, a manipulation in the light of heavenly secrets which effectively changed the manner in which believers actually lived. This was not a consequence of moral preaching so much as an exercise in communal engineering, an antecedent which has been recapitulated at varying stages in the two thousand years of Christian history.

Early Christian eschatology was able to achieve such a degree of power and authority primarily because believers expected an objective realization of their faith and hope; thus, social life in the light of such theological claims to divine knowledge was materially affected by this kind of testimony (cf. Saint Paul's various letters to the Corinthian church). Consequently,

eschatology was related, along with such themes as pneumatology and CHRISTOLOGY, to the analysis and interpretation of objective material reality. Natural as this development was, given the prevailing philosophical outlook of the historical context, it meant that acknowledged claims to an understanding of transcendent reality was accepted as authoritative *socially*. Understandable as this might have been in terms of ecclesial authority – where the responsibilities of position necessarily require some kind of higher validation – it proved deleterious to the development of Christian theology.

This problem can be identified more precisely. Given the inherently eschatological character of Christian talk about God, and the inherent (and transcendent) power and authority of eschatology, it was perhaps inevitable that this mantle of power and authority devolved on to the shoulders of the theologian, i.e. the individual (or group) required to talk about God. Effectively, this meant that eschatological power and authority became focused not only upon those who 'saw' the heavenly secrets, but also those who wrote about them. Certainly, in the New Testament it is impossible to separate, entirely, these two offices (cf. for example, the Fourth Gospel); but as the early Church progressed, canonical formulation occurred and theology became a matter of reflection upon earlier revelation rather than fresh prophecy, this phenomenon became ever more readily apparent. Thus, by the era of the great councils of the churches (Nicaea 325 CE, Constantinople 381 CE and Chalcedon 451 CE), one can say with some justification that eschatological authority, as the validation of what one writes and says about the immanence of God in the world, has devolved to the office of the theologian. This remains the case even, as with Chalcedon, when the relevant theologians acknowledge the limited speculative nature of their text.

In cases like Nicaea, Constantinople and Chalcedon, this development was endorsed by its results, which have remained central to the Christian tradition to the modern period; and the same can be said of the work of such theologians as Saint Anselm of Canterbury and Saint Thomas Aquinas. At other times, however, such eschatological authority has, arguably, degenerated into tyranny. One example of this would be the late writings of Martin Luther, where absolute conviction in one's knowledge of divine intent manifested itself in wholly prejudicial terms; similarly, Calvin's developed ECCLESIOLOGY was established in a doctrine of authority which received its own validation from a particular understanding of the communication of revelation. In both cases, important changes in the social, material circumstances of people and communities were effected because of eschatological conviction.

The objective realist worldview which substantiated this possibility, however, was attacked by the development of modern rationalism; this can be witnessed in the work of the Scottish philosopher David Hume and, decisively for modern theology, the Prussian Immanuel Kant. It was Kant, in his crucial essay 'The end of all things' (Kant 1963), who entirely demolished an understanding of eschatology which had dominated the Christian tradition for nearly eighteen hundred years.

Essentially, Kant's argument was a simple one, and rested on the theoretical position of his epistemological idealism. Kant argued that, with the advent of modernity and its vehicle, rationality, it was no longer viable for people to believe in Biblical eschatological realism, which was established in an objective distinction between a world 'below', HELL, and one 'above', HEAVEN (the crude schematic description of the problem of transcendence which, argues Kant, one finds in the New Testament; Kant's argument was adopted by, among others, Rudolf Bultmann). Instead, Kant argued that the question of immanence, *the* question of modern philosophy, is best addressed to Christian eschatology from the perspective of reason. In other words, what rational *status* can theology give to the substantive meaning of eschatology – for Kant, the immanence of God's will in space and time – if objective realism is no longer a possible level of discourse? In this way, the question of conditions of possibility overcame historical teleology, at least in Kantian (and subsequent) epistemology.

Kant's answer is the one which was *not* provided in the early Christian communities, i.e. morality. For Kant, that is, one speaks of the presence of eternity in terms of certain guiding ethical principles, which are revealed to humanity in the life and ministry of Jesus of Nazareth and which are therefore present in time as the conditions of possibility of moral conduct. Jesus, consequently, becomes for Kant the great teacher, offering individuals an intelligible programme to be implemented in their daily lives. Kant thus brilliantly addressed the principal themes of Christian eschatology: the matter of revealed knowledge, and how it is mediated, is related directly to what can be known and expressed, apparently, of Jesus's own religious existence, established by rational historical enquiry. With one basic shift, therefore, Kant is able to locate the cardinal issues of power and authority not in a vision of heavenly secrets, open solely to apocalyptic seers, but rather in the universal principle of ethical reason, a principle available, by definition, to all people.

There were three direct consequences of Kant's development in the late eighteenth century. First, it demystified, and therefore diminished, the special role of the theologian established by the previous eighteen hundred years; henceforth, the theologian became a scientist rather than a prophet, a phenomenon witnessed initially in Schleiermacher's reformed theology but subsequently becoming widespread in Europe (though opposed, in the twentieth century, by Barth). Second, Kant's analysis fostered a hundred and fifty years of theological liberalism, reaching a climax in the work of Adolf von Harnack, and having as its most far-reaching consequence the domestication and interiorization of eschatology. Third, and more obliquely, Kant's 'The end of all things' stimulated a series of contrary interpretations of the question of immanence and by extension the doctrine of eschatology. Of the three, it is the latter which is most relevant to the present article.

Kant's work established the priority of ethical reason in the modern interpretation of eschatology; but by Kantian definition this impinged directly upon individual morality alone: questions of explicitly *social* concern were addressed, if at all, solely as an extended function of subjective freedom. In the tradition which developed after Kant, however, this position was repeatedly attacked. Hegel criticized the epistemological foundations of Kant's thesis, preferring in its place his phenomenology of mind, in which the teleological development of humanity is expressed socially (and where, pointedly, Christianity as a revealed religion is only the penultimate stage in that progress). Marx, subsequently, attacked Hegel's interpretation of society, arguing that its ideal foundations were entirely inappropriate to a true understanding of the dynamics of society; famously, Marx inverted Hegel's dialectic, introducing his own understanding of materialism in place of Hegel's phenomenology of mind. Later in the nineteenth century, Nietzsche figuratively overcame both Hegel and Marx by subordinating the question of immanence to the fate of the individual alone, thereby liberating the subject from the constraints of conditioned responses. Finally in this sequence, Heidegger attempted to reject the entire Western philosophical tradition, preferring to return thoughtfully to the ecstatic event of Being in which, arguably, one recognizes the deepest meditation upon eschatology in MODERNITY; for Heidegger, any distinction between individual and SOCIETY is not simply arbitrary, but indeed meaningless, and to be ignored in favour of the more fundamental concerns of event theory. This elision of such a basic tension in modern reflection undoubtedly assisted the assimilation of Heidegger's work by fascism in the 1930s, an event [sic] which implicated Christian eschatology, to a degree, in the crimes of national SOCIALISM (something which subsequent theology has attempted to correct; cf. below).

The impetus behind these various developments was reflection upon the philosophical question of immanence, rather than eschatology *per se*; and, as noted, this provided a series of immense achievements in which the status of this question was examined and re-examined endlessly. The various results of this process, however, were by no means unanimous in articulating a specific vision of society and the presence within it, at whatever level, of universal principles. On the contrary Hegel, Marx, Nietzsche and Heidegger provide disparate impressions of the way in which reality can be interpreted. Properly understood, these interpretations are genuine alternatives to early Christian eschatology, rather than straightforward developments of it, as in Kant's original essay.

If one can speak of such a development of eschatology in the nineteenth century, then it is in terms of Schelling's philosophy of revelation of 1841–2 and, most importantly, Kierkegaard's Christian philosophy of religion. It was Kierkegaard's redescription of early Christian eschatology, not in terms of categories of analysis or conditions of possibility but in terms of encounter, that was to have a lasting influence upon such twentieth-century theologians as Karl Barth, Rudolf Bultmann and Dietrich Bonhoeffer. Bluntly stated, eschatology for Kierkegaard is a matter not of knowledge, or information, but rather of confrontation; revelation, if it occurs, is understood not in terms of the disclosure of something which was otherwise secret, but as addressed to the individual's ontological possibilities. Revelation, and its opposite concealment, consequently, are not to be experienced either objectively, or rationally, or even socially, but rather in relational encounter, specifically the relational encounter with the eschatological event, Jesus Christ. Thus, for Kierkegaard and subsequent dialectical theology, eschatology is subordinated to Christomonism.

This position dominated modern theology until the 1960s, and was characterized, ultimately, by an apolitical, asocial understanding of eschatology. Consequently, although by a radically different route, modern theology came to echo the findings of modern philosophy; it 'discovered' new states in which to locate the questions inherent to eschatology, i.e. transcendence and immanence. As a matter of historical record, it was rare for this process of relocation to incorporate society and culture; instead, the dominant theological paradigm was one of the individual Jesus encountering the individual believer, with a critical examination of the problems relevant to human existence.

Since the early 1960s, however, this almost century-long process has been reversed, principally by the efforts of political and liberation theologians who, allied to such others as feminist writers, have considerably altered the nature of contemporary theology. In particular, the publication in 1964 of Jürgen Moltmann's *Theology of Hope* and in 1977 of Johann-Baptist Metz's *Faith in History and Society* (Moltmann 1967; Metz 1980), influenced as they were by

Marxist theory and, in the former's case, explicitly by Ernst Bloch's *The Principle of Hope* (Bloch 1986), defined for contemporary theology a renewed concern for the social and political dimensions of Christian eschatology. Moltmann's early work, in comparison, for example with Wolfhart Pannenberg's (still) asocial, apolitical systematic theology, has been particularly influential in shaping the reception of eschatology over the last twenty-five years.

These theological developments in the 1960s were combined, in Roman Catholicism, with the strong ecclesial reform consequent to the Second Vatican Council (1962–5), which effectively opened the Roman Catholic Church, and its theologians, to the varied problems of contemporary society and politics. The results of this event became immediately known in the work of such leading figures as Gustavo Gutierrez, Leonardo Boff and Jon Sobrino (in South America), Edward Schillebeeckx (in Holland) and Albert Nolan (in South Africa), all of whom, to greater or lesser degrees, have attended to Marxist/socialist reflection upon society and its processes of change (*see* LIBERATION THEOLOGY). The crux of this movement was whether or not Christian belief and consequently theology could in fact address the specific socio-political context in which Christians now find themselves; the vehicle by which this vital question is being answered is, essentially, reflection upon the basic meaning of Christian eschatology and in particular the implicit concern with the *locus* of the kingdom of God. Should Christian communities so conduct themselves in the world that God's kingdom, as power and authority and therefore as the motor of change towards the eternal, becomes the present historical goal of belief and practice? This is the eschatological question which today exercises liberation and political theologians throughout the world.

As such, and importantly, these theologies have brought the question of eschatology back into the purview of natural theology, i.e. the question of the immanence of eternity within the world is now to be considered as a question *of the world*, rather than some kind of external phenomenon which is somehow imposed upon natural order. This means that the Barthian distinction between natural and revealed theology, which was so influential in the first half of the twentieth century, collapses: nature and revelation are seen to be intimately related, precisely upon the level of society and politics and, by extension, the related disciplines of ecology and the environmental sciences (cf. for example, 'GREEN' theology). What this means, effectively, is that contemporary interpretation of the eschatological dimension of Christian faith is turning towards questions which have distinct echoes in the earliest proclamation of the Gospel. Once again, in other words, the specific nature of the power and authority of divine judgement, proclaimed and expected in terms of a clear understanding of the teleology of human community, is being considered because of what changes it will bring *into* the world.

Whether or not this means that contemporary theology is moving into a kind of 'golden age' of renewed eschatological reflection, however, is unclear (although certainly the present situation is very preferable to the indulgent speculation of the earlier parts of the twentieth century); for at heart Christian eschatology is not simply *about* the world, even if it comes to expression by means of a message *to and in* the world. By this is meant that Christian eschatology is essentially about God, and God who has been to the world, and who will come again to the world: this is the Christ-shaped hope of the Christian faith. To what extent this hope can be channelled, consequently, by contemporary socio-political concerns, without simply being absorbed within them, remains debatable; it is clear, however, from the recent pronouncements of Cardinal Joseph Ratzinger on behalf of the Roman Catholic Church, that one major denomination at least is extremely concerned about the perceived usurpation of ecclesial (communal) authority by apparently secular resources and questions.

Ultimately, this remains the key question of Christian eschatology: who will exercise its special power and authority until the *eschaton* itself arrives? In this sense, the real issues are not so much *what* is known about the end time, as *who* legislates for Christian existence in society as hope awaits fulfilment. Given the peculiar nature of this eschatological hope, there can be little expectation that this situation will ever alter; on the contrary, Christianity will remain a religion in which social, teleological visions and programmes continually fall foul of those whose authority might be undermined. This, finally, must be the character of a faith which finds its ultimate foundation in the eternal, and therefore essentially mysterious, grace of Jesus Christ, one which theology would be well advised to accept with all due humility as it seeks to understand this character in both church and society.

Bloch, E. (1986) *The Principle of Hope*, 3 vols, Oxford: Basil Blackwell.

Hayes, Z. (1989) *Visions of a Future: A Study of Christian Eschatology*, Wilmington, DE: Glazier.

Hoekema, A. (1979) *The Bible and the Future*, Grand Rapids, MI: Eerdmans.

Kant, I. (1963) 'The end of all things', in *On History*, New York: Macmillan.

Metz, J.-B. (1980) *Faith in History and Society: Toward a Practical Fundamental Theology*, London: Burns & Oates.

Milbank, J. (1990) *Theology and Social Theory: Beyond Secular Reason*, Oxford: Basil Blackwell.

Moltmann, J. (1967) *Theology of Hope*, London: SCM.

Rahner, K. (1966) 'The hermeneutic of eschatological assertions', in *Theological Investigations*, vol. 4, London: Darton, Longman & Todd.

Ratzinger, J. (1988) *Eschatology: Death and Eternal Life*, Washington, DC: Catholic University of America Press.

Vahanian, G. (1977) *God and Utopia*, New York: Seabury Press.

Gareth Jones

ESPIONAGE

The term 'espionage' is from the Middle English for *espying*, that is, being a spy, or one who engages in the act of spying. Since the development of the nation state it has become closely associated with the activities of state and is frequently justified on grounds of *raison d'état*; reason of state. By extension, the term has been applied to commercial and financial activities, hence the burgeoning concern with commercial espionage. While the language of reason of state and the definition and justification of espionage in those terms stems from Machiavelli's injunction in *The Prince* that a prince needs to be deceitful, the act of spying and of deceiving both predates and is wider than the nation state. In its older and wider sense, espionage, understood as spying, deceit and deliberate dissimulation, raises issues that go right to the heart of Christian theology, secular-based morality and even to ontology; to what exists. For, as espionage plays on the pre-Socratic distinction between Being and Appearance, it is the most philosophically challenging of the Military Arts.

Tales of espionage are almost as old as written records; and deceit, more generally, has found its way into anthropogenesis. The classic mythical account of espionage is probably the use of the wooden horse of Troy as a means of deceiving the defenders of that city who were otherwise successfully withstanding a long siege. The anthropogenesis of Christian theology has mortal man and his condition arising as a consequence of the paradigmatic deceit of the serpent in the Garden of Eden. In tempting Eve to disobey the prime injunction not to eat from the fruit of the tree of knowledge, the serpent directly contradicts the warning of God that mortality would result from disobedience. 'You shall not die', it says in Genesis 3: 4, combining temptation and deception. Accounts of attempted deception are resplendent in the Hebrew Bible and indeed the Decalogue does not prohibit deception or LYING in general. There is an interdiction against bearing false witness, followed by an ordinance not to make false accusations or reports at a trial, but lying *per se*, and deception *per se* are given very little attention. Indeed Bok (Bok: 1978) makes the point that it is not until the Enlightenment, and particularly with Kant, that lying is clearly and completely interdicted. More generally, she claims, none of the major religions with the exception of late Christianity place much emphasis on the alleged fault of lying.

The archetypal spy and deceiver in the New Testament is Judas Iscariot, who having been one of the trusted apostles betrays Jesus for thirty pieces of silver. The act and the sign of betrayal was a kiss (Mark 14: 44–5), a sign of love, the motive, money. The account of the betrayal of Jesus exhibits a distinction that is often maintained between the motives of those who spy and deceive out of conviction and those who spy and deceive for mere material gain. Judas Iscariot had not even the excuse of conviction with which to mitigate his offence. Even today the motive of mere material gain is usually regarded as a poor and base reason for deception, whereas conviction and principal is a sometimes comprehensible and even, occasionally, mitigating reason for deception.

The Christian attitude to lying and deception always rests on the view that TRUTH is valued. St Augustine claims that, 'When regard for truth has broken down or even slightly weakened, all things will remain doubtful' (Bok 1978: xv, 250–5). This view is typical and comprehensible not only from a religious and theological perspective but also from a social and political perspective. Whatever other features of differing societies may be expressed in differing cultural and relativistic terms, affirmation and denial can always be found, and that there is *some* conception of truth makes the idea of espionage possible. From a different perspective it might be reasonably claimed that a society in which affirmation and denial and the comprehension of truth and truth telling failed to be consistently understood would be scarcely, if at all, viable. 'Is every lie a mortal sin?' St Thomas Aquinas asked (Bok 1978: 258ff.). The question is not merely a moral and religious question, it is also a social question. Issues of truth, lying, deception and, therefore, espionage, go right to the heart of social viability. A people that lies to itself or whose leaders systematically lie to them, is a people that endangers the internal respect required for civilized social survival.

Yet in a world where nation states have been sovereign, autonomous, greedy of the possessions of others and fearful of their own security, espionage – deception for the protection of the state – is tempting, even perhaps in some circumstances justifiable. Lying, in such cases, is primarily external, it is not to one's own people *per se* that the lie is told. It is, it is argued, rather for the benefit of one's own people, for their protection and well-being. Espionage, lying, deception are, in such cases, justified on grounds of *raison d'état*. Thus for Machiavelli a Prince may use all means at his disposal to protect his estate. By implication, that argument

can be extended to include protecting his people from external dangers. Generalized outwards, the problem indicated by Machiavelli is one of dirty hands. Is it possible to engage in the world without also engaging in dubious practices? Is it possible to instantiate, to put into practice, clean and noble thoughts while also remaining clean and unsullied? Politics, for Max Weber (Weber: 1948) is a vocation that always runs into paradoxes, the paradox of good intentions set against the reality of the world.

The problem raised by Weber is scarcely new, nor is it now redundant, it runs right through the dualism of spirit and matter. The life of the spirit pulls away from the world towards the 'just city' of Herodotus, the 'cosmic city' of Zeno, or Augustine's 'City of God'. But the life of matter pulls towards need and desire, towards the unjust city of Herodotus, or the more particularistic earthly city that the Stoic Zeno sought to overcome, or towards the earthly city of St Augustine. To attempt to engage in both cities, in both domains, while remaining clean is an ideal, but only an ideal. Nevertheless, there are limits, boundaries to what level of deception is acceptable both at a personal level and, as espionage, at the level of the state.

The clearest limit at the level of the STATE concerns its own people. There has been, and still is, a tendency of states to monitor their own people beyond what is necessary for the security of the realm. Information gathering, the intelligence aspect of security, tends to have its own imperative. Once begun, and once technically possible, it tends to be carried on for its own sake and for no further reason. At the very least this is a serious form of misguided paternalism, at the worst, it is destructive of civil society. The extreme monitoring of people, as in the totalitarian societies of the twentieth century, results in loss of initiative, continual and mutual distrust, and the breakdown of trust in social relations. Without some basic degree of trust (Giddens 1991) the fabric of society is itself threatened. Paradoxically, therefore, the extreme monitoring of a people by their own state, carried out in the interests of national security, could jeopardize the very nation it was intended to protect (*see* INTELLIGENCE SERVICES). The problem here runs not merely to formal monitoring by the intelligence community but also to the increased dogma of accountability.

The general doctrine that individuals and institutions should be accountable to the state may seem reasonable in theory. In practice, however, it often destroys a culture of trust replacing it with bureaucratically top-heavy formal structures. In Kantian terms internal compliance or morality is substituted by an external compliance or legality. External compliance depends not at all upon the heart but only on outward behaviour. There is a religious precursor to Kant's conception of morality in the moral inwardness developed in the beatitudes. The formula of formal accountability destroys the culture of inwardness and trust. It replaces it with the formality of law perceived as preceding the revolution of the beatitudes. Formal structures of accountability replace relations of trust with relations of law. In Europe and in the UK in particular this exchange of trust for accountability is characteristic of an inversion that is little more than a major cultural revolution. Notwithstanding this general inversion the security services in the UK are excused form full accountability in law. They depend instead on a culture of trust. The Security Services in the UK operate on a limited legal basis and with almost no formal accountability. They are trusted to act in the interest of the state, an interest largely defined by them. This perspective almost beggars belief, for of all institutions they trade most fully on relations of distrust.

An entirely different problem arises from competing views about what counts as a healthy and desirable political order. The problem of, and the desirability of, competing views of politics and state is healthy, but the intelligence community generally finds this view of POLITICS and this, admittedly complex, way of maintaining social order hard to comprehend. What is at issue are different accounts of what counts as acceptable political activity. On one account, which we might call, broadly, statist, it is the state that defines, and confines, political activity. That which does not take place within the state but within civil society is, by definition, social and non-political. Hence, when what appears to be political activity occurs within civil

SOCIETY, it comes to be perceived as threatening to the state and requires monitoring, possibly even suppression. On a competing account of politics, it is the state that is effectively anti-political and what takes place in civil society is a necessary counter to the limiting effect of the state: social activity, therefore, requires politicizing. Such activities are not necessarily threatening to society, they are, rather, alternative accounts of settling the agenda for society. The difficulty lies in persuading the intelligence community, charged with the protection of the state rather than the protection of the people, that political activity within civil society is not threatening but enhancing to the quality and stability of life.

A parallel problem exists where the perceived threat is external rather than internal. Frequently, but not always, the perception of a threat from another state is based on a fear of strangeness, of the alien nature of the other, rather from a genuine original threat. In Foucauldian terms, self-definition is primarily achieved through the construction of the other. The state tends to define itself, to take its own sense of identity, from other states; it characterizes its own nature by reference to what it is not. Hence a Western liberal state is defined negatively as being not communist, not totalitarian, not evil. It is instead the other state that is in Ronald Regan's phrase 'the evil empire'. This act of other definition is primarily an act of self-definition, but it has clear dangers, for this kind of self-definition may lead to the characterization of the other as enemy. Espionage, spying, even acts of de-stabilization, may then appear to be justified when the original position is not one of enmity but of strangeness. As in personal life, so it is with states; living with those like oneself, *homonoia*, is easy, living with those who are not like oneself, *heteronomia*, is hard – yet that is the real challenge, and a challenge that espionage, through its necessarily hostile recreation of the other, tends to undercut.

None of the foregoing is intended to suggest that all espionage, that all spying, is morally unworthy in all circumstances. It is, however, to circumscribe it. It is to draw attention to the dangers, and to the moral, political, social and theological ambiguities that surround the entire domain of lying in politics, of deception by the state to its own people as well as deception to other states. Sadly the problems are likely to be magnified rather than to decrease as a consequence of the electronic, biological and information gathering revolution. As the acquisition of information becomes easier and more complete, the imperatives that drive that information-gathering are likely to become more self-sufficient and compulsive. Lying in politics, deception, concealment, image-making, news and information management, and the art of the spin doctors, the advertisers and the image-makers, are likely to pull being and appearance into new areas. 'In politics', Hannah Arendt, once said, 'being and appearance are the same'. One might additionally note that in espionage, reality and appearance can be confused until the difference can no longer be untangled. The effect of taking a pre-Socratic distinction between appearance and reality, then a philosophical problem, into the practical arena of politics may well have consequences for the perception of the very world that we inhabit. In a significant way, however, espionage is not a cause but merely a symptom of the collapse of a traditional and valuable distinction. Espionage does not, of itself, collapse reality into appearance, it just systematizes that collapse on behalf of the state, and to that extent is merely symptomatic of a general malaise, a malaise neither wholeheartedly justified nor entirely condemned by our theological and religious tradition.

Arendt, Hannah 'Lying in Politics', in *Crisis in the Republic On Revolution*.

Bok, Sisela (1978) *Lying: Moral Choice in Public and Private Life*, London: Quartet.

Ellsberg, Daniel *The Pentagon Papers*.

Foucault, M. (1972) *The Archaeology of Knowledge*, trans. A.M. Sheridan Smith, New York: Pantheon.

——(1977) *Discipline and Punish*, New York: Pantheon.

Giddens, Anthony (1991) *Modernity and Self-Identity: Self and Society in the Late Modern Age*, Oxford: Polity Press.

Trilling, Lionel (1974) *Sincerity and Authenticity*, London: Oxford University Press.

Machiavelli *The Prince* (numerous editions).

Weber, Max (1948) 'Politics as a Vocation' in trans. and ed. by H.H. Gerth and C. Wright Mills *From Max Weber: Essays in Sociology*, London: Routledge and Kegan Paul.

Paul Barry Clarke

ETHICS

Ethics: the term is derived from the Ancient Greek *ethos*, where it may fairly be said that systematic thinking about ethics as a form of practical reason began. Ethics and morality are often used as interchangeable terms, although ethics is strictly the reflection upon morality. Ethical questions are, therefore, questions of scope and justification. Scope questions determine what criteria might be given to include or exclude a certain act or kind of act from the domain of ethics, for example, do the actions of doctors, scientists, businessmen and women fall under the scope of ethics? (*see also* PROFESSIONAL ETHICS). Are their actions *qua* doctor, scientist, businessman or woman actions that may be conducted according to ethical criteria? Questions of justification determine whether a particular claim to an act as a moral act can be upheld. For example, does a particular act undertaken by a businessman or woman or a scientist or a bureaucrat or a doctor that falls under the scope of ethics, count as a moral act or does it fail to meet those criteria and fail to be moral? Or, if it turns out that it falls outside the scope of morality, then the act will be non-moral. The foundation of ethics as a reflective moment is inextricably bound up with the foundation of THEOLOGY and of POLITICS. It is reasonable to think of an ethico-political theological moment: a moment that persists, at least in sedimented form, even into MODERNITY and post-modernity. Neither ethics, theology nor politics is surrendered in the sceptical pluralism of the present, on the contrary they recur with increased force. This is a conclusion that may seem surprising in a sceptical age, but it is a conclusion avoided only with difficulty.

All societies invoke some rules of conduct for their members. Indeed a settled, if possibly diverse, pattern of folkways and mores are probably an indispensable pre-requisite of SOCIETY. Such rules need not, however, be ethical in the sense of being reflectively arrived at or reflectively justified. They may be formed from habit or tradition, frequently backed up by and even integrated with religion, religious practices and a cosmological view of the place of that society in the universe. When such practices are settled and unreflective it is inappropriate to speak of that society as having ethical practices as such although it is clear that the practices they do have are equivalent to one of the prime functions of ethics; namely the ordering of society and the maintenance of its practices and its continuity. Ethics proper, however, occurs when the reflection on scope and justification becomes conscious and, more or less, deliberate. Socially this appears to have required a breakdown of traditional tribal order, or at least a weakening of the primacy of that order and intellectually a distancing from, or at least critical attitude towards prior religious frameworks. Ethics, requires a certain independence of mind and practice. It is an attempt to place the conduct of individuals and the bonds between them on a reflective and created basis rather than on those given of habit, custom, practice or religion. Ethics requires a break with tradition, not necessarily to destroy that tradition, for that tradition may be reclaimed, renewed, and affirmed as one's own, but to make it transparent. Such an act requires a break with tradition in that ethical thinking requires of traditional practices, habits, institutions, mores and folkways that they be justified according to criteria not found immediately within the practice or institution. For instance, the institution of religion can not ethically justify the religion, or the practice of SACRIFICE can not ethically justify the practice of sacrifice. A justificatory act requires, therefore, reflection upon and distance from the action, practice or institution that is under scrutiny. Ethics, so understood, is different from morality, and its emergence can, therefore, be dated as an event in western history. Understood as a distinct reflective practice in the domain of practical reason ethics is strictly western in origin, but there are some broad equivalents in other traditions. In Ancient India, and in Ancient China, for instance, there were marked breaks with past habits and traditions about 500 BCE, the period referred to by Jaspers as the axis of history. The axis of history is that time, found more or less simultaneously across a number of major regions of the world, that marked a break with the unreflective thinking of the past.

In the western tradition that break is given poetically and symbolically with Socrates,

marked out by many, Arendt for instance, as the first thinker. By this is meant the systematic questioning of existing practices and their justifications. It is represented poetically and symbolically at its sharpest in the reflective distance given by Plato to pre-existing tradition. Prior to that period there are, in the precursors to western thought, a number of codes that survive and show clear and systematic formulations of practice. They do not however, show a marked reflective justification. *The Code of Hammurabi*, in the 18th century BCE, demanded external compliance to the laws given by Hammurabi on the grounds that Hammurabi was the source of justice. The early Hebrew code of conduct, the *Decalogue*, sets out a short code of conduct for the tribes of Israel and their members but includes no justification outside the terms of its own code. Such codes are strictly legal in that they require external compliance. They are, or seem to be, externally imposed. In the case of the *Decalogue* it was brought down from on high rather than generated from the people. Codes of this kind do not require internal compliance either in the form of thoughtful compliance or as an accession of the heart to the code. It may fairly be said, that within tribal structures they are part of the mores of that society; and in that sense they are moral codes as well as legal codes, but they are not systems of ethics either formal or informal. They do not represent an inward break with the past but are rather an external sanction and reinforcement of the past.

Systems of ethics, understood as the more or less formal reflection upon practices and institutions, began with the Greeks and were fully developed as a branch of practical reason by Aristotle. In the most general terms the ethical questions of Ancient Greece revolved around the issue of how to live a virtuous life and obtain *eudaimonia*. *Eudaimonia*, the well being of the body/spirit, is a holistic notion that demands *arete* for its fulfilment. Virtue, here, or *arete*, can best be understood as excellence, and *eudaimonia*, as the well being of the spirit/body. The sense of both notions is that they can be realised only in an appropriate community context by those who show practical wisdom: *phronimos*. Aristotle had urged, that ethics, like politics, raises issues of practical reason where the central question revolves around the question, as Kant later put it, of how may *I* conduct my life? Writ large this becomes the primary political question of how may *we* conduct our lives? When the critical reflection and its relation to God was introduced into the justification for action the issues included a formally theological dimension. The first occasion when this relation was critically raised was at the point in Book II of *The Republic* when Plato introduced the term 'theology'. His concern here was how children might be taught correctly about the gods: a question that raised the issue as to how an individual and a society might judge the actions of the gods. That they could and must make such a JUDGEMENT showed that blind and uncritical acceptance of authority was not required, was even inimical to full and proper development; to *eudaimonia*. This theological moment raises large and fundamental questions about that kind of criticism and disobedience to established authority that is at the basis of individualistic ethics. Theology, ethics and politics are brought together at this point.

When ethical solutions are writ large and backed by the community as social or as political expectations or commands it raises the justiciary question of what legitimates the use of community power to enforce compliant action by individuals. It also raises the question of obligation; when must the commands of the community be obeyed and when may or even when must those commands be disobeyed, i.e., at what point does obligation to obey the directives of the community cease? Inevitably these questions are inter-linked. Questions of individual action cannot, except with great strain, and with the threat of some artificiality, be divorced from questions about political and social structures and possibilities; juristic matters of right and the limits of political obligation, and theological perspectives. As even ATHEISM is a theological perspective the ethical moment is always an ethico-political-theological moment. Within Western thought and practice, although not by any means confined to the West, there is a strong tradition of disobedience to AUTHORITY on the grounds of principled individual objections to its demands. Such objections are significant for they define not only the

individual but also the bounds of ethical questioning and the limits of political and societal power. They are further examples of the inextricable tie between ethics, politics, society and theology. Such views may be, and often are, not only individualistic or at most community based, although no less important for that, but also relativistic.

Set against the view that ethical reasoning applied to a community, and, by implication, relativistic contest the views of the Stoics, founded by Zeno of Citium, 334–262 BCE; Cleanthes 331–232 BCE and Chrysippus 280–206 BCE, emphasized universality. Zeno's *Republic*, in contradistinction to Plato's *Republic*, was an outwardly growing series of inclusive circles that gradually came to include the whole of humanity within its domain. That universalism reflected the cosmic *logos*, an idea that later became the foundation of Christian NATURAL LAW doctrines as well as that form of HUMANISM that grew to encompass the entire species. It was this universalism with respect to humanity that also came to influence the early Christians, although their cosmic community was one of equality before God, not before man. St Augustine's heavenly CITY, undoubtedly influenced by Zeno's ideas, was offset by an earthly city of great inequalities, injustices and moral defects. In Dante, and in the humanists from the thirteenth century, universalism came to include not only Christians but also non-Christians.

In the more directly Hebraically influenced tradition of early Christianity the change between pre-Christian and post-Christian ethical systems, was best represented in the change from outward manifestations of behaviour, and compliance to the law, to inner compliance. Indeed on some accounts, Immanuel Kant would be the clearest modern exemplar of the effects of this change. For Kant true morality is always and only inward; mere compliance is acting according to LAW: legality not morality. That change to inwardness demanded the inward turn of Christianity. It is best expressed in the change of emphasis from the external and legal code of the Decalogue to the inward and moral teaching of the beatitudes. Such a change is significant for several reasons not least of which is that it discovered the significance of the heart. Sins of the heart, inwardness and the sins of inwardness became central to Christianity and to much subsequent ethical thinking: inwardness became definitive of almost all ethical thinking in the western tradition.

This inwardness is not found in any significant form in Ancient Greek thought. Almost the contrary seems to have been the case. The mind was regarded as displaced. Of the terms that are available to express mind or SOUL we find that they often treat it as dispersed. *Phrenes*, and *Pneuma*, terms frequently in use to describe mind refer either to the location of *Phrenes* outside of the individual and to *Pneuma* as world spirit: a spirit in which an individual participated but which was not uniquely and unqualifiedly theirs in the sense that they alone possessed it and they alone would be responsible for it. That idea is found in the Christian idea of JUSTIFICATION not only for one's actions but also for one's thoughts.

The change is expressed in the claim of Jesus that a person who commits adultery in the heart is as guilty as one who performs the act but it is found in a more developed, if still embryonic form, in St Paul's *conscientia*, the idea that one might appeal to one's inner life as a test of the morality of an action. That idea was developed further in St Jerome's view that there was an innate capacity to distinguish good from EVIL. This was worked out remarkably in St Augustine's completion of the inward turn. That inward turn was a shift in consciousness that Taylor has called radical reflexivity (Taylor 1989). Radical reflexivity is the constant and unremitting examination of the contents of one's conscience and consciousness. Radical reflexivity places the 'I' at the centre of action and pushes the inward life of the individual to the centre of ethical questions. The roots of the idea of radical reflexivity go deep, they are found in the Delphic maxim of the fifth century BCE 'know thyself' but nowhere are they better expressed than in the beatitudes when Jesus overturns the mere external compliance of the Decalogue with the words 'and I say unto you', for those words push to the heart, to the inner life and not merely to actions, to behaviour, to compliance.

Notwithstanding the radical reflexivity of

Augustine, or even because of it, faith became a major foundation of justification for action. But the completion of that project was not possible under the order that followed Augustine. That order demanded that individual questioning be placed under the right order commanded by God. Right order here meant not only the adoption of the individual's station and its duties but also the acceptance of the order of God as command. The end point of that was the Great Chain of Being, a form of hegemony that ruled out reflexivity and ethics. For a considerable period of time Christianity suppressed the ethical INDIVIDUALISM that appeared to be at its foundation. It substituted instead an order that was so rigid that it suppressed reflexive ethics for a millennium or more.

Where mere faith dominates serious ethical thinking then demands for standards of justification that lie outside the practice or institution are significant. A significant change here is the development the view that one should try to understand what it is that one believes, a prime example of which can be found in the maxim provided by Anselm: *fides quaerens intellectum*. This maxim re-introduced serious ethical reflective thinking, for while it takes the faith as a given, the search for understanding what is given inevitably interrogates the given. The search for understanding coupled with the earlier inward turn, Jesus' edict to examine the heart, St Paul's *conscientia*, Augustine's introduction of the 'I' and the consequent radical reflexivity, emphasized the inwardness of morality. A moral act depended on, or, according to Abelard, 1079–1142 CE, at least must include, an account of the agent's intention. That intention could, it was argued, be informed by reason and by conscience. This idea was coupled with the stoic idea of natural law, universal order and Aristotle's account of practical reason. Its consequence was the view that natural law, given by God, was determinable according to the right application of reason. The most famous exponent of that view was St Thomas Aquinas, but it is also found in Hooker's *Of The Laws of Ecclesiastical Polity* and in an overtly modern and political form in John Locke's *Second Treatise of Government*.

Throughout these intellectual developments

the trend toward the breakdown of traditional structures was clear and irreversible. The clear consequence of that breakdown was that those ethical systems of thought developed against a backdrop of traditional community were strained. The response was the production of more individualistic modes of thought. Christian ethics was both a response to and a cause of that trend. The early Christians were themselves separated from traditional communities, forging their own new communities, or forgoing the company of others altogether. Inevitably the inward turn was accelerated by, if not caused by, such changes; and inevitably the question of how to behave in a community of fixed patterns was substituted by the question of how may an individual behave whether in a community or not? Ethics became, therefore, the reflection more on individual than on community conduct and the matter of community conduct became the subject of the philosophy of right. These two are inter-related. A philosophy of right is concerned with order but not with mere order. It also concerns itself with the rightness of the principles on which the order that it prescribes rests. Prior to the development of individualism, right order was understood as emanating from God or from nature, subsequent to that development it was perceived as built on individualistic principles. The most significant development in this line of thinking came with the thought of Immanuel Kant. Perhaps more than any other philosopher, Kant pursued a combination of Stoic and Christian Universalism with natural law sentiments, and Christian individuality and inwardness. Initially Kant took an individualistic line towards ethical and political questions: questions of practical reason. A moral act was one that was performed according to an appropriate maxim and that fell within the scope of morality. The emphasis on the maxim as well as the scope ensured that an act could be morally good only if it satisfied certain inward critieria. In that respect it followed Christian teaching. Those inward criteria were primarily, that it be an autonomous act, an act of the self, not done for extrinsic reward, gain or desire and that it accord with the moral law. The moral law could be encapsulated in the Categorical Imperative: 'Act only on that maxim that

you could at the same time will to be a universal law', or, in an alternative and well known formulation, 'Act always so as to treat yourself and others as an end in themselves and not as a mere means' (Kant 1953). In later works Kant argued that morality depended on the postulate of God, i.e., God had to be assumed in order to take morality as possible. He went on to consider whether it would be possible to rationally will an evil act. In this he followed the general tradition of western philosophy, if not literature, and considered such an act could not be autonomous and rational. Adopting and rationally acting on an evil maxim was impossible (Kant 1960). Satan's line in Milton's *Paradise Lost*, 'Evil be thou my good' represents a view of evil that for Kant is incoherent for here an evil maxim is adopted.

Kant's ethical thinking, indeed his thinking in general, is individualistic to the point of almost denying an independent existence to the community. In his early critical writing he seemed to regard the community as an ethical object only insofar as it was the outcome of a harmony of viewpoints and actions. In some of his later writing he does refer to the 'sensus communis', the community sense and urges that in making decisions one should consider the standpoint of others (Kant 1978). This falls short of a genuine notion of either society or community as an object in its own right with the ability to shape perceptions of self and others and the ability to shape and bind actions. This has clear consequences for the wider conceptions of ethics that might be appropriate in an age where the individual is regarded not as the creator of society but as the product of society.

Kant's ethical thinking placed the right before the good in the sense that the question of what was good for a person came as a secondary question. The prime ethical question was 'how may I conduct myself?', rather than the question of 'what is good for me?' Kant's theory is unmitigatedly deontological (*see* DEONTOLOGY) placing issues of duty and justice before issues of good and may, as a theory of right, provide criteria for testing the actions of GOVERNMENT as just or not as the case may be. A clear example of Kant's deontological approach to ethics and politics can be seen in John Rawls's *A Theory of Justice*. Set against deontological theories of ethics such as Kant's are teleological theories (*see also* TELEOLOGICAL ETHICS). Modern teleological theories place the emphasis upon questions of the search for that which is good. Jeremy Bentham's utilitarianism found in *An Introduction to the Principles of Morals and Legislation* is one of the best known examples. Bentham argues that what is good for human beings is the attainment of pleasure. What is right, therefore, and what is morally worthy and virtuous are those actions that maximize pleasure and reduce pain. Such a theory is unmitigatedly individualistic, but it too can serve as a theory of general conduct, as a theory of legislation or a theory of government. Government ought to seek to maximize the quantity of pleasure in a community and legislation should be planned and executed accordingly. This theory, in some form or other, has turned out to be powerful and influential. It turns up as cost–benefit analysis (sometimes with bizarre results as in the health care benefit notion of the QALY, the Quality Adjusted Life Year – *see* EUTHANASIA), as general appeals to benefit and, in extreme cases, as hedonism.

Objections to the theory are plentiful and telling. In its original form it eliminates agency and virtue, levelling all pleasures to the same point; it is as Nietzsche put it a 'pig philosophy' for the pleasures of a pig and the pleasures of a human count as the same. The theory was subsequently modified by John Stuart Mill (*On Utilitarianism*) who argued that different qualities of pleasure could be identified, and it has continued as preference utilitarianism where preferences rather than pleasure are taken as the basic unit. Even if these objections are allowed the theory still depends on a calculus that is difficult to perform. When the calculus is applied as proposed legislation, the boundaries of the community or society are spatially and temporally problematic to the point of arbitrariness, as is the planned effect of the action. Actions rarely stop at the merely legal boundaries of a community or state, and actions have consequences into the future that cannot be calculated. Consider, for example, the long term costs of dealing with the waste from nuclear power stations or from military reactors or nuclear weapons. Such costs are unknown, even unknowable, and are a bequest to the future for a time beyond imagination and for a spatiality beyond our knowing. Yet decisions to make and continue to make nuclear power stations are based on cost-benefit analysis and justified in consequentialist terms. This is possible only by arbitrarily designating the temporal and spatial boundaries of the consequences of the action. Nevertheless the theory, in some form or other, is remarkably persistent and influential and virtually dominant in public decision making.

Both these theories, deontological and teleological ethics and others, for example, intuitionism, the view that we intuitively know what is right or wrong; objectivism, the view that ethics is objective; naturalism, the view that goodness is to be equated with some non moral category, have come under sustained attack. Indeed the very idea of morality has been seriously challenged. If that challenge was successful then we would see the end of any possibility of ethics.

There are a number of sources for a claim that ethics is now at its end. A few are worthy of mention. First, the apparent decline of community, second, the decline of humanity, third, the so-called 'death of God', fourth, the rise of individualism, and fifth, the rise of pluralism. Not all of these claims are from the same source. There is no pretence, therefore, that they are systematically related in a single intellectual school. They are, however, probably inter-related in having developed as a consequence of extreme and far-reaching changes that are taking place in society. No ethical system can be divorced from its social and theological context and, if the social and theological context changes, so the related ethical thinking changes. The point can be developed further. If morality depends on community, and community is in decline or has died then morality and ethics too will decline.

There would appear to be some force to this claim; although it is not always clear that the outcome need be as pessimistic as is often thought. It is certainly the case that unreflective, or relatively unreflective, morality, in the form of obedience to the *mores* of a society was rooted in a stable community. Ethical thinking, however, as the reflection upon those *mores* rests on taking a distance from the *mores* of that community. It attempts to determine standards external to the practices of the mores. Hence for Aristotle the examination of the virtues is already to stand back from the virtues. In Stoicism it is to take the step yet further and seek for universalism. In Christianity the universalism is placed with God and in Kant it is found in the moral law; the Categorical Imperative. As each of these steps towards universalism developed so ethical thinking became less rooted in community practices as such and more related to abstract principles. In Christianity, for example, it became more dependent upon the postulate of God. Morality without the idea of God, was, according to Kant, inconceivable. In humanism, it became dependent on the development of an abstract conception of 'man' and humanity. The roots of that abstract conception of humanity are found in Stoic thought, and developed by Dante who turned the concept of *humanitas* from a concern with manners and civility into a membership notion. The conception of 'humanity' was given further warrant with nineteenth century biological SPECIESISM.

Conceptions of humanity and of God are closely tied together, so much so that the decline or death of one is almost certainly the decline or death of the other. The concept of humanity is the other of the Christian monoetheistic God. The concepts of a universal history, sociology, philosophy and theology that both underpin and stem from the development of the Christian conception of God is the same universal history, sociology, philosophy and theology that led to, and stems from, the development of the concept of 'man' and of humanity. There is some reason, therefore, to think that the fate of these concepts is tied together. There is also some reason to think that both concepts are under sustained attack for a variety of reasons and from a variety of sources.

The root source of the attack is in the claim made on several occasions by Nietzsche that we have killed off God or that God was dead. It is a moot point as to whether Nietzsche was, or was not, making a metaphysical claim; possibly not. He was certainly making a practical claim;

God had ceased to play a significant part in the practice of most human life. Nietzsche's claims about the death of God are well known, but that claim is sometimes stressed while forgetting that it was also Nietzsche who thought the idea of humanity a project of great difficulty. The greatest difficulty is the lack of a single source of morality combined with a variety of people and interests. His claim that, 'Hitherto there have been a thousand goals, for there have been a thousand peoples. . . . Yet tell me brothers: if a goal for humanity is still lacking is there not still lacking humanity itself' (*Thus Spoke Zarathrustra*) draws on the irreconcilability of diversity and pluralism with a single moral source of authority. The death of God is the death of morality. This seems to lead to NIHILISM and Nietzsche was certainly aware of, and fearful of, that possibility: but it may be a mistaken conclusion. It does lead to an end, to a single morality, but is it the case that this implies an end to all morality?

Much depends on the sights one sets and the perception of authority given by a single and unified conception of God and humanity. These ideas are warranted against a backdrop of the interpretation of western history as universal history. If western history is indeed universal history as Hegel, Marx and others have thought, then alternative comprehensions of moral and religious experience are subvertable to that world history: they are but chapters in a larger story rather than being stories in their own right. The difficulty here is who is to judge, and by what warrant may one judge, that someone else's religious, historical and lived experience is subservient to Western experience and is to be justified only in its contribution to a western account of world history? Any such judgement made outside that experience and imposed on others appears as hegemonic, arrogant and belittling of the lived experience of others. If that conclusion is drawn then by implication the allegedly universalistic ideas of both Christianity and of humanism turn out to be particularistic. Particularistic ideas that are given a universal expression are by definition ideological and with little claim to moral or ethical force. The paradox of Christianity and of humanism seems therefore to be, that in seeking to be the foundation of a universalistic ethic they turn out to be particularistic and ideological. Insofar as they have any universal claim it is the universality of hegemony: a hegemony that it has to be said has frequently been forceful, even brutal in its application. There are no shortage of examples from mass killings and genocides in South America, Tasmania, SLAVERY in Africa and destruction of whole peoples in wide parts of the world to show the danger of unmodified universalistic ethical ideas, whether their foundation be religious or secular (*see* GENOCIDE).

This would seem to suggest a requirement for a mode of ethics that respected pluralism and diversity. But the dangers here are also clear. A world with no universalistic ideas in it would be a world of isolated and probably warring particularities. Such particularities would not necessarily share anything except the competition for scarce resources. The outcome would be a world of perpetual conflict. To some extent this model can be seen to be ascendant. Every expression for self-determination by a people, to live their lives according to their own principles and to seek their own identities, is a rejection of universalism. Even within the same society particularistic claims are made. For example someone who rejects the language of 'mankind' in favour of man/woman, black/white, east/west or other distinctions on the grounds that the language of 'mankind' is sexist, racist, or regionalist is emphasizing difference and particularity. Sometimes that rejection is carried to the point of a denial that people have anything in common with each other. If they have nothing in common with each other then whither ethics?

The danger is certainly valid when posed in world terms, but it is also thought to flow from the particularism and individualism within societies; especially modern western societies. The individualistic ethics that followed from Christianity both before and after the Reformation might hold a community together when widely shared but when they fail the community too is in danger of failing. Nietzsche's death of God is also the death of community. His claim that 'morality in Europe today is herd animal morality' (Nietzsche 1973: 202) reduced the community to a herd. The failure of community does

not, however, mean the failure of the herd – it just pulls the last semblance of mores away from it.

Nietzsche drew attention to the dramatic turn of SECULARIZATION. He is also thought to have pointed up the radical individualism that had developed and the decline of the possibility of true community. Without community and without God, what of morality was left? Against this backdrop morality and ethics are thought by some to fade into mere subjectivism. Morality became, and, in the eyes of many, is no more than a subjective preference. Moral claims express emotional dispositions. For Alfred J. Ayer in *Language, Truth and Logic*, a moral claim is just a claim that I like or don't like something. For example the claim that 'stealing is wrong' just means 'I don't like stealing' or even 'stealing ugh!' This mode of ethics, the emotivist theory of ethics is, for Alastair MacIntyre (*After Virtue*), the dominant mode of ethical thinking today. Ethical language has fragmented and fractured, the terms good and bad, right and wrong, are there but they no longer exist in a context in which they have real validity. To have validity they would need to express some real practical way of life. They no longer do that. In consequence they are competing 'moral' claims, but those clains can never be settled, for the basic agreements on which morality needs to rest are absent. The recovery of the virtues, requires the recovery of community and values of civility within which the virtues can be cultivated.

For MacIntyre, and others of a communitarian persuasion, what is at issue is the constitution of the self. Within Kantian and most liberal theory the self is prior to the society in which it resides. This is basically secular re-working of a Christian, and before that Greek, doctrine that the soul precedes the actual material existence of the person. By contrast the communitarian model takes the self as constituted in the society of which it is a part. There are no truly a-social or pre-social individuals. If that is the case then society shapes and binds the self. Taken to its extreme society is an object of examination in its own right and ethics is just the expression of the morality found in the codes of conduct within a society. If society breaks down or becomes fragmented and/or fractured then so does morality. The absence of a higher law or notion of self/soul to appeal to that is prior to society makes a notion of morality that is higher than social arrangements difficult to sustain. Liberalism appears to offer a counter to this by taking the individual as prior to society. Here the presentation of such a pre-social individual is just an illusion, an illusion subject to hegemonic objections. The model does not fit the experience of other cultures, is confined to only a small and very recent part of western culture and seems unsustainable even in its own terms. The self that is conceived as prior to its social experience seems, in Sandel's terms, to be radically disembodied and distinct from its own ends (Sandel 1982).

Neither of these conceptions of the self seem sufficiently satisfactory to permit the development of an ethical person. In the extreme communitarian case the individual is the outcome of social forces and has no independence. In the extreme liberal case the self is conceived as sufficiently prior to its social situation as to be seriously disengaged from it. What is clear is that the moral life, and the ethical theories that arise from that, require both independence and engagement: tasks that seem difficult to the point of impossibility. It is no wonder then that these concerns taken together with the objections from Nietzsche, post Nietzschians, and communitarians, combined with the collapse of liberalism, have led to a general feeling that we have reached the end of ethics.

Such a conclusion would be understandable, it would, I think, also be premature. Further it would shy away from the possibility of creating a genuine ethics that is now open to us. The observation, made by MacIntyre and others, that moral disagreement has collapsed because community has collapsed, may be unduly pessimistic. It is clear that MacIntyre is correct that there is no single account of morality that can be given that will command universal assent. No ethical system can provide an uncontested and universal account of what counts as a moral action. Neither is there any religious system that can provide such a foundation. The voices of pluralism are too great, and too many, the world too fractured and to full of NOISE for any

single response to satisfy more than a single voice. This does not mean the end of morality, however, that conclusion is too pessimistic, nor does it mean the end of ethics. It means, instead, new challenges for the ethico-political-theological moment. In meeting those challenges it is necessary to take into account the problems that have led to the discerned collapse of ethics in the modern and post-modern world. A number of features of that collapse need to be dealt with directly. I can mention but a few.

First, the contest between individuals and community and individuals and society is no longer sustainable. Individuals are embedded in society but society while presenting individuals with structural limits is also affected by them and presents them with opportunities. Structures are necessary for action, moral and otherwise. There are no morally virtuous individuals outside social structures. Second, the real effects of society on individuals need to be recognized and dealt with as a matter of public policy. Ethical theory without action is as a 'clanging bell or a noisy' symbol/cymbal. Third, and similarly, the contest between the universal and the particular is false and based on the same error that led to the war between individual and society. Individuals may sink into particularity but they do so at great personal cost. They may also sink into universality but they do so as the expense of extra-ordinary disengagement. A balanced life equilibrates between the two, a point made fairly and strongly by Kant at the beginning of *The Critique of Judgement*. Fourth, all previously existing humanisms have failed to be genuinely humanistic; they have instead been little more than ideological and hegemonic prattle. Since Heidegger's *Letter on Humanism*, it is hard to think that humanism has reached its true potential and reached the possibilities implied in that doctrine. To parody a great Churchman who thought that your *God is Too Small* (Robinson) it seems also that your 'humanism is too small'.

There are clear theoretical implications that follow from this. There are also clear implications for public policy and public action. That is to say a society that values morality from its members and that values ethical thought and behaviour will have to take steps to nurture and safeguard that behaviour. No complete list is possible, a few pointers can be suggested. If individuals are socially embedded beings, rather than socially isolated beings, then moral behaviour will take place within a social context and their moral and ethical understanding will take place in a social setting. If ethics is a reflection on morality then situations that encourage that reflection need to be developed and encouraged. There is a deeper point to this. To be an individual is not merely to occupy a selfish first person perspective, it is also to occupy a third person perspective. The two are inseparable. But the development of that faculty requires the development of a degree of objectivity about the self. That can be done only where the self is subject to experience beyond the immediate. This broadening of experience, for that is what is entailed, often requires active intervention. It is rarely sought by individuals confined to a narrow perspective, why should it be? The narrow perspective closes down the desire for, and search for, a wide perspective. Working this through and implementing it requires social and political action for the desire to broaden the mind rarely comes from those whose minds lack breadth.

A similar point can made about the extension of humanism. What is wrong with all hitherto existing forms of humanism (to parody Marx on a different if not unrelated point) is their ideological limitation, their hegemonic programme and their inability to recognize the value of difference. That someone, or some practice, or some institution is different from some pre-conceived model of what a humanistic or civilized model should be, does not imply that it lacks civility or *humanitas*. Dante's shift in the concept of *humanitas* is significant here. That notion began in the particularity of civility and manners. In extension it retained the sedimented understanding of civility and manners. Hence if someone, or some people, failed to display the appropriate civility or manners so they exclude themselves from the inclusion membership of *humanitas* in its second sense. This was not Dante's fault, but was a consequence of taking a concept with one kind of sedimented meaning embedded in it and transforming it to a new situation. A post-humanistic humanism must break with these parochial limitations and accept diversity, difference and alterity without sinking into moral nihilism.

It is clear that while a hegemonic programme is unacceptable, the rush to parochialism is similarly unacceptable and full of dangers. Rampant particularism is so dangerous that not only might it lead to mutual incomprehension but it might also lead to a multi-world mentality in an age that requires some shared conceptions of the world in which we live and the values associated with a one world mentality. In that situation clearly some *ecumene* is required. Understandably there is a reluctance to accept the western *ecumene* with all hegemonic overtones. The difficulty is that there is nothing better on offer than will serve the purpose. On pragmatic grounds, at least, there is an urgency and necessity to take something from the shelf, and with the exception of the western *ecumene*, the common shelf is bare. For the moment at least that model with all its weaknesses, and all the caveats needed to restrict its wider possibilities, is what there is.

It is also clear that an ethics based on rampant individualism will not do on both theoretical and practical grounds. If individuals are socially embedded, a view that seems unassailable, then the actions of individuals are not always entirely of their own making. Individuals are, in the current conception, decentred. What this means is that the Pauline–Augustinian–Cartesian–Kantian–Liberal view of individuals as creators of their own society, and their own personal and social conditions, will not do. Individuals are, at most, only partially responsible for their actions and hardly at all responsible for their situation. This limits their personal and ethical responsibilities while placing some responsibility for situation and even their actions with society. The decentred individual is the outcome of social forces and has a self, that is passive with respect to society. The decentred individual has no single core. If there is no single core then, it is argued, such an individual can scarcely be held to be a moral being. The decentred human being is the outcome of a fragmented and fractured society.

If, however, society is fragmented then the cohesion that holds not only society but self and ethics together is also fragmented and broken. The implication of this would appear to be moral pluralism. There is no single principle of morality, no *arche* for either self or society, noting to hold either of these together and consequently a single conception of morality is difficult to develop and maintain. On some accounts, MacIntyre, for instance, this cannot be morality at all. For MacIntyre the moral pluralism that follows from a fragmented and fractured society is not morality at all: it is little more than emotivism.

This seems rather restrictive. Once the hegemonic conceptions of morality are removed and the self is admitted as socially embedded (a point with which MacIntyre and other communitarians would surely agree) it follows that a single conception of morality and a single theory of ethics is possible only in a society that is cohesive, self contained and antithetical to reflection. But such a society in denying, or, at least, discouraging reflection would not be a society that encouraged ethical thought. It might well be a society with a cohesive system of behaviour, with a cohesive set of practices and institutions, even a set of folkways and mores that determined the conduct of its members. It would not, however, be a society that permitted the development of ethics, for that requires reflection.

There is a deep paradox in the demand for ethical thinking. It can take place only in those societies that encourage reflection both on the society itself and on the conduct expected in that society. They are the same societies that generate the kind of critical activity that is subversive of the very society within which the ethical thought arises. To put this another way, ethics is radical and potentially subversive for it demands a questioning attitude towards the society, institutions and practices within which it finds itself. It is religiously subversive, for it demands an interrogation of the theological premises on which the society rests and it is socially subversive, for it demands an answer to the question as to why one ought to conform to given social practices.

There is still the issue as to whether the radical individualism that seems to be spawned by such conceptions can support a genuine conception of ethics. From a liberal or a communitarian perspective the answer has to be given in the negative. In either case some shared view of ethics is required. In the former case the shared view is required to be universal. In the latter case it is required that it be sufficiently shared throughout society as to create a moral community. In both cases the reality falls short of the principle.

In a diverse and multi-cultural society there will be many different conceptions of morality. The shared conceptions will frequently be so minimal as to undercut either liberal or communitarian conceptions of morality. This has led to some considerable pessimism about the nature of ethics. That it is, for example, excessively individualistic, emotivist, fragmented, lost, misplaced, that moral disagreements are irresolvable and even that morality appears to amount to little more than emotive bleating. Ethics is presumably at its end and we are now in a condition *After Virtue* (MacIntyre). It is often thought that these difficulties must lead to a decline in moral possibilities and in ethical theory. This conclusion is unwarranted and the pessimism is seriously misplaced. The world in which we now live offers greater challenges than ever before. It offers with those challenges the possibility of a genuine morality: genuine in the sense of being reflective rather than being automatic, or the result of habit, tradition, custom or just downright thoughtlessness. It does not follow from a diversity of ethical and moral viewpoints that there is no morality or that all moral preferences are little more than the subjective and emotive sighs of individuals lost in a difficult and heartless world. On the contrary, that a moral response to a situation is an individual one is at the heart of the western tradition of morality, for an individually given moral response requires thoughtfulness and commitment in a way that automatic, or merely habitual responses, do not. In that sense the individuality of moral response pre-dates modernity and individualism by a considerable time.

Nevertheless there has been shift of emphasis. Originally conceptions of ethics and of morality were significantly tied to community, later conceptions divorced individual and community sometimes to the extent of diminishing community to a mere set of individual behaviours.

Some early conceptions were so concerned with external behaviour that they left little for the individual or for the individual heart. The Greek *arete* or excellence (usually of performance of a given task), noble though it was, provided little in the way of modal inventiveness. The *Decalogue* demanded much in the way of external performance and little in the way of reflexive inwardness. The Christian emphasis on the inwardness of a virtuous act turned many away from the world. Each of these conceptions of morality has merit and each of these conceptions of morality can contribute something to an ethical perspective. Each, by itself, has for present times the inadequacy of incompleteness. For a variety of historical reasons a more complete perspective has hitherto been lacking in discussions of morality and ethics. That is not the fault of those of yester-year but it is the challenge for those of today. A fuller perspective on ethics will encompass a moderated universalism, a respect for alternative life styles, alternative communities, alternative selves, alterity, diversity while not losing sight of the need to share the planet and to communicate with each other. We do share one world yet the genuinely as opposed to hegemonically delivered ecumenic ideas on the shelf are currently limited to the point of global poverty. On pragmatic grounds, if no other, some acceptance of currently available ecumenic ideas is necessary, as a starting point, if nothing else. It does not follow, however, that the pragmatic acceptance of what is on offer warrants or justifies that model in some larger theoretical sense: clearly not.

The weakness of many ethical systems has been in their justification of externally imposed rules, mores, folkways, habits, traditions, social forms as ethical forms having universal validity. This universality is just the opposite of what they have been and are. There are two implications of this worthy of mention. First, ethical systems appear as natural. Second they appear as objective but also as alien; as objects. Both of these perceptions are at the heart of traditional conceptions of ethics. Both seem inimical to what is required for the moral life. If an ethical system appears as natural then there is no judgement to be made on it as a whole: no reflective judgement, to use a phrase of Kant's, that takes

one outside it. Such judgements as are required are what Kant called determinative judgements – judgements about how to apply this or that rule in particular circumstances. If an ethical system appears as natural, it also appears as objective, both in the sense of containing objective truths and of being an object outside of the self. In that case it appears as alien, as external, as something to which one must comply in order to be moral. But this compliance is little more than a sophisticated form of external compliance. External for it is from outside, and sophisticated for the pressure of morality is to make external rules and tests, or externally imposed order, appear as internal. The internalization of such rules or order leads not to greater morality, on the contrary, it leads to moral somnia. The counter to moral somnia is reflection on the entire condition within which an ethical system or moral code presents itself. That reflection necessarily encompasses its sociology, its history, its philosophy and its theology, each of which has to be examined against the other for each contain traces of the other as sedimented layers. When so seen, ethics and morality lose their naturalness and appear as containing multiple contingencies. But this does not bring morality to an end, on the contrary, the collapse of the unremitting appearance of the naturalness of morality brings about a collapse of its alienness.

To the moral somniac, the morally supine, the moral sleepwalker and the moral couch potato, the collapse of externally imposed moral codes leads to emotivism; and therein lies a clear danger for self and world. But for the morally prepared there is liberation from external bonds, for the morality that appears after the collapse of the alienness, appears to the self as its own morality. This reclamation of morality opens up the possibility of the self leading a truly moral life and engaging in genuinely moral action and activity.

The world as we now find it offers a greater possibility for genuinely moral action than hitherto. It also, of course offers a greater possibility for avoiding moral commitment than hitherto. That is the challenge and the danger. It is the source of the excitement and of the fear. What we need not conclude is that because the morality of one group is different to the morality of another group one, many, or all, of the groups have no moral outlook. On the contrary, for the morally wakeful, there will be moral disagreements and they will be healthy for they test one's position and prevent the onset of somnia.

All of this suggests that the world is moving towards a pluralistic conception of morality; a conception that given the roots of morality in society, and ethics in reflection is not surprising. Morality was originally community based, it was always and only local, and as early as Herodotus, there was no pretence that it be otherwise. Where the tolerance of Herodotus was lost was with the growth of universalism with its hegemonic tendencies. Universalism demands a single answer to diverse questions in diverse situations, it removes the *mores* from morality, replacing it instead with the cosmic city, or the city of God or the great chain of being or other conceptions of right order. But human beings do not live in cosmic or universal cities, or at least not in universal or cosmic cities alone. They live also in particular circumstances and develop particular identities in particular lives. That those lives and the mode in which they are acted out are not the same as some other lives, and some other mode of being, does not make them immoral or non-moral *per se*; it merely makes them contextual, as they must be if they are to develop.

Yet there is a challenge beyond mere particularism, and that challenge ensures that ethics is not yet at an end, it is rather at its very beginning. We are indeed in a condition after virtue; that is to say after its commencement.

Life after virtue's commencement requires living in, but beyond, particularities. Mere particularism, merely living out one's life in a single identity providing structure is insufficient. Mere particularism fails to provide the reflective distance within which it possible to affirm that life as one's own, rather than becoming a slave to it. It does not allow one to affirm one's morality as one's own, rather than being driven by as a external and alien force. Mere particularism in the life of the moral somniac leads to emotivism, a subjectivism that appears as inwardly driven but which is alien for it is not affirmed from a reflective vantage point. Leading the moral life after virtue requires, however, a combination of

an agonistic and an angst ridden approach to morality. This is not in any sense the morality of the ballot box or the morality of the market place, they are for the sleepwalkers and the emotivists alike. It is instead the morality of thoughtfulness and principle where the principle and the thought are one's own and not provided by some alleged authority. It is not an easy road. But the morality that emerges in one's own in the real and significant sense of being thought through and affirmed in the light of the demands and restrictions of a life that while it reaches towards universality is nevertheless and always lived out in particular circumstances.

The challenge of rising beyond mere particularism requires first, some universalistic sense, provisional though it must be, and with it some reflective judgement on, and reflecting equilibration between, different modes of being. Second, some sense of a practice of being in at least three worlds, local community, larger community, and global community and third, some sense of reaching towards eternity as well as being in time. The first of these is the role of ethical theory, the second is the function of politics and the third is the challenge for theology. All three are inter-related and all three must be taken together as the challenge of newly commencing, living and continually reliving the ethico-political-theological moment.

Ayer, Alfred J. (1971) *Language Truth and Logic*, Harmondsworth: Penguin.

Anselm (1962) *Basic Writings*, trans. S. N. Deane, La Salle: Open Court.

Aristotle *Nichomachean Ethics* (numerous editions).

Augustine of Hippo *The City of God* (numerous editions).

Bentham, Jeremy (1948) *An Introduction to the Principles of Morals and Legislation*, Oxford: Basil Blackwell.

Finnis, John (1975) *Natural Law and Natural Rights*, Oxford: Oxford University Press.

Hooker, Richard (1993) *Of the Laws of Ecclesiastical Polity*, MRTS.

Kant, Immanuel (1953) *The Groundwork of the Metaphysics of Morals*, trans H. J. Paton as *The Moral Law*, London: Hutchinson.

——(1960) *Religion Within the Limits of Reason Alone*, trans. T. M. Greene and H. H. Hudson, New York: Harper and Row.

——(1978) *The Critique of Judgement*, Oxford: Oxford University Press.

Locke, John (1982) *Second Treatise of Government*, Harlan Davidson Inc.

Macintyre, Alastair (1981) *After Virtue*, London: Duckworth.

Mill, John Stuart (1993) *On Liberty; and, Utilitarianism*, Bantam Classic.

Nietzsche, F. (1973) *Beyond Good and Evil*, trans. R. J. Hollingdale, Harmondsworth: Penguin Classics.

Plato *The Republic* (numerous editions).

Rawls, John (1971) *A Theory of Justice*, Cambridge, MA: Harvard University Press.

Sandel, Michael J. (1982) *Liberalism and the Limits of Justice*, Cambridge: Cambridge University Press.

Paul Barry Clarke

ETHNICITY

Ethnicity is derived from the Greek *ethnikos* and *ethnos*, referring to a people or nation. Today the identification of ethnicity has become an extremely confused area. The term 'ethnic group' is conventionally used to describe a group of people with some degree of coherence, people with common origins, related by shared experiences. Ethnicity and national identity are closely connected though they are not the same: nevertheless it is impossible to understand ethnicity without taking into account the formation of nations. Though the myth of origins may be rooted in a selective and inaccurate reading of history, it becomes a defining myth for nations and groups which base their identity on genealogy rather than on residence and territory. An ethnic group is usually characterized by a long shared history and by shared cultural traditions. There will normally be other features such as common geographical origin, common language, common literature or common religion, though not all of these may be present. Ethnic groups may have experienced hardship, persecution or dislocation from territory, and these experiences may strengthen, and sometimes revive, the sense of common identity. Often the term 'ethnic' is used of minorities of immigrants experiencing discrimination within a SOCIETY – thus the emergence of 'ethnic identity' and of 'ethnic groups' based on a common experience of oppression or deprivation.

In some cultures, only the upper class are seen as truly embodying ethnic purity, while the mass of the people are of diverse origins and cultures. Thus the Frankish conquerors of France in the sixth century ruled over a Romano-Gallic population. Only after many centuries was the notion of a unified French nation-state developed. In English society, ethnicity and CULTURE are closely bound up with class. In some countries (such as South Africa under APARTHEID) an ethnic minority dominates and governs the diverse majority.

Ethnic identity is closely related to the concept of nationality, and there are ethnic bases for the emergence of nations – ties, memories, myths of origin, and so on. A civic nation is a political and territorial concept, membership of which is based on residence rather than descent, real or alleged. But often NATIONALISM attempts to reconstruct a 'golden age' of ethnic purity, drawing on myths of heroes and conquests. As ideas of nation and ethnicity come together, ethnic purification or cleansing often develops. Indeed where a nation is defined in terms of origin and descent, ethnic purification is logical and perhaps inevitable. The pure body must be cleansed of foreign and alien elements.

Thus the relationship between ethnicity and nationhood varies. There may be a view of the nation which sees it as a single ethnic community, with common bonds of culture and religion – Jews, Orthodox Greeks, Sikhs, Irish Catholics and so on. Thus religion and ethnicity are often intertwined. The Greek identity for hundreds of years was inseparable from the tradition of Byzantine Orthodoxy. Migration is related to ethnic identity not only in the sense mentioned above, but also in so far as members of a community may migrate to a new country, replacing or expelling the previous inhabitants (thus the Puritan settlers in the USA *vis-à-vis* the native Americans). Subsequently other groups may enter the community. The USA, Australia and South Africa present examples of diverse communities with conflicting concepts of ethnic and national identity. Over time, notions of ethnic origin and national identity may change. There are some 40 million Americans of Irish (or part Irish) origin, of whom over 50 per cent are of Protestant background. But very few of them see themselves as Irish, and the term 'Irish' has come to be associated exclusively with Roman Catholics.

The term 'ethnics' is often used of particular minority groups, though such usage is tautological, for if some are ethnics, all are. More common in Britain is the term 'ethnic minorities', a term often used interchangeably with 'black population'. In the USA, by contrast, 'ethnics' is often used to refer to groups other than blacks – Greeks, Poles, Italians, etc. Ethnicity is central to European notions of identity, not least since the erosion of political forms of identity.

'Ethnicity' is often used as a euphemism for 'race' as in the term 'ethnic minorities'. The Race Relations Act 1976 refers to 'ethnic or national origins'. Indeed the concepts of 'ethnicity' and 'race' are often used interchangeably, yet, while there is overlap, the concepts are different (see RACISM). Race is a pseudo-biological concept, closely related to colour, and racism is a structural and cultural reality which results in discrimination and disadvantage. Ethnicity, on the other hand, defines the characteristics of a group which sees itself as distinct. Ethnicity is not necessarily related to race, colour or religion though these will often affect it. Ethnic identity will be passed from one generation to another, and may include distinct languages, religions, political and cultural styles, and so on.

Over time aspects of ethnic identity may weaken, as with many children of South Asians in Britain. However, in situations of conflict, ethnic identity may be aroused and strengthened, and may become the basis both of withdrawal into enclaves and of organizing and campaigning for improved conditions. Thus the Italians in American cities, or the Chicano movement of agricultural workers of Mexican descent in the USA are examples of such strengthening of ethnic identity. In the context of racism and deprivation, new forms of ethnic identity may emerge as in the 'African American' identity.

There is considerable concern at present that the concept of ethnicity is being appropriated in a racist form. This appropriation in its turn may be countered by a view of racism as inherent. The growth of ethnic nationalism presents a major challenge to anti-racist work. There has been criticism of 'ethnic absolutism' and the tendency to see a nation as culturally homogeneous, while some writers argue that ethnicity has replaced social CLASS as the major form of division and social stratification.

Recently there are indications that nationality and CITIZENSHIP are increasingly being understood in terms of ethnic origin. There has been a growth of ethnic exclusiveness in Germany where there has been a strong emphasis on 'stock'. While the current stress is more on customs, language, culture and institutions, such a stress is similar to the earlier concern with blood and descent, and may be identical in its effects. In Britain, there has been an increased tendency to see nationality as connected with 'patriality' and descent. More recently the concept of 'ethnic cleansing' has entered the vocabulary in the context of a fierce conflict in Eastern Europe.

Some reject the whole idea of ethnicity, arguing that race and culture are adequate categories. Some black writers, such as Cornel West and Paul Gilroy, argue for a new approach to black culture and identity which transcends the absolutism and 'essentialism' of nationalism and ethnicity.

'Ethnic monitoring' refers to the collection of statistical data based on ethnic origin. It was practised unofficially in parts of the Ministry of Labour in East London in the 1940s, but only developed on a large scale in the 1980s. It was introduced into the Civil Service and other organizations in 1985, and, in spite of early opposition, is now widely accepted in statutory and voluntary sectors. In 1991, after much debate, an 'ethnic question' was introduced into the Census.

Anderson, Benedict (1983) *Imagined Communities*, London: Verso.

Braudel, Fernand (1989) *The Identity of France*, 2 vols, London: Fontana.

Gilroy, Paul (1993) *The Black Atlantic: Modernity and Double Consciousness*, London: Verso.

Glazer, Nathan (1983) *Ethnic Dilemmas 1964–1982*, Cambridge, MA: Harvard University Press.

Glazer, Nathan and Moynihan, Daniel P. (1975) *Ethnicity: Theory and Experience*, Cambridge, MA: Harvard University Press.

Jackson, Robert (1985) 'Ethnicity', in Giovanni Sartori (ed.) *Social Science Concepts: A Systematic Analysis*, Beverley Hills, CA: Sage.

Modood, Tariq (1992) *Not Easy Being British*, London: Runnymede Trust.

Ringer, Benjamin and Lawless, Elinor (1989) *Race, Ethnicity and Society*, London: Routledge.

Said, Edward (1993) *Culture and Imperialism*, London: Chatto & Windus.

Smith, Anthony (1986) *The Ethnic Origins of Nations*, Oxford: Blackwell.

Sowell, Thomas (1983) *Ethnic America: A History*, New York: Basic Books.

West, Cornel (1993) *Keeping Faith: Philosophy and Race in America*, London: Routledge.

Kenneth Leech

EUCHARIST

The word 'Eucharist' (Greek: *eucharizesthai-*, the root of which is *charis*, grace) means 'thanksgiving'. Christ himself gave thanks when he broke the bread at the Last Supper (Matthew 26: 27; 1 Corinthians 11: 24). It has also been usual for Eucharistic liturgies to speak of the act of thanksgiving made by the faithful in the Eucharist (a 'sacrifice of praise and thanksgiving', *Church of England Book of Common Prayer*, 1549). 'Eucharist' is used in the Didache (9.1), in Ignatius (Philadelphians 4), in Justin Martyr (*Apology* 1.66) and other early texts. But other terms have been used, often with the intention of stressing a particular understanding of the Eucharist. During the late patristic (Isidore, *Etymologies* 6.xix.4; Ambrose, *Letter* 20) and medieval periods the *missa* or 'sending forth into the world' of the people at the end of the service gave rise to the word 'Mass'. In reaction against certain connotations of late medieval practice in the celebration of the Mass (see below), Protestant reformers of the sixteenth century preferred to use 'the Lord's Supper' (1 Corinthians 11: 20, as translated in the Wyclifite Bible) or 'Holy Communion'.

Four accounts of the origin of the Eucharist are given in the New Testament, one in each of the Synoptic Gospels (Matthew 26: 26–8; Mark 14: 22–4; Luke 22: 17–20) and one by Paul (1 Corinthians 11: 23–5). These describe how Jesus took first bread, which he broke, and then wine, and gave them to the disciples as he told them that these were his body and blood which were to be given for them. They were to 'take and eat' and to 'drink'. He instructed the disciples to continue to 'do this' in memory of him.

A relationship was thus set up between the institution of this Supper, Christ's death on the Cross and the future celebration of the Eucharist, which made it central to Christian life and worship. From the beginning Christians met to share bread and wine in memory of Jesus' death and RESURRECTION. Acts 2: 46 suggests that they may have done so every day. Acts 20: 7 and a number of comments in writers of the second century indicate that it was usual for the whole community to communicate at the Eucharist on Sundays. It was understood to be the supreme act of the Church making its members one body with their Lord, the bond of their peace and the expression of their unity. It is thus the supreme social act of the Church, in which the community realizes itself as one body. For the same reason, where Christian communities are divided the defining mark of their separation is that they cannot meet in one Eucharist.

Those hostile to Christianity in late antique society spread rumours that the Christians were practising cannibalism. They thus made monsters of them, alien beings, cut off from ordinary human society.

A series of controversies has arisen about the significance to individual and community of what happens in the Eucharist. At first, while there was a general sense that Christ himself was certainly really present in the consecrated bread and wine, it was possible for them to be seen as both symbols of his body and blood and in some undefinable way his actual body and blood. By the fourth century two schools of thought began to emerge: the first held that the bread and wine were actually changed by the words of consecration; the second that they became symbolic of Christ's body and blood. In the ninth century the Western monk Paschasius Radbertus wrote the first monograph on the theology of the Eucharist. He insisted that the consecrated bread was the actual body of Christ which had been born of Mary, been crucified, and resurrected and ascended into HEAVEN. This attracted criticism from Ratramnus of Corbie and Rabanus Maurus, who thought Christ's presence spiritual rather than physical. In the eleventh century Berengar of Tours raised a further difficulty. He contended that bread and wine could not really be Christ's body and blood, on the grounds that actual change was logically, physically and metaphysically impossible; and, moreover, that as a matter of historical fact Christ could not come down from heaven in his body until the Last Judgement. He was officially condemned and forced to recant at two Councils, in 1059 and again in 1079.

In reaction to what was seen as a doctrine threatening the very heart of the mystery, Lanfranc of Bec and other apologists for the Church framed the doctrine of 'transubstantiation' (so-called only from the late twelfth century). This attempts to define the physics and the metaphysics of what happens in terms of the Aristotelian *Categories*. In ordinary bread, the attributes may change (bread goes mouldy) while the substance continues to be bread. In consecrated bread the attributes remain the same (it still looks and smells and tastes like bread) but the substance is altered and becomes the actual body of Christ. In the continuing debates it was objected that one body of Christ could not be in many places at once when the Eucharist was celebrated simultaneously all over the world; nor could the sheer quantity of consecrated bread be reconciled with the size of Christ's body. This literalism reflects the comparative crudity of the concepts which were in play at this point. The late Middle Ages saw a renewal of the debate, as logic and physics became more sophisticated and it became possible to challenge the principle of transubstantiation at a technical level. But transubstantiation has remained the official doctrine of the Roman Catholic Church, although the emphasis would now perhaps be upon the fact of the change rather than upon the manner. Canon 897 of present Canon Law says that in the Eucharist 'Christ the Lord himself is contained, offered and received'. At the period of the formulation of the doctrine of transubstantiation in the West the Orthodox Churches were already divided from Rome by the events of 1054, and the doctrine was not formally adopted by the Orthodox. Nevertheless, Orthodox thinking is very close to that of the Roman Catholic Church on the physical reality of Christ's presence in the Eucharistic elements. At the Reformation in the West there was division of opinion. Luther remained

close to a transubstantiationist position, although he tended to the view that both the body of Christ himself and the bread were consubstantially present. Zwingli and the Swiss reformers saw the Eucharist as primarily a memorial and denied that any change at all took place. Calvin stood between these two positions. The major development of this period was a shift among those reformers who did not altogether deny the objective reality of Christ's presence towards talk of 'real presence' rather than 'transubstantiation'. That enabled them to continue to affirm that the Eucharist involved something more than the response of the individual worshipper who received the bread and wine 'worthily', without obliging them to speak in terms of the physics and metaphysics of an actual change in the elements. To deny the objective presence of Christ is to make it necessary to say that Christ is present only subjectively, and thus only to the true believer who receives the bread and wine 'worthily'. It also has the effect of placing an emphasis upon the individual's union with Christ rather than upon that of the whole community. Some Protestant churches have taken that view.

The establishment of the doctrine of transubstantiation had a number of implications for the way the Mass was perceived in the Middle Ages in the West. It encouraged reverence, especially for the consecrated bread, to the point where the Feast of Corpus Christi was instituted in 1264. This encouraged the simple faithful sometimes to think of the Host as having not only miraculous but magical powers, and, again, the development of a preoccupation with the consecrated bread itself to the exclusion of the 'community' action of the Eucharist. The priesthood, which had the power to 'make Christ', came to be treated with both a new respect and a new envy and resentment (which was reflected in the popular anticlerical movements of the Waldensians and others from the twelfth century). The action of the Mass could be thought of as constituting a sacrifice of Christ in its own right, like that of the Cross, and in addition to it; and consequently as having a quantifiable and directly applicable power to save in its own right. This led to the development of such practices as paying for Masses to be said for one's soul or for the souls of others (on the basis that a greater number of such Masses did more good than a smaller). That seems to have met a strongly felt pastoral need in the later Middle Ages.

The resulting separation of the action of the priest from the action of the whole community with him in the Eucharist was encouraged by liturgical changes which took place from the end of the eighth century. The consecration prayer was said increasingly quietly and eventually in silence. The priest began to stand with his back to the people (making an offering which was now seen as a propitiation to placate an angry God), instead of facing the congregation to make it clear that he and they were joining in the action. In the West the liturgy continued to be said in Latin long after Latin ceased to be understood by the congregation. The altar moved from the centre of the church to the end, away from the people. Sometimes the priest would say Mass alone, with no congregation present. The laity no longer received both bread and wine, but only the host.

Many of these changes were attacked by reformers in the sixteenth century together with the then newly-controversial notion that the Eucharist is a sacrifice not only of praise and thanksgiving but also of Christ himself. This was not in itself a new idea. It is common in the Fathers. Gregory the Great, for example, says that the words of consecration unite the Eucharistic sacrifice with that of the Passion (*Dialogues* 4. 60.2–3, SC 265.200–2). In the Middle Ages Aquinas defines a sacrifice as requiring something to be killed, poured out or eaten, and on that basis allows the Eucharist to be truly a sacrifice. Man ought to offer what God has given him. God's greatest gift to man is his Son. The perfect sacrifice is therefore Christ himself, and Christ himself connected Cross and Eucharist at the Last Supper (*Summa Theologiae* Ia2ae,q.102,a.3.c and IIIqq.83,85). Wyclif had attacked the doctrine of transubstantiation but not that of sacrifice. Lutherans had no objection to the idea that there must be satisfaction for sin. But they and other reformers rejected any implication that Christ's death on the Cross had not been sufficient for the sins of the whole world. To see the Mass as making an additional sacrifice appeared to diminish Christ's work. And to allow that the priesthood had power to 'add to' Christ's work in this way was to impute to it an authority which seemed to them a usurpation of Christ's own unique High Priestly authority (e.g. Calvin, *Institutes*, IV.18.2). It was largely for this reason that many Protestant churches refused to call their ministers 'priests' or to impute to them any 'priestly' function. In the eighteenth century, early Methodist tradition denied the priestly character of the ordained ministry, the use of an 'altar' (as distinct from a 'table') in the Eucharist, and any 'atoning or propitiatory sacrifice but the Saviour's blood' (Bowmer 1975: 227; Minutes of Conference of 1842, ix.404). Nineteenth-century Lutheran theology sustained the distinction between sacrament (God's gift to us) and sacrifice (our offering, which may include preaching). The offerings of the Church, it is still insisted, 'cannot be meritorious and atone for our offences. We must be partakers of the atoning sacrifice of Christ' (Tappert 1972: 310; Matthias Loy). The debate was revived vigorously in England in the nineteenth century. William Palmer (1803–85) published an *Origines Liturgicae* in 1832 in which he looked at early evidence that the bread and wine was seen as a sacrifice (1845: 79). The theme is sustained by Pusey in a sermon of 1841 in which he explores the ideas of the Greek Fathers. R.I. Wilberforce argues in his *The Doctrine of the Holy Eucharist* that in the Eucharist Christians participate in the mediation of Christ (1853: 347). F.D. Maurice's *The Doctrine of Sacrifice* (1854) attempts a survey from the Old Testament sacrifices to the sacrifice of Christ. One result was to bring the preoccupations of the sixteenth century once more to the forefront in evangelical circles. Nathaniel Dimock stressed in *Our One Priest on High* (1899: 84) the uniqueness and all-sufficiency of Christ's sacrifice on the Cross. Hastings Rashdall (1858–1924) revived the idea which had been current in the eleventh century that Christ's sacrifice was a ransom paid by God to Satan to free mankind (1919: 29–37; 49–56). But the notion of God as 'angry with us for what we never did' and of Christ as 'a victim laid upon the altar to appease the wrath of God' was uncongenial to Jowett (Moberly 1901: 386).

Much of the missionary endeavour which took Christianity to the New World and what is now described as the Third World was Western, although the Orthodox diaspora in the USA has created large Orthodox communities there. Missions were also denominational, and so there has been a tendency for the theology and practice of the Eucharist to reproduce that of the mother church of any given young church. There has been a strong influence of local CULTURE in some places, however, raising, for example, the question whether bread and wine ought to be replaced by the familiar local staple food and drink.

In the twentieth century the construction put upon the concept of Eucharistic sacrifice has been modified by shifts in perception and priority in society and by the pressures of the ecumenical movement. The first is nicely illustrated by Martin Luther King, who saw Christ's sacrificial act as bringing man's inward corruption out into the light where it can be healed (1964: 88). There had always been a notion of healing but it now held a stronger appeal than concepts of payment for sin by suffering and the appeasement of an angry God. In the LIBERATION THEOLOGY of South America the Eucharist is seen as the meal of liberation, betokening the freedom Christ came to bring and his kingdom in which there is no more slavery or oppression. The early Christian sense of responsibility for the poor is linked in today's thinking with the sharing of food with the hungry as something also strongly signified in the Eucharist (see CHRISTIAN SOCIALISM).

But the most significant recent advances lie in ecumenical conversations (see ECUMENICAL MOVEMENT). Here there has been an attempt to bring together the discussion of the objective reality of Christ's presence and of the sacrificial character of the Eucharist with the parallel strand of the tradition which has emphasized its character as a memorial (anamnesis). Clearly Christ intended it to be a memorial. But some of the sixteenth-century reformers, who were most anxious to avoid any suggestion that Christ's death on the Cross could be repeated or added to, pressed for the view that the Eucharist was no more than an act of 'recollection' of what Christ had done. In ecumenical statements

balance is now being restored. In the Lima Statement on *Baptism, Eucharist and Ministry* of the WORLD COUNCIL OF CHURCHES (1982) we find:

> The Eucharist is the memorial of the crucified and risen Christ, i.e. the living and effective sign of his sacrifice, accomplished once and for all upon the cross and still operative on behalf of all mankind. . . . Christ is present in this *anamnesis*, granting us communion with himself . . . . The *anamnesis* is both representation and anticipation . . . it is the Church's effective proclamation of God's almighty acts and promises.

Reformed–Roman Catholic Conversations say that 'in its joyful prayer of thanksgiving' in the Eucharist,' when the Church of Christ remembers his reconciling death . . . Christ himself is present . . . and the Church . . . becomes a living sacrifice' (Meyer and Vischer 1984: 452). The First Anglican–Roman Catholic Commission's *Final Report* says that there is 'one historical, unrepeatable sacrifice, offered once for all by Christ . . . in the celebration of the memorial, Christ in the Holy Spirit unites his people with himself . . . so that the Church enters into the movement of his self-offering' (Meyer and Vischer 1984: 69ff.).

A common Eucharist is the supreme ecumenical test that a single Church of Christ has been restored in the world. That has not yet been achieved, and complex regulations govern the admittance of communicants from one communion to the Eucharists of another. Some welcome all communicating members of other churches. Others do not.

A number of features of these developments in the understanding of the Eucharist have implications for the way society has seen itself. For more than a thousand years in medieval Europe society was made up of practising Christians. The Eucharist was the central common action of that society in its local churches. In Orthodoxy the vision of Ignatius of Antioch has been kept alive. Ignatius (*c*.35–*c*.107) gives a picture of the worshipping community gathered round a table at which the bishop presided. Sunday by Sunday he stood at the table on which were a loaf of bread and a cup of wine, and in union with his people 'made Eucharist'. This was seen as a foretaste of the very life of heaven and the bishop as the image or icon of Christ. Just as Christ draws believers into fellowship (*koinonia*) with God and one another, so the bishop becomes the focus of unity for the local church. 'Where the bishop is, there let the congregation gather, just as where Jesus Christ is, there is the catholic Church' (Ignatius, *To the Smyrnaeans*, viii.1–2; cf. ix.1). In Orthodoxy this Eucharistic focus of 'the Church in each place' remains definitive.

In the West this sense diminished, although it was never lost in principle, as the Mass gradually ceased to be a community action and became increasingly the solitary action of the priest, with the people communicating perhaps only once a year (Fourth Lateran Council, 1215, ch. 21). In an attempt to reverse this trend Protestant reformers moved to greater frequency (a minimum of three times a year in the Church of England's *Book of Common Prayer* of 1549). But their own special emphasis was upon the ministry of the Word, which they regarded as seriously neglected in the Roman Catholic Church, and so although almost all Protestant reforming communities retained the sacraments of baptism and Eucharist, their congregations came regularly to hear preaching and only comparatively infrequently met in the Lord's Supper. In recent decades of the twentieth century the Eucharist has become more consciously the central common action of the Church, e.g. in the Church of England, with the result that a 'Parish Communion' has tended to replace mattins as the main service on Sunday morning.

The question who could 'preside' at the Eucharist, i.e. say the words of consecration of the bread and wine which Christ had said, became contentious in the late medieval West. Among the Lollards some groups allowed lay persons or even women to do so. But in some congregations of today the Lord's Supper is seen as a community action in terms of a simple sharing of food and drink together by the people. But in most reforming churches of the sixteenth century and later it has been usual to insist that it should be a minister 'regularly commissioned' for the office, even if not one

given a new 'character' for life by his ordination as a priest is understood to be. Thus the image of Christ and his disciples in the motif of the pastor and people is carefully preserved.

Bowmer, J.C. (1975) *Pastor and People*, London: Epworth Press.
Dimock, Nathaniel (1899) *Our One Priest on High*, London.
Hadley, J. (1989) *Bread of the World: Christ in the Eucharist Today*, London: Darton, Longman & Todd.
King, Martin Luther (1964) *Why We Can't Wait*, New York: Signet.
Macy, G. (1984) *The Theologies of the Eucharist in the Early Medieval Period*, Oxford: Oxford University Press.
Maurice, F.D. (1854) *The Doctrine of Sacrifice*, Cambridge.
Meyer, H. and Vischer, L. (eds) (1984) *Growth in Agreement*, New York and Geneva: World Council of Churches.
Mitchell, N. (1982) *Cult and Controversy: the Worship of the Eucharist Outside Mass*, New York: Pueblo.
Moberly, R.C. (1901) *Atonement and Personality*, London.
Palmer, William (1845) *Origines Liturgicae*, 4th edn, London.
Pennington, M. Basil (1985) *The Eucharist Yesterday and Today*, Slough: St Paul Publications.
Rashdall, Hastings (1919) *The Idea of Atonement in Christian Theology*, London.
Rubin, M. (1991) *Corpus Christi. The Eucharist in Late Medieval Culture*, Cambridge: Cambridge University Press.
Stevenson, K. (1986) *Eucharist and Offering*, New York: Pueblo.
Tappert, T.G. (1972) *Lutheran Confessional Theology in America, 1840-80*, New York: Library of Protestant Thought.
Thurian, M. and Wainwright, G. (1983) *Baptism and Eucharist: Ecumenical Convergence in Celebration*, Geneva: World Council of Churches.
Wilberforce, R.I. (1853) *The Doctrine of the Holy Eucharist*, London.

G.R. Evans

EUGENICS

Eugenics is an applied science intended to improve the heritable traits of human populations. Its basic assumptions are that traits of physical and mental constitution are significantly heritable and that trait expression is subject to individual and populational variation in accordance with the laws of genetics. It is thus technically possible to breed humans using the methods of animal husbandry. This may be done by altering the frequency of a trait in a population, by enhancing or muting existing traits, by inducing new traits and by creating hybrids. The two techniques for these manipulations are the direct modification of cells (genetic engineering) and breeding.

The general aims of eugenics are usually distinguished from technical manipulations serviceable to those aims and from the implementation of eugenics measures. Any manipulation of reproduction, such as CONTRACEPTION, is potentially serviceable to eugenics, but its actual use may be eugenically random or dysgenic. Thus the current use of contraception is eugenically random since it is applied through individual choice. Yet public acceptance of voluntary contraception and other interventions in birthing indirectly promote eugenics by legitimating control of reproduction, including especially the separation of the sexual act from reproduction.

Individual reproductive choice may be channelled into eugenically directed choice. This occurs primarily through medical services, when clients accept medical advice on the advisability of MARRIAGE (genetic counselling) or of continuing a pregnancy when a birth defect has been diagnosed. The eugenic effect of these services is at present marginal because their application is limited. However, it is expected that inexpensive foetal diagnosis for a range of common genetic diseases will be integral to prenatal care within a decade. The ABORTION of most foetuses suffering impairment would perhaps have a significant eugenic effect. This service is indicative of how the eugenic concept finds technical applications and public acceptance without public canvassing of the desirability of eugenics as such. The currently accepted rationale for prenatal diagnosis is in the first instance to provide parents with the opportunity for informed choice; in the second instance it reduces claims on strained health budgets. The rationale for comprehensive prenatal diagnosis appeals in addition to the elimination of SUFFERING from genetic diseases. None of these legitimations is eugenic, but the expected outcome is.

The eugenics idea is probably very ancient. It seems to be implied by the rules of marriage that reproductively isolated aristocratic castes, and by the hygiene rules that such castes sometimes imposed. The earliest record of a proposal to apply animal husbandry to a human population occurs in Plato's *Republic*, where the breeding of a superior type is said to be necessary for the construction of a truly just political order. Aristotle rejected the proposal as impracticable but made no criticism on ethical grounds; the proposal had no uptake in the subsequent tradition of political philosophy. But there was indirect absorption through the Utopian literature that took shape in the Renaissance. In tandem with human breeding, Plato proposed to abolish the FAMILY and PROPERTY, since he held that the selfish basis of these two institutions inhibits full communal sharing (COMMUNISM). Some Christian moralists, notably St Thomas More (1477–1535), praised the abolition of property to highlight the selfless charity wanting in actual societies, but by 1800 these notions had entered the armoury of socialist thought as seriously entertained reform ideals. Their wide diffusion was part of the ferment about family and marriage characteristic of nineteenth-century progressive thought.

The term 'eugenics' was coined by Charles Darwin's cousin Sir Francis Galton (1822–1911) in 1883. Galton's idea soon became fashionable among socialists, feminists, writers, philosophers, scientists, entrepreneurs, politicians and reformers. It was deplored by conservatives and by religious faiths that opposed other social novelties. The eugenics idea quickly spread into population and public health policy formation, resulting in the advocacy of sterilization and birth control. By 1925, sterilization laws were in force in some thirty jurisdictions of nine nations. However, the Hitler government's linkage of eugenics with RACISM, and the subsequent complicity of eugenics in GENOCIDE, brought the concept into disrepute. Nevertheless, medical and scientific cadres continued to espouse voluntary eugenics measures in the postwar period. From 1960 a spectrum of procedures, notably genetic screening and abortion of foetuses with birth defects, spread through medical practice. Bench-marks for the postwar validation of eugenics are the development of genetic engineering and its commercial application to plant and animal production and to numerous medical purposes, including recently gene therapy for heritable diseases; the emergence of a consumer demand for technology-enhanced birthing options and the legitimation of these demands in law; the institutional prominence of bioethical justifications for human genetic engineering and for a variety of practices requisite to a eugenics programme, e.g. EUTHANASIA and abortion; and finally the emergence of a medico-economic concept (the quality-adjusted life year) that grades patients on a cost–benefit 'quality of life' index that identifies the point at which the withdrawal of care is indicated.

Eugenics is inherently linked to its contrary effect, dysgenics. In the last century, dysgenic phenomena were known as 'degeneration' or 'decadence'. Its study was pursued by medical scientists (B.M. Morel) and criminologists (Cesare Lombroso), who purported to demonstrate that dispositions to CRIME, disease, alcoholism, disability, mental retardation and mental illness were partly or strongly heritable. They also believed that changing reproductive patterns in modern society tended to increase the incidence of these dysgenic traits. This anxiety was heightened by recognition that infant and child mortality rates had fallen substantially in recent times, so that many 'defectives' who previously had left no progeny now produced offspring. Galton situated his quantitative studies of trait heritability in this context. 'It would be quite practical', he wrote in *Hereditary Genius*, 'to produce a highly gifted race of men by judicious marriages during several consecutive generations.' This sentiment was echoed by many, notably the philosopher Friedrich Nietzsche and the playwright George Bernard Shaw. In this century it has been affirmed by many leading biologists.

Galton's conceptual innovation consisted of unifying the evidence on inheritance with Darwin's evolutionary theory to produce eugenics as the applied science of human EVOLUTION. The core of this concept is natural selection. Darwin's theory holds that the evolution of ever more complex organization is driven by selection pressure which, like '100,000 sharp wedges', continuously deletes the weaker and maladapted. The ensuing 'struggle for existence' accumulates adaptive genetic changes that refine

species into higher types. Galton followed Darwin and Herbert Spencer in the belief that the evolution of the human species as well as the evolution of CULTURE were driven by intergroup struggle for existence in which the weak were eliminated.

These notions lead to the 'paradox of civilization' at the heart of eugenics. The paradox is that civilization tends toward its own dissolution thanks to the expansive moral sympathy characteristic of civilized law. Civilized sympathy extends sufferance or care to dysgenic individuals who in barbarous conditions are outcast, perish from disease or are executed as criminals. By staying the rigour of natural selection, sympathy enhances the reproduction of degenerate types, which in time become economic and moral burdens that return civilization to barbarism.

The eugenic response to this paradox is to replace the effects of natural selection, which are brutal, by humane, rational selection based on knowledge of inheritance. One requires in effect a comprehensive population policy aiming to control human evolution, whose two modes are the arrest of dysgenic reproduction ('negative eugenics') and the enhancement of eugenic reproduction ('positive eugenics'). The notion that all human beings are of equal worth, or are entitled to the same rights, is inconsistent with eugenics. Eugenics is also opposed to the notion that behaviour and attitudes are in the main socially learned. Galton inaugurated the science of behaviour genetics through his statistical methods for the study of inheritance, especially intelligence (IQ) and personality. He was the first to use twins and family genealogies as tests for trait heritability. His general conclusions, that variation in human performance in most skills depends significantly on inheritance, and that numerous diseases including alcoholism are genetically related, are today in some measure supported by the findings of medical and behaviour genetics.

Galton also believed, consistent with Darwin's concept of evolutionary divergence, that trait distributions change at the boundaries of breeding populations. Racial differences are one such boundary; ethnic differences are another. Galton concurred with Darwin and Herbert Spencer that the traits which had enabled

European nations to achieve world dominance were significantly heritable; accordingly, European ascendancy owed something to differential racial fitness. This founds an anthropology that grades peoples on a scale of adaptiveness to civilization. That peoples can be so graded was regarded as obvious by most anthropologists at the turn of the century. Today such views are sometimes styled 'scientific racism'. Continuing research on this question has not unequivocally demonstrated that there are significant racial differences in behavioural traits, but informed opinion does not rule out the possibility.

The rapid uptake of the eugenics idea owes much to its resonance with many streams of nineteenth-century thought. Eugenics spoke to the dread of degeneration, which was widespread despite the European ascendency. It sketched a technocratic plan for the creation of new élites to replace the class organization of the vanishing old order. It was a bold application of scientific knowledge in an age infatuated with the marvels of science and technology. It was an application of the evolutionary idea at a time when Darwinian theory was absorbed as the secular theodicy of progress. And it injected a novel scientific perspective into the extensive controversy about SEXUALITY, family and population.

The ferment of ideas together with increased social mobility and rapidly changing life possibilities stimulated openness to social EXPERIMENTATION. By mid-nineteenth century, debate on the future of the family and the status of women was commonplace, while utilitarian and socialist intellectuals were dreaming of far-reaching reform. It was appreciated that any significant change in the status of women required that each woman have technical control of her reproduction and the moral autonomy to use it. Consequently, agitation for women's equality was often accompanied by agitation for the free flow of information about contraception. This intervention separates reproduction from the natural consequences of the sexual act; such control is indispensable to eugenics. Perceiving eugenics to be an ally in disenchanting mandatory motherhood', feminists incorporated it into the campaign for sexual equality. Thus Victoria Woodhull invoked 'the scientific propagation

of the human race' to justify sex education and emancipation of women, while Margaret Sanger, the founder of the Planned Parenthood Association, extolled contraception as the key to the higher development of Western civilization. The alliance between eugenics and FEMINISM, which was cemented by 1900, was reciprocal. Darwin and Galton endorsed the emancipation of women, as did numerous eugenics popularizers. Havelock Ellis espoused eugenics and freeing sexuality from restraints imposed by marital fidelity and fear of illegitimacy. In 1924, the geneticist J.B.S. Haldane proposed extra-corporal gestation, a concept popularized in Aldous Huxley's classic eugenics novel, *Brave New World*. During the 1930s, the advocacy of eugenics was led in the USA by the Nobel geneticist Hermann Muller, who espoused the eugenic uses of artificial insemination, and in Britain by Sir Julian Huxley, who emphasized the eugenic uses of POPULATION CONTROL. Both were alarmed by the deterioration of genetic stock and by the tendency of traditional marriage customs to reinforce deterioration. As first Director-General of UNESCO, Huxley helped entrench world population control into the United Nations agenda.

The relationship of eugenics to Nazi eugenic and racial measures has been clarified by recent scholarship. It now appears that German medical science was the critical institutional link between Weimar and Nazi eugenics. In the Weimar Republic, German science was highly developed as a profession organized largely as public service cohorts in universities and health facilities. German scientific medicine thus formed cohesive professional groups capable of formulating public policy. It interpreted medicine to have, in addition to traditional responsibilities to patients, a higher responsibility to public health, which in turn enhanced national POWER. Thanks to this hierarchy of ends, health and hygiene became metaphors of renewal in a society beset by the trauma of defeat, class conflict, familial dislocation, political uncertainty and ambivalence toward technology. Health was projected as a path of duty that supplied a detailed personal and familial regimen – an ethical practice of fitness – while rehabilitating technological values by making them serve the unchallenged value of a healthy nation. Popular culture was thus linked with a scientific élite in a coalition for national solidarity. By propagating eugenic doctrine as moral duty that subordinated individuals to the future good, the structure to support Galton's hoped-for 'eugenics religion' was established.

An enduring contribution of the German medical bureaucracy was to interpret eugenics as a decision criterion in the equity of health care fund allocation. The link concept was triage – the notion that when shortness of time or resources prevent all patients receiving due care, those with the best prognosis should receive first care. Eugenicists proposed that resources should be allocated on the basis of patient health status, prognosis and likely contribution to the national genetic heritage. It was argued that involuntary eugenic sterilization and abortion were needful to relieve health budgets of avoidable burdens. Euthanasia, long recognized as a negative eugenics measure, was given a comparable socio-economic interpretation. Euthanasia was believed to be indicated for patients of low quality of life, on equity grounds, as it was also indicated by compassion for those patients themselves. Birth defects, handicaps, imbecility, senility, chronic illness and genetic disease were among the conditions for which euthanasia was indicated. The phrase 'life unworthy of life' was coined to signify this class of persons.

Eugenic advocacy was not confined to public sector health establishments in Weimar Germany. Modernist elements of the Lutheran and Catholic confessions, whose influence was exercised through their health and welfare services, were eugenics proponents. The encyclical on Christian marriage, *Casti conubii* (1930), took notice of these attitudes. While its focus was primarily on abortion, the encyclical sought a middle way with eugenics concerns. It acknowledged the legitimacy of preventative measures so long as they did not deny care to any person. Sterilization was not deemed to be consistent with charity. However, the modernists were not greatly restrained by *Casti conubii*. While they stopped short of endorsing euthanasia and abortion, they continued to use invidious distinctions, e.g. the 'inferior', 'hopeless cases', 'useless eaters', 'unworthy of life', and some maintained

that the protection of the moral law did not extend to these categories of persons. Traditionalists argued that this posture was equivalent to endorsing euthanasia.

It therefore seems that numerous conceptual, attitudinal and institutional elements of Nazi eugenics date from the Weimar Republic. Indeed, the medical and scientific personnel who manned the Nazi eugenic programme, including the extermination, were recruited from Weimar institutions. The Nazi innovation consists in three things: the implementation of a eugenics religion that related individual and social hygiene to commanding national goals; a political will for a comprehensive population policy that interpreted international relations as the fateful Darwinian struggle of nations for existence; and the identification of the Jewish people as the most dangerous of degenerates.

The discovery of the molecular structure of DNA (1953) and subsequently the development of genetic engineering fired the scientific imagination with the promise of 'boundless possibilities' for manipulating life. These innovations coincided with the widespread use of the contraceptive pill and the experiments in living associated with the sexual revolution. The popular media, recognizing the sensation of depicting science as a prime mover of unprecedented social change, gave this linkage a high profile. So did philosophers and theologians for more serious reasons. The new field of bioethics emerged from these initial debates on the ethics of eugenics, stirred by the fresh euphoria of schemes for the far-reaching modification of the human species. The key statements for this period were the encyclical *Humanae Vitae* (1968), Paul Ramsey's *Fabricated Man: The Ethics of Genetic Control* (1970) and Joseph Fletcher's *The Ethics of Genetic Control: Ending Reproductive Roulette* (1974). The first two works affirmed the unity of the procreative and sexual functions, holding that the separation of the two by eugenics or by consumer attitudes toward sex offended human dignity. Fletcher by contrast cast current eugenic thinking into the language of 'situation ethics'. The definitive human situation is that man is free to make of his future what he can and what he will. Nature provides no standards for human conduct because human action consists not least in altering and transcending nature. The highest transcendence for Fletcher is, as Nietzsche had said before, the surpassing of natural man by refashioning the species.

The decades since have largely confirmed forecasts of scientific developments. Layer after layer of behaviour and personality are being stripped back to their genetic roots. At the same time the manipulation of the roots and their offshoots in other somatic properties advances at a dizzying pace. Especially notable are advances in immune response suppression that supports an ever-expanding tissue transplantation technology, whose horizon seems to be the capacity to pair tissue at will; and the Human Genome Project (HUGO), whose objective is the complete mapping of the human genome. The knowledge acquired through this project will yield the potential for a complete genetic 'fingerprint' of each person, together with its interpretation for personality traits and life course events. It will be of great relevance in evaluating the technical feasibility of the eugenic aspiration.

The public perception of this aspiration is another matter. The central promise of the sexual revolution, the use of sexuality as guilt-free, unpossessive self-expression, now seems to have been a temporary relaxation of the emotional ties and other constraints that traditionally confined sexuality to marriage. Perhaps the most significant indicator of this change is not the restraint imposed by the AIDS epidemic but the new austerity of manners introduced by the feminists, who once spearheaded the repudiation of manners. Feminists have also turned aggressively against the reproductive technologies that formerly were emblems of emancipation from mandatory motherhood. In Germany, a coalition of feminists, Greens, anti-nuclear activists and associations for the handicapped has placed the previous experiment with eugenics back on the public agenda by strong opposition to euthanasia. Their concern is that the triage principle, which ranks people by estimated quality of life with a view to rationally administering death, threatens all the disabled.

Scientists seem to be unaware that the bid to preside over life and death lays claim to the most awesome power in human society. Medical interventions already practised and those promised for the future do not inspire confidence that the wisdom of eugenicists is more than the mechanic's flair for stunning effects. The brief experience with handling truly awesome power, nuclear energy, resulted in weapons of ultimate destruction. Opening the human genome to manipulation is a comparable power whose effects may be other than those promised.

Blacker, C.P. (1952) *Eugenics: Galton and After*, London: Duckworth.

Chamberlain, J.E. and Gilman, S.L. (eds) (1985) *Degeneration: The Dark Side of Progress*, Ithaca, NY: Columbia University Press.

Farrell, D.L.A. (1985) *The Origins and Growth of the English Eugenics Movement, 1865–1925*, New York: Garland.

Fletcher, Joseph (1974) *The Ethics of Genetic Control: Ending Reproductive Roulette*, New York: Anchor.

Hubbard, Ruth (1990) *The Politics of Woman's Biology*, New Brunswick, NJ: Rutgers University Press.

Huxley, Julian (1964) *Essays of a Humanist*, London: Chatto & Windus.

Kevles, Daniel J. (1985) *In the Name of Eugenics: Genetics and the Uses of Human Heredity*, New York: Knopf.

Nowak, Kurt (1977) *'Euthanasie' und Sterilisation im 'Dritten Reich'*, Göttingen: Vandehoeck & Ruprecht.

Ramsay, Paul (1970) *Fabricated Man: The Ethics of Genetic Control*, New Haven, CT: Yale University Press.

Sears, Hal D. (1977) *The Sex Radicals: Free Love in High Victorian America*, Kansas City, KS: University of Kansas Press.

Weindling, Paul (1989) *Health, Race and German Politics between National Unification and Nazism, 1879–1945*, Cambridge: Cambridge University Press.

Hiram Caton

EUROPEAN INTEGRATION

European integration is the process of bringing together European nation states to achieve 'an ever closer union among the European peoples'. The process aims to promote economic and social progress by securing the free movement of goods, services, capital and people within a community of nation-states. This community became the European Union in November 1993. Any European state with a democratic system of GOVERNMENT is eligible to apply for membership.

Institutionally, the European Union originated in the European Coal and Steel Community (ECSC), founded in 1951, the European Economic Community (EEC) and the European Atomic Energy Community (EURATOM), both founded by the Treaty of Rome in 1957. The three communities were merged in 1965; with the 1986 Single European Act (SEA), the communities became the European Community (EC). The founder members were France, the German Federal Republic, Italy, Belgium, The Netherlands and Luxembourg. The United Kingdom, Ireland and Denmark became members in 1973, followed by Greece (1981), Spain and Portugal (1986). Austria, Sweden and Finland will become full members by 1996. Further applications are anticipated from several recently independent East European states. Applications from Turkey, Malta and Cyprus have been unsuccessful.

As the process of European integration is intended to create a community of peoples, not an international government, a distinction is drawn between *formal integration* and *informal integration*. Formal integration is constituted in a set of supranational and inter-governmental institutions and economic agreements, along with supporting organizations and informal networks. The European Comission and the European Court are supranational institutions, charged to implement European Union treaties and policies. The Council of Ministers and the European Council are inter-governmental fora for resolving conflicts of national interests between member states. The European Parliament, the only democratic institution in the Union, has developed a vigorously supranational outlook. Informal integration refers to interactions among firms, public agencies, interest groups, communication networks and citizens of member-states. The purpose of formal integration is to promote informal integration: to attain, as expressed by Karl Deutsch, an early theorist of European integration, 'within a territory, a sense of community and of institutions and practices strong enough and widespread enough to assure, for a long time, dependable expectations of peaceful change among its population'. Together, the two processes are envisaged to create a common economic, social and political life among the citizens of the European Union.

The 'idea of Europe', as a common civilization upon which to found a unified political order, has a long history in which European unity has remained the constant objective but the underlying philosophy has undergone several transformations. The universalism of the Roman Empire and Christendom inspired early advocates, such as Abbé Dubois's proposal (1306) for an assembly of European princes and the scheme by the Duc de Sully, minister to Henry IV of France, for a 'Great Republic' of Europe. During the seventeenth century, the lawlessness of sovereign powers prompted a profusion of designs; most were the disguised hegemonic ambitions of powerful rulers. The growth of LIBERALISM and democratic ideas in the eighteenth century shifted the focus to the intellectual unity of Europe, rooted in rationalism, epitomized in Immanuel Kant's treatise *Towards Perpetual Peace* (1795) advocating a federation of free states governed by mutually agreed laws. Jean-Jacques Rousseau and Jeremy Bentham both proposed schemes for European federation; Saint-Simon's design for a European Parliament and government inspired several early peace movements. But nineteenth-century thinking about the state was dominated by nationalist ideologies, portraying the state as the embodiment of 'the nation' – leading Nietzsche to rail against 'the morbid hostility which the madness of nationalism has created among the nations of Europe' (Nietzsche 1966).

The founding of the League of Nations in 1918 signalled the beginnings of institutionalized supranationalism to secure international PEACE. But the emergence, at the same time, of several new European states, together with the drift into economic autarchy during the inter-war period, left the idea of European unity fatally vulnerable to fascist movements. Even so, the inter-war period witnessed the emergence of a myriad of loosely associated groups advocating a federation of European states to ensure the preservation of peace; the Pan-European Union, founded by Count Coundenhove-Kalergi (1923), was the most influential. With the growing strength of the American and Japanese economies, leading to fears of economic stagnation and forebodings about the survival of European civilization, integrationist thinking widened to include economic union. Amongst the plethora of literature emerging from this dispersed but vigorous European movement, Paul Valéry's influential *La Crise de l'esprit* (1919) urged a 'swift revival of the inexhaustible wealth of ideas', rooted in Greek rationalism, Roman law and the Christian gospel, which was the common heritage of the European peoples; in *The Revolt of the Masses* (1929), Ortega y Gasset extolled the 'common European stock' of ideas enjoyed by peoples of diverse language and political experience. But the European movement, confined to small sections of the intelligentsia, made little impact on the governments or political parties of the day. The presentation of the Briand Memorandum (1929) to the Assembly of the League of Nations was the first occasion that a proposal for a form of European union reached an international forum; it was swiftly smothered by Britain, Italy and Germany. Until after the Second World War, the 'idea of Europe' remained a distant ideal.

The influence of the WAR was complex. During the war, national Resistance leaders developed their visions of a new post-war order. Although operating in isolation, the common core of their designs drew on doctrines of Christian personalism to denounce nationalism as 'intellectual totalitarianism': as nation-states had proved 'instruments of disaster', European peace was to be secured by a supranational AUTHORITY, elected by the peoples of a federal Europe and committed to upholding religious and political rights. In their *Manifesto di Ventotene* (1941), Altiero Spinelli and Ernesto Rossi condemned the elevation of national sovereignty into a 'divine essence' at the expense of human dignity and individual FREEDOM; the creation of European unity was the condition for ensuring peace, HUMAN RIGHTS and personal WELFARE. Towards the end of the war, as the scale of devastation and the dominance of America and the Soviet Union emerged, and with memories of the Depression still vivid, Resistance arguments for European unity were extended to urge the creation of a common European market and the forging of a European voice in international affairs. A unified Europe was the condition for economic revitalization, the preservation of European values, and Europe's standing in the postwar world.

After the war, with the return to normal political life and the urgency of reconstruction, the influence of Resistance leaders faded. The Allied powers were preoccupied with reasserting national AUTONOMY, the containment of Soviet power and the status of a divided Germany. Britain's wartime role and Winston Churchill's several references to building a 'kind of United States of Europe' had encouraged European idealists to look to Britain to champion European union after the war; Britain chose, instead, to focus on the Empire and the 'special relationship' with the USA. By 1947, however, concerted action was demanded to rehabilitate the European economy and to secure Western Europe against the spread of COMMUNISM. In this, the influence of the USA was decisive. The Truman Doctrine (1947), pledging American support for democratic regimes, indicated a closer political relationship between the USA and Western Europe; the Economic Recovery Programme (1947), better known as the Marshall Plan, offered economic aid on the condition that European governments co-ordinated their economic planning. The Organisation of European Economic Cooperation (OEEC), the forerunner of the OECD, was created to administer the Marshall Plan, so becoming the first permanent organization charged with ensuring co-operation among West European states. The defence of Western Europe was also brought under American leadership, in the North Atlantic Treaty Organization (NATO), in 1949. Thus, the first steps in converting the 'idea of Europe' into a political reality were instigated not by the European powers themselves but by American intervention motivated by Cold War considerations.

The European ideal, however, found expression in other initiatives. The European Movement was established at the Congress of Europe (1948), leading to the founding of the Council of Europe (1949) – the first success in attempts to institutionalize political co-operation in Western Europe. Established in Strasbourg, with a Consultative Assembly and a Committee of Ministers, the Council of Europe achieved useful advances, drawing up the European Convention

for the Protection of Human Rights and Fundamental Freedoms (1950), establishing the European Court of Justice (1959) and promoting a
European Social Charter (1961). The remit of
the Council, however, due to British and Scandi-
navian insistence on nothing more than co-operation, was to foster 'greater unity' between its
members, not the economic and political union
called for by the European Movement. The
Council of Europe remains the most encompassing of several West European organizations; by
the mid-1970s, all West European states were
members, including Turkey, Cyprus and Malta.
It is also the organization most open to the new
East European regimes seeking institutional
links with Western Europe after emerging from
Soviet tutelage in 1989.

Independently of the ferment of international
linkage after the war, persisting fears of a resurgent Germany led to a unilateral French initiative to stabilize Franco-German relations by
establishing the ECSC. The Schuman Plan,
drafted by Jean Monnet, head of the French
Planning Commission, was designed to render
another war between Germany and France 'materially impossible' by pooling their coal and
steel resources under supranational control. The
opportunity for economic co-operation to sustain their fragile economies led Italy and the
Benelux countries to join with France and Germany. The goals of the ECSC were 'economic
expansion, growth of employment, and a rising
standard of living' amongst member states.
Equally significant was the ECSC's institutional
structure: a supranational High Authority with
executive power: a Council of Ministers representing national governments; a Common Assembly of representatives from member states; a
Court of Justice with jurisdiction over the High
Authority and member states. Although resistance to *dirigisme* limited the ECSC's effectiveness, it provided the blueprint for realizing
several separate initiatives, by the Council of
Europe, the OEEC, the Benelux countries, the
United States of Europe Action Committee, to
create a Common Market amongst West European states. These efforts, under Franco-
German leadership, culminated in the founding
of the EEC.

Early challenges to the EEC came from the
European Free Trade Association (EFTA), organized by Britain (1960) as a counterweight to
the EEC, and from France with General de
Gaulle's demand for a veto to protect national
interests, institutionalized in the 'Luxembourg
compromise' (1966). The enlargements altered
the internal dynamics of the EEC: British and
Danish membership brought in countries hostile
to political integration; the entry of Greece,
Spain and Portugal introduced less advanced
economies. *Negative integration*, the removal
of barriers to trade, proved relatively easy to
achieve, but the development of common economic policies – *positive integration* – has been
hampered by conflicts of national interest. The
oil crises and recessions of the 1970s provoked a
revival of protectionism. In the late 1980s, the
collapse of Soviet hegemony in Eastern Europe
led to fears about Germany's commitment to
European integration: it also encouraged Britain
to press for a 'wider' community, based on
economic co-operation to incorporate the newly
autonomous states, rather than the 'deeper'
union implied by political integration.

The SEA was a major initiative to overcome
the institutional stasis of the 1970s. It provided
for the completion of the common market, entailing the removal of all border controls on
the movement of people and goods between
member states and, under the terms of the European Monetary System and the Exchange Rate
Mechanism, the abolition of all exchange controls on the movement of capital and services.
The SEA also introduced some measure of institutional reform, especially replacing unanimity
with qualified majority voting in the Council of
Ministers and extending the competence of the
European Parliament. The Maastricht Treaty
sought to strengthen the integrity of the EC by
pushing forward towards political integration.
The treaty extended the *acquis communautaire*
beyond trade and economic policy to include
co-operation in home affairs and the development of common policies in foreign affairs and
security with the aim of arriving, eventually, at
a common defence policy. With the exception
of Britain, the treaty committed EC member
states to the completion of Economic and Monetary Union, entailing steady progression towards fixed exchange rates and a common

currency, and the implemention of the Social Chapter to protect the rights of employees and citizens.

Despite the evident success of the European enterprise, in establishing viable institutions, harmonizing the economies of member states and achieving extensive informal integration, it remains riven with tensions and contradictions. In part, these arise from the different logics governing European institutions. The supranationalism of the European Commission confronts the inter-governmentalism of the Council of Ministers and the European Council; the technocratic ethos of the Commission sits uncomfortably with the political traditions of member states and the democratic ethos of the European Parliament. The one uncontested institution is the European Court; European law supersedes national law and judgements on actors in the community are binding. Its consistent record of expansive rulings to uphold the *acquis communautaire* has rendered the Court the principal anchor of European integration. The principal objective of European institutions, to provide for common policy making, is undermined by disparities in the economic and social development of member states; accommodating these disparities, by allowing *derogations* from EC law and advancing the principle of *subsidiarity* in decision making, entails enduring fragmentation. Moreover, the boundaries of the Union and the institutional form for political union remain to be established.

European integration is similarly hampered by ideological conflicts. The Common Market is governed by the principle of *comparative advantage*, a modern expression of the liberal free-trade tradition. The economic and social costs to labour and 'loser' groups run counter to the welfare traditions of social democracy and Christian democracy; the efficiencies attained from the Common Market tend to benefit the advanced economies, exacerbating the problems of uneven development, and thereby hollowing out the concept of a community of peoples. The federal model for political union is seen by nationalists as a threat to the autonomy of the nation-state; the looser model of economic integration and political co-operation is seen by integrationists to cripple the concept of

European unity. Political leaders have relied on a rhetoric of national advantage to mobilize public support for the European Union – hence the paradox of the citizens of nation-states becoming harnessed to 'the European ideal' in the name of national identity. A coherent IDEOLOGY expressing the values and purposes of European integration remains to be articulated.

The early history of European integration was the preserve of intellectuals and visionaries inspired by great traditions in European ideas: the rule of LAW; the legitimacy of democratic institutions; respect for individual rights; the obligation to protect the weak against the strong. The pursuit of integration, however, has been dominated by economic thinking and technocratic skills. In Monnet's original scheme, economic integration was the precursor to political union: the progressive integration of the economies of 'the Six' would have 'spillover' effects, leading, in time, to political union. But as economic integration has engaged national rivalries, and the imperatives of international competition have become more urgent, political integration has come to be the condition for progress towards economic integration. Economic goals have overtaken political goals, thus rendering European integration vulnerable to economic dislocation and the enduring hold of nationalism. The revival of racism and xenophobia during the early 1990s cast dark shadows over the economic successes of European integration. Political union remains the goal of integrationist thinking but the fulfilment of the European ideal waits on further waves of idealism.

Deutsch, K. *et al.* (1957) *Political Community and the North Atlantic Area*, New York: Greenwood.

Haas, E. (1958) *The Uniting of Europe*, Stanford, CA: Stanford University Press.

Hallstein, W. (1972) *Europe in the Making*, London: Allen & Unwin.

Lipgens, W. (1982) *A History of European Integration*, vol. 1, Oxford: Clarendon.

Monnet, J. (1978) *Memoirs*, London: Collins.

Nietzsche, F.W. (1966) *Beyond Good and Evil*, New York: Vintage Books.

Nugent, N. (1991) *The Government and Politics of the European Community*, Basingstoke: Macmillan.

Ortega y Gasset, J. (1929) *The Revolt of the Masses*, reprinted London: Norton, 1963.

Urwin, D. (1991) *The Community of Europe*, London: Longman.

Valéry, P. (1919) *La Crise de l'Esprit*, Paris: *New Athenaeum*, April – May

Wistrich, E. (1994) *The United States of Europe*, London: Routledge.

Elinor Scarbrough

EUTHANASIA

The word euthanasia is derived from co-joining the Greek *eu*, good or well with the Greek *thanatos*, DEATH. Hence the word taken literally means good or well dying, its opposite is *eudaimoneia* from good or well being; a flourishing of the whole spirit-body. Within the context of a heroic or saga culture, a good death might be a violent yet heroic death in battle, whereas a death in a crippled, infirm and senile old age would not be a good death and would not be fitting for a hero. In such a culture a good death is a death fitting the life and not unfitting to it. The death of Socrates, by self administered hemlock, while premature, was fitting of the man. In modern western societies euthanasia, and the related issue of physician assisted SUICIDE, have generally been viewed with legal and moral disfavour. Currently euthanasia, while not a legal right, is tolerated in some circumstances in the Netherlands and there have been some attempts to change the law in some areas of the United States. In Washington, Initiative 119, which failed at the ballot in 1991, sought to legalize euthanasia. One year later in California, Proposition 161 sought to permit euthanasia for the competent patient with less than six months to live. In the Netherlands, an attempt to legalize euthanasia failed, but by common understanding no prosecution will be entered against a doctor who administers euthanasia according to strict guidelines. In all these cases the attempt to legalize euthanasia failed by relatively small margins. In the US attempts in the early part of the 1990s to prevent the physician Jack Kevorkian in making his well publicized 'suicide machine' available to patients failed. The book, *Final Exit*, a practical manual for suicide became a bestseller. In the UK Nigel Cox, a physician, administered a terminally ill patient a lethal dose of potassium chloride. As the body had been cremated and no post-mortem was possible he was charged with, and found guilty of, attempted homicide. He was given a one year suspended custodial sentence and allowed to continue to practice medicine. It is clear from these and other examples that euthanasia and the related issue of assisted suicide, will become prime moral issues in many western countries in the near future.

What was almost unthinkable for fifteen hundred years, that the surrender of life should be at a time of one's own choosing, has become not only thinkable but the subject of active campaigning and support by numerous people. That this should be so is due to a sea change in contemporary attitudes to life, death and SUFFERING. This has been coupled with epidemiological changes in the prime causes of death and alterations in the age distribution of western populations. It is not possible to link this sea change together with epidemiological and age range alterations as formal cause and effect, but their inter-relation is clear enough.

The sea change in attitude toward euthanasia and assisted suicide is a consequence of the growing value placed on personal AUTONOMY and mutable religious values. Objections to either euthanasia, to suicide or to assisted suicide are not universally found, and indeed not found unequivocally in the foundations of our own CULTURE. The original formulation of the Hippocratic Oath forbids a physician to take the life of a patient, but in Ancient Greece many non-Hippocratic physicians would supply hemlock when the pain and suffering of a patient was unbearable. In Rome self-inflicted death was a choice offered to some who had fallen from favour. In other cultures self-imposed death may accompany the death of a husband, as in the practice of suttee, or may accompany a loss of honour, as in the Japanese practice of Hara-Kiri. Western attitudes towards the timing of death hardened with the growth of Christianity, although as Battin has argued, this may be because Christianity among all the major religions most favours suicide and, therefore, requires stricter prohibition than might be found in other religions (Battin 1994: 206). In neither the New Testament nor in the Hebrew Bible are there clear and explicit interdictions against suicide, assisted suicide or euthanasia. Killing is interdicted frequently as at Genesis 9:5, in the Decalogue and in numerous subsequent passages, but this is always interpretable as wrongful or unjustified killing and not as killing *per se*. The failure to mention suicide or euthanasia may have been widespread at that period. Indeed Hankoff thinks that there may have been no prohibition against suicide in Early Near Eastern cultures (Hankoff 1979: 5). On some accounts suicide would not have been considered because of the tribal nature of the life of the times. Yet one of the most striking and earliest pieces of extant poetry, dating from the late second, or early third millennium BCE is the dialogue of a 'young man with his soul', recounted in Pritchard, in which the poet exhibits a personal angst and reflection on the possibility of the nearness of and appropriateness of an early death; sentiments that are familiar even now. In the final stanzas he decides in favour of prematurely ending his life and his SOUL vows that it will stay with him notwithstanding his action. That such a poem can reach across such a gap in time and culture, shows a similarity of psyche that defies some of the more relativistic readings of human being; readings that would prohibit such trans-cultural sentiments.

Early and explicit Christian interdictions against suicide, and by implication euthanasia, rest on the claim that God is the author of life. The implication of this is well represented in, for example, St Augustine of Hippo's view that it would be wrong for the authority to end one's life to be placed with oneself. On this criterion judicial killing, execution for the commission of crime, would be permissible (*City of God*, Bk. I, chap 21) but suicide and euthanasia would be wrong. The Biblical source for such specific prohibition and permissions is unclear, but Augustine may well have been influenced through Plotinus by Plato, who had certainly held that life was a gift of God. Subsequent arguments to similar effect are generally and widely found in Christian doctrine. Pope John Paul II placed such a high value on human life in the encyclical *Evangelium vitae* that not only was contraception, abortion and euthanasia regarded as immoral judicial killing, capital punishment was thought to be rarely if ever

justified. Of euthanasia the encyclical goes so far as to make it a crime,

> . . . which no human law can claim to legitimise. There is no obligation in conscience to obey such laws; instead there is a grave and clear obligation to oppose them by conscientious objection.
>
> (*Evangelium Vitae* 1995)

The respect for life found in theological doctrines have found secular counterparts in the stress on the importance of individual life found in liberal individualism. John Locke, one of the founders of the view that came to be recognized as liberalism, expressed in his 'workmanship model', the idea that life was a gift and made it the foundation of his political theory. A human may not, he argued, take their own life, for that was the absolute possession of God, but they may, indeed must, use their life to best advantage for they were sent by God to do his work and they were his property (Locke 1960). While they had control over their own body and possession over their own work this was control and possession as *use*, as trust, not as absolute and unfettered ownership; only God had that. The philosopher Immanuel Kant expanded the interdiction against suicide, and by implication euthanasia, to cover all rational beings. It was, he argued, contrary to the Categorical Imperative to take one's own life; no being could rationally will such an act for that would imply that one willed the end of all rational life, and that, he argued was rationally inconsistent. In all of these cases it is held that God, not people, is the arbiter of the end of life. Life is a trust, or a loan from God and not one's own to take. Insofar as one owns one's life it is the ownership of trust, it is not absolute: ultimately its beginning and its end belong to God and not to one's self.

Yet just as the Christian perspective fostered a view that life belongs ultimately to God so it also provided the intellectual mechanism for undercutting that claim. St Augustine's prohibition against suicide and by extension euthanasia was part of a wider view that also included the generation of the idea of FREE WILL. The arguments surrounding that and the Pelagian heresy are complex but it was a clear and strong conception of freedom of will that found its way into the model of the autonomous rational being of Kant's thought. That autonomous being was constrained from suicide and euthanasia in Kant's thought but not elsewhere, for the rationality of autonomy rather than interdicting euthanasia and suicide actually permits it. The idea of the sanctity and importance of individual life reflected in philosophical and theological thought in Western Christian culture has formed part of the foundation of the idea of personal autonomy. If a meaningful life is an autonomous life then, by extension, the final exercise of that autonomy encompasses the timing and manner of one's own death. To have a life of one's own implies that one has a death, or at least a dying of one's own and that, on some accounts, has internally exploded the patriarchal view that the manner and timing of one's death and dying are solely a matter for God, rather than for one's self.

The tendency to favour oneself in weighting decisions about the end of an autonomous life has been encouraged by the artificial prolongation of life. That artificial prolongation of life is itself often regarded as unnatural. Hence, in such cases, to take charge of it may well be in keeping with the Christian view of life rather than contrary to it. A requirement for a burdensome or excessive prolongation of life is nowhere advocated in Christian doctrine. In such cases, where life is artificially and painfully or burdensomely prolonged there is no imperative to prolong it by artificial means. In such cases it is widely accepted that treatment may, properly, be withdrawn. But, if treatment may be withdrawn in such cases, and that withdrawal leads to a painful death why, it has been argued may the life not be ended comfortably by active intervention?

The issues here have tended to rest on a number of distinctions common throughout the debates on euthanasia. A real fear in any discussion of euthanasia is based on Nazi extermination programmes; a deliberate attempt to cull a population on eugenic (*see* EUGENICS) grounds. The slippery slope argument has it that any programme of euthanasia, no matter how limited and well meaning, will slide into widespread abuse. Opponents of that view distinguish between different kinds of euthanasia; a range that includes the categories of involuntary, non-involuntary and voluntary euthanasia, and a range that includes active and passive euthanasia. The former categories indicate the degree of voluntariness involved while the latter distinguish between actively bringing a life to an end and passively refraining from intervening to prolong life. The different types of categories cut across each other with, it is sometimes argued different moral effects. It is frequently argued that there is a clear distinction between, say, the active and involuntary euthanasia of Jews, Gypsies and homosexuals in Nazi Germany and not resuscitating a person in an otherwise terminal and painful condition when that person had agreed to such non resuscitation.

All recent attempts to legalize euthanasia or permit assisted suicide have required that the termination of a person's life be at their own request i.e. voluntary. Initiative 119; Proposition 161; practice in the Netherlands; and recent discussions in the UK legislature have taken it that only voluntary euthanasia would be acceptable, if at all. Voluntary euthanasia might be active or passive.

In all Western jurisdictions competent persons may determine for themselves whether or not to have medical treatment. That right follows from the principle of personal autonomy but, depending on the jurisdiction, it may also be enshrined in legislation or may follow from the common law on assault. The latter has it that no one may be touched without their consent. As all medical treatment involves some invasion of the body the right of a rational person to refuse such treatment, even if life saving, is absolute. To refuse a life saving or life-prolonging treatment would be *autothanasia* and equivalent to voluntary passive euthanasia.

Difficulties arise when a person is not competent or, as a result of a crisis or trauma, such as a heart attack, is no longer competent. Here the decision is whether or not to withhold treatment from a non-competent patient with a terminal illness where the withdrawal of that treatment would, almost certainly, result in the death of that patient. In practice such decisions are made every day and in most cases fall under the maxim of 'thou shalt not kill but need not strive officiously to keep alive'. Heroic effort or burdensome treatment is neither morally nor legally required by doctor or patient. The Roman Catholic position in that respect is expressed well in the statement by Pius XII that while a person is obliged to stay alive they are obliged 'to employ only ordinary means . . . that is to say means which do not impose an extraordinary burden on himself [sic] or others' (1957) and has been reaffirmed in the 1995 encyclical *Evangelium vitae* which makes it clear that doctors are not required to give 'aggressive medical treatment'.

Some well known cases have arisen where someone is technically 'alive' by virtue of modern technical assistance and where it is proposed to withdraw that assistance. In 1976 the Supreme Court ruled that Karen Ann Quinlan, a young woman deep in coma and sustained only by virtue of technical assistance, could be removed from such support. In some jurisdictions, particularly the US, a declaration or 'living will' made beforehand can be taken into account should the patient be comatose or *non compos*. A 1990 Supreme Court Ruling accepted that a clear wish to have life-sustaining treatment withdrawn must be respected. A failure to express such a wish might, however, lead to the continuation of treatment of comatose patients even when that does not seem to be in their interests. This ruling gave legal and practical force to the 'living will' in the US. By contrast in the UK withdrawal of treatment or D.N.R.s ('Do Not Resuscitate' orders) are primarily seen as medical decisions thus excluding, formally at least, the wishes of patient or relatives. As medical decisions they are not subject to legal challenge if proper professional criteria have been applied. The House of Lords did, however, permit the removal of artificial feeding from Tony Bland, a patient deep in coma for some years, who was able to breathe unassisted but who required intubation. Technically this action involved the withdrawal of feeding. As the right to food cannot be withheld nor permission to withhold it be granted by the courts the court could not formally grant permission nor grant immunity from prosecution. What the court indicated, therefore, was that in the event of a prosecution being brought it would not be sustained in the House of Lords.

In jurisdictions where the prior wishes of a comatose patient are respected there are some limitations on that respect. These limitations include some or all of the following: the wish must have been expressed in a manner that shows it to be enduring and not whimsical; the decision to refuse treatment or have it withdrawn must be seen to be rational and reasonable in the circumstances; and the decision should be seen as genuinely voluntary and not made as a consequence of some external pressure.

The widespread acceptance of the right to refuse treatment and the inviolancy of the body, indicates that most moral objections arise principally not about euthanasia or suicide *per se* but about the kind of euthanasia. Voluntary passive euthanasia in the cases already discussed is already widely accepted in some form or other. Clearly there is no case for non-voluntary active euthanasia of the kind carried out by Nazi eugenic programmes; the issue of greatest practical concern, therefore, hinges on the categories of voluntary active euthanasia, and involuntary active euthanasia.

It is often argued that there is no formal distinction between active and passive euthanasia, it is just that the latter involves more suffering for the patient and less trouble for the conscience of the doctors and relatives. As the outcome is the same, the death of the patient, and the intention is the same, to bring about the death of the patient, the actions are formally the same in a moral sense. Kuhse and Singer, among others, have argued that if the actions are formally the same in a moral sense then the euthanasia might as well be active and the patient die comfortably. The counter to this rests on the Christian Doctrine of Double Effect; an act with one intention can have an outcome other than that which was directly intended. In the case of active euthanasia the intention of the lethal injection is to bring about the death of the person, whereas the intention of withdrawal of treatment is to let nature take its course. It may be that the consequence of nature taking its course is the death of the patient but this was not directly intended. The act, therefore, is one of letting die rather than killing. To some extent the Doctrine of Double Effect does modify the intention so that it might be properly said that the direct intention of withdrawal of treatment was not to kill the patient. Never the less, in many cases the death of the patient as a consequence of the withdrawal of treatment is foreseeable with as much certainty as it is granted to humans to have. In such cases reliance on the Doctrine of Double Effect has seemed to rest on excessive mental gymnastics or bad faith or both. Be that as it may unless, and until, society reaches a settled consensus on the conditions in which active euthanasia will be permitted the distinction between killing and letting die will remain crucial in this area.

Whether that social consensus will be reached and active euthanasia permitted is an open question. What is undoubtedly the case is that the issue will become the moral issue of our time in a way similar to the ABORTION issue. The social and philosophical pressures in favour of a change to permitted active euthanasia are powerful. The social pressures arise from a mix of the rising age profile in Western societies, the technological advances in medicine, and the limited economic circumstances that arise from both of these factors. The outcome is tending to be a shift to the allocation of health care resources measured against quality of life. This basically utilitarian calculation finds its formal expression in the notion of the QALY (Bell and Mendus 1988). The QALY or Quality Adjusted Life Year is a unit of measurement by which a life can be given a quantifiable value. An economically active young person scores higher on such a measure than an economically inactive elderly person who is consuming large resources. If a full return to health for the young person if ill is of relatively low cost and the cost for the elderly person high then in a time of limited resources the choice on such grounds would be clear. Sometimes, however, the choices are inverted. In March 1995 the UK courts were asked to review a decision by a hospital to withhold potentially life-saving treatment from a young girl who sought that treatment. It appeared that part of the reason for refusing to provide the treatment was cost and in the court of the first instance it was held that this was an insufficient reason to decline treatment. On appeal, however, the court held that the decision to refuse medical treatment was a purely medical matter. As a medical matter it was not subject to legal review. In the same week a 75-year-old man requiring an even more expensive treatment was provided with that treatment. In general terms, however, it is to be expected that the trend will be towards increasingly limited health care for the ELDERLY. The QALY is almost certainly ageist in its effect. It would seem a reasonable safeguard for the provider of funding for that health care to have their decisions subject to judicial review. It seems in the UK, at least, that this will not be the case as all such decisions on what will, and what will not, be funded and who will, and who will not, be funded in their health care will be exempt from judicial review: a very peculiar kind of tyranny.

These institutional and social pressures are likely to lead to an increasing number of elderly and sick people of mixed fortune. Some will have their life extended and/or their situation made comfortable by technical means that are funded by themselves or their health insurers; others will obtain care ranging from minimal to none. In both cases there may well be pressure both internally, from themselves, and externally, from others, to end their lives by peaceful and dignified means. It is hard to think that the introduction of cost–benefit analysis into health care combined with decreasing resources and increasing demand will reduce the pressures for euthanasia. In those jurisdictions that have, or have contemplated legalizing euthanasia, the reasons for the reluctance to take the final step do seem to centre less on the principle as such than on its institutionalization. The institutionalization of euthanasia is widely regarded as a slippery slope the end result of which is the unwanted but excessively easy but conveniently cost-beneficial death. It is sometimes argued that the institutionalization of euthanasia will lead to widespread abuse. Much here may depend on whether there is a systematic and well developed means of dealing with pain at the terminal point of an illness. In the UK for instance the development of hospice care and pain relief is well advanced. By contrast there is almost no hospice care in the Netherlands and almost no specialization in terminal pain relief. Where hospice care seems advanced and pain relief well developed the demand for euthanasia seems, as far as it is possible to tell, to be quite limited. There is no doubt that there are numerous people in painful, undignified and terminal conditions that merely wish their lives to be brought to a peaceful end. It is also clear that there are many people who do not wish to see the end of life *per se* but the end of pain and discomfort. Where that can be achieved they choose not to end their life but instead to have the pain and discomfort removed or alleviated.

Not all slopes are slippery but the euthanasia slope is a very slippery one indeed. For all that it is not an issue that is likely to go away. On the contrary it is likely to increase as an issue of significance on philosophical, moral, theological and social grounds. The philosophical issues take two broadly defined forms. The first, is the shift in western societies to a concern with dying rather than a concern with death. Death is rarely talked about; it is dealt with euphemistically as the wide use of expressions like 'passed over', 'gone to the other side', 'gone to sleep' and so on indicate. It is with a few exceptions a philosophically barren subject and even in religious and theological circles is rarely dealt with directly. By contrast and secondly, there is more talk about dying and the reduction of pain in dying, or about the process of dying with some semblance of dignity. Western society has attempted to control natural evil. To a large extent it has succeeded but it cannot bring death under control. It compensates by attempting to bring dying under control.

There is something inauthentic about euthanasia for it is not about death, it is about dying and it arises as a moral issue now for there is an increasing demand for control over one's life and control of one's dying and a decreasing desire to face up to the issue of death. An excessive concern with dying is part of the inauthentic response to facing up to death. But Death is Life's other. To embrace one is to embrace the other: it is the one that makes the other possible. By contrast to be overly concerned with dying is to be overly concerned with living rather than with Life. To that extent much of the moral debate about euthanasia is a poor response to the central issue of death. A mere concentration on dying is a philosophical and theological evasion tactic. This is not to say that dying is not significant, Christianity has a starting point, even a defining moment in the painful dying of its exemplary figure. It also has a starting point in the individuality, autonomy and empowerment of individuals. This is a part of the inner dynamic of Christianity, present from its inception. It is now being revealed as *alethia*, the uncovering of what is contained in Christianity. It is not surprising if that autonomy and empowerment contained within Christianity is now taken to a concern with the manner of dying. Jesus died in pain and indignity; a sacrifice too many one might think. Should his theological children also die in pain and indignity? By contrast Socrates did not die without dignity, his death was fitting of his life; should his philosophical children be granted any less?

Augustine & Hippo (1972) *Concerning the City of God against the Pagans*, trans. David Knowles, Harmondsworth: Penguin.

Battin, Margaret Pabst (1994) *The Least Worst Death: Essays in Bioethics on the End of Life*, New York and Oxford: Oxford University Press.

Bell, J.M. and Mendus, Susan (eds) (1988) *Philosophy and Medical Welfare*, Cambridge: Cambridge University Press.

Church of England Assembly Board for Social Responsibility (1959) *Ought Suicide to Be a Crime? A Discussion of Attempted Suicide and the Law*, Westminster: Church Information Office.

Clarke, P.B. and Tonti-Filippini, N. (1986) *Obligation in a Caring Profession*, Melbourne: St Vincent's Bioethics Centre.

Dworkin, Ronald (1993) *Life's Dominion: An Argument About Abortion and Euthanasia*, London: HarperCollins.

Hankoff, L.D. (1979) 'Judaic Origins of the Suicide Prohibition' in *Suicide Theory and Clinical Aspects*, L.D. Hankoff and Bernice Einsidler (eds), Littleton, MA: PSG Publishing Co.

Heidegger, M. (1980) *Being and Time*, J. Macquarrie and E. Robinson (trans.), Oxford: Basil Blackwell.

Kuhse, Helga and Singer, Peter (1985) *Should the Baby Live?* Oxford: Oxford University Press.

Humphry, Derek (1991) *Final Exit: the Practicalities of Self-deliverance and Assisted Suicide for the Dying*, Eugene, Oregon: The Hemlock Society; New York: Dell 1992.

John Paul II (1995) *Evangelium Vitae*, Vatican City: Vatican.

Locke, John (1960) *Two Treatises of Government*, ed. Peter Laslett, Cambridge: Cambridge University Press.

Pius XII (1957) 49 *Acta Apostolicae Sedis*.

Pritchard, James B. (1950) *Ancient Near Eastern Texts Relating to the Old Testament*, Princeton: Princeton University Press.

Paul Barry Clarke

EVANGELICALISM

'The term "evangelical" is a plastic one. Efforts to define it narrowly can lead to both strife among historians and battle among theologians' (Noll 1986: 1). The word is derived from the Greek noun *euangelion*, translated as 'glad tidings, good news, or gospel'. It came into use at the Reformation to identify Protestants, especially as they held to the belief in JUSTIFICATION by GRACE through faith and the supreme AUTHORITY of scripture. Subsequently, while striving to remain faithful doctrinally to the general conservative tradition of the Reformation, the doctrinal core of evangelicalism became focused on the belief that the Bible is the inerrant Word of God, the belief in the divinity of Christ and the belief in the efficacy of Christ's life, death and physical RESURRECTION (his atoning work) for the salvation of the human soul. Behaviourally, evangelicals are typically characterized by an individuated and experiential orientation toward spiritual salvation and religiosity in general and by the conviction of the necessity of actively attempting to proselytize all non-believers to the tenets of the evangelical belief system (Hunter 1987: 7).

'FUNDAMENTALISM' is a subspecies of evangelicalism which formed in the 1920s in America to combat 'modernist' THEOLOGY and secularizing cultural trends. (British evangelicals find the term 'fundamentalism' objectionable and avoid calling themselves by it.) 'Far from being a religious behemoth, simplistic in its social organization and inflexible in its social and religious conventions, [evangelicalism] is a richly diverse cultural tradition whose encounter with the twentieth century . . . has involved it in a whirl of change – change which is intensely relevant to the larger social order' (Hunter 1987: ix).

Evangelicalism, including its more rigid manifestation in fundamentalism, is a complex coalition of ideas and institutions reflecting the convergences of a number of traditions (Marsden 1980; 1987a: 191; Hunter 1983; Noll 1986). Historical roots lie in Calvinism; in seventeenth-century Puritanism and continental pietism, especially the Moravian influence on John Wesley in the mid-eighteenth century; and in the wider series of awakenings and pietist renewal movements in Protestant countries from the late seventeenth century through the nineteenth century. In England evangelicalism was manifested in METHODISM, in evangelical renewals among the nonconformists, in the founding of the Salvation Army and in the rise of the evangelical wing of the Church of England. In America the Great Awakening of the eighteenth century brought together similar movements: New England Puritanism, continental pietism, revivalist Presbyterianism, Baptist anti-establishment democractic impulses and a similar strain in Methodism.

By the early nineteenth century, evangelicals had established a network of non-sectarian 'voluntary societies' which promoted evangelism, founded Sunday schools, distributed Bibles and tracts, established schools and colleges, and brought the gospel to needy people. Guided by a postmillennial vision of spiritual and moral progress (e.g. Charles Finney (1792–1875)), they also engaged in political and social action: abolition of SLAVERY, prison reform, temperance and Sabbatarian legislation.

As the concentrated industrialism and crowded cities of the latter part of the nineteenth century overwhelmed their individualistic and voluntaristic programmes, many responded to the efforts of Dwight L. Moody (1837–99), a premillennialist who stressed rescuing the perishing from the sinking ship that was the condemned world, and who looked to the Second Coming of Christ as the only cure for the world's social and political problems (*see* MILLENARIANISM). Continuing threats to traditional conservative faith from the Enlightenment and Newton's new physics were augmented by Darwinism, the symbol of a many-faceted secular revolution which juxtaposed evolution to Genesis, and science to Biblical religion, while, indirectly threatening the fixed and absolute ethical world of conservative Christians. Whereas many liberals and 'modernists' adjusted Christian doctrine to fit the temper of the times, evangelical fundamentalists resisted.

Fundamentalism combined a militant defence of most traditional evangelical doctrines (the Trinity, the divinity of Christ, the Virgin Birth, the bodily resurrection, the miracles of Christ, substitutionary ATONEMENT, the supernatural powers of God and an inerrant Bible) with revivalist evangelical innovations of the nineteenth century (Marsden 1987b). Two innovations were particularly important. First, *dispensationalism* was a systematic scheme for interpreting all of history into seven dispensations or eras on the basis of a 'literal' interpretation of the Bible, the last to be preceded by the personal return of Jesus, the secret 'rapture' of believers, a seven-year period of wars resulting in the victory of Christ, and the establishment of a kingdom in Jerusalem where Jesus will reign for a thousand years before the Last Judgement. For their movement, inerrancy of the Bible became the key test of faith. Second, leaders of the *Keswick holiness tradition* taught that perfection could be approximated only through repeatedly being filled by the Holy Spirit. Furthermore, fundamentalism responded defensively to the revolution in values which replaced Victorian evangelical standards with the public morals of the jazz age, and to the perceived threats of Bolshevism, ATHEISM, foreign immigration and Roman CATHOLICISM. In fact, however, American fundamentalism was only the prominent edge of the larger evangelical movement. Failing in their attempts to take over the major denominations and suffering from the verdict in the Scopes Trial, the movement regrouped and developed a firmer institutional base (1925–45). It continued its evangelizing, especially through missions and the development of effective radio ministries, best exemplified by Charles Fuller's 'Old Fashioned Revival Hour'. At the same time, sharp tensions were developing within their camp: while fundamentalists added ecclesiastical separatism as a test of true commitment, the evangelicals sought to bring their movement back toward a broader definition which included a move away from dispensationalism, separatism and militancy and emphasized positive evangelism.

After the Second World War, one strain,

Harold Ockenga, Carl Henry, Edward Carnell and Charles Fuller, along with Billy Graham, co-operated in moderating fundamentalism, founding the Fuller Theological Seminary (1947) and *Christianity Today* (1956). While calling themselves the 'New Evangelicals', they still affirmed the authority (inerrancy) of the Bible, active evangelism, human depravity and individual conversion; the efficacy of the atoning death of Christ and the trace of God which justifies persons who go to him in faith and repentance, but stressed, as well, competent and comprehensive theological scholarship and certain social concerns.

Growing tensions within the New Evangelicalism were reflected in the battle over the selection of a new president for the Fuller Theological Seminary in 1962–3 (Marsden 1987a). Openness to other theological scholarship, including Karl Barth, precipitated a challenge to the meaning of 'inerrancy', a struggle won by the more progressive wing. David Hubbard, the new president, while keeping the seminary in a strong conservative theological camp, opened it up to varieties of practical ministries and to a commitment to servanthood. Fuller therefore symbolized for many evangelicals a move away from the doctrinal and moral rigidities of fundamental evangelicalism (*see* Noll 1986; Noll and Wells 1988; Packer 1990).

During the 1970s, while other Protestant groups declined, evangelicalism was growing in the USA with an estimated 40 to 50 million adherents. Being 'born again' became broadly acceptable, affirmed by celebrities in athletics, entertainment and politics, including President Carter. Evangelicalism was also a widespread international phenomenon. Two centuries of massive missionary efforts had planted evangelical communities in most of the nations of the world, many of which reaffirmed, in the Lausanne Conference of 1974, the reliability and authority of scripture and the urgency of world evangelization, along with 'the necessity of social and political concern for aiding the poor and victims of oppression' (Marsden 1987a: 195).

It is deceptive to assume that 'evangelicalism' as a consequence is a unified movement. Black evangelicals, for example, have had little to do with the historical struggles between fundamentalists and evangelicals, even though their beliefs are closely parallel. The same is true for the Southern Baptist Convention and evangelical Methodists. In fact, most holiness denominations were only tangentially related to the organized fundamentalist–evangelical movement, including the Pentecostals and charismatics who have sponsored some of the largest television ministries and who have set the tone for much of the so-called evangelical resurgence (*see* CHARISMATIC MOVEMENT). Confessional denominations, such as the Missouri Synod Lutheran and Christian Reform churches, were close allies, but always kept enough distance to preserve their distinct doctrinal heritages. In addition, many evangelicals remain in mainline American denominations. 'Such variety within evangelicalism, compounded by many denominational and regional differences, suggests that generalization about the movement is hazardous' (Marsden 1987b: 195). Further, distinctions can also be accounted for on the basis of social class and regional characteristics (Hunter 1983: 9).

It is equally difficult to generalize about the ethical and political stances of evangelicals and fundamentalists. They are often viewed by the liberal media as a hyperactive, ultra-conservative political group, not only bigoted and intolerant, by virtue of their religious convictions, but also absolutist, fanatical and the largest segment of 'potential fascists' in the USA. The reality is much more complex. Conservative in contrast to the rest of the American population, they are anything but a homogeneous political force (Hunter 1987: 125). The vast majority voted for Ronald Reagan in 1980 and 1984. They hold conservative views on the issues of ABORTION, homosexuality, the role of women, pre-marital sex and FAMILY virtues, school prayer and the teaching of creationism (along with evolution) in the public schools. They also tend to be more nationalistic, anti-communist and pro-defence, and, at certain times, have cultivated prejudices towards Catholics, Jews, blacks, political leftists and secular humanists. Compared with non-evangelicals, twice the percentage agree that 'America should do everything it can to support Israel' (Hunter 1987: 135); for its existence is viewed as the fulfilment of PROPHECY. (Hal Lindsey, *The Late Great Planet Earth* (1970),

sold 10 million copies.) But their prejudices are rarely translated into acts of aggressive, let alone violent, political activism. Political extremism, when it does surface, is typically a marginal phenomenon (Hunter 1987). In fact, the coming generation of evangelicals is more liberal than the general population, especially on gun control, defence, nuclear power and the political economy (the majority do not endorse CAPITALISM, though neither do they support SOCIALISM). On abortion, the rights of women and homosexuality, however, they remain firmly conservative.

The position of certain groups, among them Jerry Falwell's the Moral Majority (1979), the Christian Voice (1979) and the Religious Roundtable (1980), combined several long-standing fundamentalist concerns with more recent political issues. 'Sparked by the legalization of abortion in 1973, the women's movement, and the proposed Equal Rights Amendment, legislation favoring homosexuals, and general permissiveness, many fundamentalists and conservative evangelicals expressed alarm' (Marsden 1987b: 196). The Moral Majority's programme endorsed American conservative political ideals of smaller government, a larger military, superpatriotism and freedom for business, while also reviving the anti-EVOLUTION crusade by endorsing the teaching of creation science.

Marsden gives an account of the social ethical failures of the fundamentalist movement in the twentieth century (Marsden 1980) which can be read as a story of an even broader ethical failure. 'The immediate origins of fundamentalism reveal almost no systematic political thought. . . . They responded to issues haphazardly and on the basis of inherited prejudices and formulae, with next to no theoretical preparation to guide them' (Marsden 1980: 208). The New Evangelical movement that emerged in the 1940s, exemplified by Carl Henry in *The Uneasy Conscience of Modern Fundamentalists*, was a concerted effort to correct many of the defects of the older fundamentalism, but its mood was cautious, and generally compatible with traditional conservativism (Mouw and Yoder 1989: 123).

This attitude of cautious CONSERVATISM was subsequently challenged by a second wave of evangelical reform represented by the 'young evangelical' projects of the later 1960s and early 1970s, magazines such as *The Other Side* and *Sojourners*, and *The Chicago Declaration of Evangelical Concern*. These efforts strongly condemned evangelical silence in the face of RACISM, militarism and economic exploitation, and expressed a more leftist orientation. Within their discussion were the seeds of a growing *rapprochement* between two traditions which, historically, have been seen in opposition – the Anabaptists (John Yoder) and the Christian Reformed (Richard Mouw). Both communities have assumed a common starting point for moral discussion – Sola Scriptura. Both have also shared agreement about the basic sinfulness of human beings, the centrality of faith in Jesus Christ, the clear connection between personal piety and 'corporate' commitments, and the church understood in communal terms (Mouw and Yoder 1989: 130).

Although significant movement has occurred among certain groups of evangelicals–fundamentalists, its hold will probably remain strong in the USA as a source of security and certainty in times of great cultural and social change. Individualism, absolutistic value stands, a we–they understanding of their relationship to 'outsiders' and generally dichotomous thinking are strongly ingrained in fundamentalism–evangelicalism, but are also the hallmarks of much of the general American population. Future challenge lies in the direction of more systemic and communal thinking which will include thinking about individual persons as well.

Further, the progressive wing of the New Evangelicalism faces the challenge of developing a Biblical hermeneutic that takes seriously cultural change and relativity, while maintaining the authority of the Bible in such a way as to convince the evangelical community that it is not selling out to LIBERALISM.

A third historical challenge calls the mainline, 'liberal', churches to overcome their ideological blinkers in order to listen to and learn from certain evangelical concerns, especially issues of the reality of God's activity, the omnipresence of SIN, the dangers of uncritical capitulation to change and relativity, and the authority of scripture.

Evangelicalism is a potent force, not only in Anglo-American nations but also in the Third World. A more sophisticated understanding of it, and its various manifestations, can overcome simplistic thinking within the university, the media and the liberal church, promoting a more accurate awareness of its dangers and a creative response to its strengths.

Bloesch, Donald (1978, 1979) *The Essentials of Evangelical Theology*, 2 vols, San Francisco, CA: Harper & Row.

Hunter, James Davison (1983) *American Evangelicalism: Conservative Religion and the Quandary of Modernity*, New Brunswick, NJ: Rutgers University Press.

——(1987) *Evangelicalism: The Coming Generation*, Chicago, IL: University of Chicago Press.

Marsden, George M. (1980) *Fundamentalism and American Culture: The Shaping of Twentieth Century Evangelicalism 1870–1925*, New York: Oxford University Press.

——(1987a) *Reforming Fundamentalism: Fuller Seminary and the New Evangelicalism*, Grand Rapids, MI: Eerdmans.

——(1987b) 'Evangelical and fundamental Christianity', *The Encyclopedia of Religion*, vol. 5, New York: Macmillan, pp. 190–7.

Mouw, Richard J. and Yoder, John H. (1989) 'Evangelical ethics and the Anabaptists–Reformed dialogue', *Journal of Religious Ethics* 17(2): 121–38.

Noll, Mark A. (1986) *Between Faith and Criticism: Evangelicals, Scholarship, and the Bible in America*, San Francisco, CA: Harper & Row.

Noll, Mark A. and Wells, David F. (eds) (1988) *Christian Faith and Practice in the Modern World: Theology from an Evangelical Point of View*, Grand Rapids, MI: Eerdmans.

Packer, J.I. (1977) *'Fundamentalism' and the Word of God: Some Evangelical Principles*, Grand Rapids, MI: Eerdmans.

——(ed.) (1990) *The Best in Theology*, vol. 4, Carol Stream, IL: Christianity Today.

Sandeen, Ernest R. (1970) *The Roots of Fundamentalism: British and American Millenarianism, 1800–1930*, Chicago, IL: University of Chicago Press.

Stuart D. McLean

EVIL

Evil: the word comes from Old English *yfel*, which with the Middle Dutch *evel* is derived from the Teutonic *ubiloz*. In English the term is taken by the OED to mean, bad in a positive sense, as tending to do harm. The primary sense is derived from the root *up*, *over* and refers to exceeding due measure or overstepping the limits, a notion not dissimilar to the idea of sin as *hamartia*, as missing the mark. The word 'Evil' in common usage contains a complex of meanings ranging from the radical to the mildly disapproving. Interestingly it is judged by the OED to be obsolete in the strong sense when applied to persons.

It is useful to distinguish between strong and weak senses of the concept of evil. The strong sense refers to a radical principle of evil; a metaphysical or ontic understanding of evil, i.e. evil taken as real or as arising from genuinely malicious and demonic motives. The weak sense refers merely to wrong doing, to mild misfortune or to incontinence or privation. It seems that the concept of evil in the weak sense appears to be found universally, whereas the concept of radical or ontic evil is found only in certain cultures and in certain religions. Thus while some forms of Buddhism, for example, contain accounts of evil in the weak sense they do not provide any account of ontic evil, and the Fipa of south-west Tanzania to take a different kind of example, have neither a substantive sense of evil nor of good (Parkin 1985). THEOD-ICY, literally *theos dikos* God + justice, or more generally the attempt to explain SUFFERING, to bring suffering into understanding, or even to justify God are culturally specific, and not easily, if at all, generalizable. Consequently it is difficult to provide a universal or general account of conceptions of evil. Accounts of evil in Western thought do, however, have some common cultural sources and components, and do display some features recognizable across cultural and geographical gaps. It is possible, therefore, to derive some elements of a general theory of accounts of evil applicable to Western Christian cultures, and its precursors.

The most general principle of accounts of evil is that the conceptions held of God and of CREATION determine both the statement of the problem(s) of evil and the available form(s) of the solution. The theogony and cosmogony, the accounts of the coming into being of the God(s) and the universe, are related to the theodicy. By contrast if the cosmogony is comprehended in purely descriptive terms, as in contemporary scientific theory, there is no point to suffering and evil is meaningless. In the theogonic case, if the creator is conceived as directly malevolent, or even as having a dark side the difficulty in accounting for the presence of evil is different to that faced if the creator is held to be wholly good or to have no dark side.

Alternately good and evil may be held as co-existent, as in some dualistic theo-cosmogonies. In such a case the account of good and of evil is generally simpler to give than when the act of creation stems from an omnibenevolent source. Such accounts are rarely given now and almost never occur in pure form, but can be found, at least in modified form, in early mythology. Some of the earliest accounts of evil are often held as accounting for the possibility of co-equal principles of good and evil in creation, although on further examination, those accounts turn out to be more qualified than is often thought. The Sumero-Akkadian creation story *Enuma Elish*, written in the early part of the second millennium BCE, has it that the mingling of the sweet water Apsu, the begetter, and the salt water Ti'amat, who gave birth to them all, is the prime event from which the gods were formed. One of the gods thus created, Ea, later turns on and kills Apsu. In such accounts evil is already contained in the theomachy, the war between the gods. The *Zend Avesta*, the prime document of the Zoroastrian religion named after Zoroaster c.660–583 BCE, and one of the sources of the later Manicheanism, drawing on Assyro-Babylonian and pre-historic Aryanism, is often claimed to be dualistic. Ahura Mazda (Ormazd) the giver of life, light and truth, is in constant combat with Angra Mainyu (Ahriman). Thus good and evil appear to be co-equal principles. Such myths sediment, to provide the foundations of the cosmology within which a CULTURE finds its meaning. The myths surrounding conceptions of evil are, then, fundamental to a culture, for they give not only cosmological accounts of the origins and the scope of the universe but also reasons for, and meaning to, the struggles of everyday life. The dualism apparently found in Zoroastrian thought turns up in Nietzsche's attempt to show that conceptions of good and evil in Western thought have reached their end point. The figure of Zarathustra found in *Thus Spoke Zarathustra* shows how

Western 'moral' and 'religious' practice has killed off God. It is unclear, however, whether such dualistic accounts have ever been as firmly grounded as Nietzsche and others have thought.

In an extensive examination of the myths of evil, Paul Ricoeur finds four types of myth that provide accounts of the origin and the end of evil and which, while separate, can, he claims, also be viewed dynamically. First, the 'drama of creation' where good and evil are coextensive and the god(s) struggle to bring order from chaos. Second, the 'fall' as an irrational event in a creation already completed. Third, 'tragic': a tragic god who tempts, blinds, leads astray. Fourth, the 'exiled soul', where the SOUL has strayed into an earthly body. The first two types have strongly influenced Gnostic and Christian thought, while the latter seem closer to Greek tragedy and thought (Ricoeur, 1967).

A significant difficulty with the basis of this typology, however, is that while dualism is often asserted of religions the evidence for its actuality in those religions is frequently slim. In the *Enuma Elish* it is quite clear that Apsu is *theosgonia*, the begetter. The *Zend Avesta* has Ahura Mazda say to Zarathustra, 'I have created a universe where none existed', indicating a single creator – a form of MONOTHEISM before the usual ascription of monotheism. Pre-Zoroastrian forms of the myth, have it that Ahura Mazda, light, is the creator of Angra Mainyu, darkness. It is also expected that in the cosmic battle between the two, ultimately light, good, is expected to be triumphant. There appears to be no clear cut example of a true dualism. In a way this is not surprising. True dualism, if asserted, would be unsatisfactory for it would require a prior principle to explain the dualism. The provision of such a prior principle would undercut the dualism. So-called dualisms tend, therefore, to be emanationist; an evil spirit emanates from the good or from that created by the good. While it is not possible to be certain it may be that such ideas stem from onanistic principles – the view that the pantheon arises from the sperm produced by the initial masturbation of one god.

In all such accounts the good is prior to that which is evil. The good, in such accounts, usually exhibits virtue and nobility even when in conflict with that which has emanated from it. The position of Angra Mainyu, is not, in structure, unlike the position of Satan in Milton's *Paradise Lost*, or the devil in the Hungarian Saga, *Az embér tragediajá (The Tragedy of Man)*, created by, and turning away from the creator. Accounts of the origin of evil, it seems, can cope more easily with the idea of a quarrel between some aspect of that which is created and the creator i.e. a flaw in, or tension in, the creation, than with the idea of a quarrel between two independent and completely equal deities. The structure of the cosmic myth in the predecessors to Western culture has tended, therefore, towards foundational monism with an emergent dualism. It has also tended to an eventual optimism giving foundation and ultimate triumph to the principle of good. That triumph emerges, however, only after battle, tragedy and the vanquishing of that which is evil. It is not surprising, if against the background of this context, APOCALYPTIC and eschatological ideas of the end of history have come to dominate so much of western thought generally and conceptions of evil in particular. It is also scarcely surprising if against this background millenarian concerns have come to dominate the period around the end of the second millennium.

An account of evil needs to explain not merely moral evil but also natural evil. The Christian account(s) of evil contains within it the possibility of ontic or metaphysical evil applied both to actions and to nature. Thus actions can be evil, as in moral evil, but natural conditions, as in pain, pestilence and disaster, can also be evil. The ontic view of evil while sometimes retroactively imported into the ancient Hebrew tradition, as exhibited in the *Pentateuch*; the books of *Genesis, Exodus, Leviticus, Numbers* and *Deuteronomy*, seem in fact to have been absent from that lived tradition. The root Hebrew term translated into the English 'evil' is *ra* which Grayston (1950: 73) renders as conveying the 'factual judgment that something is bad ... displeasing ... or harmful. Quite generally it means anything that causes pain, unhappiness, or misery, including the discipline of PUNISHMENT sent by God'. This latter punishment from God follows from the institution of the COVENANT. Only after the giving and accepting of the Law could the relation with God be breached. The terms 'ht', 'psh', 'awon', mean respectively; missing a mark; breaking a relation or transgressing an agreement; and crooked, twisted or wrong – trespass. The force and context of these terms places significant moral evil in succession to and not precedent to the covenant, as in the later Christian reading of *Genesis*. Moral evil, furthermore, is centred on SIN and, unlike Christianity, excludes guilt.

The early theogony of ancient Greece, which is also central to the growth of Western accounts of evil, contains a pantheon descended from Gaia, EVIL and theomachy are, therefore, related. It is Plato, however, at the very point when he introduced the idea of critical reflection about God and coined the word THEOLOGY, who tells us that we must be critical of such accounts, that we must distinguish between the true and the false in telling the young about God. God is good. God is that which is good, can do no evil and is blameless:

> ... good things are far fewer with us than evil, and for the good we must assume no other cause than God, but the cause of evil we must look for in other things and not in God
>
> (*Republic* II: 379b)

God is thus exonerated from evil. As Rousseau was to put it more than two millennia later: 'God made all things good; man meddles with them and they become evil' (*Emile*).

By contrast most Christian accounts of evil generate their own internal problems by starting from two sets of premises, one: that God is omnipotent, benevolent, and the sole, transcendent, creator and two: that the problem thus generated is capable of solution in terms of a universal and de-contextualized mode of rationality. But if God is omnibenevolent from whence comes evil? That there is evil in the world, both wrong-doing and suffering, is a direct and serious challenge to the conception of an omnipotent and mono-benevolent deity. The problem, as thus expressed, is not specifically Christian. It depends rather on combining rationalistic types of expectations with the idea of a monistic deity having a particular kind of character of which expectations are high. Thus evil becomes a fundamental challenge to the existence of God. Evil places the very idea of God in jeopardy. Epicurus (341–270 BCE) in a challenge to the idea of God is reported as saying,

> God either wishes to take away evils and is unable; or He is able and unwilling; or He is neither willing nor able, or He is both willing and able. If He is willing and is unable He is feeble which is not in the character of God; if He is able and unwilling, He is envious, which is equally at variance with God; if He is neither willing nor able, He is both envious and feeble, and therefore not God; if he is both willing and able, which alone is suitable to God, from what source then are evils? Or why does He not remove them?
>
> (Hick: 1985)

Thus for Epicurus the character or nature of the concept of God, if he existed, is such as to preclude feebleness, envy and inability – God is omnibenevolent. That there is manifestly evil in the world is, therefore, a conclusive argument against the existence of God in particular and simultaneously, therefore, an argument against religion in general. This conceptualization of God and of the problem of evil that parallels it, has been taken to be a fundamental challenge to monotheism, and hence Christianity. The problem is followed throughout the Christian theology of the West from founding statements in St Paul and St Augustine through Boethius, Aquinas, and into contemporary theologies and philosophies of religion.

Proposed solutions to the problem of evil take numerous forms. These include, denying the existence of evil; placing it in a context where it is necessary either for the greater glory of God or the development of the character of humanity; and placing the fault with some characteristic of humans rather than an emanation from God. A few examples will suffice to show both the limited range of possibilities and some modern and contemporary cognates.

The Ancient Stoic solution, which has several contemporary correlates, is to treat evil as an illusion, as unreal, as merely the product of a subjective view. Events do not present themselves pre-individuated as harmful, it is rather the person upon whom the event acts who designates them as harmful, as evil. As Hamlet puts it to Rosencranz, 'for there is nothing either good or bad, but thinking makes it so' (II.ii). Remove the thought, the judgement of evil and the evil is also removed. An early modern philosophical account to a similar effect is to be found in Spinoza's *Ethics* where what is found in the world is not in itself real but an appearance constituted by the imagination. Evil is grounded in the imagination, it is appearance not reality (*see also* ESPIONAGE), the human will is not free, and humankind can neither do good nor sin (*see also* FREE WILL). Hick gives an example of a late modern account to similar effect found in Christian Science. Mary Baker Eddy, the founder of Christian Science, taught that evil is an illusion and a false belief. A recent variation on this theme can be found within some structuralist theories. For Althusser, for example, 'History is a process, without a subject'. Within the terms of this account it follows that there are either humans to act or to be acted upon or to do or to suffer evil. A postmodern account might conceivably develop this theme yet further, dissolving the subject completely. If this were so then the perception of evil would itself be illusory not for Stoic reasons, but because the subject, PERSON, individual or human being is illusory.

These kinds of accounts of evil, that evil is an illusion, falter on the simple observation that a world in which humans or imaginary subjects are so constituted as to *imagine* great suffering, such as that found at Auschwitz, to take one example, does indeed contain evil. To *imagine* that the pain of TORTURE appears to be evil is at both the metaphysical and the practical level just as evil as the pain of torture being evil. The nature of pain, as we know from Wittgenstein onwards, is such that the perception of the pain and the pain are one and the same thing. To *perceive* that one has toothache is *to have a toothache*: it is not the kind of perception about which a mistake is possible. Contrariwise, to imagine that the pains of Auschwitz do not appear as evil is itself a great evil. Someone who is able to bring themselves, or who is brought to the conception, or perceptions, that

the evils of Auschwitz are not evil, invokes or perpetuates a moral evil of the greatest sort. The thesis that evil is an illusion suffers twofold, for not only does it contain evil in the perception that constitutes the illusion, it also creates the even greater evil of distorting judgement so to deny evil where evil exists.

A variation on this idea is that of perspectivism. Here, the argument is that if one had a picture of the totality, a complete perspective, it would be evident that the evil is not so great. This kind of argument lends itself both to the excesses of rationalism and to rational calculation. In this respect the rationalist illusion of Spinoza is exceeded only in the hyper-rationalism of Leibniz's *Monadology*. In this latter view, the present world is the best of all possible worlds. God could have created many worlds, but of the worlds that were available the actual world is the best of these. If we could view the world from God's perspective, if we could see its totality, then we would see that the evils in it were small compared with other possibilities. In *Candide*, a novel inspired both by this optimism and by actual and destructive events of the day, this idea is lampooned by Voltaire. Candide, and his metaphysician companion Pangloss, embark on adventure after adventure coming into greater and ever greater difficulties and evils. As each gruesome and evil adventure develops, so the heroes of the story console themselves with the thought that 'all is for the best in the best of all possible worlds'. For Leibniz, as for Spinoza, all actions are rigidly determined, additionally all events are part of a pre-established harmony. There is no evil that cannot be justified against the perspective of the totality for each apparent evil contributes to the best of all possible worlds. The argument presented here is interesting and, in its own terms, powerful. What is also worthy of note is that it restricts the power of God. God cannot act for just any reason. God cannot create just any universe. It is always the case that God must act from the principle of sufficient reason. God it seems is, like Leibniz, a rationalist.

Rationalist solutions to the problem of evil have clear limitations, are historically specific, and find little in suffering that is ennobling to either God or humans. Not surprisingly, therefore, there is a proposed solution to the problem of evil that points up its ennobling effects. Here evil is seen as necessary to enhance either God or humanity. The greater glory of God is pointed up by the presence of evil. That which is evil, it is claimed, heightens the good of God. It is necessary that men sin in order that God may exhibit compassion and JUSTICE. In a variation of this theme life on earth is held to be a trial, a preparation for the next world, the choices made on earth affect the status of the soul and the degree of recompense in the next life. The first part of this solution is easily dismissed. It is a poor God indeed who, if omnipotent, allows, even requires suffering for self-enhancement – to point up His greater good. The idea that Auschwitz, famine, AIDS, earthquakes, Chernobyl and the greenhouse effect could be allowed or even produced by God to act as a foil to His greatness is poverty stricken. But if the premise were true it would show not that the conclusion, that the greatness of God, is true, it would show rather that the claim that his malevolence – Descartes' impossible cosmic joker – was true. The problem of evil would thus be solved by postulating a malevolent deity whose creation surpassed God in moral judgement and sensibility: a judgement that indeed Plato made of the gods, in a different way and context when he made the leap that introduced *theos logos* into the world. The second part of this kind of solution, that life is a trial, 'soul making' in Hick's phrase, is not dismissed so easily, having many adherents throughout history. Its coherence depends first, on the view that the choices that humans make are real choices, unlike the deterministic views of Spinoza and Leibniz, and second, if implicitly, that life on earth is a rehearsal, a preparation for a later life. Such accounts do, however, rob or at least diminish humans of their present life meaning, for their present life, whether good or bad, noble or base, is a means to a greater end. Structurally such accounts are not dissimilar to the crude MARXISM of the *Second International* and of subsequent Stalinist policies: it is necessary that humans should suffer now to alleviate the suffering of some hypothetical future generation. The meaning of the present is thus displaced and trivialized (*see also* DETERMINISM).

Such accounts do, additionally, have a tragic figuration, and, as such, they have the mythical structures to reinforce this imagery. If evil is necessary to enhance human beings, then humans are either less than perfect, or the producer of evil or both. Thus, while God is good, humans are, at least, a tragic, perhaps even a fallen figure, whose life on earth is necessarily one of suffering. Such a being is found in, among other places, the Adamic myth. Adam, understood as humankind, is a *motif* of little significance in Ancient Hebrew thought, being transposed from type to individual and elevated to significance in the redemptory writings of St Paul. As he has it in Romans 5:18 '. . . as one man's trespass led to condemnation for all men, so one man's act of righteousness leads to acquittal and life for all men.' As developed by St Augustine of Hippo the figure of Adam turns first into a figure of weakness and then into the figure of the FALL. In *On Free Choice of the Will* Adam's incontinence, what would have been understood as *akrasia* in Greek thought, or weakness of will in Augustinian and post-Augustinian thought, becomes the turning point for humankind as a whole. The breach of the prime interdiction, and the evil therein and therefrom, is accounted for as the freely willed outcome of this original defection from the condition given by God. Evil then is not the outcome of God's actions, it is the outcome of human's actions. To be meaningful such actions have to be unconditioned, that is to say undetermined. It is no accident, therefore, that it is in the writings of St Augustine that the moment occurs when the modern notion of FREE WILL was first fully developed and with it the counter-factual sense of, 'could have done otherwise.' This idea introduced the conception that by an act of will new modal possibilities can be created. A new modal possibility might realize itself as a different actual world. For Adam this means that he could have (anachronistically on the Pauline-Augustinian account) done otherwise, he could have resisted the temptation presented to him but he did not. To recur to the Leibnizian model there was a possible world different to, and distinct from, the actual world. The consequences of Augustine's account of evil and the notion of free will that was necessary to its development can hardly be underestimated. In one pattern of thought, as we might say, in one figuration, lies not merely a justification of evil but also the basis for the secular accounts of responsibility that came to hold sway in the west and to hold the tightest of grips on the moral and juridical structures of even contemporary times. There is no conception of personal responsibility in western jurisprudence that does not stem in whole, or in part, from such conceptions of the account of evil. And the justice or injustice that follows from that depends entirely on the correctness or incorrectness of that terminal, if not founding, moment.

The Augustinian maxim that, 'Both punishment and reward would be unjust if man did not have free will' (*On Free Choice of the Will* 1964: 36; II.I.7) holds from Augustine through to Kant, and into contemporary legal thought. Yet that same maxim came to cause Augustine some difficulty, for if evil comes from an unconditioned act of the will presumably good may be willed without aid. This Pelagian objection to Augustine's views caused him, as with St Paul, to affirm the historically real and individual person of Adam while simultaneously, and also, turning Adam into a representative figure whose tragedy is both personal and collective. Adam sinned for himself and for all humans. The Adamic myth became, therefore, the myth of the fall. From this moral turning away, and from this moral evil, natural evil, on the Augustinian account, arose. The paradise of Eden was removed and work, death and suffering followed. Evil may be freely willed but to will the good unaided was not and is not possible. It requires the assistance of God's grace. If the actual world is not to be a merely contingent world, and if the Adamic motif is a merely contingent occurrence, then the actual world has to be necessary and Adam's actions also necessary. But if Adam's actions are necessary, if he must have willed evil then an omnipotent God would have known this for all time. As God has foreknowledge of who will, and who will not be saved, so a second great Augustinian legacy is the doctrine of pre-destination and grace. Even as Augustine invented the unified, monolithic and morally responsible subject, he decentred it by limiting its capacity to will the

good without God's grace. He made the actions of the individual subject to God's foreknowledge from before the beginning of time: God was the source of moral good but humanity was the source of moral evil. Humanity was a subject in consciousness but also a subject to consciousness: no sooner invented, it seems, than simultaneously imprisoned.

Nevertheless the Augustinian legacy is that of a unified and monolithic self, having the capacity of free will. It was these notions of self and will that formed, and to a large extent still do form, the basis of contemporary accounts of moral evil, moral responsibility and ETHICS. For Kant, who developed INDIVIDUALISM and freedom of will more fully than any predecessor, humanity is, by nature, morally neutral. 'In a moral sense man is neither good nor evil, he is rather whatever he wills himself to be' (Kant 1960). Humanity is radically free, in a moral sense in a way that Augustine, at least in his later writing, had been unable to permit and the subject is firmly centred, or re-centred, at the hub of the moral universe. Nevertheless, a rational being in choosing freedom would will good. To choose freedom was to choose to act according to the moral law, the Categorical Imperative: 'Act only on that maxim which you could at the same time will to be a universal law', or one of its formal equivalents (Kant 1964). In his later writing he specifically denied the possibility of acting according to an evil principle. The exhortation, in Milton: 'Evil be thou my good' (*Paradise Lost* Bk. iii. I. 108) is rationally incoherent within a Kantian framework for it would require the adoption of an evil maxim, and that could not be rationally willed. Evil was, therefore, as with Socrates, and a long western philosophical, if not literary and theological tradition, explained in terms of privation, of turning away from good, from virtue. It was, for Kant, acting heteronomously; according to desire. No rational being could consistently will to act according to an evil maxim. Thus even what appeared as radical evil was ultimately explained as the evil of privation. This Kantian tendency, rather than the more literary and Faustian tendency expressed by Goethe as the deliberate and rational taking of the side of the devil, of selling one's soul, of adopting an evil maxim has generally predominated in philosophically oriented, if not literary oriented, intellectual thought in the West. In philosophy, at least, evil is privation, ignorance or thoughtlessness rather than the adoption of an evil principle or maxim. By contrast in the literary tradition evil is frequently regarded as the choice to follow an evil principle, to adopt the course and precepts of the DEVIL. Kant cannot conceive of the adoption of an evil maxim, Milton's Satan does just that, 'evil be thou my good' is the paradigmatic, exemplary evil maxim.

The reason for the philosophical resistance to the Faustian tendency is clear enough and may be summed as follows. First, the tradition from Plato onwards has, generally, declined to see evil as something that one would willingly choose. Second, the dominance of an omni-benevolent MONOTHEISM has eliminated any residual Manicheanism with its view of an autonomous evil principle or evil force. Third, SECULARIZATION has eliminated the demand for general explanations of natural evil and confirmed the shift, instanced most fully in the Adamic myth, of explaining moral evil as originating in the domain of the human. Moral evil thus occurs as a consequence of a fault in humankind, or as merely the product of an entirely contingent human nature – a less poetic and more secular way of making a similar structural point. Humanity is in Ricoeur's terms fallible – that is to say subject to fault, rupture, and break with what has gone before (see e.g., *Fallible Man*). Fourth, the rise of individualism has tended to confirm this break. Within individualism the source of evil is seen as centred within, and of residing within, the actions of individuals rather than without those actions. Individuals rather than structures are the source of evil. This has the merit and the convenience of removing evil from the collective and social arrangements that we make, and in which we engage, and placing its source with individuals. Evil is not on that account socially or politically inspired or encouraged, it is always a property of the individual.

Such accounts of the source of evil have considerable ideological bias and on those grounds alone must be regarded as suspect. But

there are deeper reasons for regarding them with a healthy dose of suspicion. All such explanations of evil place the source of evil in a single and unified human subject: an individual whose self is constructed along Augustinian–Cartesian–Kantian lines. Yet the modern and late modern world has highlighted a new category of evil: political and social evil. Political and social evil has its source not merely in the actions of individuals but also in social structures: this raises the issue as to whether and to what extent, if at all, individuals are responsible for the social structures in which they subsist (*see* INDIVIDUALISM). Thus when examining the evils of e.g., Auschwitz, it is not merely the actions of particular individuals that have to be judged and explained it is also the evils of the social structures and public policies involved. Specifically, and at different levels, the actions of the individual guards in administering genocidal policies; the actions of those who gave and supervised the immediate orders; the actions of those who provided the administrative back-up for the policies; the actions of those who devised the policies; and the actions of those who set the framework within which such policies seemed 'rational', need close examination. In the latter case, it does seem that the policies were 'rational' in the limited and distorted sense of being *contextually* rational.

That such a view can be countenanced at all throws doubt on the criteria of rationality employed here; its purely contextual nature, and the way in which participants in it can be swept up in the process, carried along with it and persuaded that the atrocities they were committing were rational and justifiable on those grounds. The criteria of rational bureaucratic, or administrative evil, that follows from this is a warning to us. It is not merely something of a time gone by but a perpetual possibility of bureaucratic (*see* BUREAUCRACY) and STATE structures. It remains as a possibility within such structures whenever they are found. At a social and structural level the state-bureaucratic-administrative system that incorporated genocidal goals as a 'rational' extension of its wider purposes requires new models that can meet new criteria; criteria that from the present perspective on such structures are quite radical and that are likely to meet considerable resistance.

First, it must be possible to make moral judgements about the context within which forms of rationality that are generally, or that are inclined to be destructive, are justified. Second, it is necessary to be able to make moral judgements about the actions that take place within that contextual form of rationality. Third, it must be possible to distinguish between evils that are wholly structurally generated and evils that are partly the results of the formed intentions of agents. The development of such criteria require, and still lack a coherent theory. The source of, and solution to, structural evils requires a different kind of explanation to that traditionally available. Augustine produced a model of a centred subject that could be regarded as a source of evil. In Kant that became the morally centred subject, a subject that could in a moral sense make of its moral life what it will. It could choose to become good or evil. But the very idea of, and the practice of, structural evil calls that entire model into question. Nothing is more antithetical to Christian theology, to individualism, to the idea of individual responsibility, to the idea of the centred subject and the conception of a morally responsible, centred and meaningful subject having a personally directed and meaningful life, than the idea of structural evil.

Two sorts of response to these contemporary problems can be given. The first, given by Arendt conceives structural evil as being instanced through the thoughtlessness of the evil doer. In a celebrated analysis (Arendt 1976) she argued that Adolf Eichmann, the Gestapo organizer of the 'final solution' exhibited signs of 'thoughtlessness' rather than signs of a satanic nature. Later in *The Life of the Mind* (Arendt 1978) she explored the general thesis as to whether the habit of 'thinking as such' might protect the self against being swept away by the tide of events. Arendt's approach continues the western tendency to perceive evil as privation rather than a positive force, in this case the absence of thinking. In significant respects it sides with Kant rather than Goethe, it is Platonic rather than Zoroastrian, it is Augustinian rather than Faustian, it is phenomenological rather than

intentional. In consequence it fails, of itself, to deal with the problem of evil structures and policies.

The second approach develops the idea of an Augustinian–Cartesian–Kantian conception of the subject and applies it to structures as well as individuals. This model permits a clear discrimination between centred and de-centred agents. On this model of evil, developed first by Clarke (Clarke 1980), structures do exist and they do exhibit a causal influence over individuals. In consequence it is possible to regard structural evil as something that does take place. It may seem that the existence of structural evil would eliminate agency. As developed by Clarke the model does not permit that. The existence of structural evil does not automatically absolve all agents of responsibility for their actions within those structures: the existence and reality of structures within which subjects subsist does not automatically de-centre those subjects to the point of complete absolution for their actions. Where individuals could have questioned and withdrawn from structures that embodied an evil principle, but failed to do so, they may be held responsible for bearing relevant instances of particular and evil policies. If they failed to withdraw or object when they could have done so, this does not betoken a lack of will, in the Augustinian–Kantian sense, it is rather that they elected to act heteronomously. This is the category of what Clarke has called 'heteronomous evil'. The theory of heteronomous evil permits the explanation of and judgement of the culpability of both individuals *and* of structures. For individuals involved in social and political evil the higher they are within the chain of command, and the greater the degree of flexibility permitted within the structure, the greater the degree of culpability. Hence policy makers and policy influencers are generally more culpable than those who merely execute the policy. In general terms the greatest culpability lies with those who originate and initiate the policy while the least culpability lies with those who merely execute the policy. It does not follow from this that the executors of the policy are not culpable. It is rather that maximal culpability redounds to those that originate the policy, they are the *fons et origens* of the evil in the social and political structure. They are the ones that must, therefore, bear the most culpability. The general rule in such cases is to attempt a form of personal absolution by denying that the policy was intended to harm any one in a personal sense.

There are some classic examples of this kind of double think, to the appropriate response which is to treat some allegedly impersonal policies and some allegedly impersonal structures as inherently evil. Hence the Wanasee conference in the German Third Reich that initiated the policy of the final solution produced not merely evil *actions* but also evil *policies*. The administrative and bureaucratic state structures that were subsequently generated to implement that policy can justly be regarded as evil even though they are social and political structures rather than individuals. They produce a uniquely modern feature that Clarke has called 'Administrative Evil' (Clarke 1980; 1988). At another level some structures that have a rational justification opposed to evil have evil possibilities. The doctrine of and the structures that were designed to ensure M.A.D. (Mutual Assured Destruction) in the Cold War were, within a certain context, rational; yet they contained within them the potential for a great evil: complete global destruction.

The sense of an external power that acts upon individuals is extremely common. Throughout history external forces, expressed as the Devil, Satan, the Tempter etc., have captured individual and collective imaginations and have entered into theological, literary, cultural, social and occasionally philosophical explanations of evil. Yet the sense of being guided by external forces or powers to act in ways that one would not normally act points, in social terms, towards the ALIENATION of the self and this is partly explicable in terms of Ricoeur's conception of *fallible humanity*; man subject to rupture and to break. But these faults or ruptures are found not just in humanity as phenomenological subject, they are also fault lines in social structures as well as the fault lines in Being so adeptly noted by Augustine and later Ricoeur. Being overtaken by, or being guided by, external forces is heteronomy, possibly of an elective kind, possibly not (Clarke 1980; 1988). When the heteronomy is not elective then the idea of the Augustinian–Cartesian–Kantian unified and monistic self is replaced with the idea of a dispersed subject. Here evil is decisively and primarily the property of structures and policies and only secondarily, if at all, the properties of people. In such cases there is a justification for dismantling the structures, and abandoning the policies without necessarily punishing those involved. In such cases the individuals involved have, as bearers of structures, implemented evil policies without necessarily being evil themselves in the strong agentic sense. The decision as to which category to apply in any particular case, elective heteronomy or dispersed or decentred subjectivity, is primarily an *a-posteriori* matter: a matter of evidence and argument in the light of observation.

The general theory of accounts of evil indicated briefly here covers a range of hierarchical structures from theogony, cosmogony and cosmology at one end to perceptions of the social universe and individual actions at the other. These are not disconnected. On the contrary, the relation between the most general accounts of the comprehension of the universe, its coming into being and its development, are closely related to the accounts of evil and suffering found at the micro-level. This is as true of contemporary western and apparently secular society as it is of the earliest precursors to those societies. Of course alternative accounts of evil are possible, both logically and actually. Such accounts abound in anthropological literature. But those are not the accounts that have influenced our accounts of evil. Within our accounts of evil a fairly strict hierarchy and a fairly strict relation between the various levels predominates. Those levels have not been changed nor the hierarchy changed by scientific accounts of the cosmogenesis. On the contrary the structural similarities between the earliest accounts of that cosmogenesis and the most contemporary accounts of the cosmogenesis are so close in their general isomorphy that one is lead to the conclusion that none is an extension of the other. As to which is the most meaningful, only time and personal inclination will tell. Nevertheless the isomorphism is there, and some contemporary account of evil that is subsequently found seems to follow, and possibly even seems to arise from events of four millennia or more ago. Intriguingly there has been no real change in that conception inspired by recent scientific accounts of the coming into being of the universe and the beings in it.

In those societies that have generated complex forms of mythopoesis within which the relation between upper and lower worlds, heaven and earth is close the interpenetration between the perceptions of the two levels is also quite close. Suffering and evil are explained within the over-arching mythopoesis that itself generates sub-plots: the second–third millennium BCE myth of the toothache worm, the worm that seeking its own place in the cosmos obtained the permission of the gods to live in the teeth and became the source of toothache, is a classic point (Pritchard 1950). Such cosmic myths and their sub-plots are widespread, if not universal for they attempt to explain and justify natural evil. But in the case of the toothache worm it was the gods that allowed the physical evil: to that extent it was not merely natural but God-given. A similar response to such evil is reportedly given by the people of Bali whose God Sang Hyang Widi, the highest and all embracing Divinity, is bad (*Kaon*). 'How else', according to the rapporteur, 'could there be bad in the world?' (Hobart, in Parkin 1985: 188). Here their God even has a malevolent side. But the cosmology of western society has, since St Augustine at least, freely admitted only one, omnipotent, benevolent and monistic God. Natural evil cannot, therefore, be placed with God, but must be placed with humankind. But the weakness in the argument is clear: why did God make such an incontinent humankind and then blame and punish them for their incontinence? Adam may have sinned, but why was he created so weak and why was he placed with such a monumental temptation? If God was his creator and an omnipotent creator why did God create an *akratic* man, a tempting serpent and a weak woman? When expelled from the Garden of Eden why was the punishment so severe and, given the circumstances, so disproportionate to the perfectly comprehensible crime? The challenge of natural evil remains, for the Augustinian answer is unsatisfactory. A society that places an excessive weight on de-contextualized rationality, whose God is monotheistic and whose God is omnibenevolent has remained so challenged by the problem of natural evil that either it will, as Nietzsche pointed out, kill its God, or alternatively it will kill its rationality, or both. The contemporary/post-modern West is falling towards both these possibilities. The danger that brings are accounts in which subjectivity is so decentred that no moral statements are possible. Such accounts would be both mistaken and sad. Moral evil, at least, is accountable for, in perfectly straightforward terms, as is structural evil. It is also possible, in principle, and generally in practice, to distinguish between them. Nevertheless, even in the world of late or high modernity, and in the early post-modern world it is clear that the general theory of evil still holds: namely relations between theogony, cosmogony, cosmology and social and individual actions govern and inform each other. That relation is not one of strict hierarchy; indeed its emphasis is continually changing. It is a relation that is subject to inversions and to constant processes of penetration and interpenetration and within the overall structure some components are sometimes held negatively. In Christianity, for example, the theogony is held negatively, on the grounds that God has existed for eternity. The cosmogony is held negatively by those taking a scientific world view; a positivist world view or a post-modern dislike of meta-narratives. On these views cosmogonic statements belong respectively to metaphysics, to the domain of the meaningless or to the category of the meta-narrative, a category to which the post-modern attitude is one of incredulity (Lyotard 1979). On these latter views if there is evil at all it is not metaphysical evil, and frequently the idea of natural evil is also discarded. Metaphysical evil requires a meta-narrative without which it lacks credulity and natural evil is often seen as a mere feature of an entirely contingent universe. Hence the only serious questions surround those evils that can be potentially controlled: namely moral, social and political evil and the effects of those limited natural conditions, that fall within the remit of humankind. And that is a position not too distant from that given on a text found on the side of an ancient Egyptian coffin. Dating from about 2000 BCE, some four thousand years ago, it purports to be a statement from the creator, the

All Lord, who says, 'I made every man like his fellow. I did not command that they do evil [but] it was in their hearts which violated what I had said'. It is a position that is also, and often surprisingly to those who hold it, a theological position, for the view given by the All Lord was echoed, albeit unknowingly, by Plato at the very moment of the founding of theology, when he decisively set aside an older Greek mythopoetic idea of evil as willed by a higher agency. It is this sentiment that resonates throughout those western accounts of evil that were not derailed by excessive rationalism; for 'the cause of evil we must look ... in other things and not in God' (*Republic* II: 379b). Within this statement is contained both the basic ambivalent attitude of the western theological tradition towards evil and the potential a-theology of post-modern thought. For the proffered solutions to the problem of evil we must look to the way in which the problem is posed and to the relations between the most general conceptions of the universe and the actions and events that take place within it. That way is always revealing of the self-conceptions of the society that posed the problem and provides the parameters within which a solution is regarded as acceptable. Long before the Drama of the Christian meta-narrative began the problem of evil was posed in such a way that it became insoluble within the terms provided. When Christianity borrowed and refined those terms it presented itself with a problem incapable of complete solution within its own terms. That insolubility produced a tension within which theology, ethics and politics have uneasily but, hitherto, inescapably co-existed. It has also presented a test for Christianity that it may yet fail, the problem of evil remains the Achilles heel of any religion that depends on an omnibenevolent God. Christianity falls within that category and the drama of its meta-narrative has raised considerable incredulity about its theology, its account of God or both for almost two millennia. It remains to be seen whether the first act in that drama is now at an end.

Althusser L. (1972) *Politics and History*, London.

Arendt, Hannah (1976) *Eichmann in Jerusalem: A Report on the Banality of Evil*, New York: Penguin.

——(1978) *The Life of the Mind*, 2 vols, London: Secker and Warburg.

Augustine of Hippo (1964) *On Free Choice of the Will,* trans. Anna S. Benjamin and L.H. Hackstaff, Indianapolis: Bobbs Merrill.

——(1972) *The City of God*, Harmondsworth: Penguin.

Clarke, Paul Barry (1980) 'Beyond the Banality of Evil', *British Journal of Political Science* 10, 417–439.

——(1988) *The Autonomy of Politics*, Aldershot and Brookfield: Avebury.

Descartes, René *Discourse on Method* (numerous editions).

Grayston, K. (1950) 'Evil' in Alan Richardson (ed), *A Theological Word Book of the Bible,* London: SCM.

Hick, John (1985) *Evil and the God of Love*, London: Macmillan.

Kant, Immanuel (1960) *Religion Within the Limits of Reason Alone*, trans. Theodore M. Green and Hoyt H. Hudson, New York: Harper and Row.

——(1964) *The Groundwork of the Metaphysics of Morals*, trans. H.J. Paton, New York: Harper and Row.

Leibniz, G.W. *Monadology*, Indianapolis: Bobbs Merrill.

Lyotard, Jean Francois (1986) *The Postmodern Condition: A Report on Knowledge*, Manchester: Manchester University Press.

Milton, John *Paradise Lost* (numerous editions).

Moltmann, Jurgen (1993) 'Twelve Comments on the Symbolism of Evil', *Theology Digest*, February, 40(3), 235–8.

Parkin, David (ed.) (1985) *The Anthropology of Evil*, Oxford: Basil Blackwell.

Plato *Republic* (numerous editions).

Pritchard, James B. (1950) *Ancient Near Eastern Texts Relating to the Old Testament,* Princeton: Princeton University Press.

Ricoeur, Paul (1967) *The Symbolism of Evil*, Boston.

Rousseau, Jean-Jacques *Emile* (numerous editions).

Spinoza, B. *Ethics* (numerous editions).

Voltaire, *Candide* (numerous editions).

Paul Barry Clarke

EVOLUTION

The term 'evolution' refers most specifically to the major theory of modern biology that accounts for the origin of the diverse forms of living organisms. It also refers in a specific scientific sense to the modern understanding of the entire history of life on this planet and is the central theory of modern palaeontology. Very broadly the theory of evolution holds that over the course of time new forms of life emerge and develop from older forms by a natural process of change that occurs in interaction with the environment. 'Evolution' thus refers both to the historical emergence, development and extinction of different forms of life, which can be traced in the palaeontological record of fossils, and to the scientific theory concerning the process responsible for this historical development of living forms.

Physics and astronomy apply the term 'evolution' more generally, yet with scientific meaning, to the development of the universe as a whole. In the social sciences and the humanities, 'evolution' is used loosely to refer to the historical development of human thought, cultures and societies. 'Evolution' can also have a philosophical meaning, connoting a developmental organic worldview quite opposed to any static or mechanistic view of reality.

The standard theory of biological evolution may be outlined as follows. Individuals of the same species exhibit random variations in their morphological and physiological characteristics, the occurrence of which is accounted for by genetic theory. Under environmental pressures (competition for limited resources, changing environments, etc.), some of these variations confer an advantage in the struggle for survival. The individuals possessing them are better adapted to the demands of their ENVIRONMENT, survive to produce offspring at a greater rate than those less well adapted ('the survival of the fittest') and pass on the advantageous traits to their descendants. Over the course of time, through heredity, the entire population comes to possess the new traits and a new species has developed. This process of interaction between the environment and organisms is called 'natural selection' (an analogical reference to the 'artificial selection' for desired traits by animal and plant breeders).

When applied to the history of life, evolution means that all species of living organisms have evolved from common ancestors, that the earliest multicellular organisms evolved from unicellular organisms, and that life itself evolved out of some yet unknown development in organic chemistry. Modern science understands biological evolution to occur within a more general context of cosmic evolution. Even though cosmic evolution is not yet well understood, there is widespread agreement in the sciences that the concept of 'evolution' has grasped a fundamental feature of reality.

The term 'evolution' is usually associated with the name of Charles Darwin (1809–82). Although some scientists and philosophers before Darwin had proposed ideas of evolution, he was the first to work out a systematic theory of biological evolution and present it with extensive supporting evidence. The publication of *On the Origin of Species* (1859) inaugurated a revolutionary change in Western thought. In *The Descent of Man* (1871) Darwin applied the theory of evolution to the origin and development of the human species.

Darwin was troubled by his inability to account for the random variations upon which natural selection operates. This difficulty was not resolved until the rediscovery in the early twentieth century of the genetic theory of Gregor Mendel (1822–84). The present theory of evolution, referred to as the 'modern synthesis' (or 'neo-Darwinism'), combines modern genetic theory with a modified Darwinian theory of evolution by natural selection.

There are currently debates among biologists and palaeontologists concerning exactly how evolution takes place (e.g. gradual accumulation of changes versus the theory of 'punctuated equilibrium'; whether genes are passively or actively involved in evolution, etc.). New understandings of evolution are also arising from the application of information theory and systems theory to the study of DNA and genetics. The scientific theory of evolution is still in the process of refinement. But that evolution has taken place and is the key to the history of life is not in doubt (this is what scientists mean when they speak of evolution as a 'fact').

The theory of evolution has affected all areas of thought, including philosophy, social and political theory, and economic theory. But by far its major social impact has been in the area of religion and the discipline of THEOLOGY. Darwin's theory challenged traditional Christian thought in several ways. For centuries Christianity had held that the TRUTH of Christian faith was founded in revelation and reason: the divinely revealed truth is communicated in scripture and doctrine; and reason could arrive at a 'natural theology', proving that God exists and that the world is God's creation. In Darwin's time the argument from design in nature was the most common form of 'natural theology'. Darwin's theory appeared to attack both these traditional bases of Christian faith.

The evolutionary view of the origin and history of life clearly contradicted any literal interpretation of the creation narratives in scripture and seemed to imply that scripture presented inaccurate information. This was a direct challenge to the doctrines of Biblical inerrancy, inspiration and divine revelation, as well as to the traditional historical basis of the doctrine of original SIN (the Adam and Eve narrative). The argument from design in nature claimed that the complexity of organisms and their interactions with the environment were inexplicable unless we inferred the existence of a supreme intelligence that had designed and created them (as one could infer the existence of a watchmaker by examining a watch). Darwin's theory of evolution was able to account for the supposed 'marks of design' by a wholly natural process and thus undercut both the assumptions and the conclusions of classical natural theology. Furthermore, the theory of evolution gave an intellectually acceptable, if not comforting, solution to the problem of EVIL, which had always bedeviled the argument from design: if an impersonal, unintelligent, uncaring natural process is driving evolution, then one can understand accidents, suffering, misery, death and all 'natural' evils to be the inevitable by-product. Thus the doctrines of creation, providence and even the existence of God were all called into question. The new evolutionary view of nature removed all the traditional assurances for the truth of Christian faith.

Evolution also made Christianity's traditional worldview untenable and called into question the traditional understanding of human origins and status. Christianity had long viewed the world as a fixed, static, hierarchically ordered, relatively young world, in which God's care and goodness could be observed in the design of nature. Humans were seen as special creations of God, different from all animals and endowed with an immortal soul destined for eternal life. The meaning and purpose of human life was evident from humanity's status at the top of the earthly hierarchy. Evolution now revealed a world immersed in change, a world unimaginably ancient, a world in which uncaring, impersonal forces and mere chance seem to dominate the conditions of life. It placed humans squarely within the world of nature, not above it; found human origins in lower animals, not some special and direct creative act of God; and left the meaning and purpose of life shrouded in ambiguity.

Evolution also posed a serious challenge to the basis for ethics. Christianity had taught that the basis for human conduct was in the revealed word of God. But if humans have evolved like all other animals, is not human conduct too under natural selection? Darwin and many others argued that no ethical principles could be derived from evolution ('social Darwinism' found no support in Darwin). Their age, convinced of the inevitable progress of humanity, was content to put reason in the place of divine revelation as the basis of ethics. But the twentieth century has learned how easily reason may be twisted to serve self-interest and any IDEOLOGY. The problem of the basis of social ethics is with us yet today.

Christianity has produced a wide range of responses to the challenges posed by evolution. At the most conservative end, fundamentalist and evangelical denominations have generally held that evolution conflicts with the truth of Christian faith and must be denied (see FUNDAMENTALISM). Such denominations continue to adhere to a literal interpretation of scripture and have supported such movements as 'scientific creationism', which has caused much controversy in the USA in recent years. But in all other denominations, evolution, though not the only cause, has been an important one in evoking a revolutionary change in Christian theology, perhaps the most important development since the Middle Ages. These denominations have recognized that there are different kinds of truth and that scripture was not intended to be a textbook of scientific information. They have accepted the principles of modern Biblical interpretation and have long abandoned Biblical literalism. They hold that evolution is not necessarily incompatible with Christian faith, but differ in precisely how they articulate this position.

In general theology has gone much further than the official positions of the churches in dealing with the problems posed by evolution. Some theologians have tried to insulate theology from evolution or any scientific theory by stressing the independence of science and religion, arguing that they do not conflict because they are concerned with different aspects of reality and employ different methodologies, languages and sources of data. Most theologians of the moderate and liberal demoninations have found such a solution unacceptable for methodological and philosophical reasons. Instead they have reinterpreted the key doctrines of God, revelation, creation and original sin so that they are compatible with an evolutionary worldview. New types of 'natural theology' have developed, not claiming 'proof' in the classical sense, but trying to show the reasonableness of theistic claims even in the context of an evolutionary worldview. Yet other theologians have integrated an evolutionary worldview into the very structures of their theologies, producing novel interpretations of Christian faith. The two best known examples of the latter approach are that of Pierre Teilhard de Chardin (1881–1955) and 'PROCESS THEOLOGY', which employs the philosophy of Alfred North Whitehead (1861–1947). Most Christian theology has accepted the fact of evolution and is seeking interpretations of Christian faith that are compatible with what science discovers about the nature of reality.

On the practical level, research in genetics is raising a host of ethical problems. Genetic manipulation will give us the capacity to take evolution into our hands. It will be possible to design organisms, perhaps even humans, for various purposes and environments (see EUGENICS). What ethical principles will or ought to guide the use of such technology?

Another pressing group of ethical problems concerns the human impact on other species and the physical environment. Evolution forces us to recognize our kinship with all living things and our relation to the environment. Until quite recently humans have been oblivious to the detrimental effects of their industry and lifestyles on other living things and on our common environment. We are already responsible for the extinction of many species and for having greatly accelerated the rate of extinction in the last centuries. Our continued pollution of the oceans and the atmosphere, our deforestation of the land masses, and the dangers of our nuclear weapons and power stations constitute an enormous threat to all living things. Our species must reform its conduct. Since religion has always been the most powerful expression of the deepest values and ideals, as well as the guide for living, theology must articulate the spiritual and theological basis for environmental ethics and for our treatment of animals (see ECOLOGICAL THEOLOGY; ANIMAL RIGHTS). There is a very pressing need for a persuasive theology of nature.

Although theology has already done much in this regard, continued work is needed to articulate persuasively God's relation to and action within a world understood in evolutionary terms. Evolution, especially in its cosmic and philosophical senses, blurs the classical distinction between nature, ruled by law, and history, dominated by freedom and contingency. The laws of nature themselves may evolve; freedom and contingency appear to be fundamental features of reality, not restricted to humans and their history. In working out a contemporary doctrine of creation and providence, theology must deal with the freedom that is present throughout creation. Evolution reveals the contingency of the history of life, the role of chance and accident, and the massive occurrence of suffering and death. This raises in a very powerful and novel way the ancient problem of EVIL. It also raises a profound question concerning the meaning of life and of the evolutionary history of life. Theology must continue to recast its entire interpretation of Christian faith in order to answer the questions raised by evolution and this must include a thorough revision of the doctrine of God.

Above all, theology (and Christian faith) must work to eliminate all anthropocentrism from its self-understanding and from its understanding of God's relation to the world. For millennia we have assumed that God is interested only in the human species and that nature is simply there for us to do with as we please.

But evolution forces us to recognize that all life is related. Theology must interpret this to mean that, if the human species is of value in itself and to God, then all life and all creation is of value in itself and to God. Too much theology is still cast in anthropocentric moulds and has yet to learn from Francis of Assisi's simple but most profound syllogism: if God is creator and Jesus has revealed God as Father, then all creatures are literally brothers and sisters, God's children. Christian theology must work out the implications of this vision and hold it forward as the ideal to which we are called in thought and action.

Barbour, Ian (1990) *Religion in an Age of Science*, San Francisco, CA: Harper & Row.
——(1993) *Ethics in an Age of Technology*, San Francisco, CA: Harper & Row.
Darwin, Charles (1859) *On the Origin of Species*, London: John Murray.
——(1871) *The Descent of Man and Selection in Relation to Sex*, 2 vols, London: John Murray.
Dawkins, Richard (1987) *The Blind Watchmaker: Why The Evidence of Evolution Reveals a Universe without Design*, New York: W.W. Norton.
Gilkey, Langdon (1970) *Religion and the Scientific Future*, New York: Harper & Row.
——(1985) *Creationism on Trial: Evolution and God at Little Rock*, Minneapolis, MN: Winston Press.
Greene, John C. (1959) *The Death of Adam: Evolution and Its Impact on Western Thought*, Ames, IA: Iowa State University Press.
Peacocke, Arthur (1986) *God and the New Biology*, San Francisco, CA: Harper & Row.
Simpson, George Gaylord (1949) *The Meaning of Evolution*, New Haven, CT: Yale University Press.
Teilhard de Chardin, Pierre (1959) *The Phenomenon of Man*, New York: Harper.
Whitehead, Alfred North (1929) *Process and Reality: An Essay in Cosmology*, New York: Macmillan; corrected edition, ed. David Ray Griffin and Donald W. Sherburne, New York: Free Press, 1978.

Thomas E. Hosinski

EXODUS

In the Hebrew Scriptures the Jewish people were delivered from Egyptian bondage in *c*.1300 BCE. According to the Bible, the Egyptians overwhelmed the Hebrew slaves with work; they 'made their lives bitter with hard service, in mortar and brick, and in all kinds of work in the field; in all their work they made them serve

with rigour' (Exodus 1: 14). Such affliction caused the people to cry out to God for liberation. In response God decreed:

> I have seen the affliction of my people who are in Egypt, and have heard their cry because of their taskmasters; I know their sufferings, and I have come down to deliver them out of the hand of the Egyptians.
>
> (Exodus 3: 7–8)

For the Jewish people such an experience is typologically significant; it is a paradigm of divine liberation of the oppressed and persecuted. Throughout Jewish history the Exodus continued to play a dominant role in the Jewish faith. In particular the festival of Passover was regarded as crucially important in the religious life of the people. The Passover *seder* (meal) envisages the Exodus experience as a symbol of freedom and oppression, and the whole of the *Haggadah* (Passover prayer book) is pervaded by the image of God as the Saviour of humankind. For this reason the Passover service begins with an ancient formulaic invitation to those who hunger or are in need to participate in the festival:

> This is the bread of affliction that our fathers ate in the land of Egypt. All who hunger let them come and eat: all who are in need, let them come and celebrate the Passover. Now we are here – next year we shall be free men.

Any Jew who sits down to the Passover meal and is oblivious to the call of those who are in want has missed the meaning of the celebration.

During the service the leader displays the unleavened bread to stimulate the curiosity of the youngsters at the meal. It is then the turn of the youngest child to ask about the nature of the Passover festivities. The entire RITUAL of the *seder* hinges on these enquiries. In reply the leader recites the narrative of the Exodus stressing the themes of liberation and freedom from oppression.

> We were Pharaoh's servants in Egypt; and the Lord our God brought us out thereof with a mighty hand and an outstretched arm. Now, had not the Holy One brought out our

fathers from Egypt, then we and our children and our children's children would be enslaved to Pharaoh in Egypt. Wherefore, even were we all wise men, all men of understanding, all advanced in years, all men with knowledge of the *Torah*, it would yet be our duty to recount the story of the coming forth from Egypt; and all who recount at length the story of the coming forth from Egypt are verily to be praised.

This response (based on Deuteronomy 6: 21) implies that the Passover does not simply commemorate a triumph of remote antiquity. Rather the Passover ceremony is a celebration of the emancipation of each Jew in every generation, for had it not been for the Exodus Jews would still be slaves in Egypt. The keynote of the *Haggadah* is enshrined in a central pledge of the *seder*:

It is the divine pledge that hath stood by our fathers and by us also. Not only one man has risen against us to destroy us, but in every generation men have risen against us to destroy us: but the Holy One delivereth us always from their hand.

Here Pharaoh's action is seen as a paradigm of all attempts by Israel's enemies to persecute the Jewish people. Echoes of centuries of persecution are evoked by these words, yet it is made clear that God has been, and will continue to be, on the side of the oppressed people.

In the symbols of the Passover meal, deliverance is re-enacted. Explaining this symbolism the leader states with regard to the shankbone of the lamb:

The Passover Lamb that our fathers used to eat when the Temple was still standing – that was because the Holy One, blessed be he, passed over the house of our fathers in Egypt, as it is said: 'Ye shall say, It is the sacrifice of the Lord's Passover, who passed over the houses of the children of Israel in Egypt, when he smote the Eyptians and delivered our houses.' And the people bowed the head and worshipped.

The unleavened bread is the bread of affliction, the historical emblem of the Exodus. The leader declares that it is the symbol of sympathy for the enslaved as well as that of freedom from oppression:

This unleavened bread that we eat – what is the reason? It is because there was no time for our ancestors' dough to become leavened, before the King, King of all Kings, the Holy One, revealed himself to them and redeemed them, as it is said: 'And they baked unleavened cakes of dough which they brought forth out of Egypt, for it was not leavened: because they were thrust out of Egypt, and could not tarry, neither had they prepared for themselves any victual.'

The bitter herbs, the symbol of bitterness and servitude, remind the Jews that it is their duty as descendants of slaves to lighten the stranger's burden:

The bitter herb that we eat – what is the reason? It is because the Egyptians embittered the life of our ancestors in Egypt, as it is said: 'And they made their lives bitter with hard bondage, in mortar and brick, and in all manner of service in the field, all their service, when they made them serve, was with rigour.'

The lesson of the Passover service – deeply engraved on the hearts of the Jewish nation – is that persecution and divine deliverance are realities of themselves as delivered from a perpetual enemy and they should assume responsibility for rescuing those who suffer under oppression. The Passover celebration is thus a symbolic exaltation of freedom: Jews are to rejoice in God's liberation of their ancestors in which each of them takes part.

Traditionally the motif of the Exodus has not played a central role in the life of the Christian community. Yet with the emergence of Christian LIBERATION THEOLOGY over the last few decades, the Biblical account of the Exodus from Egypt has come to the fore: like the Jewish nation these Christian theologians look to the history of the Jewish people for inspiration in their struggle against exploitation and oppression in contemporary society. As Gustavo Gutierrez wrote:

> The Exodus experience is paradigmatic. It remains vital and contemporary due to similar historical experiences which the People of God undergo. . . . It structures our faith in the gift of the Father's love. In Christ and through the Spirit, men are becoming one in the very heart of history.
>
> (Gutierrez 1973: 159)

In Egypt the ancient Israelites were exploited and oppressed. Elsa Tamez notes that this experience of oppression involved a degradation so severe that it caused the people to turn to God for deliverance (Tamez 1982). From this act of deliverance, liberation theologians derive a message of hope: if God was on the side of the poor in ancient Israel, surely he still takes sides with the downtrodden. Thus if God has a bias today, it is with the poor and oppressed. This means that God is against the Pharaohs of the modern world. Who are these Pharaohs? They are:

> the tiny minority at home who are in collusion against the great majority; they are the churches and churchpersons who give support to such oligarchies; and they are the rich and powerful from other nations who keep national oligarchies in power; thereby becoming complicit in the ongoing exploitation of the poor.
>
> (Brown 1978: 89–90)

In the view of liberation theologians, God works to liberate those who are oppressed by socioeconomic structures that are EVIL, exploitative and unjust; those who seek to be co-workers with God in creating a just SOCIETY must side with whatever forces are working for the liberation of humankind. According to these writers, the Exodus was not simply an event in the history of the Jewish people; instead it evokes a deep response on the part of the descendants of those who were liberated.

The word (Exodus) was 'recharged' with fresh meanings by successive hermeneutical re-readings up to the time that it was fixed permanently as expressing a whole world-view in the Exodus account in its present form.

> (Croatto 1981: 14)

The profundity of the Exodus therefore consists in its significance for later generations; the past holds a promise for those who understand its relevance. The Exodus is fraught with meaning. For liberation theologians it is an account of the liberation of oppressed peoples. They believe it is possible to understand the plight of those who are presently afflicted from the perspective of the Biblical Exodus – the situation of peoples in economic, political, social or cultural 'bondage'.

In this context liberation theologians stress Moses' crucial role in the process of liberation. Enrique Dussel, for example, begins his study of the history and theology of liberation by focusing on Moses' call to lead his people out of captivity (Dussel 1976). Moses fled to the desert because he killed an Egyptian. He lived comfortably as a herdsman with his wife, his father-in-law and his flocks. But one day he heard God speak to him out of a bush. 'Moses, Moses,' God cried:

> I have seen the affliction of my people who are in Egypt, and have heard their cry because of their taskmasters; I know their sufferings, and I have come down to deliver them out of the hand of the Egyptians. . . . Come, I will send you to Pharaoh that you may bring forth my people, the sons of Israel, out of Egypt.
>
> (Exodus 3: 7–10)

Liberation theologians also utilize the Exodus narrative to explain that God guides the destiny of the persecuted. In the flight from Egypt the Bible stresses that it was God who led the people. God did not take them out by way of the land of the Philistines although that was near, for God said, 'lest the people repent when they see war, and return to Egypt. But God led the people round by the way of the wilderness towards the Red Sea' (Exodus 13: 17–18). When the Egyptian army attempted to capture the Israelites, God intervened and they were saved.

Once Israel crossed the Red Sea, God sustained them in their wanderings. And not only did God deliver and protect his people, he also led them to their own land where they were no longer oppressed. The Exodus is thus a pivotal event for liberation theology; it is regarded as the salvation experience *par excellence*.

Reflecting on the significance of the Exodus, it is clear that both Jews and Christian liberation theologians have found renewed strength and hope in the Biblical account of the deliverance of the ancient Israelites from bondage. The Passover ceremony unites the Jewish people with their ancestors who endured slavery and oppression. Despite the persecution of centuries, the Jewish nation is confident of eventual deliverance and the ultimate redemption of humankind (*see* ANTI-SEMITISM). The message of the Exodus calls the Jewish people to hold steadfast to their conviction that justice and freedom will prevail throughout the world. Similarly, Christian liberationists believe that in the Exodus experience God has spoken to all human beings; in taking on the cause of the oppressed, he revealed the divine quest for the creation of a just society. Thus Jews and Christian liberationists share a common Biblical heritage and vision of the transformation of society, and the Exodus event unites them in a common hope and aspiration for the triumph of JUSTICE. Remembering the redemption of all who are oppressed – this Biblical motif thus contains a reservoir of meaning for Christians and Jews alike in their struggle to create a better world.

Brown, Robert M. (1978) *Theology in a New Key: Responding to Liberation Themes*, Philadelphia, PA: Westminster Press.

Cohn-Sherbok, Dan (1987) *On Earth as it is in Heaven: Jews, Christians and Liberation Theology*, Maryknoll, NY: Orbis.

——(1992) *Exodus: An Agenda for Jewish–Christian Dialogue*, London: Bellew.

Croatto, J. Severino (1981) *Exodus*, Maryknoll, NY: Orbis.

Dussel, Enrique (1976) *History and the Theology of Liberation*, Maryknoll, NY: Orbis.

Gutierrez, Gustavo (1973) *A Theology of Liberation*, Maryknoll, NY: Orbis.

Tamez, Elsa (1982) *Bible of the Oppressed*, Maryknoll, NY: Orbis.

Dan Cohn-Sherbok

EXPERIMENTATION

The concept of experimentation is derived from the idea of 'experience'. It refers to the controlled or intentional modification of experience with predicted but uncertain outcomes. Far from being inimical to Christian theology, as is widely thought, the notion and practice of experimentation is deeply and fundamentally tied up with that theology and with that tradition to which none the less it has an ambivalent relation. A principal foundation of western society and its precursors is the experimental imperative. It is by this imperative that it lives and it is by this imperative that it may die.

Experiment-um describes the action of trying something, of placing it before the test of experience, of empirical or other confirmatory proof. It is a test or a trial where the outcome is (possibly) predicted but is uncertain. Thus the trial by ordeal or by battle of putative offenders betokens a model of JUSTICE based on experimentation. The OED gives some of the earliest systematic references to experimentation as having roots in Christian theology. Thus in 1382 John Wyclif, the apparent originator of the English term 'experience', modified that term so that the taking of experience becomes 'xperiment' (*gen.* xlii 15) which then refers to the action of putting to the test, a trial. By 1597, in *Of the Laws of Ecclesiastical Polity*, Richard Hooker, 'the judicious Hooker', the early and major English political theologian, had spoken of 'The gathering of principles out of their owne particular experiments'. As subsequent theological and religious uses of the term 'experiment' abounded, so the idea of 'experimental religion' developed, as did Bishop Hall's idea, given in the OED that 'one practised in experimentall divinity would know how to stay a weak conscience and to raise one who had fallen' (*Epist* 1.vii 1614). By the middle of that century the idea of experimental divinity and with it the experimental divine had gained purchase as had the idea of experimental philosophy, itself concerned with an investigation of the workings of God in the laws of nature. Even before the rise of science and scientific experimentation in the early modern west, the religious idea of experimentation was firmly established.

A possible implication of this observation is not that the rise of science and experimentation provided the basis for the destruction of western religion, but that science arose from that religion. Far from being opposed to religion, western science is an extension of western religion.

The thesis that western science is an extension of western religion can be developed through an examination of four representative points in the development of the experimental imperative. First is the foundational attitude in Thales and Plato. Second is the inductive interrogation of nature, initially formalized by Bacon, that continued to the second half of the twentieth century. The third is the inductive inversion represented by the reaction of Karl Popper to the problem of induction; the failure of which signalled the end of scientific rationalism. The fourth, which emerges from this failure, is that science is partially, or wholly, a belief system or set of belief systems sustained in whole or in part by the wider belief systems from which it has emerged. On this view experimentation is not so much the interrogation of nature as the interrogation of the belief system of the community that authorizes the experimentation. Here the nature/convention distinction that is at the root of the first stage is inverted yet again so that nature becomes subordinate to convention. In a refinement of this view, science is viewed as a series of hegemonic articulations of which experimentation is a part.

All societies learn from and modify their behaviour in the light of experience and some have had quite highly developed forms of practical knowledge without ever adopting the experimental imperative that is at the heart of western SOCIETY. The roots of that imperative are parallel to the roots of THEOLOGY. When Plato wanted to know how to speak correctly about the Gods he raised two inevitable consequences of that question; how may we interrogate the gods and how may we interrogate that of which the gods have knowledge: nature? The foundation of experimentation is intended to be primarily directed at the interrogation of nature, and it is a bold, and perhaps foolish, society indeed that can adopt such interrogation as its driving force. This interrogative attitude towards nature depends upon a distinction being drawn between nature and the human mind, such that the human mind, rather than being a mere aspect of nature, stands apart from nature. When Thales, 580 BCE, returned to Greece from Egypt and Babylon he brought surveying, astronomical and numerical techniques with him but left behind, as superfluous to his needs, the consciousness of the Egyptian cosmion. This early experimental attitude when combined with the inversion in consciousness represented by the Socrates of Plato forms the foundation of experimentation. It established the right to, and the means with which to, interrogate nature *and* the gods. In Aristotle it led to the formalization of the distinction between nature and convention and permitted, even encouraged, the growth of the empirical examination of the world and an attempt to distinguish that which was given, nature, from that which was conventional, cultural and customary.

Ancient Greece contained the foundation of the experimental imperative but was not a society founded on that imperative. In consequence the effect of experimentation was limited. By contrast, Bacon challenged a form of knowledge limited in its possibilities by the stultifying effects of scholasticism. In a series of writings, between 1605 and 1623, he mocked scholastic attempts at making empirical claims and emphasized the primacy of empirical knowledge. In its extreme form, scholasticism would maintain a thesis even against empirical evidence or even deny the relevance of empirical evidence to the settlement of what would now be regarded as disputes of a clearly empirical form. Any, and all, required empirical evidence was, it was held, already contained in the ancient writings, including, importantly and ironically, Aristotle; and it was to an examination of these authorities that the scholastic turned in settling disputes. Bacon's achievement was twofold, first to re-establish the right to interrogate nature and, second, to propose a method for doing so: the inductive method.

The inductive method as postulated by Bacon consists of two distinct processes. In the first the mind is purged of anthropocentrism, personal prejudices, arguments from AUTHORITY, and all terms used are clearly defined. Similar claims were later made in philosophy by René Descartes in *Discourse on Method* (1637) and in politics by Thomas Hobbes in *Leviathan* (1651). In the second part of the process Bacon identifies four principal elements of the inductive method: empirical observation; the analysis of the empirically obtained data; the production of hypothesis from that analysis; and, finally, the verification of such hypotheses through observation and through experimentation. In short, nature, and hence God's will lying behind nature, should be interrogated. In social affairs a similar method was applied, again by Descartes and Hobbes, as the analytic-synthetic or resolutive-compositive method. It is impossible to overestimate the significance of this turn of attitude. It can best be summed up, perhaps, as the conversion of NATURAL LAW (moral) to laws of nature (scientific). Both are concerned with the workings of God in the world, but while the first confines itself to the commands of God as imperatives of eternal, divine, natural action, and its proper positive reflection in the human and moral affairs of mankind, the latter interrogates the means by which eternal, divine and natural law are implemented and examines their specification. For the first time the actions of God in the universe and in nature were systematically examined and interrogated. Underlying this interrogation was a set of rationalist principles derived from a particular view of the relation of God to the world. The attitude can best be summarized in Descartes' view first, that the self is transparent to examination by itself and second, that God would not so construct the world that it would be inaccessible to reason. In Descartes, Hobbes, Hume, Leibniz and others the rationalism spilled over into social comment and support of social experiment. As Buckle put it, 'experiment . . . is merely experience artificially modified'. It follows from rationalist principles that *if* the ground of experience is invariant then the modification of experience in experiment changes not the ground but its applicability. In a universe of limited variables, ultimately the whole is knowable and a particular possible social, moral and technical course can be charted for humankind. Auguste Comte's positivist epithet puts the point with startling clarity, 'To know in order to predict, to predict in order to control', where the control is not just of nature but also, and more significantly, of the moral world.

Not everyone was convinced either of the efficacy or of the morality of the rationalist experiment with the social world. Edmund Burke attacked the French Revolution as a grotesque experiment involving an entire society. He argued that social and political knowledge was practical knowledge and not theoretical. The application of abstract theory to the social and political world ignored the distinctive nature of practical knowledge, knowledge that was not subsumable to theoretical principles. A similar theme was echoed in the twentieth century by Michael Oakeshott who argued that the rationalism which was deep at the heart of western politics confused two different modes of experience. Political and social experimentation would be an *ignoratio elenchi*, an argument to the wrong point, literally a pearl of ignorance.

The principle challenge to the experimental imperative and its rationalist forbears comes, however, not from challenges from outside that perspective but from problems internal to that imperative and to the inductive method. The inductive method starts from experience, moves to generality and then tests the generality against experience. Thus a set of experiences E_1, $E_2 . . . E_n$ should yield laws L_1, $L_2 . . . L_n$ but no set of subsequent experiences will ever verify L_1, $L_2 . . . L_n$. Thus from the observation that the sun has risen every morning hitherto one cannot verify the claim, *ceteris paribus*, that the sun will rise tomorrow morning, nor will the fact of its rising tomorrow morning increase the probability of its rising the following morning and thereafter. A putative solution to this problem was offered by Karl Popper in 1934, although ignored for some years. Popper's argument is that no number of instances of observation will or can verify a hypothesis but a single observation may well falsify a hypothesis. Thus the function of an experiment is not to show that something is right but to attempt to show that a hypothesis is wrong. In some experimental protocols this shows itself as an attempt to disprove the null hypothesis, however this merely technical device does not deal with the serious challenge to rationalism raised by the problems of verification. Popper's second claim is that there is no clear and necessary link between experience and the hypothesis, as often as not the hypothesis is not even inspired by related experience. A notable example of this is Einstein's special theory of relativity, shattering in its impact yet conjured up through thought experiments of situations that could not have occurred in experience. On this second claim the function of experience and, therefore, experiment, is not to provide the data for the hypothesis but to attempt to disprove a hypothesis already generated. The relation of experience to the generation of that hypothesis may be slight and not itself discoverable. The effect of this mode of thinking, although not felt for some years, was profound. It wrenches context and meaning apart. While Popper would deny the claim he effectively provided a foundation for the deconstruction of the notion of induction, and with that the experimental imperative as well as the society generated alongside it has been thrown into doubt.

The fourth stage in the transformation of that experimental imperative flows as a consequence of the turn in philosophy of which Popper, and others, were unwittingly, perhaps a part. The problem as it affects science is best exhibited in the apparent claims of Thomas Kuhn. Kuhn claims that the history of science shows that science does not develop according to a linear mode of progress, but in 'paradigmatic shifts'. As a paradigm contains its own rules of evidence, there is no neutral and objective means by which one paradigm can be tested against such rules for its truth value. One possible consequence of this argument, on some readings, is that science cannot be regarded as 'progressive' for that notion requires an objective standard against which a judgement of progression can be made. Similarly it would seem that any conclusions reached by experimentation are, at best, relative and of limited validity.

The arguments to the relativity of science have been challenged but what is significant is less the validity or otherwise of Kuhn's and similar arguments than a widespread, almost generalized, lack of confidence in science and experimentation as a mode of progress. An increase in scientific and rationalistic knowledge can not be judged as progressive from an exegesis of science and rationalism. The

conclusion to progress was eisegetically placed into science from one of its major underlying meta-narratives: Christianity. It is from Christianity that the idea of temporal direction, will, cause, constancy and eschatological progress were obtained. It was Christian thinkers who, in turning to science and to experimentation hoped to discover the will of God in the natural universe.

Several conclusions follow from these observations; a few can be mentioned. First, the much-vaunted and putative clash between Science and Theology is misplaced for their roots are the same; they are but different expressions of the same underlying meta-narratives. Second, doubts exhibited in the philosophy of science go hand in hand with scepticism seen both there and elsewhere about God. As Nietzsche's view that, 'God is dead' has come to permeate philosophy, culture, and science, so theology has also, and not surprisingly, come to a crisis. Theology and science are not, and never have been, except in mistaken perceptions, in a condition of warfare; their futures are bound together. Theology is in a crisis but science, the experimental imperative and the CULTURE built upon these platforms is in crisis too. The fate of science, experimentation and theology are tied together. Third, the failure to recognize the theological underpinnings of the experimental imperative have correlated with the globe itself becoming the subject of an (uncontrolled) experiment by a dominant culture once sure of, but now doubting its hegemonic right. In that sense the very conditions of life have become part of an experiment led by a culture now incredulous towards its own principle and founding meta-narratives. That such incredulity may have come too late for the capacity, as Arendt puts it, to act into nature, to change the given, is a new and extremely alarming departure (Arendt 1958). In an awesome way we have taken our future in our own hands in a manner scarcely glimpsed at by our forebears and blurred the distinction between nature and convention set out by our predecessors. When Socrates asked 'and how may we speak correctly of the gods' he did not understand or fully appreciate the implication of the observation that we may not speak of the gods, we may speak only, and unclearly at that, of ourselves. When Stephen Hawking in introducing a new meta-narrative for a scientific age said that we will come to know the mind of God, he echoed the mistake of Socrates, for the interrogation of nature is primarily the interrogation of ourselves. We are the seeing eye which turns back on the fabric of the universe and makes of it what the dominant hegemonic articulation, in this case science, determines. This is not to say that we discover nothing, but it is to say that what we discover is predominantly driven by and shaped by dominant cultural forces and should be treated with all the scepticism, and occasional disdain, that such an outlook deserves. It is to overlook the crucial relation between our religious culture and our scientific culture, to forget that the concepts of one meta-narrative provided the foundation for the concepts of another and not entirely dissimilar meta-narrative. The experimental method in narrowing the range of permitted experiences allows us to speak, as before, principally of ourselves, but this time in the most limited, illusory, and, because of its potential consequences, the most dangerous way yet devised. There are several aspects to that danger: first, the role of Christian theology in providing some fundamental concepts within which the interrogation of nature can take place; second, its role in fostering the ethos for that interrogation; and third, in surrendering all too meekly to its world-consuming intellectual and practical drive. The effect of this has been clear and decisive. It is, as Marx said, that history repeats itself as tragedy and as farce. On this occasion the challenges are greater and the stakes are higher than Socrates could ever have imagined. Few, if any of us, can truly claim to have clean hands; what we have yet to see is whether the Socratic rupture between the gods and the human repeats itself as tragedy as farce or even as both. (*See also* VIVISECTION.)

Arendt, Hannah (1958), *The Human Condition*, Chicago IL: Chicago University Press.

Ayer, A.J. (1971) *Language, Truth and Logic*, Harmondsworth: Penguin.

Bacon, Francis (1605) *The Advancement of Learning*.

Comte, Auguste (1830–42) *Cours de Philosophie Positive* (6 vols: trans. and condensed by Harriet Martieau 1853).

Hawking, Stephen (1988) *A Brief History of Time: From the Big Bang to Black Holes*, London: Bantam Press.

Hooker, Richard (1975) *Of the Laws of Ecclesiastical Polity*, London: Sidgwick & Jackson.

Kuhn, Thomas S. (1970) *The Structure of Scientific Revolutions*, Chicago, IL: University of Chicago Press.

Oakeshott, Michael (1962) 'Rationalism in Politics', in *Rationalism in Politics and Other Essays*, London: Methuen.

Popper, Karl (1972) *The Logic of Scientific Discovery*, London: Hutchinson.

Strauss, Leo Strauss (1950) *Natural Right and History*, Chicago IL: University of Chicago Press.

Weber, Max (1930) *The Protestant Ethic and the Spirit of Capitalism*, London: George Allen and Unwin.

Paul Barry Clarke

FALL

'Fallenness' refers to the perceived gap between the universe as it now is and the universe as it was intended to be in the CREATION purposes of God. 'The Fall' refers to that event or process by which such a gap was brought about.

Any religion that believes in a Creator God who is all-good and all-powerful has the problem of explaining the occurrence of EVIL and SUFFERING in the world. The doctrine of the Fall (which has been part of the traditional Judaeo-Christian response to the problem of evil) accepts the reality of evil and suffering, asserts that they have no place in the Creation purposes or ultimate will of the Creator, and attributes them instead to the agency and operation of creatures. The doctrine of the Fall thus requires and affirms a belief in the FREE WILL of those creatures whom it regards as responsible for rebelling against the Creator, thereby disrupting the harmony and happiness which were His purpose for His Creation. The doctrine of the Fall is thus a) an affirmation of the goodness of God and a denial of His direct responsibility for evil and suffering, and b) an inherent protest against forms of DETERMINISM that undermines moral responsibility.

Within Christian theology, the *locus classicus* for understanding the Fall has traditionally been the story of Adam and Eve's disobedience in Genesis 3. There, the sociological divisions between people (3: 12, 16b; cf. 4: 1–8), the ecological divisions between people and nature (3: 16a, 17–19), and the psychological divisions between people and themselves (contrast 2: 25 with 3: 7) are presented narratively as being dependent upon the fundamental theological division between people and God (3: 8). Such divisions are characterized as being ontologically secondary, and thus the doctrine of the Fall is paradoxically, an affirmation of the essential goodness of Creation. It is also a sign of hope, for if these divisions are not intrinsic to Creation, then it is conceivable that Creation could be liberated from them.

Within Christian theology, the Fall has generally been treated as the mid-point (and the low-point) of a three-phase theological conception of human history, comprising Creation, Fall and Redemption. Any loss of confidence in the doctrine of the Fall is therefore likely to have significant consequences, not just for THEODICY (the attempt to justify belief in the righteousness of God in the face of the problem of evil), but also for any doctrine of salvation. There has been precisely such a loss of confidence in the doctrine of the Fall from the time of Darwin to the present day. The discovery that human beings evolved, and that suffering, disease, disaster and death all occurred before the emergence of humanity, made it difficult to maintain that these divisions and distortions were the consequence of human disobedience. The fossils tell us of no golden age of universal health and harmony, and the whole evolutionary hypothesis allows for no such position (*see* EVOLUTION).

Where modern theology has addressed the doctrine of the Fall at all, it has usually reinterpreted it to take account of the current scientific consensus. This has been attempted in a number of different ways. First, one trend has been to see the Fall story of Genesis 3, not as a protohistorical account (however symbolically narrated), but as a depiction of the recurring pattern of human behaviour. It is pointed out that the name 'Adam' means 'humanity', and this is taken as justification for seeing the story as being simply paradigmatic of how humans behave. This approach, circumventing as it does the scientific question, has been popular, and has even found its way into modern hymnody: 'Lord, forgive Adam, for Adam is me'. Clearly, the Fall story *is* paradigmatic, and, as a paradigm, it is highly illuminative of the human condition. However, to see it as *merely* paradigmatic has three fundamental weaknesses – theological, exegetical and theodical. The theological weakness is that is difficult to state this view in a way that avoids Pelagianism. If the Fall story is only descriptive of human experience and not in any way constitutive of it, then one must either follow Pelagius in denying that human nature is in any way tainted or morally distorted, or one has to see such distortion as a design fault which the Creator is directly responsible. The exegetical weakness of this view is that Genesis 3 seems to present itself as being both aetiological and protohistorical. Aetiologically, the story attempts to explain the origin of such evils as toil in work and pain in childbirth, which would make no sense in a merely paradigmatic reading. Protohistorically, the context of Genesis 3 in its final, canonical redaction suggests that there are chronological paths to be traced, however tenuously and tentatively, from the protohistory of Genesis 3 to the later history of the Abrahamic peoples. (See the genealogies 5 & 10.) In addition to these theological and exegetical weaknesses, there is the theodical weakness that natural evil is left unexplained.

A second trend has been to see the Fall not as a fall *away* from God's purposes for humanity, but as an upward leap *towards* them, corresponding to some crucial moment of evolutionary development. However, this view is even more difficult to square with the Biblical account and, indeed, with ethical monotheism – if the Fall was upward, then disobedience is sanctioned and rewarded – and, again, carries no theodical weight.

Thirdly, Tillich suggested that Creation and Fall, though notionally distinct, were chronologically simultaneous. The question then arises, however, to whose agency fallenness should be ascribed? If Creation and Fall are truly simultaneous, it is difficult to see how fallenness can be ascribed to any other agency than that of the Creator, in which God remains directly responsible for our fallen condition, and little theodical use would appear to be served by speaking of fallenness at all. If the Fall is creaturely – and it must be if it is to have theodical and explanatory power – then it must in some sense be historical.

These three approaches to the Fall fail to find it of any theodical usefulness *vis-à-vis* natural evil. There have, however, been three post-Darwinian approaches which attempt to explain natural evil by speaking of nature as fallen, yet still to take account of the fact that natural evil seems to have predated humanity. First, in what, astonishingly, remains the most recent major work on the doctrine of the Fall, N.P. Williams posits the pre-mundane Fall of the World-Soul, or Life-Force, and attributes the dividedness and cruelty of nature to the 'voluntary deviation of the World-Soul from conformity with the will of the Creator' (Williams 1927).

Williams rightly asserts that 'This conception of the Life-Force permeates much of the cosmological speculation of modern times'; it is not, however, part of more recent cosmological speculation, and few are likely to find it convincing today.

The second such approach is that of PROCESS THEOLOGY. This, too, accepts that nature is far from being what God would have it be (see David Ray Griffin in Davis, 1981: 111–12). It attributes this fact to the freedom which it believes every level of created reality to possess. To exist is to be free, and, if nature is not what God intended it to be, then that is the result of the accumulation of occasions on which God's advice (or 'initial aim' in process terminology) has been disregarded. The way in which this view is assessed will depend upon how plausible the idea of sub-human, and indeed sub-sentient, levels of nature making choices is seen to be, or whether the randomness of such levels can be shown to be necessary to the development of human freedom.

The third attempt to explain the fallenness of nature and to reconcile it with what we know from science, is that of the Fall of the Angels. A number of writers (e.g. Mascall, Plantinga, Davis) have drawn on the Judaeo-Christian tradition of an angelic Fall which predated the human Fall. They further suggest that this angelic Fall could have distorted the way in which Creation developed, thus explaining why natural evil pre-dates the emergence of humanity. Indeed, a closer examination of the early chapters of Genesis contradicts the initial impression that all is harmonious and happy before the human Fall. The command to 'subdue' the earth suggests opposition, the snake is clearly antipathetic to the commands of God, and Eden is only a garden – not the whole Creation. It is arguable that God's intention for humanity was that they should restore to the whole of Creation that harmony which was disrupted by the prior angelic Fall. Instead of becoming part of the solution, however, human beings compounded the problem by themselves rebelling. Genesis 3 can thereby hold humanity responsible for the divisions within Creation, without requiring that no such divisions existed prior to the human Fall. This position has a number of advantages. First, it attributes all evil and suffering to the free choices of creatures, and not to the direct will or agency of God. Secondly, it both takes account of and accounts for the fact that natural evil preceded humanity. Thirdly, it maintains a balance between the moral responsibility of human beings as actors and the mitigated responsibility of human beings as acted upon. Fourthly, it draws on and makes use of a whole strand of Biblical discourse which is arguably more prevalent than the Adam and Eve story but which is usually neglected in Christian theodical discussion. The strange beings of Genesis 6: 1–4, the watchers of Jewish intertestamental literature and the principalities and powers of the New Testament (e.g. Ephesians 6: 12) could take their place in the view that takes seriously the role of free, non-human, spiritual agents in the interactions that lie behind human experience. Fifthly, this view avoids anthropocentrism by refusing to limit fallenness to humanity. The whole of Creation is seen as being embraced by the Fall and, further, as being embraced within God's redemptive purposes. Thus, the *status quo* is not defended as being *ipso facto* the will of God. On the contrary, disease, disorder, division and death are seen as being at variance with the will of God (hence the healing and nature miracles of Christ) and as being healed in principle by the Cross (hence the Biblical visions of a future in which the wolf lies down with the lamb, and death and pain are no more).

It is here that the relevance of the doctrine is most far-reaching. If nature is fallen, then there is no straightforward line to be drawn from present reality to the purposes of God. We may not argue from the fact that a sentient being is suffering to the proposition that it is God's will that it should so suffer. We may not argue from the cruelty of nature to the assertion that God is not concerned about how we treat animals. We may not argue that the occurrence of 'natural' miscarriages legitimates planned abortions. We may not argue from a felt homosexual orientation to the conclusion 'God made me this way'. The doctrine of the Fall invalidates any argument which assumes that the *status quo* is the will of God. On the contrary, the doctrine of the Fall acts as a challenge to the *status quo*

and a mandate to join the Creator in fighting the pain, the disease, the cruelty and the sin which mar God's world, but have no essential place within it.

Nor is the fight against evil seen in Christian theology as being ultimately of fitful success and permanent duration. The Fall is seen as having been in principle undone in the incarnation, life, death and resurrection of Christ. In His healing miracles, humanity was at last beginning to fulfil its vocation to restore that harmony which was God's original purpose for His Creation. In his obedience, the disobedience of Adam was being overturned (Romans 5: 12–21). In His death, the fundamental division between us and God was being dealt with, and the principalities and powers were being disarmed (Colossians 2: 15). In His RESURRECTION is the promise of a renewed Creation in which death and suffering have no place. This eschatological vision of Creation healed is expressed in the New Testament in terms of the Fall being (at least) undone – Satan defeated (Romans 16: 20, cf. Genesis 3: 15), the curse revoked (Revelation 22: 3, cf. Genesis 3: 14, 17), access to the tree of life no longer barred (Revelation 22: 2, cf. Genesis 3: 22–24), and heaven and earth remade (Revelation 21: 1–4).

Davis, S.T. (1981) *Encountering Evil*, Edinburgh: T. & T. Clark Ltd.

Griffin, D.R. (1976) *God, Power and Evil*, Philadelphia: The Westminster Press.

Kemp, E.W. (ed.) (1969) *Man: Fallen & Free*, Hodder and Stoughton.

Linzey, A. (1987) *Christianity and the Rights of Animals*, London: SPCK.

Mascall, E.L. (1956) *Christian Theology and Natural Science*, London: Longmans, Green & Co., Ltd.

Plantinga, A.C. (1974) *God, Freedom and Evil*, New York: Harper & Row.

Tennant, F.R. (1903) *The Sources of the Doctrines of the Fall and of Original Sin*, Cambridge: Cambridge University Press.

Wenham, G.J. (1987) *Genesis 1–15* in the Word Biblical Commentary series, Waco, Texas: Word Books.

Williams, N.P. (1927) *The Ideas of the Fall and of Original Sin*, London: Longmans, Green & Co., Ltd.

Michael Lloyd

FAMILY

The term 'family' has a wide range of potential referents; as a point of departure, however, we may distinguish between a set of relationships on the one hand and a relatively bounded social group on the other. In the case of the former, we are conventionally talking about those relationships established, directly or indirectly, through MARRIAGE or through parenthood. These key terms, 'marriage' and 'parenthood', are themselves subject to a wide range of interpretation. In all cases, the important feature is the extent to which and the way in which such relationships are socially recognized and socially sanctioned. In the case of 'marriage' we are talking about socially approved sexual relationships, while in the case of 'parenthood' we are referring to those claims which are socially made and socially recognized, whether or not any actual biological relationship exists. Potentially, the number of such relationships for any one individual might be very large indeed, especially if we include ancestors and past generations, and all societies place some kind of limitations on the numbers and kinds of family and kin relationships which are seen to be significant. It is best to think of family here as a set of potential ties which may become significant in different ways and for different purposes. Thus, different considerations may influence decisions to do with inheritance, gatherings for ritual purposes, limitations on potential marriage partners or the calling upon relations in times of crisis.

The other way of considering the term 'family' is in terms of some relatively bounded group, a set of people who are recognized and who recognize themselves as 'a family'. Of course these two ways of understanding 'family' are interdependent and represent two ways of understanding the same social phenomenon. In the case of the bounded group we often understand this in spatial terms; alongside the words 'marriage' and 'parenthood' there is a third term, 'residence', and family groupings contain some mixture of all three elements. One particular term which has often been used in this context is 'household', a set of persons sharing a common residence and usually sharing at least some meals and facilities together. It is important to note, however, that, first, households may include persons other than family members (e.g. lodgers or servants) and, second and more importantly, that family relationships always cut across individual households. Thus the 'Western' practice of setting up a separate household after marriage does not preclude continuing or developing family relationships between that new household and other existing or future households.

At the heart of family relationships is a complex interplay between biology and CULTURE. Rather than seeing biology as determining the family it is more helpful to see the varying ideas of 'family' as deciding which biological relationships should be treated as being of significance. While there remains considerable room for debate and disagreement, it would seem that once widely accepted notions presenting the family as a fixed, biologically based, social institution performing relatively abiding functions on behalf of SOCIETY and the individual have been challenged by the cumulative work of sociologists, social anthropologists and social historians. There is now a much greater recognition of the variety of ways in which the 'family' is understood and experienced, by lay persons as well as by professionals, and of the importance of seeing family relationships as a process rather than as denoting some fixed entity. This entails seeing family and domestic relationships as constantly undergoing change as individuals move between and through households, as they move through their own life courses or careers and as both individuals and households themselves interact with the wider, and also changing, society. This also entails a recognition that family relationships can rarely, if ever, be studied in isolation but have to be studied in the context of wider networks of social relationships and in interaction with a variety of other social institutions.

The study of the family, therefore, is increasingly seen as a matter of some considerable complexity. Simple models of the interplays between family and society and equally simple accounts of how that family has supposedly changed from a pre-industrial form to an industrial form have been partially replaced by more finely nuanced and more variable accounts. In part this has been a question of recognizing a wider range of variations between family experiences whilst also recognizing strong themes of continuity, and in part it has been a question of recognizing differences within households.

One important difference, here reflecting the impact of feminist scholarship, has been that of GENDER. Contrary to more unitary models of marriage or the family, it is now increasingly recognized that men and women often experience these relationships in different ways, have differing understandings of the significance and nature of family ties and obligations and derive different benefits and losses from their involvements in domestic life. Further, changes in the position of women in the wider society, especially in paid employment, have been a major influence on interpersonal relationships within the household and wider family relations.

In any discussion of family relationships there are close connections between changes in actual family practices and questions of values dealing with the position of the family in the wider society and with what are understood to be the correct patterns of conduct between family members, their duties and their responsibilities. In considering such values, it can be seen that religion in general has played an important part, especially although not exclusively in the case of Christianity. It might, indeed, be supposed that the role of Christianity in relation to the family and family values has been one which is supportive of such values, as one of seeing the family as a central institution within society and giving clear endorsement to the principles of fidelity within marriage and the wider recognition and fulfilment of familial obligations. Such a model of 'the family' might appear to be a fairly traditional one although in practice it would appear to be flexible enough to allow for change and the incorporation of a recognition of, say, DIVORCE or family planning (see CONTRACEPTION).

In fact, the relationships between the Christian (and other) religions and the family have been, and continue to be, more complex than this. We may begin by considering religion and family as two important bases for individual identification. Thus, an individual might define himself or himself in terms of some family-based identity or in terms of a membership of a religious community. One conventional, and probably still quite widespread, way of understanding these two bases for identification is to see them as mutually reinforcing. A child becomes a member of a religious community through its membership of a family; many baptism ceremonies explicitly recognize this. The basic units of a religious community are seen as families rather than individuals and, reciprocally, the church is supportive, at both a general and a specific level, of family life and family values. Much of the symbolism of Christmas works through an assumed identity of religious community and ideal projections of the family.

However, this is not the whole story. Max Weber pointed to a possible tension between the more universalistic claims of the major world religions and the more particularistic values associated with families and family obligations. Here, family and religion may be understood as providing competing bases for allegiance and the investment of time and resources. This kind of competition has also been recognized closer to our own time in many mass movements such as various forms of communism, fascism and nationalism. Individuals may be called upon to sever family ties and to choose a life of CELIBACY or, less frequently, of promiscuity.

For the most part, the situation in modern societies is rarely as clear-cut as these two extremes of identity or competition may suggest. There is rarely complete overlap between family and church but there is rarely complete tension or opposition either. In a complex society, family and religion become two of a series or set of overlapping obligations and commitments which may sometimes become a source of tension under particular circumstances. What needs to be built into the discussion is a consideration of the overall place of religion in society as a whole, taking society to mean here the nation-state.

We may first consider a unitary model whereby religious community and society may be understood to be different facets of the same sets of relations located in a stable and bounded territory. Here we may find a mutually reinforcing system of community, family and religion. Clearly many so-called folk or traditional societies conform to this model and such models may often be extended, via myth and IDEOLOGY, to include the nation as a whole. Whilst a nation, unlike a local community, may not necessarily consist of members of a single faith and will certainly not consist of members of a huge extended family, the rhetoric and symbolism may seek to blur over religious, ethnic, gender and class differences in favour of some unitary model. This model may be found in some of the more authoritarian modern societies or during particular times of history such as war or in the early days of independence.

In most cases, however, we will be faced with a more pluralistic model, where there are different religious faiths and traditions within any one nation. From the perspective of an individual adherent, there may be hostility to, and boundaries erected against, the values and practices held to characterize the wider society. In some cases, the Amish and the Hutterites being prominent North American examples, family and religion will reinforce each other in some measure of opposition to the secular values of the dominant society, although over time some measure of accommodation may be reached. Or, the religious faith will cut across family obligations and the cult or sect itself may become, in rhetoric and perhaps in experience, a substitute 'family'. Many modern religious movements such as the Unification Church or the Children of God may serve as illustrations here.

However, among many of the larger, older and possibly more 'secular' religious traditions, a kind of liberal pluralism might develop, one which recognizes a variety of faiths and the rights of individuals to worship as they choose. There will be relatively weak links between religion, family and community although the tacit understanding that religion is a matter of individual choice might indirectly reinforce other wider values such as those to do with DEMOCRACY and the market economy. Further, the relegation of religion to the 'private' sphere may also reinforce a particular understanding of family and domestic life. It may also be argued that the air of tolerance and pluralism

promulgated by the dominant religions may reinforce the total or absolutist demands of the more sectarian forms within the same society.

Of course, such a schema is clearly highly abstract and cannot encompass all possibilities. It should illustrate the general point, however, that, while religion continues to be an important influence in family life and family values in modern society, this influence is by no means straightforward or predictable. Christians have, indeed, found themselves to be on opposite sides in such family-related debates as those about ABORTION, birth control, divorce and surrogate parents.

It is clear at least that family matters continue to be seen as legitimate areas of public concern for religious leaders even where there may be disagreement about the church's involvements in, say, industrial disputes or modern warfare. Certainly, throughout most Western or Christian countries there has been a range of issues, defined as 'social problems', which have demanded some kind of moral response. These include rising divorce rates, increasing rates of cohabitation and the rise in the number of single-parent households. These trends have not, of course, been uniform throughout the developed nations but they represent converging areas of concern. Also linked to these concerns are certain demographic trends, e.g. the increasing proportions of populations defined as ELDERLY, together with certain economic trends such as the increasing proportions of married women in paid EMPLOYMENT. Here one concern is whether the supposed weakened family structures can provide the range of informal care that is sometimes, often erroneously, associated with earlier generations.

As indicated above, the range of Christian responses to these problematic issues has not been uniform. One response, not confined to Christians, has been in terms of a pressure for the development of some kind of family policy, an official recognition by the STATE that family matters are a legitimate area of concern and that all aspects of legislation have some kind of family dimension to them. Another response, not necessarily distinct from this, is in terms of a moral crusade, a concern about the decline of the family and an apparent flight from marriage and about the assumed effects of such changes on the wider social order. If the approach of the former is largely in terms of the future, that of the latter involves an appeal to the past.

It should not be supposed that the responses of social scientists are any more uniform than those of practising Christians; indeed the two may often overlap. However, it is likely that the institutionalized scepticism may at least question some of the less-examined assumptions in these debates. Thus, the notion of 'decline' in family life and values is often challenged, arguing for example that households in the past were often broken by death rather than by divorce, that low or negligible divorce rates were not necessarily an indication of marital harmony and that the idea of a coherent extended family system of informal care was something of a myth. In some cases, it must be assumed, the evidence will never accumulate to the extent that we can establish any firm statements about family change. Thus, for example, it can be said that public concern about CHILD ABUSE has risen in recent years; but it cannot be argued with any certainty whether the incidence of such abuse has increased, decreased or remained stable. This is partly because the term itself is still open to a variety of interpretations and evaluations and partly because much of it takes place behind closed doors, far from the scrutiny of social scientists or statisticians.

However, this is not to say that there have been no significant changes in family living; only that such changes cannot be subsumed under labels such as 'decline' 'loss' or 'modernization'. It is possible, for example, to indicate the growing proportion of women in paid employment as both contributing to and arising out of a wider shift in gender relations especially as they affect the institution of the family. We may also indicate, as a major theme in many countries, 'privatization', a complex process that includes in varying mixes the declining availability of domestic relations to immediate public scrutiny, the identification of marriage and parenthood as major projects and the linking of such projects to wider values to do with personal development and individual fulfilment. Whether a source of approval or otherwise, these trends towards privatization of the home

represent a major *theme* in discussions about Western family life.

The word 'theme' is used to underline an important, perhaps the major, feature of family living today, and the one which perhaps contrasts most sharply with previous centuries. Whatever actual changes – demographic, economic, in terms of marital or parent–child relations – may have taken place it is almost certainly true that the family and marriage have been problematized to an extent and in a way which is different from former times. Put simply, there is now a lot more talk about 'the family' and its discontents. In part, this is reflected in a greater level of abstraction in talking about the family, in part in an increasing number of professionals with interests in family matters and in part again in an increasing focus on family relations as the source of much that is good and much that is bad about society as a whole. Christian influences have certainly played their part in this process of constructing 'the family' and 'family problems'.

Whether there will continue to be an increasing focus on the family and family relationships in the future or whether there will be a more finely tuned appreciation of familial relationships set in the context of wider networks and ties of obligation remains to be seen. It is likely, however, that religious values will continue to play a complex and sometimes contradictory part in the continuing debates about the nature and significance of domestic relations. After all, however defined, familial and marital relationships revolve around issues of sex, birth and death and these too are the abiding concerns of religions at all times and in all places.

Cheal, D. (1991) *Family and the State of Theory*, Hemel Hempstead: Harvester/Wheatsheaf.

Clark, D. (ed.) (1991) *Marriage, Domestic Life and Social Change: Writings for Jacqueline Burgoyne (1944–88)*, London: Routledge.

D'Antonio, W.V. and Aldous, J. (eds) (1983) *Families and Religions: Conflict and Change in Modern Society*, Beverly Hills, CA, and London: University of California Press.

Elshtain, J.B. (ed.) (1982) *The Family in Political Thought*, Brighton: Harvester Press.

Finch, J. (1989) *Family Obligations and Social Change*, Cambridge: Polity.

Goody, J. (1983) *The Development of the Family and*

Marriage in Europe, Cambridge: Cambridge University Press.

Morgan, D.H.J. (1985) *The Family, Politics and Social Theory*, London: Routledge & Kegan Paul.

Obelkevitch, J.J., Roper, L. and Samuel, R. (eds) (1987) *Discipline of Faith: Studies in Religion, Politics and Patriarchy*, London: Routledge & Kegan Paul.

David H.J. Morgan

FARMING

Farming is the manipulation and subjugation of the natural world, especially livestock, in order to sustain human life. Modern human society is based on the daily slaughter of millions of other creatures for food. Our practices are based on certain moral perceptions of animals which are theologically rooted and socially reinforced through language and culture (see Fiddes 1991; Willis 1990). Not surprisingly, fundamental ethical questions about farming have seldom been raised; and even doing so is still a matter of contention.

Despite the prevalence of our use of animals, the actual processes used in farming are often hidden from us or made socially invisible. Western society, spurred on by animal protection societies, has prohibited the public slaughter of animals so that, among the millions of people who consume them, only a tiny fraction have ever witnessed slaughter first hand or are aware of modern confinement methods. The social invisibility of slaughter from the later nineteenth century onwards has been paralleled by the increasing invisibility of farming processes themselves through intensification or 'factory farming'. Since the Second World War, farms have made increasing use of methods resembling production lines, for maximum financial efficiency. In the 1950s, poultry and dairy livestock began to move from pastures to confinement facilities; livestock kept for meat followed in the 1960s.

Reasons for this development include concern for the efficiency of land use and the increasing cost of farm labour. These, with general economies of scale, have led to highly specialized intensive farms, owned by large business corporations. Competition between farms has added to the drive to cut costs and increase production.

It is no longer clear that factory farming has met these needs – or at least done so in a way in which hidden costs have not outweighed its advantages. Characterizations of factory farming as a 'success' have been based on its maximizing of profit and production. Previous thinking has paid little attention to the costs manifested in potential and actual health risks and environmental degradation. These hidden costs have forced a re-evaluation of intensive practices.

For example, because of the unhealthy conditions in which many animals are kept they are prone to disease which has now become endemic within some strains, even some species. 'In 1986, more than a quarter of the samples taken [in the UK] from producers of processed animal protein were found to contain salmonella' (Johnson 1991: 88). The frequent use of antibiotics to counter disease in farm animals has led to the phenomenon of antibiotic-resistant strains of bacteria (see the Swann Report 1969–70). The outbreak of bovine spongiform encephalitis (BSE) in Britain in the late 1980s and early 1990s has been blamed on the practice of feeding animal offal to live animals, and it is unclear whether this disease will cause an outbreak of Kreuzfeld–Jacob disease amongst humans early next century.

Equally disconcerting have been the environmental effects of intensification. It is now recognized that intensive farming is not the most efficient way of utilizing crop land; while the traditional mixed-use farm was virtually energy self-sufficient, the modern farm has 'an insatiable appetite for diesel oil, electricity, synthetic fertilizers and planned-obsolescent hardware' (Johnson 1991: 169). Also, the large output of animal excrement into the waterways has led to an increase in algae, which in turn deprives other aquatic life of essential oxygen.

But the costs of intensive farming become clearest when we consider the ethical dimension of our relationship with animals (*see* ANIMAL RIGHTS). Intensive practices were first introduced when the assumption that animals could be used without limit was still without serious social challenge. The social vision which intensive farming represented was that of scientific technology enabling a world where food for humans is cheap and plentiful. As such it was the practical outworking of a scientific humanism through which, empowered by technology, humans can recreate the world to their own advantage. Because of this unexamined humanocentricity, environmental issues and the welfare of individual animals were largely disregarded. In contrast with contemporary interest in VEGETARIANISM, factory farming emerged at a time when vegetarianism was hardly considered a practical possibility (see Beardsworth and Keil 1992).

The ethical critique of factory farming may be considered under three headings.

Mechanization of animals   The Cartesian tradition viewed animals as mere machines with no rational soul and no sentience. Factory farming has turned this perspective into a social reality. Animals are treated as physiological machines which produce meat, eggs and milk – and which, with scientific ingenuity, can be adapted or even redesigned to produce even more. For example, modern milk production straddles the very limit of the cow's physiological adaptability. Kept in a perpetual state of pregnancy, the cow is milked several times per day, and when this process has exhausted her physically she is sent to the slaughter house at the age of 6 or 7 despite a normal life expectancy of 20 years. 'For many years intensive dairy systems have been developed without fully taking into account the behavioural needs of the dairy cow which has been regarded as a replaceable unit rather than a social ruminant' (David 1990: 69). Humans continue to exert great pressure on this already strained capacity – e.g. by use of a bovine growth hormone (BST) which is now utilized in the USA to boost the level of productivity even beyond current levels. Of course, it would be an exaggeration to say that mechanization has brought no benefits to animals. The proclaimed advantages of intensive farming to the animal are that a steady supply of balanced diet and sanitary water are not possible under any other system, the animals are safe from predators and the perforated floors of animal sheds keep the animals from their own excrement. Curtis argues that 'Inhumane treatments lead to unhealthy, unproductive animals, and consequently, financial losses' (Curtis 1986–7: 169). Farming, he argues, is

therefore humane as a whole. Harrison challenges this conclusion when she comments, 'cruelty is acknowledged only where profitability ceases' (Harrison 1964: 3).

The commodification of animals   The Western tradition has usually held that animals have been put here for our use – a view which has been underwritten by certain elements within the Judaeo-Christian tradition (see Linzey 1987, 1994). Beyond this instrumentalist view, factory farming treats each animal as a 'fungible' (substitutable) unit whose value is nothing other than its economic utility. The profit motive is dominant; animals are treated as replaceable units. For example, in addition to conditions of extreme confinement in battery cages (inability to spread even one wing, crowding which promotes cannibalism, and standing permanently on sloping wire mesh), mortality among battery chickens is accepted as a cost of doing business (see Mason and Singer 1980; Singer 1990). This commodification of animals ignores their intrinsic value. 'The higher animals have an economic value because of their utility; but they have a meta-economic value in themselves' (Schumacher 1974: 87).

The thingification of animals   The Catholic tradition has held that animals are not PERSONS but things: 'There are persons in our regard and there are things. ... We have no duties of any kind to the lower animals, as neither to sticks and stones' (Rickaby 1889: 248). In substituting artificial for natural environments, intensive farming necessarily involves absolute control over, and manipulation of, animal life. It typically involves a range of activities which reduce the animals to artefacts. For example, common mutilations include the debeaking of poultry, castration of pigs, dehorning of cattle and sheep, tail docking, tooth clipping, and various forms of ear punching and branding for identification purposes. One recent example of the thingification of animals is the genetic engineering (and anticipated patenting) of animal species in order to make them better meat machines (see Fox 1992; Verhoog 1992; Linzey 1994).

What is significant about this reduction of animals to machines, commodities or things is not only the cruel and unjust treatment of the animals concerned, but also the spiritual impoverishment which it represents. The very technology which reduces animals to machines at the same time reduces humans to being mere agricultural technicians devoid of any moral dimension in our relationship with other creatures. Traditional husbandry, although morally ambiguous and often insufficiently respectful of animals, did at least maintain the possibility of a humane symbiotic relationship.

'The design of systems has thus moved out of the hands of traditional stockmen and into the hands of engineers and technicians, men of great skill and ingenuity but usually with little knowledge of animals, and in particular of animal behaviour' (Carpenter *et al.* 1980: 21). What is at stake in our massive industrialization of agriculture – apart from the suffering of other living creatures – is a proper sense of ourselves in the world of creation. Factory farming therefore represents not only a reduced mechanized life for animals but also a diminished spiritual and moral life for human beings.

Beardsworth, Alan and Keil, Terea (1992) 'The vegetarian option: varieties, motives and careers', *Sociological Review* 38: 254–93.

Carpenter, Edward *et al.* (1980) *Animals and Ethics*, London: Watkins.

Curtis, S.E. (1986–7) 'The case for intensive farming of food animals', reprinted in T. Regan and P. Singer (eds) *Animal Rights and Human Obligations*, Englewood Cliffs, NJ: Prentice-Hall, 1989.

David, Graham (1990) Letter, *Veterinary Record* 126: 69.

Fiddes, Nick (1991) *Meat: A Natural Symbol*, London and New York: Routledge.

Fox, Michael (1992) *Superpigs and Wondercorn*, New York: St Martin's Press.

Harrison, Ruth (1964) *Animal Machines*, London: Vincent Stuart.

Johnson, Andrew (1991) *Factory Farming*, Oxford: Basil Blackwell.

Linzey, Andrew (1987) *Christianity and the Rights of Animals*, London: SPCK, and New York: Crossroad.

——(1994) *Animal Theology*, London: SCM and Chicago, IL: University of Illinois Press.

Mason, Jim, and Singer, Peter (1993) *Animal Factories*, New York: Crown.

Rickaby, Joseph (1889) *Moral Philosophy*, London: Longmans.

Schumacher, E.F. (1974) *Small is Beautiful: A Study of Economics as if People Mattered*, London: Abacus.

Singer, Peter (1990) *Animal Liberation*, 2nd edn, New York: Avon Books.

Swann Report (1969–70) *Use of Antibiotics in Animal Husbandry and Veterinary Medicine*, Cmd 41990, London: HMSO.

Verhoog, H. (1992) 'The concept of intrinsic value and transgenic animals', *Journal of Agricultural and Environmental Ethics* 5(2): 147–60.

Willis, R.G. (ed.) (1990) *Signifying Animals: Human Meaning in the Natural World*, London: Unwin Hyman.

Andrew Linzey
Jonathan Webber
Paul Waldau

FEMINISM

Feminism can be discussed both as an IDEOLOGY and as a social movement. As an ideology feminism is an affirmation of women's equivalent value as persons with men and a rejection of sexist ideologies that inferiorize women (*see* SEXISM). As a movement feminism is an organized effort to transform the cultural and social systems that perpetuate women's subjugation to men.

Although one may assume that there have always been some women who have personally dissented from patriarchal theories and systems of female inferiorization, male control of both EDUCATION and tradition, i.e. that literature preserved as worthy of being read, have largely succeeded in erasing these voices of dissent from the public cultural memory. Moreover, it was difficult for women who dissented from PATRIARCHY to gain a platform until there existed a counter-culture that validated such dissent as potentially correct, over against the patriarchal hegemonic CULTURE.

These conditions gradually began to develop in Western culture in the late Middle Ages. From the late fourteenth into the seventeenth century the literature of the *querelle des femmes*, largely written by men on both sides, argued pro and contra concerning the moral and intellectual equality or inferiority of women with men. One of the women to enter this debate in its earliest stage was Christine de Pisan (1363–1431), who wrote poems and treatises defending women's dignity, capacity for virtue and education over against the male detractors of women (Richardson 1929).

In seventeenth-century England two types of feminist literature developed. One, based on

Renaissance humanism, continued the arguments from the Bible and from classical and medieval literature showing that women were created equally in God's image and also had shown as much capacity for virtue and intelligence as men. A new stage of this argument is represented by figures such as Mary Astell, who began to argue for organized institutions of female education (Perry 1986). A second tradition, arising from radical Christianity, i.e. Quakers, focused on the understanding of the church as a counter-cultural community in which women were given equal prophetic gifts with men and called to decry an unjust society and established church (Irwin 1979).

However, all these early forms of feminism were limited by the assumption that patriarchy was the divinely ordained order of creation. These advocates argued for women's personal moral, spiritual and intellectual capacities *vis-à-vis* men, and for expanded opportunities in religious and educational institutions, i.e. in new forms of church and schools. But they did not seek changes in the fundamental socio-political subjugation of women.

In the late eighteenth and nineteenth centuries LIBERALISM challenged the belief that social hierarchies represent God's ordained order. The Biblical doctrine of the image of God was translated into a social theory of 'original nature', according to which all humans have the same essential capacities for reason and moral conscience. Unjust privilege, not God or 'nature', is responsible for social hierarchy. Revolutionary liberalism demanded the overthrow of aristocratic hierarchy and the creation of new societies where all 'men' were equal.

The theoreticians of the French and the American revolutions envisioned this doctrine of equality as applying only to free, propertied males, but it was soon appropriated by more radical thinkers, feminists among them, to argue for a more universal application. In the French Revolutionary Assembly in 1789 Condorcet argued that women be included in the rights of 'man and the citizen'. Olympe de Gouge made these demands more strongly in her *Declaration of the Rights of Woman and Citizen* (1791). Both protested the Terror and were executed. Mary Wollstonecraft's *Vindication of the Rights*

of Women (1792) brought these revolutionary claims to England, although with a focus on educational rather than political equality.

The 1830s saw a renewal of feminist thought in France, England and the USA, now joined with liberal constitutional movements, SOCIALISM and abolitionism (Moses 1984). In 1848 American feminists held the first Women's Rights Convention in which the claims of equal CITIZENSHIP of the American Declaration of Independence were extended to women. However, it was almost a century before these feminist movements won their goal of women's enfranchisement.

In the 1920s it seemed as if women had won the major battles of the feminist movement. They were defined as citizens with the rights to vote, hold office and engage in legal transactions in their own name. They had won access to most institutions of higher education and to the professions. Similar movements for women's civil and educational rights were proceeding under liberal or socialist auspices in Eastern Europe, Asia and Latin America. In the 1930s and 1940s a worldwide economic depression and then the Second World War demanded that women's issues take a backseat.

In 1949 Simone de Beauvoir's *The Second Sex* laid the basis for a new discussion of feminism. In the 1960s organized feminist movements sprang up in Western Europe and America, fed by the US civil rights movement and the social criticism of the New Left. These movements sought to complete the unfinished business of the earlier feminist movement, overcoming remnants of women's legal and social disenfranchisment and exclusion from education and professions. They also defined new issues that had barely been touched earlier, particularly with regard to physical and sexual VIOLENCE to women and ABORTION.

The feminist movement of the 1970s tended to divide along different lines of social theory: liberal, socialist and radical feminisms. Liberal feminism continues the traditions of the Enlightenment in defining women as having essentially the same 'nature' as men, emphasizing rationality and moral conscience. Differences between males and females are ascribed primarily to socialization. Liberal feminism seeks to reform the legal structures of society to complete the incorporation of women into the public society of paid labour and politics as equals.

In the USA the major initiative of liberal feminism was the Equal Rights Amendment which would have provided the legal basis for disallowing all federal and state laws that discriminated between males and females. In the 1960s and early 1970s it seemed as if this amendment would win easily through state by state ratification. But in 1982 backlash anti-feminist movements in American society and the churches combined to defeat the initiative.

Liberal feminism in the USA has been expressed particularly through the National Organization of Women. It has sought to promote women political candidates and has even proposed that there be a women's political party. It also focuses on women's promotion in the professions and equal pay for women in the same jobs as men.

Socialist feminism, by contrast, regards equality for women within capitalist society as impossible, since CAPITALISM itself is based on class hierarchy and the exploitation of the workers by the owners of the means of production. Women in capitalist society are seen as members of the exploited working class, both as unpaid workers in the home and low paid workers in the paid labour force. The rights of women within capitalism, therefore, can only result in the token incorporation of a few women into the management class, but not a systemic overcoming of GENDER hierarchy since this is integral to class hierarchy.

Socialist feminism tended to be stronger in Western Europe and England where there were established socialist or Labour parties and an accepted socialist intellectual tradition. This was much less the case in the USA which lacked both of these, although there were some socialist feminists associated with the New Left (Eisenstein 1979). Although socialist feminists looked to the socialist revolutions in Russia and China, and later in the Third World, i.e. Cuba, as exemplars of their theory, most had to admit that these revolutions had largely betrayed both feminist and proletarian visions of economic justice.

In contrast to liberal and socialist feminisms, radical feminism has emphasized the difference, rather than the sameness, of women and men. Women, either by 'nature' or socialization, or some combination of the two, are seen as having a different way of knowing and being in the world. Radical feminism draws on the tradition of romanticism to stress notions of female altruism and compassionate feeling for others, in contrast with the egoism and need for dominance that are seen as characteristic of males. Thus there is a distinct suggestion in radical feminism, not only of female difference, but also of moral superiority.

Radical feminists focused particularly on physical and sexual violence to women in the FAMILY and in SOCIETY and on the rights of women to protect themselves from such violence and to define their own bodily integrity. Some radical feminisms moved toward separatism and female bonding by which women would form counter-societies independent of males. Lesbian feminism as a separatist ideology falls into this perspective, although many lesbians are not separatists.

In the 1980s this feminist view of women as more 'naturally' disposed to egalitarian mutuality made alliances with anti-militarism and with ecology (see ECOLOGICAL THEOLOGY). In the ecofeminist movement there was an identification of the exploitation of women and the exploitation of nature in patriarchal societies. Not only were these two forms of exploitation compared and equated, but there was also a disposition to see the non-human world of nature itself as 'feminine', i.e. mothering and nurturing. Women and nature are seen as belonging to the 'true' reality of life-giving relationships, over against the 'unnatural nature' of masculine egoistic individualism, urge for dominance and violence (Diamond and Orenstein 1990).

This ecofeminist identification of women and nature also reflected religious perspectives that favoured renewal of the worship of the Goddess, and discounted the possibility of feminist reform of patriarchal religions (specifically Christianity). One of the characteristics of this new form of radical feminism is its interest in spirituality, in contrast to the traditional secularism of much of liberal and particularly of Marxist feminism.

Religious questions had been linked with Western feminism from its beginnings. From the late medieval *Querelle de femmes* through the struggles for suffrage in the late nineteenth century most feminists in Western Europe and North America had to deal with the fact that the Bible and the Christian churches operated as the major authorities that buttressed patriarchal society. Even among liberal feminists, such as Lucretia Mott and Susan B. Anthony (both American Quakers), it was understood that one does not dismiss the Bible and the Christian religion outright. Mott and Anthony believed that a true reading of the Biblical teaching of creation in the image of God supported women's equality in society.

Only a few feminists of this era dared to attack the Bible and the Christian religion altogether as unredeemably patriarchal: Elizabeth Cady Stanton, *The Women's Bible* (1895–8); Matilda Joslyn Gage, *Woman, Church and State* (1893). Neither was anti-religious, but they suggested the need for an alternative religion that would be genuinely pro-feminist. This idea was also developed by Charlotte Perkins Gilman, *His Religion and Hers* (1923).

Socialism, by contrast, developed an anti-religious perspective based on the Marxist critique of religion as a tool of the ruling class to pacify the worker. Religion sublimates social protest into a world beyond history. In order for revolutionary change to come about, religion must be overcome by a social scientific perspective. Socialist feminism applied this same critique of religion to the liberation of women.

However, in the 1960s more and more Christian churches were reforming their policies and ordaining women (*see* WOMEN'S ORDINATION). Women were being incorporated into theological education as students and also as professors. There began to develop in American and European Christian circles a Christian feminist theology that sought to reform the teaching of the church to be affirmative of women. Some traditions of American Judaism also were admitting women to the rabbinate. A feminist religious Judaism began to develop in these circles of American Jews (Plaskow 1990).

Christian feminism has reflected a spectrum from reformist to radical views, according to how seriously the problem of patriarchy is seen in Biblical foundations. For the evangelical reformist Christian feminists, the Bible and Christianity are essentially egalitarian, and patriarchal readings of the tradition are a distortion of the true intentions of the Biblical authors. Other more radical Christian feminists see patriarchy as much more deeply embedded in the sources of the faith. Therefore there must be a deep redefinition of Christian thought. But these thinkers also see alternative lines within the tradition that can be reclaimed for such feminist reconstruction (Fiorenza 1983).

By contrast, some formerly Christian and Jewish feminists have concluded, in the course of their struggles to change these religious institutions, that this effort is hopeless. Patriarchy is so foundational to the Bible, and the Bible is so basic to these religious traditions, that there is no use trying to reform them. One must face up to the falsehood and moral EVIL of patriarchal religions and leave them for a new pro-feminist religion. This may be seen as a religion that can be recovered from pre-patriarchal human history or a new religion that springs from feminist liberation spirituality today, or some combination of the two (Hampson 1991).

Although feminism has arisen mostly within social theory and movements in Western Europe and the USA, today it must be seen as a global movement. Liberal and socialist movements carried the feminist ideas of these traditions to the democratic, socialist and anti-colonial struggles of Latin America, the Middle East, Africa and Asia.

However, feminists in anti-colonial struggles also found themselves accused of 'bourgeois' views foreign to the 'class struggle' and also of 'Western' ideas alien to indigenous culture. The latter accusation has been particularly strong when anti-colonialism is wedded to a fundamentalist renewal of the indigenous religious culture. Thus Third World feminists have found it necessary to make their own social and cultural appropriation of feminism for their own context.

Feminists within revolutionary struggles in Latin America, Asia, Africa and the Middle East have argued that women's liberation and national liberation are not in conflict, but that women's liberation represents an additional dimension within national liberation. This has often lent itself to debates about which takes priority. Is women's liberation to be postponed until national liberation is won, or must both proceed simultaneously? Third World feminists have also sought roots of egalitarianism with their historic cultures and religions as a basis for claiming roots for a culturally indigenous feminism.

One also finds among Third World feminism divisions between those who seek a spiritual or religious base and those who reject this as counterproductive. Liberal and Marxist feminisms in Latin America have generally followed the secularism of these traditions and seen little hope in reforming the Christian churches. However, some Latin American feminists, allied with liberation theology, have sought a feminist version of this theological perspective.

Most Arab feminists have followed the secular traditions of Arab nationalism and have felt that there was little hope of a feminist reinterpretation of Islam, although a small Muslim feminist movement also exists which argues that authentic Islam is egalitarian. Africa and Asian feminisms have responded to the pluralistic religious contexts of their societies. Christian feminists in Asia and Africa are seeking to make a synthesis between holistic indigenous spirituality and what they see as liberating traditions of Christianity (Fabella and Oduyoye 1988).

In the atmosphere of sharpened conflict between rich and poor, renewed Western neo-colonial hegemony over the Third World and the fundamentalist backlash of the 1990s, feminism in all countries faces an uphill battle to gain a hearing. At the same time there is a deepened sense of the relationship between patriarchy and all forms of injustice and oppression. This insight calls for new dialogue across feminist groups, divided by culture, class, ethnicity and ideology, and a quest for a more comprehensive base for feminist theory and a networking for systemic transformation.

Diamond, I. and Orenstein, G. (1990) *Reweaving the World: The Emergence of Ecofeminism*, San Francisco, CA: Sierra Club.

Eisenstein, Z. (1979) *Capitalist Patriarchy and the Case for Socialist Feminism*, New York: Monthly Review Press.

Fabella, V. and Oduyoye, M. (1988) *With Passion and Compassion: Third World Women Doing Theology*, Maryknoll: Orbis.

Fiorenza, E.S. (1983) *In Memory of Her*, New York: Crossroad.

Hampson, D. (1991) *Theology and Feminism*, Oxford: Basil Blackwell.

Irwin, J. (1979) *Womanhood in Radical Protestantism, 1525–1675*, New York: Edwin Mellen.

Moses, C.G. (1984) *French Feminism in the Nineteenth Century*, Albany, NY: State University of New York Press.

Perry, R. (1986) *The Celebrated Mary Astell, An Early English Feminist*, Chicago, IL: University of Chicago Press.

Plaskow, J. (1990) *Standing Again at Sinai: Judaism from a Feminist Perspective*, San Francisco, CA: Harper & Row.

Richardson, L. (1929) *The Forerunners of Feminism in French Literature of the Renaissance*, Baltimore, MD: Johns Hopkins University Press.

Rosemary Radford Ruether

FREE WILL

Free will is a philosophical concept that is central to Christian Theology, social policy and judicial accounts of personal responsibility. Whether its efficacy is affirmed or denied the debates that have surrounded the concept go right to the heart of the Christian contribution to the idea of what it is to be human and what it is to be a self. While free will was first fully formulated in a theological context it is a notion that has become central to the formation of the terms of modern and contemporary secular ethical and social debates. The term is derived from a combination of the terms FREEDOM and will where freedom, in this context, means unconditioned, or uncaused, and will means to cause or bring about, as an action or event. The idea of free will at its root indicates that the will can cause some event or action while itself being uncaused. It begins a new sequence in time, or interrupts an old sequence. It is a first cause in a new sequence. When applied to the universe the first cause is Aristotle's prime mover, or the God conceived by Thomas Hobbes. When applied to the human it invokes spontaneity and AUTONOMY. Free will is opposed to DETERMINISM, where determinism implies that every action has a prior cause. Free will refers to an inner capacity to produce outer changes, whereas autonomy may be used to cover both the inner capacity of free will and the outer empirical or political and social circumstances within which actions occur.

The idea of freedom of will is specific to western culture from approximately the 4th century CE. There is no evidence that a strong and clear notion of freedom of the will is to be found either in Ancient Greek philosophy, in Hebrew sources or in Rome prior to its dissolution. Nonetheless concepts are not invented from nothing and precursor notions are to be found in Greece. Plato when considering the source of wrong doing claimed that, 'Nobody aims something which he regards as an evil at the moment he is going to act ... any failure results from lack of knowledge ... That is why nobody fails who really knows the better' (Protagoras 358). Sometimes, however, someone might be weak or incontinent: *Akrasia*. While no distinct and systematic conception of will power of an individual existed Aristotle tied intellect and practical action together in a manner that was not too distinct from that which we now understand as intentional action. Frequently, however, the order of the universe was regarded as determined. Stoics took it that choice existed only with respect to consciousness and not to actions. The source of EVIL could be ascribed to attitude rather than to actions or other sources and could be overcome by denying it as a place in the mind. Epicureans regarded humans as a mass of atoms and not able to cause events, yet for all that apparent determinism, Epicurus refers to the 'swerve' that modifies the direction of events, a swerve later mocked by Cicero as untenable.

It was Christian thought that gave a definite direction to the concept of freedom of the will. While the notion of choice had been well understood and well described, it remained as an empirical or outward notion until matched by an inner conception by which it was understood that choice could be made and could even be created. In turn this required that a significance be ascribed to the inner life. That significance initially took a moral form. It is best represented in a change from the external obedience or compliance to a law required by the *Decalogue* to the internal compliance required by early Christianity. There is no single point at which this inwardness can be said to have occurred but there a number of significant occasions of which we have knowledge. Together they make up the moment of inwardness – the discovery or even invention of the inner life. This moment of inwardness is crucial of the development of the conception of freedom of will.

Freedom of the will demands as a precondition an inner struggle, even an inner narrative such that the 'I', or subject of action, is faced with alternatives that the 'I' chooses. While Jesus has nothing to say about freedom of the will he does place emphasis on the inner state. Nowhere is this better exemplified than in the beatitudes where the state of the heart is given a central place. Thus turning away from the commandments of God is no mere disobedience or non-compliance it is a genuine inner lack, a genuine separation or ALIENATION from the life of God. The same inner notion when applied to actions of which one is doubtful developed into the notion of conscience. *Conscientia* when given force by St Paul permitted the individual rejection of the commands of others in those circumstances where conscience ran in an opposite direction. The claims of the authority of Government are to be accepted only according to conscience (Romans 13: 5) an argument that further turns the life of the mind of the Christian inward, and which leads actions as subject to an internal guide rather than an external law.

Such changes in the life of the mind did not directly produce a theory of freedom of the will, but they did provide the psychological conditions within which such a theory could be developed. The full development of that theory can be traced to many sources. Two are worthy of mention as being of particular significance. The first is that of the Cappadocian theologians of the fourth century, notably Gregory of Nyssa, the second is Augustine of Hippo. Gregory of Nyssa drew out the similarities between God and humans. Humans were able to imitate God in that they could, voluntarily, form their own moral character. The same thought was echoed later in Kant's claim that, 'in a moral sense man is neither good nor evil, he is rather what he creates himself' (Kant, 1960). However, while

Kant's point had causal overtones, Gregory's principal point was to do with character, with disposition, attitude and intellect. In the sense it was still Platonic with admittedly voluntaristic elements. Nevertheless it laid a significant foundation for the changes that were fully developed in Kant. Those changes required a second kind of conception of what it was to be human. That conception centred on the unity of the human intellect, on the unified nature of subjectivity and was provided unambiguously by Augustine and developed later by Descartes. The Greek conception of the mind was such that the idea of a unified subject was not present nor developed. Subjectivity was not fully developed thought was dispersed, thus for example *phrenes* or mind might be dispersed throughout a number of locations, in Homer for instance, it seems to have been located in the heart and lungs. Correlatively extreme passion, such as rage or unreasoning stubbornness might be externalized. Such conditions were regarded as abnormal and required a 'supernormal explanation' (Dodds 1951: 9). Such conceptions of mind effectively dissipate it in some of its most important aspects and this counts against the kind of subjectivity required for a developed conception of 'I'. Without such a conception the idea of freedom of will as the power of a person to bring about new events in the world is not possible. But a person can bring about such events if there is a clear conception of a person as one having a specific location and a specific power.

The idea of the PERSON, *prosopon*, in its earliest formation related to a role, as in a drama; it was a mask rather than some unique and individual 'I' that was underneath the mask or role (Mauss). This model of persons continued the dispersion of mind found as early as Homer. What was required as a condition of the idea of freedom of will was a single source of action and a single centre of subjectivity. The inward turn offered by Christian thought at its outset, in some of the sayings of Jesus, but more completely in the writings St Paul, laid the ground for that development. A major and striking feature of the latter is insight into the inner dynamics of the mind of Paul. It is the first systematic and extended piece of literature that reveals a distinct 'I' in the sense of a subject showing a particular location and having a distinct inner life. It is the first true autobiography in the sense that we see the world through the inner life of another.

An additional step in the development of the 'moment of the mind' was taken in the conceptualization of God as a person. The Cappadocians developed just such a concept of God and it was but a short step from that to see that humans, as made in the image of God, were also true and single persons. The doctrine of the TRINITY and the concept of the person were brought together by the Cappadocians to form a pre-cursor to the idea of the will. As Gregory of Nyssa put it, 'Thoughts are the father of the will' (Dihle 1982: 119), a view that preceded the significant breakthrough that was Augustine's concept of the will.

The achievement of Augustine in the development of the idea of the will is immeasurable. 'St Augustine was, in fact the inventor of our modern notion of will . . . he took the decisive step towards the concept of human will by reinterpreting a hermeneutical term as an anthropological one' (Dihle 1982: 144). In this he was helped by his predecessors and by the terminology of voluntariness that was developing. Nevertheless the break with the past is decisive and the outcome a new understanding of the world and the place of man within that world. In his early writing, particularly in the dialogue *On Free Choice of the Will* Augustine embraced the idea of freedom of the will wholeheartedly. His later writings back away from the concept until he eventually came to regard the idea in its Pelagian form as heretical.

The problem that Augustine came up against, once defined, is straightforward. If humans can will evil then can they not also will the good. If they can will the good can they not also will that good which is deserving of God's GRACE. But God's grace is the gift of God and can not be willed by humanity, therefore freedom of will must be asymmetric i.e. evil but not good can be willed. But freedom of will, even if willing evil, introduces new causes into the world, brings newness into the world and alters the course of world events. Yet God who created the world also created time in which it subsists. If God created time then he must stand outside time, in eternity. Yet if God stands in eternity he must know what is at the beginning of time and at the end of time, he must know the first and last days, therefore he must know what is willed in every particular case. And if he knows what is willed then that action cannot be freely willed. Even before the world was created God knew every action in the world and knew who would be saved and who would be damned.

The reasoning behind this is not as clear as might be thought and for a simple reason. To know what someone is going to do does not undercut their freedom in doing it. Foreknowledge is not determination – it is foreknowledge, no more and no less. It is frequently the case that we know what someone will do in a particular case. We might, for instance know of person 'x' that they have adopted a moral imperative with which they will lead their life. If faced with two options 'a' and 'b' where 'a' is good and 'b' is evil we know perfectly well that they will choose 'a' but it does not follow from this that their choice was determined. They were always free to choose 'b' and prior to that they were always free to choose a mode of life that did not include a moral maxim. What Augustine did, however, was to take the notion of foreknowledge and turn it into predestination which is a different doctrine altogether.

There are a variety of reasons why this turn from foreknowledge to predestination might be made but they are all led, ultimately, by the idea of redemption and grace and accompanied by an original act of will that condemned humankind and required a redemptive process. The key point is the interpretation or rather re-interpretation of the first 'man', Adam, wilfully disobeying the prime interdict not to eat from the fruit of the tree of knowledge. It was Adam's act of will that led to the fallen condition of humanity and with it the need for the parallel redemptive figure of Jesus as Christ. Of course this is hopelessly anachronistic. If Augustine invented the notion of free will and if, as is clear, there was no such notion prior to Augustine then Adam, understood as an individual as well as a representative figure, could not have such a faculty.

The Augustinian account of Adam on the face of it is incoherent and nonsensical. Yet it is also a key moment in Western development. The reason is for this is straightforward – freedom of will became the defining feature of the condition of humankind. It was that first act of will that led to the expulsion from the paradise that was the Garden of Eden and to a life of toil, struggle and suffering. It is not surprising, therefore, if Augustine drew back from it just as seen as he had found it, for will represented humanity in its fallen condition. How then could it be good? Yet it is precisely the goodness of will that became the principal feature of humanity and morality for some later thinkers: Dante, Descartes and Kant in particular.

The invention of the concept of freedom of will required a particular set of social, intellectual and theological circumstances. It was by no means a necessary development but was rather the product of certain contingent circumstances. Not every CULTURE has produced either the concept of freedom of will or cognate notions and it is clear that the notion is not necessary to a variety of forms of human life. Nevertheless it has become central to our own conception of what it is to be human and what it is to be set against the natural world with its deterministic laws. The Augustinian account depended upon the development of a unified conception of the person, able to intervene in the chain of causes and effects and begins actions anew. This distinction between nature and mind permitted Boethius to combine Greek rationalism and INDIVIDUALISM and both influenced Descartes' dualism. Here Descartes conceived of a clear distinction between the substance of mind and the substance of body. The mind was able to cause the body to act – as by free will thus beginning an act anew. Here Descartes in echoing Dante threw off the shackles of the Augustinian conception of freedom of the will and turned it into the very centre of humanity. 'Nothing gives us so much contentment as the exercise of our will.' This statement throws the past away completely. It dispenses with the sins of Adam, casts out the serpent, welcomes Eve back into the fold and defines the goodness of humanity in terms of the act that led to its FALL. It is hard to imagine a greater rupture with what had gone before, mind, will and subjectivity were brought together in a new perception of humanity – a new COVENANT – but this time with the fall.

But the new covenant is frightening. The idea that an act could begin a new causal chain in the world is both challenging and the source of much potential angst. The political philosopher Thomas Hobbes spoke for many when he dismissed the idea of freedom of will as nonsensical (*Leviathan* Ch. 5). The only freedom he was prepared to recognize was political or empirical freedom. Even now English and much American political thought takes its cue from Hobbes on this point. Thus in Mill's account of liberty (*On Liberty*) we find it explicitly stated that 'the subject of this essay is not freedom of the will . . . but social or civil liberty.' More recently the same point has been made by Christian Bay in the *Structure of Freedom*. Set against the empirical tradition of political thought has been the idea that if freedom of will does imply making new beginnings in a casual sequence then actions are not caused. If actions are not caused then they are special events whose origins can be placed within the agent. If so that makes the event unique but also the agent. It also make the agent responsible for the action. Actions that are free in this sense might then be regarded as moral actions. The most highly developed theory of this kind is to be found in the philosophy of Immanuel Kant.

Kant returned to the significance of the notion of the will in his claim that the only thing that can be regarded as unconditionally good is a good will (Kant 1964, ch. 1). All other motives or events might be contaminated. A good will is able to act according to reason rather than to some other motive. The test of a morally worthy action is that it be unconditioned by desire, that it be freely willed and that it conform to one or more of the rationally derived versions of the Categorical Imperative, the principal form of which is: 'Act only on that maxim that you could at the same time will to be a universal law' (ibid.). Thus for Kant freedom of the will is required for moral action. It is also required for integrity of personhood and for integrity of individuality. If freedom of will is lacking, either through slavery or by acting heteronomously, according to desires when that is inappropriate, then the action ceases to be moral and the self is compromised or even dissipated. Once again the act of willing is taken to be definitive of what it is to be human but it is also required for goodness – the new covenant, a covenant stemming from humanity rather than from God is yet again strengthened. Goodness is defined in terms that were characteristic of the original sin.

Kant's DEONTOLOGY represents the apotheosis not only of free will but also of the associated individualism, unity of self and personhood and the renunciation of desire. It is the Augustinian imperative carried to its logical and individualistic conclusion but with a new and expected twist in the requirement of will for goodness and the implied rejection of the Augustinian limit on will. The strength of Kant's theory is also its greatest weakness. To be effective, free will requires not only the renunciation of desires, heteronomy, but acting in accord with the Categorical Imperative, C.I., with reason alone. Only in such conditions is an action a truly moral action. But whereas Descartes had regarded the mind as transparent Kant thought it was opaque and because of the opacity of the human heart it could never be said with any certainty that an act was truly moral, or indeed that there had been truly moral act in the history of the world. Humans, in other words were capable of self-deceit; they could not be sure of their motives in acting as they did (ibid). In consequence the first duty to self was to know one's self. There could of course be no guarantees, but it seems as if the Delphic maxim 'Know thyself' was once again becoming central to human thought and action – this time in a new form.

For Kant an act that was moral was an act drawn from reason and not from empirical drives or motives. Hence human beings straddled two possible worlds, the phenomenal and the noumenal, yet the relation of any action between them remains as mysterious as with Descartes' earlier dualism. The balancing act that Kant produced was unsatisfactory for several generations of scholars. If actions had their free source in the noumenal or ideal world then they could not causally interact with the empirical world and so that world was an epiphenomena, all reality being found in ideality. Alternatively actions had an empirical basis and actions were motive and desire driven. If desire driven then either they could not be moral, or Kant's views on the constitution of a moral act were mistaken. If mistaken then some moral actions, at least, could be desire driven; a conclusion with intuitive appeal. That an action is desired does not, on the face of it, seem to prohibit its being moral. I might desire, for instance, to give alms to the poor, it does not seem to follow that my giving in to this desire and giving alms to the poor removes that action from the domain of morality. If these objections are correct then there seems to be no reason why some moral actions cannot be desire driven. In case we have to enquire into the reasons why free will, rather than desire became so central to Christian morality and to Christian conceptions of self and personhood. The significance of the notion of freedom of will in early Christianity is even more surprising given that it was the will of Adam that had led to the fall.

The basic reason for this oddity seems to go back to the almost excessive concern with sexuality and sexual desire in the early history of the Christian church. In Augustinian thought and in some of its immediate precursors, the desire that most controlled thoughts and that became central to the discussion of desire was sexual. Sexual desire, above all else, represented the pull of the flesh rather than the pull of the spirit, and it is against that background that the idea of free will as an anthropological notion, as a causal power, rather than as a hermeneutic notion was developed. Free will was continuously being tested against desire, particularly against the powerful desire of sexual attraction and the desire for sexual release. In his early writings Augustine seems to support the idea of freedom of the will but in *The City of God* he writes of the apparently independent power of the uncontrolled and uncontrollable erection. If this cannot be brought under control, then of what value is free will? The doctrine of pre-ordination dealt with one aspect of the problem but the equally dramatic doctrine of sexual renunciation and the view that sexuality was to be engaged in, with great reluctance, only for procreation, but never for co-creation was another outcome.

To follow one's desires was not only immoral,

it was to undermine the self, a unity of self copied from and contingent upon the model of God as monotheistic, as having one person, albeit expressed, on some accounts, via the trinity. It was vital that the body and its desires be brought under control. That control affirmed the spirit, affirmed will and the power of the mind over the body and limited materiality.

The Augustinian–Kantian legacy was and is immeasurable in its effects. Yet it was being eaten away at, not only in its periphery, but, also at its core and from a number of directions. The first source of attack is reasonably comprehensible and quite telling. The reasons for actions are complex and scarcely seen as residing entirely within some rationally conceived will of the agent. Factors that might influence, even cause an action, include socialization, enculturation, upbringing, character, personality, circumstances, diet, drugs, alcohol, education, opportunity, genetic predisposition, opportunity, social structure and so on. A thought Marx had in his earliest surviving essay, written as a schoolboy is apposite; in a significant sense what we are to become is determined for us even before we are born. Surely this is right, our parents, culture, language, time of birth, place of birth and much of our life chances are out of control. We are thrown into the world and in our living are always continuing the fall into it. The fall of mankind is always and at least two-fold for it refers to the fallibility or rupture expressed in the Adamic myth but it also refers to our ongoing condition of falling into the world.

As we fall into the world it becomes clear that so much of what we count as unique and self-definitional is given to us. We seem to be bound and bounded by factors outside of our control. This produces a second kind of problem for the notion of free will: the locus of the willing subject. Free will depended on the development of the concept of the person made the image of God and as having a single and definable centre. When it reached its heights, in Descartes and in Kant it was found in people who were understood as and conceived as clear individuals – the creators of their social world rather than creations of it. That idea in its strong form at least is no longer tenable. Individuals are social creations and are socially embedded. They always were and always will be, it is just that for a short period of time they appeared in an absurd and illusory form as self-positing.

But if individuals are socially embedded than what of the unified subjectivity required for a notion of freedom of will? If that is not tenable then it would seem that the notion of freedom of will is not tenable. There is a sense here in this kind of argument that we have come full circle, that the dispersal of subjectivity found in Ancient Greece and in early Christianity is upon us once again. From a practical point of view there is of course nothing impossible about that. The world existed for a long time without the notion of freedom of will and it can no doubt exist again without it. What is required to rescue the notion of freedom of will against such an attack is clear criteria of individuation for PERSONS and a clear and consistent location of subject positions. Both seem achievable. I might be thrown into the world but it is 'I' that is doing this falling. In describing that falling the description of position that includes the 'I' always locates I. In that fact at least it is quite unlike the early pre-Augustinian model or the model found in Homer for example. 'I' am able to take responsibility for and to claim mental extremes as 'mine'. In this sense subject location, subjectivity and responsibility for that are claimed and affirmed. Is there, however, a causal factor that follows from that and that relates me to an action in the relevant causal manner.

There are two broad possibilities here, both of which seem viable. The first, is to recur to the pre-Augustinian notion of *voluntas*. Here a voluntary action was understood not to mean a willed action but to mean that the action could be interpreted in a way that related the mind of the actor to the action. Was there a tie between mind and thing, *mens* and *res* that was comprehensible? From the point of view of practical reason this is perfectly satisfactory as an account of responsibility and avoids metaphysical claims of a dubious and unfashionable sort. The second, is to take a route to free will and autonomy that avoids the metaphysics normally associated with that concept. That is possible in those situations where actions are always underdetermined by factors that otherwise do bind

the agent. In those cases, cases of underdetermination, the agent's will may well become a factor in the reasons for an action. It is certainly adequate at the level of practical reason, which is all that is required. Of metaphysics we cannot speak, and as Wittgenstein said, of that which we cannot speak we must pass over in silence.

What this implies is that there is no reason whatsoever why we should abandon the notion of freedom of will. There are, however, a variety of reasons why we should regard it as but one factor in the life of people falling into the world and there are reasons why we should treat it as a practical rather than a metaphysical notion. Within the complex matrix that goes to make life and make a set of actions free will is only one factor. A person does, in Rousseau's terms, have a share in the operations of their own life, but it is a share. A life is lived within a context and against a backdrop of multiple givens. In the best cases a life can make what it will of those givens, but no one provides the givens, nor writes the givens, on a blank sheet, a *tabula rasa*.

There are two broad possibilities currently on offer and two broad types of responses that are possible. In the first the agent disappears, dissipated in a variety of causal factors that preclude the effect of free will, the grave of which is trampled or even danced upon, by those who find difficulty with the concept of agency, with the concept of free will and with its challenges. In the second, the person is celebrated. Free will is not omnipotence, on the contrary its effects depends upon the existence of pre-existing structures and pre-existing conditions for its own existence. Free will exists not in a vacuum but against the backdrop of the structures and problems within which human life is possible. Free will is not opposed to determinism, it is rather that part of the self that writes a few lines, perhaps even a few sentences or even a few words on pages already given. Free will is not omnipotence, for that is reserved to God, if anyone, it is rather, as Dante recognized when he developed the idea of common humanity and tied it to will, an opportunity to strike a blow for that which is distinctively human; to take human steps when human steps are appropriate.

Adkins, Arthur (1960) *Merit and Responsibility: A Study in Greek Values:* Oxford, Clarendon Press.

Augustine of Hippo (1964) *On Free Choice of the Will*, trans. Anna S. Benjamin and L.H. Hackstaff, Indianapolis: Bobbs-Merrill.

Brown, Peter (1990) *The Body and Society: Men, Women and Sexual Renunciation in Early Christianity*, London: Faber and Faber.

Clarke, Paul A.B (1988) *The Autonomy of Politics*, Aldershot and Brookfield: Avebury.

Dihle, Albrecht (1982) *The Theory of Will in Classical Antiquity*, Berkeley, University of California Press.

Dodds, E.R. (1951) *The Greeks and the Irrational*, Berkeley, University of California Press.

Kahn, Charles (1989) 'The Discovery of the Will: from Aristotle to Augustine' in *The Question of Eclecticism*, J.M. Dillon and A.A. Long (eds), Berkeley: University of California Press.

Kant, I. (1960) *Religion Within the Limits of Reason Alone*, trans. Theodore M. Greene and Hoyt H. Hudson, New York: Harper and Row.

——(1964) *The Groundwork of the Metaphysics of Morals*, trans. H.J. Paton, New York: Harper and Row.

Kenny, A. (1979) *Aristotle's Theory of the Will*, New Haven, NJ: Yale University Press.

Mill, J.S. (1969) *On Liberty*, J.M. Robson (ed.), John Stuart Mill: *Essay on Ethics, Religion and Society*, London: Routledge and Kegan Paul.

Peacocke, A. and Gillett, G. (eds) (1987) *Persons and Personality: A Contemporary Enquiry*, Oxford: Blackwell.

Zizoulas, J.D. (1985) *Being as Communion*, London: Darton, Longman and Todd.

Paul Barry Clarke

FUNDAMENTALISM

Fundamentalism is a modern reactive religious impulse through which conservative people attempt to ward off threats to their integrity as persons and as a people. It takes form in movements that are most visible in 'religions of the Book', such as Christianity, Judaism and Islam, but is present also in Asian and other religious cultures.

Fundamentalism, then, is not the same thing as CONSERVATISM, traditionalism, classicism or orthodoxy. Conservative movements often set out passively to conserve what they believe to be of value from the past. Traditionalists may be somewhat more aggressive about preserving presumed traditions, but they seldom make efforts to shape the world outside the religious bodies of which they are parts. Fundamentalists

are not particularly interested in determining what the classics of a tradition are: they tend to isolate one or two particular texts such as the Hebrew Scriptures, the New Testament or the Qur'an, and may show little interest in subsequent elaborations of a canon. Nor would orthodox leaders normally consider them as being simply orthodox, since most fundamentalists are quite selective as to which doctrines or practices they would stress.

From this it can be seen, then, that fundamentalisms are not encrusted or embedded vestiges of earlier religious traditions. Instead they are reactive (though not always reactionary) and in some form or other aggressive: i.e. they 'fight back'.

Fighting back means determining what it is about MODERNITY that serves as a total threat to the world as perceived by fundamentalists. Something occurs – be it the appearance of religious pluralism, the encounter with relativism, the invasion of an alien CULTURE (e.g. 'the West' in non-Western cultures) – which is regarded as an assault on the core beliefs, practices and identity of a group and of each individual that makes it up. Fundamentalists are selective about what they choose to regard as 'fundamentals' of dogma or behaviour. Normally they will choose those basic elements which they believe to be at the heart of their traditions, elements which can be employed against the real or perceived threats of modernity.

It is impossible to list the principal ideas of fundamentalism, since the fundamentals of necessity must be radically different in various traditions. Four examples will illustrate this.

For Protestants, by whom the word was invented and among whom it is most congenially applied, the fundamentals tend to be 'literal' acceptances of scripturally-based teachings which can help those who hold them stand guard against assaults. As the noted American Protestant lay leader in the 1920s, politician William Jennings Bryan, observed, liberals favoured words like 'spiritual', 'symbolic' or 'allegorical' when they dealt with classic teachings. By doing so, he averred, they 'sucked all the truth' out of them. Only literal interpretations of scriptural tenets would do.

When American Protestant fundamentalists

pioneered in selecting the doctrines for literal adherence, they chose several which they felt modernists in theology were undercutting, teachings which, if strictly retained, would shore up conservative Christianity and help it ward off erosive forces. In the eyes of most Christians of the world, be they Catholic, Orthodox, Lutheran, Anglican and more, the sacraments of baptism and the Lord's Supper or EUCHARIST would be fundamental. The fundamentalist parties in the denominations, however, never agreed on these basics. The main churchly conflict was within Baptist and Presbyterian bodies, and these stood no chance of agreeing, for instance, on the doctrine of BAPTISM.

Instead fundamentalists chose some teachings which they regarded as always having been basic in Protestantism, including the virgin birth of Jesus, his blood ATONEMENT and his physical RESURRECTION. These they felt the liberals and modernists were spiritualizing and thus compromising. To these they added more ambiguously held and controverted teachings. Decisive was support for the inerrancy of the original autographs of Biblical books, a teaching which fundamentalists supported on rationalist (Scottish Common Sense Realist) grounds. Most fundamentalists added to this, among other doctrines, 'dispensational premillennialism', a particular view of the end of history and the second coming of Jesus to begin a 1,000-year reign on earth.

In Roman Catholicism, where fundamentalism is a more recent and less defined phenomenon – few Catholics call themselves fundamentalist, but some are called this by other Catholic parties – the appeal is not made to the scriptures. Led by the late French Archbishop Marcel Lefebvre (d. 1991), a schismatic group broke with the papacy when these rebels repudiated the Second Vatican Council (1962–5). Non-schismatic groups in Italy and the Americas did not reject that Council, but with Lefebvre insisted on literal application of teachings affirmed at the Council of Trent (1546–63), the First Vatican Council (1870) and in belligerent antimodern papal documents like the Syllabus of Errors of 1864. Among the fundamentals teachings now were a return to the Mass in Latin and rejection of vernacular Masses, insistence on papal

AUTHORITY in isolation from the college of bishops, and vehement rejections of the Second Vatican Council's teachings on religious liberty.

The principal ideas of Jewish fundamentalism, as in the ultra-orthodox Haredi movement in Jerusalem and the very small but potent Gush Emunim, whose stronghold is in the occupied territories on the West Bank, at no point intersect with the basic teachings of Christian fundamentalism. The Haredim inherit a peculiar brand of Jewish orthodoxy, shaped by the experience in the Pale of Europe but firmed up especially in certain sectors of Jerusalem and, secondarily, New York City. Their movement tends to be Messianic but not Zionist; their people may live in Israel but they ordinarily reject political Israel as a working out of Biblical prophecy and rabbinic expectations. They make news by their vehement and sometimes violent action against Israelis who in their eyes profane things holy. They may destroy advertisements which they regard as lewd, or stone people who wear unapproved clothes in their sections of the city.

The Gush Emunim, or the 'Bloc of the Faithful', also takes over much of orthodoxy, though it is not moved fundamentally by the impulse to do so. Instead, its leaders take literally the Hebrew Scriptures when they license militant action on behalf of Israel and to determine the divinely chartered boundaries for modern Israel.

A fourth illustration, Shi'ite or Sunni Islam, has no substantive ties to the two kinds of Christian fundamentalism or to Jewish fundamentalism, and is less interested in doctrine or history than in practice. There the accent falls on *shari'ah*, the code of Islamic laws. Principal ideas may very well have a political import, or they may include applications of Quranic economic views which include a prohibition against the taking of interest in money-lending. The Muslims are also fundamentalistic about criminal codes and may insist on punitively cutting off the hand of the pickpocket or stoning the adulterous couple (*see* ISLAMIC FUDAMENTALISM).

From one point of view, fundamentalisms are impulses with long histories and a record of many anticipatory appearances. Thus it could be said that Hinduism has fought off 'modernisms' in most of the centuries of its development. Historians can find many parallels between some radical movements such as Anabaptism in the period of the Protestant Reformation and fundamentalism. Yet in common practice it seems advisable not to apply the term to militant traditionalisms in the past. In simplest formula, since fundamentalisms are reactive against *modernity*, it takes some form of the modern experience to trigger the response and set the impulses and movements going.

In Western Christianity, such triggering occurred thanks chiefly to two intellectual movements. One was the mid-nineteenth-century development of the theory of EVOLUTION, on models of natural selection, which began to find modified acceptance in churches in Great Britain, the USA and elsewhere. So long as evolutionary theory followed neo-Lamarckian patterns it was possible to see the process on theistic lines as being 'God's way of doing things', to quote American Protestant preacher Henry Ward Beecher. But natural selection meant that random, accidental and contingent processes were at work, and these seemed to leave no room for God as Creator. When liberal and modernist Protestants still found ways to adapt to evolution, many of their conservative colleagues reacted and reached for 'creationist' motifs in Biblical literalism to fight them off.

The second historical factor was widespread acceptance of the higher criticism of the Bible, whether in Germany, Great Britain or, latterly, the USA. During and after the eighteenth-century Enlightenment, many European scholars, some of them still retaining Christian faith, began to regard the ancient scriptures with the same literary and historical tools they would use on literature for which no supernatural claims had been made. To conservatives, such approaches threatened all historical bases for faith. They found it necessary to react.

The best case study for fundamentalism is in the USA, where early in the twentieth century many of the prestigious divinity schools were in the hands of modernists. The early ecumenical movement, which involved federations of churches (as in the Federal Council of Churches in 1908), paid little attention to cherished evangelical and evangelistic approaches, including

efforts to convert others. Between 1910 and 1912 the reactive party therefore published widely distributed booklets called *The Fundamentals*. After the First World War they began to organize interdenominationally and in 1920 a Baptist faction struggling for control of its denomination named itself 'Fundamentalist', the name which eventually came to be imposed on movements in Judaism, Islam and elsewhere.

The denominational conflicts came to a head in the mid-1920s, when fundamentalists were outmanoeuvred and defeated. To many observers it seemed as if their movement was now fossilized, a relic of an earlier but almost forgotten experience.

It remains most profitable and clarifying to concentrate on the American Protestant development after the mid-1920s. A famed legal event, the Scopes Trial, a test whether evolutionary ideas were to be permitted in the schools of Tennessee, occurred in 1925. There Bryan defended fundamentals (though he was not in every respect a strict fundamentalist) and, though his side won a legal victory, he was seen to have been disgraced nationally. But the opponents of evolution in the schools and the partisan for the fundamentals in the churches simply adopted new techniques and prospered.

First, they started denominations of their own. There were splinter Presbyterian and Baptist groups, and some of these also experienced schism as fundamentalists precisely defined their stands. Some wholly new denominations arose. Most of these were separatist or 'come-outer', as they called themselves – after a Biblical verse which urged followers of Christ to come out and be separate from others. Fundamentalists also invented other institutions. They pioneered the use of radio; they started Bible colleges and elaborate journalistic or book publishing ventures.

In the early 1940s some fundamentalists found the term stigmatizing, the movement excessive, the cause distorted, the separatism unwarranted. They formed a National Association of Evangelicals, which retained faith in most of the fundamentals but held it in somewhat more moderate and open ways. Evangelist Billy Graham became a world-renowned exemplar of this stance. Non-co-operative fundamentalism all but went underground.

Its second public wave occurred in the 1970s, partly in reaction to notable US Supreme Court decisions against prayer and devotions in government-supported schools (in 1962 and 1963) and the ruling in 1973, Roe v. Wade, which found abortion of the human foetus to be legal in many circumstances. To this might be added the increasing awareness of pluralism in a multicultural society and the jumble of pluralist and secularist signals which entered homes through pervasive media such as television. Their programmes normally neglected or demeaned conservative religion, and the fundamentalists – be it remembered, they 'fight back' – fought back with boycotts of offensive broadcasting or started their own television empires.

One can find roughly concurrent developments in Islamic fundamentalism, which arose late in the nineteenth century but found its political occasion after the Second World War, after the Western colonial powers carved up the Middle East and then abandoned it for fresh political development, or after neo-nationalist assertions elsewhere in (what scholar Marshall Hodgson called) Islamdom, as in Oceania or the subcontinent of Asia. Modern media of communication, technology and higher education exposed Muslim conservatives to both alluring and threatening teachings and practices. In the 1970s they reacted on massive scales, as in the Iranian revolution by Shi'ite Muslims under the Ayatollah Khomeini or in the Muslim Brotherhood reactions among Sunni Muslims in Egypt. In these and other cases, modernity came to be shunned under the label 'Westernization'.

Jewish fundamentalism also awaited the development of Israel in 1948 and became expressive after the Six-Day War with its threat to the survival of the nation in 1967.

Contemporary relevances of fundamentalisms appear chiefly in two areas: the cognitive/behavioural and the political.

First, the cognitive and behavioural: by this is meant the set of worldviews and strategies with which reactive fundamentalists encounter whatever they regard as a threat to their beliefs and practices. While most of them seem to be thoroughly at home with selective features of modernity, most notably as evidenced in their employment of mass media of communication, computers and sometimes weaponry, they are what sociologist Peter Berger calls 'cognitive minorities', inhabiting a sort of world apart.

Apart from what? Almost universally, they reject the normative reach of what might be called post-Enlightenment 'secular rationality'. They are more ready to assert faith in explicit supernaturalisms as these appear in their several traditions. Most of them oppose such rationality with some alternative forms of rationalism; despite many stereotypes to the contrary, most fundamentalists do not want to be seen as rejecting outright reason or science.

It turns out that in many cultures fundamentalists do not lack fellow-travellers, people discontented with prevailing naturalisms. Many of them become converts, adopting the worldviews propagated by fundamentalist teaching, writing and group experience. In fact, despite predictions from the mid-1920s that such movements would progressively wane, fundamentalisms outpace moderate, liberal and certainly modernist religious movements everywhere that they are in open competition with each other. They often contend against slightly concessive groups; in the American case, this means that fundamentalists often scorn evangelicals for having made too many compromises with modernity. A similar situation prevails in Islamic and Jewish worlds.

The second front is political. Many fundamentalisms, at least at first and especially in the Christian cases, seemed to be apolitical. They preached withdrawal from the world. The premillennial dispensational counsel was to await the coming of Christ for world transformation and not to seek it through social, economic political schemes and programmes. The mandate for conversion was to rescue people from an EVIL world which included religious compromisers.

While some fundamentalisms may remain passive and only potentially political, in most cultures there has come a time when the movements feel so threatened that they charge the followers to take aggressive counter-actions. This may mean terrorism in places where the movements are hopelessly outnumbered but feel called to express resentment and to create imbalance in systems. In other cases, as in Shi'ite

Iran, it may mean revolution and the establishment of a clerocracy or hierocracy, after its success. The image of the fundamentalist as terrorist and revolutionary, however, does not do justice to the reality of political fundamentalism. In many societies, including the USA, they have chosen to organize within the system, to pursue voluntary actions such as boycotts, to pass legislation or to change constitutions.

As director of the most ambitious comparative study yet made of fundamentalisms around the world, I have taken pains to retain a scholarly approach even where, on occasion besieged or demeaned (as a 'moderate liberal') by fundamentalists, there was an instinct to react emotionally. From that personal experience and its yields, I counsel scholarly approaches marked by equanimity unless fundamentalist onslaughts become threatening to the entire fabric of an ecclesial or political entity. Such a policy asks for at least two things: first, careful definition of fundamentalisms accompanied by an unwillingness to lump them all together in a pejorative listing and, second, a recognition that not everything in all fundamentalist reactions is destructive of human good or of some religious affirmations. Fundamentalists tend to possess good antennae; in responding to PORNOGRAPHY, threats to family life or the disdaining of all religion in pluralist cultures, they help set agenda for more moderate if also more passive types to do their own reacting. Many fundamentalists lead lives of integrity and learn to coexist with, although, of course, not to be satisfied by, the approaches taken by non-fundamentalists in their communions and cultures.

As for the future: it appears that no single all-embracing ideal of rationality, tolerance, science or progress will prevail in the modern world. Instead, there will be room for massive counter-paradigms, subcultures and cognitive minorities. They can aid in revitalizing cultures just as they serve as threats to others. Linked with tribalisms, new nationalisms and movements of resentment, they stand a chance of wreaking havoc with existing polities and governments, and sometimes of prevailing in them. In richly pluralistic societies, however, they have to settle for meliorism and compromise, even though these are not satisfying to fundamentalists who have more hegemonic and monopolistic aspirations.

Ammerman, Nancy Tatom (1987) *Bible Believers: Fundamentalists and the Modern World*, New Brunswick, NJ: Rutgers University Press.

Barr, James (1977) *Fundamentalism*, Philadelphia, PA: Westminster.

Lawrence, Bruce B. (1989) *Defenders of God: The Fundamentalist Revolt Against the Modern Age*, New York: Harper & Row.

Marsden, George M. (1980) *Fundamentalism and American Culture: The Shaping of Twentieth-Century Evangelicalism, 1870–1925*, New York: Oxford University Press.

Marty, Martin E. and Appleby, R. Scott (eds) (1991) *Fundamentalisms Observed*, Chicago, IL: University of Chicago Press (the first of five volumes on fundamentalisms).

Sahliyeh, Emile (ed.) (1990) *Religious Resurgence and Politics in the Contemporary World*, Albany, NY: State University of New York Press.

Sivan, Emmanuel (1985) *Radical Islam: Medieval Theology and Modern Politics*, New Haven, CT: Yale University Press.

Sprinzak, Ehud (1986) *Gush Emunim: The Politics of Zionist Fundamentalism in Israel*, New York: American Jewish Committee.

Martin E. Marty

GAMBLING

Gambling, involving the staking or risking of something of value, usually money, on games of chance has been the subject of enduring controversy. Historical ambivalence towards gambling is due, in part, to its rather unique status as a non-biological 'vice'. All vices contain paradoxical elements of immorality and fun:

> The term vice suggests pleasure – and popularity – as well as immorality. Murder, robbery, and theft are generally regarded as immoral, but not much fun. In contrast, gambling, illicit sex, and drug use are vices because they combine pleasure with 'evil.' The whole point about the phenomenon of vice is its duality: It is conduct that can be enjoyed and deplored at the same time. . . . Nobody has claimed to notice a sentiment among any segment of the public, favoring the legalization of murder. But people do enjoy gambling, marijuana, and illicit sex. Thus, even when such conduct is outlawed, the laws are widely violated.
>
> (Skolnick 1978: 8)

Gambling, however, allows people to take *symbolic* risks without facing the true physical risk and consequence of the activity on which the wager is based. This symbolic gesture of gambling distinguishes it from other vices and increases our confusion over its meaning and consequences:

> Games of chance may be seen as ritualization of forces over which men have no real control – in which winning is the result of 'fate rather than the personal triumph of merit over adversary'.
>
> (Abt *et al.* 1984: 210)

Societal reactions to gambling vary in terms of the culture's position on play as well as its position on thrift, industry, self-denial and God's plan for men. Puritan opposition to gambling centred, for example, on arguments that gambling prostituted divine providence to unworthy ends:

> Lotteries are appeals to providence, said

Increase Mather, and so they may not be used in trivial matters. God determines the cast of the dice or shuffle of the cards, and we are not to implicate His providence in frivolity. Like swearing, gambling debased the Lord by dragging Him into the petty vices of men.
>
> (Findlay 1986: 20–1)

Secular opponents of gambling discuss gambling in terms of social and personal pathology:

> On one side, legal commercial gambling is condemned by religious leaders who have historically equated all gambling with sin, and by secular critics, including psychiatrists professionally concerned with the treatment of 'sick' or compulsive gamblers, moral reformers, and some elected officials . . . who have established as doctrine the belief of many law enforcement professionals that illegal gambling bankrolls organized crime and is linked to various kinds of corruption.
>
> (Abt *et al.* 1985: 3)

Moreover these critics decry the gambler's reliance on 'luck' (superstition), exhibition of irrational behaviours, addiction and non-utilitarian uses of time (Shaffer *et al.* 1989). Studies of casino gambling in Atlantic City, New Jersey, have also pointed out the increase of CRIME in areas that have legalized gaming, undesirable changes within the community and the failure of casinos to stimulate redevelopment (Lehne 1986; Dombrink and Thompson 1990). On the other side of the gambling debate are those who believe that, in the words of the US Federal Gambling Commission, 'gambling is inevitable' (Kallick *et al.* 1976: 1). A variety of vested interests argue the positive social value of commercial gambling:

> Of all the vices, gambling has encouraged the least vociferous opposition, in part because its harmful effects are not easily specified and not biological in nature, but also because it serves certain functions for individuals.
>
> (Geis 1972: 2)

For instance, gambling may provide an arena for the discovery and display of decision-making skills and coolness under pressure. Gambling allows people to deal with the mystery of un-bounded chance and to reduce the feelings of anxiety over uncertainty in everyday life by turning it into a manageable game with known odds, payoff and immediate feedback to one's success or failure (Abt *et al.* 1984). Gambling, as play and entertainment, allows the partici-pant an escape from work and disciplined labour. It provides an outlet, an escape from the routine and boredom characteristic of much of modern life. Gambling introduces an element of anticipatory hope to many who otherwise see little chance to succeed. The fact that gambling blurs the distinction between well-earned and 'ill-gotten' gains is balanced by its presenting a possibility for anyone to 'make it' despite race, sex or ethnicity. In this last, gambling is a very democratic behaviour:

> The odds are egalitarian; they are unflinch-ingly stable whether the wager is large or small. The games are accessible to anyone holding the money required for a minimum bet.
>
> (Abt and Smith 1983: 65)

This peculiar 'fit' between gambling, CAPITAL-ISM and DEMOCRACY was suggested by Edward Devereaux in an early unpublished dissertation on the social functions of gambling (Downes *et al.* 1976). Devereaux argued that gambling was a kind of safety valve for the unfulfilled hopes of the lower classes. The contradiction between the ideal of equality of opportunity and the actual inequality of capitalistic economic institu-tions is obscured by gambling opportunities. Devereaux's thesis helps explain the rapid insti-tutionalization of state lotteries since the earliest state-owned lottery was legalized by voter refer-endum in New Hampshire in 1964. State lotter-ies have led the way in the contemporary expan-sion of legalized gambling in the USA (Clotfelter and Cook 1989).

While gambling appeals to people wishing to 'strike it rich' despite odds against it, it also appeals to revenue-hungry governments who have found a way to use gambling to satisfy the need for 'painless' taxes. Historically state gov-ernments have often tolerated illegal gambling but until recently they have not engaged in policies designed to increase gambling. As was noted earlier, gambling does not involve the ingestion of chemical or biological substances; therefore, as one of the 'vices', gambling is the most amenable to radical shifts in cultural mean-ing. State legislators who would never try to legalize cocaine, for example, in order to tax its use, are now willing not just to legalize existing gambling but to encourage new forms of gam-bling to satisfy the expanding revenue needs of GOVERNMENT.

Gambling is being commercialized and insti-tutionalized more rapidly than in any previous era in American history. The small illegal opera-tors who worked on a low profit margin are being overtaken by corporate big business inter-ests in gambling. The individual entrepreneurs – bookmakers and riverboat gamblers – who supplied pre-industrial America with gambling services, often with the disapproval of 'nice society', are being replaced by large-scale corpo-rate and government operators, blessed by or identical with the STATE.

Nevertheless the states have not yet estab-lished the individual's 'right to gamble' at the game of his or her choice. The states allow gambling by exception. In this way they can justify their extraordinary tax on the games 'selectively decriminalized'. This privilege tax or 'sin tax' is at a much higher rate than ordinary taxes on consumer goods or luxury activities. Clearly the state's legalization policy grows out of their own revenue needs rather than any moral or constitutional ground. The reason for this policy seems to be that if all gambling were made legal there would be no way to justify punitive taxes on commercial gambling, and the extraordinary revenues would disappear:

> The question remains whether gambling is wrong because it is illegal, or illegal because it's wrong. Even when the government does allow gambling, however, it does not respond appropriately to society's desire to gamble.
>
> (Abt *et al.* 1985: 1, 219–20)

Legalized commercial gambling games are often less advantageous to the player than illegal games and the extent of illegal gambling has often been exaggerated by state officials to rationalize their policy of selective decriminalization and monopolistic control (Reuter and Rubenstein 1978). The rapid transformation of gambling from leisure play to commercial corporate enterprises is best explained by the role of government and its historical relation to gambling in America. By latest estimates, legal commercial gambling was over $286 billion in 1990. The 1990 gross annual wager in the USA represents a 14 per cent increase in the total for 1989. Legal revenue (the dollars lost by players) was over $25 billion in 1990 (Christiansen 1991: 32–4). The billions that government derived from the direct taxation of gambling translates into thousands of incremental increases in state sales, income and local property taxes that were not made. At a time when all usual tax resources are being tapped to the point of risking taxpayer revolts, officials often see gambling revenues as 'easy money' and fail adequately to appreciate the fact that this money represents money that taxpayers no longer have to spend on other consumer or investment ventures that might encourage real growth in the 'wealth of nations'. Gambling revenues are nothing more than a transfer 'flat tax' that discriminates against the poorest, i.e. those least able to fund public expenditures who spend a disproportionate percentage of their income on state-owned or sanctioned gambling opportunities.

Many industrial countries allow commercial gambling only to the extent of supplying spontaneous, or unstimulated, demand. Great Britain's casino gaming policies and law are an example. The British Gaming Act of 1968 allows casinos 'only on the scale needed to meet the unstimulated demand for them. . . . The principle of satisfying unstimulated demand is the connecting thread which runs through the whole fabric of gaming control' (Skolnick 1978: 270, 290). Restrictions are intended to ensure that British gaming serves primarily social rather than economic purposes. As enunciated by the chairman of the Gaming Board of Great Britain, Lord Allen of Abbeydale, the Gaming Act of 1968 was intended

to purge gaming of its criminal elements, to cut out excessive profits, to ensure that

gaming was honestly conducted in decent surroundings. . . . Operators. . . were strictly controlled in such a way as to discourage socially-damaging excesses. . . . It was not a basic purpose of this act to raise revenue for the state. . . . There can certainly be no doubt that the aid (in Nevada and New Jersey) differs a great deal from what Parliament intended for Great Britain.

(Laventhol and Horwath 1980)

The philosophy which underlies the entire British Gaming Act is the principle that providing commercial gambling can only be in response to existing public demand. From 1978 to 1982 casinos operating in London were reduced from twenty-three to sixteen. Despite the great profitability and considerable economic significance of the closed casinos, the Gaming Board took the position that the gaming facilities provided by the reduced number of clubs were sufficient to meet unstimulated demand (Abt et al. 1985).

Both this policy and its rigorous enforcement are not evident in any American jurisdiction. Today American suppliers of commercial gambling are not merely supplying the naturally occurring demand for gambling opportunities, they are creating demand. Even if this were being done solely by private operators under effective state regulation it would raise serious questions of social policy. But this demand is also being created by the States themselves – by the governments that in the area of gambling policy are, for all practical purposes, sovereign. This fact adds a specifically political dimension to the issues raised by the institutionalization and legitimization of commercial gambling in America. Governments' revenue interest in gambling makes it a 'special interest' rather than a dispassionate regulator. This dual role makes American gambling even more morally questionable and ambivalent than necessary. There is no practical alternative to government as a representative of the public interest at the institutional level of SOCIETY. However, government's qualifications for this role are less than ideal. State government is an interested party – both because of its extraordinary claim on gambling revenues and because it directly operates lotteries and off-track betting. Paradoxically, typical gambling legislation appears to restrain gambling through the selective decriminalization of particular varieties of games while it simultaneously and aggressively encourages state-run commercial gambling with massive advertising campaigns.

As 'social constructions of risk', gambling decisions, forms, outcomes and society's responses to these are related to a complex, interacting matrix of factors. These factors include historical attitudes, religious morals, social and psychological influences, fiscal pressures, social change, cultural mores, the availability of gambling opportunities, government laws and enforcement policies. As such gambling presents us with a fascinating example of a human activity that incorporates social, cultural and psychological influences. Those of us interested in understanding gambling see gambling as an illustration of risk-taking, sociability, hope, despair, the relationship between work and leisure, an opportunity to study 'deviance' and 'conformity', conventional norms, social change, government influence on behaviour, as well as changing definitions of pathology and addiction. The problems and issues surrounding gambling do not have easy or complete solutions that will satisfy all the interested parties, but their examination makes fascinating social policy study.

Abt, V. and Smith, J. (1983) 'Playing the game in mainstream America', in F. Manning (ed.) *Worlds of Play*, West Point, NY: Leisure Press.

Abt, V., McGurrin, M. and Smith, J. (1984) 'Gambling: the misunderstood sport – a problem in social definition', *Leisure Sciences* 6(2): 205–20.

Abt, V., Smith, J. and Christiansen, E. (1985) *The Business of Risk: Commercial Gambling in Mainstream America*, Lawrence, KS: University Press of Kansas.

Christiansen, E. (1991) 'U.S. gaming handle up 14% in '90', *Gaming and Wagering Business* July: 32–43.

Clotfelter, C. and Cook, P. (1989) *Selling Hope: State Lotteries in America*, Cambridge, MA: Harvard University Press.

Devereaux, E. (1949) 'Gambling and the social structure: a sociological study of lotteries and horseracing in contemporary America', unpublished PhD dissertation, Harvard University.

Dombrink, J. and Thompson, W. (1990) *The Last Resort: Success and Failure in Campaigns for Casinos*, Reno, NV: University of Nevada Press.

Downes, D., Davies, B., David, M. and Stone, E.

(1976) *Gambling, Work and Leisure*, London: Routledge & Kegan Paul.

Findlay, J. (1986) *People of Chance: Gambling in American Society from Jamestown to Las Vegas*, New York and Oxford: Oxford University Press.

Geis, G. (1972) *Not the Law's Business*, Washington, DC: GPO.

Kallick, M., Suits, D., Dielman, T. and Hybels, J. (1976) *Gambling in America: Final Report of the Commission on the Review of the National Policy Toward Gambling*, Washington, DC: Government Report.

Laventhol and Howath (eds) (1980) *Second Annual Gaming Conference*, Philadelphia, PA: Laventhol & Howath.

Lehne, R. (1986) *Casino Policy*, New Brunswick, NJ: Rutgers University Press.

Reuter, P. and Rubenstein, J. (1978) 'Fact, fancy, and organized crime', *The Public Interest* 53 (Fall): 45–67.

Shaffer, H., Stein, S., Gambino, B. and Cummings, T. (eds) (1989) *Compulsive Gambling: Theory, Research and Practice*, Lexington, MA: Lexington Books.

Skolnick, J. (1978) *House of Cards: The Legalization and Control of Casino Gambling*, Boston, MA: Little Brown.

Vicki Abt

GENDER

'Gender' refers to the many aspects of human affairs concerned with the experience of being male or female in a particular CULTURE. It is a category of analysis in studies of everyday relations between women and men, especially in terms of gender inequality and hierarchy in contexts as diverse as economics and POLITICS, SEXUALITY, the FAMILY, the LAW and religion. It prompts research and analysis into the ontogeny and development of gender identity, especially associated with patterns of child-rearing and early mother–child relations; comparative studies of 'gender roles' between cultures and historical epochs; a critical examination of the portrayal of women and men in culture; and appraisals of differential qualities deemed 'masculine' and 'feminine' and their psychological and cultural manifestations.

Concern with gender as a social relation and category of personal identity arose out of feminist theory and politics, but the emergent field of critical studies of men and masculinity has further intensified the interest in this sphere. Gender studies are interdisciplinary, encompassing disciplines as diverse as anthropology, biological studies, sociology, psychology and psychoanalyis, literary theory, histories of science and medicine and philosophies of science and knowledge.

In sociological theory of the 1940s and 1950s, concern centred around the question of 'sex roles': the division of labour between women and men in the home and the economy. These were primarily regarded as a result of socialization by the family, the media and education. Theoretical clarity was added in the late 1960s by the widespread adoption of Robert Stoller's distinction between 'sex' and 'gender': the former denoting biological, physiological and reproductive difference, the latter indicating cultural, psychological and socially prescribed differences. The 'facts' of sex difference were seen as one thing – but how such facts of life were organized and perceived was claimed to be a product of human agency and therefore potentially open to change. This remained theoretical orthodoxy for at least a generation, and encouraged critical studies to focus on questions of gender attribution and enforcement on individual and structural levels. In particular, extensive studies were carried out to ascertain the true extent of gender differences, in mathematical and linguistic ability and in psychological traits. However, reviews and surveys of such studies have concluded that few significant differences could be determined, and that the evidence for definitive sex differences remains unproven (Archer and Lloyd 1982).

Furthermore, it was argued that the actual construction of research tests and measurements emphasizes gender differences at the expense of gender traits expressing considerable similarity and overlap. Such enquiries were further carried forward to challenge the notion that conclusive differences could be ascertained without due attention to the construction of knowledge and the processes by which gender divisions themselves preclude scientific neutrality or objectivity. Therefore, largely fuelled by feminist interest in the sociology of knowledge, many enquiries developed which displayed a resistance to conventional notions of scientific objectivity

as neutral records of 'facts' which speak for themselves. Instead, they must be regarded as social products, generated by human processes of enquiry, taking place in a social context that already consigns women to a lesser sphere, and rooted in particular androcentric understandings of what counts as respectable scientific knowledge (Harding 1986).

For example, researchers in the biological sciences have eschewed simple 'additive' models of sex and gender by which biology and environment (or 'nature' and 'culture') are perceived as ontologically discrete. They argue that the construction of the categories themselves cannot escape scrutiny. In particular, what we call 'nature' is itself the product of human categorization. Within the history of science and medicine, considerable attention has been paid to the socially and scientifically constructed nature of biology, sexuality and bodily configuration. It has been argued that there is no 'pure' human body unaffected by social, cultural (and often religious) interpretations. The body is never raw fact but always hedged around by associations with politics, cosmology and moral philosophy. The work of Foucault has been influential here in stressing the extent to which all knowledge of ourselves through scientific and medical discourse is harnessed to political ends (Laqueur 1990).

Anthropological studies of gender have not denied the prevalence of gender hierarchy and its symbolic association with other cultural dualisms, e.g. nature/culture, human/non-human, reason/emotion and mind/body. However, many scholars have refuted notions of gender divisions as resting upon a priori distinctions between nature and culture, and of women and men as occupying ontologically separate spheres by virtue of something called 'biological sex difference'. Instead, they have turned to alternative explanations of universal gender hierarchy, which affirm the importance of human practice in the process of making gender difference:

Women and men are products of social relations, if we change the social relations we change the categories 'woman' and 'man'. On both political and intellectual grounds we would argue that to put it at its bluntest, social relations determine sex differences rather than biological sex producing social divisions between the sexes.

(Brown and Jordanova 1982: 393)

The result of these kinds of enquiries has been that attention has turned to the elaborate and multilayered mechanisms by which gender as a social reality pervades all structures of epistemology, subjectivity and social practice. Instead of being seen as the mapping of cultural prescriptions over fixed and innately dimorphous sexual persons, it is now understood to involve a complex interplay of psyche, anatomy, culture and language. Freudian and post-Freudian psychoanalysis, especially Francophone, has been a powerful resource in this debate, as it speaks of a union of body and mind in the context of the question of what makes us cultural beings (Moi 1985).

Clearly, therefore, one of the key areas upon which debate about gender is located is a shift from what Connell (1987) terms 'categoricalism' (within both anti-feminism and radical feminism) towards a view of gender as a dialectical process, involving the material transformation of 'nature' into an integrated system of gender relations. Another reason why interdisciplinary study of gender is so crucial is the recognition that gender regimes are diverse and pluralistic: no single 'cause' – be it biology, object relations or advertising – can be held to generate gender on its own. Gender relations permeate the whole of the social structure, and only an integrated and multi-disciplinary approach can, arguably, do that justice.

In terms of gender politics, and especially within the women's movement, three basic options for change may be discerned. The first is the *assertion of gender equality* or equivalence: aiming for equality of opportunity and access for women and men, as associated with liberal feminist politics. The study and advocacy of 'androgyny' as a strategy for pursuit of gender equality is also associated with this position, the argument being that female and male psyches comprise complex interminglings of 'feminine' and 'masculine' traits and that the most healthy integrated personalities of either gender combine both sets of characteristics. Critics of this position claim that assertions of 'equality' do not adequately take account of the differentials of power and prestige that value male and masculine qualities more highly; and that psychic equality and self-actualization precludes problems of embodied being and the psychosexual influence of morphology upon gender acquisition and identity.

In response to the 'gender equality' position, radical feminists have turned to the *celebration of gender difference*, venerating female sexuality and feminine qualities as inherently superior to masculinity, often identified as pathological. Critics of this position claim that it simply inverts patriarchal gender dualism and plays into the hands of anti-feminists by perpetuating a notion of gender identity as 'essentialist' – fixed, pre-social and ahistorical. Gender, and the categories 'Woman' and 'Man', do not endure in abstract form throughout history; rather, the identities associated with male/female and masculine/feminine must be seen as historically and culturally variable and conditioned. As a result, a third analytical and political response can be discerned, which seeks to *interrogate the meaning of difference*, and not simply to take the existing points of division between the genders at face value. This position seeks to ask what the dynamics of gender differentiation are at any given point in human history, and the practical, material and embodied ways in which gender is generated (see, for example, Connell 1987). Such a 'naming' of difference is to be undertaken as a heuristic and strategic device rather than a straightforward description of reality. Gender cannot be regarded as the social expression of 'naturally' occurring dichotomies, nor the innate static qualities of 'masculinity' or 'femininity': rather, it is generated out of the raw material of reproduction, bodies, sexuality, child-rearing, subsistence, language and culture – which themselves already pre-exist in a gendered world.

Theological studies have been slow to adopt the concerns and analyses of gender studies. The following areas are suggested as potential areas for further development.

Gender Justice: disparities between women and men, especially in the economy (as in the global phenomenon of the 'feminization of POV-ERTY'), point to the systematic exclusion and oppression of women. Gender studies have indicated that this cannot be attributed to the natural or innate inferiority of women but to social and economic mechanisms. Thus the existence of gender divisions in society and issues of sexism and oppression of women, especially via control of their sexuality and reproduction and the perpetration of sexual VIOLENCE, need to be recognized as fundamental instruments of oppression of women by men. The churches have been slow in lending support to campaigns around economic and sexual justice, although work within development and aid agencies and some areas of industrial mission are beginning to address such issues and demand greater justice for women.

Christian anthropology: within feminist theology, the question of difference is implicit in critiques of theological orthodoxies surrounding certain basic categories of virtue, work, pastoral need, religious experience and the exercise of ministry, lay or ordained. Are these to be seen as universal human categories, identical for women and men? Or do women's life situations shape their experiences of these areas differently from men? Feminist theologians and ethicists have long been arguing that categories of 'service' rationalize and validate women's subordinate role, and that SIN and virtue in the Christian tradition have been defined as if maleness constituted authentic and normative humanity, to the exclusion of women's experience (Borrowdale 1989). Similarly, debates over the ordination of women centre as much on differing understandings of human nature – whether women and men are fundamentally the same kind of human being, or different – as upon theology and ECCLESIOLOGY. Yet even advocates of WOMEN'S ORDINATION are beginning to ask whether women will introduce a qualitatively different kind of ministry to that of men, and to what effect. All these issues derive from assumptions about the nature of gender difference and its expression in social contexts. They also point us towards other questions of 'difference': age, class, race, able-bodiedness, culture and ethnicity, which provide similar challenges to the notion of a single or universal human perspective.

Gender studies in the human and social sciences are careful to distinguish between the categories of biological sex, sexuality or sexual orientation, and gender. Theological anthropology must develop a similar understanding of how these three aspects of personhood are generated by different kinds of human practice. They may be linked but they do not necessarily follow inexorably from each other. Theological discourse needs also to be mindful of such fundamental philosophical and anthropological questions as whether there is a fixed 'human nature' and the degree to which we are simply the object and products of cultural discourse shaped by powers beyond our control, or whether we can choose strategies and identities freely and creatively. What is the relationship between body and mind and self to culture? How does theological discourse about women and men and religious practice (especially embodied sacramental practice) intermingle 'nature' and 'culture' in the generation of gendered identity and meanings (Bynum *et al.* 1986; Graham 1995; King 1995)?

Theology: the question of inclusive language – how to speak of, and address, God within liturgical contexts – is also of concern to many within the churches. The debate is often framed as whether God can be understood as 'Mother' as well as 'Father', and whether 'feminine' imagery is acceptable for reflecting the human experience of the Divine. Some would challenge such polarization of language, looking to develop understandings of God's relation to humanity and creation as the primary guide for 'metaphorical' language (see McFague 1982). On the other hand, use of inclusive language, in reference to God and humankind, can be seen as a step towards affirming women's experience as an avenue to the Divine; but this only serves to highlight yet again the deeper question of what the relationship is between women's and men's experience of being gendered and of living in a gendered world, and the traditional Christian claims that humankind is made in the image of God. This challenges theology to consider how human experience – being embodied, social, sexual, speaking and acting people – might be used as metaphors for further revelation of the Divine, and the role our maleness and femaleness might play in that.

The lessons from the human and social sciences would appear to be that culture and human practice must be seen as crucial to the development and formation of human personality, especially in so far as our experience of being human is always already one of being gendered. Gender as a real and constant product of social and sexual relations, rather than an abstract dichotomy beyond scrutiny and critique, must therefore remain the primary lesson for theological interrogation and response.

Archer, John and Lloyd, Barbara B. (1982) *Sex and Gender*, Cambridge: Cambridge University Press.

Borrowdale, Anne (1989) *A Woman's Work*, London: SPCK.

Brown, Penelope and Jordanova, Ludmilla (1982) 'Oppressive dichotomies: the nature/culture debate', in E. Whitelegg (ed.) *The Changing Experience of Women*, Oxford: Martin Robertson.

Bynum, Caroline Walker, Harrell, Stephen and Richman, Paula (eds) (1986) *Gender and Religion: On the Complexity of Symbols*, Boston, MA: Beacon Press.

Connell, R.W. (1987) *Gender and Power: Society, the Person and Sexual Politics*, Cambridge: Polity.

Ford, D. and Hearn, J. (1988) *Studying Men and Masculinity: A Sourcebook of Literature and Materials*, Manchester: Manchester University Press.

Graham, Elaine L. (1995) *Making the Difference: Gender, Personhood and Theology*, London: Mowbray.

Harding, Sandra (1986) *The Science Question in Feminism*, Milton Keynes: Open University Press.

Holloway, R. (ed.) (1991) *Who Needs Feminism? Men Respond to Sexism in the Church*, London: SPCK.

King, Ursula (ed.) (1995) *Religion and Gender*, Oxford: Blackwell.

Laqueur, T.C. (1990) *Making Sex: Body and Gender from the Greeks to Freud*, London: Harvard University Press.

McFague, S. (1982) *Metaphorical Theology: Models of God in Religious Language*, Philadelphia, PA: Fortress Press.

Moi, Toril (1985) *Sexual-Textual Politics*, London: Routledge.

Morgan, David H.J. (1992) *Discovering Men*, London: Routledge.

Rhode, Deborah L. (ed.) (1990) *Theoretical Perspectives on Sexual Difference*, New Haven, CT: Yale University Press.

Elaine Graham

GENOCIDE

The term 'genocide' has become increasingly used in international political discourse since the late 1960s. It has two principal meanings. The first refers to any AGGRESSION, often but not necessarily involving widespread loss of life, against an ethnic or national group. The second denotes political mass murder, whatever the character of the victims. Some writers hold that genocide is always a CRIME of states, while others treat as genocide extreme forms of ethnic conflict. The term always expresses strong condemnation. Like all political words expressing strong emotions, it is often used hyperbolically, so that the meaning of the term is stretched to cover actions which may well deserve condemnation but which may be more accurately described by less extreme terms such as 'HUMAN RIGHTS violations'.

The term was coined in 1944 by Raphael Lemkin, a Polish lawyer. He applied it to those actions of the German occupying powers during the Second World War which, in their barbarity, went beyond the scope of the existing international laws of WAR. For Lemkin, genocide was the deliberate destruction of peoples. Such destruction might be carried out by mass murder or by undermining the victims' way of life.

Lemkin's concept was transformed after the Second World War by the United Nations (UN), which adopted its Convention on Genocide in 1948. The Convention defines as genocide various acts 'committed with intent to destroy, in whole or in part, a national, ethnical, racial or religious group, as such'. The relevant acts are (a) killing members of the group; (b) causing serious bodily or mental harm to members of the group; (c) deliberately inflicting on the group conditions of life calculated to bring about its physical destruction in whole or in part; (d) imposing measures intended to prevent births within the group; (e) forcibly transferring children of the group to another group. The UN extended Lemkin's concept to peace-time actions but excluded 'cultural genocide' from the protection of the Convention. The term 'cultural genocide' has persisted in popular usage, but lawyers and social scientists have mostly held that cultural destruction and the physical destruction of peoples are conceptually distinct. Resistance to this tendency has come from anthropologists and human rights activists who have coined the term 'ethnocide' to refer to cultural destruction, with particular reference to tribal peoples.

The UN Convention has been widely criticized on two grounds. The first is its uncertain meaning. In particular, the phrases 'in part' and 'as such' are thought to be unclear. The second is the refusal of the UN to include in its definition of genocide attacks on political groups or economic classes.

Lemkin held that Nazi genocide was a reversion to ancient barbaric practices. He associated genocide with tribal and religious wars of extermination. Some scholars have followed Lemkin in treating genocide as a practice with an ancient history. Others have restricted their analyses to modern genocides.

The question whether or not 'genocide' is a generic concept denoting an ancient practice is related to an intense controversy as to whether or not the event now commonly known as 'the Holocaust', the Nazi project to exterminate the Jews, was unique or whether it may be compared with various genocides. Some scholars have held the Holocaust to be a case of genocide which may be compared with other cases, such as the Turkish genocide of the Armenians in 1915, the mass killings ordered by Stalin and the massacres carried out by the Khmer Rouge regime in Cambodia. Others have insisted on the uniqueness of the Holocaust. This controversy has been carried out in secular historical terms, the central question being whether the exterminatory intent of the Nazis was uniquely thorough-going. It has also been presented in theological terms, some writers claiming that the Holocaust raises unique problems for Jewish and Christian THEOLOGY.

The Holocaust presents a problem for Jewish theology because, although the Bible is an AUTHORITY for the idea that God punishes His chosen people for their sins, the Holocaust cannot be subsumed under this doctrine. To allow this would concede to Nazism the idea that the Jews deserved their fate. There is a consensus that this solution is unacceptable. Questions are then raised as to what the Holocaust teaches us about the nature of God and God's relationship

with the Jewish people. There is no consensus about how such questions should be answered.

According to some commentators the Holocaust also raises fundamental questions for Christian theology. The central issue is whether or not Christianity is *theologically* anti-Semitic (*see* ANTI-SEMITISM). Some Christian theologians have argued that the Holocaust requires Christians to reconsider the status of Jews, the people who rejected Christ, in Christian theology.

Those scholars who favour a comparative and historical approach to the study of genocide have been unable to agree on an appropriate methodology or theoretical framework. Sceptics have doubted whether a single theory can explain events that took place in such diverse historical and cultural settings.

Lemkin conceived of genocide as a war of extermination, a practice common throughout history. Such wars may be external or internal, or they may be carried out when the perpetrators and the victims dispute where the borders defining the internal and the external should be drawn. On this account, the Roman destruction of Carthage was an external genocide; the mass killings of the Khmer Rouge were internal; and the massacres of indigenous peoples by settler colonialists involved disputes over territorial sovereignty, i.e. over the external–internal distinction itself.

This approach links the history of genocide to the history of (external and internal) war. The principal question it raises is why some wars are exterminatory. Although knowledge of early human history is uncertain, there is reason to believe that 'primitive' tribal wars were rarely exterminatory, since both the motives and the means for genocide were unavailable. Wars of extermination are associated with the emergence of the centralized political state and urban civilization. In the ancient near East cities were both religious and political centres and struggles between would-be imperial city-states are recorded as involving the destruction of enemy cities and their inhabitants. Although the literal truth of these reports is doubtful, the records tell stories of genocide. City-destruction was the most ancient form of genocide.

The Hebrew Bible records several cases of genocidal city-destruction. This raises historical and theological problems. The literal TRUTH of these reports is called into question by modern historical scholarship. However, there is no doubt that the Hebrew Bible presents God as commanding God's chosen people to destroy other nations and reports massacres of whole populations. There is no consensus as to how Jewish and Christian theology should address this problem. Indeed, theological reflection on the problem has dwelt on the apparent contrast between the Old Testament God of war and the New Testament doctrine of PEACE rather than on the problem of genocide as such (Hobbs 1989; *see* THEODICY).

Chalk and Jonassohn (1990) have suggested a link between ancient and modern genocide based on Christina Larner's study of the witch-hunt in Scotland. Larner argued that supposed witches were persecuted for being 'enemies of God' as part of the project of establishing a new form of order required by the modern nation-state (Larner 1981). Although the witch-hunt itself was not a genocide, the persecution of real or imagined enemies of the state lies at the heart of genocidal practice. The suggestion is that there is a parallel between the persecution of supposed witches in early modern Scotland and, for example, the Khmer Rouge persecution of supposed enemies of the people in the con-struction of the new Communist order of 'Demo-cratic Kampuchea'. Similar ideological polariza-tions between the agents of (the true or chief) god and those of false or hostile gods are found in accounts of genocide in the ancient near East (Liverani 1979). On this view, genocide is moti-vated, or at least justified, by appeal to a the-ology or to a secular substitute for a theology that represents the perpetrators as agents of the ultimate source of value in the world and the victims as irredeemable enemies of the good. By contrast, theologies emphasizing peace and JUS-TICE may be, and often are, invoked to oppose this sort of lethal politics.

Some theorists argue that genocidal ideolo-gies are neither necessary nor sufficient condi-tions of genocide. They are not necessary, for genocide may be motivated by supposedly non-ideological passions such as greed. They are not sufficient, because exclusionary ideologies may persist for long periods without being actualized in genocidal practice. Several authors therefore favour a more structural theory.

Kuper (1981) has proposed that the plural society, in which mutually hostile groups with radically different cultures coexist, is a struc-tural condition of genocide. However, Kuper restricts this approach to internal genocides and it is not well suited to the analysis of the geno-cide of political groups.

An alternative approach emphasizes the role of structural crises. According to this theory, genocide is precipitated by a societal crisis, such as defeat in war. In such a crisis, a new social force comes to power with a project to create a new order. If the ideological conception of this new order excludes a particular group from membership, that group may be 'eliminated', by forcible assimilation, by deportation or by geno-cide. A further necessary condition for such a genocide is the non-intervention by external powers. This model was derived from compari-son of the Nazi and Turkish cases, but may be applicable to the USSR in the Stalinist period, to Cambodia under the Khmer Rouge and to various putative genocides in post-colonial soci-eties. The model raises two main problems. One is the vagueness of the concept of 'societal crisis'. The other is that some genocides (especi-ally those carried out in the course of imperial-istic expansion) do not seem to involve a societal crisis at all.

Although Lemkin considered Nazi genocide to be a reversion to ancient barbarism, he did recognize that it had distinctively modern fea-tures, especially in its use of bureaucratic proce-dures and industrialized means of mass murder. Some analysts have considered these features to be constitutive of MODERNITY itself and have concluded that the modern world has an inher-ently greater potentiality for genocide than earlier periods of history. The implication is not that human beings have become more or less EVIL than they were, nor is it merely that they now have more powerful means to do evil. The point is that modern SOCIETY has produced a new form of the human personality – the technical-bureaucratic – which can commit mass killing without knowing what it does and with a sense of satisfaction in the efficient perform-ance of a socially allocated task.

If modernity has increased the potential for genocide, it has also increased our resources both for understanding it and for judging it. Genocide was not a moral problem for the ancient world. It is for the modern world because moral and political values have changed. And if we understand that the modern bureaucratic-industrial state has an unprecedented potential for genocide, we know too that crisis management, democratic institutions and political cultures committed to combating RACISM and to respecting the rights of individuals and minorities are barriers to genocide.

Whether genocide is seen as a form of state tyranny or a form of ethnic conflict, perpetrators and/or victims may be distinguished by their religion. A theocratic state may persecute heretics (e.g. the mass killing of Baha'is in Iran); a secular state may destroy despised religious groups (e.g. the Khmer Rouge massacre of Buddhist monks in Cambodia); or religious groups may massacre each other (as did Hindus and Muslims in India in the aftermath of Indian independence). However, where religion apparently enters into a genocide, secular factors may be more important: this is probably true of both the Armenian and Jewish cases.

In view of the lack of consensus on the definition of genocide, it is hard to say how common it is in the contemporary world. However, Lemkin coined a term to draw attention to a distinctive form of political evil, which, even if it was manifested in its most extreme form in the Holocaust, has been repeated in various forms and magnitudes since the end of the Second World War. We live in a world of strong yet insecure states and vulnerable minorities, ethnic, national, religious and political. Those with most power to prevent genocide rarely have the will to do so. The world is thus structured for genocide. Genocide is both ancient and modern. It is motivated by the lowest passions and the highest ideals. Its relative neglect by theology is perhaps surprising.

Chalk, F. and Jonassohn, K. (1990) *The History and Sociology of Genocide: Analyses and Case Studies*, New Haven, CT: Yale University Press.

Charny, I.W. (1988) *Genocide: A Critical Bibliographic Review*, London: Mansell.

Fein, H. (1979) *Accounting for Genocide*, New York: Free Press.

——(1990) 'Genocide: a sociological perspective', *Current Sociology* 38(1): 1–126.

Hobbs, T.R. (1989) *A Time for War: A Study of Warfare in the Old Testament*, Wilmington, DE: Glazier.

Kuper, L. (1981) *Genocide: Its Political Use in the Twentieth Century*, Harmondsworth: Penguin.

Larner, C. (1981) *Enemies of God: The Witch-Hunt in Scotland*, London: Chatto & Windus.

Lemkin, R. (1944) *Axis Rule in Occupied Europe*, Washington, DC: Carnegie Endowment for International Peace.

Liverani, M. (1979) 'The ideology of the Assyrian Empire', in M.T. Larsen (ed.) *Power and Propaganda*, Copenhagen: Akademisk Forlag.

Melson, R. (1989) 'Revolutionary genocide: on the causes of the Armenian genocide of 1915 and the Holocaust', *Holocaust and Genocide Studies* 4(2): 161–74.

Wallimann, I. and Dobkowski, M.N. (1987) *Genocide and the Modern Age: Etiology and Case Studies of Mass Death*, Westport, CT: Greenwood.

Michael Freeman

GLOBAL THEOLOGY

Global theology is a relatively new way of thinking, tentative, exploratory, yet bearing a strong sense of urgency. It is an attempt to understand the present global situation from the viewpoint of Christian faith, and at the same time to interpret, or reinterpret, Christian faith in the light of this situation. Both movements are important. The world situation seems to call for a theological understanding, because its own characteristically secular way of thinking is breaking down under the impact of the crisis it has helped to bring about. There is a perceived spiritual void in the world which presents THEOLOGY with a challenge and a new opportunity. However, it is recognized that Christian theology is at present ill-fitted for the task because it has been preoccupied for too long with the relatively narrow concerns of the individual human being and the institution of the church. To 'think globally' about the meaning of Christian faith would therefore require a new way of thinking.

The first attempts by theologians to address global issues were focused on particular concerns. LIBERATION THEOLOGY developed in the

1970s as a local response, in the south, to the global issue of an unjust economic system, dominated by the north; but in the 1980s it was further developed by Balasuriya into an appropriately *Planetary Theology* (1984). Theological reflection on nuclear weapons, which began with questions of their ethical legitimacy, became fully theological with the question of how a possible nuclear holocaust should affect our understanding of God (Garrison 1982; Kaufman 1985, discussed in Race 1988). Thought about the ENVIRONMENT also developed from relatively modest reflections on 'nature' and 'stewardship' in the 1970s into more searching questions about the fate of MODERNITY, Western anthropocentrism and the ecology of the earth (Daly and Cobb 1989; Moltmann 1989; Birch *et al.* 1990; *see* ECOLOGICAL THEOLOGY). It is significant too that feminist theology has become increasingly concerned with the connections, historical and theological, between PATRIARCHY and the present threats to life on earth (Ruether 1981; McFague 1987), whilst interreligious dialogue has come to involve practical questions about our collective survival in our common earthly home (Küng 1991). Global theology can be seen as a convergence of these growing concerns.

Yet moving the discussion somewhat further, so as to include the whole globe, does take us into a new dimension of thinking. We are now having to think of the totality of our earthly existence, and of its new, or newly discovered, limits. The globe itself, as a sphere of a certain size, already symbolizes that – and by implication that which (mysteriously) transcends the limits. There is a limit to human interference with life on the globe, beyond which the globe begins to die. There is a limit to the accumulation of military defence, beyond which it becomes, paradoxically, a threat to our very existence. And there is a limit to the economic exploitation of other human beings, beyond which the global economy begins to founder and 'growth' goes into reverse. These paradoxes present us in a stark form with some new facts about our life on earth: that our mutual dependences are now truly global, that it is within our POWER as human beings to bring life on earth to an end (or, which is the obverse, to ensure

that we do not) and that the present activities of human beings, in so far as they are bent on limitless expansion, are tending in that direction. The situation is historically unique, as well as critical. It might be said that we have passed a watershed in history, since from now on it is up to us whether human life continues, whether there is a future in which our hopes can be invested.

The awareness of this situation immediately raises questions about the true *ground* of our faith and hope and LOVE, since the assumptions of our present way of life in the modern world are being systematically undermined. They lead us back to the beginnings of our history, and in particular to the sources of our spiritual traditions. But the new awareness also raises questions about how it is *possible* to have faith and hope when we ourselves are now responsible for the fate of the earth – questions which simply could not have arisen until now. God, or the holy, has become important again, but how is God, or it, to be conceived?

Again, the awareness of global mutualities and limits gives us also an awareness of how everything is related to everything else, calling for a more integrated, holistic interpretation of the world. Modern individualism and anthropocentrism are no longer appropriate. But what is to take their place? And how new will that new understanding have to be? Will it embrace or surpass Christianity? – and/or any other ancient tradition? Will it emphasize the unique role that humans will have to play in preserving and caring for the earth, as in the traditional story of Genesis, or will it, on the contrary, emphasize the relative unimportance of humans as, after all, only a part of nature? How close will the different traditions have to come in order to meet this new common challenge? And how far can theology once again become a discourse in which everyone in principle, from whatever tradition, can participate? These are some of the questions that a truly global theology will now have to address.

Ambler, R. (1990) *Global Theology: the Meaning of Faith in the Present World Crisis*, London: SCM and Philadelphia, PA: Trinity Press.
Balasuriya, T. (1984) *Planetary Theology*, London: SCM and Maryknoll, NY: Orbis.

Birch, C., Eakin, W. and McDaniel, J.B. (eds) (1990) *Liberating Life: Contemporary Approaches to Ecological Theology*, Maryknoll, NY: Orbis.

Daly, H.E. and Cobb, J.B., Jr (1989) *For the Common Good: Redirecting the Economy towards Community, the Environment and a Sustainable Future*, Boston, MA: Beacon Press; new edn, London: Green Print, 1990.

Garrison, J. (1982) *The Darkness of God*, Grand Rapids, MI: Eerdmans and London: SCM.

Küng, H. (1991) *Global Responsibility: In Search of a New World Ethic*, London: SCM.

McFague, S. (1987) *Models of God: Theology for an Ecological, Nuclear Age*. Philadelphia, PA: Fortress Press and London: SCM.

Moltmann, J. (1989) *Creating a Just Future: the Politics of Peace and the Ethics of Creation in a Threatened World*, London: SCM and Philadelphia, PA: Trinity Press.

Race, A. (ed.) (1988) *Theology against the Nuclear Horizon*, London: SCM.

Ruether, R.R. (1981) *To Change the World: Christology and Cultural Criticism*, New York: Crossroad.

Rex Ambler

GNOSTICISM

The theological designation 'gnosticism' derives from the Greek word *gnosis* ('knowledge') and was coined in the eighteenth century to refer to certain religious movements from the first two or three centuries CE whose doctrines allegedly centred around the importance of special 'knowledge'. The most well-attested of these movements were Christian, but some evidence suggests that similar movements may have existed independently of, and perhaps even prior to, early Christianity (Pearson 1990).

Before 1945, only a few writings from 'gnostics' themselves were extant, and the principal evidence for such teachings were polemical descriptions found in the writings of ancient Christian heresiologists. But the quantity of original source material was greatly increased in 1945 by the discovery near the village of Nag Hammadi in Egypt of several fourth-century CE Coptic codices whose contents included numerous writings containing doctrines of the general sort that was by then conventionally classified as 'gnostic' (Robinson 1988).

Perhaps the most famous feature in such sources is the assertion that the material cosmos was not created by the highest God but by a lower being (or a group of them). Sometimes this inferior creator is portrayed as an incompetent and devilish tyrant, who selfishly arrogates to himself POWER and AUTHORITY while only vaguely or not at all understanding that true divinity transcends him. Other sources assert merely the inferior nature, not any malevolent designs, of the creator, and in some versions he is even portrayed very sympathetically. Whatever their specific characterizations of the creator, these various strategies for removing from the true God direct responsibility for the creation of the material universe generally seem directed at a common target: the issue of THEODICY, reconciling absolute divine perfection with moral and physical deficiencies in the cosmic ecosystem. Closely associated with this concern, there are often efforts to resolve hermeneutical difficulties posed by various 'problem passages' in scripture: anthropomorphic or anthropopathic language about God; grammatical plurals that seem incongruous with monotheism (e.g. Genesis 1: 26); behaviour deemed inconsistent with divine perfection, etc. The distinction between God and cosmic creator has prompted the assertion that characteristic of 'gnosticism' was an 'anti-cosmic dualism' encouraging complete isolation from SOCIETY (Stroumsa 1992: 155). Yet there is very little evidence that persons in these movements were any less socially concerned or involved than most of their contemporaries, and in reality they sometimes display a distinct optimism about their mission within society.

A second feature is the tendency to stress a special kinship between humanity and divinity, usually expressed by an assertion that humanity bears within itself a spiritual principle or essence that derives from the realm of true divinity and that is destined to return there after release from the flesh. These speculations are often clearly indebted to Platonic traditions about the descent and ascent of the soul, but most of them also reflect a heritage concerned with Biblical creation narratives, and especially the notion that humanity was created in the likeness and image of God and that the divine spirit was breathed into the human.

Myth is a characteristic vehicle employed in these sources to articulate a symbolic framework within which anthropological, theodicean, hermeneutical and other questions are resolved. Overall, the casts of characters and the narrative elements and structures vary significantly, so that it is inappropriate to imagine all of these myths as versions of the same story. Nevertheless, some similarities among them do reflect the existence of shared school traditions and the borrowing and adaptation of mythological motifs. Several myths begin with an account of the divine realm and how it unfolded from primordial unity and transcendence into a multiplicity of mythically personified divine attributes who collectively brought the perfection of divinity into expression. The cosmic force(s) that have come to be mistaken for god(s) came into being only later, through a breach of order in the transcendent realm, an illegitimate and futile attempt by one of the entities in the divine realm to produce an image of true divinity, but which resulted in only the inferior demiurge. In other myths, the entity or entities responsible for creation are in existence from the start, and their relationship of contrast with the transcendent realm merely undergoes elaboration and definition in the course of the narrative. The various myths frequently depict how revelation is conveyed to humankind about the true origin of the cosmos, the nature of the supernal realms, and the origin, nature and destiny of humanity. A common motif is that only certain persons, the truly 'spiritual', are able to accept the revelation and experience salvation in the form of ascent to the transcendent realm. This theme, along with a tendency to speak of the spiritual as belonging to an 'elect' or special 'race' or 'class', has often been interpreted as evidence of a characteristic soteriological determinism that rendered ethical progress irrelevant. However, these are caricatures that do not do justice to most of the sources in question, where clear assumptions of provisionality and notions of moral progress can often be demonstrated (Rudolph 1983: 117).

Many of these mythic programmes amounted to grand-scale attempts at forging syntheses of presuppositions of Hellenistic-Roman cultural tradition with the religious heritage of Judaism and/or the early Jesus movement. The earliest truly systematic Christian THEOLOGY was sketched out in ambitious strokes in these circles, though such efforts were ultimately deemed heretical by what turned out to be emerging Christian orthodoxy.

In later Western thought 'gnosticism' has come to be a kind of Protean theme associated with an incredibly wide variety of theological, philosophical, literary, political and social trends – from medieval Cathars and Bogomils to the theosophy of Madame Blavatsky, the poetry of Blake or Shelley or Byron, the fiction of Herman Melville or Hermann Hesse, the psychology of Carl Jung, Marxism, Nazism, 'scientism', and a long list of further examples in these and other categories (Sebba 1981). Each association has been inspired by some point of continuity or analogy, real or imagined, between the ancient sources and some later phenomenon: a preoccupation with the evils of cosmic existence or a generally dualistic framework; a spirit of rebellion against tradition or the established order; a focus on the dynamics and implications of self-consciousness; an appeal to the esoteric or occult. On the one hand, the history of these appeals to gnosticism as hermeneutical key may be a testimony to the pervasive and enduring power of the ancient myths in question to excite the imagination. On the other hand, the application of this category to such a host of diverse phenomena has effectively emptied the label 'gnosticism' of real meaning, because it has been made to mean too much.

Perhaps one of the reasons that 'gnosticism' has turned out to be subject to such manipulation as a category is that the second- and third-century movements that it was originally invented to define were in the first place rather more diverse than the neatly constructed category would suggest.

Culiano, I.P. (1992) *The Tree of Gnosis: Gnostic Mythology from Early Christianity to Modern Nihilism*, trans. H.S. Wiesner and I.P. Culiano, San Francisco, CA: HarperCollins.

Jonas, H. (1963) *The Gnostic Religion: The Message of the Alien God and the Beginnings of Christianity*, 2nd edn, Boston, MA: Beacon.

King. K.L. (ed.) (1988) *Images of the Feminine in Gnosticism*, Studies in Antiquity and Christianity 4, Philadelphia, PA: Fortress Press.

Layton, B. (ed.) (1980) *The Rediscovery of Gnosticism: Proceedings of the International Conference on Gnosticism at Yale, New Haven, Connecticut, March 28-31, 1978*, 2 vols, Studies in the History of Religions (Supplements to *Numen*) 41, Leiden: Brill.

Pagels, E. (1979) *The Gnostic Gospels*, New York: Vintage Books.

Pearson, B.A. (1990) *Gnosticism, Judaism, and Egyptian Christianity*, Studies in Antiquity and Christianity, Minneapolis, MN: Fortress Press.

Perkins, P. (1980) *The Gnostic Dialogue: The Early Church and the Crisis of Gnosticism*, New York: Paulist Press.

Robinson, J.M. (ed.) (1988) *The Nag Hammadi Library in English*, revised edn, San Francisco, CA: Harper & Row.

Rudolph, K. (1983) *Gnosis: The Nature and History of Gnosticism*, trans. R. McL. Wilson, San Francisco, CA: Harper & Row.

Sebba, G. (1981) 'History, modernity and gnosticism', in P.J. Optiz and G. Sebba (eds) *Philosophy of Order: Essays on History Consciousness, and Politics*, Stuttgart: Klett-Cotta.

Stroumsa, G.G. (1992) *Savoir et salut*, Paris: Les Editions du Cerf.

Voegelin, E. (1957) *The New Science of Politics*, Chicago, IL: Chicago University Press.

Williams, M.A. (forthcoming) *Rethinking Gnosticism*, Princeton, NJ: Princeton University Press.

Michael A. Williams

GOVERNMENT

The modern noun 'government' derives from the Latin verb *gubernare*, to steer (originally a boat), and hence, by extension, to direct public affairs. Like many political concepts 'government' has a variety of meanings within this broad definition. In the Romance languages of Western Europe, government (*gouvernement*, *governo*, *gobierno*) is the set of persons currently directing public affairs, and contrasts with the STATE, the permanent directive apparatus. In British usage the distinction is less clearcut, owing to a less developed notion of the state, which is complicated by a wide conception of the powers of the Crown as overlapping public and private spheres. In the USA 'government' generally refers to the permanent state apparatus while the term 'administration' is preferred for the persons currently in charge.

The phrase 'forms of government' unambiguously refers to the permanent arrangements for deciding on public policy. The first systematic classification of these, made by Aristotle in the fourth century BC, has exercised a continuing influence on political discussion since it was first proposed. For Aristotle, the important distinction related to how many participated in making public decisions: Many? (DEMOCRACY) Few? (oligarchy) One? (tyranny). This was important not only for the degree of legitimacy and AUTHORITY thereby given to state policy but also, more importantly, for its quality. In the most influential Greek thinking, democracy was associated with arbitrary and inconsistent policy-making by a popular assembly; oligarchy with selfishness and class rule; and rule by a single person with tyranny. The solution was to ensure exclusive rule by the best (Plato's Philosopher King(s)), whose quality would be ensured by EDUCATION.

The medieval theologians who took over political thought from the Greeks tended to argue that the established order of authority, under the guidance of the church, was the best way of ensuring good government. They generally recognized, however, a right of resistance when a king or prince acted tyrannically. Such questioning of the powers that be was frowned upon by later theologians and theorists in reaction to the breakdown of public authority stemming from the Renaissance and Reformation (Luther, Hobbes). However, medieval concepts of limited government were increasingly reasserted during the Enlightenment (Locke, Madison). The separation of powers enshrined in the American Constitution is the most extreme mechanism for ensuring limited government, by dividing governmental authority between Congress (the many), Supreme Court (the few) and the President (the one) – and hopefully drawing on the best points of all three forms of government. Limited government also implies church–state separation – religion is one of the many areas of social life from which modern secular democracy tends to withdraw, in order to maintain overall consensus in a diversified modern world.

Modern thinking (including theological thinking) has generally endorsed democracy as the best form of government, putting its faith in the vast pool of energy and talent potentially available in modern populations, in the efficiency of a 'free market-place of ideas' (J.S. Mill) in generating the best public decisions, and in the general desirability of free discussion and free action. Modern 'representative' democracy, however, is vastly different from the assembly of all citizens of the Greeks, which decided immediately on legislation and executive action (direct democracy). In representative democracy popular participation is limited to regular elections, where the choice is essentially which political party or parties will form a government for the time being. Between elections, governments either serve for a fixed term or depend on parliamentary votes of confidence, which are conducted on partisan lines. Popular participation outside the political parties is limited to attempts to influence government thinking through media comment or interest group activity (also by the churches).

Modern support for representative democracy as the best form of government is largely based on what are perceived as the only alternatives – military rule or TOTALITARIANISM. A government dominated by or under the direct influence of the military is the norm in the developing world today. There is no evidence that it is more efficient than democracy and it often involves brutal suppression of HUMAN RIGHTS. Totalitarian forms of government (the Nazis in Germany and Stalinists in Russia) aim at total control of SOCIETY by systematic repression and terror, in the name of some single-party doctrine that absolutely guarantees the best public decisions. The defeat of Nazism in the Second World War and the internal breakdown of European Communist regimes in the late 1980s has left representative democracy without effective challenge from alternative forms of government. Its espousal of pluralism secures the support of the churches among other groups, as modern democracy does not generally seek to impose its own version of basic truths on society.

Democratic governments fall into two major categories – Presidential and Parliamentary. The major prototype of a Presidential system is the American, referred to above. Presidential systems of the American type rest on the principle of the separation of powers, with the President as head of the Executive charged with carrying through legislation passed by Congress and subject to the scrutiny of a Supreme Court which can declare both his actions and Congressional legislation unconstitutional. Presidential systems of this type are often associated with federal arrangements whereby regional governments (states) have their own sphere of action independent of the federal authorities. However, the strict independence of the various political authorities and governments can be more apparent than real, owing to

1 the increasing need for prompt action in the modern world, particularly in response to international emergencies, which tends to increase the importance of the Executive relative to the other branches;
2 the superior ability of the President to mobilize public opinion through the media;
3 the unifying bonds of party, which enable the President to gain support in Congress for the measures he proposes. Recent research has shown that the President's election priorities dominate government expenditure in the USA, with Congress appearing to have only limited initiation power.

Latin American countries, when not run by the military, generally have Presidential forms of government on the American model. Another form of Presidential government without separation of powers appears in Finland, Russia and France, where an independently elected President appoints a government which has to be approved by Parliament. This system seems likely to be adopted in the emerging democracies of Eastern Europe.

However, the major alternative to Presidential government on the American model is Parliamentary or Cabinet government, where the leaders of party(ies) with a majority in Parliament form a collective government, supported by legislative votes of confidence. In this system legislative and executive power is effectively fused under the control of the government, as party loyalty means that its measures will automatically be supported by members of the majority party(ies), at least until the government terminates.

Turning to the actual functioning of

Parliamentary governments, the phrase 'types of government' refers to the second meaning of 'government' referred to above as the persons *currently* in charge of public policy-making. The phrase is commonly used to distinguish between different sorts of Parliamentary government, primarily in terms of their party composition. This underlines the importance of the modern political party to the formation and functioning of governments and to the whole working of modern democracy.

The major types of Parliamentary governments so distinguished are single-party majority governments, single-party minority governments and coalitions – governments composed of two or more parties. Coalitions can further be broken down into surplus majority coalitions (with more parties than are absolutely needed for a Parliamentary majority), minimal winning (with only enough parties for a majority) and minority (without a majority). From 35 to 40 per cent of postwar coalition governments in Western Europe have been minimal winning; the rest have been evenly divided between minority and surplus majority. A pivotal party in most of these coalitions is the Christian Democratic Party, which because of its mixture of Catholic social doctrine with opposition to SO-CIALISM generally takes up a centre position between left and right. Distinctions between different types of coalition are important because they have consequences for the stability, effectiveness and accountability of Parliamentary governments. It is commonly argued, particularly by Anglo-American political scientists and politicians, that coalition governments are weak and internally divided, unable to agree on public policy and hence short-lived. Minority governments are likewise condemned to continual compromises to get external support in the legislature. Adverse votes of confidence are likely to cause several changes of government between elections. Single-party governments with a Parliamentary majority are almost by definition more stable and more united on policy, and more effective in carrying it through. An additional advantage of this system (often termed the 'Westminster model' after the seat of the British Parliament) is that electors can see clearly which party is responsible and accountable for policy and thus they can make a clear choice between them on policy grounds at a General Election.

Such a choice implies a two-party system in which one party gets clear endorsement by a majority of electors. In fact it is very rare to have a true two-party system under Parliamentary government (two and a half party systems are the norm). Hence Parliamentary majorities tend to be manufactured out of popular minorities by the arrangements for aggregating electoral votes into Parliamentary seats: in Britain, for example, the two largest parties get practically all Parliamentary seats even though they get less than three-quarters of the vote. Single-party majority government can thus be criticized for ensuring effective implementation of minority views. In contrast, coalition and minority governments' compromises may reflect more adequately the views of a popular majority.

Effectiveness and representativeness are thus two desiderata of democratic government which may conflict. Different types of Parliamentary government favour one above the other. There is no doubt that strict electoral accountability gets blurred under coalition arrangements. It is a mistake, however, to think that all coalitions function in the same way. Accountability and stability both vary markedly with the number of parties in government. Two-party coalitions, normal in The Netherlands, Germany and Austria, function very like single-party majority governments, and the coalition partners often campaign together in elections on their governmental record, just like a majority party. (The same may be said of minority single-party governments: the larger the party in control, the more able it is to effect policy like a majority government.)

The greater the number of parties in government (as in Belgium, Italy and Finland) the harder it is to agree and implement public policy, thus blurring accountability and leading to frequent governmental crises and breakdown. The question of when Parliamentary governments actually end is debatable. Some scholars consider that a new government forms when any of the following occur:

1 a change in party composition of the government;

2 a change of Prime Minister;

3 an election;

4 formal resignation of the government.

Others think that only a change of party composition changes a government in essential respects – another testimonial to the central role of political parties in modern government.

Indeed, the institutional differences between Presidential and Parliamentary governments are probably less consequential than differences between single- and two-party control of government on the one hand and multi-party coalitions on the other. The former offers electors reasonably stable, effective and accountable governments; the latter more internally divided and unstable governments, though through necessity they may on occasions reach a broad national consensus.

Whatever type of government emerges from electoral and party competition, however, there is no doubt that parties will be its essential building blocks. Modern democratic government is essentially party government. In almost all democracies parties are sufficiently internally united for major negotiations about government formation and composition, the distribution of ministries and policy, to be conducted between their leaders, who can be sure of supporters' compliance. As parties do try to promote the priorities laid out in their electoral programme, this fact gives electors some role in determining which set of party priorities the next government will carry through. Parties, moreover, are always eager to find popular issues, consistent with their own ideological position, which will attract votes at the next election. Hence public opinion is guaranteed some continuing influence on public policy through party competition. To the extent that democratic governments respond to popular wishes, therefore, it is through party mechanisms. Inevitably parties offer crude and sometimes unpalatable and limited choices between priorities for aggregating individual preferences and consciences into collective policies.

The classical doctrine of the party mandate sees parties as offering competing policy priorities to electors, with the one(s) that attract(s) most votes forming a government to translate these priorities into public policy. Recent research shows that this idea is still broadly relevant but has to be modified in the light of coalition and minority governments and the failure of single-party governments to obtain popular majorities. Besides a mandate gained through election, parties may have a diffuse influence on the political agenda to which governments respond – whether or not they form part of the current administration. This broader influence is important in promoting a more general responsiveness of governments to societal wishes and needs, which is very important in generating a popular consensus at a time when the state increasingly penetrates and regulates almost all areas of civil society.

Aquinas, Thomas (1959) *Political Writings*, ed. A.P. D'Entrèves, Oxford: Blackwell.

Aristotle (1958) *The Politics*, trans. Ernest Barker, London: Oxford University Press.

Budge, Ian and Hofferbert, Richard (1990) 'Mandates and policy outputs: US party platforms and federal expenditures', *American Political Science Review* 84: 111–31.

Budge, Ian and Keman, Hans (1990) *Parties and Democracy: Coalitions and Government Functioning in Twenty Countries*, Oxford: Oxford University Press.

Fredrich, C.J. and Brzezinski, Z.K. (1956) *Totalitarian Dictatorship and Autocracy*, Cambridge, MA: Harvard University Press.

Hamilton, Alexander, Jay, John and Madison, James (1911) *The Federalist Papers*, London: Dent.

Hobbes, Thomas (n.d.) *The Leviathan: Or the Matter Form and Power of the Commonwealth*, ed. M. Oakeshott, Oxford: Blackwell.

Locke, John (1947) *Second Treatise on Civil Government*, ed. E. Barker, London: Oxford University Press.

Luther, Martin (1915–32) *Works*, Philadelphia, PA: Holman.

Mill, J.S. (1910) *On Liberty* and *Representative Government*, London: Dent.

Plato (1955) *The Republic*, trans. H.D.P. Lee, London: Penguin.

Ian Budge

GRACE

The idea of divine grace has been central to Christian theology from the earliest days. Grace is God's giving of himself in love to his creation. It is thus in its most fundamental sense God's relationship to his creatures.

Grace is the self-giving of the creator, redeemer and liberator. The person of Jesus is seen by Christians as the fullest embodiment of this gift to the human race, which is why so many of the Pauline epistles end by commending their readers to 'the grace of our Lord Jesus Christ'. God's continued presence with his people is a transfiguring and transforming power, symbolized and realized by the Holy Spirit dwelling among them.

If grace is a matter of relationships it is essentially social rather than individual in its primary reference. For the Hebrews, Yahweh was seen as leading, guiding and inspiring the people of Israel. It was in the history and destiny of that people that Yahweh's grace was manifested. It was the survival of a nation that was the principal hope of Israel rather than the survival or salvation of the individual soul. God's intimate relationship with individuals, Abraham and the patriarchs, Moses, David, Jeremiah and the prophets, was always in the context of their social and political role as leaders of their people.

Grace is gratuitous. It goes beyond what is strictly required or useful, it represents an overflowing generosity. God's creation of a universe was not necessary, but is ascribed to God's abounding LOVE. In the Hebrew scriptures and above all in the sending of God's Son into the world as redeemer, God always takes the initiative, coming out to meet a fallen humanity, as the father in the story of the Prodigal Son went out to greet him on his return in penitence to the family home. Christians have insisted that salvation is to be ascribed wholly to the grace of God. Yet, believing that men and women are endowed with freedom – God has created not puppets but persons who make decisions – they must respond to God's love. Up to this point there would be general agreement among theologians of different traditions.

It is in facing the question why some respond and others apparently turn away from God's gracious offer of salvation that differences are manifested. In a classic controversy of the fifth century, Saint Augustine, the north African bishop, maintained that this positive human response can occur only when God's grace has gone ahead and liberated the human will from its bondage to SIN; this is known as 'prevenient grace' (grace which goes before). He was opposing the teachings of the British monk Pelagius, who – while accepting that salvation was by God's grace – insisted on the freedom of the individual to respond or not to God's offer. Since that time most theologians have tried to avoid the unfortunate consequences of the extreme positions, allowing both for the primacy of grace and the reality of human freedom. In its attempt to do this, much medieval theology might not unfairly be described as 'semi-Pelagian'.

Grace was frequently opposed to, or contrasted with, nature. Medieval theologians developed Stoic ideas of a natural order, which is indeed 'fallen' but with respect to which human reason, unassisted by divine (or supernatural) grace, is able to reach certain true conclusions about the existence and attributes of God and about right human conduct – by reference to a so-called NATURAL LAW. Unassisted reason, however, has definite limits and supernatural aid is necessary both to perceive the TRUTH and to do it. Grace, they held, does not destroy nature but perfects it. Grace came to be seen less as a dynamic relationship between God and God's people, however, than as a gift infused or imparted to the faithful, particularly in the sacraments, and nurtured by acts of piety and good works. Theologians distinguished between uncreated grace – the presence of God in the world – and created grace, which inspires holy actions (actual grace) or constitutes a disposition towards holiness on the part of the believer (habitual grace).

Reformation theologians, while not rejecting the distinction between nature and grace, saw in this notion of 'habitual grace' (a grace which is 'possessed' by believers) the danger of thinking that they are saved by something which is their own. Luther, in contrast to what he saw as JUSTIFICATION by good works, proclaimed justification as *sola gratia* (by grace alone) received by faith, which itself was seen as a gift (Ephesians 2: 8). Some reformers went so far as to proclaim a doctrine of 'irresistible grace', where free will played no part and humans were predestined before birth to salvation or damnation. A group of Dutch Protestant theologians, inspired by Jakob Hermandszoon (Arminius), rejected this extreme Calvinist position and reasserted the importance of free will but were condemned at the Synod of Dort (1618–19). Early Anglican reformers adopted a generally Calvinist position, but later Caroline divines moved towards Arminianism, or in the case of Jeremy Taylor even farther along the path towards Pelagianism.

Later pietistic movements developed medieval and reformation tendencies to privatize the idea of grace. It became an attribute of the individual believer, distinguishing the faithful from a wicked world and preparing them for paradise after death. Pietism also affected Catholic theology and practice. Baptism was viewed as a spiritual operation in which original sin was (at least partially) removed and the individual was translated into a state of grace. The EUCHARIST was the medicine of immortality and a tonic administered to the believer enabling him or her to survive in a hostile and oppressive world, eventually reaching the promised land. The all-sufficiency of divine grace was reflected in John Newton's celebrated hymn 'Amazing grace'. Evangelical revivals of the late eighteenth century in Britain and North America, whether Calvinist or Arminian, laid considerable emphasis on salvation by grace. CHARISMATIC MOVEMENTS, at various periods of history, have stressed the gifts of the Spirit as principal effects of divine grace in the life of believers. Particularly stressed has been the gift or grace of speaking in tongues (glossolalia); the apostle Paul, however, played down the importance of this gift (1 Corinthians 14).

Eighteenth- and nineteenth-century liberal theologians tended to emphasize, partly under the influence of neo-Platonism and later of Kant, the moral aspects of Christian life and the importance of FREE WILL and hard work. They laid correspondingly less emphasis on divine grace. A curious alliance was occasionally formed, however, between mechanistic (and later psychological) forms of philosophical determinism and divine grace. Both rejected the notion of 'free will'. Humans are formed not by the free decisions of an autonomous will but by a whole set of physical, social and psychological factors. Some Christian thinkers used this position as a basis for reasserting the supremacy of grace.

In reaction to liberal and humanist theologies, which often thought of grace in terms of progress and the education of the human race, neo-orthodox Protestants of the post-First World War era reasserted Reformation doctrines of divine 'sovereignty' and free grace. Karl Barth denounced the multiple classifications of grace in Roman Catholic theology as tending to undermine the idea of grace as simply the unmerited act of a divine sovereign. Dietrich Bonhoeffer, however, warned against a Lutheran tendency to take grace for granted and to avoid taking seriously the costliness of grace and the response of discipleship.

Eastern orthodox theologians have generally rejected the dichotomy between nature and grace which led to the conflict between Augustine and Pelagius. Nature is infused by grace. By this grace humans may share the life of God and become 'partakers of the divine nature'. This does not imply, however, a change in the essential characteristic of humanity as created being, but must be seen in the context of the Orthodox idea of divine energies – God's operations and manifestations. Humans may thus share by grace in the divine energies but not in the ineffable essence of God.

Grace must be viewed as a relationship. It is the concept that best sums up God's relationship with a fallen world, not simply with fallen individuals within it (see THE FALL). God is creator and redeemer of all things and grace is the divine mode of operation. Grace is a dynamic relationship whereby God communicates God's self to the world. This understanding of grace would reject any suggestion that grace is some kind of tonic which God offers to the world and more specifically to humans, a view reflected in the verse by J.H. Newman:

And that higher gift than grace,
should flesh and blood refine;
God's presence and his very self,
and essence all divine.

In the understanding of grace which I am here suggesting, 'God's presence and his very self' are precisely what is meant by grace.

Christians believe that men and women are made in God's image and that divine grace is able to restore that image which has been marred by SIN. God's grace is therefore a merciful, forgiving and healing presence. It is also a transfiguring and transforming presence. It is by God's grace that we are able to see beyond appearances to realities about God's self and the world in which we live. It is by the power of the Spirit that men and women are able to co-operate with God in the work of transformation, that the kingdoms of the world may become the kingdoms of our God and his Christ (Revelation 11: 15). God has enlisted us in the ministry of reconciliation (2 Corinthians 5: 18).

In this perspective the grace of baptism is seen not as an individual 'operation' to remove original sin but as the symbol of a new set of relationships into which the person is introduced. If, as Augustine maintained, sin is essentially a disordered set of relationships – of a false love of self in contempt of God and neighbour – baptism represents a new and true order which puts God at the centre and sees self and neighbour in their relationship to God. This new order is represented by the church (in its idea – in what it stands for – though sadly not in the way it often acts in history). Baptism is recruitment into God's army, to use a military analogy, in a battle against injustice and oppression in a godless world. The political and social significance of the Eucharist should also be obvious. It is seen less as a medicine of individual immortality than as a celebration in which Christ comes to his people, inspiring and strengthening them as 'workers together with him' (2 Corinthians 6: 1) in the transformation of the old order into something new. It is a feast where all bring what they have and receive what they need. These two principal sacraments remind us that the process of transformation and salvation is essentially the work of God's grace and not of our own unaided efforts, and that our job is not that of 'social reform' but a hunger and thirst for righteousness (Matthew 5: 6) which may call into question not only the status quo but also the values and assumptions of reformers. When Jesus was asked to adjudicate between two brothers on a question of property he castigated the acquisitive social order which they assumed (Luke 12: 13 f.).

A graceful life is one which avoids the arrogance of self-sufficiency, accepting the fact that humans are dependent on one another and on the grace of God. It is prepared to receive as well as to give. Such gracefulness was powerfully manifested when Jesus allowed the woman in the Gospel story to anoint his feet (Luke 7: 38) or when Peter (eventually) allowed Jesus to minister to him (John 13: 6 f.). Such gracefulness also allows for a generosity which goes beyond the limits and requirements of strict justice, and may even be in conflict with them.

By analogy we might see the politics of welfare SOCIALISM as a reflection of an Augustinian idea of grace; Thatcherite individualism is manifestly Pelagian. While in the former case there is the obvious danger that each citizen may become a merely dependent recipient of gratuitous state benefits, there is in the latter an entirely unjustified belief that each individual is (or can become) wholly self-sufficient, receiving simply what he or she deserves. The welfare state ideology, as it evolved from the 1880s in Germany and in Britain, is closely related to a liberal Protestant idea of the 'brotherhood of man' and the fatherhood of a benevolent, but somewhat indulgent, God. Combined with a bureaucratic humanism, embodied in Fabian socialism, this IDEOLOGY regarded people, particularly the poor and disadvantaged, as mere passive victims of social forces and compliant recipients of social benefits. Personal freedom of choice was regarded with suspicion by those administering the STATE, who knew much better than the recipients what was good for them.

As Augustine was reacting against the unrealistic voluntarism of Pelagius, who appeared to neglect the radical bondage of the human will to sin constituted by each person's entanglement in a whole series of EVIL institutions and relationships, the prophets of the welfare state were responding to the mid-nineteenth-century model of the self-reliant individual, who appeared in the popular writings of Samuel Smiles or in the political theory of Herbert Spencer and his followers. It is to the ideas of these men, purporting to originate with Adam Smith, that the theologians of Thatcherism looked for inspiration. It may be called political Pelagianism in its ignoring of the power of social relationships and institutions in moulding individual lives, its refusal to recognize the reality of societies other than the FAMILY, its misunderstanding of the nature of 'original sin' and its uncritical belief in 'freedom of choice'. There is little role for grace in social and political relationships conceived of in this mode.

We may, however, imagine a different relationship between God and his people on the one hand and the state and the citizen on the other. God's grace would here be seen not as opposed to or separated from nature, but as infusing the natural order. While it may be important for certain purposes to distinguish grace from nature in the realm of ideas, in terms of their actual operation they are intertwined; it may be possible to think of nature conceptually 'uncontaminated' by grace but in the real world there can be no concrete example of this. God's Spirit is present in all authentic instances of the natural. Analogically, human choice is exercised in a matrix of social relationships; as we are born (and reborn) into a specific social context, we eventually contribute to this context by the decisions we make and the actions we take. Each person, living within a structure of multiple relationships which are continually changing, for better or for worse, is able by his or her participation in this process to contribute to God's transformation of CREATION. Yet God's new order can never simply be the result of human social and political efforts. 'It is your Father's good pleasure to give you the kingdom' (Luke 12: 32). Vatican II put the complex relationship between human effort and divine grace as follows: 'Earthly progress must be carefully distinguished from the growth of Christ's kingdom. Nevertheless, to the extent that the former can contribute to the better ordering of human society, it is of vital concern to the kingdom of God' (*Gaudium et Spes* sec. 39).

Augustine of Hippo (1971) *A Select Library of the Nicene and Post-Nicene Fathers of the Christian Church*, vol. 5: *Anti-Pelagian Writings*, Eerdmans.
Barth, Karl (1960) *Church Dogmatics*, vol. 2 : 2, Edinburgh: T. & T. Clark.
Boff, Leonardo (1979) *Liberating Grace*, Orbis.
Bonhoeffer, Dietrich (1964) *The Cost of Discipleship*, London: SCM.
Calvin, Jean (1957) *Institutes of the Christian Religion*, James Clarke.
Evans, R. F. (1968) *Pelagius: Inquiries and Reappraisals*, A. & C. Black.
Haight, Roger (1979) *The Experience and Language of Grace*, Gill & Macmillan.
Rahner, Karl (1966) 'Nature and Grace' in his *Theological Investigations*, vol.4, London: Darton, Longman & Todd.
Yarnold, Edward (1974) *The Second Gift*, London: St Paul's Publications.

David Nicholls

GREEN

The colour green has become an ideological symbol, just as red is a symbol for socialism and purple is a symbol for feminism. Green is the colour of plants, the primary producers on earth; thus, green IDEOLOGY affirms the value of life on the most fundamental level, as well as human responsibility for the quality of the ENVIRONMENT. Although Greens have widely differing perceptions of green ideology, many threads hold the movement together. The German green political party, *Die Grünen*, has developed a platform based on what they call the four pillars of the Green movement. *Die Grünen* is but one of the many groups in the movement; none the less, its platform is useful for introducing the general concerns of green ideology.

The first pillar is deep ecology. Ecology is the pattern of relations between organisms and their environment. Greens are concerned with maintaining healthy relationships between humans and the environment, whether the environment consists of other humans, artificial environment or nature. Almost without exception, green ideologies are based on a metaphor of ecological interdependence. At one level or another, Greens understand that all political, economic and social actions have reactions in the human and natural environment (*see* ECOLOGICAL THEOLOGY.

Some groups, however, like *Die Grünen* hold to the tenets of what they call 'deep ecology' and contrast their position to one they call 'shallow ecology'. By deep ecology they mean a holistic and egalitarian vision of all entities and processes in the biosphere; by shallow ecology, a concern primarily for the well-being of humanity within the environment. In their view, shallow ecology attempts to cure the symptoms, whereas deep ecology attempts to address the systemic roots of problems. For example, deep ecology emphasizes care not only for the earth, but of all life. It seeks to expand the idea of self to include the rest of nature. This biocentric approach is by no means shared by all Greens.

The second pillar is social responsibility. Green ideas about social responsibility emerge from the metaphor of ecology. Because the environment is composed of interdependent parts, the whole as well as each part has worth and dignity; therefore, diversity within a well-functioning system should be celebrated and encouraged. Thus, Greens tend to promote minority and women's rights and interracial harmony. Because each component in the ecological web is important, individuals are responsible for the quality of the relationships they have with other individuals, their SOCIETY and the world as a whole. Because the successful functioning of the community and the ecosystem are important, individual actions are deemed good or bad depending on how well they contribute to the common good. This view of social responsibility is both conservative and radical. In order to preserve the integrity of the total eco-social system and the welfare of its members, it is necessary to challenge many modern social values and institutions, e.g. competitive individualism and unlimited, quantitative technological and economic growth. However, since the diversity of green concerns and the methods for addressing these concerns are many, conflicts often arise among groups within the movement.

The third pillar is grass roots DEMOCRACY. Most green organizations are ultra-democratic, rotating leadership positions among their members more frequently than is usual among other organizations. The ecological metaphor compels green groups to value the views and abilities of each member of their organizations, as each component is an important part of the system. Moreover, Greens generally favour decentralization of POWER; politically, by giving more power to small political units such as the province, county or town; economically, by various forms of worker ownership and co-management. Greens argue that in representative systems, where power is centralized, the needs of the grass roots are often pushed aside by policy-makers in upper political echelons. Furthermore, if a neighbourhood or group is responsible for its own decisions, it will have to live with them; it is unlikely to support an industry in its own backyard that will pollute its air and exploit its people. The anarchic tendencies of the Green movement have, in some cases, inhibited its political effectiveness.

The fourth pillar is non-violence. Greens argue that VIOLENCE is symptomatic of a world that does not recognize interdependences among individuals, groups and the cosmos. Therefore, green ideology tends to resist coercive exploitation of humans or nature, RACISM or WAR, through strikes, boycotts, conscientious objection, non-acceptance of state honours and civil disobedience. There are notable exceptions: a few radical Green movements have been violent in their actions, as addressed below.

Finally, the Green movement has a focus on the future. Greens prefer to see the pillars of the movement and the goals of their organizations as means and not ends, processes and not accomplishments. Greens are post-humanist in their emphasis on the biosphere, post-patriarchal in their struggle for horizontal power structures, and post-modern in their desire for non-violent change. Ernest Callenboch captures some of these elements in his futurist novel, *Ecotopia*.

The Green movement is the most recent embodiment of a long-standing movement of moral protest aimed at transforming modern mass industrial society with its associated hierarchical social organization, loss of community and personal responsibility, and ALIENATION of people from the land. Its roots lie in various nineteenth-century anarchist, populist and utopian back-to-the-land movements in Europe and the USA. This historical stream gained new life with the emergence of attitudes of fear, suspicion, anger and betrayal toward the agencies responsible for the massive post-Second World War environmental devastation. Greens felt they could no longer depend on the established political or economic structures to behave ethically. According to the Greens, the dominant powers threaten the natural environment, cause much human suffering and are leaving a poor legacy of resources for future generations. Greens argue that the alternative to dependence on an unethical establishment is an alternative establishment – one that is supported by the four pillars of the Green movement.

The first green political party was the New Zealand Values Party founded in the 1960s. The Values Party had no success in gaining seats in Parliament until 1975. Despite its demise some years later, the Values Party set a precedent worldwide that activists could become political and activate change from within the present system. Australian Greens got an early political start with the United Tasmania Group, particularly with Bob Brown's leadership in conservation work. The British Ecology Party was founded in 1973; in 1985 it changed its name to the Green Party. The first North American green party was founded in British Columbia, Canada, in 1983. Today many of the Canadian provinces have influential green parties, although as of yet there has been no action on the national front. Also, in the USA there are many local green parties, but none in the federal system, despite attempts. Green parties are active in Italy, Switzerland, Belgium, Austria, Finland, Luxembourg, Sweden, The Netherlands, Spain, Portugal and France; and green parties have members in seven European Parliaments. In fact, Austria and Finland each have two green parties: one on the Right and one on the Left.

The most successful green party is *Die Grünen* in Germany. During the 1970s some West Germans became environmentally aware, in part, through E.F. Schumacher's *Small is Beautiful* (1973) and the Club of Rome's *Limits to Growth* (1974). Small interest groups formed and banded together under umbrella organizations. Some factions were reluctant to become political, but eventually the Green Association contacted Petra Kelly and Roland Vogt to run in the European Parliament election. They won 3.2 per cent of the vote in 1979 – short of the 5 per cent necessary for representation. In 1980, *Die Grünen* won 1.5 per cent in the West German Bundestag and representation on many town councils. In 1983 they became a voice in the Bundestag with 5.6 per cent of the vote. In spite of its successes, *Die Grünen* is characterized by inner tensions. There are complaints that, despite the ecological foundation of the

party, many of the members are individualistic and sexist. Also, there is a growing rift between the Marxist and spiritual elements within the party. Furthermore, they have little sympathy for different green systems in other countries, such as the less assertive British movement.

In addition to the overt political actions of green parties around the world, green interest groups are also making political inroads to change. Organizations committed to environmental protection, such as the Sierra Club or the Garden City movement, have been active since the last century; however, it was not until the 1960s that these groups flourished to their present extent. They range in their ideologies from groups like the Royal Society for the Protection of Birds (who were reluctant to become politically active in the acid rain issue, despite their own reports that acid rain was depleting bird populations) to groups like Earth First! who consciously break laws in order to protect the environment. Green activists also protest as individuals. For example, Margaret Morgan lobbied to protect a meadow in her South Wales village of Gowerton. Her protest ended successfully, but only after a thirty-three day hunger strike.

The number of organizations, networks and journals that could be considered green goes beyond counting. Although they should not be equated with the environmental movement as a whole, Greens and green values play an increasingly significant role in environmentalism.

There are two major schisms within the movement, between (a) the Light and Dark Greens and (b) those who contest the spiritual origins of the movement.

Light Greens, while fitting well within the Green movement, tend toward what is characterized above as a shallow ecology approach to problems. They focus on single issues, such as protesting nuclear arms or preservation of particular forests or lakes, rather than on a whole system approach. They care for the environment, but also see value in the political and economic systems that are at present in place. They work to reform the establishment through many small moves, rather than trying to lead a revolution. An example of a light green organization is the Body Shop, a company which sells skin care products made from natural sources that have not been tested on animals. These products are sold in reusable containers. The company works successfully within the capitalist system and donates money to environmentally concerned organizations. The Body Shop is an example of the lightest shade of green. Slightly darker green organizations are exemplified by the World Wildlife Fund, the Pesticides Action Network and the Campaign Against the Arms Trade. In Germany the Light Greens are called realists, while the Dark Greens are called fundamentalists.

Dark Greens see themselves as radicals and visionaries in solidarity with the earth against the status quo. Dark Greens reject compromise, stating that anything less than fundamental opposition will threaten the integrity of the green project. Dark Greens go beyond preservation and conservation; they aim to restore the ecology of the earth to how it was before the Industrial Revolution. The Darkest Greens do not spend time lobbying politicians; rather, they engage in direct action. For example, Australian John Seed was one of the first Greens actually to sit in the trees destined to be cut by timber companies. His group was also the first to chain themselves to logging equipment to stop its progress. Some dark green groups rely on guerrilla theatre; Earth First! draped a great plastic mural of a crack over a hydroelectric dam during the dam's opening ceremony. Others sometimes use violence to achieve their ends; Direct Action blew up a $4.5 million Hydro Substation on Vancouver Island, in British Columbia, Canada. During the late 1970s, in the Basque region of Spain where anti-nuclear and Basque separatist movements were linked, 'ecoteurs' blew up a nuclear power station under construction at Bilbao. The explosions resulted in some deaths. Dark Greens use the warrior image: they see themselves as champions for Mother Earth, and stress the importance of individual freedom and dissent over government control.

Although the division between Light and Dark Greens has split the Green movement in Germany, it has had some unexpected advantages in Britain, Canada and the USA. Dark Green radicals make the demands of Lighter Greens sound more reasonable. For example, in the fight for the California Desert Protection Act, the Sierra Club was actually able to improve its original compromise position for acreage because of Earth First!'s extreme demands on the establishment. Furthermore, Dark Greens bring media attention to issues that might be overlooked, although the coverage is not all positive.

The second major division in the Green movement is between those who feel that the origins of the movement lie in spirituality and those that oppose this philosophy. Many Greens agree that the ecological metaphor describes a deep TRUTH of connectedness, or oneness, with all things, and that this truth is the foundation for the Green movement. Understanding this connectedness is a form of grace and leads to a belief in the intrinsic value of all living and non-living things as a part of a common existence; thus, JUSTICE for nature and society becomes imperative. Deep ecologists like Charlene Spretnak, author of *The Spiritual Dimension of Green Politics* (1986), often refer to Taoism, Buddhism, pantheism, and pre-Judaeo-Christian Goddess worship for examples of religions which celebrate this connectedness. Spiritual Greens argue that the movement must address humanity's deepest sensibilities before it can effect change, and that these deep sensibilities are spiritual.

The main fear of those that oppose the spiritual Greens is that spirituality will affect the movement's credibility and political effectiveness. This fear is of particular importance in the Green movement's most active political seat: Germany. During the Second World War Hitler used biological symbolism and the Teutonic myths to establish a feeling of national superiority. Germany is still suspicious of any pagan-like religion, and thus green spirituality is not encouraged within the German Green movement. Finally, the Marxist Greens, such as Murray Bookchin, argue that the heavy biocentrism in green spirituality directs attention from the most important cause of ecological destruction: unjust social and economic structures.

Although the division between Light and Dark Greens and the controversy over green spirituality are two of the main sources of infighting in the movement, there are many more. Charges of sexism, racism and egoism cause a tremendous amount of strife. Greens seem to have developed an attractive, if utopian, ideology, but have not yet developed the political wisdom and the ability to implement it.

Green politics act as a critique of traditional political structure in the West. In particular, the green slogan of 'Neither right nor left, but in front!' challenges the limitations of dichotomous political thinking. Both the political Right and Left are represented in the Green movement, but they are integrated in a holistic model that enables them to work together to achieve new goals in new ways. Green post-patriarchal political structures also set up a critique for traditional politics with radical democratic notions of horizontal and decentralized power structures.

Although the Greens have had little opportunity actually to implement political changes through the normal channels, there is one striking example of the Green movement stimulating green legislation. In 1971, a small Australian conservation group asked the labour union, Builders Labourers Federation, to join them in protecting a small forest. The union agreed and proceeded to strike until the forest was officially protected by the government. This was the first green ban. Between 1971 and 1975 forty-two green bans were imposed. Through these actions the grass roots stopped an extraordinary amount of development and increased legislative environmental action. The various green conservation groups and labour unions put political decision-making into the hands of the people and demonstrated just how interdependent the system really is.

The Green movement has also criticized national government dependence on the defence industry and the military. Greens suggest that both DISARMAMENT and weapons trade be controlled by the United Nations.

Finally, although green parties worldwide have had little support from voters and little political clout in governments, they have had effects on more popular and powerful parties. Both the German Social Democratic Party and the British Labour Party have become more interested in green issues since the early 1980s when *Die Grünen* received representative votes in the Bundestag.

Just as green politics provide a critique of traditional political structures, so green economics provide a critique of traditional economics in the West. Most Greens look to E.F. Schumacher for an economic model. Schumacher wrote that there was an ethically correct economics that would meet everyone's needs and exploit none. This economics would reject breakneck urbanization, heavy capital investments, mass production, centralized development planning and advanced technology. It also rejects consumerism and the push for quantitative over qualitative economic growth. Schumacher encouraged labour-intensive and decentralized economics. He stated that traditional thinking is based on the false assumptions that people are misanthropic and that the environment can provide limitless resources. These assumptions must be changed if economics are to be ethical.

The Green movement has moved beyond its original attitudes of fear, suspicion, anger and betrayal towards the dominant powers and the status quo. The Greens have developed creative new ways for people to interact with their environment and each other. They have provided alternatives to the dominant paradigm. Two questions remain. First, the methods of the Green movement are diverse and there is much infighting among factions in the movement. Is it possible for such a diffuse movement to achieve its goals? Or is a diffuse movement exactly what will be most effective in transforming society? Second, what is the role for green politics beyond the 5–10 per cent protest vote? These are issues that Greens will have to address if they are to make good on their claim to be in the front lines of the movement to a just and sustainable world.

Bahro, R. (1986) *Building the Green Movement*, Philadelphia, PA: New Society.

Hutton, D. (ed.) (1987) *Green Politics in Australia*, Australia: Angus & Robertson.

Manes, C. (1990) *Green Rage: Radical Environmentalism and the Unmaking of Civilization*, Boston, MA: Little Brown.

Porritt, J. and Winner, D. (1988) *The Coming of the Greens*, London: Fontana/Collins.

Schumacher, E.F. (1973) *Small is Beautiful: Economics as if People Mattered*, New York: Harper & Row.

Spretnak, C. (1986) *The Spiritual Dimension of Green Politics*, Santa Fe, NM: Bear.

Spretnak, C. and Capra, F. (1986) *Green Politics*, Santa Fe, NM: Bear.

J. Ronald Engel
R.J.S. Montagnes

GUILT

Dictionary definitions of guilt refer to both the fact of having committed a wrongful deed and the feeling that results from the awareness of having committed such a deed. The two meanings are interlinked and are not always clearly distinguished even in serious discussion about guilt among academics. This, it might be thought, is only to be expected, given the fact that one – the feeling – follows more or less naturally from the other. In practice, however, we often find at least the *apparent* existence of one without the other. Much of this can be explained through an examination of the concepts of legal guilt and neurotic guilt.

Legal guilt arises when a LAW is broken and does not necessarily coincide with moral guilt, because sometimes the breaking of laws is effected through morally right action. In some countries, during certain periods of history, for example, people have been guilty of helping members of minority groups to escape persecution within the law. Clearly it would be absurd to attribute moral guilt in such cases merely because an immoral law has been broken.

Whilst the concept of legal guilt is concerned chiefly with the fact of having broken a law, the concept of neurotic guilt takes us into the sphere of feelings. Feeling guilty would seem to be a normal consequence of wrongdoing, but serious problems can arise when such feelings are not the result of wrongdoing or when, a wrongful deed having been committed, their intensity is out of all proportion to the gravity of the fault. Many people suffer greatly in this way through the tyranny of the superego, that AUTHORITY figure within us which results from the internalized commands and taboos of parents and other authority figures. In childhood we learn that certain kinds of behaviour displease our parents and others who look after us. In order not to lose their affection, which is of enormous importance to us, we learn to conform to their wishes, even, eventually, when they are not physically present and transgressions could be effected in secret. Various rules and conventions are absorbed in this way, and a kind of judge is formed within us. This is the superego. It is the voice of authority and convention within us which can make us suffer, in some cases quite terribly, if we transgress its rules, even if nobody else is aware of what we have done.

The development of such a mechanism is useful in childhood as an aid to basic training. Thus we learn not to throw vases at the cat, not to wipe food from our hands on to our clothes and not to use the bed as a toilet. Sometimes, however, for a variety of reasons, feelings of rejection experienced during this process and the fear of such rejection can be very great indeed. Moreover, the effects of such conditioning can persist far beyond childhood and into old age. Unfortunately, Christianity is often presented in such a way as to increase the effects of this process. Although mention is usually made of divine mercy and forgiveness by Christian teachers and preachers, God, it seems, is often presented as a vengeful judge ready to pounce on any poor unfortunate who happens to step out of line. Fear of PUNISHMENT by this apparently not so loving Father thus becomes a controlling factor, a tool for bringing about conformity. Such was the case, it would seem, much more in past years than today, but the effects linger on in many of those who were the recipients of that kind of teaching. Some would regard themselves as unlovable, even in God's eyes. Sometimes quite amazing manifestations of neurotic guilt are encountered. A person may be convinced, for instance, that he or she alone was responsible for the outbreak of a major WAR through the commission of some minor fault about which none of the people involved in the war could possibly have known anything. In other cases, there may be quite serious complications such as, for instance, the projection of one's supposed guilt on to other people, who may then become objects of hatred.

In many cases, it is not easy to distinguish neurotic guilt from normal guilt. Traces of both, moreover, may be found in the same person at the same time. In this regard, John W. Glaser referred some years ago to the interesting phenomenon of apparently frequent transitions by some people between SIN and repentance. He cites the example of people who have what seems to them to be a habit of serious sin. In frequently confessing and receiving absolution these people experience a genuine transition from what is in reality slight sin to a state of repentance. At the same time they experience a release from the sense of guilt that results from the severity of the superego. Glaser apparently had Roman Catholics in mind in this particular case, but the principles involved can obviously be extended beyond the boundaries of any Christian group or indeed Christianity. Thus we can explain at least some cases involving apparently frequent – but unreal – movements in and out of serious states of sin.

The fact of having done wrong is, of course, an important matter. So too is one's awareness of that fact. No doubt too, a genuine and not exaggerated feeling of remorse that springs from such awareness can be helpful to the process of bringing about an improvement both internally and externally in the general moral situation of the person concerned. Indeed, many of us might be inclined to view with some alarm the absence of remorse in one who is aware of having done something dreadful. On its own, however, guilt, both as a fact and as a feeling, could well be described as little more than a morbid, negative, destructive thing. It is in this regard that a genuine preaching of the Gospel comes into conflict with that parody of Christianity which is limited to little more than threats of fire and damnation for those who stray from the straight and narrow path. Only LOVE can properly deal with guilt, and properly dealt with it must be. Forgiveness, mercy, repentance and conversion are all positive aspects or fruits of love, but guilt, real or imaginary, if left, so to speak, to its own devices, can drag the guilty person only more deeply into the depths of hatred and despair.

Having said all this, we need also to acknowledge the problems that arise from *not* admitting guilt to God, other people or oneself. This would seem to be a common enough phenomenon, but perhaps it is worth pointing out that there is a very real danger of its occurring in those of us whose claim to sanctity stems largely from our having achieved the dubious status of being 'respectable people', such 'respectability' depending largely upon our uncritical conformity to the conventions of a privileged group and our apparent inability or unwillingness to understand those – many of whom are not members of the privileged group – who cannot or will not so conform. It is also a very real danger for those of us in the so-called First World countries who live off the fat of our own and other people's lands without acknowledging any responsibility for the appalling states of POVERTY and starvation that exist in underdeveloped countries. This brings us to the thorny subject of collective guilt. We may, for instance, feel compassionate towards the poor and the starving and we may rant and rave against big companies and the governments of rich nations, including our own, because, in our opinion, they are not doing much to help. However, if we are content to live, to some extent at least, off the fruits of exploitation and immoral sales of arms, and are not prepared even to consider a drop in the standard of living of at least the most comfortable among us, we are surely deluding ourselves in trying to pin the guilt only on governments and the managers of multinational companies. After all, most democratic governments fear that they will lose the next election unless their economic policies are clearly seen to benefit the electorate, or at least a very large percentage of the electorate.

When dealing with the subject of collective guilt, however, we should use the same caution that is required when dealing with the individual variety. Take, for instance, the all too common tendency to attribute guilt to succeeding generations of an entire nation for a fault committed against one or more other nations a long time ago, in spite of the fact that many, perhaps most, people in that country regret what was done. Such uncharitable behaviour on the part of the accusers clearly does not contribute wholesomely to INTERNATIONAL RELATIONS and can have a destructive effect upon those accusers themselves, who, of course, would do well to recognize their guilt in this regard and change their ways. If, on the other hand, the accused nation benefited in some material way from the original crime and, even today, people in that country are still reaping those benefits whilst other nations are still suffering as a result of it, the people who are benefiting should, of course, do what they can to put matters right. A refusal to do so in such situations might well involve real collective guilt as in the First World–Third World scenario mentioned above.

Although it is often easy for us to say that a certain person or group of persons is responsible for a certain state of affairs because it was his, her or their action that brought about that state of affairs, we cannot with certainty, even in these cases, attribute guilt in the strictly moral sense of the word. In any one case there might be diminished responsibility or even no responsibility at all. A great deal depends upon the person's knowledge, what is really intended or what motivates that person, and the degree of freedom he or she enjoys. It occasionally happens, for instance, that, for the best of intentions, people perform acts which are objectively morally wrong but which they sincerely believe to be right. Some who indulged in anti-ecumenical activity in earlier centuries might be cited as possible candidates in this regard. Something similar may be said with regard to activity which is objectively morally right, but which is performed for a bad intention. In this regard, St Thomas Aquinas provides us with the example of a man who performs the objectively morality right act of giving alms to a beggar in a particular situation, but does so only for vain glory. As for freedom, which is necessary if we are to be held responsible for our actions, an enormous number of factors could be involved in restrict-

ing it. Examples of such factors are immaturity, genetic make-up, various psychological factors, sickness, the limits of time and space, and pressures from other people and from what are sometimes referred to as sin-filled situations. Above I listed knowledge as a separate item, but some might feel that ignorance should be included here as a limiting factor where freedom is concerned. It could, of course, be claimed that nobody is ever totally free. This may be true but, even if it is, that does not suffice to eliminate all possibility of guilt. What matters, surely, is whether or not a sufficient degree of freedom exists in any particular case for truly human action to be possible.

Even where the attributing of legal guilt is concerned, freedom, or the lack of it, should be taken into account in particular cases. This is commonly done where, for instance, certain psychological factors come into play, but it is not clear that other factors which can bring about a serious lack of freedom are given as much weight as should be attributed to them in courts of law in many countries.

Fagan, Sean (1988) *Has Sin Changed? A Book on Forgiveness*, Dublin: Gill & Macmillan.

Glaser, John W. (1968) 'Transition between grace and sin: fresh perspectives', *Theological Studies* 29: 260–74.

Rahner, Karl (1963) 'Guilt and its remission: the borderland between theology and psychotherapy', in *Theological Investigations*, vol. II, London: Darton, Longman & Todd, pp. 265–81.

Vergote, Antoine (1988) *Guilt and Desire. Religious Attitudes and Their Pathological Derivatives*, New Haven, CT: Yale University Press.

Bernard Hoose

HEAVEN

Heaven is the traditional term for the location in which believers hope to spend life everlasting as promised to them in Christian teaching.

Heaven functions as a key concept in the structure of Christian doctrine and worldview. Christian teaching includes an ideal story (or myth) of the human life. That story begins with the co-creation of the human person by parents and God; its middle part consists in the leading of a virtuous life to which belong faith in God, belief in the divine revelation in and through Jesus Christ, and church membership; life's culmination comes after DEATH: perhaps after an intermediate stay in purgatory, the human person will lead an everlasting life in heaven. The idea of heaven is closely related to and based upon belief in life after death, the immortality of the human SOUL, and especially upon the doctrine of a divine judgement, held either individually immediately after someone's death or at the end of human history. In his judgement, God or Christ determines the individual's fate as either reward in heaven or PUNISHMENT in hell. What theologians term 'ESCHATOLOGY' (everything that has to do with life after death and the divine termination of human history) has been variously elaborated and enhanced by supplementary ideas and beliefs of which the eventual RESURRECTION of the human body (and the spiritualization of that body) is the most conspicuous.

Much Christian preaching, especially medieval and Catholic preaching, has been moralistic. Typically, it was framed by the threat of eternal damnation and the promise of heavenly reward. In the words of the Council of Trent (1546): 'They [the parish priests] shall feed the people with salutary words, teaching them what they must know for salvation, telling them clearly and briefly what vices they should avoid and what virtues they should acquire in order to avoid eternal punishment and gain heavenly glory.' Meditations on 'How burdens must be borne to win eternal life' (Thomas à Kempis, *The Imitation of Christ*, 1441) and on the joys of heaven have belonged to the staple of spiritual reading among both Catholics (Francis de Sales, *Introduction to the Devout Life,* 1609)

and Protestants (Richard Baxter, *The Saints' Everlasting Rest*, 1650).

Christian beliefs about heaven can be traced back to the New Testament which reflects and elaborates beliefs taught by Jesus. The gospels indicate that Jesus shared the belief, held by some of his Jewish contemporaries, in the human person's heavenly fate immediately after death (Luke 16: 19–31). Angels would transport a deceased person's soul to a place where that person would stay 'in the bosom of Abraham,' i.e. with Israel's ancestors. In this transcendent location, human persons are no longer subject to human needs and no longer involved with an earthly social network; rather, they are like angels, i.e. like spiritual beings that live close to God and for the service of God. The marriage relationship between men and women does not continue in heaven (Luke 20: 27–40). Paul casts the Jesuanic doctrine in a more traditionally Jewish framework which includes a period of sleeping in the grave, an eventual resurrection of the body, the transformation of the resurrected body into a spiritual one, and a heavenly ascension of those who are worthy to spend life everlasting with God and Christ in heaven (1 Corinthians 15; 1 Thessalonians 4: 17). In the book of Revelation, the heavenly Jerusalem descends to earth in order to establish itself as a centre for the everlasting worship organized around the divine throne occupied by God and Christ.

The New Testament idea of heaven reflects the concerns of the early Christian community that began to form around Jesus. That community, like Jesus himself, had charismatic concerns (in the sense of Max Weber). It sought to minimize involvement with 'the world' in order to dedicate itself to the LOVE of God and the presence of Christ who was experienced in ecstatic celebrations called 'the Lord's Supper'. The theocentric (and otherwise vague) character of the New Testament heaven echoes the theocentric belief of Jesus which in turn echoes his charismatic lifestyle. In order to concentrate his life on his religious message, Jesus spurned married and occupational life while relying on the sponsorship of wealthy patronesses and patrons. Prominent early Christian leaders like Paul and John of Patmos (author of Revelation) followed

Jesus in placing religion first and in remaining celibate. With its emphasis on the worship of God (and Christ) as well as its ideal of remaining outside of the mundane bonds created by marriage and procreation, life in the Christian community anticipated important aspects of what it expected eternal existence in heaven to be like.

While belief in heaven has always held an unquestioned place in Christian preaching, popular piety and theological discourse (with the exception of twentieth-century Christianity; see below), that belief was given various contents.

The greatest revolution in the history of heaven was gradual and hidden from the eyes of Christians who, between the second and the fifth centuries, were involved with seemingly weightier doctrinal disputes. That revolution created an alternative to the stern theocentrism of the Jesuanic heaven.

Beginning with bishop Cyprian of Carthage (d. 258), an alternative to the theocentric heaven was created. By drawing upon classical Greco-Roman ideas and especially upon the Roman philosopher Cicero's dialogues *On Old Age* and *Scipio's Dream*, Cyprian envisaged a heaven in which parents and children, family and friends would be reunited in a saintly society. The idea was taken up by bishops Ambrose of Milan (339–97) and Augustine (354–430), and the latter began to speculate about a rudimentary social life in the heavenly City of God. This new and more mundane view of heaven was not only more in tune with classical Greco-Roman views and hence more acceptable in a society pervaded by pagan traditions; it was also more in tune with a church that had moved far away from its charismatic origins and its early post-charismatic phases characterized by martyrdom and ASCETICISM.

Both models of heaven – the theocentric one of Jesus, and the anthropocentric one begun in patristic times – have made an impact on the history of Christian doctrine, preaching, piety, literature and art. Whenever Christian piety renewed its theocentric focus – in medieval scholasticism, with the sixteenth-century reformers, with the Jansenists and Puritans – heaven assumed a decidedly theocentric colour.

The first to develop strong views about a heaven in which God would not occupy all the attention of saintly souls were certain medieval troubadours whom Petrarch (1304–74) joined in some of his love poetry. However, it was only Lorenzo Valla (1405–57), the great Renaissance scholar, who presented a veritable theory of social life in heaven – a life which included movement and travel which Thomas Aquinas had denied the saints, at least as a regular kind of activity. The pleasant heaven of the Renaissance assumed a graphic quality in the art of Fra Angelico, Giovanni di Paolo and Luca Signorelli whose work provides a strong contrast to the theocentric and scholastic orthodoxy of Dante's *Paradiso* (1321).

Authors of the eighteenth and nineteenth centuries vied with each other in rejecting the cold, bloodless and boring notion of the theocentric hereafter. They replaced it by ever bolder versions of an anthropocentric heaven. Among the most influential authors writing in this vein were Isaac Watts (1674–1748), Emanuel Swedenborg (1688–1772), the American novelist Elizabeth Stuart Phelps (1844–1911) and the Catholic bishop Wilhelm Schneider (1847–1909). Writers and artists like Goethe (*The Sorrows of Young Werther*, 1774), Rousseau, W. Blake, Novalis and Dante Gabriel Rossetti were often more deeply involved with expectations of meeting their loved ones in heaven than the rationalism of their time seemed to allow for. The new image of heaven was characterized by the continuation of social relationships (Phelps), including MARRIAGE (Swedenborg, Goethe, Blake, Schneider), as well as by eternal progress and activity (Watts, who was joined by nineteenth- and twentieth-century spiritualists). In heaven, earthly life in all its dimensions simply continues. Thus the deepest longings for human love (hence the insistence on 'meeting again'), for individual and social progress and for satisfactory activity can be fulfilled. While the anthropocentric heaven still haunts the imagination of twentieth-century Christian believers, theologians writing after the 1930s have largely abandoned this view as 'infantile'.

Opinion polls confirm that in our generation belief in an afterlife in heaven continues to be very strong among Christians, especially in North America, where around 70 per cent of the total population hold some form of afterlife belief (Gallup and Proctor 1984). European figures seem to be substantially smaller, but imply similar beliefs for some 30–40 per cent. The most popular view is still the anthropocentric notion of heaven as a continuation of the present life, and some minor Christian groups (Swedenborgians, Mormons) make such doctrines their official teaching. Others, while advocating theocentric notions, come close to denying 'real life' (with new developments, new experience, new challenges) in the hereafter. Karl Barth (1886–1968) and Karl Rahner (1904–84), major representatives of twentieth-century reformed and Catholic theologies, envisage a rather static eternal being in the light of God; that light, though illuminating our past earthly lives, does not allow for new decisions, new spontaneity and new adventures. More radical 'Process philosophers' and theologians (C. Hartshorne, N. Pittenger) abandon the idea of individual immortality and prefer the vague notion of God not forgetting our lives. Some prominent Christians have given up afterlife beliefs altogether (L. Tolstoy (1828–1910), Reinhold Niebuhr (1892–1971) and Rudolf Bultmann (1884–1976)), while others like John Hick experiment with reincarnation beliefs (according to which Christian souls are recycled through more than one life). In the twentieth century, the clear trends of earlier Christian history have given way to a pluralism which also characterizes other areas of intellectual life. The only general trend that can be recognized is that of minimalism. The limits of our knowledge about heavenly matters are often acknowledged in philosophical terms reminiscent of I. Kant (who is known for his devastating critique of Swedenborg and, by implication, of much theological speculation): our experience does not provide material for rational thought about the beyond. Many theologians point to the earth, rather than to heaven, as the place where Christians are to exercise their virtues. They also reject, with I. Kant, a morality based on reward (and punishment); morality, if it is to be consonant with human dignity and freedom, must stand on its own feet. Carrying its own reward in itself, it needs no external support (although such support may be helpful in education, as Kant admits in *Religion within the Limits of Reason Alone* [1793], 1960).

Notions of a hereafter have formed, and continue to form, answers to the eternal existential question people raise in the face of death. This is doubtlessly the key to their continuing fascination. Exactly *how* heaven is depicted depends on the values held by a particular Christian group, a theologian or individual thinker. People who place God first and who are prepared to sacrifice other concerns for religion have always felt attracted to theocentric notions. Others, who feel that God has created men and women to grow in knowledge, to form relationships and to be active in a world which has to be shaped, have preferred an anthropocentric view of the hereafter, sometimes coming close to neglecting the divine dimension of the other world. As far as these two leading models of heaven are concerned, Ludwig Feuerbach (*The Essence of Christianity* [1841], 1957) is certainly correct in his suggestion that the myth of heaven is Christianity's most important myth because, on a scale of importance, it ranks above the idea of God. According to the German philosopher, 'the doctrine of heaven is the final doctrine of religion, its last will and testament. What elsewhere is passed over in silence is here clearly and unashamedly explained. . . . Heaven is therefore the key to the deepest mysteries of religion', and to the deepest mysteries of the present life, of which heaven is but a projection. However, Feuerbach's key does not unlock the mysteries of twentieth-century forms of (post-?)Christianity, for one would have to conclude that at least the more radical theologians, in denying an afterlife, have little interest in the present existence. Perhaps one can suggest that those Christians who have abandoned afterlife beliefs and 'demythologized' heaven are eager followers of Feuerbach who wanted that modern men and women no longer project the wealth of their lives on to heaven but discover this wealth in their own souls, lives and communities. However, a broken myth, though appealing to some intellectuals, will hardly attract a huge following even among contemporary Christians. Most Christian believers will no doubt continue to live with more traditional and more vital ideas of the next world, into which they project their most cherished ideals.

Feuerbach, L. ([1841] 1957) *The Essence of Christianity*, trans. G. Elliot, New York: Harper.

Gallup, G. and Proctor, W. (1984) *Adventures in Immortality*, London: Corgi.

Kant, I. ([1793] 1960) *Religion within the Limits of Reason Alone*, trans. T.M. Greene and H.H. Hudson, New York: Harper & Row.

Lang, B. (1985) 'No sex in heaven: the logic of procreation, death, and eternal life in the Judaeo-Christian tradition', in A. Caquot *et al.* (eds) *Mélanges bibliques et orientaux en l'honneur de M. Mathias Delcor*, Neukirchen: Neukirchener Verlag, pp. 237–53.

——(1987a) 'Heaven on stone: eighteenth and nineteenth-century ideas about life after death as reflected in American cemeteries', in H. Becker *et al.* (eds) *Im Angesicht des Todes*, St Ottilien: Eos, pp. 603–19.

——(1987b) 'The sexual life of the Saints: towards an anthropology of Christian heaven', *Religion* 17: 149–71.

McDannell, C. and Lang, B. (1988) *Heaven: A History*, London: Yale University Press.

Wheeler, M. (1990) *Death and the Future Life in Victorian Literature and Theology*, Cambridge: Cambridge University Press.

Bernhard Lang

HELL

Such is the condition of being human that there has never been a SOCIETY or an era in which intense curiosity about and belief in life after death has not occupied a prominent place in the minds of men and women. It is only since the seventeenth century in Western European culture that radical scepticism about continued existence after DEATH has ceased to be exceptional. Some religions, at certain stages of their development, have been content with only vague pictures or abstract notions of the afterlife; in other religions curiosity about this has been satisfied by extensive and detailed descriptions. All the major world religions have developed concepts of HEAVEN and hell, and all are agreed that such concepts should properly be understood as being related, more or less directly, to the character, behaviour and beliefs of individuals in life lived before death. The idea of capricious deities arbitrarily consigning persons to places of joy or pain is excluded. Even in those religions (with the possible exception of Zoroastrianism) whose mythology places angelic beings as well as human beings in hell relate their condition of SUFFERING to a condition of wickedness. In the Judaeo-Christian tradition it is the attempted rebellion of Satan against God that is the cause of his 'fall' and subsequent occupancy of hell. The belief that the concept of hell is inseparable from the concept of divine judgement has been particularly strong in the religions of Judaism, Christianity and Islam. While it is true that in these traditions the concepts are inseparable, it should be remarked that too naïve a notion of JUDGEMENT and too literal an understanding of the torments of PUNISHMENT have often obscured whatever truth there might be in the doctrine of eternal perdition and have caused both belief in God and the notion of Hell to seem either absurd or revolting.

In the earliest strands of Jewish thought there is almost no trace of hell – as it is now understood – and very little correlation between the idea of divine judgement and that of a continued existence after death. The writings of the Hebrew Bible give no description of the state of the dead. When *Sheol*, the name given to the place of the departed, is spoken of it is described almost entirely in negative terms (Isaiah 14: 9; Proverbs 15: 24). It may be a place under the earth; it is sometimes said to be a pit; it is a place neither of reward nor punishment; existences are shadowy and insubstantial. This state of half-life is mirrored in the descriptions of the underworld that can be found in early Greek thought (*Odyssey*, Book xi). Apart from a few exceptional human beings who are translated to a semi-divine status after death, all others enter the gloom of the kingdom beneath the earth ruled over by Hades. And though Virgil's description of that world in the sixth book of the *Aeneid* written for Roman readers several centuries later is more detailed, in essence the concept of life after death is the same. These shadowy places, sometimes confusingly referred to as hell, should be regarded as progenitors of the idea that came to be established in Jewish, Christian and Muslim thought only in the sense that they sometimes provided the imagery which was to be used by the thinkers of those later traditions.

By the time of Jesus Christ the old concept of *Sheol* was disappearing from Jewish religion and was being replaced by two mutually

sive ideas. First there was the proposition suggested by the author of the book Ecclesiastes: that death meant nothing more than extinction and that speculation about the afterlife was fruitless. Second, there was the belief that each individual would have to receive the judgement of God: the righteous would achieve life in heaven and the wicked would be condemned to hell. Whether this condemnation was to be conceived as permanent or temporary remained a matter of debate. Another word, more allusive and descriptive, now came to give pictorial substance to the state of perdition: *gehenna* (gehinnon). It is the word that is used in the gospels and is usually translated into English as hell (Matthew 5: 22; 18: 9). It was the name of a specific place, a ravine to the southwest of Jerusalem in which detestable sacrifices had once been offered and which had become an area of desolation. It came to symbolize ruin and degradation and it conveniently yielded imagery of brokenness, fire and smoke. At the same time the growth of APOCALYPTIC literature was beginning to provide ever more horrible and fantastic imagery for descriptions of the place of the damned. The book of Revelation teems with this imagery, and there can be little doubt that Jesus was echoing these apocalyptic strains in his own teaching on divine judgement and life after death (Mark 9: 43–8). These are the beginnings of that branch of Christian literature that was to flower so terrifyingly and gloriously over twelve centuries later in the *Inferno* of Dante. It has embarrassed and distressed Christians in many periods of the Church's history to see Christ himself adopting what appears to be so uncompromising an attitude to the severity of the divine judgement and the possibility of hell.

There was significant resistance in parts of the early church to the inclusion of Revelation in the canon of the Scriptures, and the notion of eternal perdition became a matter of controversy. There was no possibility of returning to a belief in *Sheol*, but as early as the third century the catechetical school of Alexandria, most famously in the person of Origen, were advancing theories of apocotastasis. Hell could not be eternal; the invincible power of God's love determined that no creature, not even the devil,

could suffer unending and irrevocable loss. Against such theories the church defined its own belief in the reality of eternal damnation and therefore of hell. But it must be noted that hell and damnation received scant attention in the church's liturgy and descriptions of hell did not figure centrally in the work of most theologians. It was not until Augustine of Hippo (354–430) that we are given any substantial treatment of the subject. In his influential book *City of God* the notion is dealt with in some depth – occurring in the context of a complicated discussion on the nature of SIN, EVIL and the wrath of God. God is seen as executing a just punishment on the reprobate, angels and humans alike. As the centuries passed the church tended to turn away from the harshness of Augustine's vision and to shift the emphasis of the argument so that it became more anthropological in its basis. By the time of the great Scholastic theologians hell was being discussed in the context, not so much of God's judgement, as that of human freedom. It was argued that human creatures being free could, if they wished, choose an ultimate rejection of God; the consequence of such choice would be defined as hell. (In still later centuries English literature would provide superb artistic realizations of these choices and their consequences in Christopher Marlowe's *Doctor Faustus* and John Milton's *Paradise Lost*.) In the middle of the thirteenth century Thomas Aquinas gave classic formulation to this interpretation in his assertion that the eternity of hell was the result of the obduracy of humankind. This has remained, in essence, the position of Catholic Christendom. The Reformers, however, in advocating a doctrine of predestination and rejecting the anthropology of the Scholastic theologians tended, in their treatment of hell and damnation, to return to Augustinian precepts (cf. Council of Trent, Decree on *Justification* and *Westminster Confession of Faith*, Chapters X and XXXIII).

An interesting fact emerges: while the theological underpinning of the theory of hell and eternal perdition differed, it has often been difficult to distinguish between Catholic and Protestant representations in popular preaching. The aims of the preachers were, certainly, different, but the means by which these aims were achieved were almost identical, for despite theological divergence they used the same psychology and drew from the same sources for their imagery. Vivid descriptions of the torment of those in hell were used to terrify listeners into states of crisis and decision. This fact uncovers another: the peculiar and, at times, subversive power of imagery. The lurid descriptions of hell can obscure the very theological propositions of which they are supposed to be the expression. The literature of the Middle Ages provides ample evidence of a distance between the learned tradition of the official liturgy of the church and the work of the scholars on the one hand and popular CULTURE on the other. Hell receives only a glancing reference in one of the universally accepted creeds of the church and then only to recall Christ's descent into it, and even in masses for the dead purgatory, not hell, is the central doctrine. (The *Dies Irae* was not admitted to the Roman Rite until the beginning of the sixteenth century and in the last three decades has almost disappeared again.) The great scholars of the Christian tradition hardly ever devoted, proportionately, much time and energy to describing hell; yet the imagining of hell and speculation about the state of the damned have occupied a great deal of the time and energy of both preachers and artists. It must be admitted that with the decline of belief in the afterlife such imaginings hardly find expression in modern society; none the less the artefacts of earlier ages lie all around us and the imagery of hell still lingers evocatively in the memory of Western European culture.

It is unlikely that many would have been able, at any time in history, to give a cogent theological explanation of hell (and few would have been able to follow the subtle arguments of Thomas Aquinas or John Calvin), yet all would have had some opinion on the subject and many would have been able ·to paint a convincing picture of it. Even in our own day when it is commonplace to be sceptical about claims to knowledge of the afterlife and to regard hell as either a morally offensive concept or an obsolete metaphor ('L'Enfer. C'est les autres' – Jean-Paul Sartre), the imagery still has power to disturb the receptive imagination. Only a tiny proportion of the population of the Western world will have heard the concept discussed in serious theological terms, and most would find the notion of hell-fire preaching absurdly unconvincing; but a large proportion will have seen and wondered at artistic representations in painting, sculpture and literature from Biblical times onward. Dante's *Divine Comedy* remains one of the central books of Western civilization; and it is a fact that many modern readers find the second and third sections, *Purgatorio* and *Paradiso*, dry and difficult after the excitement of the sensuous imagery of *Inferno*. (At the same time it could be argued that the horrors of hell so graphically described by Dante are only made bearable to the reader because the imagery is held within the strong philosophical framework of the author's apprehension of the relationship between LOVE and JUSTICE.) The paradox is that while the imagery still retains a hold upon the imagination, few contemporary Christians feel themselves able to use it any more. It is true that in certain Evangelical sects it does appear in preaching and teaching, but many theologians and, perhaps, most believers are ambivalent in their attitudes to all notions of hell. Some, notably Karl Barth, have declared themselves against the doctrine of eternal perdition (*Church Dogmatics*, vol. II); others, like Nicholas Berdyaev, have been profoundly committed to it (*The Destiny of Man*). Those who embrace universalism safeguard the doctrines of an all-loving, all-powerful God, but they have the problem of reconciling their belief first with the concept of human freedom and second with the accusation that salvation for all robs decisions taken in this life of their radical seriousness. Those who retain belief in the possibility of eternal perdition, while safeguarding the notions of human freedom and the importance of choice, have to reconcile belief in hell with that of a loving God who cannot purpose the loss of any part of God's own creation.

All are aware of the scandalous way in which both the doctrine of perdition and the imagery of hell have been used; for there is no doubt that the Christian church, like every religious institution, has tried to gain tight control over the lives of its members and has used the doctrine of perdition to do so: the more terrifying the imagery the greater the possibility of achieving submission. But the misuse of a doctrine does not invalidate it and the matter cannot be resolved simply into sociological categories. Hell has been accepted as a possibility by millions who have neither been frightened into belief themselves nor had the desire to frighten others into belief or gain control over their lives. The doctrine (and its attendant imagery illustrates the point) compels even the sceptical mind to consider the extremes of human experience and the tragic depths of human existence. However demythologized, it confronts us with a consideration of the necessity of radical choice and the possibility of ultimate loss.

Barth, K. (1957) *Church Dogmatics*, vol. II, Part II, Edinburgh: T. & T. Clark.

Berdyaev, N. (1948) *The Destiny of Man*, London: Geoffrey Bles.

Camporesi, P. (1990) *The Fear of Hell*, Cambridge: Polity.

Encyclopaedia of Religion and Ethics, ed. J. Hastings, vol. XI (1920), Edinburgh: T. & T. Clark.

Gardiner, E. (ed.) (1989) *Visions of Heaven and Hell before Dante*, New York.

Hanson, A.T. (1957) *The Wrath of the Lamb*, London: SPCK.

Hughes, R. (1968) *Heaven and Hell in Western Art*, London: Weidenfeld & Nicolson.

Le Goff, J. (1953) *The Birth of Purgatory*, Chicago, IL: University of Chicago Press.

Parrinder, G. (ed.) (1983) *An Illustrated History of the World's Religions*, Feltham: Hamlyn.

Rowell, G. (1964) *Hell and the Victorians*, Oxford: Oxford University Press.

Walker, D.P. (1964) *The Decline of Hell*, London: Routledge & Kegan Paul.

Brian Horne

HERMENEUTICS

In the eighteenth century hermeneutics came to the fore as 'the art of interpretation'. The Greek word *hermeneuein* ('to interpret') recalls Hermes, the messenger of the gods. Hermeneutics retains, even among some of its modern practitioners, the sense of bearing a message. The primary focus of hermeneutics in the Enlightenment period was on texts and particularly the text of the Bible. At the beginning of the nineteenth century, the question of the conditions governing interpretation became central to hermeneutics and on that basis it ceased to be in the service of other disciplines and began to be considered a discipline in its own right. In the twentieth century, not only has it become possible to ask if and how hermeneutics contributes to social practice and the critique of IDEOLOGY, but hermeneutics has also become the title of a specific approach to philosophy and to THEOLOGY, which has had an impact on other disciplines as well, particularly the study of literature and the LAW. In consequence, the task of hermeneutics is no longer the cultivation of the art of understanding, but the provision of a theory of how understanding is possible.

The initial problem which provokes the need for hermeneutics is unintelligibility or obscurity. It is particularly acute when the task is to make an attempt at understanding that crosses linguistic, cultural and historical boundaries. Hence hermeneutics has most often understood itself as trying to overcome distance. The task of interpretation is to step in wherever the text resists understanding and supply whatever is necessary to make the text coherent.

Friedrich Schleiermacher (1768–1834) was responsible for releasing hermeneutics from the philological task of interpreting the Bible or the Greek classics. From being an auxiliary science that provided rules of exegesis, hermeneutics took on the task of developing a general theory of interpretation. Its focus was not confined to those passages in a text that could not readily be understood. Every instance of understanding was problematized. The task of hermeneutics was to refer each utterance to the work as a unity which itself was to be understood with reference to the author's life. Interpretation is possible because the interpreter shares the same human nature with the author. Furthermore, the task of reconstructing the text invites the interpreter to enter into the mind of the author and discover the rules of its production. These rules would often be hidden from the author, thereby allowing Schleiermacher to present hermeneutics as the art of being able to understand the author better than the author understood himself or herself.

Because of the fragmentary nature of Schleiermacher's writings on hermeneutics, Wilhelm Dilthey (1833–1911) served until recently as the chief mediator of his views. Dilthey portrayed Schleiermacher's theory as predominantly psychological, but this account is now considered to have overlooked Schleiermacher's recognition of the linguistic component of understanding. Dilthey himself gave a greater significance to history than any of his predecessors had done. The importance of this move was particularly apparent in some of Dilthey's later writings, where history was presented as the site of the universalization of the individual. History is conceived of by Dilthey less as an obstacle to universal knowledge than as offering a route by which one might transcend the limits of one's experience, although Dilthey is not generally thought to have succeeded in establishing how historical consciousness overcame these limits.

In *Being and Time* ([1927] 1962), Martin Heidegger (1889–1976) insisted on the importance of Dilthey's contribution rather than its limitations. Nevertheless, for Heidegger, there were two levels to hermeneutics. The study of the methodology of the human sciences, such as Dilthey envisaged, is hermeneutics only in a derivative sense. The fundamental sense of hermeneutics was to be found in the notion of the hermeneutics of Dasein or human existence, where the issue was access to one's own Being in its finitude. It might seem that Heidegger's interests were somewhat divorced from the more practical issues entertained under the title of hermeneutics, but his importance is clearly established by the subsequent history of the subject.

Heidegger's contemporary at Marburg in the 1920s, Rudolf Bultmann (1884–1976), established the basis for twentieth-century hermeneutic theology. Heidegger's influence can be clearly seen in the way that Bultmann proposed that the interpretation of scripture be directed to the understanding of human existence expressed there. More generally, although Bultmann regarded interpretation as based on the relationship that the author and the interpreter share with respect to the thing under consideration, he acknowledged the decisive role played by the interest that the interpreter brings to the issue. For Bultmann, interpretation is not only directed at an understanding of human existence, it is guided by a prior understanding of human existence. Hermeneutics does not approach the text in a vacuum. Nor does it attempt to eliminate the prior understanding that resides in the interpreter's relation to the subject-matter of the text. What one brings to a text, including most especially the questions one poses to it, opens up the claim to truth that confronts one there.

Heidegger's influence is also clearly apparent in the work of Hans-Georg Gadamer (1900–). The impact of Gadamer's *Truth and Method* ([1960] 1989) was so great that it seemed for a time that his name had become virtually synonymous with hermeneutics, as if he was the fulfilment of the hermeneutic tradition. However, that impression is somewhat misleading. Gadamer attempted to redirect hermeneutics from the Schleiermacherian model of reconstruction to that of Hegel. In so far as Schleiermacher sought only to reproduce the original purpose of a work, this still remained at the level of an external relationship with the past. Hegel's contribution was to understand the way that the past was constitutive of the present and how this established the conditions of the possibility of it being retrieved.

Hegel's concept of the unity of world history sustains Gadamer's approach to hermeneutic understanding. For Gadamer, historical consciousness does not have the task of joining independent worlds. It is made possible by what Gadamer calls 'the unity of the total tradition'. This is Gadamer's answer to the suggestion that hermeneutics is directed to avoiding misunderstanding. Misunderstanding is only possible where there is at a more fundamental level a basis of agreement from out of which the confusion arose. Openness to the tradition underlies hermeneutic understanding, just as, according to Gadamer, the prior agreement of speakers on a shared language makes dialogue possible. The unity of tradition in Gadamer plays the role that Schleiermacher gave to the unity of human nature.

Classically hermeneutics addresses an alterity that is regarded as an obstacle to be overcome. However, for Gadamer as for Heidegger, what is to be overcome is not so much the strange as the over-familiar, or, more specifically, the obviousness with which what is transmitted by the tradition presents itself. We belong to the tradition and it is always part of us. Furthermore, historical distance is to be regarded as positive, because what is distant is, for that reason alone, striking and so presents itself as a task for understanding. Understanding comes about not by transposing oneself into another time or situation, but by raising oneself to a higher universality by overcoming one's own particularity and that of the text under consideration. That is the basis on which one experiences a claim to truth, an idea that Gadamer borrowed from Bultmann's account of the claim of the *kerygma*.

Whereas Gadamerian hermeneutics seems to be genuinely instructive in its efforts to explicate the possibility of understanding within a unified tradition, it is not obvious that it is so effective at explaining how understanding across different traditions is possible. The first encounters between different cultures present a problem for Gadamer's account that he seems not to address, perhaps because he gives the history of the West the status of a universal history of humankind, if not on the Enlightenment model at least in an echo of Hegel or Heidegger.

Although there seems to be no reason for restricting hermeneutics to the understanding of texts, attempts to give it a direct practical significance are usually frustrated. Gadamer explains very well how this might be so, drawing on his reading of Aristotle's *Ethics*: a text or practical situation may call on the interpreter to change his or her life, but the directive comes from the situation and is not provided by hermeneutics itself. One can understand the work of Jürgen Habermas (1929–) in the 1960s as an attempt to overcome hermeneutics in favour of a critique of ideology. Whereas both Habermas and Gadamer acknowledge that a prior agreement underlies every misunderstanding as well as every understanding, they understand it differently. Gadamer locates this prior agreement in the dialogue that constitutes tradition, while Habermas subjects that agreement to suspicion. Consensus might perpetuate misunderstanding and pseudocommunication. It might conceal the repressiveness of a power relation that distorts the intersubjectivity of understanding. Habermas' attempt to keep intact the Enlightenment

recourse to reason as a tool with which to question the authority of tradition, however, has not been as well received as his objections against some of Gadamer's more innocent (in the sense of apolitical) formulations of the issues. Habermas' initial portrayal of a form of critical reflection that would keep the Enlightenment project alive seems to ignore the historical limitations on reason already exposed by hermeneutic understanding. In this light the result of the Habermas–Gadamer debate was that the two thinkers now seem less distant than originally thought.

Today the greatest challenge to contemporary hermeneutics comes not from Habermasian critical theory but from DECONSTRUCTION, which radicalizes and complicates the issues of reading and interpretation. The only agreement arising out of the much discussed Derrida–Gadamer debate was that no meeting of minds took place. They seemed worlds apart, even if they shared a prior consensus in the form of a disposition to use Heideggerian language. If deconstruction in the figure of Jacques Derrida (1930–) shares with Gadamerian hermeneutics a rejection of the idea that understanding consists in reconstructing the intentions of the author, it problematizes much else. Above all it no longer approaches a text anticipating coherence or even logical consistency as usually understood. Deconstructive reading does not reduce everything to the same. Rather it finds the heterogeneous within the text at hand and attempts to preserve it as such. Nevertheless, the deconstructive reading of what is foreign still defines the foreign with reference to the dominant tradition. While challenging the notion of the unity of tradition and while drawing attention to what the tradition has marginalized or excluded, it too does not provide a model for the encounter between alien cultures. In *Of Grammatology* ([1967] 1976), Derrida showed himself adept at displaying the self-defeating character of Levi-Strauss' attempt to avoid ethnocentrism. Nevertheless, Derrida himself is concerned less with what lies outside the tradition than with what the tradition has marginalized within itself. This is not simply a question of neglecting what fell outside the occidental tradition. Derrida's deconstructive strategies are a response to his recognition of the power of philosophical reason – the power of the Greek *logos* so-called – to enclose whatever is set up in opposition to it. The analysis works less well in cases where consensus is neither presupposed nor sought, as Derrida himself showed when he avoided engaging Gadamer directly.

There is every indication that the next developments in hermeneutics will be a response to the problems raised in the course of the encounter between what is identified as the tradition of the Greek *logos* and that which resists it. One might see current debates about multiculturalism and FEMINISM in this light. Afrocentrism presents itself as a challenge to the hegemony of the Occidental tradition, but does not seek hegemony for itself. Radical feminism does not attempt to meet a tradition it recognizes as having excluded the perspectives of women on terms established by that tradition. In various ways, therefore, hermeneutics today is invited to come to terms with a situation where the task is not to resolve misunderstanding by attempting to establish or uncover agreement, but to see, paraphrasing Emmanuel Levinas (1906–   ), that what presents itself as a failure to communicate can indeed be positive, an indication that the disturbance produced by the Other marks the presence of the Other as Other.

Bultmann, R. (1955) 'The problem of hermeneutics', in *Essays, Philosophical and Theological*, London: SCM Press.
Derrida, J. (1976) *Of Grammatology*, Baltimore, MD: Johns Hopkins University Press.
Dilthey, W. (1976) *Selected Writings*, ed. H. Rickman, Cambridge: Cambridge University Press.
Gadamer, H.-G. (1989) *Truth and Method*, New York: Crossroad.
Habermas, J. (1985) 'On hermeneutics' claim to universality', in K. Mueller-Vollmer (ed.) *The Hermeneutics Reader*, New York: Continuum.
Heidegger, M. (1962) *Being and Time*, Oxford: Basil Blackwell.
Michelfelder, D. and Palmer, R. (1989) *Dialogue and Deconstruction*, Albany, NY: State University of New York Press.
Ormiston, G. and Schrift, A. (1990) *Transforming the Hermeneutic Context*, Albany, NY: State University of New York Press.
Ricoeur, P. (1981) *Hermeneutics and the Human Sciences*, ed. J.B. Thompson, Cambridge: Cambridge University Press.
Schleiermacher, F. (1977) *Hermeneutics: The Handwritten Manuscripts*, Missoula, MT: American Academy of Religion.
Thiselton, A.C. (1992) *New Horizons in Hermeneutics*, London: HarperCollins.

Robert Bernasconi

HOLISM

Holism is an attitude or methodology deployed in many areas and best defined by what holists oppose. Are there real wholes irreducible to the action of their parts? Are there real parts distinguishable as separable substances from the wholes in which they are found? Are there any successful non-analytic understandings or explanations? Can analytical explanation avoid the charge that it relies on the existence of brute simples that can never be displayed by themselves? Do our descriptions, which depend on differences and distinctions, misrepresent reality?

The term's first attested use was by J.C. Smuts, Boer general and sometime Prime Minister of South Africa, who suggested that there were real emergent wholes at each level of evolutionary history which transcended any earlier capacities of their parts: atoms, molecules, cells, metazoans and societies were all more than the aggregate effect of their several parts. Similar ideas were explored, independently, by Lloyd Morgan, Teilhard de Chardin and Olaf Stapledon, and since then by Ludwig Bertalanffy and C. Waddington. In the political sphere, 'holism' has been equated with collectivism, the assumption that societies or states must matter more than the mere individuals (or lesser organisms) that make them up. Karl Popper's association of totalitarian rule with 'holism', as expressed in Plato or Hegel, was fair neither to them nor to those who actually used the term. Methodological individualists sought to explain social and political movements solely as the aggregate effect of individual action, but took the unity of the latter organisms for granted. A more deeply reductive individualism sought to explain human action as the outcome solely of biochemical events, or physical locomotion, or the flux of elementary particles. More 'holistic' commentators have denied that we could ever perform such a reductive analysis, or needed to. Even human-made machines operate as wholes, in accordance with rules that cannot be derived solely from the rules that govern their elements: they can, for example, 'go wrong', as mere locomotions cannot. Biological science in this century has generally preferred a rhetoric of reduction to any appeals to vital spirit, or the top-down effect of whole patterns. Holists would usually reject the charge of covert vitalism: living things do not differ from the non-living by the addition of an extra part, even a pneumatic or spiritual one. They differ from less organized unities (but not from all non-living processes) because the whole (and therefore its parts as well) behaves in radically new ways than the parts do on their own. This may of course only reflect our inability to perform the calculations. But there seems to be good reason to believe in dynamic patterns: one species differs from another not by arbitrary addition or reduction but by the transformation of a whole shape (as shown by D'Arcy Thompson).

Some commentators argue that the very notion of a separate and individual substance is ill-conceived. Nothing at all can be properly understood except as the consequence of the whole of which it is a part. All merely analytic understanding rests on false assumptions: the whole C is not the product of its supposed elements, A and B; A and B, as they are present in C, can only be distinguished from it in thought, and their 'separate' behaviour is not what causes C's behaviour but is instead an abstraction from the whole C. An appreciation of C's behaviour is sometimes associated with less rigorously cognitive modes of investigation: notably the 'lived reality' of a real organism's life is not to be equated with the 'mechanical product' of its parts as those are investigated by real or notional dissection. We cannot find out what a thing is by breaking it. Analysis requires us to alter one thing at a time in order to identify each element's own contribution to the whole, in the hope that the sum of such contributions will turn out to be what we first observed. But it is doubtful that we ever can alter one thing at a time, or eliminate the possibility of the whole's immediately adjusting to its loss (a three-legged dog's remaining legs do not move as once they did; a brain-damaged person need

not fail at the tasks once handled – perhaps – by the injured area of brain). If each element's behaviour is dependent on the behaviour of all the others, it may be impossible in principle to identify each bit's contribution. To suppose otherwise, some have held, is merely to project the wage principle to a wider world, as though each creature's contribution could always be identified and priced. In the theory of meaning, it is clear that no one word or sentence can have its meaning apart from the whole real or virtual context. Especially, we cannot identify a creature's beliefs and desires separately: if a brain-damaged squid no longer pursues fishes round a blind corner is this because it has forgotten they are there or because it wants them less? If nothing can have beliefs that has no desires (or contrariwise) it is pointless to suppose that its mentality could be composed of beliefs and desires conjoined. If the motion of elementary particles is the outcome of everything else that happens, that everything is not itself composed of independently moving bits.

Although there is good reason to suspect that the world is not made up of independent bits, and that there are many levels of organic unity, it may still be true that an analytic methodology is our best route to knowledge. The whole itself is not accessible to human insight: if all that we can understand are parts, we must hope to obtain some slight grasp of the totality by adding up our knowledge of the bits, even though we cannot always make that calculation and know that it must always be inadequate. At least, even if there are wholes (as it might be, the Whole Earth), an understanding of geological, meteorological and biological change must be highly particularized. Nothing happens without local changes, even if those local changes are constrained by what happens – equally locally – in the wider realm. This is why the Gaia hypothesis, that the whole earth functions rather like a living cell, still requires detailed accounts of what particular events preserve the biochemical balance. We might not look for those particular events without the conviction that the whole does matter; but the whole cannot matter without the detailed happening.

There is a constant movement, as I have already implied, between methodological and normative holism. It is one thing to say that things can only really be understood in context, in relation to a wider realm, and to oppose the notion that there are, somewhere or other, atomies that can be understood by themselves and that serve to explain the aggregates that they compose. It is quite another to suggest that we are culpably fragmented by dissociating our individual selves from the wider community or cosmos, or failing in personal integrity when we play many different, largely unrelated parts. If nothing can be understood in isolation, neither can individualists or dissociated personalities: we are no more parts of larger wholes when we socialize than when we do not. But normative holism may have some strengths: methodological holism may at least remove any reason to think that competition is the only lasting relationship. On the contrary, co-operation is the basis of existence: my interests are not bound to be at odds with those of others, because the line between myself and others is itself shifting and deconstructible. Wholeness, if it is a fact that cannot be thought away, can hardly be an ideal: but since it is fact it would be foolish to imagine that we could survive without it. The speech attributed to Chief Seattle back in 1857 (though probably composed in 1970) correctly claimed that those who spit upon the earth spit on themselves. To be at all is to be with everything; to injure 'others' is to destroy ourselves (*see* ANIMAL RIGHTS; ECOLOGICAL THEOLOGY).

von Bertalanffy, L. (1952), *Problems of Life*, London: C. A. Watts.

Birch, J. and Cobb, J. (1981) *The Liberation of Life*, Cambridge: Cambridge University Press.

Chardin, J.P. Teilhard de (1955) *The Phenomenon of Man*, London: Collins.

Lovelock, J. (1990) *The Ages of Gaia*, London: Oxford University Press.

Morgan, C. Lloyd (1923) *Emergent Evolution*, London: Williams & Norgate.

Smuts, J.C. (1926) *Holism and Evolution*, London: Macmillan.

Stapledon, O. (1946) *Death into Life*, London: Methuen.

Thompson, D'Arcy W. (1917) *Of Growth and Form*, Cambridge: Cambridge University Press.

Waddington, C. (ed.) (1968–9) *Towards a Theoretical Biology*, vols i–iv, Edinburgh: Edinburgh University Press.

Stephen Clark

HOLOCAUST

From 1933 to 1945 the Nazis carried out a systematic programme of persecution of Jews and Judaism, culminating in the 'Final Solution' adopted at Wannsee in 1942, which aimed at the physical destruction of every person who had at least one Jewish great-grandparent. The implementation of this programme is often referred to as 'the Holocaust', a term which, denoting a completely burned sacrifice, suggests a particular theological interpretation. The theologically neutral Biblical Hebrew term *Shoah* (destruction – cf. Zephaniah 1: 15), introduced by Raphael Lemkin in 1944, leaves open the question as to what meaning, if any, can be assigned to the event.

The attitudes which enabled the Nazis to 'demonize' the Jews and thus carry out their programme were already deeply embedded in the popular cultures of the nations amongst whom they operated. For so long had Christians taught that Jews were a despised people, the rejecters and killers of Christ, obdurate in their adherence to a superseded faith, that European culture was saturated with this image of the Jew. It is unique that for almost two thousand years one people has been singled out for constant and *religiously sanctioned* vilification through much of the 'civilized' world, Muslim as well as Christian (*see* ANTI-SEMITISM).

This cultural heritage underlies the *trahison des clercs*, the readiness with which academics, professionals, priests and theologians acquiesced in the destruction of the Jews.

Those Jews who found meaning in the *Shoah* did so on the basis of *halakha* (Jewish law) as well as philosophy or theology. Many *Shoah* victims regarded themselves as martyrs, yielding up their lives in an act of *Qiddush ha-Shem* (sanctification of God's name). 'I shall be sanctified amongst the people of Israel' (Leviticus 22: 32) is interpreted in the Talmud to mean that if a Jew is forced to transgress any of the major commandments of Torah, namely idolatry, adultery/incest or murder, under pain of DEATH, he should die rather than transgress, thus sanctifying God's name (codified by Moses Maimonides in *Mishneh Torah Hilkhot Yesodey Ha-Torah*, Ch. 5).

Halakha imparted meaning to such life as was possible under the *Shoah*. The range of topics of response such as those of Ephraim Oshry, compiled in the ghetto of Kovno, Lithuania, indicates how ordinary people in the ghetto, with the deep strength born of faith in God, were concerned quietly to walk in the precepts of God: 'Jews Forced to Shred a Torah Scroll', 'Sabbath Torah Reading for Slave Laborers', 'The Blessing for Martyrdom', 'Saving Oneself with a Baptismal Certificate', 'Contraceptives in the Ghetto', 'The Repentant Kapo'. No questions are so agonizing as those involving harm to the life of other victims. The Nazis did their utmost to degrade and dehumanize Jews by forcing them to destroy each other. That they often failed owes much to the spirit engendered by the *halakha* on the sanctity of life.

Classical Jewish theology distinguishes between individual and collective PROVIDENCE. In terms of collective Providence the destruction of part of the people of Israel can be interpreted as part of God's redemptive process, leading ultimately to Israel's restoration, whether or not in terms of the Land. Some orthodox rabbis, feeling deeply that modern ways of life adopted by many Jews through assimilation to 'the ways of the nations round about' have destroyed the holy world of the Jew nurtured over the centuries, have interpreted the *Shoah* as the prophesied chastisement of Israel. Individual Providence is more problematic; clearly, there were many innocent sufferers.

Many entered the gas chambers with *Ani Ma'amin* (a declaration of faith based on the Thirteen Principles formulated by Maimonides) or *Shema Israel* (Deuteronomy 6: 4–9, declaring God's unity and the duty to love Him and obey His commandments) on their lips. (*Shema Israel* is read daily at the morning and evening services and forms part of the deathbed confession.) What was happening defied their understanding, but their faith triumphed over EVIL and they were ready *in extremis* to declare the LOVE of God.

Rabbi Isaac Nissenbaum, in the Warsaw Ghetto, called for *qiddush ha-hayyim*, the sanctification of life, rather than *qiddush ha-Shem*, the holiness of martyrdom.

The sense of APOCALYPTIC, of being part of the events heralding the Messiah and the Final Redemption of Israel and the World, was strong amongst the orthodox victims of the *Shoah*. Some interpret both the *Shoah* and the strife surrounding the emergence of the State of Israel as 'birth pangs of the Messiah'.

Concepts of redemptive suffering and vicarious atonement for sin appear. As he was led to his death Rabbi Elchanan Wasserman declared:

we are being asked to atone with our own bodies for the sins of Israel. Now we really must do *teshuva* (repent) . . . we must have in mind that we will be better sacrifices if we do *teshuva*, and we may save our American brothers and sisters.

The idea of God being 'hidden' features together with the midrashic image of the *Shekhina* (divine presence) being 'in exile' with Israel, for 'I am with him in his distress' (Psalm 91: 15). Eliezer Berkovitz not merely finds the hiddenness of God compatible with God's existence, but discovers God's actual presence within His silence.

Many have found the traditional responses to suffering inadequate to confront the *Shoah*, especially if they have abandoned belief in life after death or in the authenticity of rabbinic tradition.

Elie Wiesel, in his stories of the *Shoah*, enters into its social and cultural context. He imposes no systematic structure or interpretation on reality, but creates a new myth through which the reader or hearer accesses meaning. His writings constitute a 'narrative exegesis' of the *Shoah*.

Emil Fackenheim argues that normative Judaism and Christianity act as if they were immune to all future events except Messianic ones, as if there could be no epoch-making event between Sinai and Messiah. For him, the radical challenge of the *Shoah* constitutes a new Revelation. He once proposed a '614th commandment' – to survive as Jews, to remember, never to despair of God, lest we hand Hitler a posthumous victory (*Judaism* 16 (Summer 1967): 272–3). (The earliest attribution of the popular tradition that the Torah contained 613 commandments is to the third-century rabbi Simlai (Babylonian Talmud *Makkot* 23b).) Later, he grounded his belief in *tiqqun* ('repair') in the actual resistance of *Shoah* victims to whom no realistic hope remained. This is an affirmation of life and of God, a challenge to humankind to 'mend the world'.

Richard Rubenstein was driven by reflection on the *Shoah* to reject the concept of an interventionist God.

The psychiatrist Viktor Frankl, during his time as an inmate of Auschwitz and Dachau, developed 'logotherapy'. Those unable to achieve the 'will to meaning' soon perished, he observed; those who somehow found meaning survived wherever physically possible. The visual art produced in the camps and the music of Theresienstadt are the aesthetic embodiment of this will to life and meaning.

Irving Greenberg, an orthodox rabbi, sees Auschwitz as 'a call to humans to stop the Holocaust, a call to the people Israel to rise to a new, unprecedented level of covenantal responsibility.... Even as God was in Treblinka, so God went up with Israel to Jerusalem.' Jews today, in Israel and elsewhere, have a special responsibility, in fidelity to those who perished, to work for the abolition of that matrix of values that supported GENOCIDE. Dan Cohn-Sherbok and Marc Ellis have moved from this to forms of Jewish 'liberation theology'.

For all theistic religions, age-old questions on the presence of evil, injustice and SUFFERING in God's world have acquired a new focus (see THEODICY). Yet 'at even deeper levels and in more radical ways the Holocaust is a Christian problem' (Alice Eckardt). As Gregory Baum wrote: 'The message of the Holocaust to Christian theology ... is that at whatever cost to its own self-understanding, the church must be willing to confront the ideologies implicit in its doctrinal tradition' (1976: 12).

Religious teaching both Catholic and Protestant formed the stereotypes of Jews and the emotional attitudes towards them which permeated the culture of Christian lands and made it possible for the masses in Germany and elsewhere in central Europe to acquiesce or become actively involved in the humiliation and destruction of the Jews. In Germany, there was no effective Church protest against Nazi anti-Jewish policies; even those who protested

against Nazism were diffident in specifying its anti-Jewish aspects. Indeed, the 'German Church' developed a narrowly nationalistic interpretation of Christianity which supported overt Nazi aims. Slovakian church leaders, implored to intercede on behalf of Jews being deported to the death camps, refused on the grounds that the Jews had killed Christ and deserved extermination.

As the enormity of the *Shoah* and its relationship with traditional Christian 'teaching of contempt' (Jules Isaac's phrase) was realized, many Christians addressed the task of reconstructing their theology in such a way that it could not support this teaching. For Bonhoeffer's disciple E. Bethge the Holocaust is a 'turning-point', and Franz Mussner has proclaimed: 'Without the construction of a "theology after Auschwitz" there is no genuine dismantling of Christian antisemitism'. (His paper 'What is theology after Auschwitz?' was read at the conference of the International Catholic–Jewish Liaison Committee in Prague in September 1990. An English version appears in *Christian Jewish Relations* 24 (Winter 1991), 46 f.) Peter von der Osten-Sacken writes: 'The conclusion seems to be inescapable that the latent theological and religious anti-Judaism always present just below the surface can really be overcome only if the Jewish people are no longer defined in the light of the gospel as "enemies".'

Supersessionist theology, the idea that the Church is the 'true' Israel, replacing the Jewish people, has been rejected by J. Pawlikowski, P.M. van Buren and others, and the permanence of the election of and covenant with Israel has been emphasized (H.-J. Kraus, following Calvin), sometimes on the basis of Romans 9–11. The claim of the exclusiveness of salvation through Jesus Christ has been questioned, and inclusivist (K. Rahner) or pluralist (J. Hick) models have been developed. R. Ruether's claim that anti-Semitism is the 'left hand' of Christology has stimulated formulations of Christology designed to avoid this charge.

Catholic and Protestant Church documents, pronouncements and guidelines have set the parameters for a re-evaluation of Christian attitudes to Jews and Judaism. Vatican II, in its 1965 document repudiating the collective GUILT of Jews for the death of Christ, failed to refer to the *Shoah*. Not until September 1990, at Prague, did a Vatican spokesman call for *teshuva* (repentance) on the part of the Church for its sin of ANTI-SEMITISM. The new theologies have yet to be worked out fully and to be integrated into the life of the Church through its teaching and preaching.

A number of issues and questions arise form the experience of the Holocaust. For example, are the churches willing and able to confront the ideologies implicit in traditional Christian doctrinal formulations? From the time of its separation from the Jewish people in the late first century until the modernist questioning of its doctrines Christianity consistently taught that Jews incurred special guilt for 'rejecting' Christ, that Jews were a despised people, that the Jewish religion was 'legalistic' and fossilized and that its true 'fulfilment' was Christianity. These doctrines furnished the basis for discrimination against Jews and for hatred and persecution.

The *Shoah* was not a Christian enterprise. Nevertheless, Christian teaching had permeated European CULTURE with false and malicious stereotypes of Jews and Judaism, and with an anti-Jewish IDEOLOGY which inhibited the Church from speaking up on behalf of Jews and predisposed ordinary German Christians to accept Nazi propaganda and orders.

The question thus arises, can Christianity redefine itself without denigrating Jews and Judaism? As Ruether has highlighted, this is not a marginal question but one that is integral to CHRISTOLOGY itself. After all, if it is part of your understanding of God that he was 'killed' by the Jews it is not surprising that you despise them. And if you believe that, having once been 'chosen', they rejected God's message which you accept, you are well on the way to appropriating their 'chosenness' for yourself. Once convinced that you have replaced and superseded them you will be disposed to 'triumphalism' and to denigration of their faith.

Can Christians develop a *positive* theology of Israel, as van Buren and others have attempted? Is a 'two covenant' theology to be adopted, recognizing the ongoing validity of the 'covenant with Israel'? Or would it be better to adopt a relativist position, 'normalizing' relations with contemporary Jews as with people of other religions, rather than treating them as 'theological objects' with a special status?

Certainly, Christians are not the only group with potentially dangerous ideologies. In broader terms, then, how can society prevent the permeation of culture by pernicious ideas and images arising from religious and other ideologies? How can our educational and legal systems accomplish the eradication of such ideas once they have been implanted in our culture?

How can professional ethical standards be maintained in the face of pernicious ideologies? One of the most disturbing aspects of the Holocaust was the apparent readiness of civil servants, of doctors, lawyers and priests, to comply with Nazi demands. Indeed, few if any dictators have been stopped in their tracks by the inability to procure willing persons to implement their plans.

We must learn to read the 'early warning signs' of genocidal tendencies in our society. There are no reliable means by which we can frustrate their development. Eternal vigilance is necessary, including critical examination of our most cherished beliefs and the ways they are formulated.

Baum, Gregory (1976) *Christian Theology after Auschwitz*, London: Council of Christians and Jews.

Berkovitz, E. (1973) *Faith after the Holocaust*, New York: KTAV.

Eckardt, A. Roy, and Eckardt, Alice L. (1982) *Long Night's Journey into Day: Life and Faith after the Holocaust*, Detroit, MI: Wayne State University.

Fackenheim, Emil L. (1982) *To Mend the World: Foundations of Future Jewish Thought*, New York: Schocken Books.

Fleischner, E. (ed.) (1977) *Auschwitz: Beginning of a New Era?*, New York: KTAV.

Jacobs, Steven L. (ed.) (1993) *Contemporary Christian Religious Responses to the Shoah*, University Press of America.

——(1993) *Contemporary Jewish Religious Responses to the Shoah*, University Press of America.

Kirschner, Robert (1985) *Rabbinic Responsa of the Holocaust Era*, New York: Schocken Books.

Littell, Franklin (1975) *The Crucifixion of the Jews*, New York: Harper & Row.

Marrus, Michael (1989) *The Holocaust in History*, Harmondsworth: Penguin.

Pawlikowski, J.T. (1978) *The Challenge of the Holocaust for Christian Theology*, New York: Anti-Defamation League.

Rubenstein, Richard L. and Roth, John K. (1987) *Approaches to Auschwitz: The Legacy of the Holocaust*, Atlanta, GA: John Knox Press; London: SCM.

van Buren, Paul (1980–) *A Theology of the Jewish–Christian Reality*, 4 vols, New York: Seabury Press.

Norman Solomon

HOMELESSNESS

Homelessness is a complex, multifaceted global phenomenon. Few if any nations, whether developed, developing or underdeveloped, are free from this problem. It is impossible to reflect accurately the magnitude of this global problem in human numbers. The nature of the issue precludes this. Nevertheless the perception is that homelessness is increasing worldwide and may easily total tens of millions. Estimates in the USA alone range from 1 to 5 million homeless people.

The increase in homelessness cannot be reduced to one simple underlying cause. In fact the causes of homelessness and its increase are due to a constellation of interrelated and overlapping factors ranging from natural disasters to weakened socio-economic infrastructures.

The current status and magnitude of the issue are best exemplified by the United Nations resolution adopted by the General Assembly in 1982 proclaiming 1987 as the International Year of Shelter for the Homeless (IYSH). The 1985 Report of the Secretary-General on the International Year of Shelter for the Homeless states that 'the overall conditions of shelter and related infrastructure and services for millions of poor families in the developing world and for a substantial number of families in many developed countries continued to deteriorate' (United Nations 1985: 3). The specific goals of the International Year were many but the metapurpose was to 'focus world attention on the persistent and growing shelter and settlement needs of the homeless, the poor and disadvantaged' (1985: 5).

Whatever can be said of homelessness it is clear that it is a persistent and growing problem and the human beings who compile its ranks are, with few exceptions, among the most indigent and marginalized groups in the world today. For this reason it is imperative that religious communities continue to subject this issue to ongoing analysis for the purpose of theological reflection and pastoral-political action.

In the literature that addresses the phenomenon of homelessness there is little consensus on its parameters or its defined meaning. A spectrum of definitions exists ranging from very literal to very broad. Several reasons may account for this lack of consensus. First of all, homelessness can be a very nebulous and shadowy experience determined by the fact that many homeless people are invisible as a result of social marginalization and their own intentions. This is particularly true in the case of women (single and with children) who are not safe in emergency shelters or on the streets. Second, there appear to be stages or phases of homelessness ranging from those who are at risk and whose housing situation is extremely precarious to those who fit the traditional stereotype of the single disaffiliated skid-row male. Finally, a lack of consensus is due in part to differing or conflicting political and ideological interests on the part of those who propose definitions.

An example of the literal side of the spectrum would be the definition proposed by the US Government's Department of Housing and Urban Development (HUD) in the 1984 'Report to the Secretary on the Homeless and Emergency Shelters'.

> It defined homelessness as the condition whereby nighttime residence is (a) in public or private emergency shelters which take a variety of forms – armories, schools, church basements . . . and where temporary vouchers are provided by private or public agencies, even hotels, apartments, or boarding houses; or (b) in the streets, parks, subways, bus terminals, railroad stations, airports, under bridges or aqueducts, abandoned buildings without utilities, cars, trucks, or any other public or private space that is not designated for shelter.
>
> (HUD 1984: 5)

This is a widely accepted 'working definition' in the USA. While literal definitions such as

HUD's set very exact parameters for the meaning of homelessness they do overlook two important groups of people: those who have lost their home/shelter and are forced to 'double up' with friends or relatives and those whose housing situation is so precarious that they are at serious risk of losing their shelter. In his book *Rachel and Her Children*, Jonathon Kozol contends that there could be as many as ten million people in the USA who are one lost paycheck or traumatic event (e.g. illness) from the streets (Kozol 1988: 11).

At the other end of the definition spectrum are very broad definitions an example of which would be the United Nations' definition proposed in association with the 1987 IYSH. This definition of homelessness includes two categories of people:

1) Those who have no home and who live either outdoors, in emergency shelters or hostels and 2) people whose homes do not meet U.N. basic standards. These standards include adequate protection from the elements, access to safe water and sanitation, affordable prices, secure tenure and personal safety, and accessibility to employment, education, and health care.

(Fallis and Murray 1990: 3;
Cox 1986: 14-16)

Clearly this is a very broad definition the intention of which is to link actual homelessness with substandard housing and the overall cycle of POVERTY and economic underdevelopment. This definition has much in common with 'inadequately housed' and 'at risk' definitions of homelessness.

For the purpose of this work a 'middle ground' definition of homelessness is proposed. Homelessness can be defined as the condition whereby individuals and families have no home or shelter of their own, i.e. they lack conventional and consistent access to an accepted or traditional dwelling and are forced involuntarily to seek alternative and inadequate means of shelter from public and private agencies, emergency shelters, friends, relatives or in other public and private space not intended for habitation.

These definitions are helpful because they suggest the range of homelessness and provide parameters for its meaning. They do not, however, provide insight into the subjective and phenomenological dimension of homelessness as a psycho-social phenomenon. An alternative yet complementary approach would be to define homelessness on the basis of absence of 'homefulness'. Jerome Tognoli, a psychologist, proposes six primary characteristics of home which offer an insightful framework for understanding the subjective experience of homelessness (Tognoli 1987: 657–65). These characteristics are (a) a sense of rootedness; (b) a sense of continuity and order; (c) a sense of privacy, sanctuary and ownership; (d) a sense of identity and distinction; (e) a context for social and familial relationships; and (f) a socio-cultural context (Tognoli 1987: 657–65; Fallis and Murray 1990: 17). These six aspects are profoundly absent in the phenomenon of homelessness, suggesting a complete fracturing of one's personal-social foundations as well as a debilitating lack of the necessary ingredients for a healthy sense of self and successful social relations. This approach indicates that homelessness is much more than a lack of shelter but a profound deficiency of all the positive qualities associated with having one's own private psycho-social space. It suggests an extemely bleak and broken existence.

Two issues are central to the underlying causes of homelessness. First, homelessness is often perceived as an urban problem. This is so because the bulk of services dealing with homelessness are often located in urban centres. However, homelessness is also a rural phenomenon. For example, the collapse of the FAMILY farm in North America (otherwise known as the rural farm crisis) has created an increase in homelessness in rural-agricultural regions. Most rural communities are ill-equipped to deal with this, forcing the rural homeless to urban centres for services and shelter.

Second, the homeless no longer exclusively comprise single disaffiliated males stereotypical of the skid-row vagrant. Today women, children and entire families comprise a significant percentage of the homeless population. In other words the face of homelessness has changed rather dramatically in the last ten to fifteen years. While it is difficult to track the exact causes of this, some observers point to a dramatic decrease in affordable low income housing associated with the rise of neo-conservative politics and the decline of WELFARE state social policies. This is particularly true of some Western democracies such as the USA and the UK where there were significant cuts in federal housing assistance programmes under the Reagan administration and the sale of public housing in Britain under Prime Minister Thatcher.

For the purpose of analysis the underlying causes of homelessness can be grouped into three large categories: (a) natural disasters; (b) political conflicts/WAR; and (c) socio-economic reasons. Natural disasters such as devastating storms (e.g. typhoons, tornados, etc.), earthquakes, volcanic eruptions and fires often create sudden and large-scale increases in homelessness. The homelessness created by devastating natural events is often compounded by a nation's inability to deal with sudden large-scale destruction.

Internal and external political conflicts leading to civil war and war with neighbouring states also creates significant homelessness. Refugees, created by and caught in such conflictual political conditions, not only lose their homes but are often forced to flee their native land. The unique and dreadful situation of refugees forced the United Nations to create a special department directed by the High Commissioner of Refugees in Geneva.

The third category of underlying causes, socio-economic reasons, deserves close scrutiny owing to the fact that the specific issues within this category are often debated and contested by those with different and hostile political and ideological interests. The literature on homelessness typically identifies five socio-economic factors that contribute to the phenomenon. The first, already alluded to, is the shortage of affordable low income housing. What is considered affordable housing? According to the US Government affordable housing is housing for which a family or individual pays no more than 30 per cent of income. It is estimated that in 1985 nearly 63 per cent of low income renters spent 50 per cent of their income on housing and nearly 45 per cent of these renters spent 70 per cent or more on their housing costs. This dangerous and precarious situation is in part caused and exacerbated by a shortage of federally assisted housing. According to Kozol the US Government between 1981 and 1986 cut federal funds to build or rehabilitate low income housing from 28 to 9 billion dollors (Kozol 1988). It is Kozol's view that a lack of housing is the major contributing factor to increased homelessness, particularly in the USA. This trend of reducing federal expenditures for social welfare programmes is not confined to the USA. Other governments guided by neo-conservative ideologies, such as Canada and the UK, have also sought to reduce government involvement in social welfare programmes.

The second major factor contributing to homelessness is loosely grouped under economic causes. Generally this factor indicates poorly functioning economies worldwide resulting in an unequal distribution of economic benefits. This economic situation is aggravated by recessionary cycles which in turn directly affect homelessness. Specifically these economic factors include UNEMPLOYMENT and consistently higher rates of unemployment; shifting economies from industrial to service sector production; subsequent shifts in labour MARKETS from higher to lower paying jobs; and the overall cycle of poverty. The poor, those who least benefit from inadequate economies, are the ones most typically threatened with homelessness.

The third cause of homelessness is various forms of family dysfunction. This is a relatively new observation due to the fact that dysfunction within the familial environment has received increased attention in recent years. Many observers believe that family dysfunction is the leading factor contributing to an increase in homeless women and children. Family dysfunction can take a variety of forms including drug or alcohol dependence, domestic VIOLENCE particularly directed at women and children and sexual abuse/molestation. Preliminary statistics in the USA seem to affirm the claim that increasing homelessness among women and children is directly related to increased familial dysfunction. For example some social agencies serving street youth suggest that as many as 80 per cent are victims of violence or sexual abuse. In other words many homeless youth consider the streets a safer environment than home. Also some agencies for battered women suggest that anywhere from 50 to 75 per cent of homeless women (often with children) were victims of domestic violence. The nascent research into the dysfunction factor is beginning to reveal a startling link between family dysfunction and homelessness. Preliminary research suggests that homeless adults were often homeless as children. This may indicate a developing systemic pattern suggesting that today's homeless children may become tommorrow's homeless adults.

The fourth major factor related to homelessness is drug and alcohol dependence. Most observers believe this issue to be one of the most significant contributions to the cycle of homelessness. This problem is not just relevant to the stereotypical skid-row homeless male but is a ubiquitous factor among all homeless subgroups. Debate, however, is considerable over its exact role and function in the cycle of homelessness. Many see substance abuse as a direct and major cause of homelessness while others see dependence as a 'self-medicating' response to trauma and victimization such as sexual abuse or DOMESTIC VIOLENCE. The latter group views dependence as an epiphenomenon that exacerbates an already existing condition or factor linked to homelessness. All agree, however, that drug and alcohol dependence is a significant factor in the phenomenon of homelessness.

The final contributing factor is mental illness or other related disability. In the USA estimates cover a wide range and suggest that anywhere from 25 to 50 per cent of the homeless population suffers from one or multiple psychological conditions. The root of this factor in North America can be traced to the 1960s and the process of de-institutionalization whereby many mentally ill patients were released from state and county facilities. This was to be followed by the creation of community mental health centres half of which were never built, leaving many discharged patients to fend for themselves. The failure to provide local support services for the mentally disabled has become a contributing factor in the phenomenon of homelessness.

The reader should remember that these five socio-economic factors were isolated for the purpose of analysis. In reality more than one of these factors often become linked, creating a web-like phenomenon leading to homelessness. Homelessness is rarely produced by one single socio-economic cause but by a constellation of factors which conspire to create the condition of homelessness.

Since the Second World War theological concerns have been increasingly driven by social, political and economic concerns. The impact of the HOLOCAUST forced THEOLOGY, particularly in Europe, to face its socio-political naïvety. The result was a profound interest in the social sciences and a deeper commitment to the socio-ethical dimensions of theological reflection. This turn to the social sciences gave rise to a whole new approach to theological method where social analysis, praxis, ethical-JUSTICE considerations and HUMAN RIGHTS issues moved to centre-stage in the theological enterprise. This social science/ethical perspective is most obvious among those theologies commonly referred to as political theology or the theologies of liberation.

From the perspective of these theological approaches homelessness as a specific social phenomenon would be extremely relevant. A typical procedure would be first to subject the experience of homelessness to social analysis with the aim of uncovering its systemic root causes. Homelessness would then be subjected to dialectical theological analysis for the purpose of articulating a theological response to the problem. The results of both social and theological analysis would be utilized strategically for the purpose of designing a pastoral-political response, the aim of which would be the eradication of the causes and conditions of homelessness. This theological process is sometimes referred to as the 'pastoral circle' which incorporates these movements: experience (praxis), social analysis, theological reflection and pastoral-political action (Holland and Henriot 1986: 8).

Another theological approach consistent with the one described above would be to address the issue of homelessness from the perspective of human rights theory. The global concern for human rights is perhaps best exemplified by the Universal Declaration of Human Rights adopted by the United Nations in 1948. The right to adequate shelter is specifically mentioned in Article 25. Consistent with this would be the modern Roman Catholic human rights tradition initiated by *Rerum Novarum* in 1891. Within this tradition, sometimes called the social encyclicals, the right to shelter is protected under a comprehensive rights theory first articulated in detail in *Pacem In Terris* (1963). In this tradition human rights are the minimum conditions necessary to protect and preserve the dignity of the human person.

One could also approach the issue of homelessness from a Biblical perspective. While homelessness is rarely mentioned in the Biblical text one could easily argue that the homeless, along with the resident alien, widow and orphan, are among the *personae miserabiles* of ancient Israel and are deserving of God's compassion and protection. Covenantal responsibilty, clearly and powerfully articulated in the prophetic corpus, indicates that the poor and dispossessed must be primary recipients of justice and righteousness. Perhaps the prophet Isaiah stated it best:

> This, rather, is the fasting I wish: releasing those bound unjustly, untying the thongs of the yoke; Setting free the oppressed, breaking every yoke; Sharing your bread with the hungry, sheltering the oppressed and the homeless; Clothing the naked when you see them, and not turning your back on your own.
>
> (Isaiah 58: 6–7, *New American Bible*)

Regardless of the theological perspective one embraces it is clear that the issue of homelessness is a relevant focus for contemporary theology. Whether in the academic context or in the local parish and congregation, failure to address homelessness and similar social issues places Christianity in a precarious and untenable position. Supporting the right to adequate shelter and working to alleviate the causes and conditions of homelessness is an appropriate and necessary component of lived Christian faith in the hope of building a more just and humane world order.

Cox, John E. (1986) '1987 International Year of Shelter for the Homeless', *Canadian Housing* 3(2).

Department of Housing and Urban Development (HUD) (1984) 'A Report to the Secretary on the Homeless and Emergency Shelters', US Government.

Fallis, George, and Murray, Alex (1990) *Housing the Homeless and Poor*, Toronto: University of Toronto Press.

Holland, Joe and Henriot, Peter (1986) *Social Analysis*, Maryknoll, NY: Orbis Books.

Jenks, Christopher (1944) *The Homeless*, Cambridge, MA: Harvard University Press.

John XXIII, Pope (1963) *Pacem in Terris* (encyclical on world peace), Washington, DC: National Catholic Welfare Council.

Kozol, Jonathon (1988) *Rachel and Her Children*, New York: Crown.

Leo XIII, Pope (1942) *Rerum Novarum* (encyclical on the rights and duties of capital and labour), Washington, DC: National Catholic Welfare Council originally promulgated 1891).

Momeni, Jamshid (ed.) (1990) *Homelessness in the United States: Data and Issues*, New York: Praeger.

Rossi, Peter H. (1989) *Down and Out in America*, Chicago, IL: University of Chicago Press.

Seltser, Barry Jay and Miller, Donald E. (1993) *Homeless Families: the Struggle for Dignity*, Chicago, IL: University of Illinois Press.

Tognoli, Jerome (1987) 'Residential environments', in D. Stokols and I. Altman (eds) *Handbook of Environmental Psychology*, New York: Wiley Interscience.

United Nations (1985) 'International Year of Shelter for the Homeless, Report of the Secretary-General' New York: United Nations Documents.

Russell A. Butkus

HOMOPHOBIA

Homophobia (more properly homo-erotophobia, fear of LOVE between members of the same sex) is a term of recent provenance and was coined initially within the gay and lesbian community to refer to the unreasonable fear of, and hostility toward, those of a sexual orientation or community other than heterosexuality. In particular, it is taken to mean fear of homosexuality, especially of male homosexuality. Such fear is not a rational response to a real threat but an exaggerated anxiety focused on a specific group of people. Probably the first exposition of homophobia is contained in Weinberg (1973). By the homophobic, homosexuals and bisexuals *as a group* are often viewed as pathological, potentially dangerous, probably predatory and capable and likely to corrupt and recruit others (especially the young and impressionable) to their own orientation and practices. Socio-psychologically, such prejudicial attitudes are typified by stereotyping, over-simplification and the projection of undesirable characteristics on to a minority group (much as in the case of ANTI-SEMITISM) in a mode best expounded in *The Authoritarian Personality* (Adorno *et al.* 1950).

Although not identical to it, homophobia is clearly linked to heterosexism, meaning a world-view (and practice) which considers heterosexuality not simply as normative or the most common orientation but as a privileged or the only acceptable orientation. Heterosexism not only defines other sexual orientations as deficient but excludes them as morally or legally impermissible, wrong and 'inherently disordered'. Closely akin to RACISM and SEXISM, use of the term 'heterosexism' implies a view that is cognitively over-simple, ignoring variation within other sexual communities and unprepared in principle to recognize any claim to equality before the law, or in terms of evaluation or esteem. In practical terms it also implies that resources should not be made available to non-heterosexuals, that sexual expression or behaviour other than heterosexuality (if not the propensity itself) should be legally proscribed or constrained to a significant degree, that non-heterosexuals should be forbidden to proselytize or promote their orientation. In brief, that discrimination is permissible against those who are not exclusively heterosexual in orientation.

In social science research attempts to measure homophobia (see Beere 1990) have concentrated on constructing attitude items which tap these constructs. For example, the Smith–Lumby homophobia scale (Smith 1971; Lumby 1976) covers rights of, beliefs about and reactions to homosexuals, including willingness to associate with them, with items such as the following.

- It would be upsetting for me to find out I was alone with a homosexual.
- Homosexuals should be allowed to hold government positions.
- I find the thought of homosexual acts disgusting.
- I would be afraid for a child of mine to have a teacher who was homosexual.

Although used quite extensively, the attempt to measure homophobia has been criticized on both substantive and methodological grounds. Technically, it is doubtful whether such scales are unitary (unidimensional) or measure a coherent single attitude complex. Substantively, Freudians have objected that homophobia does not meet the criteria for a classic phobia, and (on different grounds) social interactionists (see Plummer 1975) have argued that hostility towards homosexuals reflects the outcome of cultural values, beliefs, practices and social interaction rather than any abnormal psychological condition. Such criticisms do not of course diminish the extent of anti-homosexual prejudice and discrimination, nor do they impugn the utility and validity of the concepts of homophobia and heterosexism as descriptive terms, but only the attempt to use them as single explanations for what in fact is a wide variety of negative attitudes and behaviour toward non-heterosexual people (see Hencken 1982). It is significant that virtually all studies of the determinants and consequences of homophobia, however defined, pinpoint religiosity as a major and important correlate.

Traditional responses to homosexuality and bisexuality in mainstream Judaism, Christianity and Islam can certainly be characterized as heterosexist and the attitudes of many, if not most, adherents has been by and large homophobic. Indeed, Christianity could be described as even more heterosexist than it is sexist. Canon Law and Penitential codes in Western Christianity homed in on the notion of sexual activity with those of the same sex as the 'sin against nature' and carried partiality to heterosexuality as far as sanctioning execution as a punishment for homosexual activity (see Bullough and Brundage 1982).

In more recent times official mainstream Church pronouncements and teachings have shown a wide spectrum of attitude and degrees of acceptance of homosexuality, but in general an amelioration is noticeable. Initially this has often taken the form of contrasting the sinfulness of anything other than heterosexuality, but accepting legal toleration for homosexuality, followed by the adoption of a distinction between sexual 'orientation' and 'practice' – the former viewed as morally neutral, the latter as unacceptable. Contemporary positions vary considerably between the proscription of any and every form of homosexual (and auto-erotic) behaviour, combined with a recognition of homosexual orientation as neutral (the official Roman Catholic teaching, and similar to the stance adopted by conservative evangelicals), to one which accepts homosexual activity and orientation and homosexuality as subject to the same moral constraints as heterosexuality.

In contrast, fundamentalist religious organizations have become, if anything, more heterosexist, homophobic and condemnatory, whilst a few extremely liberal or specially-formed denominations (Universalist-Unitarian, Metropolitan Community Church) and special-interest groups and caucuses within established churches have promulgated positive attitudes and behaviour and acceptance of homosexual identity and sexual behaviour as entirely compatible with Christian belief.

The rational and theological debates about the acceptability (or the reverse) of homosexuality in the Christian tradition belong elsewhere (see SEXUALITY and SAME-SEX relations), but some points at issue are likely to remain contentious for some time, including

- whether there can be equality of esteem or acceptability between heterosexuality and other orientations,
- whether the distinction between orientation and practice is sufficient to encompass the complexity of (homo)sexuality – and indeed whether it is a tenable distinction,
- what role choice and preference have in determining the religious acceptability of non-heterosexual behaviour.

These issues are relevant to questions of homophobia and heterosexism both because they pinpoint the ethical issue of choice and determination of sexual orientation on the one hand, and because, if conceded, they could undermine the convenient, but ultimately empirically unsustainable, distinction between sexual activity and affective arousal upon which most theological and ethical debate in Christian circles is currently based.

The admissibility of scientific (and especially social scientific) evidence is also a necessary preliminary to such questions. Historically, and in manyfundamentalist accounts, scientific evidence of any sort is simply irrelevant. Earlier Church reports on sexuality began to accept a medical model as appropriate and accepted some psychological (usually Freudian) contentions as integral to the understanding of sexuality. Increasingly the focus has widened to include anthropological and sociological data, and to this there has been considerable resistance, often because of the (possibly justified) fear that such a perspective will relativize the question of sexuality and point to social conditioning and social construction of sexuality, which makes the exclusive and normative position of heterosexuality hard to sustain.

The distinction between orientation and behaviour was popularized by Kinsey (Kinsey *et al*. 1948), himself a biologist, to contrast the difference between the object of erotic arousal or affectivity (the feelings or dispositional component) and whether and how this was realized in behaviour. Although the two are usually congruent, the distinction made it possible to rationalize a common Christian ethical distinction between the morally neutral 'invert', who could not help acting according to orientation, and the 'pervert' who could, and was thereby condemned ethically. The underlying issue was the aetiology of homosexuality: was it caused by factors outwith a person's control? If so, it could be morally acceptable. Even the most liberal and anti-homophobic Christian positions of acceptance of homosexuality (e.g. Spong 1990) have invoked this argument, normally in the form of genetic determination.

Theological attempts to come to terms with these issues have by and large been dominated not only by the medical model but also by a clearly Western perspective. But if it no longer makes sense to enquire about the aetiology of homosexuality detached from the aetiology of all sexualities and if very different cultural forms of homosexu-ality are shown to exist which do not depend on the idea of a lifelong exclusive or predominant sexual orientation then the traditional arguments for continued discrimination against homosexuals in the Christian community become untenable.

It is probably for this reason that there is scant discussion of bisexuality in Church Reports (and, indeed, in many social science circles) because it implies that because a person is capable of heterosexual relations he or she should desist from homosexual behaviour. It is consequently viewed as more heinous than an exclusively homosexual orientation. Yet empirically bisexual behaviour is almost certainly more common than exclusive homosexuality (Tielman *et al*. 1991). In many cultures the majority of males will have had some sexual contact with other males, and in some cultures all males will have had homosexual contact, even if only for restricted period. Moreover, even among the male gay community the majority of those identifying as (male) gay have experienced vaginal intercourse (Weatherburn *et al*. 1990). Such data make the conventional categories of Christian evaluation of homosexual behaviour much more precarious, and propel the issue of choice and responsibility into the forefront of discussion.

To summarize, homophobia refers primarily to attitudinal hostility to homosexuals, and heterosexism to positive discrimination in favour of normative heterosexuality and against sexual minorities. Both terms have arisen from within the gay community and are strongly influenced (negatively) by the Judaeo-Christian tradition, which has largely created and exhibited these traits historically.

Despite occasional periods of apparent tolerance, Christian history is largely a continuous example of hostility, discrimination and prejudice against homosexuality and homosexuals (especially males). Since the nineteenth century there have been repeated and diverse attempts to define a Christian attitude to homosexuality, but all have been predicated on the unquestioned primacy and normativeness of heterosexuality and focus on the extent to which homosexuality is determined by external factors which would thereby lessen personal responsibility for its practice. The inclusion of scientific evidence and conceptualizations, and the experience of gay men and women themselves, has questioned the relevance of aetiological discussion, shown the wide prevalence of bisexual compared with exclusively homosexual behaviour and thus refocused attention on issues of choice and preference rather than determination of sexual activity and identity. The consequences of such a shift will be to undermine heterosexist opinions by questioning the tenability of exclusive heterosexuality as normative. Homophobic reactions are as likely to increase as to decrease in such a situation, and there will always be those within the Christian tradition who will disavow the relevance of scientific approaches rather than allow sexual minorities to have parity of esteem with heterosexuality. Paradoxically the shift to choice and responsibility will also undermine the liberal approaches that rely on determination and make such approaches also take direct account of gay men and women's accounts and stories in constructing a new Christian interpretation of human sexuality.

Adorno, T.W., Frenkel-Brunswick, E., Levinson, D.J. and Sanford, R.N. (1950) *The Authoritarian Personality*, New York: Harper & Row.

Beere, C.E. (1990) *Sex and Gender Issues: A Handbook of Tests and Measures*, New York: Greenwood.

Bullough, V.L. and Brundage, J. (1982) *Sexual Practices and the Medieval Church*, Buffalo, NY: Prometheus Books.

Hencken, J.D. (1982) 'Homosexuality and psychoanalysis: toward a mutual understanding', in W. Paul, J.D. Weinrich, J.C. Gonsiorek and M.E. Hotvedt (eds) *Homosexuality, Social Psychological and Biological Issues*, London: Sage.

Kinsey, A.C., Pomeroy, W.B. and Martin, C.E. (1948) *Sexual Behavior in the Human Male*, Philadelphia, PA: W.B. Saunders.

Lumby, M.E. (1976) 'Homophobia: the quest for a valid scale', *Journal of Homosexuality* 2: 39–47.

Plummer, K. (1975) *Sexual Stigma: An Interactionist Account*, London: Routledge.

Smith, K.T. (1971) 'Homophobia: a tentative personality profile', *Psychological Reports* 29: 1091–4.

Spong, J.S. (1990) *Living in Sin: A Bishop Re-thinks Human Sexuality*, San Francisco, CA: Harper & Row.

Tielman, R.A.P., Carballo, M. and Hendricks, A. (eds) (1991) *Bisexuality and HIV/AIDS: A Global Perspective*, Buffalo, NY: Prometheus Books.

Weatherburn, P., Davies, P.M., Hunt, A.J., Coxon, A.P.M. and McManus, T.J. (1990) 'Heterosexual behaviour in a large cohort of homosexually active men in England and Wales', *AIDS Care* 2(4): 319–24.

Weinberg, G. (1973) *Society and the Healthy Homosexual*, New York: Anchor Books.

Anthony P.M. Coxon

HOSPITALS

From their origins before AD 400 until the eighteenth century, hospitals were shaped and sustained by Christian concepts of charity and social obligation. Thereafter, Enlightenment views concerning personal responsibility and effective use of resources began to alter these ancient Christian institutions. During the nineteenth and twentieth centuries scientific and technological advances transformed the hospitals and created the modern medical centres that now dominate health care in Europe, America and the developing world. Because of the hospital's long history as an ecclesiastical institution, however, Christian ethical and social ideas still surround the modern medical centre, if not as guiding principles, at least as standards of constructive criticism.

For the purpose of this entry *hospital* will be defined as an institution primarily concerned with caring for the sick and, if possible, curing them. *Hospice* will be used to describe an institution which offered food and shelter to the poor, strangers and the homeless sick, but did not maintain specific services, such as the attentions of a physician, to cure the ill.

From its earliest days, Christianity demanded that its adherents aid sick and needy people. Christians believed that on the last day God would judge according to the LOVE one had shown those in need. Had one fed the hungry, sheltered the homeless, visited the sick? By the early second century bishops such as Polycarp of Smyrna expected Christian clergy to take care of the sick, orphans and widows.

Local Christian clergy were able to assist the unfortunate without any formal charitable institutions until the fourth century. Thereafter, in the eastern Greek-speaking provinces of the Roman Empire the demand for charity became so great, especially in the larger cities, that specialized institutions called *xenodocheia* (hospices) appeared. By the 320s the Church of Antioch operated a hospice to feed and shelter the poor of Syria. By mid-century, the pagan emperor Julian considered hospices a common Christian institution.

Before 360 Christian hospices did not focus attention on the sick, but by the 370s Basil, Bishop of Caesarea in Asia Minor, had opened an institution where physicians and nurses treated patients. Two decades later, Bishop John Chrysostom supervised hospitals in Constantinople where doctors tended the sick. By c.410, the monk Neilos of Ancyra considered the hospital physician a common figure in the Greek Christian world.

These early hospitals thus evolved from simpler hospices by expanding services to include free medical care for needy guests (Latin *hospes*). Hospitals met their expenses from landed endowments, donated by local bishops, wealthy laymen, and even the imperial government.

Hospitals developed most rapidly in the Eastern Roman (Byzantine) Empire, where they had first appeared. By the seventh century the Sampson Hospital of Constantinople had become a sophisticated medical centre with a staff of the city's leading physicians and a specialized ward for eye patients. By the twelfth century Byzantine hospitals had expanded the medical staff and added professional pharmacists.

Hospitals developed more slowly in the Western Roman Empire. Saint Jerome mentioned two small hospitals near Rome c.400. During the early Middle Ages, however, social conditions retarded hospital development. Barbarian invasions from the north and Muslim advances in Africa inhibited political, economic and social life. Few towns survived which could support hospitals. In Charlemagne's domains (768–814), hospitals had not evolved beyond simple hospices. As late as the thirteenth century, hospitals were rare in Europe. None of the 112 houses for the sick in medieval England provided physicians for their patients, nor did they stock any medicines.

In the twelfth century the newly formed military order, the Knights of Saint John, reintroduced into Europe specialized medical care for the sick when they constructed their renowned hospital in Jerusalem. Under Byzantine influence, they employed four doctors and four surgeons for patients. The Jerusalem hospital became famous throughout Europe and inspired new hospitals, notably the Holy Spirit Hospital in Rome and the Hôtel-Dieu in Paris (c.1210).

Only in Italy, however, did hospitals of the Middle Ages and Renaissance evolve into specialized medical centres. Around 1500 Florence supported Santa Maria Nuova, an excellent hospital served by the six best physicians of the community. On the other hand, as late as the eighteenth century many hospitals of northern Europe were still poorly equipped hospices. The deficient care available to the poor in such institutions led Enlightenment thinkers to attack hospitals as more harmful than helpful. When Jacques Tenon exposed the horrible conditions at the Hôtel-Dieu in Paris, he fuelled further criticism.

Enlightenment thinkers levelled two charges at the Christian hospitals. First, such institutions did not efficiently treat disease, partly because the latest medical discoveries were as yet imperfectly disseminated but partly too because Christian charity was motivated more by the desire of the giver to win his or her salvation than by the sincere wish to benefit the sick. Second, by providing free medical care, food and shelter, Christian hospitals encouraged laziness and wasted society's resources in rescuing the improvident from their fate. A. Robert Turgot criticized the opulent Italian hospitals as one cause of that region's economic problems.

During the nineteenth and twentieth centuries hospitals have been transformed from philanthropic, religious institutions into vast medical centres with a secular orientation. Even hospitals still run by religious denominations have experienced such a transformation. Hospitals made these changes partly in response to Enlightenment criticism but more as the natural result of medical and technological advances. As complicated surgical therapies achieved greater success, as more effective aseptic techniques were discovered to prevent infection and as new and expensive equipment proved its value, neither the doctor in his office nor the ordinary patient in his home could provide the best care. Increasingly, all patients – rich, poor, middle class – needed hospitals for complicated procedures. By 1900, hospitals were becoming the centres of the medical profession.

As hospitals supported ever more costly medical technology and burgeoning staffs, their expenses rose. Since patients increasingly belonged to more affluent classes, hospitals came to expect them to pay for their care. Government insurance plans in Europe and private insurance in the USA allowed hospitals to shift financial responsibility for care from their own endowments to patients' resources. Thus, in twentieth-century America even church hospitals expect patients to pay. In Europe, patients also pay, but through compulsory national health programmes.

We have seen that modern hospitals have turned from the initial commitment to provide free medical care and now are increasingly concerned with generating income. In the USA corporations have even begun operating specialized hospitals for profit and commercially advertising their sophisticated therapies. The majority of community hospitals, however, still consider themselves charities and insist that the profits they accrue are used only to meet the rising costs of staff salaries and of more advanced equipment. In both Europe and the USA hospital costs have, in fact, risen dramatically. In 1991, France tried to control expenses by regulating pharmaceutical prices and rejecting the demands of striking nurses for salary increases.

The costs of modern hospital care have soared, but more expensive care has brought more successful therapy. One cannot realistically demand a return to the free care of earlier institutions. Nevertheless, a civilized SOCIETY should not allow hospitals to sell their services in a free market just as restaurants and hotels do, nor should it accept physicians, nurses and other health professionals who view their work as simply another service commodity. A reconsideration of the Christian hospital tradition cannot provide ready-made solutions, but it offers some different and valuable perspectives.

From the beginning, charity was the fundamental virtue of Christian ethics (1 Corinthians 13: 13), but administering philanthropy sometimes posed problems since the unscrupulous easily feigned poverty to gain support from the Christian community. The plight of the physically ill, however, gave rise to far fewer suspicions. By the fourth century, Christian writers saw the difficult labours of caring for the sick as the very embodiment of self-sacrificing love.

This concept of charity sustained Christian hospitals from 400 to 1800. It moved Byzantine emperors such as Justinian (sixth century) and John II (twelfth century) to support lavish hospitals in Constantinople, it inspired the father of Dante's Beatrice to found Santa Maria Nuova in thirteenth-century Florence, and it fuelled the remarkable proliferation of volunteer hospitals in eighteenth-century England.

Almost as important as charity in sustaining hospitals was civic pride. According to the tradition of the Classical World, wealthy citizens had a moral obligation to provide their cities with the amenities of urban life – baths, theatres, animal shows, etc. When the Greco-Roman empire became Christian during the fourth century, bishops succeeded in channelling this traditional virtue in new directions. Christian civic pride ought not to sustain the luxuries of pagan urban life but the virtue of love for one another. One concrete expression of such love was to provide hospitals for the city's poor.

The Greco-Roman virtue of civic pride, redirected by the Christian Fathers, provided the social context for the practice of charity, a context which helped to prevent the self-centred giving so maligned by the Enlightenment critics of Christian philanthropy. In those regions of Europe where urban community spirit remained vital, hospitals were less likely to deteriorate because donors in those regions were concerned not only with their own spiritual well-being but also with the practical impact of their deeds. In sixteenth-century Florence, community pride in the city's hospitals maintained such clean and efficient medical centres that patient recovery rates reportedly reached 90 per cent.

Charity not only motivated hospital benefactors; it also inspired staff members from supervisors to kitchen help. The ninth-century Byzantine monk Theodore Stoudites described how all ranks of hospital physicians and support personnel strove to carry out the divine command of love. In founding the twelfth-century Pantokrator hospital in Constantinople, the Emperor John II reminded the staff that the sick were God's special friends and that caring for patients was more important than maintaining buildings. According to their twelfth-century rule, the Knights of Saint John were to treat patients at their hospital in Jerusalem and in their infirmaries throughout Europe just as vassals faithfully served feudal lords.

Such exhortations do not mean that medieval patients were always treated well. A poem written in Constantinople c.1300 implies that hospital employees sometimes attacked patients. In fifteenth-century England, the director of Saint Mary's Bethlehem was found guilty of terrorizing the sick and stealing valuables from the institution. Despite these aberrations, which might have been more common than the sources indicate, pre-modern hospitals offered their employees incomparable opportunities for the practice of Christian virtue.

Christian communities must revivify the concept of a divine calling, or divine opportunity, to perform the labours of charity. Physicians, nurses, orderlies and hospital maintenance personnel share a sacred mission to serve suffering humanity and the community. Hospital service embodies both the Christian ethical command to love one's neighbour and the classical concept of civic duty. Significant improvement in hospitals requires a shift away from business modes of thought and a return to Christian and classical ideals of virtue.

Today's hospital administrators have not been inclined to examine the ancient hospital traditions of Christian Europe because of the prevailing view that poorly equipped, premodern asylums for the sick have absolutely nothing in common with present-day medical centres. Such a view has its origins in Enlightenment scepticism concerning religious institutions. In 1690 John Locke contrasted the benefits science had offered to humanity with the inefficiency of charitable institutions. The preeminence of science over philanthropy became a central theme in attacks on traditional charity launched by French physiocrats and other eighteenth-century thinkers. The historical record, however, does not support such attacks. Though charitable hospitals in Northern Europe and in the English colonies offered patients minimal care, medieval and Renaissance institutions in Constantinople, Florence and other Italian cities did effectively treat the ill. With their well-trained staff physicians, Florentine hospitals c.1500 achieved remarkable cure rates. At Padua during the sixteenth century the Hospital of Saint Francis became a centre of medical studies where the best physicians of Europe supervised patient therapies.

In the Italian cities, therefore, no gulf existed between charitable hospitals and the advance of scientific medicine. In fact, hospital service formed a vital link in the training and professional development of physicians. North of the Alps this link was not forged until the eighteenth century. Only then did physicians in Northern Europe gradually realize the importance of hospitals for clinical observation of disease. That Locke and other intellectuals perceived Christian charitable institutions as opposed to the enlightened study of nature springs more from the accidents of institutional development in northern Europe than from any fundamental discord between the principles of science and the tenets of traditional philanthropy.

The central moral issue facing modern hospitals is accessibility. A cursory review of hospital history reveals how this institution has its moral grounding in charity and civic duty. Technological advances and increasing bureaucratization have obscured the hospital's obligation to treat every sick person regardless of insurance status or personal wealth. In addition, today's hospitals face other moral questions. In fact, since they have become the principal theatres of medical practice, every moral problem facing modern medicine is usually addressed in a hospital setting. Should hospitals permit ABORTION and EUTHANASIA? When can one ethically withhold nutrition and hydration from comatose patients? How far are hospitals morally obligated to provide extraordinary therapies to terminal patients? How are hospitals to handle newborns with severe birth defects? The very size of modern hospitals and their bureaucratic structures have made these many moral questions more difficult to address.

Bylebyl, Jerome J. (1982) 'Commentary', in Lloyd G. Stevenson (ed.) *A Celebration of Medical History*, Baltimore, MD and London: Johns Hopkins University Press, pp. 200–11.

Forrest, Alan (1981) *The French Revolution and the Poor*, New York: St Martin's Press.

Granshaw, Lindsay and Porter, Roy (ed.) (1989) *The Hospital in History*, London: Routledge.

Miller, Timothy S. (1978) 'The Knights of Saint John and the hospitals of the Latin West,' *Speculum* 53: 709–33.

——(1985) *The Birth of the Hospital in the Byzantine Empire*, Baltimore, MD and London: Johns Hopkins University Press.

Starr, Paul (1982) *The Social Transformation of American Medicine: The Rise of a Sovereign Profession and the Making of a Vast Industry*, New York: Basic Books.

Stevens, Rosemary (1989) *In Sickness and in Wealth: American Hospitals in the Twentieth Century*, New York: Basic Books.

Thompson, John D. and Goldin, Grace (1975) *The Hospital: A Social and Architectural History*, New Haven, CT: Yale University Press.

Timothy S. Miller

HOSTAGE

The term 'hostage' is developed from the Latin *obsid*. It is found in Middle English as *ostage*. The 'h' as 'hostage' appears to have been added to show the relation between the root term in Middle English and the terms for hospitality, where hospitality is the protection given to a stranger; to one who is an enemy; *hostis*, not *amicus*. By extension the terms 'hospital', 'hospice', 'hostice', 'hostel' are places where the stranger is given protection. The idea of hospitality is widespread, ranging well beyond Western custom and practice. In tribal or tribally based societies that lacked a state or common power, the giving of hospitality, and with hospitality protection, was fundamental. This is seen most clearly in the account in the Hebrew Bible of the fall of Sodom and Gomorrah. Here it was the failure to provide hospitality to strangers that was the fundamental error for which the cities were destroyed. Such weight on the giving of hospitality and protection even to an enemy is still seen as fundamental to the tribal cultures of the Middle East today, showing even now the basic distinction between *hostis* and *amicus*. To take a hostage, to fail to give protection even to an enemy that is within one's midst as a guest, is a fundamental breach of protocol in both ancient and modern times. In Roman times to fail to give that protection to a guest or to make a sacrifice is *host*. As Christ was given as a sacrifice the term *host* is used of him. It may refer particularly to his body as that was given as sacrifice. By transubstantiation or by symbolization (depending on belief) that body recurs in the EUCHARIST, as real or as symbol, and the term host refers to the bread or wafer offered as the body of Christ. The idea of the enemy (*echthros*) and of enmity (*echthra*) occurs frequently in the New Testament where it may be derived from the idea of the outside(r). Enmity and enemy are strictly quite distinct notions: the former relates to a disposition, the latter to a structure. To be *hostis*, enemy, was to be in a situation of public opposition; one might like someone with whom one was *hostis* whereas to be in a condition of enmity is to show an adverse disposition towards them. In that sense enmity is opposed to *agape*, to LOVE. In most interpretations, therefore, *hostis* is the public position, not the private. The distinction is important for hostages, if taken, are taken and held for public not private advantage. A person held for private advantage has been kidnapped. Hostages may, without contradiction, be personally liked by the holders and well treated. Indeed to hold a hostage with the proper honour internal to that practice is to hold the hostage well and without personal rancour. Even so the taking and holding of hostages runs counter to basic tenets of hospitality and must be regarded as both a serious breach of protocol, ancient and modern, and an act of desperation. In recent years the taking of hostages appears to have increased and moved beyond the confines of wars or conflict between states or parties in a civil war. Hostages are now held following the hijacking of aircraft, trains and other modes of transport. This has resulted in holding individuals who would otherwise have been regarded as guests and entitled, therefore, to protection. Hostages may be taken by states as by Iran or Iraq in the latter part of this century or by groups. Terry Waite, John McCarthy, Brian Keenan are well-known recent examples of individuals taken by non-state groups in an attempt to influence actions of STATE. That they have resorted to such serious breaches of protocol indicates either the breakdown of normal procedures for dealing with conflict or desperation or both. Hostages are often treated according to imperatives relating to their treatment. They are not necessarily well treated, but it is unusual for every kind of mistreatment to occur. In its own public relations the government of Iraq

declared the hostages taken immediately before the outbreak of formal hostilities between itself and the West as 'guests'. On the face of it this may seem strange but it did seem to indicate some residual, if minimal, retention of codes relating to the treatment of that which is *hostis*.

The long history of the taking and holding of hostages has given rise to a number of understandings and practices that have manifested themselves in laws and treaties. The protection in law afforded to hostages depended until recently on whether an armed conflict was in progress at the time they were taken. Until 1945, it seemed that taking hostages on occasion might be a legitimate war-time reprisal. Reprisals are breaches of the laws of war justified as countering previous breaches by the other side. During the 1870 Franco-Prussian War, when the French imprisoned officers from Prussian merchantmen, Bismarck, alleging that these actions were unlawful, ordered the imprisonment of forty citizens of occupied France. The hope was that these 'hostages' would deter further French violations (Best 1983). During the Second World War, the German army in occupied territories shot hostages as a reprisal for acts of sabotage by resistance fighters and in the post-war trials such killings were not universally condemned. Moreover, laying siege to a city, a military practice seen from the time of Troy to the time of Sarajevo, was standard military practice, even if this effectively turned its citizens into hostages. To meet this issue, the Talmudic Law of Sieges, according to the twelfth-century philosopher Maimonides, required that a city be surrounded on three sides only to allow the civilians to flee (Walzer 1977). It was only in the Nuremberg trials and in the subsequent 1949 Geneva Conventions on the Laws of War that the taking and killing of hostages, even by way of reprisal, was prohibited.

Not all hostages are taken in armed conflicts or in clearly defined armed conflicts. The United Nations Convention against the Taking of Hostages (1979) attempts to deal with this and provides for the punishment of hostage-takers. The definition of a hostage can be implied from the Convention's description of the crime. A hostage is someone who is detained and threatened with death, injury or continuing incarceration in order to compel a third party, namely, a State, an international intergovernmental organisation, a natural or juridical person, or a group of persons, to do or abstain from doing any act as an explicit or implicit condition for [the hostage's] release.

(Article 1)

According to the Preamble to the Convention, being taken as a hostage is a violation of the fundamental HUMAN RIGHTS to life, liberty and security of the person.

These legal definitions are victim-neutral, in that they do not concern themselves with the person of the hostage, whereas the general understanding of a hostage as *hostis* retains the original conception that there is no personal enmity. The hostage is personally innocent, but is being used as part of a bargain. Indeed, the very innocence of hostages, their lack of involvement in the dispute between the hostage-takers and those being intimidated, may well increase the moral pressure to submit to the various demands.

The concept of the hostage as innocent victim begs two questions. First, in time of war in the past, it may be that the person taken hostage by way of reprisal actively supported the resistance to the occupying forces. The very fact that the victims may not have been actively participating in the conflict when they were detained, that they were publicly and personally innocent, questions the justification of action against that person. Second, radical revolutionaries have argued that no-one is innocent – if one is not part of the solution through active participation in the disobedience to the state, then one is part of the problem. Nevertheless, SOCIETY has rejected such extreme views in favour of according innocence to the non-actor. Even extremists seem to accept this when they distinguish between legitimate and non-legitimate targets.

The taking of persons as hostage, as the Preamble to the 1979 Convention indicates, violates those persons' human rights, their very humanity. The definition in the 1979 Convention implies that the hostage is a mere means to an end, an asset to be used. As such, it is a denial of the idea, best formulated by Kant as recognition of human beings, of rational beings, as ends in themselves. As ends in themselves they possess dignity. To destroy that is to deny their personhood and to deny their humanity. It is to reject a significant part of God's plan for God's own creation as that has come to be understood in Christian THEOLOGY. Thomas Paine, himself a deist, wrote in the *Rights of Man* (1791) that human rights stem from the fact that 'man came [originally] from the hand of his Maker. What was he then? Man. Man was his high and only title, and a higher cannot be given him.' As Genesis 1: 27 puts it: 'So God created man in his own image'. And as William Temple wrote in 1941:

> There can be no Rights of Man except on the basis of faith in God. But if God is real, and all men are his sons, that is the true worth of every one of them. My worth is what I am worth to God; and that is a marvellous great deal, for Christ died for me.
>
> (pp. 74–5)

If reduction to a mere asset, to a mere means to some other end, undercuts the hostages' God-given image, then their innocent suffering mirrors that of Christ. The New Testament as a whole is full of references to Christ's innocence and his fulfilling of God's laws; the innocent Lamb of God slain as a ransom price for our sin. '[By] knowledge of him, my righteous servant will justify many, and he will bear their iniquities. . . . For he bore the sin of many, and made intercession for the transgressors' (Isaiah 53: 11–12 cf. Mark 15: 28). However, the analogy should not be drawn too far, for, first, the ransom spoken of in Mark 10: 45 is merely to indicate the great price that had to be paid for our salvation, and second, Christ willingly gave himself into His suffering. Nevertheless, as with many instances where Christians try to account for the problems of today, those facets of innocence and suffering seen in Christ's life will be applied to the situation of hostages.

The aspects of our CULTURE and its predecessors towards hospitality and sacrifice ensure that the taking of hostages will continue to be condemned, now as it has been for many millennia. The infinite value of human life and innocence of the victim mean that the crime of hostage-taking will not readily be eradicated – it is too effective. In this respect the attitudes of Western states have predominantly if not consistently been to refuse to deal with hostage-takers. The temptation is strong for groups that have grievances perceived by them, rightly or wrongly, as unsettlable within state structures to take hostages. Similarly the temptation of states to ignore, as best they can, the taking of their citizens as hostages is also strong. It is also not always possible for states to do this, as was seen in President Carter's failed attempt to release hostages held in Iran. All that can be hoped is that, in time of peace and war, hostage-takers will treat their hostages well, as hostage not as enemy, that those taking hostages will be punished for their crimes and that the institutional procedures of international criminal law will be in place to put this into effect.

Best, G. (1983) *Humanity in Warfare*, London: Methuen.
Milne, B. (1982) *Know the Truth*, Leicester: Inter-Varsity Press.
Packer, J.I. (1973) *Knowing God*, Downers Grove, IL: Inter-Varsity Press.
Roberts, A. and Guelff, R. (1989) *Documents on the Laws of War*, 2nd edn, Oxford: Clarendon.
Stott, J. (1984) *Issues Facing Christians Today*, Basingstoke: Marshalls.
Temple, W. (1941) *Citizen and Churchman.*
United Nations, International Convention against the Taking of Hostages 1979 (1979) 18 *International Legal Material* 1456–63.
Walzer, M. (1977) *Just and Unjust Wars*, New York: Basic Books.

Geoff Gilbert
Paul Barry Clarke

HUMAN RIGHTS

The political and cultural homogenization of the globe during the past century has placed a premium on the acceptance and implementation of norms that might give effect to a peaceful, inclusive comity of nations. The norms that today enjoy the nearly universal assent of nations are those enunciating human rights and the correlative duties of governments and citizens. This entry reviews the status of human rights in LAW and in world opinion, examines their historical origin and development, and discusses practical obstructions to their realization.

The concept of human rights derives from Western traditions concerning the dignity of PERSONS, which expanded from an initial base of civil rights to include, in recent times, social, economic and cultural rights. The commanding current perspective on human rights as the ethical and legal basis of a comity of nations is the United Nations Charter and a succession of rights declarations since the promulgation of the Universal Declaration of Human Rights (1948). These include declarations on racial discrimination, forced labour and SLAVERY, GENOCIDE, minorities and multiculturalism, civil rights, the rights of women, children, prisoners and detainees, refugees and stateless persons, and the rights of civilian populations under the rules of war. The Universal Declaration elaborates the human rights that were merely mentioned in the UN Charter. Declarations after the Universal Declaration are meant to elucidate or emphasize rights contained in the former, or else to draw out new implications not previously addressed.

In addition to UN declarations, there are a number of regional statements from African, Asian and Latin American nations. The Organization of American States proclaimed the American Declaration of the Rights and Duties of Man in 1948. An Inter-American Convention on Human Rights providing for a court of human rights was drafted in 1959 and subsequently implemented. The declaration that has enjoyed on-going institutional effect is the Council of Europe's Convention for Protection of Human Rights and Fundamental Freedoms (1950) and the European Social Charter (1961). These two declarations were linked to UN declarations as a supportive 'collective guarantee' of the UN Declaration. The Social Charter concerns primarily economic and social rights relevant to conditions of employment and work. The application of these rights is overseen by the European Commission on Human Rights and the European Court of Human Rights. In the early years of its operation, only ten of the then fifteen member states allowed citizens to petition the Commission. The Council now comprises twenty-three member states, embracing

417 million persons, most of whom may petition the Commission.

The legal status of the UN Charter and declarations is complex. The Charter was conceived as a multilateral treaty whose clauses include provision for arbitration of conflicts and sanctions against non-compliance. The Declaration, by contrast, is not a treaty but 'a common standard'. Nations interpret their obligations under the Charter and Declaration differently. The optimal relation, from the UN perspective, is that obligations incurred under treaties are binding in member nation's domestic law and hence are enforceable in domestic courts. Where this arrangement is in effect, citizens may claim relief under provisions of UN declarations. The high courts of Australia, Canada and a few other nations have indeed endorsed this relationship on specific issues, but such nations are few and the scope of such obligation is narrowly defined. Generally speaking the courts of most nations accept petitions from citizens only under domestic laws. In OECD countries, this legal obstruction has been resolved by establishing domestic human rights commissions bearing a brief drawn from the UN Declaration, or by establishing, in the case of Europe, a regional human rights commission. Such avenues of surveillance and appeal tend to be unavailable in nations where human rights violations are most serious. The UN Charter provides for sanctions, including military intervention as a last resort, against nations in flagrant violation of the UN Charter. However, decisions to use force can be taken only by the Security Council, whose five permanent members each have a veto. Owing to rivalries among the permanent members, the military sanction has been approved only twice. The General Assembly can approve economic and political sanctions, but they are also rarely invoked. The sanctions of longest duration were against South Africa for its racial discrimination laws. In addition, the United Nations and its agencies have generated a large body of treaty law by putting into effect conventions on the limited subjects mentioned above.

Since 1955, the UN Commission on Human Rights has sought to induce a process of gradual compliance by establishing reporting routines, advisory services and regional conferences on recent experience with specific rights. The reporting routine involves a triennial report by member states on progress toward safe-guarding and implementing specific rights. Members are invited to set human rights targets and to devise action programmes. The targets and action are assessed at the triennium's end and new targets are set. The objective is to engraft such procedures into the political processes of member states so that they become self-sustaining.

Progress in securing human rights can be measured in part by the support and collaboration that the United Nations has been able to attract. Regional human rights activities have been mentioned. But non-governmental organizations have played a continuing and at times decisive role in the promotion of rights. Amnesty International, founded in 1961, works closely with the United Nations. Its secretariat and large worldwide membership is dedicated to securing the release of political prisoners and to the prevention of torture and cruel punishments, including the death penalty, which it opposes. It also opposes the involvement of physicians in the administration of punishments in the guise of therapy and their involvement as executioners of death penalties. Amnesty International has highlighted the plight of political prisoners in many nations. Acting on the advice of political prisoners themselves, the organization has found that media exposure of the plight of specific individuals is often effective in securing their release and reducing abuses of others who remain in detention.

Churches have been major advocates of human rights. The Roman Church historically opposed the modern doctrine of rights because it sanctioned the separation of the STATE from the church. This attitude was comprehensively expressed in Pius IX's Syllabus of Errors, which condemned many rationalist propositions. However, this position was reversed by Leo XIII, whose *Inscrutabili* (1878) and *Libertas* (1888) laid down the fundamental principles for teaching on MARRIAGE, church–state relations, industrial relations, national self-determination and other questions. In 1938 eight racist propositions were condemned and the Church's numerous historical condemnations of slavery were reaffirmed. Such documents signify recognition that moral theology shared important practical ground with the modern doctrine of human dignity. The *rapprochement* culminated in John XXIII's *Pacem in Terris* (1963), which interpreted rights doctrine along traditional natural law lines. The Encyclical asserted the foundation for any society to be 'that every human being is a person; his nature is endowed with intelligence and free will. By virtue of this, he has rights and duties of his own, flowing directly and simultaneously from his very nature, which are therefore universal, inviolable and inalienable.' The Papal Commission, Justitia et Pax (1963), was charged with collecting evidence on human rights abuses and promoting human rights from the resources of the Church. The effects have been felt especially in Latin America, where LIBERATION THEOLOGY expressed one interpretation of *Pacem in Terris*, and in Eastern Europe, particularly the Polish Solidarity Movement.

The WORLD COUNCIL OF CHURCHES (WCC) and its member confessions have been equally committed to human rights. The Report of the Nairobi Assembly of the WCC (1974) linked the promotion of human rights with the promotion of struggles for liberation from colonial dominance in the Third World. Other WCC statements highlighted the right to life and a minimal level of economic well-being, the rights of minorities to maintain their cultural identities, and civil rights, including freedom of religion.

Human rights are the legacy of the natural rights tradition in Anglo-American and French political thought. The Petition of Right (1628), the Convention Settlement (1689), the Declaration of Independence (1776) and the Declaration of the Rights of Man and Citizen (1789) may be viewed as stages of politico-ethical development that for the moment peaks in the Universal Declaration. Its Preamble states that the 'foundation of freedom, justice and peace in the world' is 'recognition of the inherent dignity and of the equal and inalienable rights of all members of the human family'. Article 1 declares that human beings are 'born free and equal in dignity and rights', and the exercise of these rights is deemed to be incompatible with discrimination on the basis of race, colour, sex,

language, religion, political opinion, national or social origin, PROPERTY, birth or other status.

Modern rights doctrine is an outgrowth of Roman and medieval natural law teaching. Natural lawyers hold that the correct rule for conduct is found by discerning the nature of humankind, inclusive of social relationships, and the nature of the common good that the good nurture of human beings seeks to sustain. The precepts of natural lawyers were to live honestly, to harm no-one and to give each his or her due. An elaborate corpus, including a law of nations (international law), was developed from this basis. Modern rights doctrine continues the rational search of 'nature' for rules of conduct, as well as the commitment to the rule of law cherished by natural lawyers. However, Thomas Hobbes and others reconceptualized 'nature' to make it more consistent with the mechanical concept of nature and the experimental method that displaced the Aristotelian heritage. In the modern scheme, Aristotle's teleological human nature is replaced by the impetus, or force, of appetition, so that the most powerful appetites define human ends. Appetition is assessed to be selfish and non-moral. The 'state of nature' is imagined as an actual or impending chaos of competing selfish appetites, both between and within individuals. This procedure strips away all conventional distinctions of merit and status, and places each on an equal footing as self-interested individuals. This 'equality in vice' defines the common humanity. Order is brought from the chaos by methodic identification of a rational priority of appetites or wills, enumerated by John Locke as life, liberty and property (and by the Universal Declaration as 'life, liberty and the security of person'). These are called 'natural rights', meaning those desires for which human beings persistently assert themselves and call 'right'. An artificial order is imposed conceptually on the chaos by deeming that self-interested individuals contract together to secure life, liberty, property and other such liberties as are practicable. This contract legitimates the political use of force to protect the rights of each. It also establishes a cosmopolitan rule of law regime limited by the unalienable natural right of each to defend life and liberty. 'Natural right' denotes the irrepressible natural impetus of each to conserve his own life. In this way the modern doctrine replaces the natural lawyers' priorities of the human good and the common good by the priorities of individual liberty. The human good is defined by liberties, i.e. the maximum feasible realization of appetition and will. The common humanity, initially defined as selfishness, is defined in the civic state as equality in legally sanctioned liberties. This orientation displaces the natural lawyers' articulation of a prescriptive model of the virtuous life by identifying moral goodness with law-abidingness. Similarly, the common good is not a substantive notion of a community well ordered by differentiation of status and religious cohesion, but is the sum of individuals goods, meaning the maximum of liberty compatible with public order understood as protection against the appetitive invasions of others, including GOVERNMENT. This is a dynamic, open-ended concept repugnant to traditional natural law. Equality and contract undercut the identity of persons by status, age, sex, nationality and religion, and substitute a uniform concept of the individual or person as a free appetitive contracting party. The dynamism of modern personhood lies in its epistemological, experiential and political openness. Just as in natural science 'nature' is a research object whose attributes multiply as investigation progresses, so in moral and political science 'human nature' is a research object whose attributes multiply as study and experience progress. The structure of appetition that comprises the human 'nature' invoked in modern rights doctrine describes only the attributes relevant to political order. Its experiential and political dynamism is its capacity to add new attributes to the structure of desire and its amenability to individual or group interpretation. But it is opposed to the legal prescription of virtue, or the proscription of any way of life on grounds other than public safety and harm to others. This is the core of modern rights secularism.

Historically, secularism was expressed as advocacy of religious toleration, freedom of speech and opposition to prescribed conformity. The central argument for toleration was that the schism in Christendom starkly revealed the general truth that the religious community is an artifact of forced conformity. The counter argument that community is necessary for social cohesion was rebutted by the politics of interest group competition and new designs for government organization which enjoyed their efflorescence in the constitution-making of the American and French Revolutions. The American political system proved to be capable of sustaining an unprecedented rate of economic expansion and population diversity, foreshadowed in its political philosophy of rights. It is characteristic that a succession of Presidents have singled out the universality of human rights as the moral cosmopolitanism of the comity of nations.

The critique of community in the name of liberty cannot be said to have entirely succeeded intellectually or practically. A few enduring points of tension may be noted. The most conspicuous perhaps is the social paradox of the American and French revolutionary performances. Rights claims were made simultaneously in the name of individual freedom and a vision of the morally consecrated nation. American colonials beheld the vision of the incorrupt new world making a new beginning on behalf of mankind. The French vision was a mingled Christian and classical aspiration to moral regeneration. In both cases 'revolution' evoked allegiance to community goods, beginning with the right of national self-determination and extending into the higher reaches of heroic sacrifice and prescribed civic virtue. The revolution concept was adopted by movements for national independence and national salvation. In nineteenth-century Europe and Latin America, 'nation' might designate an ethno-linguistic group with no tradition of political independence. In the era of decolonialization, when many peoples lacking a political history commenced nation-building, ethnic solidarity and religion were often the main forces of national cohesion. Thus within the United Nations comity the paradox arises that the social systems for whose benefit human rights are most insistently pressed are least susceptible to the individualist rights ethos. In those settings, freedom of speech involves what is culturally perceived as BLASPHEMY or insolence toward AUTHORITY, a response particularly marked in China, Japan and the Middle East. Sexual equality is perceived nearly everywhere outside the West as unnatural, an insult to the dignity of both sexes, contrary to religion or immemorial custom, and disruptive of the established division of labour. In India, whose population is nearly one-fifth the world total, the caste system and the religious justification of ineradicable inequality and rituals of purity are wholly at odds with modern rights doctrine. Such divergence between human rights norms and the norms of most non-Western social systems encouraged Third World initiatives to develop, under the umbrella of human rights, a new style of collective rights, called 'solidarity rights'. Under solidarity rights, the human rights of individuals may be curtailed in the interest of the community. Solidarity rights are in effect the claim of non-Western cultures to persist in their ethnic patterns and practices, including the age, sex and social status differentiations typical of pre-modern societies.

The claims of community have also been raised by the many varieties of SOCIALISM that arose as a criticism of the individualist philosophy of rights. Auguste Comte, the father of Positivism and staunch defender of community, originated the idea that individualism was a necessary stage in human cultural evolution, which he associated with industrial production and the primacy of scientific method. He interpreted the Reformation as the initial manifestation of individualist rationalism. Karl Marx modified Comte by claiming that the individualist philosophy was the intellectual expression of the industrial organization of labour and associated freedom of contract. Marx accepted that modern rights doctrine was a true expression of progressive human freedom, but it remained 'abstract', conceived as the attributes of individuals in isolation from social relations. It was necessary to give this will to freedom concrete expression through the abolition of all impediments to willing created by the will in its successive objectification of previous wills; property and the law guarding it are foremost among such objectifications.

Soviet Marxism achieved power through a vehicle, the totalitarian party, that gave maximum effect to the will to destroy constraints on the will. Yet what it achieved was not what the Marxist vision of human freedom willed. In its Stalinist phase, the Soviet state was machinery for the maximum accumulation of disposable political and military force. In its post-Stalinist phase, it settled into an institutionally based patrimonial regime, dominated by elder males linked in a Byzantine maze of patronage based on the ethnic dominance of the Rus. When this regime weakened, the call for reform was expressed in the idiom of rights, including the right to ethnic self-determination. This experience indicates that the rights doctrine is not the expression of a particular social organization of work and property but is instead the articulate voice of cosmopolitan liberty audible, to some degree, in every complex culture.

INTERNATIONAL RELATIONS specialists do not generally believe that human rights provides a sufficient basis for a world order. The standards they declare are in many particulars incompatible with the social structure of Third World nations. Additionally, OECD nations experience increasing difficulty in honouring the commitment to multiculturalism, since various cultures express incompatible standards. The ABORTION issue aptly expresses the dilemma. Numerous declarations assert the sanctity of life, and the Convention on the Rights of the Child states that the right to life commences before birth. Yet the United Nations, under the influence of OECD countries, supports abortion as a means of POPULATION CONTROL. Population control is believed to be a necessity for social and environmental reasons. Thus, an extreme and cruel individual human rights violation is accepted practice for the sake of a collective good. The abortion case shows that the observance of any human right is contingent upon political judgements as to its consilience with a perceived common good.

Amnesty International Handbook 1983 (1983) London: Amnesty International Publications.

Donnelly, Jack (1989) *Universal Human Rights in Theory and Practice*, Ithaca, NY: Cornell University Press.

European Commission on Human Rights (1984) *Stocktaking on the European Convention on Human Rights*, Strasbourg: European Commission on Human Rights.

Finnis, John (1986) *Natural Law and Natural Rights*, Oxford: Oxford University Press.

Hannum, Hurst (ed.) (1984) *Guide to International Human Rights Practice*, Philadelphia, PA: University of Pennsylvania Press.

Howard, Rhoda E. (1986) *Human Rights in Commonwealth Africa*, Totowa, NJ: Rowman & Littlefield.

Laqueur, Walter and Rubin, Barry (eds) (1979) *The Human Rights Reader*, New York: New American Library.

Ramcharan, B.G. (1979) *Human Rights: Thirty Years After the Universal Declaration*, The Hague: Nijhoff.

The European Convention on Human Rights (1989) Strasbourg: Council of Europe.

Vincent, R.J. (1986) *Human Rights and International Relations*, Cambridge: Cambridge University Press.

Hiram Caton

HUMANISM

The term 'humanism' has had almost as many different shades of meaning as there have been human beings to use it. Purists use it to describe a cultural development characteristic of the European Renaissance, the period from the fourteenth to the sixteenth centuries. This humanism was in part a product of a particular kind of study of the humanities, in part a celebration of the human capacity for achievement in the arts and in the intellectual field. The 'rebirth' of intellect and CULTURE was, in great part, a recovery of the achievements of the classical Graeco-Roman era, in sculpture, in writing, in oratory, politics and philosophy. Even the sciences were not excluded from it; some of the great Renaissance figures were recoverers of forgotten facts of medicine or physics, as passionate in their concern for science as for the humanities. In art the recovery of the classical style involved also a revived delight in the beauty of the three-dimensional human form. It was in that sense that the Renaissance could also be described as a rediscovery of the joy of being human.

How far this involved putting humanity, rather than God, in the centre of everything is itself disputed. Many interpreters of the Renaissance have argued that humanism was essentially a secularizing movement which promoted an amoral INDIVIDUALISM and undermined traditional religious values. But there are other scholars who have argued that it was an authentically Christian cultural tradition.

In a sense the history of the term 'humanism' has reflected this disagreement as much as has the debate about human endeavour and divine initiative within Christian THEOLOGY itself. Thus the term is sometimes used to reject any supernaturalist view of humanity or of its place in the universe. This version of humanism is sometimes called 'scientific' humanism and essentially asserts that humanity has a dignity and worth of its own, quite independent of its being thought of as the creation of a divine creator: human beings possess, in reason, the faculty for realizing their own potential. Humanists, in this sense, regard human beings as responsible, capable of intellectual progress, and therefore competent to solve the problems of their species rationally and on its own terms. Thus the British Humanist Association is a society whose members are agnostic in matters of religious belief. Precisely which modern school of philosophical thought has been most closely associated with secular humanism is a matter of some dispute. In the twentieth century there have been both Christian and humanist forms of existentialist thought, and MARXISM by its very nature as dialectical *materialism* (rather than idealism) is humanist in the secular sense. But that humanism which treats humanity as something to be understood and explained in its own terms without reference to a divine being also has points of contact with the philosophy of such twentieth-century thinkers as A.J. Ayer and Karl Popper. These have both sought (Ayer in attempting to use the criterion of verifiability and Popper, perhaps more cogently, that of falsifiability) to make the natural sciences the model for all rationality. Since science will seek explanation in its own terms, without reference to anything outside itself, the affinity between such scienticism and a secular humanism is obvious.

'Humanist' has had other meanings, too. It has been used by some to describe those who believe that Christ was human but not divine. It has also been used as equivalent to 'humanitarian', one who is concerned for the welfare of other human beings, for JUSTICE and for HUMAN RIGHTS. This has been, to some extent, little more than a confusion of two very similar terms. But there have been varieties of humanism which have also been concerned to promote justice in SOCIETY, or to care for the poor or disadvantaged.

Like most other aspects of humanism this association with social issues is not undisputed. Within what is sometimes called the counter-reformation and sometimes the Catholic reformation, the influence of Renaissance humanism was often powerful. But it was not uniform in its effects. Some Christian humanists among the Catholic reformers believed that monastic life of extreme austerity was the only path to salvation: others, like Cardinal Contarini (a member of the preparatory commission appointed by the papacy before the Council of Trent and also someone who tried very hard to achieve a theological agreement with the Lutherans), believed that it was perfectly possible to be fully Christian while remaining in secular life. Some new religious orders and congregations originating in this period, like the oratory movement founded by St Philip Neri, which devoted themselves to caring for the sick and the poor, may have been influenced by humanism, though such devotion was, of course, traditional in Christianity. On the other hand the humanist political thought of Machiavelli is positively amoral in its application, whatever view one takes of the nature of that amorality. Some scholars think Machiavelli believed that no ruler could afford to be moral but, at the same time, that he must not pretend that he was behaving morally. In so far as Machiavelli can be regarded as a humanist, his humanism did not prevent his often treating human beings as pawns in the political POWER game.

There have always been, since the Renaissance itself, those who have claimed for themselves, with a degree of passion, the title of 'Christian' humanists. Whether this can be regarded as a legitimate claim depends, in part, on whether one is able to reconcile one's doctrine of the sovereignty of God with the value which one places upon human beings. Since the Protestant Reformation of the sixteenth century was very largely a movement which emphasized that the salvation of the human race depended not upon its own efforts but upon the divine

initiative, theologians of the Reformation tended to be theocentric in every aspect of their thought. Superficially, at least, humanism of any kind is equally likely to be anthropocentric. Renaissance and Reformation, therefore, do not merely follow one another, particularly in Europe north of the Alps, in very quick succession: but they appear to have a very complex relationship with one another. On the one hand, there is the fact that the Reformation appeared to disparage human endeavour and, in that sense, to move in a contrary direction from that of humanism. On the other hand, the Reformation obviously owed a good deal to the Renaissance. Renaissance insistence that it was important to return to original sources foreshadowed the Reformation determination to get back to what the Greek New Testament actually said, as distinct from what the medieval Church had said that it said.

Inevitably there has been disagreement among historians in their assessment of what Renaissance humanism itself stood for. Those scholars who claim that the Renaissance was concerned with style rather than content find no difficulty in reconciling the humanist concerns of the Renaissance with the theocentricity of Reformation theology. But it is not easy to maintain an absolute distinction between style and content. Many Renaissance figures, for cultural and educational reasons, favoured the study of Cicero and Aristotle. They may have been primarily concerned to develop a classical style and a logical method in which to dress their thought and so demonstrate that capacity which, above all else, distinguished humanity from the animals. But the dress in which speech was clothed could not be entirely divorced from the personal virtue or political ethics expressed through it. While it may be true that a secular amorality informs the writings of Machiavelli, it was hardly possible that churchmen who still read Augustine, and found him stylish, would cease to be influenced by his theology. And, of course, the best known of all the humanists, Erasmus of Rotterdam, was unquestionably Christian, though acidly critical of the late medieval Church. His edition of the Greek text of the New Testament and of the writings of some of the Greek and Latin Fathers prepared the way for a good deal of the theology of the reformers.

In modern times the debate about the possibility of a Christian humanism has most often taken the form of a discussion about the nature of religious TRUTH. In the nineteenth century, with the advances made by the natural sciences, truth came to be thought of as that which was at least provisionally established as a result of experiment, enquiry and exploration. Theologians who believed that truth was in some sense indivisible came to hold the view that religious truth was also that which was arrived at by the exercise of human reason and that it possessed a provisional character. This was the position associated with Liberal Protestantism on the Continent of Europe and with Broad Churchmen in England. More conservative scholars continued to maintain that religious truth was absolute and certain since it was revealed by God and guaranteed by divine AUTHORITY. In the twentieth century Karl Barth has been the most outstanding exponent of a theology which, while by no means irrationalist, does not regard human enquiry and human understanding as a satisfactory basis for religious truth. For Barth, all knowledge of God rests upon what God has revealed of the godhead, though this has not prevented him, particularly in his later writings, from championing some of the ideas more often associated with humanism, particularly the humanitarian aspects of it.

One of the most interesting of English developments is associated with the publication in 1889 of the volume *Lux Mundi* (Gore 1889). The stated object of the contributors was to attempt to relate traditional 'catholic' orthodoxy to contemporary critical and scientific thinking. The doctrine of the incarnation was to be their key concept, and it was not just that the essayists took this doctrine, in some formal sense, as the basis for understanding and interpreting various crucial aspects of Christian doctrine and life. It was specifically a kenotic understanding of incarnation, the self-emptying of the divine in order to be truly human, which lay behind their whole approach. They believed that such an understanding of the relationship of the human to the divine in Christ would enable them to arrive at a balanced understanding of the interaction of God and humanity in general. That, in turn, would permit them to combine belief in the authority of traditional dogma with a typically liberal conviction that even religious truth could legitimately be subjected to the tests of human reason.

Most defences of the Christian humanist position have not been founded on so thoroughly thought out a theoretical basis as this. For the most part they have consisted of little more than an assertion that it is

a concern for the well-being of humans that has its source in the central message of Christianity, the good news that in Jesus Christ God comes to befriend and fulfil the entire human race. Conservatives and liberals alike, non-Christians as well as Christians, have nothing to fear in opening themselves to a humanism based on Christ and the gospels.

(Franklin and Shaw 1991: 254)

That very formulation would be regarded by some conservative Christians as itself fearful and deserving of anathema. There continue to be those, however, who maintain that it is the very potential of which human personalness is capable which is the principal reason for believing in God.

Ayer, A.J. (1936) *Language, Truth and Logic*, London: Gollancz.

Barth, K. (1957) *The Word of God and the Word of Man*, revised English translation by D. Horton, New York: Harper & Row.

Berlin, I. (1972) 'The originality of Machiavelli', in M.P. Gilmore (ed.) *Studies on Machiavelli*, Florence: Sansoni.

Bouwsma, W.J. (1959) *The Interpretation of Renaissance Humanism*, New York: Macmillan.

Burckhardt, J. (1869) *Die Cultur der Renaissance in Italien*, Leipzig: Seemann.

Cameron, E. (1991) 'The late Renaissance and the unfolding Reformation in Europe', in J. Kirk (ed.) *Humanism and Reform: The Church in Europe, England, and Scotland, 1400–1643*, Oxford: Blackwell.

Franklin, R.W. and Shaw, J.M. (1991) *The Case for Christian Humanism*, Grand Rapids, MI: Eerdmans.

Gore, C. (ed.) (1889) *Lux Mundi: a Series of Studies in the Religion of the Incarnation*, London: John Murray.

Hinchliff, P. and Young, D. (1981) *The Human Potential*, London: Darton, Longman & Todd.

Hobson, A. (1985) *Modern Humanism*, Newcastle upon Tyne: Dene Books.

Kristeller, P.O. (1979) *Renaissance Thought and its Sources*, revised edn, ed. M. Mooney, New York: Columbia University Press.

McGrath, A. (1987) *The Intellectual Origins of the European Reformation*, Oxford: Basil Blackwell.

Matthews, E. (1991) *The Challenge of Secular Humanism*, Kilmarnock: Historical Society of Scotland.

Novack, G.E. (1966) *Existentialism versus Marxism: Conflicting Views on Humanism*, New York: Dell.

Packer, J.I. and Howard, T. (1985) *Christianity: the True Humanism*, Berkhamsted: Word.

Phillips, M.M. (1949) *Erasmus and the Northern Renaissance*, London: Hodder & Stoughton.

Popper, K. (1992) *The Logic of Scientific Discovery*, reprinted, London: Routledge.

Toffanin, G. (1964) *Storia dell'umanesimo*, revised edn, 4 vols, Bologna: Zanichelli.

Peter Hinchliff

HUNGER

In recent decades, most thinking has identified hunger as a concrete biological phenomenon that raises profound and general moral issues. Increasingly, students of hunger and famine are seeing these as larger social phenomena that raise very specific moral issues.

At root, hunger is the unpleasant physiological sensation that follows from failing to eat enough food. In a wider sense, the concept of hunger encompasses a range of forms of severe SUFFERING that cause poor people throughout the world to live impoverished and shortened lives. Famine is the most striking manifestation of hunger in this sense.

The core notion of undernutrition is the condition that typically arises from an inadequate consumption of food, or from debilitating disease. Acute undernutrition, due to a short but severe cutback in consumption, tends to produce a variety of symptoms, in extremity causing 'wasting' – the loss of body fat and muscle. This is characteristic of those suffering famine. Chronic undernutrition in children produces 'stunting' whereby the child fails to achieve optimal growth and in extreme cases may suffer from impairment of mental faculties. This is characteristic of prolonged severe underfeeding.

Starvation is the extreme condition under which undernutrition leads to a greatly increased risk of dying, either through lack of food or, more commonly, through increased susceptibility to an infectious disease. Beyond this, the definition of undernutrition is a matter of sometimes fierce debate among nutritionists.

Hunger – usually in the form of voluntary fasting – has a central role in many religions (*see* ASCETICISM). The Lenten fasts in Christianity and Ramadhan in Islam have very different forms (one restricts the kind of food that can be consumed, while the other restricts the hours of consumption) but have the similar avowed aim of spiritual purification and bringing the individual closer to God. The physiology of mild hunger, notably by sharpening concentration, doubtless assists in this. However, while the strenuous fasting demanded by the Ethiopian Orthodox church is said by its adherents to contribute to their ability to withstand prolonged food shortage, such controlled hunger is a fundamentally different phenomenon from famine.

The definition of famine is deeply problematic. The tendency of economists, demographers and nutritionists is to try to define it with respect to externally quantifiable indicators. Most definitions of famine hinge on a measurable increase in the death rate among a certain population, or at least a sharp measurable decline in nutritional status. Until very recently, a significant shortfall in the availability of food was also definitive of famine, and in popular usage it often remains so.

This positivistic approach to famine is a legacy of the work of the Reverend Thomas Malthus, who in 1798 wrote his *Essay on the Principle of Population*. Malthus argued that human population was increasing in geometric progression, while the resources available to sustain that population, specifically food, could increase only in arithmetic progression. Hence it followed logically that the population would at some point reach a size at which the food supplies were insufficient. If WAR or epidemic disease did not intervene to cut the population, 'gigantic inevitable famine' would do so, and 'with one mighty blow, level the population with the food of the world'. Famine thus came to play a key role in social and economic thought as a massive shortage of food and as the fall in population resulting from that by means of starvation.

Fear of uncontrolled population growth informed British famine relief policies in Ireland, when 'economic laws' were left to take their course, and in India over the following decades. This fear remains influential in much popular and journalistic thinking on famine, though no famine in the modern world has ever approached Malthus's doomsday speculations. Fortunately, by the close of the nineteenth century, colonial administrators had recognized that overpopulation could not be the cause of the famines that India was then suffering, just as mass starvation was neither their outcome nor their 'cure'. In 1880, the British Raj appointed a Famine Commission that investigated evidence concerning the repeated failure to prevent famine over the previous years, and concluded by proposing a 'Famine Code' for systematic famine prevention. At the core of this was provision of work for the able-bodied poor. These policies have proved successful and remain at the heart of India's famine-prevention system today.

The Famine Commissioners harked back to an older tradition of famine relief, one founded in Elizabethan England. A succession of famines in the late sixteenth century brought social disorder in their wake, causing the English Privy Council to recognize that the stability of the realm was closely tied in to the prevention of scarcity. The former systematic charity of the monastic orders – dissolved earlier in the century – was replaced by the Poor Laws and the Scarcity Book of Orders, which enjoined each parish to provide for vagrants. The motives were not charitable but enlightened self-interest. Modern British charity law is based upon this legislation, whose explicit aim is protection of the status quo by meeting the immediate material needs of the destitute.

The theory and practice of famine relief still reflects a fundamental tension between apolitical charity and the recognition that social justice is a prerequisite for the true banishment of hunger. This in turn reflects theological debates, notably in Christianity and Islam.

Malthus's theories not only were rejected by demographers and social scientists but also had grossly unethical implications. None the less, remarkably, Malthus's conception of famine as the ultimate apocalypse lived on. One of its most extreme manifestations was the work of the social anthropologist Colin Turnbull, who lived among the Ik of Uganda when they were suffering famine. Turnbull described the breakdown of Icien society into brutal selfishness. He made the Draconian recommendation that the Ik be dispersed elsewhere. Turnbull's book provoked a furore among professional anthropologists, who regarded his methods as unreliable and his conclusions as unethical. The Ik also objected and asked a later researcher for advice on taking out a libel suit against their ethnographer.

In the late 1970s, the view that a decline in food availability was a defining condition of famine was rejected by Professor Amartya Sen. On the basis of evidence from, among others, the 1943 famine in Bengal, Sen argued that a famine should be defined as the failure of a certain group of individuals to consume enough food, and that famines could and did occur without a decline in food availability. Instead, Sen showed that the failure of people to obtain sufficient food 'entitlements' (i.e. food produced by themselves or income to buy food) was the cause of famine. In South Asia, widespread unemployment coupled with high food prices were typically a cause of famine. Food shortfall was but one possible empirical contributor to this failure of entitlements.

By asking the question 'who starves in a famine, and why?' Sen's theory had revolutionary implications for famine relief. But while the agenda of social JUSTICE has been taken up by many international voluntary organizations when working on long-term issues such as social development, international famine relief is still locked into the tradition of palliative charity.

Sen's entitlement theory, while refuting Malthus's first claim that food supply failure is the cause of famine, did not address the second contention, that famine consists in large-scale reduction of the population through starvation. This issue was tackled by two demographers, however, Susan Watkins and Jane Menken, who analysed the demographic evidence from historical famines and concluded that famines could not account for significant population falls. Even the most severe famines caused a population fall of only a few percentage points, and those least likely to die were women of reproductive age (in all recorded famines, men have been more likely to die than women, probably because of the latter's greater physiological resilience). A relatively small loss of population could be quickly made up. In fact, in some well-known famines, such as the 1970s Sahelian famine, there is very little evidence that there were any deaths in excess of normal.

Recently, nutritional scientists have moved beyond the confines of studying malnutrition to tackle the broader problems of famine. However, this approach has also run into difficulties.

Specifically, research has shown that the 'victims' of famine do not regard hunger or malnutrition as the most serious problem they face; instead they see the threat to their future livelihoods as the greatest danger. African and Asian peasants are prepared to undergo extraordinary degrees of hunger in order to preserve vital assets such as plough oxen or farmland, or in order not to break important social taboos. The maintenance of an acceptable way of life remains an important goal during famine. Research by the social anthropologist David Turton in Ethiopia has shown how the Mursi people do not follow the ethic of 'saving every possible life' when confronted with famine; instead they try to preserve their *way of life*. Turton adds that it is not a question of valuing social norms above the lives of children, but simply that the Mursi do not know any other way to respond.

Because the Mursi have not been the objects of an international aid programme, the resulting conflict of norms between them and foreign relief agencies has not arisen. In other famines, however, mothers have been known to take their undernourished children from feeding centres in order to return to their villages to plant food for the coming year. In one remarkable instance, Ethiopian famine refugees in Sudan staged a hunger strike for the right to be able to leave to return home for the rains.

A second problem with the nutritional approach is that many famine deaths are unrelated to malnutrition *per se*. Famines involve enormous social disruption, including large-scale migration, which leads to the spread of communicable diseases that carry off the undernourished and well-fed alike.

Therefore, much recent work on famine has had the effect of unpicking the threads of Malthus's legacy and returning us to a conception of famine as primarily a social disaster, albeit one with physiological consequences for human beings. This is far more consonant with the definitions of famine espoused by those who suffer it. In Bangladesh, rural people distinguish at least three different kinds of famine; in Africa, a distinction is frequently drawn between 'famines that kill' and lesser famines. In these societies, 'hunger' is often used in an idiomatic or metaphorical sense, to express a general suffering, a lack of power, prosperity or enjoyment, as well as a lack of food consumption.

The focus on the social aspects of hunger has also led to attention being given to some important linkages between HUMAN RIGHTS and hunger. Development theorists have sometimes posited the right to food as a basic human right. More recently, social scientists have analysed the manner in which civil and political liberties can be crucial to the prevention of famine. Amartya Sen has asserted that 'indeed it is difficult to find a case in which a famine has occurred in a country with a free press and a functioning DEMOCRACY'. A free press is able to draw attention to an impending crisis and a democratically accountable government is compelled to act on such information by the demands of its electors. Given that prompt and appropriate action can prevent famine in any country, no matter how poor, this has meant that since independence India has weathered climatic adversity and severe food shortfalls without once descending into famine. Thus the often-argued case for suppressing individual freedoms in order to accelerate DEVELOPMENT and thus overcome hunger is shown to have an important shortcoming. The Chinese famine of 1958–61 was able to develop and ultimately kill 30 million people in part because of the absence of a free press and an accountable government.

The Indian experience has pointed to the

role of liberal civil and political rights, but these are only effective in overcoming hunger when a government is prepared to make major interventions in the economy. Free-market economies have shown themselves historically to be less effective at tackling chronic hunger than socialist ones. India may have escaped the appalling famine that struck China in 1958–61, but the annual toll of excess deaths due to chronic undernutrition in India, compared with China, is of the order of 5 million.

Marxist critiques of famine have centred on the 'silent violence' that is done to traditional societies in Africa and Asia, that were often fairly resistant to famine, by the encroachment of the capitalist world order and the colonial empires. Marxists argue that the development of a commercial economy undermines economic options for the poor, leading to famine. However, it is also true that the growth of peripheral CAPITALISM creates new economic niches, while socialist planning failures have been implicated in famines such as in the Ukraine, China, Ethiopia and Mozambique.

The most extreme famines are those caused by war. This has been the case throughout history, the classic case being the siege or food blockade intended to force the enemy to submit. Such actions in the Second World War by the Allies in Belgium and Greece, and the Germans in The Netherlands and Russia, contributed directly to the adoption of articles in the Geneva Conventions of 1949 outlawing the use of starvation as a weapon of war. Unfortunately, from Biafra to Bosnia, such tactics have remained common, and there have as yet been no prosecutions for the war crime of deliberate starvation.

Other means of creating famine during war, such as 'scorched earth' tactics, are also familiar from history. Of more recent provenance is the use of counter-insurgency strategies designed to force the population to choose between submission and starvation. Burning fields, bombing market-places, banning the food trade and labour migration, and forcibly resettling villagers were all used by the Ethiopian government in 1983–5, and were instrumental in creating the famine. It is a truism that in such circumstances the verb 'to starve' is transitive: people do not starve, they are starved. The government then

permitted relief agencies to feed the displaced people; those agencies that chose to operate under these conditions were making a major compromise with a brutal military regime, and it is a moot point whether some of their operations served to prolong, extend or legitimize the military actions that were so important in creating the famine in the first place. Such acute dilemmas are increasingly becoming the norm, not the exception, of relief work. Similar manipulation of humanitarian aid has been widespread in Bosnia and Somalia.

The International Committee of the Red Cross, based in Switzerland, was born out of horror at the human cost of war, and has since combined a mandate of providing for the victims of war with discrete advocacy to tighten the international law constraining the conduct of war. The British agency Oxfam was the outcome of a campaign to feed the starving in wartime Greece – the founders decided against campaigning against the ethics of the Allies' food blockade, fearing it was too political. Relief agencies working in war-famines have faced similar dilemmas ever since. Some have chosen to concentrate solely on material relief. Others, such as the church agencies in Mozambique, have combined relief with discreet peace advocacy. Rarely has aid been combined with public solidarity with victims *vis-à-vis* their oppressors. Part exceptions to the latter have been War on Want in Ethiopia in the 1980s and an array of church agencies in Biafra.

Increasingly, the agenda of international relief agencies is being set by the high profile they are obtaining in the media. The press and in particular television have a tendency to simplify and exaggerate hunger and famine, making some response imperative but also making a considered response more difficult. The public hype surrounding the operations of some Western aid agencies in Bosnia, Somalia, Rwanda and elsewhere is not only distasteful but demeaning to the supposed beneficiaries, and often misguided and unprofessional. The main organizations not subject to this trend are some church agencies, which have a natural constituency within the afflicted country and also a stronger attachment to ideals of solidarity with the suffering. Maintaining such sensitivity in the face of the growth of televisual suffering as a media commodity promises to be difficult.

At the time of writing, issues of hunger and famine are stimulating a more wide-ranging debate than ever before. The intensification of hunger, and its rapidly changing nature, has exposed the inadequacies of previous approaches to the problems, but has yet to spawn adequate responses.

Jellife, D.B. and Jellife, E.F.P. (1971) 'The effects of starvation on the functioning of the family and of society', in G. Blix, Y. Hofvander and B. Valhquist (eds) *Famine: Nutrition and Relief Operations in Times of Disaster*, Uppsala: Swedish Nutrition Foundation.

Macrae, J. and Zwi, A. (eds) (1994) *War and Hunger*, London: Zed Press.

Malthus, Thomas (1798) *Essay on the Principle of Population*, London.

Sen, Amartya (1981) *Poverty and Famines: An Essay on Entitlement and Deprivation*, Oxford: Clarendon.

Turnbull, Colin (1972) *The Mountain People*, New York: Simon & Schuster.

Turton, David and Turton, Pat (1984) 'Spontaneous resettlement after drought: an Ethiopian example', *Disasters* 8: 179–89.

de Waal, Alex (1989) *Famine that Kills: Darfur, Sudan, 1984–1985*, Oxford: Clarendon Press.

Watkins, S.C. and Menken, J. (1985) 'Famines in historical perspective', *Population and Development Review* 11: 647–76.

Watts, Michael (1983) *Silent Violence: Food, Famine and the Peasantry in Northern Nigeria*, Berkeley and Los Angeles, CA: University of California Press.

Alex de Waal

HUNTING

Hunting is the pursuit and killing of a wild animal for food or sport. The morality of hunting for food is parasitic on the morality of eating animal flesh (*see* VEGETARIANISM). Hunting foxes, deer, mink and hares for sport is legal in many Western countries, along with shooting wildfowl and angling, although other bloodsports such as cockfighting, bearbaiting, badgerbaiting, dogfighting and bullfighting are now illegal in most Western countries.

Even without appealing to a notion of the rights of animals, hunting is ethically contentious. The chief moral objection is that the (frequently painful) death of a sentient creature cannot be justified by the pleasure it may bring to hunters and spectators: comparable pleasure can be gained from activities which do not involve the death of a sentient creature. Moreover, that pleasure is derived from such 'sport' can be seen as morally undesirable in itself, not least of all because it may brutalize the human subjects: 'for the custom of tormenting and killing beasts will, by degrees, harden their [the perpetrators'] minds even towards men; and they who delight in the suffering and destruction of inferior creatures, will not be apt to be very compassionate or benign to those of their own kind' (Locke 1693: 180).

Arguments in defence of hunting include (a) the control of 'pests'; (b) the conservation of nature; (c) the traditional right to hunt, and (d) since nature is itself a predatory system, hunters are simply obeying nature's own law.

The argument that hunting is necessary to control wild animals presupposes that most, or all, wild animals need to be managed or controlled, and that, if true, hunting itself is an efficient method of doing so. The first assumption is questionable and the second is incredible. All animals breed principally in relation to the food and environment available. They naturally control their own populations, and frequent, or semi-frequent, culling reduces a percentage of the population which the species itself shortly makes up if the conditions are right (see, for example, Hewson and Kolb 1974). Quite apart from the question of whether humans have the right to determine the size of animal populations, it is questionable whether any current system of control – which fails to influence the primary factors of food availability and habitat – provides any more than short-term dents in a given animal population.

Moreover, the argument that hunting is itself a means of control lacks all credibility when it is appreciated that hunters frequently preserve 'game' for hunting, not only pheasants and grouse for shooting but also – from the earliest days – foxes for hunting. As one pro-hunting social historian frankly admits: 'Fox-hunting depended on persuading farmers to preserve foxes [for the hunt] against their better judgement' (Ridley 1990: 14).

The argument that hunters are interested in and support conservation measures carries some weight: the British Field Sports Society in the UK has identified sources of, and solutions to, river pollution since the 1940s, and taxes on sport hunting equipment in the USA currently finance wildlife restoration programmes in many States. However, as it is possible to be a conservationist without being a hunter, these actions do not in themselves legitimize hunting. Since the 'code of ethics' of the National Rifle Association requires that hunters 'support conservation efforts *which can assure good hunting for future generations*', their own claims to be altruistic conservationists or effective controllers of animal populations must be questioned (National Rifle Association 1990: ii; our emphasis).

The argument that individuals have the 'right' to hunt especially when such activities are 'traditional' confuses conventionality with moral acceptability. Iris Murdoch states the obvious: 'the fact that an activity is traditional and strongly connected to some sectional interest does not in itself show that it is worthy' (Murdoch 1960: 3). Appeals to tradition *per se* are of little moral weight; what needs to be shown is that such traditions embody practices which are themselves morally commendable. If hunting is unacceptable in itself, then the fact that it has long been practised is a condemnation of past behaviour rather than a vindication of current practice. Moreover, the claim that a practice is acceptable solely on the grounds that it is traditional endorses moral quietism through abdicating moral responsibility in favour of the status quo.

Defenders of hunting often claim that it is their legal, and political, right to hunt (see Whisker 1981) and that prohibitive legislation would deny their individual freedom. However, if hunting is morally wrong, the individual should be no more free to hunt than she or he is to pursue other morally objectionable practices, such as taking another person's property or life.

The argument drawn from obeying the 'laws of nature' raises theological as well as moral questions. It is argued that to eat and to be eaten is 'part of the blessing of God' because God ordained a predatory system; therefore it is

not wrong to act in accordance with this system (Austin 1988: 197). Indeed, some hunters claim that they are only bigger and better ecological predators (see Ritchoff 1975). However, it is doubtful whether hunters do act merely in accordance with 'nature'. Most hunting is not predatory in the natural sense – foxhunters, for example, do not eat the fox. Furthermore, specific dogs are crossbred for hunting ability and sheer ferocity; cocks are drugged and provided with artificial spurs to increase their wounding power. 'Hunters do not "imitate" the cruelties of nature: they create them' (Linzey 1994: 124).

But even allowing for some forms of aggression or wantonness or (non-moral) CRUELTY in nature, it does not follow that the natural world as it is can constitute a moral textbook. Acting morally sometimes means acting *against* nature – or what we take nature to be. Hauerwas argues that the 'natural' impulses of survival and revenge are contrary to the central Christian ethic of forgiving love, and to the Biblical vision of peaceability (Hauerwas 1984). Linzey presents a similar argument that, if predation is God's plan for humanity, the self-disclosure of God in Christ would have manifested this plan, yet the notion of a 'Predator Jesus' is diametrically opposed to the Jesus of the Gospels: 'the Predator view of Jesus is untenable' (Linzey 1994: 121). The hunter's argument from natural ecology fails to take account of the Biblical view of nature as imperfect and at variance with God's original will (see Murray 1992).

Hunting philosophy is deeply indebted to a particular social construction of nature as wild, cruel and despotic. Without denying that there are indeed morally objectionable features in nature, that we *perceive* these things to be centrally significant is itself the result of a socially constructed view of the natural world. Hunters frequently view their pastime as an antidote to over-civilization. In the words of Max Lerner: 'Every people, no matter how civilized, must have a chance to yell for blood' (Lerner 1957: 812).

But there is another, theologically grounded, perception of nature awaiting social construction. It is that what is centrally significant is that, however disordered, nature also expresses patterns of co-operation, forms of beauty and intrinsic value. What this perception should excite within us is the possibility of co-operating with what is good and bringing creation – by our own power as moral agents – to new possibilities of being. T.F. Torrance argues that our 'priestly role must take on a redemptive form' in relation to nature: 'to *save* the natural order through remedial and integrative activity, bringing back order where there is disorder and restoring peace where there is disharmony' (Torrance 1981: 130; his emphasis).

From this perspective, the hunting of wild animals and the taking of delight in their SUFFERING is a degradation of the human spirit, a practical sign that we have lost a true sense of ourselves as harbingers of the Spirit which is seeking to bring all creation currently in 'bondage to decay' into 'the glorious liberty of the children of God' (Romans 8: 18–23).

Ammon, William H. (1989) *The Christian Hunter's Survival Guide*, New Jersey: Fleming H. Revell.

Amory, Cleveland (1974) *Man-Kind? Our Incredible War on Wildlife*, New York: Harper & Row.

Austin, Richard Cartwright (1988) *Beauty of the Lord: Awakening the Senses*, Atlanta, NJ: John Knox Press.

Carpenter, Edward (1965) 'Christian faith and the moral aspect of hunting', in Patrick Moore (ed.) *Against Hunting*, London: Gollancz.

Hauerwas, Stanley (1984) *The Peaceable Kingdom: A Primer in Christian Ethics*, London: SCM.

Hewson, R. and Kolb, H.H. (1974) 'The control of foxes in Scottish forests', *Scottish Forestry* 28 (October): 4.

Lerner, Max (1957) *America as a Civilization*, New York: Simon & Shuster.

Linzey, Andrew (1994) *Animal Theology*, London: SCM and Chicago, IL: University of Illinois Press.

Linzey, Andrew and Regan, Tom (eds) (1988) *Animals and Christianity: A Book of Readings*, London: SPCK, and New York: Crossroad.

Locke, John (1693) *Some Thoughts Concerning Education*, ed. J.W. and J.S. Yolton, Oxford: Clarendon, 1989 edn; reprinted in P.A.B. Clarke and Andrew Linzey (eds) *Political Theory and Animal Rights*, London and Winchester, MA: Pluto, 1990.

Mason, Jim (1994) *An Unnatural Order: Uncovering the Roots of Our Domination of Nature and Each Other*, New York: Simon & Shuster.

Murdoch, Iris (1960) *Letter* originally published in the *National and English Review*, reprinted in *League Doings* 1 (January–March): 4.

Murray, Robert (1992) *The Cosmic Covenant: Biblical Themes of Justice, Peace and the Integrity of Creation*, London: Sheed & Ward.

National Rifle Association (1990) *The Hunter's Guide*, Washington, DC: NRA.

Ridley, Jane (1990) *Fox Hunting*, London: Collins.

Ritchoff, Jim (1975) *Mixed Bag: Reminiscences of a Master Raconteur*, Washington, DC: National Rifle Association.

Torrance, T.F. (1981) *Divine and Contingent Order*, Oxford: Oxford University Press.

Whisker, James B. (1981) *The Right to Hunt*, Croton-on-Hudson, NY: North River Press.

Andrew Linzey
Molly Baer Kramer
Jonathan Webber

IDEOLOGY

Etymologically the word should mean 'science of ideas', and it was intended to carry this meaning when it was coined, towards the end of the eighteenth century, by Destutt de Tracy, a founder and leading member of the French Institut National, and was assigned the central place in the 'Enlightenment' project to which the Institute dedicated its work. The centrality of the 'science of ideas' in any project bent on building a SOCIETY ruled by reason and composed of rationally behaving beings was argued then through a chain of simple assumptions: human conduct is guided by ideas (the corollary: one can change the world only through changing people's ideas); ideas are formed by the processing of human sensations; the processing, like all other natural processes, is subjected to strict laws; the laws can be discovered through systematic observation and experiment and, once discovered, used – like other known laws of nature – to improve on reality (in this case, to ensure that only true ideas, passing the test of reason, are formed and adopted). Itself a strict and precise science, ideology was called to occupy the central and supervisory position among all sciences; it should investigate, regulate and correct if necessary all cognitive efforts. In the words of Mercier, ideas 'are all that exist' and according to de Tracy himself, 'we exist only through our sensations and our ideas. No things exist except by ideas that we possess of them.' In practical terms, centrality of ideology among sciences meant centrality of ideologists among the constructors and stewards of enlightened society: by manipulating human ENVIRONMENT, and thus sensations likely to be aroused, and by guiding the subsequent processes of idea formation, the experts of ideology would secure the rule of reason over the whole field of human beliefs and behaviour. The theory of TRUTH in terms of which the project of ideology was argued was at the same time a theory of error; false beliefs were ascribed to the arousal of wrong sensations, prompted by uncontrolled or wrongly controlled environment, i.e. in the last account, to the absence of programmed EDUCATION or to an education programmed and conducted in defiance of the demands of reason.

Accordingly, ideology was to be a battle waged on two fronts: against ignorance, and against the wrong kind of education, in the latter case primarily against religious education, which the thinkers of the Enlightenment had charged with a major responsibility for the absence or paucity of social progress. Ideologists, the front-line operators of the new, secular knowledge élite, should take over the function of spiritual guardianship (and thus the elevated social standing which spiritual guardians deserve) from the clergy.

The first attack against ideologists, however, came from political rulers, notably Napoleon Bonaparte, who rightly sensed in the programme of ideology a thinly disguised restatement of the philosophers' bid for secular POWER. Indeed, the claimed monopoly of truth, argued by ideologists in terms of a privileged access to reason, set them on a collision course with the practitioners of state power – much as was done in the past by the Church in as far as she argued the superiority of her judgement in the name of the Revelation. Another attack against the programme of ideology came from materialistic philosophy, which gained force in the course of the nineteenth century, notably through Ludwig Feuerbach and Karl Marx, who asserted the priority of reality over ideas – an exact opposite to the ideologists' assumption: one cannot change reality by manipulating ideas; it is the reality which needs to be changed first for the change to be reflected in new ideas. In his early works, Marx confronted ideology as the major philosophical adversary, a code name for the philosophy of historical idealism, itself in his view an intellectual aberration which could only be understood as a reflection of unresolved contradiction immanent in social life; a misleading reflection – theoretical blunders could only be rectified through the resolution of practical contradictions and the reform of society.

The early attempt to establish the concept of ideology and related concerns in public discourse proved a false start. The programme advocated by ideologists (at least in the blunt and outspoken form given it by the fellows of the Institut National) failed to convince either the politicians or the philosophically informed public, and the concept itself went out of fashion and virtually fell out of use for the duration of the nineteenth century.

When the concept of ideology re-emerged in the 1920s, and then turned into one of the major concepts of political discourse and the social sciences, it carried an entirely different meaning – bearing little, if any, relation to the early-nineteenth-century precedents, by that time largely forgotten. Like its predecessor, the new concept of ideology emerged in the context of the post-Enlightenment, modern 'truth versus error', 'science versus prejudice' discourse and was meant to serve as the boundary between correct and incorrect knowledge: to separate the kernel of reliable, scientifically tested or testable knowledge from the chaff of 'mere opinions'; to reinforce the position of science as the institution and scientists as its spokesmen as the collective umpire of truth, determining the legitimacy of all knowledge. This time, however, the word 'ideology' was deployed to capture the elements of consciousness located on the wrong side of the great divide. Now 'ideology' stood for the not-yet-uprooted and not-yet-overcome, false and harmful beliefs which science had sworn to unmask, disempower and in the end eliminate from human consciousness, in the course of progress toward the undivided rule of reason. In this second phase of its history, the theory of 'ideology' intended to deal systematically with the kind of phenomena first postulated as obstacles to rational knowledge, at the dawn of the modern era, by Francis Bacon in his repeated warnings against the 'idols' of tribe, theatre or market-place.

The concept of 'ideology' in this new incarnation was conceived at the time when new profound and political divisions and the thickening clouds of intolerance and politically inspired VIOLENCE in a Europe emerging from the ravages of the First World War sapped the self-confidence of knowledge élite, casting doubt on the ultimate victory of scientific reason, by definition non-sectarian, indivisible, universal. When confronted with the world so evidently reluctant to follow the itinerary sketched in the Enlightenment scenario of reason-led progress, philosophers set themselves the twin tasks of spelling out the foolproof criteria which would set apart the true, scientifically authorized knowledge from all other opinions, and of locating the causes of the public reluctance, or inability, to accept, embrace and put in practice the verdicts of truth-testing science. Philosophers of the Wienerkreis, for instance, ascribed the resilience of false beliefs to the endemic impairment of natural languages, and saw the salvation of scientific truth in its entrenchment in an exact and precise language purified of the metaphysical or meaningless notions abounding in the messy language of daily life (as well as in the language of partisan politics). Edmund Husserl, the founder of phenomenological philosophy, doubted whether science is capable of performing the task – rooted, much as daily life itself, in the 'natural attitude', the real breeding ground of fickle opinions dressed up as true knowledge. Husserl suggested that only the Herculean effort of 'phenomenological reduction' – stripping knowledge of the successive layers of error sedimented by the narrow-sighted, locally and temporally limited circumstances in which natural attitude is confined – can allow the philosopher an insight into the non-historical, supra-cultural realm of 'transcendental subjectivity' where all pristine meanings are constituted and reside in the pure form untainted by shifting public interests and cultural fashions.

The twentieth-century concept of 'ideology' was born of similar worries and preoccupations and offered another way of accounting for the growing gap between the hopes of Enlightenment and the rising tide of irrationality in the world increasingly fragmented socially and politically; and another legitimation for the role to be played by the enlightened élite in bridging that gap. The new concept of 'ideology' fit to serve this purpose was forged by Karl Mannheim, and was apparently influenced by the idea of 'false consciousness' elaborated within the Marxist tradition by George Lukacs to account for the astonishing failure of Western working classes to rally around the cause of SOCIALISM which according to the Marxist vision of progress was both the rational expression of working-class interests and the fullest implementation of the project of rationally organized society. In Lukacs' account, without the assistance of social scientists able to raise their sights above the level of narrowly circumscribed experiences available to the workers individually or even collectively, workers will go on reflecting in their consciousness a counterfeit, falsified reality of CAPITALISM in which the truth of their plight is disguised or denied. Mannheim stretched the idea to the size of a universal principle: each group within society, separated and set apart by the particularity of its class position, national membership or professional practice, moves within a partial reality which leaves the totality out of sight. While rationally reflecting upon the truncated reality available in their experience, all groups tend to form from their own cognitive perspective their own particular distortions of 'objective' (i.e. universal for all) truth. It is such a distorted knowledge conceived within a limited cognitive perspective that was given by Mannheim the name of 'ideology'. Unlike ideology, objective knowledge (true knowledge) of social reality can only be fathomed by people unattached to any of the particular class, national or occupational divisions, people who can move freely from one group to another, gather and confront beliefs conceived from diverse cognitive perspectives and thus expose the limited, relative character of each. Such people, in Mannheim's view, were members of the intelligentsia –the educated class, the only human agents able to reach a 'generalist' vantage point from which the objective likeness of society could be gleaned and painted. Thanks to this unique social location and the unique capacity it offered, 'intelligentsia' is called to play the role of impartial critics of political practices grounded in ideological distortions, but also the role of promoters of scientific politics, founded on non-relative, objective truth. The tool which would render the proper performance of both roles feasible was to be the sociology of knowledge – the systematic study of the link between ideology and socially determined vantage points and group interests.

In Mannheim's rendering, ideology was an enemy of truth which was to be fought and could be defeated. This view implied, in agreement with widely shared ambitions of the modern scientific climate, that a fully objective knowledge – knowledge of no group in particular – is both attainable and desirable. It is the latter assumption which came to be questioned in the recent 'post-modern' climate – following, arguably, the general collapse of crusading, proselytizing cultural ambitions in the West. Another assumption has been gaining ground: that the idea of truth is itself group-based, and that it makes sense only as the unravelling of communally accumulated experience and as an aspect of on-going communal self-reflection; accordingly, no 'neutral', external point of view is conceivable from which true knowledge other than the truth of communal being could be constructed. This conception points, as to its philosophical inspirations, to Martin Heidegger's assertion of the priority of being over reflection and knowledge (before the world becomes an object of reflection, it is already given in unreflexive experience) and Ludwig Wittgenstein's presentation of language as a 'form of life' and all understanding as the 'knowledge how to go on'. In Hans Gadamer's typical rendering of both philosophical legacies, inter-group agreement is possible only as the 'fusion of horizons'. A corollary is the view of language, always a communal possession and activity, as the ultimate human reality with no 'beyond' one can visit, most radically expressed by Jacques Derrida in his blunt statement 'il n'y a pas de horstexte': questioning of any text can only be another text.

In the 'post-modern' intellectual climate the Mannheim-style negative concept of ideology is abandoned on behalf of the 'positive' concept: yes, all beliefs held in society have ideological character, all being construed and reproduced within communal practices; but this is the only character they can ever have, and this circumstance does not necessarily make them into a wrong kind of belief as there are no other beliefs which could boast 'better' grounds – and certainly not 'supra-communal' grounds. All knowledge grows from communal tradition and can exist only inside it, as an aspect of its continual reproduction. Ideologies are communal achievements. They contain set questions and answers, principles of classification, procedures of evaluation and criteria of JUDGEMENT – all conditions preceding and making possible the work of reason, and all sustained and warranted by communal traditions.

Supra-communal agreement, if at all feasible, can only be reached in the process of communication between diverse ideologically framed standpoints, reciprocal translation and negotiation: it can only be an *inter*-communal, not *supra*-communal, agreement.

Objections most commonly raised against the 'positive' notion of sociology (parallel to those voiced against programmatic cultural pluralism and the assertion of equivalence of communal worldviews in general) relate to the dangers of relativism: the refusal to distinguish between good and bad knowledge, worthy and unworthy values, good and bad taste, the moral and immoral. To these objections the proponents of the positive notion retort that choices of this kind have always been, if unknowingly, ideologically and communally engendered and that there is nothing 'relativistic' in the way communal traditions are internalized and consciously defended; though each set of beliefs held is *relative* to a communally sustained ideology, none leads necessarily to a *relativistic* attitude. The possible moral danger lies not in relativism, but in mutual intolerance or indifference between holders of diverse worldviews.

In the twentieth-century theological thought the problems struggled with by the theory of ideology found their expression in the polemics of Karl Barth and Karl Jaspers against the 'demythologizing' programme of Rudolph Bultmann: 'unwrapping' the message of the Gospel, the universal and extra-temporal truth of human condition, from its contingent temporal, culturally confined expression. Bultmann wished theologians to follow what he considered to be the practice of science aimed at the universal truth – 'the unity of the world in scientific thinking is matched by the unity of scientific thinking itself'. One may say that Bultmann's programme for theology was an equivalent of Mannheim's programme for knowledge in general – and, more generally, the reflection of the modern search for truth purified of distortions arising from local or temporal particularity. On the other hand, there is striking affinity between the views of Bultmann's critics and the strategies prevalent in post-modern time. As Barth insists, the truth of the Revelation is not 'proved' by the rationalizing efforts of religious thinkers ('man's

attempts to know God from his own standpoint are wholly and entirely futile'); the truth of God is not available to man 'before it is told him in revelation'. The truth of God cannot be grasped otherwise than from inside of received revelation – it is a miracle 'which we cannot explain apart from the faith, or rather apart from the Word of God in which faith believes'. According to Jaspers, myths do not becloud, but *carry* meanings, which are 'untranslatable into other language' and 'accessible only in the mythical element'. The task is to preserve, not to degrade the myth – 'not to demythologize, but to recover mythical thought in its original purity' which has the power to 'deepen us morally, enlarge us as human beings'.

Jaspers, Karl and Bultmann, Rudolph (1966) *An Inquiry into the Possibility of Religion without Myth*, New York: Noonday Press.
Kennedy, Emmet (1978) *Destutt de Tracy and the Origins of 'Ideology'*, Philadelphia, PA: American Philosophical Society.
Kumar, Krishan (1987) *Utopia and Anti-Utopia in Modern Times*, Oxford: Blackwell.
Larrain, Jorge (1983) *Marxism and Ideology*, London: Macmillan.
Malevez, L. (1959) *The Christian Message and Myth*, London: SCM.
Tinsley, E.J. (ed.) (1973) *Karl Barth*, London: Epworth.

Zygmunt Bauman

IMPERIALISM

Imperialism is a word with many meanings, but historians prefer to reserve the term to the period 1870–1914 when European powers greatly expanded the number and extent of their overseas territories, and when imperial dominion became a contested question in domestic politics.

One outcome of the experience with imperialism was the attempt, after the First World War, to use the League of Nations to resolve international conflicts and to promote eventual EMANCIPATION of colonies to home rule. The establishment of partially self-governing protectorates in the Middle East, and British openness to independence overtures in India, even prior to the First World War, were evidence of this intention.

Another outcome was Lenin's 'scientific'

view of it as the 'highest' stage of CAPITALISM – the stage in which capitalist 'crisis' would usher in world socialist revolution. This view became the leitmotif of Soviet foreign policy and an ideological weapon to challenge Western dominance until the recent crisis of COMMUNISM brought about its demise in Russia and Eastern Europe. National revolutions and international relations of the Cold War era were usually regarded by communists as struggle against imperialism. In the West it was usual to distinguish between ideological uses of the imperialism concept and the phenomenon as a long-term political process. The leading colonial powers accepted that the pledge of the United Nations Charter bound them to promote the self-determination of their overseas territories. Although the disengagement occurred rapidly on the historian's time scale, often independence was conceded only after strenuous contests, sometimes armed. International relations specialists in the West attempted to develop a non-Leninist theory of imperialism, but the effort was abandoned because the phenomenon could not be convincingly distinguished from colonialism, which is perennial.

Not content to be dominated by either super-power, former colonial peoples formed, in the Fifties, the 'Third World' block to assert common interests, particularly through the United Nations. One objective was to structure military and development assistance more to the advantage of recipient nations. Another was that each nation should find a culture-specific response to the all-sided mobilization of human resources common to the West and the Soviet bloc. In this context the concept of 'cultural imperialism' arose. It proved to be largely a continuation of efforts, long standing in some nations, to grapple with western influences on traditional cultures, particularly the religious organization of community life. The Catholic Church and Protestants through the WORLD COUNCIL OF CHURCHES sympathetically engaged in this process, partly because Christianity in the West was also grappling with modernity and shared a range of perceptions with peoples of the Third World. In addition, as the religion of colonial nations, Christianity had many millions of communicants in the Third World who

provided local interpretations of modernization. At a critical phase in the escalation of the Cold War, Pope Pius XII asserted the unity of the human race (*Humani generis*, 1950) and espoused the cause of colonial peoples. This was to be the consistent posture of Rome and the World Council of Churches throughout the Cold War era.

The word 'imperialism' was first used in France to chastize the grandiose aspirations of Louis Napoleon and the territorial expansion of Napoleon III. The term was soon taken up by critics of Disraeli's colonial expansion. It entered the political vocabulary when his allies accepted it as an apt designation of their aims. For them imperialism meant in part a modernization of colonial aims and administration. Claimed overseas territories were often administered by trading companies whose patents were of two centuries standing. This was a viable arrangement only because the actual territorial claims were modest. Thus before 1875, European states claimed only scattered areas along the African coasts in addition to French Algeria and British Egypt and the Cape Colony. Yet only a decade later, the whole of Africa had been claimed and boundaries were agreed internationally at the Berlin Conference (1885). During this period, the territorial extent of British overseas claims tripled.

The motives for this rapid acquisition were various. The temper of the day is conveyed in these lines from a London newspaper editorial of 1897: 'To us, and not to others, a certain definite duty has been assigned, to carry light and civilization into the dark places of the world, to give to the thronging millions, who would otherwise never know peace and security, the first conditions of human advance. To fill the wide waste places with the children of Britain and let the sound of the English tongue and the pure life of English homes give to the future of these immense regions its hue and shape – this is the task which the past has devolved upon us.' The polyvalence of this statement is typical of popular imperialist thought. Spreading the light of civilization is a 'duty' to peoples in 'dark places'. But duty's fulfilment spreads the British people, who carried the flag with them. The military, economic, technological, political and moral superiority of European civilization to all other cultures, and to Europe's own recent past, was a luminous certainty in that age of progress. It was often joined with a belief that European superiority was a product of cultural evolution, implying that non-European peoples stood on lower rungs of the evolutionary ladder; thus the racial element of imperialism enjoyed a sophisticated rationale. However, the spur to large territorial acquisition appears to have been primarily the anxieties incident to geopolitics. European powers, always conscious of political and territorial competition, were now acutely aware that national power presupposed proficiency in technology, manufacturing and trade. It was also the era when rapid advances in communications and transport technology freighted events far from Europe with strategic implications; indecision and inaction were heavy with consequences. Further to that was the population dimension. Historically colonies served European powers, as they served the ancient world, as escape valves from population growth which might also enhance commercial or military advantage. The global image in Europe's chanceries at that time revealed an earth shrinking relative to population increase, particularly in Asia. This anxiety spurred the occupation of 'empty' lands as a hedge against a crowded future.

The classic writing on imperialism was John A. Hobson's *Imperialism: A Study* (1902). Hobson, an English liberal economist, argued that the 'taproot' of imperialism was a glut of investment funds. Owing to declining profits and diminished markets in capitalist countries, financial interests had pushed governments into territorial acquisition to open new markets and new investment opportunities. True to the 'little England' tradition in classical economics, Hobson argued that colonialism actually incurred a net economic loss to the national economy, and he reprobated as dangerous to liberty the strong nationalist sentiment that imperialism aroused. His argument was taken over in its entirety by Lenin, who added the Marxist touch of economic crisis and revolution.

Hobson's argument is weakly supported by the evidence. Capital gluts are a periodic phenomenon and are unlikely to have the special

causal role attributed to them in his theory. But the telling point is that the new acquisitions made no discernible impact on either the pattern or volume of overseas investment. After 1875 it continued without significant variation into established markets in North and South America, to the Middle East, China, and Russia. Africa, where the largest acquisitions by far were made, did not attract a sudden flow of investment because markets and transport infrastructure were at levels too primitive to absorb significant investment funds. While it was recognized that Africa was rich in raw materials, it offered no essential materials that could not be obtained with less effort and more cheaply in established markets. Hobson ignored the benefits that European occupation conferred on colonies, choosing to concentrate instead on the dangers it posed to liberty in Britain and peace in Europe. Lenin categorically denied all benefits, insisting that the relation was exclusively exploitive. A more measured statement would be that colonial administrations gradually introduced the rule of law and terminated numerous cruel practices, such as *suttee*, ritual murder, cannibalism, judicial mutilation and slavery, including the slave trade in which Europeans participated for two centuries. The colonial era also laid the foundations for a global community of nations.

There is today no adequate theory of imperialism. The extensive writings of western Marxists on the subject are contrived as polemical weapons of a transient struggle and ignore the evidence of 5,000 years of territorial expansion on every continent. Imperialism is a brief episode in this long-term trend. The evidence of the longer view shows that theories which attempt to link imperialism with merely contemporary phenomena, such as the capitalist organization of society, miss the mark. Expansion and aggrandizement have been combined with the most diverse social systems and with the most diverse declared intentions. 'Cultural imperialism', equally a perennial phenomenon, has been the major avenue for the transmission of civilization. The novelty in western imperialism is not the phenomenon itself, but the overwhelming cultural dominance enjoyed by the west in virtue of its integration of science and technology with administration and production.

Crosby, Alfred (1986) *Ecological Imperialism: The Biological Expansion of Europe 900–1900*, Cambridge: Cambridge University Press.

Darwin, John (ed.) (1991) *The End of the British Empire: The Historical Debate*, Oxford: Blackwell.

Etherington, Norman (1984) *Theories of Imperialism: War, Conquest and Capital*, London: Croom Helm.

Headrick, Daniel R. (1988) *The Tentacles of Progress*, Oxford: Oxford University Press.

Hobson, J.A. (1902) *Imperialism: A Study*, London: Allen & Unwin.

Lichtheim, George (1982) *Imperialism*, New York: Praeger.

Sergeant, P. (1978) *The World Economy*, Sydney: Allen & Unwin.

Smith, W (1982) *European Imperialism in the Nineteenth and Twentieth Century*, Chicago, IL: Nelson Hall.

Hiram Caton

INDEPENDENT CHURCHES

Independent or Congregationalist churches developed in England from the late sixteenth century. They were called 'independent' because each congregation of the Church is independent of others, and 'congregationalist' because the congregation is self-governing. BAPTIST Churches are also Independent in church polity, and at first had much in common, apart from the requirement for believers' baptism. Gradually, however, they grew apart. The term is also used for African churches founded independently of missionary societies, but this usage is quite different.

The origins of Independency lie in the separatists who rejected the Elizabethan Church settlement of 1559 because the parish system compromised the purity of the Church. In the 1560s some opposed the vestments prescribed for the Church of England because of their popish associations. Royal authority in the Church was thereby challenged, and an alternative model for the authority of magistrates was found in the ecclesiology of John Calvin (1509–64), as set out in his *Institutes* (1st edn, 1536; last edn, 1559). It was affirmed that true congregations consisted of believers only, which had absolute authority under God in spiritual matters. The first known separatist congregation under Richard Fitz in London described itself in 1571 as 'a poor congregation whom God hath separated from the churches of England and from the mingled and false worshipping therein' (Watts 1988: 23). Such separatists were as unsympathetic to puritans and presbyterians as to the Church of England in general. The rejection of royal supremacy meant that early martyrs such as Henry Barrow and Robert Greenwood (both Cambridge graduates) were executed in 1593 for resisting lawful AUTHORITY.

Others laid more emphasis on the congregation as a covenanted community than on separation from the Church of England. Thus Robert Browne (1550?–1633?), elected pastor of a congregation in Norwich in 1581, wrote in the following year that 'the Church planted or gathered is a company or number of Christians or believers, which, by a willing covenant made with their God, are under the government of God and Christ, and keep his laws in one holy communion' (Peel and Carlson 1953: 253). His best-known work, *A Treatise of Reformation without Tarrying for Anie* (Peel and Carlson 1953: 150ff.), also of 1582, sums up the urgency of his plea. In the early 1600s such congregational independency was supported within the Church of England by men like Henry Jacob (1563–1624) and William Bradshaw (1571–1618). Many such ministers had to take refuge in Holland, and several sailed on the *Mayflower* for North America in 1620 in search of religious freedom.

Some returned from New England in 1640 and co-operated with the more numerous presbyterians in resisting Charles I. In the turmoil of the Civil War Independents rapidly became a significant force in Cromwell's army and gained from his military success. Independents were in a minority at the Westminster Assembly of Divines (1644–6), which produced the *Westminster Confession* and the (presbyterian) *Form of Church Government*, though the latter was not adopted in England (unlike Scotland). Their advocacy of religious liberty, seen in the work of John Goodwin (1594?–1665) and the Army debates at Putney and Whitehall (1647–9), was the main achievement of the Commonwealth period. Several Independents gained important church offices, e.g. John Owen (1616–83) who became Dean of Christ Church, Oxford, in

1651. The Preface to the *Savoy Declaration* of 1658 (itself substantially the same as the *Westminster Confession of Faith*) emphasizes the principle of liberty in church affairs, and refers to 'the Congregational Way' as 'the order which Christ himself hath appointed to be observed' (Thompson 1990: 77, 79). The annexed statement on *The Institution of Churches* provided for public maintenance of preachers, thereby moving away from strict separatism and reflecting the New England pattern.

All this collapsed at the Restoration of 1660. Even presbyterians were excluded from the Church of England by the Act of Uniformity, but two-thirds of the Independents who withdrew or were ejected from livings between 1660 and 1662 went in 1660. The persecution which followed did not end until James II's Declaration of Indulgence in 1687, although this was intended primarily to benefit Roman Catholics. The Toleration Act of 1689 permitted those of different religious persuasions to live alongside the established Church, but did not bring religious EQUALITY. Independents, like other nonconformists, were excluded from membership of municipal corporations until 1828 and from the ancient universities until the 1850s. Their isolation from the mainstream of national life after 1688 meant that theologians of the calibre of Isaac Watts (1674–1748) and Philip Doddridge (1702–51) remained denominational figures. The loss of some leading ministers to a developing theological unitarianism left Congregationalism more strongly Calvinist.

In the later eighteenth century numerical decline was arrested by the evangelical revival. Independents shared in the new evangelical zeal abroad and at home, founding the undenominational London Missionary Society in 1795 and the Home Missionary Society in 1819, often using itinerant preachers to found many new rural congregations. The County Associations gradually assumed greater responsibility for home missionary work, and a national Congregational Union was founded in 1832, which became an agency for publishing, evangelism and ministerial support. The funds needed for these developments showed that support was being drawn from the trading and manufacturing classes of the larger towns and the shopkeepers and farmers of market towns and the COUNTRYSIDE.

Congregationalists were leaders in the campaign to disestablish the Church of England and bring about the separation of CHURCH AND STATE. The London ministers in the 1830s were generally conservative, but radical initiatives came from the Midlands and the North, especially through the work of Edward Miall (1809–81), a Leicester minister who founded the *Nonconformist* newspaper in 1841 and the Anti-State Church Association in 1844. Nevertheless the shift in emphasis from the virtues of the Congregational way to the evils of an established church remained politically controversial. Moreover the nineteenth-century campaign for religious liberty was often seen as involving the relegation of religious belief from the public to the private sphere.

Later in the century several leading Congregationalists preached the necessity of the social involvement of the Church. R.W. Dale (1829–95) was renowned as an exponent of the 'civic gospel' in Birmingham, arguing that democratic local government could provide for the needs of all citizens. Andrew Mearns (1837–1925) of the London Congregational Union awakened a new concern for the social conditions of the urban poor with his pamphlet *The Bitter Cry of Outcast London* (1883).

In the twentieth century Congregationalism declined in numbers, like other Free Churches. The First World War shattered the Victorian confidence in progress and divided the churches. Some leading theologians such as P.T. Forsyth (1848–1921) supported the war; others, usually younger, such as Nathaniel Micklem (1888–1976) and Leyton Richards (1879–1948) were pacifists. Richards was secretary of the Fellowship of Reconciliation (1916–18), campaigned for DISARMAMENT between the wars and was also a pacifist in the Second World War. Social concern remained strong but the political options became more polarized with the decline of the Liberal Party in the half century after 1918. (Micklem was President of the Liberal Party in 1957–8.) The Halley Stewart Trust was founded in 1924 'for research toward the Christian ideal in social life' by Sir Halley Stewart (1838–1937), a Congregational minister, journalist, business man and politician. Housing and unemployment were the main concerns between the wars. With the coming of the WELFARE STATE after 1945 attention was given to social JUSTICE and equality (see Jenkins 1961), and also to world issues such as economic aid to poorer countries and a just distribution of the world's resources.

Congregationalists were the first of the larger English Free Churches to ordain women. Mrs Constance Coltman and her husband were ordained as assistant ministers at the King's Weigh House Church, London, in 1917, and sixteen more women were ordained in the next twenty years. In 1937 there were also thirty-eight salaried deaconesses, acting as pioneer evangelistic and social workers. The first woman to be Chairman of the Congregational Union was the Reverend Elsie Chamberlain in 1956–7. Congregationalism pioneered the 'Family Church' movement through H.A. Hamilton, who sought to involve children in the church's regular Sunday worship instead of separating them in Sunday School.

Congregationalists played a leading part in the ECUMENICAL MOVEMENT nationally and internationally. A.E. Garvie (1861–1945) was a leader in the Faith and Order and Life and Work movements between the wars. In 1967 the Congregational Union of England and Wales was reconstituted as the Congregational Church, thereby recognizing that the term 'church' could rightly be used of more than the local congregation. In 1972 the majority of congregations joined with the Presbyterian Church of England to form the United Reformed Church. (Those who stayed out formed two groups, the Congregational Federation and the Evangelical Fellowship of Congregational Churches.) The Basis of Union reaffirmed the principle of the spiritual independence of the Church under God. Despite the formal survival of the parish system, all English Churches in practice consist of gathered congregations, so the other sixteenth-century point of controversy seems less pressing. What has been less coherently worked out, however, is the basis for the Church's witness in the nation. Do its members act simply as individuals in a DEMOCRACY, or is there a role for the institution of the Church as such? How should the religious freedom which has been so important in making possible Congregationalist social and political initiatives be related to the discipline of a covenanted fellowship? The relationship of the community of the Church to the wider community of the nation remains a pressing question for the heirs of Independency.

Bebb, E.D. (1935) *Nonconformity and Social and Economic Life*, 1660–1800, London: Epworth.
Bebbington, D.W. (1982) *The Nonconformist Conscience*, London: Allen & Unwin.
Binfield, C. (1977) *So Down to Prayers*, London: Dent.
Brown, K.D. (1988) *A Social History of the Nonconformist Ministry in England and Wales*, 1800–1930, Oxford: Clarendon.
Dale, A.W.W. (1898) *The Life of R.W. Dale*, London: Hodder & Stoughton.
Davie, D. (1978) *A Gathered Church*, London: Routledge.
Jenkins, D. (1954) *Congregationalism: a Restatement*, London: Faber & Faber.
——(1961) *Equality and Excellence*, London: SCM.
Jones, R.T. (1962) *Congregationalism in England, 1662–1962*, London: Independent Press.
Mearns, A. (1883) *The Bitter Cry of Outcast London*, ed. A.S. Wohl, Leicester: Leicester University Press, 1970.
Peel, A. and Carlson, L.H. (eds) (1953) *The Writings of Robert Harrison and Robert Browne*, London: Allen & Unwin.
Thompson, D.M. (ed.) (1990) *Stating the Gospel*, Edinburgh: T. & T. Clark.
Tillyard, F.C. and Spencer, M. (1931) 'Congregationalism and social service', in A. Peel (ed.) *Essays Congregational and Catholic*, London: Congregational Union.
Watts, M. (1988) *The Dissenters*, Vol. 1, Oxford: Clarendon.
Woodhouse, A.S.P. (1938) *Puritanism and Liberty*, London: Dent.

David M. Thompson

INDIVIDUALISM

Deriving from medieval Latin *individualis* from *individuus*, the formative idea is of an indivisible or single substance, but the term has by extension come to have a number of different meanings. The term individual, at its most basic, is a logical term denoting that which can be individuated, picked out from other individual items, or from the background. In a social sense the primary idea is of human beings engaged in a form of life where the individual pursues their own valued ends. Individualism applies a principle of individuation to people that distinguishes them from tribe, clan, group, sib, FAMILY, etc. From this basic idea ethical and political individualism have been derived. Ethical individualism is a central and vital part of modern individualism that hinges on one or both of the claims that the individual is the author of and/ or is responsible for their own actions. Ethical individualism is often held to maintain that the individual has a value separate from and distinct from any value they may have as a member of a group. Human individuals have a value because they are autonomous and rational beings who are self-governing. In Kant's well known expression of the Categorical Imperative they are ends in themselves and not mere means to the ends of others. While such a view is expressed in secular terms it does historically have sacral roots. The Christian Doctrine of Man provides a divine basis for individual human life. Both representatively and individually, humans are made in the image of God and deserving of respect for that reason if no other.

Not all cultures tend to place as much weight on the concept of the individual as in contemporary western life. In totemic cultures, for instance, where nomenclature is not personal but relational, individuals take their identity from others and do not conceive themselves as having an independent existence of value. Individualism is primarily a Western notion that was fully developed by the seventeenth century CE. Prior to that, however, definite precursor notions can be traced. The roots of western individualism can be found in several sources, the most significant of which are ancient Hebrew, ancient Greek, and their transformation through the New Testament and in subsequent Christian doctrine and practice. The basis of ancient near eastern cultures was the group, whether that be empire, tribe, sib, or family rather than the individual. However, instances of individuality can be identified even before the Hebrew Bible. For example, in the ancient Egyptian poem *Dispute of a Man Who Contemplates Suicide with His Soul* (Pritchard: 405–7) we learn of the inward anguish of a man overburdened with life and conversing with his SOUL.

'To whom can I speak today?', he asks, 'Death faces me today'. His inner conversation indicates the kind of self-reflexivity that betokens the more mature individualism of Hamlet who, almost four thousand years later, agonized in a similar way.

The earliest biblical references to individuals are within a patrilineal structure, showing the prime importance of the social group. Nevertheless, even these references reveal some expression of individuality before God as when, for example, Enoch walked with God (Genesis 5: 22), or in the suffering of Job, or when David sang of his soul. Indeed, while Yahweh was the God of the chosen people, He revealed Himself not merely through the group as a whole but also through particular people. The patriarchs, e.g. Moses and Abraham, and the prophets and Kings are presented as individuals, albeit representatively.

While thought in ancient Greece developed against the backdrop of tribal life, the tribe was not altogether central. As ancient Greek philosophers gained increasing knowledge of their physical universe and the natural order of things, a higher significance and dignity was placed on the philosophers themselves. Plato's *Republic* attempts to describe the good in a communal, not an individualistic sense; philosophers, however, were individuals partly disengaged from the social world in a quest for wisdom, dignity and enlightenment. In general terms the Greek household, or individual private life was never seen as a matter for STATE intervention. Good only related to communal good, but within this framework individuality was understood and expressed outwardly in the distinctness of political action and appreciated inwardly through the Delphic maxim, 'know thyself' as well as in the Socratic dictum, 'the unexamined life is not worth living'. Notwithstanding its community basis, Greek civilization has been the principal source of the idea of the critical, reflexive, judgemental and creative individual.

The Greek philosophy of Stoicism emphasized both individual good and particularity, while developing the universalistic ideas of the law of nature and of HUMANISM. The Law of Nature gives people their station in the cosmos and in society (Troelsch, vol. 1, p. 64). The duty of the individual will is to learn this law of nature. Individuality is here combined with a sense of divine order and equality before God: individualism is merged with universalism and divine order. It is clear from the Stoic development of the law of nature, an idea that found its way into early Christianity, that the roots of individualism were contained within the very heart of Christianity itself. Individualism was not an aberration but an integral, possibly even an essential, part of Christianity. Its roots in Stoicism, in Paulian conscience, in the Law of Nature, in divine order and providence, and in the fragmentation of those components were features that laid the groundwork for the doctrine of individualism, a doctrine that was able to flourish when the social structures were appropriate.

The New Testament bears no specific reference to individualism in the modern sense but some of its central themes contain ideas that have been essential to the modern conception of the individual. The motif of Jesus Christ hovers inescapably between Jesus as individual and Christ as representative. The crucifixion is the crucifixion of both, one death to suffice for all deaths, one sacrifice individually undertaken to suffice for all sacrifices. The teachings of Jesus contain many individualistic themes; the beatitudes reverse the emphasis upon the outward compliance with the laws derived from the decalogue and emphasize the inner state, the inner compliance that was later to form the central part of individualistic morality. Even the parables show clear traces of individuality before God; 'even the hairs of your head are all numbered', and 'you are worth more than many sparrows' (Luke 12: 7).

The salvation of the individual soul was central to Christian philosophy, an essentially inner experience of the grace of God through the mediation of Christ, the personal saviour. In this way perception shifted from seeing human beings as Aristotelian political animals whose importance and value are seen in the public domain toward a more spiritual idea of an individual human that was prior to politics. When Jesus declared, 'render unto Caesar the things which are Caesar's, and unto God the things that are God's' (Matthew 22: 21) the effect was to both distinguish the political realm and the divine realm and to lay the ground for later arguments that based the political or public realm on divine will and law. The individual soul was ontologically prior to society and not constituted by it, therefore society and polity were subordinate to the divine laws itself more fundamental than positive law. Saint Augustine's *City of God* demonstrated the tension between divine and positive law in its conception of the heavenly and earthly cities, and his *Confessions* are the first systematic and sustained narrative of the inner life of a radically reflexive individual: the story of a mind rather than the story of a set of deeds.

These early conceptions of the individual took the individual as ontologically prior to society, but until the breakdown of feudal society, social and political relations were dominated by the Law of Nature and the Great Chain of Being. Individuals were conceived as individuals before God, but in social terms their station and its duties were ascribed to them and not acquired as a consequence of their own actions. Thus, on the one hand individuals had a unique place and responsibility before God, while on the other hand the circumstances and conditions of their actions were socially determined. In that tension it was the notion of the individual that came to predominate and led to the collapse of the idea of the Great Chain of Being in favour of the idea that society was a construct made by individuals. Traces of social contract thinking can be found even in some feudal relations; by the seventeenth century it was fully established. Hobbes, Locke, and Rousseau are principal representatives of social contract thinking. One of the starkest examples is found in Thomas Hobbes' *Leviathan* where Hobbes attempts to construct a commonwealth upon a systematic analysis and understanding of its constituent parts: individuals. It is the contract between individuals that authorizes the state and that in turn sustains society. Social contract theorists attempt to show that social structures are built and maintained by individuals and serve the functional purpose of fulfilling the ends of individuals. Individuals are ontologically prior to society rather than the other way around.

Parallel to the growth of social contract theory were the switch to Protestantism and changes in the pattern of justificatory belief. With the religious doctrines of Luther and Calvin, God was perceived as accessible to individual consciousness. The Catholic doctrine of the Church as mediator between individual and God was not accepted in the individualized Protestantism of the Post-Reformation period. Religion, once seen as a covenant between God and the Israelites, became individualized and transformed into a covenant between God and the newly conceived autonomous individual governed by reason. Calvinism displayed the beginnings of a marked shift in western thought and beliefs towards rationality, and individual JUSTIFICATION moved to active individual works. In the Calvinist dogma the individual actively participates in God. Thus, the elect relentlessly exercises his/her will in action, and in so doing, while absolutely subjected to God, will in actual fact participate in Him in contributing to the implementation of His designs (Dumont in Carrithers *et al.* 1985: 115). While this might seem to negate the autonomy of the individual by limiting individual freedom and FREE WILL, it subtly indicates a new perception of God, self and the nature of their relationship. Individuals, once seen as impotent in the face of God, paradoxically appeared to gain greater autonomy on earth through absolute subjection to God, through being a component constituent of His omnipotence. The shift is significant, for the great Chain of Being, the right order, breaks down, but this makes humans essentially closer to God. The self is seen as different to and distinct from the world and metaphysically more akin to the spiritual domain of God. This concept of individualism, therefore, pushes at traditional conceptions of the universe and highlights the view, always present as a possibility in early Christianity, that human value is not derived from belonging to the world, but from the essential difference of humans from it. This kind of thinking underlies the belief found in the Protestant ethic that humankind was justified in attempting to master nature, as the human being is essentially different to nature and naturally superior to it.

That mastery of nature was found not just in

episteme, in pure knowledge of science, but also in *techne* and in rationalism in economic affairs. Economic individualism is usually associated with Adam Smith's assertion that the absence of state economic regulation leads to maximized individual wealth, thus maximising the wealth of the nation. The laissez-faire attitudes, it was claimed, enlarged the private sphere of life. In Mandeville's words, private vices became public virtues. CAPITALISM itself embodied a shift away from conscious attention to the public weal to the pursuit of material WEALTH as an ethically justified occupation of the individual. The pursuit of wealth is frequently found in human affairs, but only in capitalism is it celebrated as an individual activity. Calvin had claimed that the accumulation of material wealth should be valued only as a means to personal salvation through worldly works in the name of God. Max Weber, however, argued that this gave rise to that peculiar form of self-interest that was the Spirit of Capitalism. Weber claimed the development of North European PROTESTANTISM led to the formation of social structures and individual practices and values through which the capitalist economic process could develop. Weber's account of Calvinist Protestantism illuminated the religious and moral support for individual accumulation of wealth which was gradually perceived as a divine justification for coveting material goods. Ethical individualism was dependent upon a particular form of self-reflection. The inward turn that was the unique contribution to the development of the self given by St Augustine of Hippo in the earliest days of Christianity was added to by René Descartes. Descartes' maxim 'cogito ergo sum' placed the individual at the centre of knowledge and certainty. Certainty in the world began with self-certainty, and that in turn was, for Descartes if not his predecessors, predicated upon the certainty of God's existence. Descartes' individualism began modern philosophy, taking over the idea of a monistic and unified self from Augustine and adding to it a belief in self-transparency. The self was open to reflexive inspection. That inner inspection spawned the idea that one could and should be true to one's self, that insincerity was a fault, that the inner life was itself important. The novel, a new art form, examined the world through the perceptions of the individual, ideas of individual romantic love burgeoned, and confessional literature – first seen in St Augustine's account of his search for God – was revitalized. Rousseau, in his *Confessions*, makes it clear that he thinks his enterprise novel and bold, but also that it shows that he is different:

> I am commencing an undertaking, hitherto without precedent, and which will never find an imitator. I desire to set before my fellows the likeness of a man in all the truth of nature, and that man myself. Myself alone! I know the feelings of my heart, and I know men. I am not made like any of those who are in existence. If I am not better, at least I am different.

It is the unity of individuals, as equals before God, and their narrative difference that produces tensions in individualism. Individuals as ethically autonomous place the justification of their actions with themselves and their conscience. This can lead to the end of ethical justification residing with the individual; hence Luther's exclamation: 'Here I stand, I can no more', or it can lead to a search for unversalizing principles accessible to reason and conscience. Kant's Categorical Imperative is the injunction, presented in one formulation, to 'act only on that maxim that you can at the same time will to be a universal law', or, in an equivalent formulation, as the demand to treat people, including oneself, as ends in themselves and not as a mere means.

Such imperatives reflect a deeply-held western belief that individuals have value in themselves, and that the actions of others and the actions of states towards individuals ought, therefore, to be restricted. On such an account the sovereignty and autonomy of either individuals or states may not be used to override the basic value of human individuals. The idea of universal HUMAN RIGHTS would have been inconceivable without the prior importance of individualism and its concomitant values; and that idea, like other universalizing ideas, is both a strength and weakness of individualism. The attempt to produce universalizing principles

across individual and cultural differences are the very stuff of individualism. Kant's formulation of the Categorical Imperative is a clear instance of a secularized theological claim transformed into a set of universal ethical maxims. For Kant the Categorical Imperative stands as a test of proposed actions for all rational beings in any cultural circumstances. That such principles are purely formal with regard to culture has been taken to be a weakness first by Hegel, who takes morality to be based on *Sittlichkeit*, community, and latterly by some communitarians, who see the individual as a social product. If the individual is a social product and not a natural entity then nothing can be said about individuals over and above what one could say about their CULTURE or society. Individuals subsist in society and are social products, but they are not the independent, autonomous and sovereign creators of SOCIETY. The difficulty with the notion of the individual goes deeper than this, however, running into problems at the celebration of its apotheosis in the writings of Kant. For Kant a truly moral act is an act that is done according to reason and that conforms to the Categorical Imperative. Unlike Descartes, Kant did not regard the mind as transparent, hence the motive for an action could never be known with certainty. As a corollary it could never be claimed with certainty that an action was truly moral, for, as he regarded it, 'the human heart is opaque'.

This discovery of opacity ultimately undercut the idea of the monistic and autonomous individual just as it was being celebrated. If motives could never be truly known, then the reasons for an act might not originate with the agent. Indeed the true reasons might well rest on subconscious factors *qua* Freud. The real explanation for why an individual acted in the way they did might not then rest with the agent at all but on some outside influence. If that is so then, on some accounts of the matter, it is difficult to ascribe autonomy to the agent and difficult to regard the agent as having a single and unified self. As a consequence of arguments of this kind, the area of the soul, large and dispersed in some aspects of Hellenism and large but more focused in early Christianity, was gradually confined to a single centre, that single centre, as the self, that was transparent in Descartes but opaque in Kant. Its opacity then became for Freud, and more recently for most contemporary post-modern thinkers, the point at which it lost all credibility as an idea. And, as the soul was squeezed out of play in the language of humankind, so the idea of the autonomous, self-governing individual is also being squeezed out of play in much contemporary discourse and is being replaced by post-individualistic discourse.

In a sense there is nothing surprising in the death of individualism, as with so many 'isms' it has run its course. As a doctrine, an IDEOLOGY, it had a more or less definite beginning, emerging at a particular historical point in time and representing certain underlying changes both in social structure and in ideas. As that social structure changes and as those ideas develop or run their course so one would expect to find and does find post-individualistic expressions and theories. Such theories take many forms; they might emphasize the role of the community, play down the role of subjectivity, displace the subject, locating consciousness and action elsewhere, deny the existence of subjectivity altogether or emphasize or overemphasize the forces or trends of history, as Althusser did in his claim that 'History is a process without a subject'. Such challenges to individualism are challenges that must be met by theology, if the language of the soul is to be kept in play. In Christian theology that language has given rise to and has become entangled with the language of individualism. Yet the SOUL is an idea that is not universally individualistic: it can be found in many forms. In the western experience it developed with the psyche, the breath, the wind of life. 'The psyche as the region in which transcendence is experienced must be differentiated out of a more compact structure of the soul; it must be developed and named . . . one might almost say that before the psyche man had no soul' (Voegelin 1951). But neither the development nor the naming of that soul has to be in starkly individualistic terms. Historically shifts in the conceptions of God have also shaped the development of individualism. In the early Hebrew religion God was understood monistically; in early Christianity the soul was under-

stood individualistically and monistically and God in plural, trinitarian, terms. It would not be surprising to see the idea of the soul follow a similar path. Already in post-individualistic thought the self is understood pluralistically. And so it must be, for in the very act of self enunciation, the 'I' divides in trinitarian fashion; it is the 'I' that enunciates, the 'I' that reflects on the enunciation, and the 'I' that equilibrates between the two.' If the reflective individual must be tripartite the reflective soul can be no less. If the individual really is made in the image of God, and that image is social and trinitarian, then the image of the individual can be no less. And that does not put an end to individuals as such, but it does raise new prospects and opportunities for understanding human beings and for enhancing relations of solidarity between peoples.

St Augustine (1972) *The City of God*, Harmondsworth: Penguin.
Carrithers, M., Collins, S., Lukes, S. (eds) (1985) *The Category of the Person: Anthropology, Philosophy, History*, Cambridge: Cambridge University Press.
Descartes, René *A Discourse on Method*.
Hobbes, Thomas (1946) *Leviathan*, Oxford: Blackwell.
Jaeger, Werner (1947) *The Theology of the Early Greek Philosophers*, Oxford.
Kant, Immanuel (1953) *The Groundwork of the Metaphysics of Morals*, London: Hutchinson.
Kymlicka, Will (1989) *Liberalism, Community and Culture*, Oxford: Clarendon Press.
Locke, John (1960) *Two Treatises of Government*, ed. P. Laslett, Cambridge: Cambridge University Press.
Lukes, Steven *Individualism*.
Mandeville, Bernard (1970) *The Fable of the Bees*, 1723 ed., Philip Harth, Harmondsworth: Penguin.
Pritchard *Ancient Near Eastern Texts*.
Rousseau, Jean-Jacques (1973) *The Social Contract and Discourses*, London: Dent.
Smith, Adam *The Wealth of Nations*.
Voegelin, Eric (1951) *The New Science of Politics*, Chicago: University of Chicago Press.
Weber, Max *The Protestant Ethic and the Spirit of Capitalism*.

Paul Barry Clarke
E.R. Norman

INDUSTRIALIZATION

The traditional definition of industrialization is that it represents 'the fabrication of various materials into intermediate components or finished products by primarily mechanical means dependent on inanimate sources of power' (Moore, cited in Brown and Harrison 1978). The Industrial Revolution, which first began in England in the eighteenth century, came to be characterized by the utilization of machinery, technology and scientific knowledge in the process of production. However, the preconditions for the initiation of industrialization relate more specifically to the release of labour from subsistence agriculture, the concentration of land into fewer hands and the creation of a market economy than they do to the deployment of inanimate means of production. The enclosure of the commons and of peasant farm lands, and the commercialization of agriculture in the seventeenth century, created the necessary conditions for industrialization which include the emergence of a labour market and an economy independent of land, the rise of the town and the shift of labour and capital resources from agricultural production to industrial production. It is these preconditions which explain the rise of industrialization in England before any other country (Hobsbawm 1962). Industrialization commenced in the home and in small village workshops, aided primarily by human labour and other natural sources of power including wind, water and animal power. This first phase of industrialization which involved, for example, home spinning and weaving, carpentry, iron-mongering and the like has been replicated in most industrializing countries, including the less developed countries which still manifest many of the features of this phase of industrialization, including home-working and a mix of agricultural and industrial workshop production in the same household. In many less developed countries this informal sector of economic activity remains larger than the formal industrialized economy.

The second phase of industrialization involves the systematic division of labour, the mobilization of capital in the factory system which utilizes machines and large power sources to drive the production process, and the further development of a financial and economic system independent of land and other primary commodities which has the effect of commodifying land, labour and natural resources. This second phase also requires the spread of a market for the products of industry, a market which rises as the population grows, and is increasingly urbanized.

In this second phase of industrialization the proportion of income derived from manufacturing increases sharply relative to agriculture, the proportion of labour employed in organized industry increases, and income per head also increases, though after the lapse of time and not universally. Pauperization often precedes income growth, as witness the slum and cellar dwellers of Manchester in the early nineteenth century and the more than 1 billion who are pauperized in shanty towns or landless rural poverty in the south today. The process of industrialization eventually involves the industrialization of the agricultural sector which completes the removal of labour from land and the universalization of urban culture in advanced economies. A third phase of industrialization has also been identified, variously called post-industrialism, late CAPITALISM, post-Fordism or de-industrialization, whereby labour, and a growing proportion of gross domestic product, shifts from manufacturing or the secondary sector to the tertiary or service sector which includes financial services, leisure and recreation, medical, educational, clerical and communication services. This late stage of industrialization also involves technological change whereby the proportion of machines to labour employed in manufacturing increases dramatically, and thus rising unemployment becomes a feature of advanced industrial economies.

Other important features of industrialization include URBANIZATION, population increase, the utilization of rational accounting methods, and individual entrepreneurialism. However, the development of an economic system of monetary exchange independent of labour, land or biological resources is the essential characteristic of the second and third phases of industrialization (Brown and Harrison 1978). The historical development of industrialization has been replicated internationally through IMPERIALISM in the colonial territories, and through neocolonialism and the ideologies of DEVELOPMENT and free trade in the new nations of the south. This world system reproduces in the countries of the south the enclosure of land and the commodification of labour and natural resources which first began in the countries bordering the Northern Atlantic. It also involves the internationalization of the division of labour, so that secondary manufacturing is shifting to the industrializing economies of the south where wage rates are lower than in the advanced industrial economies. The internationalization of capital and labour means that the POVERTY or WEALTH of individual countries or regions relates not only to internal political or economic conditions in particular countries, though these remain important, but also to the actions and decisions of large corporate transnational enterprises, global organizations such as the World Bank, or global currency and commodity markets whose budget or annual turnover is much larger than the gross domestic product of many smaller countries. This in turn has significant implications for the control of the industrial and economic process, and for the concept of the nation-state as a locus of sovereign and autonomous political and economic power. The apparently endemic problems of poverty, exponential population growth and environmental degradation currently being experienced by many countries in the south indicate that industrialization is not a straightforward process which is being replicated in the same way in every place, but rather that POWER and economic relations in the world system produce different patterns of industrialization and varying effects depending on the location of particular countries or regions in the global economic system (Webster 1990).

The growth of industrialization in northern Europe is associated with a decline in church-going and a decline in the social influence of religious institutions, a process known as SECULARIZATION. This decline is accounted for by various factors and theories: the alienation from the natural environment inherent in the mechanical processes and urban context of industrialism; the break-up of traditional communities and the symbolic and moral order of church and SOCIETY in local communities; urbanization itself, as the statistics indicate an inverse relation between town size and rates of churchgoing; the spread of secular ideologies such as *laissez-faire* or

market economics, socialism and communism; the development of affluent lifestyles, materialism and consumerism as represented by mass car ownership and the various sources of mass entertainment such as cinema and television.

However, this decline of organized religion has not always been accompanied by a decline in religious belief *per se*, and in any case this secularization effect seems to have been confined primarily to the industrialized countries of northern Europe. It is notable that the largest and most affluent industrialized economy, the USA, continues to experience a high degree of organized religious activity. Similarly the newly industrialized countries (NICs) of southeast Asia, Taiwan, Korea, Singapore and Hong Kong have undergone a rapid process of industrialization and rising incomes without significant reductions in religious belief or in organized religious behaviour. One theory is that it is the individualism which industrialization and capitalist development favoured in northern Europe, and on which capital formation and entrepreneurialism to a certain extent depended, which is one of the primary factors in the demise of collective religious behaviour in these countries. In southeast Asia and Japan industrialization has taken a more collective form, involving a closer partnership between state and private capital and a more collective approach to the culture of the workplace than the oppositional class system and *laissez-faire* approaches which characterized industrialization in Western Europe. This more collectivist approach to social structure and to the design and management of the industrial process, reflecting the communal ideals of Asian culture, is thought to be a factor in the economic success of the NICs and Japan relative to the industrial economies of northern Europe and North America.

CLASS conflict was also an important factor in the demise of organized religion in the countries of northern Europe. Marx asserted that religion acted as an opiate, legitimating the alienation and oppression experienced by the working classes in the division of labour and the extraction of surplus value from the working class by the owner class. However, while some have proposed that Christian influence on the trade union movement, and METHODISM in

England in particular, played an important part in the suppression of class discontent, there is much evidence that trade unionism, in asserting the rights of labour over capital, took its inspiration from the Bible and the traditions of Christian preaching and social ethics (Studdert-Kennedy 1982). None the less the role played by the established churches in England and Scotland in the enclosures and clearances which removed the peasantry from the land and prepared the way for industrialization played a significant part in the alienation of the new urban masses from established religion. Furthermore, even if the slum dweller or factory hand had the desire, or the time or energy, to attend church after the twelve- to eighteen-hour day of the early factory regime, he or she found that church accommodation was mostly rented out to the middle classes, suitable 'Sunday clothing' was too expensive, and the church building was located at some distance from the poor inner city housing areas, reflecting the fact that there were too few churches in the new towns and cities to accommodate the new urban masses (Chadwick 1975).

The response of the churches to industrialization has been varied. The loss of theological control over the economic process which occurred with the demise of the traditional prohibition on usury (Tawney 1938) was followed by a loss of ecclesial control over many other areas of human life in the new industrial culture. However, the church was able to reassert its social control and at the same time to respond to the worst social effects of industrialization – bad housing, lack of sanitation, inhuman hours of work, indebtedness, vagrancy, and child labour – by a paternalistic reproduction of a system of charitable institutions, penitentiaries and welfare which took its inspiration from the social structure of the rural parish. The parish system also needed radical revision, and town parishes were subdivided by a large programme of church building and church extension to accommodate the new urban masses.

As conditions in the industrial cities worsened so the churches began to challenge the laissez-faire economics and polity which condemned the masses to these inhuman conditions (Norman 1976). The 'slum priests' of the Anglocatholic tradition, evangelicals influenced by the ideas of William Wilberforce and the Clapham Sect, Thomas Chalmers and Patrick Brewster in Scotland, the Papal Encyclical Rerum Novarum, all in different ways sought to re-establish and represent Christian ideals of justice, community and commonwealth in the context of class conflict and the poor living conditions of the industrial classes as contrasted with the amassing of wealth by the new owner class (Charlton et al. 1986). Many of the reforms of the worst excesses of the factory system in the nineteenth century, including child labour and inhuman hours of work, were brought about under the influence of Christian ideals and leaders. Similarly in the twentieth century the universalization of medical care, welfare, unemployment benefit and education in industrialized countries took its rise from this same vein of Christian idealism and theological ideas of the common good.

As the social and charitable ideals of the Christian religion were effectively replicated in secular agencies the need for church intervention and charity declined. At the same time the alienation between industrialism and church grew all the more strongly. In response to the dechristianization of the industrial classes the churches in the twentieth century developed a new kind of ministry to industry, known as industrial mission, which originated in chaplaincies to the ordinance factories of Europe in the Second World War. The worker priest movement in France, and industrial chaplains in Britain, Germany and North America attempted to bridge the gap between the working classes and the church with varying degrees of success (Northcott 1989). The industrial mission movement has been replicated around the world in urban industrial mission, or urban rural mission, and has become an increasing locus for criticism of the globalization of industrialism through transnational corporations and banks, and its deleterious effects in terms of landlessness, pauperization, unemployment, and the enforced migration of rural peoples to shanty towns and slums on the edge of the new cities of the south. Theological criticism and social resistance to the effects of global industrialization has become focused on the movement of LIBERATION THEOLOGY which originated in Latin America. The challenge to Christian tradition and theological and social ethics, domination and oppression as experienced by the rural and urban masses in the context of the commercialization of agriculture, the rise of industrialization and the spread of the market economy has been replicated in contextual theologies around the world from Latin America to Africa and Asia.

Increasingly both in the north and the south industrialization is being criticized for its deleterious effects on the natural environment. The commodification of the natural world has resulted in the unsustainable 'mining' of natural resources including soil, water, forests and fossil fuels, and the poisoning of the natural world, the mass extinction of species, and disturbances to ecosystems including the global climate, resulting from waste products and toxins and the polluting effects of consumer goods such as automobiles. Church groups, church leaders and theologians in north and south call for restraints on affluence and consumerism, and the proper regulation of industrialism to take account of the biological limits to growth and the despoliation of the natural world, and the inequitable effects of industrial development between north and south and between urban and rural peoples (see ENVIRONMENT). While increased average incomes, the advancement of health, education and nutrition, increased leisure time and declining DEATH rates have been typical end results of the process of industrialization in many parts of the world, these human gains must be set against the global problems of environmental despoliation, the pressure imposed by increased populations in north and south, and the increasing inequities which are apparently being fostered by the contemporary pattern of industrialization in both advanced and less developed economies.

Industrialization has posed enormous problems of adaptation and response for the Christian tradition and theological and social ethics since its rise in the Industrial Revolution in Britain. There is growing evidence that, whereas the earliest phases of industrialization tended to subvert the religious patterning of human life and the Christian forms of that patterning in Europe and to a certain extent in North America,

ica, in the late twentieth century religion and traditional communities and cultures, including Christian churches and theologies, are representing a new force for criticism and change in relation to the processes and culture of industrialism. This global phenomenon is reflected in new social and ethical responses to industrialization which are being developed by Christian theologians and church communities around the world.

Brown, D. and Harrison, N.J. (1978) *A Sociology of Industrialisation: An Introduction*, London: Macmillan.

Chadwick, O. (1975) *The Secularization of the European Mind in the Nineteenth Century*, Cambridge: Cambridge University Press.

Charlton, W., Mallinson, T. and Oakeshott, R. (1986) *The Christian Response to Industrial Capitalism*, London: Sheed & Ward.

Hobsbawm, E.J. (1962) *The Age of Revolution*, London: Weidenfeld & Nicolson.

Norman, E.R. (1976) *Church and Society in England 1770–1970. A Historical Study*, Oxford: Clarendon.

Northcott, M.S. (1989) *The Church and Secularisation. Urban Industrial Mission in North East England*, Frankfurt: Peter Lang.

Studdert-Kennedy G. (1982) *Dog Collar Democracy. The Industrial Christian Fellowship 1919–1929*, London: Macmillan.

Tawney, R.H. (1938) *Religion and the Rise of Capitalism*, Harmondsworth: Penguin.

Webster, Andrew (1990) *Introduction to the Sociology of Development*, London: Macmillan.

Michael S. Northcott

INTELLIGENCE SERVICES

Government depends on information. Systems of knowing are, in Deutsch's phrase, part of 'the nerves of government' (Deutsch 1963). Governments apprehend the world of foreign policy, defence and other aspects of national security partly through the 'intelligence services' or (in recent years, in English-speaking countries) 'the intelligence community'.

The American intelligence budget in the early 1990s was unofficially estimated at about a tenth of total defence costs. In Britain the three secret agencies plus strategic military intelligence currently cost rather over a billion pounds annually – around 4% of the defence budget, or about what is spent on the Foreign and Commonwealth Office and overseas diplomacy.

The intelligence 'system' is really two linked sub-systems. One collects information by covert means, which produce 'single-source' secret intelligence and add to governments' stock of knowledge from other sources; 'secret intelligence is the continuation of open intelligence by other means' (Trevor-Roper 1968: 66). The other analyses *all* kinds of information, not just from covert sources but also from press reports, radio broadcasts, diplomatic reporting and other sources.

Intelligence has been a synonym for 'news' in English since the middle of the fifteenth century, including 'secret intelligence' from spies, informers and the interception of messages (*see* ESPIONAGE). Governments have collected 'intelligence' in this sense throughout history. The lineage of the British intelligence system is well established, dating back to Walsingham's and Thurlow's agents and postal intercepts in the sixteenth and seventeenth centuries. In the eighteenth century there were Admiralty networks of agents to give warnings of French and Spanish naval movements, and arrangements for intercepting and deciphering diplomatic dispatches. Most Continental countries had similar arrangements.

Generally *ad hoc* arrangements lasted until just after the Crimean War. But soon thereafter the technological changes of the Industrial Revolution produced bigger military forces, dispersed over wider areas, moving at greater speed, with a greater emphasis on movement and surprise. By the turn of the century most countries had introduced some form of formal structures of 'intelligence'. In Britain a War Office Intelligence Branch was formed in 1873 and an Indian Intelligence Branch in 1878. The Admiralty created a Foreign Intelligence Committee in 1882, and the first War Office and Admiralty Directors of Intelligence were appointed in 1887. In America the Navy and Army Intelligence Departments were founded in 1882 and 1885 respectively. Initially this 'intelligence' was equated with the acquisition and use of information on one's own as well as foreign forces. But 'intelligence' became increasingly identified with the study of 'Foreign Armies'.

There was an organizational parallel in the evolution of internal security. From 1815 onwards most Continental countries developed special policing for the 'exceptional crime' of domestic revolution and (later) international anarchism and communism; and in the second half of the century this developed its distinct identity. With few internal threats, Britain was late in this field. The first organization of this kind was the Metropolitan Police's Special Branch, established in 1883 after the Fenian bombings in Britain. Later fears of German spies led to the creation in 1909 of the Secret Intelligence Bureau, which became the Security Service after World War I in response to international communism. 'Security intelligence' of this kind, with espionage, sabotage, subversion and terrorism as its targets, evolved alongside the rather larger military and naval efforts on 'foreign intelligence'.

There was also a growth of specialized collection. Much of the foreign information needed by the Victorian intelligence departments was available from newspapers and military attachés' reports. But towards the end of the century technical and operational surprise became more important and secrecy increased. World War I produced an unprecedented scale of organized espionage and also saw the development of new 'technical' means of collection. Radio interception or signals intelligence (now *Sigint*) expanded the ancient art of decipherment to cope with the new targets provided by the use of radio. Aerial photography from reconnaissance aircraft (now *imagery*) similarly revolutionized the occasional earlier use of observers in balloons.

By the end of World War I some principal elements of twentieth-century intelligence were in place: military intelligence departments, internal security organizations, and professional collection agencies. The emergence of the USSR and world COMMUNISM after 1917, then World War II and the Cold War successively increased their scope and permanency. Total war in World War II needed total intelligence; the Cold War put a similar peacetime premium on integrating the military threat with the political, subversive and economic strands of Soviet activity. States which developed centralized defence planning came to need central intelligence assessments to serve it. Along with this came the idea of intelligence as a manageable, national *community*, with its own structure and overseas liaisons.

The arrangement of its building-blocks varies, but there are some Western regularities. Collection predominates; defence intelligence has its large analysis agencies and there are usually separate security intelligence organizations such as the British Security Service.

Intelligence raises issues *vis-à-vis* individual rights, the rule of law and accountability to elected governments and assemblies. The trend is to increase its public transparency and its legal framework, following the example set by arrangements for American Congressional 'oversight' developed in the 1970s. Britain in recent years has provided a statutory basis and has introduced a (limited) degree of Parliamentary accountability. But there is no easy reconciliation between democratic openness and intelligence's need for source protection. There are also practical decisions about the 'peace dividend' that might be expected to follow from the end of the cold war. On all these counts views have to be formed on intelligence's national use in the new conditions of the 1990s; and whether it makes for a better world or a worse one.

The national value of intelligence is significant. States cannot exist on intelligence alone, but it helps them to maximize other kinds of national power and influence. It has its failures, but on the whole leaders do better by listening to it than ignoring it. It may have some inbuilt 'worst' case tendencies, but leaders' own unchecked biases are worse. It is a window on a turbulent and dangerous world and there is no reason to think that intelligence will be superseded.

Covert collection is open to more debate. Much of it was devoted in the Cold War to a 'near real time' surveillance of the adversary's military forces, in a way that cannot be needed on the same scale now. American commentators argue that 'as the world becomes multipolar, more complex and no longer understandable through the prism of Soviet competition, more intelligence – not less – will be needed' (Boren 1992: 54). But the more open world surely reduces the need for secret intelligence. If CNN can see and report things instantaneously what is the need for intelligence satellites? Coverage of foreign news services must be increasingly cost-effective compared with covert sources.

But this is a matter of degree. In confused situations diplomats and the press still cannot offer everything. There are still plenty of unstable areas, secretive states, terrorist organizations and clandestine activities like arms control evasion and nuclear proliferation. There is still plenty of concealment and deception, not allayed by the unpredictability of media coverage.

Three general points are relevant. First, there is a relationship between offensive intelligence and a state's information defences. Since the eighteenth century it has been axiomatic that the best people to devise secure ciphers are a state's own cipherbreakers, and the same applies elsewhere. Second, there is the special relationship with military power. Military forces need a mass of unglamorous information; defence subjects consumed about 70% of American intelligence spending in the 1970s. The ultimate rationale for the intelligence community is as a force in being for the eventuality of war, as was demonstrated in the Gulf War. Wartime support cannot be improvised from scratch.

Third, the overall scale of intelligence still depends on how states see their threats and interests and peacetime standing. America needs foreign intelligence on a superpower scale. Britain prides herself on 'punching above her weight', with intelligence as a supporting element bound up with the transatlantic relationship. Bombs in London and Belfast give a fillip to the domestic dimension.

Intelligence has ceased to be a growth industry, but the investment in it will continue to combine states' concerns and self-images.

To this national view must be added international effects. Intelligence on the whole promotes international security. Of course it can support anti-social behaviour; states like the former Soviet Union and Saddam Hussein's Iraq get the intelligence they want and deserve. But on the whole it does something to limit the dangers of misperception.

Collection can also support international security. Arms control in the 1970s depended on photographic satellites for verification; what intelligence could see determined what arms control agreements were about. America and the USSR agreed not to impair each other's 'national technical means' (NTMs) of collection, when used for arms control 'in a manner consistent with generally recognized principles of international law' (undefined).

National collection has also served in confidence-building for others; the results of American U-2 photography were supplied to Israel and Egypt as part of the ceasefire agreement after the Yom Kippur War. There is a similar role in supporting United Nations operations, as in Bosnia. There is some talk about 'UN owned' intelligence systems for peacekeeping; but NATO experience is that an alliance cannot run secret sources securely, and has to depend on national intelligence inputs.

Most intelligence collection serves purely national interests, and on the whole its existence does not affect international security one way or the other. Photographic surveillance by American, Russian and other satellites is accepted as a fact of life. Diplomats assume that their open phone calls can be tapped by their host countries. Covert collection is for the most part accepted as part of the international game.

On the other hand not all of it is as neutral in its effect. Espionage produces feelings of intrusion and threat. Close-range technical collection in national airspace or territorial waters did the same during the Cold War, and served as a surrogate for the use of armed force. The scale and type of Soviet espionage nourished Western threat perceptions. We now have the signs that espionage cases are part of a renewed hardening of Western relations with the new Russia.

This suggests an intelligence version of the security dilemma, whereby military forces designed to promote national security have the effects of reducing it. Intelligence is collected to enhance national security. But some of it is seen by others as an intrusive threat and evokes reactions of greater secrecy and intrusive intelligence in reply, in a spiral of action and reaction.

The development of an international society of states may eventually cultivate similar standards, or a tacit intelligence equivalent of the Laws of War. Of course spies, informers and other intrusion will remain necessary, not least to counter terrorism and other non-state threats. But international security may come to demand some moderation over the circumstances and scale of intrusion: '. . . would it not be healthy to try to manoeuvre secret intelligence agencies a little more to the margin of affairs?' (Hibbert 1990: 126).

There are now said to be contacts between Russian and Western intelligence agencies concerning terrorism, policing illicit arms traffic, drug trafficking and major international crime. There may be scope for a quiet East–West dialogue on the scale of intrusion. Western intrusions around former Soviet airspaces and waters is presumably now minimal. The main issue is espionage. The recent Russian running of an agent inside CIA counterintelligence was no doubt justified as a source of information on Western espionage inside Russia. But the reaction to it calls the game into question. The principle of 'reasonable sufficiency' with respect to intelligence would require a major Russian scaling-down of the traditional communist importance of espionage vis-à-vis conventional diplomacy. But the West would need to accept that it was not an intrinsically one-sided concept.

Andrew, C. (1985) Secret Service: the Making of the British Intelligence Community, London: Heinemann.
——and Gordievsky, O. (1990) KGB, London: Hodder & Stoughton.
Berkowitz, B. and Goodman, A. (1989) Strategic Intelligence for American National Security, Princeton, NJ: Princeton University Press.
Boren, D.L. (1992) 'The Intelligence Community: How Crucial?', Foreign Affairs, 71(3).
Deutsch, K. W. (1963) The Nerves of Government, New York: Free Press.
Farson, A.S., Stafford, D. and Wark, W.K. (eds) (1991) Security and Intelligence in a Changing World, London: Cass.
Godson, R. (ed.) (1979–) Intelligence Requirements for the 1980s (Analysis and Estimates, Clandestine Collection, Counterintelligence, Covert Action, Domestic Intelligence and Elements of Intelligence), Washington, DC: National Strategy Information Center and Transaction Books.
——(1989) Intgelligence Requirements for the 1990s, Lexington, MA: Lexington Books.
Herman, M.E. (1992) 'Government Intelligence: Its Evolution and Role', Journal of Economic and Social Intelligence, 2(2).

Hibbert, R. (1990) 'Intelligence and Policy', *Intelligence and National Security*, 5(1).

Hinsley, F.H. et al. (1979–90) *British Intelligence in the Second World War*, 5 vols, London: HMSO.

Johnson, L.K. (1989) *America's Secret Power*, Oxford: Oxford University Press.

Robertson, K. G. (ed.) (1987) *British and American Approaches to Intelligence*, London: Macmillan.

Shulsky, A.N. (1991) *Silent Warfare*, London: Brassey's.

Trevor-Roper, H. (Lord Dacre) (1968) *The Philby Affair – Espionage, Treason and Secret Services*, London: Kimber.

Turner, S. (1985) *Secrecy and Democracy*, London: Harper & Row.

Michael Herman

INTERNATIONAL RELATIONS

The most widespread concepts are rarely the work of experts; one must take into account their common usage. The amalgam of sources does not always facilitate the understanding of their meaning.

Thus, although it may seem straightforward, the term 'international relations' is hampered by a triple handicap. First, it refers both to a certain category of occurrences and to their study (at least in some countries, especially Anglo-Saxon, in which the study of international relations is high on the list in academic programmes). To this first difficulty can be added a far more serious one: the term 'international', invented by Jeremy Bentham in 1780 (in *An Introduction to the Principles of Morals and Legislation*), is today widespread (e.g. *international* LAW, United *Nations* Organization, etc.). Yet 'nations', which were confused with states during the *ancien régime*, remain distinct from them in several ways, to the extent that sometimes 'nation' is opposed to 'STATE'. Nevertheless, the study of 'international' relations characterizes, more often than not, relations between states, which are the privileged subjects of international law and the principal actors on the international scene. It would therefore be more logical to speak of 'inter-state relations' instead of international relations; but scientific rigour is powerless against common usage. Finally, and above all, international relations have acquired a number of characteristics which, by

way of simplification, one tends to project on to a past of great richness and extreme complexity. To study the history of international relations would mean no less than recalling the entire human adventure, reconstructing experiences as diverse as the superposition of geological strata. A look at the past is nevertheless necessary if one wants to evaluate correctly the origin and the specific nature of international relations in the contemporary world.

No-one can know when and how the peopling of the world gave birth to the differentiation of races, languages and beliefs. However, the most ancient legends (Homer), the sacred texts (the Bible) and the works of historians (Thucydides, Herodotus) are full of sound and fury. Once they were formed into distinct societies, the peoples developed relations made up of WAR, truce and PEACE, long-lasting dominations (the Roman Empire) or short ones (Alexander's Empire), invasions and even arrangements relating to the statute of foreigners: all of which represented the manifestations of international life. Yet, do the words retain the same meaning today? Human societies are extremely diverse, not only in size and power but also in status: nomadic tribes, wealthy and dynamic cities, kingdoms of all sizes, empires, barbaric hordes have lived side by side or succeeded each other in the same area. As a general rule, relations were limited to neighbourhood and did not lead to the creation of groupings. The precariousness of living conditions and the difficulty of communication were obstacles to this, a further reason being the sacred character attributed to the exercise of POWER. 'Two cities were two religious associations which did not have the same Gods' (Fustel de Coulanges). From this probably follows – except for a few rare philosophers – the lack of conscience of a common destiny for the human species. No general design seems to have guided the progress of humanity through the advances of the most developed societies and the ruins on which civilizations have successively foundered. History is a chaotic accumulation lacking a guideline or intelligible meaning.

Paradoxically, it was the intrusion of the religious factor which was to contribute to shattering these pecularities and giving meaning to profane history. The expansion of Islam from the seventh century onwards created a vast empire, spreading from the marches of India to south of the Pyrenees. Confronted with this threat, the Christian kingdoms of Europe took some time to react. It was only at the beginning of the second millennium that Christianity was founded. At the top of the pyramid which formed the feudal structure of society were two authorities: the Emperor, in charge of temporal power, and the Pope, in charge of spiritual power. In short, medieval Christianity on a European level was the first example of an organized international society, although it is true that the permanent rivalries between these two 'swords' and the endemic uprisings of the feudal nobles frequently blighted the smooth functioning of this experience. At the same time, Christianity launched several attempts to recover the holy places occupied by Islam. The Crusades thus were the first of the great wars of religion and the first example of an intercontinental clash between two civilizations.

From the sixteenth century onwards, the scenery and the behaviour of the actors changed radically. The great naval discoveries opened up the way for colonization: the Europeans, turning away from the East, became involved in the conquest and domination of America, before spreading their supremacy to Africa. Thus, Europe became, for three centuries, the centre and driving force of a world undergoing deep transformation.

Simultaneously, Europe suffered an internal crisis of unprecedented severity. The Reformation marked the end of Christian unity and triggered wars of religion within kingdoms and between them. The Thirty Years War ended (1648) only on the basis of a compromise (*Cujus regio, ejus religio*) which established the division between Protestant and Catholic states. This religious split was to have major political consequences. The Church often remained linked to the exercise of power, but states progressively freed themselves, calling upon the principle of secularity, which enabled them to re-establish the conditions for dialogue between them. At the same time, all European states took advantage of the circumstances to cut their bonds of dependence on a superior AUTHORITY, be it temporal or spiritual, and to claim their sovereignty,

i.e. the right to decide freely on their actions concerning both internal and external matters. For sovereignty to be complete, all states, assimilated to persons, were and must be considered equal by law, irrespective of their size or power.

From then on, the state of anarchy, which had always more or less dominated international relations, acquired an explanation and theoretical justification. Opposing the jurists, who pressed to submit states to a 'NATURAL LAW' which grew more and more inconsistent as years went by, Thomas Hobbes's *Leviathan* (1677) defined the fundamental distinction between the state of SOCIETY and the state of nature. The first prevailed, within state societies, through the instauration of the Social Pact; the second subsisted in relations between those same states and was governed by the laws of preservation and self-defence alone. The theory of the 'state of nature' strengthens the pretence of states to their sovereignty and served, in the writings of well-known authors (Locke, J.J. Rousseau, Kant, Hegel, R. Aron), as a fundamental paradigm for the interpretation of international relations.

State leaders found this explanation highly suitable as it upheld their full freedom of action and the fact that the only obligations to which they accepted to be submitted, via treaties, were those to which they had previously subscribed. It was in this context that the Europeans spread their supremacy to the whole world whilst fighting among themselves to gain, one after the other, a short-lived preponderance. The rise of nationalisms during the nineteenth century only worsened rivalries, leading in 1914 to the First World War; retrospectively, it appeared as a collective SUICIDE, a foretaste of the decline of Europe (*see* NATIONALISM).

The latter was to gather momentum with ideological quarrels which reached their peak during the twentieth century. Two European countries endeavoured to overthrow the equilibrium based on the sovereign equality of states. Neither Germany under Hitler's national socialist regime nor the Soviet Union under Lenin and his successors were 'ordinary' countries. The basis of the first of these countries lay in the supposed superiority of one human race which held as its vocation to dominate, even to eliminate, the inferior races (cf. the 'final solution' to the Jewish question). This gigantic undertaking was to trigger off the Second World War in 1939 and to end in 1945 with the crushing of Germany and its allies (Japan) after hostilities had seen the major powers fighting on four continents and on the oceans of the world. For the Soviet Union, founded in 1917, it was not enough merely to be a socialist version of Russia; its aim was to become the model and instrument of a future worldwide CLASS struggle. And if circumstances initially forced the USSR to limit the construction of SOCIALISM 'to a single country', the part it played in the fight against national socialism enabled it to strengthen its situation and to position its forces with a view to initiating a world revolution. From 1945 onwards, the international scene was dominated by East–West antagonism, symbolized by the rivalry between the Soviet Union and the USA. Only through the threat of mutual destruction, illustrated by the strategy of deterrence, could a relative balance be maintained between the two blocs and the resort to nuclear weapons be avoided, the use of which would surely have signed the death warrant of civilization upon Earth.

Today, although the spontaneous collapse of the Communist system has attenuated these dangers, this does not necessarily mean a return to traditional international politics, even less the end of history.

This very succinct outline none the less provides an understanding of the many changes which have occurred, in the course of history, both in the concept and in the substance of 'international relations'. These nowadays have very little in common with the classical model drawn up by seventeenth- or nineteenth-century theoreticians.

There still persists, of course, a certain number of constants, the basic principle of which is survival and even proliferation of the state cells. The state remains the privileged subject of international law. Only agents duly mandated by governments are qualified to involve their states in relations with foreign authorities or international organizations. But is the state still the main actor in international relations? Undoubtedly, as far as major powers are concerned, which have at hand the means to ensure their independence. One should not be deluded, however, by the proliferation of the number of states following the wave of decolonization which has overswept the old European empires (including that the Soviet Union) since 1945. The United Nations amounted to fifty members when it was founded in June 1945; it includes now more than 180. And, of the 130 new states, how many have the resources, whether natural or human, which would enable them to survive? Most are merely puppets, destined to become assisted or satellites.

Even the major states are open to competition from new actors. Whether they are democratic or even authoritarian, governments must first come to terms with the internal forces which seek to influence foreign policy: the armed forces, the military-industrial complex, production cartels (both industrial and agricultural), decentralized collective bodies, public opinion (religious or ideological), all of which feel involved in the course of international relations. At the same time, states feel restrained in their initiatives under the pressure of the international, regional or universal organizations in which they participate. They are also subject to the influence of private international groups which seek to have their ideologies or interests prevail in all spheres (from churches and humanitarian movements, multinationals, to drug cartels). To get an idea of the strengthening of these international networks, one merely needs to observe that, since the beginning of the century, the number of intergovernmental organizations has multiplied by ten and that of non-governmental organizations by thirty.

The classic image of a juxtaposition of sovereign states does not correspond to reality anymore. Independence has become a myth. Those states which are not purely and simply dependent are prisoners of interdependence which greatly restricts their scope of movement.

If the situation is such, it is because technical progress, accelerated by wars, has radically changed the conditions under which international relations take place. The traditional obstacles of time and distance have been considerably reduced by new means of communication, production capacity has increased in all sectors of human activity and the volume of exchanges has grown even more rapidly. To a shrinking world, now fully explored, exploited and occupied by man, corresponds an intensification of the flux and interactions of its composing units. To continue reasoning in terms of national interest does not mean much anymore – even for the great powers. The most urgent problems for the future of humanity (population migrations, the reduction of DEVELOPMENT inequalities, arms deals, the fight against pollution and endemic diseases) have become global and, logically, call for collective decisions.

Yet, the logic which could lead to the foundation of a 'public authority of universal competence', in the words of Pope John XXIII in the Encyclical *Pacem in Terris* (1963), has already and will for a long time come up against the resistance of national peculiarities. These are exacerbated by a diffuse fear of loss of identity in a world promised to uniformity of ways of life and to a concentration of power. Even if the great ideological conflicts have been momentarily appeased, the defence of short-term interests and the visceral attachment to customs, traditions and habits, which give peoples a reason for living and dying, hinder the chances of setting up a kind of world GOVERNMENT. The Tower of Babel, the technocrats' dream, will never be built on the ruins of states and the corpses of civilizations. Yet, the timorous retreat of peoples into the galleries of a vast molehill can lead only to collective suffocation. The world is thrown back, close to the end of the second millennium, to the Hegelian dialectic of the Universal and the Particular.

Confronted with this gigantic challenge, religions cannot remain indifferent. The Christian churches (true 'internationals') have courageously opted, since 1945, for the defence of peace, development in the Third World and the reinforcement of the role of international organizations. The WORLD COUNCIL OF CHURCHES has even gone so far as to support the movements of national liberation during certain periods of decolonization. The Roman Catholic Church itself played an important part in the emancipation of Poland, which served as a prelude to the collapse of the communist bloc. Today, it is resolutely engaged in favour of the political recomposition of Europe which would regroup the Eastern and Western countries.

However, the role of the religious factor remains ambivalent. Nothing can prevent the monotheists' pretension to universality; nor can competition between their religions be avoided. Inside Christianity, the ecumenical movement is marking time and some distrust subsists between Rome and the World Council of Churches. The dialogue remains difficult to establish between Catholics and Orthodox owing to the tradition of allegiance to the political power which prevailed for a long time in Eastern Europe: the unification of Europe will not be facilitated by this. But the main issue remains the incomprehension which has arisen between the Christian religion and Islam. The religions of the Book have nevertheless certain values in common. But attempts to create a better mutual comprehension have been momentarily hindered by the politicization and radicalization of Islam, which certain fanaticized elements want to transform into the spearhead of the battle against the West. While the latter is delivered of its obsession with COMMUNISM, tensions may be transfered to the North–South axis and involve the religious forces in compromises with strategies of strength. New wars of religion are not fatal; yet there exist a number of local fires which could spread depending on the circumstances. The capacity of the world to progress beyond the egotism of inter-state relations and to engage on the path of a slow, difficult but necessary integration depends, however, at least partially, on the relations which will be established between the religious forces in the near future.

Such are the stakes and dimensions of international relations.

Aron, Raymond (1963–84) *Paix et guerre entre les nations*, Paris: Calmann-Lévy.
Baylis, John and Rengger, N.J. (1992) *Dilemmas of World Politics*, Oxford: Oxford University Press.
Deutsch, Karl (1968) *The Analysis of International Relations*, New York: Prentice Hall.
Hoffmann, Stanley (1964) *Contemporary Theory in International Relations*, New York: Prentice Hall.
Holsti, K.J. (1983) *International Politics: a Framework for Analysis*, New York: Prentice Hall.
Korany, Baghat (ed.) (1987) *Analyse des relations internationales*, Quebec: Gaetan Morin.
Merle, Marcel (1988) *Sociologie des relations internationales*, Paris: Dalloz.

Mesa, Roberto (1977) *Theoria y practica de relaciones internacionales*, Madrid: Taurus.

Morgenthau, Hans J. (1965) *Politics among Nations*, New York: Knopf.

Renouvin, Pierre (ed.) (1953–8) *Histoire de relations internationales du Moyen Age à nos jours*, 8 vols, Paris: Hachette.

——and Duroselle, Jean-Baptiste (1964) *Introduction à l'histoire des relations internationales*, Paris: A. Colin.

Reynolds, Philip (1971) *Introduction to International Relations*, London: Longman.

Rosenau, James N. (1990) *Turbulence in World Politics*, Princeton, NJ: Princeton University Press.

Truyo y Serra, Antonio (1974) *La sociedad internacional*, Madrid: Alianza.

Marcel Merle

ISLAMIC FUNDAMENTALISM

Islamic fundamentalism is an expression used, predominantly by non-Muslims, when referring to a wide variety of phenomena connected with the current resurgence of Islam. The term 'FUN-DAMENTALISM' was coined in the nineteenth century to describe a particular type of Protestant Christianity which stressed the complete inerrancy and infallibility of the Bible. It is questionable whether it is either helpful or appropriate to use it when discussing Islamic movements. However, since it is frequently employed in this context, I will examine two brands of Islam which are often dubbed fundamentalist: the Sunni Muslim Brotherhood and its various offshoots, and the Shî'ite neo-traditionalism of the late Ayatollah Khomeini. Before doing this, I will offer some general considerations concerning Muslim attitudes to the Qur'an, the origins of the traditionalist vision of Islam, and the recent history of the Islamic world.

The vast majority of Muslims are 'fundamentalist' in their approach to Scripture, in so far as they believe that the Qur'an is in its entirety the Word of God brought to Muhammad by the angel Gabriel. This is not, however, a modern development; it is the foundation of historic Islam and seems to be implied by the very structure of the Quranic discourse in which an omniscient magisterial speaker addresses a privileged individual (Robinson 1986). Moreover it is a remarkable fact that the widespread practice of accurately memorizing the Qur'an has preserved it from textual corruption in the course of transmission. Nevertheless although ordinary Muslims, who recite the Qur'an or hear it recited, may at times feel that God's authoritative Word is being addressed to them personally, much as it was first addressed to the Prophet Muhammad, they generally accept that the Quranic message needs to be interpreted by accredited religious scholars.

In addition to expertise in Arabic grammar and philology, these religious scholars draw on a vast body of traditional material. In the first place they attempt to interpret the Qur'an in the light of the Qur'an, a process which is complicated by the fact that the revelations were received piecemeal over a period of twenty-three years, that they are not arranged in chronological order, and that apparent contradictions are sometimes to be explained in terms of later revelations abrogating earlier ones. The next stage in interpretation involves confronting the Quranic text with the Sunna, i.e. with all that is reliably narrated about the Prophet: his acts, his sayings and whatever he tacitly approved. This information is preserved in the form of hadiths, each consisting of a chain of guarantors reaching back to a Companion of the Prophet, followed by a saying attributed to the Prophet himself or a statement about him. Since there is no one authoritative collection of hadiths, and since hadiths have to be graded on the basis of the strength of their attestation, due attention being paid to every link in each chain of guarantors, this aspect of Quranic interpretation requires massive erudition. After interpreting the Qur'an in the light of the Qur'an and confronting the Quranic text with the Sunna, the religious scholar may draw on traditional interpretations attributed to the Companions or, failing that, on those attributed to their pupils (Robinson 1991: 60–77).

This approach to Quranic interpretation assumes and reinforces the traditionalist vision – a vision of an authentic Islam already existing as a complete system in the time of Muhammad, perfectly understood by his Companions and scrupulously transmitted from generation to generation by an uninterrupted succession of irreproachable witnesses. Although this vision has been dominant among Muslims since the ninth century, historical investigation suggests that the thirty-year period following the death of Muhammad in 632 was in fact one of intense sectarian rivalry, and it is possible that even the contents of the Qur'an were not fixed at this stage. Moreover during the Umayyad period (661–750), when the Islamic Empire was ruled from Damascus, the influence of Greek thought encouraged speculative approaches to both theology and jurisprudence. The traditionalist vision seems to have emerged as a reaction against this, amongst the pious scholars who helped replace the Umayyad dynasty with that of the Abbasids. Although its origins are imperfectly understood, it is implicit in the approaches of all the extant Sunni legal schools, all four of which were founded in the eighth or ninth centuries, and it is very clearly articulated in the *Risâla* of Muhammad b. Idrîs al-Shâfi'î (d. 204/820), the founder of the Shâfi'ite school. Until the middle of the tenth century, religious scholars, trained according to the principles of any one of these schools, had the right of *ijtihâd*, i.e. they were entitled to make a personal effort to deduce the law from the Qur'an and Sunna when it was not self-evident. However, there then emerged a consensus that the gate of ijtihâd was closed, that there could be no new schools and that in future religious scholars would have to follow the precedents established in the school to which they belonged.

Throughout the Abbasid period religious scholars enjoyed considerable prestige, but it was in the heyday of the Ottoman Empire that they reached the apogee of their POWER. For over three hundred years, until well into the nineteenth century, they had a virtual monopoly of the administration of JUSTICE, the staffing of educational establishments and the control of religious trusts. Beginning in 1838, however, the Sultans introduced a number of reforms incorporating elements of European law into the legislative system and founding Western-style schools and colleges. As a result the power of the religious scholars was progressively undermined (Watt 1988: 24–43). The European encroachment on Islam was not restricted to the territories of the Ottoman Empire. In the course of the nineteenth century and during the first decades of the twentieth, the British, French, Dutch

and Italians colonized, created protectorates in or exerted a strong external influence on the whole of the Islamic world from Morocco to the East Indies. In most regions this led to the growth of modern cities adjoining the traditional medinas, the establishment of European schools alongside the religious madrasas and the introduction of a dual system of administration. Although the European authorities often regarded Islam as a reactionary force hindering progress they did not as a rule attempt to suppress Muslim institutions. The nationalist leaders who liberated their countries from the yoke of Western imperialism were less restrained. For instance in Turkey Ataturk abolished the Caliphate, in Iran Reza Khan introduced legislation enforcing Western-style dress for men and prohibiting the veiling of women, and in Tunisia Bourguiba opposed fasting in Ramadhan and put an end to twelve centuries of Islamic higher education by closing the Zitouna. Thus paradoxically, shortly after the armies of the colonial powers lost their last battles, their ideologies won their greatest victories. Now after several decades of independence the situation is very different. There is widespread disillusionment with the 'progressive' forces of NATIONALISM because in most instances they have failed to bring the benefits of MODERNITY to all but a tiny minority. The disillusionment is particularly rife amongst the youth, who in many countries form the bulk of the population, and it is often they who are the most zealous advocates of Islamic revival.

The common ancestor of many of the radical Sunni groups, the Muslim Brotherhood founded in Egypt in 1928, was initially a youth club which stressed moral and social reform through the propagation of knowledge about Islam. Its founder, Hassan al-Banna' (1904–49), was a primary school teacher, trained at a Western-style institution and working in Ismailiya, the capital of the Suez Canal Zone which was widely perceived as a threat to Egypt's political, economic and cultural identity. The Brotherhood gained in popularity as a result of the increase in anti-British feeling caused by Zionist activity in Palestine. In 1939, in the wake of the Palestinian Arabs' armed revolt against the British Protectorate, the Brotherhood became a political party. By the following year it had 500 branches each with its own centre, a mosque, a school and a club. The schools ran religious instruction classes and gave military training in preparation for *jihâd*. The avowed aim was to liberate Egypt and the whole Islamic homeland from alien control, and to establish a genuinely Islamic government. During the next six years anti-British feeling escalated and the Brotherhood increased tenfold, boasting half a million members and the same number of sympathizers. In 1948, when Egypt was defeated in the Arab–Israeli War, the Brotherhood blamed the political establishment and resorted to terrorism. Martial law was imposed and the Brotherhood was outlawed. Three weeks later one of its members assassinated the Prime Minister and not long afterwards Banna' was killed by security agents. Since that time the Brotherhood's fortunes have varied with periods of repression alternating with periods of official toleration. In 1954, after a failed attempt to assassinate President Nasser, 4,000 activists were goaled and many more fled to other Arab countries. A further purge took place in 1966 when several of the leaders, including Sayyid Qutb, the movement's chief ideologue, were executed. Under President Sadat, the Brotherhood flourished and its more moderate members were co-opted into the political establishment while others who became disaffected formed two breakaway groups: *al-Takfir wa 'l-Hijra* (the Denunciation and the Migration) and *Munazzamat al-Jihâd* (the Jihâd Organization). Their agents were responsible for Sadat's assassination in 1982. The Muslim Brotherhood still dominates Egypt's student unions and professional bodies. Related movements exist in all Arab countries although in some of them they are forced to operate underground. There is considerable breadth of opinion within these movements but their members share a common belief in Islam as an all-embracing system which they seek to impose by political means. They are drawn from the educated middle classes who tend to be anti-clerical, calling for a revival of *ijtihâd* in opposition to the officially accredited religious scholars whom they regard as obscurantist traditionalists hopelessly compromised with the political status quo. Many of them would endorse Sayyid Qutb's

view that Nasserist Egypt was a modern manifestation of *al-Jahiliya*, 'the period of ignorance' – i.e. the pagan Arab society which the Prophet Muhammad was sent to replace. It is this which makes them suspect to the authorities, because when the same label is attached to other Arab regimes the implication is that it is the duty of all true Muslims to strive to overthrow them, using violent means if necessary.

In 1979, the Muslims of Iran succeeded in toppling the Shah, ousting the corrupt Western-educated élite who ran their country and establishing an Islamic government. Although the leaders of the REVOLUTION were Shî'ite religious scholars the Iranian success has fired the imagination of radical Sunni activists the world over. This is partly because the Iranians have offered them assistance, playing down the specifically Shî'ite characteristics of their own brand of revolutionary Islam so as to make it appear more suitable for export. Nevertheless, although all Muslims share a common core of beliefs and practices, and although there is an additional bond between them created by the shared negative experience of European influence, there are some important doctrinal differences between Sunni and Shî'ite 'fundamentalists'.

Shî'ites hold that Muhammad was succeeded by a series of twelve infallible Imâms beginning with his cousin and son-in-law 'Alî. They further believe that the Twelfth Imâm did not die but went into occultation or hiding; he will eventually return as the Mahdi who will establish justice on earth. Like the Sunnis, most of them have a traditionalist vision of Islam but there is a subtle difference. Since the Companions failed to recognize 'Alî as Muhammad's legitimate heir, appointing three other Caliphs before he was given his turn, Shî'ites are cautious about accepting hadiths transmitted by the Companions and their pupils, preferring instead those transmitted by the Imâms. Moreover they have two law schools which differ from those of the Sunnis. Until the late eighteenth century, most of the Shî'ite religious scholars belonged to the Akhbârî school which held that the law was based exclusively on the Qur'an and hadiths as interpreted by the Imâms. At around that time the rival school of the

Usûlîs became important. They believed in the need for living *mujtahids*, who could make innovative legal judgements and who derived their AUTHORITY from the Hidden Imâm. In the course of the nineteenth century, the Usûlî school gained the upper hand. Moreover, in order to put up a united front in opposition to secularism and European interference, the Usûlî mujtahids took to designating one of their number as *marja' al-taqlîd*, to be emulated in all points of law and religious practice by all Shî'î Muslims. Without this development the influence of the Shî'ite religious scholars might well have been undermined like that of their Sunni counterparts. However, in the eyes of the faithful, the *marja' al-taqlîd* came to be regarded as less fallible than the temporal ruler. Not only was Khomeini the *marja' al-taqlîd*, he also went much further than his predecessors in teaching that it is the duty of the religious scholars to replace the corrupt temporal authorities and to rule the Muslim community on behalf of the Hidden Imâm.

Whether there will be a lasting *rapprochement* between Shî'ite and Sunni militants remains to be seen. Certainly once Iran has recovered from the war with Iraq we can expect it to play an increasingly important role internationally. Moreover, following its example, several other countries may experience Islamic revolutions. It is also possible that with the demise of the USSR and the unification of Europe we may witness the emergence of an Islamic bloc.

Burgat, P. (1988) *L'islamisme au Maghreb: La voix du Sud*, Paris: Karthala.

Carré, O. (1985) *Mystique et Politique: Lecture révolutionnaire du Coran par Sayyid Qutb Frère musulman radical*, Paris: Cerf.

Choueiri, Y.M. (1990) *Islamic Fundamentalism*, London: Pinter.

Etienne, B. (1987) *L'Islamisme radical*, Paris: Hachette.

Hiro, H. (1988) *Islamic Fundamentalism*, London: Paladin.

Kepel, G. (1985) *The Prophet and Pharaoh: Muslim Extremism in Egypt*, London: Al Saqi.

Robinson, N. (1986) 'The Qur'an as the Word of God', in A. Linzey and P.J. Wexler (eds) *Heaven and Earth: Essex Essays in Theology and Ethics*, Worthing: Churchman, pp. 38–54.

——(1991) *Christ in Islam and Christianity: The Representation of Jesus in the Qur'an and the Classical Muslim Commentaries*, London: Macmillan and Albany, NY: State University of New York Press.

Ruthven, M. (1991) *Islam in the World*, revised edition, Harmondsworth: Penguin.

Watt, W.M. (1988) *Islamic Fundamentalism and Modernity*, London: Routledge.

Neal Robinson

JUDGEMENT

In the theological sense, 'judgement' usually denotes God's evaluation of and reaction to what humans do in their freedom. It is one of the traditional topics of ESCHATOLOGY and is expressed in the notions of a 'particular judgement' of individuals immediately following DEATH and the 'last judgement' of all at the end of time. But 'judgement' is also understood to be continuing throughout history. In its larger sense, divine judgement has essential connections to the doctrines of CREATION, PROVIDENCE, revelation, SIN, GRACE, and salvation. Because of these connections, 'divine judgement' can also refer to a personal, social, or national calamity regarded as a PUNISHMENT (whether sent by God or self-inflicted) for failing to follow God's plan or commands.

The legal, philosophical and aesthetic notions of judgement interact with the theological notion. Legal judgement is the act of determining what is in conformity with the LAW and JUSTICE. It refers also to the resulting decision or opinion of a judge and the court's sentence or decree. In philosophy 'judgement' is the mental act of weighing, comparing and discriminating the evidence concerning a proposition or hypothesis in order to achieve knowledge of the TRUTH. It can also mean the discrimination of values aiming at knowledge of the good. Aesthetic judgement concerns the discernment and appreciation of beauty.

The traditional notion of divine judgement may be outlined as follows. God is creator and guides creation by God's providential plan toward the ultimate fulfilment of all God's purposes in creation. Humans are free in determining their conduct. But God has revealed God's aim and standard of judgement in God's commandments and, for Christian THEOLOGY, most especially in the person of Jesus Christ. Thus God's judgement stands over the actions of each individual life and our collective lives as families, societies, nations and world. God's judgement is continuing throughout history and can manifest itself in personal, social or national calamities whenever humans separate themselves from God in sin. There is a 'particular judgement' of each individual immediately following death, resulting in a state of eternal blessedness ('HEAVEN'), eternal damnation ('HELL') or purgation preceding blessedness ('purgatory'). At the end of time, as the last act in the consummation of history, there will be a RESURRECTION of the dead and a 'last judgement' ('final' or 'general judgement') presided over by Christ and determining the ultimate status of all in relation to God's purposes in creation and history.

The roots of the theological notion of divine judgement are in the religious and social experience of the ancient Hebrew people. The Hebrew tribes become a people, a nation, under the divine initiative, mediated through Moses. Yahweh adopts the Hebrews as 'my people' (Exodus 3: 7) and binds himself to them in a COVENANT relationship. The notion of God as judge is intimately linked to the notion of God as king in covenant relationship with Israel. Because God is king and the source of Israel's Law, which lays down the religious and social obligations of the people in the covenant relationship, it is God's duty to act as judge. God must assure justice for God's people and bring salvation and PEACE to the persecuted and oppressed. The legal and moral connotations of divine judgement stem from this context of relationship in covenant and Law. At this earliest stage divine judgement is understood to be a present and continuing activity of God in history, affecting both individuals and the nation. There is a strong interaction between the notion of God as judge, perfectly righteous and assuring justice, and the people's social experience of tribal judges and Middle Eastern kings. The idea that all judgement is God's (Deuteronomy 1: 17) acts as an ideal, a standard and a check on Israelite judges and kings; and the social experience of how tribal judges and kings act for their people influences the understanding of God.

The prophetic tradition added new dimensions to the understanding of divine judgement. As Lord of the universe and all history, God is judge of all nations, not just Israel. God communicates the divine judgements through the prophets, whose pronouncements follow the pattern of judgement on the sins of the present, threat of punishment, call to repentance and promise of deliverance. There is great stress on social justice and authentic religion as God's will. Until the late seventh century BCE, emphasis is on the collective social experience of Israel: the sins of individuals affect the nation's destiny. Israel's enemies are seen as instruments of God's judgement and military defeats are God's punishment for the nation's sins. But with Jeremiah (31: 29–30) and Ezekiel (14: 12–23; 18: 2–4) there arises a new stress on individual responsibility before God's judgement. Although there are hints of a future judgement in earlier writings, it is not until the post-Exilic period and the emergence of Messianic prophecy and expectation that we find the notion of a 'final' judgement. It is a distinctly 'this-worldly' notion, however: when Messiah comes to establish the kingdom of God, there will be a general judgement finally separating the just from the wicked and securing perfect justice and peace (as befits God's kingdom).

The emergence of APOCALYPTIC spirituality and writing in the second century BCE deeply affected the notion of judgement. Apocalyptic hope expected the 'day of the Lord' or the 'time of the end', which would be the consummation of creation and the radical transformation of the world and history. On this 'day' God would send the 'son of man' to establish and rule God's universal kingdom. God would raise the dead to life and (through the 'son of man') judge the living and the dead. The just would live everlastingly in the blessings of God's kingdom; the wicked would be consigned to everlasting punishment and disgrace. This is the notion of a general judgement of all at the end of time, history and the world (at least as we know them).

Christianity inherits this entire tradition and sees Jesus Christ as the fulfilment of Messianic hope and apocalyptic expectation. Jesus' resurrection led the first generation of Christians to believe that the 'time of the end' had begun and that Jesus Christ would soon return in judgement. Although the sense of imminence disappears by the end of the first century, the expectation of the 'second coming' of Christ 'to judge the living and the dead' remains part of Christian belief. It is affirmed in the Apostles', the Nicene and the Niceno-Constantinopolitan Creeds and in the formal liturgical prayers of many Christian churches today.

Christianity's understanding of divine judgement developed under the influence of Greek thought. While patristic theologians were not of one mind on these questions, the acceptance of the Greek notion of the immortality of the soul and reflection on the parable of the rich man and Lazarus (Luke 16: 19–31) eventually led to the dominant position that each individual SOUL is judged immediately upon the death of the body (the 'particular' judgement). On the day of resurrection these souls will be rejoined with bodies and the final judgement will take place, vindicating God's justice and righteousness. The notion of the 'particular' judgement introduced into Christian thought a preoccupation with individual destiny and a neglect of the social dimension of the tradition concerning divine judgement. This trend intensified in late patristic thought and through the entire medieval period; indeed, in the common understanding of ordinary Christians it extends well into this century.

The doctrine of predestination, which entered Christian theology as a result of the influence of Augustine (354–430), had unfortunate effects on the understanding of divine judgement. The notion that God has predestined from all eternity those who will be saved not only creates difficulties for the doctrine of free will; it also leads to thinking of divine judgement, which in the tradition is a present and future reality, as something timeless and set from all eternity. It seems to transform judgement into prejudgement, leads to an image of God as a harsh and capricious judge, and offends the human sense of justice. It also reinforced the preoccupation with individual destiny and the neglect of the social dimension of divine judgement. The doctrine of predestination was maintained in medieval theology and emphasized in the Calvinist traditions of the Reformation, but has been widely ignored and abandoned in contemporary Christian theology because it is seen as incompatible with the character of God revealed in and by Jesus.

Several important developments in twentieth-century Christian theology have affected the understanding of divine judgement. Since the rise of neo-orthodox theology (Barth, Reinhold

Niebuhr) and existentialist theology (Tillich), theology has recovered and emphasized the social and political dimensions of Christian faith. More recently, Latin American LIBERATION THEOLOGY, European and American political theology, BLACK THEOLOGY and feminist theology have all criticized current social conditions (both within the Church and in wider human SOCIETY). All are deeply motivated by a concern for social justice. This emphasis on social justice, virtually universal in contemporary theology, clearly represents a recovery of the ancient prophetic tradition's stress on God's judgement standing over human society and the course of social history. This has brought a much needed balance to the overly individualistic and otherworldly understanding of Christian faith that was so dominant for centuries.

While theology continues to stress the critical function of Christian faith in relation to society, there is also a growing consensus for the position, sometimes called 'universalism', that God saves all. Drawing on a minority tradition dating back to Irenaeus (d. *c.*200) and Origen (d. *c.*254), many theologians argue that the universal salvific will of God, the divine omnipotence (which implies that God can achieve the ends of the divine will for the salvation and fulfilment of each creature) and most especially the revealed character of God as merciful and loving saviour allow us to conclude that in the end God's love and mercy will overcome all obstacles to universal salvation. Here divine judgement and justice are being understood in terms of the divine mercy and LOVE.

Rethinking the basis for our notion of divine judgement supports this position. Especially since the medieval period, the Christian notion of divine judgement has been dominated by images and metaphors drawn from the legal sphere: God has been imagined as a harsh legal judge and both individual judgement and final judgement have been imagined as trials in God's courtroom. With such images, justice and mercy seem to be at odds. But thinking of divine judgement in terms of cognitional and aesthetic judgement, instead of legal judgement, results in a different view. If God's judgement of us individually and collectively is understood to be God's *knowledge* of what we truly are, what

we have made of ourselves and our world in our actions, then we can affirm both that God judges us and also that God in mercy forgives, loves and saves us. There is no final tension or opposition between divine justice and divine mercy and love once we get away from a legalistic understanding of divine judgement (*see* ATONEMENT).

We shall continue to see various sorts of social criticism motivated by a religious concern for social justice. The churches will continue to be active participants in discussing our common social and political concerns and debating courses of action. While there may be no explicit appeals to the doctrine of divine judgement, this is one of the notions underlying and providing the basis for criticism of church structures and the conditions in the wider society.

We are currently witnessing an extension of the concern for justice beyond human society. Environmental theology and theologies of ANIMAL RIGHTS raise the question of justice with regard to the human treatment of the entire planet and set these concerns in their proper theological context. Such theology is clearly based in the systematic relationship between the doctrines of God, creation and judgement. The emphasis on stewardship and the responsibility God has entrusted to humans leads to a recognition that we are responsible to God for what we do to the earth and its creatures. This is one of the most important developments in Christian theology today, both because of its extreme importance for the future of the planet and because it represents a very rare transcendence of anthropocentrism in Christian thought. Such theology calls for human society to give up its anthropocentric habits of thought and action and is providing the needed spiritual basis for the environmental and animal rights movements.

There are two sets of polar dimensions that must be kept together in creative interaction in thinking about divine judgement: God's judgement on individuals in contrast to God's judgement on collectives (societies, nations, history, the world); and God's present and continuing judgement (the prophetic tradition) in contrast to God's final judgement (the apocalyptic tradition). To stress one of these polar dimensions at the expense of the other in either pair is to skew the understanding of divine judgement and God's interaction with the world.

Divine judgement must not be isolated from the character of God as understood in Christian theology. It is important to recognize that divine judgement is fundamentally related to God's love and salvific activity. Far from being some isolated legal pronouncement upon us and the meting out of rewards and punishments, divine judgement is a moment in God's salvation of the world. As God takes the world's achievements and failures into God's own experience, God judges and knows us for what we have made of ourselves and our world. But the apocalyptic tradition, as well as the parables of Jesus, can be interpreted as pointing to a transformation of the world in God, so that even the EVIL in our personal and social lives – while not eradicated – is yet somehow transformed and redeemed in God. We cannot imagine what such a transformation and salvation of the world might be, but this view has been beautifully expressed by Alfred North Whitehead in his statement that God's judgement 'is the judgment of a tenderness which loses nothing that can be saved. It is also the judgment of a wisdom which uses what in the temporal world is mere wreckage' (1978: 346).

The notion of divine judgement has important functions for our understanding of self and world. It teaches us that humans are neither the originating source nor the ultimate adjudicators of value. It calls us, individually and socially, beyond self-interest. In consort with other symbols, such as the 'KINGDOM OF GOD', divine judgement functions as an ideal, urging us to be critical of the social status quo and to work for justice and the reform of social structures so that society might foster authentic fulfilment of individuals in community. Perhaps the most important function of the notion of divine judgement is to teach us that our present action or inaction has permanent significance for the universe. This conviction is the necessary background for all our sense of right and wrong, justice and injustice, achievement and failure. Without such a conviction, as Whitehead has said, 'every activity is merely a passing whiff of insignificance' (1941: 698) and no society or individual can hope and work for the future.

Several problems and questions arising from this topic concern how to express the heart of the tradition in terms of our contemporary experience and worldview. The separation of body and soul and the cosmological assumptions of the traditional notion of judgement are foreign to the contemporary mind. 'Particular' and 'last' judgement must be interpreted in categories compatible with the contemporary understanding of the human person and the physical universe. Does the notion of 'last judgement' and its associated eschatological assumptions have any reference whatsoever to physical cosmology, or must all these notions be 'spiritualized' in our contemporary interpretation? With regard to God's present and continuing judgement on individuals, societies and history, the notion of personal or social calamities as 'divine judgement' or punishment can easily lead to demonic views of God (as in the view of some fundamentalist Christians that AIDS is a divine punishment for sinful conduct). Theology must find ways of speaking about God's present and continuing judgement that do not permit such distortions and yet allow us to affirm the reality of divine providence and judgement.

A major problem arising from this and many other topics in Christian theology is how to make the riches of this tradition available to and influential within a Western society that is largely secular, explicitly non-religious in its governmental structures, and pluralistic in its convictions. Can Western societies learn from religion when these societies no longer have a common faith as a social basis? Nations are quick to 'baptize' self-interest with religious sentiments, but they resist the critical voice of religion as the attempt to impose 'private morality' on a pluralistic public. The problem of the basis of social ethics and the wider values pursued within society is a major problem confronting Western society in our age.

Arendt, H. in Beiner, R. (ed.) (1982) *Lectures in Kant's Political Philosophy*, Chicago: Chicago University Press.
Brandon, S.G.F. (1967) *The Judgment of the Dead*, London: Weidenfeld & Nicolson.
Gilkey, Langdon (1976) *Reaping the Whirlwind: A*

Christian Interpretation of History, New York: Seabury Press.

——(1981) *Society and the Sacred*, New York: Crossroad.

Hick, John H. (1976) *Death and Eternal Life*, San Francisco, CA: Harper & Row.

Küng, Hans (1984) *Eternal Life?*, trans. Edward Quinn, Garden City, NY: Doubleday.

Pittenger, W. Norman (1970) *'The Last Things' in a Process Perspective*, London: Epworth.

Suchocki, Marjorie Hewitt (1988) *The End of Evil: Process Eschatology in Historical Context*, Albany, NY: State University of New York Press.

Whitehead, Alfred North (1941) 'Immortality', in Paul A. Schilpp (ed.) *The Philosophy of Alfred North Whitehead*, LaSalle, IL: Open Court, pp. 682–700.

——(1978) *Process and Reality: An Essay in Cosmology*, Corrected edn, ed. David Ray Griffin and Donald W. Sherburne, New York: Free Press (original edition, 1929).

Thomas E. Hosinski

JUDICIARY

The judiciary is that branch of government empowered to interpret the statutory and constitutional laws of the STATE and to resolve disputes between and among governmental officials and citizens. The judiciary is often regarded as the highest protector of the rule of LAW in a community. Ideally, its judges are to be free from political pressure and personal bias, yet restrained by precedent and constitutional safeguards. Its procedures are to be public and participatory, yet insulated from the vagaries of popular opinion. An impartial judiciary is considered indispensable to a stable polity. Judicial corruption has often catalysed popular revolt.

The judiciary is a multifarious institution. It embraces various types of courts: civil and criminal, trial and appellate, permanent and itinerant. It engages various types of judges: lay and professional, appointed and elected, life-tenured and limited-tenured. It employs various procedures: inquisitorial and adversarial, legal and equitable, written and oral. The precise form and function of the judiciary turns on the legal and political climate of a given polity – the sources and forms of law that are recognized, the level of differentiation of other branches of GOVERNMENT, the range of judicial sanctions and remedies at hand, the availability of alternative forms of dispute resolution, among other factors. Most judicial systems today embrace a wide range of courts, judges and procedures.

Though the Western judiciary has a tangled and still partly uncharted history, a few common patterns can be discerned in its long development.

First, the Western judiciary has become increasingly secularized over time. The state has always exercised judicial AUTHORITY over its subjects – through separate judicial bodies or in combination with legislative and administrative functions. Religious leaders and institutions, however, traditionally also played prominent judicial roles. In ancient cultures the tribal shaman, the Egyptian priest, the Greek oracle and the Roman pontiff all participated in adjudication. After the diaspora, Jewish communities often organized themselves around rabbinic law courts, which dispensed legal opinions and adjudicated legal disputes in accordance with highly sophisticated rules of procedure and evidence. After the Papal Revolution, the Catholic Church established the first comprehensive judicial system in the West. A pan-European hierarchy of ecclesiastical courts conducted trials and heard appeals, using both adversarial and mediation procedures. Pleadings were written and court proceedings recorded. Elaborate rules of professional representation of parties, of testimonial and documentary evidence, of interrogation and inquisition were established. Church courts were courts of both law and equity empowered to order damages as well as dispensations, and to deal with both the legality and the morality of the cases before them. After the Protestant Reformation, the canon law of procedure and evidence was readily appropriated and applied by the civil courts. Church courts – though retained in some countries until the twentieth century to deal with questions of religious doctrine, liturgy, morality and family life – gave way to state courts as the principal vehicles of adjudication. During the later sixteenth through eighteenth centuries, most European nations developed elaborate new hierarchies of civil courts, with their own civil officers, their own professional bars and their own rules of written procedure, evidence and appeal. Public laws in the eighteenth and nineteenth centuries sometimes barred ecclesiastics from sitting on civil benches, and ordered that religious disputes be left to local religious communities for resolution.

Today secular civil courts and judges dominate the Western judiciary. Yet vestigial religious influence remains. State courts and legislatures respect the jurisdiction of Christian, Jewish and Muslim tribunals over their own believers and beliefs. State courts retain many of the traditional rules of procedure and evidence born of talmudic and canonical jurisprudence. State courtrooms maintain a measure of traditional religious ritual, in their formalities and ceremonies, in the dress and habits of their judges and counsel, in their oaths of veracity.

Second, the Western judiciary has become increasingly professionalized over time. The modern stereotype of the judge – a professionally trained, widely respected jurist who sits permanently and continuously on the bench – is a decidedly modern feature. Traditionally, judges were often untrained laymen who itinerated or sat intermittently to adjudicate disputes. In ancient Greece, the general assembly of Athenian citizens had plenary judicial authority, and sat in panels of more than a hundred citizens to hear ordinary cases, and *en masse* to hear important cases. In republican Rome, most civil cases were prepared for adjudication by a professional praetor, but final judgement lay with a *iudex*, a legally untrained Roman citizen. In the Germanic period, the lay folk moots heard disputes and advised the priestly and later feudal lawfinders on their final judgements. In late medieval and Reformation Germany, Scandinavia and other parts of central Europe, mixed courts of respected layman (*Schöffen*) led by one or two jurists heard the majority of civil and criminal cases. Medieval and early modern English common law courts made regular use of civil and criminal juries, and equity courts often drew upon local gentry as arbitrators. In late medieval France and portions of Iberia and Italy, generations of feudal lords and royal favourites, mostly untrained in the law, held their judicial offices as a matter of patronage and property right and often conducted their courts at considerable personal profit.

The judicial reforms of the later sixteenth through eighteenth centuries featured not only the SECULARIZATION but also the professionalization of the judiciary. Traditional forms of judicial patronage and of lay participation in adjudication were slowly discarded to prevent abuses and delay. Professionally trained judges, formal written procedures, and published judicial opinions – which had traditionally been the mark only of certain ecclesiastical and high civil courts – became increasingly the norm for the majority of courts. Courts made regular use of law professors to help adjudicate difficult and novel questions of law. To be sure, lay persons still found a place in this modern judicial system. England, America and several continental nations to this day retain jury trial for civil and criminal cases. Local magistrates and lower courts of nonrecord are still staffed principally by lay persons. But for the most part legal professionals dominate the Western judiciary.

Third, and closely related, the modern Western judiciary has become increasingly systematized and centralized. A certain level of judicial systematization and centralization, of course, can already be found in the imperial courts of the Roman Empire, in the church courts of the late medieval period and in the prerogative courts of certain early modern monarchies. But, before the reforms of the early modern period, the Western judiciary was splintered into a bewildering array of agencies and actors. Hundreds of local and specialty courts abounded in each country, with limited supervision over their activities and little realistic opportunity for appeal from their judgements. Courts of original general jurisdiction were more the exception than the rule, and a general system of appeal was nowhere fully in place.

The constitutional transformations of the eighteenth and nineteenth centuries systematized the judiciaries of many nations. The USA developed a dual track judiciary, with fifty state court systems and a concurrent federal judicial system, each enjoying both civil and criminal jurisdiction and each subject to the final authority of the United States Supreme Court. England and most Commonwealth nations developed separate hierarchies of civil law and criminal law, with final appeal in both cases to the House of Lords. A similar division of criminal and civil court systems prevails on the

Continent, often supplemented by separate courts of constitutional or public law. International judicial tribunals have also been established in the past two generations, and they promise to command greater authority and attention as the ineluctable process of globalizing law and politics matures.

An enormous literature on the judiciary has emerged in the past century. Legal historians have sought to unravel the tangled history of the judiciary. Political theorists and constitutional jurists have debated at length the value and validity of judicial review and judicial law-making. Comparativists and legal theorists have sought to account for the wide variances in styles of judicial language and reasoning among nations. Sociologists and anthropologists have assayed closely the sources of judicial decision-making in the morality, psychology and politics of judges, and have helped to trigger a great avalanche of new judicial biographies. A number of schools of legal thought have emerged around different theories of the judicial decision-making, notably 'legal formalists', who link judicial decisions to the precedents of the court and the intentions of constitutional and statutory drafters; 'legal realists', who cynically ascribe such decisions to a judge's preferences and prejudices; and 'legal pragmatists', who urge that each case be decided fairly on its own facts. These multi-disciplinary inquiries into the modern judiciary have enhanced substantially our understanding of this intriguing and indispensable legal institution.

Abraham, H.J. (1962) *The Judicial Process: An Introductory Analysis of the Courts of the United States, England and France*, New York: Oxford University Press.

Atiyah, P. and Summers, R. (1987) *Form and Substance in Anglo-American Law: A Comparative Theory of Legal Reasoning, Legal Theory and Legal Institutions*, Oxford: Clarendon.

Brunner, H. (1872) *Die Enstehung der Schwurgerichte*, Berlin: Weidmann.

Cardozo, B. (1921) *The Nature of the Judicial Process*, New Haven, CT: Yale University Press.

Dawson, J. (1960) *A History of Lay Judges*, Cambridge, MA: Harvard University Press.

Green, T.A. (1985) *Verdict According to Conscience: Perspectives on the English Criminal Jury Trial 1200–1800*, Chicago, IL, and London: University of Chicago Press.

Hall, K. (ed.) (1987) *The Courts in American Life: Major Historical Interpretations*, New York and London: Garland.

McWhinney, E. (1960) *Judicial Review in the English-Speaking World*, 2nd edn, Toronto: University of Toronto Press.

Shapiro, Martin (1981) *Courts: A Comparative and Political Analysis*, Chicago, IL: University of Chicago Press.

John Witte, Jr
Thomas C. Arthur

JUSTICE

There are two distinct sources for modern Western discourse about justice: the Greek philosophical enquiry as to a rationally coherent account of the good and constitutional arrangements which reflect and express justice; and the Judaeo-Christian search for God's justice expressed initially in the prophets' call for justice and the endeavour to embody the divine justice in the legislation and in the structure of the COVENANT community. Each of these sources has produced a tradition of reflection on justice which is very much alive today. And the two traditions have related to one another in a diversity of ways down the ages, sometimes being understood as complementary, and at other times as being in sharp opposition to one another, in tension, creative or destructive.

The Greek tradition of discussion of justice is classically rooted in the thought of Plato and Aristotle. Plato's major treatment of justice is the *Republic*. Here the discussion is located in an Athens where traditional certainties about justice, virtue and the good have been deeply shaken. No longer can fundamental questions be determined simply by reference to the tradition. In religion, morals and metaphysics, a diversity of possibilities is on offer, and those who reject an easy relativism must defend and sustain their views as more than arbitrary opinions. In the dialogue a variety of understandings of justice are examined and discarded as inadequate – Cephalus' view that justice is telling the truth and paying one's debts; Polemarchus' suggestion that justice is giving each one his due; and Thrasymachus' argument that justice is the interest of the stronger – simply a rhetorical disguise for self-interest. This last view, in progressively modifed form, is then taken over by Glaucon and Adeimantus. After this initial clearing of the ground, Socrates is pressed to present his own understanding of justice. Justice, he says, may be found both in societies and in individuals. In each it is a fundamental architectonic principle giving structure to the whole and determining the relation between the parts. As justice may more easily be described in the macrocosm, the main part of the dialogue is devoted to an account of the just STATE, which is as it were a magnification of the virtues and relationships to be found within the just individual or SOUL. In each, justice is understood as the proper harmonious ordering of parts, so that each performs its proper role and finds its own fulfilment in contributing to the good of the whole.

Aristotle's account of justice, developed most notably in the *Nicomachean Ethics*, Book V, distinguished universal and particular justice. Universal justice is directed at the good of the community as a whole, and 'is complete virtue in the fullest sense'; it is not one virtue among others, but virtue as a whole. As in Plato, this is a virtue of communities as well as individuals, the cohesive principle of a good society. Particular justice is divided into distributive justice and rectificatory justice, more or less what are known today as social justice and criminal justice. Particular justice regulates the exchange of goods and penalties among people, and while protecting the legitimate interests of the individual it assumes that all should be concerned for the common good.

The discussion of justice flowing from Plato and Aristotle gives justice a central place in morality and in the structure of the social order. It also assumes that the discussion can be pursued on a rational basis with very little if any reference to revelation or religion, although it is generally assumed that justice has a transcendent and objective grounding.

The nub of the Biblical understanding of justice has to do with faithfulness and a covenant relationship. God is proclaimed to be just (Psalms 7: 9; 103: 17; Jeremiah 9: 24, etc.), and in God's dealings with the world and with people we discover what justice is. Within the

covenant relationship God's justice is experienced and known. And God expects justice of his people (Isaiah 5: 7 etc.). Only in the doing of justice is God to be known; acting unjustly is in itself a turning away from God. God's justice demands a special concern for the weak and poor, for the widow and the stranger and the orphan (Exodus 22: 21–2; Deuteronomy 10: 18; 14: 29; 15: 7; Psalms 82: 3–4; 103: 6; 140: 12, etc.); indeed this justice is properly the heart of Israel's faith and worship, and something which is to be embodied in Israel's legislation. It is injustice above all that calls forth the prophets' protests.

In the New Testament Jesus is presented as calling people to seek first God's kingdom and his justice (Matthew 6: 33). God's justice is therefore to be made manifest in history; it is a gift of God and also a call to seek true justice. Jesus himself is the just one (Acts 3: 13 ff.; 7: 52) who has become our justice (1 Corinthians 1: 30). We therefore learn of justice from his teaching and from his life. Many of Jesus' parables proclaim a justice which is more than fairness, which contrasts sharply with wordly standards of justice. The labourers in the market-place all receive the same, no matter how long or hard they have worked (Matthew 20: 1–16); the returning prodigal receives preferential treatment, the opposite of 'his due', as his elder brother is not slow to point out (Luke 15: 11–32). Jesus' fellowship with tax collectors, prostitutes and other marginalized and despised groups suggests that God's justice reaches out to the forgotten and the excluded to affirm their worth and re-establish relationship. And when Jesus, the innocent one, stands before Pilate and is condemned, two understandings of justice are in direct opposition – the legal, expedient justice of the Roman power and the holy justice of God personified in Jesus (John 18: 28 to 19: 22). 'He was born to give testimony for justice,' wrote Hans Kelsen, 'the justice to be realised in the KINGDOM OF GOD, and for this justice he died on the cross. Thus, behind the question of Pilate, "What is truth?" arises, out of the blood of Christ, another still more important question, the eternal question of mankind: What is justice?' (Kelsen 1957: 1) The Pauline teaching on JUSTIFICATION, suggesting that while we are yet sinners God accepts us as just, indicates that God's justice is concerned with healing, reconciliation and the restoration of relationships. But the fullness of God's justice is only to be realized at the end when the kingdom is fully present.

The two traditions of understanding justice interacted from the beginning. For instance, the translators of the Septuagint and the writers of the New Testament use *dike* and its cognates to translate the Hebrew terms *tsedeq* and *mishpat*, a recognition that they are dealing with the same reality as the Greek philosophers. Augustine in *De Civitate Dei* distinguishes true justice, which must be understood in the light of the divine justice which is manifested in Jesus Christ and only fully realized in the heavenly city, from the partial and provisional justice which is the best that can be expected in the earthly city. Earthly justice must be measured against the divine justice; without a serious search for true justice a state becomes DEMONIC. Aquinas, as part of his great synthesis of Aristotle and the Christian tradition, sees the two modes of justice as largely complementary. Luther, on the other hand, sees earthly justice as often apparently, and sometimes in reality, opposed to the justice of God. Earthly justice, he argues, is God's 'strange work', which sometimes seems in conflict with his proper work. Probably some tension between the two ways of understanding justice is inevitable, or even desirable. But in pre-modern times it was almost universally assumed that justice has a transcendent grounding, that it reflects the will or nature of God, or the structure of things. This transcendent grounding has been increasingly challenged in modern times.

In recent decades there has been a remarkable flourishing of theories of justice which may be loosely labelled 'liberal'. Leading contributors to this discussion include John Rawls (*A Theory of Justice*, 1971), Robert Nozick (*Anarchy, State and Utopia*, 1974), F.A. Hayek (*Law, Legislation and Liberty*, 1982) and Brian Barry (*Theories of Justice*, vol. 1, 1991). These theories, for all their differences, share a number of important assumptions. They all claim to eschew fiduciary or metaphysical foundations, suggesting either that the argument proceeds on a purely rational basis without any recourse to assumptions or axioms about human nature, the way things are, or God, or alternatively that they are exploring the 'considered convictions' of most people in modern liberal democratic societies. There is also a tendency (most marked in Ackerman) to accept moral pluralism as a given and to reject the search for any kind of objective common good. A just SOCIETY does not propose any particular notion of the good, but provides a neutral framework within which individuals and groups may seek their own good with the minimum of interference. Rawls's argument, for instance, pivots on a situation which he calls the 'original condition' in which a group of individuals ignorant of their specific endowments and positions in society determine the principles for a fair or just society. The underlying assumptions include the belief that individuals in an unconstrained environment will operate in a self-interested way, and that individuals have some kind of priority over society, that HUMAN RIGHTS exist, and that human beings are in some sense equal.

Although liberal theorists on justice share a variety of common emphases, there are also important differences. Rawls, for instance, sees justice as 'the first virtue of social institutions' and believes that justice demands redistribution, whereas F.A. Hayek has a minimalist idea of justice as fair procedures, particularly in market transactions, and he denounces 'social justice' as a dangerous mirage and redistribution as immoral. The positions of Rawls and Nozick are particularly sharply opposed, and Alasdair MacIntyre has pointed out that in the absence of any overarching consensus about the good there are no criteria available by reference to which such conflicts might be resolved. And this, MacIntyre argues, is not only an intellectual problem but a threat to social stability and to human flourishing. We are in a condition of fundamental confusion, he suggests, about what justice is. And in such a situation justice is frequently distorted into being an ideological weapon in group conflict, no possibility being recognized of justice having an agreed or objective content.

The main critics of the liberal theorists of justice are the thinkers labelled, a little loosely, 'communitarians', notably Alasdair MacIntyre,

Stanley Hauerwas, Michael Sandel and Charles Taylor. These thinkers attack the INDIVIDUALISM, the ahistoricism and the rejection of traditions of faith on the part of the liberals. Our identity, they argue, is shaped by the communities of which we are a part; we are 'embedded' in community, and learn from the community who we are, and what the good is, and the nature of virtue. The kind of atomic individualism that the liberals assume and encourage is unreal and harmful. It also neglects the fact that peoples and communities have histories which are essential parts of their self-understanding. There is no such thing as a community or a person without a history, and to attempt to detach human beings from their specific histories is to produce a distorted understanding. The shared understandings which a community generates out of its solidarity over time should provide the basis for the principles of social ordering, especially justice. Theologians such as Karen Lebacqz and Stanley Hauerwas see a responsibility laid on the churches at this point. In a liberal society where there is profound confusion about the nature of justice, the Christian community out of the riches of its tradition should present and commend an understanding of justice which rests upon faith and safeguards virtue, and fellowship, and the common good.

Official Roman Catholic social teaching has developed a sophisticated understanding of justice, with a strong emphasis on social justice. Justice is here seen as a quality of relationships which are just in as far as they affirm human dignity and encourage mutuality and participation. There is built into this understanding of justice a priority for the poor, the excluded and the marginalized which is clearly derived from the Biblical tradition (and makes a rather surreptitious appearance in secularized garb in Rawls). This understanding of justice has been articulated in various papal encyclicals, and particularly notably in the US Catholic Bishops' Pastoral Letter, *Economic Justice for All* (1986).

But, in general, Western academic THEOLOGY has to a distressing extent abandoned an engagement with issues of justice and rarely enters into the very lively debate in social philosophy.

Two generations ago powerful voices like Barth, Brunner and Reinhold Niebuhr were widely attended to; today theology seems largely to have withdrawn from such concerns. But on the other hand communities of faith in many parts of the world are composed of the victims of injustice, or take sides with the oppressed, and cry out for justice, the justice of which they learn in the gospel. Their cry is articulated powerfully in LIBERATION THEOLOGY, which has a continuing impact on theology and also on secular life.

Christian theology rooted in the life of a community which encounters the God of justice in WORSHIP and in the experience of injustice should have a significant contribution to make to contemporary dilemmas about justice. This theology should be both critical and constructive. It is critical in as far as it enters contemporary debate armed with its story, which gives meaning and content to the community's understanding of justice, challenges injustice and encourages the doing of justice. On this basis it should seek to expose ways in which the rhetoric of justice is used to cover what is actually going on and occasions when notions of justice are used as weapons to protect the powerful. It should be constructive in as far as it offers insights into the nature of justice as contributions and clues which may help to resolve some of the contemporary confusion about what justice means, a confusion which can be profoundly harmful to people and to communities.

Ackerman, Bruce A. (1980) *Social Justice in the Liberal State*, New Haven, CT: Yale University Press.

Barry, Brian (1989) *Theories of Justice*, vol. 1, London: Harvester.

Forrester, Duncan B. (1990) 'Political justice and Christian theology', *Studies in Christian Ethics* 3(1): 1–13.

Garcia, Ismael (1987) *Justice in Latin American Theology of Liberation*, Atlanta, GA: John Knox Press.

Hauerwas, S. (1991) *After Christendom*, Nashville, TN: Abingdon Press.

Hayek, Friedrich A. (1982) *Law, Legislation and Liberty*, London: Routledge & Kegan Paul.

Kelsen, K. (1957) *What is Justice?*, Berkeley and Los Angeles, CA: University of California Press.

Lebacqz, Karen (1986) *Six Theories of Justice*, Minneapolis, MN: Augsburg.

MacIntyre, Alasdair (1988) *Whose Justice? Which Rationality?* London: Duckworth.

Nozick, Robert (1974) *Anarchy, State and Utopia*, Oxford: Blackwell.

Rawls, John (1971) *A Theory of Justice*, New York: Oxford University Press.

Duncan B. Forrester

JUSTIFICATION

Justification by faith is a central New Testament doctrine, highlighted in Paul's letters to the Romans and Galatians. The fundamental Pauline meaning is to be treated as, or to be made, righteous, even though, according to the law, one is unrighteous. The core message is that God loves/forgives human beings in spite of their unrighteousness (their SIN, not being right with God or with God's law), restoring them to a right relationship with God (righteousness). Thus, living by GRACE (God's love/forgiveness) instead of by the LAW and human achievement, Christians are empowered to love God, neighbour and themselves. In the sixteenth century Luther retrieved justification's importance in his controversy with Rome. It has continued to be a major point of difference among members of the Christian family. Its discussion is complex because, more than with any other doctrine, an adequate review includes several issues of Christian theology: law, grace, COVENANT, reconciliation, righteousness, ATONEMENT, *imago dei* and eternal life. Justification, along with these concepts, is given different meanings depending on the tradition shared, or the root metaphor employed.

The contrast between the Reformation's understanding of justification and Karl Barth's (1956, 1958) definition is highlighted by the consideration of three points: (a) the retrieval of the covenantal root metaphor, (b) the reversal of the priority of law and grace and (c) the constitution of PERSONS in terms of relationships, defined by dialogue between the persons of the Godhead and extended to the relationship of God and persons and among persons (entailed in points (a) and (b)). The language of human interaction and relationship, drama and event are employed to interpret Biblical meanings. This language has greater affinities with the social sciences, especially social psychology, and with literature than with Greek philosophy, the source of categories for most traditional reflection on the Christian faith.

For Barth, covenant is the internal basis of creation, and creation is the external basis of covenant. Thus the meaning or 'telos' of creation and history is covenant. Covenant entails God's radical binding of God's self to humankind based on free, liberating love present not only in God's electing (choosing) Israel as son/daughter/wife/family but also in the eternal covenant within God's self as the covenant of the Father with the Son as the Lord and bearer of human nature.

According to Barth covenant is an objective reality, but also is understood in terms of a God who is Subject, one who elects, loves, is faithful to and binds persons and community freely with God's self. Jesus Christ enacts and reveals this normative set of relationships in history. Thus covenant is a relational form with a dynamic event-constituted interactional content. The dialogical form of the Godhead is also present in God–person and person–person relationships (*analogia relationis*). Jesus Christ reveals both the dialogical relational *form* and the interactional *event* (LOVE, FREEDOM, GRACE) as the norm for what it means to be human (*imago dei* – real person, humanity and whole person), as well as for the character of God.

The next layer of explication is reconciliation:

> All this is from God, who reconciled us to himself through Christ, and has given us the ministry of reconciliation; that is in Christ God was reconciling the world to himself, not counting their trespasses against them, and entrusting the message of reconciliation to us.
>
> (2 Corinthians 5: 18–19)

For Barth, reconciliation is the fulfilment of the covenant partnership between God and human beings, a fellowship rejected or ignored from its human side. Within it persons are empowered to fulfil the law to love God and the neighbour as oneself. Paul's insight is that these relationships cannot be salvifically realized through the will or works of human beings, but only through receiving God's grace, the free gift of forgiving love that reconciles persons to God, to one another and to themselves. Finally, justification and sanctification are understood as aspects of reconciliation.

The doctrine of justification, as interpreted by Calvin, Luther and most classical theologians, is understood in terms of the priority and fixity of the law(s) established in creation and violated through sin (human idolatry, disobedience, etc.). In that context Jesus paid the price of our sins and brought us back into relationship with God's self and law. His righteousness was imputed to human beings even though they were unrighteous. In effect persons are forgiven, brought back into relationship with God, and empowered to obey the law(s) of creation. They are justified, treated as righteous, by God through Jesus Christ. Persons receive this reality through faith. According to this interpretation, the law of God is upheld and the reality of God's mercy (love, forgiveness) is affirmed.

For Barth, by contrast, the roles of law and grace are reversed. Grace, God's love and freedom, is primary and is understood within covenantal interrelationship. Law is subordinated to covenant and grace. God's love is understood through the covenantal form and is manifested in relationships between God and persons and persons and persons. The ongoing 'history' of this relationship, more deeply understood as a dialogue between the gift of God's grace and the human response of thanksgiving, is the 'matter' or substance of life. Definitively enacted and revealed through Jesus Christ, human beings are invited to participate in this objective reality. Here law is the *form* that follows the *function* of grace, and corresponds to the dynamic of covenantal relationships, which define what it means to be human in this relational matrix. Therefore, law is not fixed but dynamic, reflecting God's electing, covenantal love in both its vertical and its horizontal dimensions. Within this context, justification and sanctification are understood as the twin dimensions of reconciliation. In sum covenant is basic to understanding reconciliation, and the concepts of justification and sanctification are reconciliation's further explication.

Justification is defined in relationship to the activity of Jesus Christ who, embodying God's sovereign love and freedom (grace), becomes a servant (The Lord as Servant, Barth 1956: IV/1). As servant-love, Jesus Christ comes to and participates in the life of the Prodigal Son in the depths of the matrix of sin – i.e. in the pigpen, the most alienated situation conceivable to a Jew.

We are dealing with sin: . . . the determination of humanity as it has left its place as a creature and broken its covenant with God; the corruption which God has made his own; for which he willed to take responsibility in this one human being. Here in the passion in which as Judge he lets himself be judged, God has fulfilled this responsibility. In the place of all humanity he has himself wrestled with that which separates them from him. He has himself borne the consequence of this separation to bear it away.

(Barth 1956: IV/1, 247)

Love, or being *with* and *for* the Prodigal, involves taking on his sin, as both judged and Judge, hence liberating (freeing) the Prodigal to come to himself and return to his father. Appropriate (right, righteous) covenantal relationships are thus re-established. The Prodigal is redeemed (made just, justified) not primarily through his own activity but through that of Jesus Christ. Here the Prodigal's sin is pride (desire to be like God), or acting autonomously as though he can control his own destiny outside of covenantal relationships, leading to his fall. The activity of Jesus is relational and participatory (i.e. being *with* and *for* the Prodigal), as opposed to mechanistic (the transaction of Jesus Christ paying for the sins of human beings by merits gained through his perfect obedience). In Barth's definition faith becomes the acceptance of and participation in these relationships.

Sanctification is also defined in relationship to Jesus Christ in whom the Servant becomes Lord (Barth 1958: IV/2). The sin is sloth (to be more like an animal), laziness and misery, the refusal to become human in the covenantal relationships with God, others and self. Human beings are invited to participate as covenant partners with God, embodied and symbolized by Christ's relationship at God's right hand, understood as love.

In summary, reconciliation comprises the dialectical relationship between justification and sanctification which, in turn, is based on covenant. First Jesus Christ is the one who fulfils the covenant, and then, by participation in him, human beings are reconciled and given hope for redemption.

This contrast between classical Protestantism's and Barth's understanding of justification is an illustration of the importance of covenant, the priority of grace over law, and an emphasis on dialogical relationality in a contemporary interpretation of justification.

The rich history of interpretation of the meaning of 'to justify' and 'righteousness' (Hebrew, *tsedeq*, and Greek, LXX and NT, *dikaiosune*, and their cognates) is extensively explored in *The Interpreter's Dictionary of the Bible*, vol. 4, 'Righteousness in the OT', 'Righteousness in the NT'.

Historically, major controversies arose over the role of the human will in responding to God's grace. Pelagius (400–20?), in opposition to Augustine, seemed to argue that the human will was not totally destroyed by Adam's fall, and hence a person had some capacity to enter into the grace relationship. Likewise, Arminius (1560–1609) (reflected in the theology of many contemporary Methodists) rejected Calvin's form of predestination and stressed instead the ability of human beings to respond to divine grace (albeit motivated by prevenient grace). For Roman Catholics, justification literally means the making just of sinners (not just reckoning just, or imputing righteousness), i.e. justification involves the infusion of supernatural grace that blots out sin, regenerating the soul, making it worthy of the creator who made it. Finally, some Roman Catholics and Protestants believe that justification by grace alone often becomes 'cheap grace', leading to antinomianism, lawlessness, vitiating the justice and law of God.

In addition to Barth's contribution to the twentieth-century retrieval of the Pauline and Reformation understandings of justification by faith (see above), two other discussions have led to justification's contemporary relevance: (a) Paul Tillich's use of the language of acceptance, in his definition of grace, employs psychological insights about the central role of God's love for our salvation; and (b) Joe Haroutunian's employment of the dialogical categories of Martin Buber, along with George Herbert Mead's symbolic interactionism, critique atomistic individualism and faculty psychology.

First, *Paul Tillich*, in the widely read sermon 'You are accepted', translates the meaning of justification by grace through faith into the psychological language of acceptance. For Tillich, grace means that God radically accepts the person, in spite of his or her unacceptability (sin). Faith, in turn, is the openness and willingness to accept the fact of this reality. Being thus accepted (loved by God), one is enabled to accept oneself and hence is empowered to accept (love) others in spite of their unacceptability (sin). Love, for Tillich, is 'the reunion of the separated, of that which essentially belongs together'. It overcomes the alienations between God and persons, person and person, and the self from itself. While variously received by the religious community, Tillich's psychological terminology had the virtue of clarifying in contemporary language some elements of Paul's use of 'justification by grace through faith': the centrality of God's freely given love as enabling human beings to love. For Tillich, law and JUSTICE were the forms and structures which guided this drive for reunion or love.

Second, *Joseph Haroutunian*, in *God With Us*, counters the Western theological emphasis on the individual's natural capacity to respond to God's grace (modern Pelagianism). Utilizing Martin Buber and George Herbert Mead, he argues that persons are dialogical and relational beings. He says that this relationality happens between persons-in-community and, when guided by forgiveness, is, in effect, the operation of the Holy Spirit (perhaps this is a version of prevenient grace). Only when persons are motivated by the relationships and interactions of this matrix can their wills develop, so that they are enabled to decide for the objective love of God that comes to human beings through Jesus Christ. Though it may appear that an individual *decides* to accept God's grace (justification), in effect she is simply unaware of the relationships and interactions which form her as a person-with-a-will. In other words, using an understanding of selfhood influenced by social psychology and Martin Buber, Haroutunian argues that the salvific process is by grace alone, the grace that comes from God through Jesus Christ and the grace that comes from the Holy Spirit, as she moves through communities conditioned by a transcendent love and forgiveness. He argues that persons have little influence over their own salvation, for their wills are formed and shaped by the Christian community. While he grants that persons do play some part in their salvation, it is far from the simplistic understanding of individuals who 'have' wills. In effect he gives support both to the traditional understanding of justication by grace alone (*sola gratia*) and to Karl Barth's emphasis on the role of the Holy Spirit operating through the Christian community.

Once theology has been freed from a determining emphasis on law, a mechanistic view of atonement and an afterlife definition of salvation, two new issues surface: (a) a distorted focus on the interpersonal alone and (b) an emphasis on salvation which downplays creation.

First, *the focus on the interpersonal*: while the categories of relationship and interaction have contributed significantly to the enrichment of theology, such enrichment does not address the relationship of the interpersonal to the broader category of the KINGDOM (reign or network) OF GOD, recently retrieved in considerable force by Biblical and theological scholars (see Sobrino 1987). Jesus preached and enacted, not himself, but the kingdom of God. Without this broader Biblical perspective theology remains at Stage Three – the interpersonal – in terms of 'stages of faith development' (see Fowler 1981) and never reaches Stage Four (the systemic), Stage Five (the multi-systemic) and Stage Six (the universal), basically network or kingdom categories. While 'interpersonal relationship' is an essential category, and an important building block, kingdom/reign/network cannot be reduced to it. Without systemic categories faith is truncated, and significant themes of justice and love remain obscured, especially in the public and political arena.

Second, *the focus on salvation downplays the doctrine of creation*. In making creation the external basis of covenant and covenant its inner meaning, as well as centring on Christology and salvation (reconciliation, justification and sanctification), Karl Barth tilted towards salvation, and inadvertently ignored important issues of creation and the ENVIRONMENT: God's activity in and through all of creation, and oppressive interpretations of subduing and ruling the earth. While recent discussions of stewardship provide a significant antidote to the distortions of 'domination and dominion', they only partially address the problem. In addition, respect for and servant participation in creation help overcome this exploitative posture. Theology also needs to rectify the imbalance between creation and salvation in theology and preaching, not only by becoming aware of God's activity in all of creation, but also by affirming the organic root metaphor in the understanding of creation, in and through which the grace, love, creative power and glory of God operate.

Barth, K. (1956, 1958) *The Church Dogmatics* IV/1, IV/2, *The Doctrine of Reconciliation*, Edinburgh: T. & T. Clark.

Buttrick, G. (ed.) (1962) *The Interpreter's Dictionary of the Bible*, vol. 4, Nashville, TN: Abingdon (see Righteousness and Justification).

Elwell, W.A. (ed.) (1984) *Evangelical Dictionary of Theology*, Grand Rapids, MI: Baker Book House.

Ferguson, S.B. and Wright, D.F. (eds) (1988) *New Dictionary of Theology*, Downers Grove, IL: Intervarsity Press.

Fowler, J. (1981) *Stages of Faith*, San Francisco, CA: Harper & Row.

Haroutunian, J. (1965) *God With Us: A Theology of Transpersonal Life*, Philadelphia, PA: Westminster Press, Ch. 5.

Kasemann, E. (1969) *New Testament Questions of Today*, Philadelphia, PA: Fortress Press.

Küng, H. (1964) *Justification: The Doctrine of Karl Barth and a Catholic Reflection*, Philadelphia, PA: Westminster Press (2nd edn, 1981).

Sobrino, J. (1987) 'Jesus and the kingdom of God: singificance and ultimate objectives of His life and mission', in *Jesus in Latin America*, Maryknoll, NY: Orbis.

Taylor, V. (1941) *Forgiveness and Reconciliation: A Study in New Testament Theology*, London: Macmillan (2nd edn, 1946).

Tillich, P. (1948) 'You are accepted', *Shaking the Foundations*, New York: Charles Scribner's Sons.

Stuart D. McLean

KINGDOM OF GOD

In the New Testament, the kingdom of God is that divine power or reign which Jesus of Nazareth proclaims as present reality and therefore good news (cf. Mark 1: 15); consequently, it is the eschatological irruption of God's will into the world, the power of eternity which Jesus wields and which, in the achievement of MIRACLES, validates his ministry as messiah (cf. Luke 4:16–21). The kingdom of God is thus intimately related to the claims made by and for CHRISTOLOGY in the Christian tradition, specifically in relation to the encounter between church and society.

The eschatological character of the kingdom of God, particularly as found in the earliest Christian traditions, identifies its origins in the world of Jewish APOCALYPTIC; for, as Christopher Rowland has demonstrated, eschatology is one form of such apocalyptic, i.e. viewing of the heavenly secrets (cf. Rowland 1981). In this sense, specific questions which naturally address themselves to God's kingdom concern its nature, time of arrival, dimensions and locus (cf. Mark 13), all of which is held to be vital information for the believer expecting the kingdom's present inauguration. In the early Christian witness, these questions about the nature of the kingdom of God are answered in terms of Jesus Christ's person and activity during his earthly life; subsequently, questions of eschatology and Christology combined in such a way that the peculiar character of the kingdom itself was drained of specific definition: it became a cipher for certain foundationalist principles, thereby losing its fundamentally teleological appeal. This is a process which has recently been arrested by modern THEOLOGY (cf. below).

Notwithstanding this negative development, the character of the kingdom of God is defined by the POWER and AUTHORITY with which it dominates social concerns, as seen, for example, in Matthew 5 where references to the kingdom make clear its effectiveness as the expression of God's will to change and redeem human SOCIETY (cf. Matthew 5: 3, 19, 20). In the Gospels, this power is wielded solely by Jesus Christ, thereby characterizing his own unique status in the revelation of God's will; but with Pentecost and the outpouring of the Spirit upon all believers (cf. Acts 2), the determining qualities of the kingdom are opened to all, particularly the apostles. Although rarely identified as the power of the kingdom of God, the dynamic ability which enables and validates the performance of miracles by apostles such as Saint Paul and Saint Peter is entirely eschatological and therefore identical with Jesus' gospel; in this important sense, the character and definition of the kingdom of God is recognized by the manner in which it effects change in society. One might almost speak, therefore, of the kingdom of God as the cardinal point of relation between church and society in the early life of the Christian movement; it is that eschatological principle which, together with the parousia, conditions the attitudes of the earliest communities towards their social contexts.

As indicated by its eschatological and therefore apocalyptic status, however, early Christian concern with the kingdom of God was oriented towards its dimensions and its expected arrival; this is true even of the Fourth Gospel, where an arguably more 'realized' eschatology does not militate against the community's interest in the size and location of the kingdom (cf. John 14: 2; 18: 36). Questions of power, authority and dominion, consequently, entirely pertinent to the kingdom of God, are related to the *spatial* distinction which must be made between this world and that of God. The objectivist, eschatological realism which establishes and supports this distinction survived from the earliest Christian communities until the sixteenth century, when it was formulated, notably, in Martin Luther's doctrine of the two kingdoms, as a piece of theology which proved relevant to the Peasant War of 1525 and the concomitant question of the relationship between church and society (cf. below).

The advent of the modern era, however, as first indicated by the ecclesiology of John Calvin but announced, more pertinently, by the scepticism of David Hume and the epistemological idealism of Immanuel Kant in the eighteenth century, militated against eschatological realism, replacing it with a basically moralistic, individualized understanding of the power and authority of God's will. This trend can be traced back to the philosophy of Kant and the theology of Schleiermacher, becoming identified in the nineteenth century as liberal PROTESTANTISM. In the twentieth century, its two most notable advocates have been Adolf von Harnack and Rudolf Bultmann.

Harnack's theology, as best exemplified in his 1899–1900 lectures on the essence of Christianity (Harnack 1957), attempts to return to the personal religion of the historical Jesus, the famous 'kernel' which Harnack wants to distinguish from the mythical and objective rhetoric in which it is unfortunately dressed. Harnack, consequently, identifies the kingdom of God as the vital expression of God's desire that the individual change and develop into the kind of personality demonstrated by Jesus of Nazareth. In other words, in Harnack's theology the kingdom of God has lost all sense of independent reality as that divine power and authority, God's eternal model of social reality, towards which and within which every Christian community should exist; instead, the kingdom becomes for Harnack a series of liberal ethical principles which every individual should personally realize.

Although Harnack maintains the necessary effectiveness of the kingdom, therefore, its sphere of influence has been moved, decisively, away from the social towards the individual; for Harnack, that is, if one is going to speak of the kingdom of God at all, it must shed its peculiarly eschatological character; or, more precisely, the liberal post-Kantian interpretation of eschatology determines the kingdom solely in terms of its efficacy for personal conduct. This understanding of the kingdom, heavily influenced as it was by the search for the personality of Jesus, prevailed in Germany until 1919, and in Britain until the 1930s. Its consequences for European theology, particularly in the light of the First World War's destruction of bourgeois confidence in CULTURE and civilization, have been widely recognized.

One immediate reaction against this theological liberalism was the advent of Karl Barth's prophetic theology, heavily influenced by eschatological realism and with distinct materialist tendencies (cf. below); in direct succession to Harnack, however, was Barth's contemporary Rudolf Bultmann, who, although commonly regarded as a dialectical theologian, shares certain important characteristics with Harnack. Essentially, if early Christianity wants to speak of a kingdom of God *without* the world, poised to enter it at the propitious moment, and Harnack wants to speak of a kingdom *within*, to be individually realized, then Bultmann wants to speak of a kingdom both within and without, i.e. one encountered via present, temporal relationships. In modern commentary, the name given to this kind of theological discourse is existentialism.

This methodological distinction between the early tradition's realism, Harnack's liberalism and Bultmann's existentialism focuses upon the crucial philosophical question of MODERNITY, i.e. the question of immanence, which has had particular relevance for theology since Kant's crucial essay 'The end of all things' (Kant 1963). In modern philosophy, the question of immanence focuses upon the status one gives to a concept, or level of analysis, in the elaboration of one's understanding of transcendentals or universals. In theology, at least in terms of the kingdom of God, this pertains to the relationship between time and eternity, *the* universal which establishes modern discussion of all things eschatological.

Bultmann's peculiar contribution to this debate, heavily influenced by the phenomenology of Martin Heidegger, was to speak of the kingdom of God, and indeed eschatology in general, in terms of the presence of eternity within historical existence, and experienced via encounters. Overwhelmingly for Bultmann, the one encounter he was concerned with was the individual's encounter with the Risen Lord, mediated by the kerygmatic Christ; in everything he wrote, Bultmann was at pains to identify this as the only genuine understanding of Christian eschatology. By inference, for Bultmann, the kingdom of God, when 'demythologized' or interpreted in terms of its phenomenological significance, addressed the historical existence of the individual believer. In this way the claims of theological LIBERALISM were recast, rather than rejected, in a different philosophical vocabulary; but the effective function of the kingdom of God remains within the experience of the individual subject.

The consequences of this for the relationship

between Bultmann's theology and society are readily apparent; fundamentally Bultmann's theology, like Harnack's, cannot address explicitly social questions because its philosophical status will not allow such an enterprise. This situation in modern theology persisted throughout the 1930s and 1940s and into the 1950s; but with the advent of a more explicitly politicized intellectual environment in the 1960s (witness Sartre's rejection of his earlier existentialist position in favour of dialectical reason) Bultmann's theology suffered a swift decline, to be replaced by a plurality of different, more materialistic theologies. It is in this environment that contemporary reflection upon the theological and social relevance of the kingdom of God finds itself.

As noted above, Barth's early theology, specifically that of the first edition of *Der Römerbrief* in 1919, was a necessary antidote to liberalism and existentialism in modern theology, returning as it did to the eschatological realism of the New Testament. Heavily influenced by both the speculative phenomenology of Hegel, with its interpolation of universals in terms of historical processes, and its economic mediation in the work of Marx, Barth's theology opened the door to an explicitly social representation of the kingdom of God, such as had not been witnessed in Christian theology since the early church. Barth's initiative at this point has been taken up by a variety of recent writers, in particular such theologians as Johann-Baptist Metz, Jürgen Moltmann, Jon Sobrino, James Cone and Christopher Rowland.

Fundamentally, the vital question in this respect is whether one speaks of the *utopian* nature of the kingdom of God or allocates it a specific *topos* within the world of space and time. If the former, then this necessitates its relocation upon a new level of reflection, as in Harnack and Bultmann; if the latter, then one can return, with the earliest tradition, to claims relating to the kingdom's present *material* reality in space and time. The latter, essentially, is the position of the theologians identified in the previous paragraph; if it is adopted, then questions of *worldly* power and authority become intimately related to the kingdom of *God*, and Luther's well-known distinction between these two kingdoms, so influential upon modern

Protestant thought, collapses. This, effectively, is the situation in contemporary theology, where so many of the most prophetic voices are Roman Catholic and where the most pressing reflection upon the relationship between CHURCH AND STATE originates within the wide embrace of the Church of Rome.

The advantages of this approach are readily apparent: it allows the theologian to speak, in practical terms, of the hope of the Christian faith, which finds expression in both social and personal change and development. In other words, one returns to the kingdom of God some definite *content*, rather than abandoning it to the more abstract concerns of philosophical reflection. In this sense, and in socio-political contexts like El Salvador, South Africa and the black ghettos of the USA, it is irrelevant whether or not a particular theory relates to the deepest level of human intuition or its account of the status of social existence; all that matters is the practical situation which such a materialist interpretation of the kingdom of God, and other eschatological themes, addresses, and whether it addresses that situation meaningfully. On these terms, criticisms of LIBERATION THEOLOGY, or BLACK THEOLOGY, which focus on their apparently flawed methodology, essentially miss the point, which is that an appeal to a real material *topos* for the kingdom of God is not hopelessly utopian, but rather hopefully Christian.

From the evidence of contemporary theology, a line can be drawn between those, often postmodern, theologians who are increasingly turning towards pure methodology and those, often political, theologians who are increasingly prepared to accept slack theory if it is accompanied by a powerful and authoritative, eschatological and prophetic voice; pejoratively, one might locate this line on the equator between northern and southern hemispheres. If the currently eirenic status of this divide is to become more confrontational, it is hard to believe that the field will ultimately belong to methodology *per se*: arrayed against it is a powerfully conservative doctrinal position, which can call upon weighty Biblical and traditional support in its attempts to identify a dynamic future for ecclesiastically established programmes of change, in the name of the kingdom of God. The most telling implication of this possibility may well be the paradoxical one, that the much-heralded permissiveness of contemporary theology is little but a minor distraction from the far more significant onset of an essentially conservative return to the historical origins of Christianity, something which can be seen on all wings of all churches.

In fact, the debate between these divergent positions does not need to collapse into a quarrel between crude materialism on the one hand and sophisticated narrative on the other; for the real difference between these two wings of contemporary theology is one of attitude, rather than position. The future of genuine systematic theology, in other words, in any and all of its pluriform guises, depends less upon the identification of its own essence, in purely theoretical terms, and rather more upon whether or not it wishes to be truly prophetic. If it does, then it will appeal to its oldest, eschatological traditions, at the heart of which is the kingdom of God, and without which the proclamation of Christ makes as much sense as the cleaving of a head of cabbage. In this respect, the proclamation of the kingdom of God remains central to the lived experience of every Christian community which continues to witness to Jesus Christ, and which looks forward, hopefully, to the realization of his rule in the world.

Chilton, B. (1979) *God in Strength: Jesus' Announcement of the Kingdom*, Freistadt: F. Plochl.

Fierro, A. (1977) *The Militant Gospel*, London: SCM.

von Harnack, A. (1957) *What is Christianity?*, New York: Harper & Row.

de Jonge, M. (1991) *Jesus' Message about the Kingdom of God in the Light of Contemporary Ideas*, London: University of London Press.

Kant, I. (1963) 'The end of all things', in *On History*, New York: Macmillan.

Marcus, J. (1986) *The Mystery of the Kingdom of God*, Atlanta, NJ: Scholars Press.

Moltmann, J. (1981) *The Trinity and the Kingdom of God*, London: SCM.

Pannenberg, W. (1977) *Human Nature, Election and History*, Philadelphia, PA: Westminster Press.

Rowland, C. (1981) *The Open Heaven*, London: SPCK.

Sobrino, J. (1978) *Christology at the Crossroads: A Latin-American Approach*, London: SCM.

Gareth Jones

LAW

The term 'law' does not admit of easy or universal definition. Viewed in its broadest social terms, law consists of all social norms that govern human conduct and all actions taken to formulate and respond to those norms. Such norms include moral commandments, state statutes, ecclesiastical strictures, family rules, commercial habits, communal customs, forms of etiquette and various other social rules. Viewed in narrower political terms, law consists of the social enterprise by which certain norms are formulated by legitimate authorities and actualized by persons subject to those authorities. The process of legal formulation involves legislating, adjudicating, administering and other conduct by legal officials. The process of legal actualization involves obeying, negotiating, litigating and other conduct by legal subjects.

In the Western legal tradition, principal institutional responsibility for law has fallen to the multitude of royal, provincial, municipal and other civil polities that comprise the STATE. But other social institutions have also played key roles in the development of Western law – notably the church with its legal THEOLOGY and canon law, as well as monasteries, guilds, universities, mercantile leagues, manors, feudal institutions and others. This article reviews briefly the religious foundations and dimensions of Western law during certain historical watershed periods and today.

The *first* watershed period came with the Christian conversion of the Roman Emperor and Empire in the fourth and fifth centuries. On the eve of this conversion, Roman law reigned supreme throughout the West. It defined the status of PERSONS and the legal actions available to them. It punished delicts and crimes, and regulated commercial life, PROPERTY relations, the household and inheritance. It protected the public property and common WELFARE of the Roman state. Roman law also prescribed the pagan imperial cult: Rome was to be revered as the eternal CITY, ordained by the gods and celebrated in its altars and basilicas. The Roman Emperor was to be worshipped as a god and a king through the rituals of the imperial palace and the public square. The Roman law itself was viewed as the embodiment of an immutable law of nature, appropriated and applied through the sacred science of the pontiffs and jurists. The early Christian church stood largely opposed to this Roman law. Christians could not accept the imperial cult or participate in the pagan rituals required for military service, commercial relations or civil litigation. They thus organized themselves into independent communities. Church constitutions, rooted in the teachings of Christ and the apostles, set forth rules for ecclesiastical GOVERNMENT, liturgy, spiritual discipline, charity, EDUCATION, and FAMILY and property relations among Christians. The church taught obedience to the political authorities up to the limits of Christian conscience. But the clergy also urged upon their Roman rulers law reforms consonant with Christian teachings. Such legal independence and opposition by the church brought forth firm imperial edicts condemning Christianity to waves of brutal persecution.

The conversion of Emperor Constantine in 312 and the establishment of Christianity as the official religion of the Roman Empire in 381 ultimately fused these Roman and Christian laws and beliefs. The Roman Empire came to be understood as the universal body of Christ on earth, embracing all persons and things. The Roman Emperor became at once pope and king, who reigned supreme throughout Christendom. The Roman law became the perfect embodiment of Godly law and Christian morality. Such syncretic beliefs allowed the church to imbue the Roman law with its spiritual and moral teachings. By the later sixth century, orthodox Christian teachings on trinitarian doctrine, the sacraments, liturgical practices, Sunday observance, monogamous marriage, sexual restraint, benevolence to slaves, charity, education and the like were all prescribed by Roman law. But such syncretic beliefs also subordinated the Christian church to imperial rule. Roman rulers now convoked Christian councils and synods, appointed and removed clerics, founded and administered parishes and monasteries, and controlled the acquisition and disposition of church property. This 'caesaropapist' pattern of substantive influence but procedural subordination of the church to the state, and of religion to law, persisted in the Germanic era.

The *second* watershed period occurred in the twelfth and thirteenth centuries when the Catholic clergy threw off their civil rulers and established the church as an autonomous legal and political corporation within Western Christendom. The church now claimed jurisdiction over such persons as clerics, pilgrims, students, Jews and Muslims and over such subjects as doctrine and liturgy; ecclesiastical property, polity and patronage; MARRIAGE and family relations; education, charity and inheritance; oral promises, oaths and various contracts; and all manner of moral and ideological crimes. The church predicated these jurisdictional claims in part on its traditional AUTHORITY over the sacraments. In particular the sacraments of marriage, penance, ordination and last rites supported whole systems of canon law rules. The church also predicated its jurisdictional claims on Christ's delegation of the keys to St Peter – a key of knowledge to discern God's word and will, and a key of POWER to implement and enforce that word and will throughout Christendom.

The church devised an elaborate pan-Western system of canon law to support these claims. Building on earlier apostolic canons and Christianized Roman law, the Catholic episcopacy issued a welter of ecclesiastical legislation. A hierarchy of ecclesiastical courts and officials administered this law in accordance with canon law rules of procedure and evidence. A vast network of ecclesiastical officials conducted the church's executive and administrative functions. Canon lawyers dominated the new law faculties and developed a rich tradition of legal scholarship and teaching. The medieval Catholic Church became, in F.W. Maitland's famous phrase, the first true state in the West.

Canon lawyers not only imbued the individual doctrines of public and private law with cardinal Catholic beliefs. They also, together with the Romanist civilians, made lasting contributions to Western legal philosophy and science. They classified the sources of law – eternal law, Biblical and rational natural law, the law of nations, international and local customary law, canon law, civil law and common law. They developed enduring rules for the resolution of conflict of laws and contests of jurisdiction and a refined hermeneutic for the equitable application of statutes. They differentiated the concepts of legislation, adjudication and administration, and developed a rudimentary theory of the mixed constitution. They developed a good deal of the modern law of corporations and private associations as well as refined concepts of popular and political sovereignty, representation and consent, individual and corporate rights and liberties.

Though the canon law was not considered divine, it was the pre-eminent law of late medieval Christendom. Private parties preferred to litigate their claims in church courts rather than civil courts. Civil authorities readily appropriated the substance and science of the canon law in their own regimes. For the canon law was considered to be a true Christian law. It treated both the legality and the morality of social conduct, and compliance with it enabled the believer to remain reconciled to God and neighbour. Violation of the canon law was a SIN; obedience to it was conducive to salvation.

The *third* watershed period came with the transformation of canon law and civil law, and of church and state, born of the Protestant Reformation. The Protestant reformers taught that salvation comes through faith in the Gospel, not by works of the law. Each individual stands directly before God, seeks God's gracious forgiveness of sin, and conducts life in accordance with Scripture and conscience. To the reformers, the Catholic canon law had obstructed the individual's relationship with God and obscured God's simple norms for right living. The Protestant reformers further taught that the church is at heart a community of saints, not a corporation of POLITICS. Its cardinal purposes are to preach the Word, administer the sacraments, educate the young, care for the needy. To the reformers, the Catholic episcopacy's legal rule in Christendom had obstructed the church's divine mission and usurped the state's role as God's vice-regent. To be sure, the church must have internal rules to govern its own polity, teaching and discipline. The church must critique legal injustice and combat political illegitimacy. But the law is primarily the province of the state, not the church.

These new Protestant teachings transformed the Western law of the sixteenth and seventeenth centuries. Western Christendom was fractioned into competing nations and regions, each with their own religious and political rulers. The hegemony of the Catholic Church and the international rule of the canon law were permanently broken. State rulers now assumed jurisdiction over numerous subjects previously governed by the church – marriage and family relations, property and testamentary matters, education, charity, contracts and oaths, moral and ideological crimes. In Lutheran and Anglican polities in particular, the state also exercised considerable control over the clergy, polity and property of the church.

These massive shifts in jurisdiction from the church to the state did not suddenly deprive Western law of its religious influence or dimensions. The canon law remained an ineradicable part of the *ius commune* in Europe and, by reason of its sophistication and comprehensiveness, a vital legal resource throughout the West. Moreover, in Catholic polities, the legal and moral pronouncements of the papal see still held considerable sway over state legislators and judges. In Protestant polities, reformed teachings often found direct and dramatic legal application. Protestant views of lay education, charity for the deserving poor and the value of public work shaped the new social welfare laws. Protestant concepts of the deterrent, retributive and educational 'uses of law' shaped substantive and procedural criminal law. Protestant views of marriage as a public civil estate, rather than a private sacramental union, transformed the civil laws of marital formation and divorce. Protestant teachings that all persons are created equal in dignity and vocation informed the constitutional law of rights and liberties. Protestant teachings on the inherent corruptibility of the political office led to the development of such constitutional restraints as separation of powers, limited terms of office, codification of law, and restrictions on discretion and equity.

The *fourth* watershed period came with the great national revolutions born of the Western Enlightenment. The Enlightenment offered a new secular theology of individualism, rationalism and NATIONALISM to replace traditional Christian beliefs. The individual was no longer viewed primarily as a sinner seeking salvation in the life hereafter. To the *philosophes*, every individual was created equal in virtue and dignity, vested with inherent rights of life, liberty and property, and capable of choosing his own means and measure of happiness. Reason was no longer the handmaid of revelation, rational disputation no longer subordinate to homiletic declaration. The rational process, conducted privately by each person and collectively in the open market-place of ideas, was considered a sufficient source of private morality and public law. The nation-state was no longer identified with a national church or a divinely blessed covenant people. The nation-state was to be glorified in its own right. Its constitutions and laws were sacred texts reflecting the morals and mores of the collective national CULTURE. Its officials were secular priests, representing the sovereignty and will of the people.

Such sentiments were revolutionary in their time and were among the driving forces of the great national revolutions in England, America and France. These revolutions introduced sweeping changes in Western law – new constitutional laws prescribing limited government and ample civil liberties, new injunctions to separate church and state, new criminal procedures and methods of criminal punishment, new commercial, contractual and other laws of the private market-place, new laws of private property and inheritance, shifts toward a fault-based law of delicts and torts, the ultimate expulsion of SLAVERY and the gradual removal of discrimination based on race, religion, culture and GENDER. Many Western nations also developed elaborate new codes of public law and private law, transformed the curricula of their law faculties and radically reconfigured their legal professions.

The secular theology of the Enlightenment also penetrated Western legal philosophy. In the absence of traditional Christian theories of law, jurists offered a range of secular legal philosophies – often derived from earlier Christian and Graeco-Roman teachings. Eighteenth-century jurists postulated a mythical state of nature that antedated and integrated human laws and natural rights. Nationalist myths were grafted on to this paradigm to unify and sanctify national legal traditions: Italian jurists appealed to their utopic Roman heritage; English jurists to their ancient constitution and Anglo-Saxon roots; French jurists to their Salic law; German jurists to their ancient constitutional liberties. As these secular myths dissipated under the hot lights of philosophical scepticism, a triumvirate of new legal philosophies came to prominence. Legal positivists contended that the ultimate source of law lies in the will of the legislature and its ultimate sanction in political force. Natural-law theorists sought the ultimate source of law in reason and conscience and its ultimate sanction in moral suasion. Historical jurists contended that the ultimate source of law is the custom and character of the *Volk*, and its ultimate sanction is communal condemnation. These juxtaposed positivist, naturalist and historicist legal philosophies have persisted in legal academies to this day, now heavily supplemented by an array of realist, socialist, feminist and other schools of legal thought.

The budding patterns introduced in the late eighteenth and nineteenth centuries have come to full legal flower in the twentieth century. The cardinal secular beliefs of the Enlightenment have come to prominent legal expression – individualism in the constitutional and private law doctrines of privacy; rationalism in the doctrines of freedom of speech, press and assembly; nationalism in the totalitarian laws and polities of DEMOCRACY, fascism and SOCIALISM. Ambitious interpretation of the doctrine of separation of church and state has served to privatize theistic religion and to drive religious organizations from the legal and political process. The growing isolation of national laws, and the fractioning of individual bodies of law within each nation, has continued apace. These legal patterns have been offset somewhat by the growth of international law in the past half century and the effective new social and political programmes of LIBERATION THEOLOGY, post-Vatican II Catholicism and the ECUMENICAL MOVEMENT. A number of writers, however, now openly warn of a crisis of law and politics on a world scale.

Though these recent secular movements have removed traditional forms of religious influence on Western law, contemporary Western law still retains important connections with religious ideas and institutions. Even in contemporary Western society, law and religion continue to cross over and cross-fertilize each other in a variety of ways. Law and religion are conceptually related. They both draw upon prevailing concepts of the nature of being and order, the person and community, knowledge and TRUTH. They both embrace closely analogous doctrines of sin and CRIME, COVENANT and contract, righteousness and JUSTICE that invariably bleed together in the mind of the legislator, judge and juror. Law and religion are methodologically related. They share overlapping hermeneutical methods of interpreting authoritative texts, casuistic methods of converting principles to precepts, systematic methods of organizing their subject-matters, pedagogical methods of transmitting the science and substance of their craft to students. Law and religion are professionally related. Legal and religious officials and professionals are charged with the formulation, ritualization and implementation of the norms and habits of their respective fields. Analogous rules and canons govern the admission to and actions of members of these two professions. Law and religion are institutionally related, through the multiple relationships between political and religious officials and the multiple institutions in which these officials serve – in short, in the relationship of church and state.

Even in contemporary Western society, the laws of the secular state retain strong moral and religious dimensions. These dimensions are reflected not only in the substantive doctrines of private and public law that are derived from earlier Christian theology and canon law. They are also reflected in the characteristic forms of contemporary legal systems. Every legitimate legal system has what Lon Fuller calls an 'inner morality', a set of attributes that bespeak its justice and fairness. Its rules are publicly proclaimed and known, uniform, stable, understandable, non-retroactive and consistently enforced. Every legitimate legal system has what Harold Berman calls an 'inner sanctity', a set of attributes that command the obedience, respect and fear of both political authorities and their subjects. Like religion, law has authority – written or spoken sources, texts or oracles, which are considered to be decisive or obligatory in themselves. Law has tradition – a continuity of language, practice and institutions. Law

has liturgy and RITUAL – the ceremonial procedures and words of the legislature, the courtroom and the legal document that reflect and
dramatize deep social feelings about the value
and validity of the law.

Even in modern Western society, religion
maintains a legal dimension, an inner structure
of legality, which gives religious lives and religious communities their coherence, order and
social form. Legal habits of the heart structure
the inner spiritual life and discipline of religious
believers, from the reclusive hermit to the aggressive zealot. Legal ideas of justice, order, ATONE-
MENT, restitution, responsibility, obligation and
others pervade the theological doctrines of
countless religious traditions. Legal structures
and processes – the Christian canon law, the
Jewish Halakkha, the Muslim Shari'a, the
Hindu dharma – continue to organize and
govern religious communities and their distinctive beliefs and rituals, mores and morals.

The interaction of law and religion, in recent
years, has attracted a considerable body of historical and theoretical scholarship. These interdisciplinary studies will be of vital importance
to us as we continue the struggle to understand
the concepts and commandments of law, justice
and order, and as we prepare Western law and
Western culture for the emergence of a common
law of all humanity in the next millennium.

Allen, C.K. (1958) *Law in the Making*, 6th edn,
Oxford: Oxford University Press.
Berman, H. (1983) *Law and Revolution: The Forma-
tion of the Western Legal Tradition*, Cambridge,
MA: Harvard University Press.
Ellul, J. (1960) *The Theological Foundation of Law*,
Garden City, NY: Doubleday.
Fuller, L. (1969) *The Morality of Law*, revised edn,
New Haven, CT: Yale University Press.
Kelley, D.R. (1990) *The Human Measure: Social
Thought in the Western Legal Tradition*, Cam-
bridge, MA: Harvard University Press.
Pound, R. (1959) *Jurisprudence*, 5 vols, St Paul, MN:
West Publishing.
Stone, J. (1966) *Social Dimensions of Law and Justice*,
Stanford, CA: Stanford University Press.
Tierney, B. (1982) *Religion, Law and the Growth of
Constitutional Thought 1150–1650*, Cambridge:
Cambridge University Press.
Vallauri, L. and Dilcher, G. (eds) (1981) *Christentum,
Säkularisation und Modernes Recht*, 2 vols,
Baden-Baden: Nomos Verlagsgesellschaft.
Witte, J. (ed.) (1993) *Christianity and Democracy in
Global Context*, Boulder, CO and San Francisco,
CA: Westview.
Wolf, Erik (1972) *Rechtstheologische Studien*, Frank-
furt am Main: Klostermann.

John Witte, Jr

LIBERALISM

Liberalism, notably in the form 'liberal democracy', is widely regarded as the pre-eminent political doctrine of the modern world, and many
of its core ideas have the force of self-evident
truth amongst the dominant classes in Western
societies. Although the term itself was first used
in a recognizably modern political sense only in
the early nineteenth century, and there is much
debate whether any combination of ideas that
can properly be called liberal existed before the
late eighteenth century, its central position in
the public self-definition of Western democracies is now beyond question.

Despite the notable vagueness with which
the term 'liberal' and its cognates are often used
within political discussion, it is possible to make
a number of clarifying distinctions.

Classical economic liberalism, partially exemplified in nineteenth-century Britain and revived
during the 1980s, is closely connected with the
economic and political doctrines of free market
CAPITALISM. Indebted in part to the classical political economists of the eighteenth and nineteenth
centuries, it has been defended in the twentieth
century by writers such as F.A. Hayek (1899–
1992) and Robert Nozick (1938–   ). This kind of
liberalism typically advocates *laissez-faire* policies in economics, freedom of trade internationally and minimal government intervention domestically, the right of individuals to freedom
of contract, and the JUSTICE of any distributions
of WEALTH which result from free exchange.

As a response to the destructive social consequences of nineteenth-century industrial capitalism, *revisionist liberalism* from the latter part
of the century recognized the need for social
reform to accompany economic growth. This
was instrumental in bringing about the New
Deal in the USA and the postwar welfare state
in Britain, while at a theoretical level individual
liberty and social justice were coupled by political

philosophers such as L.T. Hobhouse (1864–1929) and, more recently, John Rawls (1921–). Especially in North America, this species of liberalism has come to be associated not only with redistributionist economic policies and welfarist social policies, but also with, for example, support for the civil rights movement and the rights of minorities in general; suspicion of the influence of big business on GOVERNMENT; opposition to religious FUNDAMENTALISM and moral dogmatism; a preference for non-coercive to coercive measures; and the like.

Although classical and revisionist liberals often take differing stances in particular political debates, they find common ground in a general commitment to *constitutional liberalism*. This is frequently thought to articulate the underlying rationale of Western-style political institutions, and as such to express one of the defining features of the modern Western world. It is often associated with the American and French Revolutions and (with varying degrees of historical accuracy) with writers such as John Locke (1632–1704), Baron de Montesquieu (1689–1755), Immanuel Kant (1724–1804) and the authors of *The Federalist* (1787–8). In general, constitutional liberalism attempts to provide a theoretical justification for a set of practices clustered around the principle of limited government, including most or all of the following: effective restraints on the arbitrary or tyrannical exercise of power; constitutional definition of governmental powers; the rule of LAW; government legitimated by the consent of the people; maintenance of the rights of individuals, especially their civil and political rights; official toleration of a plurality of religions and moral codes; and the legal protection of private PROPERTY. Constitutional liberalism is not the only possible defence of limited government; the particular complexion it has given that notion is illustrated by its historically most characteristic form of justification, the appeal to an actual or hypothetical social contract between consenting individuals as the basis for political authority and obligation. But the intimate association of liberalism with limited government does underline the observation that, in talk of liberal democracy, the adjective 'has the force of a qualification' (de Ruggiero 1927: 379).

All of the above are related to *liberal individualism*, which may be said (though it is disputed) to express the central values of liberalism. Broadly, liberal INDIVIDUALISM emphasizes the fundamental importance of the individual over against the claims of tradition, AUTHORITY, hierarchy or community; the equality in principle of individuals, regardless of birth, status, gender, race or creed; and above all, the liberty of individuals, with a concomitant emphasis on consent, choice and personal AUTONOMY. Beyond some version of these basic commitments, liberals differ, though liberalism is regularly associated with an 'atomist' rendition of them which depicts the individual as a sovereign chooser of his or her goals, unencumbered by any constitutive attachments, and bound by obligations and relating to others only on the basis of consent or contract; this view of the individual is in turn refracted through a mode of thought that is abstract and universalist, playing down those aspects of persons that are particular, embedded, concrete, local or historical.

There is often asserted to be a diffuse *liberal worldview* which informs each of the above in different ways. While it is difficult to enumerate its varying features precisely, those that might be attributed to it include suspicion of religion and the supernatural; optimism about the human capacity for reason, over against prejudice and passion, obfuscation and superstition; receptiveness to the claims of science; a progressivist attitude in relation to history; a temperamental dislike for conservatism and conformity, and a preference for a pluralism of lifestyles and cultural forms; and an antipathy towards the enforcement of personal morality, extending at times into moral permissiveness and a celebration of the subjectivity of values.

An indefinite variety of combinations and explications of the above can be found amongst liberal thinkers, although of course not all of these elements (e.g. classical economic liberalism and revisionist liberalism) are wholly compatible. Whether someone may properly be described as a liberal involves a judgement about the extent to which they would subscribe to an interpretation of the above; but whether they would be happy to be described as a liberal turns more on the extent of their affection for the term as a focus of allegiance. Similarly, criticisms of liberalism are liable to be criticisms of (particular features of) one version or another of it. Nevertheless, several more general criticisms are often made of liberalism.

(i) At one level, liberals are often accused of failing to live up to their ideals, or at least of not having fully followed through the implications of their ideals. Thus socialists and democrats criticize liberals for their bourgeois attitudes towards the people (reflected in the past in their limitation of voting rights to property-owning citizens) and their proclamation of the legal rights of individuals but their failure to work for the social and economic conditions that would allow the effective exercise of those rights. Likewise, feminists argue that historically liberalism has been interested principally in the political rights of male heads of households, and only secondarily in the extension of these to women or in issues of justice in the domestic sphere. In turn radicals, of whatever kind, have scorned the preference of liberals for incremental reform rather than wholesale change and their consequent tendency to accommodate themselves to the prevailing structures of power.

(ii) This line of criticism is closely connected to charges concerning liberalism's blindness to its ideological partiality and self-deception about sociological realities. Radical critics argue that liberals have been prone to make false universal claims from particular historical circumstances, failing to appreciate the significance of differences of class, race, gender and the like, and consequently masking the inequalities of power that result. Conservative critics use similar evidence to put in question the reforming aspects of liberalism, pointing to the recalcitrance of human nature as well as the opacity of society and its obdurate refusal of the demands of rationalism in politics. To the extent that these charges are justified, they may be attributed in part to the abstract universalism of the liberal mode of thought (and the middle class nature of liberalism which fosters this), and also perhaps to liberalism's occasionally exaggerated sense of its own virtue.

(iii) In general liberalism has often been insufficiently alert to the historical conditions of its own existence. In terms of economic

organization, while it is unclear whether capitalist economics inevitably leads in the long run to liberal politics, liberalism has historically ridden on the back of capitalism: it may be that there are significant limitations on the varieties of economic regime under which calls for respect for human rights (for example) can be effectually heeded. Again, with regard to the plural structure of society, although religious unity is not evidently necessary for political unity in at least some modern countries, liberals have not always been clear about what social and cultural conditions make religious and ideological pluralism possible. Nor have they sufficiently addressed the possibility that a liberal social order may depend on individuals holding moral or religious beliefs which are not themselves sustained by a secularizing liberalism. In similar vein some have argued that the atomist liberal conception of the self, with its accompanying voluntarist account of value, serves to legitimate a technological mind-set that is ultimately profoundly subversive of the values of liberty and equality.

(iv) Communitarian critics focus a number of issues concerning liberal individualism. At one level, an emphasis on community expresses the importance, both for the functioning of society as a whole and for individual human well-being, of the intermediate associations of civil society between the individual and the state, which liberalism is prone to neglect. More centrally, communitarian critics have argued (whether from sociological considerations, from philosophies inspired by Aristotle, Hegel or Wittgenstein, or from theological reflection on the Trinity and human community) for the essentially social nature of persons. This has accompanied the claim that liberals have often been insensitive to the shared values and collective goods that are intrinsic to some non-individualistic understandings of human flourishing, and have lacked a vision of the common good for a society. The ideal of state neutrality between different conceptions of the good also comes into question: not only is it doubtfully practical (with regard to religion, for example, it is unclear to what extent a public policy of neutrality can be adopted without either implicitly favouring some religions or else discriminating against all religion as such); it is also argued to be at variance with the idea that privately held conceptions of the good can only be fulfilled when given some form of public recognition.

Although these criticisms have often originated in secular thought, many of them have been shared by those working from theological premises. Christian theological reflection on liberalism also has some special concerns, particularly with regard to the liberal worldview. For example, in its affinity with doctrines of moral and social progress, there can arguably be glimpsed on occasions the spectre of liberalism as a surrogate religion offering a this-worldly ESCHATOLOGY. When coupled with its proclivity towards a Pelagian optimism about human capacities, this is liable to engender inordinate expectations of what politics can achieve, and may potentially function as a substitute for Christian salvation.

Nevertheless certain important Christian truths about the political order are preserved in liberalism. Powerful defenders in Christian thought can be found for various aspects of liberal beliefs about the value of the person, the equality and liberty of human beings made in the image of God, the limitations of the state's competence, the importance of private property, and the defence of minorities. Most notably, the liberal doctrine that religious belief and practice are not a matter of political obligation reflects the idea that political authority cannot secure salvation. No earthly order can be simply identified with the KINGDOM OF GOD: rather than being an instrument of saving grace, the public realm is composed of groups of differing beliefs and identities who are willing to co-operate concerning this-worldly matters they hold in common. One fundamental corollary of this is that no group, whether religious or secularist, can demand as a matter of right that its values be enshrined as the public values.

Recognition of these points is not tantamount to a complete theological endorsement of political liberalism, however. In separating the doctrine of limited government and the liberty and equality of individuals from the strictures of the secularizing liberal worldview, for example, Christians can begin to indicate the theological limits of political liberalism. Indeed, in general, they may also point out that the implausible liberal atomist view of the self, the sociological naïvety of many liberal conceptions, and the frequent neglect of the religious dimensions of human experience, as well as other features of the liberal worldview, all make it probable that, whatever the future fortunes of the ideal of liberal democracy, its most cogent intellectual support will not be offered by unchastened liberals.

Berlin, Isaiah (1969) *Four Essays on Liberty*, Oxford: Oxford University Press.

Bramsted, E.K. and Melhuish, K.J. (eds) (1978) *Western Liberalism: A History in Documents from Locke to Croce*, London: Longman.

Douglass, R. Bruce, and Hollenbach, David (eds) (1994) *Catholicism and Liberalism: Contributions to American Public Philosophy*, Cambridge: Cambridge University Press.

Hayek, F.A. (1960) *The Constitution of Liberty*, London: Routledge & Kegan Paul.

Hobhouse, L.T. (1911) *Liberalism*.

Kant, Immanuel (1970) *Kant's Political Writings*, ed. Hans Reiss, Cambridge: Cambridge University Press.

Locke, John (1689) *Two Treatises of Government*.

Madison, James, Hamilton, Alexander and Jay, John (1787–8) *The Federalist*.

Maritain, Jacques (1951) *Man and the State*, Chicago, IL: University of Chicago Press.

Markus, R.A. (1970) *Saeculum: History and Theology in the Theology of St Augustine*, Cambridge: Cambridge University Press.

Mill, John Stuart (1859) *On Liberty*.

Montesquieu, Charles-Louis de Secondat, Baron (1748) *The Spirit of the Laws*.

Murray, John Courtney, SJ (1960). *We Hold These Truths: Catholic Reflections on the American Proposition*, London: Sheed & Ward.

Niebuhr, Reinhold (1944) *The Children of Light and the Children of Darkness: A Vindication of Democracy and a Critique of its Traditional Defenders*, New York: Charles Scribner's Sons.

Rawls, John (1972) *A Theory of Justice*, Oxford: Oxford University Press.

——(1993) *Political Liberalism*, New York: Columbia University Press.

Raz, Joseph (1986) *The Morality of Freedom*, Oxford: Clarendon.

Ruggiero, Guido de (1927) *The History of European Liberalism*, trans. R.G. Collingwood, London: Oxford University Press.

Second Vatican Council (1975) 'Declaration on religious liberty 1965', in Austin Flannery, OP (ed.) *Vatican Council II: The Conciliar and Post-Conciliar Documents*, Northport, NY: Costello, pp. 779–812.

Robert Song

LIBERATION THEOLOGY

The use of the concept and the language of liberation as synonymous with salvation (from demonic powers, from the domination of passion or desire, from the prison of the body, from condemnation and eternal punishment or from social and political oppression) is present in most forms of religion. In the Biblical story the motif of liberation as God's salvific acts to rescue God's people from SLAVERY (the EXODUS from Egypt), from exile (the return from Babylon) or from foreign oppression (the struggles under Macedonic domination described in the books of Maccabees) is conspicuous and has been many times invoked as legitimation and symbol of liberation struggles by slaves, peasants, racially-discriminated-against or colonized peoples. In this sense one could trace a history of 'liberation theologies'. Since the 1960s, however, the term liberation theology (hence LT) has been used more strictly for the attempts to develop an understanding of the Christian faith from the point of view and the experience of social groups engaged in different forms of struggle against economic, political, social or gender oppression.

As a technical designation for this group of 'theologies', the term was first used in Latin America by Gustavo Gutiérrez in papers in 1969 and 1970 and his *Teología de la Liberación* (1972) and Ruben Alves in papers presented to SODEPAX in 1969 and the book *Religión, ¿opio o liberación?*, 1970. In the USA James Cone pointed in 1973 to the common concerns between black and Latin American LT (*see* BLACK THEOLOGY) and the expression has also been used by South African theologians in their struggle against apartheid. In Korea, 'Mingjung Theology' has also described itself as 'a theology of liberation of the people'. The feminist theology emerging also in the 1970s and 1980s (*see* FEMINISM, SEXISM) should also be included in the category of a 'theology of liberation'.

Although these 'liberation theologies' cannot be described as 'varieties' of one single type, they have certain elements in common that justify treating them as analogous. They are 'contextual' in the sense that they consciously and explicitly address a particular historical and social situation and relate to it their theological interpretations. Consequently they tend to use an 'inductive' method: to begin with the concrete facts of the condition of oppression and then 'abstract' or 'theorize' on that basis. Moreover, these theologies do not claim to adopt a neutral attitude toward the condition they are describing but understand themselves as actively 'militant' in the quest of liberation. In this sense they give a central place to the concept of 'praxis', i.e. a reflection that begins with the experience of the participation in the struggle for liberation and then, through an analysis of the realities involved in that struggle, in the light of their faith, develop a theological interpretation which, in turn, strengthens and clarifies the participation in the struggle. Finally, precisely because the theological method demands the use of analytical tools in order to understand the nature of the oppression and the strategies for liberation, these theologies are 'interdisciplinary', incorporating human sciences as sociology, anthropology or economics not merely as 'ancillary' but as constitutive of theological thinking.

Most frequently the term 'liberation theology' in the singular, without any other qualification, is understood as referring to the Latin American theological current which traces its origin to the work of Gustavo Gutiérrez, Juan Luis Segundo, Hugo Assmann, Ruben Alves, José Miguez Bonino, Leonardo Boff, Jon Sobrino and others since the late 1960s. It began with a concern for the conditions of the masses of poor people which the failure of the development plans of the late 1950s and 1960s made visible throughout Latin America. The awareness of these conditions – hearing 'the cry of the poor' as a Brazilian Catholic document put it in 1973 – raised at least three kinds of questions: what are the causes?; how can this condition of the poor be interpreted in theological terms?; what can be done about it?

The first question demands a social analysis. Latin American liberation theologians rejected the development theories and the funcionalist sociologies which had underlaid the development plans and applied instead 'the dependence theories' which understood the underdevelopment situations mainly as effects of neocolonial and imperialistic domination and the 'class analysis' of the political economists who made use of Marxist tools of interpretation. The relation of LT to MARXISM has been one of the points of debate in the 'reception' of LT by churches and theological circles both in Latin America itself and in the developed world. While liberation theologians have maintained that the use of analytical and even of some Marxian critical tools and insights – like its critique of religion – was necessary and justified, they have also insisted that this did not mean an acceptance of Marxist ATHEISM or dialectical materialism. The two letters of the Commission on Doctrine of the Vatican on the theologies of liberation ('Instrucción sobre algunos aspectos de la "Teología de la Liberación"' (1984), mainly critical; and 'Instrucción sobre Libertad Cristiana y Liberación' (1986), pointing the directions in which LT would be legitimate according to Catholic doctrine) illustrate the nature and main arguments in this debate.

In relation to the second question, several Biblical motifs became central: (a) God's particular concern for the poor, oppressed, weak and unprotected as witnessed in both the prophetic and legal tradition of the Hebrew Scriptures and in the ministry and message of Jesus; (b) the concrete and historical nature of the concept of God over against both the spiritualism and INDIVIDUALISM dominant in the prevalent religiosity and the abstract and metaphysical character of most classical theology; (c) the concept and symbol of the KINGDOM OF GOD as the new order of peace and justice which Jesus announced, incarnated and inaugurated in his ministry: the coming of the Kingdom is understood both as a promise and a task and, although it cannot be equated with any particular social order or reduced to the category of a 'utopia', it 'happens' in human history in the events and struggles of liberation and will be consummated at the end of time.

Latin American LT is particularly indebted, in its theological thinking, to some European theological developments. The Biblical renewal in the Catholic Church related to the School of Jerusalem and the Biblical studies of scholars like Gerhard von Rad, Joachim Jeremias or Ernst Käsemann who stressed the importance of history for Biblical thinking, provided a hermeneutical key to relate Biblical thought to the social and political conditions. In the same sense, the 'nouvelle théologie' and the work of Karl Rahner, von Balthasar and Schillebeeckx in the Catholic camp and the POLITICAL THEOLOGY of Jürgen Moltmann and Johannes Baptist Metz offered valuable models for a reflection on the relationship between theology and political questions. Finally, the discussions of the Vatican II Council on the one hand and the work of the ecumenical movement (WORLD COUNCIL OF CHURCHES) on the other made possible a dialogue both with North Atlantic theology and with other areas of the Third World which faced analogous problems and were developing similar insights.

Finally, the question as to what kind of praxis is involved in this theology has to be seen in the light of a fundamental premise: Christian action cannot be arbitrary, haphazard or purely conjunctural. The transformation of the condition of the poor demands a 'historical project' the broad lines of which at least, have to be designed at the social, political, economic and cultural levels. Although LT did not espouse a 'programme' or create a political organization, in general lines it favoured a democratic socialism, in which the people would have participation and control over economic resources, political institutions and cultural creation. Within these parameters, several concrete plans, strategies and tactics could be chosen and in circles related to LT the specific options were by no means unanimous.

In terms of the actual practice of people committed to this vision, three elements were particularly important. In the first place, to give central importance to the 'community of faith' as a centre of worship, reflection and action. This results in the growing movement of Base Ecclesial Communities (which had begun already in the 1950s). The ECCLESIOLOGY which emerges from this movement, with its stress on the role of the people as the active subject of Christian thinking and decision has raised some critical questions, particularly for Roman Catholic ecclesiology, as the Vatican reaction to Leonardo Boff's book *Church, Charism and Power* has shown. In the second place, the question as to what kind of 'spirituality' is involved in this theological and ecclesial renewal has been the object of theological reflection; the concern for the poor as a 'locus' for prayer, praise and Christian discipline has a history that goes back to the Hebrew Bible and the early Christian Church and has been taken up in LT in the work of Gustavo Gutiérrez, Pablo Richard, Jaci Maraschin and others. Thirdly, the question of 'means', i.e. the kinds of action in which commitment to the poor finds expression, raises ethical questions as to political action, contextual or principle ethics, the relation of Christian love – so central to LT – REVOLUTION and VIOLENCE, some of which still await adequate treatment but have been discussed in the works of Enrique Dussel, José Míguez Bonino and Hugo Assmann among others.

It has not been infrequent in the last five or six years to hear critics that predict that the crisis of the socialist regimes in Eastern Europe on the one side and the disciplinary and restrictive measures taken by the Vatican on the other will mean the decline and perhaps the end of LT. Such diagnosis seems to be an oversimplication. A theology which explicitly relates to historical conditions cannot fail to be affected by historical changes. A theology which binds itself to the condition and problematics of the people cannot remain untouched by what happens to the people. In this sense, however, LT in the Third World in general and particularly in Latin America has been challenged by changes in the region, no doubt related to the international scene but more directly affecting the conditions of the people, particularly of the poor. It is in response to these challenges that certain themes have become more central, certain new emphases are developing and new interdisiplinary avenues are being explored.

The neoliberal economic programmes which are being implemented in most Latin American countries since the end of the 1980s have raised two kinds of issues. On the one hand, the economic adjustments are creating a great concentration of economic power and a growing mass of marginalized peoples, mostly unemployed or so-called self-employed. Lacking organized political and social expressions, these masses become anomic (see ANOMIE) and develop forms of survival, not infrequently related to delinquency. The pastoral task of spiritual and social 'contention' of these people requires forms of understanding and action which, without excluding the political dimension, start from an analysis of the underlying anthropological and cultural situation. The dialogue of theology with cultural anthropology has been an important item in recent theological consultations, particularly in Peru, Mexico and Brazil.

On the other hand, the neoliberal ideology has developed a theological apologetics based on the concept of economic freedom (the so called 'free market'), competition and individual initiative as both religious and economic solutions for the problem of POVERTY and marginality. In response to this claim, theologians like Franz Hinkelammert, Hugo Assmann, Julio de Santa Ana and others have articulated a theological response showing that this apologetics in fact means an idolization of 'the market' as a miraculous subject which replaces the human subject as both subject and object of economic life. An LT has to be developed, in the first place, as 'a theology of life' over against the 'system of death' which is being implemented, sometimes precisely as a Christian answer to all human problems. In this direction, some theologians have revisited the doctrine of the TRINITY for a basic understanding of the social nature of reality (cf. L. Boff, *Trinity, Society and Liberation*, 1987) and CREATION, and also a CHRISTOLOGY based on the ministry of Jesus as a defence and restoration of life (cf. J. Sobrino, *Jesus in Latin America*, 1987; Pedro Trigo, *Creación e Historia en el Proceso de Liberación*, 1988).

Cultural anthropology has also become important in relation to the new awareness of the diversity hidden under such terms as 'poor', 'marginal', 'oppressed'. This was first raised in the 1970s by women participating in base communities and theological work and very forcefully in EATWOT (Ecumenical Association of Third World Theologians). Women do not only share the common oppression of the poor but suffer it in a particular way as women. A Theology of Liberation must also be undertaken 'from the place of women' (see the work of Elsa

Támez, Maria Clara Bingemer and Ivonne Gebara among others). An analogous questioning comes from the indigenous and black communities. Within EATWOT, both in Latin America and elsewhere in the Third World, these dimensions of oppression and liberation have been the object of theological work (cf. the EATWOT Journal, *Voices from the Third World*). The exploration of culture has underlined the importance of the religious factor, which LT tended to relegate in its early production. It is not only the analysis of religion as an instrument of domination and a potential force of liberation, which had already appeared in early work, but the significance of traditional indigenous and Afro-American religions which are inseparable from cultural identity. There is still much to be done, not only in terms of the understanding of 'other religions' of the people but also of the growing movements of 'Christian' forms of the religion of the poor, like the growing tide of Pentecostalism.

LT had been mainly articulated in doctrinal and ethical terms. At the same time, the 'popular reading of the Bible' in base communities and other Christian groups had raised important hermeneutical questions, which required more systematic work. A significant number of scholars who have actively participated in community study of the Bible have engaged in exegetical and hermeneutical work, using both the experience of 'popular reading' and socio-historical and linguistic analysis. In this respect, the work of Severino Croatto, Pablo Richard, Milton Schwantes and others are revitalizing theological thinking from the Biblical field (the Journal *Revista de Interpretación Bíblica Latinoamericano* is the best resource for approaching this work). An analogous observation has to be made in relation to historical studies that trace the history of the prophetic element in popular religion. The quincentennial events of 1992 have been the ocassion of some significant studies (Gustavo Gutiérrez, *Dios Y el Oro de las India* 1989; Fernando Mires, *La Conquista de las Almas, 1978*).

Whether liberation theologies such as were developed in the 1960s and 1970s will continue or fade away is a moot question. The theological methodology which these theologies have articulated, the theological issues that they raised and the questions that they tried to address, however, cannot be dismissed and are likely to occupy theologians at least in the immediate future.

Alves, R. (1969) *A Theology of Human Hope*, New York: World.
Boff, C. (1979) *Theology and Praxis*, Maryknoll, NY: Orbis Books.
——and Boff, L. (1987) *Introducing Liberation Theology*, Maryknoll, NY: Orbis Books.
Gutiérrez, G. (1988) *A Theology of Liberation*, Maryknoll, NY: Orbis Books (new edn).
Hinkelammert, F. (1985) *The Ideological Weapons of Death*, Maryknoll, NY: Orbis Books.
Míguez Bonino, J. (1975) *Doing Theology in a Revolutionary Situation*, Philadelphia, PA: Fortress Press.
Segundo, J.L. (1976) *The Liberation of Theology*, Maryknoll, NY: Orbis Books.
Sobrino, J. (1978) *Christology at the Crossroads*, Maryknoll, NY: Orbis Books.

José Míguez Bonino

LIBERTARIANISM

Libertarianism resembles classical LIBERALISM in holding that no human being can have AUTHORITY over any other (or over any competent adult) save by that other's free and informed consent. It is unlike classical liberalism, and like ANARCHISM, in concluding that there are no legitimate governments. Anarchists of the more familiar kind usually propose that self-governing communes could own PROPERTY and expect loyal co-operation from their members. Libertarians, although they would expect some co-operative ventures, deny that such communes could legitimately demand obedience, and resist suggestions that they might be obliged to contribute to any supposed 'common good'. The only legitimate use of coercive force is to prevent the initiation of such force against any non-aggressive individual. All human transactions should be voluntary, and the market is the most usual example of such purely voluntary transactions: in free exchange everyone gets what he or she wants. In coerced exchanges, even ones directed to 'the good of SOCIETY', unconsenting individuals are sacrificed for what others think good, or what is supposed to be good for others. It follows that taxation is equivalent to armed extortion, that WELFARE payments should only be charitable donations (which are themselves distrusted) and that no rule can be enforced but one forbidding the initiation of coercive force.

That only the consent of the governed could legitimize GOVERNMENT is a seventeenth-century idea that arose from a clearly theological context: every human individual (or at least those who were judged competent) was responsible for his or her own actions, before God, and could never excuse him or herself by claiming any duty of obedience. Every individual should do what he or she sees to be right; no individual has any right to command another's unwilling obedience; no individual should (or really could) surrender his or her God-given autonomy. No government could have any authority beyond what the governed were entitled to give it, or beyond what it had been given (whichever was the smaller class of rights). Liberals typically excused government on the plea that rational people had given or would give their consent at least to 'legitimate government', which would do nothing but enforce a civil PEACE (that might perhaps be kept by other means). Libertarians, especially in nineteenth-century USA, concluded that governments could not act to keep the peace without claiming powers that they should not have, and that actual governments actually claimed far more even than they needed. In particular, they claimed the right to apportion property: not merely to settle disputes between would-be property-owners (a task that libertarians would prefer to see performed by non-governmental mediators), but to take property away from acknowledged owners or assign it to newcomers without regard to the rule formulated by John Locke, that I can make something mine only by 'mixing my labour with it' while leaving as good material for others' work. They saw, in short, that even governments founded under the pretence of free consent quickly reverted to older habits, claiming a legitimacy that could not be, and had not been, granted. 'Anarchy is order; government is civil war.' More traditional views of government, that rulers had the mandate of Heaven to coerce the wicked and train the would-be virtuous, might have allowed governments to claim authority over the unwilling: good liberals like Locke or Jefferson had always accepted that even a government's contractual rights and duties would have to be regularly renegotiated, and that some contracts were never legitimate, or legitimating.

Anarchists of a more communitarian persuasion have sometimes decided that the agents of government (including ordinary citizens) were the legitimate targets of revolutionary VIOLENCE: they constituted a violent conspiracy, after all, against the proper concerns of the communards (see ANARCHISM). Libertarians, more suspicious of any enforced unity, including that of revolutionary armies, prefer to place their hopes in the power of market forces (freely chosen transactions) even when those transactions are illegitimately taxed by government to pay its own expenses. They are therefore sometimes called 'anarcho-capitalists', but the kind of capital they have in mind is not the artificially protected product of an alliance between Big Business and the STATE. In a truly free market large fortunes would not (they hope) develop or long remain to distort the freely chosen pattern of voluntary exchange. The larger the fortune, in any case, the less control its purported owner has over its exercise – unless governments and their armies are called in aid.

Other political theorists have also held that the legitimate powers of government were very limited or that market CAPITALISM was the best hope for general happiness. These theorists are often openly consequentialist or even utilitarian: it is because a free society ends by increasing wealth and allowing the best hope of happiness for the most people that it is preferred. True libertarians, though they may welcome this support, rest their case primarily on the 'rights' of individuals. Even if it turned out that coercive or redistributive government *did* make more people 'happy' than not (perhaps by allowing more people to be self-governing than it made into slaves), such government would still be illegitimate. No-one ought to be used as a mere means to the welfare of another, nor should anyone abandon their own view of what should be done to fit in with another's, even with a majority's. Not to do what one conceives oneself to be good merely because others reckon on another good is to be a slave. Some extreme forms of the argument, as by Ayn Rand, deny any virtue in altruism, a willingness to forgo one's own good for the sake of others. This seems to rest on a deliberate confusion between 'what one conceives good' and 'what one reckons to one's own advantage'. It is slavish, and sinful, to obey others against one's conscience: not therefore to reckon it good to benefit another at some personal cost.

Some of the plausibility of classical liberal ideas of property, that it is possible to see at once what individual would own any particular item, is lost in a long-established community where more have 'mixed their labour' than have ever been properly paid for their work. As the Russian anarchist Peter Kropotkin remarked, it is one thing to lay claim on a hut built by oneself in the forest without harming anyone, and quite another to claim the full market price of a 'hut' in the middle of Paris. There will be many occasions when it is impossible to disentangle individual contributions and best to agree that 'the whole community' owns it. But in that case there will be forms of taxation, welfare distribution and even majority rule that are not so obviously illegitimate, even if the institutions through which the common wealth is managed were once established (as they almost certainly were) by coercion. Something like Jeffersonian DEMOCRACY, whereby every matter is managed by the smallest practicable group from the Great Republic down to the family farm (or the individual hobo), may seem easier to swallow than a purely libertarian, anarcho-individualist or anarcho-capitalist form. Those with libertarian sympathies will still be profoundly distrustful of those who claim to manage the common WEALTH for the common good, and be very loath to give them POWER to accomplish even such goods as they legitimately might. The 'common good' is all too often no-one's good, or the good solely of the coercers and managers. The Ruling Ring of Tolkien's fable will corrupt even the wise and good, and what began in genuine benevolence and pity will end at last as Mordor.

Capouya, E. and Tompkins, K. (eds) (1976) *The Essential Kropotkin*, London: Macmillan.
Eller, V. (1987) *Christian Anarchy*, Grand Rapids, MI: Eerdmans.
Friedman, D. (1978) *The Machinery of Freedom*, New Rochelle, NY: Arlington House.
Krimerman, L.I. and Perry, L. (eds) (1966) *Patterns of Anarchy*, New York: Anchor.
Locke, J. (1963) *Two Treatises of Government*, ed. P. Laslett, Cambridge: Cambridge University Press.
Machan, T. (1975) *Human Rights and Human Liberties*, Chicago, IL: Nelson Hall.
——(ed.) (1982) *The Libertarian Reader*, Totowa, NJ: Rowman & Littlefield.
Martin, J.J. (1953) *Men Against the State*, DeKalb, NY: Adrian Allen.
Oppenheimer, F. (1914) *The State*, trans. J. Gitterman, Indianapolis, IN: Bobbs Merrill.
Rand, A. (1967) *Capitalism: the Unknown Ideal*, New York: New American Library.
Spencer, H. (1940) *The Man versus the State*, London: Watts & Co. (first published 1884).
Spooner, L. (1972) *Let's Abolish Government*, New York: Arno Press (reprint of two works dated 1870 and 1886).

Stephen Clark

LITURGICAL MOVEMENT

As narrowly defined the Liturgical Movement originated within the Roman Catholic Church just before the Great War, and was particularly concerned with the restoration of active participation of the laity in the official liturgies of the Church, and to promote a piety and theology flowing from the liturgical rites themselves. The movement ultimately resulted in the complete reform of the Roman rites as undertaken by the Second Vatican Council. However, similar concerns for reform and renewal can be traced in other Western Churches, and with the growth of ecumenism, there has been considerable cross-fertilization between the Churches. The term 'Liturgical Movement' has thus come to describe the whole process of liturgical renewal, reform and revision which has characterized the Western Churches in the latter part of the twentieth century. By contrast, the Eastern Churches have been little affected by this movement.

Some exponents trace the movement to the liturgical renewal pioneered at the Abbey of Solesmes in France by Dom Prosper Guéranger (1805–75), but Guéranger's interests were mainly confined to meticulous concern for rubrics and restoration of Gregorian chant. Guéranger, like the New Catholicism of Württemberg, is best viewed as a precursor.

Most exponents place the immediate origins of the movement with a paper given by Dom

Lambert Beauduin (1873–1960) of the Abbey of Mont Cesar, Louvain in Belgium, given at the Malines Conference of 1909. Beauduin had worked as an industrial chaplain before entering the Abbey at Mont Cesar. He was concerned at the apparent individualism in society, and the alienation of the working class; he saw a counterpart in the new Church, with the laity concerned with their rosaries or other individual private devotions, quite detached from the priest reciting the official prayers of the church in the Latin language. His paper of 1909 was concerned to stress the centrality of public worship for the Christian life, and he condemned the individual piety of Catholicism which had become detached from the liturgy. Beauduin believed that the active lay participation in the liturgy was essential in establishing the corporate nature of the Church as the Body of Christ. He advocated frequent communion, and encouraged a French translation of the mass to be printed in parallel columns with the Latin. He believed that this would create community in the church, which in turn could promote community and brotherhood in society. His views were more fully set out in *The Piety of the Church*, 1914. He also began a monthly bulletin, *La Vie Liturgique*, which had a pastoral orientation, and the review *Questions Liturgiques* which was more academic.

The insights of Beauduin were explored by other Benedictines in Germany and Austria, notably by Abbot Ildephons Herwegen (d. 1948) and Odo Casel (1886–1948) of Maria Laach and Pius Parsch (1884–1948) at Klosterneuberg. In German-speaking lands the dialogue mass was developed with the people responding for themselves rather than allowing a server to be their surrogate. The German High Mass was also developed, where most of the worship was in German. In the USA the movement was spearheaded by Virgil Michel at the Abbey of St John, Collegeville, and through the journal *Orate Fratres* (subsequently known as *Worship*).

The writings of these pioneers are characterized by a vision of social renewal through liturgical renewal. Instead of a collection of individuals (the Enlightenment idea of the 'Person') each buried in his or her devotions, the Church is the mystical Body of Christ, persons in community, prefiguring in some way the new community of the Kingdom of God. The Liturgy would speak of the Church's mission, and criticize the present world order – poverty, bad housing, injustice and material evils. A.G. Hebert was to put it thus:

> . . . it is the function of the Church to keep the mind of the community alive to the spiritual side; to such evils as the lack of social life in our land, the harm which is done to the rich by the sin of luxury and the class distinction which separates them from their fellow men, and the evil effects of unemployment, not merely in material poverty but in the degradation of mind and soul.
>
> (*Liturgy and Society*, p. 202)

Official encouragement towards active participation and intelligibility of the liturgy was given by Pope Pius XII in the encyclical *Mediator Dei* 1947. The document also noted that in order to achieve the renewal of the church, certain reforms in the liturgical rites may be needed. This encyclical was seen as the Magna Carta of the Liturgical Movement, and it acknowledged the work of the benedictines in the movement. As a result a number of annual liturgical congresses were held at which the leading catholic liturgists planned possible programmes of reform. A few minor reforms of the 1950s gave way to the *Constitution on the Sacred Liturgy* of Vatican II, 1963, which put the whole Catholic liturgy into the melting pot. Subsequently all the rites have been thoroughly revised to promote active participation and theological clarity which included the introduction of the vernacular. This process is still being refined.

In hindsight it can hardly be a coincidence that similar concerns can be found in other churches. In the Church of England, for example, although the attempted revision of the Prayer Book in 1928 failed, many other Anglican Provinces revised their prayer books around that date. However, already in the Christian Socialist movement of the nineteenth century, encouragement was being given to the introduction of a Parish Communion which was promoted as the main Sunday service at which people received communion as an expression of the Church as the Body of Christ. Later in England leading Anglican exponents of the ideals of the Liturgical Movement were A.G. Hebert and Henry de Candole. The latter together with some friends founded the Parish and People movement in 1949 which through the journal of that name disseminated the ideas of the Liturgical Movement in the Church of England. In the Episcopal Church in the USA the Associated Parishes movement fulfilled the same function. Renewal of liturgy has led to the modern revisions of the Book of Common Prayer, e.g. the *Alternative Service Book 1980* of the Church of England, and *The Book of Alternative Services* of the Anglican Church of Canada 1985. A similar story can be told for the Lutheran and the Reformed Churches. Indeed, churches have shared insights and scholarly findings, and there has been a remarkable growing consensus on forms of worship.

The most obvious visible results of the Liturgical Movement have been the many new liturgies which were produced after the late 1960s. However, the implications of the movement were far more than the compilation of new texts. The pioneers of the movement were concerned that worship should be an expression of, and enable the congregation to be, the Body of Christ. They saw a social dimension to a liturgy which should be available to all, regardless of education, class or race. When the Church assembles for worship, the world's divisions and structures are replaced with the 'hierarchy of diakonia (service)' of the church. The liturgy becomes a foretaste of the kingdom, and a paradigm for the world. Intelligible liturgy was regarded as the first step in building up (liturgical formation) the faith of the worshippers, and equipping them to be the church in the world. In recent years there has been a growing concern that worship should also challenge believers (and through them, the world) on issues such as social justice and human rights, and should actively champion the 'poor' and 'powerless', be it in terms of political protest, or, for example, the use of inclusive language so that women are not veiled by the liturgical texts. Another major concern at present is the whole question

of inculturation of worship. In global terms this means that Western liturgical texts and ceremonies should not be forced upon African and Asian churches, but that liturgies should be developed which express the cultural language and gestures of those places. In more local terms this means considering whether liturgy which is appropriate for a middle class suburban congregation is also appropriate for a working class congregation in an urban deprived area. The new Missal for English-speaking Roman Catholics due to be published in 1994 is an expression of 'Englishing' the Latin prayers, rather than literal translation; the Church of England's *Patterns for Worship* 1989 is an expression of concern to find forms suitable for differing types of congregations. Beneath this is the conviction that liturgy both expresses the nature of the church, and moulds the church to be what God intends it as the leaven in the world.

Balasuriya, Tissa (1979) *The Eucharist and Human Liberation*, London: SCM.

Beauduin, L. (1926) *Liturgy, Life of the Church*, Collegeville: The Liturgical Press.

Botte, B. (1988) *From Silence to Participation*, Washington: The Pastoral Press.

Constitution on the Sacred Liturgy (1963).

Fenwick, J.R.K. and Spinks, Bryan D. (1995) *Worship in Transition. Highlights of the Liturgical Movement*, Edinburgh: T. & T. Clark.

Hebert, A.G. (1935) *Liturgy and Society*, London: Faber and Faber.

Henry de Candole (1935a) *The Church's Offering: A Brief Study of Eucharistic Worship*, London: A.R. Mowbray.

——(1935b) *The Sacraments and the Church; A Study in the Corporate Nature of Christianity*, London: A.R. Mowbray.

Herwegen, I. (1929) *Christliche Kunst und Mysterium*, Münster in Westfalen: Aschendorff.

Mediator Dei (1947) (encyclical).

Michel, V. (1987) *The Social Question: Essays on Capitalism and Christianity by Fr. Virgil Michel, O.S.B.*, Collegeville: The Liturgical Press. (Reprinted Essays 1935–40.)

Bryan Spinks

LITURGY

Liturgies can be defined as the public ceremonial orders of WORSHIP of the Christian churches.

They are visible representations of invisible imperatives to re-do in remembrance the injunctions of Christ. As Christian rites, liturgies embody symbols, actions, gestures, books, music and clothing in a complex RITUAL mosaic. They are enacted in a variety of architectural settings that also express a rich cultural and theological history and tradition. The EUCHARIST, offices and the sacraments are channelled into liturgical forms, where subtle distinctions in interpretation and understanding of detail can mark differences between heresy and orthodoxy. Despite their elementary structures, liturgical forms have an enormous range of permutations of shape and resources used that almost eludes sociological grasp. These rituals also have manifold functions, of teaching, of serving as rites of passage, of acting as channels of GRACE and of forming vehicles for worship. The vast majority of Christians find their instruction and nurture within these rites which are of central importance in church life.

Cultural aspects of liturgy relate to the apparatus used, its reception and credibility, and to changes in the interpretation of ritual enactments. These facets of rite have a potential for sociological examination. The AUTHORITY and authenticity of liturgical forms gives rise to complex debate that points to an untidy relationship between sociology and THEOLOGY. The immanent and the transcendent are interrelated in a way that defies a sociological means of arbitration. Its understandings of liturgy are partial, recent and inchoate.

Prior to Vatican II, little direct reference to sociology was made in commentaries on liturgy. The objective nature of Catholic rites, such as the mass, made sociological interventions seem unnecessary. The reductionism of positivist sociology might have suggested that its interventions could be deemed hostile. The development of the liturgical renewal movement in mid-nineteenth century France gave rise to an implicit recognition of sociological aspects of liturgy, its cultural context of enactment, the nature of forms of rite and the need to animate an active participation in a community that would secure believers against the individualism of industrial society. MODERNITY generated an increased sensibility of the social basis of rite and the degree to which this was married to the theological effects its enactments were believed to secure. French sociology of religion was largely pastoral in orientation and the issue of liturgy was part of this concern.

The liturgical renewal movement sought to make rites more accessible and credible. This led to an analytical concern with forms of worship, the words used, the symbols to be deciphered and the actions to be understood. Sociology was a hidden agenda in this effort to renew rites, to give them an enhanced cultural credibility. This sociological underpinning is still not fully understood by liturgists and theologians.

In Catholicism, efforts to modernize rites in Vatican II, 1963, introduced subjective and cultural elements in understanding rites that facilitated a sociological response, but one which came after the Council. The bulk of sociological efforts to understand liturgy have arisen in relation to Catholic rites. Owing to their stress on the Word and proclamation of the text, orthodox forms of Protestant worship have attracted little sociological attention. Because of the long-standing interest in SECTS within sociology of religion, the forms of worship used by Protestant fundamentalists, house churches and charismatic assemblies have generated a small but significant sociological literature. BAPTIST, Presbyterian and METHODIST forms of worship do not use stipulated ceremonial directions, and strictly speaking their rites cannot be regarded as liturgical.

The link between sociology and liturgy in ANGLICANISM is more complex. Changes in Anglican forms of worship have been primarily textual. The crisis over the Prayer Book, 1928, which involved Parliament in liturgical revision and the introduction of the Alternative Service Book (ASB) in 1980, led to the marginalization of the Book of Common Prayer, whose civic place in English SOCIETY was much misunderstood by liturgists who sought to modernize their rites. A rather more equivocal attitude prevailed over ritual and ceremonial.

The liturgical renewal movement in the nineteenth century had a profound effect on English Anglicanism, both in its architecture and in the Romanizing of its forms of worship, where the

Eucharist was given a central place in Sunday worship. A theological suspicion of ceremonial embellishments left English Anglicans with an ambiguous attitude to sociological interventions. The civic and sacred functions of Anglican rites, their external image and reception, generate a number of sociological issues. Debates on SECU-LARIZATION, that made use of church attendance figures, did imply a recognition of liturgy but one which was never adequately developed in English sociology of religion.

Anglican efforts to modernize its rites, in the debate surrounding the introduction of the ASB, generated an unsympathetic response, paradoxically from those on the edge of the Church who supplied theologians and liturgists with a mandate for the reforms. Those sociologists who commented on the modernization of rites were uniformly unsympathetic. As was the case with Catholic efforts to modernize their liturgical forms, sociological and anthropological responses, in the 1970s, were equally hostile and traditional – much to the bafflement of liturgists. To some sociologists, it seemed as if liturgists had misunderstood the cultural basis of rites they were so eager to jettison. There is an unexpected tension between liturgists and sociologists who do not seem to speak a common language for understanding rites.

Contemporary English Anglicanism has become increasingly concerned with reforming rites to what are perceived as domain cultural assumptions. Modernity and credibility are interlinked in arguments to make these rites representative, inclusive and relevant. FEMINISM and a concern with CLASS, resulting from the report *Living Faith in the City*, embody a rhetoric that borders on the sociological, but in a way that oddly denies it a basis of intervention and analysis. Stress is on the external image of rite, its packaging for credible cultural reception. But liberal theologians and liturgists speak in generalities about society in a way that has caused efforts to renew rites to be bedevilled by bad sociology. Perhaps owing to a legacy of ritualism, little attention is paid to the internal characteristics of these rites, their order, shape, symbols and actions that mark them as autonomous religious rituals. Only sociology can supply this detailed analysis. The result of recent efforts to modernize liturgies has been an endless fragmentation of rite, whose public nature has been subsumed to the politics of local private arrangements of a particular congregation. The unexpected has become an expected part of Anglican rite. In trying to make rites available, paradoxically, Anglican liturgists have made them unavailable, especially to the working class in whose name many of these adjustments are being made. Efforts to modernize rites can have the effect of destabilizing and loosening the grip they have on adherents, who often cannot articulate why they worship in such a manner, or what is the grammar of assent they use to worship in a particular, perhaps traditional, manner. A condition of liturgical ANOMIE has emerged in Anglicanism. There is little evidence that Anglicans have learnt from some of the failures of liturgical renewal in Catholicism in the 1970s, especially in the USA.

Critical response to the liturgical reforms of Vatican II came between 1969 and 1976 from prominent English Catholic anthropologists such as Mary Douglas and Victor Turner. English social anthropology has a distinctly sacramental quality in its analytical stresses. Many of the facets it valued, such as the opacity of symbols, tracing forms of accountability in context and the thick understandings which ritual conveyed, were qualities seemingly diluted in the reforms of Vatican II. There was a tragic near miss between the stress in the documents of Vatican II on relevance, simplicity and the communal aspects of rite, which emphasized its functional significance, and a contrary anthropological approach to ritual a decade later, which stressed its meaningful, formal opaque qualities. The sacred became marginalized and treated as incredible in a liturgical consensus in the 1970s just when its credibility was being affirmed in anthropological approaches to the understanding of ritual. Although the implications of sociological and anthropological approaches to ritual and symbol were understood in the early 1970s in the USA, long before the UK, few liturgists understood the genesis of these two terms as conceived from *within* sociology. Misunderstandings were partly due to the failure of sociologists to convey to liturgists the complex methodology involved in understanding liturgies in a way that did not misunderstand their theological basis.

Liturgical forms deserve sociological study in their own right. They are condensed social expressions of complex belief systems that embody theology, philosophy and aesthetics. If religious movements have been given a sociological recognition for thriving and surviving in the sophisticated and indifferent culture of advanced industrialized societies, the capacity of liturgical forms to repeat routinely in cathedrals and churches deserves equivalent attention. Their study has some significant sociological benefits. A link needs to be developed between the sociology of religion and the theoretical reflections of the discipline as a whole. The study of liturgy can accomplish this task. Liturgical transactions embody ritual, symbol and actions that are made manifest in a structured manner. But these are ambiguous transactions playing between the determinate and the indeterminate in a way that arouses a sociological curiosity. Because they weave text, symbol and action into a pattern that fascinates, they provide an important focal point that enables sociology to use HERMEN-EUTICS to enhance understandings of complex social transactions whose meanings need to be deciphered. The notion of performance embodied in liturgy provides sociology with a means of gaining access to other disciplines such as music and aesthetics, where cultural forms are used to express an elusive content. In view of the importance of cathedrals in European culture and tourism, sociology will have to study the social transactions that embody their purpose at some stage. Failure to study these liturgies, whose format so influences many secular and civic ceremonies, leaves an analytical gap in sociology.

An implicit sociology was lodged in the liturgical reforms of Vatican II that has only recently been recognized by liturgists and theologians. Initially, a functional argument was implicit in the reforms. It was felt that simplicity of liturgical form was best suited for reception in a modern scientific culture. This untested sociological assumption has not borne fruit, as divisions of opinion over liturgical styles still persist. It is the meanings liturgies embody in their actions that count, not the relationships they

present for description. But the reforms started a sociological question, one inordinately complex that has deep theological ramifications. The Council asked an inescapable question: how can liturgical forms be modified to engage contemporary cultural sensibilities? Such a question begged sociological comment on the assumptions being used. Many of the terms used as criteria for liturgical effectiveness, such as community and active participation, were conceptually vague and were never worked into sociology in a way that would permit the necessary analytical distinctions to be made, if the forms of rite were to be credibly adjusted to contemporary cultural sensibilities. A further difficulty was that certain cultural assumptions about society, prior to 1963, were lodged in the formulation of the documents. If these were to be written in 1990, a different shape of rite would emerge. A crucial difficulty which liturgists have failed to grasp is the degree to which their insights relate to the sociology of knowledge. Religious FUNDAMENTALISM, changes in anthropological understanding of symbol and ritual and the collapse of Marxism, all came after 1963 as did the Romanticism of the counter-culture and the quest for the sacred. This crisis of meaning in culture exposed the impoverished nature of the social assumptions of Vatican II regarding liturgical enactments. The question of the nature of the link between culture and rite has arisen recently but this has been posed in terms of the indigenization of liturgies in non-European societies.

The term 'inculturation' embodies the notion of culture in rite as it relates to issues of contextualization in the use of symbols and other resources of a domestic culture. It has been argued that local cultural assumptions ought to be expressed and embodied in liturgical transactions if they are to secure a necessary credibility and assent. A representative intention, arising in a missionary context, is linked to LIBERATION THEOLOGY. Anthropological ingredients were admitted into liturgical writings, but in a way that has exposed a sociological failure to address the place of culture within liturgies in European societies.

For many reasons, feminism has had a profoundly distorting effect on the issue of the link between culture and liturgy. The question of the definition of culture it uses, the notion of POWER and reproduction it stresses, disguise issues that have wider sociological ramifications. At present there is a profound change within sociology in its approach to culture. This is partly due to debates on post-modernism and the commodification of culture in late capitalist societies. But it is also due to the growing appreciation of the writings of Pierre Bourdieu, the French sociologist, whose approach to culture has significant implications for sociological understandings of liturgy. The ideological interests of feminism, which liberal theologians take to embody the notion of culture, overshadows this important change within the domestic concerns of sociology.

Future directions for the sociological study of liturgy are difficult to predict. There are certain converging movements within theology and sociology that suggest an increased appreciation of the importance of the study of these distinctive rituals. Debates on post-modernism and the sociology of culture of Pierre Bourdieu indicate a growth of interest in symbols, the ambiguous and modes of impression management in a diversity of ritual settings. The recent and unexpected interest of sociology in aesthetics is likely to find a theological resonance in the writings of the late Swiss Catholic theologian, Hans Urs von Balthasar. The vast range of interests in his books and articles covers the full extent of European culture in a way that is unlikely ever to be emulated. He was perhaps the only major twentieth-century theologian who had a professional understanding of sociology and was familiar with the works of Georg Simmel, the noted German sociologist whose writings on culture have made a central contribution to understanding modernity.

Von Balthasar supplies a theological basis for the sociological examination of liturgy that takes into account a growing interest in issues of culture and aesthetics in sociology. The place of beauty in rite has been precarious, not least for its corrupting potential. Von Balthasar's contribution lies in giving aesthetics within rite a theological grounding it has hitherto lacked. This interest in von Balthasar relates to another trend of increasing importance: the growth of

interest in Orthodox styles of worship in the West as barriers to the East crumble. Icons, rich ceremonial forms of worship laden with symbol and gesture, present a formalized arena that offers much scope for sociological analysis. So called radical liturgies, that stress power, representation and agency, apart from being Pelagian, have always gone against the sociological grain of what the discipline understands to be language of ritual. Yet, even in liturgical circles, fashions change, and ornate rich rites that stress the sacred and contact with the invisible, with HEAVEN and HELL, that exploit a fullness of understandings and meanings in culture, harnessed into a ritual whole, are likely to come to the fore. Sociology has the analytical resources to supply theologians with an appreciation of their growing significance in modern culture.

Dalmais, Irénée Henri (1987) *The Church at Prayer, Principles of the Liturgy*, vol. 1, London: Geoffrey Chapman.

Emminghaus, Johannes H. (1978) *The Eucharist, Essence, Form, Celebration*, Collegeville, MN; The Liturgical Press.

Fenn, Richard K. (1982) *Liturgies & Trials: The Secularization of Religious Language*, Oxford: Basil Blackwell.

Flanagan, Kieran (1991) *Sociology and Liturgy: Re-presentations of the Holy*, London: Macmillan and New York: St Martin's Press.

Jones, Cheslyn, Wainwright, Geoffrey and Yarnold, Edward (eds) (1978) *The Study of Liturgy*, London: SPCK.

Living Faith in The City (1990), London: General Synod of the Church of England.

Newton, Denise (ed.) (1982) *Liturgy and Change*, Birmingham: University of Birmingham, Institute for the Study of Worship and Religious Architecture.

Perham, Michael (1984) *Liturgy Pastoral and Parochial*, London: SPCK.

Power, David N. (1984) *Unsearchable Riches: The Symbolic Nature of Liturgy*, New York: Pueblo Publishing.

——(1990) *Culture and Theology*, Washington, DC: Pastoral Press.

Schmemann, Alexander (1966) *Introduction to Liturgical Theology*, London: Faith Press.

Kieran Flanagan

LOVE

Though other religions and philosophies speak of love and of its importance, it is Christianity which is most noted for its conviction that love lies at the very heart of things. Thus Jesus declares that the law and the prophets are summed up in the double commandment to love God and neighbour (Mark 12: 30 and parallels) and Paul reiterates that 'love is the fulfilling of the law' (Romans 13: 10). Likewise, Christians believe that God, Father, Son and Holy Spirit, must be understood in terms of love, just as love must be understood in terms of God. The first epistle of John declares that 'God is love' (4: 8; 4: 16), Dante that God is 'the love that moves the sun and the other stars' (*Paradiso*), and Richard Crashaw that love is 'absolute sole Lord of life and death'.

The New Testament generally employs the one term *agape* to speak of love. So integral is this term to early Christianity that its meaning was not so much taken over from outside the tradition, as given by its use within it. The closest Greek concepts – *eros* and *philia* – have significantly different complexes of meaning and *agape* is a rare term in pre-Biblical Greek, vague and variable in sense. The Hebrew Bible notion of *ahabah* (generally translated *agape* in the LXX) has much more in common with New Testament *agape*, but in the Hebrew Bible its theological significance remains relatively undeveloped, and it is *tsedeq* ('righteousness'/'justice') rather than *ahabah* which is accorded ethical primacy.

Christian consensus about the centrality of love has not always extended to consensus about the nature of love. Matters are complicated by the fact that the word 'love' does a great deal of work in the Christian tradition. In the first place, it may have different subjects, for it may refer to God's love or to human love. Furthermore, it may have different objects, for there are many things worthy of love. Consequently, the one term 'love' may be used to speak of such diverse loves as God's love for humanity, love between the persons of the Trinity, human love for God, love for neighbour, love for money, self-love and so on.

Broadly speaking Christian accounts of love can be divided into three categories. First, there are those accounts which fail to distinguish between the different ways in which 'love' may be employed and attempt to formulate a single definition of love applicable to all its expressions. Second, there are those which note the different ways in which 'love' may be used and conclude that there is in fact not just one love, but different types of love. Usually they identify just one of these types of love as truly Christian. And third, there are those which maintain that love is indeed one, but that it may have different aspects or expressions in different contexts.

The New Testament gives little support for treating love as anything other than one. It almost always employs the one word *agape*, whatever the subject or object of love. The subjective unity of love is accounted for in Biblical terms by the belief that all love is from God. As Paul says, 'God's love has been poured into our hearts through the Holy Spirit which has been given to us' (Romans 5: 5), and as 1 John says, 'if we love one another, God abides in us and his love is perfected in us' (4: 12). Similarly, the objective unity of love, the fact that different objects are loved with the one love, *agape*, is explained by the Biblical belief that all reality has its origin and end in God. Thus the commandment to love God with '*all* your heart, and with *all* your soul, and with *all* your mind, and with *all* your strength', and to love your neighbour would make no sense if love of neighbour were not an aspect of love of God, for there would be nothing left over with which to love neighbour. Likewise, in the parable of the great assize those who love their neighbours are shown that in doing so they have also loved the heavenly Son of Man (Matthew 25: 31–46). In loving the neighbour one loves God; indeed the person who does not love the neighbour cannot love God (1 John 4: 20). Whilst the New Testament gives no abstract definition of love, it speaks in very concrete terms about love and the ways in which it is made manifest. For Christians it is not only Jesus' teachings, but the accounts of his life and death which speak of the nature of love. Very often the New Testament portrays love as benevolence, as an active desire to help those who are in some sort of need. As the parable of the Good Samaritan shows, love must be manifest in an immediate response to the neighbour's needs, whatever the cost to oneself. In the exercise of love, therefore, it may even be necessary to sacrifice one's own life: 'greater love has no man than that he lays down his life for his brother' (John 13: 2). This is not 'fair'; it is not fair to give one's coat to anyone who asks, to turn the cheek, to go the extra mile, but this is nevertheless what agape demands. There is no limit to the scope of agape: it is to be offered to the neighbour whoever he or she might be and however he or she might respond. It does not depend on the neighbour's creed or race or status (as the parable of the good Samaritan indicates), and it does not depend on the neighbour's attitude towards one (as the commandment to love one's enemy indicates). Like God's love, it is a forgiving love, offered to just and unjust alike (Matthew 5: 45).

The Bible thus has much to say about love as benevolence, and the climactic instantiation of such love in the death of Christ upon the cross has convinced many Christians that such love simply *is* Christian love. Yet the Bible knows of other expressions of love besides benevolence. For a start, the Bible knows of a love which is joyous and adoring rather than benevolent and self-sacrificing. The love of the lovers in the Song of Songs is such a love, and Christian interpreters of the Song we happy to take this as an allegory for divine love, suggesting thereby that God's love for the Church as well as the Church's love for God might be joyous and fulfilling. In addition, the Bible speaks a great deal about love which is mutual, reciprocal, and which binds people together into a unity. When the New Testament epistles speak of love, it is often love between 'the brethren', the body of Christian believers, which is spoken of, and Paul sees love as something which joins the brethren together and 'builds up' both the Church and its members. Similarly Jesus in John's gospel repeatedly commands his followers to 'love one another', and to be united with one another by such love. Again, the Bible is aware of an aspect of love which is not simply one-way benevolence.

It is perhaps a measure of just how unprecedented the New Testament's presentation and proclamation of agape really was that subsequent Christian thinkers took some time to catch up with it in their ethical and theological speculations. Not until Augustine, perhaps, does the Church produce a thinker who is able to do justice to the New Testament's understanding of agape and who insists that the double commandment must be placed firmly at the heart of Christian ethics. Augustine remains true both to the New Testament emphasis on the unity of love *and* to its sensitivity to the many aspects of love, an achievement even more remarkable in one who did not speak Greek and who found in his native Latin tongue no word equivalent to 'agape'. Given this linguistic difficulty Augustine had to make use of a cluster of Latin terms such as *caritas*, *dilectio* and *amor*, terms which he employed almost interchangeably, thus avoiding the suggestion that each named a different type of love.

For Augustine love is 'the soul's movement', the basic force which drives all human beings. Love is what attracts one to some good, and as such it has a cognitive as well as an affective aspect, for one may be mistaken about what is good and worthy of love, just as one may be mistaken about how much one should love some good, exalting lesser goods over greater ones. For Augustine God is the only proper object of the love of one's whole heart; other things, though worthy of love, should be loved only in their relation to God as made by God, loved by God, and ordered to God. Thus Augustine believes is an order of loves, with love for God and neighbour coming first, love for the rest of the created order following in due order below. 'Caritas ordinata', love set in order, is both the mark of the Godly life and the mark of God's creation, the former being for Augustine simply the intelligent and loving response to the latter.

Because of his awareness of how love is related to many different objects, Augustine was aware that, despite its unity, love could have different expressions. Love could thus be good or bad, true or false, depending on the worth of its object. Likewise, love would be affected by the nature of its relation to its object. In relation to a good which is not present, love would be manifest as desire and quest. Yet in relation to a good which is present, the same love might be manifest as delight, reverence, adoration. Augustine believed that on earth human love for God would always be a love of desire and restless qust, but that in the heavenly city its longing would be replaced by the 'unchanging love of a good attained', a love which units human beings in the enjoyment of God and of one another in God.

Though Augustine's influence on subsequent Christian understandings of love has been immense, he has rarely been without his critics. One of the earliest accurations levelled against him was that his account of love as quest and enjoyment of the good smacked of selfishness, of eudaemonist egoism. Medieval theologians like Abelard and Bernard insisted that only love which is entirely free from any thought or desire of return, recompense or reward be called Christian. This view of love is sometimes called 'ecstatic', because it sees love as a one-way outpouring, a selfless and sacrificial giving, rather than as a two-way love responsible to some good. It gained support from those who wished to stress God's total freedom (e.g. Scotus), as well as from those who wished to stress the sacrificial nature of God's love in Christ and the wholly undeserved nature of our redemption (e.g. Luther).

In the twentieth century the ecstatic view of love has found a powerful spokesman in Anders Nygren, whose *Agape and Eros* (1932) has had great influence upon subsequent Christian thought about love. Nygren is one of those Christian thinkers who believes that there are different types of love, only one of which counts as true Christian love or 'agape'. For Nygren the only love which is real is God's love, a love shown in his wholly gratuitous sacrifice of Himself upon the cross for humankind. Agape is therefore a love which flows from the goodness of its subject rather than being called forth by the goodness of its object. It is one-way, disinterested, unselfishly poured out on unworthy recipients without hope of reward. Agape is God's love, and if it is shown by Christians, that is only because they have emptied themselves to become channels of this love. Nygren does not believe that there is any Christian form of love other than agape as he describes it, and he vehemently rejects what he identifies as the Platonic/Augustinian view of love as desire for the enjoyment of some good. For Nygren such 'love' is not Christian love at all, it is 'eros', the mirror image of agape and a source of contamination in Christian ethics.

Nygren's characterization of agape as benevolent, one-way and indifferent to its object has had enormous influence in both popular and academic circles. In the former it has given rise to the idea that there is a hierarchy of different loves, with selfless agape alone at the top as the only truly Christian love, love of friends and family coming next as a poor second, and sexual desire at the bottom in the definitely sub-Christian category. (C. S. Lewis' book *The Four Loves* is often but erroneously invoked in support of this account of a hierarchy of loves.) In the academy Nygren's account has also had great influence, his interpretation of agape often accepted without demur. Even in the work of two of the most original and important postwar theorists of Christian love, Reinhold Niebuhr and Gene Outka, are aspects of Nygren's unreciprocated, *suffering* love, Outka defining agape as 'equal regard'.

One positive aspect of Nygren's legacy is that it has reawakened Christian thinkers, particularly Christian ethicists, to the importance of love in the Christian scheme of things. In very different ways Dietrich Bonhoeffer, Paul Ramsey, Reinhold Niebuhr and Joseph Fletcher have all maintained that love must be at the heart of the Christian life. One of the main issues on which they have differed is the nature of the self-sufficiency of the principle of love in the ethical life. Fletcher, for example, believed that the 'law of love' is the only LAW which is absolutely binding on Christians – other laws or principles are simply rules of thumb which may be disobeyed if following them does not seem to be the most loving option. Ramsey, by contrast, believed that there are some moral principles (e.g. 'keep promises', 'tell the TRUTH', 'do not commit adultery', 'do not kill') which are as exceptionless as the law of love. He maintained this on the ground that such principles specify in what the outworking of love regularly, and necessarily, consists. Interestingly, not only Christian ethics but also secular ethics has recently reawakened to the importance of love, even though the word itself is not always used. The work of Emmanuel Levinas has been particularly important in this regard and Levinas' characterization of the fundamental moral stance as being *for the Other* has interesting parallels with the ecstatic interpretation of Christian love.

Many recent Christian accounts of love are only really concerned with one-to-one relationships. Levinas too claims that the only moral party is the party of two. Is love really only important for the intimate realm, or may it have relevance beyond this? If one looks behind Nygren to Augustine and the New Testament one sees that love is there thought of as having unique social significance; it is love which binds human beings together. In Augustine's view even the earthly city is united by love, albeit love for itself and for its own glory, whilst the heavenly city finds a truer harmony and unity is in love for God.

But even if it is granted with Augustine and the New Testament that love may have great significance in relation to relatively small-scale communities, it is still unclear whether it can have relevance outside them, and in particular whether it can have relevance for the modern state. Is love, for example, a principle which can inform social policy? Some Christian ethicists have tried to show that it can. They admit that this means going beyond Jesus' teaching, but not that it means abandoning it. Take the situation where the neighbour needs my coat, for example. According to Jesus' teaching I should simply give it to him or her. But what if two people ask me for my coat? Then I have to work out a different solution, one still based on the belief that I must respond to the needs of my neighbour to the greatest extent possible, and that any person in need is a neighbour. Love is still the guiding principle, though now it has to adjudicate between two people's needs rather than simply responding to one person's. In such situations the notion of love clearly slides towards that of JUSTICE. Inspired by Neibuhr, some Christian thinkers have wanted to argue that justice is in fact the form which love takes when translated into a social policy, and it seems true historically speaking that our notion of justice – a justice which treats every

person as equal before it – owes a great deal to the Christian understanding of agape. But the task of stating clearly the actual and ideal relations between justice and agape is one which still faces Christian thinkers.

Burnaby, J. (1938) *Amor Dei*, London: Hodder.
Niebuhr, Reinhold (1936) *An Interpretation of Christian Ethics*, London: SCM.
Nygren, A. (1932) *Agape and Eros*, London: SPCK.
Oppenheimer, H. (1983) *The Hope of Happiness*, London: SCM.
Outka, J. (1972) *Agape: An Ethical Analysis*, New Haven, CT: Yale University Press.
Ramsey, P. (1950) *Basic Christian Ethics*, London: SCM.
Singer, I. (1966, 1987) *The Nature of Love*, vol. 1, New York: Random House; vols 2 and 3, Chicago, IL: University of Chicago Press.

Linda Woodhead

LUTHERANISM

Before we define Lutheranism, it is worth saying that the word itself is a misnomer, its use rejected by Luther as early as 1522:

> I ask that men make no reference to my name, and call themselves Christians not Lutherans. What is Luther? After all, the doctrine is not mine, nor have I been crucified for any one. St. Paul in 1 Cor. 3, would not allow Christians to call themselves Pauline or Petrine, but Christians. How then should I, a mere bag of worms, have men to give to Christ's children my worthless name? . . . Let us cast out party names and be called Christians after Him whose doctrine we hold. The Papists quite rightly bear their party name because they are not satisfied with the doctrine and name of Christ, but want also to be papist. Let them be popish, then, since the Pope is their master. I neither am, nor want to be any one's master. Christ alone is our Master. Christ teaches me, and all believers, one and the same doctrine.
>
> (WA. VIII, p. 685, 11.4–16, 1522)

The reason behind this decisive rejection of the term was because Luther sought a *re*-formation of a Christianity which, he argued, had suffered a *de*-formation for over a thousand years. He linked hands with Athanasius over the centuries. In no sense did he seek to create a party or schism, let alone a new church. This was abhorrent to him. He was orthodox and traditionalist in his theology. He differentiated himself from all previous reformers in that where they had been concerned with the reformation of scandals, which beset any institution or organization, he was concerned with the reformation of theology, that it may not deviate from the Biblical revelation. It is important to distinguish between the real idea behind the Lutheran Reformation, i.e. a summons to restore the Gospel to its central place in the *one* Church of Christ, and what the Reformation actually achieved in history, i.e. the establishment of one particular church among others. The word 'Lutheran' was used, even by men such as Thomas More, as a derogatory term for heretics. This was a profound misunderstanding. The error lives on.

When the Lutheran movement was asked to justify its existence at the Diet of Augsburg in 1530, it did so as a theological movement within the Church Catholic, dedicated to expound, safeguard and maintain the Gospel alone, the centre and circumference of which is Christ and His work for us men and for our salvation. Lutheranism came into existence to restore the liberating authority of the Bible within the Church. In a sense, it was the rejection by the Church of this movement which created Lutheranism and a Lutheran Church. True, the Council of Trent (1545–63) met to overcome the religious schism, to reform the Church, and to unite Christendom against the threatening Turk. Yet, when it did convene, it had no united mind but represented four main views: those who sought reconciliation with Protestantism (e.g. the Bishop of Trent, Contarini, Pole); the Italians, who looked to the Pope to effect reformation; the Spaniards, sharply anti-Protestant; and those who supported the Emperor in his efforts to bring about peace on the lines of the Augsburg Interim of 1548. After initial attempts to include at least some Protestants, the Council's attitude hardened and became hostile to them. As positive achievement, Trent defined and regulated the doctrines which the Reformers had attacked, but did so in a way which polarized the Church and drove Rome into a Counter-Reformation which has characterized it since, certainly up to Vatican II (1964–5). It modified the late scholastic theology, but opposed evangelical theology. It formulated its own intellectual basis, and provided a system of gradual reformation. It provided a system for the education of CLERGY. It produced an influential catechism, and the Tridentine Mass, which enshrined the doctrine of transubstantiation and the Eucharistic sacrifice. The abandonment of this Mass after 1970 and the adoption by Vatican II of some of the Reformers' principles (e.g. the vernacular in the liturgy), may be seen as meeting the Reformation in a way Trent declined to do. Vatican II is a positive and welcome development whose significance has yet to be fully assimilated, and should not be underestimated. Had Rome heeded Wittenberg, Europe might have experienced a reformation of Christendom from within itself, and Lutheranism would never have existed.

To understand Lutheranism one needs to refer to the Lutheran confessional statements of the Book of Concord 1580, which, though definitive, are cast in rather forbidding theological and intellectual terms, even scholastic is not too strong a word. For the true flavour and religious fervour of Lutheranism, one would have to read the writings of Luther: his theological works, commentaries, sermons, catechisms, liturgical writings and hymns, not least his letters (the corpus is immense, but the essential writings are now readily available in English). The confessional statements of the sixteenth century were worked out by Luther's brilliant young disciple Melanchthon (1497–1560), on the basis of Luther's groundwork, as well as by the theologians Matthias Flacius (1520–75) and Martin Chemnitz (1522–86) – statements which effectively defended Luther's theology against all modifiers and detractors. It is in these confessional statements that Lutheranism is to be found together with Luther's own writings. These are to be supplemented by the writings of a long line of Biblical and theological scholars emanating from Germany and Scandinavia.

Since the sixteenth century Lutheranism has undergone further changes in its reaction to intellectual, cultural, social and political movements. The most influential was the Pietist

Movement of the seventeenth and eighteenth centuries, a reform movement arising within Lutheranism (though now a term embracing Puritan and Wesleyan revivals, the Great Awakening and such religious renewals). The founding father was Spener (1635–1705) who was concerned about the corrupt and ineffective Lutheran Church of his day. He was a pious pastor reacting against what he considered the polemical orthodoxy and rationalistic secularism which was proving itself sterile in the face of the immorality and terrible social problems following the Thirty Years War (1618–48). He set forth his 'pious' wishes for the reformation and renewal of the Church. They were mainly (a) deep Bible study, individually and collectively; (b) committed lay discipleship; (c) practice of Christian principles, in other words, 'faith active in love'; and (d) dealing with unbelievers and heretics by prayer, dialogue and LOVE. Some historians set his significance in Lutheranism as second only to Luther's. The movement is still strong at the parish level. A theological crisis arose in Germany in 1817 when the Kaiser decreed a union between Lutherans and Reformed (Calvinists) in his kingdom. Since the war (1945) there has been a striking revival of Lutheran scholarship, not only in Germany but in Scandinavia, even in Britian, and not least in America. It is noteworthy that, as a general statement, it is true to say that almost all modern Biblical scholarship, including textual criticism, higher criticism and form criticism, originated in German Lutheran circles; it could even be argued that most modern theological scholarship originated there too (though some of it is negative and destructive, unlike Luther's). Lutheranism in Germany had undergone a revival at the beginning of the century, about 1909, and Luther studies experienced under Karl Holl (about 1926) what is still called 'The Luther Renaissance'.

This dynamic power within Lutheranism has its origin in the sheer genius of Luther: Luther is the key to Lutheranism. How can this be expressed in a few words? Perhaps Luther's prime emphasis was that Christianity was about the encounter of God with a believing person, not the human effort to find God: that the heart of the New Testament was salvation in Christ alone, graciously proffered by God, and not earned by merit, virtue, intellect, even prayer, Christ standing in for us as substitution. 'Thou hast taken upon Thyself what is mine, and hast given me what is thine: thou hast taken upon thyself what thou wast not, and hast given me what I was not.' To hear and appropriate this Word meant that there could be no place for a mediatorial or sacrificing priest: the priest yields to and is replaced by the minister of this Word. This Word of God creates and informs faith, by which alone God justifies the sinner. Luther's continual emphasis was Christ alone, faith alone, Scripture alone. These truths Luther sharpened in his distinction between Law and Gospel: the external covenant of works, and the internal covenant of Christ in the heart, bursting forth in love, joy and good works. Luther emphasized the sacraments as the visible words of this Gospel: more deeply, he saw the sacraments as an expression of the Incarnation. Baptism was the birth from above of the new life in Christ, the communion mediated in, with and under the bread and wine, Christ's very flesh and blood. Luther taught the scriptural principle of total conversion in Christ. Christ filled the whole sphere of Luther's thinking. As he said to Erasmus, 'Take Christ from the scriptures, what have you got left?' Again, 'In Christ I have the Father's heart and will.' 'Every word of the Bible peals Christ. Its entire concern is Christ.' His theology was essentially a CHRISTOLOGY. His Christology is at the root of his sacramental theology. What was received in Holy Communion was not some mysterious commodity but the very Christ Himself: that is why sacrament and word belong together. The Church could not be numbered by counting up a few cardinals' hats, nor even by any outward organization or institution. She consisted of a communion of saints known only to God, called into existence by God, and held together by the Holy Spirit, maintained under God by faithful and godly ministers through the proclamation of the Word of God and ministration of the sacraments, heard and received by believing men and women. A further word must be given to Luther's unique 'theology of the cross', which he first enunciated at Heidelberg (1519) as the mark of true theology. Closely related to

Luther's teaching on Christ's atoning work, he showed that the pattern of Christian life is the experience of God under a contrary form: living by means of dying, giving rather than receiving, serving rather than being served, the same pattern as Christ's. True life is not found in the possessions, privileges and powers, but in the tasks, trials and tribulations imposed by God: that in, through and by means of the adversity, God transmutes the suffering and affliction into the raw material of the spiritual life. These few principles express in brief through Luther's theology the nature of Lutheranism. It is recognizable the world over: the liturgical forms may vary in different lands, but generally its principal feature is a weighty Biblical evangelical sermon set in the framework of a vernacular liturgy, normally accompanied by fine music and vigorous hymn singing: whatever else, always joyous.

Germany has some 14 million Lutherans of the 37 million in Europe. When the war was over (1945), attempts were made to unite all the Lutheran churches in Germany into a United Evangelical Lutheran Church of Germany (VELKD) within the looser framework of the Federal Evangelical Church in Germany (EKD). Germany apart, it could be broadly stated that Lutheranism is the religion of Scandinavia and of Finland, though the traditional tie between Church and state has now gone. Owing to immigration and missionary work, a large constituency of Lutherans (some 8 million) exists in Asia, Africa and pockets worldwide. In North America (some 8 million), the immigrants brought their Lutheranism (and their differences) with them, to meet which differences the Lutheran World Federation was founded in 1947. The Evangelical Lutheran Church of America has some 5.5 million members, and the Lutheran Church-Missouri Synod some 2.6 million. The traditional orthodoxy of the latter brought about intense discussions on unity among Lutherans in the 1960s, culminating in a division between the conservatives and liberals in the Missouri Synod in 1973, which produced a trauma within Lutheranism and dismay in ecumenical circles. These differences have yet to be resolved, though there is still an essential unity among Lutherans. Further, it should be noted that ever since the peregrinations of Bucer in the sixteenth century Lutheran scholars have been foremost in their commitment to the wider ecumenical enterprise, not only within the WORLD COUNCIL OF CHURCHES but in conversations with the Reformed, the Anglicans and the Orthodox. These conversations have been pursued irenically at a high level of scholarship and have produced weighty and noteworthy reports. American Luther scholars have played a leading part in the scholarly quinquennial Luther World Congresses since their foundation in 1972; they have published a fifty-five volume translation of *Luther's Works*, and continue to publish a considerable amount of significant research. It is difficult to give full justice to Lutheranism in America in a few words, but a detailed and documented authoritative history of Lutheranism in America from its beginnings in the sixteenth and seventeenth centuries to 1980 is given in Clifford Nelson's *The Lutherans in North America* (1980) (with supplement).

With regard to the future, it may be suggested that Lutheranism faces two main issues: (a) how to relate to ecumenism and (b) how to relate to society. It is true that Lutheran theologians are foremost in the ecumenical enterprise and have achieved a great deal, particularly in the Protestant world. One may review some of the main achievements. The Anglican/Scandinavian conferences (begun in 1929) have formalized Eucharistic hospitality. The Anglican/Lutheran International Commission (producing the Pullach Report 1973 and the Meissen Report 1988), has resulted in inter-communion and academic and church exchanges. The Porvoo Report 1993 (Irish/Anglican/Nordic Baltic Churches) has produced further support for these advances. Lutheran/Reformed conversations have produced the Leuenberg Agreement, and French Lutheran and Reformed/Anglican conversations began in 1994. The major task, however, is the relationship with the Roman Catholic Church. The universal council, sought by Erasmus, Luther, Bucer, Calvin, Cranmer and others, never took place in the sixteenth century. True, Trent and the Counter-Reformation effected considerable reform, moral and theological; and Vatican II has met some Protestant concerns. Nevertheless, the task of mutually finding together again for our time (Orthodox, Catholic, Protestant) the true nature of the eternal Gospel, which Luther so perceptively perceived and pioneered, and relating that to contemporary society is the crux of the matter: Lutheranism may yet effect what Luther pioneered.

On the second question Lutheranism has incurred heavy criticism over the centuries for its relation to the state and to society, not unjustly. The peasants in 1525, and many others since then, criticized Luther for not concerning himself with their social revolution, which was fair and just in its demands, and not least for his harsh words during their struggle. Similarly, the twentieth century has criticized Lutheranism for its apparent neutrality to Nazism, the Hitler War, the HOLOCAUST, even for its wide support of the Hitler regime, as well for its deference to the authority of the state. This blind spot they attribute to Luther's teaching on the Two Realms, but it is only fair to say that the Church as a whole throughout history has often been blind to grave social issues, such as SLAVERY, WAR, persecution, exploitation, POVERTY. It is hardly possible to express the true position fairly in a few words, but Luther's principles are clear, and he stuck to them throughout his life against all comers. He took the position of Romans 13 and 1 Peter that the state (the 'powers that be') was a divine institution to maintain sinful mankind in justice, order, peace and morality; and to punish all evil doers who destroy this order. The Church's role was to preach the KINGDOM OF GOD, to bring souls into this realm and to sustain them there until death takes them into the eternal realm. But the Church has that further responsibility to win lost mankind to God in Christ. The problem is how to relate these two realms in any given historical situation, particularly in times of war and social upheaval. Luther's position was as follows. Where the state overreaches itself, or does not fulfil its God-appointed task, or refuses to recognize any authority other than itself, the two roles are con-fused, run into one. The Church must speak out, but be prepared to pay the price of its witness. It may never engage in intrigue, rebellion, sedition, in its resistance to the state: only disobedience, non-co-operation,

non-compliance, martyrdom. Admittedly, Lutheranism failed dismally to live up to Luther's principles of the Two Realms under Hitler, but it must be recalled that it did so in Norway and Denmark during the occupation when their preachers quoted Luther at the Nazis week by week. The resistance movement went beyond Luther's teaching when they engaged in clandestine military activity, as Bonhoeffer did in the plot to murder Hitler, but they knew what they were doing and pleaded necessity in an unredeemable plight, i.e. to act violently in the worthy effort to destroy EVIL. The danger for the Church at present is to seek to express the Gospel not in its own terms but in terms of the social needs of society in a desire to be 'relevant'. Lutheranism could well look to Luther's doctrine of the Two Realms to find a proper and creative relationship of religion to society and, in so doing, show secularized society the real purpose and nature of the state, as well as that of the Church. This could prove one of its great contributions both to the Church and the world.

Atkinson, J. (1968) *Martin Luther and the Birth of Protestantism*, Atlanta, GA: John Knox (2nd edn 1981).

Bagchi, D.V.N. (1991) *Luther's Earliest Opponents*, Oxford: Oxford University Press.

Bekenntnisschriften der Evangelisch–Lutherischen Kirche (1952) Göttingen: Vandenhoeck & Ruprecht (authoritative sources in Latin and German; for English, see Tappert below).

Bergendorf, C. (1967) *The Church of the Lutheran Reformation*, St Louis, MO: Concordia.

Bornkamm, H. (1983) *Luther in Mid-Career*, Philadelphia, PA: Fortress Press.

Brecht, M. (1985) *Road to Reformation*, Philadelphia, PA: Fortress Press.

——(1990) *Shaping and Defining the Reformation 1521–32*, Philadelphia, PA: Fortress Press.

——(1993) *The Preservation of the Church 1532–46*, Philadelphia, PA: Fortress Press.

Drummond, A. (1951) *German Protestantism since Luther*, London: Allenson.

Edwards, M.U. (1983) *Luther's Last Battles: Politics and Polemics*, Leiden: Brill.

Elert, W. (1962) *Structure of Lutheranism*, trans. W.A. Hansen, St Louis, MO: Concordia.

Fry, C.G. and Drickamer, J.K. (1979) *History of Lutheranism in America 1619–1930*, Philadelphia, PA: Fortress Press.

Gritsch, E.W. and Jenson R.J. (1978) *Lutheranism*, Philadelphia, PA: Fortress Press.

Kramm, H.H. (1947) *The Theology of Martin Luther*, London: James Clarke.

Luther, D.M. (1883–) *Werke: Kritische Gesamtansgabe, Abt. Werke*, vol. 1– , Weimar.

Nelson, E.C. (1980) *The Lutherans in North America*, Philadelphia, PA: Fortress Press.

Schlink, E. (1960) *The Theology of the Lutheran Church*, Philadelphia, PA: Fortress Press.

Tappert, T.G. (1959) *The Book of Concord* (the Confessional Statements in English), Philadelphia PA: Fortress Press.

Watson, P. (1947) *Let God be God*, London: Epworth Press.

James Atkinson

LYING

How to define a lie is part of the problem (as will be seen below) but a provisional, formal (and normal) definition would be that a lie is an intentionally deceptive statement (*see* ESPIONAGE).

The moral wrongness of lying may be distinguished from the legal (contractual) wrongness. A range of questions then opens. How is the principle of veracity to be ranked against other duties? Are there circumstances in which truth-telling does not apply? Are some intended untruths allowable or inevitable in modern society? Are there some intended untruths which are misclassified as formal lies but are fractured attempts to witness to a deeper reality?

The Judaeo-Christian scriptures are uncompromisingly opposed to lying (cf. Exodus 20: 16, the commandment against false witness; Psalms 5: 6; 1 Timothy 1: 10; Revelation 2: 15). All of these passages have a social vision. The liar is guilty not simply of individual deception but of undermining the ideal SOCIETY. In the Christian tradition, Augustine (354–430) in *On Lying* (395) defines lying (§3) as the intentional expression of a falsehood; condemns all lies (§6 and §9); offers an eightfold classification of lies (§25); and, while maintaining that all eight types are sinful, allows that one sins less seriously as one tends towards the eighth type (§42).

Faced with this blanket condemnation, which is counterintuitive, the Christian tradition explored several different approaches. One approach was to hold to a wide definition of what a lie is, but then to allow that some lies are justifiable. Thus, Aquinas (1225–74) distinguished between the helpful (officious) and the harmless (jocose) lie, neither of which are mortal sins, and the malicious lie, which is. An alternative strategy was to search for a narrower definition of a lie, from which it followed that not all falsehoods are lies. Thus, Hugo Grotius (1583–1645) argued that a falsehood is a lie only if it conflicts with a right of the person addressed. It followed that it would be permissible to say what is false to infants, insane persons and enemies. This was an attempt to distinguish a more restricted (contractual) notion of a lie.

Immanuel Kant (1724–1804) lectured on Grotius, and was critical of his approach. He allowed that legally a lie was a falsehood to the prejudice of another person. However, he argued that morally a lie was a falsehood to the prejudice of humankind. If I expressly undertake to declare my thoughts and do not, even if no individual person's right is infringed, then I have acted 'against the right of humankind, since I have set myself in opposition to the condition and means through which any human society is possible' (Kant [1780] 1949: 227). This was a basically formal argument designed to rule out any lies whatsoever. Elsewhere (e.g. *Groundwork for the Metaphysic of Morals* ([1785] 1948): ch. 1), Kant argued that I could not consistently will that my intention to tell a lie should be turned into a universal law. Ultimately, pietism may lie behind Kant's unwillingness to countenance any lies. He leaves himself without any practical way of resolving a conflict of duties. A similarly absolute (and formal) position was held by John Wesley (1703–91), who, after disposing of Aquinas' distinctions of harmless and officious lies, approvingly quotes a saying, 'I would not tell a wilful lie to save the souls of the whole world' (Wesley 1878: 42).

A strikingly different non-formal approach was taken by Dietrich Bonhoeffer (1906–45). Telling the TRUTH, he argues, means different things according to the relationship in which one stands. And we stand in many different relationships or environments. The living God has set me in a living life and the truthfulness we owe God must assume a *concrete* form in the world. So speech must be truthful, not in principle (formally), but concretely. It follows that 'telling the truth' is a matter of hard discernment and moral skill. It is being able to appreciate real situations. Bonhoeffer contrasts this to the 'cynic' who claims to speak a formal truth at all times. This, he says, destroys the 'living truth' between people. It 'wounds shame, desecrates mystery, betrays community'. What in formal terms is a lie may, in fact, be more truthful, as being more in accord with reality. For Bonhoeffer, this takes seriously both the fallen nature of humankind and God's initiative in reconciliation.

The ethics of deception have been with us for a long time. Are there any new questions at the end of the century? One might instance three areas. First, the issue of *informed* consent. The end of the century sees enormously complex political transformations (the reunification of Germany, the Maastricht Treaty). In democratic societies there are ethical issues over governmental secrecy and lies. These centre on the issue of informed consent. The people must be informed, but often are not. Similarly, in medical ethics, where there are organ transplants, maintenance of life in a persistent vegetative state and the issue of 'allowing a patient to die', informed consent is vital. Second, society is increasingly competitive. How may an individual resist the accelerating current of deception which abounds in almost every institution? Third, vast amounts of information are now stored in computer databases. The packaging of information leads to a kind of authoritarian nominalism. Persons are made to fit categories. This provokes a rejection of the categories of classification as persons make untrue statements in the name of a greater reality.

Does the existing tradition help us to address contemporary difficulties? Narrow deontological approaches (Augustine, Kant, Wesley) have proved over-inflexible and individualistic. They do not assist the resolution of moral dilemmas, nor recognize the pluralist nature of modern society. Utilitarian approaches become less satisfactory as situations become more complex. A combination of deontological and consequentialist argument is used by Sissela Bok, the most significant contemporary writer on lies. Bok insists that the perspective of the deceived be examined, and that institutional lying should be open to public examination. The most effective instrument for checking institutional dishonesty and coercive deception is fostering a free press and television documentaries. Ordinary individuals do not usually appeal to abstract principles or utilitarian calculations to solve their dilemmas concerning deception. Here, the kind of analysis offered by Bonhoeffer is perhaps most useful, as it displays the narrative base of truth-telling.

Aquinas, Thomas (1922) *Summa Theologica*, 2.2. ques. 110, arts. 2 and 4, London: Burns & Oates.

Augustine (1952) *On Lying*, in *Treatises on Various Subjects* in the series *The Fathers of the Church*, vol. 16, ed. R.J. Deferrari, New York: Catholic University of America Press.

Bok, Sissela (1978) *Lying*, New York: Pantheon.

Bonhoeffer, Dietrich (1955) *Ethics*, London: SCM (see the section 'What is meant by telling the truth?').

Kant, Immanuel ([1785] 1948) *Groundwork for the Metaphysic of Morals*, translated as *The Moral Law* by H.J. Paton, London: Hutchinson.

——([1780] 1949) 'On a supposed right to lie from benevolent motives', in *The Critique of Practical Reason and Other Writings in Moral Philosophy*, ed. and trans. Lewis White Beck, Chicago, IL: University of Chicago Press.

——(1963) *Lectures on Ethics*, New York: Harper & Row.

Wesley, John (1878) *Sermon XC – An Israelite Indeed*, in *Works*, vol. VII, London: Methodist Book-Room, pp. 37–45.

Iain Torrance

MADNESS

Throughout history, madness has been a terrible affliction, defying the powers of medicine to define and cure, yet also, through its very strangeness, a source of uncanny fascination. In such types as the holy fool, the *distrait* genius, the mystic, the prophet, mental abnormality may double insight, creativity and vision. Some have seen method in madness, a higher reason that exposes the hypocrisies and inhumanity of the sane.

Even today there is no consensus about psychiatric disorder, its causes, nature or cure. Some even question its reality. In his influential *The Myth of Mental Illness* (1961), Dr Thomas Szasz argued that to speak of insanity as a disease was a misdescription. In truth it was merely socially unacceptable behaviour. Psychiatry was thus founded upon a fiction, and 'compulsory psychiatry' (e.g. legally enforced institutionalization) was an infringement of human liberties. R.D. Laing and other 'anti-psychiatrists' were to claim in the 1960s that mental illness was not a disease but a label SOCIETY pinned on deviants. The strange behaviour of the 'schizophrenic' was perhaps a rational way of coping with an irrational society.

History shows major shifts in the understanding and treatment of insanity. Early records reveal demented behaviour regarded as possession from outside, by demons, spirits and gods. Those whom the gods wish to destroy, judged the Greeks, they first make mad. Homeric heroes are cursed and driven to frenzy by fiendish Fates and Furies.

The idea of supernatural madness was reinforced by Christianity. Church fathers saw spiritual anguish as a symptom of 'psychomachy', the war for the soul waged between God and Satan. Religious insanity could be holy, founded upon the madness of the Cross, and manifest in ecstasies, revelations and prophetic powers. But mostly it was EVIL, provoked by the DEVIL and spread through witches, demoniacs and heretics. In his illustrious *Anatomy of Melancholy* (1621), the Oxford don Robert Burton identified Satan as a key cause of depression and despair. Spiritual maladies had to be treated by spiritual means: prayer, fasting, exorcism or, amongst Catholics, visiting a shrine, like Gheel in The Netherlands, dedicated to the Irish holy woman Saint Dymphna.

The idea of madness as demonic possession underwent a major challenge (*see* DEMONIC). The new astrophysics associated with the scientific revolution of the seventeenth century portrayed the universe as regular, mechanical, governed by natural laws: little room here for satanic possession. In any case, after the ghastly disruptions of the witch-craze, the Thirty Years War and the English Civil War, public opinion turned against the religious lunatic fringe spawned by the Reformation. The ruling orders denied the 'revelations' of visionaries. Now the 'possessed' were judged simply crackbrained, suffering from brain-fever or other pathology. Early Methodists were widely diagnosed as victims of religious mania, collective hysteria or mass delusion; some were consigned to Bedlam.

A new theory of insanity became dominant, advanced by the medical profession. Dementia was increasingly explained not as an otherworldly intervention but as an organic disorder. Here doctors built upon the Greek tradition of scientific medicine. As early as the fifth century BC, Hippocrates, the father of rational medicine, had denied that epilepsy, for all its symptoms, was other than a routine natural disease. Moreover, in humoral theory, the Greeks had proposed regular, internal, physiological causes for disordered states. An excess of 'choler', or yellow bile, would cause mania, too much black bile or 'melancholy' would induce depression. Seventeenth-century physicians elaborated these ideas, and also attributed delirium and dementia to poisons in the blood, erratic movements of the womb (the cause of hysteria) and disorders of the spleen.

'Humoral medicine' itself in turn came under fire. Inspired by the new 'mechanical philosophy', anatomists saw the body too as a machine. New attention was paid to the nervous system, envisaged as a kind of hydraulic and electrical circuitry of pipes and fibres that governed sensation and motion. Within this Enlightenment model, psychiatric disorders could be attributed to the nerves or the brain. 'Neurosis' originally meant a disorder of the nervous system; only in this century has the term come to denote a mild and unspecific anxiety state, as distinct from 'psychosis'.

Organic theorists saw themselves as humane: lunacy could no longer threaten the SOUL and endanger salvation. Moreover, as a bodily affliction, insanity was expected to yield to physical treatments, drug therapies, blood-lettings, emetics, strong purges, shock treatments, rotatory chairs and, more negatively, manacles and straitjackets.

When these somatic initiatives failed, a new movement developed, around the close of the eighteenth century, arguing that madness was not, after all, an ordinary organic disorder requiring medical means, but *psychological*, the product of wretched EDUCATION, bad habits and poor socialization, and requiring distinctively psychiatric treatments, 'moral therapy'.

Again, there were long-standing traditions sanctioning the notion that sickness lay not just in the body but in the person, the self. Moralists and playwrights had analysed the passions, showing the conflicts of desire and duty, and the capacity of shame, guilt, grief to tear personalities apart. Descartes' *cogito ergo sum* ('I think, therefore I am') highlighted the role of consciousness in shaping identity; and John Locke explained madness as the product of rampant imagination or ill-disciplined thought processes. The *enfant terrible* of the Enlightenment, Jean-Jacques Rousseau, anticipated Freud's *Civilization and its Discontents* by suggesting that sophisticated civilization alienated man from his true soul, and so created a divided self.

Around 1800, influential figures like Pinel in France, Chiarugi in Italy, the Tukes in England and Reil in Germany were arguing that insanity could best be corrected by an intense inter-personal dynamics between patient and doctor, accentuating 'moral' methods – kindness, reason and humanity. The right place for this was the lunatic asylum, homely, secluded, tranquil.

In earlier centuries, treatment in madhouses had been unusual. Lunatics had mostly been kept within the family or parish, or allowed to wander. Michel Foucault has argued that this traditional liberty allowed madness to utter its own truths and engage in dialogue with reason.

Things changed from the seventeenth century. Many developments – the rise of absolutism, rationalism, the needs of CAPITALISM, the spread of literacy and education, the triumph of a glittering court and urban culture – eroded an older tolerance for strange folks and abnormal ways. The unreasonable, the irrational, the offensive and other problem people were increasingly locked away as part of what Foucault has called 'the great confinement'. Especially in the nineteenth century, the numbers of people 'shut up' (in both senses of the word) skyrocketed. In Britain, a mere 5,000 people or so were confined in asylums by 1800; this tally had leapt to about 100,000 by 1900, and to half as many again by 1950. By that date, approximately half a million deranged or defective people were confined in psychiatric institutions in the USA.

And herein lies the great irony, because the impetus and sanction for this massive (and, as we can see with hindsight, misguided) sequestration of the mad came from well-meaning reformers. Loathing traditional neglect and old brutal madhouses like Bedlam, mad-doctors argued that the insane should be handled, under legal protection, by a comprehensive system of purpose-built, fully provisioned, well-staffed institutions. With personal attention, occupational therapy and in a supportive environment, they would be cured and could be restored to society.

It was a noble ideal. It didn't work. Dispiriting experience proved that, even in well-designed new asylums, the insane rarely recovered as had been predicted. In consequence, the asylum silently changed its character, becoming the dustbin of the incurable. The more hard-bitten psychiatrists of the late nineteenth century rationalized this by arguing that insanity had proved far more intractable than imagined. Institutional care had brought to light thousands of hopeless recidivists, degenerates, alcoholics, second- and third-generation hereditary lunatics and imbeciles hitherto hidden from view. Radical critics counter-alleged that much of the madness in the asylums was, rather, the product of the 'institutionalization' that the asylums themselves begat. Almost anticipating R.D. Laing, an eminently respectable Victorian psychiatrist called a gigantic asylum a gigantic evil.

And so the optimism that created the asylum system faded. Fatalism long paralysed mental health policy. There were no great policy changes before the 1960s, when the voices of anti-psychiatrists such as Szasz and Laing, denouncing 'compulsory psychiatry' as the source of the problems for which it was supposedly a cure, chimed with other civil rights movements.

In the twentieth century, new hope has come from many quarters. Freudian psychoanalysis offered a new approach: the talking cure, the conviction that, through the method of free associations, associated repressions locked in the unconscious would be released. Freud was cautious. He insisted that only mildly disturbed people could be treated by his methods – neurotics, not psychotics or schizophrenics. Aware of the terrible pressures of civilization, and believing that mankind had a 'death wish', Freud expected no miracle cures. The close of the twentieth century finds orthodox psychoanalysis in some disarray, riven with scandals and losing ground. All the same, Freud's insights into unconscious processes, infant development and family dynamics have proved immensely fruitful for generating psychotherapeutic initiatives, particularly in the field of child and family therapy.

Others came bearing 'miracle cures'. The present century has seen a succession of hi-tech, quick-fix procedures. Insulin therapy had its hour. Wilhelm Stekel found that the reduction of blood-sugar levels induced by insulin injections would produce convulsions and coma that apparently brought remission from serious syndromes. The 1930s saw another panacea: electro-convulsive therapy (ECT). Slightly later, lobotomies and leucotomies were developed by Egas Moniz in Europe and popularized by Walter Freeman in the USA. Each produced improvements in patients whose long-term career as asylum patients was otherwise hopeless. But the trigger-happy attitudes of the promoters of such 'great and desperate cures', their violent and traumatic nature, and growing evidence of relapses and side-effects undermined confidence in them all.

That is why, from the 1950s, breakthroughs in psychopharmacology were rapturously received. There had been something quackish, primitive and destructive about shocks and psychosurgery; sophisticated scientific drugs, on the other hand, promised to do for psychiatry what penicillin had spectacularly achieved for general medicine. Neuroleptics like chlorpromozine, antidepressants and lithium (for manic-depressive conditions) had remarkable success in stabilizing behaviour. They made it possible for patients to leave the sheltered but numbing environment of the psychiatric hospital and resume life in the outside world. The drugs revolution and the patients' rights movement combined, in Britain as elsewhere, to launch the 'decarceration' trend that has gained momentum since the 1960s. We are already beginning to experience the drawbacks of this initiative.

The situation remains confused. There are hopeful signs. Many who, before the Second World War, would have been condemned to life sentences in 'museums of madness' can now look to better futures. Yet, psychiatry is a house divided against itself, and for all the vast strides made by neurology we still understand all too little about the true causes or nature of madness.

Alexander, Franz G. and Selesnick, Sheldon T. (1967) *The History of Psychiatry: An Evaluation of Psychiatric Thought and Practice from Prehistoric Times to the Present*, London: George Allen & Unwin.

Feder, L. (1980) *Madness in Literature*, Princeton, NJ: Princeton University Press.

Foucault, Michel (1961) *La Folie et la Déraison: Histoire de la Folie à l'Age Classique*, Paris: Librairie Plon; abridged as *Madness and Civilization: A History of Insanity in the Age of Reason*, trans. Richard Howard, New York: Random House, 1965.

Hunter, Richard and Macalpine, Ida (1963) *Three Hundred Years of Psychiatry: 1535–1860*, London: Oxford University Press.

Peterson, D. (ed.) (1982) *A Mad People's History of Madness*, Pittsburgh, PA: University of Pittsburgh Press.

Scull, Andrew (1979) *Museums of Madness: The Social Organization of Insanity in Nineteenth-Century England*, London: Allen Lane and New York: St Martin's Press.

——(1984) *Decarceration: Community Treatment and the Deviant – A Radical View*, 2nd edn, Oxford: Polity Press and New Brunswick, NJ: Rutgers University Press.

Skultans, V. (1975) *Madness and Morals: Ideas on Insanity in the Nineteenth Century*, London: Routledge & Kegan Paul.

Szasz, Thomas S. (1961) *The Manufacture of Madness*, New York: Harper & Row

——(1972) *The Myth of Mental Illness: Foundations of a Theory of Personal Conduct*, London:

Granada; revised edn, New York: Harper & Row, 1974.

——(1975) *The Age of Madness. The History of Involuntary Mental Hospitalization Presented in Selected Texts*, London: Routledge & Kegan Paul.

Roy Porter

MARKETS

An inescapable social problem is that of relative scarcity: this is a condition in which demands for goods and services exceed the material and human resources that would be required to produce the quantities sought. The existence of relative scarcity means that unavoidable choices have to be made as to which goods should be provided, for whom, and on the exact mode of their production. The use of markets is an answer to the challenge of relative scarcity that has faced all societies over the span of human history.

Markets are essentially information systems which make continuous use of vast amounts of decentralized knowledge spread over the minds of many agents. In generating price signals that correspond to the relative scarcities of goods and services, markets, with varying degrees of efficiency, indicate how existing and potential resources could be deployed to supply the products that are needed. In areas of economic life that rely on markets, it is through following price signals that the offerings of suppliers and the choices of consumers are brought into line with each other.

The origin of markets *as such* is obscure: they seem to be contemporaneous with the origin of civil SOCIETY itself. As the economist F.A. Hayek (1967) has described it, markets initially were not the outcome of conscious design, but rather arose spontaneously as the unintended by-product of the interactions of many individuals attempting to achieve their many different goals. Although historically not intentionally invented, once markets appeared within societies and their functioning became recognized and understood, they could then be subjected to adaptation and regulation in order that they might serve human purposes better.

In modern conditions, markets are usually associated with the institutions of private PROPERTY ownership and of free contract: the combination of these institutions constituting CAPITALISM or the free-enterprise economic system. Markets can also, however, be associated with STATE or community ownership to give what is customarily described as 'market SOCIALISM'.

Market socialism is more commonly found as a theoretical notion at academic seminars than as a functioning institution in the real world. There are a small number of concrete instances of this type of economic arrangement, however, perhaps the best known of which are the self-managed enterprises of the former Yugoslavia, created in the 1960s and 1970s by the then communist regime in an attempt to find a middle way between Western capitalism and the command economies of the former USSR. A more recent example of market socialism, surprisingly, is to be found in the self-governing Trust Hospitals of the British National Health Service of the 1990s. Here, ownership lies with the state, but the self-governing entities are meant to buy and sell medical services at market prices. Traditionally, the great weakness of market socialism has been that the managers, lacking the incentives and opportunities that face risk-taking entrepreneur-owners, perform poorly in acquiring and allocating investment capital (either to produce novel lines of goods or to replace a depreciated existing capital stock).

In the more usual context of a free-enterprise economic system, markets operate in many different areas and with varying degrees of efficiency and co-ordination with each other. At the broadest level, distinct markets exist for the goods and services bought by consumers (final product markets), for skill of different kinds (labour markets), for various types of investment capital (capital markets), and for already-issued foreign currency, company securities and real estate (asset markets). The labour and capital markets are also known as markets for factor inputs, since what is traded here, the use of skill and financial savings, is employed by firms in the productive process in order to create goods and services for sale to the final consumer. Within these wide categories, submarkets exist for particular items or, more usually, for groups of items that are considered substitutes in demand (a good, service or asset is held to be a substitute in demand for another if the level of demand for it is positively related to changes in the latter's price).

Major disagreements exist amongst contemporary economists as to the relative efficiency of different markets and on the extent to which any discerned inefficiency could be rectified by governmental intervention or otherwise. Efficiency is a term with many shades of meaning, but in this context an efficient market is one that rapidly adjusts to new information and changes in circumstances and is thus, most of the time, in a state of price-clearing equilibrium (with supply and demand being continuously equated by the ruling price). An inefficient market, in contrast, is slow to adjust to change of any kind, and is one where the usual condition is more or less permanent disequilibrium.

The most infuential economist of the twentieth century, John Maynard Keynes of the University of Cambridge, publicized the fact that an adequate explanatory theory cannot just assume that all markets are competitive and efficient. His main macroeconomic theory revolved around the key notion that many markets, if left to their own devices, do not automatically behave efficiently. In particular, Keynes (1936) stressed the vital part that inherently slow-adjusting labour markets play in the determination of persistent involuntary unemployment. To prevent the emergence of this type of phenomenon as an outcome of market inefficiency, Keynes argued that governments have a pivotal role in ensuring that aggregate demand in the ECONOMY is maintained at an appropriate level and is not permitted to fluctuate wildly. Keynes hence recommended that governments attempt to smooth out the destabilizing unevenness in cyclical patterns of private investment expenditure by themselves becoming substantial spenders on capital projects during times of recession.

It must be emphasized that while Keynes aimed to focus the attention of economists on market failure and inefficiency, he was not opposed in general to the use of markets in cases where they operated without socially destructive ramifications. His concern was simply that the repercussions for society of inefficiencies in certain important markets were far too damaging for governments to be uninvolved with the actual performance of these markets.

Possibly Keynes's greatest achievement was to demonstrate beyond doubt that what could be harmlessly assumed in theoretical economic models should not unthinkingly be identified with what happens in the real world of operating markets. Although, as the Italian economist Vilfredo Pareto (1897) was the first rigorously to prove, a perfectly competitive economy is efficient in the sense that what is supplied matches the preferences of consumers, in practice economists should be concerned with how markets behave in the context of appreciable violations of market efficiency. In reality markets function in a world of imperfectly competitive industries and where production frequently has unwanted side-effects, such as pollution, the costs of which are not borne by those generating them. A further departure from perfect competition is also occasioned by the fact that people want to be supplied with what economists call 'public goods', i.e services like street lighting and national defence. But because non-payers cannot easily be excluded from the benefits provided by the provision of public goods, such services cannot be provided in the normal way by free markets but have instead to be financed by governments using their power to tax. Yet another breach with the theoretical world of unhampered markets arises from the fact that, in most modern societies, individuals want governments to organize WELFARE programmes of various kinds and to ensure that every citizen commands a minimum income regardless of current earning capacity. (Indeed, without welfare programmes to mitigate the uncertainties and the harsh burdens on some of constant change in predominantly market-based economies, a policy of widespread reliance on markets might well not be tolerated by the voting public.)

With reference to markets that are far from efficient, economists have developed theories of the 'second best' (Lipsey and Lancaster 1956). Interestingly, and perhaps counter-intuitively, the main conclusion from this analysis is that if a market contains an unremovable distortion then *a priori* we cannot say that the most efficient outcome would result were we to confront as many of the remaining inefficiencies as possible. The theory of the second best suggests that on occasions, as empirical circumstances dictate, the most advantageous solution may be to leave removable distortions undisturbed to counter-balance, as it were, the ones that cannot be removed.

Finally, a word is in order on the topic of market morality. While we can accept that there is no realistic alternative to wide reliance on markets as a uniquely competent means of resource allocation in the circumstances of relative scarcity, this fact itself should not prevent debate on the moral aspects of particular types of market conduct. Indeed, with the spectacular worldwide collapse in the early 1990s of the command economies of COMMUNISM, the door is now open for a more dispassionate approach to ethics in the market-place.

Markets are indispensable tools for dealing effectively with the societal problem of relative scarcity, and as such are neither inherently moral nor immoral. Rather, it is the behaviour of economic agents in the milieu of markets that can appropriately be appraised on moral grounds. Fraudulent, unscrupulous and rapacious behaviour is surely just as reprehensible in the setting of markets as it would be in other areas of life, e.g. in the ENVIRONMENT of political activity. There is a growing understanding in most advanced economies, however, that the legal framework within which particular markets operate can be consciously fashioned to ensure that the opportunity for unethical activity is minimized. Good examples of this type of contextual control are the regulations prohibiting 'insider trading' in financial markets and those outlawing restrictive and anti-competitive practices in the markets for most goods and services. The emission of dangerous pollutants and the international trade in armaments are other activities within markets where unprincipled conduct can, and should, be deterred by the use of legally enforceable ground-rules.

The growing interest in universities and schools of management in the subject of business ethics is a most welcome trend (*see* BUSINESS; ETHICS). This interest is also imaginatively being extended by some into the theological realm. One such writer is Donald Hay (1989). He offers 'stewardship' as the basic organizing concept, and recommends individuals when acting as economic agents always to look upon themselves as stewards before God of the world's resources. Drawing out the precise implications of this type of approach to market behaviour, and making them applicable to real-world situations, is a most worthwhile task but one that has only just begun.

Acton, H.B. (1971) *The Morals of Markets: An Ethical Exploration*, London: Longman.

Boadway, R.W. and Bruce, N. (1984) *Welfare Economics*, Oxford: Basil Blackwell.

Bohm, P. (1987) *Social Efficiency: A Concise Introduction to Welfare Economics*, 2nd edn, London: Macmillan.

Gray, J. (1992) *The Moral Foundations of Market Institutions*, London: Institute of Economic Affairs.

Griffiths, B. (1989) *Morality and the Market Place*, London: Hodder & Stoughton.

Hay, D.A. (1989) *Economics Today: A Christian Critique*, Leicester: Apollos.

Hayek, F.A. (1949) *Individualism and Economic Order*, London: Routledge & Kegan Paul.

——(1967) *Studies in Philosophy, Politics and Economics*, London: Routledge & Kegan Paul.

Hirshleifer, J. and Glazer, A. (1992) *Price Theory and Applications*, 5th edn, Englewood Cliffs, NJ: Prentice Hall.

Keynes, J.M. (1936) *The General Theory of Employment, Interest and Money*, London: Macmillan.

Lipsey, R.G. and Lancaster, K.J. (1956) 'The general theory of the second best', *Review of Economic Studies* 24: 11–32.

Pareto, V. (1897) *Cours d'Economie Politique*, Lausanne: F. Rouge.

Varian, H.R. (1990) *Intermediate Microeconomics*, 2nd edn, New York: Norton.

Thomas S. Torrance

MARRIAGE

The human pairbond is a secular reality, part of God's creation. That statement summarizes a THEOLOGY of marriage. In English law, marriage is defined as 'the voluntary union for life of a man and a woman': and this definition is entirely acceptable to Christian theology. Canon B30 of the Church of England adds only that the definition is 'according to our Lord's teaching', and emphasizes 'for life' with the words of the wedding service, 'for better for worse, till death do them part'. Neither the secular nor the religious definition mentions the FAMILY; though, as a matter of biology, the human pairbond has evolved as the milieu in which slow-maturing human young are brought to birth and cherished; and, as a matter of history, Christian theologians and moralists have insisted so strongly upon procreation as the divine purpose of the marriage union that they have tended to belittle pleasure and reduce LOVE to duty.

Human beings, unlike apes, are pairbonding animals (Oppenheimer 1990: ch. 2). In the Judaeo-Christian scriptures marriage goes back to the Creation: 'It is not good that the man should be alone . . . . Therefore a man leaves his father and his mother and clings to his wife, and they become one flesh' (Genesis 2: 18, 24). For all the emphasis on fruitfulness, fertility is not the whole point in either of the Genesis creation stories. Procreation is blessing as much as command (Genesis 1: 27–8).

It is less easy to deny that PATRIARCHY is primary, and some feminists see this as an indictment of the Biblical tradition. Yet if one considers the vulnerability of women before reasonably reliable CONTRACEPTION was available, and the fallen condition of humankind, including the men who wrote down the scriptures, the firm conviction that women too are children of God is clear to see. In the Judaeo-Christian tradition women are not merely accessory to men and bearers of their children. Vigorous and generous-spirited women are conspicuous in their own right. Women's lives are not invisible. Women have rights which are protected, including the right to formal DIVORCE rather than arbitrary abandonment. Sexual love is a matter of celebration not disapproval. The marriage COVENANT between a man and a woman can symbolize the covenant between God and the chosen people. Susan Dowell, writing as a Christian feminist, though she rejects as inadequate some supposedly encouraging aspects of Biblical teaching, finds hope in this tradition: 'only Hebrew thought – of all the world-views of late antiquity – could expand towards an integrated ethical understanding of sexuality' (Dowell 1990: 52).

In the New Testament there can be found a theology of marriage which has not always been properly appreciated in the Christian church. According to the Gospel accounts, when Christ was asked about divorce he talked about marriage: not about 'Christian marriage', nor about offspring, but about the 'one flesh' unity of husband and wife. One can accept, without relying on dubious 'proof-texts', that Christ picked up and renewed the old teaching that the marriage union goes back to the beginnings of humanity and that faithfulness is God's will for human beings (Mark 10: 6–9).

Christ's teaching raises the question how generosity can replace the claiming of rights. Christians have substituted the question whether marriage is 'indissoluble' or 'dissoluble'. Meanwhile the recurring emphasis, in parables and in the story of the wedding at Cana, on marriage as a social reality which is fit to be celebrated goes by default. Likewise the Pauline insight, that the union of man and woman is 'a great mystery' comparable to the unity of Christ and the church (Ephesians 5: 31–2), has often been submerged in legalistic theories about marriage as an ecclesiastical sacrament. The singleness of Christ and the tradition about the virginity of his mother, instead of being interpreted as vocational, for the sake of the Incarnation, have been taken as a divine statement that CELIBACY is preferable.

The development of Christian sexual ethics can be seen as a sorry confusion of chastity with celibacy, giving unmarried men undue POWER over the lives of married men and women, though Peter Brown's fine book *The Body and Society* (1989) has shed light on positive aspects of renunciation. Sexuality, as part of God's good creation, has never been wholly repudiated; and the concept of marriage as a community of love has never been lost. The Papal Encyclical *Casti connubii* (1930) writes warmly, though in patriarchal language, of man's 'generous surrender of his whole person made to another for the whole span of life' (end of introduction).

The Eastern churches have generally taken a less anxious view of SEXUALITY than has been characteristic of Western Christianity. 'How foolish are those who belittle marriage!' said St

John Chrysostom (1986: 55). 'There is no relationship', he said, 'so close as that of husband and wife, if they are united as they ought to be' (1986: 43). He gave the example of Isaac's love for Rebecca: 'Who would not have loved such a woman, so virtuous, so beautiful, so hospitable, generous and kind, so brave in her soul and vigorous in her body?' (1986: 113).

For many, the villain is Augustine. It needs pointing out what he did and did not say. He insisted, not merely conceded, that marriage is honourable and good (*De bono conjugali* 8): 'The first natural bond of human society is man and wife' (ibid. 1). Husband and wife 'walk together, and look together whither they walk' (ibid.). This positive emphasis on the excellence of married love has been, not cancelled, but concealed from his fellow Christians by his conviction that even in marriage continence, which practically means abstinence, is best. He explains his position characteristically: 'Therefore marriage and fornication are not two evils, whereof the second is worse: but marriage and continence are two goods, whereof the second is better' (ibid. 8).

His well-known summary, 'All these are goods, on account of which marriage is a good; offspring, faith, sacrament' (ibid. 32), is governed by distrust of physical passion as loss of control. He treats sexual attraction as a divine expedient for getting the world populated; and he uses the distorting and legalistic terminology of the 'debt' owed by the spouses to one another (ibid. 4). When he writes of husband and wife feeling 'a certain gravity of glowing pleasure' (ibid. 3), it is their 'parental affection' not their sexual love which he has in mind. Marriage is best in old age, when 'there lives in full vigour the order of charity between husband and wife' (ibid. 3). With hindsight it may be said that this theology has delayed Christian understanding, not for lack of appreciation of the 'good of marriage', nor even for lack of emphasis on the relationship between husband and wife, but for failure to realize that sexual union is more than pleasure and itself builds up that relationship.

Subsequent history is tangled but by no means entirely negative. It has been complicated by a struggle between two ways in which Christians may understand marriage: as secular social reality, i.e. as human pairbond, or as a Christian sacrament controlled by the Church. This struggle continues. It has recently taken the form of an inclination to set up 'Christian marriage' as holy and inviolable, in contrast to unstable and unblessed unions of those outside the fold; and of a wish to distinguish sheep and goats more sharply by repudiating 'folk religion' and celebrating weddings only for the committed.

Christian possessiveness about marriage has not taken over, any more than the ascetic tendency in the early church to belittle marriage. Just as ASCETICISM is restrained by the firm Biblical principle that God's physical creation is 'very good', so clericalism is restrained by the principle that what makes a marriage is the consent of a man and a woman. This principle was established after much controversy about whether consent or consummation is decisive, and was no doubt influenced by the belief that the marriage of the Mother of Jesus was unconsummated (Bailey 1959: ch. IV). Be that as it may, the primacy of consent encourages an emphasis more humanist than ascetic. Two people take each other for life as husband and wife. A ceremony, religious or secular, may be desirable or even compulsory, but not essential. So the church is obliged to acknowledge the human institution of marriage. If marriage is a sacrament, the ministers of this sacrament are the man and the woman. The role of the priest is not to marry but to witness and bless in God's name. No legal or religious rite is strictly necessary for the making of a real marriage; but the ceremonies and traditions which people find life-enhancing and encouraging for witnessing, blessing and celebrating their consent need not be despised as mere 'folk religion' (*see* PARTNERING).

Nor is procreation essential: childless unions are as real and significant as marriages with children. Fertility is characteristic of marriage, not definitive. There is sociological and theological pressure to deny this, to suppose that offspring must cement the bond in theory and in practice and that divorce ought to be easier for childless couples: but such a supposition is hurtfully belittling to many good marriages, and even damaging to children if they are seen as blocking parental freedom.

Much Christian energy has been spent discussing the requirement 'for life'. Almost inevitably, marriage doctrine has developed in terms of divorce doctrine. Societies, even theocratic societies, need safety-valves for matrimonial failure. 'For your hardness of heart Moses allowed you to divorce your wives . . .' (Matthew 19: 8). If divorce is supposed to be impossible, nullity proliferates. Medieval marriages were notoriously vulnerable to annulment for remote kinship or affinity. The Reformers attended to this scandal: and Protestants accordingly had to take seriously the possibility of divorce.

They also took seriously the teaching of the New Testament. It was believed that the 'Matthaean exception' (Matthew 5: 32; 19: 9) authorized divorce for adultery; and the so-called 'Pauline privilege' (1 Corithians 7: 15) allowed a loophole for divorce for desertion. Calvin indeed believed that divorce for adultery was needful in default of the death penalty (quoted in Atkinson 1979: 51–2).

In the Church of England divorce for adultery was available, expensively, by private Act of Parliament, and the 'innocent parties' were remarried in church. The Act of 1857 began to make divorce available to the general public, still on the basis of the 'matrimonial offence'.

A combination of Biblical criticism and humane concern made it increasingly hard to justify divorces because and only because one spouse had sinned and the other refused to forgive. The grounds were widened; and then the underlying principle was questioned. In England, for example, in 1969 the law decreed, with church co-operation, that the proper reason for divorce must be the irretrievable breakdown of a marriage. This is a more Biblical understanding, but it is far from having solved the problem. Predictions that the floodgates would open have, as usual, been justified (Oppenheimer 1990: ch. 8 and Appendix).

The besetting SIN of Western theologians is legalism, of which rigorism and permissiveness are both aspects. The grass is greener on the other side of the fence, where orthodoxy emphasizes the majesty and mercy of God, who is not to be confined to human regulations. Greener grass may not transplant well. Compassion, attempted in a context still fundamentally legal, appears as softness rather than mercy. The argument continues about 'indissolubility' and the rights of grown-ups to happiness. Christian moderates may be encouraged that, while traditionalists and liberals argue, legislators are realizing that children are the real victims (Burgoyne *et al.* 1987; Law Commission 1988, 1990).

Theologians and sociologists are giving plenty of attention to marriage, but with a notable absence of co-operation. They discuss current problems in parallel, each with the assumption that the conclusions of the other are irrelevant. While theologians declare God's purpose, sociologists explain empirically what is going on (Anderson 1980: e.g. p. 43).

Various oversimplified contrasts have developed, based on the presumed difference between religious concern for God's will and humanist concern for happiness. It is asked whether marriage is sacrament *or* partnership, institution *or* relationship, as if these were mutually exclusive (Burgoyne *et al.* 1987: 84; cf. Morgan, in Clark 1991: 126–7 ff.). The plain legal concept of a 'contract conferring status', which could bridge the gap between a covenant and a 'mere' contract, is readily forgotten. It has become easy for a secular moralist to assume that pairbond means simply bond, asking whether sex, to be permissible, must 'occur within the *confines* of the institution of marriage' (Belliotto 1991: 315, emphasis mine), a question which nicely shows how LIBERALISM can be as legalistic as rigorism.

It is certainly a mistake to think in terms of a golden age, whether today in contrast to the bad old days, or in the past in contrast to modern decadence. Broken homes and 'serial polygamy' are not so new, though once it was DEATH not divorce which ended marriages early. The quoting of simplified statistics, for instance reiterating that one in three marriages breaks down, can be self-fulfilling (Oppenheimer 1990: ch. 1; Morgan, in Clark 1991: 123–6).

Like the time of Christ, like all times, the present is a time of peril *and* promise. Evidently, for good or ill, there has been a sexual revolution: not necessarily a revolution of moral values, but of the data for moral decision. Two medical developments are new facts from which new consequences are bound to follow: a longer expectation of life, and the practical possibility of separating sexual relationship from pro-creation.

Times of transition are uncomfortable: roles are confused, liberties half gained, ancient certainties lost; buried bitterness comes to the surface. But positively, ancient relentless pressure has lifted. Better appreciation of the body, smaller families, more scope for women to develop into mature human beings, wider choices for both women and men, not only allow more variegated ways of living to be recognized as responsible, but make long-term sexual fidelity less of a *faute de mieux*, more positively rewarding. What is misleading about the love story with a 'happy ending' is not 'happy' but 'ending'. A wedding, like the birth of a child, is a beginning, incomplete and needing to be 'made good' through many years. Neither romance nor family affection is new, but there is more time and space now for human relationships to develop (Stone 1979; Oppenheimer 1990: 34–7).

This discussion of marriage as secular and religious reality has not been and could not be entirely neutral. It has had the character of a theological guided tour, pointing out what appears important to a late-twentieth-century English liberal Christian. Its main point is that the seemingly parallel lines of current sociological and theological discussion could converge constructively upon the pairbond. The possibility of human marriage depends on two facts: the tendency of human beings to want to belong to one another in pairs, and the capacity of human beings, in general, to give their word and keep it and to carry on with what they start to do. Marriage can be given profound religious meaning, but only if it is founded upon this secular basis.

Of course the pairbond does not always work; but it is characteristic of our species, and when it does not work something has gone wrong. Unfaithfulness is, in philosophical terminology, a 'parasitic' concept, dependent upon the concept of faithfulness. Only a creature that could be faithful can be unfaithful. Divorce is not impossible but is akin to drastic surgery, to amputation. Husband and wife belong to one another by growing together, not by ownership. In making promises to one another human beings are truly committing themselves to an

enterprise which deserves the honour of being taken seriously. The liberalism which sits loose to commitment does not allow for the notion that commitment can itself be life-enhancing, that people can find the happiness they seek in the very permanence of their union. Stability is not cramping to human beings but conducive to their flourishing (Almond 1988; Oppenheimer 1990: ch 3; Turner 1991).

If marriage is defined as pairbond, permanence and exclusiveness need not seem tyrannical; 'personal relationships' can be appreciated but not idolized; and the dangers and stresses of today can be understood better and faced more calmly as 'swings and roundabouts', not as fearful moral deterioration. A theology of the 'one flesh' union of marriage as humanly sacramental can come into its own, shedding accumulated legalism. A sacrament is 'an outward and visible sign of an inward and spiritual grace' (The Catechism, 1662 Prayer Book). Because human beings are animal and spiritual, they need to experience and express spiritual reality by physical means. Human sexual union is more than a biological activity, whether for procreation or pleasure: it can be a means of grace, secular and divine (Oppenheimer 1990: ch. 7).

The challenge of FEMINISM is not to be repudiated. The damage done by 'patriarchy' is not negligible, but needs to be faced by women and men together in terms of generous reciprocal friendship, not in terms of gender war, which is civil war. The tyranny to be overcome is not the pairbond but the recalcitrant human tendency to force one another into stereotypes, to miss the excellent variety of which humanity is capable (Oppenheimer 1990: ch. 11).

It is no part of Christian loyalty to idolize either marriage or family. An odd result of vocal Christian anxiety about current permissiveness has been the impression that 'the family', and especially the nuclear family as we know it, is an integral part of the Christian faith: as if Christian teaching were unequivocal and one kind of family life were part of a package deal with Christmas and Easter and the Sermon on the Mount. On the contrary, marriage and family are human institutions of enormous potential, which when they go bad can be very bad. The worst is the corruption of the best. To set human love in an eternal context is to say that it needs redemption and can be redeemed. Though there is no marriage in the Kingdom of Heaven (Mark 12: 25), assuredly DEATH is the way to RESURRECTION for whatever is worth preserving in faithful sexual love (Oppenheimer 1990: 112–13).

Allchin, A.M. (1971) 'The sacrament of marriage in eastern Christianity', *Marriage, Divorce and the Church* (The Root Report), London: SPCK, Appendix.

Almond, Brenda (1988) 'Human bonds', *Journal of Applied Philosophy 5*: 1.

Anderson, Michael (ed.) (1980) *Sociology of the Family*, 2nd edn, Harmondsworth: Penguin.

Atkinson, David (1979) *To Have and to Hold*, London: Collins.

Augustine (401) *De bono conjugali (On the Good of Marriage)*.

Bailey, D.S. (1959) *The Man–Woman Relation in Christian Thought*, Harlow: Longman.

Barth, Karl (1961) *Church Dogmatics* III 1, 3, 4, Edinburgh: T. & T. Clark.

Belliotto, Raymond A. (1991) 'Sex', in Peter Singer (ed.) *A Companion to Ethics*, Oxford: Blackwell, pp. 315–26.

Brown, Peter (1989) *The Body and Society*, London: Faber.

Burgoyne, Jacqueline, Ormrod, Roger, and Richards, Martin (1987) *Divorce Matters*, Harmondsworth: Penguin.

Casti connubii, Pope Pius XI's Encyclical of 1930.

Chrysostom, John (*c.*347–407) (1986) *On Marriage and Family Life*, Sermons translated by Catharine P. Roth and David Anderson, St Vladimir's Seminary Press.

Clark, D. (ed.) (1991) *Marriage, Domestic Life and Social Change: Writings for Jacqueline Burgoyne*, London: Routledge.

Dominian, J. (1991) *Passionate and Compassionate Love: A Vision for Christian Marriage*, London: Darton, Longman & Todd, and other publications.

Dowell, Susan (1990) *They Two Shall Be One: Monogamy in History and Religion*, London: Collins.

Duby, Georges (1985) *The Knight, the Lady and the Priest*, trans. Barbara Bray, Harmondsworth: Penguin (first published 1983).

Law Commission (1988) *Facing the Future: A Discussion Paper on the Ground for Divorce*, London: HMSO.

——(1990) *Family Law: The Ground for Divorce*, London: HMSO.

Oppenheimer, Helen (1983) *The Hope of Happiness*, London: SCM.

——(1990) *Marriage*, London: Mowbray.

Schillebeeckx, E. (1985) *Marriage: Secular Reality and Saving Mystery*, 2 vols, Sheed & Ward.

Stone, Lawrence (1979) *The Family, Sex and Marriage in England 1500–1800*, abridged edition, London: Penguin (1st edn, London: Weidenfeld & Nicolson, 1977).

Turner, Philip (1991) 'Marriage and divorce', the first of the 1990 Zabriskie Lectures, 'Undertakings and promises: sexual ethics in the life of the church', *Virginia Seminary Journal*, March.

Helen Oppenheimer

MARXISM

Marx's famous dictum, 'The philosophers have only *interpreted* the world in various ways; the point is to *change* it', is an indication that we should not consider Marxism solely in its aspect as an intellectual tradition. It *is*, of course, an intellectual tradition (or, by the late twentieth century, a rather loose family of such traditions), but it also has an important historical presence as a source of revolutionary social and political critique and aspiration. Nearly all of the great radical movements of the twentieth century – the struggles against colonial domination, for women's rights, for the EMANCIPATION of oppressed racial and ethnic minorities and, more recently, for a sustainable relationship to the natural ENVIRONMENT – have drawn upon (and, in the process, transformed) the Marxian legacy. However, Marxism has also been claimed as the official philosophy of state-socialist regimes established in many parts of the world, as a result of indigenous REVOLUTION (Russia), of wars of national liberation (China, Vietnam, Mozambique) or of external imposition (Hungary, Czechoslovakia). Though this model of social and political life is now very much on the defensive, it would be premature to write it off. However, it is clear that the relationships between the doctrinal legitimations of these societies and the intellectual tradition of Marxism, not to mention the liberatory aspirations of Marxism as a revolutionary practice, are deeply problematic. Marxism should therefore be thought of in terms of three distinguishable aspects: as intellectual tradition, as revolutionary critique and aspiration, and as (in Marx's own sense) a ruling IDEOLOGY.

It is also helpful to think of the relationships

between Marxism and religion under three distinct aspects. First, Marxism as both intellectual tradition and revolutionary aspiration takes the Judaeo-Christian religious tradition as one of its most significant sources. The philosophical view of history to be found in (especially) the early works of Marx takes the form of a secular theodicy of progress toward a 'good life' for humanity whose moral character has much in common with that of a long tradition of Christian radicalism (*see* CHRISTIAN SOCIALISM). Second, Marxism as an intellectual tradition offers both a philosophical critique of religion (and of Christianity in particular) and a historical/sociological explanation of its popular appeal and functional role. Religion is therefore an *object* of Marxian analysis, as well as one of its sources. Third, Marxism as revolutionary aspiration and as ruling ideology itself has a close functional relationship with religion. In some respects Marxism competes with the various world religions for popular allegiance, and in other respects, from a broad sociological point of view, it may be viewed as itself a form of religious belief.

The founding figures of Marxism were, of course, Karl Marx (1818–83) and Frederick Engels (1820–95), but the tradition they established has been developed, revised, enriched and broadened by thinkers from many countries throughout the twentieth century. Some of these, such as Lenin, Trotsky, Mao Tse Tung and Rosa Luxemburg, were great revolutionary leaders, whereas others such as Gramsci, Althusser and Lukács are better known for their intellectual achievements than for their political activity.

The collaboration between Marx and Engels began in the early 1840s, when they were both associated with the circle of young German radicals known as the 'Left' or 'Young' Hegelians. The pervasive influence of the great German idealist philosopher G.W.F. Hegel (1770–1831) was still widely felt, and the Left Hegelians devoted themselves to developing what they saw as the critical, revolutionary side of Hegel's thought. For them, Hegel was important for the way he set philosophical questions in the context of an overall view of historical process and transformation. For Hegel, history

was to be understood as a process of spiritual development through phases of self-alienation towards an ultimate reconciliation and self-realization of 'absolute spirit'. Christianity, seen from this point of view, was a precursor of these philosophical truths, which it expressed in a more primitive and mythical or symbolic form.

The Left Hegelians commonly shared Hegel's view of Christianity and attempted to develop a more rational, secular successor-philosophy. In so far as they shared Hegel's idealist view of being, they tended to see political progress in terms of an enlarged freedom of thought and expression. However, Marx and Engels soon became impatient with what they saw as fatal limitations in this outlook. They were greatly impressed by the work of fellow Left Hegelian Ludwig Feuerbach (1804–72), who is widely credited with a 'materialist inversion' of Hegel's philosophy. This is to say, Feuerbach retained much of the *form* of Hegel's view of history as a developmental process of ALIENATION and self-realization, but substituted the human species for 'absolute spirit' as the subject and content of the process. Thought and consciousness are to be understood as activities of human beings, and it is these human beings who are the real subjects of historical development. In Feuerbach's philosophy, religion is seen as a form of self-alienation. Prevented by their material conditions of life from realizing their full human potential, people have created imaginary representations of their *own* essential powers which they have attributed to alien beings – gods – which they have set over and above themselves. Hegel's philosophy now appears, likewise, as a more rationalized form of this same self-alienation. Both religion and the idealist philosophy are to be transcended in a reappropriation within the human community of its own alienated powers.

Marx and Engels were immediately attracted to this vision, but posed two questions Feuerbach had not addressed: *what* are the conditions in material life which bring about religious and philosophical self-alienation, and *how* can they be overcome in practice? They searched for the answer to the first question in a critical review of political ECONOMY. In the course of this they came to see the modern system of private PROPERTY relations, commodity exchange, and wage-labour as both expressing and imposing upon human subjects a many-sided fragmentation of life activity. Self-alienation could now be seen as primarily a separation from nature, and from the opportunity to act freely and creatively upon it, with the consequence that relations between humans become increasingly instrumental and exploitative, and that people lose any sense of control over their own lives.

Their answer to the second question – how can alienation be overcome in practice – was suggested partly by this analysis of alienated labour and partly by their increasing experience of the conditions of industrial CAPITALISM, particularly in England, and by their contacts with socialist and communist workers' organizations in France and elsewhere. If the source of human self-estrangement is to be found in the system of private property, commodity exchange and wage-labour, then its solution must be in some radical transcendence of the material, social and cultural conditions engendered by this system. Henceforth COMMUNISM was to be the 'positive' transcendence of this system, and the looked-for context in which the communal relations of all would enable the full self-development of each. Moreover, nothing could be clearer than that the growing international self-organization and revolt of labour would be the vehicle of this great historical task.

This much Marx and Engels had achieved by the mid-1840s. For some commentators, their subsequent work should be seen as a further development and elaboration of this broad pattern of historical and philosophical ideas. It is acknowledged that in their later work Marx and Engels rarely presented the full sweep of their philosophical vision of history as the developmental process of the human species in the way they did in their early writings. Nevertheless it is argued that the value content and the still loosely Hegelian view of history remain in place as an *implicit* framework for all of the more detailed and empirical work that came later.

Opposed to this 'continuist' tradition of interpretation are many commentators who notice a marked turn from the mid-1840s onwards

towards more empirically rooted historical analysis in the name of a contrast between 'science' and 'philosophy'. In the course of their later historical investigations, their journalistic studies of contemporary political episodes and their further encounters with the established economic theories of the time, Marx and Engels came to develop a rich repertoire of new theoretical concepts, and with them an approach which came to be known as 'historical materialism'. These new concepts are developed at a level of abstraction intermediate between the earlier philosophical view of history and the more directly narrative forms of many historical studies. It is therefore possible to outline these concepts without attempting to settle the question whether they represent a decisive turning away from the earlier view.

Primacy amongst the concepts of historical materialism must go to the concept of 'mode of production'. Marx and Engels noted that all forms of social life, if they are to be sustainable, must have some institutional framework for acting upon nature so as to meet subsistence needs, and also some framework for distributing the means of subsistence thereby acquired. However, they were also aware of an immense historical and geographical *variability* in the ways in which these functions are carried out. In some cases land and instruments of production may be held in common and the products of labour shared out among the community. Elsewhere, a centralized state BUREAUCRACY or a landowning class might monopolize productive property, whilst labour might be directly coerced as in SLAVERY, or subject to taxes or rents or, as under modern capitalism, exchanged on the market as a commodity.

These different economic forms of SOCIETY were classified by Marx and Engels as so many 'modes of production'. Within each mode it was possible to make an analytical distinction between 'forces of production' and 'social relations of production'. Principal amongst the elements making up the forces of production were the labourers themselves (or their productive capacities, skills, strength, etc.), the instruments with which they worked (the 'means of production') and the raw materials upon which they worked. Though they were less clear about this,

Marx and Engels often seemed to include among the forces of production *conditions* of production, such as land or other environmental conditions, as well as relations of co-operation between workers such as are required by the task at hand (as distinct from relations arising, for example, from the need to control or discipline the workforce).

The social relations of production are, primarily, relations of property and their derivatives. Capitalism as a mode of production is distinctive in that the means of production are monopolized by one social CLASS – the capitalist class – in such a way that non-capitalists can meet their subsistence needs only by selling their ability to work to a member of the owning class. The result of this is that commodity exchange is extended to include the class of workers themselves, who acquire the status of commodities, to be bought or dispensed with as the interest of the capitalist in wealth accumulation dictates.

However, despite its moral unacceptability, and the suffering it imposes upon the wage-labourers and their dependants, capitalism was viewed as marking a 'progressive' stage in historical development. Capitalist competition itself and the antagonism between capital and labour produce an incessant demand for technological innovation. In Marxist terms, the 'forces of production' are rapidly developed. This includes both science, and its application in machinery, *and* the growing division of labour and the extent of social co-operation that goes along with it. Capitalism is also 'progressive' in that the growing contradiction between the private ownership of capital and the increasingly social and co-operative character of production gives rise to a revolutionary labour movement whose mission is to bring about the transition to a new society based on common ownership.

However, contrary to many of their more hostile commentators, Marx and Engels never supposed that the formation of a revolutionary consciousness in the working class and its translation into political change would follow directly or unproblematically from the economic dynamic of capitalism. Their more empirical and journalistic studies were full of attempts to analyse the complex relations between economic structures and interests, on the one hand, and, on the other, the various forms of the STATE and patterns of social and cultural conflicts in society. Some of their more abstract statements suggest that they viewed the state as primarily the institutional form through which the economically dominant class rules society as a whole, and also that they considered the dominant ideas in any society to be expressions of the interests of the dominant class. These do, indeed, serve as rough-and-ready first approximations to their general view, but a close reading of their historical analyses reveals a much more complex and sophisticated grasp of historical particularities.

In the twentieth century successive waves of success, defeat and disillusionment in the attempts to put these ideas into political practice have led to radical revisions of the Marxian heritage, and also to a fragmentation into numerous competing schools of thought. Success, in the shape of the Russian Revolution of 1917, both presupposed and required radical revision of Marxian doctrine. Revolution came in one of the most economically backward of the European nations, but had been expected to take place in the most advanced. Marxist internationalism had been premised upon the possibility of SOCIALISM only as a global social process, yet the Russian Revolution stood isolated. Finally, not wanting to set out Utopian 'blueprints' for the future, the early Marxists had said very little about what the new communist commonwealth would be like. Under the most desperately bleak and hostile conditions, first Lenin and then Stalin filled that absence with an oppressive dictatorship which would certainly have horrified Marx and Engels, and did horrify all but the most blinkered of socialists who lived through those times.

From the work of Rosa Luxemburg and Leon Trotsky onwards Marxists have been preoccupied with understanding the historical fate of the Soviet Union and confronting the key contemporary challenge to socialism: can the aims of sharing social wealth, and the democratic planning of social and economic life, be combined with the values of respect for individual rights and tolerance of cultural and doctrinal diversity? As unplanned global capitalist expansion threatens destructive consequences in the shape of ecological catastrophe (a situation barely envisioned by Marx and Engels themselves) this question assumes a renewed urgency.

Althusser, L. (1969) *For Marx*, London: Allen Lane/The Penguin Press.
——and Balibar, E. (1970) *Reading Capital*, London: New Left Books.
Cohen, G.A. (1978) *Karl Marx's Theory of History: A Defense*, Oxford: Clarendon.
Gerac, N. (1976) *The Legacy of Rosa Luxemburg*, London: New Left Books.
Gramsci, A. (1992) *Prison Notebooks*, New York: Columbia University Press.
Kamenka, E. (ed.) (1983) *The Portable Karl Marx*, Harmondsworth: Penguin.
McLellan, D. (1973) *Karl Marx: His Life and Thought*, London and New York: Macmillan.
——(1979) *Marxism after Marx*, 2nd edn, London and Basingstoke: Macmillan.
New Life-Review (eds) (1979) *Western Marxism: A Critical Reader*, London: New Left Books.
Trotsky, L.D. (1937) *The Revolution Betrayed*, London: Faber & Faber.

Ted Benton

MEDIA

'Media' is the plural of 'medium'. 'Media' is shorthand for 'mass media of communication' in advanced technological SOCIETY. 'Medium' refers to a single method of encoding and delivering messages to a broad public; thus, radio is a medium, television is a medium, newspapers constitute one medium; lumping together radio and television in all their forms gives us the electronic media; agglomerating newspapers and magazines gives us the print media. Both print and electronic media in all their forms make up 'the media' *tout court*. Note that this physical conception of the media is essentially technological, i.e. each of the media is not defined merely as the end product in the hands of the consumer/reader/viewer. Each medium is defined as an integrated system of invention, composition, presentation and delivery. As a mass medium, newspapers must be seen as a factory system of daily predictable output that involves brains, hands, paper, ink, steel and wheels. Borrowing from computer terminology, the media are hardware systems for handling the software

of information, enlightenment, entertainment. Generally, one speaks of the media in an all-inclusive sense that embraces both the physical system and its delivered messages, often called programming (from electronic media) or content (from print media).

'The medium is the message', a phrase of Marshall McLuhan's that the media have made universally known, should be understood therefore in two senses: first, the final display method or format of mass-mediated programming has a determining or at least limiting effect on whatever is said or shown *on the medium*; second, the integrated technological organization of a given medium invites or discourages certain types of messages, programming or content processed *through the system* because of the system's own internal needs. Thus, on a system where time is money, the sound-bite, slogan or jingle is the preferred unit of political meaning; on a system where central control is paramount, interminable speeches from the maximum leader are preferred. But given the choice, viewers will prefer the diverting jingle over the long speech because of the display capabilities of the medium. There is no market for bootlegged television speeches of Castro in New York, but MTV is worldwide and contraband videos of cause-related rock concerts are globally popular. Singapore, a centrally controlled authoritarian city-state where time is money, uses its media to enforce policy through slickly produced television minutes filled with music, handsome young people and the vacuous hope that marks product ADVERTISING in the West.

Rapid advances in communication technology have blurred the distinctions among media systems. More and more print media are processed electronically and the same kind of computer systems process words, music, images and format displays. This is reflected in ownership patterns, where the same company, like Sony, manufactures recording and display hardware and contracts musicians to own the final 'product': recorded songs or music videos. Newspaper empires often include television stations and satellite systems that can distribute not only television and radio but digitally encoded newspapers, including layout and typeface, to receiving printing plants around the world.

Cable system operators buy film studios so they can have a stock of software for their hardware.

The mass media of communication have enormous costs of maintenance which require either STATE support or commercial revenue or some combination of the two. Whatever the source of support, its size can only be justified by an equally enormous efficiency, return on investment or palpable political effects on the populace. The mass media thus tend to be servants of the established order and legitimizers of the status quo whether they glamorize British royalty, urge higher Russian production quotas or encourage smaller Chinese families or happiness-through-purchase in America.

These enormous trends toward centralization and homogeneity still do permit room for the occasional 'auteur' film of individual artistry, the profoundly critical television documentary, the journalistic exposé of corruption in high places, and other examples of independent thinking or original art. But the audience for such works is limited. The book, for so long the intellectual medium for innovation, discovery and critical awareness, has become part of the book business, which has fallen, necessarily, to the 'blockbuster syndrome'. Great books and good books are still published and some even turn a profit, but the book business is increasingly prey to the bottom line which is enhanced by the reflections of, and narrations about, celebrities from other media.

There is a significant but relatively minute counter-trend to such mainstream monoliths. New technologies centred around the increasingly more powerful personal computer are enabling smaller entrepreneurs and public interest groups to publish newsletters and produce radio and video cassettes of an 'alternative' provenance that criticizes the mainstream. GREEN, feminist, gay and some minority religious movements have made effective use of 'alternative media' in the West, as have outlawed political oppositionist movements from South Africa to Sri Lanka. By being user-friendly, communication production relying on such 'desktop' techniques demystifies the process and encourages non-professional use. But the media system is one of distribution as well as production and the former seems firmly in the control of large

entities: corporations, major religions and nation-states.

Converging ownerships, interlocking technologies and a common mass consumption all conspire to join the various media into one great media system. This is observed in the increasing legitimacy of 'media' as a singular noun, which conjures up the image of a television supermarket, with hundreds, thousands, millions of screens all showing the same picture at once, with legions of speakers playing the same rock music, all promoting a film showing in hundreds of thousands of small identical theatres worldwide on the same day. The media is the medium.

An enormous amount of research has been aimed at the media by both its exploiters and its critics. Advertisers, media owners and their managers are greatly concerned about the numbers of people they reach, about what kinds of messages move people to act the way they want, and about the inclination of those they reach to return to the same media source. Because of the presumed motives of those who commission it, this type of research is often termed 'administrative', and it is conceptually based on the transmission model of communication. A message is aimed at a specific target through a given medium with some kind of effect. A variant of this is the Harold Lasswell formula: who says what to whom with what effect? – a formula at least as old as Quintilian.

This conceptualization is result oriented and sees communication as producing effects, much as fertilizer grows grass or cue balls knock eight balls. Thus the 'effectiveness' of media campaigns to get people to buy soap or adopt birth control or vote Conservative is what is sought to be measured and the measure is tangible and finite: so many votes, so many (less) children, so many boxes of detergent. The psychological theory underpinning this kind of research is most often functionalism, which sees all voluntary human activity as motivated by the desire to find out what is going on, by the need to get along with others and by the urge to work out internal conflicts through some external symbol system. The last 'function' is explicitly Freudian in premise and much programming, self-consciously or instinctively, exploits feelings connected with sex, self-esteem or insecurity to motivate consumers.

Although administrative research still constitutes the vast bulk of media research because of the resources of BUSINESS, GOVERNMENT and other large organizations who command media, there is a growing body of research springing from an entirely different set of concerns. These are the fears and grievances of those out of the power loop of media control and the desires of social critics and intellectuals to understand the meaning and significance of media among individuals, societies and cultures. Although in fact there is no reason why the transmission model could not be used for much of this research – as it is, for instance, in studying the effects of PORNOGRAPHY on youth – the preponderant model leans away from the concern for concrete mechanical effects characteristic of the transmission model and leans toward what is loosely termed the ritualistic model. This model is more akin to anthropology and other cultural studies (as the other is closer to engineering and sociology). Here the interest is in discovering what kind of mentality is encouraged by the daily RITUAL of being exposed to mass media, with the emphasis on television, the most powerful and pervasive of the mass media in the industrialized world (and second only to radio, which it is overtaking, in the developing world). 'Mentality' embraces a broad sweep of cognate concepts: 'consciousness', 'values', 'social character', 'psychological type', 'psychographics', 'political awareness', 'leisure competence' and so forth. These in turn entail a variety of methods, including that of the literary or theatrical critic.

Because much of the pioneering work in this type of research was done by members of the Frankfurt School of social research (notably H. Marcuse, M. Hochheimer, T. Adorno, W. Benjamin), known for so-called critical theory, the great variety of this work is distinguished from the administrative by calling it critical research, following the distinction made in 1941 by Paul Lazarsfeld, a pioneer of modern administrative research.

News is a common feature of most media systems around the world and its transformations illustrate the nature of modern media systems as well as the guiding models for understanding media.

As the name implies, news is information about some recent event, deviating from expected routine. In the ancient world, official messengers brought news of military victory or defeat, natural disasters, notice of future unscheduled events. But for the most part, routine ruled human affairs and 'news' as we think we know it began with business, when trading associations in northern Europe shared information about commodity prices and other conditions that would affect profit, developing newsletters with the new print technology.

Mass media news is descended from this basic human practice of sharing and spreading information, but modern high technology and the political economy it serves have altered its nature.

First, news promulgation is now part of an industrial process which needs predictability and continuity. Thus, newspapers and news programme appear at an invariant daily, even hourly, schedule, with roughly the same amount of space and time allotted to news on a continuing basis. If there is some unprecedented cataclysm, more time or space may be allotted, but rarely is the news curtailed merely because fewer events happened. News has become a manufactured commodity, so its content is made to fit the amount of time or space routinely allotted for it. This, of course, changes the nature of news from that of the unexpected to that of the routine, for the most part. The characters may change and details may vary, but a relatively constant mix of crime, politics, entertainment and business affairs will be stretched or shrunk to fit its Procrustean medium. The designers of the format of the news, even if guided solely by system needs of predictability and control, still have had an impact on what people will think about, the categories under which they will arrange their experience and so forth. Media technology affects thought.

News programme managers, relying on administrative research, have discovered that in fact people who look at television news, for instance, do not do so in order to stay abreast of current affairs so much as to seek company and reassurance in a society that is increasingly mobile and without the market-place or water-well for friendly gossip and storytelling.

So the nature of the news programme is adjusted, now requiring attractive and friendly news-presenters, who joke and chat among themselves with an inclusive nod to the camera. They advise one on cooking, dining out, making friends, staying healthy. But these 'news teams' are paid companions, whose loyalty is not to their audiences but to their employers, who in turn are answerable to advertisers and/or the state. Their cosy personal advice thus often dovetails with advertised products or the government's current theme for public co-operation, be it paying taxes early or recycling trash or avoiding excessive cholesterol. The news has in this way become a format for socialization and acculturation in no small measure.

What is true of news is true of entertainment, EDUCATION or religion processed by the media system: the technology of the medium creates formats that are shaped for maximum effect by administrative research into a ritual whose ultimate social and cultural (and therefore moral and ethical) impact is analysed by critical research.

One must distinguish between moral and ethical issues that arise *within the context* of the media and those that are raised by *the nature of the system*.

Among the former we have a very familiar list of legitimate concerns:

- the differential rights of individuals, corporations and governments to secrecy versus the public's right to know;
- objectivity and fairness in coverage of controversial issues;
- the effects of pornography and other portrayals of objectionable or criminal acts on the impressionable;
- the validity of advertising claims and the exploitation of certain basic insecurities as a motivation for buying marginal products;
- news management and influence peddling on the part of government, business, labour, churches or any powerful interest group;
- the rights of journalists to protect their sources and their unpublished notes (in whatever medium) from unauthorized use;
- the obligations of journalists to reveal information to appropriate authority to protect life and property.

The 'morally correct' behaviour to be sought among these settings is usually obvious from commonplace sources and does not require any 'special media ethics'. Various professional guilds, trade associations and public interest groups have come up with guidelines for proper behaviour that cover most of the common cases under the above rubrics, honoured though some may be more in the breach.

Far from obvious are the ethically appropriate approaches to the problems of pornography, glamorized VIOLENCE and stereotyping of any kind, especially racial or sexual. But the moral complexity does not spring so much from the nature of media as from the nature of art and fiction: portrayal as an invitation to imitation or justification for immoral behaviour is a thorny problematic that both antedates and exceeds the context of modern media as such. In general, the transmission model has been applied here most unfruitfully, because its mechanistic presuppositions have led to the imposition or violation of taboos (nudity, *Grand Guignolism*, etc.).

In other words, almost all of the above cases can be adequately dealt with in principle within the common expectations of the system: if the media work properly, they will behave properly. It is a matter of adjustment, POWER and will – not so much understanding.

This is not true for those issues raised by the very nature of the system: when the media work properly, they may behave improperly and in some cases they may necessarily so behave.

The growing indispensability of mass media for reaching electorates, political parties, church congregations, the entire youth population and even widely dispersed intellectuals has forced not only politicians but educators, clergy and scientists to join merchants in adapting their messages to fit the exigencies of the media system. Eastern bloc politicians as well as electronic preachers have a common need for media consultants.

These media adaptations reach back into the substance of the senders and alter, in varying degrees, politics, religion, education. Even dissent and avant-gardism must now define themselves as over against mainstream media content and programming, which gives an unearned cachet to willed obscurantism.

In what senses are these developments for good or ill?

As we have seen, the techno-logic of mass media hardware is to reach larger and larger audiences. In principle, the drive of the machine is to reach everybody in the world simultaneously with the same message. The political economies within which media operate also mandate maximum use either for maximum profit or maximum control. The software must follow the hardware. And the software is nothing less than the symbolic transmission of CULTURE.

Over the years, therefore, mass media have developed a language of their own, a meta-language if you will, that may have local dialects of French or Chinese or Urdu. The curse of Babylon fragments the world audience, so it must be somehow overcome: the point of the meta-language is therefore accessibility; it must be readily understood by the largest number of people.

The image, as film distributors learned early, transcends the limitations of words. None the less, as they later learned, even images have a cultural setting. Thus, for truly international distribution, films had to have slightly different versions so as not to offend local taboos. In multi-ethnic markets, advertising agencies have set up departments to research the effects of images and words on cultural sensitivities. The Chinese, as legend has it, were thus saved from marketing a car called The Lemon and male underwear called Pansies to English-speaking cultures.

The ideal of the media meta-language, let us call it mediaspeak, is to come as close as possible to a transcultural, ahistorical, assumption-free Esperanto, that evokes no particular heritage or tradition. It aspires to be the broader equivalent of those indispensable graphic icons at international airports for toilets, luggage, cocktails, cabs and medical assistance. The export and import of consumer goods for supermarket shelves, the internationalization of personal computers with a common user icon-driven interface abet the global demand for a common reductive language.

But language is also the vehicle for morality, judgment, subtle analysis, religious tradition. The Christian cross or the Buddha are symbols; they have subtle evocative meanings, a penumbra of connotations. Airport graphics are not symbols, but signals, extensions of traffic directions for those already launched on a decided course. Mediaspeak strips language of its symbolic meanings, of its historical and traditional resonances, and pares words and pictures down to signals. It is an ideal system for selling products and a very ideal system for dictatorships and dirigiste regimes.

This single development has multiple moral effects. Vast treasures have been spent by a bankrupt United States on the Strategic Defense Initiative, an adolescent fantasy of total protection that scores of serious scientists have scorned as both dangerous and meretricious. But the cartoon graphics of 'Star Wars' in mass media have maintained sufficient support among the people to force a sceptical Congress to authorize continued billions of dollars.

The published statistics on Patriot missile effectiveness in the Middle East indicate miserable failure, but the pictures have mobilized not only cheering mass support, but serious arms sales among professional dealers.

While noting the force of images of suffering to mobilize aid for disaster victims, one must remember that the images often obscure the culprits and causes of the suffering so that symptoms are inadequately addressed while causes are blithely ignored, as in Ethiopia, Iraq, and Bangladesh.

These and other examples of the moral threat of mediaspeak in the contexts of religion, education, politics and science abound – all occasions when the media system operates as everyone expects it to.

The quotidian ethical problems of the media business require serious attention, but they are minuscule before the tidal wave of a moral deculturalization that the global media system is creating.

Barry, John A. (1991) *Technobabble*, Cambridge, MA: MIT Press.
Chomsky, N. (1991) *Deterring Democracy*, London: Verso.

Diamond, E. (1991) *The Media Show*, Cambridge, MA: MIT Press.

Entman, Robert M. (1991) *Democracy Without Citizens: Media and the Decay of American Politics*, New York: Oxford University Press.

McLuhan, M. (1989) *The Medium is the Message: An Inventory of Effects*, New York: Touchstone Books (first published 1967).

McQuail, Denis (1987) *Mass Communication Theory*, London: Sage.

——and Siune, K. (eds) (1986) *New Media Politics: Comparative Perspectives in Western Europe*, London: Sage.

Phelan, John M. (1980) *Disenchantment: Meaning and Morality in the Media*, New York: Hastings House.

——(1987) *Apartheid Media: Disinformation and Dissent in South Africa*, a Lawrence Hill Book, Chicago, IL: Chicago Review Press.

Schiller, Herbert I. (1989) *Culture, Inc.: The Corporate Takeover of Public Expression*, New York: Oxford University Press.

Schneider, L. and Wallis, B. (eds) (1991) *Global Television*, Cambridge, MA: MIT Press.

John M. Phelan

METHODISM

The Methodist movement was inaugurated by the Wesley brothers in eighteenth-century England; its roots are to be found in the serious religion of the Puritans, the Eucharistic devotion of the Non-Jurors, and the spiritual and philanthropic reforms of the evangelical revival, combined with the discipline, fellowship, devotion to Christ and missionary zeal of the Moravians. These influences were transmitted to John and Charles Wesley through early experiences: in their Epworth home, the Oxford Holy Club, in Georgia, and in religious societies in London on their return from Georgia.

In one of these in Aldersgate, London, distinctive religious experiences gave the spur to a popular preaching mission, including field-preaching and epic journeys across the whole of England. A lasting feature of their work was the development of a 'connexional' system by which those who responded to their message were linked together and submitted to a central leadership. John Wesley developed a route toward holiness for every convert through societies, classes and (an inner group of those seeking perfection) the bands. Committed to scriptural standards of Christian belief and living John Wesley made these his own through profound and distinctive insights: his emphasis that all may be saved, all may know they are saved, and all may be saved to the uttermost was given distinctiveness by his recognition of the Holy Spirit's work through 'the means of GRACE', and in a holiness and perfection summarized in the LOVE command and expressed in practical living. This resulted in a wide range of acts of service to the poor of eighteenth-century England and to a focusing of missionary work in areas where poverty was rife. John read widely and avidly on his journeys, editing a series of Christian classics which he made available to his preachers. One result of this pattern of revival was an increase in literacy and in social and political potential among the early Methodists. Reactions to early Methodism were often violent and public, sometimes associated with a fear of Jacobite influence, sometimes inspired by an anticipated threat to privilege and traditional social patterns.

When John Wesley died (2 March 1791) the frictions which had been controlled by his AUTHORITY were almost impossible to resolve. New forms of Methodism came into being, often shaped by external influences. The fissiparous character of nineteenth-century Methodism is noteworthy. American camp meetings and organization among labourers were factors in the emergence of Primitive Methodism, a movement which illustrated the Weber principle of routinization of charisma as the sect developed into a denomination (*see* SECTS). The issue of internal authority led to several divisions, not least the United Methodist Free Church, and, during the Fly Sheet Controversy, to splinter groups which still remain separate in the 1990s (e.g. the continuing Wesleyan Reform Union). Others (e.g. the New Connexion formed in 1798 under the influence of Alexander Kilham) entered the Unions which took place in 1907 and 1932. In the nineteenth century the Methodist societies in England grew with the growth of the population and the development of the towns of the Industrial Revolution. Methodist schools and colleges continued in that new context the educational role of early Methodism, often, as in the case of the teaching of the sciences, leading the field.

The international character of modern Methodism is often overlooked; Methodists number more than 60,000,000. The movement abroad began as early as 1744. The initial spread of Methodism abroad was sometimes due to army personnel (Europe; Ceylon (Sri Lanka); India). American Methodism began in a class meeting in Maryland in 1763 and has developed into the largest single part of the Methodist family. Methodism reached Canada via an itinerant preacher who emigrated in 1765 and reached the West Indies (1760) through a West Indian slave owner converted on a visit to England. Medical and educational work opened up limited developments in China (1840) and Burma. The African continent became a significant missionary field in the middle of the nineteenth century. The first Methodist Chapel in Australia dates from 1817. Work among the dates in New Zealand dates from Samuel Leigh's work in 1820. In Tonga and Fiji, as elsewhere, early martyrdoms paved the way for eventual conversions.

The twentieth century has been marked in British Methodism by the development of a Free Church identity, a deepening consciousness of social and political responsibility, and Methodist and ecumenical union negotiations. Some suggest that this interest in union negotiations is evidence of the lateral movement of a church which has ceased to advance; others see it as evidence of a new IMPERIALISM. Others (e.g. Australian Methodists now part of the Uniting Church) see the tradition of Wesley as promoting social religion and openness to the faith of others. Some claim that in the inter-church process and worldwide ecumenical discussion the kind of connexionalism which Wesley established and which has been shaped through the history just described, in which churches voluntarily submit their AUTONOMY to one another in matters of mutual concern, presents a significant ecclesiological model.

Support for Thatcherism was claimed in Wesley's advice 'Gain all you can. Save all you can. Give all you can.' However, the commitment of Wesley to the poor, which modern Methodism has transposed into the contemporary situation through its £3 million fund for 'Mission alongside the Poor', involves a sacrificial generosity not evident in all of Thatcherism's supporters. A similar interest in Methodism's role in 'preventing REVOLUTION', alleging a sublimating of revolutionary zeal, has some justification in Wesley's emphasis on conformity with public law (although his eventual opposition to the slave trade and support of the legal rights of Americans in the American War of Independence provide notable exceptions). But early Methodism may more properly be described as a pro-reforming milieu where budding reformers were educated in the techniques of organization.

Anglican–Methodist Unity (1968) London: SPCK.
Brake, G. Thompson (1984) Policy and Politics in British Methodism 1932–1982, London: Edsall.
Brewer, E.D.C. and Thumma, Scott L. (1990) World Methodism and World Issues, Atlanta, GA: Emory.
Currie, Robert (1968) Methodism Divided, London: Faber & Faber.
Heitzenrater, R.P. (1984) The Elusive Mr. Wesley, 2 vols, Nashville, TN: Abingdon.
Hempton, David (1984) Methodism and Politics in British Society, London: Hutchinson.
Rack, Henry (1989) Reasonable Enthusiast, London: Epworth.
Statements of the Methodist Church on Faith and Order 1933–1983 (1984) Methodist Publishing House.
The Constitutional Practice and Discipline of the Methodist Church (1991) London: Epworth.
Turner, John Munsey (1984) Conflict and Reconciliation, London: Epworth.
See also articles in the Epworth Review; also Histoire des Saints et de la Sainteté Chrétienne Vol. IX.

Ivor H. Jones

MIGRATION

Migration refers to movement from place to place as distinct from emigration, which means permanent departure from a country, and immigration, which means entry into a foreign country on a permanent basis. Migration includes both, but also may describe internal movements within a country and temporary movements in search of work. Migration affects the demographic fate of a country in ways that cannot always be foreseen. Thus the British population was 41 million in 1900: had there been no emigration, it would now be over 70 million. The USA had a population of 3 million at its first census of 1790: today, as a result of immigration, it has 230 million. Similarly Canada has grown from 3.6 million in 1871 to over 25 million today, and Australia from 3.7 million in 1900 to 15 million today.

Many migrations are the result of political or economic pressures, or of persecution or discrimination (as with the Huguenots in the seventeenth century, the Russian and Polish Jews in the nineteenth century, the Ugandan Asians and Bosnians in the twentieth century). But migration is also closely related to labour demands and to economic possibilities. After 1945 Britain encouraged and welcomed European labour. Between 1945 and 1951 over 300,000 workers moved to Britain under the Polish Resettlement Scheme and the European Voluntary Workers Scheme. Between 1945 and 1957 net immigration of European nationals to the UK was over 350,000. Germany has been a major receiver of migrant workers, but during the 1966–7 industrial recession around 60,000 migrant workers left the country.

West Indian labour was also recruited by Britain as a result of the labour shortage of 1951. The McCarran–Walter Act of 1952 in the USA (which virtually ended West Indian immigration) encouraged an increase in migration to the UK. Between 1954 and 1961 4,500 Barbadians were recruited by London Transport, the hospitals and the catering trades. The pattern of migration during these years shows a broad correlation with labour demands. Peach has shown how migration from the Caribbean to Britain between 1950 and 1960 followed labour needs closely.

Immigration is often seen as leading to unemployment, though this is based on the mistaken view that there is only a given amount of work to go round. In fact migrants often generate new forms of economic activity. Nevertheless, attitudes in the country of reception vary. The USA, Canada and Australia have tended to stress the economic and social benefits which accrue from immigration, while Britain has stressed the tensions and the fear of racial unrest. Some countries have suffered from massive emigration, Ireland being a dramatic example.

A major factor in migration patterns is the displacement of people through WAR, famine, POVERTY or persecution. Such dislocation is often intensified by the scapegoating of refugees who are seen as the carriers of disease, subversion or contamination. Legislation to control immigration is often the result of panic about 'undesirable aliens'. Thus in 1905 the Aliens Act was passed to control Jewish immigration from Eastern Europe. While most refugees flee from one Third World country to an adjoining one, there has in recent years been a significant increase in migration to the USA and Europe, particularly to Germany. The exceptional turmoil in Zaïre, Somalia and Angola led to increased emigration to Europe in 1991, followed by a decline in 1992. Between 1989 and 1992 the numbers seeking asylum in Western Europe doubled.

Migration patterns to, and within, Europe have been affected by the creation of the European Union and by the collapse of the communist regimes in eastern Europe and subsequent developments. There are 16 million people in the European Union whose original homes lie in 'third countries'. About 7 million have no nationality other than their country of origin. The free movement of nationals under the Treaty of Rome does not apply to such people. Rights of movement and FAMILY unity are related to work and production, not to a person's status as a human being or to CITIZENSHIP. In the aftermath of the ending of boundary controls, increased surveillance and internal controls have linked terrorism, drug traffic and illegal immigration.

Most European countries have accepted more refugees than Britain where only 3 per cent of those accepted for settlement in 1992 were refugees. But there is great concern about European policies relating to immigration and asylum, and the creation of a community of displaced persons throughout the European Union. The term 'social dumping' is often used of such processes, and the demands for tighter controls on movement into the European Union has been termed a 'Fortress Europe' policy.

There has never been any discussion about immigration policy in British history, nor has there been a coherent policy but rather a series of responses to particular pressures. British race relations policy has been based on the crude and unexamined belief that effective ('firm but fair') control is the basis of racial harmony. There were calls for immigration control as early as 1954 and these increased after racial disturbances in 1958, leading to the Commonwealth Immigrants Act 1962, originally a temporary measure. The Labour Government's 1965 White Paper was the first to establish quotas and it formed the basis for subsequent legislation. It has been called 'the keystone of modern racism' (Robert Moore). Subsequent legislation (such as that of 1968, 1971 and 1988) has led to increased restrictions on family unity and on rights of appeal. Critics of immigration policy have argued that the legislation and its implementation comes into conflict with HUMAN RIGHTS and with family life. Combined with the British Nationality Act 1981, immigration law and policy, it is claimed, has created types of second-class citizenship. Today there is very little primary immigration to the UK. In 1982 there were only 100 primary immigrants from the Indian subcontinent. In 1992 a total of 52,600 were accepted for permanent settlement of whom 35 per cent were wives of men already here.

In the USA, there was virtually unrestricted immigration from 1790 to 1874. After 1874 a series of bills controlled the entry of lunatics, idiots, paupers, polygamists, epileptics, anarchists, illiterates and subversives. Some ethnic groups were excluded (as in the Chinese Exclusion Act 1882, and the 1907 Act which prohibited the entry of Japanese and Koreans). Since 1965 there has been a more open policy, and today the USA receives more immigrants than any other industrialized nation – 1.8 million in 1991 – and contains the biggest immigrant population in the world. It took in some 9 million immigrants between 1983 and 1993. Because it is the only First World country which shares a 2,000 mile border with a Third World country, 90 per cent of immigrants to the USA are from Third World countries, particularly Mexico, which sent 3 million to the USA in that period. Recent years have seen increased anxiety about immigrants' access to welfare. It is argued that the recent North American Free Trade Agreement, by increasing prosperity in Central and South America, will in the long term reduce the pressure to immigrate to the USA.

Since migration is closely linked to CITIZENSHIP, there is a need for greater precision in this area. While 'citizen of the EU' is used in documents, its definition is imprecise. The Treaty of Rome (articles 48–57) deals with freedom of movement but this has not been linked to any clear attack on discrimination. Unless there is co-ordinated action against discrimination, the status of migrants will remain insecure and the concerns about an 'underclass' will grow.

Castles, Stephen and Kosack, Godula (1973) *Immigrant Workers and Class Structure in Western Europe*, Oxford: Oxford University Press.
Dex, Shirley (1992) *The Costs of Discriminating Against Migrant Workers*, Geneva: International Labour Organization.
Dummett, Ann (ed.) (1986) *Towards a Just Immigration Policy*, London: Cobden Trust.
Foot, Paul (1965) *Immigration and Race in British Politics*, Harmondsworth: Penguin.
Gordon, Paul (1985) *Policing Immigration*, London: Pluto.
——(1989) *Fortress Europe? the Meaning of 1992*, London: Runnymede Trust.
——and Klug, Francesca (1985) *British Immigration Control: a Brief Guide*, London: Runnymede Trust.
Hawkins, Freda (1985) *Critical Years in Immigration*, Kingston and Montreal: McGill-Queens University Press.
Macdonald, Ian (1983) *Immigration Law and Practice in the UK*, London: Butterworth.
Miles, Robert (1982) *Racism and Migrant Labour*, London: Routledge & Kegan Paul.
Peach, Ceri (1968) *West Indian Migration to Britain: A Social Geography*, Oxford: Oxford University Press.
——(1978–9) 'British unemployment cycles and West Indian immigration 1955–1974', *New Community* 7: 40–3.

Kenneth Leech

MILLENARIANISM

The definition of the term is problematic. In the Christian theological tradition, millenarianism (or millennialism or chiliasm) refers to the belief that the reign of Christ for a thousand years (the figure may be understood literally or as symbolic of a very long period), as depicted in Chapter 20 of the book of Revelation, is to be expected in the future. The millennium (the thousand-year reign of Christ and the saints) is envisaged as an ideal time, at the end of the history of this world, in which conditions of life in this world will be radically transformed. But the millennium is not the final state of collective salvation. It belongs still within the history of this world, and so has a penultimate and transitional character. It is a temporal period of earthly perfection preceding the final, eternal state of heavenly perfection. Millenarianism differs from other forms of Christian eschatology by interposing this penultimate ideal period between the present age and the eternal consummation. Of course, for millenarians the millennium, especially if it is believed to be imminent, is often the main focus of expectation. By contrast with mainstream Christian views of the final state of salvation, which have often been extremely otherwordly and disconnected from the history of this world, millenarianism envisages a thisworldly goal of God's salvific activity in history, but only as a penultimate goal.

The term may be extended to include any expectation of a penultimate ideal time, even if this belief is not based on Revelation 20. But if millenarianism is to remain a usefully precise term, it needs to be distinguished both from expectations of an ideal time which, even if it is portrayed in strongly thisworldly terms, is understood as the final state of salvation and from the kind of Utopianism which conceives of the ideal STATE in spatial rather than temporal terms (the ideal SOCIETY already exists somewhere else). However, during the last four decades, the term millenarianism has come to be used, in anthropology, sociology, religious history and the comparative study of religions, in a much less precise sense, to refer to any belief in an ideal, future, collective state of salvation in this world. For many purposes of studying groups motivated by eschatological beliefs, the distinction between a final and a penultimate ideal state may not be important, but it is integral to the Christian tradition of beliefs about the millennium and will be used to define millenarianism in this article (*see* ESCHATOLOGY).

A useful distinction can be made between two types of Christian millenarianism, known as premillennialism and postmillennialism. The distinction concerns the relation between the millennium and the second coming (parousia) of Jesus Christ. According to premillennial expectation, the parousia will precede and inaugurate the millennium. According to postmillennial belief, it will follow the millennium. This distinction can be related to, but not identified with, another distinction between passive and active millenarianism, i.e. between the belief that the millennium will come about through a purely divine act for which believers can only pray and wait, and the belief that believers can play an active part in bringing in the millennium. Premillennialism tends to be passive (because the parousia is a sheerly supernatural event of divine intervention in history) and postmillennialism active. But these correlations between premillennialism and passivity and between postmillennialism and activism are not absolute. For example, the Fifth Monarchy Men in mid-seventeenth-century England, who were premillennialists, awaited the divine signal which would call them to co-operate with the returning Christ in establishing his kingdom on earth. Many premillennialists in the modern period have believed that by preaching the Gospel to all nations the church can fulfil the major precondition for the parousia and so hasten the coming of the millennium, even though the latter is to be established by God alone. Conversely, many postmillennialists, though believing that the preaching of the Gospel and other kinds of Christian activity will be actually instrumental in establishing the millennium, have thought this could happen only when such activity is blessed by an unprecedented supernatural movement of the Holy Spirit.

Many writers associate millenarianism with sectarian groups on the fringes of mainstream Christianity and withdrawn from society. In sociological terms, millenarianism is thought to characterize groups of the sect-type, rather than the church-type or denomination-type (*see* SECTS). There is truth in this, but it is not the whole truth. It is true that, for much of Christian history, premillennialism has been regarded as unorthodox, as have some postmillennial groups, such as the Spiritual Franciscans, though postmillennialism has often been more acceptable to the mainstream. It is also true that many millenarian, especially premillennial, groups, with their expectation of an imminent divine intervention, have tended either to withdraw from worldly society or at least to show no interest in improving it. They have seen it as doomed to imminent JUDGEMENT by God and have expected it to be, not improved, but replaced by a radically different society, whether that is to be established by divine intervention alone or in part by their own revolutionary activity. But there are also counter-examples. In twentieth-century America, for example, premillennialism has become part of mainstream PROTESTANTISM, while the 'Moral Majority' movement of the 1980s, a form of conservative Christian political activism, relied on Christians of premillennial belief for much of its support. Because millenarianism envisages an ideal state of human society which highlights, by contrast, the shortcomings of contemporary society, it is almost always to some degree critical of the status quo, but such criticism may take the form of quietist withdrawal, reformist activity within the prevailing system, or activity aimed at revolutionary change. We should also remember that, like other forms of eschatological belief, millenarian beliefs may be held with varying degrees of enthusiasm and commitment. Groups whose expectation of the millennium is at first a strongly motivating feature may later give less emphasis to this aspect of their religion while continuing to hold millenarian beliefs as part of their formal belief-system.

In the second and third centuries, premillennialism, inspired not only by Revelation 20 but also by Jewish APOCALYPTIC literature, was common in the church. To a church subject to persecution and martyrdom by the empire of Caesar, it promised the reign of Christ and the restoration of paradise on earth. But the emphasis, in this millenarian hope, on ideal material conditions of life on earth led to its discrediting, in the East by a more philosophical and spiritualized eschatology influenced especially by Origen, and in the West by Augustine, who reinterpreted the millennium of Revelation 20 as the present age of the church, which would be succeeded, at the parousia, immediately by the eternal state. Under Augustine's enormous influence over Western Christianity this became the standard view and premillennialism came to be regarded as virtually a heresy.

The ideas of the twelfth-century abbot Joachim of Fiore inspired a new form of eschatological expectation which in the later Middle Ages and the Reformation period represented the major alternative to the Augustinian view. This was a form of postmillennialism. Before the end of history, there would be an age of the Spirit, a period of spiritual prosperity and peace for the church on earth, to be inaugurated by a spiritual intervention of Christ (not his bodily parousia) in the power of the Spirit. As well as inspiring some radical groups, notably the Spiritual Franciscans, in the late Middle Ages, Joachimism had a very widely diffused influence down to the seventeenth century, affecting Italian Renaissance humanists, Protestants and sixteenth-century radicals, as well as Catholics. In the early modern period it chimed in with a widespread sense of the dawn of a new age – whether because of the advance of learning, the discovery of the New World, the hope of a renewal of the Catholic church or the spread of the Protestant Gospel.

Some sixteenth-century Anabaptist leaders and groups were millenarian, though fewer than is often thought. But the Anabaptist kingdom of Münster (1535) provides the classic case of revolutionary activist millenarianism. From Münster the saints expected to go forth throughout the world killing the wicked, in preparation for the coming of Christ to establish his kingdom. The catastrophe of Münster led most Anabaptists to renounce millenarianism, and provided Catholics and Protestants with a vivid illustration of its perils.

Protestant millenarianism originated at the end of the sixteenth century and became a significant force, in both premillennial and postmillennial forms, only in the seventeenth century. Postmillennialism reflected a growing optimism about the success of the Gospel within history, and took the form either of the expectation of a period of 'latter-day glory' for the church on earth, in which the conversion of the Jews (which often features in modern millenarianism) played a prominent role, or of the more specific hope of the millennial reign of Christ. Premillennialism, though by no means limited to radical groups, often characterized them, especially during the period of political and religious revolution in mid-seventeenth-century England, when the ideas of the learned exegetes were taken up and given more militant or democratic form by popular sectarian prophets and socially radical soldiers in the parliamentary army.

The eighteenth century was the great age of Protestant postmillennialism, which played a key role in the development of missionary thinking. The British and American religious revivals were seen as the first ripples of a great movement of conversion which would engulf the world, and a view which gave human activity a significant part in God's purpose of establishing his kingdom on earth was a major stimulus to missionary activity. But the postmillennial hope was also being approximated to the growing secular doctrine of progress. In America after the Revolution postmillennialism helped to form America's sense of national destiny, with a mission to promote DEMOCRACY in the world, while in both Britain and Europe nineteenth-century postmillennialism merged imperceptibly into Protestant Liberal theology's faith in human ethical and cultural progress. It is debatable how far, as some have argued, seventeenth-century millenarianism prepared the way for the Enlightenment belief in inevitable progress in history, but it is certainly true that eighteenth- and nineteenth-century postmillennialism harnessed religious aspirations and activism to the same end.

However, premillennialism, now often embraced as a reaction against secular ideas of progress, enjoyed a significant revival in early nineteenth-century Britain, and soon blossomed into a variety of new forms, such as the dispensationalist eschatology of J.N. Darby, one of the founders of the Brethren. This version of premillennalism (which includes the idea of the 'secret rapture' of believers before the parousia) has become, in the twentieth century, a characteristic belief of American fundamentalist Christians. Many of the new Christian denominations and fringe Christian sects of the nineteenth and early twentieth centuries had their origins in British or American millenarianism and teach some form of premillennialism: the Brethren, the Christadelphians, the Seventh-day ADVENTISTS, the Jehovah's Witnesses, the MORMONS. The extent to which imminent eschatological

expectation dominates such groups – and therefore the extent to which they can be labelled millenarian movements – varies from group to group and varies over time. The early Pentecostal churches also held a premillennialist eschatology (which was often stimulated by the belief that a prophesied latter-day outpouring of the Spirit was occuring in their experience), and consequently much of the twentieth-century Pentecostal movement, including the recent Restoration movement in Britain, is premillennial.

Finally, there is a sense in which the whole project of the modern West, in its quest for a more perfect world through technology and political change, has been a kind of secular millenarianism. The ambiguity of what this project has achieved has never been more apparent. But the millenarian impulse seems hard to escape: some of the most radical ecological protest groups promise a return to paradise not unlike the millenarianism of the early church. The challenge to the contemporary church is to formulate the Christian hope in a way which (with the postmillennial tradition) promotes responsible and hopeful activity, inspired by the vision of a better world, but (with the premillennial tradition) avoids the dangerous Utopianism of believing that humanity can design and build the KINGDOM OF GOD itself.

Ball, B.W. (1975) *A Great Expectation: Eschatological Thought in English Protestantism to 1660*, Leiden: Brill.

Cohn, N. (1970) *The Pursuit of the Millennium: Revolutionary Millenarians and Mystical Anarchists of the Middle Ages*, 3rd edn, London: Paladin.

Daley, B.E. (1991) *The Hope of the Early Church: A Handbook of Patristic Eschatology*, Cambridge: Cambridge University Press.

Harrison, J.F.C. (1979) *The Second Coming: Popular Millenarianism 1780–1850*, London: Routledge & Kegan Paul.

Oliver, W.H. (1978) *Prophets and Millennialists: The Uses of Biblical Prophecy in England from the 1790s to the 1840s*, Oxford: Oxford University Press.

Olson, T. (1982) *Millennialism, Utopianism, and Progress*, Toronto and London: Toronto University Press.

Reeves, M. (1976) *Joachim of Fiore and the Prophetic Future*, London: SPCK.

Rowland, C. (1988) *Radical Christianity*, Cambridge: Polity.

Sandeen, E.R. (1970) *The Roots of Fundamentalism:*

British and American Millenarianism 1800–1930, Chicago, IL and London: University of Chicago Press.

Weber, T.P. (1979) *Living in the Shadow of the Second Coming: American Premillennialism 1875–1925*, New York and Oxford: Oxford University Press.

Richard Bauckham

MIRACLE

The concept of miracle admits of various shades of definition dependent upon the precise context within which it is employed. Thus the term may simply signify unusual events which apparently conflict with known or assumed 'laws of nature', with no specific consideration of their ultimate cause or source. More typically, however, even in discussions of a purely philosophical nature, divine or 'supernatural' agency is appealed to as bound up with the meaning of miracle – hence David Hume's classical definition: 'A transgression of a law of nature by a particular volition of the Deity, or by the interposition of some invisible agent' (Hume 1902: 121, n. 1). In the specific context of Christian THEOLOGY this teleological orientation is further refined in a soteriological and moral direction. Miracles are viewed as particular instances of divine action in the world which stand out from the general body of human experience, and which are located within the broader matrix of a revelatory and redemptive narrative from which they receive their meaning and which serves to differentiate them from mere arbitrary wonders. It has been noted that 'miracles are preeminently sociological phenomena' (Waida 1987: 548) being bound up with specific societal and fiduciary contexts in which they are recognized and acclaimed as such. A purely empirical approach to the subject is thus unlikely to generate satisfactory or decisive results, since the interpretation of the relevant evidence (whether historical, experimental or whatever) will inevitably be shaped by the plausibility structure from within which the investigation is conducted.

Inasmuch as definitions of miracle uniformly identify alleged instances on the basis of their apparent transcendence of the ordinary, one key theme in discussions of the concept (especially in the modern period) has been that of the nature and status of those alleged 'laws of nature' which are thereby seemingly transgressed, broken or interfered with. The basic framework for discussion which has prevailed in the Western tradition differentiates sharply between the 'natural' and the 'supernatural', although the precise boundaries of the former category are drawn differently by different contributors to the debate. For some, the term 'nature' is to be understood in a materialistic sense in which all that is real finds its place and is sufficiently accounted for within a closed physical system of cause and effect; thereby reality is denied to any aspect of our seeming experience which cannot be accounted for empirically and verified objectively. For others, 'nature' is to be defined more broadly, incorporating a supraphysical dimension of reality (psychical, spiritual or whatever), but still essentially perceived as a closed system in terms of which, by a process of rational analysis, all that is, is in principle explicable. The success of modern science is then frequently perceived as the successful pushing back of the boundaries of knowledge by uncovering the causal connections between events within this total system, the so-called laws of nature. The discussion of miracle centres on the question of whether or not events may be acknowledged within this system which are inexplicable within its terms and thus of 'supernatural' origin. Thus both sides in the debate often agree at least in defining the problem as one of the TRUTH or falsity of alleged interference with natural laws by some agency lying beyond the scope of the system.

Some have viewed such 'laws' as essentially prescriptive while yet corrigible. On this view, when a true counter-instance to any supposed law occurs, the proper response is not to seek some cause which transcends the system (and hence to see the law as violated) but rather to redefine and thereby refine the system itself. The law in question is shown to be inadequate; but the system remains adequate to account for the so-called miracle, which is thus granted a perfectly 'natural' explanation. A different approach views the laws of nature as essentially *a posteriori*, descriptive of what normally happens in certain circumstances, and as lacking any absolute predictive force. On this view both 'true nomologicals' and 'true counter-instances' can be tolerated, whether the agency behind the counter-instance be natural or supernatural. Yet a third view allows true nomologicals a relative prescriptive force (in so far as they are true), but insists that their function is to describe what ordinarily happens when certain circumstances arise within the pattern of nature. The point about miracle, as presented by the theologian, is that it involves the introduction of a new factor into this pattern, inexplicable in terms of the pattern itself, and thereby renders the law invalid. What occurs is thus not a violation of a law but rather a situation to which that law no longer applies. Thus miracle is better defined, it is held, as an event which is in principle inexplicable within the terms of the natural alone, rather than one which breaks nature's laws. In this case it is not the laws of nature which are violated, so much as the naturalistic or deistic assumption that God (if there is a God) never acts in such a way as to introduce such new and unlooked for influxes of creative energy into the system.

In many respects this cosmological framework itself is open to criticism. It is striking that in the Christian East, where nature is viewed not on the analogy of a closed mechanical system but as an open continuum characterized at its edges by mystery, the debate over miracle has not arisen in the same form. None the less, one need not be in the grip of a tacit deism to think of miracle as in some sense a break with the ordinary and the expected. If it were not so, there would presumably be no need to identify or single out such events for special consideration in the first place.

Miracles, or 'signs', form an integral part of the apostolic traditions concerning Jesus, where they take their place as concrete testimonies to and embodiments of the inauguration of the KINGDOM OF GOD associated with his person. In Christian understanding the incarnation itself, the very personal presence of God in the midst of human history and under the conditions of human existence, constitutes the central miracle to which all others point and by comparison with which they pale into relative insignificance. From the apostolic period until the Middle Ages it was common for miracles to be alleged to have occurred, especially in connection with sites or persons of particular religious significance. By the time of the Renaissance the nature of such claims had reached such superstitious and incredible proportions as to be in part responsible for the rationalistic backlash which ensued. Miracle was for many part of the bad old scheme of things which the new science and the intellectual liberty of the Enlightenment were helping to set aside. New-found confidence in the power of human reason and rapid advances in the natural sciences both served to encourage the view that eventually all that was mysterious and a source of wonder to humans would be fully understood. This basic attitude treated the miraculous elements of the gospel tradition in various ways. Pantheists, such as Spinoza in the seventeenth century, identified God with the order of nature discovered by the human mind, and considered any violation of this order to be tantamount to divine self-contradiction. Deists, meanwhile, insisted that God was not such as to interfere with the world having once set it on its orderly course. Some (e.g. Reimarus) proceeded to view the alleged miracles of Jesus as a sorcerer's deception of the ignorant, while others preferred a less cynical approach, presenting them as events with purely natural explanations, which were either misunderstood or misconstrued by the bystanders. In the nineteenth century, D.F. Strauss propounded the view that miracle constitutes part of the 'mythological' strand in the kerygma, and should be understood as making a theological and interpretative statement about Jesus' significance. For the most part, all but the most conservative were agreed that, however they were to be accounted for, the miracles did not actually happen.

Developments in modern science and other fields of understanding in the last fifty years have favoured a rather more open-ended perspective on reality. Both within the church and outside it there is a perceptible dissatisfaction with rationalism, materialism and numerous other associated aspects of the Enlightenment's bequest to modern humans. Perhaps it may be that, in renewed consideration of the concept of miracle within the context of a view of CREATION as an essentially open rather than closed system, there lies a potentially fruitful route to dialogue between the natural and social sciences and Christian theology, and a reintegration of theology into the mainstream of intellectual life in the West.

Basinger and Basinger (1986) *Philosophy and Miracle*, Lewiston/Queenston: Edwin Mellen Press.

Fuller, R. (1963) *Interpreting the Miracles*, London: SCM.

Hume, D. (1902) *An Enquiry Concerning Human Understanding*, 1777 edn, reprinted Chicago: Open Court.

Keller, E. and Keller, M. (1969) *Miracles in Dispute*, London: SCM.

Kelsey, M. (1972) *Encounter With God*, Minneapolis, MN: Bethany Fellowship.

Lewis, C.S. (1947) *Miracles*, London: Fount.

Polkinghorne, J. (1988) *Science and Creation*, London: SPCK.

Swinburne, R. (1970) *The Concept of Miracle*, London: Macmillan.

Waida, M. (1987) 'Miracles', in M. Eliade (ed.) *Encyclopedia of Religion*, London: Macmillan.

Wiles, M. (1986) *God's Action in the World*, London: SCM.

Trevor Hart

MISSION

The very early Christians can be seen as a movement *within* first-century Judaism. They continued to frequent both Temple and Synagogue and many of them remained 'zealous for the Law'. One of their distinguishing features, however, already prefigured perhaps in Jesus' treatment of non-Jews, was an interest in reaching out to the Gentile world with the message of the Gospel of Jesus Christ. Much of the history of the early Church and indeed of Christian doctrine can only be understood in the context of the struggle by Jewish Christians to accommodate themselves to the results of the mission to the Gentiles.

We know that at the time Judaism attracted many formal converts and many more 'God-fearers'. Some Jews may even have had a missionary concern for Gentiles (cf. Matthew 23: 15). The sheer scale and enthusiasm of the Church's Mission to the Gentiles, however, were unprecedented. The universal mandate of the Risen Christ which sent the Church to all the nations is found, in one way or another, in all

the four Gospels and in many other parts of the New Testament. From the earliest times, then, the Church seems to have understood itself as 'missionary by its very nature'.

The mission of the early Church was greatly aided by the unification of the Mediterranean world which had taken place under the Roman Empire. The pervasive influence of Hellenistic culture was also a factor in promoting cohesion in this part of the world. The *Pax Romana*, even though not perfect, facilitated the movement not only of 'missionaries' but of all kinds of Christians who travelled for trade, military or FAMILY reasons and took the Gospel with them.

We must not imagine, however, that the spread of the Christian faith was restricted to the Mediterranean world. The faith spread rapidly, for instance, in the Persian Empire (at that time the other superpower). Christians attracted as much persecution there as they did in the Roman Empire. Later, they were to be emancipated in a way very similar to their EMANCIPATION through Constantine's and Licinius' 'Edict of Milan'. Armenia became the first kingdom to describe itself as 'Christian' and Ethiopia was not far behind. Whatever the worth of the stories about St Thomas's visit to India, Christianity was well established in the south before the fifth century had ended.

One of the reasons for the rapid spread of Christianity was the capacity of the Gospel (and its purveyors) to appeal to the worldviews, thought-forms and idioms of diverse people. Lamin Sanneh of Yale has called this the 'translatability' of the Gospel. Paradoxically, however, as Christianity became more and more identified with particular cultures, Oriental or Western, its 'translatability' in respect of cultures not yet influenced by the Gospel began to suffer. In some parts of the world a stage was reached when Christianity became part of the description of communal identity for certain groups, over and against other groups who understood themselves, and were understood by others, in different ways.

The rise of Islam in the Middle East severely restricted the mission of the Oriental Churches in their own heartlands. They continued with their missionary work *outside* the world of Islam, however. The Assyrian Church of the

East (known in the West as the Nestorian Church) continued with its work in India and China, while the Coptic Church in Egypt continued to support the work of the Church in Ethiopia.

The West too was 'hemmed in' by Islamic expansion into North Africa, West Asia, southern and eastern Europe and by the domination of the sea-routes by the Muslim navies. One attempt to break out of this *impasse* took the form of the Crusades. Even in the medieval West, however, there were individuals and groups who advocated a peaceful approach to Islam. Raymond Martin (1230–84), for example, encouraged the study of Islamic literature and philosophy, while Ramon Lull (1233–1315) was a missionary in North Africa and died as a result of his labours there. Francis of Assisi's encounters with Muslims are well known.

Both the Dominicans and the Franciscans were involved in mission to Muslims during the Middle Ages. The Franciscans, moreover, had a well-developed THEOLOGY of mission. According to them, there were two 'modes of Christian presence': first, the witness of life and service which did not entail verbal proclamation and, second, proclamation which should lead to conversion and baptism. The latter mode had to await a discernment of the right time when it was appropriate to preach. The mode of presence alone was generally seen as a preparation for the mode of preaching and could last for many years.

The churches of the Reformation did not show much interest in the worldwide mission of the Church. This was partly due to the fact that the Protestant powers still did not have access to sea routes but also because the churches' identification with a particular people made it difficult for them to cross frontiers of CULTURE and race. A certain kind of dispensationalism in their theology, which sought to limit the commandment to disciple the nations to the early Church, did not help either. By contrast, the counter-Reformation in the Roman Catholic Church produced a renewed commitment to World Mission in that Church. By this time, Spain and Portugal, both Roman Catholic nations, were becoming great maritime powers. Papal decisions, moreover, which divided up the newly discovered lands in the Americas and elsewhere among them, expressly enjoined on them the obligation to spread the Catholic faith in these lands. *'Padroado'* (or official) clergy, who often travelled with the expeditions, quickly became established in the colonies and were identified with the colonial establishment. The religious orders, and particularly the Jesuits, when they arrived were often more interested in the plight of the indigenous people, in their culture and how Christianity could be made relevant for them. For these reasons, there were serious clashes between the officially established clergy and the religious orders, and sometimes between the orders themselves. The Jesuits, in particular, took the question of inculturation seriously from the very beginning. They created the so-called Indian and Chinese rites in the sixteenth and seventeenth centuries and maintained an open attitude to cultural customs such as the veneration of ancestors. Their opinions were not always upheld by ecclesiastical AUTHORITY and at least part of the reason for their suppression in the eighteenth century by Pope Clement XIV had to do with their accommodation to the cultures of indigenous peoples.

By this time the sea routes were opening up to the mainly Protestant countries of northern Europe. Along with this, Christians reading the Bible in these countries were feeling the call to mission in other parts of the world. Very often the established state churches were unwilling or unable to affirm these vocations. This led to the re-emergence of the 'voluntary principle' in World Mission. In the eighteenth century this principle had already been at work in the organization of the movement against the slave trade (and later SLAVERY itself). In the nineteenth century it would be used in various movements which sought to ameliorate the lot of the poor. Its advocates argued that the principle was to be found in the Bible, in the way some Hebrew prophets were called to fulfil a particular vocation over and against the nation and cult, for instance. It could also be seen in the ministry of prophets and evangelists in the New Testament period and in the sub-apostolic Church. We have already seen how important the religious orders have been for World

Mission. This is true not only of the Western tradition but of Eastern Orthodoxy and of the Ancient Oriental churches as well. These orders too embody the voluntary principle in a particular way.

Much of the missionary work done in the heyday of the modern missionary movement was done through the agency of voluntary societies that came into being in the eighteenth and nineteenth centuries. These societies did not only send out missionaries from their own countries but were often engaged in sending people from different parts of the world to wherever there was need of them. They also employed a considerable number of people who did not cross cultural boundaries but worked as evangelists, teachers and pastors within their own culture. In time, this was to result in the formation of indigenous churches in many different situations. Once an indigenous church had come into existence, the PROPERTY and finances of the mission agencies were often handed over to it.

Just as the early Christians had been assisted in their mission by the *Pax Romana*, so also modern mission from Europe was often *facilitated* by the structures and movements produced by European colonialism. The administration often ensured the safety of missionaries (who usually belonged to the dominant race), there was generally a network of European administrators, traders and military personnel to whom the missionary could turn for support and friendship, and the infrastructure of roads and railways established by colonial powers helped with mobility. At the same time, we need to remember that the colonial powers sometimes obstructed Christian mission if it was seen to be hostile to their interests in a particular region.

Because of the association of the modern missionary movement with Western colonialism, some Christian leaders in Asia, Africa and Latin America have argued that there should now be a moratorium on mission from the West. This would give the so-called 'younger' churches a chance to emerge with their own identities and priorities and would make for genuine partnership in the Gospel. It should be noted that political situations and GOVERNMENT policies have caused *de facto* moratoria in foreign personnel in several countries. It needs also to be acknowledged that, in at least some of these situations, the local church has been strengthened as a result and has been able to develop new ways of partnership with churches in other parts of the world.

David Barrett and others have noted the shift in Christian demography. There are now more Christians in Asia, Africa and Latin America than in 'the north'. It is not surprising, therefore, that major initiatives in Christian mission should be coming from 'the south'. This is especially so of those countries which have become wealthy in recent years and where the church has grown rapidly. But it is not confined to them and a feature of modern mission is the way in which churches in poor countries are engaging in mission across cultures, not least to countries in the richer parts of the world. Some mission agencies in 'the north' have sensed that this is God's will for the present and the future and are actively supporting the churches in 'the south' in the fulfilment of their vocation. Others, however, particularly those related to conservative churches, continue to perpetuate very traditional models of mission developed in an era which has long since disappeared.

Throughout Christian history, the Church has had ambivalent attitudes to the traditional beliefs and worldviews of people it is trying to evangelize. Sometimes it has been possible to acknowledge God's presence and work in various cultures and to relate the intellectual, moral and social achievements of these cultures to the work of the eternal *Logos* or of the Holy Spirit. At other times, the Church has had to pronounce a negative JUDGEMENT on what has been seen as error, moral failing or even oppression in particular cultures. On occasions the Gospel has been understood as *fulfilling* a people's spiritual aspirations and on other occasions it has been seen as a *replacement* for erroneous beliefs and practices. It should not be imagined, however, that these seemingly opposed stances are always mutually exclusive. It may well be that in its encounter with *each* culture the Gospel affirms certain aspects of that culture and judges others. Controversy has often occurred, however, among Christians as to which aspects of culture are affirmed and which judged in the course of this encounter.

Whatever the results of mission may have been in terms of church extension, it is clear that the modern missionary movement has made a significant social impact on many cultures, peoples and even religious traditions. The campaign against *suttee* (the custom of widows throwing themselves on their husband's funeral pyre), against Caste, as a basis for social organization, and the promotion of the rights of women in modern India, for instance, can be traced back to the influence of Christian mission. The reform of Hinduism itself and the renewed emphasis within it on social justice is not unrelated to contact with Christianity. M.M. Thomas has shown in his work *The Acknowledged Christ of the Hindu Renaissance* how this influence has been recognized by leading Hindu thinkers such as Raja Ram Mohan Roy, Rabindranath Tagore and Mahatma Gandhi. Both Julian Pettifer and Richard Bradley in their book *Missionaries* (related to a television series of the same title) and John Harris, author of *One Blood*, have shown how Christian mission was crucial in the survival of many vulnerable groups of indigenous people as they encountered MODERNITY in the form of rapacious landowners, unscrupulous traders, diseases to which they had no resistance and systematic discrimination by the colonial powers.

It is also true, however, that missionaries were and are people of their time and culture. At times they have been insensitive to the values and beliefs of other people. Sometimes, wittingly or unwittingly, they have colluded with tyrannical or oppressive authorities, colonial or indigenous. They have not always seen the real needs of the people amongst whom they have worked and sometimes they have perpetuated unsuitable structures and policies simply because these furthered their own self-interest. These are matters for confession and repentance, but they should also serve as a warning to those who have responsibility for the future of mission.

Barrett, D.B. (1982) *World Christian Encyclopaedia*, Oxford: Oxford University Press.
Bosch, D. (1991) *Transforming Mission: Paradigm Shifts in the Theology of Mission*, New York: Orbis.
DeLange, N. (1976) *Origen and the Jews: Studies in Jewish–Christian Relations in Third-Century Palestine*, Cambridge: Cambridge University Press.
Farquhar, J.N. (1913) *The Crown of Hinduism*, London: Oxford University Press.
Harris, John (1991) *One Blood*, New York: Lion Publishing.
Nazir-Ali, M.J. (1990) *From Everywhere to Everywhere: A World View of Christian Mission*, London: Collins.
Neill, S. (1964) *A History of Christian Missions*, London: Penguin.
Panikkar, R. (1981) *The Unknown Christ of Hinduism*, revised edition, London: DLT.
Pettifer, J. and Bradley, R. (1990) *Missionaries*, London: BBC Publications.
Sanneh, L. (1989) *Translating the Message: The Missionary Impact on Culture*, New York: Orbis.
Thomas, M.M. (1969) *The Acknowledged Christ of the Hindu Renaissance*, London: SCM.
Young, W.G. (1974) *Patriarch, Shah and Caliph*, Rawalpindi: CSC.

Michael J. Nazir-Ali

MODERNITY

Modernity is a term used with growing frequency to capture the unique traits of the type of SOCIETY which – beginning roughly from the seventeenth century – entrenched itself first in Europe and then was imposed, or emulated, throughout the globe; it is meant to replace other terms deployed for the same purpose, such as 'capitalist', 'industrial' or 'technological' society. The term extends to the totality of social system the quality of 'being modern', the description first introduced in European discourse to denote such spiritual endeavours and their products as stepped beyond the standards set by tradition, while confident that the transgression constitutes an improvement over the past; it implies that the lack of respect for tradition, resentment of set limits and courage to explore uncharted territories is the most seminal, as well as unique, among the attributes of that society in all its areas and functions (in science, art, economics, as much as in the patterns of human relations and identity formation). Marx's memorable phrase 'all that is solid melts into air, all that is sacred is profaned' is taken to be the motto of the modern form of life.

The obsessive urge to move beyond the

boundaries once treated as unencroachable is rooted in the pursuit of perfection: an ideal never fully satisfied by any of its present incarnations, and therefore precluding satisfaction with any achieved state. As there is always more to be done (and more that could be done once the limits to human capacity are no more recognized), there can be no excuse for stopping further efforts however impressive the successes to date. On the global-societal scale, the 'perfect STATE' was as a rule envisaged as a 'perfect order', doing away with the notorious messiness, contingency and uncontrollability of the natural state of affairs (hence the intense attention paid by modern utopias to architecture and urban planning, the two epitomes of an orderly and controlled world). On the individual scale, the search for perfection took the form of life dedicated to the implementation of a 'life project' and construction of matching self-identity; again, any achieved state was but a step on the road still leading ahead, a temporary station to be soon left behind.

Such a unique social condition, responsible for the exceptional, restless dynamism which sets modernity apart from all other historically known types of human cohabitation, emerged originally in Europe and in Europe only (only later forcing or alluring the rest of the world to follow the pattern). Roots of modernity are set deeply in European history. They reach as far as the early established European Christianity, which set the first model of transgression of the present by its unattainable ideal of godly life, moral perfection, lifelong work for spiritual salvation; and by nudging all man-made orders to try constantly – never fully succeeding – to approximate the ideal of the KINGDOM OF GOD. Of profound influence also was the Christian proselytizing urge, which in the name of spreading the word of God de-legitimized wholesale traditions and customary styles of life of the heathen world. A similarly unsettling role in the early European history was played by the stubborn presence of the 'ghost of the Roman Empire', which prompted the kings and the clerks of royal households to scour the documents of Roman Law and ancient political wisdom for the ideal patterns of which their own dominions were but pale reflections.

Between themselves, the two ideal models undermined from the very start of European history intellectual and practical respect for the limits, hallowed customs, prohibitions, so overpowering in other types of society.

Historians point to numerous and diverse developments in other fields which successively contributed to the unstoppable growth of the European urge and capacity for expansive transgression. Without hoping to make the list of factors exhaustive, one may but name the early harnessing of non-human sources of energy, beginning with water and wind; the unusual flair for mechanics, which resulted in the invention of contraptions with a revolutionary potential for work and (as in the case of clocks) the total organization of life; the rapid demographic growth of the eleventh and twelfth centuries which led to the establishment of cities and the emergence of a qualitatively new urban style of life and a new POWER base for monarchies; the institutional AUTONOMY of schools and universities; the geographical discoveries of the fifteenth and sixteenth centuries, followed by the colonization of new territories – which in view of the already achieved technological superiority of the colonizers were seen as 'empty' and served as training grounds for 'absolute beginnings', for designing and constructing a social order 'from scratch'; Reformation and Counter-Reformation, which brought the ideal models themselves, heretofore exempt from transgressive ambitions, within the horizon of a critical examination and revision; the rise of powerful state bureaucracies which sapped the custom-led reproductive mechanisms of local communities and made the day-by-day normative regulation of social life into the object of conscious policy; the expansion of the capacity, and determination, of the state powers to design, administer and supervise new artificial social orders. The accumulated multidimensional developments culminated in the eighteenth–nineteenth century political and technological revolutions, leading to the spread of democratic regimes and industrial production – both lifting the long-standing propensity for 'transgression of boundaries' to a radically higher level. Colonialism together with the intensification of worldwide physical and symbolic communication set in motion the processes of *modernization* in territories distant from the European birthplace of modernity. In the course of the twentieth century, modernity became the first civilization in history which stands a chance of becoming truly global. 'Modernization' – emulating most, if not all, the patterns set and practised by modern societies and thus sharing in the experience of modern life – has become the practice, demand and declared purpose throughout the globe, with the possible exception of the Islamic part of the world.

Theorists agree that setting free creative potential previously held in check by the iron grip of tradition, coupled with the de-legitimation of all limits once fixing the horizon of life improvement, was the secret of modernity's global success. It was also the main cause of its endemic contradictions and chronic afflictions.

Taking the lid off human desires, the prime condition of modern dynamism, has also rebounded in typically modern discontents. Pursuit of happiness promoted to the supreme objective of life efforts prevents any achieved state being judged as the state of happiness. The anxiety arising from the non-satisfaction of needs is perpetuated and exacerbated by constant creation of ever new temptations fast institutionalized as needs. Anticipations grow as a rule quicker than their implementations, standards of good life rise faster than their achievement, and hence, in Lewis Carroll's words, 'it takes all the running you can do, to keep in the same place'.

Strong on instrumental efficiency and effectiveness, modernity is much weaker on the ends instrumental skills may serve. After all purposes that human life may fulfil have been discredited one by one and rejected as happiness-constraining and hence oppressive, only self-actualization, itself a flexible and under-defined notion, is left. From the perspective of this purpose, the world has no other meanings than those of a site of individual self-satisfaction and self-expression, or the collection of obstacles for the same. Nature fell the first victim of such a perception, being cast as a raw resource meant to be given shape better fitted for human enjoyment – with consequences which come belatedly to be feared and regretted. But the instrumental posture tried on Nature has been extended over inter-human relations, with other people treated increasingly as resources or impediments for individual self-actualization. The long-term effect was the gradual erosion and weakening of institutionalized forms of human relations with MARRIAGE and the FAMILY turned into stepping-stones on the road to self-actualization, to be left behind once their uplifting potential had been exhausted.

The ultimate achievement of the modern spirit of transgression has been the undermining of the same twin resolutions it gave birth to: of the building of a human-made, perfect, rational order, obeying solely the dictate of reason, and of the challenge of self-identity construction. Experiments in social engineering on a global-societal scale (the communist adventure being a most radical among them) failed to solve any of the problems modernity set to resolve (with misery and POVERTY most notable among them). They were found instead to generate irrationality and waste instead of bringing closer the promised rational order, fell into disrepute and have been all but abandoned or are treated with considerable suspicion. Identity construction oriented to an over-arching life project has dissipated into a succession of inconclusive, inconsequential and contingent episodes. The dreams of tamed and controlled ENVIRONMENT and self-controlled life have been effectively displaced by the politics of crisis management and the life strategy of avoiding risks, this time mostly man-made and arising from unanticipated consequences and mutual incongruence of human objectives.

Modernity is notorious for the abortive attempts to ground an ethics which can be squared with the resentment of boundaries it promotes. On the one hand, the domination of instrumental attitude led to the exemption of a wide sphere of human actions from moral JUDGEMENT – declaring them 'morally indifferent'. On the other, the primacy accorded to the self-actualization among life pursuits tends to give priority to the individual rights over duties to the other, and makes it exceedingly difficult to justify the exemption of any duty (for instance, the duty to care for the less fortunate regardless of his or her merits or of own benefits) from the universal opprobrium which is the lot of constraint and oppression. Finally, assigning to the society (in practice, to its governing agencies) the sole right to legislate on ethical matters has facilitated many a genocidal excess while at the same time relieving the individual from moral concerns and responsibility.

These and other maladies balance the comparative comforts made possible by modern achievements and are increasingly regarded as a price which cannot be avoided. The ambiguity of modern achievement, projected back on the original intentions and anticipations, had prompted intellectual criticism and dissent throughout the history of modernity; indeed, one may say that, paradoxically, modern CULTURE was by and large at war with the very society it was, as cultures are, meant to service – a circumstance which further added to the intrinsic dynamism of modernity. The present stage in the development of modern society (defined by some theorists as *late modernity*, by others as *postmodernity*) is prominent, however, for the emphasis put in intellectual commentaries on the less prepossessing, even sinister outcomes of modern change and a widely held belief that the hopes of modernity are never to be fulfilled and that insisting on their fulfilment is wrong and harmful. Messiness of social arrangements, irrationalities they breed, plurality of cultures, absence of universal grounds of TRUTH, morality and artistic taste are not temporary irritants to be eventually overcome in the course of the construction of rational order, but permanent and ineradicable traits of the human condition. Their entrenchment, much like its intellectual recognition, is itself seen as an inescapable product of transformations brought about by modernity.

Adorno, Theodor and Horkheimer, Max (1979) *Dialectics of Enlightenment*, London: Verso.
Bauman, Zygmunt (1987) *Legislators and Interpreters*, Cambridge: Polity.
Berman, Marshall (1983) *All That is Solid Melts into Air*, London: Verso.
Carroll, John (1994) *Humanism*, London: Fontana.
Giddens, Anthony (1990) *The Consequence of Modernity*, Cambridge: Polity.
Hall, John A. and Jarvie, I.C. (1992) *Transition to Modernity*, Cambridge: Cambridge University Press.
Heller, Agnes and Feher, Ferenc (1991) *The Grandeur and Twilight of Radical Universalism*, New Brunswick, NJ: Transaction Publishers.
Kumar, Krishan (1978) *Prophecy and Progress*, Harmondsworth: Penguin.
Smart, Barry (1992) *Modern Conditions, Postmodern Controversies*, London: Routledge.
Turner, Bryan S. (ed.) (1990) *Theories of Modernity and Postmodernity*, London: Sage.

Zygmunt Bauman

MONETARISM

The expression 'monetarism' was first used by the economist Karl Brunner (1968). The word, however, denotes a bundle of views which have at their centre an updated version of one of the oldest ideas in economic theorizing: the notion that the overall price level is a direct function of the stock of money within an ECONOMY. This doctrine is known as the quantity theory of money.

The first clear statement of this theory appears to have been made by the French political philosopher Jean Bodin (1530–96) in his work *Réponse aux Paradoxes de Malestroit* (1569). Here Bodin explains the spectacular rise in the French price level in the first half of the sixteenth century by reference to a number of causes, the most important of which is the increased volume of gold and silver coming into France from Spain but originating from the new Spanish lands in Central and South America.

The best known, however, of the early expositions of the quantity theory is given by the Scottish philosopher and economist David Hume (1752) in his essay 'On money'. After declaring that the total stock of money has a 'natural proportion to labour and commodities' (p. 284), Hume continues as follows:

It seems a maxim almost self-evident, that the prices of everything depend on the proportion between commodities and money, and that any considerable alteration on either has the same effect, either of heightening or lowering the price. Increase the commodities, they become cheaper; increase the money, they rise in their value. As, on the other hand, a diminution of the former, and that of the latter, have contrary tendencies.

(Hume 1752: 290)

Hume's account of the quantity theory then became a central feature of classical economics, which dominated economic thought from his time until the end of the second decade of the twentieth century.

Early in the twentieth century the quantity theory was presented by the American economist Irving Fisher (1911) in the form of his famous equation

$$M V = PT$$

In this, M is the stock of money, V is the velocity or number of times each period a currency unit (a dollar or pound, etc.) is used, P is the average price of a transaction and T is the total number of transactions. But unless V is here defined precisely, the equation is a near-tautology (with V simply taking whatever value is required to equalize both sides of the equation). Fisher was aware of this point, and contended that velocity was a function of institutional factors and changed only slowly. In the short run, both V and T can therefore be treated as constant. With this established, an empirical theory emerges, namely that, in Fisher's words, 'one of the normal effects of an increase in the quantity of money is an exactly proportional increase in the general level of prices' (p. 157).

Six years after the publication of Fisher's book, Arthur C. Pigou (1917) of the University of Cambridge subtly altered the emphasis of the doctrine. First, the T in Fisher's equation (which denoted *all* transactions, including asset transactions such as sales of second-hand houses) was replaced by y standing for 'real national income' or 'output' in order to make the equation more appropriate for the dynamic wealth-creating part of the economy. Second, Pigou argued that, when market equilibrium prevails in the monetary sector, the outstanding stock of money is equivalent to the quantity of money willingly held or demanded. With monetary equilibrium, it is thus the case that $M = M^d$ (the quantity of money supplied equals the quantity demanded). Pigou then rewrote Fisher's equation as a theory of the demand for money:

$$M^d = kPy$$

where $k = 1/V$. In this form, the equation states that the stock of money demanded in nominal or cash terms, i.e. without reference to the price level, is a proportion k of nominal national income Py. The two versions of the quantity theory, as a theory of the price level and a theory of the demand for money, are not of course independent of each other. An expansion of the money stock is held to produce a rise in the general price level because the new total quantity of money is no longer willingly held, and the excess is then expended on goods and services thereby bidding up their prices.

After dividing both sides of his equation by P, Pigou obtained a theory of the demand for real cash balances:

$$M^d/P = ky$$

(The quantity of money demanded in real terms is a proportion k of real national income y.) It should be noted that Pigou, unlike Fisher, did not treat V (or its reciprocal k) as constant in the short run, but rather, to some extent, as a function of prevailing market rates of interest. The question of the determinants of k ('Cambridge k', as it came to be known), was not explored deeply by Pigou, but the matter was pursued with vigour by his able student John Maynard Keynes.

In the hands of Keynes (1930, 1936), the theory of the demand for money (or, as he calls it, the theory of liquidity preference) underwent a complete transformation. He divided the demand for money into two distinct parts: (a) a transactions demand, which was a positive function of real national income; and (b) an asset demand, which was a negative function of the market interest rate. The market interest rate is equivalent, in the simplified world of Keynes's theory, to the market yield of perpetual government bonds (by 'market yield' is meant the fixed annual sum payable as a percentage of the market price of the bond). Under this conception, which is based on the controversial assumption that the only alternative to holding excess cash balances is to acquire bonds, velocity becomes highly variable. Briefly, if the Central Bank increases the quantity of money this is used not to bid up the price of goods and services but to bid up the price of bonds, which produces a lower market interest rate; and this in turn increases the demand for money. So, on Keynes's theory, where the aggregate demand for money is highly sensitive to the market interest rate, velocity falls as money supply is increased and rises as money supply is decreased. These changes in velocity thus tend to cancel out the effects on the price level predicted by the old quantity theory. It can be seen that in the equation

$$M^d = 1/VPy$$

(where $M^d = M$ in equilibrium), if V should fall in an exactly counteracting manner as M and M^d rise, then, assuming real income y remains constant, changes in the money stock would have no *direct* effect on the price level P.

According to Keynes, the influence of money supply changes on real-world economic activity is always transmitted via changes in market interest rates. Thus, an expansion of the money stock lowers interest rates and, while this has no *direct* effect on either the price level or real income, there could be indirect effects. A fall in interest rates tends to stimulate private investment spending, and this in turn, via the multiplier mechanism, raises real income. The price level itself is not affected until real income reaches the full employment level, and only further monetary expansion after that point leads to a rise in the price level. On the stimulation of investment, it should be appreciated that Keynes himself believed that private investment spending was not particularly elastic (i.e. sensitive) to changes in interest rates. And for this reason, if an economy were stuck in a state of depression and high unemployment, Keynes advocated fiscal policy (changes in government spending and taxation) as a more effective means of raising real income and employment than the use of monetary policy (expansion of the money stock to lower interest rates with a view to encouraging private investment).

Monetarism arose in the 1950s and 1960s in opposition to Keynesian theories of the role of money in the economy. And especially, it was a reaction to the long-run inflationary consequences that appeared to be attendant in the USA and UK of governments acting upon Keynesian policy recommendations. The pioneer of monetarism was the creative and single-minded American economist Milton Friedman (who received the 1976 Nobel Prize in recognition of his contribution to theoretical economics).

If a single date is sought for the origin of monetarism as a distinctive economic doctrine, it must be the publication in 1956 of Friedman's essay 'The quantity theory of money – a restatement' in a book edited by himself and entitled *Studies in the Quantity Theory of Money*. In his essay, Friedman set out many of the themes that either he himself, in a profusion of books and learned articles, or his many followers were to refine into the theoretical system of monetarism.

Friedman (1956) takes his starting point from the quantity theory regarded as a theory of the demand for money. He then proceeds to argue that the aggregate demand for real cash balances is a stable function of a small number of variables including the level of real income, the expected rate of inflation, and the market rates of return on assets that are substitutes for money as a means of wealth-holding.

A significant element in Friedman's theory is that the demand for money is, in his words, 'highly stable' (p. 16) – not meaning constant, but rather predictably related to its determining factors. This is important, because a theory of the demand for money is also a theory of velocity, a theory that explains what stock of money will be willingly held at each level of real national income. And unless velocity can be adequately explained, the influence of changes in the quantity of money on the price level may be indeterminate. In time, much of the opposition to monetarism was to revolve around this particular point.

Friedman (1956) also expresses deep scepticism about the Keynesian claim that the demand for money could become infinitely interest-elastic, and acknowledges that the most favourable condition for his restatement of the quantity theory is when the demand for money is 'quite inelastic' (p. 15) to the interest rate and other market rates of return factors. This is an important consideration and, like the matter of stability, is a major source of contention between monetarists and their adversaries. A great deal is at stake, because a highly interest-elastic demand for money opens the door to Keynes's argument that an increase in the money stock has little direct effect because it automatically brings in its wake an accommodating increase in the demand for money.

It is a central contention of monetarists, following the restated quantity theory, that the single most important cause of changes in nominal national income is changes in the quantity of money. While monetarists accept the old classical position that in the long run 'real' economic variables (such as the level of real income, the real rate of interest, real wage rates and the volume of employment) are determined exclusively by supply-side conditions such as the state of the labour market and prevailing technology, they also argue that in the short run variations in the quantity of money can have significant real consequences. The monetarist argument here stems from Friedman (1968) in his critique of the thesis of Phillips (1958) that there is a robust long-standing trade-off between unemployment and the rate of inflation as proxied by the rate of change of money wages (the higher the rate of inflation, the lower the rate of unemployment). Friedman rejects Phillips's analysis on the grounds that wage bargainers are concerned with future real wages not just money wages, and that Phillips neglects the important role that agents' expectations of future inflation plays in current bargaining behaviour. Friedman adjusts the Phillips curve so that movement along it shows the trade-off at a given level of inflationary expectations. In the short run, an increase in the rate of growth of monetary expansion that causes the rate of inflation to rise above the rate of expected inflation leads to a temporary fall in real wages which can produce a temporary stimulus to employment. But in the long run, once inflationary expectations have fully adjusted, Friedman and Schwartz (1963) argue, variations in the quantity of money do not produce changes in real variables: they only affect the price level.

Monetarist doctrine follows pre-Keynesian economic theory in holding that the private sector of the economy is self-stabilizing and self-adjusting. For monetarists, all serious episodes of extreme fluctuation in output (for instance, the Great Depression of the early 1930s) have their origin in misguided government policies. Such policies usually take the form of either attempts to maintain aggregate expenditure by continuously fine-tuning the rate of monetary growth, or attempts to offset imagined cases of market failure by disruptive intervention with the free operation of the price mechanism. Monetarists believe that governments should eschew interventionist policies (whether in the monetary or fiscal arenas) and should instead resort to predictable rule-based behaviour. In particular, monetarists agree with Friedman (1968) who first recommended the adoption of the firm rule that monetary expansion ought to take place at a regular pre-announced rate equivalent to or around the economy's spontaneous rate of growth of real income.

On fiscal policy, as opposed to monetary policy, most monetarists would differ little from Friedman and Heller (1969) in their opposition to government endeavours to lessen the fall in employment during business recessions by undertaking countercyclical public spending financed by borrowing. The argument here is that fiscal action is unable to achieve the intended goal because any increase in government spending would tend to 'crowd out' an equivalent volume of private investment expenditure. Since monetarists believe such expenditure to be highly sensitive (negatively) to interest rate changes, such crowding out would occur, they maintain, as a direct repercussion of the rises in interest rates that substantial increases in government borrowing would produce.

It is not misleading to think of monetarism as being a theory that is composed of two distinct but closely interrelated parts: an account of the demand for money that functions as an explanation of inflation; and a theory of the overall functioning of a free-enterprise economy. The first part is summarized by the idea that in the long run inflation is a purely monetary phenomenon in the sense of being exclusively a function of the rate of growth of the money stock that is higher than the rate of growth of real income. The second part has at its heart a conception of a free-enterprise economy as an essentially self-correcting system where the predominate source of instability is erratic government policy, especially, but not uniquely, in the field of monetary policy.

The theory of monetarism rests on a number of empirical claims. The three most important are the following: the demand for money is intrinsically stable over time and exhibits a low degree of interest-rate elasticity; private investment expenditure is highly interest-elastic; and the major markets of modern free-enterprise economies, including the labour market, are *efficient* in the sense that they rapidly adjust to maintain continuous clearing at an equilibrium price in the light of new information and expectations.

These foundational propositions are crucial for the theoretical credibility of monetarism. Needless to say, however, these notions have been the objects of intense scrutiny amongst economists since Friedman restated the quantity theory in 1956. But despite the time that has passed, no clear and widely accepted verdict concerning these basic ideas has yet emerged.

Few economists would dispute that a massive and persistent monetary expansion is the straight road to hyperinflation and economic collapse. (For an outstanding analysis of the causes and economic consequences of the main hyperinflations of the twentieth century, see Cagan (1956).) What is of more interest is how well the policy precepts of monetarism can be applied in the more usual circumstances of advanced economies where annual inflation is likely to be in single percentage figures. In these circumstances, the practice of monetarism faces the twin problems of defining the 'quantity of money' and then of controlling the rate of growth of what has been defined in an environment where most of what people call 'money' consists not of banknotes and coins but interest-yielding deposits which owe their origin to credit creation by the private banking sector.

Even leaving aside the definitional problem, monetarist theorists consider that Central Banks are effortlessly able to exercise tight control over the growth of total credit within the relevant currency area. The experience of the 1980s, however, in the UK, the USA and elsewhere, is that such control is immensely difficult in a financially deregulated world where national economies are closely integrated by a high volume of international trade, banking and investment flows.

Certainly, some countries, most notably Germany, have been more successful than others. The policy of controlling an economy's credit growth appears more likely to be achieved if the Central Bank is constitutionally independent of day-to-day political direction and is accountable only to its country's legislature. Also, a necessary condition for success seems to be the existence of the institution of a fractional reserve banking system, in which the growth of private sector credit can be curtailed directly at source by the strict control of the issue of reserve banking assets which under LAW private banks are required to hold to a given fraction of their total deposits. 'Monetary targeting', of the sort practised by British governments from December 1976 onwards, where the aim is to regulate the supply of money by manipulating the *demand for credit* by adjusting short-run interest rates, is now generally regarded as a failure. In the real world, it seems, the anti-inflationary precepts of monetarism are best applied within German-style institutions.

Artis, M.J. and Lewis, M. (1991) *Money in Britain*, Hemel Hempstead: Philip Allan.

Bodin, J. (1569) *Réponse aux Paradoxes de Malestroit* (cited by E. Roll, (1938, 1961) *A History of Economic Thought*, London: Faber & Faber, p. 59).

Brunner, K. (1968) 'The role of money and monetary policy', *Federal Reserve Bank of St Louis Review* 50: 9–24.

Cagan, P. (1956) 'The monetary dynamics of hyperinflation', in M. Friedman (ed.) *Studies in the Quantity Theory of Money*, Chicago, IL: University of Chicago Press, pp. 25–117.

Congdon, T. (1992) *Reflections on Monetarism*, Aldershot: Edward Elgar.

Desai, M. (1981) *Testing Monetarism*, London: Frances Pinter.

Fisher, I. (1911) *The Purchasing Power of Money*, New York: Macmillan.

Friedman, M. (1956) 'The quantity theory of money – a restatement' in M. Friedman (ed.) *Studies in the Quantity Theory of Money*, Chicago, IL: University of Chicago Press, pp. 3–21.

——(1968) 'The role of monetary policy', *American Economic Review* 58: 1–17.

——(1991) *Monetarist Economics*, Oxford: Blackwell.

——and Heller, W. (1969) *Monetary versus Fiscal Policy*, New York: Norton.

——and Schwartz, A.J. (1963) *A Monetary History*

of the United States, 1867–1960, Princeton, NJ: Princeton University Press.

Goodhart, C.A.E. (1975) *Money, Information and Uncertainty*, London: Macmillan.

Gowland, D. (1991) *Money, Inflation and Unemployment*, 2nd edn, Hemel Hempstead: Harvester Wheatsheaf.

Hume, D. (1752) 'On money', in E.F. Miller *David Hume: Essays – Moral, Political and Literary*, Indianapolis, IN: Liberty Classics, 1987, pp. 281–94.

Keynes, J.M. (1930) *A Treatise on Money*, London: Macmillan.

——(1936) *The General Theory of Employment, Interest and Money*, London: Macmillan.

Laidler, D.E.W. (1985) *The Demand for Money*, 3rd edn, London: Harper & Row.

——(1990) *Taking Money Seriously*, Hemel Hempstead: Philip Allan.

Phillips, A.W. (1958) 'The relation between unemployment and the rate of change of money wage rates in the United Kingdom, 1861–1957', *Economica* 25: 283–99.

Pigou, A.C. (1917) 'The value of money', *Quarterly Journal of Economics* 32: 38–65.

Schwartz, A.J. (1992) *Monetarism and Monetary Policy*, IEA Occasional Paper 86, London: Institute of Economic Affairs.

Vane, H.R. and Thompson, J.L. (1979) *Monetarism: Theory, Evidence and Policy*, Oxford: Martin Robertson.

Thomas S. Torrance

MONOTHEISM

Monotheism is normally taken to refer to that conceptualization of God in Western masculinist religions (Judaism, Christianity and Islam) not only as being one but as transcending the universe, and as being omnipotent and self-subsisting. It is generally reckoned to be the highest stage of religious development, surpassing polytheism (the belief in many gods); it being held both that, on philosophical grounds, that which is ultimate cannot admit of multiplicity, and also that such a conceptualization of God represents the highest stage of moral development on the part of a SOCIETY which so conceives God. Such a God represents absoluteness rather than relationality. God is said to be separate from and other than humankind. Indeed God is classically said to have aseity, to be *a se*, complete in God's self. The implication of monotheism is that other so-called gods are in fact idols and to

worship them is BLASPHEMY. The Christian doctrine of the TRINITY is sometimes said to mitigate monotheism, in conceiving relationality as central to reality. However, this is to speak of relationality within God and still allows the concept of God to have priority in relation to humanity.

In recent years feminist scholars in particular have explored the relation between a concept of monotheism being held by a society and the pattern of social relationships pertaining within it. It is maintained that such a conceptualization of God makes for a dualistic understanding of the relationship between God and humanity, a dualism which is then repeated within human relations as men come to play the role of 'God' in relation to a humanity conceived as 'female'. Thus in the book of Hosea (and this is found running through the books of the prophets) Jahweh (or God) is understood as male and compared with the (male) prophet Hosea; while Israel which is said to have gone astray is conceived as female, indeed compared to a prostitute and vilified. Again within Christian thought, God (or Christ) is conceived as male in relation to a church symbolized as female and the bride of Christ. In each case the male has priority and is held to be good, while that which is represented as female is secondary and seen as wayward. It is supposed that AUTHORITY should lie with the male partner and obedience with the female. In Christianity humanity is often said to be represented by Mary, who casts herself as the servant of a God symbolically understood to be male.

Rita Gross (herself a Jew who has converted to Buddhism) writes:

> Monotheistic thought does tend toward dualism. The One is distinguished from all other phenomena and valued and exalted above them as supreme. The One and all else are not only distinct but separate and, more important, there is a gulf between them. The One is on high and all else is of lesser reality and value, under its control, whether that control be loving or tyrannical. Those who consider themselves to be in relationship with that One repeat these patterns, creating separations between themselves and those outside

the community, as well as within it. Awareness of variety and distinctiveness usually finds expression in relationships of hierarchy and POWER over, both in monotheistic thought and its social spillovers. The moral vision becomes one of sameness, of becoming like the One or on the side of the One insofar as possible. When sameness is not desired, possible, or allowed, hierarchical dualism is the only remaining solution. 'You shall be separate from those.' The attractions of finding the One or being the One are deep but profoundly dangerous.

Work has been done, notably by Judith Ochshorn, comparing the social structure of ancient Israel, within which monotheism developed, with its surrounding polytheistic neighbours. Ochshorn finds it indeed to be the case, as has commonly been supposed, that hand in hand with monotheism there does appear to develop a sense of moral absolutes. On the other hand within monotheism (as would be expected from the above considerations) there is a greater prominence given to GENDER (that cultural construction built on the difference in SEXUALITY between men and women). In ancient polytheistic cultures, where the divine is imaged as both female and male (indeed in which goddesses go to war and gods represent fertility) there is less propensity to see women as being 'other' and different; shown for example by less taboo surrounding their sexuality. In monotheism by contrast, where the divine has been envisaged as male, not only do women lack roles within the religion (they cannot be priestesses) but they are held to be inferior and different, closer to the earth or nature and thus also impure.

These observations have led some women of recent years to wish to overcome a male monotheism as the basic form of their religion. Sometimes 'God' has been envisaged as 'Goddess', though it has been emphasized that this is not to replace a male God with a female Goddess but rather to celebrate the earth and all her children – indeed it is questionable whether Goddess is seen to have an objectivity in the sense that this was true of the male God. It is wished specifically to celebrate variety and multiplicity. Starhawk, a well-known proponent of the Goddess movement, writes that for her 'Goddess' is equivalent to 'immanence': 'the awareness of the world and everything in it as alive, dynamic, interdependent, interacting, and infused with moving energies: a living being, a weaving dance'. Likewise Emily Culpepper writes: 'There is too much wonderful diversity, contrast and movement in the world . . . for the One to function positively as our major symbol. We need symbols for unity, but the unity of the many is very different from a collapse of all diversity into a static One.' Such a critique of monotheism is not confined to those who wish some form of 'Goddess' religion. Catherine Keller comments, of the work of H. Richard Niebuhr, author of the well-known and widely influential *Radical Monotheism*, that Neibuhr 'defeats his own pluralism: . . . that is, he construes . . . multiplicity more as threat and temptation than as an ambiguous plenum of relations'. She continues: 'Philosophically and theologically, a radical monism or monotheism too easily tempts us away from a truly multiple integrity.'

Coming out of a very different intellectual background, French thinkers likewise critique monotheism as having a singularity, completeness, non-relationality and as hierarchical. The psychoanalytic linguist and semiotician Julia Kristeva writes: 'Monotheistic unity is sustained by a radical separation of the sexes . . . . One betrays . . . one's naivity if one considers our modern societies to be simply patrilinear . . . or capitalist–monopolist, and ignores the fact that they are at the same time . . . governed by . . . monotheism . . . . Whatever attacks this radical codification of the sexual difference . . . is attacking . . . the support of monotheism and the source of its eroticism.' The conceptual construction of 'woman' as 'other', and hence the presence of an eroticism built upon difference and exploitation, is here seen as the necessary consequence of the symbolization of the divine as masculine and transcendent. Monotheism is a plank which has undergirded the SEXISM of Western CULTURE.

Interesting anthropological work has been undertaken on non-Western cultures which again suggests a relationship between the conception held of ultimate reality and societal relations. Thus Signe Howell in *Society and Cosmos* (1984), a study of the Chewong people of the Malay peninsular, concludes that the peaceable nature of that society and the relative equality between the sexes which pertains is not unrelated to the complexity of their envisaging of the divine. There seems moreover to be some correlation between those African societies which have adopted Islam and the presence of hierarchical relations within the society, and those which maintain an ancient African tribal religion which are less hierarchical. It is difficult of course to know whether it is the nature of a society which makes for a propensity to adopt a certain religious stance, or whether it is the religion which influences the nature of the society.

A critique of classical monotheism from within the male Christian establishment, which equally undercuts the traditional view of God as one, independent and supreme, is represented by Geoffrey Lampe's book *God as Spirit*. Lampe, a leading authority on patristics, believes the development of Trinitarian doctrine within Christianity to have been mistaken. A more adequate doctrine of God would, he contends, have followed from picking up on the understanding of God as spirit found within the Hebrew scriptures; that spirit being recognized to have been supremely present in Jesus of Nazareth (*see* CHRISTOLOGY). The understanding of God as spirit, as Lampe develops it, leads to a conception of God as not separate from, though infinitely more than, the human being. God is both immanent and transcendent, yet one, in that God is spirit. God is not credibly an all-powerful agent who can at will intervene in the world (e.g. through breaking the laws of the universe in effecting a RESURRECTION). The social implications of Lampe's understanding, however, remain undeveloped.

Likewise that school of twentieth-century religious thought known as PROCESS THEOLOGY, which draws upon the thought of Alfred North Whitehead, has sought to modify what its proponents consider the worst consequences of a static 'Greek' conception of God as changeless and all-powerful. God is understood as, by nature, becoming, rather than as being, and to exist in an intimate interrelationship with the world. God's power is qualified; God must also learn from the actual experience of the world, and consequently modify God's actions in relation to it. Process theologians may be attracted to the powerlessness of Christ and not simply to the image of a powerful God. Whitehead's famous line is frequently quoted that God is 'the great companion – the fellow-sufferer who understands' (Whitehead 1978: 351). It should however be noted that Process theology essentially seeks to mitigate the power of a single monotheistic God; it does not essentially change our understanding of power, so that it should be understood for example as the empowerment of others rather than as 'power-over'. The God of Process thought may moreover be thought to be paternalistic in relation to humankind.

In conclusion it is of interest to draw attention to the fact that the great detractors of religion in the modern world, Marx, Feuerbach and Freud (all from a Jewish or markedly Christian background), have taken it for granted that the deity which they contended needed to be overcome is the monotheistic supreme deity of Judaeo-Christian culture. They have seen God in anthropomorphic terms, as the 'Father' of the human race; a father-figure which must be demolished if humanity is to find maturity and come into its own. Thus for Freud, in *The Future of an Illusion* (1927), 'God' is a projection of the 'Father', whom the child saw as its chief protector in childhood, in the face of the continued neediness of adult life. It may however be the feminist challenge of recent years to the notion of a single transcendent deity, envisaged as male, which will finally mean that this understanding of divinity will be considered moribund in no longer conforming to the norms or ethos of our society (*see* FEMINISM).

Concilium 177 (1985) 'Monotheism', ed. C. Geffré and J.P. Jossua. See especially Jürgen Moltmann and (on Islam) Robert Caspar.

Culpepper, E. (1987) 'Contemporary Goddess Theology: A Sympathetic Critique', in C. Atkinson, C. Buchanan and M. Miles (eds) *Shaping New Vision: Gender and Values in American Culture*, Ann Arbor, MI: UMI Research Press.

Freud, S. (1913) *Totem and Taboo*, in J. Strachey (ed.) *The Standard Edition of the Complete*

Psychological Works of Sigmund Freud, London: Hogarth Press, vol. 13.

——(1927) *The Future of an Illusion*, in J. Strachey (ed.) *The Standard Edition of the Complete Psychological Works of Sigmund Freud*, London: Hogarth Press, vol. 21.

——(1939) *Moses and Monotheism*, in J. Strachey (ed.) *The Standard Edition of the Complete Psychological Works of Sigmund Freud*, London: Hogarth Press, vol. 23.

Gross, R. (1986) 'Contribution to "roundtable: feminist reflections on Jewish theology"', *Journal of Feminist Studies in Religion* 2(1).

Howell, Signe (1984) *Society and Cosmos*, Singapore and Oxford: Oxford University Press.

Keller, C. (1986) *From a Broken Web: Separation, Sexism, and Self*, Boston, MA: Beacon Press.

Kristeva, J. (1977) *About Chinese Women*, trans. A. Barrows, London: Marion Boyars (first published 1974).

Lampe, G. (1977) *God as Spirit*, Oxford: Clarendon.

Niebuhr, H.R. (1961) *Radical Monotheism and Western Culture*, New York and London: Faber.

Ochshorn, J. (1981) *The Female Experience and the Nature of the Divine*, Bloomington, IN: Indiana University Press.

Starhawk (1982) *Dreaming the Dark: Magic, Sex and Politics*, Boston, MA: Beacon Press.

Whitehead, A.N. (1978) *Process and Reality: An Essay in Cosmology*, New York: Free Press (first published 1929).

Daphne Hampson

MORMONS

The Church of Jesus Christ of Latter-day Saints (often referred to as the Mormon Church or the LDS Church) was founded in the USA in 1830 by Joseph Smith and a small group of believers. Between 1830 and 1846, converts to Mormonism established several different communities in the eastern and midwest regions of the USA, most notably Nauvoo, Illinois, and Independence, Missouri. Seeking freedom from religious persecution, the Mormons undertook an exodus to the western USA in 1847 where they established settlements in what are now the states of Utah, Idaho, Nevada and Arizona. As recently as 1960, 90 per cent of church membership lived in the USA – three-quarters living in the western USA. By the end of 1990, however, church membership worldwide numbered 7.8 million with only 57 per cent of the membership living in the States. The most rapid growth during the 1980s

occurred in South America, Central America and Mexico where 29 per cent of church membership live (Ludlow 1992).

The term 'Mormon' comes from the Book of Mormon, a book accepted by the Church as sacred scripture along with the Bible. Mormons believe that the the Book of Mormon is a second witness of Christ and is a record of the doctrine of Jesus Christ as it was preached on the American continent between 600 BC and AD 400. LDS theology is contained in official Church scriptures which include the King James Version of the Bible, the Book of Mormon, the Doctrine and Covenants, and the Pearl of Great Price.

Latter-day Saints affirm a belief in Christ, his ATONEMENT and RESURRECTION, the need for repentance and baptism, and the brotherhood and sisterhood of humanity. The LDS Church is a restoration of the church established by Jesus Christ and directed by his apostles after the crucifixion. In LDS theology, God has both human form and emotion. Rejecting the doctrine of the Trinity, Latter-day Saints believe that God (the Father), Jesus Christ and the Holy Ghost are three separate beings acting with one purpose and mind as the Godhead.

Perhaps most unique to Latter-day Saint doctrine is 'the plan of salvation', which describes the human experience as an existence which begins in a pre-mortal life where all humans were the spirit children of heavenly parents. Earth life is an opportunity for these spirit children to obtain a physical body and demonstrate their willingness to keep God's commandments. Jesus Christ is both older brother and redeemer, making it possible for those who yield to temptation to repent and return to God's presence. Central to the plan of salvation is the opportunity for women and men to be married for eternity. The eternal MARRIAGE ceremony is performed in a sacred building called a 'temple'. A husband and wife who are married in the temple and live lives devoted to Christ are promised that they will inherit thrones, kingdoms and powers and will thus become as God is.

In addition, church doctrine emphasizes the concept of continuing revelation and the existence of modern prophets who receive revelation from God. The President, or head, of the LDS

Church is considered a prophet of God who is able to receive revelation from God and is responsible to Jesus Christ for directing his Church on earth. The Doctrine and Covenants and Pearl of Great Price contain revelations received by Joseph Smith and subsequent prophets. Significant changes in church practices occur as a result of revelations to the prophet or head of the Church. An example of such changes include the revelation ending the practice of polygamy in 1890, and the revelation in 1978 which granted the opportunity of priesthood ordination to all worthy men, regardless of race (prior to this revelation blacks were not ordained). Mormons are well known for following a revelation given Joseph Smith in 1833 (known as the Word of Wisdom) which has been interpreted as encouraging Latter-day Saints to abstain from the use of tobacco, alcohol, tea and coffee.

The FAMILY is literally the basic unit of church organization. The emphasis on family life is a logical extension of the doctrine that all of humanity are children of heavenly parents and that women and men must marry for eternity in a temple of God. The theology teaches that marriage is ordained of God, that the marriage unit is eternal and that procreation is a commandment of God. Parents are responsible for the spiritual and emotional development of their children. Sexual purity is expected of all members since the power to create life is a gift from God. Because of the emphasis on family, Latter-day Saints are more likely to marry, less likely to be divorced (particularly low rates of divorce have been found among those married in the temple) and have a high fertility rate compared with other religious denominations.

AUTHORITY and order are central themes in the development of Mormonism. The Church of Jesus Christ of Latter-day Saints claims that it is the only true church on the earth. Through the restoration of priesthood, God has given Latter-day Saints the authority to act in his name in the performance of religious ordinances and the teaching of Christ's doctrine. Church organization is a multilayered hierarchy which links individuals and families to a central administration. In between are geographically defined units called wards (local congregation), stakes

(similar to a Catholic diocese), regions and areas. All worthy males are ordained to the priesthood and serve in many different capacities at various levels of church hierarchy. Women are not ordained but serve as teachers and administrators in local and stake organizations. Except at the highest levels of church administration, the work of the church is carried out by a lay ministry. Mormonism's success in attracting new members has been attributed to the strength of its local religious communities which encourage a high degree of commitment from the members while also providing psychological, spiritual and material support when necessary for individuals and families.

In many countries of the world, Mormonism is considered a cult or sect (see CULTS; SECTS). However, Latter-day Saints in the USA have distinguished themselves as political leaders, businessmen, scholars, athletes and entertainers. In the USA, Mormons tend to be middle class and well educated, and the LDS Church is known for its financial success. In recent years, Mormonism has become more respected. Scholars have suggested that it be studied as a new religious tradition rather than as another denomination or form of traditional Christianity (Shipps 1985; see NEW RELIGIOUS MOVEMENTS).

Allen, J.B. and Leonard, G.M. (1976) *The Story of the Latter-day Saints*, Salt Lake City, UT: Deseret Book.

Arrington, L.J. and Bitton, D. (1979) *The Mormon Experience*, New York: Knopf.

Bushman, R.L. (1984) *Joseph Smith and the Beginnings of Mormonism*, Urbana and Chicago, IL: University of Illinois Press.

Cornwall, M., Heaton, T.B. and Young L.A. (forthcoming) *Contemporary Mormonism: Social Science Perspectives*, Urbana and Chicago, IL: University of Illinois Press.

Derr, J.M., Cannon, J.R. and Beecher, M.U. (1992) *Women of Covenant: The Story of the Relief Society*, Salt Lake City, UT: Deseret Book.

Gottlieb, R. and Whiley, P. (1984) *America's Saints: The Rise of Mormon Power*, New York: G.P. Putnam's Sons.

Ludlow, D.H. (1992) *Encyclopedia of Mormonism*, New York: Macmillan.

Richards, L. (1988) *A Marvelous Work and a Wonder*, Salt Lake City, UT: Deseret Book.

Shipps, J. (1985) *Mormonism: The Story of a New Religious Tradition*, Urbana and Chicago, IL: University of Illinois Press.

Talmage, J.E. (1971) *Articles of Faith*, Salt Lake City, UT: Deseret Book.

Marie Cornwall

MULTINATIONAL COMPANIES

'Multinational company' is a generic term which gained wide currency in the 1960s to describe firms engaged in various cross-border economic activities. Although such international business operations long predated the vogue for this term, its popularity was due to an accelerating internationalization of financial, industrial and service flows, involving ever more firms, markets and countries and generating stocks of foreign direct investment. Multinational companies now comprise an increasingly heterogeneous ensemble of private, public and mixed economic agents operating in more than one national economy. They range from small and medium enterprises to giant oligopolies or monopolies; their home bases (in so far as they can still be said to have them) embrace newly industrializing economies and (post-) socialist economies as well as advanced capitalist economies. Their operations cover almost all economic fields (from mining and agriculture to high tech and producer services); and they display various organizational forms and business strategies (including nowadays joint ventures and strategic alliances). This heterogeneity makes it hard to capture the activities of multinational companies in neat statistics, to offer simple generalizations about their activities or make firm judgements about their nature and impact on the world economy, let alone their ethical implications.

Multinational companies can be traced back at least to the sixteenth century when the capitalist world system emerged (*see* CAPITALISM). Initially they were mainly 'charter' companies with trading monopolies; firms involved in indirect investment became more important in the eighteenth and nineteenth centuries; corporations involved in direct investment and transnational banks grew during the twentieth century; and strategic alliances and joint ventures (often with little measurable FDI) now play a key role in an emerging trilateral order involving Europe,

Japan and North America. Although multinational companies were initially involved mainly in the unequal exchange of raw materials from the South for northern goods in colonial or quasi-colonial blocs, the South later tended to become an export platform where cheap labour was used to produce mature goods for foreign as well as local markets. There are also increasing North–North links through cross-investment by multinational companies seeking access to markets as well as co-operation in the development of knowledge-intensive products.

A measure of the current importance of multinational companies can be gleaned from the facts that each of the largest 600 multinational companies now generate worldwide sales of over USD 1bn and together produce a quarter of gross world output. Flows of foreign direct investment (one of the key activities of modern multinational companies) grew from USD 129bn in 1970 to USD 1,435bn in 1990 (an annual growth rate of 12.6 per cent). Around two-thirds of multinational company production is still oriented to *local* markets but the remaining third is traded across borders (often within multinational companies themselves); a growing band of multinationals also pursue truly global (rather than multi-domestic) strategies. Some host countries are essentially export platforms for multinational companies, but others have large domestic markets as well as producing for export.

Recent debates often focus on the alleged responsibilities of multinational companies as key agents in the world economy and what forms of governance, if any, might hold them accountable for their actions and impact. This is related to controversies concerning whether multinational companies are oriented to the home or host countries or simply pursue their own interests. Some observers claim that it is the changing capitalist world system which forces firms to become multinational companies and then to act self-interestedly to secure market share and/or profits. Thus they both contribute to the process of internationalization and are also constrained by it. Whilst the former approach typically draws an important distinction between multinational companies and national firms, the latter downplays this distinction and criticizes capitalism (and hence all capitalist firms) in general. This concern has become more prominent in post-colonial times, as colonial political ties are cut and the market nexus becomes more important.

The initial debate on multinational companies as such was much concerned about the 'American challenge' in the 1960s, i.e. how far the new wave of predominantly US multinational companies investing in Europe promoted US economic domination and threatened the national economic interests and political sovereignty of host societies. In some cases protectionism was practised or national champions sponsored to face the US challenge; in others a commitment to the liberal postwar order led to acceptance of US inward investment. Then, as European and Japanese multinational companies developed and even penetrated the US itself, interest shifted to the more general role of multinational companies in the world ECONOMY. Their potentially adverse impact on home economies (e.g. through exporting jobs, weakening trade unionism, transferring strategic technologies and turning from innovation to cheap labour as a source of profits) was placed on the agenda alongside the issue of their impact on host economies.

A parallel debate concerned multinational companies' role in economic development. Some claimed that multinational companies helped to inhibit development of host economies (especially in the Third World and semi-peripheral countries in Europe and Australasia) by demanding excessive financial or fiscal inducements for investment, taking loans at the expense of local firms, expatriating profits rather than reinvesting and conducting research and development in the home economy. Others claim that multinational companies serve as vehicles of economic development by transferring technology, re-skilling local labour, buying local goods and services and generalizing modern managerial skills.

Another set of issues concerned the impact of multinational companies on state capacities to govern national economies – expressed in terms of 'sovereignty at bay' in headquarters and host economies alike. It was argued that the efficacy of national macroeconomic policies was being undermined by the cross-border

activities of multinational companies and that this threatened postwar policy objectives such as full employment, economic growth and stable prices. This also implied that multinational company operations escaped national control (over prices, credit, exchange rates, taxes, etc.) and that multinational companies pursued global strategies which could well contradict national economic interests. Multinational company apologists claimed it was always in their interests to act as 'good citizens' lest they be nationalized and because they needed prosperous local economies. This may be true where multinational companies are multi-domestic in form (i.e. aim to penetrate local markets with local production); it is less obviously true of multinational companies based on a global division of labour and global strategies. It is also possible that multinational companies' bargaining power varies over time. It is highest before investments are made; once sunk costs have been incurred, however, host governments and local labour tend to gain power. Another factor here is extra-territoriality, i.e. the insistence by home governments that their multinational companies obey domestic law rather than that of host countries.

Among other concerns raised by multinational companies are (a) their environmental impact whether through short-term exploitation of natural resources, through neglect of health and safety, or through polluting activities which would be illegal in the home base; (b) the disruption of traditional social institutions due to phenomena such as the feminization of the labour force in cheap labour factories or the corrosive impact of Western norms on local values; and (c) the encouragement to kleptocratic political and business élites seeking commissions or bribes. In all cases, however, it is unclear how far it is multinational companies as such or the process of capital accumulation which is at fault.

The activities of multinational companies are clearly integral to the more general process of internationalization of the capitalist economy. Moreover the collapse of the Soviet bloc and capitalist resurgence in China mean that this is now a global phenomenon. One consequence of this is that national economies are no longer 'natural' units of economic management and national states are no longer the most important political units. Over the thirty years during which multinational companies were re-discovered, their activities have been re-evaulated. Thus their success on the world market is now seen as a condition of achieving national autonomy rather than as a threat to sovereignty. States now hope to minimize the harmful domestic repercussions of internationalization and/or to secure minimum benefit to their own home-based multinational companies; and, to do so, they must get involved in creating appropriate frameworks for multinational company activities in co-operation with other nation states and multinational companies themselves. Among many activities included here are: introducing new legal forms for cross-national co-operation and strategic alliances; reforming the international currency and credit systems; promoting technology transfer; managing trade disputes; developing a new international intellectual property regime; or developing new regulatory forms for labour migration. Nor is it so self-evident that national economic space is the best starting-point for national states to pursue economic growth, technological innovation or structural competitiveness. There is growing concern with local or regional economic growth poles and with supra-national co-operation to promote growth and attract investment. The rise of regional political blocs (e.g. the European Union, ASEAN, or NAFTA) illustrates this search for new forms of economic regulation. This is linked to problems of governance linked to specific regimes for particular sets of issues (e.g. intellectual property rights, the arms trade, narcotics, telecommunications or the global commons) and attempts to secure the self-regulation of multinational companies.

Berry, Brian J.L., Conkling, Edgar C. and Ray, D. Michael (1992) *The Global Economy: Resource Use, Locational Choice and International Trade*, Prentice Hall International Paperback Editions.

Buckley, Peter J. and Casson, Mark (1991) *The Future of the Multinational Enterprise*, London: Macmillan.

Elfstrom, Gerald (1991) *Moral Issues and Multinational Corporations*, London: Macmillan.

Goldberg, Linda S. and Klein, Michael W. (1992) *Current Issues in the International Economy*, London: HarperCollins.

Helleiner, Gerald K. (1993) *The New Global Economy and the Developing Countries*, Edward Elgar.

Hoffman, Michael (1986) *Ethics and the Multinational Enterprise: Proceedings of the Sixth International Conference on Business Ethics*, October 10 and 11, 1985, University of America.

Kenwood, A.G. and Lougheed, A.L. (1992) *The Growth of the International Economy, 1820–1980*, 3rd edn, London: Routledge.

Khan, Khushi M. (ed.) (1986) *Multinationals of the South*, London: Pinter Publishers.

Negandhi, Anant R. and Welge, Martin (1984) *Advances in International Comparative Management*, Jai Press.

Reardon, John J. (1992) *America and the Multinational Corporation*, Praeger Publishers Inc.

Bob Jessop

NATIONALISM

Nationalism is so ubiquitous and varied in character that it has become difficult to provide clear definitions. In its most general usage, nationalism refers to the whole process of 'nation-building' in history. A more restricted usage equates it with 'national sentiment' or consciousness, a sense of belonging to a particular nation. Nationalism may also be treated as a particular kind of language, symbolism and mythology appropriate to a certain unit of population. Nationalism may refer to a given type of social and political movement, with recurrent goals. Most commonly, nationalism is regarded as an IDEOLOGY or doctrine of national loyalty and will.

In what follows, I shall be mainly concerned with the ideology, movement and symbolism of nationalism, and I start with the IDEOLOGY.

Of course, nationalism is much more than an ideology. It is a type of CULTURE. Nevertheless, that culture can be approached most usefully through the ideology, or what I shall term the 'core doctrine'. This may be summarized as follows:

1 The world is divided into nations, each with its own identity and destiny.
2 The nation is the source of all political power.
3 Loyalty to the nation overrides all other allegiances.
4 True freedom can only be realized in and through a nation.
5 Global PEACE and JUSTICE can only be secured through free nations.

This core doctrine is the *sine qua non* of nationalism everywhere. Yet it provides only the barest of belief-structures. In practice, nationalists must supplement the core doctrine with all kinds of 'secondary' and supporting notions and theories – e.g. the Romantic idea of Poland as a 'suffering Christ' among the nations, soon to rise again, or Zionism's belief that the Jewish people can only be reborn in their ancient, messianic homeland. In each case, however, nationalism is revealed as an ideology of the nation, not of the STATE.

The main goals of the nationalist movement – identity, unity, AUTONOMY – flow from this ideology. Nationalists strive to endow their nation with a distinctive culture or 'character', as both Rousseau and Herder proclaimed. Similarly, the unity of the nation, both territorial and social, has always preoccupied nationalists, often leading to strong centralizing policies and sometimes irredentist movements. Finally, every nationalism strives for maximum autonomy – to lead a culturally 'authentic' life, to secure some degree of economic 'autarchy', and in the end to obtain political 'home rule' or even sovereign statehood.

With these goals in mind, we can tentatively define nationalism as *an ideological movement for attaining and maintaining autonomy, unity and identity on behalf of a population, some of whose members deem it to be an actual or potential nation.*

Nationalism is an ideology of, and movement for, the nation. Though nationalists may demand independence in a state of their own, their primary concern is with the cultural–historical community of the nation. There have been many ways of defining the concept of the 'nation', some emphasizing its apparently 'natural' personality, others its artificial character, some its antiquity, others its MODERNITY, some its 'objective' features, others its purely 'subjective' character.

Nevertheless, it is possible to reconstruct the main characteristics of the nationalist concept of the 'nation' as an ideal-type stripped of all particular accretions. These include the idea that nations are communities of shared memories and mass culture, that they possess definite historic territories or 'homelands' and that they have a high degree of economic unity and shared legal norms, including rights and duties for all members.

Thus we can, again tentatively, define the nation as a *named community of shared history and mass culture, with a 'homeland' of its own, and possessing a single ECONOMY and uniform rights and duties for all members* (Smith 1991: 14, 73).

It must be stressed that these are merely working definitions. It is the symbols, language, myths and rituals of nationalism that give it the

POWER and intensity which it so often displays. Symbols like the flag, anthem, currency and passport; concepts like authenticity, self-determination and the national mission; ceremonies like military parades, remembrance services for the fallen and celebrations of historic events; above all, myths of origin, liberation and a past heroic or 'golden age'; these are what endow the belief-structures (and working definitions) of nationalism with their political, cultural and social content, and hence their popular resonance. In short, as a 'religion-surrogate', nationalism has its own specific 'dogmas, symbols, altars and feasts' (Durkheim 1915: 214).

How can we explain the power and ubiquity of nationalism in the modern world?

Most theories of nationalism are 'modernist'. They assume that nations and nationalism are wholly modern phenomena, the products of peculiarly modern conditions. This is the case with the socio-demographic school of theorists around Karl Deutsch. They chart the rise of nations through the modern processes of social mobilization and cultural assimilation, using indices like UBANIZATION, mass literacy, the mass media and voting patterns.

Elie Kedourie, on the other hand, emphasizes the ideological dimensions of nationalism. He regards it as a 'doctrine invented at the beginning of the nineteenth century', and links it to the impact of the French Revolution, the philosophy of Kant and his followers, and the exclusion of intellectuals in Germany. Ultimately, however, nationalism was the product of a *Zeitgeist*, which saw the breakdown of political habits and viable communities, so creating a restless alienated youth striving for unattainable perfection on earth (Kedourie 1960).

Later, Kedourie extended his analysis to Africa and Asia. Here European IMPERIALISM pulverized traditional societies, while European EDUCATION and scholarship rediscovered native ethnic communities. But it was colonial BUREAU-CRACY, with its discrimination against native intellectuals, that provoked the alienated discontent which demanded a 'millennial' political solution. That solution, an anti-colonial nationalism, derived its power, not just from the Enlightenment, but from a long tradition of Christian millennial strivings in Europe. Like its forebear, a secular nationalism abolished the barriers between the public and private domains, created a new purified elect and spread frenzied destruction wherever it penetrated (Kedourie 1971).

Though he may have overstated its millennial character and underestimated its auto-emancipatory optimism, Kedourie revealed an acute sense of nationalism's quasi-religious, messianic character, which can evoke such powerful sentiments of collective self-sacrifice.

Yet nationalism can also be a practical project. Indeed, for Ernest Gellner (1983), it is the political doctrine of a modern, industrial world. Past 'agro-literate' societies had no room for nations and nationalism; but a mobile industrial world requires both. Modernization has eroded traditional societies, replacing their tight structures with a literary, schooled culture. Today we are all 'clerks', and nationalism is the process by which some oral 'low' cultures are turned into literary 'high' cultures. This requires a state-supported, mass, public, standardized education system. Nations and nationalism are functional for a world of industrial cultures.

Yet there are problems. Modernization uproots villagers who flock to overcrowded cities where they compete for scarce resources with the city-dwellers. In this competition, culture plays a crucial role. It can discriminate between people of different language, colour and religion, with ensuing ethnic conflict and ethnic secession movements led by their intelligentsia.

In similar vein, Tom Nairn seeks to account for the worldwide diffusion of nationalism through the 'uneven development' of CAPITAL-ISM. The latter is brought to non-Western societies by Western imperialists, and the result is to provoke resistance by indigenous élites. Having no other resources to hand, they appeal to the masses and 'invite them into history', writing the invitation card in their language and culture. Nationalism is therefore always a populist, interclass movement, a mobilization of the masses in conditions of helplessness (Nairn 1977: chs 2, 9).

Critics have not been slow to point to the deterministic, and materialist, character of these theories. Can the close link between nationalism and economic modernization be upheld? Even if nationalism, the ideological movement, is modern, are nations too the product of capitalism and industrialism? Or would we do better by looking to cultural variables for our explanations?

In fact, Gellner had already highlighted the place of linguistic education in the genesis of modern mass nationalisms. Benedict Anderson (1983) takes this one step further by treating the nation as an 'imagined community', at once limited and sovereign. 'Imagining' and 'narrating' the nation now becomes the primary locus of explanation. This means investigating the creation of a mass reading public and focusing on the literary devices used in books, journals and newspapers to create an identification with a sociological community proceeding along an 'empty, homogeneous time'. That is why writers and intellectuals are so vital for nationalisms.

For Anderson, therefore, nations are the product of modern conditions. They are the result, not just of the decline of old sacred faith communities and dynastic realms, but also of the spread of the technology of 'print-capitalism' in sixteenth-century Europe and later. Without that technology and its commodities, books and newspapers, nations would be literally inconceivable. Nations are born on the ruins of religious traditions and faiths, yet by their appeal to the sociological imagination and the judgement of posterity they serve the same cravings for community and immortality.

How far can these various 'modernist' theories be sustained? Can we regard nations as modern communities of industrial culture?

A number of scholars have questioned these assumptions. While they cannot accept the views of an earlier generation of scholars, who sought and found nations in antiquity and treated them as primordial, they are equally sceptical of the fashionable myth of the 'modern nation'. They make several points.

1 The dating of 'nations' is problematic. If we defined the nation strictly as a 'mass' phenomenon, then most nations would only emerge with the emancipation of women (and ethnic minorities). While this might apply to the new states of Africa and Asia (but is it here the nation or the state that has a recent foundation date?), how shall we treat the histories of the core communities of the much older European states? Should we not distinguish, with Seton-Watson (1977: chs 1–3), the 'old, continuous nations' of certain (western, northern) parts of Europe from the 'nations of design' found in much of Eastern Europe, and latterly Africa and Asia?

2 Even in the new states, the 'core' population may possess a long, continuous history of shared myths, symbols, memories and traditions. The new state may be built around a relatively durable ethnic community (or *ethnie*), such as the Han Chinese, the Viet, the Burmese, the Persians, the Amhara, the Shona, or the dominant *ethnie* in the states of Eastern Europe and the former Soviet Union. How does the emergent 'new nation' relate to these ethnic cores?

3 We cannot therefore treat the political imaginings and activities of the intelligentsia or other élites, however important, as the key to grasping the growth of nations and the hold of nationalism. Nations are not simply modern constructs or discourses to be 'deconstructed' to reveal powerful élite interests. On the contrary, pre-existing ethnic ties and sentiments limit the ability of élites to manipulate mass emotions and determine which among the many traditions of 'ethno-history' will find a mass response – as Tilak discovered when he appealed to the cult of the goddess Kali to foment anti-British feelings among the Hindu masses (Armstrong 1982; Smith 1986).

4 Religious traditions, far from declining, have become revitalized in many areas, including parts of the industrial West; and much of their strength derives from an ethnic content. In many cases, there has been a symbiosis of religion and ethnicity – among Sinhalese, Sikhs, Moros, Persians, Druse, Maronites, Israeli Jews, Monophysite Amhara, Armenians, Azeris, Orthodox Serbs and Catholic Croats. Many of these ethno-religious symbioses antedate the modern era and condition the ways in which subsequent ethnic nationalisms develop.

Nationalism is also linked to pre-modern religious cultures through the SECULARIZATION of ancient myths of ethnic election. The idea of a 'chosen people', classically formulated in the Bible, was not confined to the Jews, even in antiquity, let alone the medieval world. It is found among Persians, Byzantine Greeks, Armenians and Ethiopians, as well as Russians, Poles, French, English, Irish and many other peoples. Such myths involve beliefs in the unique destiny of an ethno-religious community, a sense of collective mission, a veneration for the sacred heritage and ancestral traditions, and an equally fervent attachment to the land of those forefathers.

These are all elements that nationalism has taken up in secular form, with its emphasis on language, literature, music, the arts and popular folklore. Today, all peoples have become chosen nations, every nation is an irreplaceable elect. And the old moral and ritual obligations of chosenness have today become the duties of CITIZENSHIP and the respect for cultural diversity.

Given the many links between modern nations and much older *ethnie*, what are the prospects of a world without nations? Can humanity live without nationalism?

The late twentieth century has undoubtedly witnessed rapid, and remarkable, changes. Vast transnational companies and an international division of labour compete today with traditional national states for economic hegemony. There has also been a dramatic revolution in mass computerized information technology and communications, binding together populations with a speed and immediacy that few could have dreamt possible even two decades ago. Mass travel and communications have also awakened a more general interest in other cultures and intensified links between nations. Trade has increased, while military alliances, supra-national regional associations and global political institutions such as the United Nations have multiplied, transcending national boundaries (see Hobsbawm 1990).

Yet, as we are daily reminded, there has been little appreciable decline in national sentiments and identities in most parts of the world. If anything, ethnic nationalisms have proliferated, and the powers of national states have increased, even in democratic Western societies. The computer revolution has served to facilitate the renaissance of ethnic and linguistic nationalisms, and economic inequalities have exacerbated ethnic antagonisms handed down from earlier epochs.

Similar paradoxes attend recent attempts to forge a united Europe. On the one hand, there has been a rapid growth of economic integration and a more halting movement to political unity. Élite attitudes to 'Europe', too, though they vary from nation to nation, with Italy, Germany, Spain and the Benelux countries evincing more favourable sentiments than Britain or France, have become much more positive.

Yet no massive shift of popular identification from individual nations to the European Union has as yet been observed. At most, we may speak of the gradual evolution of a sense of European cultural kinship, based on a 'family of cultures' composed of overlapping legal, political and cultural traditions. Such a many-stranded identity must seem to be vague and nebulous compared with the vivid, accessible and deep-rooted attachments of the several national identities in Europe. Given the quite different levels of economic and political development within Europe, the many intractable ethnic problems and the continual jockeying for leadership in the Union, not to mention the problems of delimiting 'Europe', it would be premature to predict the imminent emergence, or creation, of a European identity, however conceived (Smith 1991: ch. 7).

There is a more profound reason for doubting the ability of any European project to transcend nationalism. Communities and identities require popular myths, symbols and memories; but in these respects 'Europe' (like other regional associations) is singularly lacking. It can boast no generally acceptable collective shrines, heroes and martyrs. The medieval Christian civilization of a Charlemagne or Otto is remote and at best irrelevant to modern, secular and democratic, European ideals; and heroes like Napoleon (or even Rembrandt or Beethoven) remain primarily national in their contexts and connotations. In the absence of a popular European mythology, RITUAL and symbolism, who will 'die for Europe', as so many laid down their lives for 'king and country' in two World Wars? And if they did, would we not be confronting a new, perhaps more exclusive and dangerous, 'Euro-nationalism'?

The near-universal appeal of nationalism,

suggested by this example, lies in its ability to overcome the sense of oblivion which DEATH without the hope of another world presents to mortals. By being joined to a national 'community of history and destiny', the individual becomes a link in the chain of generations stretching from distant ancestors to an unknown posterity. To this overriding need, we must add the persistence of ethnic ties and the uneven incidence of 'ethno-history' among culturally diverse populations, the conflicting interests of national states in an inter-state system, and radically divergent levels of global economic development: and the likelihood of any early super-session of nations and nationalism must appear remote.

Besides, in so many respects, nationalism (with or without religion) produces those individual and social consequences that religious faiths and sacred communities have always secured. In the words of Durkheim:

> before all else, a faith is warmth, life, enthusiasm, the exaltation of the whole mental life, the raising of the individual above himself

while for society as a whole, the symbols, rites and ceremonies of nationalism rehearse that sense of unity and unique destiny so necessary to collective existence, for

> There can be no society that does not feel the need of upholding and reaffirming at regular intervals the collective sentiments and the collective ideas which make up its unity and personality.
>
> (Durkheim 1915: 425, 427)

For these reasons, it would indeed be premature to invoke the owl of Minerva, with respect to nations or nationalism.

Anderson, Benedict (1983) *Imagined Communities: Reflections on the Origin and Spread of Nationalism*, London: Verso.

Armstrong, John (1982) *Nations before Nationalism*, Chapel Hill, NC: University of North Carolina Press.

Durkheim, Emile (1915) *The Elementary Forms of the Religious Life*, trans. J. Swain, London: Allen & Unwin.

Gellner, Ernest (1983) *Nations and Nationalism*, Oxford: Blackwell.

Hobsbawm, Eric (1990) *Nations and Nationalism since 1780*, Cambridge: Cambridge University Press.

Kedourie, Elie (1960) *Nationalism*, London: Hutchinson.

——(ed.) (1971) *Nationalism in Asia and Africa*, London: Weidenfeld & Nicolson.

Nairn, Tom (1977) *The Break-up of Britain*, London: New Left Books.

Seton-Watson, Hugh (1977) *Nations and States*, London: Methuen.

Smith, Anthony D. (1986) *The Ethnic Origins of Nations*, Oxford: Blackwell.

——(1991) *National Identity*, Harmondsworth: Penguin.

Anthony D. Smith

NATURAL LAW

Natural law generically describes ethical theories that determine what is right or wrong on the basis of the common humanity that all human beings share. A brief overview of the philosophical and jurisprudential aspects of natural law will be helpful for a better understanding of a theological discussion about natural law and its effects on SOCIETY.

Most of the classical moral philosophers in the Western tradition adopted some sort of natural law theory. In ancient times Stoics maintained that the moral life involved living in accord with nature understood as the entire natural order. Despite so many appeals to nature and natural law as the criterion of morality, natural law philosophers have not agreed on the meaning of the criterion of nature or on all the content norms proposed on the basis of a natural law theory. In modern times many contemporary philosophers have challenged a natural law approach for a number of different reasons – the very diversity among natural law thinkers themselves, cultural relativism, evolutionary development, antifoundationalism, and the naturalistic fallacy of trying to go from the 'is' to the 'ought'. Other philosophers continue to defend a natural law approach but often with a 'thin' concept of the human good which avoids claiming too much as based on a common humanity. In jurisprudence, legal positivists and others reject the natural law contention that human civil LAW and legislation must be based on natural law.

In theological ethics Roman Catholic thought has traditionally appealed to natural law to determine how Christians and all others are to live, but some Anglicans and Protestants have proposed their own version of natural law. In this context natural law involves three distinct but overlapping considerations – the strictly theological, the philosophical, and the legal.

From the theological perspective natural law involves the question of the sources of moral wisdom and knowledge for the Christian and the Christian church. Does the Christian find moral wisdom only in the Scripture and in Jesus Christ or also in human reason and experience? Natural law approaches assert that the Christian, Christian ethics and the Christian churches can find moral wisdom through human reason and on that basis can be in dialogue with all humankind. Historically Roman Catholic natural law theory has defended the role of reason to arrive at moral knowledge on the basis of its reflection on human nature. Orthodox Christianity affirms a natural law common to all based on the image of God in all humans, but the natural law provides only for a minimal social existence. Many Anglicans, Methodists and some in the Reformed tradition have given some role to the natural law or its equivalent.

The primary theological justification of natural law rests on the doctrine of CREATION. God has created human nature and human reason so that human reason can discover how human beings should act by reflecting on their own human nature. Supporters of natural law or the more generic use of reason in moral theology also appeal to Romans 2: 14 which asserts that the Gentiles who do not have the law (the Mosaic Law) do by nature what the law requires. The Roman Catholic understanding sees the natural law as a participation of the divine plan or law in the rational creature. God has formulated a plan for the world and has given human beings reason so that reflecting on the human nature made by God they can discern how God wants us to act in this world.

Many Protestants in the Lutheran tradition, some in the Reformed tradition (Karl Barth), Evangelicals, and the sects or left wing of the Protestant Reformation have strenuously opposed natural law invoking the emphasis on the Scripture alone, insisting that SIN has grievously affected both human nature and human reason, and maintaining that one can never go from the human to the divine but must start with God and God's revelation. Mainline Protestants who do not accept the natural law on theological grounds usually still find some basis for a common social morality for all human beings.

Before the Second Vatican Council (1962–5) Roman Catholic ethics and official hierarchical teachings were based almost exclusively on a neo-Scholastic natural law theory, thereby recognizing a morality common to all human beings and capable of dialogue with all others on the basis of human reason and a shared human nature, but such a morality lacked any explicit Christian dimensions. The Second Vatican Council called for a greater incorporation of Scripture, faith perspectives and explicitly theological themes in Christian ethics and life. The majority of mainstream Christians today are debating the question about the exact relationship of faith and reason in morality and how Christian and human morality are related. Many Roman Catholic theologians, while recognizing a greater role for faith and strictly theological appeals, still maintain that Christian faith does not add any unique content to morality especially in the understanding of social ethics in our pluralistic world. However, some Roman Catholic theologians today insist that faith calls for some different content in the moral life of the Christian.

The more philosophical aspect of the natural law question concerns the meaning of human nature and of human reason. The Roman Catholic teaching and tradition have consistently identified their approach as a natural law theory dependent on the work of Thomas Aquinas. Human reason can discern the plan of God by grasping the specific ends toward which we tend by nature – the ends we share with all living substances (the conservation of one's own being); the ends we share with other animals (the procreation and EDUCATION of offspring); and the ends that are proper to human beings (to know the truth about God and to live in human society). On the basis of these generic ends reason can discern (usually by deduction) the principles that should guide the moral life.

Later neo-Scholastic theologians developed this role of natural law insisting on its universality and immutability and the need to observe the God-given finalities of all the human faculties and powers. Official Catholic hierarchical teaching has employed the natural law theory to develop its moral teaching in all areas including social, biomedical and sexual morality.

Revisionist Catholic moral theologians have dissented from the official Church teaching on many sexual questions such as CONTRACEPTION, sterilization, masturbation, artificial insemination and the principle of double effect. Such ethicists criticize the neo-Scholastic natural law theory because of its physicalism (identification of the human moral act with the physical structure of the act), classicism (emphasis on the eternal, immutable, universal and unchanging) and naturalism (failure to give primary significance to the personal). Alternative ethical theories have been proposed based on other philosophical approaches (e.g. transcendental, pragmatic, relational, liberationist, linguistic, praxis oriented), but many theories constitute a revision and not a rejection of natural law. Today in Catholic theological ethics a pluralism of methodologies exists although all continue to give an important role to human reason.

The hierarchical teaching office of the Roman Catholic church continues to employ the neo-Scholastic natural law method in its official documents and teaching although that method has been modified somewhat in the area of social morality. Some theological ethicists continue to defend the neo-Scholastic natural law approach in sexual and medical ethics. Others (e.g. Germain Grisez and John Finnis) propose their own revision of natural law insisting on the existence of a number of basic human goods that one can never directly go against. Grisez, Finnis and their school generally use their revised natural law method to defend the existing hierarchical church teachings in sexual and biomedical ethics.

Discussion continues in Roman Catholicism about the third aspect of natural law – the relationship between natural law and civil law and legislation. Thomas Aquinas (d. 1274) understood civil law to be based on natural law either by accepting the conclusions of the natural law (murder is a crime) or by making specific what the natural law leaves unspecified (vehicular traffic uses the left or the right side of the road). However, no exact equation exists between natural law and human civil law or between sin and CRIME. Civil law embraces only those acts that relate to the common good of the community. Likewise the legislator must take into account human reality and not suppress all vices but only the more grievous vices from which the majority are able to abstain, especially those which are harmful to others.

As the twentieth century has progressed, Roman Catholic natural law thought has recognized the growing importance of freedom and the legitimacy of democratic political structures thus affecting its understanding of the relationship between law and morality. The Declaration on Religious Liberty of the Second Vatican Council (n. 7) enshrines the principle of free constitutional GOVERNMENT; freedom is to be respected as far as possible and curtailed only when and in so far as necessary. The STATE should and must intervene to protect the public order which includes an order of JUSTICE, of public PEACE and of public morality. Disputes both in theory and in practice continue about the relationship between law and morality with ABORTION being the primary practical issue in many countries.

Aquinas, T. (1952) *Summa Theologiae Pars I^{a}II^{ae}*, Rome: Marretti.

Battaglia, (1981) A. *Toward a Reformulation of Natural Law*, New York: Seabury Press.

Curran, C. and McCormick, R.A. (eds) (1980) *Readings in Moral Theology No. 2: The Distinctiveness of Christian Ethics*, New York: Paulist Press.

——and——(1991) *Readings in Moral Theology No. 7: Natural Law and Theology*, New York: Paulist Press.

'Declaration on Religious Freedom'(1966), in W. Abbot (ed.) *The Documents of Vatican II*, New York: Guild Press.

Finnis, J. (1980) *Natural Law and Natural Rights*, Oxford: Clarendon.

Fuchs, J. (1965) *Natural Law: A Theological Investigation*, New York: Sheed & Ward.

George, R.P. (ed.) (1992) *Natural Law Theory: Contemporary Essays*, Oxford: Clarendon.

Grisez, G. (1983) *The Way of the Lord Jesus I: Christian Moral Principles*, Chicago, IL: Franciscan Herald Press.

McBrien, R.P. (1987) *Caesar's Coin: Religion and Politics in America*, New York: Macmillan.

Charles E. Curran

NATURAL RIGHTS

According to a long tradition of political and moral philosophy, natural rights are those rights that all individuals are said to possess equally prior to their participation in civil SOCIETY and to be in some sense 'inalienable', 'imprescriptible' or 'indefeasible'. Though some commentators have expressed the view that the term 'HUMAN RIGHTS' is but a contemporary idiom for 'natural rights' (Finnis 1980: 198) the scope of the former term often embraces the sense of a society's obligation to provide its members with certain 'positive' goods such as minimally decent health care, housing, EDUCATION and the like. The more prevalent view is that natural rights are 'negative', the moral property of an individual, those traits belonging to her qua human, in virtue of which she has claim to object to or resist any unjustified interference by another (Hart 1984: 78). Though this principle has been applied by contemporary theorists in ways more or less extreme, from the radical libertarianism of Robert Nozick to the neo-Kantian liberalism of John Rawls, in virtually every case 'natural' rights are regarded as those that 'trump' all other considerations. Accordingly, in any society and under every form of GOVERNMENT, merely by virtue of their humanity, people ought to have freedom of speech and conscience; to be able to live their lives without arbitrary molestation of their persons and goods; to be treated as equal in value (though not necessarily equal in merit); to possess some form of private PROPERTY; and to be governed only by their consent.

Though the doctrine of natural rights developed from a rich interplay of theological, social and legal factors throughout the ancient and medieval worlds, its mature and most powerful expression is embodied in the writings of the great social and political theorists of the seventeenth and eighteenth centuries, figures such as Grotius, Hobbes, Locke, Rousseau and Jefferson, to name only the most prominent. In this, its classical form, which bears the indelible imprint of these thinkers and their contemporaries, the doctrine posits in the individual the existence of a private 'moral space', a sphere of personal inviolability not subject to social, communal or political control. The idea of an isolated self that has decisive AUTHORITY over its private sphere and to whom all policy must be justifiable is an indispensable tenet of Western LIBERALISM; the 'social contract' into which selves enter to secure their natural rights is the ideological basis of the modern liberal STATE.

The history of the concept of natural rights is that of the evolution of the concept of a right as something the operation of which its possessor could control himself. Roman jurists maintained a distinction between a person's *dominium* ('property'), with its implications of control and mastery, and *ius* ('right'), what is morally appropriate in a given context, something the JUSTICE of which ought to be recognized by others but in any case depended upon them. In Latin legal philosophy, thus, an *ius* was something objective, to which a claimant would appeal according to the rules of right conduct. A *dominium*, on the other hand, was subjective, constituted by humans' total control over their physical world. The distinction between the ancient notions of *ius* and *dominium* roughly parallels that, in modern moral theory, between passive and active rights. To have a passive right is to be given or allowed something by someone else; it entails duties on the part of others to secure the possessor of the right that to which he has the right. To have an active right, by contrast, is to have the right to do something oneself; to possess a right in this sense is to have that sovereignty over one's relevant moral world so as to impose a duty on others.

There are several decisive moments in the evolution of natural rights theory. The first of these was the recognition of property as a right; though this is yet the subject of controversy, there is evidence that such a development occurred in the later period of Roman jurisprudence (Tuck 1979: 12–13). In any event, by the twelfth century this transference had become well established, leading ultimately to a consistent doctrine of passive rights such as are embodied in the great natural law theories of Aquinas and others. The second crucial stage in the formation of the modern concept of natural rights was to regard rights as the natural property of their possessor, a conceptual revolution which resulted from the fourteenth-century theological conflicts between the Dominican and Franciscan orders concerning the naturalness of POVERTY.

The process by which all of a person's rights would come to be identified as his property originated in a response to the attempt by leaders of the Franciscan order to justify a systematic doctrine of apostolic poverty. Such a doctrine would permit members of the order to use all the commodities necessary for everyday life without implying the existence of property rights, matters vital if the order was to remain at once well organized and true to the ideals of its founder. Duns Scotus, who framed the Franciscan apology, argued that the *ius naturale* was incompatible with *dominium*. Common use which excluded common *dominium* was the natural state of humanity in its innocence. Therein a human being was able simply to take what he needed, and had no right to exclude another from what was necessary for him. Scotus rejected the notion, however, that such necessary use was an instance of *dominium*, for such a right was inherently private and could be defended against the claims of the indigent, violently if need be. The Franciscan doctrine was radical, and perceived as such. It advanced the view that all property was social and absent from the state of innocence; in so doing it implied that communal use, not private ownership, was a worthy ideal for all people. The papacy under John XXII opposed this doctrine in all its radicalism, supplanting it with the equally radical one of full natural rights. According to the papal response, humankind's *dominium* over their possessions and God's *dominium* over the earth were conceptually alike. Adam in the state of innocence even before the creation of Eve was said to have *dominium* over temporal things. Property was thus natural to humankind, sustained by divine law, and ineluctable. For John, all relationships between human beings and their material world were examples of *dominium*. With this conservative reaction to Scotus,

'property had begun its expansion towards all the corners of a man's moral universe' (Tuck 1979: 22). It was left to Gerson and his followers to supply the last element. By claiming that *ius* was a *facultas*, or POWER, Gerson assimilated *ius* and *libertas*, and thereby the mere assertion of will entered, for the first time, into the sphere of moral property.

The richness of its historical sources, the complexity of its development, and the robust variety of its contemporary expressions all notwithstanding, the modern doctrine of natural rights remains essentially the one postulated by the theorists of its classical period as answers to three main questions: Who is the subject of rights? What is the substance of rights? What is the basis of rights? (Shapiro 1986: 273–84).

Ultimately, the bearer of rights that could be said to be 'natural' is the Cartesian self; rational and radically autonomous. Consequently, natural rights theory maintains that the individual will is the cause of all actions, and ascribes decisive epistemic and hence moral authority to the individual over her actions, on the grounds that she has privileged access to the contents of her own mind. It is for this reason that individual consent becomes so vital to the idea of political activity. Moreover, in defining their substance, the classical theorists emphasized that natural rights were claims deduced from the principle that a person has exclusive proprietorship over her capacities and actions. Expressions of the sheer capacity for freely willed action, natural rights (as Hobbes insisted) are independent of any conception of LAW, and categorically different from every kind of law. Correlative only with the non-right of others to interfere with one's liberty, they impose no additional affirmative obligations upon others (Shapiro 1986: 277).

The assertion that individuals have rights merely as humans can only be justified by positing the existence of some uniquely human trait. The idea of natural rights implies that there is an essential human nature which determines this status and a moral order governing the relations of human beings as such, independently of the laws of all particular societies concerning their conventional relationships, as well as the Thomistic *ius naturale*. To claim rights as an individual independently of society, a person must have reached a level of self-consciousness which enables her to isolate herself in thought from her social environment; such attainment presupposes a considerable capacity for abstraction. To this extent, reason, defined as the capacity for abstraction, is the basis for natural rights, or the ability to claim natural rights. Thus, it is by possession of the specific and natural characteristic of being rational that humans resemble each other and differ from brutes (Macdonald 1984: 29). Not only do humans have rights simply by virtue of that essential characteristic which makes them human, the existence of such rights is known *a priori*; they are, in Jefferson's words, 'self-evident'.

In general terms, therefore, the doctrine of natural rights can be characterized as individualist in its conception of the self, essentialist in its definition of the moral community, and rationalist in the *a priori* manner of its justification. In each of these respects it has come under criticism from contemporary thinkers.

In defending their claim that it is the presence and actions of the state that require JUSTIFICATION, natural rights theorists assume that the model of pre-political, 'normal' human interaction takes the form of simple, voluntary transactions among isolated individuals, unmediated by any external authority structures and power relations. Yet, it has been argued that the idea of such persons is ontologically incoherent while the existence of the stipulated transactions is counterfactual. Moreover, in so far as it implies the illegitimacy of social reconstruction by means of state action, natural rights theory could be said to allow the unimpeded function of power relations embedded in the existing market system (Shapiro 1986: 289).

Since the doctrine's essentialism renders it incompatible with the moral consequences of Darwinism, it has met opposition from the growing authority of the ANIMAL RIGHTS movement, as well as from others who find the Cartesian–Kantian idea of rationality as a requirement for inclusion in the Kingdom of Ends too restrictive. While it may be true that non-human animals do not have the capacity for abstraction, neither do human infants, comatose patients or the severely mentally retarded; if brutes do not have

prima facie natural rights, then neither do the above. Moreover, if the term 'reason' is to be used more widely to include non-symbolic manifestations of intelligence ('knowing-how' as well as 'knowing that', for example), then intelligence does not posit an unbridgeable gap between humans and other creatures (Macdonald 1984: 28).

Finally, the theory of natural rights is intimately connected with a rationalism whose method of epistemic certainty aims to establish undubitable truths. Yet, the above-mentioned 'rights' need not be thought of as transcendentally justified *claims*. It is at least equally possible that the so-called 'inalienable rights' of persons are in fact no more than the cumulative *decisions* of a community concerning what ought to be as a result of human choice (Macdonald 1984: 34–40). Where such moral judgements embody the justice-seeking pragmata of everyday life unmediated by foundational discourse, the very possibility, or even need, for such axiomatic understanding of human value is problematic.

d'Entreves, A.P. (1951) *Natural Law: An Historical Survey*, London: Hutchinson.

Finnis, J. (1980) *Natural Law and Natural Rights*, Oxford: Oxford University Press.

Hart, H.L.A. (1984) 'Are there any natural rights?', in J. Waldron (ed.) *Theories of Rights*, Oxford: Oxford University Press.

Macdonald, M. (1984) 'Natural rights', in J. Waldron (ed.) *Theories of Rights*, Oxford: Oxford University Press.

Maritain, J. (1971) *The Rights of Man and Natural Law*, trans. D.C. Anson, New York: Gordian Press.

Rachels, J. (1991) *Created From Animals: The Moral Implications of Darwinism*, Oxford: Oxford University Press.

Ritchie, D.G. (1894) *Natural Rights: A Criticism of Some Political and Ethical Conceptions*, London: George Allen & Unwin.

Shapiro, I. (1986) *The Evolution of Rights in Liberal Theory*, Cambridge: Cambridge University Press.

Strauss, L. (1965) *Natural Right and History*, Chicago, IL: University of Chicago Press.

Tuck, R. (1979) *Natural Rights Theories: Their Origin and Development*, Cambridge: Cambridge University Press.

Gary Calore

NEW AGE

The New Age, sometimes known as the Aquarian Age, refers to a new cycle of existence. It is based on the concept of the astrological Great Month of 2155 years and is thus supposed to succeed the Christian era or Piscean Age.

The term itself is credited to Alice Bailey (1880–1949), a member of the Theosophical Society founded by Helena Petrovna Blavatsky in 1875. Bailey's books, particularly *Discipleship in the New Age* (1944), expand on Blavatsky's ideas, formulated in *The Secret Doctrine* (1889). These are directed towards the propagation of universal brotherhood through the analysis of Eastern and Western belief systems and an exploration of psychic phenomena.

Theosophy is a form of MILLENARIANISM, dedicated to 'the emergence of a new kingdom in nature' (Bailey 1972: 3), heralded by a last Messiah 'who will come at the culmination of the Great Cycle'. (Blavatsky 1978: 384). The dire circumstances of the modern world make the preparation of humankind for this new age a matter of prime importance, and many of the principal ideas that lie behind the New Age movement have their origins in Bailey's writings.

As a reaction to the problems created by the growth of industry and URBANIZATION in the West, the increasing sense of isolation and ALIENATION, Bailey stresses the significance of group work. The intuitive faculties are to be developed in contradistinction to the present overemphasis on intellectual, or left-brain, activity. She is concerned with 'healing the various ills of humankind – physical, mental, psychological and emotional' (Bailey 1972: 13), thus foreshadowing the holistic approach so characteristic of New Age therapies. Meditation and visualization are essential parts of the healing process, as is the development of LOVE for humankind. Bailey further advocates 'fluidity of mind' (1972: 681), the cultivation of detachment in the face of inevitable change, and the acceptance that 'men determine their own destiny' (1972: 74).

Responsibility for oneself is related to the Hindu concept of karma, the law of cause and effect, and its concomitant, reincarnation, or rebirth, which allows for reconnection with the primitive idea that people are an integral part of the planet. Human beings are part of a living universe, here to express a new spirituality of oneness with God and all life. They are co-creators with God, each reaching the Divine in their own way; thus 'you cannot impose your brand of enlightenment on anyone else' (Ferguson 1986: 451).

The New Age movement is *inclusive* in its approach. It emphasizes living in the present, and progressing through direct experience. Concern with the feminine aspects of being and creation are in keeping with its advocacy of an intuitive, synthesizing, philosophy of life.

The Theosophical Society provoked the establishment of further bodies influenced by its ideas. Among the most important are Rudolf Steiner's breakaway Anthroposophical Society (1912), which is based on his belief in the possibility of training the human intellect to a point where the individual can take part in the spiritual processes of life, and Alice Bailey's own Arcane School (1923). In their turn they have given rise to a proliferation of other CULTS and movements.

Although relatively obscure throughout the first half of this century, the growing dissatisfaction of individuals in an increasingly materialistic SOCIETY with its heavy emphasis on consumerism and the outward symbols of monetary success brought these organizations into prominence. The 1960s saw a backlash against 'CAPITALISM, mainstream Christianity, and participatory DEMOCRACY' (Melton 1990: 328), and new communities, or communes, were founded, some as a protest against what was seen as a decadent society and others in order to regenerate the spiritual aspects of people and to re-establish their harmonious relationship with the created world.

The Findhorn Community in Scotland, founded by Peter and Eileen Caddy in 1965, initially devoted itself to thoughtful cultivation of the earth, apparently inspired by nature spirits or 'devas'. One of the original New Age communes, it is now a centre running workshops and courses on the education and development of the whole person in relation to his or her ENVIRONMENT.

The Wrekin Trust, created in 1971 by Sir George Trevelyan, was another prominent body which held conferences on esoteric subjects and acted as a focal point for many New Age thinkers. Such foundations have propagated the importance of group work, the concept of HOLISM, and the empowerment of the individual to take charge of his own life.

Complementary therapies abound within the New Age movement. Homeopathy, herbalism, osteopathy, acupuncture, spiritual healing: they all affect to recognize 'the body–mind connection' (Ferguson, 1986: 108), as do the psychotherapeutic forms of treatment which use both spiritual and psychological techniques.

Interrelatedness is a dominant theme in New Age thought. Fritjof Capra's *The Tao of Physics* (1983) demonstrates links between apparently disparate explanations of reality: 'the two foundations of twentieth-century physics – quantum theory and relativity theory – both force us to see the world very much in the way a Hindu, Buddhist or Taoist sees it, and . . . this similarity strengthens when we look at . . . the properties and interactions of the subatomic particles of which all matter is made' (p. 23). James Lovelock's conception of Gaia, that the 'entire range of living matter on Earth . . . could be regarded as constituting a single living entity, capable of manipulating the Earth's atmosphere to suit its overall needs' (quoted in Bloom 1991: 166) reinforces the idea of interconnectedness in another context. The ex-Dominican priest Matthew Fox, in his book *Original Blessing* (1983), puts forward the thesis of celebratory creation-centred spirituality as opposed to the more familiar penitential fall/redemption spiritual tradition. 'It is open, seeking, and explorative of the cosmos within the human person and all creatures and of the cosmos without, the spaces between creatures that unite us all' (p. 69).

What has been described as the 'inner voice' (Bloom 1991: 41) is the most controversial aspect of the New Age. Directly related to intuitive forms of perception, the search for insight includes channelling (the bringing through of information from beings who supposedly inhabit another plane of existence) and the employment of the arts of divination. There is growing interest in pagan and druidic RITUAL involving such phenomena as standing stones, ley lines and energy fields.

Activities which enhance a sense of harmony and well-being are popular in New Age groups. Chanting and circle dancing, Hatha Yoga and T'ai Chi are all directed towards correcting the overemphasis on intellectual activity. To encourage meditative attunement there is also New Age music: avoiding recognizable melodies and abrupt changes of key or volume, it assists in the achievement of altered states of consciousness.

New Age thought sees the destructiveness of conformity and the importance of individual diversity. Egalitarian in its outlook it is typified by such organizational forms as the commune and the network, whereby people with common interests can link up with each other through directories or mailing lists.

Generally holistic in their approach, New Age movements provide a potential remedy for the alienation and stress-related ailments that typify the last years of this century. The development of intuitive insight and the exploration of non-rational forms of perception reflect on the limitations of language and the realization that we are more than the sum of our intellectual parts. Furthermore they have contributed to the increasing strength of feminist values.

New Agers are citizens of the world, personally involved in its suffering and redemption at every level of existence. Propagators of spirituality rather than organized religion, their devotion to the acquisition of enlightenment through direct experience reveals the influence of systems such as Zen and Sufism. They do not proselytize, emphasis being rather on the individual's search for a spiritual teacher and the belief that 'when the pupil is ready the master will come'.

As most New Agers have emerged from Judaeo-Christian backgrounds their attitudes and terminology draw heavily upon these belief-systems. They are therefore seen as threatening the very traditions that they have left behind: fundamentalist Christian response regards New Age ideas as savouring of black magic and the DEVIL. New Age acceptance of many roads up the mountain, its non-judgemental and inclusive stance, are diametrically opposed to fundamentalist exclusiveness. Nevertheless New Agers themselves have to guard against confusing this approach with a wishy-washy tolerance and lack of intellectual discernment.

There is also a danger of New Agers becoming as dogmatic about their teachers and their paths as the fundamentalists who regard them with such horror. There are unscrupulous gurus and false Messiahs, and groups who dabble in the occult, whose use of the New Age label to give them credibility brings the term itself into disrepute.

The great contribution of the New Age is to be found in its opposition to a male-dominated intellectual culture, its advocacy of caring and compassion made partly manifest through the healing arts, and its reminder that we are all part of one world and in destroying it we effectively destroy ourselves.

Bailey, A. (1972) *Discipleship in the New Age*, vol. 1, London: Lucis Press.

Blavatsky, H.P. (1978) *The Secret Doctrine*, vol. 1, Adyar: Theosophical Publishing House.

Bloom, W. (ed.) (1991) *The New Age*, London: Rider.

Capra, F. (1983) *The Tao of Physics*, London: Fontana.

Ferguson, M. (1986) *The Aquarian Conspiracy*, London: Paladin.

Fox, M. (1983) *Original Blessing*, Santa Fe, CA: Bear.

Melton, J.G. (ed.) (1990) *New Age Encyclopaedia*, Detroit, MI: Gale Research.

Spangler, D. (1976) *Revelation: the Birth of a New Age*, San Francisco, CA: Rainbow Bridge.

Trevelyan, G. (1984) *A Vision of the Aquarian Age*, New Hampshire: Stillpoint Publishing.

Caroline Phillips

NEW RELIGIOUS MOVEMENTS

There have, of course, always been new religious movements – all religions were new at one time; and throughout history fresh waves of new religions have been particularly visible at times of social, political or economic unrest or change, or in the wake of MIGRATION, invasion or natural disasters. More specifically, in the second half of the twentieth century the term new religious movement (NRM) has been used to cover an enormously wide variety of contemporary groups and movements which have also been subsumed under a number of other headings, such as 'alternative religions', 'unconventional religions' or 'CULTS'. Among the best-known examples are the Unification Church (popularly known as the Moonies), the Hare Krishna movement (ISKCON), the Church of Scientology, the Children of God (now known as The Family), the Rajneeshee movemement and the ill-fated People's Temple, over 900 of whose members died in Jonestown, Guyana, in 1978. But among the movements referred to as NRMs or cults one might also include the Alamo Family, Eckankar, est (the Erhard Seminars Training), the Happy, Healthy Holy Organization, Love Israel, the Church of Satan, Nichiren Shoshu Buddhism, Rastafarianism, Sekai Kyusei Kyo, The Temple ov [*sic*] Psychick Youth (TOPY), Neo-Paganism, contemporary Wicca covens, various groups pursuing Magick or Occult practices, the NEW AGE in all its manifestations – and sometimes groups associated with mainstream Christianity, such as Opus Dei or the NeoCatechumenates within Roman CATHOLICISM, and various 'Jesus' groups or House Church congregations affiliated to mainstream PROTESTANTISM.

As the foregoing catalogue might suggest, the concept of a new religious movement is not without its problems. Several of the movements can trace their roots back centuries or even millennia, and several of the movements are not obviously religious, or deny that they are religious; the Raëlians add to the confusion by calling themselves an atheistic religion. The current wave of NRMs, however, is usually taken to include movements that are new in so far as they have become visible in their present form since the Second World War, and religious in so far as they offer answers to at least some of the questions traditionally addressed by mainstream religions: What is the purpose of life? Why is there SUFFERING in the world? Is there a spiritual (or non-material) aspect of human nature that should be developed? What happens after DEATH? and so on.

Thus, although devotees in the International Society of Krishna Consciousness trace their origins to the sixteenth-century Hindu monk Chaitanya Mahaprabhu, and point to the Bhagavad-Gita as their central Scripture, ISKCON assumed its institutional existence only after His Divine Grace A.C. Bhaktivedanta Swami Prabhupada founded it in the USA in 1966. And although members of the Church of

Scientology (like some Buddhists) might not believe in a God, they have successfully fought in the Courts to prove that Scientology is a religion. On the other hand, the Science of Creative Intelligence (Transcendental Meditation) has tried, unsuccessfully, to prove in a New Jersey court that it is not a religion; and other groups, especially those associated with the Human Potential movement, may well deny that they are religions – they may none the less refer to 'the god within' and are likely to offer answers to questions about the meaning of existence or the place of the fully realized individual in the grand scheme of things (Barker 1989).

Scholars have argued that the term 'new religious movement' avoids the indiscriminately negative evaluation associated with the term 'cult', as it is employed in popular parlance and by the media. (Sociologists of religion have different, technical definitions for the term 'cult'.) An opposing position is taken by members of the 'anti-cult' lobby, who prefer to employ such terms as 'destructive cults', and who protest that to call the movements religious is dangerously misleading because the concept of religion is associated with something good, true and pure, while movements like those mentioned in the first paragraph are (a) 'bad', (b) 'wrong' or (c) 'really' a political or business enterprise. Such arguments would, however, risk our having to deny the application of the concept of religion in far more cases than the objectors would wish. First of all, history provides us with an abundance of examples of what most people would describe as 'bad behaviour' being carried out in the name of what most people would think of as 'real religions' (such as Christianity and Islam). Second, except in the case of the more liberal traditions, adherents of one particular religion are quite likely to consider that they are (at least more or less) right, while the other 'religions' are more or less wrong. And third, it is not difficult to illustrate that most traditional religions encompass in their organizational structures far more than religion – EDUCATION, businesses, WELFARE, POLITICS and numerous other functions have been within the province of religions since time immemorial, thus suggesting that it is not a case of 'either/or' but of 'both/and' being the more relevant criterion for

definitional purposes (Shupe and Bromley 1980; Robbins 1988; Barker 1989).

It is difficult, even foolhardy, to try to generalize about the current wave of new religions – although it might be noted that, unlike the situation in some of the earlier waves where the membership was drawn disproportionately from the poor and oppressed, many of the contemporary NRMs have appealed disproportionately to the middle classes. And while earlier generations of new religions in the West (more frequently referred to as 'SECTS') tended to come, at least tangentially, from the Judaeo-Christian tradition, this is no longer the case. There are, of course, numerous NRMs whose beliefs are derived from the movement's own particular interpretations of the Bible (the Jesus Army, the Vineyard Christian Fellowship, the Way International and Jews for Jesus provide some examples), but today's NRMs are just as likely to draw on Eastern religions and philosophies, such as Hinduism, Buddhism, Shintoism, Taoism, Islam, Zoroastrianism, or on polytheistic or pantheistic paganism – or syncretistic combinations of these traditions, mixed perhaps with ideas from Karl Jung, Alice Bailey, Aleister Crowley, the I Ching or science fiction. The Church Universal and Triumphant (sometimes called the Summit Lighthouse) receives messages from the Ascended Masters, channelled through the medium of its leader, Elizabeth Clare Prophet; the Aetherius Society harnesses power from Cosmic Masters in outer space; members of the Eternal Flame Foundation believe that they will not suffer physical death; disciples within the Church of Christ and the Multiplying Ministries teach not only that one cannot be a Christian unless baptized as a believing adult, but also that one may subsequently lose one's salvation and suffer eternal damnation if one does not embrace the movement's interpretation of Scripture; Sahaja Yogis believe that, with the help of Her Holiness Mataji Nirmala Devi Srivastra, they can awaken a spontaneous union with the Divine that is born within each of us; devotees of Sai Baba wonder at their guru's miraculous powers in manifesting watches and other objects; initiates of the Nessie cult venerate the Monster; Kennedy worshippers are healed by the spirit of the President who, it is

603

affirmed, gave his life for his people that they might be warned of the evil that surrounds them.

While some NRMs (such as the Asa believers in Iceland, the Damanhur community in Italy, the Winti Movement in The Netherlands or the Pucioasa New Jerusalem in Romania) have not yet travelled beyond the country of their origin, other NRMs have become multinational organizations with missionaries planted in countries all over the world. Many of the most internationally successful movements originated in the USA, frequently from the West Coast where the Human Potential movement and the 'self-religions' associated with the Esalen Institute have flourished; many more NRMs have come from the Indian subcontinent – examples would be the Ananda Marga, the Divine Light Mission (now Elan Vital), Sai Baba, Siddha Yoga and Sri Chinmoy – yet others that have had some influence in foreign lands include the Mahikari and Soka Gakkai from Japan, SUBUD from Indonesia, the Brotherhood of the Cross and Star from Nigeria, Shan the Rising Light from Denmark, the Raëlians from France, the Word of Life from Sweden, the Unification Church from Korea, the Findhorn Foundation from Scotland, the Emin and the School of Economic Science from England, and so the list could be continued.

NRMs differ not only in the origins and content of their beliefs; they differ in numerous other ways, and these ways are not necessarily aligned with the differences in either cultural or religious origins. Instances of both hedonism and ASCETICISM may be drawn from most cultures and traditions. Several NRMs expect their members to abstain from eating meat; some have rules against smoking, alcohol or any kinds of artificial stimulant; whereas a few movements, such as the Rastafarians, might use drugs for ritual purposes, many more NRMs boast that they have freed their members from a dependence on illegal substances. The Brahma Kumaris, ISKCON and Rajneeshism all come from Indian traditions, yet while the Rajneeshees have been encouraged to experiment with a wide variety of sexual practices, the most committed Brahma Kumaris remain celibate, and Krishna devotees may have sexual

relationship only within MARRIAGE for the purpose of procreation, so that couples not wanting to have children are expected not to consummate their marriage. Or, to take another example, both the Unification Church and the Children of God will justify many of their beliefs with quotations from the Old and New Testaments, but while Unificationists interpret the FALL in the Garden of Eden as a sexual event and see sex outside marriage as a dangerous and forbidden SIN, the Children of God interpret the Bible as advocating extremely liberal sexual practices, and in the 1970s and early 1980s they used to engage in 'flirty fishing', encouraging attractive young female members to be 'hookers for Jesus' in their efforts to attract outsiders to the movement. Other NRMs, such as the Church of Scientology, do not display any patterns of sexual behaviour that differ in any noticeable manner from those of the rest of SOCIETY.

Prayers can be heard and familiar liturgical forms are to be found within some of the new religions, but so are a wide variety of other practices: rituals may be newly invented by the founder or they may be adaptations of ancient scriptures or folkloric, shamanistic or magic heritages. Techniques such as sacred dance, chanting, meditation and various forms of yoga are drawn from older traditions; other exercises, such as the Scientologists' auditing with the help of E-Meters, are quite novel. Members may live in rural communes, in communal houses, with their immediate family or alone. They may work for the movement full-time, part-time or not at all. The NRM may get its money through tithing, from donations or selling literature or other objects in the streets or from door-to-door, by running businesses or charging 'clients' for courses or seminars. Some NRMs amass large amounts of wealth that may be invested or used to buy real estate or sunk into projects such as giving food to the poor (ISKCON), delivering relief aid to Third World countries (Ananda Marga), organizing conferences (the Unification Church, Emissaries of Divine Light and the Brahma Kumaris), publishing literature (ISKCON and The Family) and/ or proselytizing. It is not infrequent for leaders to become wealthy and enjoy luxurious lifestyles while members lower down the hierarchy lead a more frugal, hard-working life: Bhagwan Rajneesh, who accumulated an impressive collection of gold watches and over ninety Rolls Royces while his 'neo-sannyasins' engaged in the 'worship' that created Rajneeshpuram in Oregon, provides one example. But this is by no means a universal pattern: Dada Lekh Raj, for example, handed over his personal WEALTH to the Brahma Kumaris.

Some NRMs are organized along relatively democratic lines, others are more bureaucratic in nature, while yet others are run in an authoritarian style, possibly by a charismatic leader, unbounded by either legal rules or tradition and accountable to no-one except himself – or, occasionally, herself. The founder of an NRM may be considered by his or her followers to be an inspired leader, a teacher, an end-time prophet, a master, a Holy man, a guru, the Messiah, the Christ, a god or the God.

Lack of adequate data and disagreements over definitions means that estimates about the number of NRMs can vary enormously. It is possible, however, that between one and two thousand different movements exist in Europe and North America. It has been estimated that there are over 10,000 new religions in Africa and several thousands more in Asia and Latin America. Membership is even more difficult to estimate, but the number of fully committed individuals who devote their lives to any one of the NRMs is far smaller than is often supposed – rarely more than a few hundred, and sometimes less than a dozen. More people may have a sympathy with the movement and be 'fringe' members; others may flirt with one or two of the movements but never really convert or describe themselves as 'members'; yet others may be affected by some of the concepts (such as 'empowerment' or 'reincarnation') that have become part of the general CULTURE due, in part at least, to the activities of the NRMs. What is often overlooked when estimating membership is the very high turnover rate in most of the more visible movements – thus several hundreds of thousands may have been members of the Unification Church for a short period, but the movement has never, at any one time, had more than around 10,000 Western members (including no more than a few hundred from Britain).

The question remains as to why people join the NRMs, many of whose beliefs and practices seem strange or even repulsive to non-members. Physical coercion is rarely used by the movements – Synanon and the People's Temple are among the very rare examples where it has been – and the fact that few NRMs manage to attract and keep more than a comparatively small number of members suggests that it is difficult to sustain with much credibility sensational stories about sinister, irresistible and irreversible brainwashing or mind-control techniques being used to ensnare vulnerable victims. There is no doubt that many of the NRMs put considerable pressure on potential members, and once they have joined, people may find it psychologically or emotionally difficult to leave; but the fact remains that they can and do. Among the many attractions that the movements offer potential converts are the opportunity to lead a more religious or spiritual life, to develop a deeper relationship with God, or to explore the spiritual aspects of their own being; NRMs may offer the opportunity of living in a family-like atmosphere with like-minded people who share values which, they believe, are not shared by the rest of the world; they may offer the opportunity to contribute to making the world a better place – to bring the Kingdom of Heaven on earth – to prepare for one's next incarnation, or, in more secular vein, to develop more meaningful relations, to succeed in one's career, or even to accumulate a lot of money by chanting or placing one's faith in a 'prosperity theology'.

Needless to say, promises of simple answers to one's own or the world's problems are not always fulfilled, and life in an NRM may not turn out according to one's expectations. Sometimes converts will shrug their shoulders and move on; others will feel that, although they did not get all they wanted, they have got something from their association with the NRM; others will feel angry or bitter at having been deceived and, perhaps, exploited; yet others will be psychologically harmed by their experiences and may find it difficult to readjust to the 'normal world'. This period of readjustment may be particularly painful if, rather than leaving voluntarily, the member has been expelled by the movement – or 'deprogrammed' (Barker 1989; Bromley and Hadden 1993).

Since the 1970s, groups of people have banded together to spread warnings about the dangers of NRMs (Shupe and Bromley 1980; Beckford 1985). Members of the 'anti-cult movement', like members of NRMs, vary greatly in their beliefs and practices; some are anguished parents, some are ex-members, others are evangelical Protestants or members of other religious bodies; a few engage in the illegal practice of 'deprogramming', charging worried parents tens of thousands of dollars to kidnap adult children and hold them against their will until they renounce their commitment to their NRM – or escape and return to it.

An obvious but often forgotten feature of NRMs is that, with the passage of time, they are likely to change more rapidly than are longer-established religions. Some, like the Shiloh community, disintegrate and cease to exist. Those that continue to survive, if not to flourish, may change in a number of different ways. The variety of responses that contemporary NRMs are making to the passage of time cannot be explored here, but it may be noted that a movement composed of drop-out hippies enthusiastically following a charismatic leader in the 1960s is unlikely to have the same characteristics when, by the 1990s, the leader has died and the membership consists of young children, teenagers who may be rebelling against the movement into which they were born and brought up, and possibly worn-out and somewhat disillusioned middle-aged members who are trying to cope with an economic and social reality which has proved to be remarkably resistant to the changes they had hoped to bring about. At the same time, it should be recognized that many members claim that their lives have been, and continue to be, far more satisfactory and fulfilling than they would have been had they not joined their movement.

With the approach of the second millennium, various predictions have been made about the future of NRMs (Bromley and Hammond 1987). Some commentators point to the rise of FUNDA-MENTALISM, others to the influence of NEW AGE and the Human Potential movement as trends

that are expected to become increasingly significant. There are so many variables, however (economic, political, military, cultural), which are bound to affect the fortunes of the movements that it is unlikely that much can be said with certainty. One might none the less expect that, while the movements will be more visible at some periods than at others, in pluralist democracies which support a mass media and have high rates of social and geographical mobility, new religious movements may not enjoy the successes that they dream of, but are almost bound to continue to be with us in a multitude of different and often unanticipated guises.

Barker, E. (1989) *New Religious Movements: A Practical Introduction*, London: HMSO.

Beckford, J.A. (1985) *Cult Controversies*, London: Tavistock.

Bromley, D.G. and Hadden J.K. (eds) (1993) *The Handbook on Cults and Sects in America*, Greenwich, CT: JAI Press.

——and Hammond, P.E. (eds) (1987) *The Future of New Religious Movements*, Macon, GA: Mercer University Press.

Robbins, T. (1988) *Cults, Converts and Charisma*, London: Sage.

Saliba, J. (1990) *Social Science and the Cults: An Annotated Bibliography*, New York: Garland.

Shupe, A.D. and Bromley, D.G. (1980) *The New Vigilantes: Deprogrammers, Anti-Cultists, and the New Religions*, Beverly Hills, CA: Sage.

Stark, R. and Bainbridge, W.S. (1985) *The Future of Religion: Secularization, Revival and Cult Formation*, Berkeley, CA: University of California Press.

Wallis, R. (1984) *The Elementary Forms of the New Religious Life*, London: Routledge & Kegan Paul.

Wilson, B.R. (1990) *The Social Dimensions of Sectarianism: Sects and New Religious Movements in Contemporary Society*, Oxford: Clarendon.

Eileen Barker

NIHILISM

Nihilism (from the Latin *nihil*, 'nothing') arose in the latter half of the nineteenth century as a literature expressing a putative new historical predicament of humankind. Its intuitive sense is given in the epigrammes fashioned by nihilist and anti-nihilist writers: 'If God does not exist, everything is permitted'; 'a nihilist is a man who does not bow down before any AUTHORITY, who takes no principle, however sacred, on trust'; 'the most extreme form of Nihilism would be that *all* belief – all TRUTH assumption – is false, because there is no real world'; 'what does nihilism mean? That the highest values have devalued themselves . . . there is no answer to the question, For What?' As these quotations indicate, nihilism is experienced as a moment of insight into the illusory character of religion, moral codes, and rational beliefs. It is scepticism or unbelief carried to an extreme that rebounds in a feeling of estrangement.

Nihilism made its début as the self-description of Russian politico-philosophical anarchists who relished intimidating the bourgeoisie by saying that 'everything that exists deserves to perish'. Ivan Turgenev gave nihilism an early literary representation in *Fathers and Sons*, where the student Bazarov, who takes nothing on authority, experiences his own nothingness in a universe governed by the purposeless laws of mechanics. The experience consists of an anguished reflection on the futility of life in a universe whose vastness dwarfs the scale of human action and whose remorseless workings through the laws of force mock noble aspirations. Bazarov's response to this experience is an abiding anger at the human condition, but rather than warring on all that exists, he 'just curses' and subsequently dies of an infection caused by carelessness in his medical duties.

Nihilism was a continuing theme in the writings of Feodor Dostoievsky, for whom its core was ATHEISM. Deeply religious himself, Dostoievsky sought to confront the intellectual pretensions of fashionable atheism by exhibiting the abyss of radical freedom yawning before the godless; for in that case, Ivan in the *Brothers Karamazov* says, 'everything is permitted'. Individuals who absorb this enlightenment experiment with actions that fill the ethical abyss. Dostoievsky gave extended treatment to two violent acts expressive of anger, aimless homicide and SUICIDE. The first illustrates his belief that in an atheist society none are secure. The second illustrates the annihilation of all social bonds, since the nihilist has stripped himself of the obligation to near and dear that ordinarily constitutes a compelling reason for existence. Dostoievsky also interpreted the meaning of nihilism from the perspective of society's governors. In one of the memorable passages of modern letters, the Grand Inquisitor gives the Devil's reasons for imposing faith by gruesome means. He argues that dogma creates a meaningful world governed by moral purposes comprehensible to ordinary people. While the Christian view of the Fall and Salvation is a myth that conceals the gratuitous exploitation characteristic of the actual world, it is a transfiguring myth that saves the multitude from a fate worse than the Devil's torment – moral aimlessness. The myth does not change the world; the Inquisitor relishes his superiority as a persecuting exploiter. But the religious deceit transfigures SUFFERING and DEATH into a moral interpretation that redeems the brute ugliness of actual existence.

Nihilism reached maturity as a philosophy in the later writings of Friedrich Nietzsche (1844–1900). He held that the nihilism latent in European CULTURE was the presiding fatality of his times. The future would either tend toward degeneration, or else a new creative act would renovate European culture. Nietzsche intended his writings to prepare or constitute that creative act.

Nihilism, he thought, is a permanent human possibility apt to suggest itself to perceptive minds in transient moments. Numerous spirits in various cultures have grasped something of it, and some speculation, especially the Buddhist, is close to explicit nihilism. Nevertheless, for Nietzsche the discovery that the primary impulses driving a culture for millenia culminate in Nothing is a unique cultural event. It is then that the highest values are experienced as devaluing themselves, resulting in a loss of purpose. The Western philosophical-scientific tradition devalues itself when the search for TRUTH, after many heroic attempts, culminates in the discovery that truth is the name that a particular animal gives to the emotions that impel its life choices. Similarly, God and the Good merely name the authoritative values of PERSONS and peoples.

It is important for Nietzsche's thesis about the latency of nihilism that these outcomes really do result from the application of the rationalist and ultimately mechanistic principle to the interpretation of life. He called this interpretation of human knowledge 'perspectivism' to stress the biological conditions of animal perception. It is akin to the positivism of Ernst Mach and the conventionalism of Pierre Duhem, but Nietzsche is more explicit that Truth in the last instance rests upon the fiat, *Thus I (or we) will it*. In morals, he was an evolutionist who viewed valuation as adaptive response and values as coping strategies. His standard for judging Truth and Goodness was the 'will to power', that is, the scale of ascending and diminishing vitality. Diminishing vitality, or decadence, selects values adaptive for an organism competing defensively with stronger natures. Nietzsche believed that Christianity and Buddhism propounded decadent values, while Hinduism, Judism and Islam were religions of ascending strength. He shared Machiavelli's violent antipathy to the Christian inversion of the values of antiquity; this was the source of his anti-Christian animus.

Nietzsche believed that his philosophy overcame nihilism by incorporating it into a new human type, the Over-man (Übermensch). The Übermensch overcomes the mere man in himself, and creates a higher plateau of spirituality by accepting that Truth and Falsity, Good and Evil, are circuits composing part of the repertoire of the human animal's information-processing and motivational systems. The extreme contingency that values are episodes of animal life will terrify the decadent but invigorate strong spirits by making them acutely conscious that they are the sole authors of the worlds that they will and make. This is a variation on the central thought of German Idealism and of much European humanism. But rather than aiming at a speculative or moral fulfilment, as the humanist tradition usually did, Nietzsche aimed for the aesthetic exuberance of life in service to a cultural renewal.

The discovery of Nietzsche in France and England around 1900 was a sensation. Here was a writer of many moods, by turns witty and sombre, elevated and brutal, with a fine capacity to delineate character and riddle the secrets of the heart. Not the least of his appeal was the iconoclasm directed against the sacred cows of the cultural vanguard. DEMOCRACY, solidarity with the suffering masses, humanitarianism, LIBERALISM, SOCIALISM, utilitarianism,

the progress enthusiasm, NATIONALISM, and equality of the sexes were all teased and embarrassed by aphoristic satires. But more importantly, Nietzsche seemed to have discovered a new way of thinking that, in melting down old certainties, opened unimagined horizons. Upheaval of accustomed certainties was indeed the keynote of fin-de-siècle culture: in the plastic arts, Impressionism and Cubism; in literature, the stream of consciousness; in music, atonality; in psychology, the discovery of the subconscious and of sexuality; in physics, the paradoxes of quantum and relativity thinking. His new style of thought was, in his own phrase, 'beyond good and evil' and one may add, beyond truth and falsity. This means that one's thought is no longer in service to the Good and the True, e.g. advancing the cause of humanity and of knowledge. These categories are interrogated as motivational filters that organize the chaos of appearance into meaningful matter. As for humanity, Nietzsche's new ranking of values construes it as a 'bridge to the future', or 'matter' to be used for the creation of Übermensch; for self-overcoming.

The First World War commenced with patriotic enthusiasm in all belligerent nations. But as the drum roll of glory gave way to the meaningless carnage of trench warfare, many soldiers lost all dedication to national war aims and fought because of solidarity with comrades-in-arms. This 'nihilism of the trenches', depicted by the writers Robert Graves and Ernst Jünger, was a piquant mass experience of the highest values devaluing themselves. Among civilians too there was disenchantment with the ideals for which the war was ostensibly fought. Revolutions in Russia, Italy, and Germany confirmed the disenchantment by declaring that the old order deserved to perish. The extent to which these revolutions may have been animated by the nihilist thought remains to be assessed. The question was raised by Hermann Rauschnigg, a religious conservative who defected from the Nazis. In *The Revolution of Nihilism*, Rauschnigg concluded that all professed Nazi beliefs were excuses for a power drive that had no aim outside itself (Rauschnigg 1939). Today it is understood that Nazi policies were consistently directed toward creating a Nordic empire from the Atlantic to the Urals. The empire was to be based on a population policy which justified the destruction of competing peoples for the creation of a higher human type – aims taken by some to be consistent with Nietzsche's apparent glorification of immoralism and the 'great politics' of Übermensch. Soviet communist party cadres were, like Nazi cadres, drilled in immoralism in service to party power and the creation of the Soviet New Man. It has been suggested that the contribution of nihilism to these political furies was to facilitate the substitution of a secular impulse to perfection for the Christian vision of perfecting corrupt nature as the work of redeemed humankind. On this view, the destruction of large numbers is the purgation of the ungodly, i.e. a sacrifice to the new god of humanity.

The cultural and intellectual relativism so marked in America since the Sixties has prompted investigations of its possible sources in European nihilism. Critics of this initiative argue that relativism is a native growth from political and cultural pluralism. Not Dostoievsky and Nietzsche, but J.S. Mill, John Dewey and Margaret Mead are the relevant sources to examine if the case for a nihilist influence is to be made. Nietzsche's evaluation of English utilitarianism and of J.S. Mill in particular is consistent with this approach. He was keenly aware that utilitarianism is but one step from value relativity, and he appears to have accepted Mill's exhortation to conduct 'experiments in living' in service to self-expression. Nietzsche's chief criticism of utilitarian thinking was that its image of humankind was a diminished anthropology that denied the human 'taste' for pain, cruelty, risk, and grandeur. The American form of utilitarianism is a pragmatic orientation first popularized by Benjamin Franklin. It is a hedonic and sociable philosophy of self-realization, whose tolerance of value diversity is accepted as the rational interest of each self-realizing individual. But hedonic toleration can mutate into heroic endeavour and a lively sense of justice, as happened in the civil rights movement. Sensationalized television greed and lust, overtly nihilist youth cultures and thrill killings may be other mutations. Yet value relativism may be less a threat to Western pluralism than an expression of it. The basic pluralist idea is that liberty is to be restrained only so far as is necessary for the maintenance of public goods such as the rule of law. This because there is no objective determination of the individual good beyond the minima of life, liberty, and pursuing happiness in one's own way; or alternately, the freedom to choose and act on choice is the one good that profoundly moves most human beings.

The nihilist experience of the abyss of choice and the absurdity of life has found many echoes in popular culture. Nihilist styles are marked among the youth, who are likely to be confounded by the conflicting values impinging directly on their lives. The morbid and fragmented images, the conscious irreligion and sometimes sadistic lyrics of rock music are perhaps 'just cursing' an existence whose triviality offends the longing for a pure Good.

Bloom, Allan (1987) *The Closing of the American Mind: How Higher Education has Failed Democracy and Impoverished the Souls of Today's Students*, New York: Simon & Schuster.

Brower, Daniel R. (1975) *Training the Nihilists: Education and Radicalism in Tsarist Russia*, Ithaca, NY: Cornell University Press.

Crosby, Donald A. (1988) *The Specter of the Absurd: Sources and Criticisms of Modern Nihilism*, Albany, NY: SUNY Press.

Devine, Philip E. (1989) *Relativism, Nihilism and God*, South Bend, IN: Notre Dame University Press.

Eden, Robert (1983) *Political Leadership and Nihilism: A Study of Weber and Nietzsche*, Tampa, FL: University Presses of Florida.

Glicksberg, Charles I. (1975) *The Literature of Nihilism*, Lewisburg, PA: Bucknell University Press.

Rauschnigg, Hermann (1939) *The Revolution of Nihilism: Warning to the West*, New York: Alliance Book Corporation.

Rosen, Stanley (1969) *Nihilism: A Philosophical Essay*, New Haven, CT: Yale University Press.

Smith, C. (1987) 'Clever beasts who invented knowing: Nietzsche's evolutionary biology of knowledge', *Biology and Philosophy* 2, 1–27.

Weier, Winfried (1980) *Nihilismus: Geschichte, System, Kritik*, Paderborn: Schöningh.

Yack, Bernard (1986) *The Longing for Total Revolution: Philosophic Sources of Discontent from Rousseau to Marx and Nietzsche*, Princeton, NJ: Princeton University Press.

Hiram Caton

NOISE

The origin of the word 'noise' is unclear, it was established in its French form by the eleventh century and in English by the thirteenth century. There is some suggestion that it may have been derived from the Latin for *nausea*. The basic meaning refers to the aural effect of vibration, to sound, although it is now frequently used in a wider sense to refer to almost anything that stands out from the background. Hence there are technical references to the noise in electronic circuitry, to the residual cosmic noise left over from the Big Bang, or even to visual noise. By extension one can speak also of political noise: that concatenation of voices that in an heterogeneous and plural world demand to be heard.

Noise in the narrow sense, aural noise, is 'sound' occurring in the frequency range 20hz to 20khz, although sometimes here the term 'noise' and the term 'sound' are used interchangeably. The general trend has been to refer to unwanted sound as noise, thus giving a negative evaluation to noise. In Amos when God did not want to hear the sound of singing and of instruments he refers to it as noise, 'Take away from me the noise of your songs; to the melody of your harps I will not listen' (Amos 5: 23). When sound is wanted its effects can be positive. It may express or reveal thought as spoken prayer or as musical praise. When it is unwanted, it becomes noise or disturbance and undercuts the quietude required for a life of contemplation, the *vita contemplativa*, and fragments the mental continuity making serious thought, prayer, or reflection difficult or even impossible.

The association of noise, in its negative sense, and its opposition to all that is spiritual, is well and long established; it survives in the oldest written records. It is indeed the actions of noisy human life disturbing the peace of the gods that has, on some accounts, brought EVIL upon the world. In *The Eridu Genesis*, dating from the third millennium BCE, one of the four Gods who had created humans, Enlil, was disturbed by the noise made by humans in the earliest cities (*see* CITY). Enlil was so enraged by this that he persuaded the other gods to destroy humanity in a great flood. However, one of the gods, Enki, warned his favourite human, Ziusudra, and had him build a boat with which he, his relatives and representative animals could survive. As humans multiplied again, so did their noise which was so great at night that Enlil was kept sleepless. This time he caused a drought to bring the people to starvation and again the plot was foiled by Enki who fed the people with fish. A furious Enlil brought yet another flood, that was yet again survived by man and by representative animals (Jacobsen 1976: 114–20).

The myth shows, among other things, the clear contrast between the noisy life of world engagement and activity, all that is earthly, material and worldly, and the peace that is sought by the life of the spirit. What irked the gods of Mesopotamia, above all else, was the noisiness of their CREATION and it was for their noise, rather than for other misdeeds, that the floods were sent. In this account of the flood, an account that predates the Biblical account by some considerable time, the source of the dissatisfaction of the gods with humans was their noise rather than their general behaviour. The example is scarcely confined to such early myths for we find the Hebraic God also seeking silence, reflected clearly in the injunction to be silent when He was in His temple. When the 'LORD is in his holy temple; let all the earth keep silence before him (Habakkuk 2: 20). At another time we find it advisable for 'the prudent [to] keep silence' (Amos 5: 13) and even that, 'by doing right you may put to silence the ignorance of foolish men' (1 Peter 2: 15).

Noise is partly, if not entirely, an aspect of that which is heard. As with any aspectival phenomenon, it has a subjective, or at least partly subjective, components. As the duck, in the classical example, may be seen as a rabbit or the computer generated stereoscopic drawing as either a meaningless pattern or striking picture, so a sound may be a noise when one of its meaningful aspects has not, to use Wittgensteinian terms 'dawned' upon one. The failure to see an aspect, what has been called aspect blindness (Wittgenstein 1969), may account for some of the reasons for the appearance of sound as noise. Thus strange accents, and strange languages often seem noisy as do the participants in strange cultures. The phenomenon of aspect applied to noise has been referred to as 'Hearkening'; where one hearkens to or hears what is in the noise. As Heidegger puts it when talking of 'Hearkening',

> What we first 'hear' is never noises or complexes of sounds, but the creaking waggon, the motor cycle. We hear the column on the march, the north wind, the woodpecker tapping, the fire crackling. It requires a very artificial and complicated frame of mind to hear a pure noise.
>
> (Heidegger 1962: 207)

This aspect perception of noise introduces a subjective component into noise that forms the basis of its evaluative component. That there is an evaluative element in noise, seems to suggest that no objective criterion of noise can be given. Noise, it is often said, is merely a matter of taste; a subjective evaluation. Hence, what one person regards as a desirable sound another might regard as an unwanted and disturbing noise, one person's 'music' is another's pneumatic drill for example. Yet another, a thinker or contemplative for example, might regard almost all sound as disturbing. This apparently subjective disagreement is the source of multiple conflicts and difficulties with others; conflicts frequently compounded by a mutual and often complete incomprehension of the point of view of the other. On the basis of such arguments it might appear that no objective account of noise can be given, that it is always and only a matter of aspect or perspective. This view would be mistaken.

There is some agreement that some kinds of noise are always harmful. Extremely loud industrial noise, the noise of close aircraft, plant, cars, trucks, machinery, and occupational noise beyond a certain limit, duration, intensity or pulse is always harmful and sometimes physically painful. There is objective evidence that noise has a clear somatic effect on the human body: the 'N-response'. The N-response comprises four categories of measurable changes that occur when the body is subjected to noise. These are first, vasoconstriction, with resultant changes in blood pressure and heart rate. The vasoconstriction does not extend to the brain so the brain receives an increased blood flow. Second, under intense noise breathing becomes slow and deep. Third, there are changes in the electrical resistance of the skin and fourth, changes in skeleto-muscular tension. Additionally, gastro-intestinal motility alters, there are chemical changes in the blood and urine and startle responses to sudden and unexpected sounds or to sudden changes in background noise (Kryter 1970). Clearly any strategy for dealing with occupational noise must take account of these somatic effects and the effects of damage to hearing from long or excessive exposure to noise. The kind of noise arising from aircraft, plant, cars, trucks, machinery and so on does not, contra Heidegger, require a 'very artificial and complicated frame of mind to hear as pure noise'; that kind of noise is itself artificial, and artificial noise seems on the whole to be harder to tolerate than natural noise.

Somatic changes that result from exposure to noise are accompanied by psychological effects that vary from person to person. There is some evidence that psychological responses to noise can be grouped into three broad kinds. At one extreme there is a more or less complete indifference to noise of almost any kind. At the other extreme is a group of people who are extremely sensitive to the effects of noise and find that it disturbs their thought processes, even in extreme cases their sense of self. In between is a group of people who while disliking noise are not always disturbed by it. The subjective conflicts that arise between people about noise are often about the type of noise, but sometimes they are also merely about the noise *per se*. The worst kind of conflict is when the noise produced by people who are indifferent to the effects of noise comes to affect people who are extremely sensitive to noise. The reasons for the different response to noise are unclear although somatic variations in response to noise are clearly present as are psychological differences in aspect perception. Both these components also partly explain why the noise a person makes for themselves is usually less troublesome to them than (often even equivalent) noise made by others. Noise made by oneself is anticipated and rarely startles and, because of its expectedness, rarely produces severe somatic responses. The control that one has over one's own noise reduces its alienness and the perception or aspect that one has of it is accordingly adjusted. A noise from another source over which one does not have control is alien in all significant respects and is likely, therefore, to be at least annoying and at worst even life-threatening. These differences in response to one's own noise and the noise of others are sufficiently wide as to be the source of millions of conflicts, made all the worse by mutual incomprehension.

There are clear and wide variations between peoples' somatic and psychological attitude to noise but there is no clear and unambiguous knowledge as to the cause of the difference. The view that different types of people respond in different ways to noise is an old one. Schopenhauer who wrote how noise was a torture to him and that it has 'proved a daily torment to me all my life long' (Schopenhauer 1913: 127) went as far as to suggest that the differences in response to noise were due to physical differences. In particular he thought the source of the problem lay in brain tissue. The reason for the indifference to noise by some people he argued, 'is that the tissue of their brains is of a very rough and coarse quality' (ibid.). Such differences were not merely physical, they also had intellectual consequences, for it seemed that those who were insensitive to noise, were also insensitive to argument, or thought, or poetry. 'On the other hand noise is a torture to intellectual people' (ibid.). One may take Schopenhauer's more general observations as one will, it does seem, however, that some kinds of activity are best pursued away from excessive, somatically disturbing and psychologically fractious noise.

It is unlikely to be a mere accident that religious orders, and contemplative life-styles across a wide range of cultures, value peace and quiet and place a limit on internal noise as well as seeking to exclude extraneous noise. As the gods required peace and quiet, so it seems that the contemplation of the gods, or of God, is best undertaken against a peaceful background. That background is not necessarily complete silence. Some religious orders do require almost complete silence but, in general, WORSHIP and

religious contemplation is often thought to be assisted by sound of a soothing or gentle character. LITURGY may well be musical in form or may be accompanied by, or backed up by, plain song or evenly paced and gently modulated chant. The character of such noise avoids somatic startle effects and may assist the generation of a contemplative aspect.

That the contemporary world is full of the kind of noise that produces somatic disturbance and reduces the possibility of contemplation is not without cost and not without effect. If noise inhibits, or even prevents contemplation, then a noisy world is likely to be one that turns away from religion and from contemplation. It has been observed that the contemplative tradition, the *vita contemplativa*, replaced the *vita activa*, the life of action, after the fall of Rome (Arendt 1958). The *vita activa* is made up of labour, work, and action. It is out of the development of *Homo laborans*, and *Homo faber* that a life of action with all its human potentiality is, in principle, possible. But the increase in noise is scarcely likely to bring about a further inversion of these two traditions. It is more likely that both will be driven out in favour of a life of activity without action: the life of frenzied activity, to borrow from an observation Marx made about the breakdown of feudal society and the rise of modern society. Modern humanity has obtained a kind of inverted or distorted liberty, the liberty to engage in a frenzied activity produced by the 'unrestrained movement of the spiritual and material elements that form the content of his life' (Marx 1975: 167).

To parody on the root of the term, it would seem that the root cause of noise in the world is *Homo nausea* and a life of noise is *vita nausea*. As the components of the *vita activa* are labour, work and action so the components of the *vita nausea* are aural noise, visual noise, and economic, social and political noise.

Homo nausea is central to the world in which we live: Schopenhauer found them in a cracking of whips that tore his consciousness apart and rent it into temporally distinct and discontinuous fragments. Marx found them in that frenzied activity accompanying the social and cultural breakdown of an era and we find it in noise ranging from the pneumatic drill, the artificially extended bass of heavy metal, the deep thump of rap or jungle from the passing car to the apparently less intrusive but none the less obnoxious noise of Muzack/nauzack in the lift, store, shopping centre or other quasi-public place. Such endless noise is opposed to the thoughtful and contemplative life. It interrupts thought, breaking up its continuity, fragments consciousness, and fractures self; therein lies its appeal for *Homo nausea*. The life of *Homo nausea*, *vita nausea*, is a life of endless and frenzied activity, a life with no time or place for thought or reflection. Noise is produced to fill the vacuum of silence into which thought and thoughtfulness might otherwise enter. It is impossible for *Homo nausea* to listen, for that would be to risk silent periods and that in turn might throw *Homo nausea* inward away from *vita nausea* to *vita contemplativa* – where it might see itself, where it might be drawn to that kind of question of meaning that it must avoid at all costs. For *Homo nausea* noise is an antidote to contemporary and widespread nihilistic feelings but in avoiding the inner questions that silence raises, the NIHILISM perpetuates itself and results in yet more noise, yet more frenzy and yet more meaninglessness.

Homo nausea has never learnt the love or pleasures of silence, whether that silence be alone, or with others. The Hebraic conception of time, found in the adjunct that there is, 'a time to rend, and a time to sew; a time to keep silence, and a time to speak' (Ecclesiastes 3: 7), is unknown and alien to them. For *Homo nausea* time is not periodic and meaningful but constantly fragmented and potentially frightening – it must always be filled and always fragmented. Not for *Homo nausea* the experience of silence alone or the experience of silence with others. Not for *Homo nausea* the experience of Foucault who spoke of how he built a long lasting friendship with someone to whom he did not speak – on silence – on just being with someone (Foucault 1988). Nor for *Homo nausea* the experience of freedom that silence brings for freedom is a terrifying and dreadful abyss that *Homo nausea* cannot face, and moments of silence bring it to the edge of that abyss. The first imperative of *Homo nausea* is to avoid the fear and trembling and the dread

of Being, about which Kierkegaard wrote so powerfully and so directly, and the first mechanism by which that imperative can be fulfilled is through endless noise and the avoidance of silence.

The first love of *Homo nausea* and the foundation of the *vita nausea* is aural noise but on that base arises a vast superstructure of visual and social noise. Visual noise, visual pollution to those not caught up in the *vita nausea*, ranges from gigantic and brightly lit drinks machines set against an otherwise quiet background; the giant yellow 'M' set on a pole reaching into the sky as if it were the new tower of Babel complete with its new and trite universal language, a language generated as a clear and pathetic defiance to the dishemmination caused by the Hebraic God; the fluorescent lights of advertising hoardings; dayglo painted trucks or the dayglo coloured hairstyle shouting 'look at me', to laser lights in the sky; excessive use of city lighting that spoils the darkness for many miles and that can even be seen from far into space; to shops aimlessly displaying a thousand different televisions all flickering with a different and completely pointless lack of synchronization.

The highest activity of *Homo nausea* is to be found in distorted and quasi-political, social and economic activity. It is best represented in the shouting of demands made without pausing for long enough to listen to other voices and other concerns. *Homo nausea* turns all whims and inclinations into wants, all wants into demands and all demands into rights. Such want-rights are then used to trump, or at least to drown out, all other concerns and all other voices. Reduced to its simplest formula, the high point of the *vita nausea* is the shout of 'me too' made so loudly that it amounts to little more than 'me only'. As the politics and economics of noise, this results in the demand of multiple voices to be heard not only above others but to be heard exclusively, in an heterogeneous world. This demand and this plurality is the foundation of one of the greatest of contemporary challenges. *Homo nausea* in all its egoistic selfishness, and frenzy has finally emerged as a significant political, economic and social force in a deeply troubled world.

It is worth recalling, however, that noise is

not new and neither is adverse reaction to it. Noise may have been elevated to a discernible form of life but it seems to have been troublesome since the dawn of history. It is, perhaps, no coincidence that *The Eridu Genesis* written in the third millennium BCE, and which is our oldest account of the origin of evil, places that source with the annoyance of the gods of Mesopotamia by the noise of humankind. Noise rather than the love of money, we might say, is the source of all evil.

Arendt, Hannah (1958) *The Human Condition*, Chicago, IL: Chicago University Press.

Foucault, Michel (1988) 'The Minimalist Self' in *Politics, Philosophy and Culture: Interviews and Other Writings 1977–1984*, ed. Lawrence D. Kritzman, trans. Alan Sheridan and others, New York and London: Routledge.

Heidegger, Martin (1962) *Being and Time*, trans. J. Macquarrie and E. Robinson, Oxford: Basil Blackwell.

Marx, Karl (1975) 'On the Jewish Question', Karl Marx, Frederick Engels, *Collected Works*, vol. 3, London: Lawrence and Wishart.

Jacobson, Thorkild (1976) *The Treasures of Darkness: A History of Mesopotamian Religion*, New Haven and London: Yale University Press.

Kryter, Karl D. (1970) *The Effects of Noise on Man*, New York: Academic Press.

Schopenhauer, Arthur (1913) *Studies in Pessimism: A Series of Essays*, trans. Thomas Bailey Saunders, London: George Allen.

Wittgenstein, Ludwig (1969) *Philosophical Grammar*, trans. and ed. R. Rhees, California: University of California Press.

Paul Barry Clarke

NUCLEAR ENERGY

Nuclear energy is based on the fission of atomic nuclei. This process, whereby the nuclei of extremely heavy atoms such as uranium and plutonium split into two parts, the combined mass of which does not quite add up to the mass of the original nucleus, is accompanied by a huge amount of heat energy. If this energy is released rapidly, the result is an explosion; if it is controlled through the presence of an inert material such as carbon, the heat can be used as a source of power.

Nuclear weapons and nuclear power are therefore very closely associated, and it is this closeness which has been the source of much anxiety about nuclear power production. Although this entry will be concerned with nuclear power, the links between nuclear power and weapons must be kept in mind (*see* ARMAMENT). They are not so strong, however, as to constitute a blanket argument against nuclear power which, it will be claimed, in spite of setbacks, remains a viable future option as a source of electricity.

The social and theological implications of nuclear energy are therefore primarily about how we obtain energy, why we choose one source such as nuclear power (rather than others, such as coal) and the risks and benefits of such choices. Underlying these issues is the wider one of the extent to which human beings are entitled to use their knowledge of science and technology to meet the growing worldwide demand for more and more energy in order to achieve supposedly better standards of living. The balancing of risks, benefits and a variety of social and other factors is a matter for ETHICS; the wider questions relating to our relationship with the natural world and our neighbours, past and future, under God, are essentially theological.

There is only one naturally occurring fissionable material. This is a particular isotope of uranium with 235 protons and neutrons in its nucleus. But uranium 235 is always found in the earth's crust mixed with 140 times its quantity of uranium 238, which is not fissionable. Most conventional nuclear reactors are fuelled by either natural uranium (e.g. the Canadian CANDU) or enriched uranium in which the proportion of uranium 235 has been increased (e.g. pressurized water reactors).

In common with several other materials, uranium 235 emits radioactive particles. But it only splits (fissions) so as to produce large quantities of energy when struck by a neutron. Each fission of a uranium 235 nucleus produces at least two more neutrons with the result that a chain reaction builds up extremely rapidly. In a nuclear power generator this process is carefully controlled and the heat produced is converted into electricity.

Fast or breeder reactors use plutonium instead of uranium for fuel. Plutonium has 239 protons and neutrons in its nucleus, and is made in conventional reactors from the inert uranium 238. Thus fissionable plutonium, which does not occur naturally, is made from a non-fissionable material which would otherwise be thrown away. This reduces the pressure on limited and not particularly cheap uranium supplies, and makes the overall process so efficient from the point of view of both energy and renewable fuel that the reactor is said to 'breed' fuel.

Nuclear energy produces heat which is used to generate electricity in turbines. It first became available in the UK, France, the USA and the former USSR in the mid-1950s. By the early 1960s, Italy, Sweden, West Germany, Canada and Japan had it; by 1970 the former GDR, Holland, Belgium, Spain, Switzerland and India belonged to the nuclear club. By 1980 Czechoslovakia, Finland, Bulgaria, Taiwan, South Korea and Argentina were all producing nuclear electricity.

Nuclear technology was originally developed at the end of the Second World War to produce plutonium for military purposes. Even Britain's first commercial power station, at Calder Hall, was primarily designed for plutonium production and only secondarily to produce electricity. In 1953 US President Eisenhower announced his 'Atoms for Peace' plan which paved the way for a new emphasis on civil nuclear programmes.

From about 1970 onwards churches became increasingly concerned about the social and environmental implications of large-scale technology. In 1970 the Church of Scotland set up its Society, Religion and Technology Project under the leadership of former nuclear scientist, John Francis. M.M. Thomas, Director of the Christian Institute for the Study of Religion and Society in Bangalore, initiated discussions about the role of technology in the development of Third World countries such as India (which by 1974 had such a sophisticated nuclear programme as to be able to let off a home-made nuclear 'device').

Professor David Rose, an eminent nuclear scientist in the USA, was largely instrumental in setting up a major conference on the theme 'Faith, Science and the Future' at the Massachussets Institute of Technology in 1979 under the auspices of the WORLD COUNCIL OF CHURCHES (WCC). At this conference delegates voted for a five-year moratorium on the construction of all new nuclear power plants to enable 'wide participation in a public debate on the risks, costs and benefits of nuclear energy in all countries directly concerned'.

In Britain nuclear energy policy was the subject of a public hearing organized by the British Council of Churches (BCC) in the autumn of 1976. This was initiated by the then Secretary of State for Energy, Tony Benn, who gave evidence at the hearing. The format of the hearing and its outcome, which formed the basis for a case presented on behalf of the BCC at the Windscale Public Local Inquiry the following summer, is illustrative of the manner in which theological and social concerns can interact with one another; it will therefore be described in some detail.

The process whereby plutonium 239 is extracted from the spent fuel of a conventional reactor prior to being used in a fast reactor is a chemical one. The Windscale (now Sellafield) Inquiry was an investigation into a planning application by British Nuclear Fuels Ltd (BNFL) to build such a chemical plant, known as the Thermal Oxide Reprocessing Plant (THORP).

Prior to the Windscale Inquiry the government needed to decide whether or not to build Britain's first commercial fast reactor (CFR1). Benn's concern was that the decision should not be taken until after there had been a public debate of relevant issues, and he approached the BCC to request them to initiate one.

The hearing took the form of a cross-examination of expert witnesses by a panel representing the public interest and the fuel industries. It was chaired by Bishop Hugh Montefiore, and included the Scottish theologian Professor James Whyte. The findings of this hearing, which aroused wide public interest, were published.

The Inquiry Inspector accepted the BCC's request to present a case on the grounds that his final decision would be the outcome of a balancing of moral presumptions, some of a non-technical nature. The BCC requested him to make these explicit, and offered its own 'hierarchy of values' based on a shared British Christian and humanistic tradition to assist him with the balancing process.

The confrontational format of the inquiry made it difficult for the BCC to avoid being seen by some as anti-nuclear. But the essence of the BCC's case was that a convergence of social and environmental factors argued against the building of the reprocessing plant until several conditions had been met. These were a reduction in the level of disagreement among experts relating to relevant technical issues, the need for a satisfactory commercial solution to the safe long-term disposal of nuclear wastes, the prospect of unacceptable limitations on civil liberties and increased risks of proliferation caused by the increased use of plutonium, the foreclosing of alternative energy options, the relative insignificance of arguments for the planning proposal based on foreign earnings and employment opportunities, and the objection to embarking on a development which significantly increased the burden of responsibility and, potentially, of risk to our descendants.

It was apparent that relationships between BNFL and the local community were poor, and the BCC therefore also called for the appointment of a nuclear ombudsman to resolve this problem. The Inspector took up this suggestion in his report. But some local church members who were employed by BNFL were extremely angry at the BCC's involvement, which they interpreted as blanket opposition to one of God's potentially good gifts.

During the hearing of the previous autumn Professor Whyte had commented on what he regarded as the 'two voices' of science offering substantially different opinions about technical data. This was also evident in the case of two reports published by the Methodist Church in the early 1980s. Thus *Shaping Tomorrow*, published in 1981, adopted a fairly pro-nuclear stance, whereas *Future Conditional*, published two years later, was much more critical of nuclear power. Such divergence among experts does little to reassure the general public: some claim that it argues for caution; others believe that decisions must none the less be taken and that it is irresponsible to shelve them.

During the mid-1980s the WCC and individual churches in Canada and the USA monitored developments in the nuclear industry, which they continued to regard as an important long-term source of energy for human development. But there was at the same time a growing feeling among grass-root congregations, particularly in North America and parts of Europe, that the potential risks associated with nuclear power are incompatible with the well-being of both human populations in the vicinity of reactors and the environment generally.

The fallout from the 1986 Chernobyl disaster in the Ukraine, spreading across national boundaries and irreparably damaging plant and animal life, caused widespread concern which provoked the WCC, primarily on behalf of the Russian Orthodox Church, to call for the resolution of 'serious unresolved questions associated with reactor safety, appropriate safeguards for radiation protection and effective international standards'. It also called for 'public debate in all countries about the overall risks, costs and benefits of nuclear energy'.

It is significant that in spite of the severity of the Chernobyl accident the WCC did not adopt an anti-nuclear stance. But its attitude was increasingly shaped by the commitment of the churches at the 1983 Vancouver Assembly to covenant for Justice, Peace and the Integrity of Creation, the third part reflecting the growth in environmental awareness. At the theological level this meant that the natural world does not possess value solely in relation to humanity which has 'dominion' over it (i.e. instrumental value) but has its own intrinsic value irrespective of human beings. JUSTICE must therefore relate to the natural world, its resources and the relationships that exist between them.

Public opposition to nuclear power, heightened by accidents such as Three Mile Island and Chernobyl, plus other factors, has led to a virtual *de facto* moratorium on the construction of new nuclear reactors. But the overall problem of diminishing conventional fuel supplies (coal and oil) will not go away, and it remains to be seen how different countries will face the prospect of major energy shortfalls.

A quarter of the world's population currently consumes three-quarters of the world's primary energy. In 1980, global energy consumption stood at around 10 billion kilowatts. If use per capita were to remain at the same levels as today, by 2025 a global population of 8.2 billion would need 14 billion kilowatts (4 billion in developing countries and over 9 billion in industrial countries), a 40 per cent increase over 1980 levels of consumption. But if per capita energy consumption became the same world-wide as current industrial country levels, by 2025 the same global population would require 55 billion kilowatts, an enormous increase with drastic economic and environmental consequences.

Some thirty governments currently produce about 15 per cent of all electricity used globally from nuclear power. In 1985 some of the national percentages of electricity derived from nuclear sources were as follows: France 65; Sweden 42; the former Federal Republic of Germany 31; Japan 23; Britain 19; USA 16; Canada 13; the former USSR 10.

The Chernobyl disaster caused many countries to rethink their attitudes to nuclear power. Australia, Austria, Denmark, Luxembourg, New Zealand, Norway and Sweden continued with their 'no-nuclear' or 'phase-out' policy, and were joined by the Philippines and Greece. Finland, Italy, The Netherlands and Switzerland are still rethinking their position, and France, Britain, Germany, the USA, Russia, Poland, China and Japan have all reaffirmed their pro-nuclear stance.

As countries take stock of the various energy options open to them, they tend to take up one of three positions:

1 remain non-nuclear and develop non-nuclear sources;
2 maintain current nuclear power capacity during a period of transition to non-nuclear alternatives;
3 adopt and develop nuclear energy in the belief that associated problems and risks can be solved to a level of safety that is nationally and internationally acceptable.

Most governments agree that whichever of these routes is followed must be accompanied by the vigorous promotion of energy-efficient practices in all energy sectors, and that the promotion of safe and environmentally benign energy sources must be given top priority. In this respect nuclear power has advantages in that it does not add to greenhouse gases and takes the pressure off the demand for diminishing conventional fuel supplies which developing countries badly need.

Some of the disadvantages of nuclear power production from conventional and breeder reactors may be avoided by nuclear fusion. This is a process of merging two light nuclei to form a heavier one, with release of energy. But it is unlikely to be commercially available until the middle of the next century.

In the meantime it seems probable that most countries with a nuclear power capacity will develop and expand it, though no doubt paying constant attention to factors such as the long-term safe disposal of wastes which have caused public disquiet in the past. In Britain such a monitoring role is currently being undertaken by the Churches Energy Group (CEG), a small ecumenical committee chaired by Sir Frank Layfield who was the Inspector at the Sizewell nuclear inquiry, and the Church of Scotland's SRT Project. Early in 1994 the CEG produced a report which surveyed the various energy options and possible ways of integrating them in the light of common European policies and the 1992 Rio Earth Summit. The report contained a theological section which underlined the need to work out energy policies in the light of our concern for the natural world and long-term sustainable life styles:

> Theological consideration pitches the energy debate into a different key, although it does not provide easy solutions to every complex question. Nor does it rule out the need for pragmatism and technical data.
>
> *Rather, the vision within which the debate occurs has altered.*

When God's grounding and companionship of CREATION matters, creation itself (both human and non-human) matters. Equally, when God in Christ becomes the pattern of divine and human synergy, enhancement of life becomes the goal. To believe in God and to follow Christ is to be open to all the complexities of what is happening in the world; to be concerned over what cripples life and diminishes possibility; to contend with the selfishness which admits no responsibility and to work in synergy with God to enable creation to flourish. Thus what is to be endorsed, in the midst of the practicalities of the energy debate, is a strategy to fulfil that vision – a way of valuing creation – using it responsibly and choosing among energy options that will most enhance life on this planet of God's creation (*see* ECOLOGICAL THEOLOGY; ENVIRONMENT).

Bending, Richard and Eden, Richard (1984) *UK Energy: Structure, Prospects and Policies*, Cambridge: Cambridge University Press.

'Energy' (1993), special edition of *Christian Action Journal*, Winter, London: Christian Action.

Future Conditional (1983), London: Home Mission Division of the Methodist Church.

Gosling, David (1992) *A New Earth*, London: CCBI.

Montefiore, Hugh and Gosling, David (eds) (1977) *Nuclear Crisis: A Question of Breeding*, Prism Press.

Shaping Tomorrow (1981) London: Home Mission Division of the Methodist Church.

Solms, Friedhelm (ed.) (1980) *European Churches and the Energy Issue,* Forschungsstatte der Evangelischen Studiengemeinschaft.

David L. Gosling

OBSCENITY

'Obscenity' (Latin: *obscaenitas*, inauspiciousness, impurity, indecency) is a term which appears in a variety of contexts. People speak of the obscenity of WAR or of GENOCIDE, for example, but not without intending to give a familiar condemnation a less familiar application: *this*, they suggest, is what *ought* to shock us. Leaving aside such extensions of meaning, it is clear that 'obscenity' is most at home in relation to SEXUALITY (although the etymology of the word suggests that the connection is a contingent one). Obscenity, in normal usage, is found in actions, words or images of a sexual character which offend and disgust people. In practice, therefore, obscenity is one facet of the sexually taboo.

But more is needed, particularly because moral and legal judgements presuppose intelligible and defensible definitions. However, it is easier to identify fairly unambiguous examples of obscenity, and even to offer a broad characterization of the kind suggested above, than it is to define it as such. For instance, moralists and jurists tend to define obscenity with regard to what it *is* or to what it *does*, but each strategy has its own limitations. The former approach may degenerate into enumerating the bodily parts and functions whose public presentation or representation is deemed immoral, and perhaps wished illegal; this is the crude and arbitrary 'laundry list' procedure. The latter approach is aware that obscenity is to some extent in the eye of the beholder, and not a fixed property of certain acts, but it is in danger of an extreme subjectivism: it may degenerate into defining the obscene as whatever shocks the sexual sensibilities of each individual. Neither approach sufficiently attends to the social contexts in which claims about obscenity are made. These contexts are a reminder that the obscene cannot be isolated from wider patterns of sexual signification. (Nor should we overlook the socially conditioned character of supposedly natural and 'private' reactions to certain phenomena.)

English LAW on obscenity, which was subjected to intense scrutiny in the late 1970s (e.g. Robertson 1979, Home Office 1979, Simpson 1983), has long been dominated by a definition of the obscene in terms of what it *does*. Lord Chief Justice Cockburn's 1868 judgement (*R. v Hicklin*) suggested that a 'tendency . . . to deprave and corrupt' was the true mark of obscenity. This exact formula was incorporated into the 1959 Obscene Publications Act, although in other respects the Act attempted to improve upon older legal reasoning. In particular, it sought to distinguish art and literature from the irredeemably pornographic: a purported obscenity may be neutralized by the total effect of a publication, and/or excused through a 'public good defence' in the interests of art and learning. (In the *Lady Chatterley's Lover* case of 1960 (*R. v Penguin Books*), for example, the acquittal may have been made on one or both grounds.) Similar distinctions – aimed at separating the low brow from the high brow – were being framed in American law at about the same time. In the Roth case of 1957 (*Roth v US*), obscenity was judged to depend upon 'whether to the average person, applying contemporary standards, the dominant theme of the material . . . appeals to prurient interests' and is 'utterly without redeeming social importance.' Later to be restated in terms of 'literary, artistic, political or scientific value' – the so-called LAPS standard – the social importance qualification enabled some sexually explicit material to seek constitutional protection under the First Amendment's guarantee of freedom of expression. However, sexually explicit writings and images do not conveniently divide themselves into the worthy and the squalid, art and PORNOGRAPHY, and this is not the only area in which the law sets itself a near impossible task. It is obvious, for example, that the links between particular materials and 'prurience' or 'depravity' do not announce themselves unambiguously. Consequently, aesthetic, psychological and (above all) ethical decisions are all too easily disguised by short legal definitions. Moreover, in operating with these controversial distinctions and assumptions, the law is in a far from satisfactory condition. It is unlikely to offer a stable and useful definition of obscenity which will absolve the enquirer from further exploration.

Definitions of obscenity, for theological, moral or legal purposes, ought perhaps to take into account two basic principles which emerge from what has been said above. First, obscenity is neither purely 'objective' nor purely 'subjective': we do not have to choose between thinking the obscene a natural property of certain things and thinking it a function of individual perception. Martin Dillon's phenomenological account does justice to both poles (which are more clearly present in American than in British law) while denying that either pole can be independently determined. His account also allows us to investigate the social formation of obscenity without reducing it to being simply the operation of a *collective* subjectivity – as if communities projected the obscene, in an arbitrary way, on to acts and images value-free in themselves. The situation is much more complex than that: 'a phenomenological hermeneutic of obscenity must also attune itself to the contexts or horizons (historical, cultural, scientific, moral) within which the phenomenon emerges and which contribute to the meaning of the phenomenal theme' (Dillon 1982: 261).

The second principle is this: obscenity cannot be defined purely 'descriptively', without any reference to particular moral frameworks, since it is 'prescriptively' charged from the outset. To call something obscene, no matter how dispassionately, is to perform a complex speech-act involving a significant moral element. Doing so may not commit one to a specific course of action, legal or otherwise, but it does nevertheless express and embody some kind of moral perspective. Whether we call an image erotic or pornographic, therefore, depends upon factors over and above its material content. Similarly, in differentiating between the explicit, the indecent and the obscene, we make complex judgements which amount to a great deal more than purely 'technical' assessments.

The debate about obscenity is historically and thematically related to arguments over BLASPHEMY and sedition: it concerns the degree to which social institutions and norms (like religious and political ones) ought to be protected against dissent, 'articulate' or otherwise. In the case of sexual dissent, the variety of forms obscenity can take is itself particularly significant. The representation of the purportedly obscene – as against its presentation in actions or words – occurs in media as diverse as, novels

and films, plays and paintings, poetry and photographs. We have already seen how the law tries to distinguish 'high' and 'low' cultural productions, but aesthetic controversies can continue on both sides of that problematic divide. There is often, for instance, argument about the 'message' of a particular work; but there is also a deeper disagreement over whether works in certain media are capable of functioning as vehicles of *any* propositional content. Likewise, argument over the intended and actual 'effects' of specific works begs the question of whether this kind of reasoning has any real meaning for certain genres.

Nevertheless, despite such aesthetic complications, the issue of obscenity belongs with other issues in which social, political or religious institutions come under direct or indirect attack. As such, it is inseparable from a wider debate about the limitations, if any, to be placed upon the right to free expression. Normally there is a presumption in favour of this right, but even the most liberal societies recognize that its exercise should sometimes be waived (as a matter of ethics) and sometimes be curtailed (as a matter of law). Free expression, however highly it is valued, is still simply one value which can and does conflict with others. But the problem of free expression is itself part of a still wider debate concerning *law and morality*. They are clearly connected, but the nature of that connection is controversial. Some acts widely deemed immoral in a given SOCIETY will also, as a matter of fact, be illegal. But does the overlap go too far? Or does it not go far enough? In short, which 'sins' should be crimes? Above all, should the law seek to enforce a particular moral agenda or not? This crucial debate has been dominated, in England at least, by the celebrated Devlin–Hart debate (Devlin 1965; Hart 1963), but the analysis of the complex relations between law and morality needs to be constantly renewed in the light of scientific and social developments. (Lee (1986) provides an excellent introduction to the issues.) Moreover, despite a major contribution by a distinguished philosopher of religion (Mitchell 1967), the debate has not attracted much truly rigorous theological input.

It is in the context of this debate that the

problem of obscenity must be understood. But what was said of the wider debate applies to the specific issue too: good theological writing on the subject is hardly extensive. Religious perspectives on sexuality invariably stress the communicative, inter-personal nature of sexual activity, and its teleological dimension; together, these axioms prevent sex from being seen as a matter of individual gratification, divorced from personal and communal goals. It is not surprising, therefore, that the misuse of sex, and especially its commercial exploitation, is condemned in theological ethics. This could be the basis for a systematic critique of the obscene and the pornographic, and yet these topics (perhaps because their wrongness is taken as read) are rarely addressed as such. When they are, it is usually in terms of whether a person is justified in using written and pictorial aids to the sexual imagination – in other words, it is a question of the 'hygiene of sexual fantasy'. This seems to betray an individualistic and 'privatized' approach to sex which surfaces even in works ostensibly designed to counter it. The apparent ubiquity of the private–public distinction only underlines the extent to which theologians have set up shop in the territory of 'personal morality', fearing, perhaps, that any excursions into social policy would be branded as neo-Constantinian attempts to impose their morality on non-Christians. There are, of course, other ways in which a distinctively theological contribution could be made. But in the meantime, the social policy debate about obscenity proceeds in time-honoured paths.

Conservative approaches tend to argue that instances of obscenity, being grossly immoral, ought in general to be illegal too – unless sound counter-arguments can be produced in defence of individual cases. Although often stated with great sophistication, such approaches rely upon clusters of *moral assumptions*, *factual propositions* and *legal theories* which can be independently examined. First, conservatives rightly emphasize the role played by a shared morality in sustaining social cohesion; but they tend to confuse this *formal* observation with *substantive* claims about the content and immutability of that moral consensus, more often than not expressed in terms of 'Christian values'. The

historical, sociological and theological innocence manifested in such exhortations does much to undermine talk of 'community standards': it begins to look like the unwarranted identification of a sectional interest with community interests as a whole. Second, conservative approaches tend to assume rather than prove a causal connection between obscenity and dire social consequences. But these phenomena are a good deal more complex than populist appeals to 'what everyone can see' would suggest, and the glib dystopian rhetoric of 'floodgates' and 'slippery slopes' is just as unhelpful. Third, CONSERVATISM tends to presuppose some version of 'legal moralism', the belief that it is the job of the law to enforce a specific morality. But it is far from clear that the law should do this, even if it could, and the combination of theoretical and practical problems which arise suggests that a more nuanced account of the relation between the immoral and the criminal is needed.

Liberal approaches do not necessarily doubt that the obscene is fundamentally immoral, but they tend to argue that it falls outside the scope of the law – unless there is good reason to outlaw or restrict obscenity of certain kinds or in certain circumstances. But their moral assumptions, factual propositions and legal theories are no more above criticism than those of the opposition. First, liberals rightly stress the vital importance of freedom, but run the risk of treating individual liberty as an absolute, isolated from the social processes which in reality both generate it and limit it. Correspondingly, they concentrate on the discourse of rights, neglecting forms of moral discourse geared to duties or the virtues. So they tend, as a result, to be sceptical of appeals to 'community standards', even though such appeals reflect an important TRUTH (about ethics and social cohesion) which is unaffected by the kind of ideological takeover bids mentioned above. Second, liberal approaches are prone to doubt whether the obscene really affects society – although a readiness (in some quarters) to believe that pornography is a 'safety valve', directly reducing sex crimes, may suggest that the doubt is not evenly spread. Again, the phenomena in question will not submit to unequivocal interpretation. Third, LIBERALISM tends to appeal too innocently to the 'harm principle': in short, an individual should be free from legal interference unless her actions cause harm. But 'harm' may be taken to include not only physical injuries but also shades of moral and emotional damage; likewise, the objects of harm may be taken to include not only individual 'others' (as envisaged in the classic formulation of the principle) but also the agent herself, and even society. Precise definitions are difficult to frame, and still harder to justify, but they do determine the scope of the law's interest in obscenity. Narrowly interpreted, the harm principle might free pornography from legal interference except when models were hurt (or, of course, children were exploited) in the course of its production. But broadly interpreted, the harm principle might be used to restrict pornography: in offending those who do not like it, corrupting those who do, and damaging society, it appears (even in its distribution) to be the cause of real harm. Liberals face a dilemma here: on the one hand, the same narrow definitions which ensure freedom of expression in sexual matters might shelter all but the most blatantly violence-inciting forms of racist or homophobic speech; but on the other hand, broader definitions (designed to accommodate the actual goals of liberals) involve a level of paternalism which is indistinguishable in practice from legal moralism. It is not surprising, therefore, that liberal discussions of obscenity have generated increasingly complex and nuanced sets of legal proposals.

The theologian's first job, I suspect, is to help disentangle the moral assumptions, factual propositions and legal theories of the main approaches to obscenity. The theologian's second job is to assess them, and in so doing to raise issues which moralists and jurists might neglect. Contemporary theology is in as good a position as any discipline to advance the kinds of insights which are needed in the debate over obscenity. It can expose the complicity between conservative 'moral campaigns' and commercial pornography in their unhealthy and fantastic isolation of sex as an intrinsically 'naughty' activity. It can uncover the irreducibly communal dimensions of the sexuality we treat so individualistically – not least by revealing the deeply symbolic character of the physical body as a vehicle of

social meanings – and so bring into question the anthropologies of liberalism. Above all, perhaps, it can set an example by appropriating feminist critiques of obscenity and pornography (e.g. Lederer 1980), surely the most significant development in the debate for decades. Some feminists argue that CENSORSHIP is not the solution (e.g. Rodgerson and Wilson 1991), claiming that it would do more harm than good, and that mainstream feminist analysis has tended to confuse causes and symptoms. But the disagreement is surely subordinate to agreement on the crucial insight: that obscenity is inseparable from questions of POWER, VIOLENCE and social control. It is an insight rightly found in the best liberal discussions: 'What is truly corrupting is not sexual explicitness in itself, or even the suggestion that people should do whatever they like with a consenting partner, but the idea that they should overbear the will of another' (Robertson 1979: 13). Yet there is a long way to go before feminist perspectives are properly integrated into the debate on obscenity.

In the meantime, theologians can do much to articulate a vision, at once personal and communal, of human dignity in the midst of disorder. It is a dignity fractured and compromised by the isolation, manipulation, and negation of the erotic, for which pornography and prudery must each take some of the blame. But the manifestation of disorder in the sexual context should not blind us to its other manifestations, or we shall simply reproduce the same restrictive and destructive assumptions from which we need to escape. I began by noting that 'obscenity' is now used in many non-sexual contexts to characterize acts of violence, injustice and inhumanity; I conclude by suggesting that this usage may prove to be an unexpected but significant guide in the understanding and criticism of obscenity today.

Brown, B. (1992) 'Pornography and feminism: is law the answer?', *Critical Quarterly* 34 (2): 72–82.

Devlin, P. (1965) *The Enforcement of Morals*, Oxford: Oxford University Press.

Dillon, M.C. (1982) 'The phenomenon of obscenity in literature: the specification of a value', *Journal of Value Enquiry* 16 (4): 259–74.

Downs, D.A. (1989) *The New Politics of Pornography*, Chicago, IL: University of Chicago Press.

Dworkin, R. (1985) 'Do we have a right to porno-graphy?', in *A Matter of Principle*, Cambridge, MA: Harvard University Press.

Hart, H.L.A. (1963) *Law, Liberty and Morality*, Oxford: Oxford University Press.

Home Office (1979) *Report of the Committee on Obscenity and Film Censorship* (Cmnd 7772), London: HMSO (Williams Report).

Hunter, I. (1993) *On Pornography: Literature, Sexuality and Obscenity Law*, London: Macmillan.

Lederer, L. (ed.) (1980) *Take Back the Night: Women on Pornography*, New York: William Morrow.

Lee, S. (1986) *Law and Morals: Warnock, Gillick and Beyond*, Oxford: Oxford University Press.

Manning, R.C. (1988) 'Redefining Obscenity', *Journal of Value Enquiry* 22 (3): 193–205.

Merck, M. (1992) 'From Minneapolis to Westminster', *Critical Quarterly* 34 (2): 32–42.

Mitchell, B. (1967) *Law, Morality, and Religion in a Secular Society*, Oxford: Oxford University Press.

Posner, R.A. (1992) *Sex and Reason*, Cambridge, MA: Harvard University Press.

Robertson, G. (1979) *Obscenity: An Account of Censorship Laws and their Enforcement in England and Wales*, London: Weidenfeld & Nicolson.

Rodgerson, G. and Wilson, E. (eds) (1991) *Pornography and Feminism: The Case Against Censorship*, London: Lawrence & Wishart.

Simpson, A.W.B. (1983) *Pornography and Politics: The Williams Committee in Retrospect*, London: Waterlow.

Colin Crowder

ORGAN TRANSPLANTATION

Organ transplantation is a procedure whereby organs or tissues are transferred from one part of the body to another, or from one person to another, in the hope that those organs will survive and take over the vital function of a diseased or damaged organ or tissue in the recipient of the donation. The organs or tissues transferred include – in more or less routine therapeutic use, or more or less experimental use – bone, bone marrow, cornea, foetal tissue, heart, hormone, kidney, liver, lung, middle ear, nerve, ovary, pancreatic tissue, skin, small intestine, testicle. Combinations of transplants, e.g. heart–lung, are now feasible (*see* EXPERIMENTATION).

'Rarely has a medical procedure aroused so much emotional and public controversy as transplantation.' The modern history of transplantation began with the Bologna surgeon Gaspare Tagliacozzi (1545–99). He noted the 'force and power' of the recipient, namely the natural rejection processes. With the twentieth century, new surgical methods improved transplantation. Medewar explained how the body's immune system rejects foreign matter by producing antibodies. Tissue-typing made for better compatibility between donor and recipient. The major drug breakthrough came with cyclosporin A which can inhibit rejection without destroying host defences. Serious side-effects can still occur in drug treatment.

The 'principle of totality' is invoked to reject or approve transplantation. It can permit the amputation of a diseased limb for the good of the body as a whole. But some moralists have been less decided as to whether it is ethical to remove healthy organs from healthy donors; this would threaten the overall bodily integrity of the potential donor. However, others have argued that 'totality' can be construed in social terms and so affirm the capacity to act with, or for, others within, or even beyond, the FAMILY. None the less some moralists judge that 'the principle is too vague to support the weight of argument that has been laid upon it'.

At first sight, the maxim 'do not harm' appears to exclude transplantation of live donations because surgery may prove damaging or fatal to the donor. One necessary condition is that the donor gives informed consent. Psychological pressure placed on a family-member to donate to a recipient within the family can have very adverse consequences for the former (see the 1989 Act below).

Cadaver organ transplantation is governed, in Britain, by the Human Tissue Act (1961). There are two procedures for donation. First, PERSONS may 'contract in' by, in writing or by word of mouth, requesting their body to be used after DEATH for therapeutic purposes, medical education or research. The person lawfully in possession of the body *may* authorize action in accordance with the request. Or, second, the person lawfully in possession of the body *may*, under certain conditions, give permission for organs to be removed. The consent of surviving relatives is required. Two other recent developments outside Britain deserve mention, both motivated by the acute shortage of organs. First, by 1988, eighteen countries had promulgated 'presumed consent' where the onus is placed on positively withdrawing from availability as a donor. Second, widely spread in the USA is the 'required request' procedure that hospitals inform patients or their families about the possibility of organ donation after death.

The question of determination of death in cadaver organ donation is fundamental. Organs removed for transplant must still have life in them, and the presence or absence of such life must be demonstrable and clinically testable. Yet there must also be irrefutable evidence that the donor is truly dead. (However, the decision in the House of Lords, *Airedale NHS Trust* v *Bland* 1993, may in the long run modify this at present very firm requirement.)

The brainstem concept of death was developed in France *c*.1959 and in a 1968 report from the Harvard Medical School. This concept entails the irreversible loss of the capacity for consciousness together with the irreversible loss of the capacity for respiration and integrated organic functioning. Persons with non-functioning brainstems can be mechanically ventilated and their hearts continue to beat. Thus transplant organs can retain the 'life' necessary for transplantation.

The Human Organs Transplant Act 1989, applying only to non-regenerative organs, prohibits commercial dealings in human organs, both cadaver and live donations, and advertisements which invite persons to supply, for payment, such organs as are specified in the Act, or offering to supply such organs for payment. A counterargument claims that many who offer their organs for sale are the victims of POVERTY, disease and lack of free health care provision; it is this wider exploitation which offends. The Act's restriction of live donations (mainly) to donors and recipients who are genetically related does not help to resolve this issue. Effective legislation is needed, directed against the commercial procurers of scarce organs, not against genuine donors themselves.

There is no major theological or ethical objection to organ transplantation. It falls within the terms of 'neighbour-love' and 'bearing one another's burdens'. 'Identity' is a shared possession rooted in the image of God. Thus a narrow individualism, which would reject transplantation, should be avoided. But a prophetic critique of SOCIETY draws attention to inequity and discrimination. The criteria relating to the choice of transplant recipients should not be based on 'social worth' or social CLASS; but in practice the choice of criteria is very difficult. Some ethicists therefore commend casting of lots or first-come, first-served. Another choice is between treatment and prevention. Theologically this brings together individual and corporate stewardship of, and responsibility towards, the self which is a unitary being of body, mind and spirit. The shortage of donor organs, paradoxically brought about through greater public responsibility, e.g. by fewer road accidents, suggests a concentration upon transplants which are cheaper to perform and promise the greater longevity. There is no sound argument for anticipating death in order to secure organs from live aborted foetuses and anencephalic newborns.

Brazier, M. (1992) *Medicine, Patients and the Law*, 2nd edn, Harmondsworth: Penguin.

Capron, A.M. (1987) 'Anencephalic donors: separate the dead from the dying', *Hastings Center Report* 17: 5–8.

Gervais, K.G. (1987) *Redefining Death*, New Haven, CT: Yale University Press.

Häring, B. (1972) *Medical Ethics*, Slough: St Paul Publications.

Harris, J. (1992) *Wonderwoman and Superman*, Oxford and New York: Oxford University Press.

Lamb, D. (1990) *Organ Transplants and Ethics*, London and New York: Routledge.

Ramsey, P. (1970) *The Patient as Person*, New Haven, CT: Yale University Press.

Titmuss, R. (1971) *The Gift Relationship*, London: Allen & Unwin.

Anthony Dyson

PACIFISM

'Pacifism' is a term of recent coinage designating any position, moral or political, according to which WAR is unacceptable. At one end of the spectrum any political position can (by some) be called 'pacifist' which rejects a particular war as unjustified. The reasons may be quite pragmatic. At the other end of the spectrum is the principled rejection of all VIOLENCE, whereby the rejection of war is part of a larger moral system. In the composition of such a 'larger system' the components of moral philosophy, religious worldview and political realism vary from case to case. This review will not seek to cover purely personal, philosophical or pragmatic examples.

The central defining feature, namely the rejection of personal participation in war, seldom suffices to define a position. The wider circle of definition often includes (a) an alternative mode of public service, sometimes demanded by the authorities in lieu of obligatory armed service and sometimes performed voluntarily; (b) an explanation as to whether war is held to be wrong only for the individual (who is then often designated as 'conscientious' and his pacifism as 'vocational') or for everyone; (c) if war is held to be wrong for everyone, some alternative notion of how to defend national values non-militarily ('civilian-based defence' and/or 'alternative world order models'); (d) some moral understanding as to whether the rejection of war is contingent on providing efficacious alternative defences ((c) above) or may also call for surrender or martyrdom.

There being no one 'pacifist' worldview, and no single 'common denominator' on the level of rationale, several examples from history must be provided.

The pacifism (without the word) which marked Jewry since the age of Jeremiah was rooted in (a) drawing the negative lesson from the failure of the experiments with kingship in Israel and Judah; (b) livable experiences of surviving and even prospering as a tolerated minority among the Gentiles (Joseph, Jeremiah writing to the exiles in Babylon, Esther, Daniel, and much of later Jewish history); (c) more negative lessons from the experiences of the Maccabees and the Zealots; (d) the conviction that, since God is sovereign, if we suffer it must be that God permits it and we should not rebel against it; (e) the conviction that we shall be freed when God wills by the Messiah, and not before then or otherwise; (f) the conviction that, since there is only one God, the other nations have their place in his purposes as well; (g) the conviction that human life is sacred, so that to shed the blood of the only creature made in the divine image is uniquely sacrilegious; (h) all known empires and armies (until modern times) practised idolatry as part of military life.

The pacifism which characterized the first Christians added to this Jewish foundation, all of which they retained unchanged, the teachings of Jesus (love of enemy, renouncing retaliation, renouncing not only the lethal act but even the wish) and his example (although called to inaugurate the rule of God, Jesus renounced righteous 'zealot' violence as the way to this, and accepted innocent suffering instead). This 'early Christian pacifism' did not include expecting pagan governments to take the same path. Toward the end of the second century it did not prevent a minority of Christians from serving in the Roman army, but we have no information either about whether they ever bore arms in battle (since most soldiers administering the *pax romana* did not) or about whether their priests and bishops approved of it.

Once Christianity became the compulsory religion of the empire, the pacifist impulse was transmuted into efforts to mitigate war rather than to stay out of it. Bishops sought to mediate conflicts between princes. They decreed times (truce of God) and places (peace of God) where war could be banned. They exempted penitents, pilgrims, the clergy and women from participation in combat. There developed gradually the notion of the justified war, which would be recognized as the lesser EVIL by virtue of its meeting certain requirements as to cause, intention, authority and means.

From then on the pacifist alternative, in addition to being represented by Jewry, surfaced episodically as a critical thrust within Christendom:

1 among the *pauperes Christi*, the Franciscans and the Waldenses, in special connection with

the example of Jesus, the poor itinerant preacher;

2 in the Czech reformation (Hus, Chelcicky, *Unitas Fratrum*) accentuating the antitheses of the Sermon on the Mount as a New Law – a theme later revived by Tolstoy;

3 for Erasmus of Rotterdam, tied to his conviction that war is simply stupid, unworthy of the dignity of the human mind, or the unity of Christian Europe;

4 among the 'Anabaptists' of the Protestant Reformation, participating in the Cross of Christ through their non-violence and martyrdom;

5 in the Society of Friends (*see* QUAKERISM), trusting the power of the truth of God to illuminate even the enemy ('speaking to that of God in every person').

As other critical minorities have continued to arise, the details of the rationale have continued to vary. As Western PROTESTANTISM became more liberal and more pluralistic, so did its pacifisms.

Some use the word 'pacifist' to describe those who, while considering the just-war tradition to be ideally correct and violent self-defence to be permitted *in extremis* and in theory, can see no likely real case which would be thus justified. This was the stance of Erasmus; since the Second World War it has been held by many thinkers on the grounds of unjust means (indiscriminate or disproportional damage from nuclear, chemical or biological weapons) or unworthy causes (the defence of empire or commercial advantage). Stated by individuals in the 1950s, 'nuclear pacifism' came to be espoused by church bodies in the 1980s (*see* WORLD COUNCIL OF CHURCHES).

Such a near-categorical rejection of war can also be the conviction of an individual who, while not opposed to all wars, considers the particular wars which his GOVERNMENT is waging or is likely to wage to be unjust, and accordingly refuses to serve. This position is sometimes called 'selective conscientious objection'. Whereas most Western democracies now allow exemption from military service for thoroughgoing pacifists, they are reluctant to recognize the 'selective' variant as authentically 'conscientious'.

The other line of argument whereby persons who are not pacifist in principle none the less make common cause with pacifism in politics is the advocacy of alternative means of social struggle or 'conflict resolution' (a new branch within the social sciences), or even of non-military defence of the nation. 'PEACE studies' as an academic discipline and 'peacemaking' as a style of involvement in conflict settings bring together pacifists and near-pacifists. The same applies to the community-building resources of international agencies or even the noncombatant use of military personnel.

Under the shadow of the Second World War the pacifism both of liberal Protestants and of the free churches was abandoned by many on the ground, which seemed self-evident, that there was no alternative to violence to stop Hitler. The 'Christian realism' of that argument, articulated by Reinhold Niebuhr, dominated North American Protestant thought for a generation. That 'no alternative' argument was soon transferred to the liberation struggles of Africa and Latin America, where it was less appropriate. In that world, liberation has not been won. Since the surprising experiences of major political change achieved non-violently (Manila 1986, Eastern Europe 1989) the case against war and in favour of non-violent modes of struggle is again getting attention.

Since pacifists are an embattled minority, the best way to exposit the case for pacifism is to review its argument with majority views. Since there is no one kind of pacifism, there can be no univocal statement; it will be best to referee more than one argument, selecting those given the most attention by critics.

Reinhold Niebuhr, previously a pacifist of the liberal Christian programmatic type, characterized pacifism as being based upon an absolutized understanding of LOVE for the adversary at the expense of JUSTICE. The alternative is to see love as calling us to put in first place our responsibility for justice, even though it must be at the expense of the enemy, and therefore repentant. Pacifism still has a role, for Niebuhr, as the 'vocation' of minorities which make no claim to be socially responsible. Niebuhr became the most prominent Protestant theologian in North America in this century. His concern to refute naïve programmatic pacifism, reaching 'behind' ethics into the retrieval of Augustinian anthropology, became the most powerful motor for theological change in mid-century American protestantism. Some pacifists accepted as an honour the role Niebuhr assigned them, making their peace with a dualistic analysis which avowed their irrelevance. Others challenged his argument on Christian theological grounds. Some argued for a high view of human potential for good, challenging Niebuhr's view of the pervasiveness of SIN. Some challenged his description of Jesus as an ahistorical idealist, arguing Jesus' full and representative humanity.

Philosophers in the wake of Kant, accustomed to considering generalizability as the touchstone of moral rationality, condemn pacifism because the renunciation of killing cannot be generalized; others will continue to defend their interest by killing (or threatening to do so). As long as anyone else is ready to have recourse to violence, and the pacifist (by definition) cannot force them to renounce it, the pacifist has failed the test of rationality. The pacifist will respond that this abstract notion of rationality is odd. We do not test the case for truth-telling by asking whether by telling the truth we can keep others from LYING. The fact that other people persist in lying does not authorize us to do the same to stop them.

It cannot be a criterion for ethical consistency that a mode of behaviour should make sense for people who do not share the same assumptions. Kantian 'generalizability' can make sense if it means 'act in such a way that the rule according to which you act could be everyone's rule', but it cannot logically or morally be transmuted into 'act only in ways in which you could get people to act who do not share your values'. One set of pacifists grant that they cannot (and insist that they need not) be tested by the standards of others, and make no effort to commend their morality in alien terms. Others (see King-Hall 1958; Boserup 1975; Sharp 1985; Friesen 1986) refuse the relegation and accept the challenge of making sense of their stance in terms of the values of their neighbours.

Another less abstract argument concentrates ethical deliberation in the weighing of obvious consequences; pacifism is refuted because of the stakes involved, which only war can defend, in the massive conflicts between societies which only war can adjudicate.

At its best (i.e. when the calculation of consequences is honest and the means legitimate) this is the just-war tradition. It was convincing in the age of Niebuhr, but since then its self-evidence has lost its sheen in the analysis of hindsight; (a) the Second World War did not save Jewish lives; (b) the Second World War abandoned Eastern Europe to TOTALITARIANISM; (c) Hitler's victors went on in the next decades to justify imperialistic wars (most strikingly Vietnam) with the same rhetoric they had used against Nazism. Even further did the lesser-evil argument lose its self-evidence when it became clear that the destruction for which our weapons are designed would be massively disproportionate and uncontrollable.

The form in which 'the stakes' can be so simply argued is now no longer international conflict but 'liberation', i.e. combat against repressive regimes. The argument appears self-evident as long as 'liberty' is simply defined and ascribed incommensurate value. It is most difficult, however, really to adapt the just-war logic so as to promise 'probable success', and logically impossible to prove 'legitimate authority'. Here too pacifists respond in two ways.

1 The more 'spiritual' response in the heritage of Gandhi, Helder Camara and Dorothy Day is to engulf the consequentialism of 'liberation' rhetoric in a deep vision of the unity of ends and means. Means are to ends as the acorn to the oak. The argument that evil means could serve good ends, that war could serve peace, can be constructed in particular far-out cases, but in the long run and on average, which is the only way to reason morally, it cannot stand. The unselfcritical claim to the contrary is naïve about the facts it appeals to and about its ability to govern justly the evil means it resorts to.

2 The other school (see Sharp 1985) disproves the tacit assumption of just-war thought that violent means are effective and that there are no effective non-violent means. Recent experience has gone well beyond the early promise of the experience of Gandhi

and King in demonstrating the capacity of popular resistance to bring down unacceptable regimes. Parallel developments in political science explain that that should be no surprise.

'Peace' is not enough. On both sides of the conversation one encounters the dictum 'peace is more than the absence of war'. The just-war advocate means by that that in some cases actual war may be closer to ultimate values of justice than would be the maintenance of a tranquil but unjust situation. The pacifist, on the other hand, does not consider refraining from war as the ultimate moral duty, but merely as a prerequisite of the other components of the righteous order of *shalom*. The absence of war does not guarantee righteousness; but the presence of war makes it impossible.

Having reviewed these most typical pro-war arguments makes it possible to refocus the rest of the anti-war case.

The above pro-war arguments make assumptions conditioned by European history since the fourth century. They assume that the national community, as represented by its ruler, is the primary bearer of moral value. This 'Constantinian' vision must be challenged both practically and theologically (*see* CHURCH AND STATE). The pacifist affirms both a smaller human community (defined by particular non-coerced values) and a larger one (including the enemy, and favouring the underdog).

The above pro-war arguments assume that moral and political values are centred casuistically on test cases, quandaries, hard cost-benefit trade-offs. This misrepresents both political reality and moral discourse, which are not punctual. Moral reality is longitudinal (including past and future in a narrative thread). It is deep (constituted of dispositions and virtues). It has breadth (comprising communities and covenants). The casuistic reduction to lesser-evil reckoning is voluntarily blind to most of the moral universe.

The pro-war argument misrepresents political reality by its use of the ideal just-war schema, which does not represent what politicians and soldiers really do. Much military thought is 'realistic' in the sense that it recognizes no moral obligation beyond national interest, and no restraint on what it takes to win. Much is 'crusading' in the sense that participants believe that God is particularly on their side and that their adversaries have less than equal human status. Much is in fact 'macho', in the sense that the adversary becomes a means to prove one's manhood. Many who use the language of 'just war' do not seriously entertain the prospect of respecting the limits it imposes (eschewing illegitimate means, suing for peace when victory by licit means is impossible, prosecuting WAR CRIMES, respecting selective objection). The people who argue for the just-war option are mostly not militants, who tend to be 'realists' or 'crusaders', but intellectuals who feel that the moral claim of pacifism is too simple.

American Friends Service Committee (1982) *In Place of War: An Inquiry into Non-Violent National Defense*, New York: Grossman.

Bainton, Roland (1961) *Christian Attitudes Toward War and Peace*, Nashville, TN: Abingdon.

Boserup, Anders and Mack, Andrew (1975) *War Without Weapons*, New York: Schocken.

Brock, Peter (1960) *Pacifism in the United States from the Colonial Era to the First World War*, Princeton, NJ: Princeton University Press.

——(1972) *Pacifism in Europe to 1914*, Princeton, NJ: Princeton University Press.

——(1991) *Freedom from War; Nonsectarian Pacifism 1814–1914*, Toronto: University of Toronto Press.

Friesen, Duane (1986) *Christian Peacemaking and International Conflict; a Realist Pacifist Perspective*, Scottdale, PA: Herald Press.

King-Hall, Stephen (1958) *Defense in a Nuclear Age*, Nyack, MT: Fellowship.

Nuttall, Geoffrey (1958) *Christian Pacifism in History*, Oxford: Blackwell.

Sharp, Gene (1985) *Making Europe Unconquerable: A Civilian-Based Deterrence and Defense System*, London: Taylor & Francis.

Yoder, John H. (1985) *When War is Unjust*, Minneapolis, MN: Augsburg.

John H. Yoder

PARTNERING

Sometimes there is a well-known concept whose boundaries may need fixing with a definition: for example MARRIAGE. By contrast there is a well-bounded area, namely non-marital long-term heterosexual relations, for which most names are inexact or tendentious. However, looking for a name may clarify the concept. The terminology a SOCIETY needs says something about what that society is like.

'Cohabitation', though neutral and convenient, leaves out some long-term relationships; 'common law marriage' claims too definite a legal status; 'concubinage' includes too much social history; 'love affairs' may be transient, and sound old-world or moralistic. 'Partnership' is not neutral: it has strong connotations of camaraderie and EQUALITY, or of the efficiency of a contract. Sometimes it is used of a sexual relationship for the sake of these very connotations, as when a marriage is described as a partnership. Shed all these meanings, and the concept of a 'sexual partner' becomes too neutral: it means no more than 'bedfellow' and carries no meaning beyond the present. 'Partnering' is a neologism which can serve somewhat self-consciously as a technical term, without meaning too much or too little.

As far back in history as marriage has been formalized, that is, as far back as history goes, some people have entered into informal sexual relationships, with less or more social disapproval, and with more or less disadvantage to vulnerable women and children. The writers of ancient scripture could acknowledge concubinage as socially acceptable: from the union of Abraham and Hagar (Genesis 16), encouraged by Sarah as a bitter remedy for her barrenness, to the gorgeous but dangerous harem of Solomon (1 Kings 11: 3).

The Christian church has repudiated 'fornication' and has intended to include long-term arrangements under this reprobation. Practicality has undermined this clear moral stand in two ways. First, because motherhood is obvious and paternity harder to ascertain, it is women's chastity which has seemed all-important. The double standard has been tacitly accepted (Hume 1739).

Second, it has always been hard to make people conform to standards which they see as economically impossible. While people with PROPERTY to maintain and bequeath welcomed strong marriage laws to prevent its dissipation, and, let it be said, to protect their daughters, poor people, especially in cities, lived by their own rules, not for the sake of 'free love' but to

be married in their own way (Gillis 1985: e.g. pp. 95–100; ch. 7). Marriage is not one simple institution; arrangements which do not qualify as legal marriages have an even greater diversity.

Historically and morally, what sexual partnering means depends on the likelihood or unlikelihood of conception. Continuance of the species is the biological significance of sexual union; and until this century procreation has been its nearly inevitable result. Societies which have accepted concubinage have wanted, though not always cherished, the resulting children. Disapproval in monogamous societies for cohabitation has been based, not unreasonably, on the predictable insecurity of offspring. Today's tolerance is a complex development. Childless sexual relations can be planned with fair success: unmarried lovers need not irresponsibly bring children into the world. So the main reason for condemning informal unions has collapsed: provided that they are childless. Next, widespread acceptance of people's rights to enter into such unions has fed a growing conviction that the label of 'illegitimacy' has itself created some of the damage it deplores. So unmarried parenthood in turn acquires respectability: provided that it is based upon 'stable relationship'. Even that proviso is not sacrosanct. The only condition comes to be that 'every child must be a wanted child'. HUMAN RIGHTS, and women's rights, seem to have moved in the opposite direction from the hopes of moralists. Though matrimony is supposed now to be within everyone's reach, partnering, far from vanishing, is now a phenomenon in all social classes.

Yet the wheel comes full circle, with increased sociological awareness of the vulnerability of children when adults give priority to their own wants. While Christians set about learning greater appreciation of individual AUTONOMY, secular writers re-emphasize its risks. Gillis's conclusion, 'Living together as adult couples is properly a matter of individual discretion, but the founding of a family is not', could become received wisdom (1985: 320–1).

Religious people still find individual autonomy hard to accept. They worry about being 'conformed to this world' and ask what morality has to do with fashionable trends. They loyally pose moral questions in terms of the will of God; and the temptation to give God's answers in terms of long-understood human tradition is strong. People who fear relativism proceed to ascribe to God an inflexibility which would do no credit to a human being. The principle that right and wrong are real and yet their application changes ought not to be too difficult. The realistic possibility of separating sexual love and pleasure from procreation can make a difference to what we ought to mean by chastity. When Christian moralists cannot see this they seem, preposterously, not to care about human flourishing, missing the opportunity to place human flourishing in its true, eternal, perspective.

People who assume that unmarried partners must be 'living in SIN' give the impression of minding about respectability more than faithfulness. There is a better Christian tradition, which has rightly insisted that marriage is made by consent, not by ceremony. If this man and woman have consented to belong to one another for life, they are indeed married. The urgent questions about partnering are not about how the relationship has been authenticated but about its stability and its symmetry. If lifelong consent is withheld, is the more vulnerable partner being exploited? Who wants to keep options open, and why? There are questions here, for those who sit loose to tradition, about charity and prudence.

Conversely, there is a kind of uncharitable imprudence tempting to traditionalists, which revels in dire prophecies and makes the breakdown of tradition more thinkable and more likely. If partnering is or may be a kind of marriage which for good reasons or bad asks no blessing from church or STATE, Christians may well feel that it is a risky enterprise; but if so, what the partners need is to be sustained rather than deplored.

Anderson, Michael (ed.) (1980) *Sociology of the Family*, 2nd edn, Harmondsworth: Penguin.

Bernard, J., (1985) *Changing Family Lifestyles: Parents, Children and Change*, Arnold E. Lexington Books.

Borrowdale, Anne (1994) *Reconstructing Family Values*, London: SPCK.

Clark, David (ed.) (1991) *Marriage, Domestic Life and Social Change: Writings for Jacqueline Burgoyne*, London: Routledge, particularly Chapter 4

by B. Jane Elliott and Afterword by Jacqueline Burgoyne.

Dormer, Duncan J. (1992) *The Relationship Revolution*, One plus One.

Gillis, Robin (1985) *For Better, for Worse: British Marriage Since 1600*, Oxford.

Haskey, J. (1992) *Patterns of Marrige, Divorce and Cohabitation in the different Countries of Europe*, Population Trends no. 69, pp. 27–36.

Hume, David (1739) 'Of chastity and modesty', *A Treatise of Human Nature* II: II: XII.

Kiernan, K. and Estaugh, V. (1993) *Rise of Cohabitation and Childbearing outside Marriage*, Social Policy Research Findings no. 37, Joseph Rowntree Foundation.

McRae, S. (1993) *Long-term Cohabiting Mothers*, Social Policy Research Findings no. 42, Joseph Rowntree Foundation.

Helen Oppenheimer

PATRIARCHY

The term patriarchy means the 'rule of the father'. Patriarchy refers to systems of legal, social, economic and political relations which validate and enforce the sovereignty of male heads of families over the dependent persons in the household. In classical patriarchal systems, such as are found in Hebrew law or Roman law, these dependent persons included wives, dependent children and slaves, as well as various other groups of dependants, such as clients. In Roman law the term *familia* referred to all persons and things ruled over by the *paterfamilias*, including animals and land.

Various groups of males, such as sons and male slaves, were also ruled over by the *paterfamilias*. But women are subjugated in patriarchal societies in a more total sense than either male children or male slaves. The former could grow up to become independent householders. The latter might be emancipated and become householders. But women, first as daughters, then as wives and sometimes even as widows, were defined generically as dependent persons under the patriarch or male head of the household in which they lived. The female slave had even less protection from physical and sexual abuse, combining the status of female and slave.

Patriarchy is not to be understood as particularly Jewish, nor is it to be seen as arising primarily out of Hebrew patriarchy. As a social system, it is found in classical religions and societies around the world. Some anthropologists have believed that the patriarchal FAMILY was the aboriginal order of human SOCIETY and hence is 'natural' or inevitable. But other anthropologists have challenged this assumption. They argue that patriarchal social systems arose with the change from gardening to plough agriculture, the development of private landholding, URBANIZATION and CLASS stratification, including SLAVERY, sometime about the fourth millennium BC. Before that, and alongside these patriarchal cultures, the predominant hunter-gatherer societies which reached back to the dawn of human evolution, as well as early hunter-gardener societies that arose around the nineth millennium BC in the Ancient Near East, allowed for more equal GENDER relations, characterized by communal landholding, little or no class structure and balanced spheres of production and POWER for adult men and women.

Ancient tribal societies that were more strictly patriarchal seem to have been those nomadic animal-herding societies which lacked a major female gathering and gardening role. Strictly patriarchal religions may have developed in the Ancient Near East as nomadic animal-herding tribes invaded settled agricultural areas, conquering mother-right cultures that had developed there and co-opting and then gradually repressing religions with prominent mother-goddesses for religions with an exclusively male patriarchal God. This is true of the two major Semitic patriarchal religions, Judaism and Islam. Christianity inherited a double patriarchal culture, through both Judaism and Graeco-Roman societies, but it also inherited partially suppressed female symbols for Deity from both sources which were expressed in Wisdom images of the divine and also in Mariology.

The status of women in classical patriarchal systems contains many nuances, depending on whether remnants of mother-right remain in it and on the ways in which women remain related to their family of origin as well as to that of their husband. In addition, economic and legal changes and the spread of education can create periods of liberalization of patriarchal law, such as those which took place in the Hellenistic period and again in later Roman law. One cannot define a single system that would be true of all patriarchal societies at all times. However, it is possible to generalize about the characteristics usually found in patriarchal societies, although all may not be found in them in the same way and at the same time.

First, women are defined legally as dependants on the male head of family: their father, husband or guardian. Women lack autonomous civil status or can exercise it only in extraordinary circumstances or through a male guardian. This means that women cannot exercise legal or political power in their own right. They cannot vote, hold political office, represent themselves at law or enter into contracts in their own name.

Second, women are economically dependent. This does not mean that women do not do productive labour, but rather that their economic productivity, whether in the home or out of the home, belongs to their fathers or husbands. Restrictions are placed on women as inheritors of PROPERTY. They inherit less land or none at all compared with their brothers, and what they do receive from their families is more likely to be portable wealth. What property they inherit or the dowries given them in marriage are often managed by their husbands or male relatives.

Women in patriarchal law also suffer various restrictions of rights to their PERSONS. These may mean that they cannot decide who they will marry. This decision is made by their parents, particularly their father, and they must comply. Daughters of wealthy families with inheritances are more restricted than daughters without inherited wealth. Upon MARRIAGE women are seen as losing membership in their own families and being transferred into the families of their husbands, often with exchange of goods between the male heads of family and the payment of a bride price by the groom or a dowry by the bride's family.

Since the lineage of the children descends through the father (patriliny), female chastity is strictly guarded before and during MARRIAGE and violations on the part of the female are severely punished, in order to ensure that the wife's children will be those of her husband.

Killing a bride found not to be a virgin at marriage or an adulterous wife is common in patriarchal systems. By contrast, males are sexually free, provided they do not impinge upon the daughters or wives of 'honourable' families and confine their promiscuity to second-class women such as female servants, prostitutes and concubines. Male children are preferred to female children, and there is a sharp distinction between legitimate and illegitimate children.

Husbands are generally conceded the right to confine their wives and physically beat them, as also their children and slaves, although provision is usually made that a husband should not permanently maim or kill his wife unless she is adulterous. American law until the late nineteenth century still allowed husbands to beat their wives as long as they did not use a stick thicker than their thumb – hence the phrase 'rule of thumb'.

The husband is regarded as having unlimited sexual access to his wife, whether she desires it or not, since she is his property for SEXUALITY, reproduction and labour. (The residue of this assumption in law and custom even today makes it difficult for a woman to make a legal charge of rape against her husband.) Children also are seen as belonging legally to their father, who has the right to expose them at birth, sell them into slavery and beat them. These fates fall disproportionately on unwanted female children.

The wife is seen as having no right to interfere with the generative effects of her husband's sexual acts upon her body, by either CONTRACEPTION or ABORTION. Although knowledge of methods of contraception existed in classical antiquity, such methods were practised by prostitutes but the knowledge of them was kept from wives. The married woman's body and its 'fruits' are the private property of her husband. RAPE is seen as an offence against the property rights of the woman's father or husband, not against the woman herself. Rape of the 'loose' woman, the slave or prostitute, is not seen as an offence in the same way as the rape of a married woman or marriageable daughter. Patriarchal law also gives the husband, but not the wife, the right to divorce, particularly if the wife is adulterous or fails to produce a male heir.

Women are excluded from the exercise of public roles of power and culture and from the EDUCATION and credentials that lead to these roles. Women cannot hold political or military leadership, although there can be exceptions to this when a woman is a placeholder in a hereditary office through lack of a male heir. Women also are generally excluded from priesthoods, particularly those which pertain to the civic religions, and from professional roles that require higher education, such as lawyers, rhetors and academically trained physicians. Generally women are barred from higher education and from public leadership roles generated by higher education, such as scribes and teachers. This meant that women were excluded both from access to learning and from forming the public CULTURE although there could be exceptions to this as upper class households acquired private libraries.

This exclusion from learning and forming the public culture accounts for the almost exclusively (élite) male formation of public culture under patriarchy and the definition of women in these cultures from this male point of view. Women typically have great difficulty gaining visibility and credibility, even when they manage to gain an education and produce cultural creations of comparable quality to those of ranking males of their cultures. Since the cultural creations of women are not incorporated into the public heritage which is taught to the next generation of male students, such cultural accomplishments as women did achieve were continually lost, erased from the collective cultural memory, or survived by accident, often by being thought to be the work of a male.

Patriarchal social systems with these characteristics form the predominant background of Western civilization, in both the Hebrew and its Graeco-Roman roots. Patristic Christianity reverted to some of the stricter aspects of patriarchy, negating some of the gains for women that had developed in later Roman society, such as DIVORCE and the exercise of economic power. But Christianity modified somewhat the marriage rights of parents over daughters through the institution of CELIBACY, allowing females to resist parental demands to marry by asserting a vocation of virginity.

Christianity also supported female consent

to marriage and a single standard of sexual morality for men as well as women, rejecting concubinage, polygamy and divorce. However, medieval Christianity accepted PROSTITUTION as a necessary social EVIL, even though sinful, following the opinion of St Augustine. Yet even on matters of female consent to marriage and on divorce, the church often accommodated in practice to the dynastic needs of powerful feudal families.

European legal codes that emerged as national law in France, England, Spain and elsewhere in Western Europe in the early modern period (seventeenth century) reflected a strengthening of patriarchal principles, annulling some of the access to education, guild membership and political roles enjoyed by some women in feudal and early urban societies. In English and American society, and even longer in French society, such patriarchal law codes remained substantially intact until the early to mid-twentieth century.

It was only in the mid-nineteenth century that English and American women began to challenge the traditional legal structure that denied women higher education, civil rights and property rights. In the USA this challenge began with the first Women's Rights Convention at Seneca Falls, New York, in 1848. Over the next seventy years American women won most property rights, access to university and professional education, the right to enter professions such as medicine and law and finally the legal status of citizenship, giving them the right to vote and hold political office. Access to the ordained clergy has been even slower to open to women. Except for a few small churches in the late nineteenth century, there has been major change in this area only in the last few decades.

Although patriarchal law codes that defined women as dependants without legal status in their own right and barred them from higher education and public leadership have been largely dismantled in Western societies, remnants of this subordinate status of women remain strong even in these countries. Legal codes retain some residue of this subordinate status, such as the law that the wife takes her husband's name and thus merges with his legal identity at marriage. Patriarchal patterns of gender relations continue to be transmitted by culture and custom, particularly as sanctioned by traditional religion. Women are socialized into a subordinate and auxiliary role in the family and society by cultural patterns transmitted by the family, church and school.

The economic division of labour between public paid work done by men and unpaid domestic work done by women also makes it difficult for women to compete with men on the job. Women do the domestic support labour both for themselves and for men, while men are freed from such work by women. Hence the woman who tries to compete with men on the job is handicapped by the second 'shift' of female labour that the male generally does not have to do. Although it is becoming more common for some males to share domestic work, particularly when wives work, these cultural and economic patterns continue to be powerful ways in which patriarchal gender patterns are perpetuated, even in the absence of formal legal codes that institutionalize female subordination.

Women also continue to be subordinated by physical violence against their persons and by denial of reproductive self-determination (*see* DOMESTIC VIOLENCE). Rape and domestic battering is common even in the middle classes in Western societies. The right of birth control was conceded to women by Protestants in the 1920s–1950s, but continues to be denied by Roman Catholicism. The 1980s saw a worldwide attack on women's reproductive rights by conservative religions, particularly on legal access to abortion, although this often had the effect of diminishing access to sex education and birth control as well. Although women are present in paid employment in large numbers, they seldom hold the better paying positions or are given equal pay with men in comparable jobs.

In the 1960s a new feminist movement arose in Western Europe and North America and has spread to the countries of Asia, Africa and Latin America as well. The new feminists saw that patriarchy, far from having been eliminated by giving women access to higher education, legal and political rights and paid employment, has been redefined. Patriarchy continues in renewed forms in social structures and in culture.

Feminists sought to understand the history of patriarchy as a system and its forms of perpetuation today.

Economic hierarchy by which women do both the unpaid domestic labour and the low paid labour is a major structure that continues women's subordination. Men monopolize better paid jobs that carry power and prestige. Women's pay averages 59 per cent of male pay, while women carry the 'second shift' of housework. The poorest women are those who seek to do both jobs for themselves and their children as female heads of household without a male partner. The poorest families in all countries are those headed by females.

Also the basic psychocultural definitions of maleness and femaleness, based on dominance and subordination, continue in modern cultures. The association of masculinity with violence, both military and inter-personal, is key to this definition of gender relations. Male status is linked to the right to exercise dominating power over women and weaker men, while women are socialized to support male military violence and acquiesce to it in inter-personal relations. This culture of male violence seems infinitely capable of being revived whenever it is challenged, whether that is expressed in President Clinton throwing some additional bombs on Baghdad to prove he is not a 'wimp' or the male in the family putting his wife and children 'in their place' with his fists.

Despite the emphasis on women's development in the United Nations, current studies have shown that improvements in women's status from 1965 to 1993 have been token. There is little structural change in the basic patterns by which women in their combined labours work longer hours than men for lower pay and have far fewer economic assets. Indeed the end of the Cold War seems everywhere to have seen a growing gap between rich and poor, with women forming the major part of the growing poor. Government programmes that subsidized social needs are being dismantled, with the major burden for these losses falling on women and children.

In conclusion we can say that patriarchy, both as a psychocultural pattern and as a social and economic system, has been modified and redefined in modern industrial societies in a way that gives women formal equality of CITIZENSHIP. But it continues as a major component of the way in which social power and personal identity are defined for both men and women. Social VIOLENCE and massive injustice in society are fed in many ways at their roots by SEXISM. These patterns cannot be significantly changed without uprooting and transforming the patriarchal presuppositions which underlie them.

Ehrenberg, M. (1989) *Women in Prehistory*, Oxford: Oxford University Press.

Flexner, E. (1972) *Century of Struggle: The Women's Rights Movement in the United States*, New York: Atheneum.

Herlihy, D. (1985) *Medieval Households*, Cambridge, MA: Harvard University Press.

Lerner, G. (1986) *The Creation of Patriarchy*, Oxford: Oxford University Press.

Martin, M.K. and Voorhes, B. (1975) *The Female of the Species*, New York: Columbia University Press.

Pomeroy, S. (1975) *Goddesses, Whores, Wives and Slaves: Women in Classical Antiquity*, New York: Schocken Books.

Sanday, P.S. (1981) *Female Power and Male Dominance*, Cambridge: Cambridge University Press.

Stone, L. (1977) *The Family, Sex and Marriage in England, 1500–1800*, New York: Harper & Row.

Rosemary Radford Ruether

PEACE

Peace is the most inclusive of all virtues. Ideally it embraces the whole human race and nature as well; it is earnestly desired by the great mass of people of all religions, cultures and ideologies; it requires for its realization and maintenance the contributions of persons with all kinds of knowledge and skills; it reaches into every relationship and activity in which people are engaged.

Just because peace has this global, all-inclusive character, it has been conceived in different ways according as one aspect or another has been emphasized. This is often reflected in the language. The Greek word for peace, *eirene*, and its Latin equivalent *pax* – from which the English 'peace' is derived – denoted primarily a truce or pause in the struggle. On such an understanding, peace tends to be a somewhat negative idea, the absence of WAR. In Hebrew (with cognates in other Semitic languages) the word for peace, *shalom*, had the sense of a primary unity or wholeness. In India, however, 'peace' is expressed as *santi*, and this word stresses inward or spiritual peace.

The more negative idea of peace and the more affirmative idea seem themselves to reflect different views of human nature. If one thinks of human beings as essentially acquisitive and aggressive, then their relations among themselves will be primarily competitive and warlike. The quest for peace will be the problem of finding ways to diminish the more damaging forms of hostility, through pacts or agreements that impose restraint. A classic statement of this point of view was given by the English philosopher Thomas Hobbes in his book *Leviathan* (Hobbes 1934: 80 ff.) He held that the natural state of the human race is one of unrestricted war, everyone against everyone else. But experience teaches that a life of universal struggle is, in Hobbes's famous words, 'solitary, poor, nasty, brutish and short'. So, driven by 'fear of death, desire of such things as are necessary to commodious living, and a hope by their industry to obtain them', human beings seek peace. But peace conceived in this way is a fragile structure masking the underlying struggle. Even war is nothing exceptional but just the clear manifestation of the human condition. In the words of another famous writer on these matters, Carl von Clausewitz, 'war is nothing but a continuation of political intercourse with a mixture of other means – merely another kind of writing and language for political thought' (Clausewitz 1968: 402).

But there is a more affirmative view of peace, one closer to the Hebrew concept of *shalom*. It found expression through another English philosopher, John Locke, in his writing *Of Civil Government* (1924). He denied that the state of nature is a state of war. The state of nature, he claimed, is 'men living together according to reason'. This is the doctrine of a 'NATURAL LAW' based on a universal reason, a law which 'teaches all mankind who will but consult it, that being all equal and independent, no one ought to harm another in his life, health, liberty and possessions'.

Here we have two views of the concept of peace and of human nature itself that are in headlong collision with one another. Are we to set aside Hobbes as too cynical in his opinion of the human race? Or are we to say that John Locke was far too optimistic? The question cannot easily be decided, and we shall have to elaborate the two views more fully before trying to come to a decision between them.

By the negative view is meant the understanding of peace that we find in Hobbes and those who have thought like him, the view that human beings are incorrigibly aggressive and self-seeking, so that peace is a damage-limitation exercise superimposed on unrelenting struggle. We should not underestimate the value of efforts to reduce the level of VIOLENCE in human affairs, however for a realistic view of society is bound to concede a considerable measure of truth to the Hobbesian dictum that the state of nature is a state of war, at least in some periods of human history.

In the Middle Ages, when central governments in Europe were weak and there were many powerful private armies, attempts were made by ecclesiastics to curb unrestrained violence, and these had some merit. In 989 the Peace of God sought to exempt churches from plundering and use in war, and to extend some protection to noncombatants such as peasants and merchants. In 1027 the Truce of God extended the restrictions by forbidding fighting over weekends, the days of Christ's passion. Historian Latourette acknowledges that 'never fully enforced' these regulations 'exercised some restraint on the disorders of the time' (Latourette 1953: 475). No truly affirmative concept of peace was operative, and the irony of the situation was apparent when the Council of Clermont launched the First Crusade in 1095.

A secular interest in peace appears at the beginning of the modern era, particularly in the development of the idea of international law by Grotius and others. The most significant work coming out of this tradition was Immanuel Kant's treatise *Perpetual Peace* (1795). Kant had no illusions about the human race, and followed Hobbes in his understanding of the nature of SOCIETY and the necessity of the STATE to control the warring tendencies of individual human beings. But at the same time he shared Locke's appreciation for rationality and believed that, just as human individuals have learned or are learning to live reasonably within the state, so states must move toward some kind of federation, and he set out stages by which they could move toward such a goal, although he seems to have regarded it as an ideal rather than something that would be historically achieved.

A presupposition of such development, he held, was true DEMOCRACY in all the participating states and an absence of any secret aggressive motives in their diplomatic dealings with each other.

In this section we must also consider theories of the just war. They have their origins in Augustine and Aquinas, but are still discussed today. They deplore the unrestrained violence of war but accept that sometimes war is to be accepted as justified. The expression 'just war' is unfortunate, for, as Gibbon remarked, 'war in its fairest form implies a perpetual violation of humanity and justice' (Gibbon 1960: 474). The conditions for a just war have been variously stated but the following six points may be considered basic: (a) there must be a just cause; (b) violence is the only way left of effecting change; (c) there must be a properly constituted AUTHORITY to wage the war; (d) there must be a feasible goal; (e) the means must be appropriate to the end; (f) reconciliation is sought as the ultimate goal. It is sometimes argued that modern warfare is so destructive that condition (e) cannot be satisfied, but this is at least debatable, and in fact certain kinds of weapons have not been put to use in modern wars. So the theory of the just war has probably had some restraining effect on warlike violence and, as was clear in the Gulf War of 1990, citizens of democratic states are not likely to support a war unless they are reasonably satisfied that it can be justified. On the other hand, the nagging question must remain whether wrongs can be put right through the perpetration of fresh wrongs that are inevitable in the conduct of war.

In 1989, the ending of the 'cold war' between the USA and its allies on one side and the Soviet Union and its allies on the other was hailed, perhaps too enthusiastically, as the end of one era and the beginning of a 'new world order'. Certainly the cold war illustrates the ultimate stage in what has been called above the 'negative' view of peace, because for more than forty years, in spite of extreme rivalry between the two superpowers, overt violence was restricted to some local wars, admittedly destructive ones. That time was anxious and dangerous, but the balance of POWER or terror had the advantage of preserving an outward or negative peace. But the events of 1989 encouraged the hopes of something better, and we must now consider a more affirmative concept of peace.

As was suggested above, the prototype of an affirmative idea of peace is suggested by the Hebrew concept of *shalom*. This means a flourishing of human existence in unity and wholeness. Some of the prophets contrasted this genuine peace with a mere absence of violence, based possibly on fear or oppression. So Jeremiah complained: 'They have healed the wound of my people lightly, saying "Peace, peace", when there is no peace' (Jeremiah 6: 14). But although the vision of a deeper peace was taught by religious leaders, it was described mainly in secular terms. Peace implied material prosperity and abundance and the security needed for the enjoyments of such a state of affairs, so that, in words that have become a universal symbol of peace, spears might be beaten into ploughshares (Isaiah 2: 4; Micah 4: 3). In such an environment, people would enjoy long life and a quiet DEATH. It was even imagined that this peace would embrace non-human nature (Isaiah 11: 6–9).

Certainly this vision offers a challenge to the modern world. Can technology be harnessed in the service of peace, as it has unfortunately been made to serve war? Surely there are the means nowadays to improve agriculture and food supplies worldwide, and that would be an obvious and important step toward the spread of *shalom*. The political will has been lacking and even the United Nations has done less than might have been hoped. Fortunately voluntary agencies have stepped into the vacuum, but even so their efforts fall short of what is needed. Another point is that too little has been done to study what may be called the 'techniques' of peace. There are still many military academies where the arts of war are studied, but only a few universities (and not the best known) have departments of peace studies, specifically intended to investigate how best to help in the building of peace. So many factors and so many dimensions enter into the building and maintaining of an affirmatively peaceful world community that much study is necessary, and this calls for a suitable allocation from the vast sums that are each year contributed to research institutions.

But the problem goes beyond technology and social analysis. This is the point at which religion becomes relevant. Most religions have strongly advocated the cause of peace and have claimed themselves to bring to individuals an inward peace that heals and reconciles the conflicts that every human being experiences within. Religions too give a sense of unity to the human race through their teaching that human beings are the creatures of God, in relation to whom they are like children of one FAMILY. It is interesting to note that even in the highly sophisticated European Union the members, once at enmity with one another, have chosen as the anthem that celebrates their new unity Schiller's 'Ode to Joy' in its setting by Beethoven. It celebrates their unity as a family (*alle Menschen werden Brüder*) and this leads to the climax and ground of their unity (*überm Sternenzelt muss ein lieber Vater wohnen*). Stefan Kunze speaks of this sublime chorus as 'a vision of the harmony between human and divine-cosmic order in an age when self-alienation was already on the horizon'. Perhaps it will only be when Europe and the entire world has really appropriated such a mystical or metaphysical vision of unity that we shall have the political will to pursue with determination a truly affirmative peace for the human race.

In contrasting negative and affirmative concepts of peace, we have been careful not to suggest that one of these excludes or renders superfluous the other. The affirmative view has certainly more depth to it and in the long run holds out more promise of a genuinely peaceful future for humanity. But it was pointed out that, in an imperfect world where hostilities continue to arise, peace in the negative sense of the absence of overt violence is not always to be despised and may sometimes be the best solution available at a particular juncture of affairs. We have talked about making and maintaining peace, and this is a never-ending task. In recent years we have frequently heard the expression 'peace process', and this language makes clear what may be called the 'dynamics' of peace, a process in which there must often be a dialectical interplay of more negative and more affirmative ways of conceiving peace. The word 'peace' does suggest to most people rest, inaction, even inertia, yet the truth is that peace demands constant effort for its achievement and maintenance. Although the masses of people everywhere long for peace, the motivation behind this longing is mixed, and for many it is inspired not so much by a vision of human solidarity as simply by the selfish wish to be left to get ahead with one's private ambitions and desires regardless of what is going on in the world around. Peace does not abolish conflict, but it does try to contain it and to divert it toward constructive ends. This is especially clear in the Christian understanding of peace. The New Testament takes over the Hebrew notion of *shalom* but stresses the eschatological character of *shalom*, already taught by the prophets who associated it with a messianic kingdom of the future. Thus Jesus, while he taught non-violence or even non-resistance and promised his disciples the gift of peace (John 14: 27), realized that there would be a long struggle toward that goal and therefore had to warn them that sometimes he would bring them not peace but a sword (Matthew 10: 34). Peace cannot be the rest that leaves things just as they are but must remove everything that stands in the way of that full flourishing of human life that constitutes *shalom*. Peace, for instance, must eliminate injustice, but it will seek to do so by non-violent means. A Brazilian bishop, Dom Helder Camara, has put it very well: 'There is no doubt that Christ came to bring peace. But not the peace of stagnant swamps, not peace based on injustice, not peace that is the opposite of development' (Camara 1971: 130).

It is important that we accept that the 'natural' state for human beings is living together according to reason (Locke) or living together as a worldwide family (the Judaeo-Christian belief). It is important to believe this because our beliefs affect our conduct, and if people believe that the state of nature is a state of war and that human beings are essentially aggressive, then they will act accordingly and there will be little chance of ever achieving a true peace. Perhaps it is only religion that can give us the eschatological vision of a commonwealth of peace ('the KINGDOM OF GOD') and with the vision the political or communal will to embark on a 'peace process' directed to its realization. That process would demand all the courage, ingenuity, resources and sacrifices that have been traditionally called forth by war.

Camara, Helder (1971) *Revolution through Peace*, trans. A. McLean, New York: Harper & Row.
Childress, J.F. (1982) *Moral Responsibility in Conflicts*, Louisiana State University Press.
Clausewitz, Carl von (1968) *On War*, trans. J.J. Graham, Harmondsworth: Penguin.
Gibbon, Edward (1960) *Decline and Fall of the Roman Empire*, abridged edn, London: Chatto & Windus.
Hobbes, Thomas (1934) *Leviathan*, Oxford: Blackwell.
Kant, Immanuel (1795) *Perpetual Peace*.
Latourette, K.S. (1953) *A History of Christianity*, London: Eyre & Spottiswoode.
Locke, John (1924) *Of Civil Government*, London: Dent, pp. 119, 126.
Macquarrie, John (1990) *The Concept of Peace*, London: SCM.
US Conference of Catholic Bishops (1983) *The Challenge of Peace*.

John Macquarrie

PERSONS

The concept of the person is particularly difficult to define because it is one of those fundamental notions – like *life*, to which it is related – that resists characterization in terms of anything else. In ordinary usage person is often understood by contrast with thing while legally a person is any being having rights and duties, including collectives such as corporations. The latter fact, and its exclusion of some human beings, especially children, suggest the derivative nature of the legal conception, and the primacy of its application to divine and human being as such. Of that, two main theories are current. The first can be described as the individualistic, according to which persons are individuals, beings with certain shared characteristics, whose chief defining character is their distinction from other such beings (*see* INDIVIDUALISM). The social order corresponding to such a concept

will be that according to which persons are complete and monadic beings who enter – or refuse to enter – into relations with one another by virtue of their free will.

The second view is the relational, according to which relations with other persons are in some way intrinsic to the being of the person. Here there is a contrast between rather than an equation of the concepts of the person and the individual. A major modern exponent of the relational view of the person is the Scottish philosopher, John Macmurray: 'Since mutuality is constitutive for the personal, "I" need "you" in order to be myself' (1961: 69). An extreme version of this view will collapse persons into their relations, producing the social order known as collectivism, but that would be effectively the subversion of the relational view, which aims to guarantee and not deprive persons of their particularity. According to this view, persons are established in their particularity by their relations with one another, so that neither individualism nor collectivism eventuates, but a social order in which neither particular nor universal is submerged.

There is, similarly, much debate about the defining characteristics of persons. There is a long tradition, begun in antiquity and re-established in the modern age by Descartes, that reason is the crucial distinguishing mark. (Consider recent debates about whether a computer able to think would be a person.) It tends to be an individualistic view, concentrating attention on a quality possessed individually. A variant of the view would see in consciousness the essential mark of the person. Macmurray argued for the centrality of action: it is as agents that persons are essentially what they are. Against all such views it could be argued, without denying the secondary relevance of reason, agency and consciousness, that the distinctiveness and relational character of persons is best demonstrated in terms of a polarity of LOVE and freedom. According to the first, persons are what they are by virtue of their positive and mutually constitutive relatedness to one another. According to the second, such relatedness is personal only if it is in some way unnecessitated.

A further question concerns the extension of the term: which beings qualify to be called persons? Some modern philosophies, like those of Process, make personality a transcendental concept, applying in some way to all realities, so that even the most basic entities, the fundamental particles out of which the universe is constructed, in some way 'feel' each other (*see* PROCESS THEOLOGY). Philosophies of this kind have a particular appeal to those who believe that ecological disaster is the result of a mechanization or 'depersonalization' of the created order. At the other end of the scale there are those, like the modern philosopher Derek Parfit, who question the appropriateness of the concept even to human beings. Similarly, while there are theologians who question the attribution of personality to God, a more common view would hold that it is more appropriate to describe God and human beings as personal, but not the rest of the material world. Here, two qualifications should be made. The first is that to deny personality to the non-human world is not necessarily to condemn it to technocratic misuse. The questions remain open as to what kind of non-personal reality it is and in what forms of relation human persons are to interact with it. The second is that such a distinction does not solve without further discussion the question of the status of those realities whose full personality is for some reason in question – human foetuses, for example.

The history of the concept falls into two quite distinct phases. In times before the modern world, attention centred on the meaning of the word in relation to God; since Descartes, it is the finite person that has for the most part been under consideration. In the ancient world, the concept of the person is owed to THEOLOGY, being developed in connection with the being of God. That does not imply that pre-Christian thought had no way of conceiving the particular human being in relation to SOCIETY. For example, Plato's *Republic* contains at its heart a discussion of the relation of particular to collective in the STATE, greatly to the disadvantage, it must be noted, of the former. The point is rather that thought influenced by Plato tended to conceive the human being as a piece of mind-stuff imprisoned in essentially foreign matter, and so had difficulty in conceiving persons in their completeness and relationality.

The concept of persons as particular beings in relation came into prominence as a result of the attempt by theologians to think together the oneness and the threeness of the Christian God. Before the work of the three fourth-century Cappadocian theologians, Basil of Caesarea, Gregory of Nyssa and Gregory of Nazianzus, the Greek words *ousia* and *hypostasis* had meant very much the same, 'being' or 'reality'. The Cappadocian contribution to the development of thought about persons was to achieve what Coleridge called desynonymization: a process whereby possibilities for meaning are expanded by giving distinct significance to two words which previously meant the same. As the result of their work, the first of the terms, *ousia* came to be used for the being of the one God; *hypostasis* for the three persons in whom the being of God, according to these theologians, consists.

Previously in the Greek world, in so far as there had been a concept of the person it was found in the word prosopon, whose meaning was that of mask or face. As the debates about the person of Christ showed, it could imply that what was shown to the world was merely a mask. In this case, its use of the persons of the TRINITY would suggest that the three persons of the deity, Father, Son and Spirit, were not really the revelation of God but superficial appearances belying the real (and therefore unknown) God beneath them. By insisting that the persons were hypostases, real beings, the Cappadocians struck a blow in favour of the belief that persons are not merely appearances but concrete realities. By insisting also that the three persons were not three gods but by their inextricable relatedness constituted the being of the one eternal God, they made it possible for later thinkers to conceive that persons are relational beings: that they have their being only in relations of free and mutual reciprocity with other persons.

The development in the West was somewhat different, though in its beginnings similar. In *Against Praxeas*, written early in the third century, Tertullian took the Latin term *persona*, which is also believed to have 'mask' as one of its original meanings, and used it to develop the beginnings of a relational concept of the person. Hilary of Poitiers continued in the same tradition, using the theology of the Trinity at once to deny that God was lonely or isolated (so that for Hilary God is a relational being) and to affirm the distinctiveness and particularity of the three persons of the Godhead.

With some exceptions, the relational view of the person was not developed by later Western thinkers until quite recent times. Blame for failure to do so is sometimes laid at the door of Augustine, whose famous AGNOSTICISM about the concept of the person in God led the way for Boethius' return to a thoroughgoing Hellenic rationalism and individualism. The latter's definition of the person as an individual substance of a rational nature (*naturae rationabilis individua substantia*) has dominated discussion since, and can be seen to underlie the thought of Descartes and his successors.

Modern discussion was initiated in Descartes' conception of the person as a mind – a thinking thing – in some way contained in and controlling an essentially mechanical body. Apart from the characteristically modern mechanist emphasis, this is very much in continuity with the view of Socrates in the *Phaedo* that the human being is a soul imprisoned in matter. It initiated the modern debate about whether persons are essentially mental or material, so that it is arguable that the inadequacy of such a framework for discussion has helped to generate the agnosticism about the concept displayed in some recent writing.

Attempts to transcend the modern choice between the mental and the physical include those of Strawson and Macmurray. Strawson proposed in an influential work that the concept of the person be considered prior to the concepts of mind and matter, as being an entity to which both mental and physical predicates are to be ascribed. The immense range of modern debate is revealed by a recent Oxford symposium in which contributors take a range of positions from scientific physicalism to the more relational concept of the kind advocated in this article.

In the mean time, the nineteenth century saw the influence of romanticism and idealism, with their strong stress on personality. The era was marked by a rather individualistic concentration on the power of persons, particularly dominant or heroic persons, to shape, even to constitute

or create, their world in thought and action. But there were many variations, and the concept was called into theological service, particularly towards the end of the century, in conceptions of the creative love and power of God. J.R. Illingworth's *Personality, Human and Divine* is one important English contribution to the discussion. Although Illingworth's thesis is a Trinitarian one, the force of the idealist stress on personality works against a traditional concept of God as tri-personal, and for that reason Karl Barth argued that the concept of the person is best used of the oneness rather than the threeness of God. God is personal by virtue of his being what he is as love and freedom, and it is this that provides a model of what it is for humans to be truly personal. Barth's argument suggests that his concept of personality is deeply influenced by major strands of nineteenth-century idealism, themselves continuous with Boethian individualism.

By contrast, in some more recent discussions theological factors from the Cappadocian tradition are again becoming prominent. There are traces of them in Peacocke and Gillett, while the recent report of the British Council of Churches Study Commission gives major emphasis to the contribution of Trinitarian theology to the development of a concept of the person that is neither individualist nor collectivist. In that and other recent writings on persons the claim is made by the contemporary Greek theologian, John Zizioulas, that the Cappadocians have made philosophical and not simply theological contributions to the concept of the person.

Ayer, A.J. (1963) *The Concept of the Person and Other Essays*, London: Macmillan.

British Council of Churches (1989) *The Forgotten Trinity*, London: British Council of Churches.

Illingworth, J.R. (1899) *Personality, Human and Divine*, London: Macmillan.

Macmurray, John (1961) *Persons in Relation*, London: Faber & Faber.

Parfit, Derek (1984) *Reasons and Persons*, Oxford: Oxford University Press.

Peacocke, A. and Gillett, G. (eds) (1987) *Persons and Personality. A Contemporary Enquiry*, Oxford: Blackwell.

Schwoebel, C. and Gunton, C.E. (eds) (1992) *Persons, Divine and Human. King's College Essays in Theological Anthropology*, Edinburgh: T. & T. Clark.

Strawson, P.F. (1959) *Individuals. An Essay in Descriptive Metaphysics*, London: Methuen.
Zizioulas, J.D. (1985) *Being as Communion*, London: Darton, Longman & Todd.

Colin Gunton

PLAY

Play: the word is probably Anglo-Saxon in origin. It can be found in Beowulf (*c*. AD 700). The epic Old English literature poem shows a complex mix of pagan and Christian themes after the arrival of Christianity (AD 597). Its Anglo-Saxon meaning is primarily sport, game or pleasure although in dialect variants it can be found as either a wake or a holiday as in the expression 'play day'. Its primary meaning is still sport, game or pleasure, as in the expression to 'play a game'. In recent years the analysis of gaming and of play has extended to language itself. The implication of this is that the most basic form of play and the most basic form of game is language. If language is a game then it is difficult to see how language could represent the world. The implications of that thesis, if correct, would be far-reaching indeed.

While the word 'play' may be relatively recent the concept or idea of play or playing a game is not. The earliest ritual play, those of the Ancient Greek games, are well attested, as is their (playful) relation to theology and to ethics. The first recorded Olympic games were in 776 BC at Olympia on the Peloponnesian peninsula although it is thought the games precede that date. The first games were distinctly religious in character and were held to honour Zeus the principal god of the Greek pantheon. They were also ethical in nature.

The Greek *arete*, virtue, related primarily to excellence of performance. To do well at a task and to perform that task well was central to the moral life. To do well at a game was similarly part of moral life. So much were the games caught up in ethical and religious notions that the official spectators from another city were regarded as ambassadors of state and taken there on a sacred ship. They were the *theoroi*, and the sacred ship was the *Theoris*. The road by which they travelled was the *theodos*, and the place at which they observed the games the *theatron*. The root in all these cases is *theo*, to look or behold and supplies, as *theoria*, the basic meaning for the word theory.

The connection between *theoria* and *theos* is so close that it has led to speculation that it also serves as the root for theology. If that were so then the connection between theory, theology and play would be direct. In fact they have different roots. They do originate at about the same time, however, and play on each other, thus the connotations of theory have connotations of the gods, the god's eye perspective, the consulting of the oracle and the statesmanlike activity of *theoria*, an official spectator. The gods of the pantheon were themselves also part spectators in the drama involving human beings. Behold the human – from a god's eye perspective. By a further cross play on words, *themethla* is a foundation, a base or, even, the bottom of a mountain.

Formal play in the shape of recognized games was present not only in Ancient Greece but also Rome, where official games began in 264 BCE. In the shape of gladiatorial contests they came to take on a form that often resulted in the death of one or more of the contestants. While Roman games might have religious connotations this was not always so under the emperor Augustus, for example, the games of 17 BCE were secular. As the Roman games became more spectacular and more violent, opposition to them increased. They continued, however until the fifth century.

The period after that until the middle ages is one in which formal play and games were suppressed or even disallowed. The violence of the Roman games and the use by them at one point to target and eliminate early Christians produced a not unsurprising revulsion against play and games. In some Anglo-Saxon forms of expression play and VIOLENCE are directly linked. For example, a 'playlome' was a weapon.

Go reche me my playlome,
And I salle go hym sone;
Hym were better hafe bene at Rome,
So ever mote I thryfe.

(Chrétien de Troyes, *Perceval*, 2013)

The linkage to play and violence here is made quite clearly through Rome. Not surprisingly the collapse of Rome, blamed by Augustine on its pagan practices and its continued WORSHIP of multiple gods took the notions of play, games and sport, away from those attempting to salvage what they could out of the wreckage that was the dramatic and sudden collapse of the Roman Empire.

By 1200 CE some games of entertainment had begun to re-emerge. The French game *la soule* was a ball game somewhat like hockey. Its increasingly violent form led to it being banned in the fourteenth century. Other games rose to take its place. In the fifteenth century tennis emerged. In Shakespeare's *Henry V*, the Dauphin mocks Henry by sending him 'a tun of treasure'. The treasure turns out to be tennis balls. Shakespeare turns the reference to the playing of the game of tennis into another kind of play: a play on words. He has Henry say,

> When we have match'd our rackets to these balls,
> We will in France, by God's grace play a set
> . . . And tell the pleasant prince this mock of his
> Hath turn'd his balls to gun stones . . . (I; ii)

The development of tennis was followed by golf, football, horse racing and in the nineteenth century, with the vast growth in formal play, the revival of the modern Olympic games. In the twentieth century play, in the form of sport and games, has become a major part of life. It is an enormous income generator and an issue of personal, community and national pride. Not since the earliest games has such importance and significance been given to formally organized play.

Play, however, runs wider than formal games. And its importance may turn out to be much more significant than formal game-playing suggests. Informal and spontaneous play are part of most mammalian life. Young mammals whether they be human infants, lions or dolphins, to give just three examples, can be seen exhibiting behaviour that is clearly playful. The cause of this is partly zest and evidently so, but it may also be a means of testing themselves against others and the world, of gaining a sense of identity. A lion might be a biological lion without ever coming to know what it is to be a social lion. A dolphin may be a biological dolphin without being a social dolphin and a human infant may, as experience of feral children has shown, be a biological human without learning to be a social human. The role of play in the formation of sociality is crucial. In play the limits of the natural world, its nature and character are discovered. In play the forms of interaction that are, and are not, permitted with others are discovered.

The development of self takes place against others. A self-identity is not something that is pre-given, it is something that is obtained. Obtaining it requires interaction with others and learning to interact with others in social situations requires the understanding of rules. The rules here are not the formal rules of games, they are mostly implicit rules, knowledge of which is obtained not by consulting a rule book but by learning to play the relevant social game. The role of childhood games here is important and formative for such play teaches, again often implicitly, the nature of play and its rule-based character. It teaches a child what it is to have, hold and maintain a rule. There is a very significant sense in which play is important to the development of the adult. A child deprived of the opportunity to play will grow into an adult with, at best limited horizons and at worst, more or less a-social characteristics. Play is essential to healthy growth and development but it does not follow that any and all play is healthy. Given the significance of play in development, and in self and other conceptions, it is clear that some kinds of play could produce a strange sense of self and a strange even anti-social sense of the boundary between self and others. Interaction is necessary to sociality but it does not follow that all and any interaction is good for sociality.

The most significant kind of play in which humans engage is through language games. Shakespeare's puns on the game of tennis show one important sense of language play – punning or playing on words. Such play on words is significant and important for it is one way in which the boundaries of language are stretched.

New words come into being and new senses are given to older words. The relation between language and play is even deeper, however, than the pun suggests. It may even be that language is always play. What does a word mean? If the meaning of a word is given by that to which it refers then the correct use of a word is given by correctly relating it to the referent. On the other hand, '"When *I* use a word", Humpty Dumpty said in a rather scornful manner, "it means just what I choose it to mean – neither more nor less"' (Lewis Carroll, *Through the Looking Glass*, ch. 6).

Humpty Dumpty tears word and referent apart but it does not follow that meaning is lost. On the contrary the meaning is just what Humpty Dumpty says it is. Of course no one can go around using words in just any which way, they would run up against the use that the word was put to by others. To be understood is to use the word in a shared way. But that implies that while no one can be Humpty Dumpty all on their own there can be a coherent world of Humpty Dumpties. When *we* use a word it means just what *we* choose it to mean. In a social situation the meaning of a word is just what *we* say it is. Such a shared meaning is not one that is consciously deliberated and arrived at but it is one that is learnt, as part of what Wittgenstein called a language game. In a language game the participants learn to play by the rules. It does not follow that they know the rules, e.g., of grammar in an explicit way. It does follow that they know how to play the game. They can do it in practice even if they cannot explicitly spell out the rules. This is true of most play. Few explicitly know all the rules but they can still play the game while abiding by the rules.

In this Wittgensteinian sense play is at the heart of language. The 'meaning of a word is its use' (*Philosophical Investigations*) in the language game. Language then is just a form of play. What Henry V did with the explicit punning and explicit play on words is something that in a slightly less explicit way is common to all language. Some languages in some social situations are more open than others and so more explicit play will, or will not occur, as the case may be. In any case play, whether it be known and acknowledged or not, is at the heart of language.

Language is at the heart of human sociality. So much so that the type and structure of the language of a people has been held to determine their world outlook, their *weltanschauungen*. The anthropologist Benjamin Lee Whorf in a series of seminal studies of North American Indians showed the relation between the language of a people and the way in which a people constructs the physical world. Every language contains a world view within it. The rapid depletion of languages in the twentieth century is also the rapid depletion of world outlooks. The danger in this, according to Steiner, is that one language Amer-English could come to be the dominant language closing off all other possible world views.

If language is at the heart of human sociality then so is play. Winch has argued, on the basis of Wittgenstein's theory of language, that social institutions and social structures are constituted of rule-governed behaviour (Winch 1958). Rule-governed behaviour is behaviour that takes place in a game like manner. Social institutions and social structures are then constituted and held in place by collective play. Play, it seems, goes not only to the foundation of how we see the world but also to the foundation of the social world in which we live. The world and life is mediated always by play.

The implications of this, if correct, are far-reaching. It would not be possible, for instance, to say that one game is better than another without invoking the rules of another game and that could be justified only by invoking the rules of another game and so on. This seems to imply that all games are equal. When carried to the limit it leads to the popular but nihilistic view in which no judgements of quality (*see also* CULTURE) can be made. This seems to be patently false. All games include within them some assessment of what counts as quality within the play. That is universal to all games and not, an entirely relativistic product of a particular game. The corresponding step that judgements between games about quality of play is not an impossible one to make. It is one to be made, however, with caution, lest it become another piece of elitism or hegemony.

Play is at the foundation of all language, all social institutions, all perceptions of nature, all perceptions of the social world and all perceptions of the self. There is no perspective on self, world or others that is not mediated in some way by activities governed by play. It may be that play, albeit often disguised, is the most fundamental of our activities. We are playful beings and have turned symbolic play into the centre of our life. Many animals play, certainly all mammals play but only humans play symbolic games where the symbols then become the centre of life. As they do so, the knowledge of the play and the game fades into the background and the game becomes real. The recovery of the knowledge of playfulness at the heart of our being is necessary to well being.

One of the earliest occurrences of the word 'play' is in the Anglo-Saxon 'playday' – a holiday. The contrast makes it clear that play was then as now normally contrasted with WORK. A deeper analysis shows that both these kinds of activities referred to as work and play are ultimately a form of play. Yet some are more pleasant and some more unpleasant than others. In an ideal society what is known as 'work' and what is known as 'play' would at their best both be creative and at their best both interact. In an ideal and liberated condition work becomes recognized as a form of play and takes on the structure within which that is possible, and play comes to be seen as a kind of work, for in it we create and recreate ourselves. In an ideal world we would live in a condition beyond work and play. A condition that incorporated both without being merely either. In the meanwhile one can but note that the games which people play really is the life they lead. All of life is a game: it is just that some games are more serious than, and some games are more tedious than, others.

Steiner, George (1977) *After Babel: Aspect of Language and Translation*, Oxford: Oxford University Press.
Whorf, Benjamin Lee (1954) *Language, Thought and Reality*, New York: Wiley.
Winch, Peter (1958) *The Idea of a Social Science and its Relation to Philosophy*, London: Routledge and Kegan Paul.
Wittgenstein, Ludwig (1953) *Philosophical Investigations*, Oxford: Basil Blackwell.

Paul Barry Clarke

PNEUMATOLOGY

Pneumatology (Greek: *pneuma-*, wind or spirit, e.g. John 3: 8) is the doctrine of the person and work of God the Spirit. Central questions concern the distinctive character of the Holy Spirit and the relation of the Spirit to the other two persons of the TRINITY. Recent discussion of this topic frequently laments its neglect in THEOLOGY, especially at the expense of CHRISTOLOGY. It is sometimes countered that this is inevitable because the Spirit, as the 'self-effacing' member of the Trinity, is concerned to witness to God the Father through his revelation in his Son. It is similarly also contended that we speak from or through the Spirit, not about him. Although both points are correct, and indicate the specific character and difficulty of pneumatology, they do not on their own account for the manifest weaknesses of the dogmatic tradition in this area. As is often pointed out, regular outbreaks of MILLENARIANISM and, particularly within the past century, the growth of Pentecostal and CHARISMATIC MOVEMENTS appear to result from a marked weakness in the way that mainstream Western Christianity has perceived the Spirit.

In the Hebrew Bible the Spirit is widely seen as the vehicle of the mysterious freedom of God over and in the created world, as witnessed particularly in the vision of the valley of bones in Ezekiel 37. In relation to the creation in general he is the giver of life (Psalm 104: 30), and in relation to human creation is the one who empowers, not only in miraculous ways, but also in holding creatures in being and in enabling the prophets to speak the truth. In the New Testament the same themes are to be found, but there are more Christological and eschatological notes. The Spirit miraculously brings about the conception of Jesus, and is also the one who empowers him for mission. He is understood, after the RESURRECTION and ascension, to be the one sent by the glorified Christ to relate believers to the Father through him, and it is as such that he is the one through whom the life of the age to come is realized, the one who creates community and brings the whole of creation to its fulfilment. It must be emphasized that the Spirit is more concerned with enabling people and things to be truly themselves than with signs and wonders for their own sakes, although MIRACLES are indeed sometimes signs of the Spirit's work.

Although there was some debate about the full divinity of the Spirit, coming to a head in the fourth century, pneumatology was in general given far less attention in the patristic period than Christology. The brief evocations of his functions in the creeds – 'who spoke through the prophets'; 'the Lord and giver of life' – contrast with the careful and detailed definitions of the person and work of Christ. But there is much to be found in the work of the theologians. Four examples will suffice to set out the main developments. In contradiction to the teaching of some Gnostic sects that spirit and matter were opposed realities and that God could not be conceived to be either the creator of the material world or directly involved in it, Irenaeus of Lyons (fl. 180) contended that God was involved in the creation and redemption of the whole world not by intermediate realities but by means of his 'two hands' the Son and the Spirit, who were mediators of his activity. The Spirit's specific role is to enable believers to achieve their created destiny by enabling them to participate in the reversal of Adam's fall achieved by Christ. 'The Father approves and commands, the Son carries out the Father's plan, the Spirit supports and hastens the work' (*Against the Heresies* IV, 36, 2).

In some contrast, Origen of Alexandria (184–254) tended to see the Godhead as a hierarchy, headed by the utterly transcendent Father with the Son as a 'second god' providing a link between God and the world, in a rather Platonic scheme. The result was that the Spirit had a rather uncertain role and a doubtful divinity. But Origen did describe the Spirit as a hypostasis or particular being, and thus set the scene for later debates about the full divinity and personality of the Spirit.

The significance of the work of Basil of Caesarea (d. 379) is subject to some controversy. Because of his apparent reluctance to describe the Spirit as being, in common with the Son, 'of one substance with the Father', he is sometimes suspected of Origenist leanings, and contrasted with the more forthright Gregory of Nazianzus. But whatever be the outcome of that debate, there is no doubt that Basil made a major contribution to the identification of the Spirit, i.e. to saying something of what the Spirit's distinctive being and function are in relation to the other persons of the Godhead and to the world. He spoke of 'the original cause of all things that are made, the Father, . . . the creative cause, the Son; . . . the perfecting cause, the Spirit' (*On the Spirit* XV, 38). As the perfecting cause, the Spirit can be understood to exercise the eschatological function that is so important a feature of New Testament teaching. Thus Basil provides the basis for a development of Irenaeus' insights. At the same time, along with the other two Cappadocian theologians, he shared a theology of the Trinity as 'three hypostases (PERSONS) in one *ousia* (being)'. This offered the possibility of a development of Origen which did not place the Spirit at the foot of a divine hierarchy.

It is in his attempt to articulate, in a Western context, the meaning of that Cappadocian expression, which became in translation 'three persons in one substance', that Augustine of Hippo (354–430) became the father of Western pneumatology. Teaching that all divine actions are actions of the whole Trinity, Augustine was relatively uninterested in the question about the Spirit's distinctive mode of action, and he concentrated attention on the place of the Spirit in the inner being of God. Operating with a rather platonic scheme, he conceived the Spirit as the link between Father and Son, as 'gift' and 'LOVE'. Two features of the teaching we have reviewed so far are lost. First is the rooting of the doctrine of the Spirit in the economy of salvation (Biblically, one could equally understand the Son to be the gift and love of God). Second is the distinctive type of agency that Basil had made it possible to attribute to the Spirit. In the long run, this helped to precipitate the division of Eastern Orthodox and Western churches, which to this day disagree on whether the Spirit is 'from the Father' or 'from the Father *and the Son*' (Latin: *Filioque*).

What theological difference underlies the dispute? The Eastern argument, as exemplified by Zizioulas, is that to attribute the being of the Spirit to two sources, both the Father and the Son, invites the positing of a prior and *impersonal* source of being – 'divine substance' – behind the being of them both. It is for such reasons that Lossky tends to attribute most of the weaknesses of Western theology to this source. Eastern theology tends rather to base the being of God in the Father, a *personal* being. (The Western response to this is that it gives rise to an Origenistic doctrine of the Trinity, making both Son and Spirit subordinate to the Father. See Smail (1988) for an attempt to mediate.) Another important argument against the *Filioque* is that, if the Spirit has his being from the Son as well as the Father, he is effectively subordinate to the Son. It is sometimes argued that the doctrine of the Spirit is inadequately treated in Western theology because he is effectively relegated to doing little other than applying to the believer the benefits of Christ (see British Council of Churches 1989). (Ironically, some modern Pentecostalist and ecologically oriented conceptions go to the other extreme and conceive the Spirit independently of the Son. The same charge is sometimes made against Eastern Orthodoxy.)

This is only apparently an abstract topic, and its wider relevance is illustrated by the widespread inability of theology to do justice to the humanity of Jesus. It has been argued recently, drawing on work by the Puritan John Owen and Edward Irving (1792–1834), that the doctrine of the Spirit is the key to an understanding of the humanity of Christ. It is through his response to the Spirit, not some inbuilt divine programming, that Jesus is able to remain the one truly faithful human being. As a result of their pneumatology, Owen and Irving were able to maintain doctrines both of the incarnation and of the Spirit-led humanity of Christ, whereas it is widely held that they are alternatives (see Lampe 1977).

In contrast to these and other exceptions, the mainstream tradition has revealed an incapacity at once to give due weight to the humanity of Christ and to locate conceptually the distinctive nature and activity of the Spirit. The result has

been that the Catholic traditions of the West have tended to limit the work of the Spirit to institutional and clerical channels and have been unable to give due place to his work in the whole Christian community and beyond it in the world outside the church. Although the Reformers, particularly Calvin – 'the theologian of the Spirit' (Gordon Rupp) – broadened the conception in both respects, the later Protestant traditions, as though in reaction to supposed Catholic institutionalizing, have tended to make the equal and opposite error of locating the Spirit in human subjectivity. In the Enlightenment, the rationalist version of this approach led to a tendency to equate spirit and human reason.

A similar tendency can be seen to operate in the thought of G.W.F. Hegel (1770–1831), whose importance for this dictionary lies in the fact that he saw a close connection between spirit and social order. *Geist*, or rational spirit, was the central category of his theory of reality. From one point of view Hegel's philosophy is the most Christian of all philosophies, as a thoroughgoing theology of the third person of the Trinity. Spirit is the most real being and, as the dynamic rational process which dialectically realizes itself in history, almost the only reality. Hegel saw societies and nations as the vehicles of the progress of Spirit, and his philosophy of Spirit was an appeal to modern Western culture to develop a social order in which the oneness of the finite and the infinite in Spirit is realized. Crudely, but not wholly inaccurately put, human social CULTURE is the way by which God becomes real. How far this helped to shape modern authoritarian political orders is a matter of continuing debate.

From another point of view, Hegel's philosophy can be seen as a complete secularization of Christian categories, a tendency which Feuerbach and Marx were later to develop into full ATHEISM. By effectively reducing the Trinity to the third person, Hegel is held to have attempted to realize an ESCHATOLOGY in the present and thus encouraged excessive or even idolatrous estimates of human social potentialities. ('Hegel's only real fault was that he confused himself with the last judge; but that is quite a fault' (Robert Jenson).) Similarly, by making the Spirit an agency immanent in the human mind and human SOCIETY Hegel falsified the element of otherness in the Biblical characterization of the Spirit. Despite what is often said, it is not the function of the Spirit to become immanent in the world; that is the Son's office. The Spirit is transcendent, in the sense that he is, for example, the one who blows upon the dry bones, drives Jesus out into the wilderness, and is generally the 'other' who mediates to him his Father's will and aid, finally raising him from the dead. (For an opposing thesis, owing much to Hegel, see Lampe 1977.)

What, then, are the main features of a doctrine of the Spirit? First, *the Spirit in relation to the world*: in the New Testament, the primary work of the Spirit is the realization of human salvation by relating believers to the Father through the Son. In this, he is the mediator of freedom (2 Corinthians 3: 17). This is not conceived individualistically, however, for a major focus is the Spirit's work in creating community. That is why many links are made between the Spirit and the Church. But the emphasis is eschatological rather than institutional, so that the Spirit's distinctive mode of action is to realize in the present anticipations of the conditions of the age to come. Here, the notion of particularity is also important, for the Spirit's function is to make particular the universal work of Christ achieved on the Cross and realized through the resurrection. Though this is achieved primarily through the WORSHIP and life of the church, it would not be improper to draw from this the conclusion that the Spirit is the author of true community wherever it is achieved. (Though to be true to the New Testament, the criterion of such community would remain Christological; *see* CHRISTOLOGY.)

A similar argument could be developed, taking up themes from the Hebrew Bible and a cue from the resurrection, for the work of the Spirit in the non-personal world. The Spirit's work is to enable the whole creation to realize its own proper way of being before God. There are implications for ecology, but also for aesthetics, and it is no accident that *inspiration* is an important concept in art. The calling of the steward of creation and of the artist alike is to enable the creation to praise God in its own way. In summary, and in elaborating Basil's dictum, it could be said that, wherever created beings are enabled to achieve their particular perfection, there is the work of the Spirit.

Second, *the Spirit in the Trinity*: what doctrine of the Spirit's eternal being corresponds to the eschatological function of perfecting the creation? Here, it is possible to develop Augustine's idea of the Spirit as the link between Father and Son, but to avoid his tendency to conceive the relation as the closing of a circle of rather inward-turned love. The Spirit completes the being of God as the one who perfects the love of God as a being in communion, which means a love whose dynamic is to move outwards towards the other. From this it follows that the Spirit is the agent of the divine movement outwards, to create, redeem and perfect. The social and political implications of such a conception of dynamic community are evident, but far from simple to realize, just because they depend on the particularizing gift of the Spirit, who 'blows where it wills'.

British Council of Churches (1989) *The Forgotten Trinity*, vol. 1, *The Report of the BCC Study Commission on Trinitarian Doctrine Today*. London: British Council of Churches.

Congar, Yves (1983) *I Believe in the Holy Spirit*, 3 vols, London: Geoffrey Chapman.

Heron, Alasdair (1983) *The Holy Spirit*, London: Marshall, Morgan & Scott.

Jenson, Robert W. (1984) 'The Holy Spirit', in C.E. Braaten and R.W. Jenson (eds) *Christian Dogmatics*, Philadephia, PA: Fortress Press, vol. 2, pp. 101–78.

Lampe, G.W.H. (1977) *God as Spirit. The Bampton Lectures 1976*, London: SCM.

Lossky, Vladimir (1957) *The Mystical Theology of the Eastern Church*, London: James Clarke.

Smail, Thomas (1988) *The Giving Gift. The Holy Spirit in Person*, London: Hodder & Stoughton.

Zizioulas, John D. (1985) *Being as Communion. Studies in Personhood and the Church*, London: Darton, Longman & Todd.

Colin Gunton

POLICING

A fundamental level of social order is needed in all societies. Geographical location, the nature of economic and criminal justice systems and patterns of relationships make no difference to this social fact. Levels of social order differ from SOCIETY to society; perceptions of what amounts to stability and order vary greatly within and between societies. Individuals are capable of needlessly experiencing apprehension and fear about impending social disorder and chaos. Conversely, belief in the strength of societal stability can cloud clear evidence to challenge such a JUDGEMENT. The police is one institution with a key symbolic and instrumental role in the retention of social order (Manning 1977). Police are within the religious theme of the creation of order from chaos and, as such, have a virtual sacred status.

In industrial societies the police have developed into a distinct institution of the political STATE. The extent to which the police are seen to be acting justly and fairly should therefore be traced to the structure of the political state within which they work, not least to the basis of its law. The origins of 'the police', however, lie in custom and other forms of regulation and control. As societies became increasingly differentiated policing developed as the task of a watchman or other functionary. In industrial societies the police became a distinct institution. Historical analyses of policing have identified an evolutionary progress from 'primitive' to 'modern' forms that have retained a close relationship between police and public (Critchley 1967). Other analyses, in contrast, have discerned a development of the police consonant with increased state POWER, structured in the interest of a ruling élite or social CLASS (Brogden 1982). A more adequate history of the police has to account for the relevance of social divisions both to conflict and to social consensus (Reiner 1985).

It would be mistaken to define the police solely as that state institution mandated with AUTHORITY to enforce the LAW by the legitimate use of force. Definitions of 'police' might be widened to include members of state institutions that have a social control function – social workers, factory inspectors and tax inspectors, for example (Corrigan and Leonard 1978). A wider notion of 'police' might include the FAMILY, the school and other institutions that, for example, 'police' gender relationships (Donzelot 1980). Then there has in recent years been a proliferation of organizations concerned with private policing (Johnston 1992). Private security firms routinely patrol shops, offices, hospitals and so on.

The corporate status of the police is itself a symbol of the political state and its right to intervene in individuals' lives through the use of delegated authority and power. A uniformed police officer patrolling a street is a symbol of the political state and its potential to restrict personal liberty and, importantly, a symbol of the protective stability that the state seeks to provide (Bittner 1970). Research evidence suggests that people feel safer when police officers are seen to be patrolling their streets, despite the equally strong evidence that, as a general policy, foot patrol is no more effective in the reduction of CRIME or civil disorder than other policing strategies. The notion of trust invested in social relationships seems affected by police action, especially when personal danger is perceived (Hough and Mayhew 1985).

Social order is often thought to be directly related to the use of law. There is indeed a relationship between the two but this is not straightforward or causal. Social order can be threatened by the police use of law. In Britain and America serious social disorders have been sparked off by vigorous police law enforcement (Scarman 1981). Police states tend in the long term to be self-destructive, fostering suspicion and latent unrest (Chapman 1968). The rule of law and therefore the authority of law itself can equally be threatened by social disorder. Sensitivity to public tolerance of disorder and the use of discretion in law enforcement are fundamental to policing (Skolnick 1966).

Law is just one resource available to the police. Research studies have demonstrated that most requests for police assistance from members of the public do not require the use of law. This is more the case for rural areas than it is for inner cities. But even in large conurbations most requests for police service do not lead to law enforcement. The police have been described as a 'secret social service' (Punch 1979).

These diverse contexts of police work are complex and beg of officers 'an unknown solution to an unknown problem' (Bittner 1967) – a religious issue, indeed! There is no absolutely right answer to many problems the police deal with. If the law seems an appropriate resource for policing its precise relevance to a series of events that face an officer is rarely clear. The use of a legal power of arrest may later be interpreted as illegal by the courts. Supervisory officers may use myriad negative rules within what has traditionally been a quasi-military structure of command to manage and sanction the rank and file. Mistakes can be treacherous. People involved in an incident will provide different and at times competing accounts of events for an officer to assess. A range of available policing strategies, from the use of arrest to the offering of advice and consolation, is employed, often in private places, to seek a solution to problems. Uncertainty is a constant feature of police work. Within a setting like this a retrospective account of the content of how a police officer dealt with an incident may be difficult to determine.

One consequence of this context of police work has been the creation of a distinct rank-and-file CULTURE, the occupational culture of policing, that sustains officers' certainty about the scope of police work. An occupational culture is a body of knowledge and associated actions that are regarded as taken-for-granted, commonsensical, for the performance of work. The core of this occupational culture of policing has been documented in several studies and it has often been found to be in tension with definitions of competence written into the law, police policy and public views of the police function (Manning 1977; Holdaway 1983; Smith et al. 1986). Policing is understood by the lower ranks, for example, to be centrally concerned with crime control; to be work that is full of action and excitement; to be about the control of people through the use of authority; to be dependent upon the retention of police power to the exclusion of other factors.

In fact, policing has been found to be minimally concerned with crime control in terms of the tasks the police perform; to be a rather sporadic activity involving long periods of quiet and inaction; to require a wide range of conciliatory and related techniques; and to be dependent on a wide range of policies, institutions and individuals for effective performance. The occupational culture, however, has an interpretative function that reconstructs for the rank and file the day-to-day experience of policing into a recognizable pattern of events that accords with their apparent common sense (Berger and Luckmann 1967). Law and policy may be written to achieve particular ends but they are interpreted phenomena. If the intentions of the law or policy harmonize rather than jar with the assumptions of the police occupational culture they are more likely to be enacted. If one wants to understand why the police use law in a particular way it is therefore necessary to study how law is used in action. Law as it is written may be very different from law in action. The police occupational culture (like folk religion in relation to belief and practice) acts as a traditional source of knowledge about the practice of police work that, like much belief that is regarded as normative, is extremely resistant to change. The occupational culture is the 'Berlin wall' of policing.

This is not to suggest that the police, certainly in contemporary Britain, have not changed at all. Two trends have become increasingly evident – the development of police management and a realization of the interdependence between the police and other institutions. The evidence is patchy but notions of rational management have increasingly informed the organization and structure of police forces and the ways in which senior officers have developed policies. Terms like 'management by objectives' and 'quality assurance' are part of the vocabulary of the modern chief officer, as police services are planned on the basis of 'customer need'. In many forces chief officers have commissioned public opinion surveys about police services and used various formal fora for consultation between themselves and sections of the public. This development of management has to an extent been based upon a realization that the policing function is closely related to citizens' perceptions and needs. Most policing is in response to a call for assistance from a member of the public; most arrests are the result of information freely given to an officer by a member of the public. In this sense the public stands at the front line of the retention of social order and of crime control.

Again, although the response has been variable, there has been among many senior officers a realization that the nature and consequence of police action is closely related to the policies and practices of other institutions – the social services, the EDUCATION system, local authority housing and leisure departments, for example (Alderson 1979). The retention of law and order within a locality depends to a significant extent on the ways in which opportunities are available for constructive leisure time pursuits provided by public authorities, by the ways in which schools deal with socially disruptive behaviour, including crime, by maintaining the material fabric of a public housing area in good repair to prevent an increasing sense of disillusion among residents in the wake of vandalism and other nuisances. Here, inter-agency co-operation is aimed at crime prevention, broadly conceived. Policing and police work is therefore a shared activity; a co-operative relationship between police and people is fundamental.

These changes are very much more acceptable to senior than to rank-and-file officers and some important 'truths' are implicit within them. First, there is the realization that a powerful institution like the police cannot depend upon its own activity to fulfil its mandate to enhance social order and keep the peace. Persons and institutions are interdependent and therefore in some sense related in community. Second, when it is realized that policing is not an autonomous activity, the weakness rather than the power of the police has to be recognized. A realization of vulnerability and limitation may benefit the development of police policy.

Social order, including levels of crime, cannot be guaranteed by police action. The effects of policing are partly constrained by the broader social inequalities that abide in societies. Although there is a distinct character to police relations with minority ethnic groups, for example, these cannot be separated from wider structures of racial divisions (Holdaway 1987). When social conflict leads to large-scale social disorder the police are required to act in a militaristic manner, using very different techniques of control from those found in more routine patrol work. So acting, the police may sustain the very social inequalities that prompt the civil unrest manifest on the streets and, at the same time, strain any realization of inter-

dependence between disadvantaged groups and the police (Jefferson 1990). The balance between these competing demands remains, retaining the tension between law enforcement and peace-keeping in sharp focus. Some societies have created a specialist force to deal with civil disturbances but this is criticized as a danger to the essentially civilian rather than military character of the police function.

For these various reasons the public accountability of the police is a crucial issue in democratic states (Reiner 1991). Police need to retain a distance from the particular interests of governments while themselves being publicly accountable through procedures that permit public complaints about conduct to be lodged and an open review of their action to be undertaken. Accountability is a necessary response to individual and collective police self-interest and wrong-doing. The extent to which present systems of police accountability promote trust in the population and thereby foster a sense of personal and collective safety is an issue that should be subject to constant review. The police is one among human institutions concerned with 'making and keeping human life human' (Lehmann 1963).

Alderson, J. (1979) *Policing Freedom*, Plymouth: MacDonald & Evans.

Banton, M. (1964) *The Policeman in the Community*, London: Tavistock.

Berger, P. and Luckmann, T. (1967) *The Social Construction of Reality*, Harmondsworth: Penguin.

Bittner, E. (1967) 'The police on skid row', *American Sociological Review*, 32: 699–715.

——(1970) *The Functions of the Police in Modern Society*, Washington, DC: National Institute of Mental Health.

Brodgen, M. (1982) *The Police: Autonomy and Consent*, London: Academic Press.

——, Jefferson, T. and Walklate, S. (1988) *Introducing Police Work*, London: Unwin Hyman.

Chapman, B. (1968) *Police State*, London: Macmillan.

Corrigan, P. and Leonard, P. (1978) *Social Work Practice under Capitalism*, London: Macmillan.

Critchley, T. (1967) *A History of the Police in England and Wales*, London: Constable.

Donzelot, J. (1980) *The Policing of Families: Welfare Versus the State*, London: Hutchinson.

Holdaway, S. (1983) *Inside the British Police: A Force at Work*, Oxford: Blackwell.

——(1987) 'Discovering structure: studies of the police occupational culture', in *The Future of Police Research*, Aldershot: Gower.

Hough, M. and Mayhew, P. (1985) *Taking Account*

of Crime: Key Findings from the 1984 British Crime Survey, London: HMSO.

Jefferson, J. (1990) The Case Against Paramilitary Policing, Milton Keynes: Open University Press.

Johnston, L. (1992) The Rebirth of Private Policing, London: Routledge.

Lehmann, P. (1963) Ethics in a Christian Context, Chicago, IL: University of Chicago Press.

Manning, P. (1977) Police Work, Cambridge, MA: MIT Press.

Punch, M. (1979) 'The secret social service', in The British Police ed. S. Holdaway, London: Edward Arnold.

Reiner, R. (1985) The Politics of the Police, Brighton: Wheatsheaf.

——(1991) Chief Constables, Oxford: Oxford University Press.

Reiss, A. (1971) The Police and the Public, New Haven, CT: Yale University Press.

Scarman, R.H.L. (1981) The Brixton Disorders, 10–12 April 1981, London: HMSO.

Skolnick, J. (1966) Justice Without Trial: Law Enforcement in a Democratic Society, New York and London: Wiley.

Smith, D., Small, S. and Gray, J. (1986) Police and People in London, Aldershot: Gower.

Simon Holdaway

POLITICAL CORRECTNESS

The term 'political correctness' is of very recent origin, and seems to have arisen in the USA in the 1980s. Considered per se, it might be defined as 'adherence to language and social practice in conformity with some political ideology', so that there would be 'political correctness' in almost any SOCIETY – Marxist, Islamic, etc. However, the term is normally used (and was developed) in reference only to one particular kind of political IDEOLOGY, which has come to be very powerful in North American society and has spread from there to many countries in the Western world. In general it is fair to say that 'political correctness' is most common, both as a term in use and as a social practice, in liberal and pluralistic societies of the West.

In such societies – and again, most obviously in the USA – there is a problem about social attitudes to various groups in society, since, unlike totalitarian societies, there is no obvious official ideology which defines and enforces such attitudes. Thus, whereas in the comparatively recent past the predominant social group and the predominant mores could be described

as WASP (White Anglo-Saxon Protestant), it has been increasingly recognized in the last few decades that this may do less than JUSTICE to other groups. The criteria for identifying such groups may vary, but the most obvious candidates are racial groups (blacks, Hispanics, North American Indians, etc.); and the earliest example of politically incorrect language is the use of 'nigger' as applied to blacks. From there, however, the concept has been extended to include almost any social group against which discrimination or prejudice may be thought to exist: in particular women, but also groups with any form of handicap or disadvantage (the physically disabled, those of excessive weight or diminutive height, and so forth).

The basic idea behind political correctness is thus to enforce much greater sensitivity and care, both in language and in social practice, in dealing with members of such groups (and the groups as a whole), so that they will not feel 'inferior', or 'put down', or 'offended', or in any way victimized. It is important to note here that the groups are identified by their supposed political or social position and not by other criteria, and even then only by certain kinds of criteria (particularly race, sex and handicap). The poor, the criminal, the ungodly, the cowardly, etc., are not normally considered as candidates.

In certain parts of North America, particularly in upper middle class institutions such as universities and colleges, political correctness is now at a very high temperature. People are expected not only to conform to a linguistic code which censors a great many terms on the grounds that they may constitute 'offensive language', but also to show deference and extreme sensitivity to the relevant groups. Members of these groups may, in such institutions, be preferred as candidates for jobs and other appointments on the grounds of 'positive discrimination', i.e. to ensure that the group is adequately 'represented' in these appointments. The addition of FEMINISM to the general movement of political correctness has greatly strengthened it, since women are more likely to be omnipresent in most contexts than are other groups.

In recent years (roughly from 1990 onwards) there has been a backlash against this movement, arising chiefly from the dislike of

CENSORSHIP which it entails and the consequent restrictions on academic and other debate. It is possible to identify certain institutions as insisting on a very high degree of political correctness and others as maintaining a counter-ideology (usually based on traditional liberal values such as free speech, impersonal scholarship and other such non-political criteria). There is thus a fairly high-temperature ideological and social conflict, the result of which has yet to be determined.

The details and general flavour of political correctness at the present time may best be gained by consulting contemporary works of reference (particularly Beard 1992: see also other references); but it should be remembered that these fluctuate rapidly from time to time, and are not in force in all institutions and societies at the same time.

The basic idea of doing justice to all members of society, both individually and as group members, will commend itself to all theological and philosophical positions that believe in justice. Few do not so believe: but positions vary very widely in respect of how they construe the notion of justice both in theory and practice. Thus, to take an extreme case, there are still positions which maintain that there are groups that, by nature or divine ordinance, should occupy a politically inferior position: for instance, that women should be subordinated to men (*see* SEXISM). In general, however, at least in those societies where political correctness flourishes, both theologians and philosophers have stressed the value of political EQUALITY for all.

That, however, still leaves important problems unresolved. One problem, hinted at above, is how to *identify* those groups which merit special attention: how important are the criteria of (for instance) race, sex and handicap as against other criteria? Thus in some schools the criteria that actually go to produce unjust discrimination are more to do with the way in which certain pupils may dress, or their social class, or their awareness of the latest pop music, or even their attitude to drug-taking, than with their race or cultural background or colour. So it is far from clear what groups we need to take special care to do justice *to*: what groups are in fact being 'done down' in particular social contexts. Underlying this problem is the question

of how much weight we are to give to political or social criteria in general, against other possible criteria of a non-cultural kind. Our views on this will turn on how we conceive of the human condition generally: thus if we think that this life is inevitably unjust, a vale of tears, and that we should be primarily concerned with preparing our immortal souls for a future life, we shall be less inclined to put our money on POLITICS or 'society'. On the other hand, if – what seems to be a striking feature of much contemporary theological thinking, and practice, in the Christian faith – we see religion as essentially concerned with social justice, politics and economics, we shall take an opposite view. The former would receive support from strong strands of thought in the New Testament which stress the lesser importance of material things, and politics generally, in comparison with preparing ourselves for Christ's kingdom; the latter from the compassion which Jesus showed for the poor, the hungry, the sick and the underprivileged in general. The meaning, force and relevance of passages in the New Testament which seem related to these issues are of course much debated by scholars. Nevertheless the following passages are, at least, amongst those which would have to be taken into account, and may be thought to illustrate the points made above: Matthew 5: 3ff., 5: 38ff., 6: 19ff., 8: 2ff., 12: 10ff., 15: 14ff. (with parallels in the other Gospels).

There is also an underlying problem which concerns our attitude to dignity or social status in general. Political correctness is based on the idea that the dignity of people, particularly the underprivileged, should be reinforced: that their background, culture, sex, race, etc. should be (as it were) made much of rather than disregarded, and that we should go out of our way to avoid giving offence, adopting always an attitude of tact and yielding benevolence. This is instantiated in New Testament requirements to turn the other cheek, to 'give him thy cloak also' and in general to defer to other people. On the other hand, there is also the opposing idea (in the Beatitudes, for instance) that dignity is not important: that the meek, the persecuted, the underprivileged in general have some kind of advantage or blessing – that we should not take a stand on our rights.

However these and other passages may be interpreted, there is on any account a tension between what Strawson (1974) calls the 'reactive' and the 'objective' attitudes, i.e. between treating people as equals (with consequent emphasis on justice and rights) and treating them as clients or 'cases' (with emphasis on mercy, charity and some kind of forgiveness). It may reasonably be thought that Matthew 18: 15–17 contrasts in this respect with Matthew 5: 38 ff. This tension comes to a head in the concept of forgiveness (for a fuller discussion see Wilson 1985).

In the EDUCATION of children in particular we thus confront a choice between different messages. Political correctness demands that we do stand on our dignity and rights, and would educate children to do this – to make much of their own race, CULTURE, sex, etc. just because it is theirs, and to insist that other people respect it. The alternative message is that, so far as possible, children should not put their money on such things but should derive their security and self-esteem from transcendental values which are not at the mercy of a society which, perhaps inevitably, will be unjust. In the case of adults the problem is less stringent: we may say, perhaps, that each of us (a) ought to avoid giving offence to others and (b) ought not to take offence ourselves. But with children we have to face the question of how far we are to bring them up so that they see themselves primarily as consisting of a social identity, determined by their race, colour, sex, etc., and how far as having an identity which is more culture-free and less politically constituted.

My own views on this (see Wilson 1994) are of less importance than the very striking fact that the basic thrust of political correctness has itself made an enormous impact on theological and philosophical ideology. It is not too much to say that such ideology has yielded, rightly or wrongly, to this basic thrust: for instance, to feminist pressure on religious belief and practice. This has, in effect, not just added to or made sophisticated but dramatically changed many theologians' picture not only of religious and social values but even of God. In general this has happened uncritically, and at least partly as the result of political pressure: the

underlying questions are philosophical or (in a broad sense) methodological, and concern the general relation of religion to politics and other worldly enterprises. Perhaps unsurprisingly, political correctness has made most impact on professions especially concerned with 'caring' and 'concern': on religion, education, social work and the like. (Even the police force, in the UK, is now called 'the police service'.) Tough-minded rightwing individuals and governments may resist this, since at a certain point – notably in education – it appears to conflict with efficiency, LAW and order, and other values; here, as in religion, people may take sides with established tradition or culture-free values rather than with the demand to satisfy the tender-minded. In general, however, it is fair to say that the basic ideas of political correctness are too firmly rooted for us to expect them to be overthrown in the foreseeable future.

It is arguable that political correctness has caused, or at least correlates with, a major psychological shift in the thought and feeling of many people in the Western world. A trivial (or perhaps not so trivial) example may be found in popular videos. The authors or producers of these allow very extreme representations of sex and VIOLENCE to be incorporated, including much language that, even a decade or two ago, would have been regarded as offensive, obscene and censorable. On the other hand, they take very great care to ensure that political correctness is satisfied: that blacks and women, for instance, are fairly represented and no possible offence is given to them in the language of the videos. Thus the criteria of political correctness have become overriding in the media generally, replacing earlier criteria of what is 'taboo', 'indecent' or 'offensive', and hence suggesting a radical change in our moral values. One might hazard the guess that those who favour political correctness no longer identify themselves with any AUTHORITY or ideology which, as it were, hands down values from on high, but rather with the underdog – perhaps, unconsciously, with the young child who resents parental authority. It will, I hope, be clear from what I have said above that there are very grave philosophical, theological, psychological and ultimately political problems underlying this change of consciousness which have yet to be resolved.

In this light political correctness should perhaps be seen as just one aspect of a general ideological shift in the direction of relativism and egalitarianism. If there are no culture-free or time-free truths or principles of reason, then we shall see knowledge and values not as standing transcendentally above human life, but rather as the personal constructions and hence possessions of particular groups and individuals, and these will then engage in a power struggle to *define* what is true or right (*see* DECONSTRUCTION). On this basis the question of whether the edicts of political correctness are right or reasonable cannot even be intelligibly raised: the might of whatever group can make its will felt defines the right. Most analytic philosophers would regard this as a simple logical error: words like 'right', 'true', 'reasonable', etc., are just not used in this culture-bound way. But the movement of thought is nevertheless extremely powerful.

Sociologists might connect this with the rise of DEMOCRACY and egalitarianism. Under pressure from the masses, various authorities (admittedly themselves often unjust and unreasonable) are called into question and dismantled, and there is then no alternative but to allocate authority to all individuals and groups on a basis of equality, where each person's opinion is as valid as any other person's. (Plato describes the process in his *Republic*, Book 8, 555 ff.) Characteristically this leads to chaos and is in turn replaced by a new authority, often of a highly autocratic kind. Some aspects of this pendulum-swing may be detected in the rise of various fundamentalist ideologies at the present time, which seem to offer personal security in the face of relativism. It has finally to be noted that these matters are still under debate in all the relevant disciplines – sociology, philosophy and theology itself – and that as yet there is no sign of any consensus.

Badcock, C.R. (1987) *Madness and Modernity*, London: Routledge.

Beard, H. (1992) *Officially Politically Correct Dictionary*, New York: Grafton Books, HarperCollins.

Choi, J.N. and Murphy, J.W. (1993) *The Politics and Philosophy of Political Correctness*, New York: Praeger.

Flew, A. (1976) *Sociology, Equality and Education*, London: Macmillan.

Hare, R.M. (1992) *Essays on Religion and Education*, Oxford: Oxford University Press.

Morris, B. (1972) *Objectives and Perspectives in Education*, London: Routledge & Kegan Paul.

Plato (1888) *Republic*, trans. B. Jowett, Oxford: Oxford University Press.

Rees, N. (1994) *The Politically Correct Phrasebook*, London: Bloomsbury.

Strawson, P.F. (1974) *Freedom and Resentment*, London: Methuen.

Wilson, J. (1985) 'Is forgiveness possible?', in *Philosophy* (Spring).

——(1990) *A New Introduction to Moral Education*, London: Cassell.

——(1994) *Love, Sex and Feminism*, Aldershot: Gregg.

John Wilson

POLITICAL THEOLOGY

The first thing to be understood about political theology is that there is no one THEOLOGY that goes by the name. There are many varieties even as confined to the contemporary theological world, and many more if one takes into account the long history of doing Christian theology in the light of the 'political'.

The second thing to be understood is that a political theology is not simply the working through of the political *implications* of a theological position which in itself is 'politically neutral', as if a political theology consisted in the mere *application* of theological ideas to the political realm. Political theologies in the contemporary sense start with the political: it is theology done in conscious reflection upon the political, and more broadly social, conditions which feed into its own very constitution as theology.

It follows from this last point that 'political' options are already inscribed into any attempt to define what political theology is. There is no politically neutral definition of political theology, any more than there is any theologically neutral definition of theology. 'Political theology' is simply the recognition that all theology is political and the working out of the consequences of that recognition.

In turn a fourth point follows: since politics is an essentially contested area of human thought, there is no non-contestable definition of what political theology is. This can be seen easily with reference to the second of the preceding comments. Edward Norman, for example (*Christianity and the World Order*), denies that the utterances of Christian theology have, or can have, any political content, or can be subject to any political or social conditions as such. He rejects what he understands to be that 'politicization' of Christian theology which typifies 'liberation' theologies and, while he concedes that theological truths do have *consequences for* the political, they are only such as derive from the inherently transcendent and non-political character of Christian faith. In this he does indeed differ from the mainstream of contemporary liberation theologians, in ways which we will examine shortly. But what Norman and, say, Gustavo Gutierrez differ about in the first instance is the question of what 'political theology' is. And this means that they differ both about the nature of theology and about the nature of POLITICS.

To say that the question of what political theology is is 'essentially contested' is, fifth, to say that the disagreements over its nature are asymmetrical: contestants do not even agree about the nature of their disagreements. For Gutierrez, attempts such as Edward Norman's to define theology as *in itself* 'apolitical' can only derive from an already given, but unacknowledged political option – a conservative one, favouring the political status quo. Consequently, Gutierrez maintains that he differs from political 'neutralisms' on *political* grounds, whereas, for Edward Norman, attempts such as Gutierrez's to inscribe political options into all articulations of theology are symptomatic of a *theological* failure, a failure, that is to say, to give expression theologically to the 'transcendence' of faith. In this way political theologians and their opponents can often be said to disagree about how to describe what it is that they disagree about.

This failure to agree to differ is significant in yet a sixth connection. It explains why it is that, at least today, the major disagreements in the theological world concerning the relations between faith and politics are not, as they were in England in the mid-seventeenth century, between *rival* political theologies within a shared conception of the inherently political nature of theology. Today's theological disagreements are rather between political theologies which are nearly all on the political 'left' and 'apolitical' theologies which are, comparatively speaking, nearly all on the 'right'.

Certainly this is how the situation appears, again, to Gutierrez. For, in his view, the theological position according to which faith is politically neutral nearly always, and perhaps inevitably, issues in a conservative politics. And it *issues in* a conservative politics because it *derives from* a conservative political option which favours the established power relations.

It follows from all this that to write of contemporary political theology as if one could do so purely 'theologically' and with political neutrality is already to beg the question against it – for it is to presuppose a view of theology which political theologians of virtually any school reject. On the other hand, to write of political theologies from within the sort of political options which they presuppose is to beg the question in their favour. And there is no way out of this dilemma. Consequently this contribution to the *Dictionary of Ethics, Theology and Society* has to be written from within an option; and indeed it is written from within the standpoint, broadly, of what has come to be known as 'LIBERATION THEOLOGY' in its Latin American manifestations.

The expressions 'political theology' and 'liberation theology' as used today refer to movements of Christian thought and practice which have become prominent within the past twenty-five years or so. Sometimes the first of these, 'political theology', is used to designate the very broad spectrum of 'politicized' theologies issuing from within the northern or the southern hemispheres, so that 'liberation theology' is seen as just one, if perhaps the most significant, species of the general class. More commonly, however, 'political theology' refers to a distinctively *northern* approach to the politicization of theology, typified by the theologies of the German theologians Moltmann (*A Theology of Hope*) and Metz (*Theology of the World*), whereas 'liberation theology' is seen as a distinctively *southern* and Third World phenomenon, typified by the Peruvian Catholic, Gustavo Gutierrez (*A Theology of Liberation*), and the

Methodist, Jose Miguez Bonino. It is in this former sense that the expression is used in this contribution, with particular attention being addressed to the 'liberation theologies' of the Third World.

A few facts. Half of all Christians today live in the Third World. By the end of this century it is estimated that over half of all Roman Catholics will live in Latin America. These in themselves merely demographic 'facts' yield consequences. Most Christians live within countries which are politically authoritarian, economically impoverished, socially inegalitarian and élitist, in which the vast majority of their populations are lacking in adequate standards of education, nutrition and hygiene, are insecure (at best) in the legal establishment of HUMAN RIGHTS, in which torture is a matter of routine policing practice, in which women are 'doubly oppressed' (economically and sexually), and in which the opportunities for all these things to be changed are severely hampered by the condition of dependence in which these countries stand on the international policy interests of the most powerful nations of the north. Many in the south argue that in practice the international conditions of trade imposed by the north and embodied in World Bank policies of 'structural adjustment' (insisted upon as a condition of loans which themselves impoverish their beneficiaries) reinforce the dependence of the Third World on the north and contribute to the internal distortions of economy and politics in the dependent nations. In short, according to this view, the structure of INTERNATIONAL RELATIONS, determined by the interests of the rich northern nations, actually *underdevelops* the southern world.

These are the perceived conditions under which the majority of Christians in the late twentieth century live. Yet the theologies of the Christian Churches – i.e. the formal articulations of Christian belief and practice – are the products of the very different CULTURE of the north and so very largely of men and women who live under conditions of relative WEALTH (even of relative wealth *within* their own relatively wealthy nations); they enjoy security in human rights, and good education, hygiene, nutrition are more or less guaranteed.

For the liberation theologians, the dominant theology of the Christian Churches reflects the contextuality of those who dominate – it is academic, abstract, élitist and unself-critical. And yet, paradoxically, one of the principal ways in which it reflects its own context of domination is in the very denial that its contextuality is relevant, in its presumption of 'universality' and transcendence of particular context. Thus at one and the same time it is the product of its own contextuality and unconscious of the contextuality from which it arises. In this lies the bad faith and the self-deceit of its 'political neutralism'.

Therefore, the liberation theologian asks: given the background of wealth and security in the North, a wealth which can be sustained only by conditions which impoverish the majority nations of the south, what could the demand that theology and faith should be 'politically neutral' amount to, other than the requirement that theology ignore the background and contextuality of oppression?

It is in this connection that the liberation theologians argue that an adequate theology must be a consciously 'contextual' theology (*see* CONTEXTUAL THEOLOGY). That is, they argue that an adequate theological method requires an act of conscious reflection upon the social, economic, political and cultural conditions from which it arises, that theology should thematize and articulate those conditions within a critical analysis. And when this is done, it will be recognized that the thesis of a 'politically neutral' Christian theology and practice is one which is in harmonious equilibrium precisely with interests of the world's powerful and rich peoples. For thereby are the poor deprived of a theological voice in which to articulate the critique of their oppression. The thesis of the 'political neutrality' of theology is but the political neutralization of the poor by means of theology.

For all its civilized manners, its sophisticated scholarship and its high liberal values, northern theology therefore appears to the liberation theologian to be a theology of the oppressors. It is not claimed that northern theology is necessarily a simple, crude expression of the *desire* to oppress; indeed, it rarely is. Rather, such a 'contextless' theology is the expression of a religious consciousness alienated from its own political reality, a consciousness which 'forgets' the power relations which at once sustain it and oppress the poor. Here liberation theologians borrow, with more or less fidelity, the language of MARXISM in describing this alienated theology as essentially a form of 'IDEOLOGY'. That is, northern theology is a body of ideas and lived practices in the medium of which social agents live out a distorted, misrecognized version of their own 'reality'. They live out the inequalities of the social world in the medium of general principles of human rights; they live out 'FREE-DOM' in the distorting mirror of a market which functions efficiently only on the back of the exploitation of the economies of the Third World; they live out their spiritual and 'universalist' idealisms in the false world of a religion kept separate from the secular reality of their particular self-interest; and therefore they live out their oppression of the poor in the medium of a theology which is neutral as between the rich and the poor. And in what is perhaps the most acute and telling synthesis of the political and the theological, the liberation theologians find an important connection between the Marxist theme of 'ideology' and the Biblical (especially the prophetic) theme of 'idolatry': for, as Jose Luis Miranda argues (*Marx and the Bible*), to live in a false relation with the poor is necessarily to live in a false relationship with God. And as both he and Gutierrez put it more positively, 'to know God *is* to do justice'.

Liberation theology, therefore, aspires to be the voice of the poor, a voice in which the Word of God in Jesus Christ can alone be authentically heard. Put in other terms, liberation theology gives expression to what the Latin American bishops in a joint declaration in 1979 in Puebla, Mexico, called, 'the preferential option for the poor'.

To do theology from the standpoint of the poor and oppressed: this is the central theme of all contemporary political theologies. This standpoint requires not only a radical reassessment of theological method nor only of theological priorities, but more radically a thoroughgoing reconstruction of all the central themes of traditional theology. Thus Boff (*Ecclesio-Genesis*)

and Sobrino (*The True Church and the Poor*) have called for a new ECCLESIOLOGY founded in the theological insights and practical organization of the 'base communities' which have flourished so vigorously in Brazil particularly. Sobrino (*Christology at the Crossroads*) has attempted a 'liberationist' CHRISTOLOGY, Gutierrez a 'liberationist' reconstruction of the classical traditions of spirituality, especially of John of the Cross (*We Drink from Our Own Wells*), Miranda has shown what the implications of the Church of the poor can mean for Biblical HERMENEUTICS (*Marx and the Bible*) and, from South Africa, Albert Nolan has presented a re-reading of the Jesus of the Gospels in terms of the political options of liberationism (*Jesus Before Christianity*).

There is no doubt that the now massive literature which has issued from within the diverse schools of liberation theology owes much to the techniques and insights of the theology of the north. And in many respects, trained as most of them have been in the theological schools of Europe and North America, their literary output differs little in form or source from that of the academic writings of northern theologians. But no liberation theologian would be happy with an account of liberation theology which concentrated exclusively on its formal, literary manifestations. For the liberation theologian, theology is essentially an *act*, an engagement of faith within a practice, and the engagement of a practice by faith. It is a unity of theory and practice, for which they reserve the term *praxis*. Consequently, a theology which purports to be a 'theology of the poor' will have to be generated principally by the action of the poor, and for most liberationists the significant expressions of their theology are to be found in the new forms of ecclesial community which have flourished so vigorously in Brazil, in the new styles of catechesis which were developed by the *delegados de la palabra* in regions of Nicaragua in the face of the vicious hostility of the *Contras*, in the practical scriptural exegesis of the peasants of Solentiname, in the heroic trade union work of Rigoberta Menchu in Guatemala, and in the human rights witness of Archbishop Oscar Romero in El Salvador. As the liberation theologians conceive of it, their own literary output is but the writing up of the minutes of the meetings at which the real business was done by the self-organization of the poor by the poor.

At the heart of the project of a liberation theology is a prescription for method (doing theology 'contextually'), a concrete commitment to a priority (the 'preferential option for the poor') and the recognition of a central theological truth: that the standpoint of the poor is theologically privileged. Beyond this common ground, there are many differences between liberation theologies, even between those which have flourished in Latin America. In particular, there are really quite sharp differences over the question of the role of Marxism within the practical analysis of the determinative 'context' for theology. In Boff, the Marxism is perfunctory, which makes it all the more ironic that he should have been a principal target of Vatican strictures against liberation theology; in Gutierrez, Marxism is honoured as a tool for the analysis of SOCIETY and ECONOMY, but rejected for its 'ATHEISM'. In Miranda, the commitment to Marxism is wholehearted but eccentric, for he takes the rather patronizing view that Marx, for all his denials, was 'really' a theist. In general, the mainstream position of liberation theologians on the question of Marxism is perhaps best embodied in Gutierrez's acceptance of Marxist 'analysis' of capitalist society and rejection of the atheist ideology. The Vatican, in the Instruction *Libertatis Nuntius* of 1984, was not alone in thinking such eclecticism implausible, preferring to see the class analysis and the atheism of Marx as being inseparable. Liberal critics not necessarily sympathetic to Vatican analyses such as Nicholas Lash have argued a similar view (*A Matter of Hope*).

Others in the north, who are more ideologically sympathetic both to liberation theology and to Marxism, have also seen problems in the ambivalent relations between the two. Kee (*Marx and the Failure of Liberation Theology*) has argued that, far from being too closely allied to Marxism, liberation theology is not Marxist enough: the liberation theologians cannot, he argues, claim rights to Marx's account of ideology in its application to northern theologies without adverting to the implications of that account for their own theology. And certainly, liberation theology has paid little enough attention to the critiques which Marx and Engels directed against very similar forms of Christian 'radicalism' in the seventeenth and nineteenth centuries (see *The Communist Manifesto* and *The Peasant War in Germany*). Likewise, Turner (*Marxism and Christianity*) has argued that in rejecting 'Marx's atheism' the liberation theologians are really rejecting Feuerbach's and that there are profound lessons to be learned from the atheism of Marx which a truly self-critical theology cannot afford to neglect.

Other doubts about liberation theology and its directions come from more or less sympathetic quarters. Some streams of feminist theology owe much to liberation theology as to method, but have been sharply critical of the failure of early 'liberationism' to take up the issue of the oppression of women within their own, largely male-oriented, theological project. It is true, furthermore, that until recently liberation theologians paid scant attention to the oppression of ethnic minorities within their own countries and in South Africa the insights of liberation theology have been combined with those of James Cone and others in North America to formulate 'black' theologies of liberation (*see* BLACK THEOLOGY). Development economists have raised critical questions about the simplistic models of international exploitation and 'underdevelopment' which characterize some 'liberationist' writings. But in the last resort these are criticisms of a theological and practical movement which liberation theology should not, in principle, have much difficulty incorporating within its own methods; or else they are developments of the principle of 'contextuality' in ways fully consistent with liberationism. In any case, what these criticisms and qualifications cannot do is counter the evidence of a truly independent and authentic theological voice emerging from within the poor, oppressed peoples of the world, a voice which still threatens to match in critical energy the demographic preponderance, in Christian terms, which those people represent.

Boff, Leonardo (1986) *Ecclesio-Genesis*, New York: Orbis Books.

Galdamez, Pablo (1986) *Faith of a People*, London: Catholic Institute for International Relations.

Gutierrez, Gustavo (1973) *A Theology of Liberation*, New York: Orbis Books.

——(1984) *We Drink from Our Own Wells*, New York: Orbis Books.

Kee, Alastair (1990) *Marx and the Failure of Liberation Theology*, London: SCM.

Lash, Nicholas (1981) *A Matter of Hope*, London: Darton, Longman & Todd.

Miranda, Jose (1974) *Marx and the Bible*, New York: Orbis Books.

Moltmann, Jürgen (1967) *A Theology of Hope*, New York: Harper & Row.

Nolan, Albert (1976) *Jesus before Christianity*, David Philip.

——(1988) *God in South Africa*, London: Catholic Institute for International Relations.

Norman, E.R. (1979) *Christianity and the World Order*, Oxford: Oxford University Press.

Rowland, Christopher (1988) *Radical Christianity*, Cambridge: Polity.

Sobrino, Jon (1978) *Christology at the Crossroads*, New York: Orbis Books.

——(1984) *The True Church and the Poor*, New York: Orbis Books.

Turner, Denys (1983) *Marxism and Christianity*, Oxford: Blackwell.

Denys Turner

POLITICS

Politics: from the Greek *polis*, political community, sometimes, and somewhat misleadingly, referred to as the city STATE. Politics and THEOLOGY are closely intertwined, the experiences in thought and order that defined the conditions for the one are also the experiences that defined the conditions for the other. The inversion of thought that led to politics is the same inversion of thought that led to theology. Although the relation between politics and theology is not one of entailment, the political moment parallels the theological moment.

The term 'politics' has a number of principal senses; it may refer to an activity, to a domain or type of place where that activity occurs, or to a branch of study. As an activity politics is a particular form of world engagement, as a domain or place it takes public spaces. As a branch of study it was thought by Aristotle to belong, with ETHICS, to practical reason. As these general conditions can be partially met in many areas of life, so aspects of what appear to be political may imperfectly and widely emerge in many areas of life. Similarly, as these conditions can be partially met in many different societies, so aspects of what appear to be political may imperfectly emerge in societies whose form of GOVERNMENT is not primarily political. Politics strictly understood is a western development, exported more or less completely to other regions. In broad terms one can distinguish between prepolitical; political; statal; post-statal and post-modern expressions of politics. All political forms of world engagement contain similar basic conditions, albeit expressed differently, and all political forms of world engagement contain a theology.

The word 'politics' appeared first in its modern sense following William of Moerbecke's translation of Aristotle's treatise of practical reason *The Politics* (*ta politika*) in the middle of the thirteenth century. The word 'politics' as the nominative plural of *politic* occurs in English in the early part of the fourteenth century and this provides the primary lexical sense of *politics* as the plural of the adjective, *politic* (OED adjective and substantive). That usage also betrays an early modern concern with the study of politics as a branch of practical reason; as the proper means of the activity of applying government. In the early part of this century it has sometimes been given as a noun (OED, Webster's) and with an increasing fashion for nominalization in phrases like 'the good' (Kant 1783), 'the holy', 'the sacred' (Otto 1914), and 'the divine', where the adjective is used substantively, it has found expression in nominalized form as 'the political'. Schmitt's influential *Der Begriffe des Politischen* (1927), imperfectly translated as *The Concept of the Political*, is, deliberately and ambiguously, genitive, adjectival and substantive, reflecting both the ambiguity of the word 'politics' and the status of that which gives rise to political activity. In so far as understandings of the word *politics* are contestable and of import, a contest about its meaning is, on some accounts, political.

The form of life that was to give rise to politics was the city state common throughout the Mediterranean area and Near East from the third to fourth millennium BCE. Such knowledge that survives shows life as pre-political for humans, if not for the gods. Similarly the relation between the pre-political city states and the form of their early religion is close; a relation that in Greek hands, almost two millennia later, led to the founding and development of theology. The surviving descriptions of the pantheon of the early Mesopotamian cities show the gods exhibiting the qualities of assembly, debate and discussion and authorizing enforcement of their jointly-arrived-at decisions. In such a universe the gods were the ultimate rulers but men might sometimes partake in this, ultimately, divine and cosmic rule. In the epic *Enuma Elish* the pantheon is shown in elective mode selecting Marduk as King. It is probable that the kings of the earliest walled cities were temporary responses to particular emergencies whose success in managing ever more permanent emergencies led to the permanent institution of kingship. Individual kings were acknowledged as *soters*, saviours, and as such they became established as the heroes of epics, even challenging the gods. Prometheus was far from the first to hold this honour. In *The Epic of Gilgamesh* (Pritchard 1950), Gilgamesh showed in his actions that he was to be reckoned with even by the Gods, and if recognized by the Gods as significant then, as a human leader, he was certainly not to be challenged by other humans. As early as this the foundation of an important principle can be discerned; as the God(s) are understood so is the mode of rule. The pantheon is conducive to the creation of politics and its essay in world engagement; MONOTHEISM has generated the monism of the modern state, with its anti-political tendencies, the corrupt end form of which is TOTALITARIANISM; and SECULARIZATION, disbelief and incredulity towards all accounts of God(s), and has produced a contemporary and widespread legitimation crisis.

The relation between the pre-political life of the early city states of Mesopotamia and the Greek *polis* is undoubtedly one of influence, although the precise nature of that connection is blurred, and far from well understood. The probable original meaning of the word *polis* was the circular or ring wall of the Greek CITY.

This physical sense of the word *polis* contains within it the non-physical connotations that still form the basis of our understanding of the meaning of *politics*. The *polis* was, concretely, the wall, but it was also, symbolically, and significantly, the fortified strength and power of the community exemplified in the co-operative activity that produced the wall, maintained it, and sought safety and community within its limits. Politics was, therefore, both the activity of being engaged in maintaining that co-operation, and also the domain bounded by the wall. Even at the outset 'politics' referred to a co-operative activity producing a domain of public or common safety. The early *poleis* were warlike in structure and brutal in action, nevertheless they contained within them the seeds of trust, friendship, like-mindedness (*homonia*)· and engagement in common affairs that characterized the later political community of the mature *polis*. The trust and friendship that was the basis of the early *poleis* may well have been fostered by the coming together of members of different tribes to form the Greek hoplites. The engagement in common fighting manoeuvres provided a basis for trust that transcended the ties of tribe. Politics, at the outset, was trans-tribal and synoicistic (*synoikismos*: belonging, living together, co-habiting). In a significant sense politics can be said to have been invented in Greece as an open form of activity informed by, but not completed by, reflection, oriented towards mutual defence and the enhancement of community, and the bringing together of individuals (*see* INDIVIDUALISM) related predominantly by a trans-tribal synoicism. The *sine qua non* of politics is a substantial degree of FREEDOM and EQUALITY. Such conditions were not found either in the earlier Mediterranean city states, which were primarily the centre of tribal kingdoms, showing some pre-political patterns of activity, or in ancient Egypt, primarily a cosmic SOCIETY whose horizons were closed, rather than open, and that was dominated not by the life of the *polis* but by the demands of the *necropolis*.

The original *synoicism*, which is the first social condition of politics, is attributed by Thucydides and by Plutarch to the legendary king, Theseus, supposed founder of a unified *Attike*.

In practice the *synoicism* probably took place later than the legend suggests: at the end of the Greek dark ages. As Europe emerged from its own dark ages two millennia later, that synoicistic act was multiply repeated, in different places in north-western Europe. It is still celebrated today in Athens. The *synoicism* generates a form of belonging that is trans-tribal and generates the conditions for the public spaces within which the activity that is politics can appear. Although the *synoicism* derives from a predominantly Hellenic tradition a form of it can be found in Nehemiah. When Nehemiah brought the tribes together after the exile, in the attempt to refound Jerusalem, he attempted to unite them through allegiance to one God. They formally swore that allegiance which Nehemiah put to the re-establishment of the city. (See Voegelin 1956.) In later northern Europe the synoicism was often formal and sworn (see Weber, *Economy and Society*, for examples), but it was never, as in Nehemiah, on the basis of loyalty to one god. It was to each other, as in brotherhood, or in guild, as freemen of a city or even, occasionally, as an early form of contract (Henry Maine: *Ancient Law*). A true *synoicism* cuts across tribe, clan, or sib and finds mutuality and commonality in a trans-tribal setting. The post-exilic tribal system described in Nehemiah was not dislodged by the swearing to one god, and it must be doubted in any case whether a belief in a common God, perfectly or imperfectly held, can substitute for a trans-tribal *synoicism*. The function of the *synoicism*, or its equivalent, is to bring people together whether that be as persons, communities, friends, strangers, clansmen, tribesman, as brother or other, as *heteromonia*, and create what for Aristotle was the condition of friendship by which politics was possible; as, to use a contrasting terminology, *homonoia*. This coming together provided by the *synoicism* creates the second condition of politics, a forum; what Arendt (1958) has referred to as 'a space of appearances', a place for contest and dispute on matters common. This model of politics is dramatic, active, and agonistic. The original agonism of the old comedy in Aristophanes followed a set pattern framed by the entry of the chorus, the *parados*, and the final statement of the chorus, the *parabasis*.

The agonistic activity of politics follows a similar pattern, in that it is framed by flexible, but not infinitely so, conditions that allow a forum for contestation on matters of common concern. Where those conditions, however realized or understood, do not hold, there is no politics. At that limit point, politics ends and some other form of rule, government or mode of togetherness begins. The antithesis of the agora is found in modern totalitarianism and in absolutist states, both of which in their very nature destroy all arenas of expression and are anti-political.

The third condition of politics is equivalent to the founding moment of philosophy. This is well represented in Plato's account in *The Republic* of the bondsmen of the cave, who take as reality mere shadows flickering on the wall. They are freed, turn around to the light at the entrance of the cave and are dazzled by the truth. They now see that their previous life was but an illusion. In this moment the philosophical and the political come together. The mode of being that is political involves, indeed requires, world engagement, but it is not unreflective or uncritical, for it involves the interrogation of an existing state of affairs, placing it against alternative possible worlds. It rests on a dissatisfaction with the actual world or some of its possibilities. The philosophical moment is the *periagoge*, the turn to the light, but its political aspect is found in the judgement on the previous life and any possible attempt to persuade his fellow bondsmen of an alternate conception of being. The philosophical moment already contains a political aspect for it is not possible to merely turn to the light, to have no backward or comparative glance. And the political moment already contains a philosophical aspect, for the essay in world engagement that is politics contains some sense of a text to be written in the world.

The fourth aspect to the political moment is also the theological moment, for as in the *periogoge*, the turning around, one's past life becomes a spectacle on which judgement is passed, so in turning to the light judgement is made on the gods. And so it is not surprising that it is in Plato's *Republic* that the term 'theology' is first used in its modern sense. When Plato asks (379 b) how ought we to speak truly of the gods he not only dissociates theology from the mythology of the poetic *theologoi* of the past, but puts it in the context of politics, 'we are not poets, you and I at present,' he tells Adimantus, 'but founders of a state. . . . The true quality of God we must always surely attribute to him.' The theology and the politics are inseparable for the inversion in thought that produced the critical attitude towards the gods, and that made talk about and judgement of them possible, is the same inversion that made reflection of, and critical attitude towards, the earthly mode of life possible. And it is such an act, an act that inverts the understanding of human life as dictated principally by the actions of the members of the pantheon, that sets human life on a course dictated by its own actions, that also sets thought apart from myth and becomes the foundation of politics. It is also the foundation of theology, for only in that affirmation which takes seriously the critical Platonic question 'how may we speak correctly of the gods?' is a theology distinguished from mere myth possible. In consequence of this moment, a moment repeated in every thoughtful political act, theology is re-affirmed. As Voegelin puts it, 'When Man creates the cosmion of political order, he analogically repeats the divine creation of the cosmos' (Voegelin 1956: 16). We might add that when he takes on that task he becomes critical of, and passes judgement on, the gods and theology is born. In so far as politics is concerned with the creation of and maintenance of order it is opposed to EVIL, regarded as disorder.

Politics then is the activity of engaging in world-making, it recreates in the object of that activity the understanding of the cosmos and feeds back from that activity to the understanding of the cosmos. It contains and is predicated upon its own theology. So a strict pyramidical order, as in ancient Egypt, requires administration but not a developed politics. The assembled pantheon of Mesopotamia is an analogue for a pre-political order. The critique by which the Greek pantheon was detached from myth, by which some of its members, some of the gods, were judged and found wanting by the standards of mortals, led to a dynamic and open society. The individualism of early modern Europe reformulated the early *synoicism* as social contract

theory, and the space of the *polis* was replaced by the institution of the state. That anti-political expression of the absolutist state was preceded by the rediscovery of politics and can be seen in part as a reaction to that rediscovery. That 'politics' in its modern sense follows William of Moerbecke's translation of Aristotle's *Politics* and has tended to be reduced to state activity is no mere accident. That translation re-stated a language and a practice forgotten in the retreat from the life of the city following the sacking of Rome by Alaric in 410 CE. But the rediscovery of that forgotten form of world engagement that is politics, and the emerging early modern language for such practice, began the regeneration of the truly radical potential of politics when the distortions of a merely instrumental view of politics are set to one side. In extreme cases that distortion, best exemplified by Machiavelli's *The Prince*, reduces politics to power used instrumentally for the achievement of the self-serving ends of the power holder. Such a view of politics is common since the rise of the state as the principal political form. All hitherto existing forms of the state have tended to monopolize politics and to reduce it to state activity. Yet that is neither contained in the foundation of politics nor is it necessary to it. The state is merely the contingent arrangement which has suppressed the political impulse.

Politics may be regarded not merely instrumentally as a means to some other end but as a good in itself. In such a model politics is not merely about obtaining the good, it is itself a good, possibly a primary good for human flourishing. The first clear modern expression of this view is found in Dante's notion of *polizare*; the pursuit of humanity for its own sake, not for the sake of some other aim, but acting in a political manner with the aim of achieving human happiness through and in that manner of acting (Ullman 1975: 195). In such pure form it is a mode of being that is not divorced from the spiritual, but contains within it its own spiritual equation, for it asks the question, 'what is the true end of humankind?' and answers not merely with the catechistic response to 'worship and glorify God' but also with the proposition, 'to be engaged in the conduct of his own life'.

In such a pure form its radical potential is unbounded for being an end in its self rather than a mere instrument; it is not subordinated to any eschatological or Gnostic programme hydraulically transferred from the sacral to the secular domain.

Several responses to this radical and potentially unsettling possibility have been made. Three are worthy of mention. First, the generation of a monistic and absolutist state mirrored an omnipotent and monotheistic God. In such a condition, at its height, the divinely authorized ruler incorporated both the body politic and the rights of God on earth. Such a model of rule is anti-political: the sacral destroys the legitimacy of the secular. A second and later response is totalitarianism which, in destroying individuality, human particularity, public *fora*, and private lives, subordinates human life to the ends of the state. Dante's *polizare* is not possible in such a condition, for no action that takes human life activity as having an end in itself is permissible. A third response is liberalism, whether absolutist *qua* (e.g. Hobbes) or not. Liberal absolutism attempts to eliminate politics and *polizare* by restricting sovereignty, thus depriving attempted political expression by the people of its legitimacy and by restricting freedom to freedom in civil society; principally economic affairs. In modified form, liberalism grants the sovereignty of the people but restricts significant decisions of life and common well-being to either or both of a few ill-defined and badly instantiated representative legislative functions, and to allegedly rational and often excessively bureaucratic procedures. In both cases the role of politics and of *polizare* is at best limited, discouraged, derailed, or rendered impossible. The modern state has shifted the locus and character of politics, moving it from Dante's *polizare* to Machiavelli's statecraft, thus shifting politics from the many to the few and legitimating violence as a component of politics rather than taking violence, as Arendt has forcibly argued, as its limit point.

These responses to the early modern rediscovery of politics have tended to eliminate the radical effects of that rediscovery. Nevertheless there are some contemporary indicators that suggest a rediscovery of the political may be underway. First, the monistic state, if it ever existed other than as a legal person, is itself no longer sustainable. This parallels the decline of unchallenged and unchallengeable MONOTHEISM. In a pluralistic religious culture a state founded on monotheism is unsustainable. Second, the state is proving to be an ineffective player in some major matters of common concern, and, additionally, is seen by many as an irrelevance to the conduct of their life. Third, liberalism itself is in the process of change. Procedural LIBERALISM is anti-perfectionist, attempting merely to set the conditions in which non-political life ends can be obtained. Perfectionist liberalism, however, sees the activity of participating in the operation of one's own life, AUTONOMY, as an end worth pursuing for its own sake. In its inner dimension autonomy has led to the project of an uncertain self-discovery as a secular alternative to traditional givens and certainties. In its outer dimension it is expressed in the desire to participate in the external conditions of one's life. Taken together this is Dante's *polizare* in a contemporary guise. Fourth, both the decline and the fragmentation of religious consciousness that is symptomatic of postmodernism have produced a crisis of legitimacy. Fifth, the general fragmentation and increasing heterogeneity of contemporary western societies have created multiple new places and new spaces within which new political possibilities can be found: within which radical democratic possibilities abound (*see also* CITY).

The proper response to these possibilities is neither more nor less statism as such. In some cases it will be to treat the state as if it were a ladder up which one can climb, as a facilitator of autonomous possibilities. In other cases those autonomous possibilities will be found outside the traditional areas of state activity. The challenge of contemporary politics is, as it always was, the participation in the operation of one's own life, as *polizare*, partaking in the operation of one's own life, for its own sake. It is, as with Solon, living in a tribe while also finding ways of living alongside members of another tribe, of living with others. It is, as it was for Aristotle, stepping out of the context of the household and entering the city, however symbolically that must now be understood. It is, as with Dante, being human and enjoying that humanity for its own sake. It is standing between present and future, between particular and universal, between actual and possible and temporal and eternal as Plato's *metaxial* being. It is bringing the inner and outer aspects of one's life together, in the company of others, of continually creating and recreating the original *synoicism* of *homonia*, and in solidarity with those who are *heterhomonia* in new places and in new spaces. Such a condition is uncertain and challenging; it is also the condition of a fully realized political life. It is taking politics not as a secular activity but as a form of re-creation which contains its own theology; a theology that if separated from politics would ignore their common founding moment and result in a diminution not only in the value of politics but also in the value of theology.

Arendt, Hannah (1958) *The Human Condition*, Chicago: Chicago University Press.

Aristotle *The Politics* (numerous editions).

Bernstein, Richard (1976) *The Restructuring of Social and Political Theory*, Oxford: Basil Blackwell.

Clarke, P.A.B. (1988) *The Autonomy of Politics*, Aldershot and Brookfield: Avebury.

Derrida, J. 'The politics of friendship' in *Journal of Philosophy*, no. 11 pp. 632–44.

Fraser, Nancy 'The French Derridians; politicizing deconstruction or deconstructing the political' in *New German Critique*, Autumn, no. 33 pp. 127–54.

Ingram, David (1988) 'The retreat of the political in the modern age: Jean Luc Nancy on totalitarianism and community', in *Research in Phenomenology*, no. 18 pp. 93–124.

Jacobsen, Thorkild (1976) *The Treasures of Darkness: A History of Mesopotamian Religion*, New Haven, CT and London: Yale University Press.

Machiavelli, N. *The Prince* (numerous editions).

Maine, Henry (1917) *Ancient Law*, London: Dent.

Mouffe, Chantal (1992) 'Democratic citizenship and the political community', in Mouffe (ed.), *Dimensions of Radical Democracy: Pluralism, Citizenship, Community*, London and New York: Verso, pp. 225–39.

Otto, Rudolf (1923) *The Idea of the Holy*, London: Humphrey Milford.

Plato *The Republic* (numerous editions).

Pritchard, James B. (1950) *Ancient Near Eastern Texts Relating to the New Testament*, Princeton, NJ: Princeton University Press.

Ullman, Walter (1975) *Medieval Political Thought*, Harmondsworth: Penguin.

Voegelin, E. (1956) *Order in History*, Vol. 1: *Israel and Revelation*, Baton Rouge, LA: Louisiana State University Press.

Wolin, Sheldon S. (1960) *Politics and Vision: Continuity and Innovation in Western Political Thought*, Boston, MA: Little Brown & Company.

Paul Barry Clarke

POPULATION CONTROL

Population control is a broad policy matrix to contain population growth or, more ambitiously, to modulate population growth as the requirements of a particular nation may require. It is distinct from birth control, which is the provision of contraceptive facilities to individual families or to women. These two perspectives overlap, however. Birth control educators have usually emphasized the populational implications of family planning; and conversely, family planning by individual choice has been the means that population control advocates typically espouse. These policy choices are informed by the science of demography, which is the study of population structure and trends, based on vital statistics.

The development of population control into a worldwide policy is a post-Second World War innovation led by the United Nations' World Health Organization in collaboration with the foreign aid programmes of developed countries. Its feasibility depended on a cheap, reliable and safe chemical means of CONTRACEPTION. Since the marketing of the contraceptive pill in 1960, ABORTION laws have been relaxed in many countries, to provide a second means of averting unwanted births. The recent development of a chemical abortifacient (RU-486) is believed by some to advance dramatically the technical means of population control.

Although the feasibility of population control as a public policy depended upon advances in reproductive technology, thoughts on the subject occur early in the record of civilization. In China, which has been a populous nation since antiquity, Confucians sought to balance population to resources and formed the concept of optimum population level. In Western antiquity, observations on population fluctuations tended to link prosperity with population growth, while population decline was linked with regression. These ideas were influenced by the belief that civilized life depends on the urban hub, whose population density promotes, and is promoted by, prosperity and good government. Medieval scholars did not commonly write on these questions, but one who did, the historian Ibn-Khaldun, noted that in North Africa the association between population growth and prosperity was valid.

Population studies were revived along with other classical learning in the sixteenth century; scholars began to compile vital statistics and to explore the relation between population levels and national prosperity. In *The Interest of Holland*, a tract written in 1662 at the height of the Dutch efflorescence, Pieter de la Court argued that population growth, through births and immigration, was a prime mover of economic growth, provided that it was husbanded by good GOVERNMENT. The study of vital statistics was initiated by John Graunt's *Natural and Political Observations Upon the Bills of Mortality* (1662). Graunt's data were reports of burials and christenings in the London region.

The dissent from growth optimism was sounded by the Reverend Thomas Robert Malthus in the *Essay on the Principle of Population* (1798), a tract which laid the foundation of subsequent population control advocacy. Aware of estimates by previous writers that world population had increased greatly since recorded history, Malthus introduced a 'limits to growth' concept. It was that, while the natural rate of increase of agricultural produce is arithmetical, the natural rate of population increase is geometric. Since the number of births thus always exceeds the carrying capacity of land, human misery is permanent. Excess births, Malthus stated, are reduced by pestilence and disease, vice (infanticide and contraception), famine and war. Misery can be moderated by delayed MARRIAGE and restraint, but its bitter edge, he maintained, can never be entirely subdued. Relying on the teachings of the Anglican Church, Malthus rejected artificial contraception, abortion and infanticide as immoral methods of population control, yet he stated it as a moral duty evident to 'the humblest capacity' that 'he is not to bring beings into the world for whom he cannot find the means of support.' His utilitarian contemporaries

concluded that this duty sanctioned contraceptive practices.

The birth control and population control movements in Britain sprang in part from this contestation. Socialist writers tended to reprobate the Malthusian calculus as a 'calumny against mankind.' HUNGER was not due to insufficient fruitfulness of the earth, they insisted, but to unequal distribution of produce. This criticism was to remain the cornerstone of socialist thought on overpopulation; in this century the criticism was taken up by church leaders, theologians and the WORLD COUNCIL OF CHURCHES.

From about the 1830s the population question was increasingly integrated with the emancipation of women. The movement took its impetus from the EQUALITY idea that was spread by the American and French Revolutions, and notions of the perfectability of man that were often ingredients of equality concepts. Representative of this trend was John Stuart Mill (1806–73). In his *Principles of Political Economy* (1848) he noted that the emancipation of women and 'the increase of intelligence, of education, and of the love of independence among the working classes, must be attended with a corresponding growth of the good sense which manifests itself in prudent habits of conduct, and that population, therefore, will bear a gradually diminishing ratio to capital and employment'. His tracts *On Liberty* (1859) and *The Subjection of Women* (1869), written in collaboration with Harriet Taylor Mill, extended the legitimate domain of private liberty to include the woman's right to control her own reproduction. This logic was accepted by most socialists of the day, irrespective of their criticisms of Malthus. Socialist governments in this century have usually accepted the desirability of population control.

The effects of INDUSTRIALIZATION are of such complexity that authorities may contend either that Malthus' grim forecast has been overtaken by technology, or conversely, that overpopulation profoundly menaces human well-being.

The application of technologies to the enhancement of FARMING efficiency and to increasing crop and lifestock yields created, by the turn of the century, surpluses of produce. Today's hybrids and other technological applications

665

enable even densely populated nations such as Japan to be self-sufficient in produce. But in underdeveloped nations, where the dual pressures of land degradation and high population growth rates often occur simultaneously, malnutrition and starvation are distressingly common. Estimates of the total world population sustainable by present technologies range from 10 billion to 30 billion.

At the same time that agricultural production commenced a long period of rapid growth, around 1870 the birth rate in industrial nations entered a long period of decline (punctuated by fluctuations), which continues today. Thus for industrial nations both parts of Malthus' formula have been incorrect predictions until now. The population structure characteristic of population decline is called 'the demographic transition'. In the transition, the proportion of the population engaged in agriculture declines to the current levels of 5–10 per cent of the total. The surplus population shifts to towns and cities. Average FAMILY size decreases from about four to replacement value, and, in recent decades, below replacement value in many developed nations. At the same time, increased longevity due to improved sanitation, nutrition and health care increases the proportion of the population over 65 from about 5–7 per cent in 1900 to the present levels, in developed nations, of 14–16 per cent. Forecasts indicate that this percentage will increase to 20 per cent over the next three decades.

The revival of Malthus' prognostication despite the increase of abundance has its beginnings in reliable estimates of human population growth by Alexander Carr-Saunders (1936). The Han Empire of China and the contemporaneous Roman Empire were estimated to contain 50–100 million, but these figures fell sharply when the two empires collapsed. World population at the beginning of the Christian era was estimated at 300 million. It totalled 545 million by 1650, and 728 million by 1750. The annual rate of growth from 1750 varied greatly by continent, ranging to more than 2 per cent in Africa and Latin America. By 1950 world population had reached 2.5 billion. It had doubled by 1985, and is projected to reach 8.2 billion in 2025.

The rapid fall of doubling times indicates

Current and projected population size and growth rates

Region	Population (billion)			Annual growth rate (%)		
	1985	2000	2025	1950 to 1985	1985 to 2000	2000 to 2025
World	4.8	6.1	8.2	1.9	1.6	1.2
Africa	0.56	0.87	1.62	2.6	3.1	2.5
Latin America	0.41	0.55	0.78	2.6	2.0	1.4
Asia	2.82	3.55	4.54	2.1	1.6	1.0
North America	0.26	0.30	0.35	1.3	0.8	0.6
Europe	0.49	0.51	0.52	0.7	0.3	0.1
USSR	0.28	0.31	0.37	1.3	0.8	0.6
Oceania	0.02	0.03	0.04	1.9	1.4	0.9

Source: Department of International Economic and Social Affairs, *World Population Prospects: Estimates and Projections as Assesed in 1984*, New York: United Nations, 1986.

Medium-variant projection.

unsustainable population growth despite any imaginable technological windfall. Such alarming statistics found expression in the metaphor 'the population bomb', launched by ecologists Paul and Ann Ehrlich in 1968. Their imperative of zero population growth helped unite public unease about the risk of nuclear war, environmental degradation and mistrust of technology into the GREEN Movement, for which population control was a priority issue. Population control has since become a world priority in the post-Cold War era under the concept of a 'sustainable future'.

Population control is an audacious attempt to subdue a great natural force. The goal is to be achieved despite removing the natural checks on population growth (e.g. epidemics), and simultaneously with increasing longevity. A successful outcome would create a population structure weighted heavily toward the aged cohort claiming support from a reduced cohort of the young. Thus a new source of conflict, 'generational conflict', would arise worldwide.

Clark, Colin (1957) *Population Growth and Land Use*, New York: St Martin's Press.
Coleman, David and Schofield, Roger (1986) *The State*

of Population Theory: Forward from Malthus, Oxford: Blackwell.

Ehrlich, Paul R. and Ehrlich, Anne H. (1968) The Population Bomb, New York: Ballantine.

——and——(1991) The Population Explosion, New York: Touchestone.

Glass, D.V. (1940) Population Policies and Movements in Europe, Oxford: Oxford University Press.

Graunt, John (1662) Natural and Political Observations Upon the Bills of Mortality, London.

McEvedy, C. and Jones, R. (1978) Atlas of World Population History, Harmondsworth: Penguin.

Malthus, Thomas Robert (1798) Essay on the Principle of Population, As It Affects the Future Improvement of Society, London: J. Johnson.

Ross, John A. (ed.) (1987) International Encyclopedia of Population, London: Collier.

Soloway, R.A. (1982) Birth Control and the Population Question in England, 1877–1930, Chapel Hill, NC: University of North Carolina Press.

United Nations (1986) World Population Prospects: Estimates and Projections as Assessed in 1984, New York: United Nations.

World Commission on Environment and Development (1987) Our Common Future, Oxford: Oxford University Press.

Hiram Caton

PORNOGRAPHY

The word 'pornography' comes from two Greek words, porne (prostitute) and graphein (to write). From writing about prostitution, the word came to mean that which deals with sex or sexual activity and appeals to prurient interests or that which is obscene. In fact, for many people the distinction between OBSCENITY and pornography has become blurred. The meaning of 'pornography' today is one which lay people, as well as the courts, have struggled to define and to understand.

The controversies over pornography have waxed and waned in the twentieth century, but increasingly since 1975 or so there have been renewed discussions of this problem for several reasons. One reason is certainly the US government's stress on the notion of 'family values' and its attitude that pornography is harmful, not only to the FAMILY, but to SOCIETY in general. Another perhaps more recent factor deals with the very nature of ART itself, with modern and postmodern art as well as with popular CULTURE. The photographs of Robert Maplethorpe and various performance artists and the recordings of various rock groups and rap singers have come in for their share of criticism and, in some cases, legal attention. Finally feminist writings on pornography have vigorously presented still another viewpoint.

During the early years of the 1970s, the battlelines were clearly drawn. On the one hand were those who felt that pornography represented a real danger to society and, on the other hand, those who maintained either that pornography could not be defined adequately or that government restrictions presented a far greater danger than did pornography.

Those who held that pornography was harmful asserted that the emotional needs of children would be thwarted in a society obsessed with pornography, romantic love would disappear, and sex would be depersonalized and reduced to the mere couplings of animals, thus dehumanizing those who engaged in it. Furthermore, the no-longer sublimated sexual drive – thought to be the source of 'creative imagination' – would lead to the disappearance of a great deal of art, and perhaps even halt the progress of civilization (Mishan 1977: 250–2). Taking the word 'pornography' literally, Charles H. Keating, Jr, saw pornography as a kind of PROSTITUTION since it 'advertizes and advocates "sex for sale," pleasure for a price' (Keating 1970: 299). Sexual immorality, for Keating, 'more than any other causative factor, historically speaking, is the root cause of the demise of all great nations . . .' (p. 300).

Opposing such views were those who held that pornography was offensive but could not be clearly defined, that it had not been shown to produce actual harm and, finally, using a slippery slope argument, that the restriction of so-called pornographic material in a free society was a graver danger than the presence of such material. Finally psychologists and doctors argued that pornography was beneficial: it might aid in normal sexual development and have a positive effect on those people who might not have access to sexual relationships with a loved one.

In general, then, most of the discussions on pornography concerned whether it could be defined with any kind of clarity and whether it was, in fact, harmful since harm was considered the only sufficient reason to limit freedom. It soon became clear that in trying to weigh the dangers of restricting freedom against what some saw as the dangers of pornography, it would be necessary to define or describe pornography in relatively precise terms. Various attempts were made in the USA and various distinctions were postulated.

In 1973 Chief Justice Berger of the US Supreme Court rejected the older test, given in *Memoirs* v *Massachusetts*, that the definition of pornography should include the clause 'utterly without redeeming social value', a standard which, it might be noted in passing, would let such works as those of the Marquis de Sade, Restif de la Baron and John Cleland slip through the very net that was set to catch them. Instead Justice Berger in *Miller* v *California* tried to define pornography by giving three guidelines: one, 'whether the "average person" applying contemporary community standards would find the work taken as a whole appeals to the prurient interest'; two, 'whether the work depicts or describes, in a patently offensive way, sexual conduct'; and three, 'whether the work taken as a whole, lacks serious literary, artistic, political or scientific value'. Berger notes that to be protected by the First Amendment, a 'prurient' or 'patently offensive' work must have 'serious literary, artistic, political or scientific value'. Rosen points out that it is precisely this value of seriousness that post-modern art has rejected, along with other traditional values (Rosen 1992: 91).

These guidelines did not solve the problem for it soon became clear that they were not only subjective (for what appeals to the prurient interest of one person might not appeal to the prurient interest of another) but also vague (for who is to decide who is the average person?). Furthermore, who is to judge what is offensive and whose judgement should be considered in drawing conclusions about the literary or artistic value of various works? One has only to recall some of the books, banned in the past in the USA but now considered 'classics', to see how opinions vary. James Joyce's *Ulysses*, Henry Miller's *Tropic of Cancer* and *Tropic of Capricorn*, D.H. Lawrence's *Lady Chatterley's Lover* and so forth, were all banned at one time

or another. Consider also the many apparently hastily applied 'plaster of Paris leaves' that were once used to cover the marble genitals of innumerable ancient Greek statues in the Vatican museum in order, I suppose, to protect the delicate sensibilities of the visitor.

While discussions about pornography continued into the 1980s and 1990s, and are perhaps even more numerous than in the preceding decade, the nature of the debate has shifted and become more complex.

What happened to change the terms of the controversy concerning pornography was the view, supported by a number of feminists, that pornography does, in fact, cause harm – not vague harm to society as was claimed before, but rather harm to one-half of humanity, namely, harm to women.

Many feminists assert that pornography demeans and dehumanizes women by preserving and repeating the ancient and self-serving male myths that women really want to be raped and brutally treated. Pornography depicts women in a distorted fashion: as sexually passive, receiving pleasure from being beaten, whipped or dominated; VIOLENCE and RAPE are depicted as amusing, something to brag about – something that women enjoy, no matter what they say. Thus, pornography degrades woman by showing them as mere sexual objects – objects whose sole value lies in their ability to please men.

Some feminists argue that viewing pornography actually leads to increased male hostility and aggressive attitudes toward women and thus ultimately perhaps to an increase in rape, while other feminists see pornography as simply leading to unhealthy attitudes and stereotypical views of women.

This feminist view of pornography entails new distinctions between, for example, erotica, which might include explicit sexual descriptions but is not harmful, and pornography, which is violent, degrading or abusive. Longino makes an important distinction. Pornography is not just material that is degrading or abusive to women, but

it is material that explicitly represents or describes degrading and abusive sexual behavior so as to endorse and/or recommend the behavior . . . . The contextual features, more-over, which communicate such endorsement are intrinsic to the material: that is, they are features whose removal or alteration would change the representation or description.

(Longino 1982: 277)

Longino explains that the depiction of a rape, for example, may or may not be pornographic; it depends on the context. If a movie were made to explore the consequences of rape it might be a highly moral film, while if the same presenta-tion is given within the context of endorsing this kind of behaviour it is pornographic.

Although many feminists agree that women are unjustly stereotyped and demeaned in at least some pornographic depictions, not all agree about the best tactics to confront porno-graphy, or even about the nature of pornogra-phy itself. Some call for CENSORSHIP on the basis of a correlation between pornography and crimes of violence against women, while others would try to limit the spread of pornography by explaining how pornography exploits women and by trying to convince people not to support it financially. On the other hand, there are feminists who are critical of the antipornogra-phy position. Eisenstein asserts that

the preoccupation with pornography as a social problem is indicative of New Right politics. The belief that pornography is 'the cause' of sexual violence and promiscuity leads to a protectionist stance toward women, which allows the New Right to argue for women's protection rather than their *equality*.

(Eisenstein 1988: 162–3; my emphasis)

Women (and children) are presented as helpless creatures who need to be protected by men. Eisenstein claims that

the Reagan administration used pornography as a political issue to establish a context in which arguments for sexual freedom, sexual equality, and sexual pluralism would be cur-tailed. Through the equations of porno-graphy and sex, and sex and violence, the ad-ministration attempted to reorient the public discussion of sexual expression away from

sex equality and toward sex 'difference' in the context of phallocratic heterosexual sex.

(ibid.)

According to Eisenstein the equation of porno-graphy, sex and violence makes it difficult not to negate sex or to consider sex in 'protective terms'. Referring to those antipornography femi-nists who assert that pornography does not give just one 'message' but many, she quotes them as saying:

Pornography carries many messages other than woman-hating: it advocates sexual ad-venture, sex outside of marriage, sex for no reason other than pleasure, casual sex, anony-mous sex, group sex, voyeuristic sex, illegal sex, public sex.

(ibid., p. 171)

Eisenstein's point is clear: if pornography does not always involve the victimization of women, then condemning it creates a new prob-lem: the 'denial of the freedom to engage in multiple sexual practices' (ibid.).

It is easy to see that feminist views on porno-graphy are extremely varied and often in disa-greement with each other. It is equally clear that the problem of pornography is much more complicated and many-faceted than we once thought. At the very least, the new discussions force us to examine many of our most basic personal and social ideas and their underlying assumptions, especially our ideas about freedom and in particular a free society.

Hyperbole and exaggeration often character-ize discussions on pornography. For example, the many essays which reduce pornography to loveless sex, likening it to animal couplings, seem to know little about animal behaviour. People seem to have ignored what Desmond Morris pointed out in his book *The Naked Ape*: that the human being is the 'sexiest' animal. In comparison with humans, most mam-mals have a much more limited sex life since sexual activity is often restricted to those special periods when the female is receptive, which in some species may be only several weeks a year. Nor do those essayists who write about 'animalistic sex' consider such species as swans and geese who mate for life. Indeed, as we learn more about animal behaviour we find that, in many cases, it is not as 'mechanical' as we once thought. The courtship of many animals is sometimes extended and spectacular. We are also beginning to discover that in many species the female will not accept just any male, but makes a selection. Mary Midgely has pointed out that people are in the habit of accusing animals of behaviour that humans engage in and calling it 'animalistic' while animals do not behave in that manner at all.

Finally, the discussions on pornography, both the old and the new, are interesting for what they do not say. For example, there seems to be general agreement that pornography harms children or minors, but there is little or no discussion on why or how this happens. Nor is there much discussion about the dividing line between children and adults. Furthermore, although almost everyone agrees that child pornography – i.e. pornography involving children – also involves CHILD ABUSE since children are not old enough or mature enough to give informed consent, there are very few references to pornography involving animals, although the cases are similar in that animals are also incapable of giving consent. One wonders if pornography involving bestiality is very common. In the so-called 'roaring twenties' one of the most famous night clubs in Paris presented a show consisting of a woman supposedly having intercourse with a stallion. Consider also the fairly common incidence of sexual intercourse with various farm animals listed in the famous Kinsey report. Last but not least, in Madonna's book (1992) on sex, she is presented in photographs with animals suggesting some sort of sexual fantasies. Only a few feminists and a few animal rightists see a similarity between the exploitation of women and that of animals.

Brownmiller, S. (1975) *Against Our Will: Men, Women and Rape*, New York: Simon & Schuster.
Copp, D. and Wendel, S. (1983) *Pornography and Censorhip*, Buffalo, NY: Prometheus.
Eisenstein, Z. (1988) *The Female Body and the Law*, Los Angeles, CA and London: University of California Press.
Gould, J.L. and Gould, C.G. (1989) *Sexual Selection*, New York: Scientific American Library.
Holbrook, D. (1973) *The Case Against Pornography*, New York: Library Press.
Keating, C. (1970) 'The Statement of Charles H. Keating, Jr.', in *The Report of the Commission on Obscenity and Pornography*, Washington, DC: US Printing Office; reprinted as 'Pornography and the public morality', in T. Mappes and J. Zembaty (eds) *Social Ethics: Morality and Social Policy*, 2nd edn, New York: McGraw-Hill, 1982.
Kinsey, A.C. (1948) *Sexual Behavior in the Human Male*, Philadelphia, PA: W.B. Saunders.
Leder, L. (1980) *Take Back the Night: Women on Pornography*. New York: Morrow.
Longino, H. (1982) 'Pornography, oppression and censorship', in T. Mappes and J. Zembaty (eds) *Social Ethics: Morality and Social Policy*, 2nd edn, New York: McGraw-Hill.
Madonna (1992) *Sex*, Boston, MA: Callaway.
Mishan, E. (1977) 'The pornographic society', in T. Mappes and J. Zembaty (eds) *Social Ethics: Morality and Social Policy*, 2nd edn, New York: McGraw-Hill.
Morris, D. (1967) *The Naked Ape*, New York: Dell.
Rosen, J. (1992) '"Miller's" time', in D. Bonevac (ed.) *Today's Moral Issues: Classic and Contemporary Perspectives*, Mountain View, CA: Mayfield.
Wolf, N. (1991) *The Beauty Myth: How Images of Beauty are Used Against Women*, New York: William Morrow.

Priscilla Cohn

POVERTY

It is widely agreed that attitudes to poverty provide a major test of the moral quality of a SOCIETY. 'A decent provision for the poor is the true test of civilization', wrote Samuel Johnson, the eighteenth-century Tory, while R.H. Tawney, the twentieth-century ethical socialist, argued that 'There is no touchstone, except the treatment of childhood, which reveals the true character of a social philosophy more clearly than the spirit in which it regards the misfortunes of its members who fall by the way'. It is surely significant that both of these thinkers, for all their differences of time and of ideological commitment, were Christians and inherited a strong religious tradition of concern for the poor and for doing JUSTICE to the poor. But this moral concern does not in itself remove the problems in interpreting and responding to poverty.

There is a sense in which everyone would

claim to know what poverty is: it is a lack of the necessary resources for life, or for the good life. But it is in fact extremely hard to define or to measure poverty. For many years people sought a measure of poverty which was absolute and would apply everywhere. For example, Seebohm Rowntree's classic studies of poverty in York (1901, 1941; Rowntree and Laver 1951) sought to establish a 'poverty-line' tied to a level of income which was 'necessary to enable families . . . to secure the necessities of a healthy life'. In other words, to be in poverty is to lack the nourishment, shelter, etc. which are necessary to keep the human organism operating reasonably effectively. It was assumed that the resources required to keep out of poverty varied little from CULTURE to culture, age to age, or community to community. Poverty means not having the resources to sustain biological life: 'A family is poor if it cannot afford to eat,' wrote Keith Joseph and Jonathan Sumption (1979: 27–8). Such a measure changes little over time. And if some increase in prosperity, however little, 'trickles down' to the poor, the number of those in poverty declines sharply.

But human beings are more than biological organisms, and poverty is in fact a socially constructed idea. People are wealthy or poor in comparison with other people in the same society or culture. A society defines what is acceptable and what is unacceptable in terms of living standards, and this changes over time. A culture determines to a great extent what people need. And the experience of poverty varies vastly from one society to another. In some situations there are vital social links among the poor, so that solidarity preserves a sense of dignity and integrity even in situations of great material want. Religion sometimes accords poor people a special status within society, or alternatively teaches them that their condition is a JUDGEMENT upon them, or part of the divine ordering of society:

The rich man in his castle
The poor man at his gate
God made them, high or lowly,
And ordered their estate.

Poverty is thus commonly understood as being relative. This does not mean that we should not be deeply concerned about starvation and destitution – 'absolute poverty' – in many parts of Africa and Asia, but we should also be concerned that so many in 'prosperous societies' are poor in the relative sense, and have poor health, much reduced life expectancy, less choice and fewer life chances than the rest of the people in their societies.

Peter Townsend in his magisterial *Poverty in the United Kingdom* (1979) argued that there is an objective measure of relative poverty. He suggested that below a certain income there is a sudden and dramatic dropping off in people's participation in community life, deprivation is increased and marginalization results. Townsend argued that this measure is objective, although the precise level changes over time in relation to the relative prosperity of the society.

Others challenged Townsend by suggesting that measures of poverty must be subjective, or rather inter-subjective and socially constructed. Mack and Lansley (1985), for example, conducted a major survey to discover whether there is a consensus in Britain as to what is a decent and acceptable standard of life for people today. They asked a large sample of the population to indicate those items which they regarded as necessary. They discovered that there was in fact a strong consensus as to what is necessary for a decent and acceptable standard of living. They also found that there was an income threshold, at almost exactly the same level as that suggested by Townsend, below which it rapidly became impossible to sustain 'a decent standard of living'. Mack and Lansley thus appeared to have demonstrated that the British public accepted more or less the threshold of poverty suggested by Townsend.

Objective, subjective and consensual understandings of poverty all appear to involve value judgements (although some social scientists would deny this) and to involve imperatives, or at least suggestions as to how one should respond to poverty. Leftwingers and those who espouse relative understandings of poverty, for instance, see poverty as *inequality*, and believe that the only real solution is a more equal distribution of resources in society. They believe poverty to be disruptive of community and of human dignity; it demands a radical restructuring of society. Theorists of the New Right and those who support an absolute definition of poverty see real deprivation as something to be relieved primarily by charitable action, but they also tend to see wide differentials of resources in society as providing the necessary incentives for economic activity, and even regard poverty as a 'spur'. There is thus in Western societies today no value consensus. In a morally fragmented society it is impossible that poverty should be understood in the same way, or that there should be agreement as to how to deal with it.

But poverty is not simply a matter of lack of money and material resources. As the Anglican report, *Faith in the City* (1985) put it: 'Poverty is not only about shortage of money. It is about rights and relationships, about how people are treated and how they regard themselves; about powerlessness, exclusion and loss of dignity. Yet the lack of an adequate income is at its heart' (p. 195). The poverty issue has to do with human dignity, human flourishing and human fellowship. As David Donnison, at one time Chair of the Supplementary Benefits Commission, put it:

> To keep out of poverty, people must have an income which enables them to participate in the life of the community. They must be able, for example, to keep themselves relatively well fed and well enough dressed to maintain their self-respect and to attend interviews for jobs with confidence. Their homes must be reasonably warm; their children should not feel shamed by the quality of their clothing; the family must be able to visit relatives, and give them something on their birthdays and at Christmas time; they must be able to read newspapers, and retain their television sets and their membership of trade unions and churches. And they must be able to live in a way which ensures, as far as possible, that public officials, doctors, teachers, landlords and others treat them with the courtesy due to every member of the community.
>
> (Donnison 1982: 8)

Poverty, Donnison argues, is inseparably tied to powerlessness and pain: 'If you are concerned about pain . . . then you must also be concerned about poverty, because the poor suffer more than their fair share of pain. You must be concerned about POWER, too, because the poor are not excluded from the benefits of an affluent society by accident; they are the people whom the private sector and the STATE can most easily neglect without disaster to themselves' (1991: 27).

Such are the reasons why poverty is a profoundly spiritual matter. The Biblical documents have a pervasive concern with poverty which can fairly be described as a bias to the poor. On this basis a strong tradition emerged with three major strands. In the first place, there were frequent prophetic protests against poverty and the oppression of the poor. This persisted even when the church became wealthy: the Fathers sound very much like the Hebrew prophets when they denounce luxury, inequality and the tolerance of poverty alongside affluence. The existence of poverty was seen as an offence against God's order, and attempts to do justice were understood as contributions to the restoration of the divine ordering and the restoration to the poor of what is properly theirs: 'Not from your own do you bestow upon the poor man, but you make return of what is his. For what has been given as common for the use of all, you appropriate to yourself alone. The earth belongs to all, not to the rich. . . . Therefore you are paying a debt, you are not bestowing what is not due' (Ambrose). Such protests and calls for restitution to the poor have continued at least sporadically up to the present, and are today expressed in the 'preferential option for the poor', which is the central concern of LIBERATION THEOLOGY.

In the second place, wherever the church has had influence in society, there have been efforts to regulate the economy and protect the poor and weak from the oppression of the wealthy and powerful. These attempts at regulation found their classical expression in the theories of the just price and the just wage. The assumption was that the market on its own would not and could not provide justice for the poor and weak. A just wage must be such as to keep the worker and the worker's family at a decent standard of living. Workers must be able to live with dignity and decency, and to play their role in society. Just prices must not be dictated simply by market forces, but must be set at a level where profiteering is impossible and necessities of life are not priced out of the reach of ordinary people. This tradition was well aware how the self-interest and SIN of the powerful could distort market transactions to their advantage; it was realistically suspicious of the 'free market'. It endeavoured to protect the poor and weak, but it did not question the social order or the overall structure of economic power. In modern times a continuing concern for just prices and just wages needs to be supplemented by a search for a more just economic order.

In the third place, from very early days the Christian tradition has nurtured communities which are experiments in living by gospel values, and thereby both protests against the injustice of the world and demonstrations that another way is possible. The Jerusalem church, according to the book of Acts, was one in which Christians 'held all things in common'; Paul promoted collections to relieve the want of poor Christians and claimed that this was a basic expression of Christian fellowship and EQUALITY. The monastic communities likewise from the beginning held property in common, and the friars embraced 'holy poverty' and shared the lot of the poor as a way of being close to the Lord. They saw the poor not simply as a problem to be solved with charity or otherwise, but as those who could witness to the LOVE and generosity of God. Indeed, each congregation of God's people should see itself as a community of sharing and of concern for the poor. This surely is one of the main ethical emphases of the Lord's Supper, when believers break and share the bread which is Christ's body, given for the life of the world (John 6: 51).

The various experiences of the American 'War on Poverty' of the 1960s, of the British welfare state, of the communist regimes in Eastern Europe and of the workings of the free market all go to show that no-one has a comprehensive solution to the problem of poverty that has been shown to work. It is easy to become disillusioned. But the Christian tradition should teach pertinacity in putting the issue of poverty at the top of the ethical agenda, in affirming that the gospel is good news to the poor and in believing that doing good in minute particulars is important even in an age that has lost confidence in social panaceas. The poor may always be with us, but their cry is heard by God, and should be constantly attended to by any society with a claim to decency.

Avila, Charles (1983) *Ownership: Early Christian Teaching*, London: Sheed & Ward.

Boerma, C. (1979) *Rich Man, Poor Man – and the Bible*, London: SCM.

Boff, Clodovis and Pixley, G.V. (1990) *The Bible, the Church and the Poor*, Maryknoll, NY: Orbis.

Donnison, David (1982) *Politics of Poverty*, Oxford: Blackwell.

——(1991) *A Radical Agenda*, London: Rivers Oram Press.

Forrester, Duncan B. and Skene, Danus (eds) (1988) *Just Sharing – A Christian Approach to the Distribution of Wealth, Income and Benefits*, London: Epworth.

Gilder, George (1982) *Wealth and Poverty*, London: Buchan & Enright.

Himmelfarb, Gertrude (1984) *The Idea of Poverty*, London: Faber & Faber.

Mack, Joanna, and Lansley, Stewart (1985) *Poor Britain*, London: Allen & Unwin.

Mealand, David L. (1980) *Poverty and Expectation in the Gospels*, London: SPCK.

Rowntree, B.S. (1901) *Poverty: A Study of Town Life*, London: Macmillan.

——(1941) *Poverty and Progress*, London: Longman Green.

——and Laver, G.R. (1951) *Poverty and the Welfare State*, London: Longman Green.

Townsend, Peter (1979) *Poverty in the United Kingdom*, Harmondsworth: Penguin.

Duncan B. Forrester

POWER

The analysis of the concept of power in relation to theology and in society is fraught with difficulties. The concept of power is both complex and contextual. There have been numerous seemingly simple definitions of power, e.g. that of Bertrand Russell: 'Power may be defined as the production of intended effects. It is thus a quantitative concept: given two men with similar desires, if one achieves all the desires the other achieves, and also others, he has more power than the other' (Russell 1938: 35). Russell's renowned if somewhat problematic definition of power as 'the production of intended effects' is a notable example of the tendency of definitions of power to express, consciously or unconsciously, contextual factors or the intellectual predispositions of the writer. Thus in his subsequent argument Russell sought to discriminate between the power of the good artist and that of the mediocre (but financially successful) one in a way that reflects the usual difficulties of the British analytic and empirical tradition when its representatives attempt to differentiate between aesthetic or ethical outcomes on the basis of utility alone. The definition of the concept of power requires clarity, reflexivity and an informed contextual sensitivity; but this in itself is insufficient.

In traditional and historical terms, definitions of power and AUTHORITY are often closely correlated (Lukes 1979). This proximity is attractive to those who seek to explain and compensate for the loss of power experienced by traditional and often hierarchical organizations like churches. In the latter, there are often cyclic, unconscious and sometimes displaced struggles with the consequences of the loss of religious power as divine immediacy in the 'routinization of charisma'. Such cycles of attempted reengagement with the religious power of charisma within a given hierarchical church body may have catastrophic consequences for the organization (as in the Reformation), or these processes may be successfully incorporated and legitimated (as in forms of monasticism).

Recently, and frequently under the influence of the work of Michel Foucault, sociologists and social philosophers have replaced the quest for a definition of power with a performative and analytical description of systems of social power, what Foucault calls the 'how of power' (Foucault 1976: 229). Power is to be understood through contextual analysis on the basis of a recognition that it is, in W.B. Gallie's resonant words, an 'essentially contested concept'. Correspondingly, Stewart Clegg has argued that 'Power is not a thing but a process constituted within struggles' (Clegg 1989b: 97). It is the realization that power is to be understood within 'systems' (Talcott Parsons), 'organized

power networks' (Michael Mann) or 'frameworks of power' (Stewart Clegg) that transforms the analysis of power from the quest for essentialist definition into an interpretative procedure. Such procedures take account of the evidence of interests embodied in societal and organizational structures of surveillance and enforcement and interpret the consequent restriction or enabling of individual and collective agency within the constraints composed by the matrix of socio-cultural and economic relations constitutive of any given social context.

The history and development of the idea of power in THEOLOGY and SOCIETY presupposes a basic discrimination between power in 'religion' and power in 'theology', the latter understood as reflection incorporated into the belief system of a religious tradition. The manifestation of power in primal religion involves the categorization and analysis of the appearance of power as 'kratophany' (Mircea Eliade 1987), the essential adjunct of 'hierophany' and the appearance of the sacred. Power as the manifestation of the '*mysterium, tremendum et fascinans*' (Rudolf Otto) in religion and religious experience tends to manifest itself in terms of myth, physical metaphors and the affective language of mystical experience. Correspondingly, in contemporary terms it may be represented conceptually in a phenomenology of the numenous (following Otto and Gerhardus Van der Leeuw).

By contrast, in the Christian theological tradition (and above all in its Western Latin and Protestant forms) from very early times the question of power has tended to be enmeshed in the evolution and transformation of large-scale societal structures. For example, the original evolution of the Christian Church from obscure Jewish sect to significant social force (von Campenhausen [1953] 1969), the Constantinian transformation of Christianity (Ernst Troeltsch) and the roles of pagan religion and then Christianity in the evolution of 'ideology transcendent' in the later Roman Empire (Mann 1986: 301–40) all involve the contextualized consideration of socio-culturally embedded power. Mann categorizes this 'social power' as deriving from four sources: *transcendent* or *immanent* (ideological power), *circuits of praxis* (economics), *concentrated-coercive* (military), and centralized-territorial and geopolitical diplomatic (political) organization. All are 'promiscuous' (Mann 1986: 28) inasmuch as they interact and interpenetrate, there being no single source of ultimate power (as in classic Marxist or providential views of the historical process).

The Reformation 'turn to the subject' and correlative privatization of religious belief, combined with the principle cuius regio, eius religio, that the religion of the ruler would determine the religion of his subjects, preserved more limited societal zones of religious and theological power. But the ambiguous outcome of the Reformation achieved a new societal configuration which was inherently unstable: the disappearance of a single, all-embracing source of normative social legitimation, in effect the coercive authority and power of tradition, facilitated overt conflict. It was in Catholic Europe, and supremely in France, that the consequences of a direct confrontation between the entrenched religious power legitimating the ancien régime and an aggressive, secularizing MODERNITY took place. The French Revolution (1789 onwards) became a paradigmatic episode in the thought of Hegel and Marx: both subjected this event to universalizing theorization in schemes of thought that have informed the exercise of power throughout the subsequent period.

It was thus in Germany and notably in the early thought of Hegel that the ancestral, premodern hierarchical social order of authority and tradition was confronted by the new dynamic forms of power implicit in early modernity (Neuzeit) and nascent INDUSTRIALIZATION. Hegel rejected the banal superficiality of those strands of the Enlightenment which denied the transcendent source of tradition and put universal reason in its place. For Hegel, power was rightly seen in the 'Moments' of a cycle of changing relationships that characterized emergent human subjectivity (which comprises a dialectical straining after the absolute Other) between willing subjects and within the sociohistorical process itself.

In the parable of Lord (Herr) and Bondsman (Knecht) (Hegel [1807] 1910) Hegel paradoxically inscribed a powerful and subversive archaism upon the emergent form of the spirit of Enlightenment modernity itself. Commenting upon the dynamics of absolute power, Hegel maintains of the Lord that:

> Since he is the power dominating existence, while this existence again is the power controlling the other (the bondsman), the master holds, par conséquence, this other in subordination. In the same way the master relates himself to the thing mediately through the bondsman. The bondsman being a self-consciousness in the broad sense, also takes up a negative attitude to things and cancels them; but the thing is, at the same time, independent for him, and, in consequence, he cannot, with all his negating, get so far as to annihilate it outright and be done with it; that is to say he merely works on it. To the master, on the other hand, by means of this mediating process, belongs the immediate relation, in the sense of the pure negation of it, in other words he gets the enjoyment.
>
> (Hegel [1807] 1910: 235)

This dialectical conception of power, referred to by George Steiner (1971:46) as a theory of AGGRESSION, has undergone a pervasive and richly nuanced reception in the intervening period. Thus, for example, in Marxism and in the social theory of Max Weber, but also in FEMINISM (through Simone de Beauvoir and her development and application of J.P. Sartre's reading of the *Phenomenology of Mind* in *L'Etre et le néant*) the dialectical potential of Hegel's conception has worked its way into the consciousness of the West. A recent example is to be found in Francis Fukuyama's *The End of History* where the historic collapse of the Marxian paradigm has provoked a return both to Hegel and to Oswald Spengler's *Decline of the West*.

The historic collision between pre-modern power grounded in the coercive authority of tradition and the modernity of instrumental and technological reason is now undergoing further transformation in the context of postmodernity. The collapse of European 'grand' or 'metanarratives' (Jean-François Lyotard) and the loss of confidence in reason in the 'dialectic of Enlightenment' (M. Horkheimer and T.W. Adorno) is underlaid by the expansion of the 'free market' into cultural production, EDUCATION and human relations, a process with profound consequences. The postmodernization of influential areas of the contemporary world order has now further restricted and weakened any notions of power or authority grounded in or derived from tradition and replaced it with a complex traffic in cultural identities that are bought, sold and transmitted in a global and globalized market-place.

In the context of the modernity associated with industrialization, religious power continued its retreat into increasingly privatized and associational spheres of activity (e.g. as in Methodism and Pietism). The 'established' churches of Protestant Europe began a long and continuing struggle for 'authority' in the face of Enlightenment AUTONOMY and instrumental reason which took up concrete forms in industrialism and technology. Now, however, a worldwide resurgence of religion and religiosity in the 'condition of postmodernity' (David Harvey) might intimate a return to the analysis of power as religious power and as theological power/authority embedded in particular socio-cultural contexts.

Recent attempts in North American New Right Christianity and in Britain to re-establish religious and theological power as the 'American way of life' and 'public truth' (L. Newbiggin), respectively, imply forms of regression in the face of postmodernity. In a more sophisticated way, the English Anglican theologian Stephen W. Sykes has attempted to redefine the essence of Christianity in terms of the power/ authority problematic as confronted by a historicist modernity represented by Ernst Troeltsch's historicist reduction of the pre-critical basis of Christian belief (Roberts 1988). When placed in the framework of a post-modern understanding of society, all such attempts at the recovery of tradition face an ultimate dilemma: are they to be understood as forms of regressive FUNDAMENTALISM or could there be a benign post-modern rehabilitation of religious and theological power as legitimate dimensions of the human condition?

In a recent formal analysis of the concept of power Lukes (1974: 9) has argued for a view of power as ineradicably evaluative and both 'essentially contested' and 'empirically applicable'. Lukes advances three views of power. A 'one-dimensional model' involved the examination of decision-making in the context of·what the American behaviouralist Robert Dahl (1957) assumed to be a 'pluralist society' in which such conflict was explicit and visible. Here the conflict was 'between preferences, that are assumed to be consciously made, exhibited in actions, and thus to be discovered by observing people's behaviour' (Lukes 1974: 14). Lukes enlarges the first narrow conception of power into a 'two-dimensional' view of power which includes a more differentiated typology embracing coercion, influence, authority, force and manipulation. This is an advance on the behaviouralism of the first view, but even Dahl's critics failed to realize that actual conflict is not necessary to power; indeed, 'the most effective and insidious use of power is to prevent such conflict from arising in the first place' (Lukes 1974: 23).

Lukes proceeds to argue that 'A exercises power over B when A affects B in a manner contrary to B's interests' (Lukes 1974: 35) and that pre-emptive strategies employed by vested (for Lukes, primarily class and economic) interests may predetermine the outcome of conflicts in ways which escape forms of analysis that simplistically (or cynically) assume the efficacy of an open, pluralistic political CULTURE. Lukes' 'radical view', like those of Marx and his mentor Hegel, assumes a layered and processual complexity. Mann's view of human beings as 'goal-oriented people [who] form a multiplicity of social relationships too complex for any general theory' (Mann 1986: 30) moves beyond Lukes' more restricted decisionism. Correspondingly for Mann, 'Societies are constituted of multiple overlapping and intersecting sociospatial networks of power' (Mann 1986: 1).

The sociologist Stewart Clegg (Clegg 1989a) advances beyond both Lukes and Mann in offering a wide-ranging historical contextualization and typology of power in which he juxtaposes the figures of Hobbes and Machiavelli as proponents of power grounded in sovereignty and of power expressed in manipulation, respectively. In terms of a distinction drawn between 'legislators' and 'interpreters' (Zygmunt Bauman), Clegg sets Hobbes (and Lukes) against Machiavelli (and Foucault) and he then attempts to move dialectically beyond the duality through the exposition of a formal model of 'circuits of power' which owes much to the sociology of organizations. In the final count it is Machiavelli's 'ethnography of political action' which affords a prototype for the interpretation of power in postmodernity (Clegg 1989a: 203). Clegg goes some way in the direction of a post-modern decentring of selves when he suggests that:

> a theory of power must examine how the field of force in which power is arranged has been fixed, coupled and constituted in such a way that, intentionally or not, certain 'nodal points' of practice are arranged in this unstable and shifting terrain. ... [A] radical view of power would consist not in identifying what putative 'real interests' are but in the views and practices whereby, for instance, agents are recruited to views of their interests which align with the discursive field of force that the enrolling agency is able to construct.
>
> (Clegg 1989a: 17)

Whereas Hobbes founds a discursive framework for analysis of power as motion, causality, agency and action, and such writers as Friedrich von Hayek and Isaiah Berlin likewise remained committed to the 'indissoluble trinity' of the concepts of agency, intentionality and liberty, by contrast Clegg puts forward the 'ethnographic research method as the best means for uncovering the rules of the game' (Clegg 1989a: 31). This method is built upon Mann's insight that 'Episodic power is seen to derive from the capacities of agents grounded in resource control' (Mann 1986: 217). Clegg combines sociological acumen with a measure of ethical evaluation when he depicts the new 'iron cage' of postmodernity. This is no rigid container but an infinitely flexible and responsive system of resource movement and control (not of course confined to finance capital or goods, but of information and cultural capital as well). Unlike Marx who proposed a catastrophic reversal, Clegg argues that:

> While routinized circuits of episodic power, fixed on particular points of passage, are always open to challenge and transformation through concerted action, this is an eventual-

ity that remains in the abstract. If the organization of concerted action cannot be attempted or envisaged as a feasible form of resistance, routine relations, agencies, means, standing conditions, resources – in a word powers – will be likely to endure. The resources will be judged all too frequently and accurately to be unavailable or insufficient to overwhelm extant circuits of power.
>
> (Clegg 1989a: 222)

Successful resistance to such power has therefore to be systemic. Whilst existing structures of dominance may in principle be open to 'subsidence, disruption and innovation', subversion may not take place through negative resistance but only through 'outflanking' (Clegg 1989a: 224). Given the primacy and centrality of the market, political activity as a means of engagement with power would thus appear to be a misleading and redundant path. The 'seduction' characteristic of a dynamic and fluid market-led culture displaces the political process itself: sovereignty and legitimation have ceased to be of significance. At the present juncture in the discussion, the idea of power tends to dissolve itself into a radical and dangerously apolitical postmodernity. Such a conclusion neglects one key feature of power suggested in the realism that informs Mann's magisterial study, i.e. the acknowledgement of multiple and distinct sources of social power which resist a hegemonic and totalizing view of marketization. Furthermore, it is plausible to argue that, in a differentiated yet globalized world system, the pre-modern, the modern and the postmodern coexist at both different levels and diverse locations within the system. Thus in the aftermath of Marxism and in the face of the triumph of free-market or 'democratic CAPITALISM' (Michael Novak) the question of power needs to be reborn and not subsumed into an illusory universality ceded to postmodernity.

Arguments about authority as the successor of power are endemic in post-Enlightenment Christian apologetic traditions. Authority without coercive power to enforce is seemingly acceptable to Christians, but not to radical Muslims; the latter do not concede a systematic dichotomy between spiritual and temporal power, or between the realms or 'kingdoms'. The resurgence of ethnicity and cultural difference in the aftermath of the collapse of Marxist SOCIALISM may well imply an end to such Christian hesitance, the inauguration of a new post-liberal 'ethnic' and 'cultural cleansing', and a corresponding re-appropriation and mobilization of coercive power against the 'other'.

In conclusion, the contemporary formulation of the concept of power involves engagement with modes of conceiving power which take as their point of departure the active transition from pre-modern and modern to *post-modern* conceptions of the socio-cultural process, of which power is an all-pervasive feature, as variegated in its aspects as the differentiation of society itself. Techniques drawn from economic, management and organization theory are now being applied (given global trends towards privatization and marketization) to whole sectors of society previously consigned to the ethos of welfarism and the corporate state – and thus to forms of (albeit indirect) democratic control. The contemporary available means of constructing 'cultures' as fully internalizable fields of social power create forms of manipulation and embodiment that are now in danger of moving outside the range of effective and proper critical restraint. 'Power' and 'authority' are being subsumed into disciplinary power and practices to the extent that participation in a form of life can be understood as cultural admission through submission. The extension of this tendency towards the cultural embodiment of power is to be seen in the tribalization of post-modern society (Michel Maffesoli's *'temps des tribus'* is indicative), be it grounded in racial, ethnic, gender or other factors. These tendencies present a daunting challenge to the concerned theologian and social ethicist.

Given a fuller appreciation of the Foucauldian equivalence of power and knowledge and some acquaintance with the societal and discursive developments reviewed above, this question remains: how might Christian theology ally itself to a shared human quest for the critical oversight and responsible control of social, economic and cultural power without succumbing to the dangerous and easy temptation of regression into forms of FUNDAMENTALISM

apparently sanctioned by the pluralism of a misunderstood postmodernity?

von Campenhausen, Hans ([1953] 1969) *Ecclesiastical Authority and Spiritual Power in the Church of the First Three Centuries*, London: Adam & Charles Black.

Clegg, Stewart R. (1989a) *Frameworks of Power*, London: Sage.

——(1989b) 'Radical revisions: power, discipline and organizations', *Organization Studies* 10(1): 97– 115.

Dahl, Robert A. (1957) 'The concept of power', *Behavioural Science*, 2: 201–5.

Eliade, Mircea (1987) 'Power', in Mircea Eliade (ed.) *The Encyclopaedia of Religion*, New York: Macmillan, vol. 2, pp. 467–76.

Foucault, Michel (1976) 'Disciplinary power and subjection', in Steven Lukes (ed.) *Power*, Oxford: Basil Blackwell.

Havel, Vaclav (1987) 'The power of the powerless', in Jan Vladislav (ed.) *Living in Truth*, London: Faber & Faber, pp. 36–122.

Hegel, G.W.F. ([1807] 1910) 'Lordship and bondage', in *The Phenomenology of Mind*, trans. J. Baillie, London: Allen & Unwin, pp. 229–40.

Lukes, Stephen (1974) *Power: A Radical View*, London: Macmillan.

——(1979) 'Power and authority', in T. Bottomore and R. Nisbet (eds) *History of Sociological Analysis*, London: Heinemann and New York: Basic Books, pp. 631–76.

Mann, Michael (1986) *The Sources of Social Power*, vol. I, *A History of Power from the Beginning to A.D. 1760*, Cambridge: Cambridge University Press.

Roberts, Richard H. (1988) 'Lord, bondsman, and churchman: integrity, identity and power in Anglicanism', in C. Gunton and D.W. Hardy (eds) *On Being the Church*, Edinburgh: T. & T. Clark, pp. 156–224.

Russell, Bertrand (1938) *Power: A New Social Analysis*, London: Allen & Unwin.

Steiner, George (1971) *In Bluebeards Castle: Some Notes towards a Re-definition of Culture*, London: Faber & Faber.

R.H. Roberts

PROCESS THEOLOGY

Process theology is a relatively recent theological movement with roots dating to the 1930s at the Chicago School of Divinity, where the philosophy of Alfred North Whitehead inspired a theological movement associated with such thinkers as Henry Nelson Wieman, Charles Hartshorne, Bernard Meland, Bernard Loomer, Schubert Ogden and John B. Cobb Jr.

Process theology uses the metaphysical categories of Whitehead's scientifically informed process philosophy to re-present the Christian message for the modern world. Not surprisingly, in the development of their social ethics, process theologians tend to be concerned with the role that one's metaphysical worldview plays in the formation and resolution of social problems. The belief is that underlying most of today's social ills is an inadequate cosmology which must be transformed if there is to be social renewal.

For example, the sort of environmental ethics which has dominated political discourse, such as is found in John Passmore, grows out of a worldview in which the non-human world is understood as objects, extrinsically related to humankind and thereby having only instrumental value to humans. In such an anthropocentric worldview, environmental concern, e.g. for the spotted owl, is quickly abandoned when any human value, e.g. perceived loss of jobs for loggers, is at stake, whereas the worldview found in process theology understands all things as internally related and capable of some level of subjectivity, so that the non-human world is viewed as internally related to humankind and having intrinsic value. Thus, environmental concern cannot be subordinated to human well-being; rather, moral concern must extend to the whole web of life, human and non-human (*see* GREEN; ENVIRONMENT)

Although there are various permutations of process theology, they share several interrelated convictions that provide the framework within which a profound social ethical vision is being developed: (a) God is 'panentheistic', i.e. God is immanent in all reality – though transcending it – and thus affected by all reality while affecting it; (b) God's influence in the world is necessarily persuasive rather than coercive, by providing living beings with novel possibilities for actualization in the light of God's own experience of the world; (c) like God, all living beings are organically or 'internally related' to each other, i.e. living beings are constituted by their relations to others, so that whatever exists is affected to some degree by everything else, and in turn affects everything else; (d) each living being has some degree of subjectivity or 'feeling', i.e.

responsiveness to its environment; (e) each living being has some capacity, even if negligible, for creative self-determination, i.e. freedom; (f) human experience and freedom differ from other creatures' in degree, with humans having a greater capacity for freedom and subjectivity in the form of consciousness and self-consciousness.

Environmental ethics is certainly the social issue with which process theology is most closely identified. The works of Charles Birch and John Cobb (1981), and Jay McDaniel (1989), are the most extensive developments of a process environmental ethics. They argue that a process view of God as perfectly immanent calls forth a 'life-centred' or biocentric ethic, since 'commitment to God is inseparable to commitment to life' (McDaniel 1989: 52, *see* ECOLOGICAL THEOLOGY). Moreover, process theology points out that, even without an explicit commitment to God, the organic interrelatedness of all things requires that we depose anthropocentric ethics, since anthropocentrism alienates us not only from the non-human but also from ourselves, who are constituted by our relationships to all things, non-human as well as human. The fact that every living being has subjectivity and some capacity for self-determination means that every living being has some intrinsic value. Thus, 'Kant's doctrine of the Kingdom of Ends must be vastly expanded' (Birch and Cobb 1981: 151), and moral rights should be extended to non-human beings in proportion to their capacities for richness of experience (*see* ANIMAL RIGHTS). Finally, the role of God as a non-coercive lure to greater freedom and richness of experience in all creatures calls into question the adequacy of traditional Western notions of coercive power and domination over others, human and non-human. The ideal of process theology is non-coercive mutuality aimed at promoting richness of experience in all things, and thereby in God who eminently experiences all things in their fullness. This is an ecological ethic that goes beyond mere conservation and resource and pollution management to preservation and enhancement of the existence of wilderness, non-human species, and even protection of the rights of individual animals with complex nervous systems that support greater degrees of richness of experience and self-determination (cf. McDaniel 1989: 79–84).

In the light of process theology's re-visioning of the modern worldview, it is not surprising that its contributions to social JUSTICE have been aimed more at transformation than at reform. Thus, process theology tends to call into question fundamental industrialized, Western, male, white assumptions about the nature of economic and political well-being, EQUALITY and freedom.

With regard to economic and political justice, the works of Douglas Sturm, Herman Daly and John Cobb, and Ian Barbour point to new ways of structuring public life. Sturm's work, unlike that of other process theologians, is less concerned with global environmental issues and more focused upon political philosophy. He is especially interested in developing the significance of internal relatedness and self-determination for American political and economic life. The relational character of human existence calls forth a political philosophy that acknowledges and enhances our existence. To recognize that we exist as individuals-in-community leads Sturm to acknowledge that 'the common good is the first virtue of social institutions' (1988: 165, 169 ff.). In order to allow for self-determination within the organic interrelatedness of SOCIETY, Sturm calls for a 'social democracy', i.e. the democratization of 'all modes of social life, including the economic' (ibid. 185). Given the advent of the modern multinational corporation and the interdependence between the private and public sectors, we need a vital, participative DEMOCRACY which allows members in the community to shape the economic and political institutions which affect the common good so that these institutions are less likely to become means of oppression and domination. Thus, Sturm envisions an extension of 'public determination into the functions of allocating investment, organizing production, and distributing WEALTH with the governing intention of enhancing the quality of relationships throughout the community of life' (ibid. 185). Such a vision requires not only a change in political policies, but ultimately a transformation of worldview that understands neither the individual as existing for society, nor society existing for the individual, but each for the other (ibid. 184).

While Daly and Cobb would generally affirm Sturm's vision of economic institutions, they argue that the ecological crisis should be a critical factor in any discussion of economic development. Dominant views of economic development encourage rapid industrialization and globalization of market development, the success of which is measured by the gross national product. Cobb and Daly view INDUSTRIALIZATION and globalization as anthropocentric responses to the serious economic plight of many Third World peoples. Not only does industrialization and globalization lead to massive environmental degradation – destruction of the world's rainforests and possibly millions of species of plants and animals living there, increased pollution of air, water and soil, greater deterioration of the ozone layer, etc. – it finally does not serve the goal of human justice since such development disrupts families through increased URBANIZATION, which, in turn, is usually accompanied by increased mortality rates, lowered life-expectancy, exploitation of low cost Third World labour to provide inexpensive products for First World consumers, and ultimately destruction of the resources which might undergird any sustainable local economy. The key value that emerges here is sustainability, which not only supports environmental well-being but also better serves global economic justice. Current economic theory neglects a number of factors necessary to any sort of economic development, in particular environmental damage, resource depletion and unpaid household labour (see Daly and Cobb 1989: Appendix). Daly and Cobb propose that a sustainable and just economic theory needs to measure such factors. In order to produce better measurements in this 'index for sustainable economic welfare' we need to move away from a multinational, interdependent, market-based economy toward relatively self-sufficient regional-based systems which make use of free market mechanisms while shifting from capital-intensive to labour-intensive production (particularly in agriculture). Sustainability – as opposed to de-industrialization, which would not alleviate the SUFFERING among the Third World poor – in regional and local economies would on the one hand (amongst other things) shorten supply lines and reduce the need for fossil fuels and preservation methods in global shipping, so that use of non-renewable resources as well as pollution are reduced, and on the other require less urbanization and develop a wider range of skills among local workers, and thereby enhance job satisfaction.

While guided by the ecological values prominent in process thought, Ian Barbour goes further than any other process theologian in synthesizing a wide range of ethical perspectives into a systematic social ethics. In the second volume of his Gifford Lectures, *Ethics in an Age of Technology*, Barbour (1993) develops a matrix of nine values with which to explore the ethical implications of technology. This matrix includes the individual values of food and health, meaningful work, personal fulfilment; the social values of social justice, participatory freedom, economic development; and the environmental values of resource sustainability, environmental protection and respect for all forms of life (cf. 1993: 81). The values of justice, participation and sustainability, central to Birch and Cobb's environmental ethics, are also central to Barbour's ethical analysis of technology. For example, agriculture must be first and foremost sustainable in its development to meet human values of health and food; energy technology should be developed primarily along the path of renewable sources such as wind, solar and photovoltaic cells; and computer technology can facilitate the design of other sustainable technologies and enhance our understanding of ecosystems through modelling. In the end, the redirection of technology requires nothing less than a new social paradigm which is post-industrial, environmental, and post-materialist, i.e. one that is consistent with and can benefit by a process perspective (Barbour 1993: 258–64).

It has sometimes seemed to those committed to human social justice that environmentalism is at best a luxury and at worst a forfeiting of the needs of humans for lower creatures. For example, the sort of support for animal rights sometimes found among wealthy, white Americans is often at odds with concern about justice for the poor, persons of colour and Third World peoples. However, the real conflict here, from a process perspective, is not between a biocentric ethics and an ethics of liberation, but rather between an anthropocentric version of environmentalism and liberation that is still trapped in the worldview rejected by process cosmology. No less than liberation theologies, process theology rejects the sort of example given above, but not because it is too concerned for non-humans but because it is too anthropocentric. The First World animal rights activist who is interested in protecting animals because of their value as pets or because of their aesthetic value merely understands the value of the non-human in terms of human satisfaction and preference. This is a far cry from the environmentalism called for by a biocentric ethic which does not divorce human justice from the justice due to other forms of life. While process theology has not been appropriated in any salient way by Third World liberation theologies, it has begun to enter into self-critical dialogue with liberation theologies (cf. Brown 1981). Moreover, a number of feminist and black liberation theologians have found in process theology an agreeable perspective that enhances their own work and promises to build bridges with sympathetic white male theologians (*see* BLACK THEOLOGY; LIBERATION THEOLOGY).

Process theology has become associated with a growing number of Christian feminists, particularly Valerie C. Saiving, Sheila Davaney, Rita Nakashima Brock and Marjorie Suchocki. The non-coercive power of God, the rejection of subject–object dualism found in the organic interrelatedness of all living beings, and the continuity in value among all creatures are picked up by these feminists as a basis for an ethics of androgyny (see Saiving, in Davaney 1981: 11–31) or erotic power (Brock 1988). They find in process theology's view of internal relations and creative self-determination a metaphysical grounding for transcending dualisms such as 'humanity and nature, mind and body, reason and emotion, activity and passivity, . . . individuality and relatedness . . . [which have] in some way been correlated with the dualism of male and female' (Saiving, in Davaney 1981: 18). Moreover, since the notions of internal relatedness and creative self-determination require and enhance each other in process metaphysics, there is a basis for an androgynous rather than hierarchical, i.e. patriarchal, interpretation of relationships (Saiving, in Davaney 1981: 26). Moreover, the process view of God, who in divine affectivity operates as persuasive power in all relationships, offers an alternative vision to androcentric notions of POWER as domination (Brock 1988: 46, *inter alia*). Hence emerges a view of liberation which is positive rather than negative, community enhancing rather than individualistic, inclusive rather than exclusive.

There have been noticeably few theologians of colour who have drawn upon process theology. A recent exception is Henry James Young (1990) who finds in process theology a new paradigm capable of replacing the mechanistic paradigm which has provided the metaphysical underpinnings for 'Anglo conformity', i.e. 'the demand that minority social groups conform to the values of the white majority social group' (1990: 1). The mechanistic paradigm interprets reality as made up of externally related, self-contained substances operating according to immutable laws. Its social counterpart is expressed in competition and exploitation of others, human and non-human (1990: 23). This model does not allow for genuine social pluralism, but rather it presupposes either assimilation or exploitation of others. God stands outside this predetermined universe. For the oppressor, God has legitimated the status quo; whereas for the oppressed, God is 'on their side' as one who may intervene to restore justice. Either way, the goal is domination rather than liberation (1990: 29–31). Process theology offers a new paradigm of social relatedness and the immanence of God which undermines the notions of Anglo conformity and polarization of majority and minority social groups in favour of the ideal of social pluralism. For Young, the process view of God as the ground of novel possibilities for existence affirms the importance of celebrating cultural differences that provide alternative, novel modes of living together in society (1990: 92). Moreover, God's persuasive power provides a model of human liberation that respects and enhances the freedom of others, whereas the mechanistic view of omnipotence provides a model of liberation which coercively replaces the freedom of the dominant social group for the oppression of the minority social group (1990: 123). Finally,

the process view of God as affected by the world, 'the fellow-sufferer who understands' (Whitehead 1978: 351), means that God experiences the sufferings and joys of the oppressed and the oppressor, and God's feeling of the world is integrated into a new vision of liberated existence relevant to the present. Thus, 'the kingdom of heaven [is] existentialized with history in a dynamic manner' (1990: 132).

Barbour, Ian (1993) *Ethics in an Age of Technology: The Gifford Lectures*, vol. 2, San Francisco, CA: Harper San Francisco.

Birch, Charles and Cobb, John B., Jr (1981) *The Liberation of Life: From the Cell to the Community*, London: Cambridge University Press.

Brock, Rita Nakashima (1988) *Journeys by Heart: A Christology of Erotic Power*, New York: Crossroad.

Brown, Delwin (1981) *To Set at Liberty: Christian Faith and Human Freedom*, New York: Orbis.

Bube, Paul Custodio (1988) *Ethics in John Cobb's Process Theology*, Atlanta, GA: Scholar's Press.

Cobb, John B., Jr (1972) *Is It Too Late? A Theology of Ecology*, Beverly Hills, CA: Bruce.

——(1982) *Process Theology as Political Theology*, Philadelphia, PA: Westminster Press.

Cobb, John B., Jr and Schroeder, W. Widick (1981) *Process Philosophy and Social Thought*, Chicago, IL: Center for the Scientific Study of Religion.

Daly, Herman E. and Cobb, John B., Jr (1989) *For the Common Good: Redirecting the Economy Toward Community, the Environment, and a Sustainable Future*, Boston, MA: Beacon Press.

Davaney, Sheila Greeve (ed.) (1981) *Feminism and Process Thought: The Harvard Divinity School/ Claremont Center for Process Studies Symposium Papers*, Lewiston, NY: Edwin Mellen.

McDaniel, Jay B. (1989) *Of God and Pelicans: A Theology of Reverence for Life*, Louisville, KY: Westminster/John Knox Press.

Ogden, Schubert M. (1979) *Faith and Freedom: Toward a Theology of Liberation*, Nashville, TN: Abingdon.

Sturm, Douglas (1988) *Community and Alienation: Essays on Process Thought and Public Life*, Notre Dame, IN: University of Notre Dame Press.

Suchocki, Marjorie Hewitt (1982) *God–Christ– Church: A Practical Guide to Process Theology*, New York: Crossroad.

Whitehead, Alfred N. (1978) *Process and Reality*, corrected edn, ed. David R. Griffen and Donald W. Sherburne, New York: The Free Press.

Young, Henry James (1990) *Hope in Process: A Theology of Social Pluralism*, Minneapolis, MN: Fortress Press.

Paul Custodio Bube

PROFESSIONAL ETHICS

For an act or institution to fall into the domain of ethical consideration it must raise questions about conduct; either about how an individual or a group ought to behave, or about the conduct of a particular practice. On the face of it these two questions might be, and indeed often are, taken to be separate. Thus the question how ought one to conduct one's life and the question of what constitutes good practice in the treatment of, for example, cancer appear to be different. The first question clearly raises issues of morality, of what it is to be a good person, of what values to hold or disown, of what *general* practices to adopt or not as the case may be, of how to lead one's life. It is, in Aristotelian terms, an issue of practical reason, a question that falls into the domain of *praxis*, of that practical form of life known as the *bios praktikos*, to distinguish it from the *bios theoretikos*, the theoretical or contemplative life. In Kantian terms it centres around the question, 'What may I do?' where the 'may' is understood in the morally permissive sense i.e., what am I morally permitted to do? In utilitarian terms it raises the question of whether the consequences of an action are good or beneficial. The second question, the question of what counts as good practice in the treatment of cancer, appears to relate, however, not to *praxis*, but to *techne* or skill and beyond that to the practice of skill or technical knowledge, *techne* in already established institutions. The issue of whether being an oncologist as such is good or bad is rarely, if ever, seriously raised, for there is a settled and long-standing tradition that being a healer is good and needs no further justification. By contrast it is often held that the issue of what counts as a good or bad practice in oncology appears to be a technical and, therefore, not a moral one. Thus what counts as good practice in oncology is understood in technical terms and does not, it is frequently argued, fall into the domain of morality, although the wider life that a particular oncologist leads may well do so.

These distinctions, and they are ancient ones, persist with some modification even now, and, with some modification, still govern the domain of professional ethics. The general moral conduct of an oncologist with respect to a patient is regarded as based on a duty of care and trust. That trust involves adopting and maintaining maxims of honesty towards the patient, giving honest opinions, keeping contracts, and, in a professional sense, serving the client's best interests. In these matters the professional is generally held to be responsible to the client or, through the courts, to the state. Thus a breach of trust or dishonesty is potentially actionable in law certainly as a civil matter, and in more serious cases even as a criminal matter. In this respect professional ethics falls into the domain of *praxis*, of practical reason and is a general moral matter or even a matter for the state as the guardian of the public interest.

But the conduct of the professional goes beyond *praxis* and into the domain of technical expertise, *techne*. A professional is expected to exercise sound JUDGEMENT in their area of expertise, to show an appropriate level of skill and technical knowledge and to apply that in an appropriate way in the best interests of his or her client. Where there is no client as such, as may be the case in matters of pure research, then the professional is expected to act to the best of their ability at their task, to show sound judgement, to pursue knowledge fearlessly, not to be swayed by extrinsic factors in the use of their judgement and to be scrupulously honest in the recording of results and the drawing of conclusions. Here the conduct of the professional is not normally a matter for SOCIETY or the state but a matter for the profession itself and its governing body. *Techne*, technical knowledge, skill and its proper application, falls outside the competence of the courts. Disciplinary matters within professions are contained within professional bodies although courts can interfere in cases of loss where the professional can be shown to have acted in a manner not appropriate to the normal conduct of a reasonable and competent practitioner of that profession. Here expert testimony from other members of the profession would be needed to show that the standard of care fell short of that normally expected.

The status of the profession itself ought also, although it rarely does, fall under the domain of professional ethics concerns. A morality of practical reason permits the examination of the conduct of a particular professional with respect to the categories of trust, contract, and general conduct. By contrast the criteria related to *techne* form part of the normal scrutiny of activity within the profession i.e., was the standard of service or care delivered that which a reasonable and competent professional would be expected to give in the circumstances. But what is notable is that neither of these categories, nor current practice, permit the *profession* as such to be subject to ethical scrutiny. The profession itself, the institution and existence of that profession is not subject to scrutiny as a normal part of ethical reflection within these professions. Thus the *institution* of BUSINESS, or accountancy or ADVERTISING or banking or commerce is not the subject of professional ethics, although conduct within business might be or conduct towards clients or other businesses might be. The same point applies to virtually any profession; the scope of professional ethical questions are primarily limited to conduct within the profession or conduct towards the client but not to the activity of that profession in and of itself. These wider concerns, if raised at all, are generally regarded as the concern of society, but not of the profession. Thus, if a society permits business, banking, commerce, USURY etc., then the assumption is that business, banking, commerce, usury etc., are morally acceptable. Clearly this outlook limits the scope of professional ethics and creates a potential hiatus. Society may leave professions to govern themselves and look to their own moral conduct and status. Professions, however, tend not to look to their own moral status but only to matters of *techne* regarding the wider question as the concern of society. In consequence it may well be that the moral status of particular professions is never seriously examined. Indeed frequently it is the case that not only is there no mechanism for doing so, but such mechanisms are positively discouraged.

That professional ETHICS is limited to a concern with conduct within the profession and to conduct towards clients but not to issue of whether the profession is ethical is a direct consequence of that rupture that took place in early MODERNITY that, among other things, distinguished civil SOCIETY and the state. Civil society can be broadly understood as the economic and social relations of a people and is taken to be composed of private acts and private inter-relations which need have no overt concern for the common good. On this model questions of the common good, of the public weal, are matters for the state, a prime function of which in early CAPITALISM was to protect and preserve the WEALTH creating activities of civil society.

Professional ethics arose as a direct consequence of the self governing nature of the traditional professions. There had long been a clear model for that in the profession of the priest. The eary Hebrew religion set priests and priestly functions apart from society, and that model was followed throughout the development of the Christian church. The apostles were themselves chosen and distinguished, set apart from others, and the early fellowship of the Christian church with its emphasis on egalitarianism gave way to a distinct priestly and or monastic class. The Hebrew–Christian model of distinct priestly classes is, of course, not confined to that tradition. Ancient Egypt showed clear signs of distinct administrators and priests, and in the Ancient China of Confucius professional administrators, mandarins, were the effective rulers on behalf of their client Kings. The professions developed, particularly in early modern times, as a reaction to the feudal order and as a reaction towards the self-governing nature of those holding priestly office. The guilds that developed in early modern Europe were formations within an embryonic civil society that took sovereignty over their institutions and practices to themselves. The guilds controlled apprenticeships and entry qualifications, thus having a monopoly on membership. Their tight control over membership and their distinction from state and church made for bodies that were autonomous in their particular domain. Their control over the EDUCATION and training of their members led to the self-perpetuation of their standards, and their exclusive control over relevant knowledge made them the only appropriate judges of the professional conduct of their members. Against this backdrop it is easy to see why the subject matter of professional ethics is that of ethics within the profession and not the ethics of the institution of particular professions.

Within the limited focus of what has come to count as professional ethics certain criteria that cut across all professions can be determined. Externally, these criteria include good faith, and honesty in contractual matters with clients. Internally criteria include applying technical skill for the best interests of the client, applying best judgement and practice to the benefit of the client and not to the benefit of the professional, engaging and maintaining trust, not abusing position or knowledge, and maintaining and keeping confidences.

Internally, the application of *techne*, acting to the best of one's ability gives rise to the possibility of the Aristotelian virtues, of *arete*, of excellence. Here the motive for the practice is that of the intrinsic reward from prime performance. A professional who performs to the best of their ability in order to produce a larger fee is not acting ethically, according to *arete* for the reward is extrinsic. A professional who acts to the best of their ability for the sake of the activity itself and as an incidental consequence of that obtains a higher fee, is being virtuous, is exhibiting *arete*. The outward and visible manifestations are the same but the internal aspects are entirely different. On teleological grounds both actions are moral, even if the intentions are different. On Kantian grounds the former is not moral for it is driven by the desire for more money and, on Aristotelian grounds, it is not moral for it seeks extrinsic reward and pays no attention to the intrinsic value of acting well for its own sake.

What these examples illustrate is that there are a variety of ways of approaching professional ethics depending on the background view of morality that one takes. If extrinsic reward is significant and the activity itself has no intrinsic value then it matters not if the desire for extrinsic reward is the motive for the good performance. If, however, extrinsic reward undercuts morality then an action that is professionally moral can be so only if performed according to intrinsic criteria, for its own sake, for excellence, for the performance itself and not for pecuniary or other reward.

While professions ought to establish and debate the morality of their own existence, and not leave this to society, excellence of *techne* does indeed seem to be a matter for professions alone. The function of society at large, and by extension, the state, is not to interfere with *techne*, but to engage in a wider debate about whether particular professions are ethical or not. In fact the opposite seems to have occurred. The wider debate about the ethical status of particular professions and whether they should be allowed to continue, e.g. stockbrokers, accountants, usurers, banks, lawyers, journalists, politicians, bureaucrats, managers, traffic wardens, police, is, more or less, completely absent. Instead the state has tended to address the question of *techne* by substituting managerial efficiency and managerial modes of accounting for professional judgement, for the possibility of *arete*. The merit of the professions was that they were, perhaps, the last bastion within which the virtues could be practised; in many cases that has now been undercut and destroyed.

Professions have enjoyed a peculiar and privileged monopoly. There is, perhaps, good reason for divesting them of the monopolies and insisting that they account for themselves to a wider arena than hitherto. Monopolies are usually regrettable and frequently abusive of their position. The demands of contemporary DEMOCRACY require the maximum accountability and the maximum transparency of decision. In Europe and in the United Kingdom especially, the former, if not the latter concern has led to a wholesale attack on some traditional professions and institutions. Lawyers, doctors, teachers, universities, schools have had their autonomy stripped from them by the state and their professional judgement has been usurped by the demands of 'line' management. The difficulty is that this attack is an attack not on the status of the professions as such, but is instead an attack on their *techne* and it is this that only the professions have competence to guard. To recall a problem thrown up as long ago as Plato the guardians need guarding, but by whom shall it be? If it be the STATE then the barriers between civil society and the state collapse in some crucial ways, that would be a crucial break with all that has gone before in modern life from its very inception to the twelfth century. That something has survived for eight hundred years does not of itself make it a sacred cow, but it is worth recalling that the *techne* of the professions belongs to civil society and that a usurpation of civil society by the state has been the hallmark of every twentieth century totalitarian regime. That the state has substituted a genuine moral debate about the status of particular professions with an interference in their *techne* shows, additionally, that kind of alarming and potentially dangerous moral bankruptcy characteristic of those same totalitarian regimes.

Beauchamp, T. and Bowie, N. (eds) (1979) *Ethical Theory and Business*, Englewood Cliffs, NJ: Prentice-Hall.

Calvin, J. (1954) *Institutes of the Christian Religion*, Philadelphia, PA: Library of Christian Classics.

Drucker, P. (1979) *Management*, London: Pan.

Duns Scotus (1986) *Duns Scotus on the Will and Morality*, ed. Allan B. Walten, Washington, DC: Catholic University Press.

Durkheim, E. (1957) *Professional Ethics and Civic Morals*, London: Routledge & Kegan Paul.

Smith, A. (1950) *The Wealth of Nations*, London: Methuen.

Weber, M. (1930) *The Protestant Ethic and the Spirit of Capitalism*, London: George Allen & Unwin.

Paul Barry Clarke

PROPERTY

In a world in which most people possess very little and a few possess a great deal the subject of property is an important and highly emotive one. Sometimes the mere pronunciation of the word 'mine' can produce unpleasant overtones because what is mine, when that term is understood to indicate exclusiveness, is not yours. Even 'ours' can have the same effect if it is used to denote exclusiveness with regard to a certain privileged group. Of course, it could be pointed out that some sort of control of resources would seem to be necessary in human SOCIETY in order to avoid chaos. Even if we accept this, however, major questions remain regarding the notion of property, of claims that things are proper to me or to us, that I or we own them. What, for instance, are the limits of ownership? What kind of exclusive property rights, if any, can justifiably be claimed? What obligations does ownership bring with it?

In the Hebrew Bible there is a good deal about the ownership of land, perhaps the most controversial of all kinds of proprietorship. Like so much else in the Bible, this has to be understood within the context of the covenant that God established with the Israelites. The land was a gift which the Lord had given to them after their escape from BONDAGE in Egypt and their period of wandering in the desert. The distribution of the country among the tribes is described in some detail in Joshua 13–19. (See also Numbers 26: 52–6.) Inevitably, from time to time, things would go well for some and badly for others. The Israelites had never to forget, however, that the land was a free gift from God for all of them. Legislation was therefore introduced to protect the poor and to prevent the rich from accumulating too much. Measures were introduced, for instance, to inhibit the acquisition of more than one's fair share of land. One such measure was the jubilee year, when land which had been acquired during the previous fifty years was to be returned to its original owner, and people who had been reduced to serfdom as a result of debt were to be liberated (Leviticus 25: 8–17). Other interesting prescriptions are found in Exodus and Deuteronomy. For six years the Israelites were to sow and gather their produce. In the seventh year, however, they were to let the land lie fallow. The food it produced was to be for the poor, and what they left could be eaten by the wild animals (Exodus 23: 10–11). Even in normal years farmers were not to reap right up to the edge of their fields or completely strip their vineyards. Something was to be left for the poor and the foreigners (Leviticus 19: 9–10). At the end of every third year, moreover, tithes of harvests were to be collected in the communities so that Levites, foreigners, orphans and widows could eat all they wanted (Deuteronomy 14: 28–9). The prescriptions regarding the sabbatical year in Deuteronomy appear to go beyond matters relating to land. In that year a creditor holding a pledge from a fellow Israelite should release him from it. There should be no poor among them (Deuteronomy 15: 1–11). How well such prescriptions were adhered to at various periods in the history of the twelve tribes is a matter for debate. What concerns us, however, are the teachings and belief system on which they were based. Land was not to be sold outright because it belonged to God. The Israelites were his guests (Leviticus 25: 23–4). The land was given to them so that all could benefit from it.

Concern for the poor and the needy (*see* POVERTY) permeates the whole of the Bible, but complementary teachings which should not be ignored are those regarding the dangers inherent in the accumulation of riches. Nowhere is this stated with more insistence than in the New Testament writings attributed to Luke. There we find Jesus' disciples being told that they must be on their guard against avarice of any kind because life does not consist in possessions (Luke 12: 15). One who accumulates possessions that he does not need is a fool (12: 13–21). Jesus himself has nowhere to lay his head, and simplicity of lifestyle, it seems, is expected of his immediate followers (9: 57–8). A rich man is advised to sell all that he has and give the money to the poor (18: 18–23). The plain fact is that one cannot serve both God and money (16: 13). In general, the conclusion has to be that it is harder for a rich person to enter the Kingdom of Heaven than it is for a camel to pass through the eye of a needle (18: 24–5). In Acts we learn that those who shared the faith apparently took heed of such warnings, for they owned everything in common (2: 44–5). Without a doubt, idol worship is a large part of the problem. Paul spells that much out when he tells the Ephesians they can be quite certain that those who indulge in greed, which, he says, is WORSHIP of a false god, cannot inherit the KINGDOM OF GOD (Ephesians 5: 5–6).

Several Fathers of the Church, including such luminaries as St Ambrose and St John Chrysostom, laid stress upon the fact that the goods of the earth are for the benefit of all of us. Here and there in their writings we find quite strong language being used to convey the message that those who unnecessarily accumulate WEALTH for their own exclusive use are, in effect, stealing what belongs to the poor, even when such accumulation is brought about legally. If they then give alms, they are merely returning stolen goods. Some sort of right to private property would seem to have been acknowledged by many of the Fathers, but the notion of ownership is modified by that of stewardship. Those who have possessions are stewards or administrators of those things, and they should use them to meet the needs of others as well as their own. In this regard, it is interesting to note how John Chrysostom takes up the theme of Christ's identification with the poor and remarks on the futility of adorning church buildings and of providing golden cups for Christ's table whilst leaving him homeless, dressed in rags and starving. He also points out that the poor person in distress is more properly a temple than is a church building.

The patristic writers were well aware of the dangers that riches bring to those who possess them. Chrysostom, for instance, builds on the theme that one cannot worship both God and money. It is impossible, he writes, for an avaricious person to see the face of Christ. Cyprian refers to the danger of being enslaved by money, of being tied by the bonds and chains of avarice, so that, having been saved by Christ, one is bound anew.

Although he was also influenced by Aristotle, Aquinas kept close to the general theme of the Fathers. The community of goods, he tells us, is a part of NATURAL LAW. The *distribution* of goods, on the other hand, he goes on to say, is not a matter for natural law, but for human agreement. The individual holding of possessions is therefore a result of such agreement as an addition to natural law. Human beings, he maintains, have a twofold competence with regard to material things. One is to care for them. Bearing this in mind, we see that it is necessary for human life that people possess things. This is so for three reasons: (a) a person is more solicitous in caring for something that is his or her responsibility than for something that is held in common or by many people; (b) human affairs are organized more efficiently if each person has his or her own area of responsibility; (c) human beings live together in greater peace when all are content with their own tasks. Regarding this last point, Aquinas notes that quarrels often break out among people who hold things in common. Having thus spoken favourably about private ownership, he then turns to the second area of competence with regard to material things, which is the use and management of the resources of this world. Nobody, he says, is entitled to manage things as if they were exclusive to him or her. The interests of all should be respected, and we should all be ready to share with others in case of necessity.

Aquinas's teaching regarding private ownership has met with a good deal of agreement over the years since he wrote and, in our own days, he is still widely quoted in writings on that subject. What some might call variations on his theme however, have, appeared from time to time. It has been suggested, for example, that the development and satisfaction of certain human creative and caring tendencies can only be achieved through private ownership. Some have argued, moreover, that private ownership is necessary for, or is at least an aid in, the defence of freedom. Having their own belongings, it is claimed, gives people greater AUTONOMY and reduces the likelihood of interference by political AUTHORITY. Whatever may be the truth of such claims, it would seem to be the case that nowadays many people, perhaps the vast majority, in the Western world regard private ownership as some sort of 'natural right'. It would seem that certain philosophers have had a part to play in the development of this state of affairs. The writings of John Locke, for example, seem to have exerted a good deal of influence, perhaps most especially in the USA. He taught that there is a natural moral law which can be discovered by reason. NATURAL RIGHTS, including the right to property, derive from this natural law in Locke's scheme of things. Needless to say, numerous scholars who would claim to be reasonable have come to quite different conclusions.

The development of modern CAPITALISM and INDUSTRIALIZATION has resulted in new complications regarding the whole subject of property and property rights. Now, for instance, we hear a good deal about copyright and patents. We also come across a good deal of corporate ownership. One of the most important and controversial topics for discussion regarding capitalism, however, has been the ownership of the means of production, which are often complex, expensive and themselves difficult to produce. Not so very long ago, in countries affected by the Industrial Revolution, the means of production came to be concentrated in the hands of comparatively few people. Profits from the sale of goods went to the owner of the materials and means of production. The workers were merely paid a wage, often a mere subsistence wage. In such a state of affairs, wrote Karl Marx, workers are alienated from the products they make. Those products belong to somebody else. Workers are also alienated from their productive activity, which is not voluntary but imposed. Marx even went so far as to say that, in the capitalist system, people become less human through work and are estranged from other human beings. Such is the lot of the proletariat in societies based on private property, as capitalist societies are. In order that this state of things may be overcome, therefore, private property must be abolished (see also ALIENATION; EMANCIPATION; MARXISM).

There are some, I imagine, who feel that the failure of COMMUNISM as an economic system merely underlines the value of Aquinas's teachings on the subject of private property to which we referred above. Others, however, may be inclined to point out that the world of capitalism could also benefit from a rereading of Aquinas's words regarding the *use* of private property – and, of course, the writings of various Fathers of the Church and of numerous other Christian scholars who have written on the same subject since the time of Aquinas. Most complaints about capitalism, it would seem, concern the *laissez-faire* variety, especially when practised in an atmosphere of greed. It is possible, however, for governments to intervene in order to bring about modifications that control greed and promote the common good. Companies may be obliged by LAW, for example, to comply with certain minimum requirements regarding conditions of employment. It is also possible, of course, for companies to improve matters, with or without the help of legislation, by encouraging workers' participation in at least some aspects of decision-making and by introducing profit-sharing schemes for the work-force. All of this betrays an acknowledgement of the fact that property should not be used by the owner in an exclusive way, without due regard for other people. Governments, moreover, can, and often do, introduce monetary measures which clearly indicate a conviction that private ownership must bow to the demands of the common good. Taxation that brings about a redistribution of wealth is an obvious example. The introduction of inheritance tax is a particularly interesting way of inhibiting the accumulation of property in the hands of a few.

Governments should also keep an eye on the common good when trying to decide whether certain utilities should be in the realm of private ownership or public ownership. In the case of a particular nation, for instance, the GOVERNMENT may see that the interests of the nation would be served best by public ownership of the entities responsible for the provision of water. There may also be grounds for considering similar action with regard to the provision of gas, electricity and roads. It is, of course, possible that, because of different circumstances, public ownership of a certain utility is in the best interests of one nation but not of another. With regard to the arguments of Aquinas referred to above, it could be said that the problems associated with what we might call the absence of private ownership can be overcome by appointing responsible persons and paying them acceptable salaries.

The pressing need to protect the ENVIRONMENT provides another reason for the introduction of measures by governments to introduce restrictions regarding the holding and use of property. An obvious example concerns the use of privately owned land. Given the experience that the human race has of unsafe constructions, appalling living conditions, overcrowded areas and sheer gross ugliness which have resulted from uncontrolled building in numerous cities throughout the world, it would seem reasonable to impose some restrictions regarding the granting of planning permission. Another example is the control of the use of certain chemical substances on agricultural land and in factories when it is known that the use of such substances results in the pollution of rivers and reservoirs. Today, moreover, we hear a good deal about factors that could justify action by a government to restrict the uses of private property by its

citizens in order to defend the rights of people in other countries. A particular government might, for example, comply with an international agreement by introducing legislation to prevent citizens using their property in such a way that it causes acid rain to fall on the forests of another country. We should add that such governmental interference in the use of private property may be called for not only in defence of present-day citizens and foreigners but also in defence of future generations. Destruction of large parts of this planet by some property holders is obviously not good stewardship.

Today there is a good deal of discussion about the rights of non-human creatures. It is maintained by some, for instance, that the goods of the earth are for the benefit of all creatures, not just all humans. There is, of course, some disagreement concerning the rights of animals — and, indeed, other creatures (see ANIMAL RIGHTS). Some talk in terms of the personhood of at least some animals. Others do not put other creatures on a par with humans but accept that they do have rights. Both groups see a need to protect the habitats of non-humans. It can, of course, be argued that some such protection of habitats is necessary for the promotion of human welfare. Even those who admit of no rights for other creatures, therefore, should see that governments could be justified in introducing legislation to control the use of certain kinds of property in order that non-human species may be protected.

Malcolm Gillis has noted that deforestation and forest degradation have long been taking place primarily on land owned by governments. No doubt, it would be easy to produce quite a long list of damage caused to the environment and problems caused for the poor on land owned by governments or as a result of government legislation affecting privately owned property. Whilst we can justify some public ownership and some government interference to restrict the holding and use of property, therefore, we clearly need to do much more than make appeals for government control if we are to promote a truly Christian attitude to property. A greater emphasis in Christian teaching upon stewardship and the basic notion that the goods of creation are for the benefit of all would surely help to improve matters. A further step might be taken in the right direction if Christian organizations were to look more carefully at the ways in which they use the property they hold.

Boecker, Hans J. (1980) *Law and the Administration of Justice in the Old Testament and Ancient East*, London: SPCK.

Bormann, F. Herbert and Kellert, Stephen R. (eds) (1991) *Ecology, Economics, Ethics: The Broken Circle*, New Haven, CT: Yale University Press.

Copleston, Frederick (1959, 1963) *A History of Philosophy*, vol. V, London: Burns Oates & Washbourne, 1959; vol. VII, London, Burns & Oates, 1963.

Gonsalves, Milton A. (1985) *Fagothey's, Right and Reason. Ethics in Theory and Practice*, St Louis, MO: Times Mirror/Mosby College Publishing.

Johnson, Luke T. (1986) *Sharing Possessions. Mandate and Symbol of Faith*, London: SCM.

Locke, John (1963) *Second Treatise on Government*, in *Two Treatises of Government*, ed. Peter Laslett, New York: New American Library.

MacPherson, C.B. (1962) *The Political Theory of Possessive Individualism*, Toronto: University of Toronto Press.

Walsh, William J. and Langan, John P. (1977) 'Patristic social consciousness – the Church and the poor', in John C. Haughey (ed.) *The Faith That Does Justice. Examining the Christian Sources for Social Change*, New York: Paulist Press, pp. 113–51.

Bernard Hoose

PROPHECY

Deriving from Greek words originally used in the context of the sacred oracles in Delphi and elsewhere, 'prophecy' is generally understood as divinely inspired utterance, and the 'prophet' as the person who speaks for God, as the inspired revealer or interpreter of God's will.

In fact these terms have become important in English parlance more because of ancient Israel and the Hebrew scriptures, where the Greek words used in the Septuagint translation bring together references to several distinct categories of religious experience: the ecstatic prophets, the mystic seers, the inspired visionaries, all claiming to speak forth the message of God yet all subject to a wide, human range of self-doubt, question and opposition from others, and an endless variety of reception in the community for which their words were intended. Reaching its height in the eighth-century prophets of Israel (Amos, Hosea, Isaiah, Micah) and their slightly later successors of Judah (Jeremiah, Ezekiel), this tradition grew out of the succession of Judges as it gave way to the monarchy (Samuel, Elijah, Elisha) and ebbed after the Hebrews returned to Palestine from the exile.

Prophecy is generally seen as a specific category of human utterance, with particular attention either to its form or to its content. In terms of its form, attention is often focused on the ecstatic state in which some prophetic messages are received and spoken, on some transcendental feature of the prophet's behaviour or claim, or on the unpredictability or suddenness of the utterance, all being seen by others as to some extent indicating, or even guaranteeing, the divine origin of what is said. Not least since the great Hebrew prophets frequently spoke in critique of royalty, or of the prevailing behaviour in SOCIETY or of religious leaders, prophecy is also often associated with radical social critique.

Those who judge prophecy rather by its content will expect above all to find in the message, which already in several of the Hebrew prophets is to be seen in their life as much as in their recorded words, evidence that it is God's word and will that the prophet is transmitting. This may be found in terms of faithfulness to the known tradition of God's will, as the prophet interprets and reinterprets for the circumstances of the day what is long since accepted as God's overall purpose. It may also be, often at the same time, that prophecy, as it analyses and interprets the history of the day, offers warnings about dangers ahead or promises of reward. This is why it has come to be associated with foretelling the future. Ancient Hebrew prophecy in fact shaded over into increasingly APOCALYPTIC speech and writing (e.g. in Daniel) concerned with the coming, cataclysmic Day of the Lord.

The Hebrew tradition took a new turn with John the Baptist and Jesus of Nazareth, combining many of the features mentioned above yet with a totally new dimension added by the claims made by Jesus' followers about his RESURRECTION and about the gift of his Spirit at Pentecost, empowering and commissioning them for a worldwide mission to all nations. Within the early Church, prophecy was not unknown as a distinct gift available in certain persons, yet one which could go seriously wrong and which needed to be checked and contained within the wider disciplines of the community. In 1 Corinthians 12–14, for instance, Paul insists that the church must test prophecies in terms both of their faithfulness to the overall tradition of Christ's people and of their openness to critical discussion and reception by the church as a whole. Especially after the excesses of movements such as the Montanist in the fourth century and – no doubt – the new control over the church exercised most effectively by the imperial authorities once Constantine had made Christianity into the official religion of the empire, the gifts of prophecy seem to have been channelled into either preaching or monasticism.

Alongside the Hebrew tradition, the Middle East also knew as prophets those who founded and re-founded major religious traditions, such as Zoroaster and Mani. Then, in the seventh century of the common era, appeared Muhammad of Arabia, to whom all Muslims look as the last of the prophets. He recorded in the Qu'ran the divine messages dictated to him by an angel. These are held by Muslims to be so sacred and final that translation is at best secondary. While the Muslim community has built up over the centuries a rich tradition of interpretation of Qu'ranic teachings, this is essentially in terms of obedience to what has been laid down once and for all, not by way of adaptation or change in the light of new ideas and new circumstances.

In more recent Christian history the term 'prophecy' and the role expected of 'prophets' has been seen in several different ways. In the European Middle Ages, the theologian Joachim of Fiore and the poet Dante were both judged to be prophetic in their interpretation of contemporary history and their warnings about what could happen if humanity did not change its ways. At the Reformation the Zürich reformer Huldreich Zwingli gave the name of 'The Prophecy' to a theological institute where lay people and pastors could debate and struggle through in controversy the most appropriate and practical interpretation of the Biblical teachings for

the economic or political or military decisions facing them.

Many 'middle-of-the-road' Western Christians in modern times have come to associate prophecy with sectarian or over-intense manifestations of religion, and therefore marginalize or discount it. They have responded all too often with nothing more than prejudice, both to the many African prophets who in this twentieth century have led millions into a new freshness of Christian obedience, often combining Biblical and African traditions in a new lifestyle and spirituality, and to the various Pentecostal and CHARISMATIC MOVEMENTS which have claimed a new experience of Biblical prophecy, along with other gifts of the Holy Spirit, in their distinctively enthusiastic and committed communities.

The word has also come to be used in more secular parlance, perhaps loosely drawn from such writers as William Blake or Friedrich Nietzsche, for the message conveyed by those who speak up for some particular cause or concern against the prevailing tide, and for those who speak with passion either to warn about dangers ahead or to exhort to some particular commitment. From this the term has also come to be used in trivializing contexts, such as 'prophecies' about which horse will win the Derby, that have lost all connection with any claim to divine origin or AUTHORITY.

Among sociologists, Max Weber took a particular interest in the experience and function of prophecy in society. He is sometimes held to have expected that sociology would grow into being able to predict the patterns of interaction of different groups in society, a claim about which most sociologists today would be more reticent. More important, he pointed to the frequent tension within religious communities between the 'priest' and the 'prophet', understanding by the latter 'a purely individual bearer of charisma, who by virtue of his mission proclaims a religious doctrine or divine commandment' and whose experience is likely to be lonely, iconoclastic and often finally tragic (see *The Sociology of Religion*, pp. 65f., 1922 ET 1963 Boston: Beacon Press and London: Methuen). This distinction has helped many theologians to insist on the probability, even desirability, of a permanent and healthy tension between those, typically the professional religious leaders (priests), whose aim is to keep the community united and stable and those individuals, authorized or not, who feel they must speak God's TRUTH, however awkward and uncomfortable (prophets). In all cases, the 'truth' of prophecy can only be finally established with hindsight, in the light of how the community has come to accept or reject what the prophet taught.

Turning then to the 'relevance' of prophecy today, everything depends on the starting point for evaluation in the observer's worldview and faith commitment. A faithful Muslim will hold the message revealed to Muhammad in the Qu'ran to be every bit as vital today as ever for discovering and obeying the will of God for the life of the individual and of the social order. Those yearning for radical change in the dominant economic and/or political structures will welcome as prophecy those voices which point to new possibilities of revolutionary action. Sociologists of religion will draw discriminating attention to the continuing importance of ecstatic phenomena and to their unpredictable effects in many different cultures and political systems. Social scientists more generally will try to analyse social forces and trends with a view to setting out for voters and decision-makers various alternative scenarios and models of how society might develop, but will on the whole be wary of claiming any 'prophetic' standing for what they can offer.

An educated and widely travelled Christian will value the concept of 'prophecy' for those still frequent contributions to thinking in church and society which are marked by freshness, originality and an inspiring quality which, together with the distinctive content of what is conveyed, may be held to offer something of God's will for his creation rather than simply one person's or group's aspirations. 'Typically', writes Robert Murray (see below), 'prophecy communicates a deeper awareness of God, of fundamental values or of the responsibility of human existence; it challenges conventional beliefs by its interpretation of the world, of past history and present events and trends, and consequently it frequently describes the future and calls for a change in attitudes and behaviour.' At the same time, it will invariably deserve the most rigorous testing, along lines already laid down by Paul in 1 Corinthians 12–14. Does it serve the common good, not just the prophet and an inner circle, not just the religious community in isolation? Does it genuinely build up the community, respecting the freedoms and contributions of each and all? Is it open to the testing and critique of the wider church in other situations? Above all, does it convey the recognizably same truth, way of living and way of loving that can be seen in the record of Jesus of Nazareth, who saved the world by dying on a cross, and in the experience of the saints of his church down the centuries? Some will point to outstanding contemporary Christians such as Dietrich Bonhoeffer or Helder Camara, others will look more widely to those who have had a lasting effect in society for good, whether in political life, such as Mahatma Gandhi or Albert Luthuli, or in other spheres, such as Albert Einstein or Fritz Schumacher. In all cases, as the prophets are the first to insist, the credit, if that is the word, is not theirs but is deserved by the people who carried out their message and by God from whom they received it.

Reliable survey articles with bibliography are Sheppard and Herbrechtsmeier (1987), Wilson (1987) and Murray (1983). On the Hebrew prophetic tradition, the Christian scholar Wilson (1980) and the noted Jewish leader Heschel (1962) provide reliable discussions. For a reliable and sympathetic account of the life and role of the prophet of Islam see Armstrong (1991), while for a generous yet critical discussion of his significance beyond the Muslim community see Cragg (1984). For a variety of prophetic testimonies down the centuries see Reeves (1976), Zernov (1944), Lanternari (1963) and Sullivan (1982). For a careful discussion by a Christian theologian well versed in the social sciences, see Gill (1981).

Armstrong, Karen (1991) *Muhammad – a Western Attempt to Understand Islam*, London: Victor Gollancz.

Cragg, Kenneth (1984) *Muhammad and the Christian*, London: Darton, Longman & Todd and New York: Orbis.

Gill, Robin (1981) *Prophecy and Praxis: The Social Function of the Churches*, London: Marshall Morgan & Scott.

Hegel, G.W.F. (1979) *The Phenomenology of Spirit*, trans. A.V. Miller, Oxford: Clarendon Press.

Heschel, Abraham Joshua (1962) *The Prophets*, New York: Harper & Row.

Lanternari, Vittorio (1963) *The Religions of the Oppressed: A Study of Modern Messianic Cults*, New York: Knopf and London: MacGibbon & Fee.

Marx, K. (1859) *Preface to a Contribution to a Critique of Political Economy*.

Murray, R.P.R. (1983) 'Prophecy', in A. Richardson and J. Bowden (eds) *A New Dictionary of Christian Theology*, London: SCM and Philadelphia, PA: Westminster Press, pp. 473–5.

Reeves, Marjorie (1976) *Joachim of Fiore and the Prophetic Future*, London: SPCK and New York: Harper & Row.

Sheppard, G. and Herbrechtsmeier, W.E. (1987) 'Prophecy', in Mircea Eliade (ed.) *The Encyclopaedia of Religion*, vol. 12, New York: Macmillan, pp. 8–14.

Sullivan, F.A. (1982) *Charisma and Charismatic Renewal – a Biblical and Theological Study*, Ann Arbor, MI: Servant Books.

Wilson, Robert R. (1980) *Prophecy and Society in Ancient Israel*, Philadelphia, PA: Fortress Press.

——(1987) 'Biblical prophecy', in Mircea Eliade (ed.) *The Encyclopaedia of Religion*, vol. 12, New York: Macmillan, pp. 14–23.

Zernov, Nicholas (1944) *Three Russian Prophets*, Gulf Breeze, FL: Academic International.

Martin Conway

PROSTITUTION

Prostitution derives from *prostituere* (Latin), to offer for public sale. An ancient text provides a still important clue to understanding the phenomenon of prostitution in societies very different from one another in time and place. As Proverbs 6: 26 has it, 'a prostitute can be had for the price of a loaf'. In other words, the price for which someone (usually female) may be able to set for the sale of their SEXUALITY has much to do with their social and economic dependence on their clients, though it should be noted that the exchange of sex for money or gifts is not unique to prostitution, which marks one point on a continuum at the opposite end of which are legally sanctioned sexual unions.

In the world represented by the Biblical texts, prostitution became a metaphor for apostasy, presumably because of the analogy which may be drawn between multiple sexual partners and the religious infidelity expressed via the WORSHIP of more than one god. In the ancient world, as now, prostitutes might enjoy a certain social position, as in the case of the *hetaira* of Athens, of whom Aspasia remains the most famous example because of her association with Pericles (Pomeroy 1975).

Studies of medieval society have now begun to illuminate how prostitutes were viewed in that context, with the history of marginal social groups, of women and of sexuality prompting new interest (Otis 1985). Prostitution is associated with towns (not just seaports) where there are communities of travellers as well as large groups of married and unmarried males, tolerance of male sexual activity and spare cash. Attitudes associated with the Christian church oscillated between tolerance for what was perceived as a social necessity, the institutionalization of brothels and policies of repression, most notably associated with the period of the Reformation. It is important to note that the term 'prostitute' or its equivalents, e.g. *meretrix*, might be applied to any woman whose sexual conduct fell outside currently prescribed norms. The latter varied from place to place and depended in part on one's social position. Institutionalization in the management of brothels limited the likelihood of males being arrested for 'adultery', as well as offering some protection from VIOLENCE and extortion to prostitutes themselves. Some medieval debate about whether the church could accept almsgiving from prostitutes recognized that they and their clients were engaged in sexual SIN, but it was also clear that the women acted out of necessity (Rossiand 1988). Thus much charitable effort rightly went into trying to rescue women's social and economic position, sometimes by accommodating them in convents, hospitals and orphanages from which with assistance they might emerge as marriageable.

Prostitution is not infrequently a *transitional* state, related to a woman's economic survival or the survival of a household dependent on what she earns, and throughout the centuries the problem has remained that the 'domestic' training women were likely to receive when forcibly restricted to institutions for 'moral reform' was precisely of the kind *not* likely to render them able to earn their living without resort to prostitution unless they could be re-attached to a household group (Cohen 1992). In the Christian tradition, certain ex-prostitutes symbolized the possibility of repentance (Ward 1987), with Mary of Magdala as their patron – but significantly the patron of all, whether prostitutes or not, who were repentant (Haskins 1993).

A new phase of effort for social control of prostitutes may be identified in the seventeenth and eighteenth centuries with the establishment of 'Magdalen' homes and asylums concerned with protection, assistance, correction and re-habilitation, but the nineteenth century saw a new focus of attention on prostitution (Weeks 1981). William Acton's *Prostitution, Considered in its Moral, Social and Sanitary Aspects, in London and other Large Cities and Garrison Towns, with Proposals for the Control and Prevention of its Attendant Evils* of 1858 (second edition, 1870), was clear about on the one hand the social relationship between money and position as necessary for MARRIAGE and on the other the connection between POVERTY and prostitution (Marcus 1969). Comparable points were made by Friedrich Engels' *The Origin of the Family, Private Property and the State* of 1884 (Millett 1971). The nineteenth century was an era of attempted *police* control and registration of prostitution in Europe, which in some countries survives in the twentieth century. In Britain this control was associated with the fate of the Contagious Diseases Acts of 1864, repealed in 1886 (McHugh 1980). The campaign for repeal provided some much-needed political experience for women, some of whom were motivated by religious conviction in their determination to dislodge police control of individuals, particularly working-class women (*see* POLICING); they also raised serious questions about ineffective medical involvement in attempting to regulate public health by compulsion, and challenged the way in which the law was underpinning a double standard of sexual morality (Walkowitz 1980).

One major result of the attempt to control prostitution has been to increase the dependence of prostitutes on males acting as pimps/protectors, on groups of organized criminals and on the owners of bars, clubs, massage parlours, etc. Notwithstanding the 1949 United Nations General Assembly Convention for the Suppression of Traffic in Persons and the Exploitation of the Prostitution of Others, prostitution flourishes worldwide and continues to provide material for post-1980s studies of, for instance, Thailand, colonial Nairobi, Buenos Aires and Ethiopia to name but a few places; the literature exhibits new features, most notably attention to the POWER, GENDER, race and CLASS issues involved (Pateman 1988). Child prostitution is clearly identifiable as an important issue in discussion of the future of the world's children (Ennew 1986).

Societies may wish to subscribe to the view that it is pointless to impose penal sanctions for certain forms of sexual relationship conducted in private by responsible and consenting adults, because these sanctions are likely to be inequitable in their application and ineffective as deterrents and to give too much scope to various forms of corruption. This position leaves the question of child prostitution still to be addressed, and fails to attend to the economic, social and gender issues involved.

Anchor Bible Dictionary (1988) New York: Doubleday.

Cohen, S. (1992) *The Evolution of Women's Asylums Since 1500*, New York and Oxford: Oxford University Press.

Ennew, J. (1986) *The Sexual Exploitation of Children*, Cambridge: Polity.

Haskins, S. (1993) *Mary Magdalen: Myth and Metaphor*, London: HarperCollins.

McHugh, P. (1980) *Prostitution and Victorian Social Reform*, London: Croom Helm.

Marcus, S. (1969) *The Other Victorians*, London: Corgi.

Millett, K. (1971) *Sexual Politics*, London: Virago.

Otis, L.L. (1985) *Prostitution in Medieval Society*, Chicago, IL and London: University of Chicago Press.

Pateman, C. (1988) *The Sexual Contract*, Stanford, CA: Stanford University Press.

Pomeroy, S.B. (1975) *Goddesses, Whores, Wives and Slaves*, New York: Schocken Books.

Rossiaud, J. (1988) *Medieval Prostitution*, Oxford: Blackwell.

Walkowitz, J. (1980) *Prostitution and Victorian Society*, Cambridge: Cambridge University Press.

Ward, B. (1987) *Harlots of the Desert*, Oxford: Mowbray.

Weeks, J. (1981) *Sex, Politics and Society*, London: Longman.

Ann Loades

PROTESTANTISM

The first thing to make clear is the meaning of the term. Though the word Protestantism has now come to bear the negative meaning of anti-Roman Catholicism, it was originally used, and is still so used and understood by responsible theologians and informed church historians, in its primary positive sense of witness to the truth of the Gospel. The word itself came into being after the second Diet of Speier in 1529, some nine years after the Reformation had been launched by Luther, when the reforming party and the papal party were about equally divided: the diet allowed liberty to the Luther movement until such times as the Emperor (now abroad) should return to Germany to settle the issues in diet. Under the liberty granted in 1526, the Reformation made surging advances in Germany, so much so that the papal party flocked to the diet in 1529 to abrogate the earlier decision by out-voting the evangelicals. The reforming members withdrew, declaring their famous Protest: namely, that nothing be allowed contrary to the Word of God (afterwards enlarged to proclaim liberty of worship and doctrinal opinion). From then on they were called *Protestantes*, Protestants. True, the word does bear some negative undertone, but the Reformers used the word in the transitive positive sense just described (as Shakespeare's, 'I do protest I love thee'). The root meaning of the word is to bear witness to truth, *pro-testare*, to testify to the truth and authority of evangelical theology. Classical Lutherans and Anglicans did not use the word in contrast to Catholic practice: to them, the word signified the Catholic Faith cleared of un-Catholic additions and corruptions of the medieval Roman Church. The Caroline Divines understood the term in the same way, and called themselves Protestants. The ambiguity arose with the appearance of Dissent. It was then that Protestantism acquired the negative sense of being anti-Catholic.

The question then arises, what is Protestantism? It is argued that there were Reformers before the Reformation: that it began with Wyclif in Oxford (1324–84) and was taken up by Huss in Bohemia (1369–1415), and others, though it could not reach its full potential owing to adverse political conditions. There is some truth in that view, but the movement we call Protestantism took fire with Luther (1483–1546) in Wittenberg as a religious, intellectual, university movement, beginning with some brilliant and prophetic academic disputations, sustained by fine Biblical preaching, and developing into the famous Reformation Writings of 1520 and, eventually, the courageous stand at Worms in 1521 when he maintained his evangelical theology before Emperor and Church. From then to his death in 1546, Luther was the leading light in the Reformation movement, producing an enormous weight of books, tracts, confessional statements, letters, hymns, liturgies and writings which still influence Christendom. Zwingli (1481–1531) was working in Zürich independently at this time, and owing to his Renaissance outlook and his Republicanism, as well as his humanitarian and social interests, gave other (and permanent) features to Protestantism. Calvin (1509–64), a brilliant perceptive theologian of the next generation, entered the Reformation in its second phase. Under Luther and Zwingli the new thinking had not only broken down the old forms which had restricted enquiry, but had also positively brought about important changes to social and political life by means of sermons, conferences, writings and controversies. The response throughout German-speaking Europe was electric. Within LUTHERANISM was born the Radical Reformation (sometimes called the Left Wing Reformation), which fructified into a disturbing number of sects – the Spirituals, the Anabaptists and others. It was in the midst of all this activity that Calvin entered with his brilliant logical mind to define for the Europe of his day new forms of Christian life and work, of church and community life, all arising from his God-mastered mind with its powerful grasp of the meaning of the Bible, together with his consuming experience of the Holy Spirit. He turned the rabble of the Reformation into an army under discipline. He is seen as the great systematic theologian, but his concern was never to subject the great Biblical truths to any controlling principles of human thought or logic. His entire thinking was subject to the Word of God, which had spoken in the flesh in Jesus Christ. It was a living, active revelation, a personal encounter with the Word of God enfleshed, found and enjoyed in the living Christ, by the power of the Holy Spirit. On the relation of church to STATE, it is not accurate to say that Calvin sought to build up a theocratic state. He held a high view of the role of the state, whose responsibility was to care for the well-being of its members and support the Church; he taught obedience to civil AUTHORITY, but stressed the independence of the Church and its witness to SOCIETY.

The strength of Protestantism produced a disturbing counter-effect. Its powerful conviction of a personal experience of encounter with God, the FREEDOM of the individual to find and proclaim this, and his responsibility to create and educate a society in which these ideals may be lived out in freedom, PEACE, JUSTICE and righteousness, created doughty and independently minded men and women, but at a cost of bringing out all the fissiparous tendencies within Protestantism, as well as conflicting ideas of the nature of the Church and its role in civil and political GOVERNMENT. These problems are still with us, unsettled and unsettling.

Though the divisions within Protestantism are long-standing and have sometimes been bitter and deep, it is nevertheless possible to attempt a summary of the leading principles common to them all.

(a) The first principle suggested would be justification by faith in Christ alone, in that it was by this principle that Luther rediscovered for himself the Gospel of the New Testament and thereby inaugurated the movement. Lutherans hold it as the principle by which the Church stands or falls. JUSTIFICATION means making or being made righteous (just), i.e. restored to a right and proper relationship with God. The natural human being is a sinner and unrighteous and is therefore in a wrong relationship to the righteous God, even alienated from God, and cannot of him- or herself create the right relationship. The person can only be set into a right relationship by God and, in realizing the cause of his or her alienation, accepting pardon and acceptance by God through grace in Christ Jesus. The person is saved not by his or her own active righteousness, be it ever so good, but by an alien righteousness, the righteousness

of Christ: *justificatio propter Christum per fidem*. Still a sinner, yet right with God: *semper justus semper peccator*. No-one can attain this by prayer, intellect or good works, no matter how worthy. Faith alone justifies. But, it should be stated at once, Luther always emphasized 'faith active in love': faith is *never* without works. Roman Catholic theology seemed almost to accept this, not only during the controversies of 1517–25 but also officially at Regensburg in 1541 under the guidance of the percipient Contarini and von Pflug. The difference between the Protestant and Catholic on this point may be expressed in these words: that while the Protestant argues that the righteousness whereby the sinner is acceptable to God is not a righteousness of his or her own but the alien righteousness of Christ, a righteousness *imputed* to him, the Catholic (here the Orthodox and others may be included) speaks of a righteousness being *imparted* to the believer by grace. Put even more simply: the Protestant pleads faith without works; the Catholic does not deny this, but pleads faith with works. This is no mere splitting of hairs: the distinction clinches decisively the Incarnation as God's work, and found expression in Luther in many ways, particularly in his distinction between Law and Gospel, between Moses and Christ, following Paul and John. In the Law many works are enjoined, as Luther expressed it, all external; but in the Gospel there is only one, an internal work, and that is faith. The Law makes a righteousness which is external, but faith makes a righteousness hidden with God. Always a sinner, always penitent, always right with God (WA.LVI, 441, 15,–443, 8).

(b) All Protestants are united on the sole authority of Scripture, though not as some kind of 'paper' authority but as the living Word of God to them in their situation, the *viva vox*. The magisterial Reformers retained a high respect for tradition, as did the principal Anglican Reformers: there was no conflict – but it was admissible only in so far as it supported scriptural truth, never as an equal authority. At the Council of Trent (1545–63) many of the Fathers took the Protestant position on the authority of Scripture in relation to tradition (many modern historians and theologians still do, e.g. Lortz); nevertheless, the prevailing view of Catholicism is not Scripture *and* tradition but *both* Scripture and tradition. The Radical Reformers and sectaries took the view that Scripture was the sole authority, even discounting all tradition which was unscriptural, yet at the same time emphasized still more the direct mediation of the Holy Spirit.

(c) All the Reformers rejected any claim to political power which the Curia exercised by virtue of the spurious Donation of Constantine and the forged Decretals of Isidore, by which it was maintained that the Roman Church was the legitimate successor to the Roman Empire. The magisterial Reformers sought to instruct the secular governors on their spiritual responsibilities as rulers: Luther saw government as ordained by God (Romans 13; 1 Peter) to maintain justice, peace and social health, on which basis the spirituality could fulfil its divine role; Zwingli, with his humanist-socialist concern, tended towards involvement in society; Calvin sought autonomy for the Church but exhorted subjects to lawful obedience, seeing rulers as shepherds rather than tyrants; all Radicals sought complete separation of Church and state. Lutherans and Anglicans open themselves to the charge of Erastianism, i.e. the subjection of the Church to the state. (Thomas Erastus (1524–83) was a Zwinglian layman who opposed a ruling of the church elders at Heidelberg.) The problem is still with us in the calls for disestablishment.

(d) The priesthood of all believers – this biblical doctrine, given classical formulation by Luther, affirms the common dignity, calling and privilege of all Christians before God. By the time of Luther this doctrine had become totally obscured, so much so that the clergy and monks were thought of as one class, the spiritual, and all others, now called the laity, were of a lower status. Luther protested that baptism makes us all priests (some of whom are selected for the administration of Word and Sacraments). In general terms, the Lutheran ministry has tended to be understood in a functional rather than an ontological sense, though not so universally. The outcome of this THEOLOGY is that every Christian, prince or bishop, cobbler or farmer, has a divine role to play, in which and by

means of which they may find total fulfilment of the will of God in their common everyday life. As Luther memorably expressed it to the milkmaids at Wittenberg, 'God milks the cows, through you' (WA. XLIV. 6, summarized). This theology set every man and woman on their theological feet. It was this lay movement which occasioned the Civil War of the seventeenth century in England and compelled the Pilgrim Fathers and others to found a new kingdom in America, with all the consequences for world history such emigrations had. True, it created the Separatists, Independents, Congregationalists, Presbyterians, Quakers and the Fanatics, to dissipate the power of the Reformation.

(e) In his *Babylonian Captivity* (1520), Luther referred to the tyranny exercised by the priests with their seven sacraments, and argued that only two had dominical authority – Baptism and the Supper of the Lord. To Luther, as to Augustine, the sacraments were the Word made visible: they should not be separated. Protestants follow Luther on this (except the Quakers, who have neither ministry nor sacrament), though not all followed his teaching on the Real Presence. All rejected the Roman interpretation of the sacrifice of the Mass in favour of that given in Hebrews, where Christ offers Himself as the sacrifice. All sought communion in both kinds. There is still diversity among Protestants on the meaning of the Lord's Supper. Luther remained closer to Rome than is often assumed, in that he believed in the corporeal real presence, in, with and under the elements; Calvin interpreted the presence in spiritual terms; Zwingli, too, who also emphasized commemoration. Zwingli, of course, believed in the presence of Christ in the EUCHARIST, not His absence, and though the Eucharist was a memorial he stressed faith in Christ, who was in heaven and whose body was not in the element. Many Protestants, both Lutheran and Anglican, have tended towards the Zwinglian interpretation, though in high Anglicanism and certain sections of Lutheran and Reformed Christianity a high sacramental doctrine has been maintained. These differences are not simply differences concerning the interpretation of the the Lord's Supper, nor of scholastic terminology (e.g. the meaning of *substantia*); they relate to particular understandings of the Incarnation, the Holy Spirit and the ministry. Ecumenists still seek a common mind on these deep theological differences.

Much has happened since the Reformation of the sixteenth century. There was the terrible Thirty Years War which ended with the Peace of Westphalia in 1648. Besides many territorial decisions, the formula of the Peace of Augsburg in 1555, '*cuius regio eius religio*', was accepted as the basis of ecclesiastical settlement, which, in effect, meant that both Lutheranism and Calvinism were to be tolerated in the Empire, though not Zwinglianism. In England at this time many Separatists and ejected Anglicans emigrated to America, followed by others. Later, other emigrants went to America, as well as to Australia and New Zealand: all took their Protestantism with them, for it was largely this they sought to preserve by emigrating. At present it is estimated that there are about 58 million Lutherans, 50 million Anglicans, 48 million Baptists, 40 million Reformed, 30 million Methodists, 3 million Congregationalists (now united with the Reformed) and a growing number, difficult to estimate, of Charismatics, Pentecostalists and house and community churches. Widely divergent as these bodies are, they share a common origin. Since the Oxford Movement of the nineteenth century, high Anglicans tend to relate more to CATHOLICISM, as has been shown in the ordination of women priests in the Anglican communion, but the high Anglicans of the seventeenth century described themselves unequivocally as Protestants. A strong ECUMENICAL MOVEMENT within Protestantism in the present century has brought about union between churches, e.g. the United Church of Canada, the Church of South India and of North India, though the attempt to amalgamate Anglicanism and Methodism by Archbishop Ramsey failed.

On a higher theological and spiritual level the Anglican/Roman Catholic International Commission, following close on Vatican II, produced the Malta Report 1972 which outlined a programme for further theological discussion; this commission has produced further reports in 1983 and 1987 on central issues such as the Church and justification. Similarly, the Reformed churches are engaged in conversations with Anglicans, Baptists and Lutherans, with whom they have made the Leuenberg Agreement. The Lutheran churches of Scandinavia have held continuous discussions with Anglicans since 1909, and the German Lutherans since 1964. Many reports have been published, notably the Pullach Report 1973, the Meissen Report 1988 and the Porvoo Report 1993. The outcome of these is the recommendation for intercommunion, and plans to establish in Durham a German Protestant Library in a research centre. The same is happening in America, but of special significance is the series of discussions between Lutherans and Catholics which have produced weighty reports on Creed and Dogma, Baptism, Eucharist and Ministry.

The ecumenical movement has transformed the theological scene of the twentieth century and has created international theological discussions: Edinburgh 1910, Lausanne 1927; Edinburgh 1937 created the WORLD COUNCIL OF CHURCHES meeting at Amsterdam 1948. There followed Lund 1952, Evanston 1954, New Delhi 1961, Montreal 1963, Uppsala 1968, Nairobi 1975, Vancouver 1983; since Vatican II (1962–5), Roman Catholic observers have played a significant part. Lima 1982 attempted an agreed presentation of the Apostolic Faith for today, rather as a counter-movement to the preoccupation with economic, social and political issues which gripped the World Council of Churches.

What are the topical issues which face Protestantism today? We suggest, in general terms, that the first may be the obvious one of simple continuity: *ecclesia reformata semper reformanda*. Protestantism needs continually to encounter and experience the revelation of God given in Christ, and to express that in, to and for the context of the intellectual and societal climate of opinion of the day. This means to express it otherwise than in the ancient and medieval forms which tended to refract Biblical thought through notions borrowed from antiquity or philosophy. It does not necessarily mean to re-express the Gospel *in* the terms of contemporary culture, but rather *to* the minds and souls of people who now think and live in these terms. Liberals have long been concerned to effect this very thing. Indeed, it has been the distinguishing mark of the Church's thinkers throughout the centuries, from the Alexandrine Fathers to the present day. The danger in much contemporary apologetics unlike, for instance, Athanasius or the Cappadocian Fathers, even Luther and Calvin, seems twofold: some apologists (with strong support from the media) explain away rather than explain the central tenets of the Incarnation, the RESURRECTION and the Ascension; others, in an attempt to make the Gospel 'relevant', express theology and Gospel in political and social terms which amount to little more than humanitarian concern (see POLITICAL THEOLOGY). Protestantism must safeguard the Christian Revelation, and avoid the Scylla of radical modernism and the Charybdis of secular humanism. At the same time, it must continue to create and develop sound social doctrine to meet the demands of modern mass society.

Second, Protestantism will have to deal afresh with the problem of religious pluralism. To this problem are related the freedom of unbelief as well as the freedom to engage in anti-religious proaganda. It is not only a question of truth as represented by denominations, nor even the truth between the different faiths, but whether religious truth is truth.

Third, there is the question of ecumenical ECCLESIOLOGY – whether the pursuit of some kind of federal union is enough, or rather a religious unity rooted in the revelation of Christ. In other words, it is less a matter of churches, more the Church. Erasmus requested a General Council; Luther and Melanchthon sought it; Bucer, Calvin and Cranmer worked to this end, as did distinguished Catholics such as Contarini and von Pflug: Trent closed the door. Protestantism requires a general council to find acceptance and universal agreement.

Fourth, the Church and its relation to society – Luther thought of the Church and the state as two realms exercising *Obrigkeit* in society. Here he followed Romans and 1 Peter, and used the colourful terms 'God's Right Hand' and 'God's Left Hand'. In other words, both exercise divine authority. Zwingli and Calvin sought a closer relationship of the two realms. The Elizabethan Settlement followed Luther; the Reformed, the Independents and the Puritans followed Calvin: the Separatists opted out. The problem has grown acute in modern times with the rise of TOTALITARIANISM and the growth of SECULARIZATION. In this situation it is important for the Church to fulfil its proper role of preaching the KINGDOM OF GOD while, at the same time, not abrogating its responsibility to address, when necessary, the stewards of temporal power: to put to them their proper responsibilities while at the same time holding before the world (whether it heeds or not) the demands and promises of God's Kingship over all mankind. The two realms and the two roles must never be taken over by either party; neither must they be run one into the other.

Protestantism arose as a critical movement, and repudiates the charges of being heretical or schismatic, even though it falls out of the Catholic consensus. Catholicism has always had, and still has, its 'Protestants'. Protestantism is essentially a living, ongoing process, claiming to be activated by God, in and through our all too human institutions and our all too human understanding: *ecclesia reformata semper reformanda*. It is a pursuit of pure religious truth in the realms both of intellect and of being: it is necessarily divisive in a fallen world until the truths it emphasizes are recognized universally, or modified universally. (This principle is true of science and of theology.) Protestantism is more than a religious activity. It shoulders the responsibility of offering intellectual leadership in a secularized world: it has to out-think and out-live its pagan environment. It addresses the question of the nature of human beings and their role in the world. But, as Luther warned (and as Christ has taught us), this is no highway of glory but a veritable *via dolorosa*.

Atkinson, J. (1966) *Rome and Reformation*, London: Hodder & Stoughton.
—— (1968) *Martin Luther and the Birth of Protestantism*, Atlanta, GA: John Knox Press (2nd edn 1981).
Bainton, R.H. (1953) *The Reformation of the Sixteenth Century*, Boston, MA: Beacon Press.
Collinson, P. (1982) *The Religion of Protestants*, Oxford: Clarendon Press.
Dickens, A.G. (1966) *Reformation and Society*, London: Thames and Hudson.
Dillenberger, J. and Welch, C. (1954) *Protestant Christianity*, New York: Charles Scribner's Sons.
George, C.H. and George, K. (1961) *The Protestant Mind of the English Reformation*, Princeton, NJ: Princeton University Press.

Grimm, H.J. (1973) *The Reformation Era*, New York: Macmillan.

Lehmann, K. and Pannenberg, W. (1989) *The Condemnations of the Reformation Era*, Minneapolis, MN: Fortress Press.

Luther, D.M. (1883–) *D. Martin Luthers Werke. Kritische Gesamtansgobe, Abteilung Werke*, v.1– , Weinar (WA).

von Rohr, J. (1969) *Profile of Protestantism*, Belmont, CA: Dickinson Publishing Co.

Spitz, L. (1966) *The Protestant Reformation*, Englewood Cliffs, NJ: Prentice-Hall.

Tillich, P. (1948) *The Protestant Era*, Chicago, IL: University Chicago Press.

Whale, J.S. (1960) *The Protestant Tradition*, Cambridge: Cambridge University Press.

James Atkinson

PROVIDENCE

The idea of providence is first clearly articulated by Stoicism (third century BCE) as an essential aspect of its rational pantheism. For Stoicism the course of the universe, which is cyclical, manifests the order and reason of the Divine Word and this is *pronoia*, providence. The political implications of living in a rationally ordered universe were clearly drawn, especially by Roman thinkers such as Cicero (106–43 BCE) and Seneca (4 BCE to 65 CE). By following NATURAL LAW a political order which mirrored that of the physical world in its rationality, PEACE and stability could emerge. Stoics believed that all humans shared a spark of the Divine Word and that the individual should always respect the seed of the Word in others, regardless of class or race. Although a freed slave, Epictetus (*c*.50–138 CE), was one of Stoicism's leading teachers, Stoicism was never a radical political philosophy. Its belief in the universality of the Word was always more than balanced by its search for inner PEACE (*apatheia*) and self-control.

The Stoic idea of providence is in critical dialogue with many related ideas in the earlier Greek tradition, particularly those of *fate* (especially as expressed by the Greek dramatists), of Plato's purposeful World Reason and of Aristotle's teleology. In the Jewish and Christian scriptures by contrast there is no word for providence, but what takes its place is the idea of the lordship of God, guiding all things sovereignly for wise and loving ends. This applies as much to the realm of nature (Psalms 104, 107) as to

the historical realm where God's action is more particularly perceived. The story of Joseph illustrates how God uses human wickedness to bring salvation for many (Genesis 45: 5). The Biblical writers do not flinch from affirming that God's rule embraces EVIL as well as good (Isaiah 45: 7; Job) and can be seen in the confusion of human scheming (2 Samuel 17: 14). In the New Testament Jesus' teaching that God cares for the fall of a sparrow (Matthew 5: 26 f.; Luke 10: 29 f.) and that therefore people need 'have no care' for the necessities of life, together with the insistence that God answers prayer (Luke 11: 5 f.), became the cornerstone of much later Christian reflection. Paul echoes Plato in teaching that for those who believe all things work together for good (Romans 8: 28; cf. *Republic* 10: 612e). A philosophy of history already found in the story of the world empires in Daniel is developed by Paul into a picture of three ages, those of Abraham, Moses and Christ, which culminate in the unity and salvation of all humankind (Romans 5–11). According to this picture the church has a key role to play in God's providential scheme. For the entire New Testament, however, it is the Cross which is the paradigm of God's providence, illustrating how human SIN may be used as the means of redemption.

In the course of the second century texts such as these are understood as instancing providence (cf. Irenaeus, *Against the Heresies* 3: 25), and the Stoic concept is then personalized. Where the Stoic must seek to know natural law and live in accordance with it, the Christian must seek God's will, the exercise of which is providence. Origen (185–253) develops a THEOLOGY of providence understood as a process of EDUCATION, as fallen souls return through the spheres to the Logos. A distinction between general providence (God's rule by natural law) and special providence (guidance of some individuals) is already found in the pseudonymous Clementine *Recognitions* of about this period. Eusebius (*c*.260–340), in his *Ecclesiastical History*, saw God's providence at work in the spread of the gospel culminating in Constantine's conversion and the Christianizing of the Mediterranean world. With Augustine (354–430) the dimensions of the Christian doctrine of providence receive decisive shape. He follows Eusebius in seeing history as controlled by God's providence – even WAR is used by God, and bringing good from evil is the supreme triumph of providence (*Civ. Dei* 5.21/2); he takes from neo-Platonism the argument that evils are to be understood aesthetically, as highlighting the good (*de vera relig.* 40); most decisively providence is brought into the closest relation with predestination, God's foreknowledge and forewilling of all that will happen, including our free acts (*Civ. Dei* 5.9–11). Augustine had correctly understood that belief in fate was not compatible with providence as it excludes human free will and responsibility, but his theology of predestination is susceptible of a determinist reading. An immensely influential statement of faith in providence, close to Augustine but differing at some important points, was Boethius' *Consolations of Philosophy*, written in prison prior to his execution in 524–5 CE. Unlike Augustine Boethius preserves a role for fate, by which he means the chain of natural causes, in this following neo-Platonism. Providence is superior to fate and relates especially to God's interaction with free agents. Both Augustine and Boethius, the teachers of the medieval church as regards providence, were concerned more with the fate of the individual SOUL in the next life, and with problems of reconciling God's foreknowledge and human free will, than with any theology of history.

Augustine's arguments were followed both by Aquinas and Calvin, by both Catholic and Protestant orthodoxy. Thomism takes over Aristotelian ideas of natural law, understood as an expression of God's providential will. Although Aquinas allowed resistance to unjust rulers the political consequences of his view of providence are on the whole conservative. He is concerned to refute the millenarian views of Joachim of Fiore (1131–1202) who believed in a providential progress towards a historical eschaton, whose teaching prompted passionate hopes for a new order. Aquinas affirmed by contrast that the church exists to mediate the possibility of salvation hereafter. Change in history is relatively speaking unimportant. Although Augustinian views of history and providence could thus work conservatively, in practice belief in providence

either has often acted as a spur to action or has been invoked to legitimate action already taken, especially in Calvinist cultures. Thus seventeenth-century Holland understood the successful struggle against Spain as due to the providential selection of a new people to be a light to the nations. Cromwell invoked providence in the English Civil War, and the Boers in the Great Trek. Calvinists commonly saw God's hand in both success and disaster, the latter proving that the Lord chastens those he loves. A pagan echo of this was found in Adolf Hitler's claim that providence lay behind the rise of the Third Reich. When it comes to the individual Weber argued that Calvinists felt the need to prove their predestinate status by worldly activity: the doctrine of predestination, virtually assimilated to that of providence, was thus a driving force behind the work ethic.

Deism transposed the Calvinist belief in particular providence to a belief in divinely ordained laws which worked for the general good, a transposition which underwrote *laissez-faire* political philosophies: Malthus (1766–1834) argued that scarcity was ordained by providence to stimulate hard work; the evangelical Thomas Chalmers (1780–1847) tacitly equated Adam Smith's 'hidden hand' with providence and thus opposed both trade laws and poor relief. To intervene was to challenge God's just ordering of SOCIETY and to give free reign to the notorious licentiousness of the poor. SLAVERY was justified by Henry Irving (1792–1834) as 'a mystery of divine Providence' and Hannah More (1745–1833) believed social inequality to be part of the divine ordering of things. At the height of the Industrial Revolution, therefore, appeal to providence performed a crucial ideological function and was invoked to give divine sanction to policies deriving from Smith and Malthus.

Alongside Christian appeals to divine providence there is increasingly, from the seventeenth century onwards, a secular parallel. So Smith's capitalist is led by a 'hidden hand' to promote the common good even though he has only his own interests at heart. Hegel discerns 'the cunning of reason' at work in all historical process, leading to full secular freedom as manifested in the Prussian state. It is debatable whether this should be understood in a theistic sense. De

Tocqueville speaks of the rise of DEMOCRACY and the development of EQUALITY of conditions as 'a providential fact'. Marx speaks of class conflict as the necessary dynamic of history's evolution. For Comte the law of progressive evolution replaces the idea of providential government with 'rational prevision'. What takes the place of providence for these thinkers, in other words, is an idea of purpose in history and of progress towards an ideal STATE. The immense power of such secularized views of providence is clear in contemporary views of the peculiar 'destiny' of particular nations and peoples.

Enlightenment optimism and belief in progress was shaken by the Lisbon earthquake. The twentieth century has not only lived with far worse catastrophes but under the shadow of the nuclear threat, the threat of irreparable ecological damage and the threat of a burgeoning world population that the earth seems unlikely to be able to sustain. These facts have made belief in providence peculiarly difficult. Some scientists (Monod 1972; Dawkins 1991) have argued that the universe is characterized fundamentally by chance and were this the case belief in providence would not be possible, for wise ordering is part of its essence. Others (Bartholomew) have replied that when statistically understood chance gives rise to order and therefore they see the facts appealed to as stronger ground for faith in providence than ever before. This debate echoes classical debates about God's foreknowledge and free will. The political implications of living in an entirely contingent universe, where chance is the ruling factor, are the same as those which follow from strict determinism. Both make striving for a more just order futile. Contemporary doctrines of providence, on the other hand, which emphasize the way chaos gives rise to order, emphasize human intelligence and planning as a key product of evolution. Recent writers have gone to great lengths to show that a doctrine of providence free from the confusion of omnipotence with omnicausality is compatible with human freedom and not socially coercive.

It remains the case that the so called 'problem of evil' is in fact a problem of providence. If events are guided and ordered by a loving God, whence comes evil? The standard reply is some version of the 'free-will defence' – the argument that God seeks creatures who can freely respond in love, and that such creatures can only emerge in a rule-governed universe such as ours. Doctrines of providence have generally affirmed the possibility of miracle, of divine 'intervention'. But if God *can* intervene, why does God not do so a great deal more often, e.g. to prevent the Shoah? Some (Wiles 1986) respond to these difficulties by retreating to DEISM, and understand God as determining the initial conditions of creation but as remaining thereafter above the fray, save as we are able to relate to God in prayer. Pope's summary of Deist theology, 'The Universal Cause/Acts not by partial, but by general laws', was rejected by Wesley as being inconsistent with Scripture and it is doubtful whether Deism does justice to the Christian conception of God as loving, active and engaged. Christian prayer has taken from Jesus the command to pray for all needs, whereas for Deism prayer is more a search for self-knowledge.

The ideological use of appeals to providence makes clear the need for a HERMENEUTICS of suspicion. Belief in a God who acts makes attempts to discern God's will inevitable, but great caution is needed in proceeding to political judgements. Here as elsewhere the rule is that *crux probat omnia*, and failure to heed this rule in many classical statements of providence is their weakest point. In particular belief in providence, the belief that God is purposefully and lovingly active in the world, needs to be separated from belief in predestination and from omnipotence understood as omnicausality. Faith in God's omnipotence, properly understood, is faith that love is ultimately invincible. Belief in providence also needs to be critically separated from belief in fate, as expressed in horoscopes and other ways of divining the future, from karma and other determinist views of reality, and from trust in luck. Although belief in providence entails acceptance that there is meaning in history, it is not identical with a philosophy of history. Attempts to show that contemporary science is congenial to a theology of God's interaction with creation may have apologetic value but cannot ground a theology of providence. This remains faith in the engagement of the free God with the free creature, the God within whom all created reality exists, who sustains it in being whilst allowing it its own autonomy and freedom. That it cannot be stated without paradox does not make it irrational and it remains an essential and vital part of any living theism.

Aquinas, *Summa Theologiae 1a Qu 103–9.*
Augustine (1972) *The City of God*, Harmondsworth: Penguin.
Barth, K. (1977) *Church Dogmatics*, Edinburgh: T. & T. Clark, III/3.
Bartholomew, D. *God of Chance*, London: SCM.
Boethius (1969) *The Consolations of Philosophy*, Harmondsworth: Penguin.
Calvin, John (1986) *The Institutes of Christian Religion*, London: Hodder & Stoughton.
Cicero (1968) *De Officiis*, London: Heinemann (Loeb Classical Library).
Clementine, *Recognitions*, in J.P. Migne (ed.) *Patrologia Graeca* (1857–66), Paris: 1158–474.
Dawkins, R. (1991) *The Blind Watchmaker*, Harmondsworth: Penguin.
Hilton, B. (1988) *The Age of Atonement*, Oxford: Oxford University Press.
Löwith, K. (1949) *Meaning in History*, Chicago, IL: Phoenix.
Monod, J. (1972) *Chance and Necessity*, London: Collins.
Schama, S. (1987) *The Embarrassment of Riches*, London : Fontana.
Seneca (1985) *De Providentia*, London: Heinemann (Loeb Classical Library).
Wiles, M. (1986) *God's Action in the World*, London: SCM.

T.J. Gorringe

PUNISHMENT

Punishment is the intentional imposition of a penalty on an offender as a consequence of an offence committed. In order to distinguish punishment from revenge it is necessary that the penalty in question be imposed by an AUTHORITY entitled to do so; in order to distinguish it from acts of spitefulness and hostility it must be imposed as a consequence of a *wrongful* act. Punishment is therefore retributive by definition: it is done to a person in return for something he or she has done, usually in contravention of some rule or practice which is itself morally justifiable.

However, at least as far as the Christian tradition goes, the theological notion of punishment differs markedly from the secular concept. For God, as guardian of the moral order and creator of even the hurtful structures that SIN sets in motion, does not inflict punishments in retribution for wrongful actions, but rather allows them as expressions of God's own holy will. Since every occasion of sinning is in reality a summons to conversion, the refusal of conversion by a free agent amounts to a turning away from God. The resultant (perhaps temporary) loss of God is painful, and hence punishment is in some sense self-imposed. Thus punishment for sin in the sense captured in civil penal law is a possible, though only secondary, case of the metaphysical and theological notion of punishment which, strictly speaking, makes punitive agents and agencies superfluous. It follows that while HELL may be understood as the final estrangement and loss of God, it is not to be understood as the most drastic punitive measure of God's vengeance.

That punishment is retributive by definition settles no substantive moral questions. We must still ask whether there are good moral reasons which justify the practice of deliberately imposing distress on offenders. Do we need the practice of punishment? And if we do, why do we need it? The answers to those questions take the form of theories of punishment, each of which purports to give an account of who and what should be punished, as well as the reasons why, and what punishment is appropriate. Three principal justifications may be distinguished. The *retribution theory* of punishment claims that persons ought to get what they deserve for the wrongfulness of their actions simply because they deserve it. Thus a person must be punished if he has performed an action for which he deserves a penalty and must not be punished over and above what he has deserved, even if doing so would serve as a deterrent. Desert, therefore, is a necessary condition of a justified punishment. (It is not, however, sufficient, because of the possibility of forgiveness.) Unfortunately, the notion of desert, on which everything hangs here, is excessively vague. To say a punishment is 'deserved' seems merely another way of saying that it is 'fitting' or 'appropriate' that this person get this penalty, without explicating those terms in any satisfactory non-circular way. Perhaps the most promising further account is one which seeks to explain the appropriateness of a punishment in terms of the satisfaction of grievances: it is claimed that a punishment is fitting or deserved if it precisely satisfies the feelings of grievance the offence has given rise to. Clearly, however, such an account provides only an explanation and not a justification of the practice of punishment. That must await a convincing analysis of the concept of desert. The *deterrence theory* of punishment proceeds along quite different lines. Since punishment involves the deliberate infliction of avoidable suffering on a person it is regarded by some as intrinsically undesirable. Utilitarians, for example, demand that a punishment should serve some useful purpose other than the satisfaction of grievances. It should function to deter the offender and others from a repetition of similar offences, either by incapacitating him or by being sufficient to discourage such action by others. As it stands, however, this intention to deter is consistent with any amount of punishment and any punitive method which will effect deterrence. This may give rise to morally repugnant consequences so that, in order to ensure a necessary connection between the seriousness of a crime and the severity of its punishment, deterrence theorists have generally insisted that deterrence must be economical: a punishment is justified if it deters, if the distress caused is not greater than that which would result if the offence went unpunished and if there is no other punishment which causes less distress but produces an equally deterrent effect. Obviously, then, a utilitarian JUSTIFICATION of punishment is dependent upon the empirically verifiable claim that punishment does actually deter potential offenders and so reduce CRIME. But if it does depend on that claim, then it seems that many, if not most, current offenders are undergoing punishments of doubtful value. More fundamentally, it may be objected that punishment conceived as deterrence makes possible victimization, both of the innocent and of those who get a heavier penalty than they deserve, when doing so deters others from committing offences. This consequence contradicts our ordinary moral in-

tuition that a person may not be used merely as a means to someone else's ends, even when that end benefits SOCIETY as a whole. A third principal justification of punishment is the *reform theory*, which claims that a punishment is justified because it provides the opportunity to reform offenders. By aiming to reduce offences, punishment as reform appears to avoid the objection to retributive punishment that it enforces penalties even when no good results; by insisting reform is to be of offenders it avoids the objection to deterrence theory that it legitimates victimization. Nevertheless it remains unclear how the notion of reform could provide the entire justification of the practice of punishment since it depends on the somewhat unlikely claim that punishment itself has a reformative effect. It is probably best conceived as a part of each of the other justifications, serving to humanize them in important ways.

According to Foucault (1979), the history of punishment is the history of a movement from a focus on the body as the suitable object of punishment to a focus on the physical and psychological control of the wrongdoer. Prior to the Enlightenment, breaking the LAW was conceived of as a direct attack on the monarch, who was entitled to exact retribution for serious crimes by way of physical torture. This often disproportionate punishment of the criminal subject's body came to be seen as merely vengeful, and new 'moral technologies' were devised with the aim not to punish less but to punish better. This meant trying to establish a rational correspondence between kinds of offence and grades of punishment and reflected an attempt by the penal authorities to breed in the criminal not terror but penance. The later aim of the moral transformation of the criminal by the imposition of a regularity on her behaviour down to the very movements of her body remains a model for contemporary penal institutions.

The shift from bodily punishment to control over the wrongdoer's activity reflects changing views about who or what is wronged when a crime is committed and about the efficacy of different forms of punishment. When crime came to be regarded not as an attack on the sovereign or as an affront to God represented by the divinely appointed monarch, but rather as a breach of the social contract which jeopardized society as a whole, new methods of punishment had to be put in place which aimed to redress the wrong done to the community and restore the criminal to his proper place within it. Thus the goals of social contract theory and of utilitarianism combined to produce a degree of social control unknown in traditional societies. Still seen today, the logical development of this coalition was the 'surveillance' model of penal institution, represented in the horror of Bentham's panopticon, in which the offender becomes the subject of permanent inspection by the authorities.

The social practice of punishing individuals for offences faces various challenges today. For example, the increasing complexity of social developments and the controls necessary to regulate them, the increase in numbers of those prosecuted and the move away from purely physical punishments, all mean that the practice of punishment stands in as much need of rationalization and justification as it ever did. Yet the difficulties and weaknesses of each theory of punishment considered may suggest that each, by itself, cannot serve as a justification. Since punishment *must* be justified if it is not to be simply arbitrary, recent thinking has tended to combine the elements of each which best serve social ends, such as the stability of society. However, this move must be seen as highly questionable. For it is crucial to be clear about which principles are being employed and to keep them distinct – if only because the different approaches outlined will have very different implications for penal policy: even though retributivist and deterrence principles may occasionally agree upon a particular punishment, for instance, they are more likely most often to produce radically different decisions. For that very reason it is unacceptable to 'mix' the justifications and claim, for example, that the purpose of punishment is both to do what the offender deserves *and* to deter him and others from so acting in the future. If, for example, a retributivist allows in considerations based on deterrence then she is being unjust by her own standards – she believes X deserves a particular punishment for his offence but she then increases the amount of punishment X gets in order to deter others. Thus the application of the two principles, or a combination of them, will not have the same consequences for an offender – and, if they conflict, which one are we to apply in a particular case? This objection, some might say, is merely a pointless insistence on following rules for the sake of it. But in fact the objection raises an important issue: given that punishment is not merely a burden like other social burdens, which are to be distributed as justly as possible, but is itself an *instrument* of social JUSTICE, then an insistence on the consistent application of the principles governing it is not merely an insistence on following rules whatever they are. It is an insistence on following a rule of justice. And if justice mandates a certain practice and, as is claimed, justice claims are indefeasible, then it follows that every offender has an absolute right to a particular and identifiable form of punishment.

Second, and differently, there is a theory of human motivation and action which, if true, undermines both retributive and reform theories of punishment, and thus the very practice of punishment itself. If *determinism* is true, none of us is ultimately responsible for our actions and none of us, therefore, deserves either blame or praise. This poses a significant challenge to retributive justifications of punishment simply because it cannot be right to punish someone for something when they could not have done otherwise. Indeed, this view is already given some credence in the courts and is reflected in judgements which take into account factors such as social disadvantage. But the logical consequence of the determinist's claim that nothing is finally deserved is that retributivism should be abandoned as a justification for punishment – for even if it is acceptable in principle there is nothing to which it can apply in practice. Punishment as deterrence, however, may be justified even if determinism is true because *its* aim is simply to alter the ways in which it is in people's interests to act, rather than to assign responsibility. In this way, deterrence theory is supported by the theory of determinism because, though using different arguments, both make the notion of desert redundant. It nevertheless faces the serious problems and objections noted.

What justification of punishment we take up is a matter of the recommendation of a certain policy. That recommendation depends upon moral theory. But in dealing with matters of *justice* – and we are, since punishment is an instrument of social justice – some moral theories are more adequate than others in providing justifications. If punishment is just then it must proceed from a proper conception of justice which limits the role of 'benefit to society' and which takes account of socio-economic factors (Honderich 1989; *see* ATONEMENT; CRIME).

Bentham, J. (1843) 'Principles of penal law', in *The Works of J. Bentham*, ed. J. Bowring, Edinburgh: William Tait.

Fitzgerald, P.J. (1962) *Criminal Law and Punishment*, Oxford: Oxford University Press.

Foucault, M. (1979) *Discipline and Punish*, London: Allen Lane.

Hart, H.L.A. (1968) *Punishment and Responsibility*, Oxford: Oxford University Press.

Honderich, T. (1989) *Punishment: The Supposed Justifications*, Cambridge: Polity.

Kant, I. (1887) *Philosophy of Law*, trans. W. Hastie, Edinburgh: T. & T. Clark.

Mabbott, J.D. (1939) 'Punishment', *Mind*.

Pat Walsh

QUAKERISM

Quakers, members of the Religious Society of Friends, have no creeds. There are general assumptions, attitudes and practices, however, which characterize them. These may be said to constitute Quakerism. The basic assumption is that, as George Fox (1625–91), the founding father of Quakerism, put it, there is 'that of God in everyone' – the 'inward light', 'the Christ within', 'the seed'. By turning inwards and obeying the inward light, the believer is able to find a right relationship with God.

Originally AUTHORITY was threefold: the individual conscience as it was illuminated by the inward light; the process of testing individual conscience against the understanding of the wider Quaker community; and the teachings of the Bible. Progressively this third testing against Biblical authority has diminished as the individual conscience has been given greater weight.

WORSHIP for Quakers takes place in a context of silence where worshippers wait upon God and speak when they feel inspired to do so. Quaker business practice is a form of worship focused upon various items to be discussed. As there is no priest or minister, all decisions, be they spiritual or practical, are made by the whole group. A clerk is nominated who takes the 'sense of the meeting', but members do not vote.

Quaker social activity is characterized by 'testimony' and 'concern'. A 'testimony' is a corporate witness to a spiritual truth as it is implemented in everyday life. Thus right from the earliest days in the seventeenth century Quakers had a testimony to EQUALITY. They believed that all people were equal before God; hence they refused to use politeness codes, titles and forms of speech which divided people hierarchically. The spiritual equality of men and women was emphasized and the insights of other religious traditions were respected. Because they believed that speaking the TRUTH was an everyday requirement, they refused to take oaths as this would suggest that speaking under oath was somehow truer than ordinary speech. Many of these testimonies led to fierce persecution, imprisonment and sometimes DEATH. Quakers today still emphasize sexual and racial equality, simplicity of lifestyle, and truthfulness in word and deed.

Perhaps the best known of the testimonies is the PEACE testimony. Quakers, believing that there is that of God in all people, maintain that oppression and VIOLENCE done to others is a form of violence against God (*see* PACIFISM). This has led them to campaign against the death penalty in Britain and in a number of European countries and in favour of conscientious objection, both to serving in and paying for military institutions. In recent years many Quakers have been members of the Campaign for Nuclear Disarmament. In the United States, this peace witness led Quakers to work actively against American intervention in Vietnam and Iraq, as well as in various countries in South America. The connections they see between economic structures, oppression and social conflict have made social reform a consequence of Quaker spiritual insight. The influence of Quakers in these areas has far outweighed the smallness of the number of Quakers worldwide (which is about 220,000).

A 'concern' is an action which an individual Quaker or group of Quakers feel moved to promote or implement. A concern may become a testimony when taken up by the whole body of Quakers. For example, a number of Quakers at the beginning of the eighteenth century recognized SLAVERY as a form of human degradation. Within a few generations the whole Religious Society of Friends on both sides of the Atlantic had spoken out against slavery. Committees were formed to work for abolition and some Quakers were involved in the Underground Railroad, a scheme for helping runaway slaves. One modern form of this is the concern of some American Quakers to help refugees through the Sanctuary Movement.

The concern for EDUCATION has been reflected in the setting up of Quaker schools where the emphasis is on the development of the whole person and not just academic achievement. This concern for the whole person and individual worth is seen also in the way Quakers have made representation to government on issues such as housing, unemployment and poverty. In 1987 a statement was published by British Quakers in which they stated:

We are angered by actions which have knowingly led to the polarization of our country – into the affluent, who epitomize success according to the values of a materialistic society, and the 'have-leasts', who by the expectations of that same society are oppressed, judged, found wanting and punished.

We commit ourselves to learning again the spiritual value of each other.

Similarly reform in the areas of sexual discrimination and sexual orientation have been advocated, the latter receiving much publicity through the report 'Towards a Quaker View of Sex' which was written by a group of concerned Quakers in 1963.

Whereas in the past Quakers tended to work through their own philanthropic networks, today they work in close relationship with other Christian and non-Christian groups. They have been instrumental with others in founding Oxfam, Amnesty International and the Child Action Poverty Group, and the large Quaker Trusts, most notably set up by Rowntree and Cadbury, help finance many charitable foundations and lobbies for social reform. Many Quaker meeting houses have become centres for social action. Internationally there are Quaker offices with the United Nations and the European Union. Two areas of growth in recent years have been counselling and a care for the planet which has led to the creation of Quaker Green Concern, a network aiming to influence the larger body of Quakers in this area.

Bacon, M.H. (1986) *Mothers of Feminism, the Story of Quaker Women in America*, San Francisco, CA: Harper & Row.

Brock, P. (1990) *The Quaker Peace Testimony (1660–1914)*, York: Sessions.

Fox, G. (1975) *The Journal*, ed. John Nicholls, London: London Yearly Meeting.

Gillman, H. (1988) *A Light that is Shining, an Introduction to the Quakers*, London: Quaker Home Service; reprinted with amendments 1991.

Greenwood, J.O. (1975–8) *Quaker Encounters*, 3 vols, York: Sessions.

Isichei, E. (1970) *Victorian Quakers*, Oxford: Oxford University Press.

London Yearly Meeting (1960) *Christian Faith and Practice in the Experience of the Society of Friends*, London: London Yearly Meeting.

Punshon, J. (1984) *Portrait in Grey: A Short History of the Quakers*, London: Quaker Home Service, revised edn 1986.

Raistrick, A. (1950) *Quakers in Science and Industry*, Newton Abbot: David & Charles, reprinted 1968.

Harvey Gillman

RACISM

The concept of 'racism' depends upon that of 'race' although the two concepts are different. The existence of racism does not presuppose the truth of race as an explanatory category, but it does presuppose its existence as a concept. A 'race' denotes a group of people who are alleged to possess common physical characteristics of genetic origin. It is generally agreed that it is a misleading concept with no scientific basis. However, racism as a doctrine of superiority and inferiority is built upon the idea of race. To undermine the idea of race at an intellectual level does not necessarily affect the reality of racism in practice.

While racism as a developed doctrine was unknown in the ancient world, xenophobia and notions of 'barbarians' were common. In the Middle Ages, peasants were seen as inferior, descendants of Ham, a theme based on a Biblical text which was later to be used of black people (see APARTHEID). The word 'race' was first used in English in 1508 in a poem by William Dunbar, and first used as a biological concept by the French physician François Bernier in 1684. Carolus Linnaeus in 1735 argued for the existence of four races. Racial theory was expounded by the French anatomist Cuvier in the nineteenth century and was further developed by Arthur de Gobineau and others, though racial superiority was assumed by such writers as David Hume, John Locke and Charles Kingsley. After the appearance of Darwin's *Origin of Species* (1859), the ideas of racial contamination and degeneration were popularized through the 'science' of EUGENICS developed by Francis Galton.

In our own time the movement of sociobiology represents a fusion of evolutionary theory and modern population genetics and, whilst it is not intrinsically racist, it is often used to support racist positions. In general, however, theories of race and of racial superiority based on genetics are discredited today. There are no such realities as pure races, and this has led some writers to question the popular phrase 'race relations' as being based on a conceptual error.

The English word 'racism' was coined in the 1930s but does not appear in most dictionaries until the 1960s. *Webster's International Dictionary* included it for the first time in 1961, though Barnhart's *Dictionary of New English Since 1963* (1973) failed to do so. Both 'racism' and 'racialism' are missing from the *Oxford English Dictionary* of 1933. However, it was used by Ruth Benedict in the 1940s to refer to the IDEOLOGY and doctrine of racial superiority, and this was its original usage. Racism in this usage meant the doctrine that human behaviour is determined by stable inherited characteristics derived from separate racial stocks which have distinctive attributes and which are believed to stand to one another in relations of superiority and inferiority. Benedict saw racism as 'the new Calvinism'. In the early 1960s the term was often used to describe organized political groups ('racist organizations').

However, two changes have occurred since the late 1960s: a shift towards a structural concept of racism as embodied in institutions; and an approach which stresses cultural difference rather than superiority. This is sometimes called 'the new racism'. The idea of institutional racism owed much to Stokeley Carmichael and C.V. Hamilton, *Black Power* (1968). While it is still common to understand racism as a doctrine of inherent superiority, and therefore to deny its existence where such a doctrine is absent, crude biological notions of superiority are less common today, although they have not disappeared. Far more common are cultural ideas which stress the 'unity of the nation', defining national identity in a racialized way. Such racism is rooted in the memory of a mythical, imaginary past, a golden age of pure whiteness. The notion of purity is central to racism and is very destructive.

Accounts of racism tend to emphasize particular aspects and ignore others. Many see racism in terms of psychological models and so are inclined to take racism out of history. Others lay emphasis on racism as ignorance, and hence emphasize EDUCATION, ignoring the behavioural aspect which works through CULTURE. Emphasis on education can also ignore issues of power and economics which are central to racist practices. Some would approach racism by way of the concepts of pluralism and diversity. Roy Jenkins, when British Home Secretary in 1966, defined racial integration as 'not the flattening process of assimilation but equal opportunity accompanied by cultural diversity in an atmosphere of mutual tolerance'. The purely economistic approach tends to see racism as arising from competition in the labour market or in housing: hence, on this view, more resources, such as jobs and homes, should lead to less racism.

A reasonable working definition of racism is that it is an ideology and/or structure of actions in the public sphere, implicitly or explicitly based on a concept of racial difference as a policy category, which results in both disadvantage and discrimination for certain racially defined groups. Such a definition differentiates racism, which operates at the economic and political levels, from racial prejudice, which operates at the cultural and psychological levels. Thus discrimination in resource allocation is not simply due to the presence of prejudiced individuals but is part of a system. Racism is a feature of organizational structures. Such racism was firmly in place in Britain by the early 1950s.

Modern racism is inextricably bound up with the history of IMPERIALISM, a system of global domination with its accompanying cultural support structures. The main ethnic minorities in Britain come from a colonial background, those from the Caribbean from a colonial and slave background. In Britain since the late 1950s race relations have been linked with immigration control, and successive governments have argued that good race relations depend on tight controls.

While racism is more than racial prejudice, the extent of prejudice within a population is clearly connected with racism in its structures. The assessment of prejudice is notoriously difficult. A survey in 1984 by the Central Statistical Office, London, showed that nine out of ten people believed that Britain was a racially prejudiced society, and about 50 per cent believed that prejudice had worsened in recent years. However, high levels of prejudice in a population where the general tendency is towards EQUALITY may be less significant than low levels in a more ambivalent SOCIETY.

Race is certainly linked to CLASS but the links are complex. Much middle-class opposition to racism is of a liberal kind and avoids the realities of life in working-class communities. However, the refusal to accept the reality of working-class racism ignores the conclusions of much research. There is evidence that racial prejudice is strongest among unskilled manual workers. The election of a Fascist candidate in an East London council by-election suggests that working-class racism is a significant force in some areas.

Responses to racism vary according to the significance given to it. For some, attention to race as such evades more underlying issues and reinforces racial stereotypes. They would therefore argue for 'racial inexplicitness', focusing on economic deprivation and so on. This approach was encouraged in a book by the American sociologist William Julius Wilson, *The Declining Significance of Race* (1978), and it has been a feature of much British urban social policy. Wilson argued for the crucial importance of the urban economy and of the place of poor blacks within that economy. He urged attention to employment and social policy rather than to race as such.

For some, racism is a minority belief and attitude within a largely tolerant society. Thus Mr Justice Salmon, in sentencing offenders in the 'Notting Hill riots' of 1958, described them as 'a minute and insignificant section of the population'. Paul Gilroy has referred to this view as the 'coat of paint' view of racism: on this view, racism is an unfortunate blot on the landscape, but can be removed without fundamentally altering the shape of that landscape. Such a view tends to lead to an optimistic approach, emphasizing basic values of tolerance, goodwill and DEMOCRACY. Exponents of such an approach to racism might place emphasis on 'positive images' and on the need to oppose 'stereotypes'. They might emphasize psychological dimensions, sense of rejection, insecurity, poor self-image, the 'authoritarian personality', etc.

However, evidence suggests that racism is more deeply rooted and intertwined with the history and structures of society so that to disturb one element is to disturb the entire structure. This belief in structural racism has led to the creation of organizations to combat racism within structures. In Britain the Commission for Racial Equality, set up to implement the Race Relations Act, has developed codes of practice for employment and housing. While no British government has used the Act as a charter for racial JUSTICE, since 1981 there has been an increase in 'anti-racist strategies', promoted in the UK particularly by the Greater London Council. Such strategies include 'affirmative action' and 'contract compliance'. However, anti-racism has been criticized for encouraging the isolation of racism as a discrete and self-contained political formation, and some claim that it has exhausted its usefulness. There has been much criticism of bureaucratic anti-racism and 'managerial radicalism'. It has been claimed by some that many 'anti-racists' are mirror images of racists, with authoritarian attitudes, conspiratorial theories, etc. The MacDonald Inquiry (1988) into a murder in a school in Burnage (Manchester) was critical of 'symbolic moral anti-racism'.

The relationship of religion to race is complex. In the Hebrew Biblical tradition there is no concept of, and no word for, race in the modern sense: *ho genos ton anthropon* means the human race as distinct from animals and plants. Yet Christianity has played a central role in the growth, first, of anti-Judaism which developed into anti-semitic ideology (*see* ANTI-SEMITISM) and, second, of anti-black racism within the context of colonial slavery. It is equally clear that the Christian gospel has provided resources for resistance to racism (*see* BLACK THEOLOGY). Racism has been described as a litmus test or a barium meal, which reveals other disorders and injustices within the body politic. It therefore provides a vital area of self-scrutiny and self-criticism for religious communities and traditions.

Banton, Michael (1977) *The Idea of Race*, London: Tavistock.

Barker, Martin (1981) *The New Racism*, London: Junction.

Benedict, Ruth (1983) *Race and Racism*, London: Routledge & Kegan Paul.

Carmichael, Stokeley and Hamilton, C.V. (1968) *Black Power*, Harmondsworth: Penguin.

Cashmore, Ellis and Troyna, Barry (1983) *Introduction to Race Relations*, London: Routledge & Kegan Paul.

Davies, Alan (1988) *Infected Christianity: A Study of Modern Racism*, Kingston and Montreal: McGill-Queens University Press.

Gilroy, Paul (1987) *There Ain't No Black in the Union Jack: the Cultural Politics of Race and Nation*, London: Hutchinson.

Kovel, Joel (1988) *White Racism: a Psychohistory*, London: Free Association Books.

MacDonald, Ian *et al.* (1989) *Murder in the Playground: the Burnage Report*, London.

Smith, Susan J. (1989) *The Politics of Race and Residence*, Cambridge: Polity.

Solomos, John (1989) *Race and Racism in Contemporary Britain*, Basingstoke: Macmillan.

West, Cornel (1993) *Race Matters*, Boston, MA: Beacon Press.

Wilson, William J. (1978) *The Declining Significance of Race*, Chicago, IL: University of Chicago Press.

Kenneth Leech

RADICAL THEOLOGY

Radical theology in the USA during and after the 1960s was almost synonymous with 'death of God' theologies. The Protestant theologians Thomas J.J. Altizer, William Hamilton, Gabriel Vahanian and Paul Van Buren and the Jewish theologian Richard Rubenstein are most often associated with the appearance of radical theologies in America and John A.T. Robinson to a lesser extent in England.

Langdon Gilkey in an assessment of both the appearance and importance of radical theologies argues that the key to understanding the ferment surrounding these theologies is to comprehend '[1] the dissolution of neoorthodox theology, [2] the character, scope, and power of the secular spirit in the American cultural and so Church scene, and [3] to see the resulting radical theology as an attempt to interpret Christianity, as Bonhoeffer said, in worldly terms' (1969: 109).

The theological debate of the 1960s was more concerned about the meaning than the validity of theological discourse (Gilkey 1969: 13). One of the characteristics of all the radical theologies was that they marked a linguistic turn in theological thinking. The radical question was whether THEOLOGY was possible as a mode of meaningful discourse. This question was itself meaningful because the radical theologians could not locate within their predominately secular experience a transcendent dimension for which theological discourse was necessary for its expression and understanding. The radical theologians were united in their insistence that theology must address what is real here and now in the actuality of history. This meant nothing less than an affirmation of the unreality of God for our age. The self was understood as autonomous rather than theonomous and theological language was transformed into anthropological language (*see* AUTONOMY).

The declaration of the death of God had different meanings among these radical theologians. When Vahanian spoke of the death of God he was marking the end of Christian culture and proclaiming a new religiosity that could rise from the empty tomb of the dead God (Altizer 1967: 256). For Hamilton it was both the EVIL of the world and the absence of God in his own experience that made it impossible for him to believe in God (Gilkey 1969: 116). Van Buren did not think that any talk of God could be verifiable or falsifiable and therefore it did not meet a standard of meaningful discourse for an empirically oriented age (Gilkey 1969: 124). Altizer proclaimed a radically kenotic Christianity in which the transcendent God became fully immanent in the incarnation. The incarnation was the eternal death of the transcendent God (Altizer 1966). Rubenstein claimed: 'If there is a God of history, he is the ultimate author of Auschwitz. I am willing to believe in God, the holy nothingness . . . , but never again in a God of history' (Rubenstein 1966: 204).

These theologians are not saying the same thing but there are some common implications to their proclamations of the death of God and affirmations of the impossibility of meaningful discourse about transcendent reality. First, the human subject is privileged as an author and actor in human history. Second, the referent for theological discourse is the self in history and society. Third, history and society are secular.

Christian radical theologians turned their attention to Jesus as an ethical role model or as an exhaustive expression of the meaning of LOVE here and now. Human existence was interpreted without appeal to mythological, supernatural, suprahistorical or divine entities (Gilkey 1969: 114). The agent within theological discourse was fully human even when the discourse was centred on Jesus. Rubenstein defines the theological problem as 'how to speak of religion in an age of no God' and affirms that 'in a world devoid of God we need Torah, tradition, and the religious community far more than in a world where God's presence was meaningfully experienced' (Rubenstein 1966: 152–3). Jewish

and Christian radical theologians alike emphasized the role of the human subject within SOCIETY holding together the tenuous weave of civilization.

In John Robinson's *Honest to God*, he concludes the preface by saying that, although the book may sound too radical, 'in retrospect, it will be seen to have erred in not being nearly radical enough' (1963: 10). The course of radical theology from the 1960s to the 1990s demonstrates the prescience of his insight as it bears not only upon his work but also on the American radical theologies. What began with the proclamation of the death of God has been extended through a deconstructive hermeneutic to a displacement of the subject, the end of meaningful history and the closure of the book as a self-sufficient unity.

American radical theology that developed from or remained in conversation with the continuing work of Altizer came to ally itself with French deconstructionist philosophy. It directly confronted Jacques Derrida's claim that DECONSTRUCTION 'blocks every relationship to theology' (Taylor 1984: 6). Mark C. Taylor went so far as to claim that 'it would not be too much to suggest that *deconstruction is the "hermeneutic" of the death of God*' (1984: 6) and Carl Raschke claimed that deconstruction 'is in the final analysis *the death of God put into writing*' (Altizer *et al.* 1982: 3). What has been challenged in radical theology in its alliance with deconstructive philosophy is the whole of the Western ontotheological tradition. What is challenged is that *being* can be understood as a presence to consciousness and what is affirmed is that identity is made determinate in a play of differences.

It is clearly the writings of Jacques Derrida and Martin Heidegger that first pressured theology to contemplate its end as a correlate to the end of philosophy and the collapse of the ontotheological tradition. Heidegger had long been associated with theological thinking in the twentieth century but Derrida was not part of the theological conversation in any important way until the publication of Carl Raschke's *The Alchemy of the Word: Language and the End of Theology* in 1979, *Deconstruction and Theology* by Altizer *et al.* in 1982, followed by Taylor's very influential *Erring: A Postmodern*

A/theology published in 1984 and Charles E. Winquist's *Epiphanies of Darkness: Deconstruction in Theology* in 1986.

The questions that are persistently asked are whether theology is possible at the end of the twentieth century and, if it is possible, whether it is meaningful.

Taylor set the agenda for much of this theological discussion with his programmatic interrogation of the challenges to theological thinking in Part I of *Erring*. Part I is subtitled 'Deconstructing theology' and it is here that he argues for an intricate relationship between God, self, history and book (Taylor 1984: 7): this is then followed by analyses of the death of God, the disappearance of the self, the end of history and the closure of the book.

The metaphorics of transgression that Taylor and other radical theologians sought to articulate are not simple negations. They are not simply putting a minus sign in front of a term to create a dyadic opposition. Reversal and 'inversion, in other words, must simultaneously be a perversion that is subversive. . . . What is needed is a critical lever with which the entire inherited order can be creatively disorganized. It is at this point that deconstruction becomes a potential resource for the a/theologian' (Taylor 1984: 10).

What drove radical theological reflection into a post-modern sensibility is that the death of God is coincident with the death of the self. What is lost with the death of God is a fixed meaning of presence that grounds identity. 'In the ontotheological tradition of the West, God is virtally indistinguishable from the power of Being or Being-itself' (Taylor 1984: 36). The ontotheological tradition has construed God as the permanent substratum of things including the identity of the self.

The constituting of the self as subjectivity, an achievement of Cartesianism, privileges what is present to consciousness as the meaning of reality. But, this construction of the self is not its own ground. Just as the *I am* is grounded in the *I think*, the *I think* is implicated in the *I am*. 'The *I am*, being experienced as an *I am present*, itself presupposes the relationship with presence in general, with being as presence' (Derrida 1973: 54). That is, the *I think* means *I am*

present for which a notion of presence is a condition of its possibility. The death of God as a deferral of presence unmoors the certainty of the *cogito*. The self that first appeared to be able to stand over against God in a humanistic liberation now appears to have been implicated in the meaning of God as its own condition when inscribed within the ontotheological tradition. Both self and God are eclipsed with the deconstruction of the ontotheological tradition. The death of God and the disappearance of the self are both metaphorical expressions of the deferral of presence.

Deconstructive analyses have also been extended to the concepts of history and the book. These concepts carry with them shadows of *logocentrism* and they are theological notions.

What is intriguing in Taylor's analyses is that he sees that the death of God proclaimed by Nietzsche follows the proclamation of *absolute knowledge* by Hegel. It is Hegel's proclamation of absolute knowledge that is both the end of history and the closure of the book. Absolute knowledge is total presence. There is nowhere to go. The notion of meaningful history has come to an end and Hegel is the last philosopher of the book (Taylor 1984: 76). Logocentric full presence forms an ordered totality and is the possibility for a book of encyclopaedic proportions. With the transgression of the ontotheological tradition there is no proper book. The gathering of meaning is a dispersal.

When history ends but time continues and the book is closed but never complete, Western thought begins to drift and its centre is displaced. There can no longer be an appeal to a centred and unified subject to ground theology. Theological subjectivity is constituted as it is written into and dispersed throughout the theological text. Radical theologies are marked by an epistemological undecidability. That is, without a ground they refuse totalization and so there are always excesses that are other than the theological text and have an undecidable quality. The traces of that which is 'other' in the formulation of theological concepts will manifest themselves in fissures, gaps and incongruities on the surface of theological texts. Radical deconstructive theologies read against the grain of their own texts and the texts of tradition to open theology to the voices and force of that which is other than itself. Radical theologies are ethically implicated in rending the completeness of their own textual achievements in valuations of the 'other' and the 'other of language'.

Radical theology is not now and has never been a coherent and unified movement. There have been common themes and sometimes shared interrogative strategies in the development of a theological vision but what has not been held in common is the sense of the community to whom they are speaking and from which they are speaking. The displacement of a centred and unified subject has significant implications for the definition of community and society. The autonomous self of the early death of God theologies has now given way to a heteronomous self that does not ground a single definition of community.

The agenda of radical theology is still open to the question of whether there can be an operable community. It is open to the question of whether there can be ethical decidability in the context of epistemological undecidability. Without a transcendent referent, radical theology must understand its text as a social text and it is a social text that is a dispersion and inscription of multiple, diverse, concrete subjectivities. What is most radical in contemporary radical theologies is the sense of the 'other' not as 'wholly other' but as a 'concrete other' that matters and pressures the meaning of any theological discourse.

Altizer, T.J.J. (1963) *The Gospel of Christian Atheism*, Philadephia, PA: Westminster.
——(ed.) (1967) *Toward a New Christianity: Readings in the Death of God Theology*, New York: Harcourt, Brace & World.
——et al. (1982) *Deconstruction and Theology*, New York: Crossroad.
Derrida, Jacques (1973) *Speech and Phenomena*, trans. David B. Allison, Evanston, IL: Northwestern University Press.
Gilkey, L. (1969) *Naming the Whirlwind: The Renewal of God-Language*, Indianapolis, IN: Bobbs-Merrill.
Hamilton, W. (1961) *The New Essence of Christianity*, New York: Association Press.
Raschke, C. (1979) *The Alchemy of the Word: Language and the End of Theology*, Chico, CA: Scholars Press.
Robinson, J.A.T. (1963) *Honest to God*, Philadelphia, PA: Westminster.
Rubenstein, R. (1966) *After Auschwitz*, Indianapolis, IN: Bobbs-Merrill.
Scharlemann, R. (ed.) (1990) *Theology at the End of the Century: A Dialogue on the Postmodern with Thomas J.J. Altizer, Mark C. Taylor, Charles E. Winquist and Robert P. Scharlemann*, Charlottesville, VA: University Press of Virginia.
Taylor, M. (1984) *Erring: A Postmodern A/theology*, Chicago, IL: University of Chicago Press.
Vahanian, G. (1961) *The Death of God*, New York: Braziller.
Van Buren, P. (1963) *The Secular Meaning of the Gospel*, New York: Macmillan.
Winquist, C.E. (1986) *Epiphanies of Darkness: Deconstruction in Theology*, Philadelphia, PA: Fortress.

Charles E. Winquist

RAPE

Increasingly since the 1960s sexual intercourse without consent is taken to constitute rape in the Western world. Dictionary entries have become outdated. For not very long ago physical VIOLENCE was taken to be intrinsic to the notion of rape (from the Latin *rapere*, to seize). It was also more or less assumed that rape occurred only between strangers. Certainly, the LAW did not recognize the possibility that a wife might be raped by her husband. Now the idea of rape within marriage is no longer thought a contradiction in terms. Legislation has been changed, or is in the process of being changed, throughout the West so as to ensure that a husband can be prosecuted for raping his wife. Date-rape is increasingly also a subject of discussion within the media as well as the law courts. More and more neither the way a woman chooses to dress nor her being in certain places is considered to constitute an invitation to be raped. The former commonplaces – that women ask for it, that 'no' means 'yes', that a woman's acceptance of an invitation licenses a man to do anything he pleases to her – seem now to be widely rejected.

Within a very short time much has been achieved in changing attitudes to women in general and to rape victims in particular. The law of rape has been the subject of much revision. Police and court-room procedures pertaining to rape cases are being reassessed with a view to ensuring that rape victims are no longer treated as though *they* were the defendants, the true culprits in the matter (*see* POLICING). Many of these improvements are owed to the commitment of various feminist pressure groups, as well as to the increase in the number of women within the legal profession and politics. Much remains to be done, however. Victims of rape must be guaranteed greater protection from the prying gaze of the public; the police must ensure that its methods in rape cases are such that no-one will be deterred from reporting the CRIME; rapists must not only be prosecuted but must receive appropriate sentences; and so on. Moreover, trends can change, the course of public opinion by no means always follows the enlightened path. Prejudices can return with renewed rigour after seemingly irrevocable periods of EMANCIPATION as, for instance, the history of European Jews demonstrates all too clearly.

To be sure, rape has always been considered a great EVIL and, though the nature of the penalty varied from period to period, it has been thought to deserve the severest of punishments for millennia. Defined as the unlawful carnal knowledge of a woman by force and against her will, rape, as Antony Simpson has noted, was a capital crime already in early Anglo-Saxon times. Moreover, it was deemed a crime even where legal codes said nothing of it. Thus, natural rights theorists, such as the Chevalier de Jaucourt (1704–80), one of the main contributors to the *Encyclopédie* (1751–72), used rape as an example in his article 'Naturel' (vol. XI) to illustrate the difference between positive and NATURAL LAW. Jaucourt cited the argument which Cicero (106–43 BC) had made in *De Legibus* (*c*.46 BC) that

even if there was no written law against rape at Rome in the reign of Lucius Tarquinius, we cannot say on that account that Sextus Tarquinius did not break that eternal Law by violating Lucretia, the daughter of Tricipitinus! For reason did exist, derived from the Nature of the universe, urging men to right conduct and diverting them from wrongdoing, and this reason did not first become Law when it was written down, but when it first came into existence; and it came into existence simultaneously with the divine mind.
(II. iv. 10)

Nor should it be thought, as it used frequently to be claimed in the early stages of feminist debates about rape, that the issue of rape was somehow silenced in the past and that it took the late twentieth century to place it on the political agenda. Nothing could be further from the TRUTH. Though they mostly considered rape not so much from the point of view of individual women but from that of society as a whole, political theorists warned princes of the consequences of rape. Machiavelli (1469–1527), for one, stressed the political danger it presented. 'Among the primary causes of the downfall of tyrants,' he argued in *The Discourses* (*c*. 1516–18), 'Aristotle puts the injuries they do on account of women, whether by rape, violation or the breaking up of marriages ... absolute princes and rulers of republics should not treat such matters as of small moment, but should bear in mind the disorders such events may occasion and look to the matter in good time, so that the remedy applied may not be accompanied by damage done to, or revolts against, their state or their republic' (III, 26).

Amongst those who wrote about rape, some like St Augustine (AD 354–430) stressed that the victim of rape was untainted by it. 'There will be no pollution, if the lust is another's; if there is pollution, the lust is not another's,' he contended in the *City of God* (413–26), adding, 'while the mind's resolve endures, which gives the body its claim to chastity, the violence of another's lust cannot take away the chastity which is preserved by unwavering self-control' (I, 18). Critical of Roman culture and the importance it gave to honour, St Augustine criticized Lucretia for taking her life following her rape by Tarquin. Christian women, St Augustine argued, 'did not take vengeance on themselves for another's crime' (I, 20). The public gaze did not unduly concern them, for they knew themselves to be chaste in the sight of God. In the seventeenth century, the jurist Samuel Pufendorf (1632–94) was one of the many authors who reiterated St Augustine's point, although he stressed that this did not impinge on the right of women to kill their aggressors in the course of defending themselves (*Of the Laws of Nature*, II, 5, 11). Commenting on *The Laws*, Jean Barbeyrac (1674–1744) drew attention to the fact that, under several ancient legal systems, seducers were actually thought worse than rapists, because they violated not only the body of their victims but effectively their mind as well, and hence exercised power over their whole person and over their family (ibid.).

To recognize that we are by no means the first to attend to the issue of rape is not to presume, however, that rape is a timeless or universal feature of social existence. Women have not always lived in fear of rape, at least not to the extent to which they now do in some parts of the Western world. Anthropological and historical studies reveal some societies and ages to be far more 'rape-prone' than others. In 'Rape and the silencing of the feminine' (in Tomaselli and Porter 1989) Peggy Reeves Sanday has compared societies which respect nature and protect the vulnerable and those which do not and has found that in the former women are almost entirely safe from rape, whereas they live under its constant threat in the latter. Similarly, while rape was not an infrequent fictional topic in the eighteenth century (e.g. Samuel Richardson's *Clarissa*, 1747–8), there is good reason to believe that women had remarkably little grounds to fear travelling extensively, even on their own. Rape thus seems to admit of a history over and above the history of the law pertaining to it.

In fact, it was during the eighteenth century that conjectural histories of woman were first put forward which provided an account of how the advent of civil SOCIETY and development of civilization had emancipated women from the physical tyranny of men. A number of thinkers, including Jean-Jacques Rousseau (1712–78) who collaborated with Louise-Marie-Madeleine Dupin (1706–99) in this project, as well as Denis Diderot (1713–84), outlined theoretical histories of woman to parallel the theoretical histories of man which underpinned contemporary views of the nature of modern commercial society. These presented mankind as moving ever further from the state of nature. While some authors, most notably Rousseau, thought of this process in terms analogous to the FALL – since man, in entering civil society, lost his original innocence, alienated himself from his true nature and chained himself to a spiral of needs – no-one

thought of the rise of civilization in anything but a positive light when they considered the history of mankind from woman's point of view. The reason for this was that on all accounts the condition of women, however deplorable in civil society, was incomparably worse in the state of nature. Prior to society, men knew no restraint on their behaviour and, being physically stronger than women, oppressed women at their will. As one woman was as good as another to any one man, there was no incentive for men to be pleasing. They simply satisfied their lust. They did not seek the desire of the other. Only with the beginnings of society and civilization did men learn to desire being desired as they found themselves having particular objects of desire. This enticed them to become attractive to women and hence to treat them with respect and decorum. Men ceased raping. They used language where they had previously used force and each individual sought to distinguish himself from the rest of his sex. Women therefore gained by the growth of INDIVIDUALISM and all that went with it, according to these theories, such as the establishment of private PROPERTY, the institution of the FAMILY and of MARRIAGE, the development of manners and politeness, the urge to shine in the eyes of others – in other words, everything which Rousseau and others after him thought as making for the enslavement of men. The liberty of women was thus grounded on the subjection of men to the taming influence of CULTURE. Indeed, it was a characteristic view of the Enlightenment that the condition of women in any society constituted a thoroughly reliable index of its level of civilization.

Whatever one's reservations about theoretical history in general or its eighteenth-century version in particular, applying this model to society in the twilight of the twentieth century highlights some of the contradictions peculiar to our times. As our ignorance of the history of women recedes, it is becoming clear that at various times some women have made great contributions in all fields of knowledge and in every profession. Nevertheless, it is indisputable that never have so many been able to do so much as at present. Slow and painful though the process may be, it would seem that equality of opportunity in every sphere is within our daughters' or granddaughters' grasp. What is far more uncertain is whether they will enjoy as much freedom from violence and violation as the generations before them. However respected women might be in their professional or working capacity, or again within the circle of their family and friends, very many in the West also inhabit a world which is terrifyingly similar to the state of nature depicted in Enlightenment conjectural histories of women. Large numbers of women live in fear of rape and there is little sign that this will change.

Theorists who consider all heterosexual intercourse as rape have nothing to contribute to any debate about what is to be done, except to suggest the complete segregation of the sexes and realignment of sexual preferences within a society of test-tube babies. The rest must place their trust in the power of culture. Somehow it is failing to civilize at least a sizeable proportion of males. Some men, it would seem, do not aspire to the desire of the other. They treat women as though they were mere things. The question therefore is: 'What is it about our culture that it allows men, even only some men, to consider women as nothing but things?'

At least part of the answer to this question is by no means novel. A society which constantly presents women as commodities, as objects of lust, whether in pornographic films and magazines or in seemingly more acceptable media, which shies from inculcating morals, which discourages all talk of restraint and self-control, which glorifies acquisition and the satisfaction of appetites regardless of their nature, such a society encourages men to think of women as things. Indeed, it encourages women to see themselves as things. Such a society has no possible remedy for rape. It may, thanks to the continued efforts of feminists and women in the legal profession, have a legal system which expresses loudly and clearly the contempt in which it holds rapists. It may encourage women to acquire techniques and instruments of defence. It may even have relatively efficient means of catching rapists; but it will not put an end to rape. Insightful though eighteenth-century theories about the condition of women might be, it is

obvious that its improvement cannot be left to the passing of time.

In *The Genealogy of Morals* ([1887] 1956), Friedrich Nietzsche (1844–1900) wrote:

No act of violence, rape, exploitation, destruction, is intrinsically 'unjust', since life itself is violent, rapacious, exploitative, and destructive and cannot be conceived otherwise. Even more disturbingly, we have to admit that from the biological point of view legal conditions are necessarily exceptional conditions, since they limit the radical life-will bent on power and must subserve, as means, life's collective purpose, which is to create greater power constellations. To accept any legal system as sovereign and universal – to accept it, not merely as an instrument in the struggle of power complexes, but as a *weapon against struggle* (in the sense of Dühring's communist cliché that every will must regard every other will as its equal) – is an anti-vital principle which can only bring about man's utter demoralization and, indirectly, a reign of nothingness.

(XI)

Those who, like Cicero, endorse a NATURAL LAW theory and who believe natural law to be the expression of God's will have no difficulty in arguing what is wrong about rape. Nor should they face too much difficulty in making a case for a moral community which enforces certain ideals of conduct with respect to others and themselves. Those who do not ground their moral theories in a theocentric framework will have to come to terms with the fact that liberty is not an empty ideal, a licence for anything, and that the liberty of women is conditional on the struggle against their being considered in any way men please, in other words that, as Nietzsche contended, wills cannot be regarded as equal. The law is indeed an instrument of struggle; it is one of the means by which society struggles against barbarism. Others must be deployed to make for a culture in which sex is not conceived as something individuals have a right to, nor independently of personal relationships and the duties and responsibilities they entail. This will not be the reign of nothingness, it will be the assertion of the will of civilized women, and men.

Augustine of Hippo (1972) *Concerning the City of God against the Pagans*, trans. David Knowles, Harmondsworth: Penguin.

Barnes, Toronto L. (1977) *Rape: Bibliography 1965–1975*, New York: Whitson.

Brownmiller, Susan (1975) *Against Our Will: Men, Women and Rape*, New York: Simon & Schuster and London: Secker & Warburg; republished Harmondsworth: Penguin, 1977.

Cicero (1977) *De Re Publica, De Legibus*, trans. Clinton Walker Keyes, Cambridge, MA: Harvard University Press (Loeb Classical Library).

Donaldson, Ian (1982) *The Rapes of Lucretia: A Myth and its Transformation*, Oxford: Clarendon.

Groth, Nicholas (1979) *Men Who Rape*, New York: Penguin.

Nietzsche, Friedrich (1956) *The Birth of Tragedy and The Genealogy of Morals*, trans. Francis Golffing, Garden City, NY: Doubleday.

Pufendorf, Samuel (1759) *Le Droit de la Nature et Des Gens ou Système Général des Principes les Plus Importants de la Morale, de la Jurisprudence, et de la Politique*, trans. Jean Barbeyrac, Leiden: Wetstein.

Simpson, Antony E. (1987) 'Vulnerability and the age of female consent: legal innovation and its effect on prosecutions for rape in eighteenth-century London', in G.S. Rousseau and Roy Porter (eds) *Sexual Underworlds of the Enlightenment*, Manchester: Manchester University Press, pp. 181–205.

Tomaselli, Sylvana and Porter, Roy (eds) (1989) *Rape: An Historical and Social Enquiry*, Oxford: Basil Blackwell.

Sylvana Tomaselli

REALISM

Realism is a wide-ranging term that is found in metaphysics, in epistemology and in political theory, particularly contemporary international relations theory. As a philosophical doctrine its clearest and best known foundation occurs in Plato's theory of forms, the view that what appears participates in some ideal form or set of forms – hence that which is phenomenal is appearance and that which is real is not immediately apparent to us but needs to be exposed through philosophical investigation. Latterly realism in philosophy has come to refer to any doctrine that holds that there is a world independent of the theories that are held about it and/or that there is a world that can be discovered rather than constituted by theory, language or sign. As a claim about what exists it is a metaphysical doctrine, and as a claim about what can be known it is epistemological. In politics realism refers to that body of thought best represented in Machiavelli and which maintains that the actions of Princes should be effective oriented towards their own and best interests and not to some ideal or Utopian vision. In international relations theory this view is extended to treat the state rather than individuals as actors. It is accompanied by the normative claim that states ought to act in their own best interest in international affairs rather than in the collective interest. The Nixon–Kissinger attitude towards US foreign affairs is a clear modern exemplar. In theology realism centres around the claim that God exists independently of the claims that are made about him, but can nevertheless be discovered. Discovery is by revelation. Realism in all these cases is opposed to idealism, the claim that the world does not exist independently of the theories, ideas or linguistic formulations that are held about it, or that individuals not states are actors or that God does not exist independently of the way in which he is understood.

All complex discourse is to do with the manipulation of signs, whether verbal, symbolic or numeric. Realism is interested not in the sign as a thing in itself, but in that to which it refers, and in the adequacy of its reference. If a sign's reference is too adequate, then it may substitute for that to which it refers, and here realism would turn into its opposite and become an idealism, substituting a *phenomenology* for an *ontology*. In practice, this might well lead to formalism in science and FUNDAMENTALISM in THEOLOGY. Alternatively, if the relation between the sign and that to which it refers is loose, questions of the correspondence of TRUTH to reality fall away and are replaced by criteria of effectiveness or by a coherence theory of truth. In practice, this might lead to pragmatic instrumentalism in science and to moralizing exhortation in theology. If realism is to refer to an independent reality, under the correction and control of that reality, then it must be self-critical and always aware of its own inadequacy.

This illustrates that in theology at least

realism is not a substantive doctrine but an epistemological claim which may occur in many different areas. As an epistemological claim it only occurs as part of an *ecology*, and operates in contrast to idealism, which itself encompasses empiricism and rationalism. Under certain circumstances, extreme realism can invert and, as shown, become its opposite, a kind of idealism. At a more basic level, it must be noticed that the context in which an epistemological view is located is of fundamental importance. Modern idealism has flourished where there is an overall context in which the human observer has evolved theoretical structures (theories) that take appearances as basic. Realism in theology will only flourish where there is a context of *unitary* thinking, i.e. where the human observer allows theoretical structures to evolve in dialogue with concrete experience of reality. So the possibility of realism is located in the more ultimate question of the absence of dualism. This will be illustrated next.

The modern debate over realism in theology begins with the Reformation and Renaissance. The Italian humanists of the fourteenth and early fifteenth centuries were hostile to the scholastic method and its procedure of deductively unpacking what was already known. This was a concentration on theory in abstraction from concrete experience. Lorenzo Valla in *Dialecticae disputationes contra Aristotelicos* (1499) attempted to devise a new way of framing questions so that what was genuinely new could be allowed to emerge. He was followed by the Renaissance lawyers Rodolph Agricola of Heidelberg and John Calvin of Geneva. Calvin applied this to the interpretation of scripture, becoming the first 'modern' Biblical scholar. Francis Bacon applied it to the interpretation of nature, becoming the initiator of modern empirical science.

What we seen here is an attempt both in empirical science and in theology to understand their object through its own self-disclosure, and not in accordance with received authorities (church traditions) or abstract rationalist assumptions. This was unitary or integrative thinking in which the theoretical element of knowledge was integrated with actual experiential contact. It was in contrast to a dualist method in which the theoretical element was separated from experiential contact, and there was the attempt to state in advance how we know in the abstract from what we know.

However, through Galileo's (1564–1642) and Descartes' (1596–1650) separation of primary and secondary qualities, where primary qualities alone were subject to mathematics, and Newton's (1643–1727) distinction between absolute and relative time and space, the idea re-emerged, even more powerfully, that knowledge is what is mathematically determinate, and so the separation between the theoretical (which yielded knowledge) and the experiential (which yielded only what was uncertain) reopened.

Into this arena David Hume (1711–76), who believed that we only have knowledge of immediate sense impressions, threw his bombshell that the principle of causality corresponded to nothing in reality but was merely a convenient habit of mind. This forced Immanuel Kant (1724–1804), attempting to save the foundations of Newtonian science, to ask under what conditions knowledge is possible. Kant argued that if anything is to be an object of human knowledge in a public world, it must necessarily fall under certain categories (which included cause and effect) and be within time and space. This was his 'Copernican revolution' in which, rather than the mind gradually evolving principles out of nature, the mind imposed them upon it.

Kant's philosophy was immensely influential and set the agenda for all who came after him. By making an absolute distinction between the unknowable thing in itself and the processed thing which is known, Kant made it literally meaningless to ask what something can be in itself. It followed that it was impossible even to state realism. Faith was removed from the realm of rational thought, and a mechanistic science was directed down the path of technology. This raised the question of whether his system was philosophically sound. By giving a methodological primacy to the human knower, Kant made knowledge always a knowledge-for-us. A realist will ask: may we ever see past the intrusive human observer? Many will reply: do we want to? Even if Kant's system was flawed (and it is), many would see his anthropocentrism as an enduring and valuable legacy. This in turn raises the late-twentieth-century issue of different styles of doing theology.

Theologically, the most trenchant defender of realism this century has been Karl Barth (1886–1968). In a reversal of Kant's programme, he insisted that God should allowed to be God: 'the procedure in theology ... is ... to begin with the certainty of God without waiting for the validating of this beginning by self-certainty' (Barth 1975: 196). To Barth, if knowledge of God is to be of *God*, then it cannot be drawn from a human capacity or deduction. It must be a gift, coming by GRACE from God's self-disclosure. Theology, then is rooted in WORSHIP, listening and actual engagement. Yet the realism which results from this engagement is never naïve. God's grace exposes human SIN and the distortions of human thinking. The human theologian must work with open concepts, constantly revising them under the impact of the encounter with God.

Kant's mechanistic science foundered on the electromagnetic field and then the theories of Einstein (1879–1955), which developed not deductively through the application of abstracted law but out of a reintegration of theory and experience, thus ushering in a new realism in the physical sciences. Realism in physical science was also espoused by Karl Popper (1902–94), who rejected what he called essentialism and instrumentalism in favour of an experimental method for developing theory. Michael Polanyi (1891–1976), a chemist, through an analysis of skills, developed an influential realist epistemology in which theory and practice were reintegrated and a positive role was found for the subjective element in knowing.

In theology, Thomas F. Torrance (1913–) is the most consistent modern exponent of critical realism. Drawing on Athanasius, Calvin, Barth, Einstein and Polanyi his contribution has been to bring classical theology into dialogue with modern physics, and to point the way to the transformations needed as theology lets go of its old dualisms.

In philosophy most realist views have come under sustained attack following the linguistic turn. This view is represented in several areas of thought. In the later Wittgenstein it follows from the observation that the meaning of a word is given by its use. Consequently a word cannot refer to some object independent of the context of use. In Saussurean linguistic theory the sign is shown to be arbitrary and the signifier is itself part of a linguistic structure, hence reference is always reference to some part of language and not to some independently existing object or 'world'. In social thought realism has come under sustained attack in the post-Hegelian world. Following Hegel and, later, Schutz's attack on Weber human consciousness is seen as intersubjective; hence society itself is a set of self-constituting meanings. In consequence there is no social reality outside of the theories, linguistic patterns, meanings etc. that are found within that society. In international relations theory realism is coming up against the decline of the nation-state as a sovereign entity that can act solely in its own interests without regard to global interests. Theological realism has itself been challenged by this linguistic turn by, for example, Cupitt who has argued that claims about God can be understood only in the context in which they occur. The linguistic turn has provided challenges to theological realism no less than any other kind of realism. It will have to respond to this major intellectual turn if it is to survive and much is at stake.

In theology realism is an epistemological outlook, not a substantive doctrine. Its concern with truth means that it sees itself as having a vital prophetic role. Against the theological right it deplores the lapse of theology into a closed system of formalism either of dogma or text. Hence it is the critic of any false authoritarianism, acknowledging only the authority of the truth towards which scripture points but which can never be encapsulated and frozen in human concepts. Against the theological left, where the old dualism between the thing in itself and the world as it appears to us is still fostered, realism will deplore the conversion of statements about God into statements about human feelings, emotivism, or merely human ideas, theological idealism. It will stand as a corrective to sexist theology which attempts to project gender into God. It will point to the hidden Kantian assumptions behind much Biblical study (the alleged impossibility of ever passing behind the appearances to the historical Jesus). It will have much to contribute to ecumenical theology, showing the different traditions where their witness is perverted by being frozen into non-essential cultural additions from their past.

Barth, Karl (1975) *Church Dogmatics*, 2nd edn, vol. 1, Part 1, ch. 1, §6, Edinburgh: T. & T. Clark.
Einstein, A. (1954) *Ideas and Opinions*, New York: Bonanza Books.
——and Infeld, L. (1938) *The Evolution of Physics*, New York: Simon & Schuster.
Kant, I. (1964) *Critique of Pure Reason*, trans. Norman Kemp Smith, London: Macmillan.
Polanyi, M. (1958) *Personal Knowledge*, London: Routledge & Kegan Paul.
Popper, K. R. (1965) *Conjectures and Refutations*, London: Routledge & Kegan Paul.
Torrance, T. F. (1969) *Theological Science*, London: Oxford University Press.
——(1984) *Transformation and Convergence in the Frame of Knowledge*, Grand Rapids, MI: Eerdmans.

Iain Torrance
Paul Barry Clarke

RECIPROCITY

Very few concepts link theological and sociological discussions more directly and clearly than 'reciprocity', and few have greater significance for the religious lives of individuals. Reciprocity (Latin: *reciprocus*, returning the same way; *re*-back, *pro*-forward) is the process of giving and receiving objects or services which establishes particular kinds of relationships and obligation between people.

The principal ideas behind reciprocity include acts of (a) giving and (b) receiving, involving (c) motives, and resulting in (d) obligations and (e) alliances between different parties. A fundamentally important dimension of reciprocity is (f) the fact that the human species is intrinsically social and inevitably caught up in relationships with others. Reciprocity is a fundamental way of creating, sustaining and marking the nature of these relationships. Reciprocal relationships also characterize (g) the way people think of their gods and of their own salvation, especially in terms of merit. The idea of (h) ethical vitality provides one important focus for the religious significance of reciprocity.

Christian THEOLOGY has long been concerned with the nature and quality of relationships both between God and humanity and between human beings. Christianity's Jewish roots were also firmly bedded in a covenant relationship between God and humanity which itself is a form of mutual obligation, as is the ethical golden rule that we should do to others what we expect others to do to us. Paul's New Testament writings often argue about the relationship between merit earned by individuals and faith in Christ who alone possesses real merit. This argument over the source of salvation was developed in the fourth-century debate between Augustine and Pelagius, and came to lie at the very centre of the Reformation and Martin Luther's stress on faith and God's saving act and his denunciation of indulgences as a source of merit and salvation.

In sociological thought the idea of reciprocity was first spelled out clearly by Marcel Mauss (1872–1950) in his study of gift-giving first published in French in 1925. Mauss argued that gifts – interpreted in the broadest sense – are not inert but have a kind of POWER demanding that they be repaid in some way. He realized that gifts express relationships between people involving bonds of mutual obligation. Gifts are not, in fact, free because obligation follows receipt. The donor may even use a gift to put someone under obligation. Mauss showed that many forms of human behaviour have a reciprocal basis to them as, for example, in the case of SACRIFICE. With Henri Hubert, Mauss wrote on sacrifice in 1898, arguing that sacrifice involved a reciprocal process of communication between humanity and the gods.

Mauss showed how gifts could serve many ends. They could increase the status of donors and, in a sense, could even be used as weapons in the status war between people, as in the Potlatch ceremonies of the Kwakiutl Indians of northwest America. This reflected the idea of 'conspicuous consumption' advanced by Thorsten Veblen.

Mauss's idea of reciprocity has been developed in contexts as different as urban Canada, where Cheal found that women were much more likely to be involved in gift-giving than were men, and Nepal, where Ortner showed how the Sherpas used reciprocity in their dealings with each other and their gods. More theoretically, David Riches argued that people give because of their own interests but explain their action in terms of their obligations. In an important speculation on reciprocity Riches suggested that very able people are given prestige in SOCIETY in return for the benefit they give to society.

The significance of reciprocity for a theological understanding of society is far reaching, extending from doctrines of salvation to ethics and poverty.

Reciprocity links world religions in a particularly clear way. In Hinduism, Buddhism and Sikhism the idea of *karma* is central and refers to a process through which individuals reap the rewards of their actions. Good acts will bring good rewards, bad acts EVIL consequences. This system of reciprocity acts according to its own logic through some process unknown to us. It brings to sharp focus the idea of merit. In sociological terms merit is a benefit gained by those who act in accordance with the rules of society, including religious laws.

In Eastern and Western religions ideas of merit and behaviour are closely linked with salvation. This can be grasped through the concept of ethical vitality, which describes the power of behaviour to generate merit or accrue de-merit and is important in understanding the idea of salvation. In his important essay, 'The ideology of merit', the anthropologist S.J. Tambiah described how, in some Buddhist traditions, boys become monks for limited periods of time; observing Buddhist rules they sacrificially renounce their own desires to make merit to use to offset de-merit in the lives of their family. Tambiah speaks of this gain as ethical vitality which can counter *karma* and suffering (1968: 105).

Christianity radically changes the emphasis on ethical vitality and merit-making. Instead of each individual being involved in gaining merit for their own salvation, it is the person, Jesus Christ, who becomes the source of all merit (*see* GRACE). Living fully in accordance with God's will, when still in the prime of life he gave himself to DEATH. The merit generated by his perfect life which is finally yielded up in death is enough to count against all the lack of merit of the rest of humanity. In the teaching of Paul there is another application of ethical vitality directed to those who have already become Christians through the merits of Jesus Christ and not through their own efforts. Paul addresses believers in this way:

I appeal to you therefore, brethren, by the mercies of God, to present your bodies as a living sacrifice, holy and acceptable to God, which is your spiritual worship.

(Romans 12: 1)

Because Christ's merit has already won salvation for believers, they can now devote their own ethical vitality to other ends, not to achieve salvation but to live out their Christian lives expressing salvation through service to their neighbour. This ethical outlook derives from the belief that people should LOVE each other in response to God's love for them.

For Christian theology, an understanding of the deep influence of reciprocity upon human nature is important in the development of spirituality and the nature of faith. Christians need to consider to what extent they project their social ideas of reciprocity on to God. This touches on the problem of evil because it is easy for some people to think that when evil befalls them either it is their due, as God pays them back for some earlier transgression, or it is unfair because they have done nothing worthy of misfortune. Either way this approach to life fails to enter into the nature of faith as a life of trust in God in a world which often operates in ways which cannot be mastered or controlled through simple formulas.

Cheal, D. (1988) *The Gift Economy*, London: Routledge.
Furer-Haimendorf, C. (1967) *Morals and Merit*, London: Weidenfeld & Nicolson.
Humphrey, C. and Hugh-Jones, S. (eds) (1992) *Barter, Exchange and Value*, Cambridge: Cambridge University Press.
Mauss, M. (1990) *The Gift*, London: Routledge.
Ortner, S. (1978) *The Sherpas Through Their Rituals*, Cambridge: Cambridge University Press.
Riches, D. (1981) 'The obligation to give – an interactional sketch', in L. Holy (ed.) *The Structure of Folk Models*, London: Academic Press.
Tambiah, S.J. (1968) 'The ideology of merit', in E.R. Leach (ed.) *Dialectic in Practical Religion*, Cambridge: Cambridge University Press.
Veblen, T. (1899) *The Theory of the Leisure Class*, London: Macmillan.

Douglas J. Davies

RESURRECTION

The word 'resurrection' is a transliterated Latin word which means 'rising again'. It is used to translate the Greek word *anastasis* which means 'standing up again'. In both languages the term originally articulated the belief that at some point in the future God would reassemble and revivify the human corpse. For many centuries the belief was taken absolutely literally and this literal view continues to be the 'official' stance of historic Judaism, Christianity and Islam. However, in practice many contemporary believers use the term in a less literal sense to express a hope for continued personal life after DEATH without necessarily implying that the buried or cremated corpse will in fact be raised up.

Belief in bodily resurrection came into being relatively late in the development of Hebrew thought. Throughout most of the period of the writing of the Hebrew Bible there was no expectation of any worthwhile human continuance after death. The earliest explicit affirmation occurs in what is thought to be a later interpolation into the text of Isaiah found in chapter 26: 19: 'Thy dead shall live, their bodies shall rise.' The only other unequivocal affirmation in the Hebrew Bible comes in Daniel 12: 2: 'And many of those who sleep in the dust of the earth shall awake, some to everlasting life, and some to shame and everlasting contempt.' In both cases the hope of resurrection emerged in response to a time of crisis. In the case of the Daniel quotation the crisis was an intense persecution of faithful believers by Antiochus Epiphanes where it became clear that only belief in life beyond death could vindicate continuing belief in a righteous God who cares for those who trust in him.

During the inter-testamental period belief in bodily resurrection became common, though not universal, among the Jews. Its essential foundation was belief that if God truly loves and cares for each individual then God will not allow death to have final dominion but will use his creative power to restore the person to life.

In Christianity belief in the bodily resurrection of Jesus was of crucial importance in confirming and revitalizing this Jewish belief. Scholars are divided as to how the events of the first Easter morning should be interpreted, but what is not disputable is that by the end of the first century it was all but universally understood in terms of Jesus having conquered death by rising physically from his tomb leaving it empty. What happened to Jesus then was seen as a foretaste of what will happen to all at the end of time. At that point, according to early Christian teaching, the 'particles composing each individual's flesh' will be collected together, the 'sea will give up its dead', the 'cannibal will give back the flesh he has borrowed' and 'the identical structure which death had previously destroyed' will be restored (for documentation see Badham 1976: 47). This wholly literal doctrine of the 'Resurrection of the Flesh' was incorporated in the Apostles' Creed; it was declared *de fide* by the Fourth Lateran Council for the Catholic Church; it was expounded as the official viewpoint of Eastern Orthodoxy by John of Damascus, of ANGLICANISM by Hooker, and of the main Protestant traditions by Luther and Calvin (for documentation see Dahl 1962: 37). Within Rabbinic Judaism bodily resurrection was so central a belief that Maimonides taught that a person who did not believe it could not be regarded as an adherent of Judaism (cf. Bowker 1991: 70). In Islam, bodily resurrection is taught throughout the Qur'an where the argument is repeatedly used that God is as able to recreate the person as he was to create him initially.

In recent centuries belief in a literal resurrection of our present fleshly bodies has declined. One reason for this is that, historically, this understanding of resurrection was linked to beliefs about a physical HEAVEN in the sky to which the bodies of the saved would ascend and a physical HELL beneath the earth (of which volcanoes are the vent-holes) into which the damned would descend. With the rise of modern cosmology such beliefs became impossible, and hence the understanding of what might be implied by resurrection was rethought. In the English-speaking world Cranmer's decision to amend the Apostles' Creed to read 'body' instead of 'flesh' aided such rethinking even though Cranmer himself remained content with the older understanding.

Among most contemporary Christians, resurrection is understood to mean that after death we will be given new and glorious 'spiritual bodies' suited for a life in heaven beyond our comprehension. This view was expressed very clearly by the Archbishop of Canterbury's Commission on *Doctrine in the Church of England* (1938):

> We ought to reject quite frankly the literalistic belief in a future resuscitation of the actual physical frame which is laid in the tomb ... none the less in the life of the world to come the soul or spirit will have its appropriate organ of expression and activity ... what is important when we are speaking of the identity of any person's 'body', is not its physico-chemical constitution, but its relation to that person.

Comparable developments have taken place among many Jews and some Muslims. In the Islamic case the fact that the Qur'an justifies belief in resurrection by saying that God 'has power to create the like of them' (Sura 17: 99) may be used to suggest that the resurrection body will be 'like' but not necessarily identical to the bodies we at present inhabit.

One problem with the reinterpretation of resurrection outlined above is that talking of the person receiving a spiritual body for life in heaven implies acceptance of body–mind duality, where personhood is identified with continuity of mind or SOUL rather than with one's physical constituency. Since dualism has been much criticized in contemporary philosophy, John Hick has tried to present a new interpretation of resurrection which avoids this understanding. He suggests that resurrection be understood as the creation of an exact psycho-physical replica in another space (Hick 1976: ch. 15). This hypothesis has been much discussed, but the overall consensus seems to be that, for this psycho-physical replica to be truly 'me', some continuity of mental life between the present and the future bodies remains necessary, and hence a dualism of mind and body continues to seem inescapable in any understanding of resurrection other than belief in the literal reconstitution of the corpse.

For some Christians talk of resurrection in terms of personal life after death has become too problematic to take seriously. One response has been to reinterpret resurrection to mean simply that we will live on in the eternal memory of God. This, however, seems a very radical change in understanding since to be remembered, even by God, is very different from actually rising to a new life after death!

Other Christians are even more extreme and reject wholly any identification between resurrection and life after death. Instead resurrection is seen as relating wholly to a new experience of life in the here and now. The ground for this reinterpretation is that the New Testament talks of the existential consequences of Resurrection Faith in terms of living life now in a new way. Arising from this Rudolf Bultmann and many others have sought to give a wholly existential interpretation of what resurrection really means. This approach has two difficulties: first that the exponents of the theory differ profoundly in what they see as being the characteristics of the claimed 'new life', and second that there appears to be no obvious connection between such a viewpoint and the historic resurrection belief.

Among those who claim an 'objective' meaning to the concept of resurrection there is often a profound inconsistency. For themselves, almost all contemporary Christians understand resurrection as a way of expressing their hope for some kind of continuance after the total extinction of their present bodies, which they do not expect to get back. However, they ground this hope on belief in the resurrection of Jesus Christ which they continue to understand as entailing the literal uprising of Jesus' corpse and the emptiness of his tomb. The internal tension caused by these disparate beliefs causes press controversy every Easter concerning what Christians ought or ought not to affirm concerning the resurrection of Christ.

In the present century a weakening of belief in the resurrection of our present bodies has psychologically helped the trend towards cremation rather than burial (*see* DISPOSAL). In the olden days the notion of ultimate physical reconstitution led to a sense of the dead as 'sleeping' in the churchyard awaiting the sound of the last trump! In some churchyards, clergymen were deliberately buried in the opposite direction to their flock so that they would rise again facing them. This pattern of belief and behaviour has now all but vanished, but there is no consensus about what should replace it.

From the perpective of religion and society a firm belief in resurrection has been a dynamic force in human history. In the second century BCE, it played a crucial role in the willingness of Jews to fight to the death and to die as martyrs in the Maccabean revolt which led to the re-establishment of a Jewish state and the preservation of their religious inheritance.

Within Christianity, the New Testament makes it clear that belief in Christ's resurrection was the central message of the first Christians. The certainty this gave them about a future life enabled them to die willingly as witnesses (in Greek 'martyrs') to their convictions, and to convert others to their faith. The coming into existence of Christendom and the worldwide spread of the Christian Gospel are both testimonies to the social impact of resurrection faith. Although confidence has declined in recent centuries, Easter remains the main Christian festival and the sense that Christians should lead a new life as 'The Easter People' continues to have social consequences. The best contemporary example is the LIBERATION THEOLOGY movement which seeks to transform society in Latin America and elsewhere.

In Islamic history resurrection faith played a comparable role in a willingness to fight to the death for the cause of Islam, or for a cause believed to be sacred. The most recent example was the willingness of thousands of young Shia Muslims to go to almost certain death in the recent Iran–Iraq war (*see* ISLAMIC FUNDAMENTALISM).

Few beliefs have the same dynamic for changing people's values than the conviction that this life is not all, but that we can rise to life anew through the power of God (*see* ESCHATOLOGY; SOUL).

Badham, P. (1976) *Christian Beliefs About Life After Death*, Basingstoke: Macmillan.
——and Badham, L. (1982) *Immortality or Extinction?*, Basingstoke: Macmillan.
Bowker, J. (1991) *The Meanings of Death*, Cambridge: Cambridge University Press.
Bultmann, R. (1985) *New Testament Theology*, London: SCM.
Carnley, P. (1987) *The Structure of Resurrection Belief*, Oxford: Clarendon.
Dahl, M.E. (1962) *The Resurrection of the Body*, London: SCM.
Daley, B.E. (1991) *The Hope of the Early Church*, Cambridge: Cambridge University Press.
Davies, S.T. (1989) *Death and Afterlife*, Basingstoke: Macmillan.
Harris, M.J. (1983) *Raised Immortal*, Basingstoke: Marshalls.
Hick, J. (1976) *Death and Eternal Life*, Basingstoke: Macmillan.

Paul Badham

REVOLUTION

Revolutions are radical, extra-constitutional changes in the forms of governments or structures of states and/or in the structures of societies. Political can be distinguished from social revolutions, and revolutions from rebellions. Revolutions are political if they change the structures of governments or states; they are social if they change the structures of societies. Rebellions are extra-constitutional protest movements that do not necessarily intend nor achieve radical changes in governments, states or societies.

It is commonly said that revolutions are by definition sudden and violent. However, radical political and/or social changes may result from protracted or non-violent extra-constitutional struggles. Some authors define revolutions in terms of popular revolts, but it is useful to distinguish between revolutions from above and popular revolutions. Traditionally, a distinction was made between revolutions, which by definition were 'progressive', and counter-revolutions, which were 'reactionary'. This distinction, however, rested on some theory of progress, and such theories are now widely rejected.

All known societies have produced ideologies of order and obedience. These have often been expressed theologically. Many religions represent gods as *rulers*. Some official ideologies have represented earthly rulers either as gods or as deputies of gods. According to such ideologies, rebellion and revolution are sacrilege.

The first scientific analysis of revolutions was made in the classical Graeco-Roman period. Unlike most of the ancient peoples known to

Western history, the Greeks were familiar with political forms other than theocratic monarchy. Plato was impressed by the tendency of political forms to decay and to change into other forms. Aristotle produced an explanation of revolutions in terms of struggles for EQUALITY and inequality. Polybius placed revolutions in the framework of a cyclical view of history (Calvert 1970: ch. 2).

The MONOTHEISM of the Hebrew Bible introduced a potential theological basis for rebellion. While obedience to God was absolutely required, the secular monarchical STATE was theologically problematic. The basis for the religious critique of the state was laid. In the New Testament the instruction of Christ to render to Caesar the things that are Caesar's and to God the things that are God's (Matthew 22: 21) appeared to leave no space for a theological JUSTIFICATION of rebellion. However, conflicts arose between early Christian religious practices and the AUTHORITY of the state, and the development of the Christian state and the Christian church opened up the possibility of conflict between the two and of a theological justification of resistance to anti-Christian state POWER. The classic medieval statement was that of St Thomas Aquinas who, with considerable caution, held resistance to tyranny permissible in some circumstances.

The Protestant Reformation was itself a sort of revolution. Nevertheless, both Martin Luther and John Calvin commanded absolute obedience to secular authority. Some Lutherans, however, rejected Luther's position, some Anabaptists adopting a revolutionary attitude to existing political authority (Skinner 1978: 73–81). Calvinism made a greater contribution to the theory of resistance in France, Scotland and The Netherlands. In England the Puritan 'revolution of the saints' developed important ideological and organizational components of the modern revolutionary party (Walzer 1969).

A transition from theological to modern secular justifications of resistance and revolution was initiated by John Locke in his *Two Treatises of Government* (1690). Locke based his theory of revolution on the idea of God-given NATURAL RIGHTS. The purpose of GOVERNMENT was to secure these rights. A ruler who

systematically violated such rights might be resisted. In such circumstances the people might reject the existing government and form another. Such a revolution was a defence of the divine order against its violation by the tyrant.

In the American and French revolutions of the late eighteenth century the right of resistance to tyranny was asserted as a natural right while its foundation was gradually shifted from the ordinance of God to the will of the people. Revolution was now justified less as the restoration of the divine order than as the creation of a new, secular-democratic regime. Revolution became a Promethean project, emancipatory and noble to its friends, hubristic and even sacrilegious to its enemies. The French Revolution became paradigmatic for modern revolutionaries, counter-revolutionaries, philosophers and social scientists. The expression of high political aspirations in the secular, rationalist discourse of the Enlightenment, the drama and violence of its events, and the disillusion and horror at its outcome left a legacy to political reflection that is still not exhausted.

In the late eighteenth and the nineteenth centuries the idea of revolution came to be associated less with a natural order of rights and more with the idea of inevitable progress. The most important proponent of the new thinking was Karl Marx, whose view of revolution was derived from the French example but who analysed revolutions in terms of CLASS conflict on the basis of a materialist transformation of Hegel's theory of history. The problematic of the right to revolution was replaced by a doctrine of its historical necessity. Although Marx's theory was explicitly atheistic, his critique of CAPITALISM, identification of the proletariat as the liberators of humanity and vision of a conflict-free communist future have been read as a secularized THEODICY and ESCHATOLOGY (Gunnemann 1979). These aspects of Marx's theory became highly problematic when, in the name of Marxism, the Bolsheviks seized power in Russia in 1917, anti-imperialist revolutions were launched in many non-European societies, and Communist regimes were established in Eastern Europe after the Second World War. To critical observers, these revolutions did not seem to be proletarian nor did their outcomes seem to be emancipatory.

The transfer of the legitimating basis for revolution from God to the people in the French Revolution produced a close association between DEMOCRACY (the sovereignty of the people) and NATIONALISM (the self-determination of the nation). In the nineteenth century various movements for national self-determination, many of them not at all democratic, adopted revolutionary programmes. In the twentieth century the anti-imperialist revolutionary movements employed the popular-nationalistic IDEOLOGY of the French Revolution, sometimes combined with Marxism–Leninism. Nationalist revolutions have also taken the extreme anti-democratic form of fascism. At the end of the twentieth century the nationalist revolutionary idea seems to have lost none of its force.

The ideas of progress and national self-determination have led to revolutionary projects of modernization. Whereas the classic French and Marxist theories envisaged revolutionary modernization as a democratic process, many twentieth-century modernizing revolutions have been imposed from above.

The revolutionary optimism, which for many was the legacy of the French Revolution and for some of Marxism, inspired the so-called 'youth revolution' in the rich countries of the West during the 1960s, but the failure of advanced capitalist societies to succumb to popular revolutions, the failure of radical-popular movements in the Third World, the authoritarianism of post-colonial regimes and the repressive stagnation of the supposedly Marxist regimes of Eastern Europe caused this revival of the revolutionary spirit to wane. Elsewhere, however, revolutions continued to erupt. The last quarter of the twentieth century saw an Islamic revolution in Iran, which inspired various forms of Islamic protest around the world, liberal-democratic transformations in many countries, especially in southern Europe and Latin America and the collapse of COMMUNISM in Eastern Europe. There has been speculation that the influence of the classic French model of revolution may be over. Late twentieth-century revolutions have either been illiberal or cautiously liberal. The

age of APOCALYPTIC, 'progressive' optimism appears to have ended.

Recent explanatory theories of revolution have passed through four main phases. At first, an attempt was made to describe the 'natural history' of the 'Great Revolutions'. Under the influence of the empiricist turn in political science, attention was diverted from the small number of Great Revolutions to more ambitious generalizations about rebellions, revolutions, internal wars, political VIOLENCE, etc. Then disillusion set in about the alleged vacuity of wide-ranging generalizations and there was a return to the analysis of world-historical revolutions with more attention to problems of explanatory methodology and theory construction (Skocpol 1979; Taylor 1984). After this approach was in its turn subjected to critical scrutiny, some writers have attempted to develop a theoretical framework that can give an explanatory account of a wide range of revolutions while acknowledging their great diversity (Goldstone et al. 1991).

From these developments no agreed explanatory theory of revolution has emerged but there is a considerable consensus on a number of significant points. Oppression, exploitation and poverty do not themselves explain revolutions, for these conditions are common and revolutions are rare. Similarly, psychological states such as ALIENATION, ANOMIE, frustration and relative deprivation explain little because they are compatible with non-revolutionary situations. However, attempts to replace psychological with structural explanations are also unsatisfactory in so far as they neglect the diverse ways in which potential revolutionary actors can interpret the structured situations in which they find themselves.

There is some consensus that explanations of revolutions wholly by reference to intra-societal factors (such as class conflict) are defective because societies and their regimes may be undermined by international forces. No single model of the internal and external causes of revolutions has been successfully applied to diverse revolutions, but recent theories have given greater weight to the geopolitics of revolution.

Although it is not denied that revolutions may have their roots in social conflict, recent theory has attached more importance to the role of political élites and political struggles to reconstitute the state. In the explanation of popular revolt less emphasis is now placed on the causes of discontent than on the social conditions conducive to solidaristic and disciplined popular organization. Revolutions are understood as crises of the state in which political élites are divided, popular mobilization for change may have been possible and the state coercive capacity weakens by some combination of external pressure, internal loss of legitimacy and, in particular, failure of loyalty of the state's coercive agencies.

Revolutions are therefore failures of state control and/or social order, but they are also reconstitutions of control and order. The form of the new regime will be explained by the conditions that produced the crisis of the old, the dynamics of the revolutionary struggle, and the external environment of the new regime. The ideas of revolutionary leaders and of popular forces may affect the outcomes of revolutions, but these outcomes are shaped by many forces beyond the revolutionaries' control. There is thus a complex relation between the ideas that are proposed to justify revolutions, the explanation of their outcomes and the evaluation of revolutionary projects.

Revolutions are explicable after the event yet hard to predict. The factors facilitating and inhibiting revolutions are better understood than they were, but the balance of such factors in particular situations is a matter of JUDGEMENT and not of precise measurement. Revolutions of the future may well contain novel features that will require further revisions in explanatory theory.

Revolutions aim to liberate people from injustice and to construct more human political and social orders, yet they often involve highly destructive violence. Throughout history religion has been deployed more often for conservative than for revolutionary purposes. However, religion has been used to justify revolution. Since the late 1960s LIBERATION THEOLOGY has attempted a *rapprochement* with secular radicalism, although its relation with violent revolution has been uncertain and controversial. Similarly, the issue of revolutionary violence has divided Islamic theologians.

The modern revolutionary tradition has been morally ambiguous. It has generated a complex record of success and failure. Many of the principles of the French Revolution are now widely accepted. Many twentieth-century revolutions have brought disasters. The causes of revolutions and of revolutionary outcomes are fairly well understood but are hard to control. Where revolutions have proved to be inadequate solutions to deep social and political problems, nonrevolutionary solutions have also often failed. Revolutions are ambiguous dramas about the intractability of the problem of EVIL.

Calvert, P. (1970) *Revolution*, London: Pall Mall.
Cohn, N. (1970) *The Pursuit of the Millennium*, revised edn, New York: Oxford University Press.
Dunn, J. (1989) *Modern Revolutions: An Introduction to the Analysis of a Political Phenomenon*, 2nd edn, Cambridge: Cambridge University Press.
Goldstone, J.A., Gurr, T.R. and Moshiri, F. (eds) (1991) *Revolutions in the Late Twentieth Century*, Boulder, CO: Westview Press.
Gunnemann, J.P. (1979) *The Moral Meaning of Revolution*, New Haven, CT: Yale University Press.
Gutiérrez, G. (1988) *A Theology of Liberation*, revised version, London: SCM.
Lewy, G. (1974) *Religion and Revolution*, New York: Oxford University Press.
Sigmund, P.E. (1990) *Liberation Theology at the Crossroads*, New York: Oxford University Press.
Skinner, Q. (1978) *The Foundations of Modern Political Thought*, vol. 2, *The Age of Reformation*, Cambridge: Cambridge University Press.
Skocpol, T. (1979) *States and Social Revolutions: A Comparative Analysis of France, Russia and China*, Cambridge: Cambridge University Press.
Taylor, S. (1984) *Social Science and Revolutions*, New York: St Martin's Press.
Walzer, M. (1969) *The Revolution of the Saints*, New York: Atheneum.

Michael Freeman

RITUAL

'Ritual' is a word we usually (and rightly) associate with CULTURE at its most cultural, and hence some readers will be surprised to discover that it originates in nature – and not, moreover, amongst our nearer kin such as the monkeys but way back, amongst the reptiles, birds and insects.

As a definition I would propose 'Any action

which proceeds invariably according to a set sequence may be said to have been ritually performed'. What we have learned in this century from ethologists and evolutionary biologists is that, even amongst rudimentary creatures, many activities surrounding courtship and aggression tend to proceed along set sequences, and hence are said to be 'ritualized'. The function seems to be basically threefold: (a) to communicate clearly a potentially dangerous state of arousal (for sex or fighting); (b) to facilitate bonding or imprinting (male to female or mother to infant); and (c) to provide a 'theatrical' way of defusing intra-specific aggression.

What is important here for students of human culture to notice is not only that we come honestly by our strange disposition to ritualize, but also that it originates in Mother Nature's desire for her children occasionally to communicate clearly and forcefully with each other: in short, if it is important that your message get through, if it is to carry the stamp of AUTHORITY and finality, *ritualize* it.

Why should this be so? The evolutionary answer is straightforward. If you were designing a perceptual apparatus to govern and trigger some animal's deepest instinctual responses, you would construct a simple code whose grammar would make it stand out somewhat from the other messages coming in; a code which, once received, would automatically call forth the desired response.

Thus can we see that Durkheim's famous distinction between the 'sacred' world that ritual opens and the 'profane' quotidian in fact originates in the animal kingdom. When Mother Nature wants one of her creatures to be truly shaken, awakened from the humdrum and memorably called unequivocally to bear witness to its profound simplicities, she calls upon it with ritual. And will this not do fairly well for a description of humankind's religious rituals? In short, the line of development from Nature to culture is continuous, and in this fact a version of the ontological argument for God's existence can be discerned: if man is the ritual-making animal, and if these rituals in every culture lay down avenues for access to divinity, from what privileged standpoint could one find the whole business risible and mistaken? The answer, of course, is 'from a book-bound PROTESTANTISM' (of which more presently), and the answer looks very shaky. Rituals were laid down by Mother Nature in the beginning for the guidance of her creatures: books were invented late last night and their transcendental credentials are by no means obvious. The difference between man's rituals and those of the other animals is that the latter are 'given' and the former must be made – which means that they vary a good deal from culture to culture. It is upon this variation that the relativist-nihilist brigade (so noxiously ubiquitous in our time) base their scoffing. The answer to them (as both Plato and Aristotle knew) is that 'In the beginning is Nature (*phusis*), and who are we to question her ordinances?' The fact that some cultures build wonderful roads to heaven and others do not is simply part of the lottery life becomes when man becomes free to choose his way.

There is one more scientific point I would make. As mammal turns to human, the codes of instinct and the rituals which govern them are gradually unbolted as the brain's neocortex grows to supplant them; and the human becomes free to fall into the most profound confusion. In order to avoid doing so he tends, in primitive days, to ritualize all his important activities (which is to say, virtually all his activities). As his life becomes more orderly and he achieves better terms with his neocortex, he can afford to allow more free play into his day; but he still clothes his most important moments (such as the initiation of child into adult) in the most solemn rituals.

Part of the reason for this has to do with memory. Once our life is no longer encoded by Nature but constructed in culture, our morals and metaphysics and even our aesthetics are lodged in the long-term memory, and recent research on the neurophysiology of the brain suggests that they get there by being repetitively 'dreamed in' over a period of three years. We dream in images not words and our culture-bearing images are the stuff of ritual, usually harrowing, to get things off to a good start with the long-term memory. For a discussion of this 'dreaming in' process see Winson (1985).

And so to the gods. It goes without saying that the morals and metaphysics and aesthetics of the primitive human are utterly bound up in transactions with divinity; and hence that all his most solemn rituals (what one might call his nominative fictions) will be concerned with calling forth the ancestors and gods to bless, renew and reconsecrate that body of lawfulness which constitutes and animates the cosmos. Such calling is a re-calling (since it is one of our important 'legal fictions' that our rituals have been performed just so since day one) and to re-call is to re-member, which literally means to replace the skeleton of the body politic. 'Shall these bones live?' is a phrase that resonates in several dimensions.

Religious ritual is a kind of serious play, and it is quite like a play, not far from theatre. Like a play it is concerned with representing exemplary or constitutive actions; and like all acts of serious representation its intent is magical: through mimesis actually to re-*present* 'the thing done' (Greek *dromenon*) in the beginning. To re-call the gods into our presence is a manifestly dangerous undertaking, and hence we attend with care to the *form* of the ritual which will contain the sacred power: if it spills over we will not be renewed but polluted.

Our first rituals take place on the dancing ground where we call upon the spirits of our animal masters to come amongst and enliven us. By degrees gravity will have its way with us, the ballet will give ground to unmusical movement, and in time 'the thing done' will be accompanied by 'the thing said' (Greek *legomenon*), and the *dromenon* will be moving towards the *drama*.

As Mircea Eliade has taught us to remember, in his many exemplary works, religious ritual was thought by the primitive human to take us out of the here and now into some other where. Where? Not a where so much as a when; for though the dancing ground is set aside in serious ritual, marked off from 'here' and reserved to the performers, this is even on day one a kind of make-believe, a convention. What is altogether less whimsical are the powers and realities attested and summoned therein, and they are thought to reside in another time, *that* time (*illud tempus*), sacred time, sempiternal time, now, then and always. We contact it by re-membering, and this bit of primitive wisdom

has been secured for modern humanity by the Greek heroes and philosophers who knew that immortality is achieved through being *remembered* by others – 'now in the mind indestructible' as Ezra Pound put it. The Greek verb for remembering is *anamimneskomai*, which means (more or less) 'to bear or call up and back and preserve through mimesis'. (What a language!)

I have said that the primitive human's rituals are concerned with divinity (virtually his only narrative subject), and there is an important distinction to be made. Divinity (by which I mean all the invisible powers that gather and scatter and blow in the wind) *presents itself* in storms and drought and pestilence and birth and DEATH, whereas in the carefully controlled sequences of ritual it is re-presented. Ah, but is it *really* there in such mimesis? This, as the reader will have gathered, is the question of Protestantism, about which to generalize briefly is idiotic: suffice it to say that cultures vary in their anxiety over the dangers involved in rituals improperly performed, and that this variation might be an index to their sense of dramatic irony.

I also said earlier that at a certain point in the EVOLUTION of culture the thing done (*dromenon*) will be accompanied by the thing said (*legomenon*). This is a very important moment to consider, for it points forward not only to the mythologies of the dream-time and the *drama* (the tragic theatre of the classical Greeks) but on to the philosophy of Plato, where ritual disappears more or less totally in the scholar's meditation on knowledge. For Socrates this meditation required at least the active interlocutory presence of others (hence dialogical and almost dramatic) but for Plato a human alone with his book may be able to remember the gods (Protestantism again). From this appalling moment we have never fully recovered, though Plato does repent somewhat in the *Laws*, as does Aristotle (on Plato's behalf) in his *Ethics*. And what of Jesus? Some of us think he instituted a counter-revolution whose energies have not yet been exhausted.

What to say? There is at least some consolation in knowing that our contemporary perplexities are nothing new, but a replay of what our forebears went through. For Jesus to win us from Plato he had to relocate the point of access to divinity (the heart, not the head); and this he did. And yet, to my mind he is mostly a Protestant too, building upon and extending the Platonic position more than counteracting it: the book, the myth, the word, the holy spirit, the thing imagined, *not* the law and the prophets ritually renewed. The writings of Augustine seem to me to suggest that he thought so too; and yet Augustine also provided the words from which medieval Christianity built its massive body of ritual. Is this not one of the great and inexhaustible historical ironies?

One might put it this way: when Socrates went cheerfully off to die, snubbing his snub nose at the jurors, he went off with his *daimonion* to 'a world elsewhere'; and this dealt a lethal blow to our belief in the power of ritual (even though Gilgamesh and some others had done it, rather differently, before). And when Jesus of the gospels went off, not altogether dissimilarly, he reinforced the point, which much of Plato's writing had extended and cerebralized: SOCIETY, which renews itself in acts of communal ritual, is not the last word.

Part of this massive shift in the location of reality is in the relocation of eternity. I suggested earlier that when primitive man ritualizes he calls the eternity of 'that time' into his presence to renew the life of today; and though all the tribe may disappear into that time when they die, to help the ancestors renew the present, it is not an 'afterlife' *per se*, but only an endless turning and returning to the here and now, whose consecration is *all that matters*. With Socrates and Plato, however, comes the idea that the timeless time of eternity is a realm that tries and *fails* to illuminate the here and now (whether through ritual or learning), and hence the sooner one can leave the stage with dignity the better. Thus does eternity become a world elsewhere and better, in opposition to the here and now, and this leads to (among other things) the altogether regrettable vulgarity of the dead Christian harping upstairs with the angels.

These last few paragraphs have been manifestly tendentious (slightly Nietzschean) and I hope that those offended will at least find them worth disagreeing with. My aim has only been to suggest where we might look to address our current ambivalence about ritual. On the one hand, in my view, we still largely belong to (the Protestant sides of) Plato and Jesus, never more than half-moved by civil ceremony and religious rite. On the other, we long to restore not only ceremony and manners to our daily existence, but ritual access to a transcendent something most other ages and cultures have enjoyed.

Moreover, we recognize that our lack of ritual is certainly tied to the aetiolation and bodilessness of modern life. When the ethologists tell us that Mother Nature endowed the animals with ritual performance in order to foster and govern the expression of sexual and aggressive energies, we listen with interest and a touch of envy. And when the anthropologists tell us that primitive man actually managed to escape the nightmares of 'history' and commune with the gods through elaborate thumpings on the dancing ground, we listen to that too. Who knows, we may be getting back to it.

On the whole, as Hegel's Owl of Minerva attests, one only philosophizes when a way of life has grown cold; hence the best work on ritual has been done in this century. For a genial introduction to ritual in the animal kingdom see Lorenz (1952, 1966). On the neurophysiology of dream see Winson (1985). On the sacred and the profane see the pioneer Emile Durkheim (1915) but more importantly the works of Mircea Eliade (e.g. 1954, 1964). For a scholarly but imaginative introduction to Greek ritual, Jane Harrison is still the one (see Harrison 1911). For a general guide to primitive spirituality (more myth than ritual) see Campbell (1959). To think about what Plato did to and for Western spirituality, is there a better starting point than Augustine's *Confessions* (1966)? For an extensive discussion of ritual amongst the chimpanzees and primitive man, see Young (1991).

Augustine (1949) *Confessions*, trans. E.B. Pusey, New York: Random House.
Campbell, Joseph (1970) *Primitive Mythology*, New York: Viking.
Durkheim, Emile (1915) *The Elementary Forms of the Religious Life*, London: Allen & Unwin.
Eliade, Mircea (1954) *The Myth of the Eternal Return*, New York: Bollingen Pantheon.
——(1964) *Myth and Reality*, London.
Harrison, Jane (1911) *Themis*, London; new edition, Merlin, 1963.

Lorenz, Konrad (1952) *King Solomon's Ring*, London: Methuen.
——(1966) *On Aggression*, London: Methuen.
Winson, Jonathan (1985) *Brain and Psyche*, New York: Doubleday.

Young, Dudley (1991) *Origins of the Sacred*, New York: St Martin's Press.

Dudley Young

SABBATARIANISM

Derived from the Hebrew word *šā-bat* ('cease, desist, stop'), the term refers to observance of the seventh day of the week (Saturday) as the day of rest and religious observance by Jews and some Christians, especially Seventh-day ADVENTISTS. It can also can be applied to Christian observance of the first day of the week (Sunday) as the memorial of Jesus' RESURRECTION.

According to the Priestly Creation account the Sabbath was built into the structure of the universe from the beginning: 'So God blessed the seventh day and hallowed it, because on it God rested from all the work that he had done in creation' (Genesis 2: 3). Attempts to explain the origin of the Sabbath in the Kenite observance of the day of Saturn, ancient Mesopotamian lunar calculations or Canaanite agricultural practices are more suggestive than probative. The Sabbath commandments in the Decalogue (Exodus 20: 8–11; Deuteronomy 5: 12–15) agree that the seventh day is a Sabbath to the Lord for the entire household. However, they appeal to different theological roots: creation (Exodus 20: 11), and the exodus from Egypt (Deuteronomy 5: 15). The reason for the Sabbath rest is basically humanitarian (Exodus 23: 12), though the command appears once in a 'cultic' context (Exodus 34: 21).

In New Testament times the Sabbath was an essential part of Jewish life and piety. The chief matter of controversy was what constituted 'work' on the Sabbath day of rest. The group represented in the *Damascus Document* (probably early Essenes) laid down very strict rules – far stricter than those later codified by the rabbis. This debate is reflected in various Gospel episodes (Matthew 12: 1–14; Mark 2: 23 to 3: 6; Luke 13: 10–17; John 5: 1–18; 7: 19–24; 9: 1–41). There Jesus appears as respectful of the Sabbath yet having the AUTHORITY to do what more strict observers might not allow.

As the first century AD progressed, Sunday became a more important and distinctively Christian institution. The theological root was Jesus' resurrection on Easter Sunday and his appearances to the disciples. The first day of the week (the 'Lord's Day') became a time for Christians to gather for prayer, the EUCHARIST, and collections (1 Corinthians 16: 2; Acts 20: 7; Revelation 1: 10; *Didache* 14: 1). Jewish Christians probably continued to observe the Saturday (Jewish) rest and the Sunday (Christian) worship-fellowship. But in the early second century Ignatius of Antioch urged that Christians 'no longer observe Sabbaths but fashion their lives after the Lord's Day' (*Magnesians* 9: 1).

Jews continue to observe the Sabbath from sunset on Friday to sunset on Saturday. In Jewish piety the Sabbath is a day of joy, rest and prayer in the home and the synagogue. The rabbinic tractates *Shabbat* and *Erubin* delineate what constitutes work and the 'Sabbath resting place' respectively. From the exile in the sixth century BC to the present, Sabbath observance has served as a sign of Jewish identity. Attempts by the Reform Jewish movement in the nineteenth century to move synagogue services to Sunday morning had little or no popular appeal.

For early Christians Sunday was primarily a time for WORSHIP. Following the Constantinian Sunday Law of AD 321, however, church leaders often appealed to the Biblical Sabbath commandment and applied it to the observance of Sunday as a day of rest from work. Medieval theologians defended this transfer by interpreting the basic Sabbath law in the Decalogue as a moral precept and disregarding its ceremonial features (including Saturday observance). The Reformers held different views about the Sunday Sabbath: a day of worship (Luther), a day of worship and cessation from labour (Calvin) and a day equivalent to the Biblical Sabbath in every respect (English Puritans). The 'radical Reformation' spawned various Sabbatarian (Saturday observing) groups. The most prominent Christian Saturday-observers today are the Seventh-day Adventists. They point to the clear teaching of the Hebrew Scriptures on the Sabbath and look on the Sabbath as a sign of creation, hope for future redemption, and the transcendence of God.

Sabbath observance involves interrupting regular patterns of work and everyday activity. It provides physical rest, spiritual refreshment and social space for its observers. It fosters social solidarity especially where observers (Jews in the Diaspora, Seventh-day Adventists) form a minority. It can lead to economic, legal and cultural tensions where the majority hold to the different practice.

The Sabbath remains the Jewish day of rest and worship. Whatever debate there may be in Judaism about the Sabbath concerns its practice, not so much its THEOLOGY. Seventh-day Adventists have developed an elaborate theology of the Sabbath and situate their observance in that context. Mainline Christian churches reflect the tensions that have accompanied the matter from New Testament times: Should Sunday be primarily a day of worship, or is it also a day of rest? To what extent should Old Testament Sabbath regulations be transferred to Sunday?

Karl Barth in *Church Dogmatics* (3/1: 213–28; 3/4: 47–72) sought to rethink the Sabbath for Christian theology. With particular attention to the Priestly Creation account in Genesis 1: 1 to 2:3, Barth found, in the first Sabbath teachings about God's satisfaction with creation, freedom *vis-à-vis* creation and loving concern for creation. Barth viewed the Sabbath as a lens for understanding God's GRACE, ethical responsibility, the meaning of work, and ESCHATOLOGY (the eternal Sabbath).

Contemporary discussion about the Sabbath often relates to SECULARIZATION and ecology. In 'Christian countries' the Sabbath regulations imposed on Sunday are rapidly disappearing through legal and political processes. However inevitable this trend is and whatever economic and social benefits it may bring, many people wonder about physical and psychological exhaustion in societies in which one day is the same as every other. Those concerned with ecology find in the Sabbath concept a rich resource for giving the earth a 'rest' and thinking about the 'environmental Sabbath'. Their interest, however, seems to be with the basic idea of Sabbath rest rather than with Biblical-theological foundations and traditional observances.

Bacchiocchi, S. (1977) *From Sabbath to Sunday: A Historical Investigation of the Rise of Sunday Observance in Early Christianity,* Rome: Gregorian University Press.

——(1980) *Divine Rest for Human Restlessness: A Theological Study of the Good News of the Sabbath for Today,* Rome: Gregorian University Press.

Carson, D.A. (ed.) (1982) *From Sabbath to the Lord's Day: A Biblical, Historical, and Theological Investigation,* Grand Rapids, MI: Zondervan.

Dawn, M. (1989) *Keeping the Sabbath Wholly: Ceasing, Resting, Embracing, Feasting,* Grand Rapids, MI: Eerdmans.

Eskenazi, T.C., Harrington, D.J. and Shea, W.H. (eds) (1991) *The Sabbath in Jewish and Christian Traditions,* New York: Crossroad.

Parker, K.L. (1988) *The English Sabbath: A Study of Doctrine and Discipline from the Reformation to the Civil War,* Cambridge: Cambridge University Press.

Primus, J.H. (1989) *Holy Time: Moderate Puritanism and the Sabbath,* Macon, GA: Mercer University Press.

Rordorf, W. (1968) *Sunday: The History of the Day of Rest in the Earliest Centuries of the Christian Church,* Philadelphia, PA: Westminster.

Daniel J. Harrington

SACRIFICE

In common English 'sacrifice' is the offering of a slaughtered animal to a god; deriving from this is the more common meaning of giving up something to obtain a greater good. In the social sciences, significant discussion of sacrifice arises principally in the fields of social and cultural anthropology. When the word is used by anthropologists, the emphasis has been on the taking of life in a RITUAL context.

Such a phenomenological definition has limitations. It brings together rituals which give widely different symbolic meanings to the act of slaying. It includes rituals in which the act of slaying may be peripheral to the symbols acted out, and excludes closely related rituals such as offerings of agricultural products.

In Christian THEOLOGY, the term 'sacrifice' has been applied principally to the DEATH of Christ and to its commemoration in the EUCHARIST. This Christian concept of sacrifice derives from sacrifices in the Hebrew Bible, which link into anthropological studies.

De Vaux (1964) shows how the ancient Hebrews incorporated into their religion of Yahweh a variety of sacrifices from the peoples around them, including the Passover commemorative sacrifice, holocausts, communion sacrifices and expiatory sacrifices, the last developing particularly in the later period. A focus on

WORSHIP developed in the written tradition, which emphasized morality over ritual performance (Thompson 1974).

In some respects, Christ did away with the offering of sacrifices and the old priesthood; but ideas involved in Hebrew Bible sacrifices were taken up in New Testament times: expiation and ATONEMENT, communion, commemorative celebration, and particularly homage to God. The crucifixion of Christ becomes interpreted as a sacrifice, Christ being both priest and victim. Christian life could also be interpreted as sacrifice, in the sense of an act of homage to God. The Roman Catholic tradition in particular has emphasized this theme, presenting the symbolic offering of Christ in the Mass as sacrifice and extending the meaning to ways in which individual Christians can offer themselves to God (see Daly 1978; also, in the Protestant tradition, Young 1974). This has involved the development of a concept in a particular tradition in a way which cannot easily be applied to other symbolic systems.

A number of attempts have been made to unravel the essential meaning of sacrifice, understood loosely to incorporate Christian concepts and ritual killings generally. Early accounts simply regarded sacrifices as a way of giving gifts to gods, the destruction of the victim ensuring that the gift is irrevocable.

Robertson Smith (1889), drawing from accounts of a wide range of cultures, argued that sacrifice among the ancient Semites was originally essentially a meal for the god, with the human community sometimes participating. A secondary idea was the substitution of the life of a person or a domestic animal for a life that was in some way threatened, which developed into expiatory sacrifices. In such sacrifices, what cannot be eaten remains sacred and must be disposed of in some other way. While this analysis has some merits for particular sacrifices, and even traditions, the meal is not of central importance in all traditions.

Hubert and Mauss (1898) argued that all sacrifices have an essential structure involving someone who benefits, a victim that is first consecrated and then immolated, and finally a process of purification to allow the participants back into ordinary life. These authors argued

that sacrifice mediates between the sacred world of social values and the profane world of individual interests. It achieves this by taking a victim, in some way related to the person making the sacrifice, and consecrating it, bringing it into the sacred, moral sphere. The problem with this analysis is the assumption of a radical divide between the sacred sphere of social values and the profane sphere of everyday life, a division which is not applicable to all cultures.

Evans-Pritchard (1956) emphasized expiation and propitiation in the sacrifices of the Nuer people of Southern Sudan. The sacrifices he pays most attention to were performed in times of danger, and involved propitiating spirits and restoring the moral order. He argued that the consecration of the victim suggests an identification between the victim and the person offering the sacrifice, and the substitution of the victim's life for threatened human life. There was an element of gift exchange, but gift giving is not simply a transfer of material property: it involves personal commitment. Ideally, valued cattle should be offered; but a poor person could offer a goat, or even symbolically sacrifice a wild cucumber, and the gods would accept it. Evans-Pritchard points out that a wide range of ideas may be found in Nuer sacrifices, any of which may be emphasized in a particular context. Variations of essential meaning are even more relevant cross-culturally.

Girard (1972) argued that sacrifice is essentially a means to comprehend and contain the VIOLENCE that is instinctive in any animal species. The victim is associated with the group concerned, yet in some way alien to it. Through the violent elimination of the victim, the instinct for violence within the group is appeased and put to rest. Girard's ideas may throw light on specific sacrifices, particularly where a scapegoat is involved, but a single central meaning cannot cover the diverse institutions of sacrifice in different societies and different contexts.

De Heusch (1985) used structuralism to produce a general theory of sacrifice in Africa. He pointed out that in any sacrifice a particular animal is used (or substituted for within limits): the symbolism of the victim must therefore be examined, and within the symbolic system of the CULTURE concerned. De Heusch noted that the killing of the animal is only one part of a ritual sequence that may be very long and elaborate. He also observed the difference between sacrifice in the domestic sphere and sacrifice involving kings and rulers, each of which involves a different symbolic system. Nevertheless, he tried to generalize: sacrifice involves the taking of life, and de Heusch argued that it is primarily an attempt to outwit death.

Some approaches in anthropology have paid attention to the material factors involved in sacrifice, such as the need for meat in a ritual meal or who bears the expenses of providing victims and perhaps employing priests. Such factors may on occasion be important to the participants (especially in societies where meat is only eaten on ritual occasions). But material considerations cannot penetrate the symbolic meaning of rites within their cultural contexts, and can be of little importance to theologians concerned with meanings. Even outside the Christian context, we occasionally find people performing sacrificial rites using a valueless substitute for the normal victim: in such cases, economic factors are at most incidental to an understanding of the sacrifices.

The problem for social anthropologists is that death, which is irreversible and in the human context upsets the social order, is a powerful symbol that can acquire a variety of meanings. Ritual killing can be associated with irretrievably presenting a gift to god, for appeasement or in order to obtain some favour or in joyous thanksgiving. Ritual killing can be associated with the fine smell of cooked food, bringing people together for a meal. It can be associated with the spilling of blood, a symbol of both life and death, or more generally with the release of vitality in healing rituals. Death can be associated with the removal of various types of EVIL. POWER over life and death can be a symbol of political power and status. Such power might include evil, occult powers. The association of domestic animals with people can involve an element of substitution in sacrifice. In a particular cultural context, any of these and other factors may come into play in determining the symbolic meaning of particular sacrifices. Indeed, the taking of life need not be central

to the symbolic meaning of the ritual as a whole.

If sacrifice is to be defined in terms of the ritual taking of life, there can be little future in attempts to elucidate a general meaning of sacrifice. Similarly, it cannot be shown that sacrifice is a response to a fundamental human religious urge. Nevertheless, there is room to explore the characteristics of sacrifices in particular cultures with their particular deities and symbolic contexts; we may expect to find that some of these characteristics are common to a variety of contexts.

For Christian theology, there is a question of relevance. It appears to many that the ritual taking of life is no longer meaningful in the modern world. Even in the 'modern' parts of the world, however, we can see that the ritual taking of life is part of our human history, and that certain sacrifices provide a framework for understanding the Gospel story and its message.

Many Christians live in societies where animal sacrifices are common, often offered to local deities for material ends. The task for Christian theology in such contexts is to relate the Biblical symbols of sacrifice to the meanings of non-Christian sacrifices, whether to incorporate ideas of such societies into Christian thinking or clearly to explicate the differences between Christian and other traditions.

Bourdillon, M.F.C. and Fortes, M. (eds) (1980) *Sacrifice*, London and New York: Academic Press. This volume contains a number of anthropological and theological perspectives, resulting from a meeting of theologians and anthropologists.

Daly, R.J. (1978) *The Origins of the Christian Doctrine of Sacrifice*, London: Darton, Longman & Todd.

Evans-Pritchard, E.E. (1956) *Nuer Religion*, Oxford: Clarendon, ch. 8: 'Sacrifice'.

Girard, R. (1972) *La Violence et le sacré*, Paris: Bernard Grasset.

de Heusch, L. (1985) *Sacrifice in Africa: A Structuralist Approach*, Manchester: Manchester University Press.

Hubert, H. and Mauss, M. (1898) 'Essai sur la nature et la fonction du sacrifice', *L'Année sociologique* 29–138.

Smith, W. Robertson (1889) *Lectures on the Religion of the Semites*, London: A. & C. Black.

Thompson, P.E.S. (1974) 'The anatomy of sacrifice', in M.E. Glasswell and E.W. Fasholé-Luke (eds) *New Testament Christianity for Africa and the*

World: Essays in Honour of Harry Sawyer, London: SPCK.

de Vaux, R. (1964) *Studies in Old Testament Sacrifice*, Cardiff: Wales University Press.

Young, F.M. (1974) *Sacrifice and the Death of Christ*, London: SPCK.

M.F.C. Bourdillon

SAME-SEX RELATIONS

Same-sex relations are almost always now referred to by the neutral term 'homosexuality', a term first used in 1897 to describe those who have sex with, or are sexually attracted to, others of the *same* (Greek *homos*) sex. The term 'homophile' has sometimes been adopted to give a general and less sexual connotation to erotic attraction within the same sex. Having sexual relations with *both* sexes is referred to as 'bisexuality' (Latin: *bi-*, two), a term of earlier provenance (1824) (Tielman *et al.* 1991).

Many cultures have colloquial terms to denote a homosexual person (usually a male), most of which are derogatory. In the West, the most acceptable term to refer to male homosexuals is 'gay' and to female homosexuals 'lesbian'. It is the fact that the partner in sexual activity is of the same sex which is definitive of homosexuality, and not other contingent factors. In particular, homosexuality is to be distinguished from effeminacy (having mannerisms and behaviour typical of the female GENDER), paedophilia (attraction to young children of either sex), transvestism (dressing in the clothes of the opposite sex) and transsexuality (a change, or desire to change, from an initial biological sexual status to the other), all of which may apply equally to heterosexuals and to homosexuals.

Different cultures deal with same-sex relations in dramatically different ways, and much of what modern SOCIETY understands by the term is in fact peculiar to the recent past of industrial societies. In particular, the ideas that one's sexual preference should form the basis for a recognized social identity – let alone a person's main identity – or that this identity is a lifelong one are very recent and Western notions.

Homosexuality is best thought of as an orientation or disposition to behave sexually in a certain way. It includes three distinct components, which in a given individual may or may not be congruent.

- Homosexual *behaviour* refers to performing certain sexual activities with a member of the same sex.
- Homosexual *arousal* occurs if a person is sexually aroused by (or attracted to) a member of the same sex.
- Homosexual *identity* means that a person willingly labels or identifies himself or herself as 'homosexual' (or 'gay' etc.).

Empirically, the most typical progression among young people is from *suspecting* one is homosexual to *identifying* oneself as one, and usually only then to having homosexual *experience*.

Christianity has developed a very distinctive view of sexuality in general (see SEXUALITY), and a largely negative view of homosexuality, which has had profound effects on LAW, ETHICS and social attitudes.

The most influential modern treatment of the Biblical treatment of homosexuality in the English-speaking world (Bailey 1955) appeared at a time when the issue of legalizing homosexuality was under discussion in England prior to the 1967 Sexual Offences Act, which legalized certain forms of male homosexuality (female homosexuality has never been illegal in the UK). He re-examined the Biblical texts popularly believed to condemn homosexual behaviour, bringing recent Biblical scholarship and some social science to that task. In particular, he interpreted the story of the destruction of Sodom and Gomorrah (the *locus classicus* for condemning 'sodomy' in the Latin tradition) in a radically new way, arguing that it referred primarily to breaches of hospitality to strangers and only peripherally to any sexual issues. The proscriptions of male-with-male sexual activity in the Purity/Holiness Code in Leviticus 11–26 have also been subject to anthropological reinterpretation (Countryman 1989) as referring to reinforcing culturally defined categories and defining 'purity' as behaviour which conforms to such category systems and thus functions to express national identity. Mixing of categories (such as eating animals with cloven hooves or using clothing with mixed materials) produces moral or legal proscription, as in most cultures. A range of sexual proscriptions occurs in the context of impurity/category mixing: sex with a menstruating woman and taking a woman and her sister into a man's harem occur, as well as homosexual intercourse.

Bailey also examined Biblical words which are translated into English bearing a homosexual connotation (such as 'sodomite'), and in particular the Pauline terminology of *malachoi* and *arsenokoitai* in 1 Corinthians 6: 9 and 1 Timothy 1: 10, rendered respectively as 'catamite/sodomite' (JB), 'effeminate/abusers of mankind with themselves' (AV), 'sensual/given to unnatural vices' (Chicago Bible), 'effeminate/liers with mankind' (Douai); the RSV (1st edition) renders both as 'homosexuals' (McNeill 1976). This provides an excellent example not only of the difficulty of translation, but also of the intrinsic ambiguity of meaning, since other more exact words existed to describe the class of males engaging in sexual activity with other males. It also exemplifies the ease with which modern assumptions are read back; indeed, Boswell (1980: App. 1) argues that *arsenokoitai* cannot have referred to homosexuals.

Sexuality in the early Christian tradition up to St Augustine was dominated by a highly specific view of permanent sexual renunciation ('continence, CELIBACY and lifelong virginity'), in part against the prevailing Graeco-Roman culture (Brown 1988) in which homosexual sex did not merit especial attention. In a detailed study which reversed many previous assumptions, Boswell (1980) showed that the assumption of 'unremitting hostility [of the Church] to the "sin of sodomy"' is untenable, and that the period up to the twelfth century was characterized by phases of general tolerance, only to be reversed, drastically, in the fourteenth century.

This period, characterized by an immense increase in the number of legal documents, not surprisingly also witnessed a rapid increase in the growth of 'Penitentials', which flourished once homosexual acts (and indeed solitary masturbation) came to be linked to heresy and defined as preeminently *contra naturam* (similar acts performed heterosexually being treated no differently). Dating from sixth-century Ireland,

the Penitentials provided advice (and normally appropriate time-specified penance) for confessors for all types of sins but came to be dominated in the eleventh century by sexual sins, and by homosexual activities in particular. Papal concern to enforce celibacy on clerics and campaigns to reform monastic life naturally led to a further concentration on penitents in Holy Orders, and the combination led to one of the most significant source documents of this period, a Penitential by St Peter Damian (1007–72) entitled *Book of Gomorrah* (Payer 1982), which called upon Pope Leo IX to depose any clerics proved in this manner to be sodomites. The success of the opus is unsure; it may well have received little but a polite acknowledgement from Leo IX, but its value as a manifestation and legitimation of the repressive judgements which formed the Christian thought of subsequent centuries is undoubted.

In the modern period, the work of sexologists and social scientists had scant effect on Christian thinking about homosexuality (as opposed to, say, contraception), until the moves to distinguish 'SIN' from 'CRIME' were applied to sexuality in the 1950s. Although Christian opinion was overwhelmingly hostile, some began to take a more liberal (if still traditional) line, and one of the few innovative contributions was 'Towards a Quaker View of Sex', published by The Society of Friends in 1963, which advanced the (then) radical thesis that:

> We see no reason why the physical nature of a sexual act should be the criterion by which the question whether or not it is moral should be decided.

More recent times have seen reports from virtually all mainstream denominations. Typically they have a similar structure:

- examination and evaluation of Biblical texts apparently condemning homosexual behaviour;
- a statement of theological consensus and dissensus within that church's tradition;
- a statement of the ethics of sex and its application to homosexuality, with consideration of pastoral issues;

- evaluation of medical, psychological and sociological approaches to homosexuality, and their relevance.

Fundamentalist denominations and SECTS generally take the view that homosexuality (in all its aspects) is sinful. Virtually all other reports adopt the distinction between the 'condition' and the 'practice' of homosexual acts – the former being morally neutral (usually because it is believed to be involuntary, or practically so). Considerable dissensus exists over whether (and if so, under what conditions), the physical expression of the 'condition' of homosexuality is permissible or acceptable and whether 'out' gay and lesbian people may be ordained. Broadly speaking, traditionalist churches (including the Roman Catholic, Orthodox and Evangelical traditions) reject the acceptability of homosexual behaviour, and Reformed and mainstream Protestant churches are more accepting. Anglicans, as is their wont, are divided. However, official pronouncements rarely reflect the considerable internal dissension that also exists.

Male homosexual behaviour became legally proscribed in England and Wales with the 1885 Labouchère Amendment to the Criminal Law Amendment Act, and a number of states and nations followed this lead. Shortly afterwards, and into the opening years of this century, medical practitioners in Europe and the USA increasingly advanced the theory that homosexual behaviour was more adequately and 'scientifically' considered as a pathology than as moral degeneracy or turpitude (even Oscar Wilde described his condition as 'a disease') and works such as Krafft–Ebbing's *Psychopathia Sexualis* (1886) and Havelock Ellis's *Sexual Inversion* (1897) led to widespread acceptance of the idea that 'inversion' (equals homosexuality) and other sexual 'abnormalities' were the result of excessive masturbation and/or inherited abnormalities of the nervous system. Such ideas were often welcomed by male homosexuals themselves and formed an important basis for Magnus Hirschfeld's epoch-making work on sexual behaviour in Germany, before its suppression by the Nazis. This 'medicalization' of homosexuality as a pathology was virtually unanimously accepted and had a profound (and, at the time, quite a liberating) effect on social science theorizing about homosexuality, on professions concerned with it (including some clergy) and even on those beginning to be overt about their 'condition'.

A pathology invites examination of its aetiology, and much effort was then exercised on discovering or theorizing about the 'causes of homosexuality'. The fact that few indeed of the empirically testable aspects of these theories have been verified on ordinary homosexuals (as opposed to those in psychoanalytic therapy, prison or psychiatric hospital) has not affected their popularity, and not until the late 1950s did Evelyn Hooker's findings begin to be accepted that, when *non-institutionalized* homosexuals were matched with equivalent heterosexuals, no significant differences remained in the tests supposedly discriminating or 'pathologizing' them. Subsequent work by anthropologists and sociologists repeatedly confirmed this finding, and in 1973 the American Psychiatric Association removed homosexuality from the roster of 'mental disorders', deplored discrimination against homosexuals and supported their civil rights (see West 1977). Although not all psychiatrists accepted the decision, its effects have been profound. Contemporary thinking holds that the pursuit of aetiology is at best misleading and at worst discriminatory, and that if aetiology has a place it lies in examining the causes of sexual orientation in general, of whatever variant.

The exact detail of how genetic and social learning affect the determination of sexual orientation is still problematic. Brain hemispheres (Krafft–Ebbing), chromosomal abnormalities and hormonal abnormalities have been postulated as (sole) causal agents, but the samples used have often been highly abnormal and no consistent evidence has been adduced. Even the evidence from monozygotic ('identical') twin studies is far from compelling. In a review of such studies, West (1977) concludes that results emphasize not only the critical interdependence of both genetic and environmental factors in final sexual orientation, but also that hereditary factors seem less important in determining the sexual orientation of those who are adjusted to their sexual orientation.

Freudian theories postulate bisexuality as the basic sexual orientation, and look to pathogenic parent–child relations as a determinant of homosexual orientation. None the less in a famous letter in 1935 to a concerned mother he states the surprisingly positive view that

> homosexuality is assuredly no advantage, but it is nothing to be ashamed of, no vice, no degradation, it cannot be classified as an illness; we consider it to be a variation of the sexual development.

Once again, evidence of such FAMILY pathology (and especially of the hypothesized influence of a possessive, dominant mother) is scant and contradictory, as is the impact of any later factors in adolescence. In general, it seems most consistent with findings from reliable studies among samples of non-pathological self-identified (male) homosexuals that sexual orientation is quite stably and irreversibly fixed in early childhood and is only rarely susceptible to change after that point, even where motivation is high and external social pressure is strong.

Same-sex relations are a universal phenomenon of all recorded societies. Attitudes toward sexual activity with the same sex, and especially to males who have sex with males, range from tolerance (and even social prescription) to outright condemnation and legal proscription. Attitudes towards sexual activity between women have generally been quite different, and where lesbianism is acknowledged (Queen Victoria is reputed to have been of the opinion that it was not possible) it is often subsumed under nonsexual terms, such as the 'close friendship' in the nineteenth century of 'The Ladies of Llangollen'. In the West, current attitudes and behaviour have been overwhelmingly influenced by the Judaeo-Christian tradition, which has had a strong impact on both legal codes and social attitudes. In other societies, provision for homosexuality has often been radically different (Blackwood 1986), including the social definition of an approved third GENDER role (e.g. the Indian *Hijra* and the American Indian *Berdache* 'men women').

There has been a rapid increase in historical, anthropological and sociological research in recent decades. These findings radically complicate and relativize much received wisdom about same-sex (and, indeed, other-sex) relations, and put in doubt the extent to which we can be said to be dealing with the 'same' phenomenon cross-culturally and trans-historically. In non-Western and pre-industrial societies, homosexuality has been far more clearly restricted and homogeneous than modern Western homosexuality. In many cultures, words apparently equivalent to, or synonyms of, 'homosexual' (such as *bichas* – 'worms' – in Brazil) refer only to those engaging in *passive anal intercourse* and often only to those exhibiting 'feminine' traits. Their 'active' sexual partners are felt to impugn neither their heterosexual status nor their masculinity.

Anthropological and sociological theories of (homo)sexuality have always been sensitive to the danger that the Western Judaeo-Christian conceptualization of sexuality be taken as defining normality and how this has dominated scientific thinking about sex. Consequently they have attempted to 'de-construct' the categories used to define sexuality. Thus, other societies may lack our categories of 'homosexuality' and 'homosexual', or have no notion of homosexual identity. Unlike the modern Western notion of lifelong (homo)sexual identity, other societies define homosexual behaviour as age and role specific, as in ancient Greece (Dover 1978), where the older/active man often acted as mentor to the younger/passive one, and in Melanesia (Herdt 1984), where insemination of boys in a given age-peer by older men formed a ritualized (and obligatory) initiation into manhood.

Another instructive example is the social construction of 'pederasty'. It can only be unequivocally defined by reference to legal age of consent, sexual maturity, attitudes to intergenerational sex – all of which are culturally specific. Moreover, responses to it vary enormously; pederasty can be almost universally disapproved (as in many Western societies), or approved, or approved subject to conditions (as in classical Greece) or required (as in Melanesian ritualized homosexuality). Under the influence of Foucault (1980, 1987, 1988), such historical and transcultural diversity has been taken as axiomatic, and questions are increasingly asked about how sexual identity and categories are socially constructed rather than how a given 'essence' (e.g. 'homosexuality') expresses itself.

A definitive study in the USA entitled *Homosexualities* (Bell and Weinberg 1978) well expresses the individual, social and cultural diversity of the phenomenon. In Western societies homosexuality is most often a lifetime identity, but it can also be specific to a given setting (often where the opposite sex is absent, as in prisons, single-sex schools and the armed forces). It can also be carried on in parallel with heterosexual behaviour or identity; an estimated 2 per cent of married men have significant (and sometimes exclusively) homosexual experience ('married gays'), and about 12 per cent of gay men have been married.

The estimation of the prevalence and incidence of homosexual behaviour and arousal is methodologically complex, since the term has shifting definitional content, the 'population' cannot be conventionally sampled, and there are strong pressures to lie about any non-heterosexual identity. Since estimates crucially depend on what is to count as a homosexual, numbers will change as the definition is widened. The pioneering study by Kinsey *et al.* (1948, 1953) in the USA in the 1930s–1940s introduced the seven-category mixture scale between exclusively heterosexual [0] and exclusively homosexual [6] (*see* SEXUALITY). Despite considerable methodological criticism, their estimates still provide fairly robust (but probably somewhat high) estimates of the percentage prevalence of homosexual experience in North American and European populations. His estimates of homosexuality in the male population range (according to the restrictiveness of the criterion) from

- 4 per cent (lifelong, exclusively homosexual activity) through
- 25 per cent (continued homosexual experience over three years between 15 and 55) to
- 37 per cent (some significant, overt homosexual activity to orgasm during sexually active life)

and recent studies converge on a figure between 6 and 12 per cent for those men who are exclusively or predominantly homosexual for most or all of their sexually active life. The corresponding figures for female homosexuals are considerably lower (2 per cent, 13 per cent, 28 per cent respectively), with 2–10 per cent as predominantly homosexual for most of their life. Recent national studies (Johnson *et al.* 1994) give a lower prevalence rate of male homosexual activity (averaging 1.8 per cent in the last year and 4.8 per cent in the lifetime), although these are likely to be underestimates. Estimates of the number of lesbians are consistently half those of male homosexuals.

The sexual lifestyle of homosexual men and women has been little charted before this century, and before definitive research could be done the appearance of HIV infection among male homosexuals in the West dramatically changed that lifestyle.

Anal intercourse has usually been taken to be the definitive homosexual activity, but this is a mistaken assumption; many (indeed, probably most) male homosexuals do not engage in it, and a significant fraction of heterosexual couples do, either for its own sake or as a method of birth control. Among male gays, the incidence of anal intercourse has dropped rapidly with the adoption of 'safer sex' since the beginning of the AIDS/HIV pandemic. Whilst a high fraction (*c.*85 per cent) will have engaged in anal intercourse at some stage of their sexual life, recent World Health Organization international studies (Coxon 1992) show that under one-half will have done so in the last month.

The most common single sexual activity is solitary masturbation, followed by (active, passive and mutual) masturbation and (active, passive and mutual) fellatio. Together these activities account for over three-quarters of sexual acts of homosexual men. Perhaps the most significant difference compared with heterosexual activity is that approximately twice as many sexual sessions of homosexual men are 'reciprocal' (taking the active and passive roles in turn) than are 'role/power' based, where each partner adopts a consistent modality role throughout.

Relationship-type is also an important component of homosexual lifestyle. In many societies the idea of a continuing, domestically based homosexual relationship is totally foreign and sometimes (as in the UK until 1967) legally proscribed. Consequently, casual encounters or non-cohabiting relationships have necessarily been far more common, and the universal Christian (and well-nigh universal legal) proscription of homosexual 'marriages' mean that there can be no equivalent of 'monogamy'. In those nations where homosexuality is not legally proscribed there has been a considerable increase in pair-bonded relationships and a move toward a pattern of 'serial monogamy'. This trend has accelerated in the last decade, but probably the majority of gay men at any given time have no regular relationship. Lesbians, by contrast, tend to have a much higher proportion of close-coupled cohabiting relationships.

Although homosexuals do not form a 'community' in any sociological sense, male homosexuals in particular form a recognizable 'constituency' in most Western countries and more overt members tend to be well-organized politically. In most countries there is an urban 'scene', usually based upon bars and clubs and often including voluntary social, counselling and special-interest organizations.

Christian definitions of, and attitudes towards, homosexuality have been definitive in the Western tradition. Social science has had to struggle against this hegemony in order to understand how sexuality is constituted and expressed. Theologians in seeking the *Sitz im Leben* of Biblical and other texts and in understanding the contexts within which doctrine is formulated and expounded have used similar perspectives and asked similar questions.

For the institutional churches, prospects for change in the future are less promising. On any criterion, the influence of Christianity on sexuality, and upon homosexuality in particular, has been little short of disastrous. It has promoted abstention or a narrow (procreationist) marital ethic, and excluded all other alternatives. It has pursued a single-minded and vindictive homophobia throughout almost all its history, and it has shown few signs of listening to those with homosexual experience. The dilemma involved in changing Christian thinking is real; if one appeals to Biblical texts they refer to something which cannot be equated with modern homosexuality, but if social science perspectives are invoked this will mean reconstructing virtually the whole of the theology of sexuality and of the body. If sexual orientation is not simply genetically determined, conventional liberal ethics based on the presumption of non-culpability will have to allow for the justification of the choice to be homosexual. Some have begun this enterprise with vigour (Nelson 1978; Spong 1990), but the generally highly negative reaction to such work among Christian folk emphasizes how deep-rooted the older interpretations are; homosexuals may be tolerated, but homosexuality by and large is not. The rethinking of homosexuality may well have to wait upon, or be part of, the Christian rethinking of human sexuality itself.

Bailey, D.S. (1955) *Homosexuality and the Western Christian Tradition*, London: Longman.

Bell, A.P. and Weinberg, M.S. (1978) *Homosexualities: A Study of Diversity Among Men and Women*, New York: Simon & Schuster.

Blackwood, Evelyn (ed.) (1986) *The Many Faces of Homosexuality: Anthropological Approaches to Homosexual Behavior*, New York: Harrington Park Press.

Boswell, John (1980) *Christianity, Social Tolerance and Homosexuality: Gay People in Western Europe from the Beginning of the Christian Era to the Fourteenth Century*, Chicago, IL: University of Chicago Press.

Brown, Peter (1988) *The Body and Society: Men, Women and Sexual Renunciation in Early Christianity*, London: Faber & Faber.

Brundage, James A. (1987) *Law, Sex and Christian Society in Medieval Europe*, Chicago, IL: University of Chicago Press.

Coxon, A.P.M. (1992) *Homosexual Response Studies: International Report*, Geneva: World Health Organization, Global Programme on AIDS.

Dover, Kenneth J. (1978) *Greek Homosexuality*, Cambridge, MA: Harvard University Press.

Foucault, Michel (1980, 1987, 1988) *The History of Sexuality*, vol. 1, *An Introduction* (Harmondsworth: Penguin Books); vol. 2, *L'Usage des plaisirs* (Paris: Gallimard); vol. 3, *Le souci de soi* (Paris: Gallimard).

Greenberg, David E. (1988) *The Construction of Homosexuality*, Chicago, IL: University of Chicago Press.

Herdt, G.H. (ed.) (1984) *Ritualized Homosexuality in Melanesia*, Berkeley, CA: University of California Press.

Johnson, A.M., Wadsworth, J., Wellings, K. and Field, J. (1994) *Sexual Attitudes and Lifestyles*, London: Blackwell Scientific Publications.

Kinsey, A.C., Pomeroy, W.B. and Martin, C.E. (1948) *Sexual Behavior in the Human Male*, Philadelphia, PA: W.B. Saunders.

——,——,——and Gebhard, P.H. (1953) *Sexual Behavior in the Human Female*, Philadelphia, PA: W.B. Saunders.

McNeill, SJ, John J. (1976) *The Church and the Homosexual*, Kansas City, KS: Sheed Andrews & McMeel.

Nelson, James B. (1978) *Embodiment: An Approach to Sexuality and Christian Theology*, Minneapolis, MN: Augsburg.

Payer, P.J. (trans.) (1982) *Book of Gomorrah: An 11th Century Treatise Against Clerical Homosexual Practices*, Waterloo, Ont.: Walter Laurier Press.

Spong, J.S. (1990) *Living in Sin: A Bishop Re-thinks Human Sexuality*, San Francisco, CA: Harper & Row

Tielman, R.A.P., Carballo, M. and Hendricks, Aart C. (eds) (1991) *Bisexuality and HIV/AIDS*, Buffalo, NY: Prometheus.

West, D.J. (1977) *Homosexuality Re-examined*, 4th revised edition, London: Duckworth.

Anthony P.M. Coxon

SECTS

Sects are separated bodies of dissentient believers within one major religious tradition. Strictly speaking, the concept has a distinctly Christian provenance and was a term of *odium theologicum* used by churchpeople to disparage dissident minorities. The exclusivist commitment of Christianity tolerated neither dual allegiances nor doctrinal deviation and, in consequence, sects were excoriated in much harsher terms than those applied to distinct schools or parties within other religious traditions (Hinduism, Buddhism, Judaism and Islam) where a wider degree of tolerance has traditionally been accorded to most such separatists. It is therefore inappropriate and potentially misleading to use the term 'sects' for the various subdivisions which prevail in other religions, although this is not uncommon in popular usage.

From the very beginnings of the church, sects began to emerge, and the first expositor of a theory of sects, Ernst Troeltsch (1865–1923), based his work on historical as well as contemporary cases of Christian sectarianism. Although the idea of the sect had been earlier employed by theologians, it was Troeltsch who established the concept as a descriptive, sociological and non-evaluative category. He saw the sect as an alternative form of religious organization to that of the church, and traced its roots to the Gospels. Following Troeltsch, sociologists have used the word as a technical term. In academic use – as distinct from popular and journalistic use – it is today employed without the pejorative connotations that were a part of its earlier theological legacy.

Since Troeltsch set up his dichotomous distinction of sect and church, the concept of the sect has been subject to further refinement. It has become more clearly differentiated from other forms of religious organization, in particular from the denomination and the cult. Whilst some of the elements which Troeltsch saw as distinguishing features of the sect (such as the essentially lower class origin which he attributed to sects) have today, in the face of considerable contradictory empirical evidence, been relinquished, a set of distinct criteria are generally accepted as characteristic of the sect. Whilst not all of these indicia are necessarily found in each individual case, they constitute a constellation of associated variables of a probabilistic kind and make up an ideal-type construct which is advanced as an extended hypothesis and proximate definition. Thus, the sect is an on-going organization of separated believers who stand in some measure of protest against the dominant religious system and against at least some aspects of the prevailing secular CULTURE. Members see themselves as a specially chosen élite. They believe their movement to enjoy a monopoly of the complete TRUTH as a divinely designated custodian of that faith (even if they allow that some other religious bodies might have partial access to aspects of that truth). They are essentially voluntary bodies, to belong to one of which the individual must make his or her own specific and unequivocal commitment: there are no in-born members. Membership is by some proof of merit, usually by attested knowledge of doctrine and rectitude of moral life. The sect embraces, in more extreme intensity, the exclusivism inherent in the Christian tradition, and tolerates neither dual memberships nor divided allegiances even with ostensibly like-minded movements. The sect provides not only the necessary and sufficient knowledge and facilities for salvation, but admits of no extra-sectarian sources of virtue. The movement requires total commitment and virtuoso moral performance from all members. As a lay organization, the sect affirms at least the formal equality of all adherents, and condemns in particular the sacerdotal claims of religious leaders of other organizations, usually rejecting the validity of any sort of distinctive ordained ministry or pastorate. There are exacting standards of discipline, with the ultimate sanction of expulsion (under such designations as 'disfellowshipping' or 'putting out') of the doctrinally errant or the morally wayward. The individual's identity as a sectarian is primary to all other bases of social identity (whether of ethnicity, nationality, social class or even family membership): the sectarian is a sectarian before he is anything else.

The sect differs from the denomination in that the latter accommodates the secular culture. The denomination has often (albeit not always) begun as a sect which, over time and with the recruitment of the second and subsequent generations, has come to relax its rigour and to exhort adherents only to conventional, rather than perfectionist, standards of moral performance, accepting its place as one among a number of more or less equally legitimate variations of religious orientation. From the cult, the sect is differentiated by its insistence on its own exclusivity, its monopoly of truth, its epistemological authoritarianism and the firmness of its own boundaries.

Until the Reformation, sects were often no more than local, unorganized and essentially ephemeral manifestations of social disquiet expressed in religious form. They were generally persecuted and suppressed by the Roman Catholic Church, and few contemporary sects can trace their origins back beyond the seventeenth century – the Waldensians in northern Italy and the Hutterian Brethren (originating in central Europe but, after a sojourn in Russia, settled principally in Canada and the USA) being exceptional survivors. The Reformation facilitated the emergence of a congeries of religious movements, and sects such as the Baptists and the Congregationalists appeared first as tolerated Nonconformists and later as settled denominations in Britain but sometimes, especially in the case of the Baptists, persisted as sectarian splinter movements, particularly in the USA.

The Quakers and Muggletonians were among sects of the post-Civil War period which survived into the twentieth century whilst retaining the general characteristics of sectarianism (see QUAKERISM). The Methodists, who in Britain at least were in their beginnings less a fully fledged sect than an independent dissentient movement organized eventually in several schismatic free churches, more rapidly relinquished their sectarian attributes to become, like the main body of BAPTISTS, a recognized denomination (see METHODISM). Most contemporary sects originated not earlier than the last century, and almost all of them are to be described as Protestant sects, since only in Protestant countries was there sufficient toleration to allow such movements to persist. Conspicuous among the movements arising in Britain were the Southcottians or Christian Israelites, the Brethren and the Salvationists, whilst in America there emerged a wider variety of movements, including the MORMONS, the Seventh-day ADVENTISTS, the Christadelphians, Jehovah's Witnesses, various Holiness movements, Christian Scientists and, in the early twentieth century, a diverse assortment of Pentecostal bodies. Almost all of the aforementioned bodies have suffered internal subdivision, giving rise to mutually opposed fraternities. The process has been particularly marked among movements which seek to operate with a minimal organizational structure (sometimes denying that they have any formal organization at all) in which informal leadership has given rise to struggles for influence. The phenomenon has been particularly marked among the Brethren and the Christadelphians.

Sects represent a distinct genus of religious organization, but despite evident similarities among them there are also manifest differences which have led to attempts to establish typological distinctions. Seven subtypes have been postulated principally with respect to the way in which the sect is oriented to the world. The adventist (or revolutionist) sect emphasizes the EVIL nature of the wider society which God will overturn. Human beings are seen as entirely dependent on God; their end is predestined; and salvation is at the will of God. The sect is mortalist (denying the existence of an immortal SOUL); salvation will occur with the RESURRECTION of the body. This type of sect holds strongly to Biblical PROPHECY, has a strong cognitive orientation, requires of its members clear knowledge of scripture, and preaches its message as an urgent matter for human obedience. Jehovah's Witnesses approximate this type.

The introversionist sect concentrates on the maintenance of holiness within its own community, where the sect escapes from the evil world. Although it holds strongly to the idea of the advent and subsequent millennium, it is more concerned that its members separate from the world. The sect prosecutes a cognitive but quietistic faith, conceiving of salvation as almost already achieved by the elect within the sanctified community. New members are accepted but not sought and sometimes are initially almost objects of suspicion. Exclusive Brethren and various American communitarian movements such as the Rappites and the Shakers exemplify this type of sect. A third type is the Gnostic (or manipulationist) sect, which espouses a special interpretation of scripture that transforms understanding. For these sectarians, the world only *appears* to be evil: true knowledge will allow men to work out their own salvation, which can be realized here and now. The sect claims esoteric knowledge and special wisdom which will lead the individual to salvation. There is little community orientation, and new members are readily accepted when they show themselves ready to become adepts. Christian Science and New Thought movements illustrate this type.

Conversionist sects are closest to the doctrinal emphases of evangelical PROTESTANTISM, but literal belief is accompanied by emphasis on emotional experience. Although the world is evil, people's dispositions can be changed by their free-will choice to accept salvation, which is by faith. The soul's migration to HEAVEN is the way salvation is conceived, attested by profound 'heart experience' by which new members are converted and recruited. Holiness and Pentecostal groups are prominent examples of this type.

The three further types, the thaumaturgical, reformist and Utopian, are less common. The thaumaturgical orientation claims special powers to overcome specific evils and to obtain temporal benefits by random wonder working, effected by agents who contact supernatural forces. Such sects have a minimal structure based on a client–practitioner relationship on an *ad hoc* basis. The reformist sect perceives the world as imperfect but capable of improvement if human beings, as vessels of divine enlightenment and conscience, seek to use their God-given insights to change the social order. Salvation is primarily in this world, and the style is strongly ethical inclining to the rationalistic. The emphasis is on social concern to which members are conscientiously directed. The Utopian sect sees the social word as evil and in need of radical reconstruction on the lines of God's plan for salvation in this life, not in the world, but in the enclosed perfected community. To this end life is closely regulated, goods are often held in common, and would-be entrants are carefully scrutinized. Spiritualists come close to the thaumaturgical response; contemporary Quakers to the reformist; and various community movements flourishing in nineteenth-century America, such as the Oneida Community, to the Utopian orientation.

The response to the world and conception of salvation of any sect may change over time, and the thesis postulated by H.R. Niebuhr was that every sect was valid for only one generation: thereafter, especially by recruitment of the second generation, its destiny was to develop, butterfly-like, into a denomination. Whilst this thesis may be exemplified, particularly in the case of certain late nineteenth-century sects in the USA – the Disciples of Christ and the Church of the Nazarene being examples – it is far from being a valid universal proposition, as the persistence over several generations of sects such as Jehovah's Witnesses, Christadelphians and Exclusive Brethren makes plain. Niebuhr's thesis holds best for sects of the conversionist type. The orientation of other sects may also change over time, typically from adventist to introversionist (evident in the case of the Christadelphians) or from introversionist to reformist (true of Quakers), but also into a mixed conversionist and reformist response as found in the Salvation Army.

Although the prevailing stereotype of the sect is of a small, schismatic movement, in actuality contemporary sects are often sizeable bodies with an international distribution and with their origins in some process other than that of schism (e.g. as the development of a group of seekers, as followers of a charismatic or quasi-charismatic leader, or as a result of sponsored revivalism). Thus, the Church of Jesus Christ of Latter-day Saints (Mormons) originated in the revelations to Joseph Smith, Jr, and, despite schisms, that body in itself could claim over 6 million adherents in 1990. The Seventh-day Adventists, who also originated in America in the mid-nineteenth century, began not as a schism but as a movement of those who believed that the second advent would occur in 1843 or 1844. With nearly half a million adherents in the USA, the movement had nearly 6 million believers worldwide in 1990. At about half that size, Jehovah's Witnesses are another sect the origins of which lie not in schism but rather in seekership. The congeries of Pentecostalism have certainly manifested numerous internal schisms, but taken as a whole the Pentecostal movement is basically the product of revivalism (*see* CHARISMATIC MOVEMENTS). Overall, the number of Pentecostalists is probably incalculable, but the larger individual sects among them are of considerable size – among them the Assemblies of God which, in the USA alone, has claimed nearly one and a half million members.

All of these aforementioned sects, and many others, originated in the USA. Except for some of the smaller Pentecostal bodies, all have evolved highly rational patterns of organization and make extensive use of uniform distribution of literature throughout the world. Mormons, Adventists, Witnesses and Christian Scientists all use important texts which supplement, augment or interpret the Bible. In all of these four movements there is strong centralized AUTHORITY with very limited AUTONOMY for the local congregation. In their common rejection of sacerdotalism (which may be said despite the designation, in Mormonism, of all adult males as priests), all have adapted secular styles of leadership and management. Although there is hostility towards the secular state on the part of Mormons, Adventists and Witnesses, all of them, together with Christian Scientists are markedly American in style, and maintain that style in spite of their international diffusion.

The relation of sects to the wider society, and in particular to the STATE, is marked by considerable tensions since sects, as dissentient movements, reject at least some aspects of the general culture and the normal obligations of citizens. Adventist and introversionist sects in particular see their CITIZENSHIP as not of this world, and whilst their members are generally punctilious in 'rendering unto Caesar' in such matters as paying taxes, they normally maintain conscientious objection to compulsory military service. Christadelphians and Exclusive Brethren seek exemption from jury service, and both these sects and several others avoid membership of trade unions or any circumstance of being 'unequally yoked' with unbelievers. Witnesses and Exclusive Brethren commonly disdain all EDUCATION beyond the age of compulsory schooling. All sects favour, and some require strict, endogamy of their members, and contravention of this principle is likely to result in expulsion from fellowship. The wider society becomes concerned at allegations that sects cause family break-up, a circumstance which arises when contravention of sect mores leads to disfellowshipping and the severance of relationship between family members.

Despite contentious issues, sects now enjoy steadily increasing toleration in Western countries, and some sects have taken legal action in different countries to secure the extension of HUMAN RIGHTS on a variety of issues on behalf of their adherents. The major sects generally continue to show sustained growth, particularly in the Third World, despite some persisting persecution (particularly of Jehovah's Witnesses). These Christian sects have been by no means superseded by the emergence, in recent decades, of NEW RELIGIOUS MOVEMENTS, many of them of exotic provenance, which, whilst certainly identifiable as deviant minorities, are not strictly to be defined as sects in the now-established sense of the term.

Beckford, J.A. (1975) *The Trumpet of Prophecy: A Sociological Study of Jehovah's Witnesses*, Oxford: Blackwell.

Kanter, R.M. (1972) *Commitment and Community: Communes and Utopias in Sociological Perspective*, Cambridge, MA: Harvard University Press.

Moore, R.L. (1986) *Religious Outsiders and the Making of Americans*, New York: Oxford University Press.

Schwartz, G. (1970) *Sect Ideologies and Social Status*, Chicago, IL: University of Chicago Press.

Troeltsch, E. (1931) *The Social Teachings of the Christian Churches*, trans. O. Wyon, New York: Macmillan.

Wallis, R. (ed.) (1975) *Sectarianism*, London: Peter Owen.

Whitworth, J. McK. (1975) *God's Blueprints: A Sociological Study of Three Utopian Sects*, London: Routledge & Kegan Paul.

Wilson, B.R. (ed.) (1967) *Patterns of Sectarianism*, London: Heinemann.

——(1970) *Religious Sects*, London: Weidenfeld & Nicolson.

——(1990) *Social Dimensions of Sectarianism*, Oxford: Oxford University Press.

B.R. Wilson

SECULARIZATION

Secularization is the process of social change in which religion loses social significance. That process may be many-sided and may occur over a shorter or longer time period. Its major manifestation occurs as religious agencies lose the social functions which, in traditional societies, they have typically fulfilled. More obviously, secularization also occurs when religious bodies lose control of PROPERTY and resources; when religious personnel diminish in number and undergo loss of social status; when religious ideas and beliefs are increasingly relinquished by the general population; and with the growing neglect of religious practices. Whilst popular conceptions of secularization focus primarily on religious practice, particularly on the decline in recent decades in church attendance, this is no more than one facet of the process and by no means the sole or even the salient criterion of secularization.

The term itself is first recorded in use in the arrangements made under the Treaty of Westphalia following the Thirty Years War, when considerable church property was sequestered and placed under the control of the secular authorities, although the phenomenon as such had occurred in earlier periods of history, notably in the dissolution of the monasteries in England. Such expropriations were conscious and deliberate examples of secularization: in general, however, the concept also applies, and in modern circumstances applies more particularly, to social developments that are neither conscious nor planned, but which affect the character and operation of the social system.

Secularization is a neutral term describing a particular pattern of social development. It should be sharply distinguished from secularism, with which, in loose usage, it is sometimes confused. Secularism is an IDEOLOGY which advocates the abolition of religion and the transfer of the ancillary social functions of religion to secular agencies. In contrast, secularization is a non-evaluative term describing empirically established social trends. Secularism may, in certain respects, have forwarded the processes of secularization, but there are other non-ideological forces at work which have more directly and significantly influenced its course.

Examples of secularization are documented in numerous historical and sociological studies, even when that concept is not explicitly deployed. Various aspects of social change may be identified as constituent elements of secularization. Chief among these has been the rationalization of social, economic and political organization, and the supersession of traditional procedures in which religious practices and beliefs were often entrenched: the increased division of labour is an example discussed below. Laicization, which is the transfer of particular responsibilities and functions from a sacerdotal class to laymen, is clearly closely bound up with secularization and has usually been a more overtly conscious form of it. A typical example would be the replacement of priests and religious in schools by lay teachers, which, in different circumstances, occurred in both England and France. The privatization of religion, a process by which religious agencies have relinquished or reduced significant aspects of their erstwhile social and public performances and confined themselves to servicing private needs, is equally seen as one facet of the more general secularization process, and one of its more recent manifestations in Western society.

Although the focus of interest in secularization lies principally in the last two centuries of Western history (since, that is, the French Revolution and the creation of two consciously secularized regimes, in France and in the USA), longer-term trends can be readily discerned. The effect of the great religions, particularly of Judaism and Christianity, was to discipline and rationalize the numerous random and local agencies which sought to invoke the supernatural. If religion is broadly defined to include all manifestations of belief in and supplication to supernatural sources, then it can be said that these great religions brought order and unity into religious dispositions and actions, thereby establishing a secular realm from which the religious was clearly demarcated. The sustained onslaught against magic and paganism by the Christian churches was no less a way of circumscribing and rationalizing access to the supernatural, and hence of considerably secularizing certain areas of social relationships and activities.

In recent Western history, secularization has occurred as religion has lost its former presidency over other institutions. In times past, secular authorities were legitimized by religious agencies (residually evident in coronations), whilst the endorsement of religious leaders was regularly sought for the pursuit of particular social policies, including even warfare. Social control was sustained by the repertoire of supernatural threats (of HELL, purgatory and limbo) and promises (of HEAVEN). Knowledge ('religion and true learning') and the institutions in which it was purveyed, the universities, were the domain of theologians and church leaders. The SOCIALIZATION of children was primarily in the hands of the clergy. Even in the maintenance of health, religious ministry was prominent, both in the diaconal office and in the provision of infirmaries and hospitals. And the Church sought, too, to regulate recreative activities. In all of these institutional areas, religious authority has given place to secular mandates. GOVERNMENT is now legitimized by democratic procedures and authenticated by rational–legal structures of election and appointment. Social

policy is endorsed by popular manifesto. The maintenance of social control is the concern of a wide variety of specialist agencies of the judiciary and the police, who have recourse to a battery of electronic and bureaucratic devices, from data retrieval systems and traffic lights to fiscal records and, in some countries, identity cards. Knowledge is increasingly scientific, validated by empirical and analytical procedures and subsumed into rational structures of tested theory, whilst for the EDUCATION and socialization of children, reliance is placed on professional, secular experts. Health, similarly divested of its religious connotations, is no longer dependent on divine sanction or intercessorial supplication. Popular recreation has become the concern of several related industries and is no longer subject to religious constraints, and religious bodies themselves are today responsible for only a minor and amateur part of the provision of recreational facilities. This general process of the structural differentiation of the various sections of the social system has been accompanied by the separation of religious and secular concerns, and the virtual disappearance of religious influence from these other areas of social organization.

The decline of influence in public affairs has had the effect of focusing religious activity on the private lives of those who accept its ministrations. Religion has become increasingly more a matter of private predilection than of public responsibility. This process of privatization has placed emphasis on the functions of religion as a source of celebration, solace and reassurance. Simultaneously, as religion has been extruded from its earlier role in reinforcing constitutional, political, social and cultural arrangements, so the opportunity has arisen for the churches to criticize and even to challenge the policies and activities of governments. Some church spokesmen see the process of structural differentiation as altogether salutary in allowing the churches, now freed from extraneous entanglements, to present a less compromised spiritual message.

Privatization is the restriction of the influence of religion to the private lives of individuals, but even in this limited sphere religion no longer has free rein. The operation of modern SOCIETY increasingly depends on refined division of labour and a structure of roles, particularly in economic activities. The expansion of role systems has been a major manifestation of rationalization, as human activities have become more and more specialized and co-ordinated as an essentially impersonal system of relationships. This development has extruded from modern forms of social organization much of the personal affectivity by which relationships were characterized in more communally organized societies. Religion was readily capable of infusing with spiritual values the relationships that prevailed in that older order, but that capacity diminished once society had become role-articulated. Rationalization, by which men are reduced to the equivalent of machine-parts, has been a powerful agency of secularization at an individual level.

The secularization thesis has been disputed on various grounds. Noting that secularization posits a decline in religiosity, some critics have asked when, exactly, was the great age of faith which the thesis implies. In support, they point to the registration, over many centuries, of the complaints of bishops in many dioceses about lax religious practice and absence from communion. However, once it is appreciated that the thesis does not treat solely of Christianity but encompasses in its definition of religion all kinds of recourse to the supernatural, this argument is easily rebutted. There is no doubt about the extent to which people in traditional societies entertained a wide variety of superstitions, belief in witchcraft, magic, charms and relics, as well as, or in lieu of, orthodox religious ministrations. Such promiscuous religiosity does not amount to a great age of faith as conceived by the churches, but past ages were times of vibrant belief in the supernatural, which is all that the longer-term application of the secularization thesis needs to contend.

Other critics have taken as the test of secularization the evidence provided by statistics of church attendance. Whilst not only in relative but even in absolute terms these figures have steadily declined in most advanced societies in recent decades, none the less, they vary considerably from one country to another, and in some of the most advanced societies, such as the USA, attendances have remained at higher levels than elsewhere. The fallacy of supposing secularization to be manifested merely by attendance figures reposes in the behaviouristic assumption that the act of going to church can be taken as a unitary item of account with a uniform cultural meaning no matter in what society or in what denomination it occurs. In practice, there may be culturally specific factors which encourage church-going when, for example, religion serves to reinforce ethnic identity or when, in the absence of long-settled, natural community life, the church becomes a surrogate focus of local attachment. Alternatively, there may be culturally specific deterrents to church attendance, such as a long history of religious obligation and coercion against which, once religious toleration prevails, a negative reaction may occur.

The decline in voluntary allegiance to religious beliefs and support for religious organizations provides some evidence of secularization, even though it is not the central part of the phenomenon. In Britain, and in Europe generally, there has been in recent decades a decline in the numbers professing belief in God (and even more particularly belief in a personal God) and in an afterlife. Confessions, confirmations and baptisms have decreased per head of the eligible population in almost all countries, albeit at different rates. In Britain, many Anglican and nonconformist churches have closed, whilst the number of CLERGY has fallen both absolutely and relative to population. Anglicans and Catholics alike find new entrants difficult to recruit and, once recruited, to retain, so that the average age of clergy in Western Europe is steadily rising.

Sociologists have developed the concept of the internal secularization of religion, alluding to the departure from older doctrinal, liturgical and ethical traditions. Thus, the idea of God as exacting father and judge and of people as inherently sinful has lost currency as the secular culture has shifted from paternalism to fraternalism. The high cultural form of liturgy has been replaced by use of the vernacular in WORSHIP and freedom for spontaneous ecstatic expression in charismatic renewal – a movement sharing something of the ethos of the simultaneously emerging secular hippy movement, which also originated in California. The traditional ascetic ethic which encouraged men and women to forsake gratifications in this world in order to accumulate reward in the next has given way to teachings better accommodated to the hedonism of contemporary secular society.

The dominant contention of the secularization thesis is that whereas religion once fulfilled latent functions in all the institutional areas of society, today those functions are increasingly supplied by deliberate and calculated rational action which makes no reference to the supernatural. The modern social system, unlike traditional societies, operates increasingly on the assumption that the social order is human-made rather than God-given. Associated with this process there appears to have been a considerable diminution of the free-will recourse to traditional religious patterns of thought and practice of, and attendance at, public religious rites and ceremonies. The atrophy of religious culture, as the religious coloration of natural life and social institutions fades, renders religion an increasingly private concern. Support for established religious institutions, ideals, teachings and values was formerly forthcoming from society at large (and in many cases from the state itself). As that support diminishes, so personal faith rather than public performance becomes the primary *locus* of whatever religious commitment remains. Once a relatively integrated religious culture fragments, those who do persist in seeking a religious orientation to the world enjoy unrestricted private choice from a diversified range of often newly-emergent and socially-unrooted beliefs and practices that offer personal reassurance or therapeutic or compensatory benefit. Widespread indifference; the privatization of much of such religious expression as does persist; and the emergence of new movements and cult practices may be regarded as usual accompaniments of the secularization process.

Berger, Peter L. (1969) *The Social Reality of Religion*, London: Faber.
——(1979) *The Heretical Imperative*, New York: Anchor Press.
Bruce, Steve (ed.) (1992) *Religion and Modernization: Sociologists and Historians Debate the Secularization Thesis*, Oxford: Clarendon.
Dobbelaere, K. (1981) 'Secularization; a multi-dimensional concept', *Current Sociology* 28: 2.
Fenn, Richard K. (1978) *Toward a Theory of Secularization*, Storrs, CT: Society for the Scientific Study of Religion.
Martin, David A. (1978) *A General Theory of Secularization*, Oxford: Blackwell.
Sommerville, C. John (1992) *The Secularization of Early Modern England*, New York: Oxford University Press.
Weber, Max (1965) *The Sociology of Religion*, London: Methuen.
Wilson, Bryan (1982) *Religion in Sociological Perspective*, Oxford: Oxford University Press.

B.R. Wilson

SEXISM

Sexism refers to the inferiorization of women because of their 'sex' or, more properly, their GENDER, i.e. the socially constructed view of who they are as women. It might be argued that males also can be inferiorized by gender, and so the term should include both males and females. But, in fact, when this happens it is generally a spill-over from the inferiorization of females. Males experience hostile verbal assaults that suggest that they are not fully 'masculine', but 'sissies' (sisters) or 'effemininate'. Such assault is based on the assumption that men become 'masculine' by negating identification with qualities and roles assigned to females.

Inferiorization of homosexuals because of their sexual orientation is often assumed to relate to their lack of 'masculinity', in the case of males, or 'femininity', in the case of females (*see* SAME-SEX RELATIONS). Thus HOMOPHOBIA is related to sexism. However, this is properly a separate subject, namely 'heterosexism', and so it will not be treated here. This entry will focus on the central meaning of sexism, namely the inferiorization of women as women.

Sexism is expressed in personal psychology and inter-personal relations, but it cannot be defined in only individualist terms. It is part of a social and cultural system with a long history. This system is generally called *patriarchy*. It has shaped the legal, economic and political systems, as well as the cultures, of most of the societies of the world. PATRIARCHY is a broader concept than sexism. It refers to social systems in which the male head of the FAMILY is seen as exercising collective sovereignty over wives, children, slaves and servants, animals and land. Public political power is held by the collectivity of male heads of family: *patres familiae.*

This system does not seem to have existed throughout human social evolution. It arose in close association with plough agriculture, SLAVERY and early URBANIZATION, displacing more egalitarian societies (in terms of both gender and CLASS) in the gathering and gardening stages of economy (Lerner 1986). Although patriarchy includes various other categories of subjugated people – children (including young adults) and slaves or servants – females are the most central category of subjects. Male children can grow up and male slaves become emancipated. Only females remain permanently subjugated. Thus patriarchy is the larger system that shapes sexism as a social and cultural pattern.

Patriarchy shaped not only the classical societies of the Ancient Near East, Greece and Rome, but also those of India and China. It is beyond the scope of this entry to do a comparative world history of the development and characteristics of patriarchy. Suffice it to say that patriarchal societies have generally restricted women in the following variety of ways.

Women were defined as legal dependents on the male head of family, their father, husband or guardian. They lacked autonomous civil status or exercised it only in extraordinary circumstances or through their male guardian. They could not exercise legal or political power directly, i.e. vote, hold office, represent themselves in LAW or enter into contracts in their own name.

Women were economically dependent. This did not mean that women did not do productive labour, but rather that their productive labour, whether in the home or out of the home, belonged to their fathers or husbands. Restrictions were often placed on women as inheritors of PROPERTY. Such property as they inherited or the dowries given them in marriage were often managed by male guardians.

Women suffered restrictions of rights to their PERSONS. They might be forced to marry against their will. At MARRIAGE they were seen as leaving membership in their own family and becoming a subjugated member of their husband's family. There was a sexual double standard in which women must be virgins at marriage and chaste within it, while males were sexually free. Husbands had a right to beat their wives and to have unrestricted sexual access to them (*see* RAPE). Women's bodies, in terms of labour, sexuality and reproduction, were seen as belonging to their husband. Forbidding women birth control or ABORTION is part of this picture.

Women were excluded from the exercise of public roles of POWER and from the EDUCATION and credentials that led to such roles. This meant that women could not hold political or military office, although exceptions might be made for female heirs in the absence of a male heir. Women were generally excluded from priesthoods, especially those of the civil religion, from professional roles, such as lawyers, professors and physicians, and from the higher education that led to such roles. Thus women were excluded from forming the dominant public CULTURE.

Variations on these patterns shaped Western civilization in its classical roots in Ancient Near Eastern, Hebrew, Greek and Roman societies. These patterns continued in the Middle Ages and early modern Europe and America. A partial breakdown and redefinition of the patterns of classical patriarchy took place in the nineteenth and early twentieth centuries with industrialization and the shift from a household economy to a collective industrialized ECONOMY owned and run outside the household. It was these shifts that shaped the system of sexism in its modern form.

With the collectivization of the economy outside the family, household productive labour from wives, children and servants was no longer needed. It became possible to abolish slavery and to emancipate women. Neither of these developments happened easily. In England, the United States and Western Europe there were organized feminist movements in this period that sought to give women equal civil status to men, making women legal persons, with the rights to hold property, make contracts, vote, serve on juries and hold office. Access to higher education and professions were also goals of this first stage of feminism (Flexner 1972).

Most of these goals were achieved by the

1920s in England, North America and Western Europe. However, there remained significant remnants of traditional patriarchal practices toward women. In many codes of law there continued to be restrictions on women's full legal autonomy, in matters such as making contracts, having credit for borrowing money and holding property. The legal name of the married woman as Mrs plus the name of her husband continued the patriarchal assumption that the married woman 'disappears' as a person into the collective legal identity of her husband.

Some universities and professional schools still barred women from study, and many passed new laws that restricted the percentage of women students that could attend. Custom reinforced many of the limits that were no longer present in law. Women found it difficult to establish themselves in more than token numbers and only at the lower end of most professions, such as law, medicine and university teaching. The churches were even slower to open ordained ministry to women. Significant change began to happen in this profession only in the 1960s–1970s.

Physical VIOLENCE to women in the form of rape and domestic battering continued (see DOMESTIC VIOLENCE). The right to birth control was won among Protestants in the 1950s, but continues to be rejected by the Roman Catholic church. The 1980s saw worldwide attack on women's reproductive rights by conservative religion, primarily by restrictions to the right to abortion but often having the effect of diminishing sex education and access to birth control as well (see CONTRACEPTION). Although women were allowed paid employment, they seldom had access to the better paying positions or equal pay with men in those jobs they could obtain.

In the 1960s a new feminist movement arose in Western Europe and North America which sought to address these remaining issues of sexism. They saw that patriarchy, far from being eliminated by giving women legal access to the public sphere of political and economic activity, had been redefined. It continues in renewed form as social structure and culture (see FEMINISM).

The major structural aspect of women's economic inferiorization is the dichotomization of unpaid housework and paid labour. Paid work is organized in time and social location on the assumption that males are the normative paid workers, and they are 'freed' for such work by women doing the unpaid labour of the household. Women are socialized to do this unpaid labour, and men not to do it, as a matter of gender identity. So women who hold jobs also do the unpaid household labour, both for themselves and for the men and children of their household. This makes it extremely hard for women to compete with men in the paid labour force.

The basic pattern of industrial labour is that the better paid jobs with authority and status go to men. Women on average earn about 59 per cent of male wages whilst also carrying most of the 'second shift' of unpaid family labour. Some couples seek to share this labour, but in most Western societies (other than Scandinavia) there is little social support to help them do so. Socialist societies have sought to aid women to work by providing state child care, but this has been resisted in the USA particularly. But these helps do not fully alter the basic gender asymmetry. All working women who have families labour under some elements of this handicap of the 'second shift' from which males are largely exempt.

In addition, the basic psychocultural definition of maleness and femaleness, based on dominance and subordination, continues in modern cultures. The association of masculinity with violence, military as well as personal, is key to this definition. Male status is linked to the right to exercise dominating power over women and other weaker persons, while women are socialized to support and acquiesce in male violence. This culture seems to be revived whenever it is challenged, whether it is expressed in the American President Bush bombing Third World countries to prove that he is not a 'wimp' or in the male batterer putting his wife and children 'in their place'.

Despite the emphasis on women's development in the United Nations and in the WORLD COUNCIL OF CHURCHES current studies suggest that improvements in women's status in the last thirty years have been token. There has been little structural change in the basic patterns by which women work longer hours than men for much lower pay and have far fewer economic assets. The culture of violence to women that supports social violence has not been ameliorated. Indeed both of these patterns may be becoming worse in the 1990s as societies face the stresses of increased population, growing UNEMPLOYMENT and mass POVERTY.

What role has religion played in this history of inferiorization and violence to women and what should it be playing today? Most of the classical world religions – Confucianism, Hinduism, Judaism, Christianity and Islam – have validated patriarchal societies (Sharma 1987), defining them as divinely ordained and the mirror of the cosmic order. Sometimes they have moderated family violence against women by suggesting limits within which men could beat their wives or insisting on the right of the bride to consent to a marriage. But generally patriarchal religions have provided the sacral justifications for the patriarchal patterns described above.

In the 1990s these patriarchal religions also provide a major element in the backlash movements against women's emancipation, expressed in various forms of 'FUNDAMENTALISM'. Fundamentalist movements are found in Judaism, Christianity and Islam, Confucianism, Hinduism and Buddhism. All such movements see the subjugation of women to male familial authority and power as a central expression of their 'return to fundamentals' (Marty and Appleby 1991).

There also exist liberal sectors of Christianity in particular that have supported the ordination of women and the emancipation of women in society. Such Christians have been fairly well represented in leadership sectors of liberal denominations and in the World Council of Churches. For these Christians, overcoming sexism, the equality of women and men in the church and in society, is a faith position, not simply an accommodation to secular society. They regard sexism as sin. The affirmation of the full humanity of women, in mutuality with men, is redemptive and the authentic obedience to divine will. In Christianity (and to some extent in Judaism) there is a conflict between

fundamentally opposed ethical visions in regard to the moral status of sexism.

In conclusion, we can say that sexism, both as personal psychology and as social, economic and cultural systems, has been modified and redefined in modern industrial society. But it continues as a major component by which social power and personal identity are defined for both men and women. Social violence and massive injustice in society are in many ways fed at their roots by sexism. These patterns cannot be significantly changed without uprooting and transforming sexist modes of relationship.

DeCrow, K. (1974) *Sexist Justice*, New York: Vintage.

Dobash, R. (1979) *Violence Against Women*, New York: Free Press.

Flexner, E. (1972) *Century of Struggle*, New York: Atheneum.

Hare-Mustin, R. and Marecek, J. (1990) *Making a Difference*, New Haven, CT: Yale University Press.

Hartsock, N. (1983) *Money, Sex and Power*, London: Longman.

Lerner, G. (1986) *The Creation of Patriarchy*, Oxford: Oxford University Press.

Marty, M. and Appleby, R.S. (eds) (1991) *Fundamentalisms Observed*, Chicago, IL: University of Chicago Press.

O'Brien, M. (1983) *The Politics of Reproduction*, London: Routledge & Kegan Paul.

Ruether, R. (1983) *Sexism and God-talk*, Boston, MA: Beacon.

Sharma, A. (ed.) 1987 *Women in World Religion*, Albany, NY: State University of New York Press.

Rosemary Radford Ruether

SEXUALITY

Sexuality is a concept with notoriously fuzzy borders; it is evaluatively laden and its exact sense and reference are often culturally specific. The narrowest definition of *permitted* sexual activity (characterizing the Judaeo-Christian position in many centuries) is

- vaginal intercourse (behaviour)
- between a male and female who are adults and married (age/gender/relational aspect)
- who have intercourse with the express intention of procreation (intentional aspect).

But sexuality in general covers an immeasurably larger area, not only of other behaviours (e.g. specific acts such as kissing, fondling and 'petting', masturbation, oral–genital cunnilingus and fellatio and less common ones such as anal intercourse, oral–anal contact, inter-femoral intercourse), but also of other relational/gender aspects (between two members of the same sex, or between an adult and a child or between a human and an animal). Sexuality is often defined to include more subtle aspects such as attraction and arousal and to cover the legal, ethical and social mores which will circumscribe or evaluate such activity. The exact form of such evaluation differs dramatically and what is permitted in one CULTURE may be proscribed in another (thus, all societies prescribe incest taboos but they differ widely in what counts as incest; some societies proscribe homosexual relations, others make it obligatory in some contexts (see SAME-SEX RELATIONS)). This complexity makes it impossible to offer a single definition of 'sexuality' and underlines the point that it is a social constructed and changing concept.

Certain distinctions are useful to differentiate common aspects of sexuality. In the past sex *versus* gender has been understood as differentiating the biological and physical basis of sex (male *versus* female) from the social and psychological beliefs and aspects of behaviour appropriate to a person of a given sex, i.e. masculinity *versus* femininity. In recent years 'gender' has been used especially in feminist contexts to refer to all the aspects of female identity (see GENDER).

Sex identification is made biologically, usually at birth from inspection of the genitals, and is defined genetically by the X and Y sex-determining chromosomes to form XX (female) and XY (male) identity. (There are also a number of rare 'intersex' viable alternatives, such as X, XXX, XXY and XYY, whose holders are usually sterile.)

Sexual orientation refers to how a person relates and behaves sexually to members of the same and the opposite sex. Kinsey *et al.* (1948) define orientation as a dispositional continuum (later a seven-point mixture scale) from

[0] exclusively heterosexual (Greek: ἕτερος:

héteros, the other, of two; hence those who have sex with the opposite sex) and through

[3] bisexual (Latin: *bi*-, two, i.e. those who have sex with both sexes) to

[6] exclusively homosexual (Greek: ὁμός, homós, the same; hence those who have sex with the same sex).

The intermediate categories have 'Predominantly X, only incidentally Y' and 'Predominant X, but more than incidentally Y' as qualifiers. This 'Kinsey scale' of 'psychologic reactions and overt experience' is still extensively used in sexual research (*see* same-sex relations for a discussion of homosexuality and bisexuality). This entry will refer primarily to Western and recent studies of heterosexuality.

Because the Judaeo-Christian tradition has had such a strong impact on thinking about sexuality in Western societies it is important to trace its origins and contrast it with other traditions and cultures.

The two stories of Creation in Genesis contain an important divergence in accounting for sexuality. The later Priestly account (1:1–2:4) stresses the reproductive; male and female are made simultaneously and are commanded to 'be fruitful, multiply, fill the earth and subdue it' (Genesis 1: 28, JB). In the earlier Yahwistic account (2: 4 ff.), God forms man from the dust, and afterwards forms woman from his rib to be 'a helper suitable for man' (Genesis 2: 20, JB). The subsequent tension between the reproductive and companionate/pleasure aspects of sexuality are reflected here. Later Judaism developed a strong commitment to procreation and propagation, and never developed the notion of CELIBACY as preferable, or even as good. Whilst pre-marital virginity of the woman was viewed as necessary, male virginity was not viewed as especially meritorious, though 'fornication' was reprimanded and RAPE merited death. Probably the most heinous sexual sin was adultery, especially by the woman, since this had consequences for property transmission. The Levitical Holiness Code forbade in differing degrees a number of sexual practices, including transvestism, bestiality and male (though not expressly female) homosexual intercourse.

Members of the early Church both in New

Testament times awaiting the parousia and into succeeding centuries quickly gained a reputation as ascetics and celibates, exceeded often only by their heretical rivals, including the dualist Gnostics, the radically anti-sexual and anti-marriage Marcionites and later the Manichees, who numbered St Augustine (b. 354) among their converts. The Manichees had a distinctively double attitude (Brown 1988): sexuality was a powerful and dark, fearful force; sexual desire and procreation stood in stark contrast to true CREATION, polluting the Kingdom of Light. But the sexual impulse and desire could be for ever transcended and banished, and the Adept or Elect (to whom marriage was forbidden) could achieve total freedom from its dark and disturbing power. The more lowly catechumens, the Auditors, by contrast were not thus bound, and young Augustine, aspiring to be an Adept, still wrestled with his sexual desires and kept his mistress. After his conversion to Catholic Christianity in 387, Augustine brought with him and into his writings much of this Manichaean heritage and it cast a long shadow over the subsequent history of Western philosophy and theology of sexuality.

Virginity and celibacy were lauded and elevated to place of honour, and MARRIAGE was simply permitted to those who could not thus aspire. The downgrading of marriage as second-best received its most trenchant statement in Canon 10 of the Council of Trent's twenty-fourth session: 'Virginity and celibacy are better and more blessed than the bond of matrimony.' The detail of the highly elaborate sex-negative prescriptions are well illustrated by 'The Penitentials', confessors' handbooks that developed with the rise of private auricular confession from the sixth century onwards (Brundage 1987). In itself, intercourse was EVIL, an animal lust, and only in marriage (and then only in a circumscribed manner) did it become acceptable, since procreation was its only permitted intention and goal. All other sexual activity (and indeed intercourse in marriage where the aim was not procreation) was sinful; the Penitentials at various points also forbade sex in Advent, Lent, on Wednesdays, Fridays, whilst the wife was pregnant or menstruating, in daylight, naked . . . (ibid., Figure 4.1). Obviously, anything which frustrated procreation was

equally sinful, and non-vaginal intercourse, masturbation, *coitus interruptus*, ABORTION and primitive (if largely ineffective) CONTRACEPTION fell under this heading.

Moreover, the position of woman was hardly flattering. She is cause of the FALL and origin of sexual temptation, and has few rights in either PROPERTY or sexuality. The fact that 'Eva' is reversed into 'Ave' in the growing Marian cultus during this same period poses problems of its own (Warner 1976). The conjunction of Virgin *and* Mother corresponds all too well to the normally incompatible sexual goods of chastity *and* procreation, and whilst none can truly emulate her, the ideal she presents and the devotion she is given (promulgated in large part by male clerics) came to act as a major focus for the values of chaste motherhood and feminine submission. The somewhat dangerous principle of '*Potuit, decuit, ergo fecit*' ('[God] could, it was fitting that He should, so He did') when applied to aspects of Mary's life and death meant that she was elevated into a uniquely exalted position, and hence came to typify the desired female virtues to an exaggerated degree. Woman's position was at the same time demoted through an over-literalist interpretation of the Yahwist Genesis account of the woman as man's helper, reinterpreted as his subordinate. This subjugation of woman to man was expressed particularly baldly by St Thomas Aquinas:

> In a secondary sense the image of God is found in man, and not in woman: for man is the beginning and end of woman; as God is the beginning and end of every creature.
> (*Summa Theologica* I, 93, 4 ad. I)

This culture of ASCETICISM and anti-eroticism became the prevalent and indeed the ruling orthodoxy for many centuries, even if more liberal and sex-accepting voices and opinions were occasionally heard. However unpalatable it is to the Christian tradition, it cannot be denied that this highly distinctive, and disturbing, perspective still permeates much of Christian thinking and pronouncement about sex and gender.

What the 'secret history' of the lives of ordinary folk in this period was is harder to fathom, since there are few sources. Clerical celibacy was becoming (somewhat fitfully) the norm in the West, and local CLERGY and peripatetic friars certainly left little doubt in the minds of the faithful about the Church's official teaching. But actual behaviour was often radically different (Flandrin 1975), even among the clergy. Probably (Parrinder, in Geer and O'Donohue 1978) marriage was a prime concern of the laity, but in most countries in Europe the transmission of property demanded that there be a male heir, and couples would often not seek marriage until pregnancy (to prove fertility and the possibility of male offspring) or until the sex of the newborn had been established. If offspring were to be avoided, methods such as *coitus interruptus* and anal intercourse were often used. Since infant mortality was very high, women's lives were often taken up almost entirely with pregnancy, birth and upbringing.

Up to the Council of Trent marriage needed neither Church nor priest to be valid; the exchange of vows between the man and wife constituted the sacrament. Surprisingly, PROSTITUTION was often viewed as a 'necessary vice', and what evidence there is from folk sources indicates fairly earthy reaction to the pretensions and hypocrisy of many clergy and religious. Although the notion of 'romantic love' (in origin the highly stylized and élitist – but essentially unconsummated – longing of the Troubadour for the Lady) took centuries to diffuse to ordinary folk, the belief that 'Fornication is no sin if accompanied by love' has long been prevalent. The liberating spirit of the Renaissance, with its return to concern for and sensuous appreciation of the body, also remained a minority concern, but equally came to influence all (Foucault 1980: I).

Reformation and counter-Reformation brought surprisingly little change to Christian views of sexuality. Certainly marriage of Western clergy was a major change (or reversion) and may have forged a bond of sympathy between clergy and laity, and the virtual abandonment of virginity and celibacy as 'preferred states' in the Reformed tradition contrasted starkly with the continued Catholic practice. But the aims and legitimacy of such marriage differed little from the earlier tradition, and

continued virtually unchanged until this century.

In the West, INDUSTRIALIZATION brought about a series of changes which were ultimately to change the traditional attitudes towards sex and gender drastically. Initially, however, the growth of modern medicine seemed largely to support traditional values. Over-indulgence in sexual activity and masturbation were repeatedly identified medically as the causes of many physical pathologies (and later, conditions identified as psychological pathologies), and the ravages of syphilis from the sixteenth century (whose actual three-stage progression was not understood until the nineteenth century) understandably, if erroneously, was attributed to sexual promiscuity, which led to the delayed, but lethal, third stage (Bullough 1976). Right up to the mid-1940s, when penicillin was discovered to be an effective cure, medicine and religion joined to lay at the door of sexual activity (and especially pre- and non-marital or illicit sexual activity) the cause not only of these 'venereal diseases' but a goodly number of other conditions (Brandt 1985). In our day, AIDS is an heir to this tradition. An important variant of this medicalization of supposed sexual pathologies occurred following Tissot's theories from the 1750s that wastage of vital fluids from the body could (and ultimately would) be lethal. Semen was especially implicated due to excessive sex (especially when not engaged in for reproduction) and particularly through masturbation, at whose door was laid a series of outcomes from madness to rheumatism. Women were implicated in this pathology, and old echoes sounded in William Acton's warning in 1871 that 'God had created females indifferent to sex in order to prevent the male from losing his vital energy through senseless sexual activity' (Bullough 1976).

With the eruption of Darwinism and technological advances in the nineteenth century, the claims of medical science to diagnose and cure organic and psycho-pathologies, the growth of psychotherapy (and especially psychoanalysis) and the birth of social sciences such as political economy and demography, interest in sexual activity increased dramatically, and not without major opposition. In the nineteenth century the vocabulary for sexuality began to escape theological terminology, and widespread professional acceptance of Freud's assertions that sexual issues concerned with childhood underlay all neuroses shifted attention to sexual matters in a dramatic fashion.

With a rapidly declining death rate after *c.*1850 (and continued high birth rate) the catastrophic overpopulation foreseen by the Reverend Thomas Malthus in the eighteenth century began to become a reality, and increasing material aspirations of the middle class led to sufficient motivation to adopt contraception (*see* POPULATION CONTROL). Vulcanization of rubber and the development of feasible methods of contraception involving the new condom made this possible, but not without bitter opposition from clergy and a number of notorious and bitterly fought court cases (such as the Bradlaugh–Besant trials). With increasing use of condoms, and later of the contraceptive pill, it became possible for the first time for the size and spacing of families to be planned, releasing women from constant child-bearing and allowing the idea of sex for pleasure to become a permanent reality.

Knowledge of the sexual behaviour and attitudes of other cultures was scant indeed in the West. Freer Graeco-Roman lifestyles were certainly known and bitterly opposed by earlier generations, but known in any detail only to the classically educated fraction of the population. Even then, even the most reliable texts were subject to editorial 'Bowdlerization' to disguise different practices (and/or blatant gender change in the case of homosexual practices). Frazer's *The Golden Bough* began to describe and popularize the ways in which other historical cultures dealt in radically different ways with sexuality, and from the 1930s anthropologists such as Ruth Benedict and Margaret Mead (1949) described how the Western equivalencing of sex role and gender (aggressive 'masculine' males and submissive 'feminine' women) was dealt with in totally different (and possibly more stable) ways in other cultures. Malinowski's classic study of sexuality among the Trobriand islanders, *The Sexual Life of Savages in North-Western Melanesia* (1929), served the double purpose of providing a comparative ethnography

of a totally different sexual culture and questioning the supposed universality of Freud's postulated Oedipus complex. Although earlier accounts have been criticized, much detailed, extensive and reliable historical, anthropological and sociological evidence is now becoming available; an excellent, though dated, summary is given in Ford and Beach (1948). What such studies have done is show how contingent Western sexual arrangements are and how limited and ethnocentric Western views of sexuality are (*see also* SAME-SEX RELATIONS). Anthropological studies have shown that sexual activity and attitudes divorced from their cultural contexts are either meaningless or readily subject to misinterpretation when thus abstracted (Davenport, in Geer and O'Donohue 1978).

Sociological studies show equally that not only conceptions of the body, procreation, etc. but sexuality is itself a social (and often a historical) construction (Foucault 1980, 1987, 1988); some argue that an 'essentialist' position (that sexuality is an inherent 'given') is consequently untenable. They have argued that sexuality needs to be seen not only in a given cultural setting but also as an interactional and relational negotiation (Gagnon 1977).

Empirical studies of sexual behaviour are at an interstitial stage. Kinsey's pioneering social–biological work mapped the detail of male and female sexual behaviour and its social determinants, using the notion of 'sexual outlet' to understand the repertoire of sexual behaviour in which an individual engaged whose outcome was orgasm. In the case of males, he divided these (somewhat idiosyncratically) into masturbation, nocturnal (involuntary) emission, petting, vaginal intercourse, homosexual activity, animal contact and 'spontaneous' outlets. This was found to vary by educational level, social class, ethnic group and religious identification. (Least sexually active are Orthodox Jews, devout Catholics and active Protestants – his adjectives – and most sexually active are those least religiously active, Jewish, Catholic and Protestant.) The findings received with greatest astonishment (and condemnation) were those for homosexual incidence (*see* SAME-SEX RELATIONS), which provided estimates far in excess of those currently accepted. Although the methodology has (rightly) been subject to detailed criticism, many of his estimates are still acceptable and have not been bettered. Later studies by Masters and Johnson (1966) of the (primarily physical) sexual *response* were based upon clinical and laboratory studies. They argue that male and female sexual excitation follows a standard four-phase pattern (Excitement, Plateau, Orgasmic and Resolution), and that functionally heterosexual and homosexual responses have more similarities than differences. These and similar studies monitored and exemplified the post-Second World War moves toward greater sexual experimentation and openness, and a concern with behaviour and performance. Sexual mores were slower to change, but with the advent of the contraceptive pill that made coition entirely free from fear of pregnancy, behaviour and attitudes began to change from the younger end upwards, with considerable demographic consequences. Premarital sexual activity (and intercourse) and cohabitation before marriage became widespread during the 1960s among younger people, and serial (virtual) monogamy and divorce became a common pattern. Even among Roman Catholics (and especially among middle-class members), 'artificial' birth control has become very widespread indeed, and the number of children and the life-span devoted to procreation and upbringing have declined systematically.

The coming of AIDS/HIV infection has had disastrous consequences among heterosexuals in Africa, and is beginning to grow among already socially disadvantaged groups in inner-city areas, especially in the Americas. Whether it is self-sustaining in the heterosexual population in Europe is still subject to debate, but the balance of opinion is strongly that it will become so. Whether the sexual behaviour of heterosexuals will change (as sexual behaviour has among homosexual men) and whether AIDS/HIV infection will be seen as a threat is yet to be found out; careful probability-sample surveys of sexual behaviour of the general population are now under way in many Western countries (Johnson *et al.* 1994).

The contributions of psychology, biomedical science and social sciences such as anthropology and sociology have had an immense impact on thinking about sexuality, as has Biblical and historical criticism, and, whilst there is continuity, most of these contributions conflict dramatically with historical Christian positions. Churches have made pronouncements which take this material into account, but the Roman Catholic (and Orthodox) hierarchies and fundamentalist evangelical churches maintain a virtually unchanged position of approving only procreative sexuality and condemning not only sex for pleasure but also contraception, abortion, homosexuality and even masturbation. Anglicans have moved slowly and somewhat more cautiously than some liberal Protestant churches, but still remain very conventional in sexual attitude.

Whilst many professionals and lay Christians take views at variance with the official positions (an increasingly common phenomenon) there has been little evidence of any systematic rethinking in theological terms, perhaps because to do this involves the development of radically different starting points. Examples might include views delineated by Dr Jack Dominian (1987), an influential Roman Catholic psychiatrist, in his reply to the encyclical *Humanae Vitae* in 1958, where he defined sexual morality on the basis of 'the concept of the person, in terms of human wholeness, and LOVE', though there are precedents as early as the seventeenth century when Bishop Jeremy Taylor commended marriage as 'the queen of friendships', husband and wife as the best of friends; marriage given 'for the order of nature and the ends of God', including desire for children, lightening the cares of household life and 'to endear each other' (Parrinder, in Geer and O'Donohue 1987).

Whilst traditional modes of thinking remain most common, radical rethinking of a THEOLOGY of sexuality is taking place. Particularly influential is Nelson (1978), whose starting positions include the inherent goodness of sexual pleasure, the recognition of God working in the complexity and chaos of human relationships, the need to understand and learn from sexual minorities, the need to create a 'sexual theology' and new sexual ethics based upon sex as God's gift and hence to begin to think of the church as a sexual community.

The development of any new sexual theology or ETHICS has to take account not only of tradition but especially of the insights and impact of the human sciences on thinking about sexuality, but their implicit (and necessary) heuristic relativism does not provide a means of deciding on moral issues involved in a sexual relationship or action. Historically, Christian thinking on sexuality has been largely negative and continues to be so. An adequate theological rethinking is beginning; it is not clear that it will find acceptance.

Brandt, Allan M. (1985) *No Magic Bullet: A Social History of Venereal Disease in the United States since 1880*, New York: Oxford University Press.

Brown, Peter (1988) *The Body and Society: Men, Women and Sexual Renunciation in Early Christianity*, London: Faber & Faber.

Brundage, James A. (1987) *Law, Sex and Christian Society in Medieval Europe*, Chicago, IL: University of Chicago Press.

Bullough, Vern L. (1976) *Sexual Variance in Society and History*, Chicago, IL: University of Chicago Press.

Dominian, Jack (1987) *Sexual Integrity*, London: Darton, Longman & Todd.

Flandrin, J.-L. (1975) *Les Amours paysannes: Amour et Sexualité dans les campagnes de l'ancien France (XVI–XIXe siècles)*, Paris: Gallimard/Julliard.

Ford, C.S. and Beach, F.A. (1951) *Patterns of Sexual Behavior*, New York: Harper & Row.

Foucault, Michel (1980, 1987, 1988) *The History of Sexuality*, vol. 1, *An Introduction* (1980); vol. 2, *The Use of Pleasure* (1987); vol. 3, *The Care of Self* (1988), Harmondsworth: Penguin.

Gagnon, John H. (1977) *Human Sexualities*, Glenview, IL: Scott Foreman.

Geer, James H. and O'Donohue, W.T. (eds) (1978) *Theories of Human Sexuality*, London: Plenum.

Johnson, A. M., Wadsworth, J., Wellings, K. and Field, J. (1994) *Sexual Attitudes and Lifestyles*, London: Blackwell Scientific Publications.

Kinsey, A.C., Pomeroy, W.B. and Martin, C.E. (1948) *Sexual Behavior in the Human Male*, Philadelphia, PA: W.B. Saunders.

——,——,——and Gebhard, P.H. (1953) *Sexual Behavior in the Human Female*, Philadelphia, PA: W.B. Saunders.

Malinowski, Bronislaw (1929) *The Sexual Life of Savages in North-Western Melanesia*, London: Routledge & Kegan Paul.

Masters, W.H. and Johnson, V.E. (1966) *Human Sexual Response*, London: Churchill.

Mead, Margaret (1949) *Male and Female*, New York: Morrow.

Nelson, James B. (1978) *Embodiment: an Approach to Sexuality and Christian Theology*, Minneapolis, MN: Augsburg.

Spong, J.S. (1990) *Living in Sin: a Bishop Re-thinks Human Sexuality*, San Francisco, CA: Harper & Row.

Warner, Marina (1976) *Alone of All Her Sex: The Myth and Cult of the Virgin Mary*, London: Weidenfeld & Nicolson.

Anthony P.M. Coxon

SIN

Sin is a central category of Christian theological discourse and has been so from the beginning. Its roots lie in the THEOLOGY of the Hebrew Bible and in the religion of Israel and the Jews. It functions as part of the grammar of Christian understandings of the human condition and of Christian understandings of GRACE and salvation. In general terms, sin denotes separation from God, a falling away from a relationship of faithfulness to God expressed in concrete acts of disobedience to the divine will. The following treatment will concentrate on two areas: Biblical hermeneutics and contemporary understandings.

The Bible is concerned throughout with the problem of sin and its consequences. In both Testaments there is an extensive lexicon of terms for sin, as the standard Biblical dictionaries make clear (e.g. Brown 1978). From Genesis on, there are myths and legends which constitute profound reflections on the nature of the human condition as sinful, tables of commandments which identify specific fundamental transgressions of the divine will, histories and prophetic traditions which recount God's love for a people in spite of its frequent rebellion, psalms – the classic is Psalm 51 – which acknowledge personal GUILT and constitute confessions of sin, wisdom traditions which grapple with human experiences of radical EVIL in the world and the problem of THEODICY, gospels which proclaim a messiah who announces the divine forgiveness and JUDGEMENT, epistles which reflect on how the Christ overcomes sin, and apocalypses which herald and envision the ultimate triumph of God and the overthrow of sin.

The main features of the Biblical conception of sin include the following. First, sin is a universal, though not inevitable, aspect of the human condition. A corollary of the doctrine of the universality of sin is the doctrine of human freedom and responsibility. This is the presupposition of the story of the Flood (cf. Genesis 6: 5–7). It is also a central conviction of the theology of Paul: 'all have sinned and fall short of the glory of God' (Romans 3: 23). Second, sin finds expression in acts of unfaithfulness to God and a breaking of the covenant relation with God established in the CREATION of the world, the election of a holy people and the giving of the commandments. Third, sin is both individual and corporate, and fundamentally disorders human relationships – with God, between men and women, within households, within and between nations, and between humankind and the natural environment. The narrative of Genesis 1–11 exposes this dimension of sin in a masterly way, especially in the Garden of Eden story (cf. Moberly 1988). Fourth, sin does not just consist of individual acts of transgression: it is not just a moral or juridical concept, but a religious one. The human situation is more serious than the individual sins indicate. For, without being deterministic or fatalistic, sin is understood also as the condition into which human beings are born and the POWER which holds all creation in bondage. The classic Biblical exploration of this dimension of sin is by Paul in Romans 1–8. In orthodox theology, this aspect was developed subsequently, especially by Augustine, into the doctrine of 'original sin'. Fifth, sin is neither the whole nor the end of the Biblical story. Although it provokes the divine wrath, it provokes even more the divine mercy. So in the Hebrew Bible, God repeatedly renews his covenant relationship with his people and provides the means – in acts of repentance and in the sacrificial cultus – for ATONEMENT and reconciliation. In the New Testament, God sends his own Son to reconcile humankind to God by atoning through his death for the sins of the world, and freeing humankind from the power of sin by raising Christ from the dead.

This Biblical legacy is fundamental for contemporary theological reflection on sin. Furthermore, there is a widespread popular and scholarly consensus that the Ten Commandments of the Hebrew Bible and the Sermon on the Mount of the New Testament provide basic guidance both on what constitute manifestations of human sinfulness and what constitutes a moral framework for life in community under God. At the same time, recent developments in Biblical interpretation and hermeneutics have helped to foster new directions in understanding sin. The following examples are noteworthy.

The story of the FALL, in Genesis 3, has been a *locus classicus* for the Christian doctrine of sin and for the strong association in the Western tradition of sin and SEXUALITY, as well as for the tendency to make a scapegoat of the woman – what Elaine Pagels (1988) aptly calls 'the politics of Paradise'. Precedent for this occurs even within Scripture itself: 'I permit no woman to teach or to have authority over men; she is to keep silent. For Adam was formed first, then Eve; and Adam was not deceived, but the woman was deceived and became a transgressor' (1 Timothy 2: 12–14). On the one hand, Phyllis Trible (1978) has given a feminist rhetorical reading of Genesis 3 which effectively rebuts misogynist, scapegoating interpretations and shows that the disobedience of the woman and the man in the garden was shared. On the other hand, Jouette Bassler (1988) has made a sociohistorical study of the use of Genesis 2–3 in the Pastoral Epistles, showing that it was the ecclesiastical politics of the pastor's own day which best explains his insistence on the subordination of women by making 'Eve-the-Easily-Deceived' the archetype, not merely of all women, but of all heretics as well. Such feminist and sociocritical reinterpretations of Biblical texts are important. They strip from our conception of sin associations and ideas which are themselves pernicious and have a long history, witnessed to vividly by Tertullian's notorious statement concerning woman as Eve: 'You are the Devil's gateway. You are the unsealer of that forbidden tree. You are the first deserter of the divine law. You are she who persuaded him whom the Devil was not valiant enough to attack. You destroyed so easily God's image man. On account of your desert, that is death, even the Son of God had to die' (*de Cultu Feminarum* 1:1).

As a second example, attention may be drawn to work done on the Biblical idea of sin as impurity, pollution or defilement. This idea is common in both testaments, where holiness is defined, on its negative side, as the avoidance of impurity. In the levitical laws of the Hebrew Bible, this includes dietary prohibitions, rules of taboo for women concerning menstruation and child-birth, rules about skin diseases like leprosy, incest taboos, MARRIAGE rules prohibiting exogamy, and so on (cf. Leviticus 11 ff., Deuteronomy 14). In the New Testament, the cultic purity rules tend to be set aside or internalized and holiness is defined primarily in terms of the avoidance of spiritual impurity (e.g. Mark 7: 1–23; Romans 1: 24–32); but the imagery of sin as contagious defilement remains, as do rules prohibiting marriage outside the company of the faithful (e.g. 2 Corinthians 6: 14–7: 1). Historically, such imagery has had extremely deleterious effects, however unintended originally. The psychological power of images of stain or pollution sometimes creates neuroses of guilt and obsessional concerns about cleanliness. At the socio-political level, the latter aspect is exemplified in the doctrines and practices of APARTHEID, ANTI-SEMITISM and 'ethnic cleansing'. Taboos about menstruation and child-birth contribute still to the subordination of women, as well as to attempts to control women's bodies and exclude women from the public domain (cf. Ruether 1990). Taboos about sex contribute to the denial of the body in some quarters or to sexual promiscuity in others.

Considerable enlightenment on this imagery of sin and its effects has been gained through the social sciences. Mary Douglas (1966, 1973), in particular, has shown that 'natural symbols' like food or the body are potent media for defining group identity and maintaining group boundaries, and that notions of holiness and defilement have to do, respectively, with what constitutes the integrity and wholeness of the social order and what threatens to destroy it. Her exposition is important in drawing attention to the socio-political dimension of images of sin. It has been applied recently to the interpretation of Biblical sexual morality by William Countryman (1989). In the light of such work, sin and images of sin are not just matters of private morality: they are also matters of public, corporate identity and belonging. Israel's purity rules and holy wars attempted to maintain Israel's separation from the heathen Gentiles, and Christianity's purity rules and holy wars

have attempted to maintain a separation between believers and unbelievers. The VIOLENCE directed at 'sinners', whether in Biblical times or since, is a violence directed at those whom a SOCIETY or group regards as anomalous and therefore threatening to the group's purity (cf. on homophobia, Barton 1989). History bears witness, with tragic irony, to the ways in which conceptions of sin, especially that of sin as impurity, may be used to serve sinful ends.

A third example of recent critical reflection on Biblical ideas of sin focuses on the imagery of sin as captivity, enslavement or bondage. Such imagery is all-pervasive in the Bible and takes its rise from the hierarchical nature of power relations in the ancient world and the universal practice of SLAVERY. Amongst the many powerful evocations of sin or evil as enslavement and salvation as liberation, there are the stories of the EXODUS and the Exile in the Hebrew Bible and, in the New Testament, the gospel exorcisms like that of Legion (Mark 5: 1–20) and above all Paul's analysis of the human condition as one of universal enslavement to sin, in Romans 6: 12–7: 25. The strengths of this conception of sin are manifest. In the twentieth century it has a powerful existential appeal in the context of worldwide experiences of oppression, imperialistic aggression, economic inequality and the human abuse (through domination) of the ecosystem. Nevertheless, it is open also to misinterpretation. Mary Grey (1994) has pointed out that the strong tendency in some religious circles to give a spiritualizing, privatized interpretation to the idea of being in bondage tends to obscure the situation of people who are enslaved in one form or another by the political and economic system. It can, in other words, engender a false consciousness where what people interpret as freedom from the bondage of sin is really an escape from responsible, embodied commitment to just action in church and society.

In fact, greater recognition of the systemic aspects of sin has developed in contemporary Biblical interpretation. Liberation theologians have emphasized ways in which Israel's exodus from enslavement in Egypt can be interpreted as a political act, 'a mass act of CIVIL DISOBEDIENCE' (cf. Fierro 1983), as well as ways in which the teaching and practice of Jesus can be interpreted as provocative socio-political engagement (cf. Rowland 1988; *see* LIBERATION THEOLOGY). Walter Wink (1984) has argued that the mythic language to do with power and 'the powers' in the New Testament has a human and structural dimension to it as well as a spiritual dimension. Dale Martin (1990) has provided a sophisticated socio-historical study showing that an adequate understanding of Paul's language of slavery (to Christ) as salvation is possible only in the context of a familiarity with the ambiguities of slave status in Graeco-Roman social relations. Finally, Bruce Malina (1983) has brought the insights of cultural anthropology to Biblical studies in such a way as to provide a powerful antidote to anachronistic, individualizing interpretations. He shows that sin in the Biblical world is a violation of one's loyalties to the group and that honour and shame are the pivotal values in such a context, not guilt. Such studies, in their various ways, offer a corrective to images of sin as bondage which apply too narrowly and atomistically to the realm of the personal and the individual.

Apart from attempts to make broad generalizations and appeals to summary tables like the Ten Commandments, it is not possible to define what sin is in essence. For, as has been recognized increasingly in theologies influenced by MODERNITY and postmodernism, what sin is or how sin is described is bound up inextricably with who is doing the defining, in what social and communal context it is taking place, and to what end. Defining and describing sin is a political matter, not just a theological matter. Even the commonly held Western, bowdlerizing view that effectively reduces sin to sexual immorality is related directly to the SECULARIZATION of Western society and the consequent privatization and trivialization of religion and morality to matters of the bedroom. Sin will mean different things, therefore, according to one's place in the world, including one's GENDER, race, CLASS, history and geography.

Feminist theologies have made a significant contribution here. They have argued that, until very recently, sin has been defined by male theologians in a universalistic fashion which not only overlooks the fact that women and men sin in gender-specific ways and interpret sin differently, but also casts women and womanhood in a negative light – with disastrous consequences for both women and men. Thus, in her now classic essay of 1960, 'The human situation: a feminine view', Valerie Saiving argued that Reinhold Niebuhr's universalizing interpretation of sin as pride, the will-to-power, exploitation and self-assertiveness ignores completely the experience of women. She says: 'For the temptations of woman *as woman* are not the same as the temptations of man *as man*, and the specifically feminine forms of sin ... have a quality which can never be encompassed by such terms as "pride" and "will-to-power." They are better suggested by such items as triviality, distractibility, and diffuseness; lack of an organizing center or focus; dependence on others for one's own self-definition; tolerance at the expense of standards of excellence; inability to respect the boundaries of privacy; sentimentality, gossipy sociability, and mistrust of reason – in short, underdevelopment or negation of the self' (Saiving 1979: 37).

Of course, Saiving can herself be criticized for her own generalizations about the experience of women. In subsequent intra-feminist criticism, therefore, the point has been made that the understanding of sin held by white middle-class women does not necessarily hold true for working-class women, black women, Third World women and so on. Nevertheless, to the extent that Saiving successfully differentiated 'a feminine view' of sin, the way was opened up for what Mary Grey describes as a 'positional' approach to sin, according to which the imagery of sin is interpreted through lenses of gender, race and class, and attempts at abstract, universalizing definitions are seen as the rhetorical weapons of a predominantly Western, male cultural élite.

Saiving's own analysis was developed by Judith Plaskow in her *Sex, Sin and Grace* of 1980. In dialogue with Niebuhr and Tillich, Plaskow argues that, from the viewpoint of women's experience, sin is not a kind of Promethean rebellion against God and human finitude; rather it is the opposite, the acceptance of passivity and the position of the victim, and 'the failure to take responsibility for self-actualization' (p. 3). She suggests paradoxically that the traditional Christian virtues of SACRIFICE, humility and obedience are what constitutes 'women's sin' – because, in specific cultural contexts of male domination, such virtues only reinforce the subordination of women and inhibit the attainment of true selfhood.

More recently still, Susan Thistlethwaite (1990) has advocated a further important qualification from the viewpoint of the experience of black women, arguing that discussions of sin and selfhood often assume a white Western, individualistic model of the self quite inappropriate to understandings of the self in black cultures: 'For the black woman ... sin is being outside the community and the life-sustaining bread of survival that this community bakes and passes from one generation to the next. ... The besetting sin of black women consists in turning away from their community and their ancestors, in denying their heritage of social responsibility to their people and to oppressed women everywhere' (pp. 82, 85; see BLACK THEOLOGY). This kind of observation reinforces the point made earlier that there can be no unitary definition of sin and that sin cannot be defined independently of specific notions of the self worked out in relation to gender, race and class. For the black woman, identity and power relations in society are blighted by SEXISM and compounded by RACISM. Her understanding of sin will relate quite specifically, therefore, to her sense of being 'other' on both of these fronts.

The other major reinterpretation of sin based on a HERMENEUTICS of suspicion is that of theologies of liberation. Here, emphasis is placed on the contextual nature of theology over against theologies not rooted sufficiently in history and society; and theology is understood as critical reflection on practical engagement in the struggle for the liberation of the oppressed, over against theologies which encourage escapism and naïve optimism. Thus, Gustavo Gutierrez (1974) defines sin in the following terms:

[I]n the liberation approach sin is not considered as an individual, private, or merely interior reality – asserted just enough to necessitate a 'spiritual' redemption which does not challenge the order in which we live. Sin is regarded as a social, historical fact, the absence of brotherhood and love in relationships among men, the breach of friendship with God. . . . Sin is evident in oppressive structures, in the exploitation of man by man, in the domination and slavery of peoples, races, and social classes. Sin appears, therefore, as the fundamental alienation, the root of a situation of injustice and exploitation. It cannot be encountered in itself, but only in concrete instances, in particular alienations.

(pp. 175–6)

Such an analysis constitutes an important corrective to previous understandings of sin. First, it helps to counteract the tendency towards anthropological pessimism in the orthodox doctrine of original sin defined so profoundly by Augustine and developed with such intensity by Luther, Calvin and the Protestant tradition after them. Second, it offers a corrective to the personalism of liberal theology which, with Schleiermacher, defines sin as lack of love, a cutting of oneself off from the feeling of 'absolute dependence', but which leaves sin at the level of personal deficiency and fails to make room for the embodiment of sin in structures of domination and socio-economic relations. Third, it challenges the evolutionary optimism of the theology of Teilhard de Chardin and more recent theologies of human progress like those of the NEW AGE movement. In place of evolutionary optimism, the focus of LIBERATION THEOLOGY is much more that of Biblical ESCHATOLOGY, of hope-filled struggle in history and society for the realization of the KINGDOM OF GOD inaugurated by Christ the liberator. A clear expression of the latter, eschatological option is The Kairos Document (1985), written as a theological response to the political crisis in South Africa occasioned by the persistence of apartheid.

Gutierrez's early analysis of sin is deficient in giving no attention to oppression based on gender. But more recently, in a book entitled significantly Against Machismo (Tamez 1987), he acknowledges explicitly that women in Latin

America are 'doubly oppressed and marginalized' by their POVERTY and sex. The way has opened up, therefore, for an important dialogue between liberation and feminist theologies. This dialogue has been taken some distance already by Dorothee Sölle (1990), who draws for her understanding of sin on both the Marxist idea of ALIENATION and the feminist critique of PATRIARCHY.

There can be little doubt that one of the impressive features of the Judaeo-Christian tradition is its attempt to grapple with the reality of sin and evil, even if those attempts remain flawed in the face of what, theologically speaking, is a mystery of existence where humankind finds itself, tragically, to be both victim and perpetrator. Today, our awareness of sin is not only individual and personal: it is societal as well. It is not just an alienation at the spiritual level: it is rather a breakdown of relationships at every level. At the present time, the ecological dimension of this breakdown is attracting attention, if not concerted action (cf. Primavesi 1991). Related to this are the deep moral ambiguities and uncertainties generated by the phenomenon of nuclear power and the possession of nuclear weapons of mass destruction. As Sallie McFague (1987) puts it: 'The threat of a nuclear holocaust symbolizes the ultimate sin of which human beings are capable. That we are truly capable of such sin is manifest in the other holocaust, the Jewish one. We stand between these two holocausts, which witness to the depths of human evil and illuminate the nature of sin as such: it is the desire to be like God, with control over good and evil, life and death' (p. 139).

No ready-made formula can provide a solution to the problem of sin and evil. But there are a number of ways forward. First, at the theological level, and depending on what is appropriate contextually, we need a concept of God which relates God and the world in a much more holistic, non-dualistic, non-hierarchical way: God as 'lover' rather than (or in addition to) God as 'lord'. Against this backdrop, sin would be understood, not so much as a turning from God to the self and the world, but as a turning away 'from interdependence with all other beings, including the matrix of being from whom all life comes' (McFague 1987: 139).

Second, at the methodological level, we need to develop ways of doing theology which are more local and contextual, more attuned to the experience of the oppressed, the abused and the marginalized, and more oriented on action for what the WORLD COUNCIL OF CHURCHES has termed 'peace, justice and the integrity of creation'. Third, at the ecclesiological level, we need to develop a sharper critique of the systemic evil within the church's own history, structures and organizations (cf. Boff 1985), not least its oppression of women, Jews and sexual minorities. Such a critique could provide the basis for a renewed understanding of the catholicity of the church and of the sacramental and prophetic aspects of the church's call. Fourth, at the liturgical level, liturgies are needed, both in church and society, which permit the acknowledgement in much more profound ways of the flawed, tragic dimensions of existence and which foster also the formation and celebration of more just, truthful and 'connected' forms of life (cf. Ramshaw 1987; see LITURGY). Finally, at the personal and political level, individuals, groups and societies need to accept responsibility for the God-given stewardship in creation which is theirs (cf. Maimela 1989). A doctrine of sin must certainly expose the brokenness and corruption of humankind but not so as to induce inertia, paralysis and despair which only compound the problem. For, in a Christian perspective, the doctrine of sin is inseparable from the doctrine of grace, and recognition of sin is the basis for that turning in love to God, the neighbour and the world which constitutes repentance and brings the hope of salvation.

Barton, S.C. (1989) 'Homosexuality and the Church of England', *Theology* 92: 175–81.

Bassler, J. (1988) 'Adam, Eve, and the pastor', in G.A. Robbins (ed.) *Genesis 1–3 in the History of Exegesis*, Lewiston, ME: Edwin Mellen, pp. 43–65.

Boff, L. (1985) *Church: Charism and Power*, London: SCM.

Brown, C. (1978) 'Sin', *Dictionary of New Testament Theology*, vol. III, Exeter: Paternoster, pp. 573–87.

Countryman, L.W. (1989) *Dirt, Greed and Sex*, London: SCM.

Douglas, M. (1966) *Purity and Danger*, London: Routledge & Kegan Paul.

——(1973) *Natural Symbols*, 2nd edn, London: Barrie & Jenkins.

Fierro, A. (1983) 'Exodus event and interpretation in political theologies', in N.K. Gottwald (ed.) *The Bible and Liberation*, New York: Orbis, pp. 473–81.

Grey, M. (1994) 'Falling into freedom: searching for new interpretations of sin in a secular society', *Scottish Journal of Theology* 47: 223–43.

Gutierrez, G. (1974) *A Theology of Liberation*, London: SCM.

Kairos Document, The (1985), London: Catholic Institute for International Relations.

McFague, S. (1987) *Models of God*, London: SCM.

Maimela, S. (1989) 'A theological view from the non-nuclear world', in R.J. Bauckham and R.J. Elford (eds) *The Nuclear Weapons Debate*, London: SCM, pp. 16–28.

Malina, B. (1983) *The New Testament World*, London: SCM.

Martin, D.B. (1990) *Slavery as Salvation*, New Haven, CT and London: Yale University Press.

Moberly, R.W.L. (1988) 'Did the serpent get it right?', *Journal of Theological Studies* 39: 1–27.

Pagels, E. (1988) *Adam, Eve, and the Serpent*, London: Weidenfeld & Nicolson.

Plaskow, J. (1980) *Sex, Sin and Grace*, Washington, DC: University Press of America.

Primavesi, A. (1991) *From Apocalypse to Genesis: Ecology, Feminism and Christianity*, London: Burns & Oates.

Ramshaw, E. (1987) *Ritual and Pastoral Care*, Philadelphia, PA: Fortress Press.

Rowland, C. (1988) *Radical Christianity*, Oxford: Polity.

Ruether, R.R. (1990) 'Women's body and blood: the sacred and the impure', in A. Joseph (ed.) *Through the Devil's Gateway*, London: SPCK, pp. 7–21.

Saiving, V. (1979) 'The human situation: a feminine view', in C.P. Christ and J. Plaskow (eds) *Womanspirit Rising*, San Francisco, CA: Harper & Row, pp. 25–42.

Sölle, D. (1990) *Thinking About God*, London: SCM.

Tamez, E. (1987) *Against Machismo*, Oak Park, IL: Meyer Stone Books.

Thistlethwaite, S. (1990) *Sex, Race, and God*, London: Geoffrey Chapman.

Trible, P. (1978) *God and the Rhetoric of Sexuality*, Philadelphia, PA: Fortress Press.

Wink, W. (1984) *Naming the Powers*, Philadelphia, PA: Fortress Press.

Stephen C. Barton

SLAVERY

Most societies have had forms of slavery. Some still do. The League of Nations and the United Nations defined current forms of slavery as follows.

1 *Chattel slavery*: 'the status or condition of a person over whom any or all of the powers attaching to the right of ownership are exercised' (LNP, A104, 1926, VI, 1).

2 *Serfdom*: 'the tenure of land whereby the tenant is by law, custom or agreement bound to live and labour on land belonging to another person and render some determinate services to such other person, whether for reward or not, and is not free to change his status' (UN, 19 sess, 9 Feb, 1955, E/2673, 26).

3 *Debt bondage*: 'the status or condition arising from a pledge by a debtor of his personal services or those of a third person under his control for security for a debt where the value reasonably assessed of those services rendered is not applied towards the liquidation of the debt or the length and nature of those services are not respectively limited and defined' (UN, 19 sess, 9 Feb, 1955, E/2673, 26).

Slavery in the West has been justified by the Abrahamic faiths, the Greeks, the Church Fathers and most of the world's religious and secular leaders up to the nineteenth century. 'You may keep [slaves] as a possession for your children after you, for them to inherit as property' (Leviticus 25: 46). Moses, David, Jesus and Paul did not speak out against the institution of slavery, although I will argue that they laid groundwork for change. Many of the ancient Greeks believed in the intellectual inferiorities of some peoples and that they needed to be bound. Plato understood slavery as a microcosm of the hierachical pattern that pervaded SOCIETY and the entire universe – the body is the 'slave' of the SOUL. He approved of slavery though not of Greeks taking Greeks (*Republic*, V, 269). Aristotle said that a good and wise man who happens to be a slave is never 'really' a slave but is 'really' free. The true slave is one bound to his own faults and lusts (*Politics*, 1255; *Ethics*, Book 8). Something similar might have been in Paul's mind when he wrote:

There is no longer Jew or Greek, there is no longer slave or free, there is no longer male and female; for all of you are one in Christ Jesus.

(Galatians 3: 28)

This text was not interpreted by the church as a statement against the institution of slavery, but was spiritualized similarly to Aristotle's comments. Clearly male and female, Jew and Greek, slave and free still existed although relations between them might be altered by LOVE, as was the case in Paul's letter to Philemon about a slave that he himself loved (cf. Philemon).

Both Augustine and Ambrose argued that slavery was good for the slave – the lower one's station in life, the more exalted the virtue. Augustine claimed that slavery was the result of original sin and excessive human greed, but also that slavery is a rod of discipline in the hands of God (*City of God*, 19, 15). Among the famous popes, Pope Gregory the Great said 'it is against nature for one man to have dominion over another' (*Pastoral Rule II*, 6) but he revoked previous laws which had permitted slaves to hold office in the Church. Only a few other voices were heard during the centuries that spoke against slavery.

> Tell me this: who can buy a man, who can sell him, when he is made in the likeness of God, when he is ruler over the whole earth, when he has been given as his inheritance by God authority over all that is on the earth?
>
> (Gregory of Nyssa,
> *Studio Patristica*, vol. XVIII, p. 334)

Aquinas argued that slavery was against nature, but it was introduced as a punishment for SIN (*Summa Theologica*, Q. 52).

Many in the nineteenth century believed that slavery was part of the grand design for the progress of society and the advance of civilization. With slaves the wildernesses could be conquered, the world could be fed and clothed, and industrial prosperity would benefit all, including the slaves. Slavery was also seen as a way of Christianizing the dark races though many assumed that they were inferior to whites.

Perhaps torture, sexual abuse, murder, as well as forced family breakups were so numerous that people who knew became immune to them, although the mass of people probably were kept in ignorance. The British public were finally galvanized in 1781 when *HM Zong* dumped 132 sick slaves overboard in order to save the healthy ones for sale, and they were able to claim insurance on them if thrown overboard but not if they died on ship. People started to ask questions and demand answers.

How did the abolition of serfdom, chattel slavery and debt bondage finally come about? Some argue that it was largely economic changes that brought freedom and people would not easily give up their slaves unless they found them a burden. In 1776 Adam Smith wrote:

> The late resolution of the Quakers in Pennsylvania to set at liberty all their negro slaves, may satisfy us that their number cannot be very great. Had they made any considerable part of their property, such a resolution could never have been agreed to.
>
> (1937: 366)

Others argue that there is evidence that slavery was actually economically viable and Britain's long and expensive crusade to stamp out the oceanic slave trade was at odds with its commercial interests. In Manchester, artisans were the most vocal anti-slavers, perhaps because they were also uprooted from their homes and could sympathize. It can be argued that politicans and churchpeople followed, not initiated, the abolitionist trends among the ordinary people in society. But there are many individual examples, especially among the evangelical and dissenting Christians, of people who risked their careers and livelihoods for the cause of abolition. David Livingstone went to Africa to bring Christianity and commerce, and he thought both would help to eradicate slavery. However, there is one interpretation of these events that claims that Britain's high moral ground in Africa was in reality an IDEOLOGY to show up the Islamic slave-trading Arabs and therefore to gain favour with the people for future trading purposes. Whatever the accuracy of this point, there are few instances of ethical purity in the history of the abolition of slavery.

It could be argued that there are other forms of oppression that are close to the UN definitions of slavery. Examples are the status of some wives, concubines, children, animals, and those forbidden to hold PROPERTY, to vote or to give legal testimony. Many spoke of 'the slavery of sex' when describing married women's legal subservience to their husbands and, in a broader sense, the imprisonment of all women within the traditional concept of a woman's proper sphere. An Ohio woman in 1848 said: 'Slaves are we, politically and legally'. Aristotle mentioned that the wage-labourer is similar to a slave because of a helpless dependence on various employers. On the international scene, many point out that the rich nations are subjecting the poorer nations to a form of subservience that they will find difficult to solve. It is true that these examples are beyond the accepted UN definitions, but they are similar enough to debt bondage to merit consideration.

We could note psychological states of slavish mentalities, and it may well be that with Karl Marx we can still see that certain forms of industrial work are a cause of slave-like fetishism (see ALIENATION). One could argue that 'false wants' brought on by advertising and the general attitudes toward possessions ('born to shop') induce a slavish stance. These are conjectural ideas but need to be discussed widely.

Many have pointed to the spiritual resources that are inherent within Abrahamic faiths that can be utilized for criticizing forms of slavery, even if the religious institutions have not been very assiduous in following their own ideals. At the heart of Judaism is the EXODUS from Egypt, celebrated yearly in the Passover. God said to Moses:

I have observed the misery of my people who are in Egypt; I have heard their cry on account of their taskmasters. Indeed, I know their sufferings, and I have come to deliver them.

(Exodus 3: 7–8a)

Jesus quoted Isaiah when stating part of his own mission for the Kingdom:

He has sent me to proclaim release to the captives . . . to let the oppressed go free . . .

(Luke 4: 16)

Many have used these and similar texts to build up various forms of liberation theologies. An example was the Puritan justification of the American founding where the Exodus tradition played a major role, creating a justification for escaping the oppression and some said, the 'slavery' of England. In our time Latin American theologians have combined these texts with various tools of social analysis to criticize the oppression of existing societies. In a broader sense, the Western faiths brought self-esteem, self-expression and images of a better life. These doubtless helped raise the consciousness of the underclasses and may have even affected the ruling classes. So today we can find many radical activists who are members and leaders of their local synagogues, churches, base communities or mosques.

THEOLOGY cannot deal with these problems in a vacuum, but congresses, parliaments or multinational corporations cannot do so either. The connections between religion, race, CLASS, GENDER, POLITICS and economics form the ideology of any given CULTURE. This applies to slavery as well as other social problems. Moral sensitivity toward the remaining forms of slavery and oppression in the world today must be related to how the nations or cultures perceive themselves and why. Then religions and their various liberation theologies can help motivate individuals and nations to do something about it.

Archer, Leonie (ed.) (1988) Slavery and Other Forms of Unfree Labour, London: Routledge.

Bolt, Christine and Drescher, Seymour (eds) (1980) Anti-Slavery, Religion and Reform, Folkestone: Dawson.

Davis, David Brion (1966) The Problem of Slavery in Western Culture, Ithaca, NY: Cornell University Press.

——(1984) Slavery and Human Progress, Oxford: Oxford University Press.

Drescher, Seymour (1986) Capitalism and Antislavery, London: Macmillan.

Marx, Karl (1963) Early Writings, ed. T.B. Bottomore, London: C. A. Watts.

——and Engels, Friedrich (1931) The German Ideology, London: Lawrence & Wishart.

Patterson, Orlando (1982) Slavery and Social Death: A Comparative Study, Boston, MA: Harvard University Press.

Smith, Adam (1937) The Wealth of Nations, New York: Modern Library (first published 1776).

de Ste Croix, G.E.M. (1981) The Class Struggle in

the *Ancient Greek World from the Archaic Age to the Arab Conquests*, London: Duckworth; corrected reprint 1983.

Troeltsch, Ernst (1931) *The Social Teachings of the Christian Church*, London: Allen & Unwin.

Walvin, James (1983) *Slavery and the Slave Trade: A Short Illustrated History*, London: Macmillan.

——(1992) *Black Ivory: A History of British Slavery*, London: HarperCollins.

Williams, Eric (1944) *Capitalism and Slavery*, Chapel Hill, NC: University of North Carolina Press.

Charles Brock

SOCIALISM

The early history of the term 'socialism' is somewhat obscure. Everyone seems to agree that the ideas which animated it gradually emerged during the course of the eighteenth and nineteenth centuries and that the word itself was first coined during the early nineteenth century in either Britain or France. According to Kolakowski (1981: 183) the invention of the term was claimed by Pierre Leroux, a follower of Claude Henri, Comte de Saint Simon (1760–1825), who first used it publicly in 1832. Berki (1975: 12), on the other hand, suggests that it first appeared publicly in English in 1827 to describe the movement inspired by the English industrialist Robert Owen (1771–1858), and that it then appeared in French in 1835 in connection with the Saint Simonians. Cole (1975: 79), by contrast, dates its use from the second half of the 1820s. Whatever the case, however, it is difficult to disagree with Berki (1975: 12) that such facts do not, in themselves, tell us very much about socialism in its contemporary meaning; to which one might add that they tell us nothing about the complex and deeply ambivalent relationship between socialism and religion.

The more interesting and significant problem in this context is that it is impossible to define socialism in any simple way or to capture its meaning by investigating the ideas of one or another socialist. At its core are a number of very general unifying propositions about values and institutions that can be readily identified. At the institutional level, everyone is agreed that socialists are, at base, opposed to the capitalist system of private enterprise and free market competition and want to replace it with a system based on 'common' or 'public' ownership of the means of production which, at minimum, would ensure a just and equal distribution of WEALTH, while at the level of values there is also general agreement that socialism 'stands for . . . freedom, EQUALITY, community, brotherhood, social justice, the classless society, co-operation, progress, PEACE, prosperity, abundance, happiness'; or, alternatively, that it is opposed to 'oppression, exploitation, inequality, strife, WAR, injustice, POVERTY, misery and dehumanization' (Berki 1975: 9). However, although these propositions have generally served to unite socialists in a (more or less) critical approach to the capitalist order, they have not served to produce any unity on the question of organizational alternatives to it. On the contrary, as Berki points out, all the values to which socialists claim allegiance as well as the principle of public ownership itself are susceptible to different, and often contradictory, definitions and interpretations, or are 'too indiscriminate to have any concrete meaning' (1975: 10). The result has been the development of widely divergent theories and practices. For example, for some socialists equality may mean 'equality of opportunity' while for others it means 'equality of remuneration'. 'Freedom' has also been variously interpreted, for instance as 'the freedom to follow one's natural inclinations' or as the 'freedom to follow one's reason and to strive for self-improvement' (ibid.). Equally, 'public ownership' can refer to a variety of different institutional arrangements: e.g. total state ownership of all resources and central planning; the nationalization of key industries only; state shareholding in private enterprise; workers' control; producers' co-operatives; etc. (ibid.). Nor, as this list implicitly suggests, have socialists been uniformly and unremittingly hostile to the capitalist system. At one extreme, socialists have sought to reform and 'civilize' CAPITALISM from within (social DEMOCRACY in the British and German traditions, for example). At the other extreme socialists have sought its revolutionary overthrow (the communist movements). This diversity is reflected in the numerous derivative 'isms' that have emerged under the general rubric of socialism, for example,

Utopian Socialism, CHRISTIAN SOCIALISM, Fabianism, Social Democracy, Democratic Socialism, Market Socialism, MARXISM, COMMUNISM, to name only the most obvious.

A similar diversity is visible in the relationship between socialism and religion. This relationship is deeply ambivalent on both sides. At one end of the spectrum, socialism has been, and remains, deeply hostile to all forms of religion and religious practice. And the hostility has been reciprocated. The most extreme example is the bitterly antagonistic relationship that has prevailed between modern communism and religion which, as in the Soviet case, resulted in the anathematization and excommunication of each side by the other, although the brute question of survival eventually forced the churches involved to capitulate to the demands of the STATE. At the other end of the spectrum, however, there has over time been something of a confluence between socialism and religion, largely because they share many of the same moral and ethical objections to the social evils of the capitalist system.

From the socialist side the overtly moralistic overtones of much of the critique of capitalism in terms of its cruelty, inhumanity and injustice has produced some close affinities with Christian principles (see below). In the nineteenth century, for example, the German Wilhelm Weitling (1808–71), a prominent revolutionary figure in the 1840s and himself a worker by origin, advocated a revolutionary socialism, or better a primitive evangelical communism, based on Christian principles that promoted complete equality (Kolakowski 1981: 212; also McGovern 1984: 94). In France, the Utopian socialist Etienne Cabet (1788–1856) advocated a form of non-revolutionary communism as the teaching of Christ and went on to found a fully egalitarian community (called Icaria) in the USA in the 1850s (Kolakowski 1981: 213 ff.). More importantly, however, Saint Simon, accounted the founder of modern theoretical socialism by Kolakowski because he took an extremely positive view of historical development and therefore of the new industrial order of early capitalism (1981: 187 ff.), nevertheless looked to religion, or what he called 'the New Christianity', to provide the moral and ethical

principles that could alone underpin modern industrial society and counter the more pernicious consequences of the rampant self-interest that it promoted (Berki 1975: 45; also Kolakowski 1981: 189).

Similar processes have also been discernible in the twentieth century. For example, modern social democracy, particularly its British variety in the form of the Labour Party, has been heavily imbued by a moralism that in many ways derives from the values of Christianity or, in the case of individual politicians, has been overtly Christian in origin. Its preoccupation with ideals like social JUSTICE, goodwill and compassion, its appeals to mutual help and individual responsibility to the community and its calls for CLASS co-operation and reconciliation are precisely those socialist values with which professing Christians can most easily identify without fear of self-contradiction (Berki 1975: 26; also p. 101).

From the religious side there has also been something of a 'convergence' over the course of the last two centuries (see McGovern (1984) for a useful and detailed account).

At the outset, the Christian ecclesiastical hierarchies (especially Catholic and Protestant) anathematized socialism in general as promulgating anti-Christian doctrines and practices. During the nineteenth century the key reasons for this antagonism (see McGovern 1984: 93) were, first of all, that religion appeared to be a major target for the socialist and communist movements which threatened church AUTHORITY and property with destruction. Second, socialism appeared to be the culmination of ideas that had already proved destructive of religion. For example, the Reformation had challenged the authority of the Catholic Church, the Enlightenment had introduced pervasive processes of secularization, and the French Revolution had subordinated the Church to the state and wrought tremendous destruction against French Catholicism. As McGovern notes, 'Socialism seemed bent on carrying these disruptive ideas to their radical conclusion' (ibid.). Finally, there appeared to be an irreconcilable philosophical difference between the two. Religion preached original sin and individual redemption and therefore saw its mission as the achievement of personal salvation, whereas socialist ideas focused on environmental and systemic factors as the primary causes of EVIL (hence presumably the name 'socialism'). The social issues that preoccupied socialists were therefore deemed either irrelevant or purely the responsibility of the state by the established churches, or appeared as an exculpation of individual responsibility. Individual clergy and small Christian groups in most of the countries of Europe did attempt to alert the established churches to the miserable state of the working classes and some of them positively advocated socialism. For example, a significant Christian socialist movement from within the Protestant tradition emerged in England during the 1840s under the leadership of two clergymen, F.D. Maurice and Charles Kingsley (McGovern 1984: 94). But such efforts had little influence on official church policy at the time, although over the long term they did succeed in sowing the seeds of Christian socialism as a possible alternative to capitalism (see McGovern 1984: 95).

Religious attitudes to socialism and social issues have undergone a considerable sea-change, however, during the course of this century. There have been a number of reasons for this.

To begin with, by the turn of the century the established churches could no longer ignore the social destructiveness of the capitalist ethic. The acquisitive and competitive individualism generated by the profit motive, the endless accumulation of wealth for its own sake and the excessive materialism of capitalist society not only had grotesquely debilitating effects on the majority of society (those actually producing the wealth) but threatened central Christian values – community, brotherly love and so on – with complete dissolution. Consequently, although the established churches did not condemn the capitalist system *per se* they increasingly, and vigorously, condemned its abuses.

Second, and related, the established churches also realized that they could no longer remain entirely disengaged from the realities of the earthly world. The period of the 1960s in particular saw dramatic changes in this regard. For example, on the Catholic side Pope John XXIII and the Second Vatican Council adopted new attitudes towards the secular which put great emphasis on the importance of transforming *this* world, and that resulted in a new ESCHATOLOGY that 'stressed no longer heaven alone but "a new earth where justice will abide"' (McGovern 1984: 110). This new social teaching was to give enormous impetus to the Christian–Marxist dialogues that were to follow in subsequent years (McGovern 1984: 111ff.). Equally, on the Protestant side there was a growing preoccupation with social issues and, in particular, with the processes of REVOLUTION that were sweeping the post-colonial world, as evinced for instance at the World Conference on Church and Society in 1966 (McGovern 1984: 115).

Third, the increasing differentiation between the various 'brands' of socialism in the course of the century, between, for example, moderate, non-Marxist social democratic movements on the one hand and radical communist movements on the other, made it much easier for the established churches to adopt a nuanced approach to the question of their relationship to socialism. Although they continued to oppose communism and Marxism as atheistic and materialistic creeds which sought to impose their version of the 'truth' once in power (as had occurred in the Soviet Union and China), there was nevertheless a tacit recognition of the justice of many socialist demands that was visible not so much in positive approval but in the absence of many earlier criticisms of socialism in papal encyclicals and other official church documents.

This process was also encouraged by the final factor, which was the growing radicalism of many ordinary Christians and lower-ranking clergy during the 1960s and 1970s. Profoundly 'disturbed by the enormity of poverty and powerlessness in most of the world and frustrated by efforts or promises of reform' many Christians have increasingly begun 'to question the whole socio-economic system of capitalism' (McGovern 1984: 117). This development was most noticeable in Latin America where Catholic priests began actively to advocate Marxism both as a tool for the critical analysis of capitalism and as providing a vision of the new society – classless, without exploitation or pain – which 'far from appearing inimical to the faith, seemed to them much more consistent with the Christian message than corporate capitalism'

(McGovern 1984: 118). This new 'LIBERATION THEOLOGY' as it has been loosely called also spread to Europe and into Africa. The debates which it has generated within the established churches are as yet far from over.

It is now necessary to investigate more precisely why socialism has been so ambivalent in its attitudes to religion.

Berki (in a perceptive book on which this analysis has relied heavily) locates socialism's ambiguities and contradictions in the heterogeneity of its origins and in the consequent heterogeneity and contradiction of the 'Promethean tasks' that it has set itself. He isolates four key tendencies which are to be found, to a greater or lesser degree, in all forms of socialism, and all of which *inter alia* carry implications for the socialist relationship to religion.

The first is egalitarianism. This, according to Berki, 'is the *classical* principle of socialism' because the early socialists derived some of their inspiration from the model of the Greek city-state (1975: 25) and because it is in many ways socialism's founding principle. It is primarily concerned with the question of 'equality'. This must be understood, however, in its purest form as advocating the 'self-transcendence' of the individual through his or her membership of the community and the consequent primacy of community over individuals. As Berki puts it, 'Equality must lead logically to community.' Egalitarianism consequently 'expresses the aspiration for a return to a 'public or communal way of life' (ibid.). The egalitarian principle is militantly opposed to capitalism because of the antagonistic divisions that it has imposed on the community, notably the division between rich and poor (ibid.). It is ambiguous, however, on the question of religion. On the one hand, it must be opposed to the highly authoritarian hierarchies of power and control that have come to dominate the established churches. On the other hand, it shares with Christian theology its preoccupation with community and fellowship and its values of voluntary self-sacrifice, courage and devotion (Berki 1975: 26). In this respect it could be argued that the egalitarian principle also harks back to the primitive communism of the earliest Christian communities. Certainly, the egalitarian principle has provided one of the points for discussion and the meeting of minds between socialists and Christians.

The second tendency isolated by Berki is moralism. This 'constitutes the Christian principle of socialism', not in the narrow sense but in so far as it derives from the values of Christianity (ibid.). Its chief values are 'social justice, peace, co-operation, brotherhood' (ibid.). Its critique of capitalism consequently focuses on the system's inhumanity in setting 'man against man in the guise of free competition'; and on its fundamental injustice in exploiting and inflicting suffering 'on the very people who produce society's wealth' (ibid.; *see* ALIENATION). As already indicated it is in this moral and ethical aspect that socialism and religion most closely coincide and are most able to talk to one another. However, it is also a source of the most trenchant socialist critique of the established churches. As Berki points out, socialism's moral principle seeks to turn 'the professed moral values' of capitalist society (as enunciated by the churches) 'into really operative principles to be followed in daily life, instead of leaving them as mere façades' (1975: 29). Since the established churches have generally tended to side with the capitalist order and frequently with the most powerful classes and have often manifestly failed to uphold Christian values in any meaningful way, socialists, and for that matter militant Christians, have justly been able to condemn them for their hypocrisy.

Berki's third tendency is rationalism. This derives directly from the Enlightenment of which socialism is the chief heir (1975: 17). Its key values are, in Berki's words, 'individual happiness, reason, knowledge, efficiency in production, the rational, purposeful organization of human society in the interests of progress' (1975: 27). The rationalist principle is not opposed to capitalism *per se* but seeks to build on and 'rationalize' its productive capacity in order to bring about the final 'EMANCIPATION' of man which is what the capitalist order originally promised but failed to deliver (1975: 30). What the rationalist critique of capitalism consequently 'decries most [is] the chaos and waste involved in capitalist production, and its continued enthronement of ignorance and dark superstition' (ibid). The rationalist principle is therefore, on the whole, profoundly hostile to religion as a primary source of ignorance and superstition and a key obstacle to progress, although this has not prevented some rationalists (e.g. Saint Simon) from appealing to religious values like the injunction to 'love one another' when faced with the consequences of unfettered self-interest.

The final tendency, possibly the most extreme and least productive, is LIBERTARIANISM. Berki dubs this socialism's 'romantic principle'. It centres on the ideal of freedom 'in the sense of the total absence of restraints, external or internal' and it seeks to liberate humankind 'from rationality as well as convention' and to return it to its 'natural' and 'authentic' condition (1975: 28). Its critique of capitalism focuses on its 'oppressive character, its systematic smothering and falsification of human desires' (ibid.). This tendency is consequently also entirely hostile to organized religion.

Taken together as an organic whole, these tendencies help to explain socialism's deep ambivalence towards capitalism and the extraordinary inner tensions, divisions and often bitter conflicts over theory, strategy and tactics that have characterized its internal development. They also help to explain, *inter alia*, socialism's equally deep ambivalence towards religion. The affinities over moral and ethical issues have enabled cross-fertilization but, by the same token, have also helped to generate or perpetuate the antagonism that often characterizes the relationship between closely related ideas or systems of thought. This equally applies to the affinities and conflicts concerning the ultimate vision, and achievement, of the ideal. As I have remarked elsewhere (*see* COMMUNISM) the socialist vision of the ideal society is in many ways simply an earthbound version of the Christian Utopia called HEAVEN. Socialism's strongest suit against Christianity has always been to enquire why it has done so little to improve humanity's lot on earth, while Christian antagonism towards socialism has sometimes reflected the fear that were socialists ever to succeed religion would lose its *raison d'être*.

Berki, R.N. (1975) *Socialism*, London: J.M. Dent.

Chambre, Henri (1960) *Christianity and Communism*, trans. R.F. Trevett, New York: Hawthorn.
Cole, G.D.H. (1975) 'What is socialism?', in A. De Crespigny and J. Cronin (eds) *Ideologies of Politics*, Cape Town: Oxford University Press Southern Africa.
Dussel, Enrique (1976) *History and the Theology of Liberation*, trans. J. Drury, New York: Orbis.
Hall, Gus (1964) 'Catholics and Communists, Elements of a Dialogue', *Political Affairs*, June.
Kolakowski, Leszek (1981) *Main Currents of Marxism*, vol. 1, Oxford: Oxford University Press.
McGovern, Arthur F. (1984) *Marxism: An American Christian Perspective*, New York: Orbis.
Oestreicher, Paul (ed.) (1969) *The Christian–Marxist Dialogue*, Toronto: Macmillan.
Tawney, R.H. (1938) *Religion and the Rise of Capitalism*, London: Pelican Books.
West, Charles C. (1958) *Communism and the Theologians, Study of an Encounter*, Philadelphia, PA: Westminster.

Rachel Walker

SOCIALIZATION

Socialization is the process by which individuals internalize the values, standards and mores of SOCIETY at large. It typically refers to the patterns of nurture and EDUCATION through which children enter the adult world. A distinction is sometimes made between primary socialization (nuture up to the age of about five years) and secondary socialization. If the FAMILY is the locus of most primary socialization, wider organisations (schools, peer groups, clubs, churches, etc) are important for secondary socialization. Socialization, or sometimes re-socialization, can also refer to the ways adults are 'converted' through example, propaganda or social coercion.

Functionalist approaches in sociology tend to focus upon the material or behavioural aspects of socialization. For example the work of Emile Durkheim, especially *The Elementary Forms of the Religious Life* (1912), has encouraged sociologists of religion to focus upon the power of RITUAL and communities. Religion is seen as eminently social. It binds society together and is typified in beliefs and rituals which unite people into a single moral community. Through such beliefs and rituals children are inducted into the adult social world.

On this approach, socialization in tribal societies often involves elaborate rituals. Boys and girls nearing puberty undergo crucial and on occasions painful rituals. So, boys are sometimes separated from the tribe, living together and passing through various tests of manhood. Social anthropologists such as Victor Turner have identified this as a 'liminal' stage of socialization. It marks a point of transition, after which young people become adult members of the tribe. They have successfully internalized the values, standards and mores of their society. In contrast, 'deviants' are ostracized. Turner extends the concept of liminality to include such forms of religious behaviour as pilgrimages – individuals undertaking sometimes highly arduous journeys to sacred places and being changed in the process.

In advanced industrial societies such puberty rituals of socialization are seldom so explicit. Nevertheless, in many churches confirmation, or reception into communion, is seen as an important part of religious development. Individuals internalize promises often made for them as infants and are confirmed as adult members through touch. Religious socialization of children may involve a lengthy process of baptism, Sunday school attendance, religious education in schools, and religious example at home. But at confirmation it changes from education to adoption and internalization. The injunction at confirmation of 'Receive the Holy Spirit', in theory at least, becomes the apex of this process.

Functionalist approaches to sociology have again been widely used to analyse the techniques through which NEW RELIGIOUS MOVEMENTS, CULTS and SECTS seek to make new members. Socialization here typically refers to adult 'conversion'. Radical conversionist sects, such as the Jehovah's Witnesses, have carefully planned techniques. They proselytize in pairs for mutual protection and influence, arguing on doorsteps to identify potential recruits, and then subjecting those so identified to a systematic campaign of indoctrination. Their literature is carefully controlled and members are allowed little deviation from it. They rigorously exclude 'deviants', replacing them with new members, who in turn must themselves proselytize on doorsteps. They

also offer an unusually strong community of beliefs and values to members.

Those sociologists who adopt an interactionist or humanistic approach to socialization typically focus more upon cognition. Socialization is seen as the process through which individuals adopt a *Weltanschauung*, world-view or meaning-system. On this approach, ideas play an important social role; ideas change the behaviour of individuals and through them shape surrounding society.

If Durkheim has been the seminal writer for functionalists, Max Weber has been the seminal writer for sociologists of religion adopting this second approach. His major work *The Protestant Ethic and the Spirit of Capitalism* (first published in 1905) offered the startling thesis that Protestant theology was an important factor in generating the values that underlay the origins of CAPITALISM. The this-worldly emphasis of PROTESTANTISM, combined with a stress upon the individual and upon thrift and hard work, acted as a significant contrast to CATHOLICISM. Protestant socialization unwittingly made an important contribution to the rise of Capitalism within the West.

Although Weber's specific 'Protestant Ethic' thesis has been widely contested, his stress upon the social role of ideas is still highly influential amongst sociologists of religion. Studies of both SECULARIZATION and resurgent FUNDAMENTALISM in the world today have often concentrated more upon belief than upon behaviour. Through the writings of sociologists such as Peter Berger and Bryan Wilson, cultural secularization has often been held to be the dominant religious pattern in the West. Religious belief has been viewed as increasingly epiphenomenal and religious socialization has consequently become a decreasing and marginal activity.

However, under the influence of movements such as post-modernism, the theory of secularization has itself become more contested. Resurgent fundamentalism and neo-orthodoxy, especially in ethnic minority groups, has suggested that religious socialization may still be an important factor in society. In some Western countries there has been increasing pressure to allow special schooling for religious minorities. There has been increasing criticism of liberal, secular humanism, and religious groups themselves have frequently claimed that moral socialization is inextricably linked to religious socialization.

In modern theology an important analysis of theological socialization is sometimes termed the Tracy/Lindbeck debate. Most of those involved in this debate seem to agree that we live in a post-modern or post-liberal age. They assume that the secularist assumptions that once predominated in the intellectual world – based upon rationalist individualism and positivism – are now under attack. George Lindbeck's highly influential *The Nature of Doctrine* maintains that this is a radical cultural-linguistic phenomenon which implies that there is no longer any common rational discourse, there are only specific communities which share languages and assumptions (*see* DECONSTRUCTION). The Christian theological community for him is based upon, and fashioned by, Scripture. In that sense it is quite distinct from other communities and, as society at large becomes less Christian or, at least, less fashioned by Scripture, so Christian theologians will become increasingly distinctive and distanced from other intellectuals in the academy.

In contrast, David Tracy's *The Analogical Imagination* argues for a more complex understanding of faith traditions and theological socialization. He is not finally convinced by Lindbeck's stress upon culture at the expense of propositions and experience in faith traditions even within a post-modernist age. For Tracy, both modernist and post-modernist elements are inescapably part of our inheritance and theology responds in many different and complex ways to them. Theology is not deduced simply from Scripture – it involves imagination, interpretation, analogies and experience. For Sallie McFague this implies that Scripture is not the sole means of theological socialization. It is necessary for Christian communities, at times, also to reform and remould Scriptural tradition – for example, in the light of the feminist critique.

Viewed in interactionist terms, theological education is itself a form of religious socialization. Individuals are inducted into patterns of criticism and learning which may radically change their perceptions of faith. It is not just the seminarian who is socialized, but theology

and religion students more generally. They engage in a literature which may expand their religious horizons. Denominational theology was consciously designed to mould perceptions. Inter-denominational and multi-religious theology may transform them.

Berger, P.L. (1967) *The Sacred Canopy*, New York: Doubleday; English edition, *The Social Reality of Religion*, London: Faber.
——*The Heretical Imperative*, New York: Anchor/Doubleday and London: Collins.
Durkheim, E. (1912: trans. 1954) *The Elementary Forms of the Religious Life*, Glencoe: Free Press.
Gill, R. (1977) *Theology and Social Structure*, Oxford: Mowbrays.
——(1987) *Theology and Sociology*, London: Chapman.
Kaufman, Gordon (1981) *The Theological Imagination: Constructing the Concept of God*, Philadelphia, PA: Westminster Press.
——(1988) 'Models of God: Is Metaphor Enough?', *Theology Today*, April, vol. 45, no. 1.
——(1993) *In Face of Mystery: A Constructive Theology*, Cambridge, MA: Harvard University Press.
Lindbeck, George (1984) *The Nature of Doctrine: Religion and Theology in a Postliberal Age*, Philadelphia, PA: Westminster Press and London: SPCK.
McFague, Sallie (1975) *Speaking in Parables: A Study of Metaphor and Theology*, Philadelphia, PA: Fortress.
——(1982) *Metaphorical Theology: Models of God in Religious Language*, Philadelphia, PA: Fortress.
——(1987) *Models of God: Theology for an Ecological, Nuclear Age*, Philadelphia, PA: Fortress and London: SCM.
——(1993) *The Body of God: An Ecological Theology*, Minneapolis, MN: Fortress.
Ruether, Rosemary R. (1988) 'Models of God: Exploding the Foundations', *Religion and Intellectual Life*, Spring, vol. 4, no. 3.
Tracy, David (1981) *The Analogical Imagination: Christian Theology and the Culture of Pluralism*, New York: Crossroad.
——(1987) *Plurality and Ambiguity: Hermeneutics, Religion, Hope*, San Francisco, CA: Harper & Row.
——(1988) 'Models of God: Three Observations', *Religion and Intellectual Life*, Spring, vol. 5, no. 3.
——(1991) *Dialogue with the Other: The Inter-religious Dialogue*, Grand Rapids, MI: Eerdmans.
——and Cobb, John B., Jr (1983) *Talking about God: Doing Theology in the Context of Modern Pluralism*, New York: Seabury Press.
——and Küng, Hans (eds) (1989) *Paradigm Change in Theology: a Symposium for the Future*, New York: Crossroad.
Turner, V. (1978) *Image and Pilgrimage in Christian Culture*, New York: Columbia University.

Weber, M. (1930) *The Protestant Ethic and the Spirit of Capitalism*, London: Allen & Unwin, first published 1905.

Wilson, B.R. (1982) *Religion in Sociological Perspective*, Oxford: Oxford University Press.

——(1990) *The Social Dimensions of Sectarianism*, Oxford: Clarendon.

Robin Gill

SOCIETY

Society: the term is derived from the Latin *societas*, *socius* + *tas*, where the root *socius* is being in and maintaining company with another, as being in partnership or being in association in *collegium* or battle. *Societas* is an association formed for a common aim or goal; an alliance. The earliest usage probably dates from Etruscan law, subsequently repeated in the law of old Rome, and appears to refer to the principle by which PROPERTY was governed and its use shared in the dominant familial situation of the time (*see also* freedom).

Society is now commonly used in three different and principal ways, first, and most generally, to cover any group of people enjoying some form of association and identity. In this sense it covers groups as wide in size and nature as the membership of empires, *poleis*, tribes, clans, sibs etc. When used in this way the term is often used interchangeably, and confusedly, with community; by extension it may even be used loosely and interchangeably with nation or people. Second, the term may refer to high society (*see* CULTURE), an elitist notion, that distinguishes between the general population and a selected group taken to be representative of the cultural and social achievements of an age. Third, since the rise of INDIVIDUALISM, it is common to distinguish, FAMILY, civil society, and the STATE. Society, on this view, consists in the set of relations, often, but not exclusively, economic and contractual that are carried out by individuals and groups coming under the jurisdiction of a state, but excluding political and familial relations. On this understanding the term 'society' would include the constitution and membership of churches and religious groupings. The term 'society' would exclude individual and group relations undertaken as, or constituting, part of the mechanisms of state, e.g., the judiciary, the police, and the bureaucratic apparatus. It would also exclude those actions or aspects of those actions otherwise belonging to some other domain that were a part of the conformation to state regulations.

Some general relations between society in its widest sense, and ETHICS and THEOLOGY can be determined. The first is one of interdependence; hitherto every society has presupposed a theology, every theology has presupposed a society and both presuppose and generate mores that when reflected on becomes ethics. In general terms an absolutist theology goes with an absolutist society, together with its associated mores and practices. A closed theology goes with a closed society with its closed mores, practices and ethical reflections; an open theology goes with an open society, while a diverse theology goes with a diverse society. Any attempt to modify this linkage is fraught with difficulty. To take one example, an absolutist and closed theology will not sit well with an open society or an open ethical outlook.

Second, if, as may happen in the late modern and post-modern world, a cohesive and clearly individual society becomes impossible so a cohesive and clearly delimited theology becomes impossible. Social, cultural and ethical pluralism will not sit well with a closed theology for as the boundaries of social practices and the boundaries of ethical practices change and break down so the boundaries of theology are stretched. An important question in such circumstances is what kind of theology is appropriate when society itself is in the process of being transcended, when society itself becomes impossible, when, 'there is no such thing as society'? Third, and conversely, as ethics and theology comes under strain so society becomes strained. If, as Nietzsche had one of his characters in Zarathustra say, 'You have killed God', (Nietzsche 1978) then is the foundation of society itself destroyed? And if it is what, if anything, is the role of ethics and the role of theology in that destruction?

Fourth, without ethics, and without theology is the continuance of society possible?

Conceptions of theology contain within them conceptions of society. At a surface level this can readily be seen. If, for instance, the idea of a plural society is highly valued, then a theology, an ethic, and a political conception, that reflects, sustains and supports this, will be more appropriate and more relevant than a theology an ethics or a political conception that flies in the face of that value. Conversely a theology that is opposed to cultural diversity in a diverse society is either, not speaking to the concerns of that society, or contains presuppositions akin to those of social engineering. At a deeper level, dealing with these issues turns on the conditions for the persistence of societies, the criteria for their individuation, and the uniqueness of contemporary western understandings of society.

The continuance and persistence of every society depends upon, among other things, biological reproduction, cultural reproduction and development, and the sustenance of institutions and structures sufficient to meet the material, security and psychological needs of its members. A wide variation in the manner and inventiveness with which these tasks are met is possible: hence an infinite number of variations in social forms seems possible. It does appear, both on intuitive and on empirical grounds, correct to assert that social forms furnish the mechanisms by which meaning in life is realized. All known hitherto existing societies have contained some means by which meaning is given to the life of its members. Without such meaning, life, suffering and EVIL would make no sense and there would be no reason, beyond mere biological instinct, to struggle with the adversities of life. Indeed entire societies do appear to have come to an end as a result of ennui (Aberle 1950). In social terms the role of religion, and its intellectual correlates expressed in the theology of the society, is to provide the architectonic meaning structures within which life can be understood and borne. The role of ethics is to provide, among other things, a justification for the normative practices of a society and to bring those practices into question where appropriate. Ethics may depend on a social base for its formation and realization, but it then turns against that base and provides a foundation for its interrogation. The relation between society and religion is similar to the relation between society and ethics. Both are inter-related yet theology can interrogate the social form within which it finds itself. It is a reflective and reflexive practice that contains at its best the potential to look back onto, even into the social foundation that helped spawn it.

It follows from the close inter-relation between religion, theology and society that there is no single architectonic meaning principle valid for all societies and nor should we expect to find one. This does not mean that some broad generalizations are impossible, although they are necessarily tentative and revisable. Ideal-typically, it is possible to distinguish three models relating the society and its religious architectonic. First, societies that regard themselves as participating in an aspect of some drama of the gods; here the gods and life, are understood mythopoetically. Second, societies that see themselves as distinct from, yet connected to and, usually, created by, a god or gods, here Christianity serves as a clear example. Theology in such a case, arises from the critical concern with the reflective and interrogative connection between created and creator. Third, and logically possible, a society divorced completely from any conception of a god or gods; a truly secular society (see SECULARIZATION). As yet we have only a very partial experience of this latter form of society: indeed it may not be completely possible. Systematic attempts to instantiate such possibilities as in the Stalinist Soviet Union were markedly unsuccessful and the current drive in the West towards secularization, expressed best in Nietzsche's claim about the death of God, must be regarded as experimental (see EXPERIMENTATION).

Mythopoetic societies that regard themselves as participating in some drama of the gods have been historically and globally the most pervasive form of social organization. They have been extremely successful at solving internal conflicts and, in some cases, coping with external problems. Their stability has been matched by immense durability: sometimes tens of thousands of years. They range from the empires of the Ancient Near East, the Sumero-Akkadian social organizations of Mesopotamia, the necropolitical empires of Egypt, to traditional and tribal societies of immense lineage such as that found among the Aborigines of Australia.

The religious architectonic that accompanies such societies can be and often is wide ranging, even complete. The surviving instructions of the Vizier Ptah-Hotep of the 5th Dynasty 2450 BCE in Ancient Egypt, for example, range from the most extensive and basic claim that, 'Justice is great, and its appropriateness is lasting; it has not been disturbed since the time of him who made it, (whereas) there is punishment for him who passes over its laws . . .' (Pritchard 1955: 234) to the apparently mundane statement that 'the eating of bread is under the planning of God'. Such claims reveal a conception of a universe of bounded horizons within which every action has significance on grounds residing outside of that action: of its place in the cosmos. To break a LAW, or to act against the mores or folkways is to break with cosmic and divinely given right order.

That order became *oikonomia*, and was expressed as the ecumenic and divinely ordained drive that led to attempts to dominate the known world. To break that order was to risk divine retribution and to impose it was justified by some grand conception of society and its place in the macrocosmos (Voegelin 1987). In modern times, and by a strange inversion *oikonomia*, the model of divine order became ECONOMY, what Arendt called housekeeping (Arendt 1958). To impose on divine grounds a social order on others, later became part of western hegemony, an hegemony inspired by, and justified by, conceptions of right order and universal world history.

In societies where divine or right order was dominant to break that order was to risk divine retribution. Nowhere is this idea put better than by Solon two thousand years after the claims of Ptah-Hotep. As Archon of Athens 594 BCE Solon was appointed to deal with a crisis in Athens. The ills of Athens could not be blamed upon the Gods. It was rather that her citizens had failed to follow the canons of justice, of right order, 'The destruction of our city,' he says, will be brought about not by the direct will of the gods but by the people who have acted without restraint,

They have ignored the firm foundations of divine Justice, who, though now quiet, is

mindful of all that is now happening and that which has happened in times gone by. In due time she will undoubtedly come to seek appropriate penalties. . . . When evil falls upon public life its scourge invades the private lives of all men. A man who thinks it can be escaped by hiding within the jurisdiction and confines of his own home is not secure, for even his house fails to furnish him with security. Such public evil vaults over the wall of his courtyard however high that wall may be, and finds him out, even should he turn and run and conceal himself in the deepest recesses of his own apartments.

(Clarke 1994: 38)

The later distinction formed in Europe from the seventeenth century CE that distinguished the public and private domains, or between civil society and the state is markedly absent in Ancient Greece. Nevertheless there was a distinction between household and public place but one that Solon indicates is not sufficient here. Any action that is an action against the right order that underpins society is an action whose consequences cannot be avoided by slinking off into the private domain. Right order percolates to the very recesses of shared life and divine justice knows no artificial boundaries and no privileged private domain.

Similar accounts of the close relation between cosmic understanding and social life are so widely found that they might be regarded almost as the norm until recently. As an example, and from a completely different context, and from within, in many ways, a different kind of society, the Aboriginal 'Tale of the Dreamtime', both explains creation and gives meaning to life and death.

. . . the Lord God, Baiame walked on the earth he had made, among the plants and animals, and created man and woman to rule over them. He fashioned them from the dust of the ridges and said 'These are the plants you shall eat – these and these, but not the animals I have created.' All was well until the rain ceased to fall and in desperation a man killed some kangaroo rats and shared them with his wife. In consequence of this disobedience death came into the world . . . but the Southern Cross is a sign to men that there is a place for them in the limitless regions of space, the home of the All-Father himself and that beyond death lies a new creation.

(Reed 1978: 14–16)

It is a mythopoetic account of the relation of society to the cosmos that compares in general structure with Genesis in which the sin of Adam in disobeying the prime interdiction is followed by mortality and suffering for all humanity (*see* FREE WILL). The difference is that Genesis does not directly deal with redemption and afterlife. That required subsequent events, particularly the mission of Jesus and a subsequent interpretation and intellectualization of that mission, particularly the theology of St Paul and his successors in that respect. It required also a different type of society, to complete the circle between the interdiction and the redemption.

The second type of relation between society and its *theos logos* is one in which the process of intellectualization has been firmly established and where that intellectualization has been placed at the service of relating *ratio*, *theos*, and social order. It is found most clearly in the inversion in the perception of being that turns myth to thought. Such inversions are widely found; the thought of Confucius, Buddha, and Socrates are clear examples. In the western tradition it is represented, paradigmatically, in both the Platonic discussion of correct speaking about the gods in *Republic* II and in the *periagoge* of the cave in *Republic* VII. In the former, Plato, when discussing how children are to be best educated, says to Adimantus, 'and how are we to speak correctly of the gods?' (*Republic* II). Here in placing a critical purchase on talk about the gods he places a critical purchase on the gods themselves: man becomes the judge of the good, the idea of the good is no longer taken as merely received; it is obtained by critical examination.

This is the point at which the word and concept of theology, as we came to understand that, was introduced into discourse and thought. It is simultaneously the founding moment of

society as an order of community that is consciously perceived as such. The republic was to be an ordered arrangement, a strictly ordered one at that, but its initial order was subject to critical reflection on its religious architectonic. In a poetic sense, at least, philosophy, and theology – as correct yet critical talk about the gods; and the conception of a formally ordered society based on principles accessible to reason, came into being simultaneously. But one contains the seeds of the destruction of the other within it. For a critical theology is ultimately bound to turn against the very society that spawned it. In reaching beyond the present towards that which is eternal it then returns bringing a perspective from beyond the immediate and the momentary to bear on the present, on the merely secular and transitory. Again there is a moment in Plato that draws this out, not in this case of theology but of philosophy. In particular it is that moment in western thought that discovers or invents – we will never know which – the distinction between that which is real and that which is merely apparent.

That founding moment is found in the parable of the Cave. Here the flickering shadows appear as reality to the bondsmen. But one of them turns around, towards the light. In the turning around, the *periagoge*, the bondsman (*see* BONDAGE) is directed to the light and the truth. What has passed before is seen as an illusion, and the new burst of *noetic* reasoning is placed at the service of the world whose realities become exposed as illusions and whose certainties collapse into myths. In the *periagoge* appearance and reality are split apart with staggering consequences for ethics, society and theology.

There are numerous dimensions to the Platonic moment. Most significant, perhaps, is that after Plato all that appears is but a pale participant in a deeper, more fundamental reality. For Plato that reality was not, however, completely inaccessible. For subsequent thinkers it is a matter of debate as to whether any deeper reality that might lie under appearance, or behind appearance, is ever discernible. St Paul put one such view well when he said 'we see as through a glass darkly'. Yet another view is put in the image that humankind has 'a glassy essence', that it is transparent. And yet another view is put that the human mind is opaque, subject to deception and counter deception without ever knowing its true motives for acting or the real foundation of its thought.

There is a significant sense in which all of these views stem from the interrogative form of inquiry represented so well in Plato's critical talk of the gods. That possibility leaves open much lesser possibilities. If we can bring ourselves to challenge the gods then we can certainly bring ourselves to challenge our own ethical practices and our own social arrangements. There is a sense in which the social interrogation, that became sociology in the nineteenth century, has its roots in the interrogative attitude and the appearance–reality distinction found in the fourth century BCE.

A second significant feature of the Platonic moment is that the irruption or burst of reason, of *noesis*, provided part of the cause for the ultimate collapse of that kind of mythopoetic conception of society (Voegelin 1978) and brought about a requirement for a new and more intellectualized conception of the relation between social structure and meaning. *Noesis* as a form of thought is so powerful, so radical and revolutionary that the mythopoesis that is found prior to it, crumbled under the weight of this irruption of reason. *Noesis* requires as its object that which is noetic but that cannot be the gods of yore for they cannot carry either the weight of the task demanded of them or the critical thought with which they are faced. It is not surprising then that it is in the kind of questioning descended from Plato that we find the possibility of deep criticism, a criticism that in the right hands can be used to penetrate to the very foundation of society.

Of course the critical perspective on society and the critical theology that went with it is placed with Plato in a paradigmatic sense only. But it is also significant that Plato, the founder of the possibility of radical questioning, sought also to confine and limit the questioning to but a few and sought to construct a society of such rigid order that it could not effectively be questioned by its ordinary members. The point is not a trivial one, for if everyone questions social arrangements and the gods all the time, there is

a real danger to the continuance, persistence and even the very existence of society. In a closed society such radical and ongoing questioning and interrogation is unlikely to take place. If it is sucessfully closed, the interrogation will be so completely interdicted, consciously or not, as to limit horizons for a considerable period of time.

The Roman Empire provided a satisfactory ecumene for some time, but after its collapse, that had to be re-established. The form that took was to draw on the Stoic conception of laws of nature and right order. The effect of that was to create a society in which the people in it had and knew their station and its duties. That model of order was remarkably successful for more than a millennium. It was a social order that was in accord with the structure of the cosmos given by god. At its best it was intended that in its positive it would mirror natural, divine and eternal law. And human beings lay between angels and beasts in the order of things. Within the society itself, the social order was perceived to be natural and, therefore, God given, or sanctioned by God. It is a period that was limited in its ethical, theological and social reflection and interrogation. Not surprisingly – the order was successful, was perceived as natural and right and the interrogative climate was discouraged or even suppressed. Cosmic order and society were in harmony. The world, the western Christian world at least, was a microcosm of the larger cosmos. It was a recipe for a stable social arrangement that would last for a considerable period of time and, in general terms it did. The most stable of all known societies are microcosmic societies. Left undisturbed they can, as with the Australian Aborigines, persist with little change for thousands of years. Indeed it seems, in some cases, that it is only external changes that bring about internal changes.

The western microcosmic society that developed after the fall of the Roman empire contained within it, however, the seeds of its own destruction in the form of contradictory tendencies. Those contradictions necessarily produced an internal dialectic the outcome of which was radical change. Two tendencies are worth mentioning. First, the interrogative tradition, while suppressed, was not completely dead. Second, the stress on immortality and individual justification, that is at the heart of Christianity sits ill with the notion of right order. If the order and commands are given then in what way, except the trivial sense of mere obedience, is an individual to be justified?

The completion of the critical theme required a distinction between, and a separation or ALIENATION between, society and its members and the breakdown of right order. In medieval terms society was well understood and well intellectualized in the structures of Christian theology as part of right order. But the Christian value of individual life, individual redemption, a clear conception of a monistic self, and the immortality of the single soul, are values that count against strict notions of right order. The value they place on independence of action and judgement are sufficiently great to eat away at the medieval order. Those values when fully articulated are values, as Weber pointed out, appropriate to the Protestant post-feudal order of individual economic independence (Weber 1930). It is this view of economic and ontological independence of individuals that was the foundation of civil society in its distinctively modern sense, an independence aptly described by the jurist Henry Maine as arising out of, 'the movement from status to contract' (Maine 1861).

In MODERNITY the concept of society is often regarded as being opposed to the concept of the individual. A principal issue is whether society is composed of individuals or whether individuals are produced by, or constituted by, social relations. A clear and forceful expression of the individualist point of view is to be found in Thomas Hobbes' claim that society is the outcome of individuals rationally seeking to maximize their safety through the mechanism of state. On this view individuals are prior to both society and the STATE, and the state is prior to society. In contrast to the Aristotelian view, that man was *zoon politikon*, a political animal, Hobbes took it that man was not naturally political but naturally a-social. Individualism rather than sociality was the natural condition of mankind.

The priority of the individual as a self-contained rational being able to posit and· make their own world, is shown in a variety of writings from Robinson Crusoe to Immanuel Kant and beyond. All these cases are merely representative of what was the dominant mode of thought from the seventeenth century to the late nineteenth century. In the nineteenth century the view that individuals were prior to society was challenged from a number of directions. The problem with extreme individualism is that it tends towards scepticism and is unable to account for the reality of others. The best known example is Descartes' *cogito ergo sum*, I think, therefore I am (1968: 54). Descartes' scepticism led him to the view that he could be sure of his own existence, as a thinking substance, and he could be sure of the existence of others, only because God would not fool him into believing that others existed if they did not. God was not a cosmic joker. If others do not exist, or at least can be sufficiently doubted, then society as a constitutive component of individuals does not exist. In consequence of this sceptical train of thought such social argument as can be found from Descartes to the nineteenth century treat individuals as self positing beings who make, but are not made by, society. The sceptical line of reasoning seems to eliminate others, justifying, if not generating, an egoism that undercuts society. In this case the interrogation was carried to the point of doubting self, doubting others and doubting society. That others and that society existed at all, could be justified only through an argument to God. Once again the relation between society and its religious architectonic seemed clear with, in this case, the proviso that the religious architectonic was on the very edge of collapse. Descartes' solution to the problem of scepticism was unsatisfactory in several respects, not least of which is that an argument that depends on God's will and grace to establish the reality of others, seems weak. In an age of increasing secularization it turned out to be catastrophic. The rationalist argument to the corrigibility of sensation that forms the basis of Descartes' argument seemed sound, but the rationalist argument to the existence of God seemed weak, hence the existence of others, especially other minds became, and, in some traditions of western thought, still is, regarded as a major problem.

Nevertheless the problem of other minds remained as a major difficulty in philosophy until Hegel's argument, best developed in the dialectic of Lordship and BONDAGE in *The Phenomenology of Mind*, showed that mind required otherness for its development. Hegel's argument is both powerful and anti-sceptical. Consciousness requires for its development an other consciousness. A mind on its own in an otherwise empty universe would not develop. By extension, human minds can be assumed to develop as a consequence of their interaction with others. The implications of this line of argument are clear and significant. Cartesian scepticism is misplaced and the minds of others do, exist. The fact that we have a sense of our own mind and a sense of our own existence is, for Hegel, proof that others do exist, and exist as mental beings. Human consciousness is always mediated consciousness, mediated through the consciousness of others. Individuals are, therefore, beings who are not self positing beings. Such an idea is mistaken and merely the product of historical time and circumstances. The point was picked up by Marx when he wrote that modern bourgeoisie society was the product of the breakdown of feudalism and that feudalism broke down into the frenzied activities of egoistic individuals (Marx 1975: 166).

One possible consequence of Hegelian and quasi-Hegelian type argument is that individuals come to be recognized as the products of society. Either individuals exist as products of society or they do not exist at all, instead there are only societies, social relations and their expressions. It is perfectly reasonable to think that individuals are but expressions of societies that are constituted in a certain way at a certain time. The end of the nineteenth century marked the development of some significant strands of thought that recognized society as an entity in its own right. At the very least society had a significant effect on individuals. At the most it constituted individuals. Central to such arguments has been the view that there are such things as social facts. Thus, for Durkheim SUICIDE, apparently the most personal of acts, was to be explained not in personal terms but in social terms. By contrast all terms that refer to social institutions and so called social facts are,

for Watkins (Watkins 1973), merely shorthand for that which can ultimately be described in terms of individual actions and dispositions.

What is at issue here seems to be the reducibility of so called social facts. If a social fact, an institution say, or an institutional practice of some kind, can be restated in terms that relate entirely, and only, to the actions of individuals then it would seem that there are no social facts. Such rediscriptions seem, however, to be fraught with difficulty. One might, for instance, attempt to explain the institution of banking in terms of individual actions. Hence the cashing of a cheque can be explained by the actions of the cashier etc., an entirely individualistic explanation. The difficulty is that the actions of a 'cashier' make sense only against the institution of banking and the related practices.

Another way of expressing this point is through descriptions of an action. An action is behaviour that is intended. But it can be intended only if there is a social matrix within which the intention makes sense. Put another way an action, as opposed to aberrant or random behaviour, is always meaningful. But there can be no meaning without social context. Hence no social action is completely describable in individualistic terms. The further description of the individual's intention and meaning always requires a description of the social context. Additionally, it is probably the case that terms that refer to formal institutions are substance sortal terms. 'Bank', 'state', 'bureaucracy' and so on and are not, therefore exhaustively reducible to merely individualistic terms; they have their own validity and their own imperatives (Clarke 1988). This does not deny the reflexive aspects of either society or individuals. That some social terms are substance sortal terms does not exclude the clear observation that such institutions are also reflexive. Indeed, in a critical and self-interrogative society the degree of reflexivity can be extremely high. For such a society that means it is continuously in change and for individuals it means that agency terms, terms that refer to the power of individuals to affect their social environment, do have some force. Individual and society interpenetrate each other and co-subsist. The swing from extreme conceptions of right order to extreme individualism can be reasonably corrected. Both are possible in some limited sense, but neither are right or natural in some larger sense.

This swing can most clearly be seen consequent to the breakdown of feudalism. In feudalism the role and power of the individual was minimal, neither society nor individual were significantly reflexive in a critical mode. The dissolution of the medieval circle, however, freed individuals and gave them powers and modes of reflection hitherto not available to them. Initially this was perceived as individualism: the thesis that individuals constituted their social world. Latterly it has been perceived as a dyadic and reflexive relation; a relation in which individuals are constituted by and constitute social structure and their own identities. This model is well expressed by Giddens' theory of structuration (Giddens 1984) but it has precedents in Marx's view that 'men make history, but they do not make it in circumstances of their own choosing', or 'the dead hand of history weighs heavily on the living'. All such views express a similar sentiment: human beings make their social world, but they make it on a canvas already given to them; they have the capacity to act freely, and within given constraints, they do have the capacity to make what they will of their own lives. This does not mean that they have an omnipotent capacity to choose a social *tabula rasa* into which to be born (*see also* FREE WILL and DETERMINISM). Society is not, therefore, composed of bare individuals. It has certainly come in late modernity to constitute individuals, but those individuals, while having marked powers with respect to society always act against the given backdrop; and to act effectively they have to act on it and not against it. Individuals subsist in society but are not constitutive of society (*see also* INDIVIDUALISM). The relation between society, in its most general sense, and the individuals that have come to subsist in it is like the components of the TRINITY. It is one of internal relations. Both society and individuals do exist and are real and substantial. But society and individuals are also reflexive: they have a duality that can be hypostatized as one pole or another, but all such hypostatizations place needless limits and needless horizons in the way of human life.

The reality of society or the reality of individuals is not one that rests on a pre-existing independence that has come to be related to something already present. It is rather that, as a consequence of contingent features of western social development, individuals have come to internally subsist in social relations. Individuals are, therefore, real and not reducible, but rather than being a natural unit, they are a reflexive and created unit of western social systems. Once so created and once so reflexively constituted they come to have a substantive being that is not readily dismissed or undercut. The implication of this is that in a significant and important sense society is prior to the individual. The historical evidence for this is quite clear. Prior to the breakdown of the mediaeval circle individualism was extremely limited; society, expressed as some kind of distinct and clear order was dominant. The primary form of that dominance was the notion of right order, a direct descendant of the Ancient Greek conception, and prior to that, the right order of Mesopotamia expressed in the code of Hammurabi or in the laws of, Vizier Ptah-Hotep of the 5th Dynasty in Egypt. In broad terms some direct relation between macrocosmos and the microcosmos lasted from the third millennium BCE until the period of the twelfth to the fifteenth century CE. The details are subject to considerable change and variation but the broad structure is the same. The conception of the macro-cosmos determines and is determined by the structure of the micro-cosmos. The religious architectonic determines and is determined by the society. That period has now come to an end.

The religious architectonic is in the process of collapsing. The social architectonic is fracturing and a coherent and single ethical conception has come to its end. From this we might well conclude, and many have, that there is no society, no theology and no ethics.

Such a view would be hasty. It is certainly premature, although not, perhaps, by a great deal. It is not a view without some foundation. There has indeed been a significant rupture between feudal and modern times. It is tempting, therefore to place the source of the rupture with the breakdown of feudalism. This overstates the significance of the 'ditch' that is sometimes placed at the beginning of modernity, separating it from what went before.

In some more than trivial ways, the roots of that rupture can be placed with the beginning of the critical perspective. Once appearance and reality became separated, and a critical purchase against the gods permitted, even obligatory, then it is almost as if the rest was merely a matter of time. The order required to permanently contain that critical perspective as it developed and grew in Christian thought and individualism was probably not possible.

The critical perspective that poetically at least can be placed with Plato's discussion with Adimantus, and his parable of the cave, is twofold. It invents theology and it invents philosophy. The invention of the former removes mere meekness and subservience in the sight of the gods and the invention of the latter was part of the pre-condition for the invention of ethical thinking. The relation here is intriguing, for the criticism of society came into being at the same time as the criticism of the gods and the criticism of conduct. The criticism of society was a direct and immediate consequence of the invention of theology and ethics. We might say that the theo-ethico-political moment is the root cause of the end of society. Theology and Ethics are inimical to Society.

There is a sense in which this is right. A critical perspective on the gods is bound to lead to a critical perspective on the religious architectonic of society – how could it be otherwise? And that critical perspective is bound to be subversive, again, how could it be otherwise? Theology properly carried out just is subversive.

The same is true of ethics. Ethics brings into account the taken for granted practices and institutions of a society and demands that they be justified by criteria not derived internally, from within themselves. A clear and sad example of a failure of ethics in this respect is so-called PROFESSIONAL ETHICS, a rather poor parody of ethics, that deals primarily with internal criteria of the institution in question and does not bring external criteria to bear on the professional institution as such. Ethics properly, and ruthlessly pursued, interrogates not merely practices and institutions but their very social

foundation. Ethics, like theology, is subversive of society.

The subversive effects of theology are there in its founding moment. It is part of the inner contradiction of that moment that in considering how to deal with the religious architectonic for an ideal society the ways and manners of the gods had to be questioned. But the evidence for the general point about the subversiveness of theology is not confined merely to its internal contradiction. It is found clearly in the actual end of the traditional social order in the period of the twelfth to the fifteenth century CE. It was at that point that theology after a period of marginalization was rediscovered. Its first major rediscovery brought empiricism to bear on traditional questions, shaking the foundations of traditional authority. Here St Thomas was the archetypal figure. Its second major rediscovery was the return to the original biblical sources. Here Luther is the archetypal figure. Its third major rediscovery was in working out the implications of the imperatives of a new age for individual justification. Here Calvin is the archetypal figure. Its fourth major rediscovery was the idea of a religion based on reason rather than on revelation. Here Kant was the archetypal figure. In all these cases the effect of the theological imperative was the elimination of the conditions within which society as a coherent and monistic unity of inter-relations could continue to develop. The very features of society that these theological movements intended to foster – a unified society – were made impossible by those same movements. The new rise of theology was subversive of society for it destroyed the religious architectonic.

But subversion does not necessarily mean nihilism. It can also mean TRANSCENDENCE in the sense of rising above, of supersession, *aufgehoben*, of going beyond while incorporating what has gone before.

What has gone before in the sense of recovering a single and monolithic society or a single and monolithic theology or a single and monolithic ethics is not possible. Nor is it desirable to seek to recover it. The past is never recoverable in any clear sense and to seek to do so is, at best, to pointlessly whistle into the hurricane of change, at worst, it is to damage the future.

The past has, however, brought some values with it that are worth preserving, even fostering. The direction of Christian theology and doctrine, has been to encourage, even foster, the emergence of individualism. In itself this is no bad thing. It is unfortunate only when it fails to recognize the social embeddedness of individuals and to treat them as both God given and natural. Individuals are valuable but it does not follow from that observation that individuals are self-positing beings that create, or at least maintain, society as a consequence of rational choices. That conception of individuality downplays the role of society in the formation of individuals.

By contrast, the emergence of the couplet 'society and individual' recognizes the significance of society on the individual and the significance of the individual on society: it treats them as mutually reinforcing in their shared reflexivity. That shared reflexivity could lead to mutual destruction and to shared nihilism but it need not. If it does not it will require a change and development in theology and in ethics as part of the sustenance of society. The contemporary world breaks with all hitherto known conceptions of the relation between theology, ethics and society. The relation between theology and society can be understood in a variety of ways but, hitherto at least, it has always been understood in some way. By contrast the social self-understanding of the contemporary world is an entirely secular self understanding, lacking those *koinonetic* features, in which God is regarded as revealed in the social world.

That understanding has revealed itself variously. It is found in the tribal lineage of the Hebrew Bible: from the account of the social beginnings, through the social devices of the decalogue to the synoicism of lineage and to the fealty to one god insisted upon by Nehemiah when he brought the tribes together after the exile. It is revealed in the New Testament not as mere *societas* but as community, as fellowship or partnership, exhibited in Acts 2: 42, Galatians 2: 9, as participation in and sharing in knowledge of the Son of God, as in 1 Corinthians 1: 9, or as participation in the holy spirit, as in 2 Corinthians 13: 14. It continued through Augustine's conception of the society of God,

through the idea of harmony and NATURAL LAW as found in Aquinas and the natural law successors, and into the idea of natural rights. It is found in the Protestant traditions from Luther and Calvin through to Anglicanism, Episcopalianism, non-aligned Churches and NEW RELIGIOUS MOVEMENTS.

It does not, however, form any part of the self-understanding of modern society, of its workings, or individual actions, of offical pronouncements or actions of, except nominally, state functions or structures. Society is effectively secularized and that SECULARIZATION arises not merely because of a general incredulity towards meta-narratives (Lyotard 1986) of which religious meta-narratives are prime examples, but because such religious sentiment that does exist is, like society itself, diverse and pluralistic. The pluralism and *heteronomeity* of contemporary late modern society, and which is its principal defining feature, as well as its principle challenge, is mirrored in the contemporary pluralism and heterogeneity of theology.

When the relations between individuals are perceived, as in Maine's conception of modernity, as primarily contractual, then the view of society that flows from that is the conception that society does not, of itself, exist but is merely the sum of individual arrangements. Two consequences of note follow from that perspective. The first is that society itself, as a single and unified meaning endowing, and meaningful, structure, loses its significance. It comes to be replaced by a plurality of social forms in which human beings multifariously subsist. The second is that a single meaningful and shared religious practice, a single and unified theological understanding of that practice, a single ethical conception and a single political conception becomes problematic even impossible.

Of the first conception, that society is just the sum of individual arrangements we can be clear that it is mistaken. There are no de-contextualized and individual, yet social, actions; and there are no formal social institutions that are not partially substantive as well as reflexive. We can in short guarantee some sociality. Of the second point we can say that there is no such thing as society, if by that we mean a single, coherent, cohesive, monolithic, monistic substantive entity. If there ever was such a thing theology and ethics saw it off. And if they had not done so it would have generated the ethics and theology that did see it off. The internal contradictions within western society and its precursors guaranteed that it would be challenged. They also guaranteed that the primary basis of the challenge would come from ethics and from theology.

This does not mean that there is something that we cannot call society. It is, however, a strange beast. It is rather like the duality of light, which is both wave and particle, uncertain in its appearance; for it appears as simultaneously substantive and as reflexive. As substantive it appears definable and fixed, as reflexive it appears fluid and without boundaries for no sooner are those boundaries imagined then they have changed. Those boundaries might be imagined by ethics or by theology but no sooner are they imagined than society changes. This implies that the relation between ethics, society and theology is one of constant challenge, interpenetration, change and fluidity. They gather together briefly in a moment, but no sooner is the moment grasped than the grasping changes the relation and destroys the moment. So it is with reflexive relations.

This has considerable implications for contemporary theology and contemporary ethics. Most importantly, that no single conception of either is realistically possible. To imagine a condition is already to change it. In an open society the variety of imaginings is unlimited and the changes and variety of change unlimited and uncontrollable. But this is not the end of society, or of ethics, or of theology; it is rather the foundation for their true beginning. Hitherto these were givens. Givens in the strong sense that if not liked they could not be rejected. They were givens also in that no other option, and no other vision was possible. No variant was permitted. They were indeed the cosmic architectonic writ small in the minds of subjects. But that is not a genuine religion a genuine ethic or even a genuine society. It may be a social order together with given thoughts about how it is to be regarded, but it is imposed not chosen. By contrast for the first time there is the possibility of developing for one's self, with

others, an ethic, a theology, and a social form within which to express it. Such a perspective might be regarded as weak theology, weak ethics and weak society on the grounds that it has to be developed ground up rather than imposed top down. That is indeed a break with the past. But it cannot be otherwise, for the best theology is always and when fully expressed, always has been, radical with respect to society. Participation in one's own life, values, ethics and theology is the only way in which those values can become one's own in a meaningful sense and society is far too diverse to ever return to the past.

There are, however, startling and possibly disturbing consequences of this plurality of society. The effect of social plurality is that each individual becomes the judge of God. It is God that requires justification for actions in the world rather than individuals whose actions require justification before God. There is nothing new in this. When Plato introduced the idea of theology he also introduced that critical perspective on God which when overly intellectualized led to that dismissive saying of the aborigines of Australia that, 'White man got no dreaming'. It also led to Zarathustra saying of the joyful man in the forest, 'Could it be that he has not heard that God is dead' (Nietzsche 1978). To this we might add the codicils, 'Has the Aborigine not heard that there are dreams and visions a-plenty' and has the man in the forest not also heard, 'that society is dead and that a social, theological, ethical and political pluriverse has risen from its ashes'.

Aberle, D.F. *et al.* (1950) 'The Functional Prerequisites of Society', *Ethics*, January.

Arendt, Hannah (1958) *The Human Condition*, Chicago, IL: University of Chicago Press.

Augustine of Hippo (1967) *Concerning The City of God against the Pagans*, trans. Henry Bettenson, Harmondsworth: Penguin.

Clarke, Paul Barry (1988) *The Autonomy of Politics*, Aldershot and Brookfield: Avebury.

——(1994) *Citizenship*, London and Boulder, CO: Pluto Press.

Descartes, René (1968) *Discourse on the Method of Properly Conducting One's Reason and of Seeking the Truth in the Sciences*, Harmondsworth: Penguin.

Durkheim, Emile (1951) *Suicide: A Study in Sociology*,

trans. J.A. Spalding and G. Simpson, New York: Free Press.

Giddens, Anthony (1984) *The Constitution of Society; Outline of the Theory of Structuration*, Cambridge: Polity Press.

Hegel, G.W.F. (1931) *The Phenomenology of Mind*, trans. J.B. Baillie, London: Allen and Unwin.

Hobbes, Thomas (1968) *Leviathan*, Harmondsworth: Penguin.

Luther, Martin (1952) *Reformation Writings of Martin Luther*, trans. and annotated by Bertram Lee Woolf, Lutterworth.

Lyotard, Jean-François (1986) *The Post Modern Condition: A Report on Knowledge*, Manchester: Manchester University Press.

Maine, Henry (1959) *Ancient Law* (1861), London: Dent.

Marx, Karl and Engels, F. (1975) *Collected Works*, vol. 3, London: Lawrence and Wishart.

Nietzsche, Friedrich (1978) *Thus Spoke Zarathustra*, trans. Walter Kaufmann, New York: Penguin.

Parsons, Talbot (1949) *The Structure of Social Action*, Glencoe: The Free Press.

Pritchard, James B. (1955) *Ancient Near Eastern Texts Relating to the Old Testament*, Princeton: Princeton University Press.

Reed, A.W. (1978) *Aboriginal Myths: Tales of the Dreamtime*, Franchise Forest, NSW: Reed Books.

Seager, Richard Hughes (ed.) (1993) *The Dawn of Religious Pluralism: Voices From the World's Parliament of Religions*, London: Open Court.

Tönnies, Ferdinand (1955) *Community and Association*, trans. C.P. Loomis, London (originally *Gemeinschaft und Gesselschaft*, Leipzig 1887).

Voegelin, Eric (1978) 'About the Function of Neosis' in *Anamnesis*, trans. and ed., by Gerhardt Niemeyer, Columbia and London: University of Missouri Press, pp. 206–13.

——(1987) *Order and History: In Search of Order*, Louisiana: Louisiana State University Press.

Watkins, J.W.N. (1973) 'Methodological Individualism: A Reply' in John O'Neill (ed.) *Modes of Individualism and Collectivism,* London: Heinemann.

Weber, Max (1930) *The Protestant Ethic and The Spirit of Capitalism*, London: George Allen and Unwin.

Paul Barry Clarke

SOUL

The idea of the soul is that the essence of human personhood is not to be solely identified with one's physical being but with a spiritual component. This spiritual component normally fully interacts with body and brain to form the unified human person, but it is in principle separable, and at the moment of DEATH this separation happens. The concept of the soul is to be found in many religious and philosophical traditions although there are significant differences both in the way it is understood as existing and in the relationship it is held to have with the human body and brain.

In Western philosophy there are broadly three traditions concerning the soul. One tradition claims the authority of Plato (though Plato's own position is complex and disputed). In this tradition the soul pre-exists the body, comes to live in the body as in a prison, ought ideally to be influenced as little as possible by the body's activities, but should devote itself to the contemplation of eternal things, prior to its liberation from the body at death. In the Aristotelian–Thomist tradition the soul is the animating or formative principle of the body, essential to the body's life and necessarily linked to a particular body as its 'vital force'. For Descartes, the soul as a 'thinking substance' is logically distinct from the body, but in practice it interacts with the body at all times to form a single person.

In recent centuries it has become apparent that the soul, if it exists, certainly interacts with the body at all times. Hence the Platonic understanding seems no longer viable. It has also become clear that 'vitalist' explanations for the body's actions are superfluous, so the Aristotelian–Thomist view tends to be discarded. This means that some variant of Cartesianism seems to be the only form of dualism with any serious philosophical support today, though even that is very limited. Nevertheless Cartesianism may be an option in that it can fully accept everything that modern neurology and biology says concerning the intimate and exact correlation between the thinking and feeling of the mind on the one hand and the physicochemical condition of the human body and brain on the other.

However, for the majority of contemporary philosophers even a Neocartesianism understanding of the soul is rejected, because it seems to them simpler to account for the correlation between mind and brain either by asserting their identity or by saying that the mind is merely an epiphenomenon arising from an ultimately physical substratum. The physicalist position is supported by the fact that any concept of the soul is difficult to integrate with a full acceptance of the theory of EVOLUTION, or with what is now known concerning the imperceptibly gradual development of the human foetus.

During the 1950s and 1960s the 'Biblical theology' movement drew attention to the similarity between the modern physicalist position and the psychosomatic understanding of human beings to be found in much of the Hebrew Bible. Consequently many Biblical scholars came to reject the concept of the soul as a hellenistic intrusion into the Judaeo-Christian tradition. This movement has been weakened in recent decades by a growing awareness that developments within Judaism itself led to an acceptance of dualism by many Hebrew thinkers in the inter-testamental period, quite apart from the influence of Greek thought and language. It has also been realized that the understanding of Biblical revelation is itself rooted in human religious experiences and that reflection on such experience may lead to the view of St Paul that 'spiritual things are spiritually discerned' (1 Corinthians 2: 14).

The argument is that if human beings are believed to encounter God through religious or mystical experiences some concept of a soul seems necessary. For it is axiomatic that these experiences are not mediated through the senses. No one literally 'sees' God with the eyes. Hence if religious 'vision' is to be regarded as veridical, then it must happen directly between God and the soul rather than being mediated through the normal neural pathways of the brain. Likewise religious hopes for a life after death seem to depend on supposing that selfhood can pass to a new life through the continuity of spiritual and mental identity. For even concepts of RESURRECTION depend on a continuity of selfhood between the two lives. According to Pope John Paul II, 'The Church affirms that a spiritual element survives and subsists after death, an element endowed with consciousness and will, so that the "human self" subsists, though deprived for the present of the complement of its body. To designate this element the Church uses the word "soul", the accepted term in the usage of

Scripture and Tradition' (Neuner and Dupuis 1983: 691).

Islam holds a comparable view of the soul. This derived partly through its common semitic inheritance of thought which was then modified by the impact of hellenistic philosophy upon Islam when the writings of Plato and Aristotle were rediscovered and safeguarded by Arab scholars. John Bowker sums up the Islamic view thus: 'Muslims believe in the soul as immortal, bestowed by God and temporarily inhabiting this body. Although it may be separated from the body at death, it will be reunited with the body on the Day of Resurrection' (Bowker 1991: 109).

Hinduism may be characterized as teaching an even more extreme version of the soul's independence from the body than Christian Platonism. For in Hinduism the 'atman' is held to exist as an unchanging and undying entity passing from life to life unaffected by the essentially unreal vicissitudes of the body. This view seems difficult to reconcile with modern knowledge, and indeed with ancient knowledge too as the Buddha pointed out when he repudiated the speculative view that '. . . I shall be atman after death – permanent, abiding everlasting, unchanging and that I shall exist as such for eternity' (Rahula 1967: 59). This and other texts are sometimes interpreted as if Buddha repudiated any concept of the soul, but since he explicitly taught a doctrine of rebirth and denied extinction at death this seems unlikely. What seems more plausible is that, for the Buddha, any understanding of our true identity must do justice to the fact of constant change and development which we know to be the characteristic of all life. This would seem reconcilable with a Neocartesian concept of the soul which stresses the importance of its interaction with the environment for human growth and development.

As to whether the soul is a reality or not the prevailing consensus of philosophy and neurophysiology is overwhelmingly negative, despite the arguments of some outstanding individual thinkers. One major problem is to relate the concept of the soul with what is now known of the genetic heritage of human life. The problem is most acute in the case of the official Roman Catholic position, as defined at the first Vatican

Council, namely that the soul is directly created by God and infused by God into the developing human embryo, presumably at the moment of conception. The genetic problem is less acute for those who see the soul as emerging into being in the process of our living, so that this life is quite literally what Keats called it metaphorically, 'a vale of soul-making' (Ward 1985: 149; cf. Bowker 1991: 221).

Some believe that reports from people who have been resuscitated from apparent death are relevant to the concept of the soul, because such reports often include a claim to have gone 'out of the body' and to have observed the resuscitation attempts from above. Since the observations appear to be accurate and to reflect what would have been seen by an agent looking down from above, such reports suggest that, at the point of death, consciousness actually does come apart from the body. If this is true, then the possibility exists that the soul may indeed be a reality, and the religious hope for a life after death may be at least thinkable.

From the perspective of SOCIETY the concept of the soul has been criticized as leading to an individualistic concern for mental and spiritual goods rather than with a wider involvement with society and with an acceptance of the value of the physicality and SEXUALITY of the human person. It should be noted, however, that such criticisms apply more to 'Platonic' concepts of the soul than to the notion of the soul as such.

In the ethical sphere the concept of the soul continues to influence public debate concerning *in vitro* fertilization and ABORTION. This is because on the Roman Catholic view of the soul being infused into the embryo at the moment of conception it can be argued that the foetus is already a person and therefore entitled to full protection. Such an argument would not of course apply if the soul is thought of as developing throughout life.

Badham, P. (1976) *Christian Beliefs About Life After Death*, Basingstoke: Macmillan.
——and Badham, L. (1982) *Immortality or Extinction?*, Basingstoke: Macmillan.
——and——(eds) (1987) *Death and Immortality in the Religions of the World*, New York: Paragon House.
Bowker, John (1991) *The Meanings of Death*, Cambridge: Cambridge University Press.
Davis, S.T. (1989) *Death and Afterlife*, Basingstoke: Macmillan.
Edwards, Paul (ed.) (1992) *Immortality*, New York: Macmillan.
Hick, J. (1976) *Death and Eternal Life*, Basingstoke: Macmillan.
Kenny, A. (1989) *The Metaphysics of Mind*, Oxford: Clarendon.
Neuner, J. and Dupuis, J. (1983) *The Christian Faith in the Doctrinal Statements of the Catholic Church*, London: Collins.
Rahula, W. (1967) *What the Buddha Taught*, Bedford: Gordon Fraser.
Swinburne, R. (1986) *The Evolution of the Soul*, Oxford: Clarendon.
Ward, Keith (1985) *The Battle for the Soul*, London: Hodder.

Paul Badham

SPECIESISM

Speciesism is the arbitrary favouring of one species' interests over the interests of others. As a concept, speciesism challenges the exclusivist claims of humanocentric ethics which allow humans to discriminate against non-human species on morally irrelevant grounds.

Pivotal to speciesist thinking is the use of the notion of 'species' – rather than the individual within the species – to make assessments of their ontological or moral worth. For example, one recent theologian argues that if we 'look at a herd of cattle, we can pick out individual cows from the mass'. But, he continues, 'no cow has a "history" ... although cattle, like human beings, live individual lives which are extended throughout time, there is no particular significance which resides in the individual life-course of each' (O'Donovan 1984: 51). Note how the notion of *species* is here attributed to animals whilst their *individuality* (analogous to human species' individuality) is denied. In a situation where the interests of individuals from differing species conflict, if a decision regarding whose interests should prevail is made *on the ground of species membership alone* – rather than on the relative merits of the individuals involved – that decision is speciesist.

The Judaeo-Christian tradition has variously reinforced, if not originated, strong speciesist tendencies drawn from its varying theologies of humans as made in the image of God, alone bearers of rationality, and alone possessors of an immortal SOUL. These ideas have been bequeathed to Western tradition in ways that have justified arbitrary and unjust treatment of non-human creatures. The idea, for example, that animals are 'here for our use' has been – and still is – socially illustrated and reinforced by a range of institutional practices – in FARMING, in research and in sport – where animals are regarded as only means to human ends (*see* HUNTING; VIVISECTION).

Anti-speciesist thinking gathers around two issues: first, the arbitrariness of the species distinction so central to Western thought. Note that this view is logically distinct from claiming either that there are no non-trivial differences between species or that biological relatedness of a high degree, such as membership of a family, is irrelevant to justifications for differential treatment. Second, many traditional arguments for human superiority are unfair. The classical arguments for human superiority rely on views of rationality, intelligence, language and moral sense which frequently proceed on the basis of familiarity with humans and relative ignorance of non-humans.

Moreover, they use traits which are self-evidently human to assess the value of non-humans. Comparable traits in non-humans are ignored (such as the possession of intelligence and language analogues), as are distinctive traits which might confer value if assessed without reference to a hidden human model of evaluation. Examples of relevant characteristics include sentience, individual personalities, self-awareness, family life, socially complex interactions and, generally, the possession of interests.

Speciesism is predicated on an essentialist understanding of species which is itself contentious. An essentialist view holds that there is some property which all *and only* members of that species possess. But distinguishing characteristics are by no means consistent within populations of animals or humans. Biology has largely shifted from essentialist to populationist modes of thinking (see Dupre 1981).

The very term 'species' then is problematic to some degree. Speciesism requires that members of the human species – if not all species – be thought of as sharing a common essence which is distinctive. In particular, individual humans are seen as having the human 'essence' even if they are otherwise deprived of the normal traits associated with the species. An example is a mentally handicapped human who has an incompletely formed brain from birth such that there is no hope whatsoever that functions associated with normal human adult behaviour (such as rational thinking, use of language or the acceptance of responsibility for one's actions) will ever be attained. Such instances have come to be referred to as 'marginal cases' (Linzey 1976; Narveson 1977; Regan 1979).

Marginal cases have traditionally been treated in human ethical systems as possessing the essence of the species and to be favoured when compared with members of other (non-human) species. They have thus been given rights (such as freedom from experimentation, or being killed voluntarily, or eaten) even though members of other species, who are not granted these rights, surpass 'marginal' humans in areas historically claimed to be the province of humans alone, such as intelligence, language ability, rationality and the ability to enter into interpersonal relationships.

On the other hand, some theologians (see Linzey 1994) hold that some notion of the integrity of species is vital not least of all to prevent the genetic engineering of animal species for human benefit. If there is no 'essential' or 'intrinsic' nature appropriate to animals or humans, on what basis can we oppose the development of genetically redesigned animals such as 'geeps' (sheep/goat hybrids) or indeed human/animal hybrids? What needs to be wrestled with, from a theological perspective, is the status of what is 'given' as 'good' in creation, on one hand, and the God-given capacity of humans to change what is 'given', on the other. Those who argue against genetic engineering maintain that there is – at the very least – a 'nature' appropriate to animals which is intrinsically valuable and worthy of respect.

The term 'speciesism' was first used by Richard Ryder (Ryder 1970, 1975, 1981) and was popularized by Peter Singer in *Animal Liberation*. Singer argued that the pattern of discrimination in both RACISM and speciesism was 'identical in each case' (Singer 1976: 9). While in a limited way this analogy to other instances of arbitrary exclusiveness has been appreciated (Diamond 1978; Steinbock 1978; Midgley 1984; Rachels 1991; Klug 1995), it has been challenged as to its accuracy and effectiveness.

There are several conceptual problems in relying heavily on any analogy to human discrimination against other humans (whether in the form of racism, SEXISM or SLAVERY). The exclusions of intrahuman discrimination are viewed as problems primarily because they are a negation of the central idea of humanocentric or normative ethics, namely that there is an essence which each human has which is unique and which entitles the human in question to be within the moral circle. It is possible to be completely against racism, sexism or slavery while completely affirming humanocentrism in ethics. The differences in the logical structures of speciesism and the various forms of intrahuman discrimination can be seen in the fact that opposition to speciesism challenges the very basis of what historically has been the core of opposition to racism, namely inclusion of all members of the human species within the moral circle (rather than just those favoured by the racist) because they are uniquely special such that the exclusion of them from the moral circle, and treatment of them 'like animals' is wrong *per se*. The fact that opposition to racism can be premised on an affirmation of the very view which speciesism is opposing reveals how limited any analogy to intrahuman discrimination can be.

Another reason for caution in relying on any parallel with racism is the vagueness of that notion itself. According to Midgley racism is an 'impenetrably obscure concept, scarcely capable of doing its own work' (Midgley 1984: 99). Midgley has in mind the problems of defining racism in such a way that it does not invalidate acts of reverse discrimination, and concludes that the ambiguity of the concept renders it 'quite unfit to generate a family of descendants which can be useful elsewhere' (ibid). Midgley may be over-cautious here. After all, the strength of a moral case cannot *solely* rely on the clarity of ethical language, however desirable that may be.

Nevertheless, intrahuman analogies to speciesism are bound to be logically dissimilar and therefore partial. Accepting this overall limitation, they can be used to point out the pervasiveness of systematic exploitation of 'others', human or non-human; they can also be used to highlight that discrimination relying on biological criteria can be illicit if premised on morally irrelevant criteria. Most importantly, the development of speciesism as a concept has been tied to intrahuman discrimination no doubt because these analogies were used to generate moral condemnation. It is here in the political and pragmatic use of the notion that its true value may lie: it alerts its hearers to the possibility of oppression beyond humanocentric definitions of injustice.

But there is a far more radical challenge to anti-speciesist thinking and that is embodied in the theology of the Christian tradition. According to Christian theology, humans *are* the divinely favoured species. From this perspective, speciesism has a metaphysical and ontological basis: God has become incarnate as a member of the human species. In the famous words attributed to Karl Barth: 'Man is the measure of all things, since God became man' (Barth, in Gutierrez 1971: 6). Not only in the doctrine of the incarnation is God's favouritism expressed. According to Pinches, the creation of 'each according to its kind' in Genesis represents a divine endorsement of the category of species beyond the value of individual creatures (Pinches 1993). Allied to these doctrines of CREATION and incarnation is a third, namely redemption. Humans who are uniquely made in the image of God and befriended in the incarnation are – according to mainstream doctrine – exclusively the subjects of redemption as well. In short: God as Creator, Reconciler and Redeemer is wholly speciesist.

Whether this rendering of mainstream doctrine is – or is likely to remain – the most dominant form of Christian thinking is as yet unclear, but it cannot be doubted that, historically at least, it is the form that has attracted the majority of intellectual adherents in the West. Is Christian theology then irredeemably speciesist and Christian praxis similarly so? In the same way that some theologians hold that feminism is incompatible with Christianity – since it is grounded in a historical narrative irreducibly patriarchal (see Hampson 1990) – are we also to conclude that theology is inexorably tied to a view of the cosmos that is neglectful of claims for justice beyond the human sphere?

Some 'animal theologians' have tried to show how it is possible to recast traditional doctrines in ways which are inclusive of animal welfare and rights or, at the very least, offer a definition of the human 'species' which is eco- and animal friendly. It is highly questionable whether the Hebrew Bible with its strong emphasis upon a sovereign creator is unambiguously humanocentric; e.g. the covenant in Genesis is strikingly inclusive of all living beings (Genesis 9: 3 f.) as is the promise of redemption (Isaiah 11: 1–9). One theologian has argued that human 'dominion' or power over the world of animals needs to take as its model 'the Christ-given paradigm of lordship manifest in service', and that humans should regard themselves not as the master species but as the 'servant species' (Linzey 1994: ix). Moreover, it is possible to interpret the incarnation not just as God's Yes to the human species but generally as an affirmation of the whole of creation.

But there is one more urgent reason why theology should take the debate about speciesism with special seriousness. It is found in the critique advanced by Feuerbach to the effect that 'theology is anthropology' nothing less than the deification of the human species itself. 'Man is the beginning, the middle, and the end of religion' (Feuerbach 1957: xv, xix). To answer this critique, theology must show that its dogmatic and moral theology is more than the self-aggrandizement of the human species. In so many presentations of theology the revealing Word is severed from the world in which that Word is revealed, so that everything that is non-human appears as otiose or mere theatre to the real revelation that happens within the human species. The challenge to theology is to expand its ancient comprehension of the *Logos* so that the Word which becomes flesh is also revealed as the *Logos* which unites and sums up all living beings.

In this sense, speciesism is a direct result of the failure of the Christian tradition to give a sufficiently full, even unprejudiced, account of the concerns of God the Creator which are infinitely greater than the preservation and redemption of one species alone. In supposing a God exclusively concerned with humanity, theology has rendered itself parochial (*see* ANIMAL RIGHTS).

Diamond, Cora (1978) 'Eating meat and eating people', *Philosophy* 53: 465–79; reprinted in *The Realistic Spirit: Wittgenstein, Philosophy, and the Mind*, London: Bradford, 1991.

Dupre, John (1981) 'Natural kinds and biological taxa', *Philosophical Review* 40(1).

Feuerbach, Ludwig (1957) *The Essence of Christianity*, ed. and trans. George Eliot, introduction by Karl Barth, foreword by H. Richard Niebuhr, New York: Harper Torchbooks.

Gaita, Raimond (1991) *Good and Evil: An Absolute Conception*, London: Macmillan.

Gutierrez, Gustavo (1971) *A Theology of Liberation*, ed. and trans. Caridad Inda and John Eagleson, London: SCM.

Hampson, Daphne (1990) *Theology and Feminism*, Oxford: Basil Blackwell.

Klug, Brian (1995) 'Speciesism: some skeptical remarks about prejudice against animals', in *Tradition, Technology, Responsibility: Essays on the Philosophy of Hans Jonas*, ed. Harold P. Sjursen, Chicago, IL: University of Chicago Press.

Linzey, Andrew (1976) *Animal Rights: A Christian Assessment*, London: SCM.

——(1987) *Christianity and the Rights of Animals*, London: SPCK and New York: Crossroad.

——(1994) *Animal Theology*, London: SCM and Chicago, IL: University of Illinois Press.

Midgley, Mary (1984) *Animals and Why They Matter: A Journey Around the Species Barrier*, Athens, GA: University of Georgia Press.

Narveson, Jan (1977) 'Animal rights', *Canadian Journal of Philosophy* 7: 161–78.

O'Donovan, Oliver (1984) *Begotten Or Made?* Oxford: Clarendon.

Pinches, Charles (1993) 'Each according to its kind: a defence of theological speciesism', in Charles Pinches and Jay B. McDaniel (eds) *Good News for Animals? Christian Approaches to Animal Well-Being*, Maryknoll, NY: Orbis.

Rachels, James (1991) *Created From Animals: The Moral Implications of Darwinism*, Oxford and New York: Oxford University Press.

Regan, Tom (1979) 'An examination and a defense of one argument concerning animal rights', *Inquiry* 22 (1–2): 189–219.

Ryder, Richard D. (1970) *Speciesism* (booklet), Oxford.

——(1975) *Victims of Science: The Use of Animals in Research*, London: Davis-Poynter.

——(1989) *Animal Revolution: Changing Attitudes Towards Speciesism*, Oxford: Basil Blackwell.

Singer, Peter (1976) *Animal Liberation: A New Ethics for Our Treatment of Animals*, London: Jonathan Cape.

Steinbock, Bonnie (1978) 'Speciesism and the idea of equality', *Philosophy* 53: 247–56.

Williams, Bernard (1985) *Ethics and the Limits of Philosophy*, London: Fontana.

Andrew Linzey
Paul Waldau

STATE

State: the word is developed from the Latin for *estate*, or *status*, standing, or *stasis*; the term may be used widely, and generally, to describe a sovereign organization of rule for any society. In such a case the term encompasses any form of rule whether that be the Ancient Greek *polis*, the Roman Empire or an African Tribe. In this wide sense no distinction is made between the form of legitimacy or the general nature of the structure. It may embody secular or theocratic principles, be popular or élitist, traditional or customary. The term may also be used more precisely to refer to that distinct form of rule that emerged alongside the growth of INDIVIDU-ALISM in Europe after the late middle ages as a secular and national organization having complete control over its own jurisdiction. The classic definition of the modern state is given by Max Weber, as an autonomous body having territorial jurisdiction and a monopoly of coercive force within that jurisdiction. This second model is rooted in Christian theology and ethics to the extent that it cannot be separated from those conceptions. If those conceptions are set aside, or seen as contingent features of a particular history and set of experiences, there is no over-riding intellectual reason to prefer the second model to the first. Yet the second model has come to displace the first. The contradictions in the second model are deep and fundamental. This and its widespread hegemonic application have led to a worldwide crisis in the institution of the state, the outcome of which is a general crisis of rule.

This second model of the state has grown to become the dominant, if not exclusive, form of rule in the twentieth century. It has displaced all cases of alternate forms of rule wherever they have been found. There is no one that is not touched by the institution of the nation state in some way or other. It is also in a period of major transition or even terminal decline. Given the absolutist claims of the modern state and the effectiveness of the destruction by it of all other forms of rule, it is to be expected that its decline will leave a power vacuum that will produce considerable disruption and VIOLENCE. It is often the case that when the institutions of an era come to an end some will do so violently, dangerously and dramatically. In this case the world has put too many eggs in one institutional basket to expect to emerge unscathed.

The developed institution of the nation state is closely tied to western theology and western ethical conceptions. Indeed there is a view that all concepts of the modern state are secularized theological concepts. There is considerable truth in this claim. It is almost certainly also true that the challenges and changes placed on western ETHICS, western theology and western SOCIETY will result in challenges and changes to the western concept of the state: the world wide effect of the conclusion of the state is likely to be dramatic.

The rise of the modern western concept of the state is usually placed in the emerging secular discourse of state developed between the thirteenth and the fifteenth centuries. That discourse was, however, built on some clear theological and philosophical pre-conditions. The Greek *polis*, the Roman Empire and the Hebraic tribe were religious forms of rule. Not formally theocratic but always anchored firmly in some religious concept. Thus a *polis* as a CITY or city state would have a god or goddess, as Athens had Pallas Athene. To be loyal to the city was to be loyal to the god, to be loyal to the god was to be loyal to the city. The distinction between these is not made. The Hebraic account of their history is redolent with quarrels about the acceptance of the God of the covenant and staving off alternate gods, Baal for instance, as in 1 Kings. The category of the 'secular' had there no meaning and no place. The causes of the generation of the split between earthly life and spiritual life are complex. Criticism of minor gods in Greece was common in literature and comedy. In larger themes when Prometheus defied the gods he brought judgement on them. Long before that Gilgamesh had consorted with the gods raising human themes and human concerns as distinct from sacred concerns. Adam and Eve, in a myth that in Christian interpretation personalized these general figures, defied the prime interdiction of God. Such events distinguish gods and people but they also provide the basis for a domain that is distinctly human. It is the perception of such a domain that provides the basis of the secular.

The justification for such a domain is given in Christianity in Jesus' response to questioning, 'Render unto Caesar that which is Caesar's', he responds, and 'unto God that which is God's.' St Paul too, the first Christian theologian, makes it clear that unthinking obedience is not required. Conscience, *conscientia*, what one might even now call the 'still small voice' of God (1 Kings) may always be there demanding disobedience to the state, and such disobedience, once again establishes two domains – CHURCH AND STATE. The Christians that were fed to the lions bore witness to two domains. They also made it clear which domain had prime hold on them. The theme of two domains is massively represented in St Augustine's *City of God*. Among other themes Augustine deals with the problem of how a single person with a single soul can subsist in two separate domains. The conflict can threaten to pull someone apart. It is a conflict that runs right through western accounts of political life as the problem of dirty hands. How is it that a person of honour and goodness can engage in the world without acting dishonourably. It appears to require a twin ethic as Machiavelli, Weber and countless others have argued. For Augustine the choice is clear enough Christians are in two cities, the Kingdom of light and the Kingdom of Darkness, but they are always facing the light and are always saved from the beginning of time.

The Christian model accepted that there are two domains but places the sacral above the secular. It still does that, with some, admittedly limited, success (see e.g., *Evangelium vitae* 1995). Indeed the development of the nation state, its rise and imminent decline can be seen

as a continuing struggle with its theological foundations with how to deal with the relation between the two cities. The Christian *problematique* was how to be law abiding while following the dictates of God. One model was to attempt to subordinate the state to the church. Pope Nicolas I (858–867) for instance took it that what followed from Augustine's doctrine of the two cities was the papal dominance of secular power. Hildebrand, as Gregory VII, took it that the secular power was to be directed by the sacral power and even excommunicated Henry IV until such time as Henry sought and obtained personal absolution, which he did in 1077.

The dominance of the church was most successful and complete in intellectual matters. This made independent political theory and, therefore the development of an independent language and theory of secular GOVERNMENT impossible. The language of state had, therefore, to be dragged from the language of church and the institutions of state had to be modelled on the institutions of church. After more than a thousand years of a complete absence of significant political theory it was inevitable that the language of state was drawn from the language of church; that theology provided the basis for the development of the modern state. The modern state is an institution developed from the split between church and state from the thirteenth century onwards. In the contest between sacral and secular that has been characteristic of Christianity the modern nation state is a direct consequence of the failure of the church to hold its own position. Correlatively the development of the structure, institutions and constitution of the nation state follows directly from the experience and knowledge of ecclesiastical structures and theological forms of argumentation.

There are several features to the development of the state worthy of mention. First, the reassertion of two domains. Second, the extent of powers in a domain. Third, the justification of the state. Fourth, the distinction between personage and institution, and fifth the moral status of the state.

The effect of the Nicolas–Hildebrand position was to undercut the two domains or two cities. Augustine's doctrine always contained that possibility within it, but only as a perversion. The basic Christian position had seemed to be clear enough, 'render unto Caesar that which is Caesar's', seems to specifically legitimate the secular domain. The first stirrings of a church–state split of some intellectualized significance are found in the works of Dante and Marsiglio. Dante Alighieri argued in *De Monarchia* (1308) that in the *Respublica Christiana* ('Republic of Christendom') there are two powers, one, the Holy Roman emperor who obtains authority from the Roman emperor Augustus, two, the spiritual pope who obtains his authority from Saint Peter. Both operate in quite distinct spheres, but by operating in harmony they will together bring Christianity and the idea of the republic together to produce a Christian Republic (*De Monarchia*, 1308). In *Defensor Pacis*, Marsilius of Padua, 1275–1342, argued that all the authority of the state derives from the people. Yet the church derives all its authority, spiritual and temporal, from the state. He thus inverted the Nicolas–Hildebrand position and attempted to subordinate Church to State. He also added limitations on the state by arguing that its authority was derived from the people.

The limitations on state power that Marsilius insists on are quite marked and his work is one of the most significant turning points in the development of theories of the modern state. Those limitations were rarely accepted however, and in the period of the time and until the twentieth century it was more usual to find some form of absolutism linked to the state. Bodin and Hobbes are representative. By contrast with Marsilius the state receives no laws or commands from its subjects, it can 'give laws unto all and every one of its subjects'. It is absolute. The sovereign was the creator of positive law and was, therefore, beyond such law. But this did not mean he could act in any way that he chose, for he was subject to NATURAL LAW. Similar constraints rested upon the sovereign as construed by Hobbes. The function of Hobbes' sovereign was the preservation of peace and life. He was absolute within his domain but, contrary to popular misconceptions, Hobbes does not licence any kind of order. He expects the sovereign to exercise his absolute POWER according to natural law, to reason, and

for the benefit and well-being of the subjects. In both cases the state may be absolute but such absoluteness does not warrant bestial, savage or uncaring behaviour on the part of the sovereign. Indeed so much does Hobbes charge the sovereign with the maintenance of peace within which civil society can develop that he can be fairly considered a founder of liberalism.

These concerns spill over into the justification of the state. Hobbes is perhaps the clearest example. It is to preserve the life of members of society. In the absence of society life is one of continual conflict. It is a 'war of every man against every man'. The end result of that is a life that is 'nasty, brutish and short'. The rational solution to this, Hobbes argues, is the surrender of all of one's individual powers to a sovereign. The sovereign is not part of the contract and remains, therefore, in the state of nature. It may consequently impose peace by whatever means it sees fit. Order is paramount and it is, primarily a secular order. Behind it may lay natural law but it is the natural law of cause and effect rather than the natural law of a moral order. By contrast it is just that natural law of a moral order that justifies the state for Locke. A state that does not act according to the natural law, that acts tyrannically, has not authority and may be removed by the people. Here the people are sovereign not the state. With some modifications the Lockean model is predominant in contemporary times.

The fourth point is the distinction between personage and state. Here, perhaps more than in any other area, the struggle to conceptualize the modern state was most marked. The reason for this is not hard to comprehend. The modern state as we now understand it is an abstract entity. Abstract entities, particularly abstract entities that concern people, are difficult to understand and difficult to conceptualize. On the face of it people seem concrete and real. How then can an institution that is a King or prince be anything other than real? And why should a King or prince cede the principle that they do not personally own the kingdom? Again theology provides the model. The pope was not Christ continued. The pope was not the Church. To claim either of these would be to claim that the pope was God incarnate. That claim could be reserved for Christ only. The pope might be the descendant of Peter, with all the authority that appeared to come from that office, but to claim to be the descendant of Christ was inconceivable. What this implied was that the pope was the holder of an office – a representative rather than God incarnate; concepts that are remarkably different. The implications of this are staggering, for it introduces the idea of holding an office, or playing a role or being a representative right at the foundation of the known world. These are now familiar concepts but they were, at the time new and radical concepts. The implication for the secular domain is clear enough. If the pope is an office holder, then so surely is the prince or king.

The idea of a king or prince distant from, and separate from, the office that they held and the powers that they exercised was, and to some extent still is, difficult to grasp. To have a power yet not to own it is a concept of some complexity and in early modern political theory one that was struggled with rather than revealed in the blinding light of a conversion. It is not clear when, how and who made the necessary jump from person to office. There are clear references in Machiavelli that indicate that the state of the Prince and the person of the Prince might be distinguished. In Machiavelli we see, if embryonically, the idea of the modern state; an abstract and legal concept whose roots are to be found in the idea of autonomy within a certain territory. Even in some early thinking it was coupled to the view that the state belongs to no person in particular. Such a view of the state is ultimately subversive to the idea of any particular personage having unfettered autonomy over the lives of the people. On this view, a view that took some time to be fully developed, a King may be a symbol of the state, but is not the state. The claim of Louis XIV that 'L'état, l'état c'est moi', the state, the state is me, is wrong headed, anachronistic and muddled.

For all that there are clear references in early modern thought that indicate that the prince might act for what we now call reasons of state, raison d'état. This language and conception does distinguish between two types of morality, the morality required by the imperatives of state and personal morality. The significance and importance of the former can be seen in the ease with which reasons of state are given and accepted as an excuse for performing acts that would be regarded a personally immoral. To perform an act that is otherwise immoral because it is in the interests of the state is widely given and accepted. It is part of that political theory that in INTERNATIONAL RELATIONS is expressed as REALISM, the view that state concerns over-ride individual concerns, that state imperatives over-ride individual morality. It is a view that is still dominant in many parts of the world and in much contemporary thought.

The state when so construed is an autonomous institution distinct from the sacral domain and acting according to its own imperatives. Those imperatives might override individual morality. Indeed at times to be divorced from all conceptions of morality: to be an institution without moral constraint or restraint. That would be a fair portrait of the absolutist and completely sovereign state of the nineteenth and twentieth centuries. It is that portrait that led to Weber's definition and to Hobbes' much earlier claim that princes stand like gladiators, poised for battle. It was in short a realist conception of the state that removed it so completely from the moral and sacral domains that its absolutism was effectively unchallenged for over a century. Its imperatives were those of its own survival and the pursuit of its own interests.

The challenge, when it came, was radical, primarily the state was partisan, it served not the interests of the people as a whole but a section of the people. As Marx put it:

The State's law of gravitation was discovered around the same time as Copernicus' great discovery of the true solar system. The state's focus was found to reside within itself, and with the initial shallowness of practice, the various European governments started to apply this result to the system of the balance of power. In a parallel way, people like Machiavelli and Campanella and later Hobbes, Spinoza, Hugo Grotius and finally Rousseau, Fichte and Hegel began to perceive the state through human eyes and to develop its natural laws from reason and experience rather than from theology, just as Copernicus was not impressed by Joshua's telling the sun to stand still at Gideon and the moon to remain at the valley of Ajalon.

(*Rheinische Zeitung*, 14 July 1842)

Against this backdrop the state appeared to have no moral status. If it was but the representative of powerful interests then it was, and is, no more than a partisan mechanism of control and hegemony. Marx's point is a theoretical one in the first instance, but it has empirical backing. Those who controlled the mechanisms of state at its peak were drawn from a single CLASS and represented a single focus of interests. In such a case the state can scarcely be regarded as representative of the people. Marsilius we might think would turn in his grave.

Marx's solution is radical; it is the abolition of the state and its replacement by face to face relations. The solution seems impractical, if noble in outlook. Another kind of solution is to bring the state under moral control. There is a clear precedent here in the work of Hegel who regarded the state as the embodiment of rationality and reason. Following Hegel, the English idealists similarly regarded the state as a moral institution capable of embodying and expressing the highest moral ideas. In this respect the state, now separate from the sacral domain, came to be contained by its own moral imperatives. Ideally it required limits set from within. Green, Bosanquet and Bradley argued in various ways that the state could embody moral ideals of the highest kind.

In practice this seems to have been an ideal that never found a sponsor. The development of the European nation state in the late nineteenth and early twentieth century is the tale of a hegemonic monster set on the single minded course of bringing the world under its antiquated model of right order. In this, it was remarkably successful. So much so that the end of the period up to about 1950 saw the universal and enforced application of the idea of the nation state with all the difficulties that went with that.

At its worst the nation state was absolutist, sovereign and unrestrained by anything other than alternate nation states. It was in Hobbist terms poised like a gladiator in combat. Combat or threatened combat was its forté. Morality was not in its remit.

Such a monster could neither continue nor be allowed to continue. Fortunately there were the vestiges of some kind of restraint. The first were internal, the second external. The internal restraints derived from the source of the state in Christian theology. Christian theology for all its weaknesses was not, and is not, without a tradition of moral reflection. Insofar as the state was derived from theological and ecclesiastical sources it took over some of that reflection. The external restraints resulted primarily from the effects of two world wars brought about by the alleged and assumed rights of states to do as they pleased. But doing as they pleased led to conflicts that were destructive and seemed to breach laws more fundamental than those made by nation states. The upshot has been a series of events that has led to a general and generalized crisis for the institution of the nation state. Those events can be divided into two broad types. First, those that impinge on the nation state directly, whether from inside or outside. Second, those that directly or indirectly have come to outrun or bypass the remit of the nation state.

The first kind of event arises from limits placed on the absolutism of the nation state. These are sometimes formal, sometimes informal and a consequence of a change of attitude that has led to a widespread legitimacy crisis for the institution of the state in many parts of the world. The limits on the absolutism of the state have many sources but include among the most significant, appeals to higher laws; alternate and plural demands outwith the western concept of the state; and a decline of western hegemony.

The claim to absolutism runs through the foundation of the state in its conflict with the church. The absolutist demands of the church were met with absolutist claims by the state. It peaked in theory with the arguments of Bodin and Hobbes. It peaked in practice with the full development of the European nation state in the nineteenth century. Absolutism is not TOTALITARIANISM. The absolutist claims merely that the authority is singular rather than plural. There is one source of power. The totalitarian claims that, *and* attempts to control every aspect of life. Absolutism is predicated on individualism and, usually, permits the individual to do as they will providing it does not conflict with commands of the sovereign. The totalitarian state destroys civil society taking it into itself. The absolutist state permits the growth and development of civil society reserving the right to regulate it where it sees fit. The hallmark of the absolutist state is, therefore, not the absolute control of daily lives but the claim to be the sole source of power in a jurisdiction. There can, therefore, be no conflict of interest, no dual loyalties. The state has an absolute claim on loyalty and obedience.

A clear consequence of absolutism is that such states claim that municipal law, that is to say their own law is higher than any other law, and that such laws have a complete and total claim on their members. Such laws over-ride any other claims. Yet in 1942, in Germany, the final solution, the destruction of the Jewish people, was adopted at the Wannsee conference as a matter of policy. It was subsequently claimed at Nuremberg that the Führer Principle gave the word of Hitler the force of law and anyone falling under that principle had a legal duty to follow it, even if that resulted in over-riding other laws or treaties. In other words, municipal or state law over-rode all other considerations. So it would, if the absolutism of the state was accepted. The judges at Nuremberg refused to accept any defence based on the over-riding claims of municipal law, or any claims, as was submitted by General Jodl, for instance, that obeying a state law, or obeying orders was a sufficient reason for acting in a manner that could reasonably be taken as a CRIME against humanity.

The decision here is significant. It introduced a limit on the commands of the state. The new crime, 'crimes against humanity', was held to be higher than state or municipal law. That limit was placed on the actions of state, notwithstanding the fact that such a crime and such a charge was new and novel. There was not, and had not been, any such crime on the statute books, or expressed in international treaty or law prior to its application at Nuremberg, yet it was expressed and applied at Nuremberg. In the

process of doing so the limit of the nation state was clearly stated: it could not demand of its members that they breach fundamental laws that they ought as human beings be capable of knowing. There was, in short, a higher form of law than the law of the nation state. In this judgement we see, to some extent practically, but certainly symbolically, the demise of the absolutism of the nation state. The establishment of the United Nations continued the theme. The United Nations is composed of nation states and only of nation states but, formally at least, they are bound to respect each other, their members and the charter to which they are subject. Formally at least, they limited their autonomy, and increasingly so as they agreed to new declarations, new restrictions on their autonomy and new international treaties.

The United Nations accepts as its members peoples that have obtained statehood and who agree to be bound by the Charter and its instruments. Herein lies its strength and its weakness.

Its strength is that it does provide, at least the outline of, a new ecumenical order, ecumenical in its original sense of all-embracing, of bringing disparate groups together under one order or principle. The original *ecumene* was the Roman Empire, a body that united numerous factions and peoples. Its weakness is that the new *ecumene* of the United Nations embodies the ideas and IDEOLOGY that developed from the old *ecumene*; from the Roman Empire and its theological, ethical and political successors.

Membership of the United Nations is restricted to States. The aim of the United Nations is to bring the peoples of the world together and unite them. But peoples that are not members of a nation state, or do not feel comfortable with membership of a nation state, or are in a state of rebellion against a nation state have no direct voice. In itself this might not be a problem. Clearly some degree of representation is required. Not every person on the planet can be present at the General Assembly. Even if, in some electronic future, every person could directly vote on issues brought to the assembly it is not necessarily the case that this would be a good thing.

The problem thrown up in the new *ecumene* is not, therefore, representation as such but the kind of representation. It is a form of representation confined to the state; and this is a western concept developed from western theology and applied worldwide. Similarly the institutes, charters and declarations of the new *ecumene* are western based, derived from western social and political experience, western theology, and western ethics. There is no part of the so-called 'new world order' that is not irredeemably based on western order. This sufficed when the hegemony of western order was at its strongest, when entire cultures, outlooks, perceptions could be and were shaped by the west. That condition, however, has weakened considerably. There are new outlooks, new voices, new perceptions, new experiences and they do not necessarily want to be shaped and packaged by what they regard as the old world order. From the perspective of the new voices, the so-called new world order, is just the last gasp of the old world order.

The second sort of challenge to the state comes from the change in its component parts, in particular the growth of organizations and activities that have come to outrun or bypass the writ of the nation state. This might be due to the growth of civil society; the growth of alternate political forms of organization; or the result of a recursion to earlier models of rule.

The modern state was the appropriate form of rule for individuals. It came into being at the same time as individuals, and developed and grew together with individuals. It provided the security within which they could make those economic and social arrangements that became the basis of civil society. Hobbes provides the classical model. He conceived of a society of individuals so in competition with each other that they are held from harming each other only by the state. It is the state that is the foundation of society, for without the state individuals would be at war with each other. It is necessary that the state have absolute power in order to control the warring potential in society. The state and civil society in this model are closed, and synchronically congruent.

The demands of state and civil society, however, outgrew their boundaries. Economic and entrepreneurial activities led to the growth of IMPERIALISM. While growth in both state and civil society was possible, as in the age of imperialism, there was little difficulty in the state retaining control over civil society. The difficulty arises when autonomous states reach their mutual limits. Here states either follow entrepreneurial demands or relinquish control. If they take the former course they risk WAR, if they take the latter course they surrender their absolutism. This tension was at its least in the nineteenth century. Maximum growth in state and civil society with minimal risk was then possible. The nineteenth century represents the peak of the absolutist nation state. However, once the world was carved up, any further attempt to expand would result in conflict. The massive wars of the twentieth century can be explained partly as a consequence of tensions at the very heart of the European concept of the absolutist nation state.

But while it was contradictions in the concept of the nation state that led to the conditions that could produce massive war, there is now a further contradiction once satisfactory mechanisms for conflict resolution are in place. That contradiction is that the demands of civil society and entrepreneurial activity do not stop at national borders, yet those borders define the limits of the writ of the state. The very mechanisms that limit state activity and expansion tears apart the synchronic congruence of the state and civil society found in the classic model. As it does this so civil society outruns the state. The practical effects of this are seen multifariously; in multinational corporations and transnational companies whose activites are difficult, if not impossible to regulate; in trade agreements that undercut the autonomy and sovereignty of the state. Prime examples are the emerging European Union, following from the Maastricht Treaty, and the North American Free Trade Association. In both cases political arrangements are necessary to keep up with the demands of civil society, for instance freedom of movement without let or hindrance in Europe; a goal that implies and has produced the fact of dual CITIZENSHIP. In both cases we see clear examples of POLITICS chasing economics. We see the nation state desperately attempting to keep up with economic reality and, in each case, surrendering its sovereignty as that was classically understood. Taken more widely it is unlikely that the nation state can do more than nominally control and regulate civil society. Economic arrangements are global, run well beyond the influence and power of the nation state and have run its claimed absolutism to the ground.

The same general point applies to communications. Once entirely under the control and regulation of the nation state they are now understood globally. No nation state can prevent, or prevent for long, people in its domain accessing information available elsewhere. The fax machine, E-mail and the internet have moved the *samizdat* into a completely new domain. What was once a risky form of distribution of information can now no longer be controlled at all. The same point can be multiplied endlessly. Satellite TV, Cable TV, digital compression techniques and instant global communication, in general, have split the synchronicity of the nation state and civil society. As they have done so, they have undercut the absolutist model of the state and left it floundering: searching for a role, looking for a place in a world that has passed it by.

The ability of the state to control legal organizations such as MULTINATIONALS or transnationals is limited almost to the point of being miniscule. How much more so then its ability to control illegal organizations? Illegal organizations simply ignore all state regulation, bypassing it and caring not at all about its claimed legitimacy. Here classic examples are the activities of organized crime. Such organizations might range from major organizations, such as the Mafia; the Mob; the Chinese Triads down to relatively small instances, the local boss, the drug dealer, the street bully and so on. All merely ignore the state. For them it has no legitimacy, no writ and no authority. It may have some residual power of a limited kind. But this can be dealt with under the terms of the 11th Commandment: Thou shall not be found out. The success of such activities can be seen in Italy, in Colombia, in the US, in the UK and so on. That such activities are successful is a direct consequence of the state attempting to deal with something at which it is bound to fail. The state will lose, for instance, 'the war on drugs', for every state activity in such an area points up the contradictions within the state. Every success of the state in the war on drugs is yet another nail in the coffin of the state. Yet lemming like it must head towards its own doom.

A major aspect in the decline of the state is the growth of alternate forms of political organizations. This might indeed include the Mafia or the Mob, for in a wide sense at least, they are a form of government and a form of rule having a hold on and the loyalty of their subjects. More significantly on the global stage, at least, it is found in those forms of political organization or political unit that do not have the status of a nation state. Clear examples here are the Palestinians and the Kurds, both of whom have made a political claim while not fulfilling the formal criteria required for recognition of, and membership of, the UN. Such peoples seem to be in a kind of *Catch 22* situation for they cannot be heard at the UN unless they are a people defined in terms of the Charter of the UN. And they cannot be a people so defined unless recognized by the United Nations as such a people. They cannot achieve that status for it is denied it by a state that has met that criteria and that will not release them.

The examples can be multiplied endlessly and tragically. In what was once Yugoslavia, in Rwanda, in what was once the Soviet Union, indeed in what is, even now the Russian Republic, in Australasia, in North America, in Europe, in China, in Asia, in South America and in wide areas of Africa, there are peoples clamouring to be heard and clamouring to live their lives in their way. In many cases they wish to live their lives and to be heard, however, not as nation states but as distinct peoples having a distinct identity that does not necessarily fall under the description of statehood. Nation states are too individualistic a form of government for any traditional non-individualistic forms of life. Nation states are too buried in the history and pre-history of Europe to serve as a natural unit of government for many peoples. Often they will seek statehood and pretend to aspire to that condition. But often that aspiration is driven by the need to meet criteria for formal recognition; statehood is not their mode of being. It is an imposition born unhappily and, for pragmatic reasons, necessarily.

The pre-history of the state is found in the synoicism of the *polis*; that act of bringing together peoples from different tribes that swear fealty to themselves thus breaking the overriding hold of the tribe. It is echoed in the Roman Empire as an ecumenical association that attempted to include a number of diverse groups and diverse points of view. It was repeated in the cities, guilds and corporations of early Europe, a repetition that brought individuals together after the collapse of feudalism. That those individuals could be so united was due to both the ethical conceptions of individualism and the theological background that provided both the unit of the individual and the model of absolutism on which the state was predicated.

The state is a markedly European institution exported to the rest of the world in the aftermath of imperialism. And to that world it is notably and strikingly alien. The experience that led to its success in Europe was not present elsewhere. Where the shared experiences of people are different, then institutions from afar born of alien experiences, will not take hold, put down roots and bear fruit. It is this that lies at the basis of the breakdown and the supercession of the nation state.

It is both a breakdown and a supercession, for the state is shifting in two directions. At one level a new tribalism appears to be on the ascendant. At another level new forms of political organization are arising from the remnants of the state. These two aspects to the crisis of the state are not necessarily separated – they may, in some cases, co-exist. It is not possible to say, therefore, with any confidence what will come after the state. At its best there will be new forms of co-operation and new organizations that reveal the shallowness and limitations of the traditional state. There will be restrictions on state power and state absolutism together with a wide acceptance that power descends only insofar as legitimacy ascends. At its worst there will be breakdown, tribalism, ethnic cleansing, GENOCIDE and the arbitrary brutality associated with a new feudalism. The latter is not the sole province of peoples outside Europe or North America. On the contrary developed

nations may be subject to both, the demands of the post-nation state and the demands and threats of the new feudal barons. The difficulty for the state or the post-state, whatever it might turn out to be called, is that it can no longer police its claimed territory; that it does not have, in Weber's terms, the absolute monopoly of the means of coercion within a given territory. It fails to meet its basic definition. But it fails in that respect in a peculiar manner, a manner that produces a *paradox of oppression*.

The paradox of oppression arises as a direct consequence of the failure of the state to produce conditions of safety for its otherwise law abiding citizens. Such citizens accept the legitimacy of the state, obey its edicts, pay their taxes and conform to the expectations of the state both formal and informal. They are in short obedient. Nevertheless they are at risk if they stray from policed areas or come into contact with those who are generally disobedient. For here the state offers them no protection and no effective redress. By contrast those who have adopted a maxim of disobedience and lawlessness are effectively immune from state edicts, and taxes and do not accept its legitimacy. The law abiding citizen thus comes under two forms of rule: the legitimate rule of the state and the illegitimate banditry of the lawless. The paradox and irony is that the state, in order to appear effective, directs the majority of its edicts at the activities of the lawful. As it is in their nature to obey so they do and the state appears to be effective. The reality is that it is being bypassed and ignored in substantial and important ways. The failure of the nation to grasp this and deal with it is part of its failure of vision.

Without doubt the state is in a crisis. There is nothing surprising in this. The state emerged in certain quite specific social, historical, theological, ethical and geographical circumstances. It was a form of government for Christian individuals. Those circumstances have changed and the conditions on which the state rested and out of which it emerged have changed. As they have changed so the conditions and requirements of the state have changed. The success of the state for so long was to impose a specific concept of state, the modern European state on the world and over-ride earlier, wider and more basic conceptions of state. The failure of the European nation state was to impose itself on the world without realizing that such an imposition was historically, ethically, socially and theologically hegemonic; that it was alien, largely unwanted, and was bound to end in tears. We are now seeing the tears.

All institutions have beginnings and all institutions have ends. As the dominance of western modes of thought are coming to an end so the nation state is coming to an end. The end of the nation state is nigh! This is not the end of the world, but it is the end of an era and the beginning of a new age.

Augustine of Hippo (1972) *Concerning the City of God against the Pagans*, trans. David Knowles, Harmondsworth: Penguin.
Aristotle (1941) *The Basic Work of Aristotle*, New York: Random House.
Dante (1904) *De Monarchia*, London: Dent.
Hobbes, Thomas (1968) *Leviathan*, Harmondsworth: Penguin.
Machiavelli, N. (1925) *The Prince*, London: Philip Allen.
Oakeshott, Michael (1991) 'The Idea of a European State' in Michael Oakeshott, *On Human Conduct*, Oxford: Clarendon Press.
Plato (1961) *The Collected Dialogues of Plato*, Princeton, NJ: Princeton University Press.
Skinner, Quentin (1979) *The Foundations of Modern Political Thought*, Cambridge: Cambridge University Press.
Weber, Max (1948) 'Politics as a Vocation' in H. Gerth and C. Wright Mills, *From Max Weber: Essays in Sociology*, London: Routledge and Kegan Paul.

Paul Barry Clarke

STIGMA

Stigma is the Greek word for the mark made by piercing the skin with a pointed instrument, thus a brand or tattoo, more generally a wound or spot, and metaphorically a moral blemish or mark of dishonour. In the ancient world, animals were regularly branded to indicate ownership; slaves were similarly marked in the Orient, but in Greece and Rome this practice was restricted to those who had committed serious crime or to military deserters – hence the negative connotation of the metaphorical usage.

Herodotus (1, 790) records an instance of a runaway slave who took refuge in an Egyptian temple and was tattooed with the mark of the deity to prevent his recapture and punishment. The ambiguity of this stigma, signifying at the same time social disgrace and divine protection, recalls the Hebrew Bible story of the mark of Cain (Genesis 4: 15) and the mark on the forehead of both saints and servants of the beast in the New Testament Apocalypse (Revelation 7: 2; 14: 9 f.). Apart from the mark left by circumcision, Jewish tradition prohibited tattooing (Leviticus 19: 2); the Church endorsed this officially in AD 787, but apparently no longer enforces it.

The word stigma occurs only once in the New Testament, at Galatians 6: 17 where St Paul claims to carry in his body the stigmata of Jesus. This is unlikely to be a reference to the mystical phenomenon which is unknown before the thirteenth century; equally, accidental acquisition of wounds precisely like those of crucifixion is hard to credit, as is the theory that Paul was tattooed with the sign of the cross at his baptism. It is most likely, therefore, that the reference is general, to the scars of Paul's suffering as an apostle, particularly his beatings in the synagogue at the hands of Pharisaic opponents (2 Corinthians 11: 24). These would be marks of dishonour from the Jewish point of view, but for Paul they were proof of his allegiance to the true Messiah (Philippians 3: 10). There may also be a secondary allusion in Galatians to the demand being made by the same opponents for the stigma of circumcision to be imposed on gentile Christians (6: 12 f.), to which Paul's answer is the simple sufficiency of solidarity with the Crucified (6: 14). Since crucifixion was a particularly humiliating punishment, reserved for slaves and rebels, the 'stigmata of Jesus' probably has the double meaning of both physical wounds and social disgrace. It is noteworthy that the record of Jesus' ministry in the Gospels also emphasizes Jesus' friendship with stigmatized persons in Palestinian society (the disabled, the unclean, prostitutes and quislings), even though the early church was soon to become socially more conformist.

Devotion to the Passion in medieval Christianity saw the rise of the phenomenon of mystical stigmata. The earliest and best known case is that of St Francis of Assisi, who after a vision on 14 September 1224 received a precise replica of the wounds of Christ (i.e. nail heads in his palms and nail points on the back of his hands); these never healed and remained till his death. They were understood by his followers as proof of his sanctity and vindication of his teaching. In subsequent centuries a large number of other cases was reported, amounting to over 300 by the end of the nineteenth century, of whom sixty-two had been beatified or canonized. According to Roman Catholic teaching, stigmata are not alone sufficient to demonstrate sainthood, but they may be a contributory factor. Some cases in the twentieth century have been thoroughly investigated, especially those of Therese Neumann and Francesco Forgione (Padre Pio). There is considerable variation in the forms of religious stigmatization: it may include marks on the forehead and back as well as the classic five wounds; they may bleed at regular intervals, Fridays or Lent, or bleed irregularly or not at all; the wounds may be impervious to medical treatment, and resist inflammation or septicaemia or not; they may even be invisible as in the case of St Catherine of Sienna, whose humble prayer was granted that her stigmata should have no physical manifestation, thus incidentally demonstrating the intellectual superiority of Dominican over Franciscan piety!

Different explanations of the phenomenon have been offered: that such wounds are self-inflicted either by deliberate fraud or in unconscious states of trance; that they are the psychosomatic effect of religious hysteria, since they occur most frequently in women (!) and are often accompanied by glossolalia, clairvoyance, anorexia, etc.; or that they are a divine gift granted to a select few of sharing physically in the sufferings of Christ (cf. Colossians 1: 24). The latter is the official view of the Roman Catholic Church but it raises theological problems, such as the doubt it might cast on the all-sufficiency of the atoning work of Christ; and the problem that, while Jesus suffered at the hands of the ungodly, stigmatics are afflicted directly by God. What is most significant, however, for present purposes is the way that this Western mystical tradition eclipses the original connotation of stigmata as marks of social dis-

honour and turns them into the badges of extraordinary piety.

In several modern sciences, like botany, medicine and entomology, stigma has been adopted as a technical term with precise meanings. In social science, it refers to 'a deeply discrediting attribute and the relationship its possessor thereby has with the rest of SOCIETY' (Goffman 1963: 13). Examples of stigma would be gross physical handicap or deformity; socially deviant behaviour such as criminality, drug addiction or homosexuality; and the 'tribal stigmas' of minority race, nationality or religion. Evidently the degree of immediate visibility may vary; so may the possible techniques of concealment ('passing' in Goffman's terminology) or conformity to the behaviour of the majority ('covering'). But among others of their own kind, stigmatized persons also develop distinctive patterns of in-group behaviour designed to normalize their abnormality.

Since the 1960s social scientists have tended to speak less about objective stigma, i.e. the discreditable attribute itself (with the one possible exception of smoking), and more about the societal process of stigmatization, commonly now referred to as 'labelling'. That the majority in society should feel the need to deny certain rights to stigmatized groups, and turn them into scapegoats, is a revealing indicator of its own insecurities. Social scientists have also studied the process of de-stigmatization ('coming out') by which such groups organize politically and assert their demand that the majority respect the legitimacy of their minority status as a basic question of HUMAN RIGHTS (Kallen 1989).

In certain cases of social stigma, the Christian churches today have spoken out officially against the persecution of minorities; but in others they are just as likely to to side with the majority and justify stigmatization as a means of enforcing standards of decent behaviour. That there might be some connection between religious stigmata and social stigma is hardly ever perceived, nor is any inference drawn.

Amann, E. (1941) 'Stigmatisation', *Dictionnaire de Theologie Catholique*, Paris, 14.2, cols 2616–24.
Becker, H. (1963) *Outsiders: Studies in the Sociology of Deviance*, New York: The Free Press.

Edgerton, R. (1967) *The Cloak of Competence: Stigma in the Lives of the Mentally Retarded*, Berkeley, CA: University of California Press.

Goffman, E. (1963) *Stigma: Notes on the Management of Spoiled Identity*, Englewood Cliffs, NJ: Prentice-Hall.

Kallen, E. (1989) *Label Me Human: Minority Rights of Stigmatized Canadians*, Toronto: University of Toronto Press.

Kinloch, G.C. (1979) *The Sociology of Minority Group Relations*, Englewood Cliffs, NJ: Prentice-Hall.

Ruffin, C.B. (1982) *Padre Pio, The True Story*, Huntingdon, IN: Our Sunday Visitor.

Steiner, J. (1967) *Therese Neumann: a Portrait based on Authentic Accounts, Journals and Documents*, Staten Island, NY: Alba House.

Thurston, H. (1952) *The Physical Phenomena of Mysticism*, London: Burns, Oates & Washbourne.

John Muddiman

SUFFERING

The theological problem of suffering can be posed in terms of the following question: what is it to say that the pain and suffering of innocent beings (whether human or otherwise) is to be construed as a 'sign' which seemingly tells against God's righteousness or existence?

The Hebrew Bible and the New Testament do not provide anything like a comprehensive or systematic answer to this question. The book of Job, however, is a classic study of unwarranted suffering, a narrative of one individual's attempts to read the 'signs' that are embodied in his afflictions. Job, an upright and pious servant of God, enjoys good fortune. Suddenly, this is taken away from him. Job undergoes a spiritual crisis; he begs God to show him why he has been visited by such calamities. His friends seek to comfort him by advancing reasons for his plight, but Job repudiates their arguments. His relationship with God in crisis, Job finds himself moving beyond the comforting and 'comfortable' faith of his fathers to hope in a God who speaks 'out of the whirlwind'. His experience compels him to tread the path of unknowing: God refuses to give Job the explanations he craves, and Job has to work towards a faith beyond all purely personal concerns. He learns he has to LOVE and WORSHIP this hidden and terrible God for God's own sake. This, if anything, is 'the lesson' of the book of Job.

The New Testament displays a similar lack of interest in an abstract explanatory scheme when dealing with issues of pain and suffering. It gives these issues a Christological gloss: the suffering of Jesus *is* the suffering of God. THEODICY in a metaphysical sense is clearly displaced by a THEOLOGY of the Cross or a doctrine of the ATONEMENT. This God does not need to be vindicated by creaturely beings (the heart of the enterprise of 'theodicy'); rather the God who suffers on the Cross of Christ is a God who is self-justified. And this divine self-justification, God's 'assumption' of the pain of the world, is inextricably bound up with the redemption of CREATION.

Later Christian traditions, especially those which sought to address the philosophical concerns associated with the European Enlightenment, certainly sought to provide treatments of the problems of EVIL and suffering with a less emphatically Christological focus. Here it is necessary to mention a strand of thought that extends from Leibniz (1646–1716) up to present-day theodicists and proponents of a FREE-WILL defence, most notably John Hick, Alvin Plantinga and Richard Swinburne. The two basic notions underlying these theodicies are that evil and suffering are consistent with an already existing belief in God, or that it is possible to demonstrate the plausibility of belief in God, given the presence of evil and suffering in the universe. Opponents of these approaches to the problem of evil charge them with rendering rational and reasonable that which is so often unspeakable and mind-stopping. Their proponents, however, maintain that it is always desirable to seek a response to evil and suffering which carries intellectual conviction, and that this is precisely what an adequate philosophical theodicy purports to do.

Another noteworthy aspect of Christian reflection on the problems of evil and suffering has been a tendency in some traditions to glorify suffering. This tendency is invariably an extension of doctrines which, whether directly or indirectly, uphold an instrumental view of suffering. Suffering, on this view, is a discipline which moves the one who is afflicted to repentance (and thus can be said to be an essential component of a 'pedagogy' of salvation) and/or a visible manifestation of true discipleship when undertaken in the spirit of the *imitatio Christi*, since the devout sufferer in such instances is following in the footsteps of Christ ('the figure-head'). The former strand of thought, which tends to emphasize the infliction of suffering on others ('for their own good'), can be said to find its classical expression in the writings of Calvin. The latter perspective, which stresses the value of taking-on for oneself the burden of faithful suffering, is to be found in various parts of the New Testament – the Book of Acts, the First Letter of Peter, the Letter to the Hebrews and the Letter of James evince in some way an instrumental view of suffering according to which an agony borne in the 'spirit' of Christ is characterized as an exemplary act of disciple-ship. It is impossible to make a straightforward adjudication of these understandings of suffer-ing. One the one hand, the Church survives because of the deeds of its martyrs, who nearly always have to suffer excessive and unbearable pain in the course of bearing their witness. On the other hand, the precept that Christians should willingly submit themselves to suffering has been used to justify acquiescence to many injustices and oppressions (though it goes virtu-ally without saying that theological tradition is unqualifiedly opposed to the victimization of innocents – Christ for it being the holiest of innocents).

It is a commonplace that attitudes to suffer-ing are decisively shaped and constrained by historical circumstances and social configura-tions. Here the nineteenth century can be said to represent a crucial conjuncture in Western thought. For the Victorian era saw the wide-spread growth and development of movements to alleviate suffering, a phenomenon profoundly connected with the increasingly prevalent convic-tion that suffering, both 'human' and 'animal', was gratuitous and repulsive (*see* CRUELTY). This conviction was arguably a deliverance of the era's dominant IDEOLOGY of progress, com-fort and betterment, an ideology whose benefi-cial effects were of course selectively and un-evenly manifested. This optimism was reflected in what was undoubtedly the seminal work of that age, Darwin's *On the Origin of Species* (1859). Darwin followed Paley and Malthus in

stressing the significance of conflict in nature. Nevertheless, he maintained that each adapta-tion is beneficial: 'Natural selection will never produce in a being anything injurious to itself, for natural selection acts solely by and for the good of each. No organ will be formed as Paley has remarked, for the purpose of causing pain or for doing an injury to its possessor.' The inescapable implication of this view is that pain is contrary to the 'nature' of the organism and therefore not finally conducive to its well-being.

The theologies of this time share in this spirit of optimism and satisfaction. There was a proliferation of theodicies invoking notions of progress and development and viewing nature as a domain fundamentally congenial to the enhancement and well-being of its creatures (or *homo sapiens* at any rate). Thus Alexander Campbell Fraser, in his Gifford Lectures of 1894-6, sought to present a 'conception of man as at present in physical progress towards a happy millennium', and A.B. Bruce, in the same lecture series for 1897–8, opined that Christ's 'watchwords were: Nature God's instrument; and, Growth the law of the moral as of the physical world'. The First World War discred-ited this ideology of progress and the reassuring theologies sanctioned by it.

The catastrophes of the twentieth century seemingly have not curtailed the quest for a life that is free of pain, a quest whose rationale is derived in large part from a socially/culturally legitimated disposition, at least in North America and Europe, to achieve 'perfect' control over 'nature'. Very significant developments have taken place in numerous biomedical and biotechnological fields. Some of these have had a profound social impact. (In the USA, for instance, the average life expectancy, at birth, has doubled since 1900.) The proposition that the human 'state' is biotechnologically modifi-able is now virtually uncontested. 'Nature' is itself perceived to be an inherently problematic and unstable category: the standard, age-old, opposition between 'nature' and 'CULTURE' or 'the biological' and 'the social' has effectively broken down. Such terms as the 'biosocial'/'bio-cultural' now constitute a dominant idiom in scientific accounts of human development. Like-wise, the category of the 'human' has itself been problematized, both in respect of that which is alleged to separate *homo sapiens* from other species and in regard to that which allegedly is specific and even unique to 'humankind'. It is difficult now to have settled convictions about where the boundaries of 'humanity' lie. It is perhaps significant that few if any theologians have attempted fully to 'theorize' these transformations and their implications. This task appears to be left to those who work in new, paradisciplinary fields which blur any distinction between philosophy, the history of ideas, social theory, cultural studies and (what is called these days) 'literary theory'.

Particularly noteworthy here has been the work of the historian of science Donna Haraway. Haraway has attempted to construct 'an ironic political myth' around the image of the cyborg. The cyborg is a being whose 'identity' is no longer specifiable in terms of the traditional oppositions physical/non-physical, animal/human, organism/machine, nature/culture. The cyborg is 'the biological organism' *as* 'biotic system' (though the semiotic registers of these two sets of terms effectively displace each other). The 'human' is now, potentially if not actually, an amalgam of prosthetic devices (a cyborg in other words). The cyborg myth poses interesting and important questions for the theologian and philosopher of religion. What is it to say that cyborgs can suffer? Or that they can be redeemed (or 'need' a redeemer)? Or does this obviation of the 'human' imply a concomitant repudiation of the 'divine'? What is the import of this myth for a doctrine of creation? For a theological ETHICS? For theodicy? Or has theodicy, even as a dream, become dispensable? But what then of 'our' (cyborgian or otherwise) seemingly unvanquishable propensity to be cruel and destructive? The questions of pain and suffering, one senses, will continue to present themselves, albeit in forms that we are perhaps unable to anticipate.

Fiddes, P. (1990) *The Creative Suffering of God*, Oxford: Clarendon.
Haraway, D. (1991) *Simians, Cyborgs, and Women*, London: Routledge.
Hick, J. (1968) *Evil and the God of Love*, London: Fontana/Collins.
Soelle, D. (1975) *Suffering*, London: Darton, Longman & Todd.
Surin, K. (1986) *Theology and the Problem of Evil*, Oxford: Blackwell.
Tilley, T. (1991) *The Evils of Theodicy*, Washington, DC: Georgetown University Press.
Young, R. (1985) *Darwin's Metaphor: Nature's Place in Victorian Culture*, Cambridge: Cambridge University Press.

Kenneth Surin

SUICIDE

Suicide, on the surface the most personal of acts, must always be understood in its social and cultural context. Although we personalize its meaning through autobiographical filters, the SOCIETY we live in constructs the social meanings of suicidal acts. These social meanings, which include religious views of suicide, define the terms in which intrapsychic debates take place. These meanings influence not only the way potential suicides view their acts, but the way in which suicide survivors, those left behind by a suicide, view the suicide and are viewed, and either supported or unsupported, by others.

Suicide has a straightforward meaning in everyday discourse but a vastly more complex one in the social and behavioural sciences – not because in academic disciplines the task seems often to be to make something easy look difficult (unlike ballet where the task is to make something difficult look easy) but rather because any scientific definition of suicide must be precise, and must take into account the psychological and sociological complexity of the act itself. The definition must make analytical sense.

In everyday language, suicide is the taking of one's own life, for example by overdosing on barbiturates, and attempted suicide is the failed attempt to take one's own life, for example by taking more than the prescribed number of barbiturates but failing to die. Imagine, however, the following scenarios leading to the outcome of a self-inflicted DEATH. A person may decide to kill himself or herself, take a fatal dose of barbiturates with the knowledge that that dose will be fatal, and then die. A person may decide to kill himself or herself, take an overdose of barbiturates, change his or her mind, crawl to the telephone to call for help, not be able to make it, and die. In a third case, a person may take what they believe is a non-fatal dose of barbiturates as a dramatic gesture to elicit the sympathy of a spouse who is expected to return shortly, but misjudge the dosage necessary to just barely pass out and misjudge the time of arrival, and then die instead. If that were not complicated enough, it is clear from research that a potential suicide may be ambivalent about dying, may in fact not want to die but simply want to escape intolerable SUFFERING, may, in David Bakan's (1969) interpretation, want to achieve immortality by choosing the time of death to demonstrate that if they had not so chosen they would have lived forever (a piece of emotional, not Aristotelian, logic). Or, finally, what is to be done with the person who eats himself or herself to death over a number of years knowing full well that obesity combined with an unfavourable family cardiac history, his or her own diabetes, etc. makes a 'premature' death a likely, though perhaps long-range, outcome?

In the face of this complexity, suicide as intentional, self-inflicted death has little validity except as a description of the common-sense view. Perhaps the most satisfactory definition of suicide in the behavioural and social sciences, because it takes into account both the personal and social dimensions of meaning, is Edwin Shneidman's (1985: 203):

> Currently in the Western world, suicide is a conscious act of self-induced annihilation, best understood as a multidimensional malaise in a needful individual who defines an issue for which the suicide is perceived as the best solution.

Shneidman (1985: 17–22) suggests that *attempted suicide* should be used only in cases where the person was clearly trying to die, for example by shooting himself or herself in the head, but lived anyway. Following Kreitman *et al.* (1969), he suggests the term *parasuicide* be used to describe all those seemingly suicidal instances in which the intention to die was not clear, often reflected in the non-lethal means selected. Finally, he (Shneidman 1985: 20–2) suggests that when people engage in self-destructive behaviour whose long-range consequence may be death the terms *subintentioned death* or *indirect suicide* (Farberow 1980) should be used.

Shneidman (1981: 151) points out that all suicidal and parasuicidal situations have at least two dimensions: *perturbation*, how agitated the individual is, and *lethality*, how potentially deadly his or her state. High lethality, often fuelled by high perturbation, is the usual precursor of suicidal acts. This distinction has great therapeutic and analytical utility. Practically, workers in suicide prevention centres or therapists working with suicidal patients can attempt to assess how seriously suicidal the people they work with are. It is also useful in understanding variations in some suicide rates. One reason the suicide rates of police officers in the USA have tended to be so high is the constant availability of lethal means should their level of perturbation begin to rise to a point where there is a risk of using them, i.e. they carry loaded guns on and off the job (*see* POLICING).

There are a number of possible relationships between religious ideas and suicide that highlight the importance of the meaning of suicidal acts for suicides and their survivors. The most important are the following.

A distinction has often been made between martyrdom and suicide. This question may have theological currency, but from a psychological point of view Shneidman (1985: 209) has laid it to rest, so to speak, by pointing out that whether people go to their death for religious reasons, cultural reasons or reasons of personal unhappiness, i.e. whatever the degree of social grounding, the common thread in the scientific examination of these acts is the attempt to understand what was in the minds of the individuals who committed them.

However, the distinction has had an important place in many religions, and consequently has a reality that must be recognized in any attempt to understand suicide. Whether individuals think of their death as a suicide or different from suicide may make a difference in their psychology. In addition, the view of their community on what kind of death has occurred certainly influences the reactions of survivors and the treatment (shame, sympathy or celebration) that survivors receive from the community.

For analytical purposes, the definition of suicide is seen by some social scientists to be produced by the practice of those in a society who have the legitimate right to make those judgements. In the cases of barbiturate overdose mentioned above, in many societies it is the coroner who sorts out such cases, deciding that some are clearly suicides and some are not. Atkinson (1978) studied coroners' decisions in England and came up with a list of rules, sometimes latent, sometimes acknowledged, that coroners use to make decisions at inquests. Some of the rules may seem arbitrary, for example the coroner who mentioned that clothing neatly folded on the beach in the case of a drowning usually indicates a suicide. None the less, in a practical sense, suicide rates are made up not by people killing themselves as much as by those who officially designate some deaths as suicides and some deaths as not suicides.

A second analytical approach is to look at the death retrospectively, focusing on the mental condition of the deceased in order to reconstruct the psychic events leading up to the suicide. The technique is called the *psychological autopsy* (Litman *et al.* 1963; Shneidman 1981: 133–48).

There are two basic questions in the study of suicide: Why does a particular individual commit suicide (the psychological question)? And why do suicide rates vary from group to group (the sociological question)?

In an interesting study, Boldt (1982–3) points out that changes in the suicide rate can be seen as the result of increases or decreases in factors that move people toward suicide, the usual approach, but can also be understood as the result of the strengthening or weakening of barriers to suicide. Because the meaning of suicide is *socially constructed*, i.e. constructed by people in societies, it changes as societies change. Currently suicide in Western countries is becoming a less unacceptable alternative. For better or worse, people find more and more comprehensible the decision of some elderly people, beset with financial and health problems, to end their lives. In effect, one of the barriers to suicide is weakening (*see* EUTHANASIA).

Although religion is sometimes linked statistically to variations in the suicide rate, it is perhaps in greater part the degree of religious commitment rather than simple religious affiliation that socially supports or fails to support an individual through what might turn out to be a suicidal crisis (Stack 1983). In addition, religion may make suicide seem an acceptable or at least a less unacceptable alternative in at least four ways. In some religious SECTS or CULTS, suicide may be seen as the right thing to do under some circumstances (see, for example, Black (1990) on the mass suicides in Jonestown, Guyana). Heroic deaths in battle may be sanctioned using religious grounds ideologically to justify those deaths in the name of religion. Martyrdom may also be supported by religion (although the line between heroic death and martyrdom is sometimes difficult to draw). Finally, religion may indirectly encourage suicide by making it less unacceptable. For example, the Roman Catholic Church's *Codex Iuris Canonici* of 1917 prohibits a suicide from being buried in consecrated ground without a bishop's approval whereas *Codex Iuris Canonici* of 1983, by failing to mention suicide specifically, implies that a person cannot be *denied* burial in consecrated ground without a bishop's approval. Although the official position may represent only one view within a religion and although there may be a gap between doctrine and practice, the official view carries a certain weight and, at the very least, must be taken into account by all members of that religious community.

Similarly, the secular, but religiously relevant, phenomenon of near-death experiences, i.e. the almost always pleasant experiences that some people near death report (sometimes involving religious visions) *may* make death seem less frightening and consequently remove the obstacle of fear of the unknown from the restraints on a person near the edge.

Religious sanction may have an enormous effect on suicide survivors, those left behind by a suicide. If religious doctrine affects attitudes toward a suicide, it exercises equal power over the attitudes of survivors and the attitudes of others toward survivors. A religious proscription against suicide may complicate the grieving process of survivors by defining the deceased as an object of shame. There is often a gap between religiously defined STIGMA and the unconditional support families receive from people around them. This disparity seems to be universal (for example, see Headley 1983). Certainly, a prohibition against burial in consecrated ground presents a number of practical problems for families of suicides no matter how much other support they receive. Families sometimes lie about the circumstances of death or collude with members of the CLERGY to define the deceased as not having been of sound mind, traditionally in many religions a mitigating circumstance in assigning full stigma to a suicidal death. At best, this accomplishes the relief afforded by a respectable burial complicated by private and official deceit.

The issue of suicide is likely to become even more important as the possibilities of medical intervention increase and the economic strain of supporting life beyond the limits of what people define as life worth living grows, as the wave of FUNDAMENTALISM sweeping the Islamic world makes battlefield martyrdom more likely, as the issue of assisted death is addressed more aggressively, and as the AIDS pandemic continues to rage, creating an almost ideal suicidogenic confluence of quality-of-life issues debated against a backdrop of economic strain. In sum, if these conditions persist, suicide will probably become more common, and consequently may become more important as a social issue in many societies. Of course, history instructs us to consider the opposite possibility: that, as suicide becomes more common, it may be taken more for granted.

In either eventuality, the precise role of religion remains an open question. Religion has stood or been stood on both sides of the question of suicide. It has been both a significant and an insignificant factor in suicide's aetiology and in the experiences of survivors. Religions contribute to social change and in turn change in response to changes in society. In any case, the place of religion near the heart of the issue will remain secure.

Alvarez, A. (1971) *The Savage God*, London: Weidenfeld & Nicolson.
Atkinson, J.M. (1978) *Discovering Suicide*, London: Macmillan.
Bakan, D. (1969) 'Suicide and immortality', in E.S. Shneidman (ed.) *On the Nature of Suicide*, San Francisco, CA: Jossey-Bass.
Black, A. (1990) 'Jonestown – two faces of suicide: a Durkheimian analysis', *Suicide and Life-Threatening Behavior* 20: 285–306.
Boldt, M. (1982–3) 'Normative evaluations of suicide and death: a cross-generational study', *Omega* 13: 145–57.
Douglas, J.D. (1967) *The Social Meanings of Suicide*, Princeton, NJ: Princeton University Press.
Dunne, E.J., McIntosh, J.L. and Dunne-Maxim, K. (eds) (1987) *Suicide and its Aftermath*, New York: Norton.
Durkheim, E. (1951) *Suicide*, trans. J.A. Spaulding and G. Simpson, New York: Free Press.
Evans, G. and Farberow, N.L. (1988) *The Encyclopedia of Suicide*, New York: Facts On File.
Farberow, N.L. (ed.) (1980) *The Many Faces of Suicide*, New York: McGraw-Hill.
Headley, L.A. (ed.) (1983) *Suicide in Asia and the Near East*, Berkeley, CA: University of California Press.
Kreitman, N., Philip, A.E., Greer, S. and Bagley, C.R. (1969) 'Parasuicide', *British Journal of Psychiatry* 115: 746–7.
Leenaars, A.A. (ed.) (1991) *Life Span Perspectives of Suicide*, New York: Plenum.
Litman, R.E., Curphy, T., Shneidman, E.S., Farberow, N.L. and Tabachnick, N. (1963) 'Investigations of equivocal suicides', *Journal of the American Medical Association* 184: 924–9.
Maris, R.W. (1981) *Pathways to Suicide*, Baltimore, MD: Johns Hopkins University Press.
Menninger, K.A. (1938) *Man Against Himself*, New York: Harcourt, Brace.
Shneidman, E.S. (ed.) (1967) *Essays in Self-Destruction*, New York: Science House.
——(1981) *Suicide Thoughts and Reflections, 1960–1980*. New York: Human Sciences Press.
——(1985) *Definition of Suicide*, New York: Wiley.
Stack, S. (1983) 'The effect of religious commitment on suicide: cross-national analysis', *Suicide and Life-Threatening Behavior* 11: 362–74.

Jack Kamerman

SURROGACY

When a woman bears a child for another person, she is called a surrogate mother. However, since the term 'surrogate' generally refers to a substitute, it is not an entirely suitable expression since in many cases the surrogate mother is in fact the real mother.

In the past, a person had only two parents: a father and a mother. There was no problem about what these terms meant: a 'mother' was the woman whose ovum was fertilized and who gave birth and a 'father' was the man whose sperm fertilized the mother's ovum. Any other parents were godparents or step-parents. Now with the success of modern reproductive technology one might have a total of five parents: a genetic mother (the woman who contributes the ovum), a gestational or birth mother (the woman in whose uterus the ovum develops), a nurturing or social mother (the woman who raises the child), a genetic father (the man who contributes the sperm) and a nurturing or social father (the man who raises the child).

Modern reproductive techniques are so new that the terminology is not yet firmly established. For instance, one sometimes reads about the 'biological mother' or 'natural mother', although it is not clear whether these expressions refer to what I have called the genetic mother or to the gestational mother or whether it refers to one woman who performs both functions. In general, however, the terminology attempts to distinguish between these different forms of surrogacy. Similarly, the sperm donor is sometimes referred to as the real father. In England the terminology is slightly different.

The problems raised by surrogacy are not primarily terminological, however, but involve a massive number of important ethical, legal and social questions. For example, is surrogacy a form of baby selling? Should surrogacy contracts be legal or should the practice be outlawed? Should surrogacy be permitted, but fees outlawed? Can such contracts be enforced? Does surrogacy lead to the view that women are mere commodities that can be, if not bought and sold, at least rented? Might surrogacy lead to the exploitation of poor women or women from Third World countries? If it is shown that surrogacy is exploitive, is that a sufficient reason to prohibit it or is a surrogate contract simply another kind of contract? Does the pre-implanted embryo have any moral or legal status, and if so who determines it: the parents (the 'gamete sources') or the doctors and researchers? The latter question arises because some of the *in vitro* fertilization techniques involve fertilizing more eggs than are implanted. Once the child is born, who gets custody if there is a dispute? What happens if neither genetic parent wants the infant? Does the genetic father have rights equal to the genetic mother or do his rights

have priority since the genetic mother has already agreed to give up her child? Is surrogacy simply a continuation of the right to reproduce as some have claimed? Should only married or heterosexual couples be permitted to use these reproductive techniques or should male homosexual or lesbian couples also be allowed to employ surrogates? Should single people be allowed to hire surrogates? Should there be limitations or conditions, such as age or having already borne a child, concerning who can become a surrogate? Should a woman be allowed to become a surrogate only once? Finally how will the various decisions that are made about surrogacy affect society in general?

Most of the objections to surrogacy are based on the notion that either the surrogate mother or the child is exploited and comes to be considered as a commodity. Reinforcing such views is the media attention paid to some of the less successful cases of surrogacy, such as the 1987 Baby M case which involved the unhappiness of the genetic mother in giving up her child and the 1982 Stiver–Malahoff case which involved the birth of a microcephalic baby which neither genetic parent originally wanted. Such problems could be solved by detailed contracts which would take into consideration all possible consequences if the child was not normal, and which would also give the genetic mother a limited amount of time in which to change her mind, as happens with adoption and with many other kinds of contracts.

A slightly different objection is raised by Herbert Krimmel, who finds nothing wrong in a woman acting as surrogate if she simply bears an already fertilized egg. He sees this situation as analogous to a foster mother or wet-nurse. On the other hand, he finds troubling the woman who provides the ovum for he holds that this involves 'the separation of the decision to create a child from the decision to parent it . . .' (Krimmel 1983: 62–3). Krimmel adds that children should be desired for their own sake and not for some benefit they may provide for their parents. These criticisms assume, first, that all children are planned, which is certainly not the case, and second, that not only is it possible to understand one's motivation for wanting a child – a questionable assumption – but that such motivation is suspect if it involves, for example, a desire that the child care for its parent in the latter's old age and so forth. Such assertions do not provide a telling argument against surrogacy.

Some feminists would like to see surrogacy prohibited because they find it exploitive of the surrogate mother, while others maintain that to outlaw surrogacy, particularly on the basis that it exploits women, is to present women as less than mature adults capable of making responsible decisions. These feminists claim that the stereotypical image of women as dependent beings requiring protection is only strengthened by paternalistic laws prohibiting surrogacy.

Other authors feel that many of the problems concerning surrogacy arise because we confuse the act of surrogacy with its commercial aspects. They maintain that prohibiting the payment of money to surrogate mothers would solve the problem concerning the exploitation of poor women. With nothing to gain financially, women who chose to become surrogates would do so freely without the pressures of economic incentives. On the other hand, a surrogate mother presumably has additional medical expenses and takes certain risks. Should she be compensated for these expenditures? Such payments, it is said, are not equivalent to 'renting a womb', nor are they a reward for the woman; the exchange of money in this case is simply a payment for the woman's inevitably incurred expenses. I have not seen it suggested that one way to avoid the exploitation of poor women might be to charge sufficiently large sums for surrogacy so that, for example, a Third World or poor woman would be able to earn enough to gain financial independence for at least a number of years.

The real problem is not, I think, one of exploitation for many practices in modern society by their very nature are exploitive. The author who writes a book often needs a literary agent to publish the book and pays part of the royalties to such a person although the agent takes no part in the literary creation. Is that not also a kind of exploitation? Indeed, there are those who claim that any form of taxation is a kind of exploitation.

Nor are there any facts or statistics that corroborate the notion that surrogacy leads to viewing children as a commodity – those who hire a surrogate often desperately want a child and value the child as well as the surrogate highly.

The real questions, which are not often raised in discussions of surrogacy, involve something quite different. Why is there this great emphasis on having one's own genetic child when there are children that can be adopted?

The facile explanation of this question is historical, namely that the preference for one's 'own' child is traditional. From Biblical times, procreation has been praised and men have wanted to produce their own children. Consider God's promise to Abraham: 'I will make your descendants countless as the dust of the earth' and 'Your heir shall be a child of your own body. Look up into the sky and count the stars if you can. So many shall your descendants be' (Genesis 13: 16; 15: 5 respectively). We find references in the story of Abraham and Isaac concerning the social importance of having one's own children as opposed to adopted ones. This story also presents us with an example of surrogacy, although it is a slave who, impregnated by the husband, is to bear a child that the legal wife will then raise as her own. The story of Jacob and his two wives also involves the notion of surrogacy. In this story the beautiful Rachel plaintively cries to her husband, 'Give me sons or I shall die'. Notice that she asks, not for children, but for male children, and notice furthermore her extreme distress at her apparent infertility. (Of course, we know now that the sex of the child depends on the male, not the female.) These Biblical stories emphasize not only the importance of procreation but also the importance for the child to be of one's own flesh rather than adopted. It is not surprising if we retain these values.

These stories and the continued importance of such values raise the question whether the desire to have a genetically related child is biologically determined or culturally conditioned. Gena Corea argues that there are a number of ways in which such desires are culturally conditioned. If this is the case, then these values could be altered.

As we begin to realize that the human species

is one of the most successful animals in terms of reproduction, we begin to worry not about being fruitful and multiplying, but rather about how to control the human population of the planet and how to avoid the dire consequences that are predicted to come about as the result of continued and unlimited increases in population. We are told that the inevitable consequences of overpopulation are mass starvation, lack of drinking water, overcrowding and so forth.

In the light of these dire predictions, we might ask if there is a right to procreate. Most people assume that there is such a right, and indeed it was argued in the Baby M case that surrogacy simply allows for 'the furtherance of [a couple's] constitutionally protected right to procreation' (Schneider 1987). Clearly, if there is no right to procreate, then the argument attaching surrogacy to such a right fails.

If the predictions concerning overpopulation are correct or even probable, it is not the case that procreation does not harm anyone for the opposite would be true: continued and perhaps unlimited procreation harms everyone and, as such, it would be difficult to view it as a right. Moreover, is it not inconsistent to spend huge sums of money to make it possible for infertile men and women to reproduce when we are actively encouraging members of the Third World not to do so? Is it not somewhat peculiar to spend large amounts of money in research to 'cure' infertility as if it were a disease, when the medical profession is faced with AIDS, drug-resistant tuberculosis and so forth? This is, of course, the old question of how we allot limited resources. We have to ask what portion of our resources, if any, we ought to put into fertility research when only a small percentage of people have such problems and an even smaller percentage of people will ever be able to afford the technologies available.

Finally the question of surrogacy raises the much larger question of technology itself – of a technology that seems to have developed a life of its own and such a powerful life that no-one can stop it and ask whether the continuation of this or that research or technology is really for the betterment of society.

Andrews, L. (1989) *Between Strangers: Surrogate Mothers, Expectant Fathers and Brave New Babies*, New York: Harper & Row.

Chadwick, R.F. (1987) *Ethics, Reproduction and Genetic Control*, London: Croom Helm.

Corea, Gena (1985) *The Mother Machine: Reproductive Technologies from Artifical Insemination to Artificial Wombs*, New York: Harper & Row.

——(1988) 'What the king cannot see', in E.H. Baruch, A.F. D'Adamo, Jr and J. Seager (eds) *Embryos, Ethics and Women's Rights: Exploring the New Reproductive Technology*, New York: Harrington Park Press.

Field, M.A. (1988) *Surrogate Motherhood: The Legal and Humane Issues*, Cambridge, MA: Harvard University Press.

Fletcher, J. (1988) *The Ethics of Genetic Control*. Buffalo, NY: Prometheus Books.

Hull, R. (1990) *Ethical Issues in the New Reproductive Technologies*, Belmont, CA: Wadsworth.

Krimmel, N.T. (1983) 'The case against surrogate parenting', *Hastings Center Report* 13(5); in T. Mappes and J. Zembaty (eds) *Social Ethics: Morality and Social Policy*, New York: McGraw-Hill, 1992.

Schneider, K. (1987) 'Mothers urge ban on surrogacy as a form of slavery', *New York Times*, September 1; quoted by R. Macklin, 'Is there anything wrong with surrogate motherhood: an ethical analysis', in *Taking Sides: Clashing Moral Issues*, 3rd edn, Sluice Dock, CT: Duskin.

Singer, P. and Walter, W.A. (1982) *Test-Tube Babies: A Guide to Moral Questions, Present Techniques and Future Possibilities*, Oxford: Oxford University Press.

Priscilla Cohn

TELEOLOGICAL ETHICS

For some ethical systems, actions are right or wrong, good or bad (or answer to some other predicates which provide their most basic evaluation of actions, such as rational or irrational) according to whether they conform to a certain system of rules; for other ethical systems they are so by virtue of the goodness or badness of their actual or likely consequences. The former systems are called deontological, the latter consequentialist. Teleological ethical systems may be regarded as a subclass of consequentialist systems, distinguished by the fact that the relevant consequences are a matter of an action's promotion or hindrance of just one particular goal. However, since the singleness of a goal is none too clear a concept, there is in practice no hard and fast line between teleological and other types of consequentialist system. Both will be considered in this entry.

The main goals, movement towards or away from which have been the determinants of right and wrong for some ethical systems, are (a) happiness, (b) self-realization, (c) virtue, (d) personal salvation or union with God and (e) the improvement of the human race.

(a) Systems for which the promotion of *happiness* and prevention of unhappiness are the relevant goals are known as *hedonistic systems* when happiness is identified with (in J.S. Mill's phrase) 'pleasure, and the absence of pain' and unhappiness with 'pain and the privation of pleasure'. Personal hedonism holds that actions are right or wrong according to their effects on the agent's own happiness and unhappiness. (I substitute 'personal' for the more usual 'egoistic' to avoid the dyslogistic flavour of the latter.) In contrast, universalistic hedonism, otherwise known as hedonistic utilitarianism, holds that actions are right or wrong according to whether they promote or otherwise the happiness of all affected by them, the 'all' sometimes seeming to be confined to members of the human race but usually meaning all sentient creatures. Epicurus (341–270 BC) is particularly associated with the thesis that it is one's own happiness which is the proper end of conduct and that actions are to be evaluated for promoting or hindering this end. Such classical utilitarians as Jeremy

Bentham (1748–1832), J.S. Mill (1806–73) and Henry Sidgwick (1838–1900) are the main representatives of the view that it is effects on the general happiness which are the criterion of right and wrong.

Mention should be made of various forms of *non-hedonistic utilitarianism*. The ideal utilitarianism of Hastings Rashdall (1858–1924) and G.E. Moore (1873–1958) held that the criterion is the effects of action in increasing the amount of intrinsic value (counting intrinsic disvalue as a negative quantity of this) and claimed that the intrinsically valuable included things other than happiness (and negatively of unhappiness). Moore, for example, held that certain sorts of personal relationship and the enjoyment of beauty possessed an intrinsic value not simply a matter of their pleasurableness. However, if any system is consequentialist without being teleological, it is this, for its whole point is to stress the diversity of the consequences which make an action right or wrong.

Eudaimonistic systems make happiness, whether individual or general, the criterion of right and wrong but repudiate a purely hedonistic account of it. Aristotle's (384–322 BC) ethics seems a form of personal eudaimonism: right action is recommended for its promotion of the agent's happiness (which, however, importantly includes acting properly to others). Most forms of teleological ethics, in fact, tend to justify their peculiar goal as either the best means to, or the best form of, happiness, in some sense or other, but how exactly happiness relates to pleasure is often problematic.

(b) F.H. Bradley (1846–1924) is perhaps the chief proponent of a form of *self-realization ethics*. Taking it for granted that self-realization is every rational individual's goal, he evaluates a series of moral stances (hedonism, the pursuit of virtue, satisfactory fulfilment of one's role in the community, associated loosely with each of Mill, Kant and Hegel respectively) for the extent to which we can reach self-realization through them and decides that none is quite adequate, though the third is the best. By self-realization, though he does not quite put it so, he seems to mean becoming what one can be enduringly pleased to be. T.H. Green (1836–82) and other British idealists of the period had much the same idea, though with Green self-realization was more determinedly identified with moral virtue, and there is more emphasis on the intrinsic need of a virtuous person to see the increase of virtue in his community as a desideratum.

Spinoza's (1632–77) ethics is in effect a form of self-realization ethics. He speaks indeed of mere survival as being the proper end of a rational man by which he will judge his actions as good or bad, but by survival he means the actualization of one's individual essence in as strong and powerful a form as possible.

(c) Green, as has been seen, could be classified as a teleological ethicist for whom virtue, both of the agent himself and of all members of his community, are the good. Kant is the prime example of a deontological ethicist but there are in fact strands of a teleological ethics of virtue in his work. Historically, the most systematic form of *virtue ethics* was that of the Stoics (founded by Zeno of Citium, 342–270 BC). (They reached this via the claim that virtue was the only genuine form of happiness or *eudaimonia*, but this was not meant to be an end to which it was a mere means.)

(d) Distinctively *religious ethical outlooks* are likely to be teleological in one way or another. For some Christians and Muslims what ultimately makes an action the right one is that by pleasing God it promotes one's own salvation, while for Buddhists and Hindus it may be that it reduces the load of karma thus assisting a final escape from the cycle of rebirths.

(e) A fairly pure example of a philosopher for whom the criterion of right and wrong ought to be (though it has failed to be during the Christian era) *the improvement of the human race* was Nietzsche (1844–1900). For him the goal of conduct should be the production of the superman or *Übermensch* either in one's own person or in that of others. It was not, however, that Nietzsche looked for a race of supermen. Rather the human race was to be justified, so far as it could be, by the existence of a sufficiency of supermen serviced in their needs by a race of lesser men whose point would be simply to provide the appropriate infrastructure. Nietzsche's ideas, or what were thought to be such, were used in support of Nazi IDEOLOGY, but Nietzsche's supermen were not to be members

of some special superior race but simply some few isolated great individuals whose existence would give point to their societies.

Both J.S. Mill and Bradley, and many others, took the improvement of the human race, in a much more pervasive way, as the main mediate goals of the best human endeavour. So also have some proponents of so-called *evolutionary ethics*, though its most famous partisan, Herbert Spencer (1820–1903), seems to have thought rather that actions are right or wrong in so far as they already anticipate the progress of human evolution towards a state in which there would be a maximum of co-operative human heterogeneity.

The main alternatives to teleological ethics are the following.

(1) In some types of consequentialist ethics the consequences are too various to be easily classified as constituting some single end of conduct, e.g. Moore's ideal utilitarianism. But, as already emphasized, it is difficult to distinguish between unity of verbal expression and real unity or diversity of relevant consequences.

(2) There are various ethical outlooks for which it is their motivation which makes actions right or wrong, e.g. Hutcheson's view that it is the degree of benevolence shown which determines the moral quality of an action, and Schopenhauer's view that an action is right, indifferent or wrong according to whether it exhibits compassion, ordinary egoism or excessive egoism or even malice.

(3) Some forms of Christian ethics seem to repudiate teleological ethics. The view that actions are right or wrong according to whether they express sufficient love of God or one's neighbour is another form of motive ethics. Religious critics of ABORTION are likely to be ranged against typical forms of modern consequentialism, but whether they are deontic or teleological in some ultimate way must depend on the ultimate JUSTIFICATION. The simple view that actions are right or wrong according to whether God commands or forbids them is presumably deontological, but the alternative simple view that they are right or wrong according to their effects on one's own relationship with God is personally teleological.

(4) Deontic ethics, where what matters is

conscious conformity to a rule, is the most obvious alternative to consequentialism. Kant is the most famous deontic ethicist. For him an action is right or wrong according to whether the agent could possibly wish the maxim which inspired it universalized or, supposedly in the end equivalently, treats every instance of humanity as an end in itself. In this century the best form of deontic ethics was that advocated by W.D. Ross who considered the right act that which conformed to that of various *prima facie* duties (such as promise keeping, beneficence, truth telling) which was most stringent in the current circumstances.

Much current discussion centres round a distinction between agent-relative and agent-neutral moral requirements. An agent-neutral requirement bids everyone attach a certain degree of importance to the forwarding of some state of affairs, varying only with their power to influence it, irrespectively of any other relation in which they stand to it. Thus it would be an agent-neutral requirement that everyone attaches a certain degree of importance to the decrease of LYING, no matter who is to tell the lies, whether myself, my personal associates or merely strangers. On such a view to tell one lie to prevent others telling several must in principle be right. On an agent-relative view, in contrast, it may be my peculiar duty not to tell lies (or perhaps not to let my family do so) whatever the effects on the amount of lying in general.

Consequentialism, and thus teleological ethics, is usually thought of as agent neutral in this sense and deontic ethics as agent relative. For Kant, famously, I must not lie to a potential murderer as to where his victim is hidden, whereas for Bentham this would be obviously right. It is to be noted that personal forms of teleological ethics are intrinsically agent relative. If my task is to make myself happy or virtuous there may be things I should not try to bring about, as making me unhappy or vicious, even though others may legitimately seek them at the cost of my misery or moral degradation.

More important, perhaps, than most of these distinctions is that between what might be called historical teleological ethics, which judges an individual life for its part in some long historical progress, and systems for which its moral

significance turns on its character at its own time and place. For a certain type of evolutionary ethics and for (the largely discredited) Marxist ethics, the main task of human beings *now* (for however long that lasts) is to work for some much better state of human affairs in the far future, while for self-realization ethics, and for Kant, it is a matter of what I do here and now with my life that matters, whatever may or may not happen in the future. Utilitarian ethics tends to fall, not discreditably, between these two schools. However, few serious moral philosophers can be neatly placed precisely in one of the pigeonholes provided in an article like this.

Consequentialists and teleologists, implicitly or explicitly, take the concept of good and bad as characterizations of states of affairs or things as basic, while deontological ethics take right and wrong as predicates of action as more basic. For the consequentialist it seems irrational to stick to a rule except in so far as in the particular case it is a means of achieving the best possible results (including under these whatever value pertains to the doing of the deed itself together with the reinforcement of desirable traits of character). For the deontologist this fails to do justice to such things as the peculiar duties binding on us in virtue of our special personal relations to particular people. Granted consequentialism, a teleological version thereof tends to recommend itself to those who think the notion of a mere plurality of good and evil consequences, as determinants of desirable action, too lacking in any dominating focus to be the basis of an examined life.

Bradley, F.H. (1962) *Ethical Studies*, Oxford: Clarendon (1st edn 1876).

Green, T.H. (1903) *Prolegomena to Ethics*, ed. A.C. Bradley, 5th edn, Oxford: Clarendon (1st edn 1883).

Kant, I. (1964) *The Groundwork of the Metaphysic of Morals*, ed. H.J. Paton, New York: Harper & Row.

Moore, G.E. (1903) *Principia Ethica*, Cambridge: Cambridge University Press.

Parfit, D. (1984) *Reasons and Persons*, Oxford: Clarendon.

Scheffler, S. (1982) *The Rejection of Consequentialism*, Oxford: Clarendon.

Sidgwick, H. (1907) *The Methods of Ethics*, 7th edn, London: Macmillian (1st edn 1874).

T.L.S. Sprigge

THEOCRACY

The term 'theocracy' was first coined by the Jewish historian Josephus (*Against Apion* 2.165) at the end of the first century to describe the form of government favoured in the Hebrew Scriptures. The Greek term *theokratia* denotes the exercise of the rule of God, and in the ancient world Josephus found this in its purest form amongst the Jews, contrasting it with the monarchies, oligarchies and republics found elsewhere. He claims that according to Mosaic principles of government all rule (*archē*) and exercise of power (*kratos*) belong to God. This gives rise to a model of society in which the total ordering of the people's life discloses the salvific will of God. Although the rule of God can be mediated by a charismatic leader, a monarch or a priest the Hebrew Bible can also look forward to an eschaton in which the JUDGEMENT of God will be immediate and direct (Isaiah 2).

Theocracy, however, is a term which has never been precisely defined either in subsequent THEOLOGY or in social theory. Its usage since the nineteenth century has often been pejorative, referring to societies in which there is a close alignment of CHURCH AND STATE or, more specifically, a ruling priestly group (the term hierocracy is more properly used in the latter context.) John Calvin's Geneva is perhaps the most frequently cited illustration of a theocracy. Here there is a liaison of church and state in which the civil ruler(s) has the responsibility of suppressing idolatry in the church and maintaining purity of religion. It is no accident that in this context Reformed theologians (particularly John Knox in Scotland) could appeal to Old Testament precedents in attempting to construct societies in which the Reformed religion was part of the social fabric. None the less, in Calvin's writings there remains something of Luther's two kingdoms theory in which there is a sharp distinction between the form and means of power in the civil and spiritual realms. This largely prevented the CLERGY from holding both civil and spiritual office.

Later Reformed theology, however, particularly in the USA, felt the need of a much sharper distinction between church and state than had obtained in Geneva. Here the case for religious toleration, freedom of WORSHIP and religious pluralism became effective. The inner conscience of the individual cannot be invaded by the civil order; consequently, true religion and a just social order will always respect the independence of the other. It is significant that in response to the cogency of these arguments the chapter on the civil magistrate in a leading Reformed confession, the Westminster Confession (1647), was redrafted in late eighteenth-century America. This approach had the undoubted merit of preventing an imperialism of any one religious group and thus of negating the old dictum *cuius regio eius religio*. None the less, its inherent danger is that it divorces the spiritual from the political, hence relegating religion to a private domain with little direct impact upon public affairs.

Late twentieth-century ecclesiastical pronouncements, often influenced by the role of the Confessing Church in Nazi Germany, have tended to strike a balance between theocratic and apolitical models of religion by providing critical support for the civil state. Here there is recognition that the state has a divinely appointed task, and that the Christian witness to the KINGDOM OF GOD is of its very nature a political witness. Nevertheless, there cannot be a total alignment of the civil and religious. The state must guarantee the peaceful coexistence of different religious groups and freedom to worship must be recognized. At the same time, the church is called upon to criticize the civil order both positively and negatively on the basis of the divine revelation to which it must witness. 'By preaching the truths of the Gospel and clarifying all sectors of human activity through its teaching and the witness of its members, the Church respects and encourages the political freedom and responsibility of the citizen' (Vatican II, *Gaudium et Spes* 76). Here, as elsewhere, the radical departure from theocratic ways of thinking is apparent.

Theocratic patterns of thought have been detected in other religious traditions such as Tibetan Buddhism. But the clearest manifestation of theocracy in recent times has been in ISLAMIC FUNDAMENTALISM influenced by the writings from the 1920s of Muhammed Rashid Rida. Especially in Iran, Islamic fundamentalism has been marked by a rejection of Western SECULAR-IZATION and by the attempt to model SOCIETY on the principles of the Sharia. Here Christian distinctions between the separate provinces of the civil and religious are largely irrelevant. With the alignment of temporal and spiritual GOVERN-MENT, and the political rule of the Supreme Imam, the term 'theocracy' has found a contemporary reference. (Historically Islam has always been a more theocratic religion than either Judaism or Christianity.) While the close relationship perceived between divine and human justice may awaken Christian theology to the dangers of their dissociation, the religious monism of Islamic fundamentalist society is unlikely to win intellectual support in the increasingly pluralist West.

Breslow, M.A. (ed.) (1985) *The Political Writings of John Knox*, London: Folger.
Eichrodt, Walter (1961) *Theology of the Old Testament*, vol. 1, London: SCM.
Hiro, Dilip (1988) *Islamic Fundamentalism*, London: Paladin.
Höpfl, Harro (ed.) (1991) *Luther and Calvin on Secular Authority*, Cambridge: Cambridge University Press.
Little, David (1992) 'Reformed faith and religious liberty', in D.K. McKim (ed.) *Major Themes in the Reformed Tradition*, Grand Rapids, MI: Eerdmans, pp. 196–213.
Symposium on Theocracy (1981) *Reformed Review* 34 (Winter).
Taubes, Jacob (ed.) (1987) *Theokratie*, Munich: Wilhelm Fink.
Wallace, Dewey D., Jr (1987) 'Theocracy', in *Encyclopedia of Religion*, New York: Macmillan, pp. 427–30.
World Council of Churches (1978) *Church and State: Opening a New Ecumenical Discussion*, Geneva: World Council of Churches.

David A.S. Fergusson

THEODICY

The term 'theodicy', constructed from the Greek words for 'god' and 'justice', refers to any attempt to exhibit in a positive way the relationship of God, especially God's justice and goodness, to EVIL. The term is sometimes used even more broadly to mean any interpretation of evil and human existence which enables people to find meaning and purpose in life in spite of the presence of evil in the world. However, the tradition of modern philosophical and theological theodicy, as well as the term itself, originate roughly with the publication in 1710 of Leibniz's work, *Theodicy: Essays on the Goodness of God, the Freedom of Man and the Origin of Evil*. Arising in the context of Enlightenment theistic apologetics, this tradition of modern theodicy construction has conceived the nature of theodicy more narrowly as the attempt to reconcile God's power and goodness with the existence of evil by providing a true and reasonable explanation of evil, based on God's morally sufficient reasons for permitting evil.

On this view a successful theodicy should both explain evil and exonerate God's decision to permit or cause it. Modern theodicists have for the most part addressed atheist or agnostic critics of theism, attempting either to defend or to demonstrate the logical consistency and rational plausibility of a broadly theistic interpretation of human existence and the evils it contains. John Hick, a leading contemporary theodicist, distinguishes three main types of modern theodicy: Augustinian, Irenaean and modern process theodicy. In his *Philosophy of Religion* (1990) he gives a concise presentation of the distinctive content of each type of theodicy. I shall discuss the common features and logical structure of this Leibnizian tradition of modern theodicy construction and will outline an alternative view of the theodicist's task.

Modern theodicists accomplish their twofold task of explaining evil and exonerating God by appealing to the Greater Good Principle. According to this principle, evil exists because it is in some way necessary for God's realization of a good which outweighs or defeats it. This greater good has the following main elements, which are explained in different ways by the different types of theodicy: the good of individual human existence and experience, and especially the FREE WILL essential to human personhood; the good of a created or natural order which can be understood by its human participants but not altered by them; and finally, certain higher order goods which emerge historically from the actions and interactions of God and human PERSONS within the context of the created or natural order. These higher order goods are broadly moral, involving a community of LOVE in which human individuality is both affirmed and transcended. This community of love, or KINGDOM OF GOD, is the end which fulfills the goods embodied in human freedom and the natural order. The evils the world contains are viewed as necessary conditions or inevitable, if divinely unintended, consequences of the process whereby the previously mentioned goods are realized.

Critics have argued that many actual evils seem unnecessary for the supposed greater, justifying goods and that the actual goods we see being realized in the struggle between good and evil are not sufficient to justify permitting the amount and type of evil the world contains. The world, they argue, contains many *apparently gratuitous evils*. By 'gratuitous evil' is meant any evil God could remove and whose actual removal would make the world better. The issue here is not the logical consistency of God's existence and evil, the so-called logical problem of evil. According to many recent critics the primary and most cogent form of the problem of evil is instead the so-called evidential or empirical problem of evil. According to this version of the problem of evil, the presence of apparently gratuitous evil constitutes evidence against the existence of God, renders God's existence improbable, and makes our belief in God's existence implausible. If you were God, the argument sometimes seems to suggest, would you have allowed so much and such terrible evil to accomplish such meagre results.

Modern theodicists argue in response that, from a theistic point of view, the world may contain evils human beings are not able to explain but it does not contain apparently gratuitous evils. They insist that the *total* evidence, including evil, does not render God's existence improbable and our belief in it implausible. In this context the concepts of evidence and total evidence are particularly difficult to clarify. and make the dispute particularly difficult to adjudicate.

Leibniz supported the reasoning of the theodicists by claiming that, since God is omnipotent and absolutely perfect, the world he created, the actual world, must be the best of all logically possible worlds. God's desire to maximize good provides a morally sufficient reason for every evil in the world because, should God remove even the smallest evil, the resulting world would be a different possible world and, by hypothesis, one which is not as good as the actual world. Many modern theodicists have adopted a modified version of this reasoning which enables them to distinguish two concepts of gratuitous evil. They argue that the actual world may not be the best of all possible worlds but is instead the best world God is able to actualize. Thus the actual world does contain evils which are gratuitous in the sense that their removal *by someone*, say you or me, would make the world better but it contains no evils which are gratuitous in the sense that their removal *by God* would make the world better. My free decision not to murder my neighbour, for example, would have improved the world, even though God's preventing the murder by taking the choice out of my hands may well *not* have made the world better.

On this view such evils should be regretted and there may well be no morally sufficient reason for them as such, even though there is a morally sufficient reason for God's decision to permit them.

Modern theodicists have also argued that they need not be able to produce explanations of God's morally sufficient reasons for permitting particular evils in order to construct successful theodicies. Even though such explanations are in principle possible, they are likely to be too complicated for human beings to understand. It is enough, they suggest, to provide a plausible account in global, general terms of God's morally sufficient reasons for permitting various *kinds* of evil. Such theodicies have tried to exhibit in a general way God's goodness to the world taken as a whole rather than to exhibit God's special goodness to human agents as they engage in their struggle with particular evils.

This broadly Leibnizian framework for understanding the problem of evil and the nature of theodicy has been criticized by both theists and non-theists. Terrence Tilley (1991), for example, has argued that such theodicies misconceive the problem of evil and inhibit a proper response to actual evils. Such theodicists inevitably play the role of Job's friends who try to silence Job's protests with explanations of his situation which make him responsible for what is happening to him. Modern theodicies try to put the world's evils in proper perspective, thereby assuring us that all evil fits into a larger pattern whose perfection somehow explains evil and justifies God. Tilley argues that constructing such theodicies is tantamount to constructing a tranquillizing rationalization which not only inhibits moral protest but also prevents us from identifying with sufferers who need to be supported and given a voice rather than silenced and suppressed. Modern theodicies efface the actual evils the world contains and make it difficult for people to confront them honestly and realistically. Indeed the phrase 'the problem of evil' is seductive in this regard because it tempts one to think there is a single general problem of evil which can be abstracted from the concrete conditions within which evil actually occurs and then 'solved' theoretically by deducing its occurrence from the divine nature and the structure of the universe.

In a similar but more ironic way Marilyn McCord Adams (1986) suggests that the framework within which philosophers and theologians discuss the problem of evil needs to be changed and our understanding of the task of the theodicist adjusted accordingly. That framework has been dominated by the following questions:

1 Why does God not do more than he does to prevent or eliminate evils?
2 Why did God make a world in which there are evils of the amounts and kinds found in this world instead of one with fewer or less severe kinds?
3 Why did God make a world such as this instead of one entirely free from evils?

Our understanding of the world and its evils is far too incomplete to produce any answers to these questions, other than the global, abstract answers offered by Leibniz and other modern theodicists.

Adams suggests that the problem of evil can be contextualized and the content of theodicy construction focused on exhibiting God's agent-centred goodness to those struggling with actual evils by approaching these issues from a Christian point of view through the question

4 How can I trust (or continue to trust) God in a world like this (in distressing circumstances such as these)?

This question will be answered in part, she believes, by addressing the following question:

5 How does God fit evils, of the amounts and kinds we find in the world, into his redemptive purposes?

On this view the theodicist has a role to play in the process whereby people overcome evil by reflecting on what God is actually doing to overcome evil and encouraging the believer to identify in faith with that process. The purpose is to achieve a practical understanding of God's relationship to evil which gives a believer hope in her own struggle to overcome evil. This approach encourages formulation of the problem of evil itself in terms of questions which reflect the situations and conditions within which people actually confront evil. Furthermore, it encourages the theodicist to examine and articulate the broad range of resources people actually rely upon in their efforts to overcome evil.

Such theodicies display a more distinctly religious content, whether that content be drawn from the Christian tradition or some other religious tradition, and are less apologetically oriented than the broadly theistic theodicies developed within a Leibnizian framework. In fact, Jürgen Moltmann (1980) argues that theologians should develop a distinctively Christian theodicy based on a Trinitarian concept of God which has at its centre the SUFFERING of God revealed in Jesus Christ. On the latter point there has been a great deal of debate, both earlier in this century and recently, about whether or not an adequate Christian theodicy must affirm that God suffers because of the evil the world contains. The issue of divine suffering is likely to continue to be important in future discussion of theodicy and the problem of evil.

In conclusion, I believe that the different approaches to theodicy outlined here can be viewed as complementary rather than contradictory. The modern, Leibnizian approach has clarified the key logic concepts involved in understanding the problem of evil, especially those related to the Greater Good Principle. That principle does help us understand why human beings permit or cause events which in themselves are evil. But when the same principle is applied to God's relationship to evil the results are misleading because we lack an adequate understanding of God's power and goodness. The Greater Good Principle successfully explains evil only when the concepts of power and goodness are given clear boundaries. Leibniz tries to do this for God with his concept of a single best possible world; other modern theodicists try to do the same thing with their concept of a best world God is able to actualize; and modern process theodicists try to do it with their understanding of the metaphysics of freedom and power. Criticism has shown, however, that while these approaches may enable one to defend the consistency of theism in general they do very little to clarify the actual relationship between God's goodness and the world's evils. The theoretical and apologetic gains made possible by these approaches with respect to the consistency and reasonability of theism in general often occur at the expense of the relevance of the theodicy project for the practical task of really understanding and overcoming actual evils. On the other hand, the practical, religiously oriented approach to theodicy construction discussed above is broad enough to embrace the apologist's concern to respond to theism's critics without undermining the overall relevance of theodicy construction to the important task of confronting and overcoming the evils our world actually contains. Thus, I believe such a framework is more useful for understanding the nature of theodicy and for guiding theodicists in the work of theodicy construction.

Adams, Marilyn McCord (1986) 'Redemptive suffering', in Robert Audi and William Wainwright (eds) Rationality, Religious Belief and Moral Commitment, Ithaca, NY: Cornell University Press.
Augustine of Hippo, 'The free choice of the will', in Saint Augustine: The Teacher, the Free Choice of the Will, Grace and Free-Will, trans. Robert P. Russell, OSA, The Fathers of the Church vol. 59, Washington, DC: Catholic University of America Press, 1967.
Hick, John H. (1978) Evil and the God of Love, revised edition, San Francisco, CA: Harper & Row.
——(1990) Philosophy of Religion, 4th edn, Englewood Cliffs, NJ: Prentice-Hall.
Hume, David (1779) Dialogues Concerning Natural Religion, ed. Norman Kemp Smith, Indianapolis, IN: Bobbs Merrill, 1947.
Leibniz, G.W. (1710) Theodicy, Essays on the Goodness of God, the Freedom of Man and the Origin of Evil, trans. E.M. Huggard, ed. Austin Farrer, London: Routledge & Kegan Paul, 1952.
Moltmann, Jürgen (1980) The Trinity and the Kingdom, trans. Margaret Kohl, San Francisco, CA: Harper & Row, 1981.
Plantinga, Alvin (1974) God, Freedom and Evil, New York: Harper & Row.
Rowe, William L. (1986) 'The empirical argument from evil', in Robert Audi and William Wainwright (eds) Rationality, Religious Belief and Moral Commitment, Ithaca, NY: Cornell University Press.
Tilley, Terrence W. (1991) The Evils of Theodicy, Washington, DC: Georgetown University Press.

Henry Schuurman

THEOLOGY

Theology may be defined as human logia concerning the Word (logos) of God (theos). Theology, therefore, is not simply discourse about God, or even about a Christian notion of God as such, but discourse about the God already revealed in the Logos. Its logia or discourse is tied to the Logos: 'Theology itself is a word, a human response: yet what makes it theology is not its own word or response but the Word which it hears and to which it responds' (Barth 1963: 20; original emphasis).

From this perspective, theology apparently depends – humanly speaking – on an impossibility. Humanity cannot summons God and insist that God speaks. That God speaks in any way, or at all, is a concrete fact of grace. It is astonishing that God should speak to humanity and that humanity should answer. No good theology should want to disguise this fact or take away the scandal which (humanly speaking) its whole endeavour and discipline represents. 'If anyone should *not* find himself astonished and filled with wonder when he becomes involved in one way or another with theology, he would be well advised to consider once more, from a certain remoteness and without prejudice, what is involved in this undertaking.' Barth continues '. . . I have finally and profoundly become a man made to wonder at himself by this wonder of God' (Barth 1963: 61–70; original emphasis).

There are obvious dangers in such a bold, yet traditional, conception of theology, and theological work, that should be recognized. The first danger is idolatry. If theology has sometimes claimed too little (see later), there is the opposite danger that it claims too much – at least of itself. As Barth rightly warns: 'Theology is *modest* because its entire logic can only be a human *ana-logy* to that Word; analogical thought and speech do not claim to be, to say, to contain, or to control the original word' (Barth 1963: 21). Theology always degenerates when it seeks to become more than response to the Word; it destroys itself when it sets arbitrary boundaries beyond which God cannot speak or humans cannot listen. Because of this, even the most robust theology – warning of the dangers of infidelity or wickedness – will always understand the necessary provisionality which must characterize its endeavours.

The second danger is FUNDAMENTALISM. 'Fundamentalism', wrote Tillich, 'has demonic traits' (Tillich 1951: 3). This is necessarily so because it *absolutizes* human agency, authority, or creed above that of God. Infallibility properly applies to God alone. Barth's well-known distinction between religion and revelation is relevant here. All religion – in the sense of being human-made systems which seek to set themselves above God – is sinful. In the words attributed to Martin Buber: 'Nothing is apt to mask the face of God so much as religion'. Theology when true to itself must exercise a critical function in relation to all religious systems not only, as Barth recognized, non-Christian religious systems but also – even especially, Christian ones as well. The meeting of religious needs does not of itself constitute encounter with the living God. Perhaps we should say that all religion which cannot admit that it *may* be DEMONIC *is* demonic.

The third danger is parochialism. Although many theologians make a strong and necessary connection between theology and the church, it is vital that theology distinguishes between service and servility. 'Theology, as a function of the Christian church, must serve the needs of the church' wrote Tillich (Tillich 1951: 3). But this service slides into servility if it becomes bound to the maintenance of religious or Christian positions *per se* rather than to the seeking out of God's truth. Coleridge's famous aphorism may be relevant here: 'He who begins by loving Christianity, better than truth, will proceed by loving his own sect or church better than Christianity, and end in loving himself better than all' (Coleridge 1825: 101). Far from being a defence of individual autonomy, Coleridge here defends the Christian vision of truth as social. As D.W. Hardy explains: '. . . loving truth was primary, as a co-ordination of will and reason, and this brought a correspondence of man's will and reason with those of God, the Trinity' (Hardy, in Gunton and Hardy 1989: 22–31).

From the standpont of society and ethics, there are five dimensions to theology which need to be addressed. The first is that all *theology is historical theology*. Theology takes as its starting point what has been given in history, supremely in the life and person of Christ (*see* CHRISTOLOGY). Here, as Barth would have it, is nothing less than the 'centre' of theology itself. The Word is historical, that is, it is set within a sequence and pattern which we interpret as historical or with historical meaning. In this sense we may speak of the word 'made flesh', as come among us, in time and history. God becomes enfleshed in history. Incarnation is both enfleshment and 'inhistorization'. Alongside this characterization needs to go the recognition that the incarnation is the embodiment of how God eternally is. God not only becomes fleshly, God takes fleshly existence into Godhead. To affirm the Logos as the centre of God is to affirm both spiritual and material existence at the heart of ultimate reality.

Such a conception might suggest that theology is forever destined to be looking backwards – to its primal beginning. In one sense this is true, but only in one sense. A theological system, according to Tillich, should serve two needs:

'the statement of the truth of the Christian message and the interpretation of this truth for every new generation'. There is for Tillich, as with Barth though in a different way, an essentially dialectical nature to theology. 'Theology moves back and forth between two poles, the eternal truth of its foundation and the temporal situation in which the eternal truth must be received' (Tillich 1951: 3).

There is a theological basis for these two apparently contradictory emphases – one that is rooted in the Christian doctrine of God itself. For the experience of the triune God is the starting point for understanding who God is (see TRINITY). A 'revelational' understanding of God as proposed by Barth and which is necessarily centred on what is disclosed in the life and work of Christ – can sometimes obscure the fact that the triune God consists of Father, Son, *and Holy Spirit*. In other words, God, as defined by traditional formulae, is not only a God who has revealed in the past but also continues to do so in the present through the Spirit. 'For if we place absolute or near-absolute authority on what is given in Christ to the neglect of the third person of the Trinity, namely the Spirit, we actually weaken, seriously if not terminally, the fullest understanding of God's self-presentation' (Linzey 1988: 51).

The Spirit is 'to lead us into all truth' for 'there are things we cannot bear now' (John 16: 12–15). According to this scriptural perspective, the dual task of the Spirit (see PNEUMATOLOGY) is both to bear witness to that which has been given in Christ and also at the same time to bring new life to bear. The Spirit does not of course obliterate what is given in Christ but makes it new. It follows from this that there is bound to be a certain tension in theological formulations which purport to speak of the truth that is given while remaining open to the new things of God which are to be revealed in our own time. For Hans Küng, theology has no 'elitist, privileged access to the truth'. Its work consists primarily in 'scholarly reflection upon its object' (i.e. God). Küng argues that the 'method' of theology is 'to be proved by results ... the rules of the game in theological science are not in principle different from those of the other sciences ... For serious theology is not a question of rewarding simple faith or cementing an ecclesiastical system but – always and everywhere – of seeking the whole and entire truth' (Küng 1978: 87). At face value, Küng's claim that theology is an 'open' search for truth appears incompatible with the view that truth is given in revelation. But, on deeper reflection, it seems that both emphases are not just compatible with but also required by trinitarian orthodoxy.

The historical nature of the Word made flesh and the present work of the Spirit in witnessing to that Word means that to theologize is to do so within an historical tradition. Christian theology comes out of a tradition shaped by what is given and interpreted anew. This tradition in turn is sustained by a community, the church, and the theologian is called to theologize, to articulate, refine, develop – and not least of all, criticize – the faith of that community to which he or she belongs and of which he or she is a representative. The historical responsibility of theology, and theologians in particular, is forcefully expressed by E.L. Mascall: 'The Church's tradition is a great living inheritance of thought and life, most of whose content has hitherto been undiscerned and most of whose potentialities have hitherto been unactualized. It is by bringing this great living inheritance into impact upon the world in which we live that our task towards that world will be achieved' (Mascall 1977: 62).

Secondly, all *theology is social theology*. Seen from one perspective, Jesus Christ appears as one solitary man in history. And yet early Christian reflection was driven to an estimate of Jesus in more than individual terms. This is what C.F.D. Moule describes as the 'extraordinary conception of the Lord Jesus Christ as a corporate, a more-than-individual personality' (Moule 1967: 21). Pauline theology speaks variously of how individuals experience Christ from within, of being 'in Christ', even incorporated into his Body through baptism (see e.g., 1 Corinthians 12: 6; 2 Corinthians 13: 3; Ephesians 3: 20; Philippians 2: 13; Colossians 1: 29, and 3: 16). This remarkable language testifies to the early conviction that what was happening in Christ was a 'new creation'. Indeed the triune description of God as Father, Son and Holy Spirit continues and develops this conception of sociality. God is the centre of true communion, a society of equal persons. To be drawn to God is to be brought into a new relationship not only with the divine but with all God's creatures. As St Basil put it, 'The *nature* of God is communion' (cited in Zizioulas 1985: 134; discussed in Gunton and Hardy 1989: 66; original emphasis).

It is not difficult to see how the shape of this trinitarian theology provides a strong theoretical framework for social vision. It is not accidental that many social movements, notwithstanding pietism and MILLENARIANISM, have appealed to trinitarian formulations of faith (*see* CHRISTIAN SOCIALISM). For example, Stewart Headlam who founded the Guild of St Matthew in 1877, made the incarnation his rallying point for social action: 'You are literally, as he himself said, feeding, clothing, housing Jesus Christ when you are feeding, clothing, housing any human being; bad food, ugly clothes, dirty homes, not only injure the body, but injure the soul; nay more they do great injury to God himself' (Headlam 1882: 84; discussed in Leech 1985: 247).

More important than these straightforward appeals to Christ-like charity, is the explicit rejection of the distinction between the secular and the sacred. Any trinitarian theology must view the world as embraced by God and as the theatre of God's redeeming and enlivening activity. Such a view stands in contrast to the increasing privatization of religious belief that has characterized our century (*see* SECULARIZATION). The withdrawal of theology from the realm of social life, including social debate and policy making, has reduced churches to the role of managers of religious affairs. 'Nothing can at first sight be more attractive than the attempt to restrict the claims of Christianity to those departments of life in which they might be expected to encounter least resistance' argued R.H. Tawney (Tawney, in Runcie 1988: 20–21). But what is often overlooked is that this process of withdrawal also makes trinitarian theology itself increasingly unintelligible.

C.N. Cochrane, in his study of the development of the Logos doctrine, maintained that: 'In Christ, therefore, they [early Christians] claimed to possess a principle of understanding superior to anything existing in the classical world. By this claim they were prepared to stand or fall' (Cochrane 1944: vii). Without such a doctrine, theology in our own day becomes marginalized from intellectual culture and lacks the power and confidence to speak beyond its own self-imposed religious boundaries. There is always the ironical possibility that the community of the Word itself comes to think that Word irrelevant to the world through which it came to be. The contrary view is well expressed in this line attributed to John Henry Newman: 'In truth, the Church was framed for the express purpose of interfering (or as irreligious men would say) meddling with the world'.

And yet a note of caution is necessary here: to extol the rightness of social theology based in turn on the sociality of God cannot justify uncritical social – and political – engagement. Christians need to reflect on the fact that theology has often been used to bolster up oppressive regimes and that the church has often been a willing provider of ideological support for those in power. Napoleon argued that: 'I hold . . . that apart from the precepts and doctrines of the Gospel there is no society that can flourish, nor any real civilization.' His reasoning should act as a perpetual reminder of how easily appeals to the Gospel can be socially manipulated: 'What is it that makes the poor man take it for granted that ten chimneys smoke in my palace while he dies of cold – that I have ten changes of raiment in my wardrobe while he is naked – that on my table at each meal there is enough to sustain a family for a week? It is religion which says to him that in another life I shall be his equal, indeed that he has a better chance of being happy there than I have' (Napoleon in Vidler, 1961: 19).

The truth is that all theology is not only social but also POLITICAL THEOLOGY. There is no neutral theology. Theology is, inevitably, to some degree a product of the society to which it speaks and conversely the society to which it speaks has also – negatively and positively – been shaped by theology itself. It is naïve to deny the significance of context in all theological formulations (*see* CONTEXTUAL THEOLOGY). If, as Tillich suggested, theology moves between two poles: 'the eternal truth of its foundation' and 'the temporal situation in which the eternal truth must be received' then there is a delicate balance to be struck. Theology must guard against the abandonment of insights simply because they are unfashionable, and yet it must also guard against the rejection of new truths simply because they are new. The very need for theology to minister to the here and now can become a slavish desire to follow the pattern of the age, and yet the failure to discern God's truth can position the church against the movement of the Spirit.

Thirdly, all *theology is moral theology*. It is sometimes overlooked that the Logos is the supreme revelation of God's moral will. That revelation, according to Christian theology, both completes and actualizes the revelation on Mount Sinai. To be drawn to God is not only to be drawn into communion but also into holiness. Given this starting point, there can be no articulation of theology devoid of moral content or without moral significance. The various practical injunctions found within the New Testament are quite secondary to the realization that in Christ is 'new creation': that in Christ the divine image in us is renewed. That renewal is nothing short of a moral transformation. '. . . now that you have discarded the old nature with its deeds and have put on the new nature, which is being constantly renewed in the image of its Creator and brought to know God . . . put on the garments that suit God's chosen people, his own, his beloved: compassion, kindness, humility, gentleness, patience . . . you must forgive as the Lord forgave you. To crown all, there must be love, to bind all together and complete the whole' (Colossians 3: 9–16).

Such a vision of human perfection is an inseparable part of Christian theology. It means that Christians are called to be signs of the Gospel, that is, of the moral regeneration willed by God. Moreover, it follows that the tradition contains a moral critique of itself. In this regard, we can see the failure of theology (and especially of the church) most clearly when we look back at its moral record. Sadly it now seems incontrovertible that theology has better served the oppressors than the oppressed whether these oppressors be slave-owners, antisemites, homophobes, male-chauvinists or despotic governments. In these matters it is not just that theology has reflected only too well the social norms of the day but most especially that it has seldom reflected that dynamic of moral generosity demonstrated in the earthly life of the Logos. Such historical excursions should give us some pause. If theology has in previous ages so misread the signs of God's Spirit, how shall its current record be judged by future generations? A theology of the Word must be guided by the Spirit. There is an urgent agenda for theology represented by many of the ethical issues covered in this Dictionary. Some of the new kinds of theology currently emerging – whether they be GREEN, feminist, black, gay, animal or global – are testimony to the gnawing anxiety that traditional theology has failed to hear voices that belong to its own moral response to the Word.

Unsurprisingly, theologies which are sensitive to the poor moral record of Christianity have drawn strength from ideas of EXODUS, of liberation and, latterly, of the Cross itself. From these perspectives, the Exodus is the paradigmatic experience of liberation in which the oppressed find deliverance. The God of Isaac, of Jacob, of Abraham, and of Jesus Christ is the God of liberation especially on the side of the poor, the marginalized and the oppressed. Gutierrez writes movingly (and surely rightly) of how those who live in squalor and poverty 'feel keenly' that believers 'cannot claim to be Christian without a commitment to liberation' (Gutierrez 1974: 81) (*see* LIBERATION THEOLOGY). Such appeals make sense because the Cross of Christ can properly be interpreted as God's own self-identification with the vulnerable, the unprotected and the defenceless. Moreover, the Cross highlights the horror of innocent suffering (*see* CRUELTY). As Bonhoeffer once remarked: 'Only a suffering God can help'. To affirm the Cross – from this perspective, is to affirm a way of redemptive suffering, a final way out of human misery, because God is a co-participant in all our suffering.

Theology has yet to face the full force of the moral critique raised by the Gospel against itself. If full weight is given to the experience of Exodus and the Cross, it must be postulated that any theology which desensitizes us to suffering or which serves the forces of oppression ceases to be Christian theology. There is much still to be done in the direction of refocusing theology as a means of humanization and liberation (*see* HOMOPHOBIA, PATRIARCHY, SEXISM and SPECIESISM). Equally urgent perhaps is the need for a theologically adequate doctrine of GRACE that recognizes the role of the Spirit in empowering social life as well as individual moral discernment.

Fourthly, all *theology is ecological theology* (*see* ECOLOGICAL THEOLOGY). 'Ecology' means the study (logos) of the world as our 'oikos' (home). Although now a largely secularized discourse, ecology picks up a clear Christologically based, 'this-worldly', theme in scripture and tradition. The Logos made flesh is the one and the same Logos that, according to St Athanasius, 'orders and contains the universe' illuminating 'all things visible and 'invisible, containing and enclosing them in himself' (Athanasius 1971: 113–15). Moreover, the incarnation has a cosmic purpose: 'When the Word visited the holy Virgin Mary, the Spirit came to her with him, and the Word in the Spirit moulded the body and conformed it to himself desiring to join and present *all* creation to the Father, through himself, and in it to reconcile *all* things, having made peace, whether things in heaven or things upon the earth' (Athanasius, in Torrance 1969: 14; my emphases). This vision of the Logos as summing up and containing all things derives of course from the great cosmic verses in Ephesians and Colossians. The universal, cosmic significance of Christ's work is a theme which runs through the writings of many of the Church's earliest thinkers like St Basil the Great, St Gregory Nazianzen, St Maximus the Confessor, St Cyril of Jerusalem and St Gregory of Nyssa. 'For when he considers the universe, can anyone be so simple-minded as not to believe that the Divine is present in everything, pervading, embracing and penetrating it?' asks St Gregory of Nyssa. 'For all things depend upon Him who is, and nothing can exist which does not have its being in Him who is' (Gregory of Nyssa 1964: 124). From this perspective, the Logos is both the origin and destiny of all that is.

Theology needs to sensitize itself to its own vision of the Logos as the sustaining principle of earthly ecology. Contemporary debates about ANIMAL RIGHTS, speciesism and green issues generally focus on the inadequacy of humanocentric perspectives as a basis for discerning the worth and value of non-human beings. We reach here perhaps a critical point in theology's own development. Can theology be true to its own vision of the Cosmic Christ, uniting and sustaining all life, or will it continue to maintain a humanocentric morality that unfairly eclipses God's providential concern into a presumed divine disregard for all creatures save the human ones? Feuerbach's critique is directly relevant here: If theology is more than the selfish projection of the interests of the human species, then humanity must respect the God-given worth of other living creatures. Indeed, according to scriptural accounts there is nothing less than a divine commission to care for the earth and its non-human inhabitants (Genesis 2: 5, 15). Our special vocation is to live on this earth not as the master species but as the 'servant species' (Linzey 1994: 45).

Fifthly, all *theology is eschatological theology* (*see* ESCHATOLOGY). There appears to be a contradiction between the 'this-worldly' and the 'other-worldly' emphases within the Christian tradition. And there is no getting away from it, the same tradition which contains a vision of a world sustaining and embracing Logos has also generated movements, such as ASCETICISM, CELIBACY and monasticism, which have negated the life of the flesh and limited social and political engagement. If such movements have any justification at all (and they may not), they can be justified only on the basis that they have prepared individuals for another world in which the demands of God's JUSTICE will be met in full. For Christian theology as a whole is inescapably eschatological in orientation: human beings, and indeed the whole creation, are made for an end, namely the freedom of the Sabbath and there to enjoy with their Creator the blessings of God for all eternity (Genesis 2: 1–2; Romans 8: 18–24).

Perhaps the enemy of theology has never been human fallibility or even social oppression but rather a practical and philosophical nihilism which quenches hope and denies our CITIZENSHIP of two worlds (*see also* CITY). Almost the entire moral and social agenda of theology fails to make sense unless there is ultimate judgement and redemption. All nihilistic movements – of which DECONSTRUCTION is the latest but surely not the last – have this in common: a denial of the ultimate possibility of justice. According to deconstructionist theory, words are *only* words; they do not point beyond themselves, and in this they only mirror the sad state of humankind for ever locked into self-enclosed positions from which there is no escape. There is no doubting it: nihilism is a formidable enemy, not only of theology, but all social and ethical theory and practice. It *could* be true, but if true it is as true for nihilistic theory as for all else: it must follow that it is as meaningless to adopt nihilism as it is to reject it.

John Robinson, following Paul Tillich, once offered the now well-known definition of the subject matter of theology as 'that which concerns us ultimately'. From this perspective: 'A statement is "theological" not because it relates to a particular being called "God", but because it asks *ultimate* questions about the meaning of existence: it asks what at the level of *theos*, at the level of its deepest mystery, is the reality and significance of our life' (Robinson 1963: 49; original emphases). In retrospect such a definition will strike us as optimistic, for it presumes precisely what *cannot* be assumed in nihilistic thinking, namely that there *are* 'ultimate concerns' which can bind and reinforce our humanity.

Against NIHILISM stands the Gospel, and the faltering attempts of theology to understand it and, even occasionally, to practise it. Christian theology is offered as a way of making moral sense of the world which (precisely because it is creation and not Creator) cannot make sense of itself. Western society as we know it has been fashioned through a variety of exchanges, some fruitful, some less so, with a vision of human living which owes much to a specifically theological reckoning of ultimate ends and goals. Whether a society less indebted, if at all, to its theological and moral heritage can survive – or survive as well – has yet to be seen. In this sense the line attributed to William Temple equally serves for the future of western society: 'Theology is still in its infancy'.

Athanasius, St (1971) *Contra Gentes and De Incarnatione*, ed. and trans. by Robert W. Thompson, Oxford: Clarendon.

Barth, Karl (1936) *Church Dogmatics*, 1/1, *The Doctrine of the Word of God*, trans. by G.T. Thompson, Edinburgh: T. & T. Clark.

——(1963) *Evangelical Theology*, trans. by Grover Foley, London: Weidenfeld and Nicolson.

Boff, Leonardo (1978) *Jesus Christ Liberator: A Critical Christology for Our Time*, New York: Orbis Books.

Bracken, Joseph A. (1991) *Society and Spirit: A Trinitarian Cosmology*, foreword by John B. Cobb Jr, New York: Susquehanna University Press/Associated University Presses.

Cochrane, Charles Norris (1944) *Christianity and Classical Culture: A Study of Thought and Action from Augustus to Augustine*, London and New York: Oxford University Press.

Coleridge, S.T. (1825) *Aids to Reflection in the Formation of A Manly Character*, London: Taylor & Hessey.

Danielou, Jean (1967) *Prayer as a Political Problem*, trans. by J.R. Kirwan, London: Burns and Oates.

Eliot, T.S. (1939) *The Idea of a Christian Society*, London: Faber and Faber.

Gunton, Colin E. (1993) *The One, The Three and the Many: God, Creation, and the Culture of Modernity*, Cambridge: Cambridge University Press.

Gregory of Nyssa, St (1964) 'Address on Religious Instruction' in E.R. Hardy and C.C. Richardson (eds) *Christology of the Later Fathers*, vol. III, London: SCM Press.

Gutierrez, Gustavo, *A Theology of Liberation: History, Politics and Salvation*, trans. by Caridad Inda and John Eagleson, London: SCM Press.

Headlam, Stewart D. (1882) *The Service of Humanity and Other Sermons*, London.

Hardy, Daniel W. (1989) 'Created and Redeemed Sociality' in Colin E. Gunton and Daniel W. Hardy (eds), *On Being the Church: Essays on the Christian Community*, Edinburgh: T. & T. Clark, pp. 21–47.

Hopkins, Richard (1994) 'Salvation Through Trinitarian Politics', *The Oxford International Review*, Winter Issue, pp. 53–57.

Irenaeus of Lyons (n.d.) 'Against Heresies' in *The Writings of Irenaeus*, trans. by A. Roberts and W.H. Rambaut, Ante-Nicene Christian Library, 2 vols, Edinburgh: T. & T. Clark.

John of the Cross, St (1974) *The Complete Works*, ed. and trans. by E. Allison Peers, Wheathampstead, Hertfordshire: Anthony Clarke.

Küng, Hans (1978) *On Being a Christian*, trans. by Edward Quinn, London: Collins.

LaCugna, Catherine (1991) *God For Us: The Trinity and Christian Life*, San Francisco, CA: HarperCollins.

Leech, Kenneth (1985) *True God: An Exploration in Spiritual Theology*, London: Sheldon Press.

Linzey, Andrew (1989) 'On Theology' in Paul Barry

Clarke and Andrew Linzey (eds) *Theology, the University and the Modern World*, London: Lester Crook Academic Press, pp. 29–66.

——(1994) *Animal Theology*, London: SCM Press; Chicago: University of Illinois Press.

Lossky, Vladimir (1957) *The Mystical Theology of the Eastern Church*, trans. by the Fellowship of St Alban and St Sergius, Cambridge: James Clarke.

Lyons, J.A. (1982) *The Cosmic Christ in Origen and Teilhard de Chardin: A Comparative Study*, Oxford Theological Monographs, Oxford: Oxford University Press.

Mascall, E.L., *Theology and the Gospel of Christ: An Essay in Reorientation*, London: SPCK.

Milbank, John (1990) *Theology and Social Theory: Beyond Secular Realism*, Oxford: Blackwell.

Moltmann, Jürgen (1981) *The Trinity and the Kingdom of God*, London: SCM Press.

Moule, C.F.D. (1967) *The Phenomenon of the New Testament: An Inquiry into the Implications of Certain Features of the New Testament*, Studies in Biblical Theology, Second Series, London: SCM Press.

Norris, Richard A. (1966) *God and World in Early Christian Theology: A Study in Justin Martyr, Irenaeus, Tertullian and Origen*, Studies in Patristic Thought, London: A. and C. Black.

Owen, H.P. (1969) *The Christian Knowledge of God*, London: The Athlone Press.

Reckitt, Maurice B. (ed.) (1945) *Prospect for Christendom: Essays in Catholic Social Reconstruction*, London: Faber and Faber.

Robinson, J.A.T. (1963) *Honest to God*, London: SCM Press.

Runcie, Robert A.K. (1988) 'Theology, the University and the Modern World' in Paul Barry Clarke and Andrew Linzey (eds) *Theology, the University and the Modern World*, London: Lester Crook Academic Press, pp. 13–28.

Scott, Peter (1994) *Theology, Ideology and Liberation: Towards a Liberative Theology*, Cambridge: Cambridge University Press.

Sobrino, Jon (1981) *The True Church and the Poor*, New York: Orbis Books.

Tillich, Paul (1951) *Systematic Theology*, Parts I and II, London: SCM Press.

Torrance, T.F. (1969) *Theology in Reconstruction*, London: SCM Press.

——(1981) *Divine and Contingent Order*, Oxford: Oxford University Press.

Vidler, Alec R. (1961) *The Church in An Age of Revolution: 1789 to the Present Day*, Harmondsworth: Pelican Books.

——(1964) *A Century of Social Catholicism 1820–1920*, London: SPCK.

Ward, Keith (1994) *Religion and Revelation*, Oxford: Oxford University Press.

Wilder, A.N. (1956) 'Kerygma, Eschatology and Social Ethics' in W.D. Davies and D. Daube (eds) *The Background of the New Testament and its Eschatology*, Cambridge: Cambridge University Press, pp. 509–36.

Zizioulas, John D. (1985) *Being As Communion: Studies in Personhood and the Church*, London: Darton, Longman and Todd.

Andrew Linzey

TOLERATION

Toleration is the virtue of a preparedness to accept for the sake of a higher good – especially the well-being of human SOCIETY – behaviour and convictions that are believed to be mistaken. It implies disapproval of what is tolerated, and is distinguished from the personal quality of tolerance by virtue of the fact that it refers to the public policy whereby religions, groups or opinions which are believed to be contrary to official policy or doctrine are allowed existence. It is superficially paradoxical in theory, apparently involving acquiescence in error and immorality, but can be argued to be necessary for higher reasons such as human freedom to dissent and the value to society of the diversity of opinions. It tends also to be selectively applied in practice because it involves fine judgements about what measure of diversity a society can tolerate without dissolution. The Roman Empire, for example, was from one point of view religiously tolerant, in that it allowed a pluralism of religious practice, but in another repressive, persecuting religions which did not belong on its list of officially approved religions.

The concept of toleration, like many aspects of Western culture, has a double origin. One dimension comes from Athens and is a fruit of her democratic institutions. The funeral speech placed by Thucydides on the lips of the Athenian politician Pericles claims tolerance to be among the virtues of their democratic society. The somewhat idealized picture is complemented by the portrayal of the fallibility and finitude of the human condition by the great dramatists of Athens, both tragic and comic, where the gods indicate firmly the limits human capacity – a major consideration for later defences of toleration. It was called into question, however, by the later political philosophy of Plato which advocated a more monolithic society, arguing that social order can be secured against dissolution only by the rule of those who know, i.e. philosophers. The social order sketched in *The Republic* is intolerant of all deviation from official norms.

The second historical root of toleration is to be found in the Christian gospel. Historic Christianity combines a form of intellectual exclusiveness – a strong commitment to the truth of its fundamental confession – with an equally strong commitment to ecclesiastical and political toleration which derives from two doctrines. The first, which is stressed by theologians of the first three centuries, is that the Christian gospel must be accepted freely and that any form of coercion – as distinct from argument and the employment of churchly sanctions like excommunication – is foreign to it. The second is the teaching of human fallibility, finitude and sinfulness. The history of the church shows that these two doctrines have often been more honoured in the breach than in the application, but it can be argued that politicized forms of Christianity of the kind that long reigned in Europe represent an aberration. The social situation of Christianity after the conversion of the Emperor Constantine discouraged the development of the insight that Christianity must be accepted freely. The Christian Church, in different ways in East and West, became the guarantor of a society with a rather monolithic structure, and consequently involved in the repression of dissent. But both forms of argument for religious toleration have recurred, especially since the Reformation.

The history of Christianity's place in Western society has meant that until very recent times discussions of toleration centred on religion. The political after-effects of the Reformation, especially in England, with its rival forms of Christian polity, fostered the development of pleas for toleration, especially by Dissenters. Early among them was *A Short Declaration of the Mistery of Iniquity* (1612) by Thomas Helwys, a Baptist, who argued that earthly rulers had no AUTHORITY in matters of religion. Later that century the Puritan John Owen, Cromwell's chaplain, argued a somewhat more subtle case which did not deny the duties of rulers in matters of religion but firmly repudiated any form of violent or civil sanction.

Owen's case depends in part on his Congregationalist conception of Christianity which, like Tertullian's in the second century, makes strong appeal to the voluntary nature of allegiance to the church, but also on a Biblical and theological appeal to the character of Christianity's God.

The chief question arising in this context concerned whether dissent from the established church should be tolerated, and it produced what has become the classic discussion, John Locke's *A Letter Concerning Toleration*, written from exile in tolerant Holland in the years leading up to the Revolution of 1688. John Locke was a member of Christ Church, Oxford, whose head Owen had been. He remains in the tradition of Owen – for example, he repeats Owen's definition of the church as a voluntary society – even though he has become the father of what in more recent times is an increasingly secular case for toleration. Locke argues from Scripture that toleration is the chief character of the true church, and proceeds to posit, after Helwys, a strong dualism of church and commonwealth. Because the one is concerned with inward and otherworldly matters, the other with civil and this-worldly concerns, there is to be no confusion of the authority of CLERGY and magistrates, who must also strictly limit their activities to their own realm.

Alongside the theological arguments is to be found a more characteristically modern appeal to the wide diversities of opinion on matters of religion, and the consequent limitation in claims to knowledge that religious authorities may make. Locke undermines the two bases of religious intolerance in Christendom until his time: the church's identification with a particular social order and state, on the one hand, and, on the other, the authoritarian and rationalist form its claims to knowledge had tended to take. It is to be noted, however, that there are limits to the toleration Locke will recommend: excluded are opinions adjudged to be contrary to the preservation of civil society, religions whose members are in effect in the service of a foreign prince, and atheists. (It is around the first of those that modern discussions of tolerance are likely to centre: for example, on the effect on social order of PORNOGRAPHY or racialist literature.)

The Toleration Act of 1689 was the outcome of the 'Glorious Revolution' of 1688 and 'gave orthodox Dissenters statutory freedom to worship in their own way, but it did not give them civil equality' (Watts 1978: 260). The latter, and the removal of disabilities for Roman Catholics and unbelievers, had to await the nineteenth and twentieth centuries. In other countries, the after-effects of the Reformation, and in particular the religious wars that its political arrangements fostered, led to a revulsion against religion that encouraged the view that Christianity was essentially an enemy of toleration. In France, doctrines of toleration shaped by Enlightenment rationalism helped to foment the Revolution. In Britain in the nineteenth century J.S. Mill saw religious bigotry as a chief cause of intolerance, and the view continues to be widespread.

In the late twentieth century it is less easy than it once was to see in religion the essential cause of intolerance. Consciously anti-religious regimes have ruthlessly repressed dissent, and it is more reasonable to suggest that some religions and theologies aid the development of toleration while others work in the opposite direction. More important than scoring historical points is an enquiry into the underlying intellectual questions. At the heart of the matter are at least the following.

First are fundamental beliefs about the nature of God and reality. It has been argued that a one-sided stress on the divinity of Christ at the expense of his humanity transforms the suffering Christ into an authoritarian ruler, and that this was one of the theological developments that accompanied the development of institutional Christian intolerance from around the fourth century. The point could also be made that a loss of the centrality of the Jewish humanity of Jesus has been one of the contributory causes of the still existing scandal of ANTI-SEMITISM. With respect to the doctrine of God, it has similarly been argued that a tendency to conceive God in monist rather than Trinitarian or relational categories encourages monist and intolerant politics or social order. (David Hume, in his *Natural History of Religion*, had claimed that polytheist religions were superior to monotheist in respect of toleration.) The German theologian Erik Peterson (1935) argued during the time of Nazi Germany that Trinitarian forms of theology are more likely to encourage the development of open forms of social order than monist ones, a point that has been developed recently by Jürgen Moltmann (1981).

The second important predisposing factor to toleration is the estimate that is made of human rational and moral powers. Sir Karl Popper, identifying Plato, Hegel and Marx as enemies of what he called the open society, saw the root of much intolerance in overestimation of human rational powers, thus echoing an argument of Voltaire two centuries earlier. Just as it might appear that religiously grounded intolerance derives from an overconfidence in the possession of the final truth by churchly authorities, so the characteristic repressiveness of some modern political ideologies derives from overconfidence in the powers of a political group to direct history and plan social order. Similarly, Paul Tillich located the root of intolerance in idolatry, and held that 'the symbol of the Cross stands against the self-elevation of a concrete religion to ultimacy, including Christianity' (1958: 122).

In recent times, discussions of toleration have moved from the chiefly religious sphere to the general question of the rights of dissenting minorities in what is often claimed to be the distinctively pluralistic character of modern CULTURE. A question that occurs in many discussions, especially Mill's, concerns the distinction between the toleration of opinions and the toleration of actions. The former are generally held to require less legal restriction than the latter, as impinging less directly on the freedom of others. One of the apparently paradoxical features of the logic of toleration is the fact that doctrines of relativism, which are apparently intellectually tolerant in giving equal epistemic rights to all opinions, have historically, according to Popper, generated social intolerance. The classical defences of toleration have depended on the denial of human infallibility but not of the existence of objective TRUTH. The argument that truth is more likely to emerge through the free discussion of both truth and error is the heart of J.S. Mill's case in *On Liberty*, and it depends upon an assumption that there is truth to be discovered.

Accordingly, the crucial question today concerns the justification of toleration and its defence especially in the face of the increasing fragmentation of modern thought and society. The controversy over Rushdie's *Satanic Verses* suggests that modern liberal thought, lacking the confidence of Locke and Mill in the unity of truth, lacks also the conceptual equipment to deal with some of the adversarial trends in modern culture. The resurgence of religious ideologies which deny Locke's separation of church and commonwealth, and therefore one important historic basis of toleration, is also likely to prove problematic. On the other hand, Lord Scarman has argued that it may be necessary to impose toleration by law, e.g. of minority religious groups (*see also* BLASPHEMY).

Thought is also required about the character and basis of a society that is plural without the fragmented pluralism that invites authoritarian unification. Related to this is the question of whether a society can flourish if it has no theology at all, in the sense of a widely shared conviction of a unitary basis for human community, however diversified and plural we may wish that to be. If the 'higher reasons' for toleration cannot be given some clear expression, what is to counter outbreaks of the moral, political or religious authoritarianism – the Platonic reaction to real or imagined social decay – that have fed the fires of intolerance in most periods of human history? It has yet to be shown that a social order which shares no broad religious or philosophical basis can maintain the delicate balance between order and diversity which is required for toleration to exist.

Hume, David (1757) *The Natural History of Religion*.

Locke, John (1688) *A Letter Concerning Toleration* 1st edn.

Mendus, Susan and Edwards, David (eds) (1987) *On Toleration*, Oxford: Clarendon. See especially the contributions by Mendus and Popper.

Mill, J.S. (1974) *On Liberty*, Harmondsworth: Penguin (1st edn 1859).

Moltmann, Jürgen (1981) *The Trinity and the Kingdom of God*, trans. M. Kohl, London: SCM.

Owen, John (1862) 'On toleration', *Works*, vol. VIII, Edinburgh: T. & T. Clark, pp. 163–206.

Peterson, Erik (1935) *Der Monotheismus als politisches Problem. Ein Beitrag für Geschichte der politischen Theologie im Imperium Romanum*, Leipzig: J. Hegner.

Tillich, Paul (1958) *Dynamics of Faith*, London: Harper.

Voltaire, F.M. (1763) *Traité sur la Tolerance*.

Watts, M. (1978) *The Dissenters*, Oxford: Oxford University Press.

Colin Gunton

TORTURE

Torture means any act by which severe pain or SUFFERING, whether physical or mental, is intentionally inflicted on a person, usually for such a purpose as the obtaining of information or a confession. Other purposes are listed under the Convention against Torture and Other Cruel, Inhuman or Degrading Treatment or Punishment. The legal definition also includes such treatment imposed for any reason when it is based on discrimination. In international LAW, ill-treatment can only constitute torture when it is inflicted by or at the instigation of or with the consent or acquiescence of a public official or other person acting in an official capacity. This is a product of the system of enforcement, which generally only operates against states. An exception is personal liability for the commission of WAR CRIMES; where the torture constitutes a war crime, the individual can be held responsible. The legal definition expressly excludes pain or suffering arising only from, inherent in or incidental to lawful sanctions.

Key elements in the definition include the severity of the suffering, the notion that it is imposed on a person by someone having control over him or her and that it is a means to an end and cannot be an end in itself. Whether one analyses the situation from the point of view of both the perpetrator and the victim or merely the victim may affect the relevance of the question of the underlying purpose. It may be necessary to distinguish between purpose and motive. It is not clear whether ill-treatment can constitute torture if the victim consents to it.

In international law, the prohibition of torture is absolute, in contrast to other HUMAN RIGHTS norms, including fundamental ones. In certain, very limited, circumstances, it is recognized that state officials may even be justified in killing a person. In no circumstances is torture legally justifiable.

The theological issues include whether torture is always immoral. If so, is that on account of the perpetrator, the victim or both? If not, in what circumstances is it not immoral? In particular, does the 'excuse' only legitimate such action on the part of an AUTHORITY and, if so, does it matter which and whether it is accountable? If not, is it sufficient to make out the legitimating ground or must some further requirement be satisfied?

Torture has been practised from the earliest times to the present day. The Hebrew Bible is replete with references to treatment which nowadays would constitute torture. Some of the punishments envisaged in the Qur'an, such as the stoning in public of adulterous wives and the amputation of the hands of thieves, might be regarded as torture. Most adherents of one faith have been tortured by the adherents of another faith at some time or other (see HOLO-CAUST). This is also true within a particular faith (e.g. Catholics and Protestants). When international law developed, it prohibited the ill-treatment of the victims of WAR (see WAR CRIMES) and of foreigners, under the law of state responsibility. It was not until the Universal Declaration of Human Rights that international law prohibited the torture of a state's own citizens. All major human rights treaties on civil and political rights prohibit torture in all circumstances. That rule cannot be derogated from, even in a national emergency or war. Torture also forms the subject of two specific treaties. The European Convention for the Prevention of Torture is designed to prevent situations arising in which there is a particular risk of ill-treatment.

A deontological approach would condemn torture in absolute terms. The victim is made in the image of God, as is the perpetrator. The ill-treatment seems as objectionable in either case. Dualism, on the other hand, may be particularly vulnerable to the practice of torture. Where the body and SOUL are seen as distinct, harm to the body is either irrelevant or a positive good if it is for the good of the soul. The inquisition is an example of the possible, if not inevitable, result of such an approach.

The consequentialist argues that the end justifies the means. This leads him to grapple with the doctrine of double effect. The torture may be a regrettable (contrast the dualist position) product of a legitimate end. If torture can only be legitimated as the lesser of two evils, it follows that the infliction of torture as an end in itself is immoral.

The kind of purpose envisaged by the consequentialist must then be positively good, rather than merely neutral, in order to justify the harm caused by the ill-treatment. The usual reasons given for the infliction of torture appear to be materially different from one another. The first type of alleged excuse is the extraction of a confession regarding an act of which the victim or a third person is suspected of being guilty. The act in question is past. The torture cannot be justified as preventing the harm brought about by the act. It could only be justified as deterring the commission of similar acts by others or as necessary for the punishment of crime. As a justification, that is different in kind from the attempted prevention of a specific greater harm. The obvious example is where a person is known or believed to have information regarding an imminent criminal action which will result in the death of many people. If this is seen as, in principle, capable of justifying torture, it might be thought to justify the torture of a person alleged to be planning the assassination of a ruthless dictator who routinely orders mass murder. In other words, assessing the balance of the greater good may itself be far from straightforward. The justifications advanced for torture are particular to each case. The routine use of torture as a normal method of interrogation would seem unjustifiable as an administrative practice and that would call into question the legitimacy of individual acts of torture perpetrated within such a regime. A further difficulty in the consequentialist approach is that, even if the victim and the perpetrator were applying the same criteria, they might well reach different conclusions!

Those reluctant to accept Utopian absolutism, on account of humankind's SIN making the absolute ends unattainable, prefer a system of checks and balances. This may lead to a certain paradox. If all absolute claims are suspect, is this equally applicable to invariable means and to absolute ends? In that case, in the name of humankind's inherent sinfulness, there could be no absolute prohibition of torture as a means. That is contingent upon relativism being applicable not only to positive actions but also to prohibitions. This problem does not arise for those who consider that only ends and not means are absolute.

A Christian realist might regard the saving of innocent lives as the universal good to which may be harnessed apparently sinful acts, such as torture, produced by people's self-interest. The converse presents a difficulty. Can knowingly violating a prohibition of torture ever represent moral self-giving? That is to make sin a virtue, where it is done for proper ends but it assumes that such ends can be recognized. If the virtue lies in the self-giving, it is not clear that the end matters. In that case, it would be right to torture, even if it were in the service of immoral group selfishness, on condition that the torture represented self-giving.

There is a need to distinguish the perspective of the perpetrator and the victim. If it is better to suffer oneself in order to spare others, then this would require that the victim not give information about others, even at the price of being tortured. Such a refusal to give information could, in some circumstances, be an allegedly legitimating factor for the perpetrator. The torturer's imperative to torture meets the wall of the victim's obligation not to disclose the information. A focus on the victim also raises the problem of a sought-after martyrdom, whether on religious or ideological grounds. Starvation could constitute torture. A hunger-strike might lead to the same result but can a person inflict torture on himself or herself? Can an individual consent to the infliction of torture by another?

From reliable reports from organizations such as Amnesty International, it appears that a significant number of states routinely resort to torture. It is particularly prevalent in states experiencing armed rebellion in one form or another. International law is ill-equipped to address the question of the responsibility of insurgent movements and other armed groups for the torture which they perpetrate. This raises the issue of the types of authority, if any, which may legitimate the use of torture and the relationship between the lawfulness of the cause and the lawfulness of the means.

This entry has been written by a lawyer. It is perhaps not surprising that the author takes the view that torture is always morally unacceptable, even though that is not necessarily the case with killings. It is possible to kill persons without thereby denying their being made in the image of God or their humanity. It is not possible to torture persons without seeking to destroy their individual integrity and identity or using means calculated to produce that result. That is to deny both that the victim is a unique human being and also that he or she is made in the image of God. To that extent, it is an assault on God. In addition to the argument of principle, it should be noted that, at a practical level, it cannot be guaranteed that any information extracted will be accurate. That is particularly likely to be the case where the victim is innocent. The victim must invent the information which the torture is designed to extract. For the author, it is the obligation of the perpetrator not to assault God, rather than the right of the victim not to be tortured, which makes torture, but not necessarily killings, morally unacceptable in all circumstances.

For provisions dealing with torture in human rights treaties, see the following:
Convention against Torture and Other Cruel, Inhuman or Degrading Treatment or Punishment.
European Convention for the Prevention of Torture.
Ireland v. *United Kingdom*, Eur Ct HRs, Series A, No. 25.
Sieghart, P. (1983) *The International Law of Human Rights*, Oxford: Clarendon, Section 14.3.
The Greek Case, *Yearbook of the European Convention on Human Rights*, 1969, vol. 12 *bis*.

Amnesty International (1984) *Torture in the Eighties*, London: Amnesty International.
Barth, K. (1981) *Ethics*, Edinburgh, T. & T. Clark.
Bonhoeffer, D. (1955) *Ethics*, London: SCM.
Niebuhr, R. (1954) *Christian Realism and Political Problems*, London: Faber.

Françoise J. Hampson

TOTALITARIANISM

According to Leonard Shapiro 'totalitarianism' was the invention of Italian Fascism. The term was originally coined by Giovanni Gentile, the official philosopher of Fascist theory, who first described Fascism as 'a total conception of life' in March 1925 (Shapiro 1972: 13). Thereafter it became one of Mussolini's favourite terms for describing the system he wanted to create, which he generally called *lo stato totalitario*, the 'totalitarian State' (ibid.).

Of the three systems which are generally considered to have approximated totalitarianism most closely, namely Mussolini's Italy, Hitler's Germany and Stalin's USSR, only the first used the term as a positive self-description – ironically, since Mussolini's attempts to create such a state were the least successful of the three. In Germany, the term *total* or *totalitar* never became popular. There were some attempts to develop a National Socialist conception of the 'totalitarian state' at the beginning of the 1930s. Hitler, however, never liked the term, largely Shapiro surmises because of its Italian origins, preferring the word *autoritar* instead (ibid.: 13–14). Consequently, it fell into disuse. In the USSR, by contrast, 'totalitarianism' never acquired any positive connotations. It was first used in 1940 but was then, and subsequently, applied exclusively to Fascist regimes. Soviet officials always rejected the term as a description of the USSR, contending that it was simply an instrument of Cold War propaganda (ibid.: 14).

Beyond the boundaries of these three regimes, however, the term 'totalitarianism' swiftly acquired considerable notoriety from 1925. On the one hand, it rapidly became a pejorative term for dictatorial regimes both during the inter-war years amongst liberal opponents of Fascism and, more particularly, after the Second World War when its use became widespread in political and journalistic circles. Inevitably its application became increasingly indiscriminate. As Shapiro notes, it was applied not just to the Stalinist and Fascist regimes but was also used to describe ' "movements", "parties", "leaders", "processes", "ideals" ', as well as systems as diverse as Tsarist Russia and ancient Sparta (ibid.: 15). On the other hand, political scientists also sought to systematize the concept more rigorously as a model of a particular form of regime. One of the first attempts was G.H.

Sabine's application of the term to one-party states, including the USSR, which appeared in the 1934 edition of the *Encyclopaedia of the Social Sciences* (ibid.: 14). Much the most influential, however, was the work of Carl J. Friedrich who, in 1954 and again in 1956 (jointly with Z. Brzezinski), endeavoured to isolate the key characteristics of 'totalitarianism' as a new and unique form of political rule. In what became known as the 'six-point syndrome', Friedrich isolated the following factors as being common to all modern totalitarian regimes: an official, millenarian IDEOLOGY to which everyone had to conform; a single mass party led by one man; a technically conditioned near-monopoly of the means of coercion; a similarly conditioned near-monopoly over all means of mass communication; a system of terroristic police control; and central control and direction of the entire economy (see Shapiro 1972: 18). This model was to remain dominant despite all the criticisms that were subsequently levelled against it.

Such attempts to systematize the concept, as well as the increasing lack of discrimination in its popular use, inevitably resulted in a great deal of contention concerning both its substance and its application, with Friedrich's 'syndrome' coming in for particular criticism. Almost from the outset there was argument as to whether totalitarianism could rightly be said to apply to both Fascist and Communist regimes, given the differences between their political and economic systems. There was considerable debate as to whether totalitarian systems were as unique as they were claimed to be. Above all, the disappearance of Nazi Germany and Fascist Italy in 1945, followed by the death of Stalin in 1953 and subsequent attempts to reform the Soviet system, raised the question of whether the concept had any relevance at all in the postwar world – a question that is even more germane now that the USSR itself has disappeared.

None of these arguments has been fully resolved but neither has the idea of 'totalitarianism' entirely lost its appeal. Undoubtedly, this owes something to the Cold War, since it provided Western politicians with a convenient way of condemning COMMUNISM whenever it suited them. It also, no doubt, owes something to a tacit consensus that the regimes of Stalin and Hitler at least had, indeed, produced unique forms of rule. Above all, though, it could be argued that the idea of totalitarianism has retained an appeal because it has served to express a general apprehension that there are systems of thought and organization which, if not exactly 'totalitarian' in Friedrich's sense, nevertheless contain a 'totalitarian impulse' in terms of wanting to impose a 'total conception of life' on their adherents and/or on humanity at large. As Shapiro notes, for example, there is an affinity between the modern concept of totalitarianism and Utopian thinking which has always been centrally preoccupied with creating the conditions for total order and complete social harmony at whatever cost to the individual (1972: 85 ff.): both Stalinist and Nazi ideology provide modern examples in this respect. Another, more immediately relevant, example is provided by religion. The great religions, CATHOLICISM in particular, have not only sought to assert the absolute truth of their theological interpretations of both the Divinity and the secular world, through the medium of papal infallibility and at an incalculable cost in individual lives over the centuries; they have also sought to impose rules for everyday living that have often extended well beyond the religious and moral spheres narrowly defined. Indeed, in terms of the POWER and control it has exercised, in POLITICS and social matters especially, and the number of adherents from whom it has exacted unquestioning obedience to the pronouncements of one 'infallible' leader, the Catholic Church cannot be bested.

The example, and the threat, of organized religion was not lost on the Soviet Communist Party (CPSU) nor on the German National Socialist Party (NSDAP).

From the ideological point of view both parties endeavoured to exploit the popular effect of religious language, forms and symbols in order to exact a similarly unquestioning faith in their goals, and total obedience to their Supreme Leaders, not only on the part of party members but from the population as a whole. In the case of the NSDAP there was a deliberate, and entirely cynical, attempt to create a 'positive Christianity' based on an 'ersatz theology', in Conway's words, that built on Nazi theories of race; manipulated Christian (particularly Catholic) concepts of the CREATION, the FALL, redemption, salvation and the Day of Judgement (Conway 1968: 145); and blended these with neo-pagan, theistic symbols that had their origins in German culture. The CPSU, by contrast, was less deliberately exploitative of religious symbolism, partly because its militantly explicit ATHEISM dictated a much more confrontational approach to religion in all its forms. Nevertheless, religious imagery was used, especially during the 1930s, to deify Stalin as the 'new God' and was quite cynically exploited during the Second World War in order to rally the population against the Nazi invaders.

On the negative side, however, organized religion was also seen as representing an immediate threat to the power and control of the two regimes. At the practical level, religion provided both an alternative source of individual loyalty and the basis for organized institutional opposition, neither of which could be tolerated by parties that sought to hegemonize and transform SOCIETY as a whole. As a result, the religious establishments in both cases were subjected to sustained attack in order to eliminate them as sources of opposition and harness them to the goals and propagandistic activities of the regime. In the Soviet case, the attack on religion was devastating, more so than its German counterpart. It amounted, in effect, to an attempt to bring about the wholesale physical destruction of religion in all its forms; and when this failed brought the religious establishments of Russian Orthodoxy and Islam under the direct control of the party-state through a 'concordat' that granted them an official existence as long as they abided by official policy in all matters and gave up any pretensions to AUTONOMY. Smaller non-conformist denominations were driven underground as were the religious beliefs of all but the most ardent and determined. The situation in Germany, by contrast, was more complex but the end result was not dissimilar. Hitler effectively bound both the Catholic and Protestant churches to the Third Reich by offering the first a 'Reich concordat' that guaranteed its existence in return for obedience, while attempting in the case of the second to create a unified Reich church for all German Protestants that would be fused with the Reich state. The consequence for German Catholicism was complicity with the crimes of the Nazi regime that the Church has yet to confront adequately. The consequence for German Protestantism was chaotic disintegration at the time which nevertheless allowed a few courageous pastors to stand out as symbols of Christian resistance against the Nazis (Scholder 1987: II, 90).

The church reaction in both cases, inevitably, was to seek accommodation with the new authorities. The underlying motivations for each church, however, were different. For Russian Orthodoxy accommodation really was a brute question of survival, since not only was it identified as an 'alien ideology' but its clergy were classified as 'class enemies' who had to be eliminated along with the remnants of the old ruling class. Moreover, as an autocephalous church it lacked organized external support. In these circumstances there was no room for compromise, total submission was the only available course. For the two great German churches, Catholicism and Lutheran Protestantism, on the other hand, the situation was more complex. In both cases, there were some doctrinal and cultural grounds for compromise. There were also considerable organizational differences. In the Catholic case, its adherents could, and many did, concur with the Nazi anathemas on 'Communism, Liberalism, Atheism, Relativism and Permissiveness' (Grunberger 1971: 439). They could sympathize with some aspects of Nazi eugenics to the extent that these dovetailed with Catholic views on the family and the healthy life. They could also sympathize with Nazi ANTI-SEMITISM since this was both a Catholic prejudice and deeply rooted in German culture. Moreover, the Catholic Church was the more easily compromised because it was keen to assert its German patriotism against chauvinistic criticism of its allegiance to Rome (ibid.: 437). These points of contact did not prevent Nazi attacks on the Church, but they did enable the rapid negotiation of the 'Reich concordat' (signed in June 1933), which granted recognition and limited autonomy to the Church in return for its obedience and papal recognition of the Reich. The Catholic Church was organizationally in a strong position, however, because it had a compact, autonomous and extremely authoritative hierarchy and because, of course, it was able to receive considerable external support from the Vatican. The NSDAP, therefore, was never able to destroy its cohesion entirely. The Protestant Church, by contrast, was much more vulnerable to Nazi manipulation because both Lutheranism and National Socialist ideology shared common roots in German history and culture. This was not just a question of their common anti-Semitism and anti-communism, German Protestantism also resonated with similar nationalist themes (in response to the same causes – Versailles and Weimar) and conceived of itself as the Church Militant in defence of God and country. German Protestantism did not, however, speak with one voice. It was highly decentralized, consisting of twenty-eight regional churches (or *Landeskirchen*). It was also very confessional and individualistic in its theological approach. Regional responses to the Nazi regime therefore varied considerably. By the same token, however, German Protestantism was easy prey for ambitious politicians (both clerical and civil) and the NSDAP adopted a very deliberate, and successful, policy of 'divide and rule' in order to subdue it.

Neither Stalin nor Hitler was able to destroy religion. This is testimony, in part, to the enduring nature of spiritual belief. It is also testimony, however, to the intuitive appeal of meta-narratives that seek to explain and order the whole of social and natural existence. Although very different in some of their premises and presuppositions both Stalinist and Nazi ideology and the religions they sought to repress shared a homologous structure that for want of a better word can only be called totalitarian or 'totalizing'. They have all endeavoured to sacralize TRUTH and the truth-giver – whether in the form of God and/or the 'Supreme Leader'. They have all sought to explain history in teleological terms, positing either HEAVEN, or heaven on earth, for the chosen people as the foreordained outcome. They have all attempted to establish rules and precepts for everyday living that were intended to permeate both the public and the private spheres. And all of them have anathematized or de-humanized those who disagreed with them (either consistently or intermittently).

This presents us with a philosophical difficulty. On the one hand, a condition of absolute universalism is not possible, however intuitively appealing it might be, except at the expense of all human difference and individuality, a condition that cannot be sustained. On the other hand, human beings cannot live in a state of total relativism and complete particularism either since this would eliminate the social sphere without which individuals cannot survive: totalizing meta-narratives have frequently been a response to such perceived 'breakdowns' of the social order. Religion has been permeated with the conflict between individual conscience – the search for individual redemption – the human need for fellowship and the exigencies of power. So has politics. Democratic theory has sought to find a middle way between these polarities but in the late twentieth century it is an open question whether it has succeeded.

Arendt, Hannah (1958) *The Origins of Totalitarianism*, New York: Meridian Books.

Binchy, D.A. (1941) *Church and State in Fascist Italy*, London: Royal Institute of International Affairs.

Bracher, Karl D. (1971) *The German Dictatorship. The Origins, Structure and Effects of National Socialism*, trans. Jean Steinburg, London: Weidenfeld & Nicolson.

Conway, J.S. (1968) *The Nazi Persecution of the Churches 1933–45*, London: Weidenfeld & Nicolson.

Friedrich, Carl J. and Brzezinski, Zbigniew (1966) *Totalitarian Dictatorship and Autocracy*, 2nd edn, New York: Praeger.

Grunberger, Richard (1971) *A Social History of the Third Reich*, London: Weidenfeld & Nicolson.

Mosse, George L. (1966) *Nazi Culture. Intellectual, Cultural and Social Life of the Third Reich*, London: W.H. Allen.

Scholder, Klaus (1987) *The Churches and the Third Reich*, vol. 1: *1918–1934*; vol. 2: *The Year of Disillusionment 1934*, trans. John Bowden, London: SCM.

Shapiro, Leonard (1972) *Totalitarianism*, Key Concepts in Political Science, London: Macmillan.

Steeves, Paul (1989) *Keeping the Faiths. Religion and Ideology in the Soviet Union*, New York: Holmes & Meier.

Rachel Walker

TOURISM

The Barbarian of yesterday is the Tourist of today.

(Nancy Mitford,
Encounter, 13 October, 1959)

By the end of the century tourism will be the largest industry in the world, in terms of both EMPLOYMENT and economic value. Its effects on economic, social and cultural life are immense. In particular this is because it channels enormous flows of people through other areas of the same SOCIETY or increasingly through other societies. The temporary migrations involved are more substantial and more profound than any previously experienced. There is a range of moral issues which such collective forms of travel raise, in terms of both social and environmental consequences. In the 1970s the Greek Orthodox Church recommended a new prayer: 'Lord, Jesus Christ, Son of God, have mercy on the cities, the islands and the villages of this Orthodox Fatherland, as well as the holy monasteries which are scourged by the worldly touristic wave'.

Tourism is a leisure activity which presupposes its opposite, namely regulated and organized work. Acting as a tourist is one of the characteristics of life in modern society, a marker of CITIZENSHIP. Tourist relationships arise from the movement of people from their normal place of residence and work to another place or places. It is presumed that the move is temporary and that there is a clear intention to return 'home'; that the move has been made for non-pecuniary reasons; and that socialized forms of provision are available in the destination area to cope with the collective forms of movement involved. It is also necessary that people anticipate, through daydreaming and fantasy, that when they are away they will encounter intense pleasures, either of a different scale or involving different senses from those customarily encountered.

Central to tourism is that otherwise mundane social activities are located within a distinctive or unusual visual context (see Urry 1990). When people go away they look upon the physical or built ENVIRONMENT with curiosity and interest.

It speaks to them. There is in other words a 'tourist gaze', or rather a whole variety of different gazes. Such gazes are socially organized, in part by professionals, they are authorized by various discourses, and they have tremendous consequences both for the places and people being gazed upon and for the social practices of those doing the gazing.

Three further points should be noted about the tourist gaze. First, a particular tourist gaze depends upon what it is contrasted with – the non-tourist forms of practice and perception. It is these which set off the place being visited, although there are numerous ways in which such contrasts between the everyday and the extraordinary are established and sustained. A crucial role in this is played by guide books which serve to construct the sacred quality of various physical and man-made objects (as Roland Barthes has shown in the case of the Guide Bleu).

Second, people do not gaze upon landscapes and townscapes in an unmediated fashion. The tourist gaze is constructed semiotically. Indeed the tourist might be principally understood as the collector of signs, such as the typical German beer-garden, the characteristic British pub or 'timeless, romantic Paris' (as evidenced by seeing two people kissing by the banks of the Seine).

Third, there are a number of typical forms taken by the tourist gaze. These are the *romantic*, solitary, sustained and auratic appreciation typically of 'nature'; the *collective*, shared encounters gazing with others at the familiar; the *spectatorial*, brief glances and collection of many different signs; the *environmental*, sustained and didactic scanning to surveil, inspect and if necessary collectively organize; and the *anthropological*, sustained immersion to scan and actively interpret a CULTURE.

Early social theory on the analysis of tourism was mainly concerned with the authenticity of the tourist experience. Daniel Boorstin, anticipating Umberto Eco (1986) and Jean Baudrillard, argues that Americans could not experience reality directly but thrived on pseudo-events, such as being a tourist. Isolated from the host environment and local people, the mass tourist travels in an 'environmental bubble' and finds pleasure in inauthentic and contrived attractions. Over time the images generated constitute a closed and self-perpetuating system of illusions. Somewhat similarly Turner and Ash (1975: 292) argue that 'the pursuit of the exotic and diverse ends in uniformity'.

Erik Cohen argues against this pessimistic position. He employs distinctions drawn in the sociology of religion to suggest that there are a variety of tourist types or modes of tourist experience. The 'experiential', the 'experimental' and the 'existential' tourist types do not rely upon wholly artificial 'environmental bubbles'.

Dean MacCannell (1976) accepts the inauthenticity and superficiality of much modern life but maintains that all tourists embody a quest for authentic experiences. This quest he sees as a contemporary version of the universal human concern for the sacred. He sees tourists as contemporary pilgrims, seeking authenticity in other 'times' and 'places' away from their patterns of everyday life. Particularly salient objects of such pilgrimages are the 'real working lives' of others. These real lives can only be observed backstage. And it would clearly be intrusive if such backstages were immediately visible to all those who wished to peer into them. Hence, MacCannell says the people being observed and local tourist entrepreneurs gradually come to construct backstages in an artificial and contrived manner – what he terms 'staged authenticity'.

Two further points from MacCannell are important to note. First, unlike the religious pilgrim who pays homage to a single centre, the tourist pilgrim may pay homage to a wide variety and types of centre, including some which might be thought to be somewhat unexpected: Parisian sewers, Welsh coalmines, New England mills, Japanese prisoner-of-war camps, Liverpool football stadia and so on. Second, each of these centres involves complex processes of production. A natural or cultural artefact has to undergo sacralization in order to render it a revered object of the tourist RITUAL. There are a number of stages of this process: naming the sight, framing and elevation, enshrinement, mechanical and visual reproduction, and social reproduction as new sights name themselves after the 'original'.

Some writers have developed the tourist

metaphor of pilgrimage through using the work of Victor Turner (1974). Three stages are identified: social and spatial separation from the normal place of residence and from conventional social ties; the liminal zone where people find themselves in an anti-structure out of time and place and where an intensive bonding or 'communitas' is experienced; and reintegration, where individuals are reintegrated with the previous social group, albeit at a higher social level (higher status from having visited the right place and claimed via the holiday snapshots?). What this analysis points to is that in much tourism there is licence for permissive and non-serious behaviour and the encouragement of a relatively unconstrained social togetherness. Shields (1991) provides an exemplary demonstration of this with regard to Brighton beach. This shifted in the nineteenth century from a medicalized beach to be a liminal zone, a zone of pleasure and also of carnival. The beach became noisy and crowded, full of unpredictable social mixing and involving the inversion of social hierarchies and moral codes.

This last comment also demonstrates that large-scale tourism is a relatively recent phenomenon and that it is necessary to examine its historically changing character. It has already been suggested that being a tourist is one of the key characteristics of the modern experience. This is the ability and right not merely to move around within cities as described by Baudelaire or Simmel, but to be mobile between cities and between cities and the seaside and countryside. Not to 'go away' is like not possessing a car or a nice house. It is a marker of status, a right of citizenship and something deemed necessary to good health. It is firmly embedded within three discourses, of consumerism, social rights and health promotion.

However, this is not to suggest that the features that we now characterize as 'tourist-related' were unknown before the nineteenth century. There were five main historical precursors: tourism for the Roman élite often involving the development of a complex infrastructure along the main routeways; religious pilgrimage in both the Christian and Muslim religions (see Eickelman and Piscatori (1990) on the latter); the Grand Tour for the sons of the European landed classes which often involved a pilgrimage to Italian religious painting and architecture; populist forms of fair and circus linked to the holding of markets; and spa tourism based on the development of specialist urban centres dedicated to élite forms of residential/medicinal tourism.

But although these were of some importance the developments beginning in the nineteenth century have been on a quite different scale and have involved, at least in the case of Western Europe and north America, the extension of travel and holiday opportunities to most of the population. Furthermore, some of this large-scale movement has involved travel abroad and so the consequences have been internationalized.

Some contemporary issues relating to large-scale international tourism will be outlined. These are the issues which are going to structure the debate about tourism for the rest of the century.

First, it is becoming clear that tourism has exceptionally profound environmental consequences. These problems range from the design of hotels, the destruction of 'natural' phenomena, the congestion and overcrowding of roads, airports and footpaths, the increased use of fossil fuels transporting international visitors, threats to water supply and so on. However, the environmental effects are not wholly negative. Much of the current GREEN consciousness stems from the increased awareness by tourists of the various environmental alternatives and from their attempts to implement conservation. Recently the organization *Tourism Concern* has started to promote a 'green tourism'.

Second, some of the apparently most destructive forms of tourism are becoming less appealing. The 'packaged' holiday to southern Mediterranean resorts, which produced so much scorn from middle class 'travellers', is rapidly declining in popularity. Visitors increasingly reject the mass consumption pattern and might be said to be more flexible and post-modern in their preferences. It has even been suggested that some visitors might be viewed as 'post-tourists', people who are ironic, playful and fully aware that 'tourism' is a game with multiple texts and scripts.

Third, tourism has important effects in

relation to different patterns of social inequality. In the nineteenth century in Britain seaside resorts developed different social tone depending on the social CLASS of the typical visitor. More recently whole countries have lost their place in the social hierarchy of tourist destinations as the social status of their visitors has declined. This has happened in particular in the case of the Mediterranean countries. It is also important to note that some tourist areas depend upon the exploitation of relatively weak sections of the labour force, such as young people, blacks or women. In certain cases the 'exotic' nature of indigenous peoples has led to so-called 'sex-tourism'.

Finally, since tourism is increasingly viewed as a major social phenomenon, there is a growing interest in its political and moral consequences. The following points should be noted: that the demand to visit other countries has become an important citizenship claim, one which seems to have partly motivated the revolutionary changes in Eastern Europe; that the effects of worldwide tourism will be to introduce 'Western' moral codes into otherwise 'traditional' societies, the effects of which, as Iran showed, may occasionally be to re-emphasize fundamentalist religion; that because of the scale of the phenomenon it is imperative to establish just what 'the good tourist' should do and how she or he should avoid the crassest forms of insensitive appropriation of other cultures; and that moral changes occur anyway and it is not reasonable to blame 'tourists' for all the negative social and moral consequences of contemporary life.

Barthes, R. (1972) *Mythologies*, London: Cape.
Boorstin, D. (1964) *The Image*, New York: Harper.
Cohen, E. (1979) 'A phenomenology of tourist types', *Sociology* 13 : 179-201.
Eco, U. (1986) *Travels in Hyper-Reality*, London: Picador.
Eickelman, D. and Piscatori, J. (eds) (1990) *Muslim Travellers*, London: Routledge.
Lumley, R. (ed.) (1988) *The Museum Time-Machine*, London: Routledge.
MacCannell, D. (1976) *The Tourist*, London: Macmillan (2nd edn 1989).
Shields, R. (1991) *Places on the Margin*, London: Routledge.
Turner, L. and Ash, J. (1975) *The Golden Hordes*, London: Constable.
Turner, V. (1974) *The Ritual Process*, Harmondsworth: Penguin.
Urry, J. (1990) *The Tourist Gaze*, London: Sage.
Wood, K. and House, S. (1991) *The Good Tourist*, London: Mandarin.

John Urry

TRADE UNIONS

Trade unions are combinations of workers to promote and defend rights, wages and working conditions within the relevant industry or organization. Although modern trade unions are a product of INDUSTRIALIZATION, there were earlier groupings of workers such as the medieval craft guilds which must be seen as part of the history of the organized workers' movement. Modern workplace organizations were established in Britain by 1789. The Combination Acts of 1799 banned union organizing until their repeal in 1824. The history of trade unions is marked by struggles for legal recognition. Unions were illegal in France until 1884 and in Germany until 1890. The oldest legal unions were in Britain and Germany, in both cases the result of lengthy struggles. The Trades Union Congress (TUC) was formed as early as 1868. In Britain, unions secured a legal footing in the mid-1870s, but the right to strike and picket, the two fundamental elements of union rights, were not guaranteed until 1906. By 1910 British unions had 2.6 million members, higher than anywhere except Germany. By the mid-1870s over half of trade union members were in cotton and mining. The cotton spinners were organized as early as the beginning of the nineteenth century. By 1880 union members formed about 4 per cent of the population. Concern about the power of the unions was expressed by the Conservative leader Arthur Balfour as early as 1912.

The later years of the nineteenth century saw new unions and new formations. The Amalgamated Society of Engineers was formed in 1851. The Trade Union Act of 1871 recognized unions as legal corporations. From 1888 to 1918 union membership grew rapidly, and by 1918 membership stood at 6.5 million. Between 1900 and 1925 membership grew from 12 per cent of the workforce to 45 per cent, but declined to 22 per cent by 1933. The inter-war years led to a decline in membership but an increase in socialist activity in the unions. In 1979 52 per cent of the workforce were members of unions but this was followed by further decline. By 1982 there were 142 unions affiliated to the TUC with over 10.5 million members.

While it is true that union membership has been predominantly male, there were some early examples of female-dominated unions. The Manchester Spinners Society, formed in 1798, consisted mainly of women. Women have remained marginal to the trade union movement. The machinery to improve wages and conditions has not accommodated the needs of women. Trade union bargaining has been based on the right of the male 'family wage'. However the increase in women workers since 1939, and particularly since the 1960s, has led to an even greater increase in women's membership in unions (largely due to the growth of unions in the service sector). Several large unions (e.g. teachers and local government) joined the TUC in the 1960s. In fact the recent increase in union membership has been among women and white collar workers. Between 1960 and 1980 women members of unions affiliated to the TUC trebled to 3.7 million.

While the strongest union growths have been in western Europe, unions existed throughout the Soviet bloc, though strikes were illegal and in most countries the unions were controlled by the Communist Party, the Solidarity movement in Poland in the 1980s being an exception. Recent years have seen the formation of new independent trade unions in Eastern Europe.

The relationship of trade unions to SOCIALISM has been ambiguous. Engels wrote on the role of unions in cotton and coal, and saw the unions as 'schools of war'. But he was critical of the narrow base of union negotiations (higher wages, shorter hours). Engels, Marx and Hyndman saw the unions as an obstacle to socialism, and there was considerable tension between socialists and the TUC throughout the 1880s. The socialist presence in some unions increased in the late 1880s, and the alliance of socialism and the union movement which Kier Hardie wanted to see did eventually happen. The election of George Barnes as general secretary of the Amalgamated Society of Engineers (later the Amalgamated Engineering Union) in 1896 was a turning point. In 1899 the TUC approved a motion for the election of Labour Members of Parliament. Another turning point was the decision of the House of Lords in 1901 in relation to the Taff Vale Railway Strike that strike action might lead to major financial damages, a decision which was reversed by the Trade Disputes Act 1906.

Union support for the Labour Party increased after the strikes began in 1910. The increased power of the unions was an integral factor in the emergence of the Labour Party as a centralized organization after 1918. Ernest Bevin claimed that the Labour Party 'emerged out of the bowels of the trade union movement'. But the relationship of the trade unions to the Labour Party has been a matter of dispute since the Trade Unions Act 1913. From 1920 onwards amalgamations led to the emergence of bigger unions. The Trade Disputes Act 1927 made financial support for the party more difficult. Between 1969 and 1979 three prime ministers found their policies were prevented by union actions.

The tension between reform and REVOLUTION has affected unions since early days. Some unions, such as the Catholic unions in Europe, accepted the capitalist system but worked for changes within it. Most unions have been reformist in their practice though often revolutionary in their rhetoric. Unions in the USSR were agencies of the productive drive. Anarcho-Syndicalists saw unions as revolutionary, and the Industrial Workers of the World ('Wobblies') argued for 'one big industrial union'. Down to the present day many unions are content with collective bargaining, while others are insisting on a greater say in management. The movement for workers' control of industry has been important, but marginal to the union movement as a whole.

The abortive General Strike of 1926 was a major setback to the movement, and since then there have been no 'political strikes' on such a scale. The election of the Labour Government in 1945 led to a closer alliance with the TUC which accepted wage freezes and anti-strike policies. The Labour Party document *In Place of Strife* (1969) attempted to curtail union power, as did the Conservative Government of 1970–4 which set up Industrial Relations Courts. They were abolished by the Labour Government of 1974–9. It was incomes policies which led to increased militancy on the part of dockers, engineers and health workers, as well as the miners, and confrontation with the miners brought about the fall of the Heath Government in February 1974. From the coming to power of Margaret Thatcher in 1979, the attack on the unions became fiercer and more ideological. The importance of the miners' strike of 1984 is interpreted in varied ways. Many see it as a final defeat for organized union power.

Since the 1970s more middle class professional groups have become unionized. Technical and design workers have joined unions especially those in engineering and computer technology. There have been changes too in approaches to negotiation, as in the Lucas Aerospace struggle in the mid-1970s. Again the globalization of the major corporations has affected union strategy. Workers at Ford Motors were ahead of other unions in developing international mechanisms for policy making. However, union membership has fallen in Britain to below 40 per cent of the workforce (in the USA it is as low as 15 per cent). The TUC is weaker today, and unions have declined throughout Europe, particularly in France.

From its beginnings, the trade union movement was influenced by Christians, particularly by Methodists. The Tolpuddle Martyrs of 1829 were led by George Loveless, a local preacher. Unions were strongly defended by Pope Leo XIII in *Rerum Novarum* (1891) which became known as 'the workers' charter'. The Church of England was ambivalent towards the unions. In the House of Lords debate on the Trade Disputes Act of 1906 only the Bishop of Southwark supported the unions. Yet the stress on solidarity, on collective action, on discipline and, in spite of criticisms of it, the 'closed shop' are seen by many to have roots in the radical nonconformist Christian movements (*see* CHRISTIAN SOCIALISM).

Bain, G.S. (1970) *The Growth of White Collar Unionism*, Oxford: Oxford University Press.
Boston, S. (1980) *Women Workers and the Trade Unions*, Davis Poynter.
Davis, M. (1993) *Comrade or Brother?*, London: Pluto Press.
Flanders, A. (1970) *Management and Trade Unions*, London: Faber.
Hutt, A. (1979) *British Trade Unions: A Short History*, Lawrence & Wishart.
Lovell, J. (1977) *British Trade Unions 1875–1933*, London: Macmillan.
McIlroy, J. (1988) *Trade Unions in Britain Today*, Manchester: Manchester University Press.
Mortimer, J.E. (1971) *Trade Unions and Technological Change*, Oxford: Oxford University Press.
Pelling, H. (1963) *A History of British Trade Unionism*, London: Penguin.
Pimlott, B. and Cook, C. (eds) (1991) *Trade Unions in British Politics*, London: Longman.
Rule, J. (ed.) (1988) *British Trade Unionism 1780–1850*, London: Longman.
Taylor, R. (1993) *The Trade Union Question in British Politics*, Oxford: Blackwell.
Wearmouth, R.F. (1937) *Methodism and the Working Class Movements in England 1800–1850*, Epworth.
——(1959) *Methodism and the Trade Unions*, Epworth.
Webb, B. and Webb, S. (1898) *The History of Trade Unionism*, Chiswick Press.

Kenneth Leech

TRANSCENDENCE

Whenever the concept of transcendence appears in any discussion it is almost invariably accompanied by a reference to immanence. Neither has a single meaning; rather it is in the clarification of their relationship that the specific meaning of the terms emerges. Thus it might be said that God is transcendent and not immanent: God is distant from the material world and not directly involved in it. This would distinguish MONOTHEISM from pantheism and deny the divinity of the natural world. But the same assertion, that God is transcendent and not immanent, might not deny that God is involved in the material world. Rather it might assert an ontological distinction between God and the world such that while God is constantly active within the events of human history 'God' is not simply a name for historical movement. The meaning of the term is therefore clarified positively and negatively, through asserting what it is and, by association with immanence, denying what it is not. A line is drawn between the two, and transcendence always refers to that which is 'beyond'.

Transcendence can therefore have a metaphysical meaning, referring to a dimension which lies beyond the human, the material, the mundane. Frequently this way of speaking is mythological, expressing a qualitative difference in quasi-geographical terms. The qualitative distinction can also represent a value judgement, favouring the spiritual over the material. In the aphorism *soma sema* the ancient Greeks described the body as a prison house of the SOUL. In this case transcendence is the escape of the soul, the liberation of the higher spiritual element from the lower, material element. In an ontology imbued with this valuation it would be inconceivable that God could be immanent, a contradiction in terms. Thus the Christian doctrine of incarnation would be 'foolishness to the Greeks', as Paul says.

In Western thought the concept of transcendence has been largely dominated by its use in Christian THEOLOGY, but that theology has been dominated in turn by Greek metaphysics, first Platonic and then Aristotelian. Transcendence has been regarded as a divine attribute. The rise of critical philosophy in the West has been marked by the criticism of religion, which has expressed ALIENATION from such a transcendent being, and indeed has questioned the existence of God. This century has seen a renewed interest in transcendence as a human attribute. This has in turn led some theologians to ask whether in its loyalty to Greek philosophy theology has not developed an understanding of transcendence quite out of keeping with the Biblical doctrine of God.

Twentieth-century philosophy has been indebted to the work of the phenomenologist Martin Heidegger. His *magnum opus, Being and Time*, begins with a critique of Greek ontology. His own fundamental ontology attempts to break with the tradition of objectifying thinking which Heidegger found everywhere present in European thought from Aristotle. As a phenomenologist he observed that human beings do not have attributes, but existentialia, modes of existence. Their nature – or better, their character – is not an expression of a fixed essence but the actualization of various possible modes of existence. The question might then be raised whether transcendence, instead of being a divine attribute, is a possible mode of human existence. To this point we shall return, but Heidegger's

fundamental ontology does raise the question whether divine transcendence should be approached as an attribute or whether it should refer to a mode of divine existence. Does transcendence refer to the divine essence or to the manner of God's being towards humankind?

The concept of transcendence is central to the philosophy of Karl Jaspers, in his understanding first of natural science and then of religion. He was concerned about immanence as a worldview, the assumption that only that which can be established scientifically is knowledge, and therefore real. But for Jaspers human existence transcends scientific knowledge. He gave science its place, and put it in its place. Our knowledge begins with the scientific and then transcends it. Science, especially medical science, objectifies human beings and knowledge thus derived is part of the immanent world. But it would be false and dehumanizing to suppose that there is nothing more to be said about human existence. It transcends the purely objective: there are dimensions which cannot be treated objectively, notably human freedom and choice.

It is tempting to ask Jaspers for a definition of transcendence, but to define anything is to objectify it, to control it, to reduce it to available knowledge. Thus transcendence is not amenable to definition. 'I lose transcendence when I anticipate it and think I already have it in some intelligible world.' It is not difficult to see why Jaspers is grouped with the existentialist philosophers: he was much influenced by Søren Kierkegaard, the Danish philosopher and theologian, often regarded as the father of existentialism. Yet Jaspers, like Heidegger, was concerned with human existence only in a wider ontological context. The individual transcends the limits of objective life, but experiences transcendence in relation to other people. And beyond this, transcendence is real and makes sense because it is already there: it is not simply a human experience. 'In every true attitude toward transcendence lies a sense of being independent of me. My historicity does not produce it; it produces me, my self, as I become aware of it.'

In this century much existentialism has been humanist, even atheist, and it is therefore of some interest that Jaspers speaks of the two sides of the experience of transcendence. 'Transcendence is more than it is for me.' Since religious experience has the same two sides to it, Jaspers' ontology seems to offer a philosophical basis for returning to religion and belief in God. This is not entirely true, although like previous philosophers, such as Hegel, he is prepared to use religious language at times to illustrate his point. 'Transcendence beyond the world or before the world is called God.' However, this way of speaking is merely an aid along the way to his own philosophical faith: 'what we refer to in mythical terms as the soul and God, and in philosophical language as *Existenz* and transcendence. . . .' Herein lies his criticism of religion. A mythical mode of speaking is an objectifying mode. In his famous programmatic essay on demythologizing Rodolf Bultmann provided an imprecise though suggestive definition. 'Mythology is the use of imagery to express the other worldly in terms of this world and the divine in terms of human life, the other side in terms of this side.' In Bultmann's terms religion – at least in its mythological form – eliminates the 'beyond' which we have already associated with transcendence. Thus in Genesis God walks in the garden in the cool of the day, the serpent speaks to woman, man and woman eat the fruit of the tree which gives knowledge of good and EVIL. Bultmann's call for demythologizing was to find a method of interpretation which would allow the reader to pass 'beyond' the objectifying language of the text to its profoundly religious meaning. But what Bultmann claimed about mythological religion Jaspers asserts about religion as such. Religion represents the objectifying process by which the transcendent is named, described, made available, controlled, guaranteed – in short, made part of this world.

Religion has a particular value for Jaspers' philosophy. 'Philosophy appears to need religious soil to grow in.' Religion maintains an awareness of transcendence, a witness to it, a sensitivity towards and an expectation of the possibility of transcendence in a CULTURE or SOCIETY. Jaspers' criticism is that through literalism the ciphers or symbols of religion come to be taken literally. Thus the symbol that 'God was in Christ' eventually becomes the Chalcedonian statement of the two natures of Christ. The mystery is reduced to a quasi-physiological definition, the transcendent faith reduced to pseudo-scientific knowledge. Like Feuerbach before him Jaspers is not alienated from religion, but rather from its theological expressions. Theology represents the 'mundanization of transcendence'. On this view transcendence is not a neutral, philosophical way of speaking about God; rather, God is a cipher of transcendence. Truly understood the doctrine of God 'beyond' this world is a cipher which witnesses to the experience of transcendence which carries us beyond the immanent world. The Buddhist is advised to kill the Buddha if he meets him in the street: an objective Buddha would be the death of transcendence. Thus in philosophical faith it may be necessary to deny God. This would not be a descent into immanence, but rather an affirmation of transcendence.

As noted earlier, Christian theology was developed in dialogue with Greek philosophy and incorporated many assumptions from that source. This approach is often contrasted with Hebrew thought forms and a distinction is made between Biblical religious thought and later doctrinal forms. Thus Jaspers was able to claim that his position took seriously the second commandment. 'You shall not make for yourself a graven image, or any likeness of anything. . . .' People in the modern world are not much given to making model calves out of gold and bowing down before them and therefore seem to be entirely innocent in this respect. However, a more subtle reading of the text would expose to condemnation any objectification of God, whether in material form or not.

This point is made at length by the Mexican liberation theologian Jose Porfirio Miranda in his book *Marx and the Bible*. The subtitle, 'a critique of the philosophy of oppression', refers to what Miranda considers to be an objectifying tendency in European culture. It reduces subject peoples to objects. But in our context we should note that it also objectifies God. Miranda begins with the observation that 'the Bible wishes to emphasize the transcendence of God'. This does not mean moving from the already known, in an Aristotelian sense, nor does it simply mean that God is not to be identified with things, material images. The God of the Bible makes himself known in his words, in his commandments and above all in his requirement of JUSTICE. This is illustrated in God's words to the young king Josiah:

Did not your father eat and drink and do
justice and righteousness?
Then it was well with him.
He judged the cause of the poor and the
needy;
then it was well.
Is not this to know me? says the Lord.

Miranda describes this as 'antiontological actualism'. God does not exist in some ontological way such that he can be known objectively, his existence debated and his nature analysed. God is only known in the doing of his will. 'Transcendence does not mean only an unimaginable and inconceivable God, but a God who is accessible only in the act of justice.' This lies behind the anticultic statements of the eighth-century prophets. According to Amos God declares 'I hate, I despise your feasts, and I take no delight in your solemn assemblies.' Instead, God declares 'let justice roll down like waters, and righteousness like an ever-flowing stream.' There are not two ways of knowing God, a cultic and an ethical. The supposed cultic route is one of religious objectification, but it avoids the demands of justice. Miranda quotes Levinas with approval. 'Ontology, as a fundamental philosophy which does not call into question the self, is a philosophy of injustice.' It is an objectifying approach which attempts to seek God while ignoring the neighbour. This is the philosophy of oppression, so much a part of Western thought and practice according to Miranda, and so far removed from the Biblical call to love God in caring for the widow, the orphan and the migrant. 'True transcendence situates us beyond the categories of being and all the extrapolations of being. Yahweh is not among the entities nor the existings nor in univocal being nor in analogous being, but rather in the implacable moral imperative of justice.'

It is therefore not possible to give a precise definition of transcendence. Nor is it possible to say in advance how any writer is going to use the term. In a Wittgensteinian sense we must let the meaning emerge from the way in which the term is used in any text. It is possible to use it in the exposition of classical theism, as the basis of a critique of religion and even as the perspective from which to defend true religion. In this century it has also become an important point in maintaining the humanist dimension of MARXISM.

What follow here are simply some illustrations of the importance of the term transcendence for revisionist Marxists. Far from being considered a theological term with no concrete application, it was used by Herbert Marcuse in a practical, empirical sense. It is the very opposite of that which impacts on our lives from elsewhere. 'It is opposed to all metaphysics by virtue of the rigorously historical character of transcendence.' He can even refer to the 'praxis of transcendence'. Karl Mannheim had used the term in writing of Utopia. 'Only those orientations transcending reality will be referred to by us as utopian which, when they pass over into conduct, tend to shatter, either partially or wholly, the order of things prevailing at the time.' Marcuse makes the same contrast between IDEOLOGY and Utopia, referring to an idea which cannot be contained within an ideological system and which transcends it. 'This transcendence speaks not against, but for, its truth.' We see the same approach to transcendence in the work of Ernst Bloch. Transcendence is not an ontological category, a synonym for God. In Bloch it is rescued from reification and restored as a human mode of existence. 'What is decisive; to transcend without transcendence.' It was the contribution of the French Marxist Roger Garaudy to attempt to rescue Marxism from a dehumanizing materialist mould into which orthodoxy pressed it. Like Jaspers he praised religion for maintaining a witness to this subjective dimension. He reckons that Marxism owes a debt to Christianity 'as a contributing factor in the exploration of the two essential dimensions of man: subjectivity and transcendence'. He does not pretend that the two systems understand the term in the same way. 'For a Christian, transcendence is the act of God who comes towards him and summons him. For a Marxist, it is a dimension of man's activity which goes beyond itself towards its far-off being.'

Both in religion and in HUMANISM transcendence can be a critical term in the attempt to open up closed theological or ideological systems. At one stage in the debate we might pose the question, does transcendence lie beyond, or rather does it lead beyond? But after Jaspers these might be but two sides of the same coin. Does the experience of transcendence lead beyond simply because in the commitment to the life of justice transcendence meets the transcendent?

Anderson, R. (1975) *Historical Transcendence and the Reality of God*, London: Chapman.

Bonnet, N. (1987) *Immanence et Transcendence chez Teilhard de Chardin*, Montreal: Editions Bellarmin.

Bultmann, R. (1961) 'New Testament and mythology', in H.-W. Bartsch (ed.) *Kergyma and Myth*, New York: Harper & Row.

Daly, G. (1980) *Transcendence and Immanence*, Oxford: Clarendon.

Garaudy, R. (1970) *The Turning-Point of Socialism*, London: Collins.

Heidegger, M. (1962) *Being and Time*, London: SCM.

Jaspers, K. (1967) *Philosophical Faith and Revelation*, London: Collins.

——(1969) *Philosophy*, Chicago, IL: University of Chicago Press.

Johnson, W.A. (1974) *The Search for Transcendence*, New York: Harper & Row.

Lorant, H. (1991) *A Study in the Concept of Transcendence in Contemporary German Theology*, Edinburgh: Rutherford House.

Mannheim, K. (1972) *Ideology and Utopia*, London: Routledge & Kegan Paul.

Marcuse, H. (1964) *One-Dimensional Man*, London: Routledge & Kegan Paul.

Miranda, J.P. (1974) *Marx and the Bible*, Maryknoll, NY: Orbis.

Wilezek, G. (1992) *Die Frage nach der Transcendenz*, Eichstatt: Bronner & Daentler.

Alistair Kee

TRINITY

An encounter with the divine Mystery lies at the root of all religious doctrine. This encounter evokes a deep experience embracing all our humanity: emotions, reason, will, desire and heart. The first reaction, an expression of pleasure, is praise, worship and proclamation. After that comes the task of appropriating and translating this experience-encounter, the task of devout reasoning. This is the stage at which doctrines and creeds come into being.
(Boff 1988: 1)

The earliest Christians experienced God as 'Father', 'Son' and 'Holy Spirit'. (The traditional divine names are given in quotation marks here and elsewhere in this article to indicate their metaphorical nature, and the non-sexist intent of the author.) Only afterwards did the Apologists and other early Christian theologians begin to wrestle with the theoretical issues involved in worshipping God as simultaneously three and one. The doctrine of the Trinity as set forth first at the Council of Nicaea in 325 and then in more elaborate form at the First Council of Constantinople in 381 was the eventual result of their theological reflection. Here the Church Fathers solemnly declared Jesus Christ as the 'Son' of God to be consubstantial with the 'Father' in the possession of divinity; likewise, they declared the 'Holy Spirit' to be likewise God and to have proceeded from the 'Father' (DS 125, 150).

Subsequently, in the High Middle Ages, the great Dominican theologian Thomas Aquinas set forth what has come to be accepted in the Western Church as the classical explanation of the doctrine of the Trinity. In Questions 27–43 of the First Part of the *Summa Theologiae*, he proposed that there is one God with two processions, namely, begetting and spirating, corresponding to the operations of knowing and loving within the divine being. As a result of these two processions there are four real relations in God: begetting and being begotten, spirating and being spirated. Finally, three of these four real relations are subsistent as divine PERSONS. That is, the personal identity of the 'Father' consists in begetting the 'Son' and, together with the 'Son', spirating the 'Spirit'. The personal identity of the 'Son', on the other hand, consists in being begotten by the 'Father'; while the personal identity of the 'Spirit' consists in being spirated by the 'Father' and the 'Son'.

William Hill comments that Aquinas thus makes relationality intrinsic to being: 'at the very heart of being as such, of all being, there resides a mysterious *respectus ad alterum*. A certain inner-relationality is revealed in the depths of reality that is not merely incidental' (Hill 1982: 73). Reality, in other words, is intrinsically social. Individual entities do not first exist in themselves and then later amalgamate into groups on a secondary or purely operational level. Rather, like the divine persons, if they are to exist at all, they must exist in dynamic interrelation. If a given social grouping fails, then the individual members of the group must either reorganize or face extinction.

There is, to be sure, some doubt whether Aquinas himself realized the full import of this insight into the intrinsic sociality of being since he took for granted (and indeed most of his followers to the present day still take for granted) that the world of CREATION is ultimately made up of individuals who exist in relation to other entities, but whose very being or essence is not constituted by those same relations. The image of the Trinity in which the three divine persons exist only in virtue of their dynamic relation to one another is seen, in other words, as the exception, not the rule. Rather, the implicit paradigm for life in this world is the individual as an entity existing in its own right, what Aristotle in the *Metaphysics* referred to as individual substance (*Metaphysics*, 1028a). Even in formulating his doctrine of the Trinity, Aquinas clearly had Aristotle's notion of individual substance in mind. For, he described the divine persons as subsistent relations. As relations, they inhere in an underlying substance; as subsistent relations, they are identical in being with the substance. But the net effect is that God is still one individual entity, one supra-substantial reality, rather than a community as the analysis of persons-in-relation might otherwise suggest.

In recent years, however, there has been an upsurge of interest in the social analogy for the Trinity from various quarters. As I shall indicate below, European thinkers like Jürgen Moltmann and Heribert Mühlen have implicitly joined forces with Latin American liberation theologians like Juan Luis Segundo and Leonardo Boff in rejecting the traditional understanding of God as a transcendent individual entity and embracing a communitarian model for the relations of the divine persons with one another. Likewise, Thomistically inspired theologians like William Hill, Bernard Lonergan and John

O'Donnell have sought ways to think of the Trinity in terms of divine intersubjectivity. Furthermore, the influential Greek Orthodox theologian John Zizioulas urges that, if the life of God is a communion of persons, then the very notion of Being should be reconceived in interpersonal terms. Yet, if Being is thus intrinsically relational, is it not likewise inherently processive? Not only the Latin American liberation theologians but others as well have argued that the three divine persons are necessarily involved with their creatures in the ongoing history of humankind and indeed of the cosmos. Finally, in the light of the same social analogy for the doctrine of the Trinity, still other theologians have speculated whether the divine names for the persons of the Trinity should continue to be exclusively masculine or rather should be both masculine and feminine.

I will begin this survey of recent theological reflection on the Trinity with the Latin American theologians Juan Luis Segundo and Leonardo Boff. In *Our Idea of God*, Segundo initially claims: 'Our falsified and inauthentic ways of dealing with our fellow men are allied to our falsifications of the idea of God. Our unjust SOCIETY and our perverted idea of God are in close and terrible alliance' (Segundo 1974: 7–8). In his view, the traditional understanding of God as a transcendent individual being who creates the world by a simple act of the will and who is in no way dependent upon it for God's own happiness or welfare has indirectly fostered among human beings the illusory ideals of personal self-sufficiency and total independence of others (pp. 66–9). Rather, what the Bible itself reveals to us about God and what is surely needed by the majority of human beings in their struggle for liberation from political and economic oppression is the image of God as a community of divine persons who are actively involved with their human creatures in the creation of a new social order. God the Father is 'God before us', leading human beings to the goal of a new social order. Jesus as the Incarnate Son of God is 'God with us' and the Holy Spirit is 'God within us' in the struggle to attain that same ideal (pp. 21–31).

A decade later, the Brazilian theologian Leonardo Boff in *Trinity and Society* echoed many of the same themes. Relying heavily upon the writings of Augustine in the West and of the Cappadocian Fathers and St John Damascene in the early Greek-speaking Church, Boff develops the notion of the Trinity as a communion of three persons who reciprocally interpermeate one another's being and activity (Boff 1988: 54–7, 83–5, 123–54). But, like Segundo, he too sees the pragmatic value of this communitarian model of divine life for the hopes and aspirations of human beings today, above all those in the Third World. 'In the Trinity there is no domination by one side, but convergence of the Three in mutual acceptance and giving. . . . Therefore a society that takes its inspiration from trinitarian communion cannot tolerate CLASS differences, dominations based on POWER (economic, sexual or ideological)' (p. 151). Moreover, to combat an implicit sexual domination of men over women in virtue of the traditional masculine names for the persons of the Trinity, he suggests that trans-sexual names be used for the persons of the Trinity: e.g. God as maternal Father and/or paternal Mother. He then concludes: 'God seen as communion and co-existence can be both masculine and feminine, giving us a more complete and integrating experience of God' (p. 122).

Turning now to the work of the two German theologians, Heribert Mühlen and Jürgen Moltmann, we note that they, too, seem anxious to describe the relations of the divine persons to one another in strictly interpersonal terms. Mühlen, for example, speaks of three *Urworte*, personal pronouns which are foundational for all intersubjective communication: namely, I, Thou and We. 'Without a Thou, there is no I' (Mühlen 1966: 56). But likewise, without Thou and I together, there is no We. Mühlen then argues that God the 'Father' is the subsistent I- Relation, God the 'Son' is the subsistent Thou-Relation and God the 'Holy Spirit' is the subsistent We-Relation. There are, to be sure, difficulties with this approach. Are the 'Son' and the 'Holy Spirit', for example, likewise in their own persons an 'I', or is the 'Father' alone a self in the strict sense of the word? But the principal merit of Mühlen's approach is still intact: namely, that the divine persons are thus not only seen as subsistent relations, as in the past, but as subsistent *interpersonal* relations.

Similarly, Jürgen Moltmann begins his treatise on *The Trinity and the Kingdom* with the observation that the notion of God as Absolute Substance in the theology of Thomas Aquinas and other medieval thinkers and the notion of God as Absolute Subject in the thought of Hegel and the other German Idealists are inadequate for a proper understanding of the Trinity since they both result in 'abstract MONOTHEISM' rather than genuine Trinitarian theology (Moltmann 1981: 16–20). Rather, like Boff, he has recourse to the writings of the Greek Fathers, in particular their doctrine of *perichoresis*, the 'dancing around' of the three divine persons or their mutual interpermeation of one another's being and activity. The divine persons are thus neither three separate individuals who subsequently enter into association with one another nor simply three modes of being for the one God as Absolute Subject. Rather they exist as individuals only in terms of their dynamic relationship to one another within the divine life. Moltmann concludes: 'The unity of the triunity lies in the eternal perichoresis of the trinitarian persons' (p. 175). Likewise, with the Latin American liberation theologians, Moltmann recognizes that the Trinity understood as a community of co-equal persons provides a potentially revolutionary model for the restructuring of GOVERNMENT both in the church and in civil society. 'The three divine Persons have everything in common, except for their personal characteristics. So the Trinity corresponds to a community in which people are defined through their relations with one another and in their significance for one another, not in opposition to one another, in terms of power and possession' (p. 198).

As already noted, theologians who are basically oriented to the thought of Thomas Aquinas on the Trinity have likewise sought to introduce an intersubjective dimension into their explanation of the doctrine. Bernard Lonergan, for example, in his lectures on the Trinity at the Gregorian University several decades ago argued that 'Father, Son and Holy Spirit are in virtue of one real consciousness three subjects conscious of themselves, of one another, and of their act [of being] both notional and essential' (Lonergan 1964: II, 186). There are, to be sure, problems with this explanation since the three divine persons would thus have to be aware of themselves as essentially only one self even as they are personally or 'notionally' three separate selves. William Hill concedes the difficulty, noting that in God consciousness is both essential and personal: 'the former establishes the persons in their unity, the latter establishes them in their distinction' (Hill 1982: 270). At the same time, he seems to resolve the difficulty by conceiving the essential consciousness of God as a *shared* consciousness. 'The persons in God thus constitute a divine intersubjectivity. Father, Son, and Spirit are three centers of consciousness in community, in mutual communication. The members of the Trinity are now seen as constituting a community of persons in pure reciprocity, as subjects and centers of one divine conscious life' (p. 272). John O'Donnell, in his overview of recent theological speculation on the doctrine of the Trinity, concurs with Hill on this point although he cautions that each of the divine persons is an 'I' or centre of consciousness only in an analogous sense (O'Donnell 1989: 110).

John Zizioulas, on the other hand, representing the Greek Orthodox tradition in Trinitarian theology, is critical of Western theologians in their claim that the unity of the Trinity is grounded in the underlying divine nature or substance. For, in this way the three divine persons are ontologically subordinate to an impersonal principle or structure within the divine being (Zizioulas 1985: 17–18). In his view, the Cappadocian Fathers located the unity of the divine being in the person of the Father 'who is the "cause" both of the generation of the Son and of the procession of the Spirit' (pp. 40–1). One could counterargue, of course, that Zizioulas is thereby implicitly neglecting the ontological implications of the Cappadocian doctrine of *perichoresis* for the relations of the divine persons to one another. For, within this dynamic understanding of the divine life, relationships of origin for the divine persons would seem to be ultimately subordinate to relationships of EQUALITY within the 'dancing around' which is their common life. Even more importantly, however, Zizioulas seems to have missed the deeper implications of his own thesis that Being is communion. Logically, communion should be grounded

in a process of communing between co-equal persons, not in the person of the 'Father' who causes the other two divine persons to exist in dynamic relationship to 'Himself'. There are, in other words, rival paradigms for the relationship of the One and the Many operative here. Zizioulas follows the classical paradigm in which the One (the 'Father') is productive of the reality of the Many (the 'Son' and the 'Spirit'). The notion of Being as communion, on the other hand, seems to imply another paradigm in which the Many (all three divine persons) are by their dynamic interrelation productive of the reality of the One (community or communion).

What Zizioulas has in mind, to be sure, is to overcome the determinism implicit in the classical notion of 'cosmos', a world governed by fixed law and unvarying essential relationships, and replace it with the notion of a world order governed by persons acting out of freedom in their interrelationships. But this, in turn, raises the question whether the process-relational metaphysics of Alfred North Whitehead would not better serve as an underlying conceptuality for the notion of Being as communion and, in particular, for the Cappadocian doctrine of Trinitarian *perichoresis*. Whitehead, to be sure, basically conceived God in unipersonal rather than tripersonal terms. But his thought is grounded in the notion of self-constituting subjects of experience in dynamic interrelation. Hence, the ultimate constituents or 'building blocks' of reality are not individual entities which first exist in themselves and then are related to one another externally in space and time, but momentary subjects of experience ('actual entities') whose individual existence is intrinsically bound up with the existence and activity of other such momentary subjects of experience, past, present and future. Thus 'the actual world is a process', and 'the process is the becoming of actual entities' in dynamic unison with one another (Whitehead 1978: 22).

What is evidently missing from Whitehead's presentation, however, is due recognition of the equiprimordiality of the notion of 'society' with the notion of actual entity. That is, the actual entities invariably aggregate into various objective unities called 'societies' which correspond to the persons and things of common-sense experience. Apparently, in his preoccupation with working out the dynamics of the internal self-constitution of actual entities, Whitehead paid too little attention both to what happens as a result of this clustering of actual entities at any given moment and to what endures as an objective reality once a given set of actual entities has 'perished' and a new set is still in process of formation. As a result, his philosophy has been criticized as atomistic or overly individualistic, even though the entire thrust of his worldview is with respect to the intrinsic sociality or relationality of all entities with one another.

Furthermore, the same lacuna in his thought is quite possibly the deeper reason why Whitehead did not better grasp the value of the doctrine of the Trinity for reinforcing his own philosophy of universal intersubjectivity. That is, because his doctrine of societies was relatively undeveloped, he had no way to affirm the objective unity of God at any given moment as a community of actual entities (divine persons) in dynamic interrelation. What is needed, accordingly, as I have pointed out elsewhere (Bracken 1991: 123–60), is a Trinitarian reinterpretation of Whitehead's metaphysical scheme whereby the three divine persons co-constitute with their creatures a constantly expanding, all-embracing community which perdures through time and into eternity. In this way, the proposal that Being is communion will be verified, not simply on the level of the divine life or even of human life in its better moments, but on all levels of existence and activity within the cosmos, wherever actual entities as momentary subjects of experience are dynamically interrelated with one another.

Yet even this process-relational approach to the mystery of the triune God does not solve the problem posed by the traditional masculine names for the persons of the Trinity. As Leonardo Boff commented above, God seen as both masculine and feminine gives human beings a more complete and integrating experience of God. Hence, it is important not only for women but also for men to address God as 'Mother' as well as 'Father' and to sense the latent feminine aspects of the 'Son' and the 'Spirit'. For some,

to be sure, the answer lies in referring to the divine persons in somewhat neutral terms as respectively Creator, Redeemer and Sanctifier. But these names still carry an implicitly masculine tone. There seems to be, accordingly, no alternative but consciously to use feminine images for God both in theological discourse and in public worship until one is completely comfortable with feminine as well as masculine imagery for the divine persons. Moreover, as Sallie McFague points out (McFague 1987: 21–8), use of feminine names and images for God indirectly makes clear the metaphorical character of all language about God. Thus, through the conscious use of both masculine and feminine imagery for God, one may be led more deeply into the experience of God as Divine Mystery, which, as Boff noted, is both the beginning and the end-point of all theological reflection on the reality of God.

Boff, L. (1988) *Trinity and Society*, trans. P. Burns, Maryknoll, NY: Orbis.

Bracken, J.A. (1991) *Society and Spirit: A Trinitarian Cosmology*, Cranbury, NJ: Associated University Presses.

Hill, W.J. (1982) *The Three-Personed God: The Trinity as a Mystery of Salvation*, Washington, DC: Catholic University of America Press.

Johnson, E. A. (1992) *SHE WHO IS: The Mystery of God in Feminist Discourse*, New York: Crossroad.

LaCugna, C.M. (1991) *God for Us: The Trinity and Christian Life*, San Francisco, CA: Harper Collins.

Lonergan, B.J.F. (1964) *De Deo Trino*, 2 vols, Rome: Gregorian University Press.

McFague, S. (1987) *Models of God: Theology for an Ecological, Nuclear Age*, Philadelphia, PA: Fortress.

Moltmann, J. (1981) *The Trinity and the Kingdom: The Doctrine of God*, trans. M. Kohl, San Francisco, CA: Harper & Row.

Mühlen, H. (1966) *Der heilige Geist als Person*, 2nd edn, Munster: Aschendorff.

O'Donnell, J.J. (1989) *The Mystery of the Triune God*, New York: Paulist.

Segundo, J.L. (1974) *Our Idea of God*, trans. J. Drury, Maryknoll, NY: Orbis.

Whitehead, A.N. (1978) *Process and Reality: An Essay in Cosmology*, corrected edition, D.R. Griffin and D.W. Sherburne (eds), New York: Free Press.

Zizioulas, J.D. (1985) *Being as Communion. Studies in Personhood and the Church*, Crestwood, NY: St Vladimir's Seminary Press.

Joseph A. Bracken

TRUTH

We use the word 'truth' in our everyday conversation without difficulty. Yet if we look at the history of thought we find that there are many different conceptions of truth. In a lengthy article on truth Ferrater Mora (1979: 3397) tells us that this term is used primarily in two senses: to refer to the truth of a proposition or statement and to refer to a reality. When it is said that a proposition is true, this notion is opposed to that which is false. When it is said that a reality is true, this notion is opposed to what is apparent, illusory, unreal, non-existent and so forth.

The ancient Greek philosophers, according to Ferrater Mora, identified truth as a permanent reality, regardless of whether this reality was thought to be material substance, numbers, primary qualities or ideas. As that which is permanent, truth was contrasted with what is changing, which is only apparently true, although not necessarily false. The Greeks often maintained that truth was accessible only to thought. They conceived of truth as pertaining to the discovery of what a thing is, to its essence. Truth as *aletheia* was the uncovering of being, which is hidden by appearances.

The *locus classicus* of truth understood as the truth of propositions or statements is found in Aristotle: 'To say of what is that it is not, or of what is not that it is, is false, while to say of what is that it is, and of what is not that it is not, is true' (*Metaphysics* 7, 1011 B 26–8). This statement does not differ greatly from what Plato had already said in the *Cratylus* where Socrates asks if 'a true proposition says that which is, and a false proposition says that which is not' (385 B; see also *Sophist* 240D–241A and 263 B).

Another quite early view of truth, according to Ferrater Mora, was that developed by the 'classical' Hebrews who viewed truth ('*emunah*') as that which is faithful or which keeps or will keep its promise, namely God. This means that, in contrast with the Greek idea, truth for the Hebrews was not something static, not found in things: 'it was this people's consciousness of possessing a truth that must be transmitted; its consciousness that it existed in order to bear witness to that "future" truth –

among the great powers and, if need be, against them' (Ferrater Mora 1957: 54).

Ferrater Mora's work shows that one could view the entire history of thought according to the different theories concerning truth. Varying formulas and theories were propounded not only in the ancient world but during the Middle Ages and in the modern as well as in the contemporary period.

Probably the best known theory of truth and that which seems most commonsensical to the general public is the so-called correspondence theory of truth, which in its simplest form involves the correspondence between what one says and what is talked about, namely between the proposition or statement and things, or, as it is sometimes expressed, between a statement and reality.

During the medieval period this notion of truth was discussed in great detail. Truth was seen not only as the correspondence or conformity of things with the mind, which meant that things were intelligible, but also as the conformity of the mind with things. For example, St Anselm (1033–78), following the Aristotelian tradition, discusses truth as the truth of statements, but he also asserts that the truth of things corresponds to their ideas in the mind of God, the 'supreme truth', and cause of all other truths. God, the supreme truth, then, is the cause that makes the correspondence between things and the mind possible. Maintaining a similar view, but giving greater emphasis to the truth residing in statements, Thomas Aquinas defines truth as *adequatio rei et intellectus*.

A correspondence theory of truth does not necessarily include such notions about God. For example, the theory developed by the modern logician Tarski, known as the semantic conception of truth, is a form of the correspondence theory. Tarski maintains that the expressions 'is true' and 'is false' are metalogical. In an artificial language, the correspondence is between the meta-language and the object language.

Another well-known theory of truth is the coherence theory upheld by idealists, where single statements are only partial truths. In its more extreme versons, these partial judgements are 'absorbed' or synthesized into a whole, so that, for example, Hegel can say that the truth is the whole.

Theories of truth and refinements on these theories abound. William James, for example, developed the so-called pragmatic theory of truth which involves the notion that a statement is true if it works, is able to predict something, solves other problems in science, can be validated and so forth.

These different theories show that truth can be conceived in a variety of ways: absolute or relative; eternal or changing, and so forth.

Perhaps some of the most provocative and influential views on truth have been those developed by nineteenth- and twentieth-century thinkers who reject the traditional notions of truth as correspondence, as intellectual, and who deny that there is a straightforward antithesis between truth and falsity.

Consider the notions of Nietzsche who asks on what basis we can talk about truth if the traditional source of all truth, namely God, is dead. Nietzsche links the ideas of truth and goodness to that which encourages or causes life to flourish while falsity is that which stifles life. 'The falseness of an opinion is not for us any objection to it.' To him, 'The question is, how far an opinion is life-furthering, life-preserving, species-preserving, perhaps species-rearing' (Nietzsche 1927: 384). This biological or evolutionary view of truth maintains that struggle, delight in one's own power, exploitation, is life-furthering, while the so-called altruistic values, maintained by the Judaeo-Christian tradition, of chastity, meekness, 'turning the other cheek', concern for one's neighbour and so forth are thought to be a denial of life. Viewing life as a struggle to survive and to assert oneself, Nietzsche apparently did not consider the value of co-operation – a characteristic that at least some biologists consider responsible for the great reproductive success of the human species.

Heidegger also rejects the traditional view of truth, although he claims that he is going back to the original Greek understanding. In *Being and Time* Heidegger tries to show that the correspondence theory of truth is a development of a more primordial truth which is truth as *aletheia* or uncovering. Heidegger claims that those entities which are uncovered in the world are true but only in a derivatory sense. What is primarily true, what is truth, is Dasein itself –

the term Heidegger uses to refer to human reality. Thus rejecting the idea that truth is a value found primarily in statements made by man, Heidegger claims that 'Dasein is "in the truth"'. These ideas are reformulated by Heidegger in his essay 'On the Essence of Truth' where he asserts that '*The essence of truth is freedom*' (Heidegger 1977: 125). He acknowledges that this sounds strange since freedom is usually considered a human property, but he holds that 'Freedom now reveals itself as letting beings be'. i.e. freedom 'lets beings be the beings they are' (ibid.: 127). This letting-be can be and has been understood in different ways – it could be interpreted, for example, as a way of behaving that would please environmentalists, but it is still a rather puzzling theory to be held by a thinker who supported the political rise of Hitler.

In so far as he expressed a kind of contempt or distinterest in the correspondence theory of truth, Heidegger was in agreement with his Danish predecessor Søren Keirkegaard, who also dismisses the traditional correspondence theory of truth, which he calls 'objective truth'. Kierkegaard rejects any kind of truth that involves the detachment of the person seeking the truth. Thus he rejects the importance of mathematical and scientific truths, precisely those branches of knowledge which are generally thought to be the most certain. He has little interest in scientific or objective truth since he considers that this 'truth is always abstract'. Objective truth or knowledge for Kierkegaard is 'accidental' and its 'degree and scope is essentially indifferent' (Kierkegaard 1941: 177). Sooner or later objective truth is reduced to a tautology, to the logical form 'a or not a' or 'not both a and not a'. One must then turn one's back on objective truth, which means one must reject the supreme principle of objectivity, namely the law of non-contradiction.

Kierkegaard does not deny the certainty of objective truth, but the truth he seeks is precisely that truth which is based on objective uncertainty, what he calls 'essential truth' or 'subjectivity'. He claims that 'All essential knowledge relates to existence' (ibid. 176). For Kierkegaard, knowledge must have a relationship to the knower and the knower is the existing individual. Such knowledge is limited to ethical and ethical–religious knowledge. According to Kierkegaard, *'The objective accent is on WHAT is said, the subjective accent on HOW it is said'* (ibid. 181). Now this 'how' does not express the manner in which a person expresses a truth; it concerns rather the relationship between the individual and this truth. Kierkegaard asserts:

Objectively the interest is focused merely on the thought-content, subjectively on the inwardness. At its maximum this inward 'how' is the passion of the infinite, and the passion of the infinite is truth.

But the passion of the infinite is precisely subjectivity, and thus subjectivity becomes the truth . . . . Here is such a definition of truth: *An objective uncertainty held fast in an appropriation-process of the most passionate inwardness.*

(ibid.: 181–2)

What does all of this mean? For Kierkegaard, objective truth is something indifferent, something outside of the individual, something that can be learned and understood once, while subjective truth cannot be learned in this way since it is not a truth which resides in sentences. Indeed, we do not learn subjective truth, but we must 'appropriate' it. By choosing it continually we make it our own – it is not something we merely have or possess, but we become truth or, what is the same thing, it becomes a part of our existence, we live this truth.

Furthermore, we must make this truth our own with passion even if this truth is objectively uncertain, involving paradox and absurdity. But this description of truth is Kierkegaard's understanding of Christian faith.

The absurdity of Christianity, for Kierkegaard, is that the infinite becomes finite, the eternal came into being in time. The paradox of faith is precisely that, if one is capable of objectively proving what one believes, then faith has disappeared and become (objective) knowledge. In order to preserve one's faith, one must hold on to what is actually repulsive to objective understanding. This is also the risk involved in faith. In fact, Kierkegaard goes so far as to say that 'The absurd is precisely by its objective repulsion the measure of the intensity of faith in

inwardness' (ibid.: 189). Faith involves a further paradox since it is only when one feels oneself to be nothing before God that one becomes – to the greatest extent possible – a (true) individual.

Once one has faith or becomes an individual, then since the individual is 'higher than' or superior to the universal, which refers to universal ethical rules, then one can, in 'fear and trembling', suspend the universal. To explain his meaning, Kierkegaard uses the Biblical story of Abraham and Isaac. For Kierkegaard, this story shows

what a tremendous paradox faith is, a paradox which is capable of transforming a murder into a holy act well-pleasing to God . . . for faith begins precisely where thinking leaves off.

(Kierkegaard 1955: 64)

This story illustrates what Kierkegaard calls the 'teleological suspension of the ethical'.

One might agree with Kierkegaard in differentiating faith from knowledge and in pointing out that faith contains an element of doubt. One might also agree that religious faith contains a higher truth than scientific truth. So far, Kierkegaard might be saying nothing more than Thomas Aquinas, who maintained that certain truths, like that of the Trinity, cannot be understood by human reason but are a matter of revealed truth, the highest truth, a mystery. But Aquinas would not, I think, argue that the truth of these beliefs depends on the fact that they cannot be understood by reason; it just so happens that human reason, being finite, cannot fully understand them. Kierkegaard, on the other hand, seems to be saying that it is precisely because such truths are by their very nature not intelligible that they are true. He has, I think, carried the distinction between knowing and believing too far and with his dismissal of all that is rational, and his belief that in certain circumstances – even if these are very special and unusual circumstances – one can 'suspend' the ethical, he opens the door for the justification of all kinds of abuses.

Anselm (1929) 'Dialogue on truth [Dialogus de veritate]', in *Medieval Philosophers*, ed. and trans.

R. McKeon, vol. I, New York: Charles Scribner's Sons.

Aquinas, T. (1952) *Truth* [*Quaestiones Disputatae De Veritate*], trans. R.W. Mulligan, SJ, Chicago, IL: Henry Regnery.

Aristotle (1941) 'Metaphysics', in *The Basic Works of Aristotle*, ed. R. McKeon, New York: Random House.

Ferrater Mora, J. (1957) *Man at the Crossroads*, Boston, MA: Beacon Press.

——(1979) *Diccionario de filosofía*, Madrid: Alianza Editorial.

Hegel, F. (1949) *The Phenomenology of Mind* [*Phanomenolgie des Geistes*], trans. J.B. Baille, 2nd edn. London: Allen & Unwin and New York: Macmillan.

Heidegger, M. (1962) *Being and Time* [*Sein und Zeit*], trans. J. MacQuarrie and E. Robinson, New York and Evanston, IL: Harper & Row.

——(1977) 'On the essence of truth [*Vom Wesen der Wahrheit*', in *Martin Heidegger: Basic Writings*, ed. D.F. Krell, New York: Harper & Row.

James, W. (1909) *The Meaning of Truth: A Sequel to Pragmatism*, New York: Longmans, Green.

Kierkegaard, S. (1941) *Concluding Unscientific Postscript*, trans. D.S. Swenson and W. Lowrie, Princeton, NJ: Princeton University Press.

——(1955) *Fear and Trembling and The Sickness Unto Death*, trans. W. Lowrie, Garden City, NY: Doubleday, Anchor Books.

Nietzsche, F. (1927) *Beyond Good and Evil* in *The Philosophy of Nietzsche*, New York: Random House.

Plato (1961) 'Cratylus' and 'The Sophist', in *The Collected Dialogues of Plato*, ed. E. Hamilton and H. Cairns, Princeton, NJ: Princeton University Press, Bollingen Series LXXI.

Tarski, A. (1956) *Logic, Semantics, Metamathematics: Papers from 1923–1938*, trans. and ed. J.H. Woodger, Oxford: Oxford University Press.

Priscilla Cohn

UNEMPLOYMENT

In 1975 the number of unemployed people in Great Britain reached 1 million and there was a widespread feeling of panic up and down the country. From then on unemployment continued to rise relentlessly to a peak of just over 3¼ million, 12 per cent of the working population, at the beginning of 1986.

Between 1971 and 1990, however, nearly 3¼ million more people entered the labour force, many of them young people leaving school and married women looking for part-time work. But British industry and commerce has not grown enough to offer them the employment they want. The persistence of large numbers of people out of work has continued to be a matter of major concern to the public and to politicians.

Unemployment is not just a matter of the ups and downs of the trade cycle; it also has structural features. During the twenty years since 1971 manufacturing industry has declined by over a third, while the service sector has grown by a third, particularly in banking, finance and insurance. The nature of available employment has therefore changed substantially. Those who lost their jobs in heavy engineering, for example, have often found it impossible to retrain for newly emerging work in offices equipped with microelectronic technology.

There have also been a number of disturbing underlying features. Long-term unemployment has increased. In 1991 more than a quarter of men and a fifth of women were out of work for a year or more, and 10 per cent of the men were unemployed for more than three years. Ethnic minority unemployment has been high. The rate for West Indian and Guyanese people has been nearly double, and for Pakistanis and Bangladeshis nearly three times that for white people. Unemployment for men under twenty has also been double the average male rate.

The basis on which the official unemployment figures have been compiled has been frequently revised, however, with a major change in 1986 that reduced the total by around 200,000, and this has made comparisons difficult from one year to another.

The official GOVERNMENT response to unemployment in Britain has shown various elements.

Strenuous attempts have been made to restructure and revive the economy and to make it more competitive at an international level, so that more jobs could be opened up. Numerous grants and subsidies have also been made available for small businesses and for those starting up in employment.

In the early 1970s the government set up the Manpower Services Commission (MSC) to develop special programmes for the unemployed. Up to half a million people have been taken out of the unemployment figures at any one time as a result. But constant changes to the schemes, and uncertainty about what people would do afterwards if there was no job to go to, brought some dissatisfaction. Among the larger schemes were the Job Creation Programme, the Special Temporary Employment Programme, the Community Programme, the Youth Opportunities Programme and the Youth Training Scheme. More recently the work of the MSC has been absorbed into the Department of Employment and a greater emphasis has been given to training rather than to the provision of temporary employment itself.

Unemployment in its modern form is a feature of an advanced industrial society and is therefore a fairly recent phenomenon. It would be wrong to look for any discussion of it in the tradition of Christian thinking in former periods. In this century, however, it has quickly been seen by the churches as a major issue of concern. In *Christianity and Social Order*, for example, first published in 1942, Archbishop William Temple declared: 'Unemployment is the most hideous of our social evils'. Long-term unemployment, he continued, creates in the unemployed 'a sense that they have fallen out of the common life'. That they are not wanted 'has power to corrupt the soul of any man not already far advanced in saintliness' (1976: 33–4).

With the rise in unemployment in the 1970s after a long postwar period of growth and near full employment, the churches took up this issue again. Immediate responses centred around the counselling of those made redundant, offering advice about coping with the psychological experience, about claiming unemployment benefits and about taking steps to find alternative employment. Companies making people redundant were also advised about the most caring methods to use. In 1982 the ecumenical organization 'Church Action with the Unemployed' was founded to encourage churches to develop an informed and effective practical response. A leaflet circulated to 30,000 churches urged three main activities: pastoral care, the provision of work experience, and job creation. A network of contact people covering the whole country was set up to give local help to those wanting to get into action.

The practical experience of responding to widespread unemployment also led to deeper reflection. In 1977, *Work or What?*, a report from the British Council of Churches, for example, described the crisis in some detail and gave examples of a variety of government and church responses. It also questioned the continuing relevance of the work ethic in the rapidly changing world of new technology, and argued for its replacement with a 'life' ethic. Such an ethic would set work in the wider context of human fulfilment, of respect for creation and of a better balance with leisure, and would clarify the ends of economic activity, ensuring that the means used were consistent with them.

Some dramatic voices at the time even spoke of the collapse of work and the introduction of a leisure society in which machines would replace human labour altogether.

Two years later a further report, *Work and the Future*, produced by the Church of England, argued for experiment with new products and services, for the development of new small companies and new forms of industrial organization, for new opportunities for activities outside paid employment and for new opportunities for leisure.

Other voices called for a greater sharing of work among those competing for what was available. In *Work in Crisis*, published in 1982, Roger Clarke argued for a range of work-sharing options such as earlier retirement, longer periods of training for young people before they entered the labour market, a different pattern of relationship between paid employment, unemployment and retirement, and less systematic overtime.

Clarke proposed a 'contribution' ethic, rooted in the 'belief that our humanity does find fulfilment in doing things for others'. He continued, 'Part of the heresy of the Work Ethic was to emphasise the importance of the occupational at the expense of the informal, the convivial, the world of FAMILY and friends, the spheres of festivity and recreation, the blessedness of unstructured time' (1982: 196, 198). A contribution ethic would give a greater significance to these other aspects of life.

Developing the same theme in *The Future of Work*, published in 1984, Charles Handy put forward the idea of 'portfolios' of work, a mixture of paid job work, marginal work, including small private home-based jobs, craft and personal service activities, and gift work, such as housework, Do-it-Yourself and caring, done without any money changing hands.

All these responses from church sources accepted the revolution being brought about by new technology, and the apparently inevitable decline in the amount of paid employment available. Society had to accommodate these developments, to diversify into other activities and to find equitable ways of sharing the available work and the wealth created by it. Without such responses society was in danger of what Clarke called 'the fracture of fellowship'. Paid employment was to be seen as one activity among many in a full human life.

Further Christian reflection on the persistence of high unemployment led to a deeper study of the workings of the ECONOMY itself. Keynesian and monetarist economic theories were examined, and critical voices were raised about any system that had the effect of dividing people into 'haves' and 'have-nots', rich and poor, powerful and powerless.

But the practical realities of BUSINESS and employment soon brought a greater emphasis on the virtue of the wealth-creating process itself. Products and services could not be provided without work; WEALTH had to be created before it could be distributed. Economic efficiency was increasingly accepted as a legitimate goal, provided that it was kept within certain limits. In *The Creation of Wealth*, published in 1984, Brian Griffiths argued that 'Wealth creation within a market economy bounded by a concern for justice is compatible with Christian faith' (p. 117). Griffiths attributed unemployment to four factors: high inflation, structural changes in the world economy, the rising cost of labour, and high welfare benefits. Freeing up the market seemed to be the most hopeful way of creating more jobs and more wealth.

From its peak in 1986 unemployment in Britain declined by more than half before turning up again in mid-1990. As a result unemployment programmes were reduced in scope and the debate about a future leisure society declined in significance. It seemed that the management of the economy to increase competitiveness had indeed proved to be the most important and the most effective response. Earlier warnings of fundamental change were shown to be unfounded.

But the effects of sustained unemployment on the individual and on society have continued to cause concern. HOMELESSNESS and mental health problems, for example, often compound unemployment to produce a multi-faceted problem for society as a whole. The poverty that comes with inadequate access to money and to participation in normal society has been increasingly seen as the fundamental issue for public policy.

The ecumenical organization 'Church Action on Poverty', set up in 1982, has attempted to focus this perception into research and political campaigning to secure changes in policy and practice to help the least well-off. The Anglican report *Faith in the City*, published in 1985, also made numerous recommendations for action by government as well as for action within the churches.

Three features have characterized Christian reflection on unemployment in recent years. The basic importance of work, both for individuals and for society, has been firmly recognized, and the loss of employment has been seen as an important matter of concern. The immediate provision of personal care for unemployed people has been a natural initial Christian response.

This has quickly led, secondly, to a deeper examination of the social and structural causes of unemployment and to the attempt to engage with them. Questions have been raised about the means and the ends of all economic activity, and its place in life as a whole. A recognition of the basic goodness and importance of the

creation of wealth has been balanced with a concern about the equitable distribution of that wealth.

The values, thirdly, of community, fellowship, sharing and interdependence have formed the ethical basis of Christian thinking and action on these matters. The adequate provision of paid employment has not been seen just as a question of economic management, but as a fundamental part of the structure of a caring society as a whole.

If the numbers of people out of work remain high, and effective steps are not taken to provide work for all who reasonably want it, serious questions about the morality, and the future, of society will become increasingly important.

Bleakley, David (1983) *Work: The Shadow and the Substance*, London: SCM.

British Council of Churches and Church of England General Synod Board for Social Responsibility Industrial Committee (1977) *Work or What? A Christian Examination of the Employment Crisis*, London: CIO.

Church of England the Archbishop of Canterbury's Commission on Urban Priority Areas (1985) *Faith in the City*, Church House Publishing.

Church of England General Synod Board for Social Responsibility Industrial Committee (1979) *Work and the Future: Technology, World Development and Jobs in the Eighties*, London: CIO.

Clarke, Roger (1982) *Work in Crisis: Dilemma of a Nation*, Edinburgh: St Andrew Press.

Griffiths, Brian (1984) *The Creation of Wealth*, London: Hodder & Stoughton.

Moynagh, Michael (1985) *Making Unemployment Work*, Tring: Lion Publishing.

Seabrook, Jeremy (1982) *Unemployment*, London: Quartet Books.

Sinfield, Adrian (1981) *What Unemployment Means*, Oxford: Martin Robertson.

Temple, William (1976) *Christianity and Social Order*, London: Shepheard Walwyn/SPCK (first published 1942).

Paul Brett

UNITARIAN

Unitarianism is closely affiliated with the modern Western movement toward religious, political and intellectual freedom of thought and association. Initially, it denoted a religious view which denied the doctrine of the TRINITY.

Modern Unitarianism has evolved to include a much wider expression of religious experience and affirmation: the use of reason in religion, tolerance, belief in continuous revelation and in the moral obligation of individuals and communities for the common good.

Unitarians claim their roots from independent movements originating in Poland, Transylvania, England and the USA. Michael Servetus' *Errors of the Trinity* (1531) and the Socinian Polish Brethren's *Racovian Catechism* (1605) set the foundations of the Continental movement. They described the unity of God and the humanity of Christ and stated that eternal life was available through faith in conjunction with critical interpretation and understanding of scripture. Furthermore, these works emphasized that individuals have inherent goodness and the ability to make moral choices.

In Transylvania, at the Diet of Torda (1568), King Sigismund legalized Unitarianism as a part of the Reformed Church in Transylvania. The tolerant Sigismund was succeeded by the Báthorys who imprisoned and killed the Unitarian Francis Dávid (1510–79) for preaching against the worship of Jesus. Dávid's non-adorantist teachings remain in Transylvanian Unitarian Churches today. Dávid's struggle is representative of Unitarian commitment to freedom of conscience throughout the movement's history.

In England, records exist from as early as the fourteenth century of anti-Trinitarian martyrs, but the movement did not begin in earnest until John Biddle (1615–62) published *Twelve Arguments Drawn Out of the Scripture* (1647) and other works. Biddle gathered a small congregation which survived past his death and through numerous bouts of severe persecution linked to the political instability of England in the sixteenth and seventeenth centuries. Although Unitarians were excluded from the Act of Toleration (1689), they persisted in the Church of England and among Dissenting Churches. In 1719, dissenting ministers met at Salter's Hall to discuss whether ministers should conform to confessional statements or to scripture alone. The group taking the second view later moved towards Unitarianism. As William Chillingworth said: 'The Bible, the Bible, I say, the Bible only is the religion of Protestants.'

During the eighteenth century, the British and American forerunners of Unitarianism were fed by the Enlightenment renewal of classical thought and natural theology. Lord Herbert's Deism, John Locke's *The Reasonableness of Christianity*, John Tillotson's 'Natural religion', William Paley's *Evidences of Christianity*, David Hume's empiricism and Dugald Stewart's 'Common sense' philosophy provoked and excited liberal religionists to carve out their own theological niche between Old Light Calvinism and full-blown anarchic DEISM. The optimism and success of these liberals were demonstrated in the nineteenth century when Thomas Jefferson, a self-claimed Unitarian, asserted, 'I trust there is not a young man now living in the United States who will not die a Unitarian'.

Unitarianism was first organized into a congregational setting in England in 1774. Theophilus Lindsey (1723–1808) left his position in the Church of England, over a dispute of the Athanasian Creed, to found the Essex Street Chapel. Lindsey's successor, Thomas Belsham, and Joseph Priestley (1733–1804) led the Unitarian Church towards a Biblically based, Enlightenment theology augmented by reasonable enquiry into scripture, a firm belief in truth as experienced through the senses, and 'the simple humanity of Christ'. James Martineau (1805–1900) developed Unitarian thought further when he emphasized personal experience as a source of truth. In 1844, the Dissenter's Chapels Act was approved by Parliament, thus making the Unitarian Church an official religious presence in England.

American Unitarianism emerged from the families of the Puritans that left England in the hopes of building a Christian society in the New World. During the Great Awakening of the eighteenth century Charles Chauncey opposed Jonathan Edwards on the role of free will in regeneration. Some of those who followed Chauncey adopted the name 'Unitarian' after William Ellery Channing (1780–1842) delivered his sermon 'Unitarian Christianity' (1819). Channing stressed a critical approach to scriptural interpretation, the unity of God and the moral perfection of God and Christ. The movement was sparked by Channing's willingness to give its theology a name, and in 1825 the American Unitarian Association (AUA) was formed.

Channing was followed by two other seminal Unitarian thinkers: Ralph Waldo Emerson (1803–82) and Theodore Parker (1810–60). Emerson's 'Divinity School Address' (1838) lifted up personal experience as the core of all religion, while Parker's 'The Transient and the Permanent in Christianity' (1841) stated that church form and doctrine were transitory in relation to human innate knowledge of God, the moral law and the immortality of the SOUL.

In 1961 the AUA merged with the Universalist Church of America to form the Unitarian Universalist Association (UUA). The Universalists, who hold a doctrine of universal restoration, had been following a liberal religious path, parallel to that of the Unitarians, since their beginnings in the eighteenth century. The UUA, which also includes the Canadian Unitarians, is by far the largest Unitarian organization worldwide, although there are Unitarians in Transylvania, England and parts of Asia and Africa.

Unitarians have been committed to civil and religious liberty since the days of Servetus and the Polish Brethren; figures like Theodore Parker and Robert Wilberforce in the anti-slavery movement, Mary Wollstonecraft and Susan B. Anthony crusading for women's rights, Richard Price in prison reform, and John Haynes Holmes in conscientious objection to mandatory military service, continued the fight for freedom. More recently Unitarians have become involved in global issues such as the ENVIRONMENT and HUNGER. The denomination has also maintained its connections with science, empiricism and reason that it gained through Enlightenment figures like Priestley and Thomas Jefferson.

Unitarians are creedless; however, in 1985 the UUA adopted the following seven principles to guide their faith: 'the inherent worth and dignity of every person; JUSTICE, equity and compassion in human relations; acceptance of one another and encouragement to spiritual growth in our congregations; a free and responsible search for truth and meaning; the right of conscience and the use of the democratic process within our congregations and in society at large; the good of the world community with PEACE, liberty and justice for all; and respect for the interdependent web of all existence of which we are a part'. Unitarians draw on personal experience, the words and deeds of prophetic men and women, the world's religions (especially Judaeo-Christian) and humanist teachings for religious inspiration. Although Unitarianism began as a movement against a single doctrine, it has evolved into a religion which emphasizes method of belief and common values over doctrine.

Ahlstrom, S.E. and Carey, J.S. (1985) *An American Reformation: A Documentary History of Unitarian Christianity*, Middletown, CT: Wesleyan University Press.

Holt, R.V. (1958) *The Unitarian Contribution to Social Progress in England*, London: Lindsey Press.

Robinson, D. (1985) *The Unitarians and the Universalists*, Westport, CT: Greenwood Press.

Wilbur, E.M. (1945) *A History of Unitarianism: Socinianism and its Antecedents*, Cambridge, MA: Harvard University Press.

——(1977) *A History of Unitarianism in Transylvania, England, and America*, Boston, MA: Beacon Press.

Wright, C. (1986) *Three Prophets of Religious Liberalism: Channing, Emerson, Parker*, Boston, MA: Unitarian Universalist Association.

J. Ronald Engel
R.J.S. Montagnes

URBANIZATION

In everyday terms urbanization refers to an increase in the proportion of population living in settlements defined as cities or towns. Associated with this basic concept of a shift from country to town are ideas about changes in the economy, social organization and political structure, as well as contemporary CULTURE. Urbanization has also been interpreted as the diffusion of urban, commercial, culture into rural areas.

To be more precise, urbanization can be defined in terms of societal changes in demography (the ratio of urban to rural population deriving from the two elements of reproduction and migration); ECONOMY (the location of wealth generative capacity and the stimuli to further wealth generation); social organization and culture (the norms of FAMILY, neighbourhood, religion, work unit, political representation and STATE rights, as well as attitudes to MODERNITY); political structure (the relationship between state institutions and those governed).

There is also the environmental aspect. To be 'urban' is to live in a society dominated by the problems of a densely built environment. These include the provision of food and water, transport systems, pollution, EDUCATION and housing provision and public health needs, as well as those of MARKETS in property. Lewis (1965) defined urbanization in terms of these services and the people's access to them. On these criteria very large settlements, such as refugee camps, might have very low 'urban' ratings, and very many urban residents are not 'urbanized'.

The first sociologists associated urbanization with the transition from pre-industrial SOCIETY to modern industrial society. The earliest writers such as Marx and Engels in the 1840s had associated the great cities with industrialization and the emergence of a working CLASS capable of radical political organization. The dominance of capitalist social relations was assured by urbanization. A second wave of scholars – Tonnies, Simmel and Weber in Germany, Durkheim in France – in the period 1880–1920 linked urbanization with the emergence of the centralized nation-state, the predominance of the money economy, BUREAUCRACY and the rationalization of modern society, and the shift to a society in which social consensus was ceasing to depend on traditional institutions.

An essay by Simmel (1904), 'Metropolis and mental life' (Sennett 1969), presented sociological attitudes to urbanization. He traced the connection between the expansion of the money economy, urban growth, and the development of a 'metropolitan type of individuality'. In the CITY 'man' had to adapt to an existence founded on calculation, precision in personal affairs and daily discipline. In addition, 'man' had to become more sophisticated – reserved in dealing with others, blasé in attitude to daily affairs, capable of reacting intellectually to the stimuli of urban life. He argued that modern cities caused a high level of individuation: style and personality were both exaggerated in a social world in which the traditional markers of status – birth, place and religion – had been superseded.

These ideas were transmitted by Park (1915) to Chicago, then a centre for the new academic discipline of sociology. As the USA became the world's premier industrial economy, so the cities expanded at unprecedented rate. Migrants from the 'Old World' competed for jobs and living space in cities whose lifestyle contrasted starkly with those of the farms and small towns of rural America. In this context urbanization was assigned a progressive role in the creation of a new society. The imagery was that of the city as a melting pot in which different ethnic and religious groups would be assimilated into the culture of the American Dream. Mobility and the market processes which channelled urban residents into dense inner city ghettoes and then towards the outer suburbs in which mass-produced commodities became the symbols of status were the crucial elements in the process of urbanization.

Park and his pupils Wirth (1938) and Redfield (1947) made specific predictions as to urban and rural culture (see Sennett 1969 for key statements). These can be summarized as follows: family ties would be weakened so that birth rates would fall and small households would predominate; the local neighbourhood would lose significance; social participation would be through work, commercial entertainment or voluntary groups; and political association would increasingly derive from class-status alignments rather than those of ethnic or religious loyalties. In the city no one group could call on an individual's allegiance. Typically, social interaction would be segmented, i.e. in many different settings without cross connection. Therefore the mass MEDIA would be crucial in establishing public opinion. In more modern terminology, urbanization was seen as 'privatization' – a social and political culture in which people jealously safeguard the rights to privacy and individual determination of needs, and in which public, collective life is restricted.

The relevance of this concept of urbanization to the world's affluent societies is disputed. There are tendencies in modern urban life that confirm this analysis: affluence has allowed family members to live apart in small households; widespread car-ownership permits regional rather than neighbourhood association; friendship and professional networks may be maintained on an international scale; political life is increasingly conducted through the medium of television rather than public meetings or local associations. Conversely, one can point to the resilience of family ties, the ongoing involvement with neighbourhood affairs and the salience of ethnic identities in society and politics. North American cities never became the social melting pots predicted, and the relatively homogeneous and secular societies of Europe are coming to terms with the pluralism caused by labour migration, assertive claims to national recognition and religious FUNDAMENTALISM. In these respects they are becoming more similar to the post-colonial societies of North Africa, the Middle East and South Asia where urban politics has been patterned by ethnic competition (Alavi 1991). Ethnic identities are defined and redefined as groups contend for access to privileged positions. Urbanization is increasingly associated with ethnic conflict and the revival of religious legitimacy to state power.

As more came to be known about urbanization outside Europe and North America there was scepticism about the assumptions as to modernization and the rupture of traditional allegiances. Some of the most interesting analyses of urban MIGRATION derive from research in Southern Africa in the 1950s (Mitchell 1956; Mayer 1961; Epstein 1969). There the towns had been developed as nodes within a circulatory system of labour migration in which urban workers were able and encouraged to retain connections with their birthplaces to which they returned in times of economic stress and at various stages in the life-cycle. A labour migrant's life and labour history could alternate between town and country as the worker moved in and out of urban employment to satisfy kinship obligations. Town and country had to be seen as one 'social field' in which migrants maintained networks.

Several conclusions followed from this approach: (a) urbanization and rural development were inextricably linked, not opposing social situations; (b) the migrant experienced urban social life as a complex of networks of social association; (c) these networks permitted the reconstitution of 'traditional' social institutions within the limits of the formal order of the town and the restrictions of spatial separation from the districts of origin; (d) urbanization did give migrants a certain choice of career and lifestyle: they might remain encapsulated in close-knit networks enforcing conformity to 'tribal' morality, or adopt a culture which tolerated receptivity to industrial European institutions (Mayer 1961).

In East London (Cape Province) Mayer had identified two distinct groups of Xhosa migrants. One, which he termed 'School', was receptive to Christianity and formal education; the other, termed 'Red', 'seemed to reflect a wish to remain bound by the structure from which their migration could have liberated them. Their way of organising themselves amounts to voluntarily rebuilding something as like the home system as possible.' The split was evident even among brothers and sisters – ultimately these lifestyles were personal decisions.

These insights into migration have proved valuable in studying urbanization elsewhere, notably in Latin America, but also in Britain. Studies of migration to Britain from Pakistan, Kashmir or the Punjab (see Ballard 1987) emphasize the connections between the economy and culture of origin and that of residence. Household strategies for work, investment, marriage and retirement straddle the continents. Modern technology permits close contact between the towns and villages of South Asia and the neighbourhoods of British towns so that urbanization is not the decisive move experienced a century ago. Therefore the people from South Asia have experienced all the cleavages of their homelands – class, caste, region, political faction, religion and sect – as well as those fostered in the response to the alien and largely hostile environment of the British city.

It is now accepted that urbanization is a much more complex process of social change than that predicted by the early sociologists. The freedoms of the modern society, epitomized in the anonymity of the big city, include the freedom to affiliate to the past, re-enact older moralities and re-create 'tradition' in a modern, urban, idiom. Accordingly, one of the features of urban residence may be enhanced religiosity. This may be seen, for instance, in disputes over control of a mosque or gurdwara, or the greater discipline imposed on the activities or dress of women. Various writers have noted that women may be more oppressed in modern cities than in villages or small towns (Alavi 1991). Women's withdrawal from the labour force and their seclusion in the house are a mark of family success and urban respectability. The same tendency towards greater religious discipline in town was also noted by Lewis in Mexico City.

The other world region in which urbanization has been a focus of study is Latin America. There has been persistent interest in the self-help housing initiatives which transformed the cities into the sprawling shanty-town aggregates of, for example, Rio or Mexico City, and in the political processes by which élites maintained power and these new suburbs, housing peasant migrants, were incorporated into the urban system. Castells (1983) and Friedmann (1989) have emphasized the radical potential of these 'barrio' movements. Their informal work organization, self-build housing and community initiatives, their co-operative ethos and reliance on relationships of trust, are interpreted as an alternative to the bureaucratic formal model of urbanization. It is argued that the barrio movements, supported by other interests (such as the liberation theologians of the Catholic Church), are claiming citizen rights which will form the basis of an 'autonomous' rather than a 'dependent' urbanization. Other writers (Roberts 1977) remain sceptical about the radicalism of the barrios, stressing their reliance on political patronage, the dependence of informal economies on core institutions and the inclusion of these enclaves into the property markets and formal politics of the city. There has been little discussion of the role of the churches. The main issues have been the rapidity of INDUSTRIALIZATION and urban development and the denial of CITIZEN-SHIP rights to the mass of the population.

In conclusion, the early writers believed that there was an inevitable change in the people who came from a small-scale 'folk' culture into the culture of the city. This change might have several stages – from a receptivity to Christian teachings in a 'bush' mission, for example, or curiosity about Western consumer culture, through the move to work in a town, encapsulation in a kin/ethnic network, to, finally, the internalization of 'urban' norms of conduct,

consumption and culture. Urbanization was a social process with a definite end. That end was modernity: a world of individual freedoms limited by the rule of law, the operation of a market economy, the discipline of bureaucratic organizations, and the social constraints of a class-status hierarchy whose ordering principle was that of individual achievement. Recent writers, with the benefit of more systematic detailed research and awareness of historical variation, are more cautious about this paradigm of social change. Its limitations are most apparent in Islamic societies where urbanization is now associated with a resurgence of religious fundamentalism.

The growth of cities and economic modernization intersect with religious beliefs very differently in particular societies in specific historical epochs. Therefore there is recognition that instead of a universal process labelled 'urbanization' there are many studies of aspects of urban migration and social change which contribute to an understanding of religious organization and belief.

Alavi, H. (1991) 'Pakistani women in a changing society', in D. Hastings and P. Werbner (eds) *Economy and Culture in Pakistan*, London: Macmillan.

Ballard, R. (1987) 'The political economy of migration', in J. Eades (ed.) *Migration, Workers and the World Order*, London: Tavistock.

Castells, M. (1983) *The City and the Grassroots*, London: Arnold.

Epstein, A. (1969) 'Urbanisation and social change in Africa', in G. Breese (ed.) *The City in Newly Developing Countries*, New York: Prentice-Hall.

Friedmann, J. (1989) 'The Latin American "barrio" movement', *International Journal of Urban and Regional Research* 13.

Lewis, O. (1965) 'Further observations on the folk–urban continuum', in P. Hauser and D. Schnore (eds) *The Study of Urbanisation*, New York: Wiley.

Mayer, P. (1961) *Townsmen or Tribesmen*, Oxford: University Press; extract reprinted in G. Germani (ed.) *Modernization, Urbanization and the Urban Crisis*, Boston, MA: Little, Brown, 1973.

Mitchell, J.C. (1956) 'Urbanisation, detribalisation and stabilisation in Southern Africa'; reprinted in P. Meadows and E. Mizruchi (eds) *Urbanism, Urbanization and Change*, New York: Addison Wesley, 1976.

Roberts, B. (1977) *Cities of Peasants*, London: Arnold.

Sennett, R. (1969) *Classic Essays in the Culture of Cities*, New York: Appleton Century Crofts.

Rosemary Mellor

USURY

The taking of interest in either goods or money is found from the beginning of recorded history. The Code of Hammurabi (*c.*1700 BC) has many provisions relating to interest aiming at preventing unfair enforcement. In the Hebrew Bible the taking of interest between fellow Israelites is prohibited, but it is allowed with non-Jews (Exodus 22: 25; Deuteronomy 23: 19–20; Leviticus 25: 36–7; Ezekiel 18: 8; Psalms 15: 5). The Deuteronomists wanted full remission of debts every seven years (Deuteronomy 15), and the authors of Leviticus every fifty (Leviticus 25), in order to prevent debt SLAVERY, a common feature of Ancient Near Eastern civilizations.

Usury is not condemned as such in the New Testament, but Jesus put remission of debt at the heart of the prayer he taught his disciples, and condemned ruthless creditors (Matthew 18). There are the severest warnings against riches (Mark 10: 25; Luke 6: 24, 18: 23; James 5), and money is called 'the root of all evil' (1 Timothy 6: 10). This helps to explain why many of the Church Fathers condemn usury outright on the ground that it contravenes Scripture and breaks all the laws of charity (Tertullian C. Marc 4.17; Cyprian Strom 2.18; Chrysostom Hom 57 on Matthew; Nyssa Oratorio c Usuarios). Augustine regards it as a CRIME (Augustine, on Psalms 128). The Council of Nicea (325) ordered usurious clergy to be deposed, and the Council of Carthage (345) condemned its practice by laity. Later Councils reiterated this, the third Lateran Council (1179) denying usurers the sacrament or Christian burial and the second Council of Lyons (1274) forbidding the letting of property to foreign usurers.

The economy of Europe began to grow in the eleventh century with greater political stability. As states became centralized so rulers, and even popes, found the need to borrow money. Aquinas, in the thirteenth century, set the tone for much later teaching in repeating Aristotle's condemnation of usury as unnatural. Money is made for exchange, and to lend it on interest is to sell what does not exist. This leads to inequality and is contrary to JUSTICE (*Summa Theologiae* 2.2 Qu 78, Art. 1; Aristotle, *Politics* 1.3, 1.10). Though usury is sinful, it is not sinful to take a loan so long as this is done for a good cause (78, Art. 4). This prevarication enabled Jewish moneylenders to be simultaneously employed and vilified. Developing economies soon made it difficult to exist without taking interest. In the fifteenth century Franciscan schemes to help the poor found it necessary to charge a small amount of interest to cover expenses. Despite this the medieval canonists all condemn usury and place it alongside adultery, theft and murder. It was allowed only to cover actual losses, or the profit forgone by making the loan.

In 1524 Luther's great tract *On Trade and Usury* appeals to the medieval tradition. Usury is 'grossly contrary to God's word, contrary to reason and every sense of justice, and springs from sheer wantonness and greed'. Twenty years later, however, and writing from the merchant city of Geneva, Calvin argued that the Biblical texts relating to usury have to be understood in their context, that conditions have changed and that restrictions on usury were too severe. Both Protestants and Catholics now distinguished between loans for production and loans for consumption, and argued that in the former case capital was productive. Usury was neither contrary to Scripture nor to NATURAL LAW, but must be used only under the strictest conditions so that the poor are not oppressed. Benedict XIV reiterated scholastic warnings against usury in 1745, and usury laws remained on the statute books throughout Europe for another two centuries (in England until 1854), but fell everywhere into desuetude. Within PROTESTANTISM attacks on usury ceased and the marketplace came to be seen as a moral battlefield where the righteous could prove their mettle. When Bentham wrote his *Defence of Usury* in 1787 he felt no need to offer a moral defence of it. Money he regarded as on a par with any other form of goods. When usury is not legalized it forces people into criminal practices, and the usury laws expose a useful CLASS of people to unnecessary SUFFERING and disgrace.

The principal justification of usury is

pragmatic. Appeals are made to the tremendous advances achieved by CAPITALISM. These could not have happened, it is argued, without interest, which is necessary to attract investors to make their capital available. Interest can be regarded as a charge on services, or a kind of danger money for putting capital at risk. Moral objections, however, remain cogent. According to the labour theory of value it is labour which creates value. Under the system of interest, however (stocks and shares), money accrues to the rich where no labour is involved. Such earnings are therefore parasitic. More importantly, Aquinas' contention that usury leads to the growth of inequality has been confirmed by careful contemporary studies. The present operations of interest lead to a systematic transfer of WEALTH from those who have less to those who have more. This occurs within northern hemisphere economies, but has reached catastrophic proportions in the relation between southern hemisphere economies and the International Monetary Fund and the World Bank. Countries such as Brazil pay more on interest per annum than their entire gross national product. The present indebtedness of Third World countries is a major threat to world ecology, as the attempt to meet interest payments leads to the reckless consumption of natural resources. Interest-free economies have been envisaged for many years. Proudhon (1809–65) wished to replace interest by worker co-operatives with their own banks. The need to have sufficient capital for research and development is clear, as is the need for some mechanism for saving, but moving beyond the present framework of interest and debt has been recognized as an urgent contemporary task.

Aquinas (1967) *Summa Theologiae*, vol. 38, *Injustice*, London: Eyre & Spottiswoode.
Clavero, B. (1984) *Usura: del uso economico de la religion en la historia*, Madrid: Tecnos.
Divine, T.F. (1959) *Interest: An Historical and Analytical Study*, Milwaukee, WI: Marquette University Press.
George, S. (1992) *The Debt Boomerang*, London: Pluto.
Green, F. and Sutcliffe, B. (1987) *The Profit System*, Harmondsworth: Penguin.
Jones, N.L. (1989) *God and the Moneylenders: Usury and the Law in Early Modern England*, Oxford: Blackwell.
Luther, M. (1962) *On Trade and Usury*, Luther's Works, vol. 45, Philadelphia, PA: Muhlenberg Press.
Nelson, B.N. (1949) *The Idea of Usury: From Tribal Brotherhood to Universal Otherhood*, Princeton, NJ: Princeton University Press.
Noonan, J.T. (1957) *The Scholastic Analysis of Usury*, Cambridge, MA: Harvard University Press.
Robertson, J. (1990) *Future Wealth*, London: Cassell.
Tawney, R.H. (1964) *Religion and the Rise of Capitalism*, Harmondsworth: Penguin.
Weber, M. (1976) *The Protestant Ethic and the Spirit of Capitalism*, London: Allen & Unwin.

T.J. Gorringe

VEGETARIANISM

Vegetarianism has become a generic term for a family of related dietary restrictions grounded in a variety of ethical and other concerns. 'Demi-vegetarians' abstain at least from red meat, and some also from white meat. 'Vegetarians' abstain from both red and white meat as well as fish and, usually, from slaughterhouse by-products such as leather and gelatine. 'Vegans', or 'pure vegetarians', abstain not only from all products and by-products of slaughter, but also from other animal products such as milk and honey. The coherence of each position is dependent upon the concerns in which it is grounded. There are four main areas of such concerns.

Health Until comparatively recently, the consensus amongst health specialists was that some form of animal protein was required in order to live or live well. This consensus has been shaken by the increasing number of studies which extol the medical value of animal-free diets. Studies have identified lower rates of diet-related cancer, especially colon and rectal cancer, and prostate cancer among vegetarians (see Giovannucci *et al*. 1993; Chang-Claude and Frentzel-Beyme 1993). Coronary heart disease is more common among non-vegetarians than among vegetarians, probably a result of the latter's lower serum cholesterol levels (see Hostmark *et al*. 1993). Other health advantages include reduced rates of obesity, hypertension and diabetes (see, for example, Sciarrone *et al*. 1993). Current knowledge indicates that a balanced vegetarian diet incurs no specific health risks and offers some significant advantages.

'Do you not know that you are God's temple and that God's Spirit dwells in you? If any one destroys God's temple, God will destroy him. For God's temple is holy, and that temple you are' (1 Corinthians 3: 16–17). These and other scriptural verses (1 Corinthians 6: 19 and Ephesians 2: 22) are sometimes interpreted as a warning not only against SUICIDE but also against any 'defilement' of the body including intoxication and other activities harmful to the body – hence, for example, the long-standing vegetarianism of Seventh-day ADVENTISTS who have also been pioneers in health food reform. Given that a balanced vegetarian diet is healthier than a non-vegetarian one, not only can vegetarians coherently hold this position but also anyone who uses this argument for any purpose must be vegetarian in order to be consistent. However, the modern world presents insuperable problems with the demand of non-defilement of the body: widespread air, land and water pollution mean that even breathing, eating and drinking can be in some measure harmful to the body.

Spiritual or ascetic Within Eastern culture, vegetarianism has an established place, especially within Jainism and, to a lesser degree, within Buddhism and Hinduism. Jainism is perhaps the clearest example of a religious tradition fully committed both to non-violence and to ASCETICISM; following the path of purification involves the total renunciation of VIOLENCE to all life forms. Despite a strong ascetic ideal within Christianity, it has never formally endorsed vegetarianism, although some strands affirm the spiritual value of abstention from meat. For example, the Rule of St Benedict forbade the eating of 'the flesh of four-footed animals' except by 'the sick who are very weak' (1976: 46). This qualification indicates that vegetarianism was not regarded as inherently wrong in itself but rather that it should be pursued as part of an ascetic regime. The spiritual gain of such self-denial has been variously affirmed within Christianity (see Sorrell 1988).

Contemporary vegetarianism draws upon this ascetic motif in terms of developing the notion of human responsibility for the well-being of the ENVIRONMENT. Meat-eating, it is sometimes claimed, is the 'rich man's food' obtained through unfair trading relations in which cash crops are bought at low prices in the Third World in order to provide animal foodstuffs in the First (see Lappé 1982). (Interestingly enough it is now suggested by some New Testament scholars that the rich/poor distinction may lie behind part of the food controversy concerning meat in, for example, Paul's letter to the Romans (see, for example, Ziesler 1989; and the Matthean critique of privilege, Matthew 23–5).) Animals are seen as protein machines in reverse consuming vital crops which could themselves sustain indigenous populations.

Vegetarianism is sometimes urged as a moral restraint in the face of an increasingly indulgent Western lifestyle.

Ecological There are two specific arguments from ecological concerns to vegetarianism. The first concerns the present system of intensive FARMING which is efficient in short-term (cash) costs but highly inefficient in the long term since it is energy-intensive rather than labour-intensive and hence contributes to the pollution of our planet (see Johnson 1991). The second argument coincides with ascetic appeals (see above) and maintains that, if enough Westerners became vegetarians, worldwide food distribution will become more equitable. It is estimated by vegetarian societies that to produce one tonne of beef requires on average ten tonnes of grain. It is also calculated that the biosphere could support around 6 billion people if they all had a vegetarian diet, but if 15 per cent of our calories came from animal products the biosphere could support only 4 billion people. If 35 per cent of our calories came from animal products, as in North America today, the figure would fall to 2.5 billion (see Meyers 1990). If these calculations are correct, it means that the practice of producing meat has a direct negative effect on the health and life-expectancy of a fair proportion of the world's population.

Such calculations, however, fail to acknowledge the complexity of existing trading arrangements based on inequitable systems of supply and demand. Despite the evident increase in vegetarianism from the 1970s onwards, it is unclear that the political will exists to pioneer alternative economic and food production policies. Morally, however, it is debatable whether the fact that the rest of the world may refuse to change its habits justifies (or exculpates) the individual's participation in those habits.

Animal-centred Animal-centred – or 'ethical' – vegetarianism is the abstention from the products of the exploitation of non-human sentient life. Its different varieties derive from different extensions of the notions of 'exploitation' and 'sentient life'. For demi-vegetarians, 'exploiting' is eating, and 'sentient life' covers mammals and, for some, birds. For vegetarians, 'exploiting' is killing, and 'sentient life' includes mammals, birds and fish. For vegans, 'exploiting'

involves killing and other uses such as the 'perpetual pregnancy' method of milk production, and 'sentient life' is seemingly inclusive of all but plant life.

Christianity's view of the status of animals has comprised both negative and positive strands (*see* ANIMAL RIGHTS). Aquinas' conviction that animals are not possessed of immortal souls laid the groundwork for the Cartesian view of animals as non-sentient, non-conscious automata, and therefore worthless (see Descartes, 'Discourse on Method', 1965). On the other hand, it is the seemingly non-rational, non-communicative nature of animals that moved St Richard of Chichester to pity 'innocent creatures' who have done nothing to deserve death at our hands, and cannot even complain (see Butler 1946: 157). The negative strand has unquestionably dominated systematic and moral theology to the point that Christianity has never formally endorsed animal-centred concerns. Indeed, Calvin wrote of the 'insupportable tyranny' of ethical vegetarianism which closed up God's own storehouse 'by mortal man, who is not able to create even a snail or a fly' (Calvin 1847: 199–200).

There have been a minority of Christians throughout the centuries, however, who have advocated vegetarianism for ethical reasons. Christian notions of generosity and charity informed the founding of animal protection societies, including the SPCA (as it then was) in 1824, and generally assisted the rise of sensibility towards animals throughout the nineteenth and twentieth centuries. As early as 1809, the Bible-Christian Church, founded by an Anglican priest, William Cowherd, made vegetarianism compulsory among its members. Drawing inspiration from Genesis 1: 29, its church leaders maintained that vegetarianism represented the purity of diet which God had commanded at the beginning of creation (see *History of the Philadelphia Bible-Christian Church*, 1922). There has been a long history of Christian appreciation of the inherent worth of other creatures because of their divine creation. The origins of this outlook are manifest in the early and medieval periods (see Sorrell 1988), most typically expressed in the life of St Francis of Assisi. This viewpoint has begun to receive systematic expression in modern times in terms of reverence for life or life-centred ethics (see Schweitzer 1967; Linzey 1976, 1987, 1994; McDaniel 1989; Birch *et al.* 1990).

The ambivalence of the Christian tradition towards vegetarianism may stem from contrasting views within the Bible. In the Hebrew Bible, humanity is given 'dominion' over the rest of creation including other animals (Genesis 1: 26–9) and prescribed a vegetarian diet (1: 29–30); only after the Flood did God's command include the taking of animals for food when necessary (9: 3). Humans are still held accountable for any blood shed (9: 4–5). The right to take animal flesh as food appears as a concession to human sinfulness and hence there arose the continuing hope of final peace and harmony among creation (cf. Hosea 2: 18; Isaiah 11: 6f.; Ezekiel 34: 25f.; see also Baker 1975). It seems that vegetarianism is the ideal presented in the Hebrew Bible (see Linzey 1994) and some modern Jewish vegetarians (e.g. Kook 1979) argue that abstention from meat is one step towards realizing the peaceable kingdom of the prophets. The Hebrew Bible, then, views meat eating as a departure from God's original will, a necessary evil, and looks forward to a peaceable age when it will no longer be necessary.

However, the New Testament seems to accept meat eating as ethically justifiable. Jesus is not presented as a vegan or vegetarian; the gospel accounts record that he ate fish, and if the passover meals he ate were traditional ones he would have eaten red meat. Furthermore, the early church debates over meat (Romans 14 and 1 Corinthians 8–9) concern what sort of meat could be eaten, not whether meat eating is itself ethically justifiable. Some theologians hold that contemporary vegetarianism represents a Christ-like response to the evils of modern animal exploitation and can be justified on theological grounds: 'since animals belong to God, have value to God and live for God, their needless destruction is sinful' (Linzey 1987: 146). The consumption of meat may have been necessary for survival in first-century Palestine (and so was not an issue), but in the modern Western world a vegetarian diet can easily be pursued without medical or nutritional disadvantage.

A theological argument against vegetarianism can be constructed along the lines of natural law ethics, similar to a line of argument used by some secular environmental ethicists: because nature is a predatory system, it is natural for humans, as well as animals, to consume sentient life. Humans must live in accordance with the workings of their natural (divinely ordained) environment and human nature (Ferre 1986; Rolston III 1988). However, few theological ethicists are convinced that the current natural order is as God intended, which is why NATURAL LAW ethics has moved from 'physicalism' to 'personalism' in the last fifty years. A natural law argument against vegetarianism fails to take account of the Biblical account of the FALL (see, especially, Genesis 6: 11–14) and the prophets' vision of a future peaceable kingdom (see, especially, Isaiah 11: 1–9), as well as ignoring the evidence that the planet cannot adequately support the number of people currently living on it (not to mention estimates of future populations) while vegetarianism is still so comparatively rare.

Baker, John Austin (1975) 'Biblical attitudes to nature', in Hugh Montefiore (ed.) *Man and Nature*, London: Collins.

Birch, Charles and Eakin, William McDaniel Jay B. (eds) (1990) *Liberating Life: Contemporary Approaches to Ecological Theology*, Maryknoll, NY: Orbis.

Bonaventure, St (1978) *The Life of St Francis*, London: SPCK.

Butler, Alban (1946) *Lives of the Saints*, revised by Herbert Thurston and Donald Attwater, New York: Kennedy.

Calvin, John (1847) *Commentaries on the First Book of Moses*, vol. 1, Edinburgh: Calvin Translation Society.

Chang-Claude, J. and Frentzel-Beyme, R. (1993) 'Dietary and lifestyle determinants of mortality among German vegetarians', *International Journal of Epidemiology* 22(2): 228–36.

Descartes, René (1965) 'Discourse on method', in *Philosophical Works of Descartes*, vol. 1, ed. and trans. E.S. Haldane and G.R.T. Ross, Cambridge: Cambridge University Press.

Dombrowski, Daniel A. (1985) *Vegetarianism: The Philosophy Behind the Ethical Diet*, Boston, MA: University of Massachusetts Press and London: Thorsons.

Ferré, Frederick (1986) 'Moderation, morals and meat', *Inquiry* 29: 391–406.

Giovannucci, E. *et al.* (1993) 'A prospective study of

dietary fat and risk of prostate cancer', *Journal of the National Cancer Institute* 85(19): 1571–9.

History of the Philadelphia Bible-Christian Church, 1817–1917 (1922), Philadelphia, PA: J.P. Lippincott.

Hostmark, A.T. *et al.* (1993) 'Reduced plasma fibrinogen, serum peroxides, lipids and apolipoproteins after a 3-week vegetarian diet', *Plant Foods and Human Nutrition* 43(1): 55–61.

Johnson, Andrew (1991) *Factory Farming*, Oxford: Basil Blackwell.

Kook, Abraham Isaac (1979) 'Fragments of light: a view as to the reasons for The Commandments', in *The Lights of Penitence, The Moral Principles, Lights of Holiness: Essays, Letters, and Poems*, ed. and trans. Ben Zion Bokser, London: SPCK.

Lappé, Frances M. (1981) *Diet for a Small Planet*, 2nd edn, New York: Ballantine.

Linzey, Andrew (1976) *Animal Rights: A Christian Assessment*, London: SCM.

——(1987) *Christianity and the Rights of Animals*, London: SPCK and New York: Crossroad.

——(1994) *Animal Theology*, London: SCM and Chicago, IL: University of Illinois Press.

——and Regan, Tom (eds) (1989) *Animals and Christianity: A Book of Readings*, London: SPCK and New York: Crossroad.

McDaniel, Jay B. (1989) *Of God and Pelicans: A Theology of Reverence for Life*, Louiseville, KY: John Knox/Westminster.

Myers, Norman (1990) *Mass Extinctions: Palaeography, Palaeoclimatology, Palaeoecology*, Amsterdam: Elsevier.

Rolston III, Holmes (1988) *Environmental Ethics: Duties to and Values in the Natural World*, Philadelphia, PA: Temple University Press.

Rule of St Benedict (1976) ed. and trans. Justin McCann, Spiritual Masters Series, London: Sheed & Ward.

Schweitzer, Albert (1967) *Civilization and Ethics*, ed. and trans. C.T. Campion, 2nd edn, London: Unwin.

Sciarrone, S.E. *et al.* (1993) 'Biochemical and neurohormonal responses to the introduction of a lacto-ovovegetarian diet', *Journal of Hypertension* 11(8): 849–60.

Sorrell, Roger D. (1988) *St Francis of Assisi and Nature: Tradition and Innovation in Western Christian Attitudes toward the Environment*, Oxford: Oxford University Press.

Ziesler, John (1989) *Paul's Letter to the Romans*, London: SCM.

Andrew Linzey
Jonathan Webber

VIOLENCE

In the same way that one person's 'terrorist' is another person's 'freedom fighter', so one person's 'violence' is another person's 'just order'. These counter understandings or definitions are embodied in narratives that opposing sides tell in conflicts in many parts of the world. Thus, attempts to define 'violence' outside of any context of language and culture-in-use must be considered sorely inadequate.

Certain actions, such as killing another person, are generally thought of as 'violent'. Yet, this leaves much unexplained and many distinctions and disagreements masked. For instance, those killed in automobile accidents are not said to have died violent deaths in the same way as those shot to death in, say, a robbery attempt.

The same holds true with 'coercion'. Although violent acts are generally considered 'coercive', not all coercive acts are thought of as violent. For example, a criminal and a police officer may commit the same act, and yet their differing status leads us to call the former 'violence' and the latter 'enforcement of the law'. Their actions may be equally coercive, and yet assigned radically different moral status. Thus we see that our very descriptions of some rather than other acts as 'violent' or 'coercive' presumes prior commitments to certain kinds of acts which we wish to justify.

One of the commitments that greatly influences society's understanding of what constitutes violence is the commitment to uphold 'order' (however we define it); societies tend to equate upholding order with the preservation of PEACE, and thus cannot imagine that 'upholding order' might be inherently violent. For example, from an Israeli perspective, if there are no disturbances or riots in the West Bank, then one presumes a state of peace. On the other hand, from a Palestinian perspective, which involves a very different understanding of 'order', the very occupation of the West Bank by the Israeli army is a continual state of 'violence'. From a Palestinian perspective, the lack of disturbances or riots at any one point in time in no way makes the current 'order' in the West Bank less violent. Thus, when Palestinians employ specific acts of violence against the Israeli forces, they justify their acts of violence by claiming that their actions are a response to and an attempt to change the 'violence' of the current occupation in the West Bank and to install a regime of order and peace. This example should serve to remind us of the context-dependent nature of concepts such as 'violence'. For the meaning of 'violence' will often depend on who is doing the defining.

The same issues arise in distinguishing 'violence' from 'POWER'. In matters of CIVIL DISOBEDIENCE, those committed to 'non-violence' will distinguish the use of power from the use of violence and employ non-violent forms of power. They will argue that power need not always be viewed negatively as inevitably violent. Hannah Arendt develops a compelling theoretical account distinguishing violence from power, arguing that people resort to violence when they are stripped of any other source of power. According to Arendt, appropriate exercises of power depend upon consent and co-operation, and the rise of violence is an indication that those forms of power have been lost.

Christian conceptions of what is 'violent' and their approach to dealing with violence will often be at fundamental odds with the definitions of violence and the practices of other communities. For example, some societies have laws which recognize the state's right to execute its political opponents. The same societies may deny that a person raping their spouse is violence, or deny that executing those who renounce military service is violence. Such views about violence cannot be reconciled with Christian practices.

The Christian community will always live in tension with any SOCIETY which demands they accept violence as necessary for order. As long as human societies assume a role for violence which is contrary to Christian peaceableness, intrinsic to the Christian community's practices of forgiveness, reconciliation and LOVE, this tension remains. Describing violence rightly will be a major task and constant struggle for the Christian community which strives to live faithful to the gospel.

How one describes 'violence' will influence greatly how one envisions the sources of violence. If, for example, one assumes that all 'order' is but disguised forms of violence, then one will see sources of violence to be located in the very constitution of power structures of societies and/or of human nature. For example, on a Hobbesian model, one could view all life as a struggle for survival, in which some are subjugated to others in the interests of this continual survival. On this view, violence is part of the essential character of human existence as people whose lives are destined to death. Acquiescence to this 'order', which is acknowledged to be coercive and violent, is achieved on the assumption that it is better to have controlled rather than uncontrolled violence and that such 'order' makes our lives less nasty, brutish and short.

Other accounts of violence give it a less foundational character, ascribing violence to specific injustices. For instance, one could argue that those who are violent are responding to inequities in the economic and/or political system. WAR, terrorism, CHILD ABUSE, HOLOCAUST, RACISM, RAPE, REVOLUTION, political and economic oppression, DOMESTIC VIOLENCE, ecological destruction – theorists have depicted all of these as causes of and/or responses to various perceived injustices. Some theorists will try to account for these various forms of violence by rooting them in 'deeper' social, psychological or physiological dysfunctions, lust for power and so on. Those who attribute the sources of violence to such causes often do so on the assumption that if we could eliminate such injustices we could thus eliminate the cause of violence.

Christian theologians have avoided giving any one explanation for violence. Rather violence is understood as SIN, i.e. rebellion from God's ordering of the world as a world of peace. The ultimate expression of the violence of the world is to be seen in the world's rejection of God's love in crucifying Jesus Christ.

Justifications of violence are as varied as understandings of the nature and sources of violence. The realist view rejects theoretical justifications of violence, maintaining that violence simply exists, justified or not. Rather than justifying violence, the realist strives to harness violence to serve worthier ends than those to which it is usually assigned. According to the realists, the goal of JUSTIFICATION is in the final analysis irrelevant; the acceptability of violence depends on whether it is being used in a smart and productive fashion.

Many theories of violence adopt a bifurcated approach and justify only certain forms of violence. For instance, a 'two kingdoms' view distinguishes state violence from the violence used by individuals. This view is based on the presumption that the state can use violence in an impersonal and controlled fashion in a way that an individual cannot. The police function of the state is justified because it is thought to exercise an impartial and thus just authority (see POLICING). Similarly, war fought by states is distinguished from other forms of mass violence, because it is thought to be done with legitimate AUTHORITY and in an organized fashion, which makes it appear capable of minimal rational control.

St Augustine justified state violence on the basis of the Christian duty to protect the innocent. Augustine argued that Christians could use violence to defend the empire because Christian charity required the protection of the innocent neighbour even if such protection required the death of the attacker. Interestingly, Augustine did not believe that Christians could kill in self-defence. If one was attacked, one could attempt to defend oneself in a non-lethal manner, but it was better to be killed than to kill. Augustine's defence of just war was a theory of exceptions to the Christian norm of acting non-violently. Augustine's primary goal was not to justify war, but to limit its practice among the new mass of converts following Constantine.

Some contemporary theorists argue that just-war theory is a theory *justifying* state violence against other states, thus fundamentally changing the theory's original purpose as an attempt to *limit* state violence in war. This transformation is not surprising, because the just-war criteria, which make a moral distinction between forms of violence used by an established authority versus violence done without such authority, can easily be co-opted by those in power to prove that their use of violence is legitimate because they constitute an established authority.

Christian reflection on the justification of violence has ranged from realist presumptions to those that disavow all use of violence on the part of Christians. It is often pointed out that the Bible is a book of extraordinary violence, true of both the Old and New Testaments. The Israelites are ordered by God to annihilate their enemies. The Psalmist prays for death and destruction for his enemies (Psalms 35, 55, 58, 59, 69, 109). Jesus died a violent death.

Christian attitudes to the possibility of acting violently also have been shaped by their understanding of Christian witness to the wider society (see CHURCH AND STATE). Those who have understood the place of Christians as being faithful witnesses while being perpetual outsiders and critics of society have understood violence differently from those Christians who have understood their role as ruling their society. In a related way, Christian attitudes have been shaped by whether they believe that their primary call is to live as Jesus does in the midst of violence, or whether their call is to (possibly) do violence in order to reduce the amount of violence.

One of the great ironies of Christian tradition is that the justification of violence that many Christians advocate would legitimate the execution of Jesus by the Roman authorities. However, most Christians have continued to maintain the centrality of the Cross in a manner that has always sustained a tension between Christian convictions and the legitimation of violence. Certainly the portrait of Jesus Christ in the New Testament shows that he dealt with violence by calling into question the very presumption of the necessity or the efficacy of violence.

Nowhere is this displayed more eloquently than in the Pauline accounts of Jesus' confrontation with the Powers. In confronting the Powers, Paul shows that the proper source of power for the Christian community lies in the life, death and resurrection of Jesus Christ and in the church's faithful embodiment of that power. Jesus is born into a society of violent power. His very birth evokes a genocidal reaction from Herod the Great (Matthew 2). At the inauguration of his ministry Jesus is tempted to express his power unfaithfully, is tempted to violence (Luke 4: 1–13). Christ defeats the powers and principalities, not through the avenues that the devil advocated or those which society expects, but through forgiveness, reconciliation and love, as they are defined in the light of the Cross and resurrection. In doing so, Jesus repudiates that society's conception of power. The rejection of the use of the power of violence is most clearly displayed by Jesus in the Garden of Gethsemene. When Jesus tells Peter to put away his sword, Christ shows all Christians that His way, and thus their way, is not the way of violence (Matthew 26: 47–56). It is in the power of the Cross and resurrection that Jesus effects salvation. The salvation Christ brings is liberation from the powers of the world, powers existing from the fall to the eschaton.

Jesus' peaceable salvation wrought in the Cross and resurrection is the culmination of his peaceable life, whose purpose is to call his followers to the KINGDOM OF GOD. The kingdom of God is the new society inaugurated by Jesus and governed and sustained by the Holy Spirit, who gives birth to the Christian community at Pentecost (Acts 2). In the power of Christ and of the Holy Spirit, the Christian community strives to live the Biblical vision of the kingdom of God. Radically different from any worldly kingdom, the kingdom of God is shown in the peaceableness of creation where all humans and animals live at peace with one another, and is envisioned in Isaiah's (ch. 11) and Hosea's (ch. 2) prophecy, in St Paul's discussion of the yearning of all creation for liberation from the bondage of this world (Romans 8) and in St John's vision of that time when 'They will hunger no more, and thirst no more; . . . And God will wipe away every tear from their eyes' (Revelation 7). The Christian community's faithfulness to the gospel will not consist merely of an absence of violence, but in the active embodiment of the peaceableness of the kingdom of God.

Violence is with the world until the return of Christ. Yet the message of the gospel seems to make doing violence contradictory to all basic Christian convictions. So for the Christian community, the first and primary question with regard to violence must be not whether violence is *per se* right or wrong, or whether violence by Christians can be justified, but how Christians are to live peaceably in a violent world.

In the same way that the Christian community must struggle to maintain a faithful conception of violence, so must it struggle to maintain a faithful conception of peaceableness. For instance, there are pacifists who define peace in largely negative terms, as an absence of overt violence (*see* PACIFISM). Such pacifists often think that war in the modern age is unthinkable as a moral option; it is impossible to justify war anymore on purely utilitarian grounds given the existence of nuclear weapons. These 'liberal' pacifists understand their mission as one of protecting the world from war. Similarly, the role of the state 'is often seen as one which protects its citizens from violence. Certainly the Roman Empire understood its task as one of bringing peace and order to otherwise anarchic and barbaric regions. Thus the Roman Empire spoke of its *Pax Romana*. Yet it is clear that this *Pax Romana* is not the same as the *Pax Christi*, the peace of Christ.

Jesus says 'my peace I give to you; not as the world gives do I give to you' (John 14: 27). That Jesus' peace is different from that of the world is embodied clearly in Jesus' Cross. For Jesus does not come to protect Christians from suffering violence, but to give them strength to live faithfully to the gospel, whatever its demands may be. The history of the early church and its martyrs makes it clear that the *Pax Romana* could never be and will never be the *Pax Christi*.

For the *Pax Romana* is merely ordered violence, reinforcing the social structures that further the interests of the Empire. That the interests of society are inevitably at odds with the *Pax Christi* is clear from the example of Jesus. For it was the high priest Caiaphas who wanted to preserve *Pax Romana*, the world's peace of undisturbed status quo, and the world's peace meant that Jesus had to be edged out of this world to the Cross. To protect the *Pax Romana*, it will sometimes be necessary that some persons should die for the good of the whole people, (John 18: 14). If Christians are to proclaim the *Pax Christi*, they must not expect their society to accept their peace anymore than it did the peace of Jesus Christ.

If the Christian community recognizes the peace of Christ as an active power confronting the *Pax Romana* with the gospel of forgiveness, reconciliation and love, then it will never confuse its pacifism with what might be called 'passivism'. The Christian community will proclaim that 'Blessed are you who are poor', but will never separate that from the corresponding 'But woe to you who are rich', and will never accept such beatitudes as calling for passivity (Luke 6: 20–6). For example, the 1968 Medellín document, published by the Latin American Catholic bishops, speaks of the violence done to the poor by the maintenance of the institutions which maintain the majority of the population at a subsistence level (or less) while a small percentage of the population lives in relative opulence. If the Christian community speaks for the side of wealthy by simply accepting the status quo as 'ordained by God', then it is unfaithfully proclaiming the violent *Pax Romana* and has failed in its task to bring the gospel of *Pax Christi* to these people. Someone like Dorothy Day who could say 'blessed are the poor' and yet work to assist the poor and down-trodden is on their way to understanding Jesus' beatitudes.

Similarly, with respect to the problem of domestic violence, if the church adopts society's all-too-common conception of the issue as merely a 'private affair' to be worked out at home, or worse, advocates that this is rightful 'submission' of the wife, then the church perverts the gospel and denies the obligation to seek true reconciliation. In this instance, the Christian community might appropriately separate the batterer from his wife and children by taking one or other into their homes, confront the batterer with his actions and tell him that he must repent of his actions and show his peaceableness before he will be allowed to live with his spouse and children.

Arendt, Hannah (1970) *On Violence*, New York: Harcourt Brace Jovanovich.
Brown, J.C. and Bohn, C.R. (eds) (1989) *Christianity, Patriarchy and Abuse*, New York: Pilgrim Press.
Ellul, Jacques (1970) *Violence*, London: SCM.
Hauerwas, Stanley (1983) *The Peaceable Kingdom*, Notre Dame, IN: University of Notre Dame Press.
Merton, Thomas (1968) *Faith and Violence*, Notre Dame, IN: University of Notre Dame Press.
Niebuhr, Reinhold (1932) *Moral Man and Immoral Society*, New York: Scribner's.
Ramsey, Paul (1961) *War and the Christian Conscience*, Durham, NC: Duke University Press.
Shaffer, Jeremy (ed.) (1971) *Violence*, New York: David McKay.
Williams, Rowan (1983) *The Truce of God*, New York: Pilgrim Press.
Yoder, John Howard (1972) *The Politics of Jesus*, Grand Rapids, MI: Eerdmans.

Stanley Hauerwas
John Berkman

VIVISECTION

Vivisection comes from the Latin words *vivus* (living) and *sectio* (cutting), though it is now used generally to describe any painful experiment performed on a living animal which may or may not involve incision. Living animals are used in experiments not only to aid basic scientific research but also in product testing, behavioural research, for instructional purposes, in *in vivo* tests and for emergency medicine. In product testing – to take only one example – a wide range of substances are tested for their toxicity including 'insecticides, pesticides, antifreeze, brake fluids, bleaches, Christmas tree sprays, silver and brass polish, oven cleaners, deodorants, skin fresheners, bubble baths, freckle creams, eye makeup, crayons, inks, suntan lotions, nail polish, zipper lubricants, paints, food dyes, chemical solvents, and floor cleaners' (Gendin 1986: 16).

The practice of dissecting live animals as a method of scientific enquiry dates back to the beginning of Western medicine. About 300 BC, the author of the Hippocratic text *On the Heart* 'cut the throat of a pig which was drinking coloured water, in order to study the act of swallowing' (Maehle and Tröhler 1987: 15). Human unease with the practice, at least when certain animals were used, is also ancient. The Stoic physician Galen of Pergamon found the expression of apes when vivisected 'unpleasant' and recommended using pigs or goats instead (Maehle and Tröhler 1987: 15). The use of vivisection fluctuated in succeeding centuries, and then proved influential in the development of physiology in Europe in the mid-nineteenth century. British scientists were slow to adopt vivisectional techniques partly for reasons of scientific tradition (see French 1975) though it is likely that concern about animal suffering also prevented the quicker adoption of the practice. Though animal experimentation had 'increased greatly' after the publication of the English translation of Descartes's *Discours de la Methode* in 1649 (which espoused the theory that animals were incapable of feeling pain or pleasure), even Cartesian experimenters expressed some empathy for their animal subjects (Shugg 1968: 228). Indeed Robert Boyle held that animals possessed the 'Beame of Diuinity' [Divinity] like humans (see Oster 1989: 151) and later on, in his famous 'air-pump' experiments, refused to perform more than one experiment on each animal. His colleague, Robert Hooke, hesitated to perform his respiration experiments in view of the 'torture of the creature' involved and wished for an 'opiate' which would render the creatures senseless (Shugg 1968: 238).

The Royal Society was known to reject applicants if their experiments proved too cruel, as in the case of Dr Philip, whose petition was denied in 1816 owing to the 'great offence' felt at the mere description of his experiments on living animals. Joseph Banks recorded that 'during the reading of his paper, many of the auditors left the room' (Dawson 1958: 506). As late as 1863, a report in the London *Times* described 'tortuous experiments' on live horses at a French veterinary college which prompted opposition from English scientists: the *British Medical Journal* stated that 'destroying animals for mere experimental research' was not justified 'under any circumstances' while 600 English veterinarians signed a memorial to encourage their French colleagues to adopt the English practice of 'using only dead carcasses for the exercises of students' (Ryder 1989: 198; Cobbe 1894: II, p. 247). In a set of recommendations drafted in 1870, the British Association discouraged its members from using vivisection for the purposes of illustration or exhibition, or to better operative skill, and encouraged the use of anaesthesia in such experiments (Cobbe 1894: II, pp. 250–1). Meanwhile, the Royal Society for the Prevention of Cruelty to Animals (RSPCA), led by its secretary John Colam, appealed to Napoleon to help end the French experiments and attempted to prosecute a French physiologist, Eugene Magnan, for CRUELTY to animals when he publicly operated on two living dogs in England in 1874 (Cobbe 1894: II, pp. 247, 253–4).

However, as Continental scientists continued to make important discoveries, scientific (and popular) opinion on vivisection began to turn: many English scientists became convinced that, in Sir William Jenner's words, 'in this land alone ... Science walks in fetters' (French 1975: 270). The RSPCA, feeling pressure from some of its pro-science supporters, announced in 1875 that the Society was now 'not so entirely unanimous' on the subject 'to desire the passing of any special legislative enactment' restricting the practice of vivisection (Cobbe 1894 II, p. 265). Isaac Barrow described the scientific 'curiosity' which claimed the lives of animals as 'a perfectly innocent cruelty' (Shugg 1968: 277). The numbers of animals used annually in experiments began to rise every year, from fewer than 800 in 1876 to over 5.5 million in 1970 in the UK. Current estimates for the USA 'range as low as 15 million to as high as 200 million'; the world estimate is 500 million (Gendin 1986: 15, 54).

In 1880, Baron Ernst von Weber, a leading German anti-vivisectionist, offered his opinion as to why the movement against vivisection had taken root so quickly and deeply in England. The most prominent reasons for English support, he believed, were 'the religious tendency of the English nation' and 'the warm sympathy of the ... clergy' (French 1975: 235). In his examination of the early anti-vivisection movement, historian Lloyd Stevenson found that 'religious feeling – religious certainly in origin' had 'permeated the whole issue of animal experimentation' (Stevenson 1956: 125). Though few organized churches lent official support to the anti-vivisection agitation in the nineteenth century, an impressive number of their representatives did: among those active in the Victorian cause were Cardinal Manning, Dr Thompson (Archbishop of York), Marcus Beresford (Primate of Ireland), Lord Chief Justice Coleridge, and the Bishops of Winchester, Exeter, Salisbury, Manchester, Bath and Wells, Gloucester and Bristol, Hereford, St Asaph and Derry (Ryder 1989: 174; Cobbe 1894: 255, 274). Most committed and active were Cardinal Manning (Archbishop of Westminster) and the philanthropist and reformer Lord Shaftesbury. He and Manning founded one of the earliest – and certainly the most influential – anti-vivisection society in the world, the Victoria Street Society, with Frances Power Cobbe and Dr George Hoggan in 1876. Shaftesbury continued to wield great influence in the movement until his death in 1885. Cobbe wrote later, 'Lord Shaftesbury never joined the Victoria Street Society; it was the society which joined Lord Shaftesbury' (Cobbe 1885: 3).

With hindsight, we can now see that early, and subsequent, debates about vivisection brought into focus a number of competing – and probably incompatible – perceptions not only of animals and human responsibility but, most strikingly, of the nature of moral progress itself. Unsurprisingly, they touched issues of religious sensibility since all of them concern deeply held theological convictions. We can separate them out into three major areas.

Progress versus idolatry This tension went to the heart of Victorian society for that society was both unashamably religious and also increasingly enthralled by the prospect of progress, not least of all in the field of science. For some religious anti-vivisectionists, legal cruelty was evidence of the threat that science posed to the position of religion in society: vivisection was 'idolatry', potentially dethroning religious faith and replacing it with a 'materialism' that offered no moral guidance and was, in fact, immoral (Shaftesbury n.d.: 4). Even the benefits of vivisection could not outweigh this threat: many thought it more important 'that tender and just and compassionate feelings should grow and abound than that a cure should be found for any *corporeal* disease' (Cobbe 1889: 5; our emphasis). Claude Bernard, the 'father of modern physiology', expressed this offence directly with his view that, when increasing knowledge was the goal, causing SUFFERING was little more than an occupational hazard: the 'true physiologist', he opined, 'does not hear the animal's cries of pain. He is blind to the blood that flows. He sees nothing but his idea, and organisms which conceal from him the secret he is resolved to discover' (Leffingwell 1895: 3).

Doubtless, Bernard's view was extreme, even for the time, but it encapsulated a disregard for emerging zoophily which some regarded as nothing less than an attack upon divine providence. The 'necessity' of vivisection denied the idea of

a 'just and merciful God': in a sermon delivered in Westminster Abbey in 1889, the Bishop of Durham, Dr Westcott, found it 'absolutely inconceivable' that 'He should have arranged the avenues of knowledge' such that we should only discover truths 'through the unutterable agonies of beings which trust in us' (Cobbe 1889: 1–2; Wescott n.d.). The notion that vivisection is 'idolatrous' may strike us as extreme as Bernard's view that suffering is nothing more than an occupational hazard, and yet in the intervening years from the 1880s to the present when experimentation has triumphed so completely as a method of scientific enquiry, we may now be in a better position to grasp the deification of humanity which such methods presuppose. Human life and well-being, we now commonly accept, justifies the institutionalized use of millions of animals. 'Do not animals now suffer in our laboratories to make our life easier, to help prolong our lives, to fulfil our therapeutic wants, even if the benefit concerned is as trivial as a new face cream, lip stick or nail varnish? Are not animals now sacrificed for a species that increasingly takes to itself God-like powers and who regards its own interests as unquestioningly the goal and purpose of creation itself?' (Linzey 1994: 40).

Utility versus cruelty 'We decline to accept the Vivisectors' tenet that cruelty is justifiable provided it be useful ... we are confident that practice which is spiritually repulsive and morally deteriorating cannot be scientifically necessary.' This article of the anti-vivisectionists' 'Credo' adopted in 1908 (Westacott 1949: 197) highlighted the dilemma of the movement. Given a divinely sanctioned moral order in the universe, cruelty should not prosper, and pain should not bring reward, but the growing advances in science and medicine at the turn of the century – and since – have made it difficult to doubt that vivisection is useful, no matter how cruel. The Credo ends by desiring a 'complete' dissociation from scientific research and 'from participation in the use of the alleged "benefits" of vivisection' (Westacott 1949: 197). Such a strategy built on non-participation in all the medical and scientific benefits from EXPERIMENTATION was doomed from the start. From the 1900s onwards, it was necessary only for scientists to point to the utility of vivisection to decisively win their argument, and such arguments have continued in abundance ever since (see, for example, Halsbury 1973; Frey 1984; Paton 1984).

In two ways, however, the Credo was prophetic. First, the claim that utility can justify cruelty was to lead to the growth of experimentation not only on animal subjects but on human ones too. Lewis Carroll in 1875, and C.S. Lewis in 1947, both argued that the logic of experimentation, if morally valid, should extend to human subjects: 'no argument for experiments on animals can be found which is not also an argument for experiments on inferior men' (Lewis 1947: 9–10). The same century which has witnessed an exponential growth of animal experiments has also seen experiments on various human subjects including Jews, blacks, prisoners of war and patients in mental hospitals. Second, while anti-vivisectionists in failing to make a distinction between 'gains' and 'ill-gotten gains' made a fateful strategic error, it is nevertheless true that some claims for experimentation have been exaggerated and other paths to reducing disease have been underrated. This has led to a scientific questioning of animal experimentation as an appropriate model for the study of human disease (see, for example, Rowan 1984; Sharp 1988, 1994).

Hierarchy versus mercy   The view that humans are superior to animals so long nurtured by the Christian tradition laid the ideological foundation for the growth of vivisection. The difference between humans and animals has been the rallying cry of vivisectors until the present day: 'man . . . is so radically different from animals that he is to be regarded differently' (Paton 1984: 13). But this appeal to difference is capable of being interpreted differently. Our 'very superiority', claimed Lewis, 'ought partly to *consist in* not behaving like a vivisector: that we ought to prove ourselves better than the beasts by the fact of acknowledging duties to them which they do not acknowledge to us' (Lewis 1947: 8; original emphasis). Cobbe herself admitted that 'the relationship of the brutes to God' was the 'humblest' but thought this should 'move us to an emotion the reverse of such callous contempt' (Cobbe 1863: 506). Thus

the scene was set for two rival interpretations of hierarchy: one set by the dictum of Thrasymacus that 'might is right', and the other that greatness warrants *noblesse oblige*.

In this one respect alone the debate which vivisection has historically engendered provides a continuing moral agenda. Are humans to see themselves as set over creation as a theological right, or is their function within the creation only as stewards, even servants, of God's moral will? If the former, divine providence favours the preservation and well-being of humanity even at the expense of the rest of creation. If the latter, then there must be fundamental moral limits to what we can do in creation – and to other creatures. Chief among these limits must be the moral rejection of the infliction of pain and suffering on innocents. In Cardinal Manning's words, humans 'owed it to God, whose creatures they are, to treat them mercifully' (Cobbe 1894: 171–2).

Carroll, Lewis (Charles L. Dodgson) (1875) *Some Popular Fallacies about Vivisection* (Oxford: private circulation), June.

Cobbe, Frances Power (1863) 'The rights of man and the claims of brutes', *Fraser's Magazine* (November): 588–602.

——(1885) *In Memoriam. The Late Earl of Shaftesbury, K.G. First President of the Victoria Street Society*, London.

——(1889) *A Controversy in a Nutshell*, London: Victoria Street Society.

——(1894) *Life of Frances Power Cobbe by Herself*, 3rd edn, London: Richard Bentley & Son.

Dawson, Warren R. (1958) *The Banks Letters*, London: Quaritch.

French, Richard (1975) *Anti-vivisection and Medical Science in Victorian England*, Princeton, NJ: Princeton University Press.

Frey, Raymond G. (1983) *Rights, Killing, and Suffering: Moral Vegetarianism and Applied Ethics*, Oxford: Basil Blackwell.

Gendin, Sidney (1986) 'The use of animals in science', in Tom Regan (ed.) *Animal Sacrifices: Religious Perspectives on the Use of Animals in Science*, Philadelphia, PA: Temple University Press, pp. 15–60.

Halsbury, Lord, (1973) 'Ethics and the exploitation of animals', Paget Lecture, *Conquest* 164: 2–12.

Leffingwell, Albert M.D. (1895) *A Dangerous Ideal*, Providence, RI: American Humanitarian League.

Lewis, C.S. (1947) *Vivisection*, foreword by George R. Farnum, Boston, MA: New England Anti-vivisection Society.

Linzey, Andrew (1987) *Christianity and the Rights*

of Animals, London: SPCK and New York: Crossroad.

——(1994) Animal Theology, London: SCM and Chicago, IL: University of Illinois Press.

Maehle, Andreas-Holger, and Tröhler, Ulrich (1987) 'Animal experimentation from antiquity to the end of the eighteenth century: attitudes and arguments', in Nicolaas Rupke (ed.) Vivisection in Historical Perspective, London and New York: Routledge.

Orlans, F. Barbara (1993) In the Name of Science: Issues in Responsible Animal Experimentation, New York: Oxford University Press.

Oster, Malcolm R. (1989) 'The "Beame of Diuinity": animal suffering in the early thought of Robert Boyle', British Journal for the History of Science 22: 151–80.

Paton, William (1984) Man and Mouse: Animals in Medical Research, Oxford: Oxford University Press.

Pratt, Dallas (1976) Painful Experiments on Animals, New York: Argus Archives.

Rollin, Bernard (1989) The Unheeded Cry: Animal Consciousness, Animal Pain, and Science, Oxford: Oxford University Press.

Rowan, Andrew N. (1984) Of Mice, Models and Men: A Critical Evaluation of Animal Research, Albany, NY: State University of New York.

Ryder, Richard (1975) Victims of Science: The Use of Animals in Research, London: Davis-Poynter.

——(1989) Animal Revolution: Changing Attitudes Towards Speciesism, Oxford: Basil Blackwell.

Shaftesbury, Anthony Ashley Cooper, 7th Earl of (n.d.) Quotations from Great Thinkers, London.

Sharpe, Robert (1988) The Cruel Deception: The Use of Animals in Medical Research, Wellingborough: Thorsons.

——(1994) Science on Trial: The Human Cost of Animal Experiments, Sheffield: Awareness Books.

Shugg, Wallace (1968) 'Humanitarian attitudes in the early experiments of the Royal Society', Annals of Science 24(3): 227–38.

Stevenson, Lloyd G. (1956) 'Religious elements in the background of the British anti-vivisection movement', Yale Journal of Biology and Medicine 29 (November): 125–57.

Westcott, Dr, Bishop of Durham (n.d.) Quotations from Great Thinkers, London.

Westacott, E. (1949) A Century of Vivisection and Anti-vivisection, Rochford: C.W. Daniel.

Molly Baer Kramer
Andrew Linzey

WAR

War has been present in virtually all human societies but its manifestations, as well as its specific practices, have taken on myriad forms. Its abiding features are that it is an organized form of VIOLENCE or coercion and that it takes place in the public or political domain. To this extent war is conceptually distinct from private resorts to force. By the seventeenth century, the idea was becoming dominant that war was a political activity carried out only by states and was indeed the legal expression of their unique competence to do so.

Historically, war has been conceived in many different ways, reflecting the various means by which war is thought to be 'caused' or what its essential nature is deemed to be. To many analysts, war is simply a demonstration of an instinctive behaviour – a natural propensity to fight as with other animal species. Theologically, the tradition of Christian pessimism has tended to transcribe this notion into one of moral failure: war is the mark of humankind's sinning nature.

The problem with such notions is making sense of ideas predicated upon individual traits to explain what is deemed to be a social phenomenon. Is it not some feature of organized societies that makes wars possible or necessary? Rousseau, for instance, was insistent that war is a relation 'not between man and man, but between State and State'. If this is so, what do notions of instincts for aggression or of original SIN tell us about the social structure of behaviour? Accordingly, many theories stress instead the compulsions of NATIONALISM, the nature of the political STATE and its genesis in the quest for military efficiency, the anarchical setting of INTERNATIONAL RELATIONS and the dynamics of international economic competition to explain the onset of war.

War may be thought to have 'purposes' as well as causes. To the Roman mind, and subsequently to the medieval, war appeared to be a form of divination or legal trial. It was a means of putting a claim to the test to discover the favour of the gods and seek a divine verdict. In a wider philosophical sense, war may be thought to be part of a historical test to bring out the best in individual nations or, in Kantian terms, as part of nature's didactic purpose for mankind's improvement.

The importance of such diverse approaches to an understanding of war is that each separate concept entails different conclusions for normative JUDGEMENT or for remedial action. If war is itself deemed to be an improving process, as in the view of Hegel, it scarcely invites moral censure nor prophylactic action. By contrast, if war is akin to a disease, the dominant tendency will be to seek for a remedy or a cure to overcome its afflictions, whilst if war is viewed, by analogy, as some kind of natural disaster or cataclysm, it cannot be cured but humanity may seek for palliatives to minimize the destruction and suffering caused by it. In short, the analysis of war entails a complex interrelationship uniting its (social) essence, its causes or functional requisites, and normative judgements.

Notions in all three areas have shifted considerably as the idea of war, and associated prescriptions of how to respond to it, have evolved. War itself has, of course, undergone immense changes in response to political, economic and technological transformation. Historical limits on the size of armies were set by such considerations as the raising of taxes to pay for them, and the logistics of feeding and moving such forces. Politically, the solution to this problem was found in the heady mixture of democratic CITIZENSHIP and NATIONALISM which offered a supply of military personnel hitherto unimaginable. Economically, the efficiency of the modern state in managing the practice of war and in securing the funds for its prosecution contributed to the 'totality' of wars of the past century. Indeed, war has increasingly become a form of economic competition rather than a narrowly military struggle. Technologically, increases in fire power, coupled with aerial bombardment techniques from aircraft to missiles, have rendered the hard shell of protective states vulnerable to an unprecedented extent, as well as posing with fresh urgency questions about the distinction between combatants and noncombatants. Technology, from the railroad to aircraft carrier, has also made it much easier to project military power at a distance. To this extent it is evident that war serves as a precise barometer of wider social and technological changes while, in turn, also becoming itself a potent source of these changes.

Attitudes towards war have evolved accordingly. From a realist perspective, war was accepted as an inescapable instrument of the anarchic system of international relations. Starting from the quintessential expression of this view by Carl von Clausewitz in his *On War*, there solidified the notion that states engaged in war as an extension of normal political intercourse. There was therefore no need for solutions to the problem of war, nor should war be regarded as an abnormal nor diseased condition. This combined with doctrines of legal positivism during the nineteenth century to assert the incapacity of international LAW to itself make judgement about the state's entitlement to resort to war.

By contrast, a more critical social perspective on war had emerged powerfully during the Enlightenment. Its view of history as movement gave rise to a sense of historical change and, concomitantly, of progress and this view was brought to bear by the *philosophes* and others in their analysis of war. Increasingly, war was criticized as part of a wider indictment of the structure of contemporary SOCIETY and of its political organization: war was a product of the international relations of princes and would be cured by a more genuinely international relation of peoples. In this process, the development of Republican constitutions, as well as of mutually beneficial commerce, would have their parts to play.

From this critical or liberal tradition developed at least three separate strands of reformist strategy. The first embraced the view that the most effective way of controlling war was through a system of legal regulation. In the positivist context of the nineteenth century, this meant regulating the means and the conduct of war rather than the state's fundamental right to resort to it. Accordingly, various conventions and protocols, from Geneva in 1864 to St Petersburg in 1868 and finally The Hague in 1899 and 1907, sought to institute codes of practice to ensure a degree of humanity in warfare. A second, and opposed, approach was to seek for war's abolition rather than its legal regulation

which might seem too much like a code for the toleration of warfare. From an abolitionist perspective, the scourge was to be removed either by outright PACIFISM, or in the Kantian and Wilsonian idea of democratization of states themselves, or finally by schemes for world federation or world GOVERNMENT. The latter relied on a 'domestic analogy' form of reasoning which assumed that authoritative government had pacified states domestically and would do likewise for the wider international society.

In between the two, much international practice has concentrated its efforts neither upon legal regulation nor upon abolition but instead upon diplomatic management. While war is seen and accepted as the *ultima ratio* for settling international disputes, its incidence can be reduced by intelligent statesmanship and by resort to such diplomatic means as the exercise of a managerial role by the major powers (as in the Concert of Europe or in the United Nations Security Council), by the manipulation of the balance of power to avoid the emergence of instabilities and by specific techniques of crisis diplomacy and management, thought to have been developed by the superpowers during the confrontations of the Cold War.

These critical notions developed apace in the present century, stimulated in large measure by the disastrous experiences of the First World War. It was the most momentous consequence of this war to call into question the prevalent assumption that international society could tolerate an untrammelled resort to war on the part of individual states, and since 1919, as further developed by the United Nations' Charter, a more restrictive notion is now the international legal norm whereby states can legally go to war only for purposes of self-defence or in exercise of a duly authorized enforcement action by the international community.

Theological opinion over the centuries has both accepted the institution of war and contributed towards the more critical analysis of it. Its most impressive legacy is the substantial, if varied, body of opinion known as the just-war tradition. The central ambivalence of theological encounters with war is perfectly captured in this tradition in that just-war thinking embodies both an acceptance of war (since some resorts to war are deemed permissible) and a quest for its restriction (since it also excludes various acts of war from the realm of legitimacy). Just-war thinking has normally been classified into two components which are none the less interrelated in complex ways. The first is the *ius ad bellum* which is concerned with the just reasons for initiating war; the second is the *ius in bello* which is concerned with the just means of conducting war once it has already been entered into. The two sets of questions are at once separate and interconnected. For instance, equal restrictions apply to both belligerents regardless of which side might be thought to enjoy JUST-ICE in *ius ad bellum* terms; alternatively, the justice of a war, established on the merits of its cause, may subsequently be eroded by its breach of *ius in bello* considerations.

At once, it can be seen that just-war thinking applies only within the confines of a particular conception of war. In contrast to the view, professed by General Sherman, that 'war is Hell' and in which no extrinsic rules apply beyond the necessities of securing military victory, a just-war conception immediately asserts a view of war that is rule-governed. Indeed, it is central to this notion that it is the existence of these rules which make it war at all, rather than simply a form of massacre or butchery. The object of the exercise is then to establish the philosophical bases for asserting the restrictions which need to be observed both in the resort to war and in its subsequent conduct.

Just-war thinking has a long and complex history and involves more than theological debate: it has drawn also from notions of chivalry, from military practice and from incipient legal norms. However, in the Western tradition, it had its beginnings in the Christian Church's abandonment of a posture of pacifism. As elaborated by Augustine of Hippo, just-war doctrine was almost exclusively concerned with the *ius ad bellum* and not with war's actual conduct. Viewing war as primarily a temporal form of punishment of the evil-doer, Augustine could scarcely develop restrictions on its mode of prosecution. Even in the medieval period, writers such as Aquinas referred to *ius in bello* restrictions implicitly if at all. Aquinas' main contribution was to draw together systematically the main elements of a just war which he presented as requiring proper AUTHORITY, just cause and right intention.

However, during the course of the eighteenth and nineteenth centuries, just-war doctrine became less assured of its capacity to resolve vexed issues of just cause, involving as they did the claims of sovereign states each with equal capacity to resort to the instrument of war. This entailed a progressive slide towards the notion of simultaneous ostensible justice whereby both sides might be thought to have an equal claim to justice: in secular terms, international law became disinterested as far as issues of cause were concerned. Simultaneously, the quest for restriction in war came to express itself more in *ius in bello* terms: if the state's right to go to war could not be restrained, it might none the less be possible to encourage a humane practice of warfare.

It is only in the twentieth century that we have witnessed a revival of both elements of just-war doctrine. As noted, reaction to the First World War stimulated renewed attempts to delimit the right to go to war. Although the language was legalistic and sought to distinguish between aggressive and defensive wars, this comes close to earlier notions distinguishing between just and unjust wars. Moreover, in wider social and theological debate, just-war language and concepts have made a dramatic resurgence since the 1950s. The reasons for this are relatively clear. Initially, writers such as Paul Ramsey in the USA developed just-war concerns in the context of the new agenda about nuclear weapons and nuclear deterrence and there was some related retrospective discussion of strategic bombing issues during the Second World War. A further stimulus was provided by disenchantment with the USA's war in Vietnam which drew attention to diverse matters such as just cause and WAR CRIMES, but also to more specific concerns such as the justice of insurgency warfare and the role of conscientious objection. Finally, in the late 1970s a new wave of anxiety about nuclear matters encouraged a plethora of studies about the justice of nuclear warfare. Uniting all these discussions is the shared perception that the placing of limits upon warfare is all the more essential given the increased destructiveness of the means of war.

To the debate about the justice of initiating a particular war has been added a number of amplificatory conditions. Various thinkers have insisted that for a war to be deemed just all other means of resolving the issue should have been exhausted before resort is made to armed force. Others again have made a just war conditional upon reasonable prospects of success. In addition, some have made it a requirement that there be due proportionality between the grievance giving rise to the war and the likely cost of prosecuting it. This notion of cost has been expanded to encompass the long-term environmental effects which might result from a war.

The main issues in the area of the *ius in bello* are those pertaining to discrimination, proportionality and humaneness of methods. Discrimination may be viewed as essential to any notion of war as war. It stipulates that war may only be conducted against legitimate targets and the traditional form of discrimination is between combatants and noncombatants. Unhappily, the tendency of twentieth-century warfare has been to erode these contours of discrimination because of the importance of domestic production (the home front) and because of the nature of aerial bombardment. The main object of discussion has therefore been to try to establish the relevance of noncombatant immunity in conditions of otherwise potentially indiscriminate warfare.

Rules of proportionality enjoin that the selection of any one particular military means should be proportionate to the objective sought. Military necessity is not in itself a sufficient criterion but must be tempered by appeal to some such rudimentary standard. In turn, the means of war have been approached from the point of view of trying to prohibit weapons that are considered inhumane in their effects. The relevant consideration here is thought to be the avoidance of unnecessary suffering beyond that required to terminate armed resistance. Such a categorization of military weapons and means has, of course, become a matter of international law as well as of just-war discourse.

One of the major intellectual challenges of the postwar era has been the attempt to explore the role of nuclear weapons from a just-war perspective. This offered unpalatable choices. On the one hand, there has been unsurprising reluctance to employ just-war concepts such as discrimination and proportionality in a context to which they might be thought radically inappropriate. On the other, there was unease about the utility of a moral discourse about war that eschewed engagement with the dread prospect of nuclear war. When the debate was entered, the major point of disagreement centred upon the significance of the role of deterrence for moral assessments. Given that the role of nuclear weapons, from the point of view of their adherents, was avowedly to prevent war, their moral status ought to be regarded as different from that of weapons actually used. From this starting point, complex analyses have evolved about the precise relationship between deterrence and use. On the one side, it is attested that deterrence prevents much greater evils and is therefore a 'clean-hands' strategy; on the other it is insisted that deterrence expresses a conditional intention to employ nuclear weapons in specified circumstances and therefore this is the relevant consideration in passing judgement upon the strategy.

It is impossible to generalize from the experience of recent wars as to the directions it might be taking and the kind of judgements to which it is subject. For eight years from 1980, Iran and Iraq engaged in a First World War-style war of attrition with large-scale casualties amongst armed personnel: cities were attacked by inaccurate missiles and gas was used in the course of the conflict. By contrast, the Gulf War of 1991 was subject to intensive media scrutiny and was conducted in such a way as to foster the impression that high-technology war could be fought in order that noncombatant casualties could be minimized. It is possible that this experience may have generated unrealistic expectations about the degree of precision and clinicality possible in the conduct of future wars.

As a matter of international politics, there is no convincing reason to anticipate a decline in the incidence of war: the diminution of conflicts related to the Cold War will almost certainly be counterbalanced by the outbreak of wars in regional settings now liberated from Cold War-induced restraints. While the United Nations may be expected to play a more prominent role in seeking to defuse conflicts, its involvement is likely to be selective and its effectiveness variable. As a matter of theory and normative judgement, the principal problems of warfare are therefore likely to be abiding in nature.

Three specific issues appear set to loom larger, however, in future attitudes to war. The first, as indicated, will be the difficulty of reconciling, in the developed world at least, a continuing concept of just war with a marked growth of unwillingness to accept any appreciable level of military casualties, especially since the Gulf War has established a new benchmark of expectations, however unrealistic these may be. Second, just-war thinking needs to move beyond the simple assertion of a right to noncombatant immunity and address such painfully hard choices as the extent of the personal danger which must be accepted by armed forces in the avoidance of civilian casualties: how much risk must they be expected to bear to save enemy civilian lives? Finally, the analysis of the social, political and economic roots of war must be continued with a view to finding political solutions to conflicts. Without this, efforts to restrict the incidence of war or to regulate its conduct, welcome as they are, must be regarded as attempts to treat the symptoms rather than the causes.

Best, G. (1980) *Humanity in Warfare*, London: Weidenfeld & Nicolson.

Clark, I. (1988) *Waging War: A Philosophical Introduction*, Oxford: Oxford University Press.

von Clausewitz, Carl (1976) *On War*, ed. M. Howard and P. Paret, Princeton, NJ: Princeton University Press.

Howard, M. (ed.) (1979) *Restraints on War*, Oxford: Oxford University Press.

Keegan, J. (1976) *The Face of Battle*, London: Jonathan Cape.

Khadduri, M. (1955) *War and Peace in the Law of Islam*, Baltimore, MD: Johns Hopkins University Press.

Ramsey, P. (1968) *The Just War*, New York: Scribner's.

Waltz, K. (1959) *Man, the State, and War*, New York: Columbia University Press.

Walzer, M. (1977) *Just and Unjust Wars*, New York: Basic Books.

Wright, Q. (1942) *A Study of War*, 2 vols, Chicago, IL: University of Chicago Press.

Ian Clark

WAR CRIMES

'War crimes' are breaches of the laws and customs of war (*ius in bello*). In international law there are three types of war crime. 'Grave breaches' of the Geneva Conventions of 12 August 1949 and Protocol I of 1977 involve serious ill-treatment of the 'victims of war', defined as the wounded and sick, shipwrecked, prisoners of war and civilians in occupied territory. The limits on conduct do not involve restrictions on the conduct of hostilities. Protocol I added to the list serious breaches of the rules designed to protect all civilians from the effects of hostilities. This necessarily sets limits to the conduct of the fighting. The second type of war crime involves 'serious violations' of the Geneva Conventions and Protocol I. The category is not defined but such actions are within the jurisdiction of the International Fact-Finding Commission, established under Protocol I. The final category includes any other breach of the laws and customs of WAR which regulate the conduct of hostilities, even between the fighters *inter se*, and set limits on the weapons that may be used and how they may be used.

War crimes must be distinguished from the other heads of the indictments served on the defendants in the International Military Tribunal at Nuremberg: crimes against PEACE and crimes against humanity. Crimes against peace are breaches of the law on the resort to armed force (*ius ad bellum*). Only the political leaders of a state can properly be tried for crimes against peace. Crimes against humanity are actions which would now be regarded as breaches of HUMAN RIGHTS law and possibly as GENOCIDE but which, at the time of the Nuremberg trial, were arguably not breaches of the then laws and customs of war.

The concept of war crimes inevitably involves the notion that certain actions are not unlawful in war although they would be in peacetime. This necessarily assumes that war itself can be lawful; if not, all actions forming part of the war would be unlawful. There is therefore a relationship between the resort to armed force and the conduct of hostilities. One of the conditions of a just war is that it is fought justly. War crimes imply rules, the breach of which represent crimes. The conduct proscribed by the just-war doctrine includes the infliction of unnecessary SUFFERING on the fighters and of any suffering on the innocent, including the wounded and sick and civilians. The doctrine of double effect is applicable to foreseeable but unintentional innocent victims. Similar criteria constitute the underlying principles of the international law rules regulating the conduct of war.

The concept of rules of war pre-date the just-war doctrine. The earliest account is probably that of Sun Zu, 'The Art of War', about 500 BC. One of the earliest trials recognizable as a war crimes trial was that of Peter von Hagenbach, acting under orders of Charles, Duke of Burgundy, who was tried in 1474 for the ransacking of Breisach. He was accused of 'trampling underfoot the laws of God and man'. He sought to rely on the defence of superior orders but that was rejected in principle on the grounds that it would be contrary to the law of God, since it would elevate the claims of the military superior above those of the law of God.

Whilst the just-war doctrine has played a vital role in shaping the concept of war crimes, other influences have also made a contribution. The rules of chivalry helped form those rules which apply between the fighters themselves. As a code, it was limited to members of the same class. That changed into the concept of honour, whose principles were not confined to fighting but were still seen as confined to a particular class. The claims of personal honour were seen by some as higher even than those of God (e.g. duelling).

The development of the nation-state contributed to Rousseau's sense that war was not fought between men but between states. This meant that, once captured or wounded, the fighter ceased to be a threat and could be seen as an individual. The evolution of the nation-state, however, and its relationship to the development of international law resulted in a distinction being drawn between matters internal to the state and those concerning its relations with other states. Only the latter were regulated by international law.

Instructions for the Government of Armies of the United States in the Field (1863), known as the Lieber Code, was one of the first codifications of rules for the benefit of land forces. It was in fact produced for the forces of the Union fighting in the American Civil War. Treaty rules on the conduct of warfare regulate principally inter-state conflicts. Codification of the rules of conduct started in the nineteenth century and developed rapidly in the early years of the twentieth century with the adoption of The Hague Conventions of 1907, including the Regulations on the Laws and Customs of War on Land, annexed to The Hague Convention IV. The rules on the conduct of warfare were updated in 1977 and partially merged with the updated Geneva Conventions of 1949.

In origin the rules were seen as very European in orientation, whether on account of the Judaeo-Christian heritage or eighteenth-century political philosophy. The Japanese, for example, are alleged to have thought that any person taken prisoner would want to be humiliated, since the Japanese themselves would so have reacted if the roles had been reversed. Such an attitude seems to be based on a particular cultural manifestation of the notion of honour.

Crimes involve the possibility of trial and punishment (see CRIME). Different procedures apply to the three types of war crime. In the case of 'grave breaches' of the Geneva Conventions and Protocol I, every state is under a legal obligation to try alleged perpetrators, irrespective of the nationality of the alleged offender or the victim and of the place where it happened. The offences are seen as universal and, by some states, as of such a nature that no time limit should apply to their prosecution. There is no permanent international tribunal. The International Military Courts established at Nuremberg and Tokyo were exceptional. More recently, *ad hoc* international tribunals have been established for the trial of war crimes and crimes against humanity (former Yugoslavia) and genocide (Rwanda). Since 1992, the International Fact-Finding Commission has jurisdiction to investigate alleged serious violations by the state, or by persons for whose actions it is responsible, but the body is not a court and it cannot try individuals. Further, the state complained against must have accepted its jurisdiction. States are expected to try alleged perpetrators of 'grave breaches' in their own criminal or military courts. In the case of 'serious violations', there is no obligation to prosecute but it would seem that a state is free to do so if, under its domestic law, its courts have jurisdiction. In the case of other war crimes, the state will be delictually responsible to the injured state. The individual may be subject to the criminal or military law of his or her own state but states do not usually try foreigners for such actions.

Since 1945, it would appear that there is no defence of superior orders but the plea may be relevant in mitigation of sentence. The test appears to be whether the defendant had a moral choice.

It used to be thought that, in non-international armed conflicts, there was no scope in international law for the concept of 'war crimes', which imply a conflict between two or more states. In a non-international armed conflict, the actions are judged according to domestic law and subject to the limits of human rights law. If a soldier kills a civilian without legal justification, he should be tried by court martial or under the criminal law. If a 'rebel' kills anyone, be it soldier or civilian, he can be charged with murder. Where the state recognizes the rebels as belligerents, the law of international armed conflicts becomes applicable, as it does where a people is fighting in the name of self-determination against colonial domination, alien occupation or a racist regime. The ad hoc War Crimes Tribunal for the former Yugoslavia may establish liability for war crimes for actions committed in a non-international conflict. In moral terms, the distinction between such conflicts is only relevant if the only authority which can call upon people to fight in a just cause is a state (just war, just rebellion). The justice of an individual killing, within the context of a just war, would seem to depend on the same factors, whether the conflict is international or non-international.

The contemporary importance of war crimes trials was highlighted during and after the conflict in the Gulf in 1991. The soldiers who liberated the Second World War concentration camps saw what happened to those responsible at the Nuremberg trial. Those who saw the devastation wrought in Kuwait have seen the atrocities go unpunished. There is concern as to the impact of the lack of actual legal accountability on the future conduct of currently law-abiding forces. Concern that trials should be seen to be fair gives rise to problems where the vanquished are tried by the victors. This would have been a particular difficulty if Saddam Hussein had been tried by Americans, Canadians and Britons. This suggests the need for a permanent international criminal court, at least for war crimes.

Three important problems which have not been resolved include the difficulty of ensuring the trial of alleged war criminals where there has not been a complete surrender; the issue of the regulation of non-international conflicts; and the tension between the demand for justice, which points to the need for trials, and the search for international and national reconciliation, which some claim requires amnesties but gives rise to the issue of impunity.

Best, G. (1980) *Humanity in Warfare*, London: Weidenfeld & Nicolson.

Fotion, N. and Elfstrom, G. (1986) *Military Ethics*, London: Routledge & Kegan Paul.

International Military Tribunal (1946) *Judgement of the International Military Tribunal for the Trial of German Major War Criminals*, London: HMSO.

Johnson, J.T. (1981) *Just War, Tradition and the Restraint of War*, Princeton, NJ: Princeton University Press.

Lachs, M. (1945) *War Crimes: An Attempt to Define the Issues*, London: Stevens.

O'Brien, W.V. (1981) *The Conduct of Just and Limited War*, New York: Praeger.

Oppenheim/Lauterpacht (1952) *International Law*, vol. II, 7th edn, London: Longman.

Ramsey, P. (1961) *War and the Christian Conscience: How Shall Modern War be Conducted Justly?*, Durham, NC: Duke University Press.

Schwarzenberger, G. (1968) *The Law of Armed Conflict*, London: Stevens.

Walzer, M. (1992) *Just and Unjust Wars*, 2nd edn, New York: Basic Books.

Françoise J. Hampson

WEALTH

Wealth is nominally a superfluity of goods required for subsistence, but the character of these goods varies with the use of wealth. To the consumer in a market ECONOMY wealth is property, savings, and disposable income, all of which may be assigned a money value. For the economist, however, national wealth is the sum of the tangible assets plus the net foreign balance. This sum is computed from the flows of exchange in a given time (usually a year) and the stocks of assets at any time. These computations yield the nominal monetary value of a national economy, but it is not a realistic assessment of wealth or of wealth potential. It excludes all assets for which there is no market evaluation (military assets, works of art), natural resources, and human resources. Thus in practice national wealth can hardly be measured from the balance sheets of sectors of an economy. An apt demonstration of this circumstance is the economic performance of Germany and Japan in the aftermath of the Second World War. In 1945, both economies were 'in ruins'. Their credit and manufacturing installations were destroyed, personal PROPERTY and dwellings had been severely reduced, and they were beholden to conquerors who might extract what they will. Yet these countries recovered rapidly; in four decades, Japan had become the world's leading creditor while the victorious United States had become the leading debtor nation. Such changes of fortune are characteristic of wealth acquisition and dissipation.

The components of wealth are related to a context of use. For hunter-gatherers, money and property are of no value while offspring are of high value; for the subsistence farmer, arable land, good seasons, and security of tenure are valuable because they are conditions of production. Until now most human beings have lived in one of these two conditions. Societies with a flourishing trade and extensive MARKETS date to about 1000 BC, yet most of the population of these societies lived in agrarian settlements. This remained the pattern even in industrial Europe until well into this century. Thus, the ascendancy of urban wealth is recent, while the ascendancy of industrial forms of wealth are but a

moment's duration relative to the antiquity of the human species. Industrial forms of wealth dominate economic thought today, but experience of the intractability of Third World societies to economic planning show that they do not elucidate the human relation to other forms of wealth. The reason for this mismatch is that modern forms of wealth depend on two factors that are unique to recent times. One of these is the development of a monetized market economy; the other is the extensive exploitation of natural resources by technological means.

While barter and exchange are found in all societies, markets are a distinctive development correlated with civilizing trends. Markets are a vehicle of exchange on the basis of price, independently of other considerations. They require a stable medium of exchange (money), security of property and contract, accounting methods, and a 'critical mass' in population density. Price competition is implicit in markets, since in a purely economic exchange consumers tend to prefer the lowest price for commodities of equal quality. A market in which buyers and sellers are free to exchange on this basis is a 'free market'. Such exchanges over a given time establish the monetary values of commodities and services. Wherever markets are relatively well developed, the values they generate tend to penetrate and mould the ambient value system. This probably occurred in parts of ancient China and India, in the civilizations of the Fertile Crescent, especially Phoenicia, Carthage, Athens and Rome. Late medieval European economic development was led by cities engaged in trade and manufacture.

Markets and the values they introduce are in some respects deeply contrary to pre-urban values that continue to support community sociability in civilized conditions. The conflict and its characterization is documented in the practices and moral persuasion of numerous premodern cultures, in the difficulties of Third World development and in the history of industrializing Europe. The core of this conflict may be stated in terms of competing kinds of wealth. For hunter bands and agricultural settlements, the most important wealth is group solidarity. Livelihood can be attained only on the condition of the ordered co-operation of the adult group members and the docility of the offspring. Assistance in times of distress is available only from other members of the group. The single most significant standing cost of such groups is reproduction and nurturing the young. Thus MARRIAGE is typically the most important type of exchange, since it establishes a life-long sequence of exchanges and obligations of care. The reality of community solidarity is kinship; 'community' means the 'tribe' or reproductive group. The values of such groups are the 'natural' values of kin association. In the anthropological documentation these values include the apportionment of status by age and sex; paternalism, or male dominance of the group; maternalism, or female dominance of the household; egalitarianism stemming from sibling solidarity and rivalry; the inclusion of all group members in the obligation to care stemming from parental dominance of the social order. The aesthetics, religious belief and practices of natural communities reiterate these values. Obligations between parent and child are sacred; exchanges are conditional upon their consistence with personal attachments; great ceremonial importance is attached to birth, puberty, marriage, and DEATH; property and social status are held on sufferance of continuing group sanction.

Anthropological economics seems to indicate that group solidarity opposes not merely market values, but any personal accumulation of wealth. Contrary to Karl Marx, who characterized 'primitive accumulation' as naked exploitation by force, anthropologists find that it consists of accumulation of prestige by enterprising individuals who organize exchanges, usually valued food. To illustrate, among the !Kung bushmen, Hxaro is a network of reciprocal obligations that enables any individual to call upon the assistance of his or her Hxaro-related individuals. As a result, any superfluity of food or other reserves possessed by an individual is promptly demanded by Hxaros, who say that they are hungry. As this request cannot be refused, no accumulation is possible. It is not surprising that the !Kung spend about 20 hours a week in work and the remainder of their time cultivating Hxaro relations. The transition to accumulation is illustrated by the Tee ceremonial exchange in New Guinea. 70,000 persons are linked in a cycle of ceremonial exchange in which pigs and other goods are circulated. The exchanges are not directed toward accumulation but toward cementing affiliative relationships between groups for purposes of territorial defence and marriage. The 'entrepreneurs' in the Tee system have no capital except their persuasive skill. They create chains of 'finance' by securing a multitude of agreements to specific payment at the Tee festival. Distribution of the goods is done publicly so that all can see that agreements were kept. Archaeology suggests that the domestication of plants and animals was not for subsistence but to obtain items for use in ceremonial exchanges. Élites of 'accumulators' may arise in this way.

Pre-modern markets have apparently in all cases been constrained by moral limits, such as the ecclesiastical concepts of 'just price' and 'just wage'; they were a compromise between a free market and some counterpart of Hxaro exchange that give preference to nepotistic economic exchange paralleling kin obligations. State and ecclesiastical organization were consistently used to redistribute wealth in accordance with perceptions of equity, prestige and magnificence. The historical record of the uses of wealth shows a consistent preference for non-functional extravagance, monumentalized in architecture and art, both civic and religious.

Modern economic thinking, inaugurated by Adam Smith in *The Wealth of Nations* (1776), would maximize accumulation because a general increase of wealth benefits all members of society. The maximization goal dictates that the market be 'free', this is, be based on price competition and cleared of all legal and moral impediments that secure advantage or provide protection against competition. While acknowledging that the free market would result in closing uncompetitive employments, classical economists believe that this consequence is more than compensated by the advantages, which are chiefly the elimination of the exploitive advantage of economic élites, and the new employments that are added by the stimulus of economic growth. Critical to classical economic thought is the belief that individual initiative at all levels of society is the great lever of economic growth.

This system has never been fully implemented anywhere because of its incompatibilities with kin affiliation and because a free market will reveal morally obnoxious demands, e.g. for slaves, babies and child prostitutes. The WELFARE state is a conscious compromise between kin affiliation and the market principle. In this scheme the state assumes a broad paternalistic obligation to redistribute wealth to assure subsistence and minimum dignity to all, this being the common good as understood in natural communities.

The most severe conflicts over wealth, however, have not issued from the market system but from the technological exploitation of natural resources which is the primary cause of the unprecedented growth of wealth since the industrial revolution. The industrial system created the urbanizing process and in so doing disrupted natural community. An abiding sense of estrangement or personal jeopardy has been the price paid for endless opportunities for upward social mobility.

Boulding, K. (1981) *Evolutionary Economics*, Beverly Hills, CA: Sage Publications.

Caton, Hiram (1988) *The Politics of Progress: The Origins and Development of the Commercial Republic 1600–1835*, Gainesville, FL: University of Florida Press.

Chao, K. (1986) *Man and Land in Chinese History: An Economic Analysis*, Stanford, CA: Stanford University Press.

Hayden, Brian and Rob Gargett (1990) 'Big Man, Big Heart?: A Mesoamerican view of the emergence of complex society', *Ancient Mesoamerica* 1: 3–20.

LeGoff, J. (1980) *Time, Work, and Culture in the Middle Ages*, Chicago, IL: University of Chicago.

Ovitt, G. (1987) *The Restoration of Perfection: Labour and Technology in Medieval Culture*, New Brunswick, NJ: Rutgers University Press.

Rostow, W.W. (1975) *How it All Began*, New York: McGraw-Hill.

Wrigley, E.A. (1988) *People, Cities and Wealth: The Transformation of Traditional Society*, Oxford: Blackwell.

Hiram Caton

WELFARE

A concern for the welfare of others, especially the poor, the oppressed, the sick and the excluded, is close to the heart of the Christian and Biblical tradition. Widows, orphans and strangers have rights within Israel according to the law books of the Hebrew Bible. And the obligation to care for the welfare of the weak is not only binding on individuals, it also applies to rulers and to nations. Princes are to be shepherd-kings, caring tenderly for their flocks; the prophets call the nations to account for their treatment of the weak; and in Matthew 25 it is the nations who are summoned before the throne to hear JUDGEMENT pronounced on how they have treated the sick, the HOMELESS, the naked and the prisoners. The issue here is not simply one of charity, but rather of JUSTICE as the restoration of God's ordering of human relationships. And the concept of welfare is reformulated in terms of *shalom* as one of the major features of the messianic age. Thus the concepts of welfare and of salvation become closely related.

On this basis from a very early stage the church sponsored what today would be called welfare agencies; indeed it was itself a welfare agency. Through hospitals, schools and measures for the relief of POVERTY the church became a major provider of welfare. In many contexts the parish was seen as a community which was responsible for the welfare of its own members. With the growth of the cities and the increasing SECULARIZATION of SOCIETY the church's monopoly of welfare provision could not survive, and in the nineteenth century there emerged on the one hand a multitude of voluntary welfare agencies, many of them church-related, and on the other hand a steady increase in state provision of welfare.

The modern welfare state has its roots in these developments. With the industrial revolution came vast misery and hardship among the urban working classes, and also economic theories which suggested that poverty and hardship were usually the result of individual fecklessness or depravity. Only those who were 'deserving' were entitled to 'relief', which must even so be set at a level which would discourage people from becoming dependent on it. Private charity was expected to take the bulk of the load, and state provision only came in as a last resort. Bismark's bureaucratic state in the late nineteenth century produced a kind of prototype of the modern welfare state, whereas in Britain similar proposals were made somewhat later, initially by Sidney and Beatrice Webb.

Two formative experiences led to the formal establishment of some kind of welfare state in most western democracies in the aftermath of the Second World War. These were the Depression of the 1930s, and the experience of the war itself. The first furnished memories of hardships and aroused the determination that they must never be repeated; the second generated a new sense of solidarity and common purpose, and bred a confidence in the state as the disinterested guardian of the common good. Sir William Beveridge caught the public imagination with his call to do battle with the giants of ignorance, want, disease, squalor and idleness. Beveridge crystallized the hopes of large numbers of people. And the Beveridge vision was enthusiastically endorsed by the churches – most notably by Archbishop William Temple (who declared of Beveridge's report on social security and allied services that it was the first attempt ever to embody the whole spirit of the Christian ethic in an act of parliament!) and by Principal John Baillie in Scotland.

In the late 1940s under the post-war Labour government the basic fabric of the British welfare state was established – a National Health Service in which health care is provided free at the point of need; a policy of full employment; a comprehensive system of social security, with certain benefits like Child Allowances and Old Age Pensions available to all; a radical restructuring of the educational system to provide greater opportunity for all; and a policy of providing massive amounts of modern housing for those to be moved from the decaying inner-city slums. The advent of this welfare state was greeted with tremendous enthusiasm, and it has continued to enjoy massive popular support despite criticisms and acknowledged problems, not least from the Christian churches which have tended to regard it as essentially Christian in its concern for the welfare of all.

Many of the problems that the welfare state ran into in the 1960s and the 1970s had to do with inflated expectations and the insatiability of some basic human needs. Some people accused the welfare state of trying to play God, by attempting to make the human condition unproblematic. The demand for health care in particular seemed to have no limits, as life span

enlarged and increasingly expensive and sophisticated forms of treatment were developed. Western democracies began to wonder whether their economies could stand the escalating costs of the welfare state. Furthermore, there were on the one hand increasing worries that existing patterns of welfare provision lead to an enervating dependency on a 'nanny state' and the erosion of economically vital incentives, and on the other hand it was demonstrated by a variety of researchers that the middle classes benefitted disproportionately from health care, education, and housing in particular. A welfare state which was based on egalitarian and communitarian ideals was clearly not working as it should. Such criticisms came mainly from the Left, while the Right argued not only that the welfare state had become prohibitively expensive, but that it was making healthy economic development impossible and serving the interests of the welfare BUREAUCRACY more than meeting the needs of the poor and the weak.

In the 1970s the right wing launched an all-out assault on the welfare state as it had been established in the 1940s, attempting to move towards market provision of welfare, allowing more choice to the client, and replacing universal provision with the provision of a 'safety net' of 'targetted' benefits for the weakest and the poorest. The extreme Left had all along seen the welfare state as a palliative which obstructed the possibility of radical change by obscuring the harmful effects of a market ECONOMY. The moderate Left continued to see the welfare state as a tool of social engineering rather than a safety net, but sought more cost-effective, decentralized and participative ways of providing welfare.

A mediating critique from a theological angle was provided by Bishop Lesslie Newbigin. He saw both Right and Left as sharing Enlightenment assumptions. Both speak in terms of individual rights: the Right assert each individual's right to define and pursue a specific good without interference on the grounds of a higher common good; the Left affirms that every person has a right to have basic needs met by the community. Each of us, according to the Enlightenment world-view, has the right not only to pursue happiness and fulfil our needs,

885

but to decide what is our good, and what our needs are, for ourselves. There is no way of establishing as 'public truth' some understanding of human beings and the goal of human life which would allow us to affirm some agreed or objective understanding of human needs or the good for human beings. In short, 'if there is no publicly accepted truth about the end for which human beings exist, but only a multitude of private opinions on the matter; then it follows, first that there is no way of adjudicating between needs and wants, and second that there is no way of logically grounding rights either in needs or in wants'. As a consequence, Newbigin asserts that the concept of human nature assumed in capitalist economics is false, and that underlying the modern welfare state seriously inadequate. A Christian view must be in tension with both, he suggests, and it will provide a critique of the past and some clues as to the way forward:

> Justice means giving to each what is due, but it is of the essence of the fallenness of human nature that I overestimate what is due to me and underestimate what is due to others. Thus we fight one another for justice with all the fervour of a moral crusade, and it eludes us while we tear the fabric of society to shreds. But if what is really due to each person is to be loved and honoured as made in God's image and for God's love, then the struggle for justice (which is always necessary among sinful human beings) is protected from that demonic power which always takes over when I identify justice for me with the justice of God. We struggle for more justice in a world where absolute justice cannot be, but we live by grace as debtors to the charity of God; and the stigmas has been borne by another.
>
> (Newbigin 1985: 182)

From a more secular angle, Michael Ignatieff gives a complementary treatment of human needs in his remarkable book, *The Needs of Strangers*. In a secular society, he suggests, the whole concept of need has been narrowed; no longer do people understand the notion of spiritual need so only material and social needs are left, and since these are isolated from any kind of metaphysical or religious framework, there is no way of ranking them or determining priorities. Furthermore, what might be considered human beings' fundamental need for a framework of meaning cannot be met. The welfare state was and is an attempt to create and sustain community in the absence of agreement about what is good. It has attempted 'to create fraternity by giving each individual a claim or right to common resources'. Yet this material sharing, good as it is in itself, has not created fellowship, it has simply in a fundamentally materialist society redoubled the scramble for scarce status goods. Yet here, too, the neighbour who is a stranger continues to have a claim on one, and one may not abandon the search for fellowship and for justice.

These are indeed penetrating critiques. But they do not give much help to Christians and others as to how to act in a world in which there is precious little agreement about ends and goals and the good. That is why many Christians feel that the welfare state, as a serious and considered attempt at the communitarian provision of care with a special concern for the most vulnerable, deserves to be defended even by those who are well aware of its problems and inadequacies. The institutions of the welfare state have shown that they are capable of expressing to some extent Christian insights into human beings as beings-in-relation, and into the need for community in sharing joys, problems and resources. Christian motivation can well be expressed in the anonymous transfer of resources to needy strangers through the workings of the tax and benefits systems. There is, of course, cause for concern even in the very Utopian hopes which initiated the welfare state: such utopianism again and again has served as a disguise for power-play and the aggrandizement of some at the expense of others.

Newbigin is right: there are more possibilities than the polarized debate between Left and Right would suggest. Christians have a perennial responsibility to wrestle with the questions, 'Who is my neighbour?' and, 'How should we respond to our neighbour's needs and claims?' And when they come up with provisional answers they have also to translate these answers into the language of public policy and commend them to the broader society.

Church of England Board for Social Responsibility (1987) *Not Just for the Poor*, London: Church House Publishing.

Donnison, David (1991) *A Radical Agenda*, London: Rivers Oram Press.

Forrester, Duncan B. (1985) *Christianity and the Future of Welfare*, London: Epworth.

Ignatieff, Michael (1984) *The Needs of Strangers*, London: Chatto & Windus.

Mishra, Ramesh (1984) *The Welfare State in Crisis*, London: Wheatsheaf.

Newbigin, Lesslie (1985) 'The Welfare State', *Theology*, May.

Titmuss, Richard (1976) *Essays on 'The Welfare State'*, 3rd edn, London: Allen & Unwin.

Walter, Tony (1985) *All You Love is Need*, London: SPCK.

Duncan B. Forrester

WOMEN'S ORDINATION

The question as to whether women can be ordained to the Christian priesthood and ministry is the point at which the clash between the nature of a religion which has come out of a patriarchal world and the values of the modern age has become the most evident. The greater part of Christendom, the Catholic, Orthodox and some Anglican churches, still refuse to ordain women – in an age in which women have held the position of head of state in many diverse countries. Women themselves are divided as to whether they wish to seek admission to the Christian church on equal terms with men or whether they think that there is no point in tinkering with a male religion which is by definition biased against women.

The ordination of women is not a question which is new to the twentieth century. Thomas Aquinas, writing in the thirteenth century, considers it, as do many theologians of the later Middle Ages. Thomas is ambivalent, remarking that orders pertain to the SOUL not the body (which is the same in women as in men) – a point which he then fails to answer. He concludes, however, against – the ground for the negative conclusion being that ordination signifies 'AUTHORITY' and a woman cannot signify

authority for she is 'in a state of subjection'. His evidence for the latter is the Aristotelian biology which he has adopted, whereby the female of the species is a distorted form of the male, rather than (as we now know) neither sex being biologically normal for humanity. (It is presumably with this in mind that the 1976 Vatican Declaration against the ordination of women refers to arguments which are now discredited.)

That only men have been admitted to the threefold ministry of the church, of bishop, priest and deacon, has always been the case (with the probable exception of women deacons in the early centuries before the office became defined). The fact that such an ordained ministry can however in no way be said to go back to the time of Jesus or to have been set up through his command, opens up the matter. It is now generally recognized (through Biblical scholarship of the last hundred years) that Jesus' intention in 'calling' the twelve was not to consecrate twelve bishops but rather, in all probability, to signal that he saw himself as the Messiah; for it was said of the Messiah that he would gather in the twelve tribes of Israel. Any symbolic representation of the tribes had to be in the form of (circumcised) males. Moreover the concept of ministry in the earliest church appears to have been extremely fluid; it can in no way be said that the twelve went out from Jerusalem 'ordaining' others and so founding the church.

The question therefore arises as to whether it has been a purely sociological matter, reflecting the inferior position of women in society, that men alone have been ordained. In which case, now that the sociological reasons for not doing so have been removed and women are doctors, lawyers and prime ministers, it is without further ado appropriate to ordain women. Indeed further, many Christian women (and men) have said that it belongs to the very essence of the Christian gospel that women should not be discriminated against. The famous verse of St Paul in Galatians is quoted, that 'in Christ' there is 'neither Jew nor Greek, nor bond nor free, there is no more male and female'. Paul would seem to be referring back to the verse in Genesis where it is said 'male and female' created he them: in which case his meaning is that in Christ the subordination of women to men (which in Genesis is said to be woman's punishment for the FALL) is overcome. If indeed this division is abolished in baptism, it can be argued, then it is illogical and against the Christian gospel to introduce it again in ordination.

Furthermore it may well be argued that in the patristic period, in which the doctrine of the Incarnation was worked out, the philosophical background to THEOLOGY was that of neo-Platonism, such that the 'universal', rather than particular instances of it, was held to be 'reality'. Thus God in Christ is said to take on 'humanity'; it is not the case that an individual instance of humanity, the man Jesus of Nazareth, is, in a second nature, God. Women then bear the same relation as do men to Jesus as the Christ (as saviour) for they, equally, are members of humanity, and no mileage is to be made from the fact that the particular instance of humanity in which God was incarnate was male. Indeed, in the patristic period, nothing was made Christologically either of Jesus' maleness or his Jewishness, which to have done would have undermined the universal nature of the redemption which he was said to have accomplished.

On the other hand, now that the issue has been raised it is argued that Christ was of necessity male. It is said that, far from it being chance that God was incarnate in the form of a male, this belongs to and reflects the whole nature of CREATION. God is to be construed by humans as 'male' (and has revealed this to us); humanity in the form of the church is to be conceived as 'female' and receptive. Again, Christ is the 'bridegroom', the church the 'bride'. The form of the logos, the symbolism through which Christ came to be understood as Christianity entered the Greek world, and is said to be active and outgoing; that which receives, passive. Mary, who is female, represents humanity at its highest in her response to the initiative of the (male) God. Thus for the priest who not only represents humanity to God but also at the altar God to humanity, to be female would be to upset a whole symbolic universe which is fundamental to our psyche and which has been revealed by God. Symbols run deep and are not interchangeable.

Thus the current stance of the Vatican, in its encyclical of 1976 *Inter Insigniores*, is that only a man can 'represent' Christ. The response to this on the part of those in favour of ordaining women may be that the EUCHARIST is not a play about the Last Supper (in which case the actor playing the part of Christ should presumably be male, Jewish and bearded), but a retelling, in a way which is, however, new each time, of God's one act of redemption in Christ. It is Jesus as the Christ, the saviour of humanity, and not the man Jesus of Nazareth, who is represented. Nevertheless it may be noted that even in some churches which have admitted women to their ordained ministry, such as churches in the Reformed (Presbyterian) tradition, the staging of the Eucharist, with elders sitting round the table seemingly representing the disciples who are supposed to have been present at its inauguration, does in some sense seek to recreate a historic occasion.

Other Christians, notably those of an evangelical disposition, object to the ordination of women on the grounds of 'male headship', which they believe to be commanded by scripture. Karl Barth, arguably the greatest theologian of the twentieth century, notoriously declared woman to be to man as 'B' to 'A'. Woman, on this view, can only find her fulfilment as she stands in the place ordained for her by God in what is conceived as a covenantal relationship between God and humanity, and man and woman. Such reasoning would seem to dictate against women being allowed to preach and it would certainly follow that women may not be in charge of a parish where they would have authority over men, quite as much as prohibiting their celebration of the Eucharist.

For more radical feminists on the other hand, for women to wish to be ordained in the Christian church is mistaken. They would argue that to say that women are equal 'in Christ' cannot be held to be a gender-neutral statement, for Christ was a man and the symbolism remains male. Moreover the whole context within which the Eucharist arose was that of a patriarchal society. Through continuing to celebrate this feast and to read texts from a patriarchal age, the bias of past religion is propelled into the present, continuing to distort human relationships. From this perspective there is no particular point in women gaining admission to the priesthood and ministry of the church, for it will never be possible for women to be the equals of men within Christianity. The ordination of women may indeed serve to hide (and can never solve) what is a more fundamental problem.

Church of England General Synod (1984) *The Ordination of Women to the Priesthood: Further Report* [*A background paper by Christian Howard*], GS Misc198, London: General Synod of the Church of England.

——(1988) *The Ordination of Women to the Priesthoood. A Second Report by the House of Bishops of the General Synod of the Church of England*, GS 829, London: General Synod of the Church of England.

Edwards, Ruth (1989) *The Case for Women's Ministry*, London: SPCK.

Hampson, Daphne (1990) *Theology and Feminism*, Oxford: Basil Blackwell.

Jewett, Paul (1980) *The Ordination of Women: An Essay on the Office of Christian Ministry*, Grand Rapids, MI: William Eerdmans.

Leonard, Graham (1984) 'The ordination of women: theological and Biblical issues', *Epworth Review* 11(1) January.

Norris, Richard (1976) 'The ordination of women and the "maleness" of Christ', *Anglican Theological Review*, Supplementary Series 6 (June), pp. 69–80, reprinted in M. Furlong (ed.) *Feminine in the Church*, London: SPCK, 1984.

Stendahl, Krister (1966) 'The Bible and the role of women' (pamphlet), Philadelphia, PA: Fortress Press, Facet Books, Biblical Series 15.

Swidler, L. and Swidler, A (eds) (1977) *Women Priests: A Catholic Commentary on the Vatican Declaration*, New York: Paulist Press. Includes the Vatican Declaration of 1976 *Inter Insigniores*.

Wijngaards, John (1977) *Did Christ Rule Out Women Priests?* Great Wakering, Essex: Mayhew-McCrimmon, revised edn, 1986.

Daphne Hampson

WORK

Work: the term may well be one of the oldest in European vocabulary. It appears to have been derived from the Proto Indo-European *worg*. If so it pre-dates even ancient European cultures. The term, in some variation or other, seems to have been central to that great swathe of languages and peoples that spread across the northern Indian sub-continent, and north of the Mediterranean passed into Europe and to parts of northern Asia. It entered into Ancient Greek as 'erdo' (ἐρδω), and 'ergon' (ἐργον), from which the Old English *wyrcan*, *worch* and then, work, appear to have been derived. It turns up in a variety of Indo-European forms. It is found as, *verk* in Old Norse, *werk* in Old Spanish, *werk*, in Dutch and German, for example. In English the word *wyrcan* seems to have developed in *worch* from where the modern form 'work' is derived. The oldest etymological sense to which we have relatively clear access indicates that the Greek *ergon*, from which we also derive *ergonomic*, relates to the performance of a deed or act. According to Arendt who makes labour, work, and action, as the *vita activa*, central to *The Human Condition* (Arendt 1958) all European languages distinguish between work and labour, where the former is a creative act and the latter one of mere necessity or need. This distinction may well be true of all those European languages derived from the proto Indo-European form. Whatever the linguistic facts may be, it is certainly the case that the importance of the distinction between labour and work goes deep into collective mythology. This, and the importance attached to the idea of work, indicates some deep rooted aspect in these cultures that relates work, and conceptions of the condition of humanity. That mythology has in turn come to affect theological and ethical accounts of what counts as valued activity and immeasurably influenced the structure of western society.

The mythological turning point between labour and the generation and creativity of work, is found both in Christian cosmogenesis and in its anthropogenesis. Work is at the centre of the western originary. The act of CREATION, of the making of the world, is referred to as God's work. 'Thus the heavens and the earth were finished, and all the host of them. And on the seventh day God rested from all his work which he had done in creation' (Genesis 2). By contrast, the function that God gave to Adam in the Garden of Eden was to 'till it and keep it' (Genesis 2: 15) which, by virtue of its repetitive nature, is more akin to the activity of labour, *homo laborans*, than work, with its creative sense, *homo faber*. Subsequently in the principal EVIL act, the breaking of the interdiction against eating from the fruit of the tree of knowledge, Adam is told that the ground beneath him is cursed and, 'in toil you shall eat of it all the days of your life' (Genesis 3: 17) and be banished from the garden of Eden. God is concerned that in the eating of the fruit of the tree of knowledge, mankind obtains knowledge of self that is exhibited in shame. Adam and Eve have changed their prime qualities moving from innocence to knowledge. 'You have become like one of us' God tells them.

Becoming like one of us seems to refer to the act of self-reflection. The sense of self that is produced. But it also extends to creativity. In leaving the garden of Eden, not only is it necessary to toil and labour, it is also possible and desirable to work, to engage in creative activity. That creativity activity was not denied even to Cain who having slain his brother Abel, was told that his labour would be meaningless for, 'when you till the ground it shall no longer yield to you its strength, you shall be a fugitive and a wanderer on the earth'. Nonetheless, Cain engaged in an act of God-like creativity, of work, for he founded a city. As he founded a city, and as Adam and Eve were required to leave paradise, so they became human in the sense that we now understand that term. Their humanity depended on reflexivity and a sense of self, but also on creativity, on work.

There is some suggestion that the concept of work was of sufficient importance in early Christianity to be regarded as a means of JUSTIFICATION. James (2: 14–26) has it that, 'What does it profit, my brethren, if a man says he has faith but has not works (εργα)?', a claim that seems, on the face of it, to offset the claim of St Paul that Justification might be by faith without works, or by works alone. The disagreement is probably more apparent than real. When Paul says that 'in Christ Jesus neither circumcision nor uncircumcision is of any avail but only faith working through love' (Galatians 5: 6), he seems to be referring to work in the sense of external compliance to the religious LAW, but if that were required membership of the body of Christ would be limited to those of the Jewish faith. Paul does make it clear that faith will manifest itself in good deeds. A point James emphasizes when he says that while faith apart from works

is barren it is in works that faith manifests itself and is completed (James 2: 18–22). Nevertheless the claim that, 'man is justified by works and not by faith alone' was later interpreted to imply that the faith required work as its visible sign. The faith of the couch potato, it might be said, is of little value.

Much here of course depends on what is meant by work. For the Rabbinical Paul, attempting to show the significance of the break with the external compliance of mere RITUAL it meant compliance with the law. But it had already been given a wider interpretation for Jesus, himself, had engaged in work. He had proclaimed the kingdom of God, expressing God's final saving act through his own word and work (Mark 1: 14; Matthew 12: 28). For James work means acts of charity and LOVE towards others, actions, deeds and visible signs and expressions of faith. Faith required the giving of such signs for its realization and full expression.

In none of these cases had work, and here the Greek form of the proto Indo-European – given as *ergon* – is always found, was it implied that work was to be regarded as an economic activity. In the hearts and minds of some INDIVIDUALS of the Northern European Reformation, however, it did receive that rather narrower than original interpretation. Justification by work meant primarily justification by economic activity. This restricted scope of work and justification was far from universal throughout the reformation. Luther relying on what he thought was biblical authority, unmediated by church doctrine took it that salvation was by grace alone, and that was dependent on God but required faith. Mere external signs alone or mere external activity could not substitute for faith. Faith was the means to justification. Calvin, however, emphasized the outward signs being in the body of the church, a doctrine that led to the Protestant ethic and, it has been claimed, the development of Capitalism.

The Protestant ethic places considerable importance on individual work and economic reward. But the economic value thus obtained is not for ostentatious and personal gratification. On the contrary it also requires thrift and self-discipline. The internalization of these values became a distinct ethic, an ethic with clear implications for economic activity. The relation between that ethic and economic activity led Max Weber to argue in *The Protestant Ethic and the Spirit of Capitalism* that PROTESTANTISM had led to capitalism. In Calvinism individuals could not be sure of their state of grace. Hard, economically directed work, was an attempt to deal with this difficulty. That work could be justified even further if it was accompanied by a sense of vocation or a call. Such a call was the voice of the deity. But rewards were not personal they were to be fed back into society as further investment. Such attitudes and such activities were just what was required for capitalism. Calvinists made good capitalists and in work they could seek justification. Weber's theory is attractive; it is not, however, without its criticisms. Two are significant.

Weber's theory seems to depend on a casual relation between ideas and the world, *idealfaktoren* and *realfaktoren* that places ideas ahead of states of affairs. Ideas cause real economic changes in the world. Outside of some grand speculative metaphysical system it is unclear what the basis of such a claim could be. On the contrary, according to Marx, it is not the consciousness of people that determines their being but their being that determines their consciousness. In other words it is the real economic and material relations within which people are engaged that leads to the beliefs they have. The rise of the Protestant ethic is, therefore, primarily, although not exclusively, consequent upon the economic circumstances in which people find themselves. Those circumstances were fed largely by the rise of INDIVIDUALISM, that in turn had resulted from the breakdown of feudalism; a breakdown fed by internal contradictions in the mode of production of that economic form. Newly emergent individuals in that alienated form of being, would develop the appropriate and compensatory forms of consciousness. Individual work would come to be valued for that would justify the mode of being that existed.

A second sort of objection to Weber came from Richard Tawney. For Tawney there was some form of embryonic capitalism before the Reformation. The Reformation and capitalism had developed together, but one was not the cause of the other.

There are problems with both of these accounts. Marx's argument, at least in its cruder form, depends on placing economic circumstances (at least in the last instance as Engels was to put it in a letter to Joseph Bloch) prior to consciousness. This is just as speculative and unprovable in some larger sense as the alternative claim. It too cannot be sustained without some large metaphysical framework within which to support it. Tawney's argument depends on a clear conception of what counts as an embryonic capitalist form of exchange, before the institution of capitalism existed within which it can be understood and defined. It is far from clear that such an account could easily be given. That said, there is certainly widespread evidence of changes in individual relations that precede either the Reformation or the growth of capitalism that would have been supportive of both those ideas.

The political and ethical implications of the work ethic were of enormous significance in the west. PROPERTY, Locke argued, derived from work. The world, he said, belonged to the 'industrious and the rational and not to the quarrelsome and contentious' (Second Treatise). Whether he intended it or not, this was a doctrine that influenced and justified settlement in other lands. It also justified the industrious and the rational taking prime control of GOVERNMENT the function of which was the preservation of the property of their person and their goods. People had been made by God, they were the 'workmanship of one omnipotent and sovereign master sent about the world to do his business.' In this as in all their conduct they were governed by the NATURAL LAW. Whether Locke intended it or not (that is a matter of disputed interpretation) it led to a clear natural right to take the property of one's labour and work as private property. In this manner work could be used to justify the partition of the world.

Justification before God was by work, but work justified social, political and ethical structures and inequalities – all backed up it seemed by the force of God and appearing, therefore, as natural rather than as what they are, conventional.

Given what, for so many, was the oppressive nature of work in the industrial revolution, it is not surprising if the value of the concept of work went into decline. Within the Protestant ethic the sign of virtue was good works. Within the latter days of the industrial revolution the sign of value was to be freed from work: to lead a life of leisure. There is a history to this that, if not as long as work, is certainly of some lineage. Ancient Greek SOCIETY depended for the development of its POLITICS and its thought on SLAVERY. It was slaves and those in BONDAGE that produced the freedom and LEISURE within which political and scholastic modes of life could develop. To be free of work and to engage in leisure was to be *skole* a term from which we derive our present conception of the scholar. It is, even now, widely accepted that the scholarly life is not compatible with a life of labour, and probably not with a life of work, where that is narrowly understood. Thought requires some degree of freedom from meniality. So in Ancient Greece political activity required a similar degree of freedom. Arendt makes this crucial to the human condition. The human condition requires freedom, and freedom requires freedom from necessity, that is to say labour and work. Only then will action arise. Only in action can the space of appearances develop and only in the space of appearances is the self-revelation characteristic of freedom possible.

The model presented by Arendt is attractive. But only within the confines of a perspective that takes the public life of action as the life of freedom. An alternative, widely canvassed is to agree with Arendt that while freedom certainly includes freedom from necessity, that freedom is neither for work not action but for leisure. Freedom is exhibited and found in a life of leisure, a life free from work, free from labour, and free from public participation. The impact and significance of that latter model can hardly be underestimated. In bourgeoise society freedom is leisure – what the Greeks called *skole*, but is not necessarily pointful *skole*, on the contrary it can be pointless and meaningless – it might indeed be the *skole*, but not of the scholar but of the social and ethical couch potato. And herein lies the weakness of the conception of freedom developed by *Homo prostratus*.

Homo prostratus works not at all, creates not at all, but has the uncreative freedom of the do-nothing backed up by *ex cathedra* pronouncements on what those that do engage in work ought to be doing to further his, if not their interests. In this model the freedom of leisure is but a sad sign of moral decrepitude. By contrast the strongest secular claim on work was made by Marx. Allegedly an atheist, he made work central to human development. Capitalism alienated the worker from the product of his own work: that was a fault. It led to ALIENATION from self, species being and others. But what is significant here is not that work was evil *per se* but rather that the way in which it was structured, generated and exploited led to evil consequences. Properly managed work could be liberating, and meaningful, for in work that was properly managed, a kind of freedom could be achieved; the freedom of negating the given of making the world in which we live rather than being passive recipients of that world; of being active with respect to the world rather than subject to it.

This has left us with two traditions. In one work is the very opposite of freedom. Freedom can be obtained only by transcending it, by leaving work behind. The true domain of freedom begins where work ends. It is then that the truly human can emerge. In the other, work is central to what it is to be human. In work we recreate the original act of creativity, in work we become not so much like God, 'as one of us' as Yahweh had it as that which is definitively human. The expulsion from the garden of Eden was the point at which, poetically, at least, we became human rather than mere tillers of that which God had provided. The expulsion from the garden of Eden made work definitive of what it is to be human. And is this so surprising? If 'as one of us' we recreate in work the creation then we do indeed define ourselves as made in the image of God. If, in times of personal crisis, we say as with Candide 'Let us go and work in the garden' it is because in that simple activity there is something that is deeply satisfying.

Can we say, however, as with Weber, or with Tawney or with Marx that the emphasis on work is merely the outcome of some development in individualism and in capitalism? All of these claims have some force, therein lies their attractiveness. They are also all weak in some respects. This weakness is in different ways but there is one way in which they share a similar weakness. Their vision is too small. It is a vision that needs extending. The very importance and prevalence of the term work, variously defined though it may be and its relation to some religious conceptions of humanity and justification is clear. That relation in such a far-reaching form is so specific to Christianity and its originary that a connection of some sort between that doctrine and the social practices of capitalism is evident. It is also possible that the very prevalence, centrality and significance of the term work, variously interpreted as it might have been in Indo-European languages, has conditioned an outlook towards work of which the Protestant Ethic is merely a completion or end point. It may even be as Vere Gordon Childe argued in *The Prehistory of European Society* that the roots of the work ethic go back to the third millennium or more BCE. Such a conclusion would not be surprising. The idea of work, its importance, its significance, its conceptualization and its relation to creation, recreation and the founding act and prerogative of the deity, run very deep indeed. No society can take such a concept so deeply into itself and emerge unaffected by it.

The founding myth, the originary, remains instructive. It is a myth of course but it is a defining one for it pushes us into some of our deepest and most enduring self conceptions. And self-conceptions are, to a large extent, self defining. The importance of work and its persistence in the founding myths shows that the act of creativity that is possible in work is central to the way in which the human condition has come to be conceptualized. By contrast, of course, should that creative possibility be denied then a distinctive aspect of deeply held self conceptions of what it is like to be human would be undercut. In work the best and the worst is possible. At its worst it is the crudest and most unforgivable form of exploitation of one human being by another. At its worst is a form of bondage of the kind that in Fordism turned work into labour and dehumanized it for millions. At its best it is a form of creation

and recreation that continually lives and relives a founding moment in the originary of the western universe. In work we may become tied as in bondage or we become indeed as Yahweh said, like 'one of us'. We become in short, if not gods, at least human. It seems to follow that the denial of, or absence of creative work denies something crucial to western conceptions of what it is to lead a meaningful life, conceptions that well up from the deepest historical, ethical, psychological and theological core of some shared ideas of what it is to be human. All work and no play may make Jack a dull boy but without meaningful work as well as play it seems that Jack will be nothing at all.

Arendt, Hannah (1958) *The Human Condition*, Chicago, IL: Chicago University Press.
Childe, V. Gordon (1958) *The Prehistory of European Society*, Harmondsworth: Pelican.
Locke, John, *Two Treatises on Government*, Cambridge: Cambridge University Press.
Marx, Karl and Engels, Friedrich (1975) *Karl Marx, Friedrich Engels: Collected Works*, London: Lawrence and Wishart.
Tawney, R.H. (1926) *Religion and the Rise of Capitalism*.
Voltaire (1980) *Candide*, London: W.W. Norton.
Weber, Max (1948) *The Protestant Ethic and the Spirit of Capitalism*, London: Allen and Unwin.

Paul Barry Clarke

WORLD COUNCIL OF CHURCHES

The World Council of Churches (WCC), now based in Geneva, formally came into existence in Amsterdam in 1948. Its origin arose from the interplay of many factors, one of the most important of which was the World Missionary Conference at Edinburgh in 1910. Not only was there a concern for doctrine and THEOLOGY at that conference which led to two major world conferences for the churches on faith and order issues (Lausanne 1927 and Edinburgh 1937) but, as R.H. Preston (1973) has pointed out, the concern of the ecumenical movement for the renewal of the Church as well as its unity meant that 'life and work' issues were as important as those of 'faith and order'. The experience of world war, economic depressions and the reaction of the Third World against Western domination was the background against which many of the churches jointly began to work out their social theology.

The two world conferences on life and work (Stockholm 1925 and Oxford 1937), together with the faith and order conferences referred to above, provided the background which led to the merging of those two movements and to the inaugural assembly of the WCC at Amsterdam in 1948 as a 'fellowship of churches which accept our Lord Jesus Christ as God and Saviour'. A more explicit Trinitarian reformulation of the WCC basis was adopted by the United Assembly (New Delhi 1961) as: 'a fellowship of churches which confess the Lord Jesus Christ as God and Saviour according to the scriptures, and therefore seek to fulfil together their common calling to the glory of the one God, Father, Son and Holy Spirit'.

As Konrad Raiser reminds us 'Theology in the Ecumenical Movement', in Lossky et al. 1991: 992), not only has the ECUMENICAL MOVEMENT been shaped by theology, but the movement itself has in turn influenced developments in theology and not least in the interaction between theology and social thought. In particular, the increasingly global emphasis of the WCC has led in recent years to the bringing to bear of specific contextual approaches to theology (e.g. Asian and Pacific Theology, Minjung (South Korea)) as well as the now more broadly based liberation and political theologies which have sought to make much clearer the social dimension of the Christian gospel and feminist theologies which take seriously the experience of women in different socio-political contexts.

However, social theology in the early days of the ecumenical movement was largely influenced by Western conceptions of the theological enterprise. The 1925 Stockholm conference referred to earlier (the first Protestant ecumenical conference on social ethics), for example, tended to oscillate in its theological approach to social issues between Anglo-Saxon social gospel, KINGDOM OF GOD perceptions and more European (two kingdom) views. It was not until the Oxford conference on church, community and state in 1937 that a different approach – that of

'middle axioms' (after J.H. Oldham) – was found which also provided a theological basis for criticism of the social, political and economic order in the 1948 WCC Assembly at Amsterdam. The middle axioms approach sought to identify middle ground between Christian views offering no general directions on social, political and economic issues and views which attempted to use scripture in too direct a fashion and to identify the mind of Christ too simply with specific social, political and economic programmes (see Preston 1973: Appendix 2). The middle axioms approach crystallized in the concept of the 'responsible society' at Amsterdam where a middle course was being steered between SOCIALISM and *laissez-faire* CAPITALISM. The 'responsible society' was characterized as

One whose freedom is the freedom of men who acknowledge responsibility to justice and public order and where those who hold political authority or economic power are responsible for its exercise to God and to the people whose welfare is affected by it.

(Visser't Hooft 1949: 77)

Such ideas on the interaction of ethics, theology and SOCIETY featured in the work of the WCC for the following twenty years, making their final appearance at the fourth assembly in Uppsala in 1968. However, they were much criticized at the 1966 Geneva conference of the Church and Society subunit of the WCC, especially by the large number of non-Western representatives, as in practice simply endorsing Western ideals of representative government, the liberal or mixed economy and the economic dependence of many non-Western and non-European countries. It was also felt that such approaches concentrated on social, political and economic problems within states rather than between states. At this time the WCC, bringing together as it did most of the non-Roman Catholic churches, including the Orthodox communion, was also stimulated in its global and social thinking by parallel developments in the social theology of the Roman Catholic Church in a succession of important social encyclicals from *Rerum Novarum* (*Workers Charter*), 1891; *Quadragessimo Anno*, 1931; *Mater et Magistra*,

1961; *Pacem in Terris*, 1963; *Gaudium et Spes*, 1965; *Populorum Progressio*, 1967). Co-operation and good relations between the WCC and the worldwide Roman Catholic Church has continued to ensure a cross-fertilization of ideas in social theology and other areas to the mutual benefit of both organizations.

The 1966 Church and Society Conference of the WCC in Geneva had used the concept of the responsible society, but together with other programmes of the WCC it began to stress the theological understanding of human nature, its future and purpose. This led to the foundation of the 'Humanum' project at the WCC. Together with a growing emphasis on an ethic of JUSTICE and an affirmation of a concern for participatory decision-making, this marks the first stage of a move to the WCC's concept of a 'just, participatory and sustainable society'.

A growing understanding of the importance of ecological issues in the WCC's social thought also led to the realization that justice and participation in future societies was closely linked to wise stewardship of resources in the present. Indeed, the Church and Society world conference in Bucharest in 1974 defined the sustainable society as a long-term goal for social ethics. The New Delhi (third) Assembly of 1961 had already drawn attention to the need for an understanding of the relationship between God, humanity and nature in the WCC's thinking, and the Nairobi Assembly (1975) expressed its social ethic as 'the struggle for a just, participatory and sustainable society' against a background of the increasing importance of science and technology in the modern world and the need to work out a doctrine of CREATION which was sensitive to the insights of science and technology (see Shinn 1980).

During the last fifteen years, the interaction between ethics, theology and society in the work of the WCC has been largely focused on the development of a conciliar process for justice, peace and the integrity of creation (JPIC), formulated in the 1983 Vancouver Assembly and articulated more fully in the World Assembly on JPIC, Seoul, 1990. As Emilio Castro (former General Secretary of the WCC from 1984 to 1992) has pointed out (Castro 1992: 291) the necessity to incorporate peace into the

conciliar process follows from the realization that the present generation is the first to have the capacity to destroy the whole of creation. The term 'integrity of creation' is new for the Christian churches. The report of a WCC ecumenical discussion on this topic in Granvollen, Norway, in 1988 stressed several interrelated dimensions of the term: dependence on the Creator, the interrelatedness of 'all that is', wholeness, stewardship, commitment, hope, solidarity and fulfilment.

The 1991 Canberra Assembly clearly wished the JPIC conciliar process to continue and be deepened in future work and the recent restructuring of the units of the WCC has provided an opportunity for that to occur in the establishing (1993) of the new programme Unit Three on Justice, Peace and Creation. Whilst specific areas of focus are identified in this Unit – RACISM, indigenous peoples, ETHNICITY, POVERTY, ECONOMY, ENVIRONMENT, HUMAN RIGHTS, conflict resolution, women and youth issues – the interrelationships between concerns will be given particular attention in future work.

The newly restructured programme units of the WCC (Unit One: Unity and Renewal; Unit Two: Mission, Education and Witness; Unit Three: Justice, Peace and Creation; Unit Four: Sharing and Service) no doubt will allow other Unit concerns (in addition to those discussed above) such as community and justice, health and healing, gospel and culture, the theological significance of religions (Unit Two) and meeting urgent human need (e.g. refugee issues, advocacy and action with the poor) (Unit Four) to be explored in creative new ways. What seems to be certain is that the WCC in all its varied programmes will continue to be fully committed to the working out in society of a CONTEXTUAL THEOLOGY which is rooted in Biblical witness, is shared by and accountable to the life of the Christian community, and which belongs to the whole people of God (see Lossky *et al.* 1991: 992–7).

Castro, E. (ed.) (1985) 'Church and society, ecumenical perspectives, essays in honour of Paul Abrecht', in *The Ecumenical Review* 37(1), Geneva: World Council of Churches.
——(ed.) (1991) 'The ecumenical future and the WCC – a dialogue of dreams and visions', in *The*

Ecumenical Review 42(1), Geneva: World Council of Churches.

——(1992) 'JPIC: A Conciliar Process', *The Ecumenical Review* 44(3), Geneva: World Council of Churches.

Gosling, D. (1992) *A New Earth – Convenanting for Justice, Peace and the Integrity of Creation*, CCBI.

Limouris, G. (ed.) (1990) *Justice, Peace and the Integrity of Creation – Insights from Orthodoxy*, Geneva: World Council of Churches.

Lossky, N., Bonino, J.M., Pobee, J.S., Stransky, T.F., Wainwright, G. and Webb, P. (1991) *Dictionary of the Ecumenical Movement*, Geneva: World Council of Churches.

Metz, J.B. and Schillebeeckx, E. (1991) *No Heaven without Earth* (Concilium 1991–4), London: SCM.

Preston, R.H. (ed.) (1971) *Technology and Social Justice*, An International Symposium on the Social and Economic Teaching of the World Council of Churches from Geneva 1966 to Uppsala 1968, London: SCM.

——(1973) *Church and Society in the Late 20th Century: The Economic and Political Task*, London: SCM.

——(1994) *Confusions in Christian Social Ethics: Problems for Geneva and Rome*, London: SCM.

Shinn, R.L. (ed.) (1980) *Faith and Science in an Unjust World*, vols 1 an 2 of the Report of the World Council of Churches Conference on Faith, Science and the Future, Geneva: World Council of Churches.

Visser't Hooft, W.A. (1949) *The First Assembly of the WCC: The Official Report*, London: SCM.

Barry Thompson

WORSHIP

Worship is the simplest and most basic constitutive element of religion, and virtually coextensive with it. In its primary sense, it designates the response evoked by that which is recognized as the source of all order and energy in existence. The response is not self-generated but elicited by the quality of what or who is recognized, by a glory whose plenitude elevates the human faculties responding to it. In its secondary sense, it is the activity of bringing all life into relation to that which has such abundance of being and other perfections as to make it constitutive for life itself, to allow it to be shaped thereby. In the one sense, worship is the manifestation of ultimate plenitude, in the other it is the reconstitution of all proximate life by reference to this plenitude.

The first sense follows the strict designation of the English term worship (from the Old English *weorthscipe*, 'the condition [in a person] of deserving, or being held in, esteem or repute' [OED]). The term signifies the having of worth or positive value, or the honour or dignity which is *inherent* in the one in whom it is found, and is therefore recognized by others. The second sense becomes more widespread in the humanistic climate which has prevailed since the European Renaissance, and is further accentuated in twentieth-century developments, where worship is assimilated to the human task of constructing a full life. But more usually, worship incorporates the acknowledgement of a fullness of being, truth, goodness and beauty which is constitutive for all else, and the human responsibility to be formed through the deepest possible relation to this plenitude.

Worship escapes the possibility of full or complete definition, for several reasons. Firstly, its concern with plenitude and the idea of God makes it expansive and self-transforming, reaching always for the yet fuller being which lies beyond present conceptions and practices, and lifting human faculties beyond confinement by such categories and forms. While it is not contentless or formless, this plenitude always exceeds grasp by human conceptions and practices no matter how far their reach is extended. In this way, it is fundamentally opposed to *idolatrous* substitutes for this fuller being and *magical* attempts to dominate and manipulate it.

Second, however, at its profoundest level worship is both a *synchronic* and a *diachronic* activity. On the one hand, it is stimulated by intimations of the possibility of the ultimate unity and meaning of all things, and also by convictions of the presence of this unity and meaning for and in all things, its engagement with them and with us. But, on the other hand, these are only developed and confirmed through the ongoing rediscovery of their presence in the order of things and in history; and history will be complete when all fully acknowledge the Lord (Revelation 15: 4).

Third, worship is linked to all the features of life in the world and activates them in relation to their infinite and abundant source. As such, it includes and activates all other forms of religious understanding and practice such as RITUAL, symbols, doctrine, moral practices, and also forms less directly associated with religion, such as the reason, understanding, ethical behaviour, etc. It is by the placing of these others in the dynamic of worship that they achieve their proper standing and empowerment. The ancient Christian principle *lex orandi, lex credendi* acknowledges this for belief.

Full understanding of worship requires close attention to its very conception and dynamics, and the widely varying means by which it occurs. Because it is so closely interwoven with all the most basic features of human understanding and agency, life in the world and the nature and purposes of the primary reality called God, a full account of it would require analysis of all theololgy, human understanding and practice. This article only outlines the basic dynamics of worship together with a variety of historical practices which exemplify it, and the ways in which worship is made problematic – and may be enriched – in modern understanding. It does not attempt to trace all (or even most) of the ways in which it is found either in wider human understanding and practice or the forms and practices of liturgical worship.

The same three issues which affect the task of defining worship show important aspects of its conception and dynamics. They deserve further consideration.

First, we recall that worship is fundamental to the fuller appreciation of the transcendent source of order and energy upon which the cosmos and human salvation depend. In it a primary and transformative impulse is recognized as creative of all the ingredients of life, as they are ordered and energized within an ever-transcendent sphere of reference, which accords them a fundamental orientation and frees them for the fullest possibility which is their. It is within this recognition, concentrated in the dynamics of worship, that the development of human understanding of the 'nature' of the transcendent source occurs and continues.

Such worship, and the understanding in which it results, embraces both mystery and illumination. In 'apophatic theology' such as that emphasized in Eastern Christian thought, for example, it is only within a divine darkness like that which Moses entered on Sinai in meet-

ing God, and through the purification of the senses, intellect and words, that God is found in a union of 'pure prayer' (Evagrius Ponticus, sixth century AD). 'Cataphatic theology', however, seeks to move toward God through the understanding of aspects of creation, while still recognizing that God is beyond the very things – 'Being', 'the Good' and 'Life' – by which he is called through the use of notions from the created world. 'With these analogies we are raised upward toward the truth of the mind's vision, a truth which is simple and one. [Then] we leave behind us all our own notions. We call a halt to the activities of our minds and, to the extent that is proper, we approach the ray which transcends being' (Pseudo-Dionysius, sixth century AD). Both apophatic and cataphatic are ways of approaching God, in the one case through divine darkness and purification, and in the other through being raised upward through the mind's use of concepts from the created world. Contrasting emphases on mystery and illumination coexist in approaching the divine plenitude through the 'field of relations' – darkness and light – established by it.

Second, appreciation of this abundant or all-sufficient source is appropriately achieved only in accordance with its nature and purpose. This gives rise to a particular dynamic of acknowledgement which – *synchronously* considered – has five aspects.

Because this source is the infinite plenitude of being, truth, goodness and beauty, worship is offered primarily as *adoration* and *praise*, expressions of gladness for the very being and love of this God, in attitude and language refined to exalt God. It looks beyond creatureliness and creaturely thought to the very source of this plenitude, both unknowable in splendour (the *apophatic* element) and also self-conferring (the *cataphatic* element) in such a way that human beings can – at least provisionally – adore and praise God.

The adoring and praising of God brings to light the shortcomings of those who do so. A second aspect is therefore the *confession* of the faults by which they have distorted their relation to God and those around them. For Christians, this is not simply an expression of penitence, but opening themselves to the goodness by which God overcomes these sins in Jesus Christ.

When the infinite plenitude of God is conferred upon human beings, and particularly in their salvation ('O come let us sing unto the Lord; let us heartily rejoice in the strength of our salvation' Psalm 95), the appropriate response (the third aspect) is *thanksgiving*. This is a responsive movement of the hearts of those touched by the movements of God toward them, by which they show gratitude for God's acts.

It is equally important, however, that the world and these human beings be shaped through God's movements toward them. As regards 'the world' in its various dimensions, God's actions are to be related to people and issues in the world through *intercessory prayer*, the fourth aspect. For Christians, this is a sharing in the work of Jesus Christ which holds together God and the world in his own suffering and dying, and a proclamation of God's infinite mercy as it is to be found everywhere. It is necessarily very specific, and requires involvement in the needs and pains of others. As regards those who worship, the movements of God's life are to be brought to bear on their lives – and all their details – in *petition*, the fifth aspect.

This synchronic analysis of the dynamics of worship is intimately associated with the *diachronous*. Worship always draws from, and in turn sharpens, elevates and enriches the historical recognition of the nature of the plenitude whose movement toward human beings enables their adoration, praise, thanksgiving and petition. All of these involve the recalling (*anamnesis*) of the historical events by which divine plenitude has formed the basis of human wellbeing. The basis for worship is not (as Feuerbach thought) a metaphysical absolute which confines humankind in an alienated personification of himself ('God'), thereby dissipating his energies, but One whose history with humankind fulfills and energizes it.

Appreciating this history – a history which is not only historical but theological in its incorporation of God's benevolent purposes within the texture of historical events and interpretation – requires a readiness to traverse it within worship, as can be seen in the prominence given to biblical history in Jewish and Christian worship, where memories of God's action in history are read and celebrated as indicative of the decisive and continuing purposes of God for the present. For example, the rehearsal of the Biblical witness to the Exodus is the means of recalling the still valid act by which God saved his people, just as the Eucharist is the remembrance of the Lord's death and resurrection as an accomplished fact present for the worshipper today.

Third, as we have seen, worship naturally incorporates all the features of life in the world and activates them in relation to their infinite and abundant source. The way in which it typically does so is to focus on situations in which God's actions and purposes are intertwinded with crucially important events, features and institutions of human life in the world. Hence, for example, Hebrew worship concentrated on divine presence and action in the immediacies of human life, flesh and blood (in the practice of sacrifice), social institutions (covenant, law and monarchy), myths and rituals (feasts), personal behaviour (tithes and offerings, hospitality), crucial events in time (exodus and passover), particular spatial locations (shrines, the ark of the covenant, altars and temples), specially-endowed representative personages (prophets, priests and kings), etc. Through these, and later through the relocating of worship in the synagogue, with carefully-legislated practices of scripture-reading and prayer and a carefully-trained class of experts, there were the possibilities of the presence and self-conferral of God in determinate circumstances, with attendant purifications and blessings. In many cases, these had their origins in particular historical and social circumstances, but that is much less important than the successive transformations which they underwent in being made the vehicles for the understanding of this God present for these people in a tradition of sacred history.

While these three aspects of the dynamics of worship – the recognition of the source of all plenitude, the synchronic and diachronic dimensions of worship, and its realization of the divine presence and activity in the immediacies of life – are found in most worship, they take on a distinctive form in different traditions. Hence the same features as are found in Hebrew worship are continued but radically transposed in

Christianity, primarily through their comprehensive reshaping in relation to Jesus Christ. The very activity of God's blessing is seen to have occurred through God's relation with the world in Jesus Christ, through whom God chose his people even before creation – destining them to be holy and blameless, his sons in Christ, redeemed by his own blood from their trespasses to live in his grace and praise him. In effect, therefore, the fullness of worship occurs in Christ, and by being incorporate into Christ.

The implications of this transposition are extremely deep. The very plenitude of God is seen in a new light, as decisively turned toward humanity in history for the fullest blessing, whose form is redemption of humankind from the sin which blinds them to God and distorts all existence. It is through the very movement of God's holiness toward humankind in the life, suffering, death and resurrection of Jesus Christ that mankind is purified and redeemed. Hence the very synchronic and diachronic character of worship is changed into 'remembering the Lord's death until he comes'. And finally, God is fully knotted together with humankind – in the Holy Spirit re-ordering and re-energizing humankind for a new history with God, thereby conferring a new fullness of interactivity between human beings in their life together. All the ways in which the immediacies of life are incorporated in worship – institutions, rituals, personal behaviour, events of sacred history, etc. – are transformed through being refocused on the fullness of God's work in Christ and the Holy Spirit, and given new norms. All of life is so intimately united to the life of Jesus Christ in the Holy Spirit that it serves to honour, adore and glorify the Father.

In one sense, the significance of worship for religious life, and even for that outside of religion, is quite clear. Within the dynamic of worship is found ever-fuller relationship with the God who is fullest being, truth, goodness and beauty, and this is concentrated in determinate forms of understanding and practice which provide ways for human beings more fully to realize the movements of this God with and for them. Even where there is no explicit awareness of God, but only a striving for the realization of such fullness, there is an implicit concern with worship.

In another sense, however, the significance of worship – for religion and non-religious life alike – has yet to be fully appreciated. The problems which have arisen for it in modern times are closely associated with distortions of the dynamic which is proper to worship.

Viewed analytically, worship is a dynamic and inclusive activity attracted by the fullness of God's life toward (a) appropriate recognition of this fullness as source of all things, (b) determinate means by which this recognition is best concentrated, and (c) adequately disciplined behaviour – outward and inward – of agents. In the more specific forms of religion which we have reviewed, worship includes concentrated (synchronic) attempts to grasp the nature of the plenitude of God coupled with (diachronic) remembrance through which the economy of God's life and activity is recalled through performative re-enactment both corporate (which requires the constitution of leaders for it) and individual. Both make use of particular features of the world, its history and its life, and are undertaken through the dedicated activities of human beings.

Worship as such involves all three simultaneously – source, media and agents. Since the source which it realizes is infinite and all-encompassing, however, by the nature of the case worship locates it in determinate media in which the performance of human beings assumes definite shape. Given their purpose of locating the infinite and all-encompassing, the media employed in worship are both wide and complex (seen, for example, in the liturgical actions characteristic of Christianity). And they, in turn, rely on the intelligible incorporation of features of the natural world, human social life, rationality, culture, language, etc. Their use, however, requires their coordination in relation to the fullness of being whose presence in nature, history and human life which they are to show.

The decline in the significance of worship in modern times is largely attributable to the transportation of the dynamic interplay between its elements – the fullness of God in determinate media enacted by human beings – into the media themselves or into the performance (whether conscious or ethical) of human agents.

One feature of the decline is that the very

notion of a plenitude of being, truth, goodness and beauty in God is seen as problematic. Many reasons are cited, to such an extent that God's fullness is displaced by 'God the problem'. Those most often rehearsed are: the confusion of God with rival claims to loyalty (idols), the difficulty of framing criteria for distinguishing ultimate fullness from proximate forms, the emergence of powerful alternative forms of explanation in the natural and human sciences, the regularity with which devotion to God has provided particular social realities with justifications for order and the illegitimate exercise of power, etc.

In response to such complex difficulties, one common strategy has been to recast worship as the critical consideration of the ways in which human beings find their bearings in the world, including the imaginative visions (including statements about God) which provide them with the most effective orientation. In effect, therefore, worship is reconstrued as the pragmatics of the media in which human lives are lived most fully. No longer the plenitude upon which all else rests, God is relegated to the position of a mystery beyond the reach of all human insight and understanding, 'the name for that, whatever it might be, which serves to transform and correct – all our relativities, biases, and corruptions' (Kaufman).

Examples of the transposition of the fundamental dynamic of worship into a preoccupation with determinate media abound in modern times. As religious communities struggle to maintain their identities in an increasingly complex social situation, they harden their points of difference, in practices of worship (word or sacrament), tradition, ecclesial form, bible, doctrine, and practice, as well as in views of the place of history, reason, experience, religion and social concerns. They argue these differences – which are essentially differences in the use of determinate media in worship – to such an extent that the fundamental dynamic of worship is lost. In doing so, they follow the tendencies of modernity, for which worship has become eloquent didacticism.

The transposition of the dynamic of worship into dissonance about the media of worship is the chief agenda to be confronted by those who would restore worship today. It is best answered by reaching more deeply into the plenitude which meets human beings *in* the media and *in* the exercise of their agency, rather than by supposing that this plenitude is a mystery somehow distanced from them. The Christian view of the presence and activity of God in the immediacies of human life is of crucial importance in this task.

Aune, D.E. (1992) 'Early Christian Worship' in *Anchor Dictionary of the Bible*, vol. VI, 973–89, Garden City, NY: Doubleday.

Bouyer, L. (1956) *Life and Liturgy*, London: Sheed and Ward.

Corbin, J. (1988) *The Wellspring of Worship*, New York: Paulist Press.

Halbertal, M. and Margalit, A. (1992) *Idolatry*, London: Harvard University Press.

Hardy, D.W. and Ford, D. F. (1983) *Jubilee: Theology in Praise*, London: Darton, Longman & Todd.

Peterson, D. (1993) *Engaging with God*, Grand Rapids, MI: William B. Eerdmans.

Schmemann, A. (1988) *The Eucharist*, Crestwood, NY: St Vladimir's Seminary Press.

Torrance, T.F. (1975) *Theology in Reconciliation*, London: Geoffrey Chapman.

Wainwight, G. (1980) *Doxology: The Praise of God in Worship, Doctrine and Life*, New York: Oxford University Press.

Westermann, C. (1981) *Praise and Lament in the Psalms*, Atlanta, GA: John Knox Press.

Daniel W. Hardy

ZOOS

A zoological park is a collection of animals kept for purposes other than companionship or immediate human needs. While in common usage we call many different kinds of collections of animals a zoo, the current paradigm is a large collection of animals permanently housed on a dedicated piece of land and managed on a budget generated by visits from humans seeking entertainment.

Zoos are an ancient institution dating back to at least the third millennium BC. They were found in ancient Egypt, China, Mesopotamia, Greece, Mexico and perhaps most notoriously in ancient Rome where animals were held captive prior to slaughter in the infamous games. Collecting and holding animals continued into medieval times in European and Asian countries, and eventually developed into the more modern notion of municipal zoos. Zoological collections – whilst declining in popularity – are still common. In 1987 there were 198 zoos in the UK, and in the USA they run into many hundreds (Kew 1991; Jamieson 1985).

Controversy concerning the moral propriety of zoos arose as early as the eighteenth century in England and France (see Thomas 1983). But despite occasional sensitivity to appalling conditions of captivity in the late nineteenth and early twentieth centuries, few of the major institutions carried out projects which provided animals with a natural or satisfactory habitat. The twentieth century has seen an increased awareness of both the technical and ethical issues posed by permanent captivity. Justifications for zoos have historically been given after the fact; only comparatively recently in the history of ethics has the issue received serious attention (see Jamieson 1985; Linzey 1987; McKenna et al. 1987; Bostock 1993).

The lateness of ethical reflection has been due in part to the only gradual appreciation of the harm done to animals by permanent captivity. Early animal protection campaigns were directed principally at physical CRUELTY; that animals could suffer mentally was sometimes assumed but was always difficult to demonstrate. Various studies of animals have indicated the complexity of animal awareness (see, for example, Dawkins 1980, 1993; Griffin 1981). Minimum standards for managed animals (see FARMING) have been recommended which recognize the full range of animals' emotional as well as physical needs. These include freedom to perform natural physical movement, association with other animals, and facilities for comfort activities, e.g. rest, sleep and body care (Carpenter et al. 1980: 38). Poor welfare indicators include sterotypèd or stereotypical behaviour patterns (frequently seen in captive animals) which are the result of stress or neurosis. The Zoo Licensing Act of 1981 in the UK laid down some minimum standards. However: 'conditions are largely unspecified; no minimum amount of space for individual species; no minimum qualifications for zoo staff' (Kew 1991: 129).

Allied to an increased ethological sensitivity to the conditions of captivity has gone a radical questioning of the right of humans to capture and constrain other sentient creatures. There are two kinds of critique: one drawn from theological considerations and the other from philosophical considerations. The theological critique maintains that animals have the right to be animals, i.e. to live free of human control wherever possible and in accordance with their own natural conditions of life. 'We need to free animals from our own desire to control them and from our attempts to humanise them' (Linzey 1976: 68; 1987). While nature is not perfect, wild animals are as their Creator intended; their very 'wildness' is an inherent part of their being as free creatures. Since it is an inherent characteristic of all wild things to be free, to deprive them of their liberty is to deprive them of their God-given nature.

The philosophical critique is similar. There should be a 'moral presumption' against keeping wild animals in captivity since this necessarily involves depriving them of 'a great many goods'. Chief among these 'goods' are the satisfaction of their biological needs and their own ties of kinship and society. 'If we are justified in keeping animals in zoos, it must be because there are some important benefits that can be obtained only by doing so' but, without such justification, the case for zoos fails (Jamieson 1985: 109).

Partly in response to these and similar criticisms, zoo defenders have sought to identify the benefits of captivity and, in particular, have developed two main justifications: education and conservation.

At face value, the education argument appears strong, although some studies have questioned the educational effectiveness of zoos (see the discussion in, for example, Jamieson 1985: 111; Linzey 1987: 132). There is clearly an educational potential since humans can see animals in captivity which otherwise would not be seen. But such a justification assumes that humans who have *seen* animals in a zoo can *appreciate* them. One distinctive disadvantage of using captive animals to educate young humans is the unavoidable message that we can – and should – view animals instrumentally, and that they are not important enough as individuals or groups to leave in their wild state. It is true that zoos pass on values, but are they values concerning the *intrinsic worth* of the individual captives? It seems most likely that through a visit to a zoo we are educated more fully about our dominance of animals than about what non-humans are truly like in their own worlds.

Further, if education is the major justification for zoos, the educational aspect should be given priority over others, whereas it is seldom more than a rationalization for a practice already established and justified on other – usually commercial – grounds (see Jordan and Ormrod 1978). To establish that zoos happen to educate is not to accept that their existence is justified by their educational potential alone.

It is sometimes argued that animals are better off in zoos – even that animals are not in fact 'really free' in the wild (Hediger 1964). It is true that human engineering can cancel the harsher aspects of 'wild' existence, but that cancellation comes with heavy tradeoffs in terms of the quality of the individual animals' lives, e.g. through capture, transport and loss of social relationships. Alternatively, some have argued that 'really good captivity is not, to all intents and purposes, captivity at all' (Bostock 1993: 44). Zoos which meet at least some of the behavioural needs of animals and offer 'enriched semi-naturalistic enclosures' (Bostock 1993: 104) are to be preferred, but it may still be questioned

whether this really constitutes a 'good' life for non-humans. Some have argued that only 'good zoos are good news' (Bellamy 1988: 10) but without detailed ethical criteria such claims are vacuous. Although naturalistically designed zoos can ameliorate the harm done by captivity, they cannot remove the fundamental offence which captivity itself constitutes.

One example of the problematic nature of even 'good' captivity may help here. It is normal behaviour for animals to develop filial relationships and to breed. Successful breeding is sometimes cited as practical evidence of humane zoo management. But it comes at a high cost for the individual animals themselves because surplus animals are invariably sold to other zoos or killed. Although precise figures are not available, there is of necessity a dark side to zoo management: controlling animal lives means also necessitating their death.

The conservation argument, including justifications for benign research and preservation, also appears strong at first. From the outset, it should be noted that this argument, whatever its validity, is not a justification for all zoo practices, still less the existence of zoos generally, for only *some* species need conservation or can benefit from even benign research. Even if one is convinced that some confinement is validated by the need to research, or preserve, threatened species, we need to be clear that zoos generally cannot be justified by references to one recently identified benefit of a traditional practice established for, and still dominated by, other purposes. In short: the conservation argument at best offers only *limited* justification for very particular circumstances of *temporary* animal confinement, not a blanket defence of zoos.

Zoo conservation involves formidable technical problems, including the creation of a gene pool of adequate size, the maintenance of conditions conducive to possible reintroduction into the wild and the increased health risks posed by artificially created environments, especially proximity to other species. Even if these problems can be overcome, there is a fundamental ethical issue raised by the nature of the utilitarian calculations exemplified by conservation programmes. For almost all these programmes are predicated on a respect for the species rather than a concern for the *individuals within* that species. Individual animals are frequently viewed merely as carriers of the gene pool but without individual rights or intrinsic value. Thus even the most enlightened programmes within zoos necessarily adopt the view that the interests of individual sentients should be subordinated to the interests of the species, or biodiversity, or ecosystem (*see* SPECIESISM).

Overall, the evidence invites the conclusion that zoos are not in themselves essential for conservation. Some preservation programmes may require the temporary confinement of individual animals, but if the preservation of species is our goal, arguably the most morally enlightened way forward is the protection of their lives *as individuals* in the wild and the protection of their natural habitat (see Linzey 1987).

Underlying the conservation argument is an even deeper question. It is whether humans have the right to manage the whole earth and its animal populations according to their own utilitarian calculations. While theology has presupposed an active role for humans in the care and maintenance of the planet, this traditional view has certain limits. It does not follow that we have an absolute right to decide what species should live or die, or indeed *where* they should live and die. Conservation programmes are frequently indebted to a purely humanistic view that presupposes that humans always have the right and always know best.

Our conclusion is that moral theology should at least question the view which places humanity in such an absolute position without any corresponding sense of human limitations or divine-like responsibilities. Jamieson concludes that 'Zoos teach us a false sense of our place in the nature order,' and that 'because what zoos teach us is false and dangerous, both humans and animals will be better off when they are abolished' (Jamieson 1985: 117). Perhaps the history of zoos is testimony to a way of viewing our-selves in relation to animals that has become morally objectionable and theologically otiose (*see* ANIMAL RIGHTS).

Bellamy, David J. (1988) 'Good zoos are good news', in Miranda Stevenson (ed.) *Edinburgh Zoo*, published to commemorate Edinburgh Zoo's 75th Anniversary, Edinburgh: Royal Zoological Society of Scotland, pp. 10–11.

Bostock, Stephen St C. (1993) *Zoos and Animal Rights: The Ethics of Keeping Animals*, London and New York: Routledge.

Carpenter, Edward, *et al.* (1980) *Animals and Ethics*, London: Watkins.

Clark, Stephen R.L. (1979) 'The rights of wild things', *Inquiry* 22(1–2): 171–88.

Dawkins, Marian Stamp (1980) *Animal Suffering: The Science of Animal Welfare*, London and New York: Chapman & Hall.

——(1993) *Through Our Eyes Only? The Search for Animal Consciousness*, Oxford and New York: W.H. Freeman/Spektrum.

Griffin, D.R. (1981) *The Question of Animal Awareness*, New York: Rockefeller University Press.

Hediger, H. (1964) *Wild Animals in Captivity*, New York: Dover Publications.

Ironmonger, John (1992) *The Good Zoo Guide*, London: HarperCollins.

Jamieson, Dale (1985) 'Against zoos', in Peter Singer (ed.) *In Defence of Animals*, Oxford: Basil Blackwell, pp. 108–17.

Jordan, Bill and Ormrod, Stefan (1978) *The Last Great Wild Beast Show: A Discussion on the Failure of British Animal Collections*, London: Constable.

Kew, Barry (1991) *Animal Facts and Figures*, London: Green Print.

Linzey, Andrew (1976) *Animal Rights: A Christian Assessment*, London: SCM.

——(1987) *Christianity and the Rights of Animals*, London: SPCK and New York: Crossroad.

——(1994) *Animal Theology*, London: SCM and Chicago, IL: University of Illinois Press.

McKenna, Virginia, Travers, Will and Wray, Jonathan (eds) (1987) *Beyond the Bars: The Zoo Dilemma*, Wellingborough: Thorsons.

Thomas, Keith (1983) *Man and the Natural World: Changing Attitudes in England 1500–1800*, London: Allen Lane.

Andrew Linzey
Paul Waldau

INDEX

Note: **bold** page numbers refer to main entries in the Dictionary.